Joel Whitburn PRESENTS

Billboard®

TOP 10 ALBUM CHARTS

1963-1998

Chart Data Compiled From *Billboard's* Top Pop Album Charts.

ISBN 0-89820-132-2 (Hardcover)
ISBN 0-89820-133-0 (Softcover)

Record Research Inc.
P.O. Box 200
Menomonee Falls, Wisconsin 53052-0200 U.S.A.

Phone: 414-251-5408
Fax: 414-251-9452
E-Mail: record@execpc.com
Web Site: http://www.recordresearch.com

CONTENTS

AUTHOR'S NOTE

I am pleased to introduce to you the first-ever collection of more than 1,800 individual Top 10 charts from *Billboard* magazine's weekly Top Album charts. **Billboard Top 10 Album Charts 1963-1998** begins with the Top 10 of *Billboard's* first all-encompassing albums chart, Top LPs, dated August 17, 1963. Previously, *Billboard* concurrently published two separate stereo and mono charts. The first consolidated albums chart was published just prior to the music industry's shift in emphasis from the single to the album. Five months after its debut, the Top LPs chart met The Beatles, the heroes of the British invasion who very quickly redefined the role of the album in western popular culture.

Over the years, *Billboard's* Top Albums chart has reported exactly what the hottest-selling music in America is, week in and week out. As you travel through these pages you'll revisit a diversity of music trends, from the soul, bubblegum and psychedelic rock of the '60s, to the soft rock and disco of the '70s, to the new wave and heavy metal '80s, to the rap, grunge, country and R&B of the '90s. Perhaps the most intriguing aspect of this chart is that many genres of music come together on common ground.

Billboard Top 10 Album Charts 1963-1998 is both the subject of study and entertainment. Recently as I flipped through these Top 10 charts, I jotted down the tidbits listed below. As you read on, you too will engage in some fascinating and some frivolous discoveries of your own.

April 2, 1966	Herb Alpert & The Tijuana Brass accomplished the incredible and unsurpassed feat of claiming FOUR (!) spots in the Top 10: #2, #3, #9 and #10.
May 18, 1968	*The Birds, The Bees & The Monkees* is followed by *The Good, The Bad And The Ugly*.
March 27, 1971	The #1 and #3 positions belonged to Janis Joplin and Jimi Hendrix, whose deaths in 1970 were 16 days apart. Coming between their albums at #2 was the soundtrack to *Love Story*, a movie about a young person dying.
October 2, 1971	After The Beatles disbanded, their two principle songwriters met once more in the Top 10: Paul McCartney with *Ram* and John Lennon with *Imagine*.
November 22, 1975	After their split in 1971, Simon & Garfunkel reunited in the Top 10 with Paul Simon's *Still Crazy After All These Years* and Art Garfunkel's *Breakaway*.
June 19, 1976	*Rastaman Vibration* became the only album to enter the Top 10 for superstar reggae legend Bob Marley.

February 4, 1984	Half of the Top 10 had numerical titles: *Colour By Numbers, 1984, 90125, Seven And The Ragged Tiger*, and *Rock 'N Soul, Part I.*
January 16, 1988	Seven of the Top 10 albums had one-word titles: *Faith, Tiffany, Bad, Whitesnake, Whitney, Hysteria,* and *Kick.*
February 3, 1990	The seven veteran acts of the 1970s who claimed a majority of the Top 10 were Billy Joel, Quincy Jones, Aerosmith, Tom Petty, The B-52's, and Phil Collins.
October 27, 1990	No rivalry existed among these sibling acts in the Top 10: The Vaughan Brothers, Wilson Phillips, AC/DC, and INXS.
October - November, 1996	The 10th and 11th months of the year are typically a hot time for new superstar releases. In the eight weeks between October 12 and November 30, 1996, 21 new albums debuted in the Top 10; the only album to remain on the chart during this rapid turnover was *Falling Into You* by Celine Dion. Jump ahead to the eight-week period between December 21, 1996, and February 8, 1997, when no new albums made their chart debut within the Top 10!
July 11, 1998	The sound offerings of the visual media dominated the Top 10 with five movie soundtracks plus albums by two TV stars.

JOEL WHITBURN

KEY TO THE TOP 10 ALBUM CHARTS

Billboard Top 10 Album Charts is a comprehensive, week-by-week history of the Top 10 of *Billboard* magazine's *Top Pop Albums* chart. It contains more than 1,800 individual Top 10 charts from over 35 years of *Billboard* Top Album charts, beginning with the August 17, 1963 "Top LP's" chart — *Billboard's* first consolidated, all-encompassing albums chart — right through "The Billboard 200" of December 26, 1998.

In keeping with the original chart format, each week's current and previous chart positions are shown, along with weeks on chart, the artist and original label and number.

TW: this week's *Top Albums* chart position

LW: last week's *Top Albums* chart position

WK: total weeks charted on the *Top Albums* chart

If an album re-entered the Top 10 after several years, its original weeks charted are included with its current weeks charted.

❸: chart bullet

Billboard indicates albums that made substantial gains for the week by showing their chart positions in reverse type. *Billboard* changed its methodology for awarding bullets over the years, giving out fewer bullets during the early years and more in later years.

PEAK POSITIONS

In a departure from the original chart, all titles at their peak positions are shown in **boldface** type. At a glance, you can see exactly when each title was at its peak of popularity.

ALBUM TITLES / ARTIST NAMES

Please note that the album titles and artist names are listed exactly as they appear on the actual albums. Unfortunately, the charts were not always as precise; and, therefore, you will occasionally notice a difference in the way an album title or artist name is listed in this book versus the original *Billboard* charts.

ALBUMS FROM *TOP LP's MONAURAL & STEREO* CHARTS

Prior to the first all-encompassing *Top LP's* chart of August 17, 1963, *Billboard* published the Top 150 *Top LP's – Monaural* chart and the Top 50 *Top LP's – Stereo* chart. The following eight albums were in the Top 10 during the first few weeks of the new all-encompassing *Top LP's* chart, but reached their peak on the previously mentioned monaural or stereo album charts:

Live At The Apollo...James Brown (peaked on 8/3/63)
Ramblin' Rose...Nat "King" Cole (peaked on 11/3/62)
Peter, Paul and Mary...Peter, Paul & Mary (peaked on 10/20/62)
(Moving)...Peter, Paul & Mary (peaked on 3/30/63)
The Barbra Streisand Album...Barbra Streisand (peaked on 7/27/63)
Cleopatra...Soundtrack (peaked on 7/27/63)
Lawrence Of Arabia...Soundtrack (peaked on 4/27/63)
West Side Story...Soundtrack (peaked on 5/5/62)

The following two albums were in the Top 10 during the first few weeks of the new all-encompassing *Top LP's* chart and returned to the same peak position they previously reached on the monaural or stereo album charts:

Joan Baez In Concert...Joan Baez (peaked on 11/17/62)
Days of Wine and Roses...Andy Williams (peaked on 5/4/63)

YEAR-END CHARTS 1976-PRESENT

Due to holiday constraints, *Billboard* has not published an issue during the last week of each year since 1976. To account for the missing charts from 1976 through 1991, one week is added to the total weeks charted for each entry on the next chart published. Since 1992, *Billboard* has compiled *The Billboard 200* chart for the unpublished week and has made it available through their on-line services. The Top 10 of those on-line, year-end charts are in this book.

TW	LW	WK	Billboard® AUGUST 17, 1963	TOP LP's
①	1	18	**Days of Wine and Roses**	*Andy Williams*...Columbia 8815
❷	5	6	Little Stevie Wonder/The 12 Year Old Genius	*Stevie Wonder*...Tamla 240
③	4	95	West Side Story	*Soundtrack*...Columbia 2070
④	3	31	(Moving)	*Peter, Paul & Mary*...Warner 1473
❺	15	5	Trini Lopez At PJ'S	*Trini Lopez*...Reprise 6093
⑥	6	69	Peter, Paul and Mary	*Peter, Paul & Mary*...Warner 1449
⑦	2	8	Live At The Apollo	*James Brown*...King 826
❽	11	6	Shut Down	*Various Artists*...Capitol 1918
⑨	8	9	Cleopatra	*Soundtrack*...20th Century 5008
⑩	9	17	Bye Bye Birdie	*Soundtrack*...RCA 1081

TW	LW	WK	Billboard® AUGUST 24, 1963	TOP LP's
①	2	7	**Little Stevie Wonder/The 12 Year Old Genius**	*Stevie Wonder*...**Tamla 240**
❷	5	6	**Trini Lopez At PJ'S**	*Trini Lopez*...Reprise 6093
③	1	19	Days of Wine and Roses	*Andy Williams*...Columbia 8815
④	4	32	(Moving)	*Peter, Paul & Mary*...Warner 1473
❺	90	2	My Son, The Nut	*Allan Sherman*...Warner 1501
⑥	3	96	West Side Story	*Soundtrack*...Columbia 2070
⑦	8	7	**Shut Down**	*Various Artists*...Capitol 1918
⑧	7	9	Live At The Apollo	*James Brown*...King 826
⑨	10	18	Bye Bye Birdie	*Soundtrack*...RCA 1081
⑩	6	70	Peter, Paul and Mary	*Peter, Paul & Mary*...Warner 1449

TW	LW	WK	Billboard® AUGUST 31, 1963	TOP LP's
❶	5	3	**My Son, The Nut**	*Allan Sherman*...Warner 1501
②	2	7	**Trini Lopez At PJ'S**	*Trini Lopez*...Reprise 6093
③	1	8	Little Stevie Wonder/The 12 Year Old Genius	*Stevie Wonder*...Tamla 240
④	4	33	(Moving)	*Peter, Paul & Mary*...Warner 1473
⑤	3	20	Days of Wine and Roses	*Andy Williams*...Columbia 8815
⑥	6	97	West Side Story	*Soundtrack*...Columbia 2070
⑦	10	71	Peter, Paul and Mary	*Peter, Paul & Mary*...Warner 1449
⑧	9	19	Bye Bye Birdie	*Soundtrack*...RCA 1081
⑨	7	8	Shut Down	*Various Artists*...Capitol 1918
⑩	13	11	Cleopatra	*Soundtrack*...20th Century 5008

TW	LW	WK	Billboard® SEPTEMBER 7, 1963	TOP LP's
①	1	4	**My Son, The Nut**	*Allan Sherman*...Warner 1501
②	2	8	**Trini Lopez At PJ'S**	*Trini Lopez*...Reprise 6093
③	3	9	Little Stevie Wonder/The 12 Year Old Genius	*Stevie Wonder*...Tamla 240
④	4	34	(Moving)	*Peter, Paul & Mary*...Warner 1473
⑤	8	20	Bye Bye Birdie	*Soundtrack*...RCA 1081
⑥	6	98	West Side Story	*Soundtrack*...Columbia 2070
⑦	7	72	Peter, Paul and Mary	*Peter, Paul & Mary*...Warner 1449
⑧	5	21	Days of Wine and Roses	*Andy Williams*...Columbia 8815
⑨	9	9	Shut Down	*Various Artists*...Capitol 1918
⑩	17	28	Lawrence Of Arabia	*Soundtrack*...Colpix 514

TW	LW	WK	Billboard. SEPTEMBER 14, 1963	TOP LP's
1	1	5	**My Son, The Nut**	*Allan Sherman*...Warner 1501
2	2	9	**Trini Lopez At PJ'S**	*Trini Lopez*...Reprise 6093
3	5	21	Bye Bye Birdie	*Soundtrack*...RCA 1081
4	4	35	(Moving)	*Peter, Paul & Mary*...Warner 1473
5	7	73	Peter, Paul and Mary	*Peter, Paul & Mary*...Warner 1449
6	3	10	Little Stevie Wonder/The 12 Year Old Genius	*Stevie Wonder*...Tamla 240
7	6	99	West Side Story	*Soundtrack*...Columbia 2070
8	8	22	Days of Wine and Roses	*Andy Williams*...Columbia 8815
9	16	5	Sunny Side!	*The Kingston Trio*...Capitol 1935
10	11	12	Live At The Apollo	*James Brown*...King 826

TW	LW	WK	Billboard. SEPTEMBER 21, 1963	TOP LP's
1	1	6	**My Son, The Nut**	*Allan Sherman*...Warner 1501
2	2	10	**Trini Lopez At PJ'S**	*Trini Lopez*...Reprise 6093
3	3	22	Bye Bye Birdie	*Soundtrack*...RCA 1081
4	5	74	Peter, Paul and Mary	*Peter, Paul & Mary*...Warner 1449
5	4	36	(Moving)	*Peter, Paul & Mary*...Warner 1473
6	7	100	West Side Story	*Soundtrack*...Columbia 2070
7	9	6	**Sunny Side!**	*The Kingston Trio*...Capitol 1935
8	10	13	Live At The Apollo	*James Brown*...King 826
9	27	4	Ingredients In A Recipe For Soul	*Ray Charles*...ABC-Paramount 465
10	6	11	Little Stevie Wonder/The 12 Year Old Genius	*Stevie Wonder*...Tamla 240

TW	LW	WK	Billboard. SEPTEMBER 28, 1963	TOP LP's
1	1	7	**My Son, The Nut**	*Allan Sherman*...Warner 1501
2	2	11	**Trini Lopez At PJ'S**	*Trini Lopez*...Reprise 6093
3	3	23	Bye Bye Birdie	*Soundtrack*...RCA 1081
4	4	75	Peter, Paul and Mary	*Peter, Paul & Mary*...Warner 1449
5	5	37	(Moving)	*Peter, Paul & Mary*...Warner 1473
6	9	5	Ingredients In A Recipe For Soul	*Ray Charles*...ABC-Paramount 465
7	7	7	**Sunny Side!**	*The Kingston Trio*...Capitol 1935
8	6	101	West Side Story	*Soundtrack*...Columbia 2070
9	8	14	Live At The Apollo	*James Brown*...King 826
10	12	24	Days of Wine and Roses	*Andy Williams*...Columbia 8815

TW	LW	WK	Billboard. OCTOBER 5, 1963	TOP LP's
1	1	8	**My Son, The Nut**	*Allan Sherman*...Warner 1501
2	3	24	**Bye Bye Birdie**	*Soundtrack*...RCA 1081
3	6	6	Ingredients In A Recipe For Soul	*Ray Charles*...ABC-Paramount 465
4	4	76	Peter, Paul and Mary	*Peter, Paul & Mary*...Warner 1449
5	2	12	Trini Lopez At PJ'S	*Trini Lopez*...Reprise 6093
6	5	38	(Moving)	*Peter, Paul & Mary*...Warner 1473
7	9	15	Live At The Apollo	*James Brown*...King 826
8	8	102	West Side Story	*Soundtrack*...Columbia 2070
9	7	8	Sunny Side!	*The Kingston Trio*...Capitol 1935
10	10	25	Days of Wine and Roses	*Andy Williams*...Columbia 8815

Billboard. OCTOBER 12, 1963 — TOP LP's

TW	LW	WK			
1	1	9	**My Son, The Nut**	*Allan Sherman*	Warner 1501
2	3	7	**Ingredients In A Recipe For Soul**	*Ray Charles*	ABC-Paramount 465
3	5	13	Trini Lopez At PJ'S	*Trini Lopez*	Reprise 6093
4	2	25	Bye Bye Birdie	*Soundtrack*	RCA 1081
5	4	77	Peter, Paul and Mary	*Peter, Paul & Mary*	Warner 1449
6	7	16	Live At The Apollo	*James Brown*	King 826
7	6	39	(Moving)	*Peter, Paul & Mary*	Warner 1473
8	11	14	Shut Down	*Various Artists*	Capitol 1918
9	12	5	Elvis' Golden Records, Volume 3	*Elvis Presley*	RCA LSP-2765
10	8	103	West Side Story	*Soundtrack*	Columbia 2070

Billboard. OCTOBER 19, 1963 — TOP LP's

TW	LW	WK			
1	1	10	**My Son, The Nut**	*Allan Sherman*	Warner 1501
2	2	8	**Ingredients In A Recipe For Soul**	*Ray Charles*	ABC-Paramount 465
3	3	14	Trini Lopez At PJ'S	*Trini Lopez*	Reprise 6093
4	5	78	Peter, Paul and Mary	*Peter, Paul & Mary*	Warner 1449
5	4	26	Bye Bye Birdie	*Soundtrack*	RCA 1081
6	7	40	(Moving)	*Peter, Paul & Mary*	Warner 1473
7	9	6	Elvis' Golden Records, Volume 3	*Elvis Presley*	RCA LSP-2765
8	11	6	The Second Barbra Streisand Album	*Barbra Streisand*	Columbia 8854
9	10	104	West Side Story	*Soundtrack*	Columbia 2070
10	8	15	Shut Down	*Various Artists*	Capitol 1918

Billboard. OCTOBER 26, 1963 — TOP LP's

TW	LW	WK			
1	4	79	**Peter, Paul and Mary**	*Peter, Paul & Mary*	Warner 1449
2	5	27	**Bye Bye Birdie**	*Soundtrack*	RCA 1081
3	1	11	My Son, The Nut	*Allan Sherman*	Warner 1501
4	6	41	(Moving)	*Peter, Paul & Mary*	Warner 1473
5	8	7	The Second Barbra Streisand Album	*Barbra Streisand*	Columbia 8854
6	2	9	Ingredients In A Recipe For Soul	*Ray Charles*	ABC-Paramount 465
7	7	7	Elvis' Golden Records, Volume 3	*Elvis Presley*	RCA LSP-2765
8	9	105	West Side Story	*Soundtrack*	Columbia 2070
9	3	15	Trini Lopez At PJ'S	*Trini Lopez*	Reprise 6093
10	13	12	**Blue Velvet**	*Bobby Vinton*	Epic 26068

Billboard. NOVEMBER 2, 1963 — TOP LP's

TW	LW	WK			
1	12	2	**In The Wind**	*Peter, Paul & Mary*	Warner 1507
2	1	80	Peter, Paul and Mary	*Peter, Paul & Mary*	Warner 1449
3	6	10	Ingredients In A Recipe For Soul	*Ray Charles*	ABC-Paramount 465
4	7	8	Elvis' Golden Records, Volume 3	*Elvis Presley*	RCA LSP-2765
5	5	8	The Second Barbra Streisand Album	*Barbra Streisand*	Columbia 8854
6	4	42	(Moving)	*Peter, Paul & Mary*	Warner 1473
7	9	16	Trini Lopez At PJ'S	*Trini Lopez*	Reprise 6093
8	2	28	Bye Bye Birdie	*Soundtrack*	RCA 1081
9	8	106	West Side Story	*Soundtrack*	Columbia 2070
10	3	12	My Son, The Nut	*Allan Sherman*	Warner 1501

TW	LW	WK	Billboard. NOVEMBER 9, 1963	TOP LP's
1	1	3	**In The Wind**	*Peter, Paul & Mary*...Warner 1507
2	5	9	**The Second Barbra Streisand Album**	*Barbra Streisand*...Columbia 8854
3	3	11	Ingredients In A Recipe For Soul	*Ray Charles*...ABC-Paramount 465
4	4	9	Elvis' Golden Records, Volume 3	*Elvis Presley*...RCA LSP-2765
5	7	17	Trini Lopez At PJ'S	*Trini Lopez*...Reprise 6093
6	2	81	Peter, Paul and Mary	*Peter, Paul & Mary*...Warner 1449
7	6	43	(Moving)	*Peter, Paul & Mary*...Warner 1473
8	10	13	My Son, The Nut	*Allan Sherman*...Warner 1501
9	17	31	The Barbra Streisand Album	*Barbra Streisand*...Columbia 8807
10	8	29	Bye Bye Birdie	*Soundtrack*...RCA 1081

TW	LW	WK	Billboard. NOVEMBER 16, 1963	TOP LP's
1	1	4	**In The Wind**	*Peter, Paul & Mary*...Warner 1507
2	2	10	**The Second Barbra Streisand Album**	*Barbra Streisand*...Columbia 8854
3	4	10	**Elvis' Golden Records, Volume 3**	*Elvis Presley*...RCA LSP-2765
4	5	18	Trini Lopez At PJ'S	*Trini Lopez*...Reprise 6093
5	3	12	Ingredients In A Recipe For Soul	*Ray Charles*...ABC-Paramount 465
6	7	44	(Moving)	*Peter, Paul & Mary*...Warner 1473
7	10	30	Bye Bye Birdie	*Soundtrack*...RCA 1081
8	6	82	Peter, Paul and Mary	*Peter, Paul & Mary*...Warner 1449
9	11	108	West Side Story	*Soundtrack*...Columbia 2070
10	12	6	Painted, Tainted Rose	*Al Martino*...Capitol 1975

TW	LW	WK	Billboard. NOVEMBER 23, 1963	TOP LP's
1	1	5	**In The Wind**	*Peter, Paul & Mary*...Warner 1507
2	2	11	**The Second Barbra Streisand Album**	*Barbra Streisand*...Columbia 8854
3	3	11	**Elvis' Golden Records, Volume 3**	*Elvis Presley*...RCA LSP-2765
4	4	19	Trini Lopez At PJ'S	*Trini Lopez*...Reprise 6093
5	5	13	Ingredients In A Recipe For Soul	*Ray Charles*...ABC-Paramount 465
6	8	83	Peter, Paul and Mary	*Peter, Paul & Mary*...Warner 1449
7	14	7	**Surfer Girl**	*The Beach Boys*...Capitol 1981
8	54	3	The Singing Nun	*The Singing Nun*...Philips 203
9	6	45	(Moving)	*Peter, Paul & Mary*...Warner 1473
10	10	7	Painted, Tainted Rose	*Al Martino*...Capitol 1975

TW	LW	WK	Billboard. NOVEMBER 30, 1963	TOP LP's
1	1	6	**In The Wind**	*Peter, Paul & Mary*...Warner 1507
2	8	4	The Singing Nun	*The Singing Nun*...Philips 203
3	2	12	The Second Barbra Streisand Album	*Barbra Streisand*...Columbia 8854
4	4	20	Trini Lopez At PJ'S	*Trini Lopez*...Reprise 6093
5	6	84	Peter, Paul and Mary	*Peter, Paul & Mary*...Warner 1449
6	3	12	Elvis' Golden Records, Volume 3	*Elvis Presley*...RCA LSP-2765
7	7	8	**Surfer Girl**	*The Beach Boys*...Capitol 1981
8	13	9	**Sinatra's Sinatra**	*Frank Sinatra*...Reprise 1010
9	10	8	**Painted, Tainted Rose**	*Al Martino*...Capitol 1975
10	12	34	The Barbra Streisand Album	*Barbra Streisand*...Columbia 8807

TW	LW	WK	Billboard. DECEMBER 7, 1963 TOP LP's
1	2	5	**The Singing Nun** ... *The Singing Nun*...Philips 203
2	1	7	In The Wind ... *Peter, Paul & Mary*...Warner 1507
3	3	13	The Second Barbra Streisand Album ... *Barbra Streisand*...Columbia 8854
4	5	85	Peter, Paul and Mary ... *Peter, Paul & Mary*...Warner 1449
5	4	21	Trini Lopez At PJ'S ... *Trini Lopez*...Reprise 6093
6	6	13	Elvis' Golden Records, Volume 3 ... *Elvis Presley*...RCA LSP-2765
7	12	111	West Side Story ... *Soundtrack*...Columbia 2070
8	8	10	**Sinatra's Sinatra** ... *Frank Sinatra*...Reprise 1010
9	10	35	The Barbra Streisand Album ... *Barbra Streisand*...Columbia 8807
10	13	15	Ingredients In A Recipe For Soul ... *Ray Charles*...ABC-Paramount 465

TW	LW	WK	Billboard. DECEMBER 14, 1963 TOP LP's
1	1	6	**The Singing Nun** ... *The Singing Nun*...Philips 203
2	2	8	In The Wind ... *Peter, Paul & Mary*...Warner 1507
3	3	14	The Second Barbra Streisand Album ... *Barbra Streisand*...Columbia 8854
4	5	22	Trini Lopez At PJ'S ... *Trini Lopez*...Reprise 6093
5	6	14	Elvis' Golden Records, Volume 3 ... *Elvis Presley*...RCA LSP-2765
6	10	16	Ingredients In A Recipe For Soul ... *Ray Charles*...ABC-Paramount 465
7	4	86	Peter, Paul and Mary ... *Peter, Paul & Mary*...Warner 1449
8	13	10	Surfer Girl ... *The Beach Boys*...Capitol 1981
9	7	112	West Side Story ... *Soundtrack*...Columbia 2070
10	12	48	(Moving) ... *Peter, Paul & Mary*...Warner 1473

TW	LW	WK	Billboard. DECEMBER 21, 1963 TOP LP's
1	1	7	**The Singing Nun** ... *The Singing Nun*...Philips 203
2	2	9	In The Wind ... *Peter, Paul & Mary*...Warner 1507
3	3	15	The Second Barbra Streisand Album ... *Barbra Streisand*...Columbia 8854
4	4	23	Trini Lopez At PJ'S ... *Trini Lopez*...Reprise 6093
5	5	15	Elvis' Golden Records, Volume 3 ... *Elvis Presley*...RCA LSP-2765
6	7	87	Peter, Paul and Mary ... *Peter, Paul & Mary*...Warner 1449
7	11	8	Washington Square ... *The Village Stompers*...Epic 26078
8	8	11	Surfer Girl ... *The Beach Boys*...Capitol 1981
9	6	17	Ingredients In A Recipe For Soul ... *Ray Charles*...ABC-Paramount 465
10	18	61	**Joan Baez In Concert** ... *Joan Baez*...Vanguard 2122

TW	LW	WK	Billboard. DECEMBER 28, 1963 TOP LP's
1	1	8	**The Singing Nun** ... *The Singing Nun*...Philips 203
2	2	10	In The Wind ... *Peter, Paul & Mary*...Warner 1507
3	3	16	The Second Barbra Streisand Album ... *Barbra Streisand*...Columbia 8854
4	4	24	Trini Lopez At PJ'S ... *Trini Lopez*...Reprise 6093
5	7	9	**Washington Square** ... *The Village Stompers*...Epic 26078
6	5	16	Elvis' Golden Records, Volume 3 ... *Elvis Presley*...RCA LSP-2765
7	6	88	Peter, Paul and Mary ... *Peter, Paul & Mary*...Warner 1449
8	12	114	West Side Story ... *Soundtrack*...Columbia 2070
9	9	18	Ingredients In A Recipe For Soul ... *Ray Charles*...ABC-Paramount 465
10	13	50	(Moving) ... *Peter, Paul & Mary*...Warner 1473

TW	LW	WK	Billboard. JANUARY 4, 1964 TOP LP's	
1	1	9	**The Singing Nun**	*The Singing Nun*...Philips 203
2	2	11	In The Wind	*Peter, Paul & Mary*...Warner 1507
3	3	17	The Second Barbra Streisand Album	*Barbra Streisand*...Columbia 8854
4	6	17	Elvis' Golden Records, Volume 3	*Elvis Presley*...RCA LSP-2765
5	4	25	Trini Lopez At PJ'S	*Trini Lopez*...Reprise 6093
6	8	115	West Side Story	*Soundtrack*...Columbia 2070
7	12	8	**Maria Elena**	*Los Indios Tabajaras*...RCA 2822
8	11	5	Joan Baez In Concert, Part 2	*Joan Baez*...Vanguard 2123
9	7	89	Peter, Paul and Mary	*Peter, Paul & Mary*...Warner 1449
10	13	9	Little Deuce Coupe	*The Beach Boys*...Capitol 1998

TW	LW	WK	Billboard. JANUARY 11, 1964 TOP LP's	
1	1	10	**The Singing Nun**	*The Singing Nun*...Philips 203
2	2	12	In The Wind	*Peter, Paul & Mary*...Warner 1507
3	3	18	The Second Barbra Streisand Album	*Barbra Streisand*...Columbia 8854
4	18	4	Fun in Acapulco	*Elvis Presley/Soundtrack*...RCA LSP-2756
5	6	116	West Side Story	*Soundtrack*...Columbia 2070
6	9	90	Peter, Paul and Mary	*Peter, Paul & Mary*...Warner 1449
7	7	9	**Maria Elena**	*Los Indios Tabajaras*...RCA 2822
8	8	6	Joan Baez In Concert, Part 2	*Joan Baez*...Vanguard 2123
9	10	10	Little Deuce Coupe	*The Beach Boys*...Capitol 1998
10	12	52	(Moving)	*Peter, Paul & Mary*...Warner 1473

TW	LW	WK	Billboard. JANUARY 18, 1964 TOP LP's	
1	1	11	**The Singing Nun**	*The Singing Nun*...Philips 203
2	2	13	In The Wind	*Peter, Paul & Mary*...Warner 1507
3	4	5	**Fun in Acapulco**	*Elvis Presley/Soundtrack*...RCA LSP-2756
4	6	91	Peter, Paul and Mary	*Peter, Paul & Mary*...Warner 1449
5	5	117	West Side Story	*Soundtrack*...Columbia 2070
6	3	19	The Second Barbra Streisand Album	*Barbra Streisand*...Columbia 8854
7	8	7	**Joan Baez In Concert, Part 2**	*Joan Baez*...Vanguard 2123
8	10	53	(Moving)	*Peter, Paul & Mary*...Warner 1473
9	9	11	Little Deuce Coupe	*The Beach Boys*...Capitol 1998
10	34	4	The Presidential Years 1960-1963	*John Fitzgerald Kennedy*...20th Century 3127

TW	LW	WK	Billboard. JANUARY 25, 1964 TOP LP's	
1	1	12	**The Singing Nun**	*The Singing Nun*...Philips 203
2	2	14	In The Wind	*Peter, Paul & Mary*...Warner 1507
3	3	6	**Fun in Acapulco**	*Elvis Presley/Soundtrack*...RCA LSP-2756
4	5	118	West Side Story	*Soundtrack*...Columbia 2070
5	4	92	Peter, Paul and Mary	*Peter, Paul & Mary*...Warner 1449
6	6	20	The Second Barbra Streisand Album	*Barbra Streisand*...Columbia 8854
7	7	8	**Joan Baez In Concert, Part 2**	*Joan Baez*...Vanguard 2123
8	8	54	(Moving)	*Peter, Paul & Mary*...Warner 1473
9	9	12	Little Deuce Coupe	*The Beach Boys*...Capitol 1998
10	10	5	The Presidential Years 1960-1963	*John Fitzgerald Kennedy*...20th Century 3127

Billboard — FEBRUARY 1, 1964 — TOP LP's

TW	LW	WK	Title	Artist...Label
①	1	13	**The Singing Nun**	*The Singing Nun*...Philips 203
②	2	15	In The Wind	*Peter, Paul & Mary*...Warner 1507
③	3	7	**Fun in Acapulco**	*Elvis Presley/Soundtrack*...RCA LSP-2756
④	5	93	Peter, Paul and Mary	*Peter, Paul & Mary*...Warner 1449
⑤	9	13	Little Deuce Coupe	*The Beach Boys*...Capitol 1998
❻	12	6	That Was The Week That Was	*John Fitzgerald Kennedy*...Decca 9116
⑦	4	119	West Side Story	*Soundtrack*...Columbia 2070
⑧	10	6	**The Presidential Years 1960-1963**	*John Fitzgerald Kennedy*...20th Century 3127
⑨	7	9	Joan Baez In Concert, Part 2	*Joan Baez*...Vanguard 2123
⑩	8	55	(Moving)	*Peter, Paul & Mary*...Warner 1473

Billboard — FEBRUARY 8, 1964 — TOP LP's

TW	LW	WK	Title	Artist...Label
①	1	14	**The Singing Nun**	*The Singing Nun*...Philips 203
②	2	16	In The Wind	*Peter, Paul & Mary*...Warner 1507
❸	92	2	Meet The Beatles!	*The Beatles*...Capitol 2047
④	5	14	**Little Deuce Coupe**	*The Beach Boys*...Capitol 1998
⑤	6	7	**That Was The Week That Was**	*John Fitzgerald Kennedy*...Decca 9116
⑥	4	94	Peter, Paul and Mary	*Peter, Paul & Mary*...Warner 1449
⑦	3	8	Fun in Acapulco	*Elvis Presley/Soundtrack*...RCA LSP-2756
⑧	8	7	**The Presidential Years 1960-1963**	*John Fitzgerald Kennedy*...20th Century 3127
⑨	7	120	West Side Story	*Soundtrack*...Columbia 2070
⑩	11	22	The Second Barbra Streisand Album	*Barbra Streisand*...Columbia 8854

Billboard — FEBRUARY 15, 1964 — TOP LP's

TW	LW	WK	Title	Artist...Label
①	3	3	**Meet The Beatles!**	*The Beatles*...Capitol 2047
②	1	15	The Singing Nun	*The Singing Nun*...Philips 203
③	2	17	In The Wind	*Peter, Paul & Mary*...Warner 1507
④	4	15	**Little Deuce Coupe**	*The Beach Boys*...Capitol 1998
⑤	9	121	West Side Story	*Soundtrack*...Columbia 2070
⑥	6	95	Peter, Paul and Mary	*Peter, Paul & Mary*...Warner 1449
⑦	11	57	(Moving)	*Peter, Paul & Mary*...Warner 1473
⑧	12	11	Joan Baez In Concert, Part 2	*Joan Baez*...Vanguard 2123
⑨	10	23	The Second Barbra Streisand Album	*Barbra Streisand*...Columbia 8854
⑩	16	22	Honey In The Horn	*Al Hirt*...RCA 2733

Billboard — FEBRUARY 22, 1964 — TOP LP's

TW	LW	WK	Title	Artist...Label
①	1	4	**Meet The Beatles!**	*The Beatles*...Capitol 2047
②	2	16	The Singing Nun	*The Singing Nun*...Philips 203
❸	22	3	Introducing...The Beatles	*The Beatles*...Vee-Jay 1062
④	3	18	In The Wind	*Peter, Paul & Mary*...Warner 1507
⑤	10	23	Honey In The Horn	*Al Hirt*...RCA 2733
❻	12	9	**Charade**	*Henry Mancini & His Orchestra/Soundtrack*...RCA 2755
⑦	8	12	**Joan Baez In Concert, Part 2**	*Joan Baez*...Vanguard 2123
⑧	6	96	Peter, Paul and Mary	*Peter, Paul & Mary*...Warner 1449
⑨	11	10	Fun in Acapulco	*Elvis Presley/Soundtrack*...RCA LSP-2756
⑩	4	16	Little Deuce Coupe	*The Beach Boys*...Capitol 1998

Billboard — FEBRUARY 29, 1964 — TOP LP's

TW	LW	WK		
1	1	5	**Meet The Beatles!**	*The Beatles*...Capitol 2047
2	3	4	**Introducing...The Beatles**	*The Beatles*...Vee-Jay 1062
3	4	19	In The Wind	*Peter, Paul & Mary*...Warner 1507
4	2	17	The Singing Nun	*The Singing Nun*...Philips 203
5	5	24	Honey In The Horn	*Al Hirt*...RCA 2733
6	6	10	**Charade**	*Henry Mancini & His Orchestra/Soundtrack*...RCA 2755
7	9	11	Fun in Acapulco	*Elvis Presley/Soundtrack*...RCA LSP-2756
8	7	13	Joan Baez In Concert, Part 2	*Joan Baez*...Vanguard 2123
9	13	6	**The Wonderful World Of Andy Williams**	*Andy Williams*...Columbia 8937
10	11	25	The Second Barbra Streisand Album	*Barbra Streisand*...Columbia 8854

Billboard — MARCH 7, 1964 — TOP LP's

TW	LW	WK		
1	1	6	**Meet The Beatles!**	*The Beatles*...Capitol 2047
2	2	5	**Introducing...The Beatles**	*The Beatles*...Vee-Jay 1062
3	5	25	**Honey In The Horn**	*Al Hirt*...RCA 2733
4	3	20	In The Wind	*Peter, Paul & Mary*...Warner 1507
5	4	18	The Singing Nun	*The Singing Nun*...Philips 203
6	13	7	Yesterday's Love Songs/Today's Blues	*Nancy Wilson*...Capitol 2012
7	6	11	Charade	*Henry Mancini & His Orchestra/Soundtrack*...RCA 2755
8	25	3	Hello, Dolly!	*Original Cast*...RCA 1087
9	9	7	**The Wonderful World Of Andy Williams**	*Andy Williams*...Columbia 8937
10	12	6	There! I've Said It Again	*Bobby Vinton*...Epic 26081

Billboard — MARCH 14, 1964 — TOP LP's

TW	LW	WK		
1	1	7	**Meet The Beatles!**	*The Beatles*...Capitol 2047
2	2	6	**Introducing...The Beatles**	*The Beatles*...Vee-Jay 1062
3	3	26	**Honey In The Horn**	*Al Hirt*...RCA 2733
4	6	8	**Yesterday's Love Songs/Today's Blues**	*Nancy Wilson*...Capitol 2012
5	8	4	Hello, Dolly!	*Original Cast*...RCA 1087
6	5	19	The Singing Nun	*The Singing Nun*...Philips 203
7	7	12	Charade	*Henry Mancini & His Orchestra/Soundtrack*...RCA 2755
8	53	3	The Third Album	*Barbra Streisand*...Columbia 8954
9	4	21	In The Wind	*Peter, Paul & Mary*...Warner 1507
10	10	7	There! I've Said It Again	*Bobby Vinton*...Epic 26081

Billboard — MARCH 21, 1964 — TOP LP's

TW	LW	WK		
1	1	8	**Meet The Beatles!**	*The Beatles*...Capitol 2047
2	2	7	**Introducing...The Beatles**	*The Beatles*...Vee-Jay 1062
3	3	27	**Honey In The Horn**	*Al Hirt*...RCA 2733
4	5	5	Hello, Dolly!	*Original Cast*...RCA 1087
5	8	4	**The Third Album**	*Barbra Streisand*...Columbia 8954
6	4	9	Yesterday's Love Songs/Today's Blues	*Nancy Wilson*...Capitol 2012
7	9	22	In The Wind	*Peter, Paul & Mary*...Warner 1507
8	6	20	The Singing Nun	*The Singing Nun*...Philips 203
9	11	9	**The Wonderful World Of Andy Williams**	*Andy Williams*...Columbia 8937
10	7	13	Charade	*Henry Mancini & His Orchestra/Soundtrack*...RCA 2755

Billboard — MARCH 28, 1964 — TOP LP's

TW	LW	WK			
1	1	9	**Meet The Beatles!**	*The Beatles*	Capitol 2047
2	2	8	**Introducing...The Beatles**	*The Beatles*	Vee-Jay 1062
3	3	28	**Honey In The Horn**	*Al Hirt*	RCA 2733
4	4	6	Hello, Dolly!	*Original Cast*	RCA 1087
5	5	5	**The Third Album**	*Barbra Streisand*	Columbia 8954
6	7	23	In The Wind	*Peter, Paul & Mary*	Warner 1507
7	6	10	Yesterday's Love Songs/Today's Blues	*Nancy Wilson*	Capitol 2012
8	11	9	**There! I've Said It Again**	*Bobby Vinton*	Epic 26081
9	17	101	Peter, Paul and Mary	*Peter, Paul & Mary*	Warner 1449
10	9	10	The Wonderful World Of Andy Williams	*Andy Williams*	Columbia 8937

Billboard — APRIL 4, 1964 — TOP LP's

TW	LW	WK			
1	1	10	**Meet The Beatles!**	*The Beatles*	Capitol 2047
2	2	9	**Introducing...The Beatles**	*The Beatles*	Vee-Jay 1062
3	3	29	**Honey In The Horn**	*Al Hirt*	RCA 2733
4	4	7	Hello, Dolly!	*Original Cast*	RCA 1087
5	5	6	**The Third Album**	*Barbra Streisand*	Columbia 8954
6	6	24	In The Wind	*Peter, Paul & Mary*	Warner 1507
7	7	11	Yesterday's Love Songs/Today's Blues	*Nancy Wilson*	Capitol 2012
8	8	10	**There! I've Said It Again**	*Bobby Vinton*	Epic 26081
9	9	102	Peter, Paul and Mary	*Peter, Paul & Mary*	Warner 1449
10	11	15	Charade	*Henry Mancini & His Orchestra/Soundtrack*	RCA 2755

Billboard — APRIL 11, 1964 — TOP LP's

TW	LW	WK			
1	1	11	**Meet The Beatles!**	*The Beatles*	Capitol 2047
2	2	10	**Introducing...The Beatles**	*The Beatles*	Vee-Jay 1062
3	3	30	**Honey In The Horn**	*Al Hirt*	RCA 2733
4	4	8	Hello, Dolly!	*Original Cast*	RCA 1087
5	5	7	**The Third Album**	*Barbra Streisand*	Columbia 8954
6	10	16	**Charade**	*Henry Mancini & His Orchestra/Soundtrack*	RCA 2755
7	6	25	In The Wind	*Peter, Paul & Mary*	Warner 1507
8	7	12	Yesterday's Love Songs/Today's Blues	*Nancy Wilson*	Capitol 2012
9	8	11	There! I've Said It Again	*Bobby Vinton*	Epic 26081
10	19	3	Dawn (Go Away) and 11 other great songs	*The 4 Seasons*	Philips 124

Billboard — APRIL 18, 1964 — TOP LP's

TW	LW	WK			
1	1	12	**Meet The Beatles!**	*The Beatles*	Capitol 2047
2	2	11	**Introducing...The Beatles**	*The Beatles*	Vee-Jay 1062
3	3	31	**Honey In The Horn**	*Al Hirt*	RCA 2733
4	4	9	Hello, Dolly!	*Original Cast*	RCA 1087
5	5	8	**The Third Album**	*Barbra Streisand*	Columbia 8954
6	10	4	**Dawn (Go Away) and 11 other great songs**	*The 4 Seasons*	Philips 124
7	7	26	In The Wind	*Peter, Paul & Mary*	Warner 1507
8	6	17	Charade	*Henry Mancini & His Orchestra/Soundtrack*	RCA 2755
9	13	5	**Sweet & Sour Tears**	*Ray Charles*	ABC-Paramount 480
10	11	8	**Pure Dynamite! Live At The Royal**	*James Brown*	King 883

Billboard — APRIL 25, 1964 — TOP LP's

TW	LW	WK	Title	Artist	Label
1	1	13	**Meet The Beatles!**	*The Beatles*	Capitol 2047
2	2	12	**Introducing...The Beatles**	*The Beatles*	Vee-Jay 1062
3	3	32	**Honey In The Horn**	*Al Hirt*	RCA 2733
4	4	10	Hello, Dolly!	*Original Cast*	RCA 1087
5	5	9	**The Third Album**	*Barbra Streisand*	Columbia 8954
6	6	5	**Dawn (Go Away) and 11 other great songs**	*The 4 Seasons*	Philips 124
7	41	3	Glad All Over	*The Dave Clark Five*	Epic 26093
8	7	27	In The Wind	*Peter, Paul & Mary*	Warner 1507
9	9	6	**Sweet & Sour Tears**	*Ray Charles*	ABC-Paramount 480
10	23	3	Kissin' Cousins	*Elvis Presley/Soundtrack*	RCA LSP-2894

Billboard — MAY 2, 1964 — TOP LP's

TW	LW	WK	Title	Artist	Label
1	16	2	**The Beatles' Second Album**	*The Beatles*	Capitol 2080
2	1	14	Meet The Beatles!	*The Beatles*	Capitol 2047
3	4	11	Hello, Dolly!	*Original Cast*	RCA 1087
4	2	13	Introducing...The Beatles	*The Beatles*	Vee-Jay 1062
5	3	33	Honey In The Horn	*Al Hirt*	RCA 2733
6	10	4	**Kissin' Cousins**	*Elvis Presley/Soundtrack*	RCA LSP-2894
7	7	4	Glad All Over	*The Dave Clark Five*	Epic 26093
8	5	10	The Third Album	*Barbra Streisand*	Columbia 8954
9	6	6	Dawn (Go Away) and 11 other great songs	*The 4 Seasons*	Philips 124
10	8	28	In The Wind	*Peter, Paul & Mary*	Warner 1507

Billboard — MAY 9, 1964 — TOP LP's

TW	LW	WK	Title	Artist	Label
1	1	3	**The Beatles' Second Album**	*The Beatles*	Capitol 2080
2	2	15	Meet The Beatles!	*The Beatles*	Capitol 2047
3	3	12	Hello, Dolly!	*Original Cast*	RCA 1087
4	7	5	Glad All Over	*The Dave Clark Five*	Epic 26093
5	5	34	Honey In The Horn	*Al Hirt*	RCA 2733
6	6	5	**Kissin' Cousins**	*Elvis Presley/Soundtrack*	RCA LSP-2894
7	4	14	Introducing...The Beatles	*The Beatles*	Vee-Jay 1062
8	8	11	The Third Album	*Barbra Streisand*	Columbia 8954
9	9	7	Dawn (Go Away) and 11 other great songs	*The 4 Seasons*	Philips 124
10	11	5	**Days Of Wine And Roses, Moon River, and other academy award winners**	*Frank Sinatra*	Reprise 1011

Billboard — MAY 16, 1964 — TOP LP's

TW	LW	WK	Title	Artist	Label
1	1	4	**The Beatles' Second Album**	*The Beatles*	Capitol 2080
2	3	13	Hello, Dolly!	*Original Cast*	RCA 1087
3	2	16	Meet The Beatles!	*The Beatles*	Capitol 2047
4	4	6	Glad All Over	*The Dave Clark Five*	Epic 26093
5	5	35	Honey In The Horn	*Al Hirt*	RCA 2733
6	6	6	**Kissin' Cousins**	*Elvis Presley/Soundtrack*	RCA LSP-2894
7	7	15	Introducing...The Beatles	*The Beatles*	Vee-Jay 1062
8	13	3	Funny Girl	*Barbra Streisand*	Capitol 2059
9	8	12	The Third Album	*Barbra Streisand*	Columbia 8954
10	10	6	**Days Of Wine And Roses, Moon River, and other academy award winners**	*Frank Sinatra*	Reprise 1011

Billboard — MAY 23, 1964 — TOP LP's

TW	LW	WK		
1	1	5	**The Beatles' Second Album**	*The Beatles*...Capitol 2080
2	2	14	Hello, Dolly!	*Original Cast*...RCA 1087
3	4	7	**Glad All Over**	*The Dave Clark Five*...Epic 26093
4	8	4	Funny Girl	*Barbra Streisand*...Capitol 2059
5	3	17	Meet The Beatles!	*The Beatles*...Capitol 2047
6	5	36	Honey In The Horn	*Al Hirt*...RCA 2733
7	6	7	Kissin' Cousins	*Elvis Presley/Soundtrack*...RCA LSP-2894
8	7	16	Introducing...The Beatles	*The Beatles*...Vee-Jay 1062
9	9	13	The Third Album	*Barbra Streisand*...Columbia 8954
10	13	31	In The Wind	*Peter, Paul & Mary*...Warner 1507

Billboard — MAY 30, 1964 — TOP LP's

TW	LW	WK		
1	1	6	**The Beatles' Second Album**	*The Beatles*...Capitol 2080
2	2	15	Hello, Dolly!	*Original Cast*...RCA 1087
3	4	5	Funny Girl	*Barbra Streisand*...Capitol 2059
4	18	3	Hello, Dolly!	*Louis Armstrong*...Kapp 3364
5	5	18	Meet The Beatles!	*The Beatles*...Capitol 2047
6	6	37	Honey In The Horn	*Al Hirt*...RCA 2733
7	3	8	Glad All Over	*The Dave Clark Five*...Epic 26093
8	21	4	The Academy Award Winning "Call Me Irresponsible"	*Andy Williams*...Columbia 8971
9	9	14	The Third Album	*Barbra Streisand*...Columbia 8954
10	8	17	Introducing...The Beatles	*The Beatles*...Vee-Jay 1062

Billboard — JUNE 6, 1964 — TOP LP's

TW	LW	WK		
1	2	16	**Hello, Dolly!**	*Original Cast*...RCA 1087
2	3	6	**Funny Girl**	*Barbra Streisand*...Capitol 2059
3	4	4	Hello, Dolly!	*Louis Armstrong*...Kapp 3364
4	1	7	The Beatles' Second Album	*The Beatles*...Capitol 2080
5	8	5	**The Academy Award Winning "Call Me Irresponsible"**	*Andy Williams*...Columbia 8971
6	5	19	Meet The Beatles!	*The Beatles*...Capitol 2047
7	6	38	Honey In The Horn	*Al Hirt*...RCA 2733
8	7	9	Glad All Over	*The Dave Clark Five*...Epic 26093
9	12	8	**Today**	*New Christy Minstrels/Soundtrack*...Columbia 8959
10	9	15	The Third Album	*Barbra Streisand*...Columbia 8954

Billboard — JUNE 13, 1964 — TOP LP's

TW	LW	WK		
1	3	5	**Hello, Dolly!**	*Louis Armstrong*...Kapp 3364
2	2	7	**Funny Girl**	*Barbra Streisand*...Capitol 2059
3	1	17	Hello, Dolly!	*Original Cast*...RCA 1087
4	4	8	The Beatles' Second Album	*The Beatles*...Capitol 2080
5	5	6	**The Academy Award Winning "Call Me Irresponsible"**	*Andy Williams*...Columbia 8971
6	7	39	Honey In The Horn	*Al Hirt*...RCA 2733
7	6	20	Meet The Beatles!	*The Beatles*...Capitol 2047
8	8	10	Glad All Over	*The Dave Clark Five*...Epic 26093
9	9	9	**Today**	*New Christy Minstrels/Soundtrack*...Columbia 8959
10	10	16	The Third Album	*Barbra Streisand*...Columbia 8954

Billboard — JUNE 20, 1964 — TOP LP's

TW	LW	WK	Title	Artist	Label
1	1	6	**Hello, Dolly!**	Louis Armstrong	Kapp 3364
2	2	8	**Funny Girl**	Barbra Streisand	Capitol 2059
3	3	18	Hello, Dolly!	Original Cast	RCA 1087
4	4	9	The Beatles' Second Album	The Beatles	Capitol 2080
5	5	7	**The Academy Award Winning "Call Me Irresponsible"**	Andy Williams	Columbia 8971
6	6	40	Honey In The Horn	Al Hirt	RCA 2733
7	10	17	The Third Album	Barbra Streisand	Columbia 8954
8	11	5	Cotton Candy	Al Hirt	RCA 2917
9	7	21	Meet The Beatles!	The Beatles	Capitol 2047
10	8	11	Glad All Over	The Dave Clark Five	Epic 26093

Billboard — JUNE 27, 1964 — TOP LP's

TW	LW	WK	Title	Artist	Label
1	1	7	**Hello, Dolly!**	Louis Armstrong	Kapp 3364
2	3	19	Hello, Dolly!	Original Cast	RCA 1087
3	2	9	Funny Girl	Barbra Streisand	Capitol 2059
4	4	10	The Beatles' Second Album	The Beatles	Capitol 2080
5	7	18	**The Third Album**	Barbra Streisand	Columbia 8954
6	8	6	**Cotton Candy**	Al Hirt	RCA 2917
7	5	8	The Academy Award Winning "Call Me Irresponsible"	Andy Williams	Columbia 8971
8	6	41	Honey In The Horn	Al Hirt	RCA 2733
9	9	22	Meet The Beatles!	The Beatles	Capitol 2047
10	11	5	**Today, Tomorrow, Forever**	Nancy Wilson	Capitol 2082

Billboard — JULY 4, 1964 — TOP LP's

TW	LW	WK	Title	Artist	Label
1	1	8	**Hello, Dolly!**	Louis Armstrong	Kapp 3364
2	2	20	Hello, Dolly!	Original Cast	RCA 1087
3	3	10	Funny Girl	Barbra Streisand	Capitol 2059
4	4	11	The Beatles' Second Album	The Beatles	Capitol 2080
5	5	19	**The Third Album**	Barbra Streisand	Columbia 8954
6	6	7	**Cotton Candy**	Al Hirt	RCA 2917
7	14	5	Getz/Gilberto	Stan Getz/Joao Gilberto	Verve 8545
8	7	9	The Academy Award Winning "Call Me Irresponsible"	Andy Williams	Columbia 8971
9	11	13	Glad All Over	The Dave Clark Five	Epic 26093
10	10	6	**Today, Tomorrow, Forever**	Nancy Wilson	Capitol 2082

Billboard — JULY 11, 1964 — TOP LP's

TW	LW	WK	Title	Artist	Label
1	1	9	**Hello, Dolly!**	Louis Armstrong	Kapp 3364
2	2	21	Hello, Dolly!	Original Cast	RCA 1087
3	3	11	Funny Girl	Barbra Streisand	Capitol 2059
4	7	6	Getz/Gilberto	Stan Getz/Joao Gilberto	Verve 8545
5	4	12	The Beatles' Second Album	The Beatles	Capitol 2080
6	11	4	The Dave Clark Five Return!	The Dave Clark Five	Epic 26104
7	5	20	The Third Album	Barbra Streisand	Columbia 8954
8	6	8	Cotton Candy	Al Hirt	RCA 2917
9	8	10	The Academy Award Winning "Call Me Irresponsible"	Andy Williams	Columbia 8971
10	10	7	**Today, Tomorrow, Forever**	Nancy Wilson	Capitol 2082

TW	LW	WK	Billboard. JULY 18, 1964 TOP LP's		
1	1	10	**Hello, Dolly!**	*Louis Armstrong*	Kapp 3364
2	2	22	Hello, Dolly!	*Original Cast*	RCA 1087
3	3	12	Funny Girl	*Barbra Streisand*	Capitol 2059
4	4	7	Getz/Gilberto	*Stan Getz/Joao Gilberto*	Verve 8545
5	6	5	**The Dave Clark Five Return!**	*The Dave Clark Five*	Epic 26104
6	7	21	The Third Album	*Barbra Streisand*	Columbia 8954
7	5	13	The Beatles' Second Album	*The Beatles*	Capitol 2080
8	8	9	Cotton Candy	*Al Hirt*	RCA 2917
9	9	11	The Academy Award Winning "Call Me Irresponsible"	*Andy Williams*	Columbia 8971
10	11	44	Honey In The Horn	*Al Hirt*	RCA 2733

TW	LW	WK	Billboard. JULY 25, 1964 TOP LP's		
1	12	2	**A Hard Day's Night**	*The Beatles/Soundtrack*	United Artists 6366
2	2	23	Hello, Dolly!	*Original Cast*	RCA 1087
3	1	11	Hello, Dolly!	*Louis Armstrong*	Kapp 3364
4	3	13	Funny Girl	*Barbra Streisand*	Capitol 2059
5	4	8	Getz/Gilberto	*Stan Getz/Joao Gilberto*	Verve 8545
6	5	6	The Dave Clark Five Return!	*The Dave Clark Five*	Epic 26104
7	8	10	Cotton Candy	*Al Hirt*	RCA 2917
8	6	22	The Third Album	*Barbra Streisand*	Columbia 8954
9	7	14	The Beatles' Second Album	*The Beatles*	Capitol 2080
10	10	45	Honey In The Horn	*Al Hirt*	RCA 2733

TW	LW	WK	Billboard. AUGUST 1, 1964 TOP LP's		
1	1	3	**A Hard Day's Night**	*The Beatles/Soundtrack*	United Artists 6366
2	2	24	Hello, Dolly!	*Original Cast*	RCA 1087
3	3	12	Hello, Dolly!	*Louis Armstrong*	Kapp 3364
4	5	9	Getz/Gilberto	*Stan Getz/Joao Gilberto*	Verve 8545
5	4	14	Funny Girl	*Barbra Streisand*	Capitol 2059
6	6	7	The Dave Clark Five Return!	*The Dave Clark Five*	Epic 26104
7	7	11	Cotton Candy	*Al Hirt*	RCA 2917
8	8	23	The Third Album	*Barbra Streisand*	Columbia 8954
9	9	15	The Beatles' Second Album	*The Beatles*	Capitol 2080
10	10	46	Honey In The Horn	*Al Hirt*	RCA 2733

TW	LW	WK	Billboard. AUGUST 8, 1964 TOP LP's		
1	1	4	**A Hard Day's Night**	*The Beatles/Soundtrack*	United Artists 6366
2	4	10	**Getz/Gilberto**	*Stan Getz/Joao Gilberto*	Verve 8545
3	3	13	Hello, Dolly!	*Louis Armstrong*	Kapp 3364
4	2	25	Hello, Dolly!	*Original Cast*	RCA 1087
5	5	15	Funny Girl	*Barbra Streisand*	Capitol 2059
6	6	8	The Dave Clark Five Return!	*The Dave Clark Five*	Epic 26104
7	8	24	The Third Album	*Barbra Streisand*	Columbia 8954
8	7	12	Cotton Candy	*Al Hirt*	RCA 2917
9	9	16	The Beatles' Second Album	*The Beatles*	Capitol 2080
10	10	47	Honey In The Horn	*Al Hirt*	RCA 2733

Billboard — AUGUST 15, 1964 — TOP LP's

TW	LW	WK			
1	1	5	**A Hard Day's Night**	*The Beatles/Soundtrack*	United Artists 6366
2	2	11	**Getz/Gilberto**	*Stan Getz/Joao Gilberto*	Verve 8545
3	3	14	Hello, Dolly!	*Louis Armstrong*	Kapp 3364
4	5	16	Funny Girl	*Barbra Streisand*	Capitol 2059
5	4	26	Hello, Dolly!	*Original Cast*	RCA 1087
6	125	2	Something New	*The Beatles*	Capitol 2108
7	13	3	All Summer Long	*The Beach Boys*	Capitol 2110
8	11	19	**The Pink Panther**	*Henry Mancini & His Orchestra/Soundtrack*	RCA 2795
9	6	9	The Dave Clark Five Return!	*The Dave Clark Five*	Epic 26104
10	8	13	Cotton Candy	*Al Hirt*	RCA 2917

Billboard — AUGUST 22, 1964 — TOP LP's

TW	LW	WK			
1	1	6	**A Hard Day's Night**	*The Beatles/Soundtrack*	United Artists 6366
2	6	3	**Something New**	*The Beatles*	Capitol 2108
3	2	12	Getz/Gilberto	*Stan Getz/Joao Gilberto*	Verve 8545
4	7	4	**All Summer Long**	*The Beach Boys*	Capitol 2110
5	3	15	Hello, Dolly!	*Louis Armstrong*	Kapp 3364
6	4	17	Funny Girl	*Barbra Streisand*	Capitol 2059
7	5	27	Hello, Dolly!	*Original Cast*	RCA 1087
8	8	20	**The Pink Panther**	*Henry Mancini & His Orchestra/Soundtrack*	RCA 2795
9	9	10	The Dave Clark Five Return!	*The Dave Clark Five*	Epic 26104
10	10	14	Cotton Candy	*Al Hirt*	RCA 2917

Billboard — AUGUST 29, 1964 — TOP LP's

TW	LW	WK			
1	1	7	**A Hard Day's Night**	*The Beatles/Soundtrack*	United Artists 6366
2	2	4	**Something New**	*The Beatles*	Capitol 2108
3	3	13	Getz/Gilberto	*Stan Getz/Joao Gilberto*	Verve 8545
4	4	5	**All Summer Long**	*The Beach Boys*	Capitol 2110
5	21	3	Everybody Loves Somebody	*Dean Martin*	Reprise 6130
6	6	18	Funny Girl	*Barbra Streisand*	Capitol 2059
7	5	16	Hello, Dolly!	*Louis Armstrong*	Kapp 3364
8	7	28	Hello, Dolly!	*Original Cast*	RCA 1087
9	12	4	Rag Doll	*The 4 Seasons*	Philips 146
10	10	15	Cotton Candy	*Al Hirt*	RCA 2917

Billboard — SEPTEMBER 5, 1964 — TOP LP's

TW	LW	WK			
1	1	8	**A Hard Day's Night**	*The Beatles/Soundtrack*	United Artists 6366
2	2	5	**Something New**	*The Beatles*	Capitol 2108
3	5	4	Everybody Loves Somebody	*Dean Martin*	Reprise 6130
4	4	6	**All Summer Long**	*The Beach Boys*	Capitol 2110
5	3	14	Getz/Gilberto	*Stan Getz/Joao Gilberto*	Verve 8545
6	6	19	Funny Girl	*Barbra Streisand*	Capitol 2059
7	7	17	Hello, Dolly!	*Louis Armstrong*	Kapp 3364
8	15	4	Peter, Paul and Mary In Concert	*Peter, Paul & Mary*	Warner 1555
9	9	5	Rag Doll	*The 4 Seasons*	Philips 146
10	8	29	Hello, Dolly!	*Original Cast*	RCA 1087

Billboard — SEPTEMBER 12, 1964 — TOP LP's

TW	LW	WK			
1	1	9	**A Hard Day's Night**	*The Beatles/Soundtrack*	United Artists 6366
2	2	6	**Something New**	*The Beatles*	Capitol 2108
3	3	5	Everybody Loves Somebody	*Dean Martin*	Reprise 6130
4	4	7	**All Summer Long**	*The Beach Boys*	Capitol 2110
5	5	15	Getz/Gilberto	*Stan Getz/Joao Gilberto*	Verve 8545
6	8	5	Peter, Paul and Mary In Concert	*Peter, Paul & Mary*	Warner 1555
7	7	18	Hello, Dolly!	*Louis Armstrong*	Kapp 3364
8	9	6	Rag Doll	*The 4 Seasons*	Philips 146
9	6	20	Funny Girl	*Barbra Streisand*	Capitol 2059
10	10	30	Hello, Dolly!	*Original Cast*	RCA 1087

Billboard — SEPTEMBER 19, 1964 — TOP LP's

TW	LW	WK			
1	1	10	**A Hard Day's Night**	*The Beatles/Soundtrack*	United Artists 6366
2	2	7	**Something New**	*The Beatles*	Capitol 2108
3	3	6	Everybody Loves Somebody	*Dean Martin*	Reprise 6130
4	4	8	**All Summer Long**	*The Beach Boys*	Capitol 2110
5	6	6	Peter, Paul and Mary In Concert	*Peter, Paul & Mary*	Warner 1555
6	5	16	Getz/Gilberto	*Stan Getz/Joao Gilberto*	Verve 8545
7	8	7	**Rag Doll**	*The 4 Seasons*	Philips 146
8	7	19	Hello, Dolly!	*Louis Armstrong*	Kapp 3364
9	9	21	Funny Girl	*Barbra Streisand*	Capitol 2059
10	10	31	Hello, Dolly!	*Original Cast*	RCA 1087

Billboard — SEPTEMBER 26, 1964 — TOP LP's

TW	LW	WK			
1	1	11	**A Hard Day's Night**	*The Beatles/Soundtrack*	United Artists 6366
2	2	8	**Something New**	*The Beatles*	Capitol 2108
3	3	7	Everybody Loves Somebody	*Dean Martin*	Reprise 6130
4	5	7	**Peter, Paul and Mary In Concert**	*Peter, Paul & Mary*	Warner 1555
5	4	9	All Summer Long	*The Beach Boys*	Capitol 2110
6	6	17	Getz/Gilberto	*Stan Getz/Joao Gilberto*	Verve 8545
7	8	20	Hello, Dolly!	*Louis Armstrong*	Kapp 3364
8	9	22	Funny Girl	*Barbra Streisand*	Capitol 2059
9	10	32	Hello, Dolly!	*Original Cast*	RCA 1087
10	7	8	Rag Doll	*The 4 Seasons*	Philips 146

Billboard — OCTOBER 3, 1964 — TOP LP's

TW	LW	WK			
1	1	12	**A Hard Day's Night**	*The Beatles/Soundtrack*	United Artists 6366
2	2	9	**Something New**	*The Beatles*	Capitol 2108
3	3	8	Everybody Loves Somebody	*Dean Martin*	Reprise 6130
4	4	8	**Peter, Paul and Mary In Concert**	*Peter, Paul & Mary*	Warner 1555
5	5	10	All Summer Long	*The Beach Boys*	Capitol 2110
6	18	5	How Glad I Am	*Nancy Wilson*	Capitol 2155
7	6	18	Getz/Gilberto	*Stan Getz/Joao Gilberto*	Verve 8545
8	8	23	Funny Girl	*Barbra Streisand*	Capitol 2059
9	9	33	Hello, Dolly!	*Original Cast*	RCA 1087
10	17	9	Keep On Pushing	*The Impressions*	ABC-Paramount 493

TW	LW	WK	Billboard. OCTOBER 10, 1964	TOP LP's
1	1	13	**A Hard Day's Night**	*The Beatles/Soundtrack*...United Artists 6366
2	2	10	**Something New**	*The Beatles*...Capitol 2108
3	3	9	Everybody Loves Somebody	*Dean Martin*...Reprise 6130
4	4	9	**Peter, Paul and Mary In Concert**	*Peter, Paul & Mary*...Warner 1555
5	5	11	All Summer Long	*The Beach Boys*...Capitol 2110
6	6	6	How Glad I Am	*Nancy Wilson*...Capitol 2155
7	7	19	Getz/Gilberto	*Stan Getz/Joao Gilberto*...Verve 8545
8	10	10	**Keep On Pushing**	*The Impressions*...ABC-Paramount 493
9	9	34	Hello, Dolly!	*Original Cast*...RCA 1087
10	8	24	Funny Girl	*Barbra Streisand*...Capitol 2059

TW	LW	WK	Billboard. OCTOBER 17, 1964	TOP LP's
1	1	14	**A Hard Day's Night**	*The Beatles/Soundtrack*...United Artists 6366
2	2	11	**Something New**	*The Beatles*...Capitol 2108
3	3	10	Everybody Loves Somebody	*Dean Martin*...Reprise 6130
4	17	3	People	*Barbra Streisand*...Columbia 9015
5	6	7	How Glad I Am	*Nancy Wilson*...Capitol 2155
6	4	10	Peter, Paul and Mary In Concert	*Peter, Paul & Mary*...Warner 1555
7	5	12	All Summer Long	*The Beach Boys*...Capitol 2110
8	9	35	Hello, Dolly!	*Original Cast*...RCA 1087
9	8	11	Keep On Pushing	*The Impressions*...ABC-Paramount 493
10	7	20	Getz/Gilberto	*Stan Getz/Joao Gilberto*...Verve 8545

TW	LW	WK	Billboard. OCTOBER 24, 1964	TOP LP's
1	1	15	**A Hard Day's Night**	*The Beatles/Soundtrack*...United Artists 6366
2	4	4	People	*Barbra Streisand*...Columbia 9015
3	3	11	Everybody Loves Somebody	*Dean Martin*...Reprise 6130
4	2	12	Something New	*The Beatles*...Capitol 2108
5	5	8	How Glad I Am	*Nancy Wilson*...Capitol 2155
6	7	13	All Summer Long	*The Beach Boys*...Capitol 2110
7	6	11	Peter, Paul and Mary In Concert	*Peter, Paul & Mary*...Warner 1555
8	8	36	Hello, Dolly!	*Original Cast*...RCA 1087
9	9	12	Keep On Pushing	*The Impressions*...ABC-Paramount 493
10	15	8	The Animals	*The Animals*...MGM 4264

TW	LW	WK	Billboard. OCTOBER 31, 1964	TOP LP's
1	2	5	**People**	*Barbra Streisand*...Columbia 9015
2	3	12	**Everybody Loves Somebody**	*Dean Martin*...Reprise 6130
3	1	16	A Hard Day's Night	*The Beatles/Soundtrack*...United Artists 6366
4	4	13	Something New	*The Beatles*...Capitol 2108
5	5	9	How Glad I Am	*Nancy Wilson*...Capitol 2155
6	6	14	All Summer Long	*The Beach Boys*...Capitol 2110
7	10	9	**The Animals**	*The Animals*...MGM 4264
8	9	13	**Keep On Pushing**	*The Impressions*...ABC-Paramount 493
9	15	6	The Great Songs From "My Fair Lady" and other Broadway hits	*Andy Williams*...Columbia 9005
10	8	37	Hello, Dolly!	*Original Cast*...RCA 1087

TW	LW	WK	Billboard. NOVEMBER 7, 1964 TOP LP's
①	1	6	**People** ... *Barbra Streisand*...Columbia 9015
②	2	13	**Everybody Loves Somebody** ... *Dean Martin*...Reprise 6130
③	3	17	A Hard Day's Night ... *The Beatles/Soundtrack*...United Artists 6366
④	4	14	Something New ... *The Beatles*...Capitol 2108
⑤	5	10	How Glad I Am ... *Nancy Wilson*...Capitol 2155
⑥	6	15	All Summer Long ... *The Beach Boys*...Capitol 2110
⑦	7	10	**The Animals** ... *The Animals*...MGM 4264
⑧	9	7	The Great Songs From "My Fair Lady" and other Broadway hits ... *Andy Williams*...Columbia 9005
⑨	8	14	Keep On Pushing ... *The Impressions*...ABC-Paramount 493
⑩	11	14	The Best Of Jim Reeves ... *Jim Reeves*...RCA 2890

TW	LW	WK	Billboard. NOVEMBER 14, 1964 TOP LP's
①	1	7	**People** ... *Barbra Streisand*...Columbia 9015
②	2	14	**Everybody Loves Somebody** ... *Dean Martin*...Reprise 6130
③	3	18	A Hard Day's Night ... *The Beatles/Soundtrack*...United Artists 6366
④	5	11	**How Glad I Am** ... *Nancy Wilson*...Capitol 2155
⑤	4	15	Something New ... *The Beatles*...Capitol 2108
⑥	6	16	All Summer Long ... *The Beach Boys*...Capitol 2110
⑦	7	11	**The Animals** ... *The Animals*...MGM 4264
⑧	8	8	The Great Songs From "My Fair Lady" and other Broadway hits ... *Andy Williams*...Columbia 9005
⑨	10	15	**The Best Of Jim Reeves** ... *Jim Reeves*...RCA 2890
⑩	11	13	Sugar Lips ... *Al Hirt*...RCA 2965

TW	LW	WK	Billboard. NOVEMBER 21, 1964 TOP LP's
①	1	8	**People** ... *Barbra Streisand*...Columbia 9015
②	2	15	**Everybody Loves Somebody** ... *Dean Martin*...Reprise 6130
③	3	19	A Hard Day's Night ... *The Beatles/Soundtrack*...United Artists 6366
④	4	12	**How Glad I Am** ... *Nancy Wilson*...Capitol 2155
⑤	6	17	All Summer Long ... *The Beach Boys*...Capitol 2110
⑥	5	16	Something New ... *The Beatles*...Capitol 2108
❼	44	3	Beach Boys Concert ... *The Beach Boys*...Capitol 2198
⑧	8	9	The Great Songs From "My Fair Lady" and other Broadway hits ... *Andy Williams*...Columbia 9005
⑨	10	14	**Sugar Lips** ... *Al Hirt*...RCA 2965
⑩	9	16	The Best Of Jim Reeves ... *Jim Reeves*...RCA 2890

TW	LW	WK	Billboard. NOVEMBER 28, 1964 TOP LP's
①	1	9	**People** ... *Barbra Streisand*...Columbia 9015
❷	7	4	Beach Boys Concert ... *The Beach Boys*...Capitol 2198
③	2	16	Everybody Loves Somebody ... *Dean Martin*...Reprise 6130
④	3	20	A Hard Day's Night ... *The Beatles/Soundtrack*...United Artists 6366
⑤	4	13	How Glad I Am ... *Nancy Wilson*...Capitol 2155
⑥	6	17	Something New ... *The Beatles*...Capitol 2108
⑦	8	10	The Great Songs From "My Fair Lady" and other Broadway hits ... *Andy Williams*...Columbia 9005
⑧	5	18	All Summer Long ... *The Beach Boys*...Capitol 2110
⑨	9	15	**Sugar Lips** ... *Al Hirt*...RCA 2965
⑩	11	29	Hello, Dolly! ... *Louis Armstrong*...Kapp 3364

Billboard — DECEMBER 5, 1964 — TOP LP's

TW	LW	WK			
1	2	5	**Beach Boys Concert**	*The Beach Boys*	Capitol 2198
2	1	10	People	*Barbra Streisand*	Columbia 9015
3	3	17	Everybody Loves Somebody	*Dean Martin*	Reprise 6130
4	4	21	A Hard Day's Night	*The Beatles/Soundtrack*	United Artists 6366
5	14	4	Roustabout	*Elvis Presley/Soundtrack*	RCA LSP-2999
6	7	11	The Great Songs From "My Fair Lady" and other Broadway hits	*Andy Williams*	Columbia 9005
7	6	18	Something New	*The Beatles*	Capitol 2108
8	13	12	Where Did Our Love Go	*The Supremes*	Motown 621
9	12	9	My Fair Lady	*Soundtrack*	Columbia 2600
10	5	14	How Glad I Am	*Nancy Wilson*	Capitol 2155

Billboard — DECEMBER 12, 1964 — TOP LP's

TW	LW	WK			
1	1	6	**Beach Boys Concert**	*The Beach Boys*	Capitol 2198
2	2	11	People	*Barbra Streisand*	Columbia 9015
3	11	5	**12 x 5**	*The Rolling Stones*	London 402
4	5	5	Roustabout	*Elvis Presley/Soundtrack*	RCA LSP-2999
5	6	12	**The Great Songs From "My Fair Lady" and other Broadway hits**	*Andy Williams*	Columbia 9005
6	9	10	My Fair Lady	*Soundtrack*	Columbia 2600
7	8	13	Where Did Our Love Go	*The Supremes*	Motown 621
8	4	22	A Hard Day's Night	*The Beatles/Soundtrack*	United Artists 6366
9	3	18	Everybody Loves Somebody	*Dean Martin*	Reprise 6130
10	7	19	Something New	*The Beatles*	Capitol 2108

Billboard — DECEMBER 19, 1964 — TOP LP's

TW	LW	WK			
1	1	7	**Beach Boys Concert**	*The Beach Boys*	Capitol 2198
2	4	6	Roustabout	*Elvis Presley/Soundtrack*	RCA LSP-2999
3	3	6	**12 x 5**	*The Rolling Stones*	London 402
4	2	12	People	*Barbra Streisand*	Columbia 9015
5	5	13	**The Great Songs From "My Fair Lady" and other Broadway hits**	*Andy Williams*	Columbia 9005
6	6	11	My Fair Lady	*Soundtrack*	Columbia 2600
7	7	14	Where Did Our Love Go	*The Supremes*	Motown 621
8	14	12	Mary Poppins	*Soundtrack*	Buena Vista 4026
9	16	6	**The Door Is Still Open To My Heart**	*Dean Martin*	Reprise 6140
10	8	23	A Hard Day's Night	*The Beatles/Soundtrack*	United Artists 6366

Billboard — DECEMBER 26, 1964 — TOP LP's

TW	LW	WK			
1	1	8	**Beach Boys Concert**	*The Beach Boys*	Capitol 2198
2	2	7	Roustabout	*Elvis Presley/Soundtrack*	RCA LSP-2999
3	3	7	**12 x 5**	*The Rolling Stones*	London 402
4	4	13	People	*Barbra Streisand*	Columbia 9015
5	7	15	Where Did Our Love Go	*The Supremes*	Motown 621
6	8	13	Mary Poppins	*Soundtrack*	Buena Vista 4026
7	10	24	A Hard Day's Night	*The Beatles/Soundtrack*	United Artists 6366
8	20	3	The Beatles' Story	*The Beatles*	Capitol 2222
9	9	7	**The Door Is Still Open To My Heart**	*Dean Martin*	Reprise 6140
10	6	12	My Fair Lady	*Soundtrack*	Columbia 2600

TW	LW	WK	Billboard ❂ JANUARY 2, 1965 ❂ TOP LP's
①	2	8	**Roustabout** .... *Elvis Presley/Soundtrack*...RCA LSP-2999
②	1	9	Beach Boys Concert .... *The Beach Boys*...Capitol 2198
③	3	8	**12 x 5** .... *The Rolling Stones*...London 402
④	6	14	Mary Poppins .... *Soundtrack*...Buena Vista 4026
⑤	5	16	Where Did Our Love Go .... *The Supremes*...Motown 621
⑥	7	25	A Hard Day's Night .... *The Beatles/Soundtrack*...United Artists 6366
⑦	8	4	**The Beatles' Story** .... *The Beatles*...Capitol 2222
⑧	4	14	People .... *Barbra Streisand*...Columbia 9015
⑨	9	8	**The Door Is Still Open To My Heart** .... *Dean Martin*...Reprise 6140
⑩	10	13	My Fair Lady .... *Soundtrack*...Columbia 2600

TW	LW	WK	Billboard ❂ JANUARY 9, 1965 ❂ TOP LP's
❶	98	2	**Beatles '65** .... *The Beatles*...Capitol 2228
②	1	9	Roustabout .... *Elvis Presley/Soundtrack*...RCA LSP-2999
③	5	17	Where Did Our Love Go .... *The Supremes*...Motown 621
④	4	15	Mary Poppins .... *Soundtrack*...Buena Vista 4026
⑤	2	10	Beach Boys Concert .... *The Beach Boys*...Capitol 2198
⑥	6	26	A Hard Day's Night .... *The Beatles/Soundtrack*...United Artists 6366
⑦	7	5	**The Beatles' Story** .... *The Beatles*...Capitol 2222
⑧	3	9	12 x 5 .... *The Rolling Stones*...London 402
⑨	10	14	My Fair Lady .... *Soundtrack*...Columbia 2600
⑩	8	15	People .... *Barbra Streisand*...Columbia 9015

TW	LW	WK	Billboard ❂ JANUARY 16, 1965 ❂ TOP LP's
①	1	3	**Beatles '65** .... *The Beatles*...Capitol 2228
②	3	18	**Where Did Our Love Go** .... *The Supremes*...Motown 621
③	4	16	Mary Poppins .... *Soundtrack*...Buena Vista 4026
④	5	11	Beach Boys Concert .... *The Beach Boys*...Capitol 2198
⑤	6	27	A Hard Day's Night .... *The Beatles/Soundtrack*...United Artists 6366
⑥	2	10	Roustabout .... *Elvis Presley/Soundtrack*...RCA LSP-2999
⑦	7	6	**The Beatles' Story** .... *The Beatles*...Capitol 2222
⑧	9	15	My Fair Lady .... *Soundtrack*...Columbia 2600
⑨	8	10	12 x 5 .... *The Rolling Stones*...London 402
⑩	10	16	People .... *Barbra Streisand*...Columbia 9015

TW	LW	WK	Billboard ❂ JANUARY 23, 1965 ❂ TOP LP's
①	1	4	**Beatles '65** .... *The Beatles*...Capitol 2228
②	2	19	**Where Did Our Love Go** .... *The Supremes*...Motown 621
③	3	17	Mary Poppins .... *Soundtrack*...Buena Vista 4026
④	4	12	Beach Boys Concert .... *The Beach Boys*...Capitol 2198
⑤	5	28	A Hard Day's Night .... *The Beatles/Soundtrack*...United Artists 6366
⑥	8	16	My Fair Lady .... *Soundtrack*...Columbia 2600
⑦	7	7	**The Beatles' Story** .... *The Beatles*...Capitol 2222
⑧	6	11	Roustabout .... *Elvis Presley/Soundtrack*...RCA LSP-2999
⑨	10	17	People .... *Barbra Streisand*...Columbia 9015
⑩	9	11	12 x 5 .... *The Rolling Stones*...London 402

Billboard JANUARY 30, 1965 TOP LP's

TW	LW	WK	Album	Artist	Label
1	1	5	Beatles '65	The Beatles	Capitol 2228
2	2	20	Where Did Our Love Go	The Supremes	Motown 621
3	3	18	Mary Poppins	Soundtrack	Buena Vista 4026
4	4	13	Beach Boys Concert	The Beach Boys	Capitol 2198
5	6	17	My Fair Lady	Soundtrack	Columbia 2600
6	5	29	A Hard Day's Night	The Beatles/Soundtrack	United Artists 6366
7	11	14	Fiddler On The Roof	Original Cast	RCA 1093
8	8	12	Roustabout	Elvis Presley/Soundtrack	RCA LSP-2999
9	9	18	People	Barbra Streisand	Columbia 9015
10	10	12	12 x 5	The Rolling Stones	London 402

Billboard FEBRUARY 6, 1965 TOP LP's

TW	LW	WK	Album	Artist	Label
1	1	6	Beatles '65	The Beatles	Capitol 2228
2	2	21	Where Did Our Love Go	The Supremes	Motown 621
3	3	19	Mary Poppins	Soundtrack	Buena Vista 4026
4	5	18	My Fair Lady	Soundtrack	Columbia 2600
5	4	14	Beach Boys Concert	The Beach Boys	Capitol 2198
6	15	7	My Love Forgive Me	Robert Goulet	Columbia 9096
7	7	15	Fiddler On The Roof	Original Cast	RCA 1093
8	9	19	People	Barbra Streisand	Columbia 9015
9	11	6	Coast To Coast	The Dave Clark Five	Epic 26128
10	8	13	Roustabout	Elvis Presley/Soundtrack	RCA LSP-2999

Billboard FEBRUARY 13, 1965 TOP LP's

TW	LW	WK	Album	Artist	Label
1	1	7	Beatles '65	The Beatles	Capitol 2228
2	3	20	Mary Poppins	Soundtrack	Buena Vista 4026
3	2	22	Where Did Our Love Go	The Supremes	Motown 621
4	4	19	My Fair Lady	Soundtrack	Columbia 2600
5	5	15	Beach Boys Concert	The Beach Boys	Capitol 2198
6	6	8	My Love Forgive Me	Robert Goulet	Columbia 9096
7	9	7	Coast To Coast	The Dave Clark Five	Epic 26128
8	17	10	Goldfinger	Soundtrack	United Artists 5117
9	10	14	Roustabout	Elvis Presley/Soundtrack	RCA LSP-2999
10	18	4	You've Lost That Lovin' Feelin'	The Righteous Brothers	Philles 4007

Billboard FEBRUARY 20, 1965 TOP LP's

TW	LW	WK	Album	Artist	Label
1	1	8	Beatles '65	The Beatles	Capitol 2228
2	2	21	Mary Poppins	Soundtrack	Buena Vista 4026
3	8	11	Goldfinger	Soundtrack	United Artists 5117
4	3	23	Where Did Our Love Go	The Supremes	Motown 621
5	10	5	You've Lost That Lovin' Feelin'	The Righteous Brothers	Philles 4007
6	6	9	My Love Forgive Me	Robert Goulet	Columbia 9096
7	7	8	Coast To Coast	The Dave Clark Five	Epic 26128
8	5	16	Beach Boys Concert	The Beach Boys	Capitol 2198
9	4	20	My Fair Lady	Soundtrack	Columbia 2600
10	9	15	Roustabout	Elvis Presley/Soundtrack	RCA LSP-2999

Billboard — FEBRUARY 27, 1965 — TOP LP's

TW	LW	WK			
1	1	9	**Beatles '65**	*The Beatles*	Capitol 2228
2	3	12	Goldfinger	*Soundtrack*	United Artists 5117
3	2	22	Mary Poppins	*Soundtrack*	Buena Vista 4026
4	5	6	**You've Lost That Lovin' Feelin'**	*The Righteous Brothers*	Philles 4007
5	6	10	**My Love Forgive Me**	*Robert Goulet*	Columbia 9096
6	7	9	**Coast To Coast**	*The Dave Clark Five*	Epic 26128
7	4	24	Where Did Our Love Go	*The Supremes*	Motown 621
8	9	21	My Fair Lady	*Soundtrack*	Columbia 2600
9	8	17	Beach Boys Concert	*The Beach Boys*	Capitol 2198
10	11	18	Fiddler On The Roof	*Original Cast*	RCA 1093

Billboard — MARCH 6, 1965 — TOP LP's

TW	LW	WK			
1	1	10	**Beatles '65**	*The Beatles*	Capitol 2228
2	2	13	Goldfinger	*Soundtrack*	United Artists 5117
3	3	23	Mary Poppins	*Soundtrack*	Buena Vista 4026
4	4	7	**You've Lost That Lovin' Feelin'**	*The Righteous Brothers*	Philles 4007
5	5	11	**My Love Forgive Me**	*Robert Goulet*	Columbia 9096
6	8	22	My Fair Lady	*Soundtrack*	Columbia 2600
7	7	25	Where Did Our Love Go	*The Supremes*	Motown 621
8	9	18	Beach Boys Concert	*The Beach Boys*	Capitol 2198
9	6	10	Coast To Coast	*The Dave Clark Five*	Epic 26128
10	13	23	People	*Barbra Streisand*	Columbia 9015

Billboard — MARCH 13, 1965 — TOP LP's

TW	LW	WK			
1	3	24	**Mary Poppins**	*Soundtrack*	Buena Vista 4026
2	2	14	Goldfinger	*Soundtrack*	United Artists 5117
3	1	11	Beatles '65	*The Beatles*	Capitol 2228
4	4	8	**You've Lost That Lovin' Feelin'**	*The Righteous Brothers*	Philles 4007
5	6	23	My Fair Lady	*Soundtrack*	Columbia 2600
6	7	26	Where Did Our Love Go	*The Supremes*	Motown 621
7	5	12	My Love Forgive Me	*Robert Goulet*	Columbia 9096
8	8	19	Beach Boys Concert	*The Beach Boys*	Capitol 2198
9	10	24	People	*Barbra Streisand*	Columbia 9015
10	9	11	Coast To Coast	*The Dave Clark Five*	Epic 26128

Billboard — MARCH 20, 1965 — TOP LP's

TW	LW	WK			
1	2	15	**Goldfinger**	*Soundtrack*	United Artists 5117
2	1	25	Mary Poppins	*Soundtrack*	Buena Vista 4026
3	3	12	Beatles '65	*The Beatles*	Capitol 2228
4	4	9	**You've Lost That Lovin' Feelin'**	*The Righteous Brothers*	Philles 4007
5	6	27	Where Did Our Love Go	*The Supremes*	Motown 621
6	5	24	My Fair Lady	*Soundtrack*	Columbia 2600
7	12	7	L-O-V-E	*Nat "King" Cole*	Capitol 2195
8	9	25	People	*Barbra Streisand*	Columbia 9015
9	8	20	Beach Boys Concert	*The Beach Boys*	Capitol 2198
10	7	13	My Love Forgive Me	*Robert Goulet*	Columbia 9096

TW	LW	WK	Billboard. MARCH 27, 1965 TOP LP's
1	1	16	Goldfinger ... *Soundtrack*...United Artists 5117
2	2	26	Mary Poppins ... *Soundtrack*...Buena Vista 4026
3	3	13	Beatles '65 ... *The Beatles*...Capitol 2228
4	7	8	L-O-V-E ... *Nat "King" Cole*...Capitol 2195
5	5	28	Where Did Our Love Go ... *The Supremes*...Motown 621
6	4	10	You've Lost That Lovin' Feelin' ... *The Righteous Brothers*...Philles 4007
7	12	10	Blue Midnight ... *Bert Kaempfert & His Orchestra*...Decca 74569
8	6	25	My Fair Lady ... *Soundtrack*...Columbia 2600
9	9	21	Beach Boys Concert ... *The Beach Boys*...Capitol 2198
10	8	26	People ... *Barbra Streisand*...Columbia 9015

TW	LW	WK	Billboard. APRIL 3, 1965 TOP LP's
1	1	17	Goldfinger ... *Soundtrack*...United Artists 5117
2	2	27	Mary Poppins ... *Soundtrack*...Buena Vista 4026
3	3	14	Beatles '65 ... *The Beatles*...Capitol 2228
4	4	9	L-O-V-E ... *Nat "King" Cole*...Capitol 2195
5	5	29	Where Did Our Love Go ... *The Supremes*...Motown 621
6	7	11	Blue Midnight ... *Bert Kaempfert & His Orchestra*...Decca 74569
7	8	26	My Fair Lady ... *Soundtrack*...Columbia 2600
8	6	11	You've Lost That Lovin' Feelin' ... *The Righteous Brothers*...Philles 4007
9	9	22	Beach Boys Concert ... *The Beach Boys*...Capitol 2198
10	11	15	My Love Forgive Me ... *Robert Goulet*...Columbia 9096

TW	LW	WK	Billboard. APRIL 10, 1965 TOP LP's
1	2	28	Mary Poppins ... *Soundtrack*...Buena Vista 4026
2	1	18	Goldfinger ... *Soundtrack*...United Artists 5117
3	3	15	Beatles '65 ... *The Beatles*...Capitol 2228
4	4	10	L-O-V-E ... *Nat "King" Cole*...Capitol 2195
5	20	8	Introducing Herman's Hermits ... *Herman's Hermits*...MGM 4282
6	6	12	Blue Midnight ... *Bert Kaempfert & His Orchestra*...Decca 74569
7	7	27	My Fair Lady ... *Soundtrack*...Columbia 2600
8	8	12	You've Lost That Lovin' Feelin' ... *The Righteous Brothers*...Philles 4007
9	14	10	The Return Of Roger Miller ... *Roger Miller*...Smash 67061
10	5	30	Where Did Our Love Go ... *The Supremes*...Motown 621

TW	LW	WK	Billboard. APRIL 17, 1965 TOP LP's
1	1	29	Mary Poppins ... *Soundtrack*...Buena Vista 4026
2	2	19	Goldfinger ... *Soundtrack*...United Artists 5117
3	5	9	Introducing Herman's Hermits ... *Herman's Hermits*...MGM 4282
4	9	11	The Return Of Roger Miller ... *Roger Miller*...Smash 67061
5	6	13	Blue Midnight ... *Bert Kaempfert & His Orchestra*...Decca 74569
6	16	5	The Rolling Stones, Now! ... *The Rolling Stones*...London 420
7	3	16	Beatles '65 ... *The Beatles*...Capitol 2228
8	4	11	L-O-V-E ... *Nat "King" Cole*...Capitol 2195
9	7	28	My Fair Lady ... *Soundtrack*...Columbia 2600
10	8	13	You've Lost That Lovin' Feelin' ... *The Righteous Brothers*...Philles 4007

Billboard® — APRIL 24, 1965 — TOP LP's

TW	LW	WK	Title	Artist	Label
1	1	30	**Mary Poppins**	*Soundtrack*	Buena Vista 4026
2	3	10	**Introducing Herman's Hermits**	*Herman's Hermits*	MGM 4282
3	2	20	Goldfinger	*Soundtrack*	United Artists 5117
4	4	12	**The Return Of Roger Miller**	*Roger Miller*	Smash 67061
5	6	6	**The Rolling Stones, Now!**	*The Rolling Stones*	London 420
6	5	14	Blue Midnight	*Bert Kaempfert & His Orchestra*	Decca 74569
7	14	99	Ramblin' Rose	*Nat "King" Cole*	Capitol 1793
8	9	29	My Fair Lady	*Soundtrack*	Columbia 2600
9	7	17	Beatles '65	*The Beatles*	Capitol 2228
10	21	5	The Beach Boys Today!	*The Beach Boys*	Capitol 2269

Billboard® — MAY 1, 1965 — TOP LP's

TW	LW	WK	Title	Artist	Label
1	1	31	**Mary Poppins**	*Soundtrack*	Buena Vista 4026
2	2	11	**Introducing Herman's Hermits**	*Herman's Hermits*	MGM 4282
3	3	21	Goldfinger	*Soundtrack*	United Artists 5117
4	10	6	**The Beach Boys Today!**	*The Beach Boys*	Capitol 2269
5	5	7	**The Rolling Stones, Now!**	*The Rolling Stones*	London 420
6	11	7	The Sound Of Music	*Soundtrack*	RCA 2005
7	7	100	Ramblin' Rose	*Nat "King" Cole*	Capitol 1793
8	4	13	The Return Of Roger Miller	*Roger Miller*	Smash 67061
9	8	30	My Fair Lady	*Soundtrack*	Columbia 2600
10	20	4	Dear Heart	*Andy Williams*	Columbia 9138

Billboard® — MAY 8, 1965 — TOP LP's

TW	LW	WK	Title	Artist	Label
1	1	32	**Mary Poppins**	*Soundtrack*	Buena Vista 4026
2	2	12	**Introducing Herman's Hermits**	*Herman's Hermits*	MGM 4282
3	6	8	The Sound Of Music	*Soundtrack*	RCA 2005
4	4	7	**The Beach Boys Today!**	*The Beach Boys*	Capitol 2269
5	10	5	Dear Heart	*Andy Williams*	Columbia 9138
6	3	22	Goldfinger	*Soundtrack*	United Artists 5117
7	5	8	The Rolling Stones, Now!	*The Rolling Stones*	London 420
8	8	14	The Return Of Roger Miller	*Roger Miller*	Smash 67061
9	9	31	My Fair Lady	*Soundtrack*	Columbia 2600
10	15	5	A Song Will Rise	*Peter, Paul & Mary*	Warner 1589

Billboard® — MAY 15, 1965 — TOP LP's

TW	LW	WK	Title	Artist	Label
1	1	33	**Mary Poppins**	*Soundtrack*	Buena Vista 4026
2	2	13	**Introducing Herman's Hermits**	*Herman's Hermits*	MGM 4282
3	3	9	The Sound Of Music	*Soundtrack*	RCA 2005
4	4	8	**The Beach Boys Today!**	*The Beach Boys*	Capitol 2269
5	5	6	Dear Heart	*Andy Williams*	Columbia 9138
6	6	23	Goldfinger	*Soundtrack*	United Artists 5117
7	9	32	My Fair Lady	*Soundtrack*	Columbia 2600
8	8	15	The Return Of Roger Miller	*Roger Miller*	Smash 67061
9	7	9	The Rolling Stones, Now!	*The Rolling Stones*	London 420
10	10	6	A Song Will Rise	*Peter, Paul & Mary*	Warner 1589

Billboard MAY 22, 1965 **TOP LP's**

TW	LW	WK	Title	Artist...Label
1	1	34	**Mary Poppins**	*Soundtrack*...Buena Vista 4026
2	3	10	The Sound Of Music	*Soundtrack*...RCA 2005
3	2	14	Introducing Herman's Hermits	*Herman's Hermits*...MGM 4282
4	4	9	**The Beach Boys Today!**	*The Beach Boys*...Capitol 2269
5	5	7	Dear Heart	*Andy Williams*...Columbia 9138
6	6	24	Goldfinger	*Soundtrack*...United Artists 5117
7	7	33	My Fair Lady	*Soundtrack*...Columbia 2600
8	10	7	**A Song Will Rise**	*Peter, Paul & Mary*...Warner 1589
9	8	16	The Return Of Roger Miller	*Roger Miller*...Smash 67061
10	14	6	Girl Happy	*Elvis Presley/Soundtrack*...RCA LSP-3338

Billboard MAY 29, 1965 **TOP LP's**

TW	LW	WK	Title	Artist...Label
1	1	35	**Mary Poppins**	*Soundtrack*...Buena Vista 4026
2	2	11	The Sound Of Music	*Soundtrack*...RCA 2005
3	3	15	Introducing Herman's Hermits	*Herman's Hermits*...MGM 4282
4	5	8	**Dear Heart**	*Andy Williams*...Columbia 9138
5	4	10	The Beach Boys Today!	*The Beach Boys*...Capitol 2269
6	6	25	Goldfinger	*Soundtrack*...United Artists 5117
7	7	34	My Fair Lady	*Soundtrack*...Columbia 2600
8	8	8	**A Song Will Rise**	*Peter, Paul & Mary*...Warner 1589
9	10	7	Girl Happy	*Elvis Presley/Soundtrack*...RCA LSP-3338
10	11	5	Bringing It All Back Home	*Bob Dylan*...Columbia 9128

Billboard JUNE 5, 1965 **TOP LP's**

TW	LW	WK	Title	Artist...Label
1	1	36	**Mary Poppins**	*Soundtrack*...Buena Vista 4026
2	2	12	The Sound Of Music	*Soundtrack*...RCA 2005
3	3	16	Introducing Herman's Hermits	*Herman's Hermits*...MGM 4282
4	4	9	**Dear Heart**	*Andy Williams*...Columbia 9138
5	5	11	The Beach Boys Today!	*The Beach Boys*...Capitol 2269
6	39	3	My Name Is Barbra	*Barbra Streisand*...Columbia 9136
7	6	26	Goldfinger	*Soundtrack*...United Artists 5117
8	8	9	**A Song Will Rise**	*Peter, Paul & Mary*...Warner 1589
9	9	8	Girl Happy	*Elvis Presley/Soundtrack*...RCA LSP-3338
10	10	6	Bringing It All Back Home	*Bob Dylan*...Columbia 9128

Billboard JUNE 12, 1965 **TOP LP's**

TW	LW	WK	Title	Artist...Label
1	1	37	**Mary Poppins**	*Soundtrack*...Buena Vista 4026
2	2	13	The Sound Of Music	*Soundtrack*...RCA 2005
3	6	4	My Name Is Barbra	*Barbra Streisand*...Columbia 9136
4	5	12	**The Beach Boys Today!**	*The Beach Boys*...Capitol 2269
5	4	10	Dear Heart	*Andy Williams*...Columbia 9138
6	3	17	Introducing Herman's Hermits	*Herman's Hermits*...MGM 4282
7	7	27	Goldfinger	*Soundtrack*...United Artists 5117
8	9	9	**Girl Happy**	*Elvis Presley/Soundtrack*...RCA LSP-3338
9	10	7	Bringing It All Back Home	*Bob Dylan*...Columbia 9128
10	11	36	My Fair Lady	*Soundtrack*...Columbia 2600

Billboard — JUNE 19, 1965 — TOP LP's

TW	LW	WK	Title	Artist	Label
1	1	38	**Mary Poppins**	*Soundtrack*	Buena Vista 4026
2	3	5	**My Name Is Barbra**	*Barbra Streisand*	Columbia 9136
3	2	14	The Sound Of Music	*Soundtrack*	RCA 2005
4	4	13	**The Beach Boys Today!**	*The Beach Boys*	Capitol 2269
5	5	11	Dear Heart	*Andy Williams*	Columbia 9138
6	6	18	Introducing Herman's Hermits	*Herman's Hermits*	MGM 4282
7	7	28	Goldfinger	*Soundtrack*	United Artists 5117
8	8	10	**Girl Happy**	*Elvis Presley/Soundtrack*	RCA LSP-3338
9	9	8	Bringing It All Back Home	*Bob Dylan*	Columbia 9128
10	10	37	My Fair Lady	*Soundtrack*	Columbia 2600

Billboard — JUNE 26, 1965 — TOP LP's

TW	LW	WK	Title	Artist	Label
1	1	39	**Mary Poppins**	*Soundtrack*	Buena Vista 4026
2	2	6	**My Name Is Barbra**	*Barbra Streisand*	Columbia 9136
3	3	15	The Sound Of Music	*Soundtrack*	RCA 2005
4	5	12	**Dear Heart**	*Andy Williams*	Columbia 9138
5	4	14	The Beach Boys Today!	*The Beach Boys*	Capitol 2269
6	6	19	Introducing Herman's Hermits	*Herman's Hermits*	MGM 4282
7	7	29	Goldfinger	*Soundtrack*	United Artists 5117
8	10	38	My Fair Lady	*Soundtrack*	Columbia 2600
9	8	11	Girl Happy	*Elvis Presley/Soundtrack*	RCA LSP-3338
10	9	9	Bringing It All Back Home	*Bob Dylan*	Columbia 9128

Billboard — JULY 3, 1965 — TOP LP's

TW	LW	WK	Title	Artist	Label
1	1	40	**Mary Poppins**	*Soundtrack*	Buena Vista 4026
2	2	7	**My Name Is Barbra**	*Barbra Streisand*	Columbia 9136
3	3	16	The Sound Of Music	*Soundtrack*	RCA 2005
4	26	3	Herman's Hermits On Tour	*Herman's Hermits*	MGM 4295
5	5	15	The Beach Boys Today!	*The Beach Boys*	Capitol 2269
6	4	13	Dear Heart	*Andy Williams*	Columbia 9138
7	6	20	Introducing Herman's Hermits	*Herman's Hermits*	MGM 4282
8	8	39	My Fair Lady	*Soundtrack*	Columbia 2600
9	7	30	Goldfinger	*Soundtrack*	United Artists 5117
10	15	8	Whipped Cream & Other Delights	*Herb Alpert's Tijuana Brass*	A&M 110

Billboard — JULY 10, 1965 — TOP LP's

TW	LW	WK	Title	Artist	Label
1	48	3	**Beatles VI**	*The Beatles*	Capitol 2358
2	4	4	**Herman's Hermits On Tour**	*Herman's Hermits*	MGM 4295
3	1	41	Mary Poppins	*Soundtrack*	Buena Vista 4026
4	2	8	My Name Is Barbra	*Barbra Streisand*	Columbia 9136
5	3	17	The Sound Of Music	*Soundtrack*	RCA 2005
6	5	16	The Beach Boys Today!	*The Beach Boys*	Capitol 2269
7	7	21	Introducing Herman's Hermits	*Herman's Hermits*	MGM 4282
8	6	14	Dear Heart	*Andy Williams*	Columbia 9138
9	9	31	Goldfinger	*Soundtrack*	United Artists 5117
10	10	9	Whipped Cream & Other Delights	*Herb Alpert's Tijuana Brass*	A&M 110

TW	LW	WK	Billboard — JULY 17, 1965	TOP LP's
①	1	4	**Beatles VI**	*The Beatles*...Capitol 2358
②	2	5	**Herman's Hermits On Tour**	*Herman's Hermits*...MGM 4295
③	3	42	Mary Poppins	*Soundtrack*...Buena Vista 4026
④	4	9	My Name Is Barbra	*Barbra Streisand*...Columbia 9136
⑤	5	18	The Sound Of Music	*Soundtrack*...RCA 2005
⑥	7	22	Introducing Herman's Hermits	*Herman's Hermits*...MGM 4282
⑦	8	15	Dear Heart	*Andy Williams*...Columbia 9138
⑧	6	17	The Beach Boys Today!	*The Beach Boys*...Capitol 2269
⑨	10	10	Whipped Cream & Other Delights	*Herb Alpert's Tijuana Brass*...A&M 110
⑩	12	18	The Rolling Stones, Now!	*The Rolling Stones*...London 420

TW	LW	WK	Billboard — JULY 24, 1965	TOP LP's
①	1	5	**Beatles VI**	*The Beatles*...Capitol 2358
②	2	6	**Herman's Hermits On Tour**	*Herman's Hermits*...MGM 4295
③	3	43	Mary Poppins	*Soundtrack*...Buena Vista 4026
④	5	19	The Sound Of Music	*Soundtrack*...RCA 2005
⑤	4	10	My Name Is Barbra	*Barbra Streisand*...Columbia 9136
⑥	7	16	Dear Heart	*Andy Williams*...Columbia 9138
⑦	6	23	Introducing Herman's Hermits	*Herman's Hermits*...MGM 4282
⑧	9	11	Whipped Cream & Other Delights	*Herb Alpert's Tijuana Brass*...A&M 110
❾	13	8	Today-My Way	*Nancy Wilson*...Capitol 2321
⑩	10	19	The Rolling Stones, Now!	*The Rolling Stones*...London 420

TW	LW	WK	Billboard — JULY 31, 1965	TOP LP's
①	1	6	**Beatles VI**	*The Beatles*...Capitol 2358
②	2	7	**Herman's Hermits On Tour**	*Herman's Hermits*...MGM 4295
③	4	20	The Sound Of Music	*Soundtrack*...RCA 2005
④	3	44	Mary Poppins	*Soundtrack*...Buena Vista 4026
⑤	5	11	My Name Is Barbra	*Barbra Streisand*...Columbia 9136
⑥	6	17	Dear Heart	*Andy Williams*...Columbia 9138
⑦	9	9	**Today-My Way**	*Nancy Wilson*...Capitol 2321
⑧	7	24	Introducing Herman's Hermits	*Herman's Hermits*...MGM 4282
⑨	10	20	The Rolling Stones, Now!	*The Rolling Stones*...London 420
⑩	8	12	Whipped Cream & Other Delights	*Herb Alpert's Tijuana Brass*...A&M 110

TW	LW	WK	Billboard — AUGUST 7, 1965	TOP LP's
①	1	7	**Beatles VI**	*The Beatles*...Capitol 2358
②	2	8	**Herman's Hermits On Tour**	*Herman's Hermits*...MGM 4295
③	3	21	The Sound Of Music	*Soundtrack*...RCA 2005
④	4	45	Mary Poppins	*Soundtrack*...Buena Vista 4026
⑤	5	12	My Name Is Barbra	*Barbra Streisand*...Columbia 9136
❻	12	7	**Mr. Tambourine Man**	*The Byrds*...Columbia 9172
⑦	9	21	The Rolling Stones, Now!	*The Rolling Stones*...London 420
❽	48	3	Summer Days (And Summer Nights!!)	*The Beach Boys*...Capitol 2354
⑨	6	18	Dear Heart	*Andy Williams*...Columbia 9138
⑩	11	20	The Beach Boys Today!	*The Beach Boys*...Capitol 2269

TW	LW	WK	Billboard. AUGUST 14, 1965	TOP LP's
1	1	8	**Beatles VI**	*The Beatles*...Capitol 2358
2	2	9	**Herman's Hermits On Tour**	*Herman's Hermits*...MGM 4295
3	93	2	Out Of Our Heads	*The Rolling Stones*...London 429
4	8	4	Summer Days (And Summer Nights!!)	*The Beach Boys*...Capitol 2354
5	3	22	The Sound Of Music	*Soundtrack*...RCA 2005
6	6	8	**Mr. Tambourine Man**	*The Byrds*...Columbia 9172
7	5	13	My Name Is Barbra	*Barbra Streisand*...Columbia 9136
8	4	46	Mary Poppins	*Soundtrack*...Buena Vista 4026
9	11	12	**Just Once In My Life...**	*The Righteous Brothers*...Philles 4008
10	13	16	Bringing It All Back Home	*Bob Dylan*...Columbia 9128

TW	LW	WK	Billboard. AUGUST 21, 1965	TOP LP's
1	3	3	**Out Of Our Heads**	*The Rolling Stones*...London 429
2	1	9	Beatles VI	*The Beatles*...Capitol 2358
3	4	5	Summer Days (And Summer Nights!!)	*The Beach Boys*...Capitol 2354
4	2	10	Herman's Hermits On Tour	*Herman's Hermits*...MGM 4295
5	5	23	The Sound Of Music	*Soundtrack*...RCA 2005
6	6	9	**Mr. Tambourine Man**	*The Byrds*...Columbia 9172
7	7	14	My Name Is Barbra	*Barbra Streisand*...Columbia 9136
8	8	47	Mary Poppins	*Soundtrack*...Buena Vista 4026
9	9	13	**Just Once In My Life...**	*The Righteous Brothers*...Philles 4008
10	10	17	Bringing It All Back Home	*Bob Dylan*...Columbia 9128

TW	LW	WK	Billboard. AUGUST 28, 1965	TOP LP's
1	1	4	**Out Of Our Heads**	*The Rolling Stones*...London 429
2	2	10	Beatles VI	*The Beatles*...Capitol 2358
3	3	6	Summer Days (And Summer Nights!!)	*The Beach Boys*...Capitol 2354
4	4	11	Herman's Hermits On Tour	*Herman's Hermits*...MGM 4295
5	5	24	The Sound Of Music	*Soundtrack*...RCA 2005
6	7	15	My Name Is Barbra	*Barbra Streisand*...Columbia 9136
7	10	18	Bringing It All Back Home	*Bob Dylan*...Columbia 9128
8	8	48	Mary Poppins	*Soundtrack*...Buena Vista 4026
9	9	14	**Just Once In My Life...**	*The Righteous Brothers*...Philles 4008
10	11	9	Sinatra '65	*Frank Sinatra*...Reprise 6167

TW	LW	WK	Billboard. SEPTEMBER 4, 1965	TOP LP's
1	1	5	**Out Of Our Heads**	*The Rolling Stones*...London 429
2	3	7	**Summer Days (And Summer Nights!!)**	*The Beach Boys*...Capitol 2354
3	5	25	The Sound Of Music	*Soundtrack*...RCA 2005
4	2	11	Beatles VI	*The Beatles*...Capitol 2358
5	59	3	Look At Us	*Sonny & Chér*...Atco 177
6	4	12	Herman's Hermits On Tour	*Herman's Hermits*...MGM 4295
7	7	19	Bringing It All Back Home	*Bob Dylan*...Columbia 9128
8	8	49	Mary Poppins	*Soundtrack*...Buena Vista 4026
9	6	16	My Name Is Barbra	*Barbra Streisand*...Columbia 9136
10	10	10	Sinatra '65	*Frank Sinatra*...Reprise 6167

TW	LW	WK	Billboard SEPTEMBER 11, 1965	TOP LP's
❶	61	3	**Help!**	*The Beatles/Soundtrack*...Capitol 2386
❷	5	4	**Look At Us**	*Sonny & Chér*...Atco 177
③	1	6	Out Of Our Heads	*The Rolling Stones*...London 429
④	3	26	The Sound Of Music	*Soundtrack*...RCA 2005
⑤	2	8	Summer Days (And Summer Nights!!)	*The Beach Boys*...Capitol 2354
⑥	6	13	Herman's Hermits On Tour	*Herman's Hermits*...MGM 4295
⑦	8	50	Mary Poppins	*Soundtrack*...Buena Vista 4026
⑧	4	12	Beatles VI	*The Beatles*...Capitol 2358
⑨	10	11	**Sinatra '65**	*Frank Sinatra*...Reprise 6167
⑩	7	20	Bringing It All Back Home	*Bob Dylan*...Columbia 9128

TW	LW	WK	Billboard SEPTEMBER 18, 1965	TOP LP's
①	1	4	**Help!**	*The Beatles/Soundtrack*...Capitol 2386
②	2	5	**Look At Us**	*Sonny & Chér*...Atco 177
③	3	7	Out Of Our Heads	*The Rolling Stones*...London 429
④	4	27	The Sound Of Music	*Soundtrack*...RCA 2005
⑤	6	14	Herman's Hermits On Tour	*Herman's Hermits*...MGM 4295
❻	12	6	The In Crowd	*The Ramsey Lewis Trio*...Argo 757
⑦	5	9	Summer Days (And Summer Nights!!)	*The Beach Boys*...Capitol 2354
⑧	7	51	Mary Poppins	*Soundtrack*...Buena Vista 4026
⑨	8	13	Beatles VI	*The Beatles*...Capitol 2358
⑩	10	21	Bringing It All Back Home	*Bob Dylan*...Columbia 9128

TW	LW	WK	Billboard SEPTEMBER 25, 1965	TOP LP's
①	1	5	**Help!**	*The Beatles/Soundtrack*...Capitol 2386
②	2	6	**Look At Us**	*Sonny & Chér*...Atco 177
③	4	28	The Sound Of Music	*Soundtrack*...RCA 2005
④	6	7	The In Crowd	*The Ramsey Lewis Trio*...Argo 757
⑤	3	8	Out Of Our Heads	*The Rolling Stones*...London 429
⑥	5	15	Herman's Hermits On Tour	*Herman's Hermits*...MGM 4295
⑦	7	10	Summer Days (And Summer Nights!!)	*The Beach Boys*...Capitol 2354
⑧	8	52	Mary Poppins	*Soundtrack*...Buena Vista 4026
⑨	10	22	Bringing It All Back Home	*Bob Dylan*...Columbia 9128
⑩	9	14	Beatles VI	*The Beatles*...Capitol 2358

TW	LW	WK	Billboard OCTOBER 2, 1965	TOP LP's
①	1	6	**Help!**	*The Beatles/Soundtrack*...Capitol 2386
②	2	7	**Look At Us**	*Sonny & Chér*...Atco 177
③	4	8	The In Crowd	*The Ramsey Lewis Trio*...Argo 757
④	3	29	The Sound Of Music	*Soundtrack*...RCA 2005
⑤	5	9	Out Of Our Heads	*The Rolling Stones*...London 429
⑥	6	16	Herman's Hermits On Tour	*Herman's Hermits*...MGM 4295
⑦	9	23	Bringing It All Back Home	*Bob Dylan*...Columbia 9128
⑧	8	53	Mary Poppins	*Soundtrack*...Buena Vista 4026
⑨	7	11	Summer Days (And Summer Nights!!)	*The Beach Boys*...Capitol 2354
⑩	10	15	Beatles VI	*The Beatles*...Capitol 2358

Billboard® — OCTOBER 9, 1965 — TOP LP's

TW	LW	WK	Title	Artist...Label
1	1	7	Help!	*The Beatles/Soundtrack*...Capitol 2386
2	2	8	Look At Us	*Sonny & Chér*...Atco 177
3	3	9	The In Crowd	*The Ramsey Lewis Trio*...Argo 757
4	4	30	The Sound Of Music	*Soundtrack*...RCA 2005
5	5	10	Out Of Our Heads	*The Rolling Stones*...London 429
6	7	24	Bringing It All Back Home	*Bob Dylan*...Columbia 9128
7	8	54	Mary Poppins	*Soundtrack*...Buena Vista 4026
8	15	8	More Hits By The Supremes	*The Supremes*...Motown 627
9	6	17	Herman's Hermits On Tour	*Herman's Hermits*...MGM 4295
10	9	12	Summer Days (And Summer Nights!!)	*The Beach Boys*...Capitol 2354

Billboard® — OCTOBER 16, 1965 — TOP LP's

TW	LW	WK	Title	Artist...Label
1	1	8	Help!	*The Beatles/Soundtrack*...Capitol 2386
2	2	9	Look At Us	*Sonny & Chér*...Atco 177
3	3	10	The In Crowd	*The Ramsey Lewis Trio*...Argo 757
4	4	31	The Sound Of Music	*Soundtrack*...RCA 2005
5	28	3	Highway 61 Revisited	*Bob Dylan*...Columbia 9189
6	8	9	More Hits By The Supremes	*The Supremes*...Motown 627
7	5	11	Out Of Our Heads	*The Rolling Stones*...London 429
8	12	23	Whipped Cream & Other Delights	*Herb Alpert's Tijuana Brass*...A&M 110
9	7	55	Mary Poppins	*Soundtrack*...Buena Vista 4026
10	11	22	My Name Is Barbra	*Barbra Streisand*...Columbia 9136

Billboard® — OCTOBER 23, 1965 — TOP LP's

TW	LW	WK	Title	Artist...Label
1	1	9	Help!	*The Beatles/Soundtrack*...Capitol 2386
2	2	10	Look At Us	*Sonny & Chér*...Atco 177
3	4	32	The Sound Of Music	*Soundtrack*...RCA 2005
4	5	4	Highway 61 Revisited	*Bob Dylan*...Columbia 9189
5	3	11	The In Crowd	*The Ramsey Lewis Trio*...Argo 757
6	6	10	More Hits By The Supremes	*The Supremes*...Motown 627
7	7	12	Out Of Our Heads	*The Rolling Stones*...London 429
8	8	24	Whipped Cream & Other Delights	*Herb Alpert's Tijuana Brass*...A&M 110
9	9	56	Mary Poppins	*Soundtrack*...Buena Vista 4026
10	11	11	Elvis For Everyone!	*Elvis Presley*...RCA LSP-3450

Billboard® — OCTOBER 30, 1965 — TOP LP's

TW	LW	WK	Title	Artist...Label
1	1	10	Help!	*The Beatles/Soundtrack*...Capitol 2386
2	2	11	Look At Us	*Sonny & Chér*...Atco 177
3	3	33	The Sound Of Music	*Soundtrack*...RCA 2005
4	4	5	Highway 61 Revisited	*Bob Dylan*...Columbia 9189
5	5	12	The In Crowd	*The Ramsey Lewis Trio*...Argo 757
6	8	25	Whipped Cream & Other Delights	*Herb Alpert's Tijuana Brass*...A&M 110
7	7	13	Out Of Our Heads	*The Rolling Stones*...London 429
8	9	57	Mary Poppins	*Soundtrack*...Buena Vista 4026
9	6	11	More Hits By The Supremes	*The Supremes*...Motown 627
10	13	20	Herman's Hermits On Tour	*Herman's Hermits*...MGM 4295

Billboard ● NOVEMBER 6, 1965 ● TOP LP's

TW	LW	WK	Title / Artist
①	1	11	**Help!** .... *The Beatles/Soundtrack...*Capitol 2386
❷	5	13	**The In Crowd** .... *The Ramsey Lewis Trio...*Argo 757
③	4	6	**Highway 61 Revisited** .... *Bob Dylan...*Columbia 9189
④	3	34	**The Sound Of Music** .... *Soundtrack...*RCA 2005
⑤	2	12	**Look At Us** .... *Sonny & Chér...*Atco 177
⑥	6	26	**Whipped Cream & Other Delights** .... *Herb Alpert's Tijuana Brass...*A&M 110
⑦	7	14	**Out Of Our Heads** .... *The Rolling Stones...*London 429
⑧	8	58	**Mary Poppins** .... *Soundtrack...*Buena Vista 4026
⑨	10	21	**Herman's Hermits On Tour** .... *Herman's Hermits...*MGM 4295
⑩	12	25	**My Name Is Barbra** .... *Barbra Streisand...*Columbia 9136

Billboard ● NOVEMBER 13, 1965 ● TOP LP's

TW	LW	WK	Title / Artist
①	4	35	**The Sound Of Music** .... *Soundtrack...*RCA 2005
②	1	12	**Help!** .... *The Beatles/Soundtrack...*Capitol 2386
③	2	14	**The In Crowd** .... *The Ramsey Lewis Trio...*Argo 757
④	6	27	**Whipped Cream & Other Delights** .... *Herb Alpert's Tijuana Brass...*A&M 110
⑤	3	7	**Highway 61 Revisited** .... *Bob Dylan...*Columbia 9189
⑥	5	13	**Look At Us** .... *Sonny & Chér...*Atco 177
⑦	7	15	**Out Of Our Heads** .... *The Rolling Stones...*London 429
⑧	8	59	**Mary Poppins** .... *Soundtrack...*Buena Vista 4026
⑨	10	26	**My Name Is Barbra** .... *Barbra Streisand...*Columbia 9136
⑩	9	22	**Herman's Hermits On Tour** .... *Herman's Hermits...*MGM 4295

Billboard ● NOVEMBER 20, 1965 ● TOP LP's

TW	LW	WK	Title / Artist
①	1	36	**The Sound Of Music** .... *Soundtrack...*RCA 2005
②	4	28	**Whipped Cream & Other Delights** .... *Herb Alpert's Tijuana Brass...*A&M 110
③	2	13	**Help!** .... *The Beatles/Soundtrack...*Capitol 2386
④	3	15	**The In Crowd** .... *The Ramsey Lewis Trio...*Argo 757
⑤	6	14	**Look At Us** .... *Sonny & Chér...*Atco 177
⑥	5	8	**Highway 61 Revisited** .... *Bob Dylan...*Columbia 9189
❼	39	3	**My Name Is Barbra, Two** .... *Barbra Streisand...*Columbia 9209
❽	19	6	**Going Places** .... *Herb Alpert & The Tijuana Brass...*A&M 112
⑨	7	16	**Out Of Our Heads** .... *The Rolling Stones...*London 429
⑩	11	10	**You Don't Have To Be Jewish** .... *Various Artists...*Kapp 4503

Billboard ● NOVEMBER 27, 1965 ● TOP LP's

TW	LW	WK	Title / Artist
①	2	29	**Whipped Cream & Other Delights** .... *Herb Alpert's Tijuana Brass...*A&M 110
❷	7	4	**My Name Is Barbra, Two...** .... *Barbra Streisand...*Columbia 9209
③	1	37	**The Sound Of Music** .... *Soundtrack...*RCA 2005
④	3	14	**Help!** .... *The Beatles/Soundtrack...*Capitol 2386
⑤	4	16	**The In Crowd** .... *The Ramsey Lewis Trio...*Argo 757
⑥	6	9	**Highway 61 Revisited** .... *Bob Dylan...*Columbia 9189
⑦	8	7	**Going Places** .... *Herb Alpert & The Tijuana Brass...*A&M 112
⑧	5	15	**Look At Us** .... *Sonny & Chér...*Atco 177
⑨	10	11	**You Don't Have To Be Jewish** .... *Various Artists...*Kapp 4503
⑩	9	17	**Out Of Our Heads** .... *The Rolling Stones...*London 429

TW	LW	WK	Billboard. DECEMBER 4, 1965 TOP LP's
①	1	30	**Whipped Cream & Other Delights** .... *Herb Alpert's Tijuana Brass*...A&M 110
②	2	5	**My Name Is Barbra, Two...** .... *Barbra Streisand*...Columbia 9209
③	3	38	The Sound Of Music .... *Soundtrack*...RCA 2005
④	4	15	Help! .... *The Beatles/Soundtrack*...Capitol 2386
⑤	7	8	Going Places .... *Herb Alpert & The Tijuana Brass*...A&M 112
⑥	5	17	The In Crowd .... *The Ramsey Lewis Trio*...Argo 757
❼	16	3	The Best Of Herman's Hermits .... *Herman's Hermits*...MGM 4315
⑧	8	16	Look At Us .... *Sonny & Chér*...Atco 177
⑨	6	10	Highway 61 Revisited .... *Bob Dylan*...Columbia 9189
❿	61	2	"Welcome to the LBJ Ranch!" .... *Various Artists*...Capitol 2423

TW	LW	WK	Billboard. DECEMBER 11, 1965 TOP LP's
①	1	31	**Whipped Cream & Other Delights** .... *Herb Alpert's Tijuana Brass*...A&M 110
②	2	6	**My Name Is Barbra, Two...** .... *Barbra Streisand*...Columbia 9209
③	3	39	The Sound Of Music .... *Soundtrack*...RCA 2005
❹	10	3	"Welcome to the LBJ Ranch!" .... *Various Artists*...Capitol 2423
⑤	5	9	Going Places .... *Herb Alpert & The Tijuana Brass*...A&M 112
⑥	7	4	The Best Of Herman's Hermits .... *Herman's Hermits*...MGM 4315
⑦	4	16	Help! .... *The Beatles/Soundtrack*...Capitol 2386
⑧	6	18	The In Crowd .... *The Ramsey Lewis Trio*...Argo 757
❾	14	3	Beach Boys' Party! .... *The Beach Boys*...Capitol 2398
⑩	11	8	**Farewell, Angelina** .... *Joan Baez*...Vanguard 79200

TW	LW	WK	Billboard. DECEMBER 18, 1965 TOP LP's
①	1	32	**Whipped Cream & Other Delights** .... *Herb Alpert's Tijuana Brass*...A&M 110
②	3	40	The Sound Of Music .... *Soundtrack*...RCA 2005
③	4	4	**"Welcome to the LBJ Ranch!"** .... *Various Artists*...Capitol 2423
④	2	7	My Name Is Barbra, Two... .... *Barbra Streisand*...Columbia 9209
⑤	5	10	Going Places .... *Herb Alpert & The Tijuana Brass*...A&M 112
⑥	6	5	The Best Of Herman's Hermits .... *Herman's Hermits*...MGM 4315
⑦	9	4	Beach Boys' Party! .... *The Beach Boys*...Capitol 2398
⑧	8	19	The In Crowd .... *The Ramsey Lewis Trio*...Argo 757
⑨	7	17	Help! .... *The Beatles/Soundtrack*...Capitol 2386
⑩	11	6	Harum Scarum .... *Elvis Presley/Soundtrack*...RCA LSP-3468

TW	LW	WK	Billboard. DECEMBER 25, 1965 TOP LP's
①	1	33	**Whipped Cream & Other Delights** .... *Herb Alpert's Tijuana Brass*...A&M 110
②	2	41	The Sound Of Music .... *Soundtrack*...RCA 2005
③	3	5	**"Welcome to the LBJ Ranch!"** .... *Various Artists*...Capitol 2423
④	5	11	Going Places .... *Herb Alpert & The Tijuana Brass*...A&M 112
⑤	6	6	**The Best Of Herman's Hermits** .... *Herman's Hermits*...MGM 4315
⑥	4	8	My Name Is Barbra, Two... .... *Barbra Streisand*...Columbia 9209
⑦	7	5	Beach Boys' Party! .... *The Beach Boys*...Capitol 2398
❽	13	3	December's Children (and everybody's) .... *The Rolling Stones*...London 451
⑨	8	20	The In Crowd .... *The Ramsey Lewis Trio*...Argo 757
⑩	10	7	Harum Scarum .... *Elvis Presley/Soundtrack*...RCA LSP-3468

Billboard — JANUARY 1, 1966 — TOP LP's

TW	LW	WK	Title	Artist	Label
1	1	34	**Whipped Cream & Other Delights**	*Herb Alpert's Tijuana Brass*	A&M 110
2	2	42	The Sound Of Music	*Soundtrack*	RCA 2005
3	3	6	**"Welcome to the LBJ Ranch!"**	*Various Artists*	Capitol 2423
4	4	12	Going Places	*Herb Alpert & The Tijuana Brass*	A&M 112
5	8	4	December's Children (and everybody's)	*The Rolling Stones*	London 451
6	7	6	**Beach Boys' Party!**	*The Beach Boys*	Capitol 2398
7	5	7	The Best Of Herman's Hermits	*Herman's Hermits*	MGM 4315
8	10	8	**Harum Scarum**	*Elvis Presley/Soundtrack*	RCA LSP-3468
9	6	9	My Name Is Barbra, Two...	*Barbra Streisand*	Columbia 9209
10	13	12	My World	*Eddy Arnold*	RCA 3466

Billboard — JANUARY 8, 1966 — TOP LP's

TW	LW	WK	Title	Artist	Label
1	60	3	**Rubber Soul**	*The Beatles*	Capitol 2442
2	2	43	The Sound Of Music	*Soundtrack*	RCA 2005
3	1	35	Whipped Cream & Other Delights	*Herb Alpert's Tijuana Brass*	A&M 110
4	5	5	**December's Children (and everybody's)**	*The Rolling Stones*	London 451
5	4	13	Going Places	*Herb Alpert & The Tijuana Brass*	A&M 112
6	7	8	The Best Of Herman's Hermits	*Herman's Hermits*	MGM 4315
7	10	13	**My World**	*Eddy Arnold*	RCA 3466
8	8	9	**Harum Scarum**	*Elvis Presley/Soundtrack*	RCA LSP-3468
9	9	10	My Name Is Barbra, Two...	*Barbra Streisand*	Columbia 9209
10	3	7	"Welcome to the LBJ Ranch!"	*Various Artists*	Capitol 2423

Billboard — JANUARY 15, 1966 — TOP LP's

TW	LW	WK	Title	Artist	Label
1	1	4	**Rubber Soul**	*The Beatles*	Capitol 2442
2	2	44	The Sound Of Music	*Soundtrack*	RCA 2005
3	3	36	Whipped Cream & Other Delights	*Herb Alpert's Tijuana Brass*	A&M 110
4	4	6	**December's Children (and everybody's)**	*The Rolling Stones*	London 451
5	5	14	Going Places	*Herb Alpert & The Tijuana Brass*	A&M 112
6	6	9	The Best Of Herman's Hermits	*Herman's Hermits*	MGM 4315
7	7	14	**My World**	*Eddy Arnold*	RCA 3466
8	11	22	September Of My Years	*Frank Sinatra*	Reprise 1014
9	12	10	Golden Hits	*Roger Miller*	Smash 67073
10	9	11	My Name Is Barbra, Two...	*Barbra Streisand*	Columbia 9209

Billboard — JANUARY 22, 1966 — TOP LP's

TW	LW	WK	Title	Artist	Label
1	1	5	**Rubber Soul**	*The Beatles*	Capitol 2442
2	3	37	Whipped Cream & Other Delights	*Herb Alpert's Tijuana Brass*	A&M 110
3	2	45	The Sound Of Music	*Soundtrack*	RCA 2005
4	4	7	**December's Children (and everybody's)**	*The Rolling Stones*	London 451
5	5	15	Going Places	*Herb Alpert & The Tijuana Brass*	A&M 112
6	6	10	The Best Of Herman's Hermits	*Herman's Hermits*	MGM 4315
7	7	15	**My World**	*Eddy Arnold*	RCA 3466
8	8	23	September Of My Years	*Frank Sinatra*	Reprise 1014
9	9	11	Golden Hits	*Roger Miller*	Smash 67073
10	10	12	My Name Is Barbra, Two...	*Barbra Streisand*	Columbia 9209

TW	LW	WK	Billboard. JANUARY 29, 1966 TOP LP's
①	1	6	**Rubber Soul** .... *The Beatles*...Capitol 2442
②	2	38	Whipped Cream & Other Delights .... *Herb Alpert's Tijuana Brass*...A&M 110
③	3	46	The Sound Of Music........ *Soundtrack*...RCA 2005
④	5	16	Going Places .... *Herb Alpert & The Tijuana Brass*...A&M 112
⑤	6	11	**The Best Of Herman's Hermits**........ *Herman's Hermits*...MGM 4315
⑥	4	8	December's Children (and everybody's)...... *The Rolling Stones*...London 451
⑦	8	24	September Of My Years .... *Frank Sinatra*...Reprise 1014
⑧	9	12	Golden Hits........ *Roger Miller*...Smash 67073
⑨	10	13	My Name Is Barbra, Two........ *Barbra Streisand*...Columbia 9209
⑩	7	16	My World .... *Eddy Arnold*...RCA 3466

TW	LW	WK	Billboard. FEBRUARY 5, 1966 TOP LP's
①	1	7	**Rubber Soul** .... *The Beatles*...Capitol 2442
②	2	39	Whipped Cream & Other Delights .... *Herb Alpert's Tijuana Brass*...A&M 110
③	4	17	Going Places .... *Herb Alpert & The Tijuana Brass*...A&M 112
④	3	47	The Sound Of Music........ *Soundtrack*...RCA 2005
⑤	5	12	**The Best Of Herman's Hermits**........ *Herman's Hermits*...MGM 4315
⑥	7	25	September Of My Years .... *Frank Sinatra*...Reprise 1014
⑦	9	14	My Name Is Barbra, Two........ *Barbra Streisand*...Columbia 9209
⑧	8	13	Golden Hits........ *Roger Miller*...Smash 67073
⑨	6	9	December's Children (and everybody's)...... *The Rolling Stones*...London 451
⑩	10	17	My World .... *Eddy Arnold*...RCA 3466

TW	LW	WK	Billboard. FEBRUARY 12, 1966 TOP LP's
①	1	8	**Rubber Soul** .... *The Beatles*...Capitol 2442
②	2	40	Whipped Cream & Other Delights .... *Herb Alpert's Tijuana Brass*...A&M 110
③	3	18	Going Places .... *Herb Alpert & The Tijuana Brass*...A&M 112
④	4	48	The Sound Of Music........ *Soundtrack*...RCA 2005
⑤	7	15	My Name Is Barbra, Two........ *Barbra Streisand*...Columbia 9209
⑥	5	13	The Best Of Herman's Hermits........ *Herman's Hermits*...MGM 4315
⑦	8	14	Golden Hits........ *Roger Miller*...Smash 67073
⑧	6	26	September Of My Years .... *Frank Sinatra*...Reprise 1014
⑨	9	10	December's Children (and everybody's)...... *The Rolling Stones*...London 451
❿	13	8	A Man And His Music .... *Frank Sinatra*...Reprise 1016

TW	LW	WK	Billboard. FEBRUARY 19, 1966 TOP LP's
①	2	41	**Whipped Cream & Other Delights** .... *Herb Alpert's Tijuana Brass*...A&M 110
②	1	9	Rubber Soul .... *The Beatles*...Capitol 2442
③	3	19	Going Places .... *Herb Alpert & The Tijuana Brass*...A&M 112
④	4	49	The Sound Of Music........ *Soundtrack*...RCA 2005
⑤	5	16	My Name Is Barbra, Two........ *Barbra Streisand*...Columbia 9209
⑥	8	27	September Of My Years .... *Frank Sinatra*...Reprise 1014
⑦	7	15	Golden Hits........ *Roger Miller*...Smash 67073
⑧	6	14	The Best Of Herman's Hermits........ *Herman's Hermits*...MGM 4315
⑨	10	9	**A Man And His Music** .... *Frank Sinatra*...Reprise 1016
❿	13	11	**The 4 Seasons' Gold Vault of Hits** .... *The 4 Seasons*...Philips 196

Billboard® — FEBRUARY 26, 1966 — TOP LP's

TW	LW	WK	Title	Artist...Label
1	1	42	**Whipped Cream & Other Delights**	*Herb Alpert's Tijuana Brass*...A&M 110
2	2	10	Rubber Soul	*The Beatles*...Capitol 2442
3	3	20	Going Places	*Herb Alpert & The Tijuana Brass*...A&M 112
4	4	50	The Sound Of Music	*Soundtrack*...RCA 2005
5	6	28	**September Of My Years**	*Frank Sinatra*...Reprise 1014
6	7	16	**Golden Hits**	*Roger Miller*...Smash 67073
7	5	17	My Name Is Barbra, Two...	*Barbra Streisand*...Columbia 9209
8	14	14	**Going To A Go-Go**	*Smokey Robinson & The Miracles*...Tamla 267
9	9	10	**A Man And His Music**	*Frank Sinatra*...Reprise 1016
10	10	12	**The 4 Seasons' Gold Vault of Hits**	*The 4 Seasons*...Philips 196

Billboard® — MARCH 5, 1966 — TOP LP's

TW	LW	WK	Title	Artist...Label
1	3	21	**Going Places**	*Herb Alpert & The Tijuana Brass*...A&M 112
2	1	43	Whipped Cream & Other Delights	*Herb Alpert's Tijuana Brass*...A&M 110
3	2	11	Rubber Soul	*The Beatles*...Capitol 2442
4	4	51	The Sound Of Music	*Soundtrack*...RCA 2005
5	5	29	**September Of My Years**	*Frank Sinatra*...Reprise 1014
6	6	17	**Golden Hits**	*Roger Miller*...Smash 67073
7	7	18	My Name Is Barbra, Two...	*Barbra Streisand*...Columbia 9209
8	8	15	**Going To A Go-Go**	*Smokey Robinson & The Miracles*...Tamla 267
9	12	16	The Best Of Herman's Hermits	*Herman's Hermits*...MGM 4315
10	11	13	**Thunderball**	*Soundtrack*...United Artists 5132

Billboard® — MARCH 12, 1966 — TOP LP's

TW	LW	WK	Title	Artist...Label
1	53	3	**Ballads of the Green Berets**	*SSgt Barry Sadler*...RCA 3547
2	2	44	Whipped Cream & Other Delights	*Herb Alpert's Tijuana Brass*...A&M 110
3	1	22	Going Places	*Herb Alpert & The Tijuana Brass*...A&M 112
4	3	12	Rubber Soul	*The Beatles*...Capitol 2442
5	4	52	The Sound Of Music	*Soundtrack*...RCA 2005
6	5	30	September Of My Years	*Frank Sinatra*...Reprise 1014
7	6	18	Golden Hits	*Roger Miller*...Smash 67073
8	9	17	The Best Of Herman's Hermits	*Herman's Hermits*...MGM 4315
9	7	19	My Name Is Barbra, Two...	*Barbra Streisand*...Columbia 9209
10	8	16	Going To A Go-Go	*Smokey Robinson & The Miracles*...Tamla 267

Billboard® — MARCH 19, 1966 — TOP LP's

TW	LW	WK	Title	Artist...Label
1	1	4	**Ballads of the Green Berets**	*SSgt Barry Sadler*...RCA 3547
2	2	45	Whipped Cream & Other Delights	*Herb Alpert's Tijuana Brass*...A&M 110
3	3	23	Going Places	*Herb Alpert & The Tijuana Brass*...A&M 112
4	4	13	Rubber Soul	*The Beatles*...Capitol 2442
5	5	53	The Sound Of Music	*Soundtrack*...RCA 2005
6	6	31	September Of My Years	*Frank Sinatra*...Reprise 1014
7	8	18	The Best Of Herman's Hermits	*Herman's Hermits*...MGM 4315
8	7	19	Golden Hits	*Roger Miller*...Smash 67073
9	9	20	My Name Is Barbra, Two...	*Barbra Streisand*...Columbia 9209
10	10	17	Going To A Go-Go	*Smokey Robinson & The Miracles*...Tamla 267

Billboard — MARCH 26, 1966 — TOP LP's

TW	LW	WK	Title	Artist	Label
1	1	5	Ballads of the Green Berets	*SSgt Barry Sadler*	RCA 3547
2	2	46	Whipped Cream & Other Delights	*Herb Alpert's Tijuana Brass*	A&M 110
3	3	24	Going Places	*Herb Alpert & The Tijuana Brass*	A&M 112
4	5	54	The Sound Of Music	*Soundtrack*	RCA 2005
5	4	14	Rubber Soul	*The Beatles*	Capitol 2442
6	19	7	The Best Of The Animals	*The Animals*	MGM 4324
7	20	8	Just Like Us!	*Paul Revere & The Raiders*	Columbia 9251
8	7	19	The Best Of Herman's Hermits	*Herman's Hermits*	MGM 4315
9	6	32	September Of My Years	*Frank Sinatra*	Reprise 1014
10	11	42	The Lonely Bull	*Herb Alpert's Tijuana Brass*	A&M 101

Billboard — APRIL 2, 1966 — TOP LP's

TW	LW	WK	Title	Artist	Label
1	1	6	Ballads of the Green Berets	*SSgt Barry Sadler*	RCA 3547
2	3	25	Going Places	*Herb Alpert & The Tijuana Brass*	A&M 112
3	2	47	Whipped Cream & Other Delights	*Herb Alpert's Tijuana Brass*	A&M 110
4	4	55	The Sound Of Music	*Soundtrack*	RCA 2005
5	7	9	Just Like Us!	*Paul Revere & The Raiders*	Columbia 9251
6	6	8	The Best Of The Animals	*The Animals*	MGM 4324
7	5	15	Rubber Soul	*The Beatles*	Capitol 2442
8	14	4	Boots	*Nancy Sinatra*	Reprise 6202
9	11	39	South Of The Border	*Herb Alpert's Tijuana Brass*	A&M 108
10	10	43	The Lonely Bull	*Herb Alpert's Tijuana Brass*	A&M 101

Billboard — APRIL 9, 1966 — TOP LP's

TW	LW	WK	Title	Artist	Label
1	1	7	Ballads of the Green Berets	*SSgt Barry Sadler*	RCA 3547
2	3	48	Whipped Cream & Other Delights	*Herb Alpert's Tijuana Brass*	A&M 110
3	2	26	Going Places	*Herb Alpert & The Tijuana Brass*	A&M 112
4	4	56	The Sound Of Music	*Soundtrack*	RCA 2005
5	8	5	Boots	*Nancy Sinatra*	Reprise 6202
6	6	9	The Best Of The Animals	*The Animals*	MGM 4324
7	7	16	Rubber Soul	*The Beatles*	Capitol 2442
8	9	40	South Of The Border	*Herb Alpert's Tijuana Brass*	A&M 108
9	5	10	Just Like Us!	*Paul Revere & The Raiders*	Columbia 9251
10	12	23	My Name Is Barbra, Two	*Barbra Streisand*	Columbia 9209

Billboard — APRIL 16, 1966 — TOP LP's

TW	LW	WK	Title	Artist	Label
1	3	27	Going Places	*Herb Alpert & The Tijuana Brass*	A&M 112
2	1	8	Ballads of the Green Berets	*SSgt Barry Sadler*	RCA 3547
3	2	49	Whipped Cream & Other Delights	*Herb Alpert's Tijuana Brass*	A&M 110
4	4	57	The Sound Of Music	*Soundtrack*	RCA 2005
5	5	6	Boots	*Nancy Sinatra*	Reprise 6202
6	8	41	South Of The Border	*Herb Alpert's Tijuana Brass*	A&M 108
7	6	10	The Best Of The Animals	*The Animals*	MGM 4324
8	11	9	Spanish Eyes	*Al Martino*	Capitol 2435
9	9	11	Just Like Us!	*Paul Revere & The Raiders*	Columbia 9251
10	15	8	The Dave Clark Five's Greatest Hits	*The Dave Clark Five*	Epic 26185

TW	LW	WK	Billboard® APRIL 23, 1966 TOP LP's		
①	1	28	Going Places	Herb Alpert & The Tijuana Brass	A&M 112
②	2	9	Ballads of the Green Berets	SSgt Barry Sadler	RCA 3547
③	3	50	Whipped Cream & Other Delights	Herb Alpert's Tijuana Brass	A&M 110
④	4	58	The Sound Of Music	Soundtrack	RCA 2005
⑤	5	7	Boots	Nancy Sinatra	Reprise 6202
❻	67	3	Color Me Barbra	Barbra Streisand	Columbia 9278
⑦	7	11	The Best Of The Animals	The Animals	MGM 4324
⑧	8	10	Spanish Eyes	Al Martino	Capitol 2435
⑨	11	6	I Hear A Symphony	The Supremes	Motown 643
⑩	10	9	The Dave Clark Five's Greatest Hits	The Dave Clark Five	Epic 26185

TW	LW	WK	Billboard® APRIL 30, 1966 TOP LP's		
❶	1	29	Going Places	Herb Alpert & The Tijuana Brass	A&M 112
②	3	51	Whipped Cream & Other Delights	Herb Alpert's Tijuana Brass	A&M 110
❸	6	4	Color Me Barbra	Barbra Streisand	Columbia 9278
❹	24	3	Big Hits (High Tide And Green Grass)	The Rolling Stones	London 1
⑤	4	59	The Sound Of Music	Soundtrack	RCA 2005
⑥	2	10	Ballads of the Green Berets	SSgt Barry Sadler	RCA 3547
⑦	5	8	Boots	Nancy Sinatra	Reprise 6202
⑧	9	7	I Hear A Symphony	The Supremes	Motown 643
⑨	10	10	The Dave Clark Five's Greatest Hits	The Dave Clark Five	Epic 26185
❿	28	8	If You Can Believe Your Eyes And Ears	The Mama's & The Papa's	Dunhill 50006

TW	LW	WK	Billboard® MAY 7, 1966 TOP LP's		
①	1	30	Going Places	Herb Alpert & The Tijuana Brass	A&M 112
②	2	52	Whipped Cream & Other Delights	Herb Alpert's Tijuana Brass	A&M 110
③	3	5	Color Me Barbra	Barbra Streisand	Columbia 9278
④	4	4	Big Hits (High Tide And Green Grass)	The Rolling Stones	London 1
⑤	6	11	Ballads of the Green Berets	SSgt Barry Sadler	RCA 3547
⑥	5	60	The Sound Of Music	Soundtrack	RCA 2005
❼	10	9	If You Can Believe Your Eyes And Ears	The Mama's & The Papa's	Dunhill 50006
⑧	8	8	I Hear A Symphony	The Supremes	Motown 643
⑨	7	9	Boots	Nancy Sinatra	Reprise 6202
⑩	9	11	The Dave Clark Five's Greatest Hits	The Dave Clark Five	Epic 26185

TW	LW	WK	Billboard® MAY 14, 1966 TOP LP's		
❶	1	31	Going Places	Herb Alpert & The Tijuana Brass	A&M 112
②	2	53	Whipped Cream & Other Delights	Herb Alpert's Tijuana Brass	A&M 110
③	4	5	Big Hits (High Tide And Green Grass)	The Rolling Stones	London 1
❹	7	10	If You Can Believe Your Eyes And Ears	The Mama's & The Papa's	Dunhill 50006
⑤	3	6	Color Me Barbra	Barbra Streisand	Columbia 9278
⑥	6	61	The Sound Of Music	Soundtrack	RCA 2005
⑦	5	12	Ballads of the Green Berets	SSgt Barry Sadler	RCA 3547
⑧	8	9	I Hear A Symphony	The Supremes	Motown 643
❾	12	3	Soul & Inspiration	The Righteous Brothers	Verve 5001
⑩	9	10	Boots	Nancy Sinatra	Reprise 6202

TW	LW	WK	Billboard® MAY 21, 1966		TOP LP's
①	4	11	**If You Can Believe Your Eyes And Ears**	*The Mama's & The Papa's*	Dunhill 50006
❷	60	2	What Now My Love	*Herb Alpert & The Tijuana Brass*	A&M 4114
③	3	6	**Big Hits (High Tide And Green Grass)**	*The Rolling Stones*	London 1
④	1	32	Going Places	*Herb Alpert & The Tijuana Brass*	A&M 112
⑤	5	7	Color Me Barbra	*Barbra Streisand*	Columbia 9278
⑥	6	62	The Sound Of Music	*Soundtrack*	RCA 2005
⑦	9	4	**Soul & Inspiration**	*The Righteous Brothers*	Verve 5001
⑧	2	54	Whipped Cream & Other Delights	*Herb Alpert's Tijuana Brass*	A&M 110
⑨	8	10	I Hear A Symphony	*The Supremes*	Motown 643
⑩	11	15	The Best Of The Animals	*The Animals*	MGM 4324

TW	LW	WK	Billboard® MAY 28, 1966		TOP LP's
①	2	3	**What Now My Love**	*Herb Alpert & The Tijuana Brass*	A&M 4114
②	1	12	If You Can Believe Your Eyes And Ears	*The Mama's & The Papa's*	Dunhill 50006
③	3	7	**Big Hits (High Tide And Green Grass)**	*The Rolling Stones*	London 1
④	5	8	Color Me Barbra	*Barbra Streisand*	Columbia 9278
⑤	6	63	The Sound Of Music	*Soundtrack*	RCA 2005
⑥	4	33	Going Places	*Herb Alpert & The Tijuana Brass*	A&M 112
⑦	7	5	**Soul & Inspiration**	*The Righteous Brothers*	Verve 5001
⑧	8	55	Whipped Cream & Other Delights	*Herb Alpert's Tijuana Brass*	A&M 110
⑨	10	16	The Best Of The Animals	*The Animals*	MGM 4324
⑩	9	11	I Hear A Symphony	*The Supremes*	Motown 643

TW	LW	WK	Billboard® JUNE 4, 1966		TOP LP's
❶	1	4	**What Now My Love**	*Herb Alpert & The Tijuana Brass*	A&M 4114
②	2	13	If You Can Believe Your Eyes And Ears	*The Mama's & The Papa's*	Dunhill 50006
③	5	64	The Sound Of Music	*Soundtrack*	RCA 2005
④	6	34	Going Places	*Herb Alpert & The Tijuana Brass*	A&M 112
⑤	4	9	Color Me Barbra	*Barbra Streisand*	Columbia 9278
⑥	8	56	Whipped Cream & Other Delights	*Herb Alpert's Tijuana Brass*	A&M 110
⑦	3	8	Big Hits (High Tide And Green Grass)	*The Rolling Stones*	London 1
⑧	7	6	Soul & Inspiration	*The Righteous Brothers*	Verve 5001
❾	33	12	Doctor Zhivago	*Soundtrack*	MGM 6
⑩	12	13	Boots	*Nancy Sinatra*	Reprise 6202

TW	LW	WK	Billboard® JUNE 11, 1966		TOP LP's
①	1	5	**What Now My Love**	*Herb Alpert & The Tijuana Brass*	A&M 4114
②	2	14	If You Can Believe Your Eyes And Ears	*The Mama's & The Papa's*	Dunhill 50006
③	3	65	The Sound Of Music	*Soundtrack*	RCA 2005
④	4	35	Going Places	*Herb Alpert & The Tijuana Brass*	A&M 112
⑤	6	57	Whipped Cream & Other Delights	*Herb Alpert's Tijuana Brass*	A&M 110
⑥	7	9	Big Hits (High Tide And Green Grass)	*The Rolling Stones*	London 1
⑦	5	10	Color Me Barbra	*Barbra Streisand*	Columbia 9278
⑧	9	13	Doctor Zhivago	*Soundtrack*	MGM 6
⑨	8	7	Soul & Inspiration	*The Righteous Brothers*	Verve 5001
⑩	11	11	**Daydream**	*The Lovin' Spoonful*	Kama Sutra 8051

Billboard — JUNE 18, 1966 — TOP LP's

TW	LW	WK			
1	1	6	**What Now My Love**	Herb Alpert & The Tijuana Brass	A&M 4114
2	2	15	If You Can Believe Your Eyes And Ears	The Mama's & The Papa's	Dunhill 50006
3	5	58	Whipped Cream & Other Delights	Herb Alpert's Tijuana Brass	A&M 110
4	3	66	The Sound Of Music	Soundtrack	RCA 2005
5	4	36	Going Places	Herb Alpert & The Tijuana Brass	A&M 112
6	6	10	Big Hits (High Tide And Green Grass)	The Rolling Stones	London 1
7	8	14	Doctor Zhivago	Soundtrack	MGM 6
8	7	11	Color Me Barbra	Barbra Streisand	Columbia 9278
9	20	6	The Shadow of Your Smile	Andy Williams	Columbia 9299
10	11	12	The Shadow Of Your Smile	Johnny Mathis	Mercury 61073

Billboard — JUNE 25, 1966 — TOP LP's

TW	LW	WK			
1	1	7	**What Now My Love**	Herb Alpert & The Tijuana Brass	A&M 4114
2	2	16	If You Can Believe Your Eyes And Ears	The Mama's & The Papa's	Dunhill 50006
3	3	59	Whipped Cream & Other Delights	Herb Alpert's Tijuana Brass	A&M 110
4	7	15	Doctor Zhivago	Soundtrack	MGM 6
5	4	67	The Sound Of Music	Soundtrack	RCA 2005
6	9	7	**The Shadow of Your Smile**	Andy Williams	Columbia 9299
7	5	37	Going Places	Herb Alpert & The Tijuana Brass	A&M 112
8	6	11	Big Hits (High Tide And Green Grass)	The Rolling Stones	London 1
9	10	13	**The Shadow Of Your Smile**	Johnny Mathis	Mercury 61073
10	20	8	Lou Rawls Live!	Lou Rawls	Capitol 2459

Billboard — JULY 2, 1966 — TOP LP's

TW	LW	WK			
1	1	8	**What Now My Love**	Herb Alpert & The Tijuana Brass	A&M 4114
2	2	17	If You Can Believe Your Eyes And Ears	The Mama's & The Papa's	Dunhill 50006
3	5	68	The Sound Of Music	Soundtrack	RCA 2005
4	4	16	Doctor Zhivago	Soundtrack	MGM 6
5	3	60	Whipped Cream & Other Delights	Herb Alpert's Tijuana Brass	A&M 110
6	6	8	**The Shadow of Your Smile**	Andy Williams	Columbia 9299
7	10	9	Lou Rawls Live!	Lou Rawls	Capitol 2459
8	7	38	Going Places	Herb Alpert & The Tijuana Brass	A&M 112
9	14	6	Wonderfulness	Bill Cosby	Warner 1634
10	11	6	**Pet Sounds**	The Beach Boys	Capitol 2458

Billboard — JULY 9, 1966 — TOP LP's

TW	LW	WK			
1	1	9	**What Now My Love**	Herb Alpert & The Tijuana Brass	A&M 4114
2	2	18	If You Can Believe Your Eyes And Ears	The Mama's & The Papa's	Dunhill 50006
3	19	4	Strangers In The Night	Frank Sinatra	Reprise 1017
4	5	61	Whipped Cream & Other Delights	Herb Alpert's Tijuana Brass	A&M 110
5	4	17	Doctor Zhivago	Soundtrack	MGM 6
6	3	69	The Sound Of Music	Soundtrack	RCA 2005
7	7	10	Lou Rawls Live!	Lou Rawls	Capitol 2459
8	9	7	Wonderfulness	Bill Cosby	Warner 1634
9	8	39	Going Places	Herb Alpert & The Tijuana Brass	A&M 112
10	6	9	The Shadow of Your Smile	Andy Williams	Columbia 9299

TW	LW	WK	Billboard. JULY 16, 1966 TOP LP's
1	1	10	**What Now My Love** .... *Herb Alpert & The Tijuana Brass*...A&M 4114
2	3	5	Strangers In The Night .... *Frank Sinatra*...Reprise 1017
3	4	62	Whipped Cream & Other Delights .... *Herb Alpert's Tijuana Brass*...A&M 110
4	2	19	If You Can Believe Your Eyes And Ears .... *The Mama's & The Papa's*...Dunhill 50006
5	7	11	Lou Rawls Live! .... *Lou Rawls*...Capitol 2459
6	5	18	Doctor Zhivago .... *Soundtrack*...MGM 6
7	9	40	Going Places .... *Herb Alpert & The Tijuana Brass*...A&M 112
8	8	8	Wonderfulness .... *Bill Cosby*...Warner 1634
9	6	70	The Sound Of Music .... *Soundtrack*...RCA 2005
10	14	6	Midnight Ride .... *Paul Revere & The Raiders*...Columbia 9308

TW	LW	WK	Billboard. JULY 23, 1966 TOP LP's
1	2	6	**Strangers In The Night** .... *Frank Sinatra*...Reprise 1017
2	18	3	"Yesterday"...And Today .... *The Beatles*...Capitol 2553
3	1	11	What Now My Love .... *Herb Alpert & The Tijuana Brass*...A&M 4114
4	5	12	**Lou Rawls Live!** .... *Lou Rawls*...Capitol 2459
5	19	3	Aftermath .... *The Rolling Stones*...London 476
6	7	41	Going Places .... *Herb Alpert & The Tijuana Brass*...A&M 112
7	4	20	If You Can Believe Your Eyes And Ears .... *The Mama's & The Papa's*...Dunhill 50006
8	8	9	Wonderfulness .... *Bill Cosby*...Warner 1634
9	6	19	Doctor Zhivago .... *Soundtrack*...MGM 6
10	10	7	Midnight Ride .... *Paul Revere & The Raiders*...Columbia 9308

TW	LW	WK	Billboard. JULY 30, 1966 TOP LP's
1	2	4	**"Yesterday"...And Today** .... *The Beatles*...Capitol 2553
2	1	7	Strangers In The Night .... *Frank Sinatra*...Reprise 1017
3	5	4	Aftermath .... *The Rolling Stones*...London 476
4	3	12	What Now My Love .... *Herb Alpert & The Tijuana Brass*...A&M 4114
5	4	13	Lou Rawls Live! .... *Lou Rawls*...Capitol 2459
6	6	42	Going Places .... *Herb Alpert & The Tijuana Brass*...A&M 112
7	8	10	**Wonderfulness** .... *Bill Cosby*...Warner 1634
8	9	20	Doctor Zhivago .... *Soundtrack*...MGM 6
9	7	21	If You Can Believe Your Eyes And Ears .... *The Mama's & The Papa's*...Dunhill 50006
10	10	8	Midnight Ride .... *Paul Revere & The Raiders*...Columbia 9308

TW	LW	WK	Billboard. AUGUST 6, 1966 TOP LP's
1	1	5	**"Yesterday"...And Today** .... *The Beatles*...Capitol 2553
2	2	8	Strangers In The Night .... *Frank Sinatra*...Reprise 1017
3	3	5	Aftermath .... *The Rolling Stones*...London 476
4	4	13	What Now My Love .... *Herb Alpert & The Tijuana Brass*...A&M 4114
5	8	21	Doctor Zhivago .... *Soundtrack*...MGM 6
6	6	43	Going Places .... *Herb Alpert & The Tijuana Brass*...A&M 112
7	20	4	Somewhere My Love .... *Ray Conniff & The Singers*...Columbia 9319
8	12	65	Whipped Cream & Other Delights .... *Herb Alpert's Tijuana Brass*...A&M 110
9	10	9	**Midnight Ride** .... *Paul Revere & The Raiders*...Columbia 9308
10	9	22	If You Can Believe Your Eyes And Ears .... *The Mama's & The Papa's*...Dunhill 50006

TW	LW	WK	Billboard. AUGUST 13, 1966 TOP LP's
①	1	6	**"Yesterday"...And Today** .... *The Beatles*...Capitol 2553
②	3	6	**Aftermath** .... *The Rolling Stones*...London 476
③	4	14	What Now My Love .... *Herb Alpert & The Tijuana Brass*...A&M 4114
④	2	9	Strangers In The Night .... *Frank Sinatra*...Reprise 1017
⑤	5	22	Doctor Zhivago .... *Soundtrack*...MGM 6
⑥	7	5	Somewhere My Love .... *Ray Conniff & The Singers*...Columbia 9319
⑦	6	44	Going Places .... *Herb Alpert & The Tijuana Brass*...A&M 112
⑧	8	66	Whipped Cream & Other Delights .... *Herb Alpert's Tijuana Brass*...A&M 110
⑨	10	23	If You Can Believe Your Eyes And Ears .... *The Mama's & The Papa's*...Dunhill 50006
⑩	12	74	The Sound Of Music .... *Soundtrack*...RCA 2005

TW	LW	WK	Billboard. AUGUST 20, 1966 TOP LP's
①	1	7	**"Yesterday"...And Today** .... *The Beatles*...Capitol 2553
②	2	7	**Aftermath** .... *The Rolling Stones*...London 476
③	3	15	What Now My Love .... *Herb Alpert & The Tijuana Brass*...A&M 4114
④	4	10	Strangers In The Night .... *Frank Sinatra*...Reprise 1017
⑤	5	23	Doctor Zhivago .... *Soundtrack*...MGM 6
⑥	6	6	Somewhere My Love .... *Ray Conniff & The Singers*...Columbia 9319
⑦	7	45	Going Places .... *Herb Alpert & The Tijuana Brass*...A&M 112
⑧	8	67	Whipped Cream & Other Delights .... *Herb Alpert's Tijuana Brass*...A&M 110
⑨	10	75	The Sound Of Music .... *Soundtrack*...RCA 2005
⑩	9	24	If You Can Believe Your Eyes And Ears .... *The Mama's & The Papa's*...Dunhill 50006

TW	LW	WK	Billboard. AUGUST 27, 1966 TOP LP's
①	1	8	**"Yesterday"...And Today** .... *The Beatles*...Capitol 2553
②	3	16	What Now My Love .... *Herb Alpert & The Tijuana Brass*...A&M 4114
③	4	11	Strangers In The Night .... *Frank Sinatra*...Reprise 1017
④	5	24	Doctor Zhivago .... *Soundtrack*...MGM 6
⑤	6	7	Somewhere My Love .... *Ray Conniff & The Singers*...Columbia 9319
⑥	7	46	Going Places .... *Herb Alpert & The Tijuana Brass*...A&M 112
⑦	2	8	Aftermath .... *The Rolling Stones*...London 476
⑧	9	76	The Sound Of Music .... *Soundtrack*...RCA 2005
⑨	8	68	Whipped Cream & Other Delights .... *Herb Alpert's Tijuana Brass*...A&M 110
⑩	10	25	If You Can Believe Your Eyes And Ears .... *The Mama's & The Papa's*...Dunhill 50006

TW	LW	WK	Billboard. SEPTEMBER 3, 1966 TOP LP's
①	2	17	**What Now My Love** .... *Herb Alpert & The Tijuana Brass*...A&M 4114
②	1	9	"Yesterday"...And Today .... *The Beatles*...Capitol 2553
③	4	25	Doctor Zhivago .... *Soundtrack*...MGM 6
④	5	8	Somewhere My Love .... *Ray Conniff & The Singers*...Columbia 9319
⑤	3	12	Strangers In The Night .... *Frank Sinatra*...Reprise 1017
⑥	7	9	Aftermath .... *The Rolling Stones*...London 476
⑦	8	77	The Sound Of Music .... *Soundtrack*...RCA 2005
⑧	9	69	Whipped Cream & Other Delights .... *Herb Alpert's Tijuana Brass*...A&M 110
⑨	10	26	If You Can Believe Your Eyes And Ears .... *The Mama's & The Papa's*...Dunhill 50006
⑩	11	7	Best Of The Beach Boys .... *The Beach Boys*...Capitol 2545

TW	LW	WK	Billboard. SEPTEMBER 10, 1966	TOP LP's
1	45	2	**Revolver**	*The Beatles*...Capitol 2576
2	3	26	Doctor Zhivago	*Soundtrack*...MGM 6
3	1	18	What Now My Love	*Herb Alpert & The Tijuana Brass*...A&M 4114
4	4	9	Somewhere My Love	*Ray Conniff & The Singers*...Columbia 9319
5	7	78	The Sound Of Music	*Soundtrack*...RCA 2005
6	5	13	Strangers In The Night	*Frank Sinatra*...Reprise 1017
7	2	10	"Yesterday"...And Today	*The Beatles*...Capitol 2553
8	8	70	Whipped Cream & Other Delights	*Herb Alpert's Tijuana Brass*...A&M 110
9	9	27	If You Can Believe Your Eyes And Ears	*The Mama's & The Papa's*...Dunhill 50006
10	10	8	Best Of The Beach Boys	*The Beach Boys*...Capitol 2545

TW	LW	WK	Billboard. SEPTEMBER 17, 1966	TOP LP's
1	1	3	**Revolver**	*The Beatles*...Capitol 2576
2	2	27	Doctor Zhivago	*Soundtrack*...MGM 6
3	3	19	What Now My Love	*Herb Alpert & The Tijuana Brass*...A&M 4114
4	4	10	Somewhere My Love	*Ray Conniff & The Singers*...Columbia 9319
5	5	79	The Sound Of Music	*Soundtrack*...RCA 2005
6	8	71	Whipped Cream & Other Delights	*Herb Alpert's Tijuana Brass*...A&M 110
7	6	14	Strangers In The Night	*Frank Sinatra*...Reprise 1017
8	7	11	"Yesterday"...And Today	*The Beatles*...Capitol 2553
9	10	9	Best Of The Beach Boys	*The Beach Boys*...Capitol 2545
10	12	49	Going Places	*Herb Alpert & The Tijuana Brass*...A&M 112

TW	LW	WK	Billboard. SEPTEMBER 24, 1966	TOP LP's
1	1	4	**Revolver**	*The Beatles*...Capitol 2576
2	2	28	Doctor Zhivago	*Soundtrack*...MGM 6
3	4	11	**Somewhere My Love**	*Ray Conniff & The Singers*...Columbia 9319
4	5	80	The Sound Of Music	*Soundtrack*...RCA 2005
5	3	20	What Now My Love	*Herb Alpert & The Tijuana Brass*...A&M 4114
6	6	72	Whipped Cream & Other Delights	*Herb Alpert's Tijuana Brass*...A&M 110
7	7	15	Strangers In The Night	*Frank Sinatra*...Reprise 1017
8	9	10	**Best Of The Beach Boys**	*The Beach Boys*...Capitol 2545
9	11	12	Aftermath	*The Rolling Stones*...London 476
10	12	10	Blonde On Blonde	*Bob Dylan*...Columbia 841

TW	LW	WK	Billboard. OCTOBER 1, 1966	TOP LP's
1	1	5	**Revolver**	*The Beatles*...Capitol 2576
2	2	29	Doctor Zhivago	*Soundtrack*...MGM 6
3	3	12	**Somewhere My Love**	*Ray Conniff & The Singers*...Columbia 9319
4	4	81	The Sound Of Music	*Soundtrack*...RCA 2005
5	5	21	What Now My Love	*Herb Alpert & The Tijuana Brass*...A&M 4114
6	6	73	Whipped Cream & Other Delights	*Herb Alpert's Tijuana Brass*...A&M 110
7	9	13	Aftermath	*The Rolling Stones*...London 476
8	7	16	Strangers In The Night	*Frank Sinatra*...Reprise 1017
9	10	11	**Blonde On Blonde**	*Bob Dylan*...Columbia 841
10	8	11	Best Of The Beach Boys	*The Beach Boys*...Capitol 2545

TW	LW	WK	Billboard® OCTOBER 8, 1966 TOP LP's	
1	1	6	**Revolver**	*The Beatles*...Capitol 2576
2	2	30	Doctor Zhivago	*Soundtrack*...MGM 6
3	3	13	**Somewhere My Love**	*Ray Conniff & The Singers*...Columbia 9319
4	5	22	What Now My Love	*Herb Alpert & The Tijuana Brass*...A&M 4114
5	4	82	The Sound Of Music	*Soundtrack*...RCA 2005
6	6	74	Whipped Cream & Other Delights	*Herb Alpert's Tijuana Brass*...A&M 110
7	7	14	Aftermath	*The Rolling Stones*...London 476
8	8	17	Strangers In The Night	*Frank Sinatra*...Reprise 1017
9	10	12	Best Of The Beach Boys	*The Beach Boys*...Capitol 2545
10	13	8	Sinatra At The Sands	*Frank Sinatra*...Reprise 1019

TW	LW	WK	Billboard® OCTOBER 15, 1966 TOP LP's	
1	1	7	**Revolver**	*The Beatles*...Capitol 2576
2	2	31	Doctor Zhivago	*Soundtrack*...MGM 6
3	3	14	**Somewhere My Love**	*Ray Conniff & The Singers*...Columbia 9319
4	4	23	What Now My Love	*Herb Alpert & The Tijuana Brass*...A&M 4114
5	12	4	The Supremes A' Go-Go	*The Supremes*...Motown 649
6	6	75	Whipped Cream & Other Delights	*Herb Alpert's Tijuana Brass*...A&M 110
7	5	83	The Sound Of Music	*Soundtrack*...RCA 2005
8	21	3	The Mamas & The Papas	*The Mamas & The Papas*...Dunhill 50010
9	10	9	**Sinatra At The Sands**	*Frank Sinatra*...Reprise 1019
10	7	15	Aftermath	*The Rolling Stones*...London 476

TW	LW	WK	Billboard® OCTOBER 22, 1966 TOP LP's	
1	5	5	**The Supremes A' Go-Go**	*The Supremes*...Motown 649
2	1	8	Revolver	*The Beatles*...Capitol 2576
3	2	32	Doctor Zhivago	*Soundtrack*...MGM 6
4	8	4	**The Mamas & The Papas**	*The Mamas & The Papas*...Dunhill 50010
5	4	24	What Now My Love	*Herb Alpert & The Tijuana Brass*...A&M 4114
6	3	15	Somewhere My Love	*Ray Conniff & The Singers*...Columbia 9319
7	6	76	Whipped Cream & Other Delights	*Herb Alpert's Tijuana Brass*...A&M 110
8	7	84	The Sound Of Music	*Soundtrack*...RCA 2005
9	13	10	And Then...Along Comes The Association	*The Association*...Valiant 5002
10	14	15	The Impossible Dream	*Jack Jones*...Kapp 3486

TW	LW	WK	Billboard® OCTOBER 29, 1966 TOP LP's	
1	1	6	**The Supremes A' Go-Go**	*The Supremes*...Motown 649
2	2	9	Revolver	*The Beatles*...Capitol 2576
3	3	33	Doctor Zhivago	*Soundtrack*...MGM 6
4	4	5	**The Mamas & The Papas**	*The Mamas & The Papas*...Dunhill 50010
5	5	25	What Now My Love	*Herb Alpert & The Tijuana Brass*...A&M 4114
6	18	4	The Monkees	*The Monkees*...Colgems 101
7	9	11	And Then...Along Comes The Association	*The Association*...Valiant 5002
8	13	8	Lou Rawls Soulin'	*Lou Rawls*...Capitol 2566
9	10	16	**The Impossible Dream**	*Jack Jones*...Kapp 3486
10	6	16	Somewhere My Love	*Ray Conniff & The Singers*...Columbia 9319

Billboard® NOVEMBER 5, 1966 — TOP LP's

TW	LW	WK	Title	Artist...Label
1	3	34	Doctor Zhivago	*Soundtrack*...MGM 6
2	6	5	The Monkees	*The Monkees*...Colgems 101
3	1	7	The Supremes A' Go-Go	*The Supremes*...Motown 649
4	4	6	The Mamas & The Papas	*The Mamas & The Papas*...Dunhill 50010
5	2	10	Revolver	*The Beatles*...Capitol 2576
6	5	26	What Now My Love	*Herb Alpert & The Tijuana Brass*...A&M 4114
7	7	12	And Then...Along Comes The Association	*The Association*...Valiant 5002
8	8	9	Lou Rawls Soulin'	*Lou Rawls*...Capitol 2566
9	10	17	Somewhere My Love	*Ray Conniff & The Singers*...Columbia 9319
10	11	11	The Kinks Greatest Hits!	*The Kinks*...Reprise 6217

Billboard® NOVEMBER 12, 1966 — TOP LP's

TW	LW	WK	Title	Artist...Label
1	2	6	The Monkees	*The Monkees*...Colgems 101
2	1	35	Doctor Zhivago	*Soundtrack*...MGM 6
3	3	8	The Supremes A' Go-Go	*The Supremes*...Motown 649
4	4	7	The Mamas & The Papas	*The Mamas & The Papas*...Dunhill 50010
5	6	27	What Now My Love	*Herb Alpert & The Tijuana Brass*...A&M 4114
6	7	13	And Then...Along Comes The Association	*The Association*...Valiant 5002
7	8	10	Lou Rawls Soulin'	*Lou Rawls*...Capitol 2566
8	5	11	Revolver	*The Beatles*...Capitol 2576
9	9	18	Somewhere My Love	*Ray Conniff & The Singers*...Columbia 9319
10	10	12	The Kinks Greatest Hits!	*The Kinks*...Reprise 6217

Billboard® NOVEMBER 19, 1966 — TOP LP's

TW	LW	WK	Title	Artist...Label
1	1	7	The Monkees	*The Monkees*...Colgems 101
2	2	36	Doctor Zhivago	*Soundtrack*...MGM 6
3	3	9	The Supremes A' Go-Go	*The Supremes*...Motown 649
4	4	8	The Mamas & The Papas	*The Mamas & The Papas*...Dunhill 50010
5	6	14	And Then...Along Comes The Association	*The Association*...Valiant 5002
6	5	28	What Now My Love	*Herb Alpert & The Tijuana Brass*...A&M 4114
7	8	12	Revolver	*The Beatles*...Capitol 2576
8	9	19	Somewhere My Love	*Ray Conniff & The Singers*...Columbia 9319
9	10	13	The Kinks Greatest Hits!	*The Kinks*...Reprise 6217
10	11	88	The Sound Of Music	*Soundtrack*...RCA 2005

Billboard® NOVEMBER 26, 1966 — TOP LP's

TW	LW	WK	Title	Artist...Label
1	1	8	The Monkees	*The Monkees*...Colgems 101
2	2	37	Doctor Zhivago	*Soundtrack*...MGM 6
3	3	10	The Supremes A' Go-Go	*The Supremes*...Motown 649
4	4	9	The Mamas & The Papas	*The Mamas & The Papas*...Dunhill 50010
5	6	29	What Now My Love	*Herb Alpert & The Tijuana Brass*...A&M 4114
6	10	89	The Sound Of Music	*Soundtrack*...RCA 2005
7	5	15	And Then...Along Comes The Association	*The Association*...Valiant 5002
8	7	13	Revolver	*The Beatles*...Capitol 2576
9	11	12	Sergio Mendes & Brasil '66	*Sergio Mendes & Brasil '66*...A&M 4116
10	8	20	Somewhere My Love	*Ray Conniff & The Singers*...Columbia 9319

TW	LW	WK	Billboard® DECEMBER 3, 1966	TOP LP's
1	1	9	**The Monkees**	*The Monkees*...Colgems 101
2	2	38	Doctor Zhivago	*Soundtrack*...MGM 6
3	3	11	The Supremes A' Go-Go	*The Supremes*...Motown 649
4	4	10	**The Mamas & The Papas**	*The Mamas & The Papas*...Dunhill 50010
5	5	30	What Now My Love	*Herb Alpert & The Tijuana Brass*...A&M 4114
6	8	14	Revolver	*The Beatles*...Capitol 2576
7	6	90	The Sound Of Music	*Soundtrack*...RCA 2005
8	7	16	And Then...Along Comes The Association	*The Association*...Valiant 5002
9	9	13	Sergio Mendes & Brasil '66	*Sergio Mendes & Brasil '66*...A&M 4116
10	12	13	Lou Rawls Soulin'	*Lou Rawls*...Capitol 2566

TW	LW	WK	Billboard® DECEMBER 10, 1966	TOP LP's
1	1	10	**The Monkees**	*The Monkees*...Colgems 101
2	2	39	Doctor Zhivago	*Soundtrack*...MGM 6
3	3	12	The Supremes A' Go-Go	*The Supremes*...Motown 649
4	7	91	The Sound Of Music	*Soundtrack*...RCA 2005
5	4	11	The Mamas & The Papas	*The Mamas & The Papas*...Dunhill 50010
6	5	31	What Now My Love	*Herb Alpert & The Tijuana Brass*...A&M 4114
7	9	14	**Sergio Mendes & Brasil '66**	*Sergio Mendes & Brasil '66*...A&M 4116
8	14	61	Going Places	*Herb Alpert & The Tijuana Brass*...A&M 112
9	6	15	Revolver	*The Beatles*...Capitol 2576
10	10	14	Lou Rawls Soulin'	*Lou Rawls*...Capitol 2566

TW	LW	WK	Billboard® DECEMBER 17, 1966	TOP LP's
1	1	11	**The Monkees**	*The Monkees*...Colgems 101
2	2	40	Doctor Zhivago	*Soundtrack*...MGM 6
3	4	92	The Sound Of Music	*Soundtrack*...RCA 2005
4	3	13	The Supremes A' Go-Go	*The Supremes*...Motown 649
5	12	6	Parsley, Sage, Rosemary and Thyme	*Simon & Garfunkel*...Columbia 9363
6	6	32	What Now My Love	*Herb Alpert & The Tijuana Brass*...A&M 4114
7	5	12	The Mamas & The Papas	*The Mamas & The Papas*...Dunhill 50010
8	8	62	Going Places	*Herb Alpert & The Tijuana Brass*...A&M 112
9	10	15	Lou Rawls Soulin'	*Lou Rawls*...Capitol 2566
10	17	5	Je m'appelle Barbra	*Barbra Streisand*...Columbia 9347

TW	LW	WK	Billboard® DECEMBER 24, 1966	TOP LP's
1	1	12	**The Monkees**	*The Monkees*...Colgems 101
2	2	41	Doctor Zhivago	*Soundtrack*...MGM 6
3	12	3	S.R.O.	*Herb Alpert & The Tijuana Brass*...A&M 4119
4	5	7	**Parsley, Sage, Rosemary and Thyme**	*Simon & Garfunkel*...Columbia 9363
5	3	93	The Sound Of Music	*Soundtrack*...RCA 2005
6	10	6	Je m'appelle Barbra	*Barbra Streisand*...Columbia 9347
7	8	63	Going Places	*Herb Alpert & The Tijuana Brass*...A&M 112
8	4	14	The Supremes A' Go-Go	*The Supremes*...Motown 649
9	7	13	The Mamas & The Papas	*The Mamas & The Papas*...Dunhill 50010
10	6	33	What Now My Love	*Herb Alpert & The Tijuana Brass*...A&M 4114

TW	LW	WK	Billboard® DECEMBER 31, 1966	TOP LP's
①	1	13	**The Monkees**	*The Monkees*...Colgems 101
②	3	4	**S.R.O.**	*Herb Alpert & The Tijuana Brass*...A&M 4119
③	2	42	Doctor Zhivago	*Soundtrack*...MGM 6
④	4	8	**Parsley, Sage, Rosemary and Thyme**	*Simon & Garfunkel*...Columbia 9363
⑤	5	94	The Sound Of Music	*Soundtrack*...RCA 2005
⑥	6	7	Je m'appelle Barbra	*Barbra Streisand*...Columbia 9347
⑦	7	64	Going Places	*Herb Alpert & The Tijuana Brass*...A&M 112
⑧	8	15	The Supremes A' Go-Go	*The Supremes*...Motown 649
⑨	9	14	The Mamas & The Papas	*The Mamas & The Papas*...Dunhill 50010
⑩	11	11	**Golden Greats**	*Gary Lewis & The Playboys*...Liberty 7468

Billboard® — JANUARY 7, 1967 — TOP LP's

TW	LW	WK	Title	Artist	Label
1	1	14	**The Monkees**	*The Monkees*	Colgems 101
2	2	5	**S.R.O.**	*Herb Alpert & The Tijuana Brass*	A&M 4119
3	3	43	Doctor Zhivago	*Soundtrack*	MGM 6
4	5	95	The Sound Of Music	*Soundtrack*	RCA 2005
5	6	8	**Je m'appelle Barbra**	*Barbra Streisand*	Columbia 9347
6	7	65	Going Places	*Herb Alpert & The Tijuana Brass*	A&M 112
7	4	9	Parsley, Sage, Rosemary and Thyme	*Simon & Garfunkel*	Columbia 9363
8	11	5	Born Free	*Roger Williams*	Kapp 3501
9	8	16	The Supremes A' Go-Go	*The Supremes*	Motown 649
10	10	12	**Golden Greats**	*Gary Lewis & The Playboys*	Liberty 7468

Billboard® — JANUARY 14, 1967 — TOP LP's

TW	LW	WK	Title	Artist	Label
1	1	15	**The Monkees**	*The Monkees*	Colgems 101
2	2	6	**S.R.O.**	*Herb Alpert & The Tijuana Brass*	A&M 4119
3	3	44	Doctor Zhivago	*Soundtrack*	MGM 6
4	4	96	The Sound Of Music	*Soundtrack*	RCA 2005
5	5	9	**Je m'appelle Barbra**	*Barbra Streisand*	Columbia 9347
6	6	66	Going Places	*Herb Alpert & The Tijuana Brass*	A&M 112
7	8	6	**Born Free**	*Roger Williams*	Kapp 3501
8	11	6	Winchester Cathedral	*The New Vaudeville Band*	Fontana 27560
9	9	17	The Supremes A' Go-Go	*The Supremes*	Motown 649
10	10	13	**Golden Greats**	*Gary Lewis & The Playboys*	Liberty 7468

Billboard® — JANUARY 21, 1967 — TOP LP's

TW	LW	WK	Title	Artist	Label
1	1	16	**The Monkees**	*The Monkees*	Colgems 101
2	2	7	**S.R.O.**	*Herb Alpert & The Tijuana Brass*	A&M 4119
3	3	45	Doctor Zhivago	*Soundtrack*	MGM 6
4	4	97	The Sound Of Music	*Soundtrack*	RCA 2005
5	8	7	**Winchester Cathedral**	*The New Vaudeville Band*	Fontana 27560
6	11	6	**got Live if you want it!**	*The Rolling Stones*	London 493
7	7	7	**Born Free**	*Roger Williams*	Kapp 3501
8	5	10	Je m'appelle Barbra	*Barbra Streisand*	Columbia 9347
9	9	18	The Supremes A' Go-Go	*The Supremes*	Motown 649
10	10	14	**Golden Greats**	*Gary Lewis & The Playboys*	Liberty 7468

Billboard® — JANUARY 28, 1967 — TOP LP's

TW	LW	WK	Title	Artist	Label
1	1	17	**The Monkees**	*The Monkees*	Colgems 101
2	2	8	**S.R.O.**	*Herb Alpert & The Tijuana Brass*	A&M 4119
3	3	46	Doctor Zhivago	*Soundtrack*	MGM 6
4	4	98	The Sound Of Music	*Soundtrack*	RCA 2005
5	5	8	**Winchester Cathedral**	*The New Vaudeville Band*	Fontana 27560
6	6	7	**got Live if you want it!**	*The Rolling Stones*	London 493
7	12	7	The Temptations Greatest Hits	*The Temptations*	Gordy 919
8	16	5	That's Life	*Frank Sinatra*	Reprise 1020
9	7	8	Born Free	*Roger Williams*	Kapp 3501
10	14	90	Whipped Cream & Other Delights	*Herb Alpert's Tijuana Brass*	A&M 110

Billboard — FEBRUARY 4, 1967 — TOP LP's

TW	LW	WK	Title	Artist	Label
1	1	18	**The Monkees**	The Monkees	Colgems 101
2	2	9	**S.R.O.**	Herb Alpert & The Tijuana Brass	A&M 4119
3	3	47	Doctor Zhivago	Soundtrack	MGM 6
4	4	99	The Sound Of Music	Soundtrack	RCA 2005
5	5	9	**Winchester Cathedral**	The New Vaudeville Band	Fontana 27560
6	7	8	The Temptations Greatest Hits	The Temptations	Gordy 919
7	8	6	That's Life	Frank Sinatra	Reprise 1020
8	6	8	got Live if you want it!	The Rolling Stones	London 493
9	10	91	Whipped Cream & Other Delights	Herb Alpert's Tijuana Brass	A&M 110
10	15	6	The Spirit Of '67	Paul Revere & The Raiders	Columbia 9395

Billboard — FEBRUARY 11, 1967 — TOP LP's

TW	LW	WK	Title	Artist	Label
1	122	2	**More Of The Monkees**	The Monkees	Colgems 102
2	1	19	The Monkees	The Monkees	Colgems 101
3	2	10	S.R.O.	Herb Alpert & The Tijuana Brass	A&M 4119
4	3	48	Doctor Zhivago	Soundtrack	MGM 6
5	6	9	**The Temptations Greatest Hits**	The Temptations	Gordy 919
6	4	100	The Sound Of Music	Soundtrack	RCA 2005
7	7	7	That's Life	Frank Sinatra	Reprise 1020
8	5	10	Winchester Cathedral	The New Vaudeville Band	Fontana 27560
9	10	7	**The Spirit Of '67**	Paul Revere & The Raiders	Columbia 9395
10	8	9	got Live if you want it!	The Rolling Stones	London 493

Billboard — FEBRUARY 18, 1967 — TOP LP's

TW	LW	WK	Title	Artist	Label
1	1	3	**More Of The Monkees**	The Monkees	Colgems 102
2	2	20	The Monkees	The Monkees	Colgems 101
3	3	11	S.R.O.	Herb Alpert & The Tijuana Brass	A&M 4119
4	4	49	Doctor Zhivago	Soundtrack	MGM 6
5	6	101	The Sound Of Music	Soundtrack	RCA 2005
6	5	10	The Temptations Greatest Hits	The Temptations	Gordy 919
7	7	8	That's Life	Frank Sinatra	Reprise 1020
8	8	11	Winchester Cathedral	The New Vaudeville Band	Fontana 27560
9	9	8	**The Spirit Of '67**	Paul Revere & The Raiders	Columbia 9395
10	10	10	got Live if you want it!	The Rolling Stones	London 493

Billboard — FEBRUARY 25, 1967 — TOP LP's

TW	LW	WK	Title	Artist	Label
1	1	4	**More Of The Monkees**	The Monkees	Colgems 102
2	2	21	The Monkees	The Monkees	Colgems 101
3	3	12	S.R.O.	Herb Alpert & The Tijuana Brass	A&M 4119
4	4	50	Doctor Zhivago	Soundtrack	MGM 6
5	6	11	**The Temptations Greatest Hits**	The Temptations	Gordy 919
6	7	9	**That's Life**	Frank Sinatra	Reprise 1020
7	5	102	The Sound Of Music	Soundtrack	RCA 2005
8	8	12	Winchester Cathedral	The New Vaudeville Band	Fontana 27560
9	11	94	Whipped Cream & Other Delights	Herb Alpert's Tijuana Brass	A&M 110
10	9	9	The Spirit Of '67	Paul Revere & The Raiders	Columbia 9395

Billboard® — MARCH 4, 1967 — TOP LP's

TW	LW	WK			
1	1	5	**More Of The Monkees**	*The Monkees*	Colgems 102
2	2	22	The Monkees	*The Monkees*	Colgems 101
3	21	3	Between The Buttons	*The Rolling Stones*	London 499
4	3	13	S.R.O.	*Herb Alpert & The Tijuana Brass*	A&M 4119
5	4	51	Doctor Zhivago	*Soundtrack*	MGM 6
6	6	10	**That's Life**	*Frank Sinatra*	Reprise 1020
7	5	12	The Temptations Greatest Hits	*The Temptations*	Gordy 919
8	7	103	The Sound Of Music	*Soundtrack*	RCA 2005
9	9	95	Whipped Cream & Other Delights	*Herb Alpert's Tijuana Brass*	A&M 110
10	10	10	The Spirit Of '67	*Paul Revere & The Raiders*	Columbia 9395

Billboard® — MARCH 11, 1967 — TOP LP's

TW	LW	WK			
1	1	6	**More Of The Monkees**	*The Monkees*	Colgems 102
2	3	4	**Between The Buttons**	*The Rolling Stones*	London 499
3	2	[illegible]	The Monkees	*The Monkees*	Colgems 101
4	4	14	S.R.O.	*Herb Alpert & The Tijuana Brass*	A&M 4119
5	5	52	Doctor Zhivago	*Soundtrack*	MGM 6
6	6	11	**That's Life**	*Frank Sinatra*	Reprise 1020
7	7	13	The Temptations Greatest Hits	*The Temptations*	Gordy 919
8	8	104	The Sound Of Music	*Soundtrack*	RCA 2005
9	10	11	**The Spirit Of '67**	*Paul Revere & The Raiders*	Columbia 9395
10	13	24	The Mamas & The Papas	*The Mamas & The Papas*	Dunhill 50010

Billboard® — MARCH 18, 1967 — TOP LP's

TW	LW	WK			
1	1	7	**More Of The Monkees**	*The Monkees*	Colgems 102
2	2	5	**Between The Buttons**	*The Rolling Stones*	London 499
3	3	24	The Monkees	*The Monkees*	Colgems 101
4	5	53	Doctor Zhivago	*Soundtrack*	MGM 6
5	4	15	S.R.O.	*Herb Alpert & The Tijuana Brass*	A&M 4119
6	12	5	**The Supremes sing Holland-Dozier-Holland**	*The Supremes*	Motown 650
7	8	105	The Sound Of Music	*Soundtrack*	RCA 2005
8	7	14	The Temptations Greatest Hits	*The Temptations*	Gordy 919
9	6	12	That's Life	*Frank Sinatra*	Reprise 1020
10	9	12	The Spirit Of '67	*Paul Revere & The Raiders*	Columbia 9395

Billboard® — MARCH 25, 1967 — TOP LP's

TW	LW	WK			
1	1	8	**More Of The Monkees**	*The Monkees*	Colgems 102
2	2	6	**Between The Buttons**	*The Rolling Stones*	London 499
3	3	25	The Monkees	*The Monkees*	Colgems 101
4	4	54	Doctor Zhivago	*Soundtrack*	MGM 6
5	5	16	S.R.O.	*Herb Alpert & The Tijuana Brass*	A&M 4119
6	6	6	**The Supremes sing Holland-Dozier-Holland**	*The Supremes*	Motown 650
7	7	106	The Sound Of Music	*Soundtrack*	RCA 2005
8	8	15	The Temptations Greatest Hits	*The Temptations*	Gordy 919
9	9	13	That's Life	*Frank Sinatra*	Reprise 1020
10	20	4	My Cup Runneth Over	*Ed Ames*	RCA 3774

Billboard — APRIL 1, 1967 — TOP LP's

TW	LW	WK			
1	1	9	**More Of The Monkees**	The Monkees	Colgems 102
2	2	7	**Between The Buttons**	The Rolling Stones	London 499
3	3	26	The Monkees	The Monkees	Colgems 101
4	4	55	Doctor Zhivago	Soundtrack	MGM 6
5	5	17	S.R.O.	Herb Alpert & The Tijuana Brass	A&M 4119
6	11	3	The Mamas & The Papas Deliver	The Mamas & The Papas	Dunhill 50014
7	10	5	My Cup Runneth Over	Ed Ames	RCA 3774
8	6	7	The Supremes sing Holland-Dozier-Holland	The Supremes	Motown 650
9	7	107	The Sound Of Music	Soundtrack	RCA 2005
10	8	16	The Temptations Greatest Hits	The Temptations	Gordy 919

Billboard — APRIL 8, 1967 — TOP LP's

TW	LW	WK			
1	1	10	**More Of The Monkees**	The Monkees	Colgems 102
2	6	4	**The Mamas & The Papas Deliver**	The Mamas & The Papas	Dunhill 50014
3	3	27	The Monkees	The Monkees	Colgems 101
4	4	56	Doctor Zhivago	Soundtrack	MGM 6
5	7	6	My Cup Runneth Over	Ed Ames	RCA 3774
6	2	8	Between The Buttons	The Rolling Stones	London 499
7	5	18	S.R.O.	Herb Alpert & The Tijuana Brass	A&M 4119
8	8	8	The Supremes sing Holland-Dozier-Holland	The Supremes	Motown 650
9	9	108	The Sound Of Music	Soundtrack	RCA 2005
10	11	7	**Georgy Girl**	The Seekers	Capitol 2431

Billboard — APRIL 15, 1967 — TOP LP's

TW	LW	WK			
1	1	11	**More Of The Monkees**	The Monkees	Colgems 102
2	2	5	**The Mamas & The Papas Deliver**	The Mamas & The Papas	Dunhill 50014
3	3	28	The Monkees	The Monkees	Colgems 101
4	4	57	Doctor Zhivago	Soundtrack	MGM 6
5	5	7	My Cup Runneth Over	Ed Ames	RCA 3774
6	6	9	Between The Buttons	The Rolling Stones	London 499
7	11	5	The Best Of The Lovin' Spoonful	The Lovin' Spoonful	Kama Sutra 8056
8	9	109	The Sound Of Music	Soundtrack	RCA 2005
9	7	19	S.R.O.	Herb Alpert & The Tijuana Brass	A&M 4119
10	10	8	**Georgy Girl**	The Seekers	Capitol 2431

Billboard — APRIL 22, 1967 — TOP LP's

TW	LW	WK			
1	1	12	**More Of The Monkees**	The Monkees	Colgems 102
2	2	6	**The Mamas & The Papas Deliver**	The Mamas & The Papas	Dunhill 50014
3	4	58	Doctor Zhivago	Soundtrack	MGM 6
4	5	8	**My Cup Runneth Over**	Ed Ames	RCA 3774
5	3	29	The Monkees	The Monkees	Colgems 101
6	6	10	Between The Buttons	The Rolling Stones	London 499
7	7	6	The Best Of The Lovin' Spoonful	The Lovin' Spoonful	Kama Sutra 8056
8	8	110	The Sound Of Music	Soundtrack	RCA 2005
9	9	20	S.R.O.	Herb Alpert & The Tijuana Brass	A&M 4119
10	11	10	The Supremes sing Holland-Dozier-Holland	The Supremes	Motown 650

TW	LW	WK	Billboard® APRIL 29, 1967	TOP LP's
①	1	13	**More Of The Monkees**	*The Monkees*...Colgems 102
②	2	7	**The Mamas & The Papas Deliver**	*The Mamas & The Papas*...Dunhill 50014
③	3	59	Doctor Zhivago	*Soundtrack*...MGM 6
❹	7	7	The Best Of The Lovin' Spoonful	*The Lovin' Spoonful*...Kama Sutra 8056
⑤	4	9	My Cup Runneth Over	*Ed Ames*...RCA 3774
⑥	5	30	The Monkees	*The Monkees*...Colgems 101
⑦	6	11	Between The Buttons	*The Rolling Stones*...London 499
⑧	8	111	The Sound Of Music	*Soundtrack*...RCA 2005
⑨	12	20	The Temptations Greatest Hits	*The Temptations*...Gordy 919
⑩	9	21	S.R.O.	*Herb Alpert & The Tijuana Brass*...A&M 4119

TW	LW	WK	Billboard® MAY 6, 1967	TOP LP's
①	[illegible]	14	**More Of The Monkees**	*The Monkees*...Colgems 102
②	2	[illegible]	**The Mamas & The Papas Deliver**	*The Mamas & The Papas*...Dunhill 50014
③	4	8	**The Best Of The Lovin' Spoonful**	*The Lovin' Spoonful*...Kama Sutra 8056
④	5	10	**My Cup Runneth Over**	*Ed Ames*...RCA 3774
⑤	3	60	Doctor Zhivago	*Soundtrack*...MGM 6
⑥	6	31	The Monkees	*The Monkees*...Colgems 101
⑦	8	112	The Sound Of Music	*Soundtrack*...RCA 2005
⑧	7	12	Between The Buttons	*The Rolling Stones*...London 499
⑨	9	21	The Temptations Greatest Hits	*The Temptations*...Gordy 919
⑩	11	25	**A Man And A Woman**	*Soundtrack*...United Artists 5147

TW	LW	WK	Billboard® MAY 13, 1967	TOP LP's
①	1	15	**More Of The Monkees**	*The Monkees*...Colgems 102
②	2	9	**The Mamas & The Papas Deliver**	*The Mamas & The Papas*...Dunhill 50014
③	3	9	**The Best Of The Lovin' Spoonful**	*The Lovin' Spoonful*...Kama Sutra 8056
④	4	11	**My Cup Runneth Over**	*Ed Ames*...RCA 3774
⑤	5	61	Doctor Zhivago	*Soundtrack*...MGM 6
⑥	7	113	The Sound Of Music	*Soundtrack*...RCA 2005
⑦	6	32	The Monkees	*The Monkees*...Colgems 101
❽	12	6	I Never Loved A Man The Way I Love You	*Aretha Franklin*...Atlantic 8139
⑨	9	22	The Temptations Greatest Hits	*The Temptations*...Gordy 919
⑩	10	26	**A Man And A Woman**	*Soundtrack*...United Artists 5147

TW	LW	WK	Billboard® MAY 20, 1967	TOP LP's
①	1	16	**More Of The Monkees**	*The Monkees*...Colgems 102
②	2	10	**The Mamas & The Papas Deliver**	*The Mamas & The Papas*...Dunhill 50014
③	5	62	Doctor Zhivago	*Soundtrack*...MGM 6
④	3	10	The Best Of The Lovin' Spoonful	*The Lovin' Spoonful*...Kama Sutra 8056
❺	8	7	I Never Loved A Man The Way I Love You	*Aretha Franklin*...Atlantic 8139
⑥	6	114	The Sound Of Music	*Soundtrack*...RCA 2005
⑦	7	33	The Monkees	*The Monkees*...Colgems 101
⑧	4	12	My Cup Runneth Over	*Ed Ames*...RCA 3774
⑨	9	23	The Temptations Greatest Hits	*The Temptations*...Gordy 919
⑩	11	8	**Temptations Live!**	*The Temptations*...Gordy 921

Billboard — MAY 27, 1967 — TOP LP's

TW	LW	WK	Title	Artist	Label
1	1	17	**More Of The Monkees**	*The Monkees*	Colgems 102
2	5	8	**I Never Loved A Man The Way I Love You**	*Aretha Franklin*	Atlantic 8139
3	20	3	Revenge	*Bill Cosby*	Warner 1691
4	2	11	The Mamas & The Papas Deliver	*The Mamas & The Papas*	Dunhill 50014
5	3	63	Doctor Zhivago	*Soundtrack*	MGM 6
6	6	115	The Sound Of Music	*Soundtrack*	RCA 2005
7	7	34	The Monkees	*The Monkees*	Colgems 101
8	4	11	The Best Of The Lovin' Spoonful	*The Lovin' Spoonful*	Kama Sutra 8056
9	8	13	My Cup Runneth Over	*Ed Ames*	RCA 3774
10	16	10	Surrealistic Pillow	*Jefferson Airplane*	RCA 3766

Billboard — JUNE 3, 1967 — TOP LP's

TW	LW	WK	Title	Artist	Label
1	1	18	**More Of The Monkees**	*The Monkees*	Colgems 102
2	2	9	**I Never Loved A Man The Way I Love You**	*Aretha Franklin*	Atlantic 8139
3	3	4	Revenge	*Bill Cosby*	Warner 1691
4	4	12	The Mamas & The Papas Deliver	*The Mamas & The Papas*	Dunhill 50014
5	5	64	Doctor Zhivago	*Soundtrack*	MGM 6
6	6	116	The Sound Of Music	*Soundtrack*	RCA 2005
7	10	11	Surrealistic Pillow	*Jefferson Airplane*	RCA 3766
8	8	12	The Best Of The Lovin' Spoonful	*The Lovin' Spoonful*	Kama Sutra 8056
9	7	35	The Monkees	*The Monkees*	Colgems 101
10	22	4	Born Free	*Andy Williams*	Columbia 9480

Billboard — JUNE 10, 1967 — TOP LP's

TW	LW	WK	Title	Artist	Label
1	1	19	**More Of The Monkees**	*The Monkees*	Colgems 102
2	2	10	**I Never Loved A Man The Way I Love You**	*Aretha Franklin*	Atlantic 8139
3	3	5	Revenge	*Bill Cosby*	Warner 1691
4	101	2	Sounds Like	*Herb Alpert & The Tijuana Brass*	A&M 4124
5	4	13	The Mamas & The Papas Deliver	*The Mamas & The Papas*	Dunhill 50014
6	10	5	Born Free	*Andy Williams*	Columbia 9480
7	7	12	Surrealistic Pillow	*Jefferson Airplane*	RCA 3766
8	5	65	Doctor Zhivago	*Soundtrack*	MGM 6
9	15	5	**Greatest Hits**	*Paul Revere & The Raiders*	Columbia 9462
10	8	13	The Best Of The Lovin' Spoonful	*The Lovin' Spoonful*	Kama Sutra 8056

Billboard — JUNE 17, 1967 — TOP LP's

TW	LW	WK	Title	Artist	Label
1	4	3	**Sounds Like**	*Herb Alpert & The Tijuana Brass*	A&M 4124
2	3	6	**Revenge**	*Bill Cosby*	Warner 1691
3	2	11	I Never Loved A Man The Way I Love You	*Aretha Franklin*	Atlantic 8139
4	1	20	More Of The Monkees	*The Monkees*	Colgems 102
5	6	6	**Born Free**	*Andy Williams*	Columbia 9480
6	197	2	Headquarters	*The Monkees*	Colgems 103
7	5	14	The Mamas & The Papas Deliver	*The Mamas & The Papas*	Dunhill 50014
8	7	13	Surrealistic Pillow	*Jefferson Airplane*	RCA 3766
9	9	6	**Greatest Hits**	*Paul Revere & The Raiders*	Columbia 9462
10	11	7	**Bob Dylan's Greatest Hits**	*Bob Dylan*	Columbia 9463

TW	LW	WK	Billboard	JUNE 24, 1967	TOP LP's
1	6	3	**Headquarters**	*The Monkees*	Colgems 103
2	1	4	Sounds Like	*Herb Alpert & The Tijuana Brass*	A&M 4124
3	2	7	Revenge	*Bill Cosby*	Warner 1691
4	3	12	I Never Loved A Man The Way I Love You	*Aretha Franklin*	Atlantic 8139
5	5	7	**Born Free**	*Andy Williams*	Columbia 9480
6	8	14	Surrealistic Pillow	*Jefferson Airplane*	RCA 3766
7	4	21	More Of The Monkees	*The Monkees*	Colgems 102
8	-	1	Sgt. Pepper's Lonely Hearts Club Band	*The Beatles*	Capitol 2653
9	7	15	The Mamas & The Papas Deliver	*The Mamas & The Papas*	Dunhill 50014
10	11	67	Doctor Zhivago	*Soundtrack*	MGM 6

TW	LW	WK	Billboard	JULY 1, 1967	TOP LP's
1	8	2	**Sgt. Pepper's Lonely Hearts Club Band**	*The Beatles*	Capitol 2653
2	1	4	Headquarters	*The Monkees*	Colgems 103
3	2	5	Sounds Like	*Herb Alpert & The Tijuana Brass*	A&M 4124
4	4	13	I Never Loved A Man The Way I Love You	*Aretha Franklin*	Atlantic 8139
5	6	15	Surrealistic Pillow	*Jefferson Airplane*	RCA 3766
6	3	8	Revenge	*Bill Cosby*	Warner 1691
7	5	8	Born Free	*Andy Williams*	Columbia 9480
8	7	22	More Of The Monkees	*The Monkees*	Colgems 102
9	10	68	Doctor Zhivago	*Soundtrack*	MGM 6
10	9	16	The Mamas & The Papas Deliver	*The Mamas & The Papas*	Dunhill 50014

TW	LW	WK	Billboard	JULY 8, 1967	TOP LP's
1	1	3	**Sgt. Pepper's Lonely Hearts Club Band**	*The Beatles*	Capitol 2653
2	2	5	Headquarters	*The Monkees*	Colgems 103
3	3	6	Sounds Like	*Herb Alpert & The Tijuana Brass*	A&M 4124
4	4	14	I Never Loved A Man The Way I Love You	*Aretha Franklin*	Atlantic 8139
5	5	16	Surrealistic Pillow	*Jefferson Airplane*	RCA 3766
6	6	9	Revenge	*Bill Cosby*	Warner 1691
7	7	9	Born Free	*Andy Williams*	Columbia 9480
8	8	23	More Of The Monkees	*The Monkees*	Colgems 102
9	9	69	Doctor Zhivago	*Soundtrack*	MGM 6
10	10	17	The Mamas & The Papas Deliver	*The Mamas & The Papas*	Dunhill 50014

TW	LW	WK	Billboard	JULY 15, 1967	TOP LP's
1	1	4	**Sgt. Pepper's Lonely Hearts Club Band**	*The Beatles*	Capitol 2653
2	2	6	Headquarters	*The Monkees*	Colgems 103
3	3	7	Sounds Like	*Herb Alpert & The Tijuana Brass*	A&M 4124
4	4	15	I Never Loved A Man The Way I Love You	*Aretha Franklin*	Atlantic 8139
5	5	17	Surrealistic Pillow	*Jefferson Airplane*	RCA 3766
6	6	10	Revenge	*Bill Cosby*	Warner 1691
7	7	10	Born Free	*Andy Williams*	Columbia 9480
8	9	70	Doctor Zhivago	*Soundtrack*	MGM 6
9	8	24	More Of The Monkees	*The Monkees*	Colgems 102
10	17	17	The Doors	*The Doors*	Elektra 74007

TW	LW	WK	Billboard — JULY 22, 1967 — TOP LP's
1	1	5	**Sgt. Pepper's Lonely Hearts Club Band**....... *The Beatles*...Capitol 2653
2	2	7	Headquarters.. *The Monkees*...Colgems 103
3	3	8	Sounds Like .... *Herb Alpert & The Tijuana Brass*...A&M 4124
4	4	16	I Never Loved A Man The Way I Love You .... *Aretha Franklin*...Atlantic 8139
5	6	11	Revenge .... *Bill Cosby*...Warner 1691
6	5	18	Surrealistic Pillow... *Jefferson Airplane*...RCA 3766
7	7	11	Born Free..*Andy Williams*...Columbia 9480
8	8	71	Doctor Zhivago.. *Soundtrack*...MGM 6
9	10	18	The Doors.. *The Doors*...Elektra 74007
10	9	25	More Of The Monkees .... *The Monkees*...Colgems 102

TW	LW	WK	Billboard — JULY 29, 1967 — TOP LP's
1	1	6	**Sgt. Pepper's Lonely Hearts Club Band**....... *The Beatles*...Capitol 2653
2	2	8	Headquarters.. *The Monkees*...Colgems 103
3	3	9	Sounds Like .... *Herb Alpert & The Tijuana Brass*...A&M 4124
4	6	19	Surrealistic Pillow... *Jefferson Airplane*...RCA 3766
5	5	12	Revenge .... *Bill Cosby*...Warner 1691
6	4	17	I Never Loved A Man The Way I Love You .... *Aretha Franklin*...Atlantic 8139
7	7	12	Born Free..*Andy Williams*...Columbia 9480
8	8	72	Doctor Zhivago.. *Soundtrack*...MGM 6
9	9	19	The Doors.. *The Doors*...Elektra 74007
10	10	26	More Of The Monkees .... *The Monkees*...Colgems 102

TW	LW	WK	Billboard — AUGUST 5, 1967 — TOP LP's
1	1	7	**Sgt. Pepper's Lonely Hearts Club Band**....... *The Beatles*...Capitol 2653
2	2	9	Headquarters.. *The Monkees*...Colgems 103
3	4	20	**Surrealistic Pillow**...................................... *Jefferson Airplane*...RCA 3766
4	19	3	Flowers.. *The Rolling Stones*...London 509
5	9	20	The Doors.. *The Doors*...Elektra 74007
6	3	10	Sounds Like .... *Herb Alpert & The Tijuana Brass*...A&M 4124
7	6	18	I Never Loved A Man The Way I Love You .... *Aretha Franklin*...Atlantic 8139
8	7	13	Born Free..*Andy Williams*...Columbia 9480
9	5	13	Revenge .... *Bill Cosby*...Warner 1691
10	8	73	Doctor Zhivago.. *Soundtrack*...MGM 6

TW	LW	WK	Billboard — AUGUST 12, 1967 — TOP LP's
1	1	8	**Sgt. Pepper's Lonely Hearts Club Band**....... *The Beatles*...Capitol 2653
2	2	10	Headquarters.. *The Monkees*...Colgems 103
3	4	4	**Flowers**.. *The Rolling Stones*...London 509
4	3	21	Surrealistic Pillow... *Jefferson Airplane*...RCA 3766
5	5	21	The Doors.. *The Doors*...Elektra 74007
6	7	19	I Never Loved A Man The Way I Love You .... *Aretha Franklin*...Atlantic 8139
7	6	11	Sounds Like .... *Herb Alpert & The Tijuana Brass*...A&M 4124
8	12	9	**Up, Up And Away** .... *The 5th Dimension*...Soul City 92000
9	9	14	Revenge .... *Bill Cosby*...Warner 1691
10	8	14	Born Free..*Andy Williams*...Columbia 9480

Billboard — AUGUST 19, 1967 — TOP LP's

TW	LW	WK	Title	Artist	Label
1	1	9	**Sgt. Pepper's Lonely Hearts Club Band**	*The Beatles*	Capitol 2653
2	2	11	Headquarters	*The Monkees*	Colgems 103
3	3	5	**Flowers**	*The Rolling Stones*	London 509
4	5	22	The Doors	*The Doors*	Elektra 74007
5	4	22	Surrealistic Pillow	*Jefferson Airplane*	RCA 3766
6	7	12	Sounds Like	*Herb Alpert & The Tijuana Brass*	A&M 4124
7	6	20	I Never Loved A Man The Way I Love You	*Aretha Franklin*	Atlantic 8139
8	8	10	**Up, Up And Away**	*The 5th Dimension*	Soul City 92000
9	10	15	Born Free	*Andy Williams*	Columbia 9480
10	12	10	Release Me	*Engelbert Humperdinck*	Parrot 71012

Billboard — AUGUST 26, 1967 — TOP LP's

TW	LW	WK	Title	Artist	Label
1	1	10	**Sgt. Pepper's Lonely Hearts Club Band**	*The Beatles*	Capitol 2653
2	2	12	Headquarters	*The Monkees*	Colgems 103
3	3	6	**Flowers**	*The Rolling Stones*	London 509
4	4	23	The Doors	*The Doors*	Elektra 74007
5	5	23	Surrealistic Pillow	*Jefferson Airplane*	RCA 3766
6	7	21	I Never Loved A Man The Way I Love You	*Aretha Franklin*	Atlantic 8139
7	6	13	Sounds Like	*Herb Alpert & The Tijuana Brass*	A&M 4124
8	10	11	Release Me	*Engelbert Humperdinck*	Parrot 71012
9	8	11	Up, Up And Away	*The 5th Dimension*	Soul City 92000
10	14	6	Insight Out	*The Association*	Warner 1696

Billboard — SEPTEMBER 2, 1967 — TOP LP's

TW	LW	WK	Title	Artist	Label
1	1	11	**Sgt. Pepper's Lonely Hearts Club Band**	*The Beatles*	Capitol 2653
2	2	13	Headquarters	*The Monkees*	Colgems 103
3	3	7	**Flowers**	*The Rolling Stones*	London 509
4	4	24	The Doors	*The Doors*	Elektra 74007
5	5	24	Surrealistic Pillow	*Jefferson Airplane*	RCA 3766
6	18	4	Groovin'	*The Young Rascals*	Atlantic 8148
7	8	12	**Release Me**	*Engelbert Humperdinck*	Parrot 71012
8	10	7	**Insight Out**	*The Association*	Warner 1696
9	6	22	I Never Loved A Man The Way I Love You	*Aretha Franklin*	Atlantic 8139
10	16	4	With A Lot O' Soul	*The Temptations*	Gordy 922

Billboard — SEPTEMBER 9, 1967 — TOP LP's

TW	LW	WK	Title	Artist	Label
1	1	12	**Sgt. Pepper's Lonely Hearts Club Band**	*The Beatles*	Capitol 2653
2	2	14	Headquarters	*The Monkees*	Colgems 103
3	3	8	**Flowers**	*The Rolling Stones*	London 509
4	4	25	The Doors	*The Doors*	Elektra 74007
5	5	25	Surrealistic Pillow	*Jefferson Airplane*	RCA 3766
6	6	5	Groovin'	*The Young Rascals*	Atlantic 8148
7	7	13	**Release Me**	*Engelbert Humperdinck*	Parrot 71012
8	10	5	With A Lot O' Soul	*The Temptations*	Gordy 922
9	8	8	Insight Out	*The Association*	Warner 1696
10	20	3	Aretha Arrives	*Aretha Franklin*	Atlantic 8150

Billboard — SEPTEMBER 16, 1967 — TOP LP's

TW	LW	WK	Title	Artist	Label
1	1	13	**Sgt. Pepper's Lonely Hearts Club Band**	*The Beatles*	Capitol 2653
2	4	26	**The Doors**	*The Doors*	Elektra 74007
3	2	15	Headquarters	*The Monkees*	Colgems 103
4	3	9	Flowers	*The Rolling Stones*	London 509
5	5	26	Surrealistic Pillow	*Jefferson Airplane*	RCA 3766
6	6	6	Groovin'	*The Young Rascals*	Atlantic 8148
7	7	14	**Release Me**	*Engelbert Humperdinck*	Parrot 71012
8	8	6	With A Lot O' Soul	*The Temptations*	Gordy 922
9	10	4	Aretha Arrives	*Aretha Franklin*	Atlantic 8150
10	9	9	Insight Out	*The Association*	Warner 1696

Billboard — SEPTEMBER 23, 1967 — TOP LP's

TW	LW	WK	Title	Artist	Label
1	1	14	**Sgt. Pepper's Lonely Hearts Club Band**	*The Beatles*	Capitol 2653
2	2	27	**The Doors**	*The Doors*	Elektra 74007
3	4	10	**Flowers**	*The Rolling Stones*	London 509
4	3	16	Headquarters	*The Monkees*	Colgems 103
5	6	7	**Groovin'**	*The Young Rascals*	Atlantic 8148
6	5	27	Surrealistic Pillow	*Jefferson Airplane*	RCA 3766
7	9	5	Aretha Arrives	*Aretha Franklin*	Atlantic 8150
8	8	7	With A Lot O' Soul	*The Temptations*	Gordy 922
9	60	2	Ode To Billie Joe	*Bobbie Gentry*	Capitol 2830
10	7	15	Release Me	*Engelbert Humperdinck*	Parrot 71012

Billboard — SEPTEMBER 30, 1967 — TOP LP's

TW	LW	WK	Title	Artist	Label
1	1	15	**Sgt. Pepper's Lonely Hearts Club Band**	*The Beatles*	Capitol 2653
2	9	3	Ode To Billie Joe	*Bobbie Gentry*	Capitol 2830
3	2	28	The Doors	*The Doors*	Elektra 74007
4	3	11	Flowers	*The Rolling Stones*	London 509
5	4	17	Headquarters	*The Monkees*	Colgems 103
6	7	6	Aretha Arrives	*Aretha Franklin*	Atlantic 8150
7	8	8	**With A Lot O' Soul**	*The Temptations*	Gordy 922
8	5	8	Groovin'	*The Young Rascals*	Atlantic 8148
9	6	28	Surrealistic Pillow	*Jefferson Airplane*	RCA 3766
10	10	16	Release Me	*Engelbert Humperdinck*	Parrot 71012

Billboard — OCTOBER 7, 1967 — TOP LP's

TW	LW	WK	Title	Artist	Label
1	1	16	**Sgt. Pepper's Lonely Hearts Club Band**	*The Beatles*	Capitol 2653
2	2	4	Ode To Billie Joe	*Bobbie Gentry*	Capitol 2830
3	3	29	The Doors	*The Doors*	Elektra 74007
4	4	12	Flowers	*The Rolling Stones*	London 509
5	6	7	**Aretha Arrives**	*Aretha Franklin*	Atlantic 8150
6	5	18	Headquarters	*The Monkees*	Colgems 103
7	13	6	The Byrds' Greatest Hits	*The Byrds*	Columbia 9516
8	8	9	Groovin'	*The Young Rascals*	Atlantic 8148
9	9	29	Surrealistic Pillow	*Jefferson Airplane*	RCA 3766
10	12	7	Are You Experienced?	*Jimi Hendrix Experience*	Reprise 6261

Billboard® OCTOBER 14, 1967 TOP LP's

TW	LW	WK	Title	Artist	Label
1	2	5	**Ode To Billie Joe**	*Bobbie Gentry*	Capitol 2830
2	1	17	Sgt. Pepper's Lonely Hearts Club Band	*The Beatles*	Capitol 2653
3	15	3	Diana Ross and the Supremes Greatest Hits	*Diana Ross & The Supremes*	Motown 663
4	3	30	The Doors	*The Doors*	Elektra 74007
5	5	8	**Aretha Arrives**	*Aretha Franklin*	Atlantic 8150
6	7	7	**The Byrds' Greatest Hits**	*The Byrds*	Columbia 9516
7	6	19	Headquarters	*The Monkees*	Colgems 103
8	8	10	Groovin'	*The Young Rascals*	Atlantic 8148
9	16	5	Vanilla Fudge	*Vanilla Fudge*	Atco 224
10	10	8	Are You Experienced?	*Jimi Hendrix Experience*	Reprise 6261

Billboard® OCTOBER 21, 1967 TOP LP's

TW	LW	WK	Title	Artist	Label
1	1	6	**Ode To Billie Joe**	*Bobbie Gentry*	Capitol 2830
2	3	4	Diana Ross and the Supremes Greatest Hits	*Diana Ross & The Supremes*	Motown 663
3	2	18	Sgt. Pepper's Lonely Hearts Club Band	*The Beatles*	Capitol 2653
4	4	31	The Doors	*The Doors*	Elektra 74007
5	5	9	**Aretha Arrives**	*Aretha Franklin*	Atlantic 8150
6	6	8	**The Byrds' Greatest Hits**	*The Byrds*	Columbia 9516
7	8	11	Groovin'	*The Young Rascals*	Atlantic 8148
8	7	20	Headquarters	*The Monkees*	Colgems 103
9	9	6	Vanilla Fudge	*Vanilla Fudge*	Atco 224
10	14	4	The Four Tops Greatest Hits	*Four Tops*	Motown 662

Billboard® OCTOBER 28, 1967 TOP LP's

TW	LW	WK	Title	Artist	Label
1	2	5	**Diana Ross and the Supremes Greatest Hits**	*Diana Ross & The Supremes*	Motown 663
2	3	19	Sgt. Pepper's Lonely Hearts Club Band	*The Beatles*	Capitol 2653
3	4	32	The Doors	*The Doors*	Elektra 74007
4	1	7	Ode To Billie Joe	*Bobbie Gentry*	Capitol 2830
5	5	10	**Aretha Arrives**	*Aretha Franklin*	Atlantic 8150
6	6	9	**The Byrds' Greatest Hits**	*The Byrds*	Columbia 9516
7	10	5	The Four Tops Greatest Hits	*Four Tops*	Motown 662
8	9	7	Vanilla Fudge	*Vanilla Fudge*	Atco 224
9	7	12	Groovin'	*The Young Rascals*	Atlantic 8148
10	8	21	Headquarters	*The Monkees*	Colgems 103

Billboard® NOVEMBER 4, 1967 TOP LP's

TW	LW	WK	Title	Artist	Label
1	1	6	**Diana Ross and the Supremes Greatest Hits**	*Diana Ross & The Supremes*	Motown 663
2	2	20	Sgt. Pepper's Lonely Hearts Club Band	*The Beatles*	Capitol 2653
3	3	33	The Doors	*The Doors*	Elektra 74007
4	4	8	Ode To Billie Joe	*Bobbie Gentry*	Capitol 2830
5	5	11	**Aretha Arrives**	*Aretha Franklin*	Atlantic 8150
6	7	6	The Four Tops Greatest Hits	*Four Tops*	Motown 662
7	8	8	Vanilla Fudge	*Vanilla Fudge*	Atco 224
8	6	10	The Byrds' Greatest Hits	*The Byrds*	Columbia 9516
9	9	13	Groovin'	*The Young Rascals*	Atlantic 8148
10	10	22	Headquarters	*The Monkees*	Colgems 103

TW	LW	WK	Billboard. NOVEMBER 11, 1967 TOP LP's
1	1	7	**Diana Ross and the Supremes Greatest Hits** .... *Diana Ross & The Supremes*...Motown 663
2	2	21	Sgt. Pepper's Lonely Hearts Club Band .... *The Beatles*...Capitol 2653
3	3	34	The Doors .... *The Doors*...Elektra 74007
4	100	2	Strange Days .... *The Doors*...Elektra 74014
5	6	7	The Four Tops Greatest Hits .... *Four Tops*...Motown 662
6	4	9	Ode To Billie Joe .... *Bobbie Gentry*...Capitol 2830
7	7	9	Vanilla Fudge .... *Vanilla Fudge*...Atco 224
8	9	14	Groovin' .... *The Young Rascals*...Atlantic 8148
9	5	12	Aretha Arrives .... *Aretha Franklin*...Atlantic 8150
10	11	87	Doctor Zhivago .... *Soundtrack*...MGM 6

TW	LW	WK	Billboard. NOVEMBER 18, 1967 TOP LP's
1	1	8	**Diana Ross and the Supremes Greatest Hits** .... *Diana Ross & The Supremes*...Motown 663
2	2	22	Sgt. Pepper's Lonely Hearts Club Band .... *The Beatles*...Capitol 2653
3	4	3	**Strange Days** .... *The Doors*...Elektra 74014
4	3	35	The Doors .... *The Doors*...Elektra 74007
5	5	8	The Four Tops Greatest Hits .... *Four Tops*...Motown 662
6	7	10	**Vanilla Fudge** .... *Vanilla Fudge*...Atco 224
7	6	10	Ode To Billie Joe .... *Bobbie Gentry*...Capitol 2830
8	11	13	Bee Gees' 1st .... *Bee Gees*...Atco 223
9	10	88	Doctor Zhivago .... *Soundtrack*...MGM 6
10	8	15	Groovin' .... *The Young Rascals*...Atlantic 8148

TW	LW	WK	Billboard. NOVEMBER 25, 1967 TOP LP's
1	1	9	**Diana Ross and the Supremes Greatest Hits** .... *Diana Ross & The Supremes*...Motown 663
2	2	23	Sgt. Pepper's Lonely Hearts Club Band .... *The Beatles*...Capitol 2653
3	3	4	**Strange Days** .... *The Doors*...Elektra 74014
4	5	9	**The Four Tops Greatest Hits** .... *Four Tops*...Motown 662
5	4	36	The Doors .... *The Doors*...Elektra 74007
6	6	11	**Vanilla Fudge** .... *Vanilla Fudge*...Atco 224
7	7	11	Ode To Billie Joe .... *Bobbie Gentry*...Capitol 2830
8	8	14	Bee Gees' 1st .... *Bee Gees*...Atco 223
9	9	89	Doctor Zhivago .... *Soundtrack*...MGM 6
10	10	16	Groovin' .... *The Young Rascals*...Atlantic 8148

TW	LW	WK	Billboard. DECEMBER 2, 1967 TOP LP's
1	29	2	**Pisces, Aquarius, Capricorn & Jones Ltd.** ... *The Monkees*...Colgems 104
2	1	10	Diana Ross and the Supremes Greatest Hits .... *Diana Ross & The Supremes*...Motown 663
3	3	5	**Strange Days** .... *The Doors*...Elektra 74014
4	2	24	Sgt. Pepper's Lonely Hearts Club Band .... *The Beatles*...Capitol 2653
5	5	37	The Doors .... *The Doors*...Elektra 74007
6	6	12	**Vanilla Fudge** .... *Vanilla Fudge*...Atco 224
7	8	15	**Bee Gees' 1st** .... *Bee Gees*...Atco 223
8	9	90	Doctor Zhivago .... *Soundtrack*...MGM 6
9	4	10	The Four Tops Greatest Hits .... *Four Tops*...Motown 662
10	12	15	Are You Experienced? .... *Jimi Hendrix Experience*...Reprise 6261

TW	LW	WK	Billboard® DECEMBER 9, 1967 TOP LP's
1	1	3	**Pisces, Aquarius, Capricorn & Jones Ltd.**... *The Monkees*...Colgems 104
2	2	11	Diana Ross and the Supremes Greatest Hits ... *Diana Ross & The Supremes*...Motown 663
3	3	6	**Strange Days** ... *The Doors*...Elektra 74014
4	4	25	Sgt. Pepper's Lonely Hearts Club Band... *The Beatles*...Capitol 2653
5	14	5	**Farewell To The First Golden Era** ... *The Mamas & The Papas*...Dunhill/ABC 50025
6	5	38	The Doors... *The Doors*...Elektra 74007
7	6	13	Vanilla Fudge ... *Vanilla Fudge*...Atco 224
8	10	16	Are You Experienced? ... *Jimi Hendrix Experience*...Reprise 6261
9	8	91	Doctor Zhivago ... *Soundtrack*...MGM 6
10	7	16	Bee Gees' 1st... *Bee Gees*...Atco 223

TW	LW	WK	Billboard® DECEMBER 16, 1967 TOP LP's
1	1	4	**Pisces, Aquarius, Capricorn & Jones Ltd.**... *The Monkees*...Colgems 104
2	2	12	Diana Ross and the Supremes Greatest Hits ... *Diana Ross & The Supremes*...Motown 663
3	4	26	Sgt. Pepper's Lonely Hearts Club Band... *The Beatles*...Capitol 2653
4	3	7	Strange Days... *The Doors*...Elektra 74014
5	5	6	**Farewell To The First Golden Era** ... *The Mamas & The Papas*...Dunhill/ABC 50025
6	7	14	**Vanilla Fudge**... *Vanilla Fudge*...Atco 224
7	8	17	Are You Experienced? ... *Jimi Hendrix Experience*...Reprise 6261
8	14	144	The Sound Of Music ... *Soundtrack*...RCA 2005
9	9	92	Doctor Zhivago ... *Soundtrack*...MGM 6
10	10	17	Bee Gees' 1st... *Bee Gees*...Atco 223

TW	LW	WK	Billboard® DECEMBER 23, 1967 TOP LP's
1	1	5	**Pisces, Aquarius, Capricorn & Jones Ltd.**... *The Monkees*...Colgems 104
2	2	13	Diana Ross and the Supremes Greatest Hits ... *Diana Ross & The Supremes*...Motown 663
3	3	27	Sgt. Pepper's Lonely Hearts Club Band... *The Beatles*...Capitol 2653
4	4	8	Strange Days... *The Doors*...Elektra 74014
5	5	7	**Farewell To The First Golden Era** ... *The Mamas & The Papas*...Dunhill/ABC 50025
6	9	93	Doctor Zhivago ... *Soundtrack*...MGM 6
7	8	145	The Sound Of Music ... *Soundtrack*...RCA 2005
8	7	18	Are You Experienced? ... *Jimi Hendrix Experience*...Reprise 6261
9	6	15	Vanilla Fudge ... *Vanilla Fudge*...Atco 224
10	13	6	**Dionne Warwick's Golden Hits, Part One** ... *Dionne Warwick*...Scepter 565

TW	LW	WK	Billboard. DECEMBER 30, 1967 TOP LP's
①	1	6	**Pisces, Aquarius, Capricorn & Jones Ltd.**.... *The Monkees*...Colgems 104
②	2	14	Diana Ross and the Supremes Greatest Hits .... *Diana Ross & The Supremes*...Motown 663
③	3	28	Sgt. Pepper's Lonely Hearts Club Band .... *The Beatles*...Capitol 2653
❹	157	2	Magical Mystery Tour .... *The Beatles/Soundtrack*...Capitol 2835
❺	29	2	Their Satanic Majesties Request .... *The Rolling Stones*...London 2
⑥	6	94	Doctor Zhivago .... *Soundtrack*...MGM 6
⑦	7	146	The Sound Of Music .... *Soundtrack*...RCA 2005
⑧	5	8	Farewell To The First Golden Era .. *The Mamas & The Papas*...Dunhill/ABC 50025
⑨	4	9	Strange Days .... *The Doors*...Elektra 74014
⑩	10	7	**Dionne Warwick's Golden Hits, Part One** .... *Dionne Warwick*...Scepter 565

Billboard — JANUARY 6, 1968 — TOP LP's

TW	LW	WK	Title	Artist...Label
1	4	3	**Magical Mystery Tour**	*The Beatles/Soundtrack*...Capitol 2835
2	5	3	**Their Satanic Majesties Request**	*The Rolling Stones*...London 2
3	1	7	Pisces, Aquarius, Capricorn & Jones Ltd.	*The Monkees*...Colgems 104
4	2	15	Diana Ross and the Supremes Greatest Hits	*Diana Ross & The Supremes*...Motown 663
5	3	29	Sgt. Pepper's Lonely Hearts Club Band	*The Beatles*...Capitol 2653
6	6	95	Doctor Zhivago	*Soundtrack*...MGM 6
7	7	147	The Sound Of Music	*Soundtrack*...RCA 2005
8	8	9	Farewell To The First Golden Era	*The Mamas & The Papas*...Dunhill/ABC 50025
9	9	10	Strange Days	*The Doors*...Elektra 74014
10	11	8	Love, Andy	*Andy Williams*...Columbia 9566

Billboard — JANUARY 13, 1968 — TOP LP's

TW	LW	WK	Title	Artist...Label
1	1	4	**Magical Mystery Tour**	*The Beatles/Soundtrack*...Capitol 2835
2	2	4	**Their Satanic Majesties Request**	*The Rolling Stones*...London 2
3	3	8	Pisces, Aquarius, Capricorn & Jones Ltd.	*The Monkees*...Colgems 104
4	4	16	Diana Ross and the Supremes Greatest Hits	*Diana Ross & The Supremes*...Motown 663
5	5	30	Sgt. Pepper's Lonely Hearts Club Band	*The Beatles*...Capitol 2653
6	6	96	Doctor Zhivago	*Soundtrack*...MGM 6
7	7	148	The Sound Of Music	*Soundtrack*...RCA 2005
8	15	4	Herb Alpert's Ninth	*Herb Alpert & The Tijuana Brass*...A&M 4134
9	8	10	Farewell To The First Golden Era	*The Mamas & The Papas*...Dunhill/ABC 50025
10	10	9	Love, Andy	*Andy Williams*...Columbia 9566

Billboard — JANUARY 20, 1968 — TOP LP's

TW	LW	WK	Title	Artist...Label
1	1	5	**Magical Mystery Tour**	*The Beatles/Soundtrack*...Capitol 2835
2	2	5	**Their Satanic Majesties Request**	*The Rolling Stones*...London 2
3	3	9	Pisces, Aquarius, Capricorn & Jones Ltd.	*The Monkees*...Colgems 104
4	4	17	Diana Ross and the Supremes Greatest Hits	*Diana Ross & The Supremes*...Motown 663
5	8	5	Herb Alpert's Ninth	*Herb Alpert & The Tijuana Brass*...A&M 4134
6	5	31	Sgt. Pepper's Lonely Hearts Club Band	*The Beatles*...Capitol 2653
7	15	7	Disraeli Gears	*Cream*...Atco 232
8	10	10	**Love, Andy**	*Andy Williams*...Columbia 9566
9	9	11	Farewell To The First Golden Era	*The Mamas & The Papas*...Dunhill/ABC 50025
10	13	10	The Turtles! Golden Hits	*The Turtles*...White Whale 7115

Billboard — JANUARY 27, 1968 — TOP LP's

TW	LW	WK	Title	Artist...Label
1	1	6	**Magical Mystery Tour**	*The Beatles/Soundtrack*...Capitol 2835
2	2	6	**Their Satanic Majesties Request**	*The Rolling Stones*...London 2
3	3	10	Pisces, Aquarius, Capricorn & Jones Ltd.	*The Monkees*...Colgems 104
4	4	18	Diana Ross and the Supremes Greatest Hits	*Diana Ross & The Supremes*...Motown 663
5	5	6	Herb Alpert's Ninth	*Herb Alpert & The Tijuana Brass*...A&M 4134
6	6	32	Sgt. Pepper's Lonely Hearts Club Band	*The Beatles*...Capitol 2653
7	7	8	Disraeli Gears	*Cream*...Atco 232
8	8	11	**Love, Andy**	*Andy Williams*...Columbia 9566
9	9	12	Farewell To The First Golden Era	*The Mamas & The Papas*...Dunhill/ABC 50025
10	10	11	The Turtles! Golden Hits	*The Turtles*...White Whale 7115

TW	LW	WK	Billboard® — FEBRUARY 3, 1968 — TOP LP's
1	1	7	**Magical Mystery Tour** .... *The Beatles/Soundtrack*...Capitol 2835
2	2	7	**Their Satanic Majesties Request** .... *The Rolling Stones*...London 2
3	4	19	Diana Ross and the Supremes Greatest Hits .... *Diana Ross & The Supremes*...Motown 663
4	3	11	Pisces, Aquarius, Capricorn & Jones Ltd. .... *The Monkees*...Colgems 104
5	5	7	Herb Alpert's Ninth .... *Herb Alpert & The Tijuana Brass*...A&M 4134
6	6	33	Sgt. Pepper's Lonely Hearts Club Band............... *The Beatles*...Capitol 2653
7	10	12	**The Turtles! Golden Hits** .... *The Turtles*...White Whale 7115
8	7	9	Disraeli Gears .... *Cream*...Atco 232
9	9	13	Farewell To The First Golden Era .. *The Mamas & The Papas*...Dunhill/ABC 50025
10	14	7	**The Last Waltz** .... *Engelbert Humperdinck*...Parrot 71015

TW	LW	WK	Billboard® — FEBRUARY 10, 1968 — TOP LP's
1	1	8	**Magical Mystery Tour** .... *The Beatles/Soundtrack*...Capitol 2835
2	2	8	**Their Satanic Majesties Request** .... *The Rolling Stones*...London 2
3	3	20	Diana Ross and the Supremes Greatest Hits .... *Diana Ross & The Supremes*...Motown 663
4	5	8	**Herb Alpert's Ninth** .... *Herb Alpert & The Tijuana Brass*...A&M 4134
5	48	3	John Wesley Harding .... *Bob Dylan*...Columbia 9604
6	4	12	Pisces, Aquarius, Capricorn & Jones Ltd. .... *The Monkees*...Colgems 104
7	7	13	**The Turtles! Golden Hits** .... *The Turtles*...White Whale 7115
8	8	10	Disraeli Gears .... *Cream*...Atco 232
9	9	14	Farewell To The First Golden Era .. *The Mamas & The Papas*...Dunhill/ABC 50025
10	10	8	**The Last Waltz** .... *Engelbert Humperdinck*...Parrot 71015

TW	LW	WK	Billboard® — FEBRUARY 17, 1968 — TOP LP's
1	1	9	**Magical Mystery Tour** .... *The Beatles/Soundtrack*...Capitol 2835
2	5	4	**John Wesley Harding** .... *Bob Dylan*...Columbia 9604
3	2	9	Their Satanic Majesties Request .... *The Rolling Stones*...London 2
4	4	9	**Herb Alpert's Ninth** .... *Herb Alpert & The Tijuana Brass*...A&M 4134
5	3	21	Diana Ross and the Supremes Greatest Hits .... *Diana Ross & The Supremes*...Motown 663
6	6	13	Pisces, Aquarius, Capricorn & Jones Ltd. .... *The Monkees*...Colgems 104
7	7	14	**The Turtles! Golden Hits** .... *The Turtles*...White Whale 7115
8	36	10	Blooming Hits................................ *Paul Mauriat & his orchestra*...Philips 248
9	8	11	Disraeli Gears .... *Cream*...Atco 232
10	9	15	Farewell To The First Golden Era .. *The Mamas & The Papas*...Dunhill/ABC 50025

TW	LW	WK	Billboard® — FEBRUARY 24, 1968 — TOP LP's
1	1	10	**Magical Mystery Tour** .... *The Beatles/Soundtrack*...Capitol 2835
2	2	5	**John Wesley Harding** .... *Bob Dylan*...Columbia 9604
3	8	11	Blooming Hits................................ *Paul Mauriat & his orchestra*...Philips 248
4	24	3	Axis: Bold As Love .... *Jimi Hendrix Experience*...Reprise 6281
5	5	22	Diana Ross and the Supremes Greatest Hits .... *Diana Ross & The Supremes*...Motown 663
6	3	10	Their Satanic Majesties Request .... *The Rolling Stones*...London 2
7	4	10	Herb Alpert's Ninth .... *Herb Alpert & The Tijuana Brass*...A&M 4134
8	7	15	The Turtles! Golden Hits .... *The Turtles*...White Whale 7115
9	15	27	Are You Experienced? .... *Jimi Hendrix Experience*...Reprise 6261
10	9	12	Disraeli Gears .... *Cream*...Atco 232

Billboard — MARCH 2, 1968 — TOP LP's

TW	LW	WK	Title	Artist	Label
1	3	12	**Blooming Hits**	*Paul Mauriat & his orchestra*	Philips 248
2	2	6	**John Wesley Harding**	*Bob Dylan*	Columbia 9604
3	1	11	Magical Mystery Tour	*The Beatles/Soundtrack*	Capitol 2835
4	4	4	Axis: Bold As Love	*Jimi Hendrix Experience*	Reprise 6281
5	33	2	Aretha: Lady Soul	*Aretha Franklin*	Atlantic 8176
6	7	11	Herb Alpert's Ninth	*Herb Alpert & The Tijuana Brass*	A&M 4134
7	9	28	Are You Experienced?	*Jimi Hendrix Experience*	Reprise 6261
8	6	11	Their Satanic Majesties Request	*The Rolling Stones*	London 2
9	5	23	Diana Ross and the Supremes Greatest Hits	*Diana Ross & The Supremes*	Motown 663
10	10	13	Disraeli Gears	*Cream*	Atco 232

Billboard — MARCH 9, 1968 — TOP LP's

TW	LW	WK	Title	Artist	Label
1	1	13	**Blooming Hits**	*Paul Mauriat & his orchestra*	Philips 248
2	2	7	**John Wesley Harding**	*Bob Dylan*	Columbia 9604
3	4	5	**Axis: Bold As Love**	*Jimi Hendrix Experience*	Reprise 6281
4	3	12	Magical Mystery Tour	*The Beatles/Soundtrack*	Capitol 2835
5	5	3	Aretha: Lady Soul	*Aretha Franklin*	Atlantic 8176
6	6	12	Herb Alpert's Ninth	*Herb Alpert & The Tijuana Brass*	A&M 4134
7	10	14	Disraeli Gears	*Cream*	Atco 232
8	9	24	Diana Ross and the Supremes Greatest Hits	*Diana Ross & The Supremes*	Motown 663
9	7	29	Are You Experienced?	*Jimi Hendrix Experience*	Reprise 6261
10	13	16	**The Lettermen!!!...and "Live!"**	*The Lettermen*	Capitol 2758

Billboard — MARCH 16, 1968 — TOP LP's

TW	LW	WK	Title	Artist	Label
1	1	14	**Blooming Hits**	*Paul Mauriat & his orchestra*	Philips 248
2	5	4	**Aretha: Lady Soul**	*Aretha Franklin*	Atlantic 8176
3	3	6	**Axis: Bold As Love**	*Jimi Hendrix Experience*	Reprise 6281
4	4	13	Magical Mystery Tour	*The Beatles/Soundtrack*	Capitol 2835
5	2	8	John Wesley Harding	*Bob Dylan*	Columbia 9604
6	6	13	Herb Alpert's Ninth	*Herb Alpert & The Tijuana Brass*	A&M 4134
7	7	15	Disraeli Gears	*Cream*	Atco 232
8	8	25	Diana Ross and the Supremes Greatest Hits	*Diana Ross & The Supremes*	Motown 663
9	11	16	**History Of Otis Redding**	*Otis Redding*	Volt 418
10	10	17	**The Lettermen!!!...and "Live!"**	*The Lettermen*	Capitol 2758

Billboard — MARCH 23, 1968 — TOP LP's

TW	LW	WK	Title	Artist	Label
1	1	15	**Blooming Hits**	*Paul Mauriat & his orchestra*	Philips 248
2	2	5	**Aretha: Lady Soul**	*Aretha Franklin*	Atlantic 8176
3	3	7	**Axis: Bold As Love**	*Jimi Hendrix Experience*	Reprise 6281
4	114	2	The Graduate	*Simon & Garfunkel/Soundtrack*	Columbia 3180
5	5	9	John Wesley Harding	*Bob Dylan*	Columbia 9604
6	4	14	Magical Mystery Tour	*The Beatles/Soundtrack*	Capitol 2835
7	18	5	**Greatest Hits, Vol. 2**	*Smokey Robinson & The Miracles*	Tamla 280
8	8	26	Diana Ross and the Supremes Greatest Hits	*Diana Ross & The Supremes*	Motown 663
9	9	17	**History Of Otis Redding**	*Otis Redding*	Volt 418
10	10	18	**The Lettermen!!!...and "Live!"**	*The Lettermen*	Capitol 2758

TW	LW	WK	Billboard — MARCH 30, 1968 — TOP LP's		
1	1	16	**Blooming Hits**	*Paul Mauriat & his orchestra*	Philips 248
2	4	3	The Graduate	*Simon & Garfunkel/Soundtrack*	Columbia 3180
3	2	6	Aretha: Lady Soul	*Aretha Franklin*	Atlantic 8176
4	3	8	Axis: Bold As Love	*Jimi Hendrix Experience*	Reprise 6281
5	5	10	John Wesley Harding	*Bob Dylan*	Columbia 9604
6	6	15	Magical Mystery Tour	*The Beatles/Soundtrack*	Capitol 2835
7	7	6	**Greatest Hits, Vol. 2**	*Smokey Robinson & The Miracles*	Tamla 280
8	12	4	Valley of the Dolls	*Dionne Warwick*	Scepter 568
9	11	5	**Once Upon A Dream**	*The Rascals*	Atlantic 8169
10	10	19	**The Lettermen!!!...and "Live!"**	*The Lettermen*	Capitol 2758

TW	LW	WK	Billboard — APRIL 6, 1968 — TOP LP's		
1	2	4	**The Graduate**	*Simon & Garfunkel/Soundtrack*	Columbia 3180
2	1	17	Blooming Hits	*Paul Mauriat & his orchestra*	Philips 248
3	3	7	Aretha: Lady Soul	*Aretha Franklin*	Atlantic 8176
4	5	11	John Wesley Harding	*Bob Dylan*	Columbia 9604
5	15	74	Parsley, Sage, Rosemary and Thyme	*Simon & Garfunkel*	Columbia 9363
6	13	3	The Dock Of The Bay	*Otis Redding*	Volt 419
7	8	5	Valley of the Dolls	*Dionne Warwick*	Scepter 568
8	4	9	Axis: Bold As Love	*Jimi Hendrix Experience*	Reprise 6281
9	9	6	**Once Upon A Dream**	*The Rascals*	Atlantic 8169
10	10	20	**The Lettermen!!!...and "Live!"**	*The Lettermen*	Capitol 2758

TW	LW	WK	Billboard — APRIL 13, 1968 — TOP LP's		
1	1	5	**The Graduate**	*Simon & Garfunkel/Soundtrack*	Columbia 3180
2	2	18	Blooming Hits	*Paul Mauriat & his orchestra*	Philips 248
3	3	8	Aretha: Lady Soul	*Aretha Franklin*	Atlantic 8176
4	6	4	**The Dock Of The Bay**	*Otis Redding*	Volt 419
5	5	75	Parsley, Sage, Rosemary and Thyme	*Simon & Garfunkel*	Columbia 9363
6	7	6	**Valley of the Dolls**	*Dionne Warwick*	Scepter 568
7	4	12	John Wesley Harding	*Bob Dylan*	Columbia 9604
8	14	19	Disraeli Gears	*Cream*	Atco 232
9	8	10	Axis: Bold As Love	*Jimi Hendrix Experience*	Reprise 6281
10	16	10	The Good, The Bad And The Ugly	*Soundtrack*	United Artists 5172

TW	LW	WK	Billboard — APRIL 20, 1968 — TOP LP's		
1	1	6	**The Graduate**	*Simon & Garfunkel/Soundtrack*	Columbia 3180
2	2	19	Blooming Hits	*Paul Mauriat & his orchestra*	Philips 248
3	3	9	Aretha: Lady Soul	*Aretha Franklin*	Atlantic 8176
4	4	5	**The Dock Of The Bay**	*Otis Redding*	Volt 419
5	5	76	Parsley, Sage, Rosemary and Thyme	*Simon & Garfunkel*	Columbia 9363
6	6	7	**Valley of the Dolls**	*Dionne Warwick*	Scepter 568
7	10	11	The Good, The Bad And The Ugly	*Soundtrack*	United Artists 5172
8	8	20	Disraeli Gears	*Cream*	Atco 232
9	23	3	To Russell, My Brother, Whom I Slept With	*Bill Cosby*	Warner 1734
10	11	8	Once Upon A Dream	*The Rascals*	Atlantic 8169

Billboard — APRIL 27, 1968 — TOP LP's

TW	LW	WK	Title	Artist	Label
1	1	7	**The Graduate**	*Simon & Garfunkel/Soundtrack*	Columbia 3180
2	2	20	Blooming Hits	*Paul Mauriat & his orchestra*	Philips 248
3	3	10	Aretha: Lady Soul	*Aretha Franklin*	Atlantic 8176
4	4	6	**The Dock Of The Bay**	*Otis Redding*	Volt 419
5	5	77	Parsley, Sage, Rosemary and Thyme	*Simon & Garfunkel*	Columbia 9363
6	7	12	The Good, The Bad And The Ugly	*Soundtrack*	United Artists 5172
7	6	8	Valley of the Dolls	*Dionne Warwick*	Scepter 568
8	9	4	To Russell, My Brother, Whom I Slept With	*Bill Cosby*	Warner 1734
9	8	21	Disraeli Gears	*Cream*	Atco 232
10	12	22	History Of Otis Redding	*Otis Redding*	Volt 418

Billboard — MAY 4, 1968 — TOP LP's

TW	LW	WK	Title	Artist	Label
1	1	8	**The Graduate**	*Simon & Garfunkel/Soundtrack*	Columbia 3180
2	2	21	Blooming Hits	*Paul Mauriat & his orchestra*	Philips 248
3	3	11	Aretha: Lady Soul	*Aretha Franklin*	Atlantic 8176
4	71	2	Bookends	*Simon & Garfunkel*	Columbia 9529
5	6	13	The Good, The Bad And The Ugly	*Soundtrack*	United Artists 5172
6	5	78	Parsley, Sage, Rosemary and Thyme	*Simon & Garfunkel*	Columbia 9363
7	8	5	**To Russell, My Brother, Whom I Slept With**	*Bill Cosby*	Warner 1734
8	4	7	The Dock Of The Bay	*Otis Redding*	Volt 419
9	9	22	Disraeli Gears	*Cream*	Atco 232
10	13	37	Are You Experienced?	*Jimi Hendrix Experience*	Reprise 6261

Billboard — MAY 11, 1968 — TOP LP's

TW	LW	WK	Title	Artist	Label
1	1	9	**The Graduate**	*Simon & Garfunkel/Soundtrack*	Columbia 3180
2	4	3	Bookends	*Simon & Garfunkel*	Columbia 9529
3	2	22	Blooming Hits	*Paul Mauriat & his orchestra*	Philips 248
4	5	14	**The Good, The Bad And The Ugly**	*Soundtrack*	United Artists 5172
5	3	12	Aretha: Lady Soul	*Aretha Franklin*	Atlantic 8176
6	6	79	Parsley, Sage, Rosemary and Thyme	*Simon & Garfunkel*	Columbia 9363
7	7	6	**To Russell, My Brother, Whom I Slept With**	*Bill Cosby*	Warner 1734
8	8	8	The Dock Of The Bay	*Otis Redding*	Volt 419
9	9	23	Disraeli Gears	*Cream*	Atco 232
10	10	38	Are You Experienced?	*Jimi Hendrix Experience*	Reprise 6261

Billboard — MAY 18, 1968 — TOP LP's

TW	LW	WK	Title	Artist	Label
1	1	10	**The Graduate**	*Simon & Garfunkel/Soundtrack*	Columbia 3180
2	2	4	Bookends	*Simon & Garfunkel*	Columbia 9529
3	80	2	**The Birds, The Bees & The Monkees**	*The Monkees*	Colgems 109
4	4	15	**The Good, The Bad And The Ugly**	*Soundtrack*	United Artists 5172
5	3	23	Blooming Hits	*Paul Mauriat & his orchestra*	Philips 248
6	5	13	Aretha: Lady Soul	*Aretha Franklin*	Atlantic 8176
7	83	2	The Beat Of The Brass	*Herb Alpert & The Tijuana Brass*	A&M 4146
8	8	9	The Dock Of The Bay	*Otis Redding*	Volt 419
9	6	80	Parsley, Sage, Rosemary and Thyme	*Simon & Garfunkel*	Columbia 9363
10	9	24	Disraeli Gears	*Cream*	Atco 232

TW	LW	WK	Billboard® MAY 25, 1968 TOP LP's
1	2	5	**Bookends** ... *Simon & Garfunkel*...Columbia 9529
2	1	11	The Graduate ... *Simon & Garfunkel/Soundtrack*...Columbia 3180
3	3	3	**The Birds, The Bees & The Monkees** ... *The Monkees*...Colgems 109
4	7	3	The Beat Of The Brass ... *Herb Alpert & The Tijuana Brass*...A&M 4146
5	6	14	Aretha: Lady Soul ... *Aretha Franklin*...Atlantic 8176
6	4	16	The Good, The Bad And The Ugly ... *Soundtrack*...United Artists 5172
7	13	6	Honey ... *Bobby Goldsboro*...United Artists 6642
8	10	25	Disraeli Gears ... *Cream*...Atco 232
9	9	81	Parsley, Sage, Rosemary and Thyme ... *Simon & Garfunkel*...Columbia 9363
10	12	15	Music From "A Fistful Of Dollars" & "For A Few Dollars More" & "The Good, The Bad And The Ugly" ... *Hugo Montenegro*...RCA 3927

TW	LW	WK	Billboard® JUNE 1, 1968 TOP LP's
1	1	6	**Bookends** ... *Simon & Garfunkel*...Columbia 9529
2	2	12	The Graduate ... *Simon & Garfunkel/Soundtrack*...Columbia 3180
3	3	4	**The Birds, The Bees & The Monkees** ... *The Monkees*...Colgems 109
4	4	4	The Beat Of The Brass ... *Herb Alpert & The Tijuana Brass*...A&M 4146
5	9	82	Parsley, Sage, Rosemary and Thyme ... *Simon & Garfunkel*...Columbia 9363
6	7	7	Honey ... *Bobby Goldsboro*...United Artists 6642
7	5	15	Aretha: Lady Soul ... *Aretha Franklin*...Atlantic 8176
8	6	17	The Good, The Bad And The Ugly ... *Soundtrack*...United Artists 5172
9	8	26	Disraeli Gears ... *Cream*...Atco 232
10	10	16	Music From "A Fistful Of Dollars" & "For A Few Dollars More" & "The Good, The Bad And The Ugly" ... *Hugo Montenegro*...RCA 3927

TW	LW	WK	Billboard® JUNE 8, 1968 TOP LP's
1	1	7	**Bookends** ... *Simon & Garfunkel*...Columbia 9529
2	2	13	The Graduate ... *Simon & Garfunkel/Soundtrack*...Columbia 3180
3	3	5	**The Birds, The Bees & The Monkees** ... *The Monkees*...Colgems 109
4	4	5	The Beat Of The Brass ... *Herb Alpert & The Tijuana Brass*...A&M 4146
5	5	83	Parsley, Sage, Rosemary and Thyme ... *Simon & Garfunkel*...Columbia 9363
6	6	8	Honey ... *Bobby Goldsboro*...United Artists 6642
7	8	18	The Good, The Bad And The Ugly ... *Soundtrack*...United Artists 5172
8	7	16	Aretha: Lady Soul ... *Aretha Franklin*...Atlantic 8176
9	11	14	Look Around ... *Sergio Mendes & Brasil '66*...A&M 4137
10	10	17	Music From "A Fistful Of Dollars" & "For A Few Dollars More" & "The Good, The Bad And The Ugly" ... *Hugo Montenegro*...RCA 3927

TW	LW	WK	Billboard® JUNE 15, 1968 TOP LP's
1	2	14	**The Graduate** ... *Simon & Garfunkel/Soundtrack*...Columbia 3180
2	1	8	Bookends ... *Simon & Garfunkel*...Columbia 9529
3	4	6	The Beat Of The Brass ... *Herb Alpert & The Tijuana Brass*...A&M 4146
4	3	6	The Birds, The Bees & The Monkees ... *The Monkees*...Colgems 109
5	6	9	**Honey** ... *Bobby Goldsboro*...United Artists 6642
6	5	84	Parsley, Sage, Rosemary and Thyme ... *Simon & Garfunkel*...Columbia 9363
7	9	15	Look Around ... *Sergio Mendes & Brasil '66*...A&M 4137
8	8	17	Aretha: Lady Soul ... *Aretha Franklin*...Atlantic 8176
9	13	43	Are You Experienced? ... *Jimi Hendrix Experience*...Reprise 6261
10	10	18	Music From "A Fistful Of Dollars" & "For A Few Dollars More" & "The Good, The Bad And The Ugly" ... *Hugo Montenegro*...RCA 3927

Billboard — JUNE 22, 1968 — TOP LP's

TW	LW	WK	Title	Artist	Label
1	1	15	**The Graduate**	*Simon & Garfunkel/Soundtrack*	Columbia 3180
2	2	9	Bookends	*Simon & Garfunkel*	Columbia 9529
3	3	7	The Beat Of The Brass	*Herb Alpert & The Tijuana Brass*	A&M 4146
4	4	7	The Birds, The Bees & The Monkees	*The Monkees*	Colgems 109
5	5	10	**Honey**	*Bobby Goldsboro*	United Artists 6642
6	7	16	Look Around	*Sergio Mendes & Brasil '66*	A&M 4137
7	9	44	Are You Experienced?	*Jimi Hendrix Experience*	Reprise 6261
8	6	85	Parsley, Sage, Rosemary and Thyme	*Simon & Garfunkel*	Columbia 9363
9	11	29	Disraeli Gears	*Cream*	Atco 232
10	10	19	Music From "A Fistful Of Dollars" & "For A Few Dollars More" & "The Good, The Bad And The Ugly"	*Hugo Montenegro*	RCA 3927

Billboard — JUNE 29, 1968 — TOP LP's

TW	LW	WK	Title	Artist	Label
1	2	10	**Bookends**	*Simon & Garfunkel*	Columbia 9529
2	1	16	The Graduate	*Simon & Garfunkel/Soundtrack*	Columbia 3180
3	3	8	The Beat Of The Brass	*Herb Alpert & The Tijuana Brass*	A&M 4146
4	9	30	**Disraeli Gears**	*Cream*	Atco 232
5	5	11	**Honey**	*Bobby Goldsboro*	United Artists 6642
6	6	17	Look Around	*Sergio Mendes & Brasil '66*	A&M 4137
7	4	8	The Birds, The Bees & The Monkees	*The Monkees*	Colgems 109
8	7	45	Are You Experienced?	*Jimi Hendrix Experience*	Reprise 6261
9	10	20	**Music From "A Fistful Of Dollars" & "For A Few Dollars More" & "The Good, The Bad And The Ugly"**	*Hugo Montenegro*	RCA 3927
10	11	21	The Good, The Bad And The Ugly	*Soundtrack*	United Artists 5172

Billboard — JULY 6, 1968 — TOP LP's

TW	LW	WK	Title	Artist	Label
1	1	11	**Bookends**	*Simon & Garfunkel*	Columbia 9529
2	2	17	The Graduate	*Simon & Garfunkel/Soundtrack*	Columbia 3180
3	3	9	The Beat Of The Brass	*Herb Alpert & The Tijuana Brass*	A&M 4146
4	4	31	**Disraeli Gears**	*Cream*	Atco 232
5	12	8	A Tramp Shining	*Richard Harris*	Dunhill/ABC 50032
6	6	18	Look Around	*Sergio Mendes & Brasil '66*	A&M 4137
7	7	9	The Birds, The Bees & The Monkees	*The Monkees*	Colgems 109
8	5	12	Honey	*Bobby Goldsboro*	United Artists 6642
9	8	46	Are You Experienced?	*Jimi Hendrix Experience*	Reprise 6261
10	11	87	Parsley, Sage, Rosemary and Thyme	*Simon & Garfunkel*	Columbia 9363

Billboard — JULY 13, 1968 — TOP LP's

TW	LW	WK	Title	Artist	Label
1	1	12	**Bookends**	*Simon & Garfunkel*	Columbia 9529
2	3	10	The Beat Of The Brass	*Herb Alpert & The Tijuana Brass*	A&M 4146
3	2	18	The Graduate	*Simon & Garfunkel/Soundtrack*	Columbia 3180
4	5	9	**A Tramp Shining**	*Richard Harris*	Dunhill/ABC 50032
5	6	19	**Look Around**	*Sergio Mendes & Brasil '66*	A&M 4137
6	4	32	Disraeli Gears	*Cream*	Atco 232
7	15	11	**God Bless Tiny Tim**	*Tiny Tim*	Reprise 6292
8	9	47	Are You Experienced?	*Jimi Hendrix Experience*	Reprise 6261
9	8	13	Honey	*Bobby Goldsboro*	United Artists 6642
10	7	10	The Birds, The Bees & The Monkees	*The Monkees*	Colgems 109

TW	LW	WK	Billboard. JULY 20, 1968 TOP LP's
①	1	13	**Bookends** .... *Simon & Garfunkel*...Columbia 9529
②	2	11	The Beat Of The Brass .... *Herb Alpert & The Tijuana Brass*...A&M 4146
③	3	19	The Graduate .... *Simon & Garfunkel/Soundtrack*...Columbia 3180
④	4	10	**A Tramp Shining** .... *Richard Harris*...Dunhill/ABC 50032
⑤	5	20	**Look Around** .... *Sergio Mendes & Brasil '66*...A&M 4137
⑥	6	33	Disraeli Gears .... *Cream*...Atco 232
⑦	7	12	**God Bless Tiny Tim** .... *Tiny Tim*...Reprise 6292
⑧	8	48	Are You Experienced? .... *Jimi Hendrix Experience*...Reprise 6261
⑨	9	14	Honey .... *Bobby Goldsboro*...United Artists 6642
❿	15	7	Honey .... *Andy Williams*...Columbia 9662

TW	LW	WK	Billboard. JULY 27, 1968 TOP LP's
①	2	12	**The Beat Of The Brass** .... *Herb Alpert & The Tijuana Brass*...A&M 4146
❷	28	3	Wheels Of Fire .... *Cream*...Atco 700
③	1	14	Bookends .... *Simon & Garfunkel*...Columbia 9529
④	4	11	**A Tramp Shining** .... *Richard Harris*...Dunhill/ABC 50032
⑤	3	20	The Graduate .... *Simon & Garfunkel/Soundtrack*...Columbia 3180
⑥	5	21	Look Around .... *Sergio Mendes & Brasil '66*...A&M 4137
⑦	8	49	Are You Experienced? .... *Jimi Hendrix Experience*...Reprise 6261
❽	29	3	Aretha Now .... *Aretha Franklin*...Atlantic 8186
❾	52	3	Time Peace/The Rascals' Greatest Hits .... *The Rascals*...Atlantic 8190
⑩	10	8	Honey .... *Andy Williams*...Columbia 9662

TW	LW	WK	Billboard. AUGUST 3, 1968 TOP LP's
①	1	13	**The Beat Of The Brass** .... *Herb Alpert & The Tijuana Brass*...A&M 4146
②	2	4	Wheels Of Fire .... *Cream*...Atco 700
③	3	15	Bookends .... *Simon & Garfunkel*...Columbia 9529
④	5	21	The Graduate .... *Simon & Garfunkel/Soundtrack*...Columbia 3180
❺	8	4	Aretha Now .... *Aretha Franklin*...Atlantic 8186
❻	9	4	Time Peace/The Rascals' Greatest Hits .... *The Rascals*...Atlantic 8190
⑦	7	50	Are You Experienced? .... *Jimi Hendrix Experience*...Reprise 6261
⑧	4	12	A Tramp Shining .... *Richard Harris*...Dunhill/ABC 50032
⑨	11	35	Disraeli Gears .... *Cream*...Atco 232
⑩	10	9	Honey .... *Andy Williams*...Columbia 9662

TW	LW	WK	Billboard. AUGUST 10, 1968 TOP LP's
①	2	5	**Wheels Of Fire** .... *Cream*...Atco 700
②	4	22	The Graduate .... *Simon & Garfunkel/Soundtrack*...Columbia 3180
❸	6	5	Time Peace/The Rascals' Greatest Hits .... *The Rascals*...Atlantic 8190
④	1	14	The Beat Of The Brass .... *Herb Alpert & The Tijuana Brass*...A&M 4146
⑤	5	5	Aretha Now .... *Aretha Franklin*...Atlantic 8186
⑥	3	16	Bookends .... *Simon & Garfunkel*...Columbia 9529
⑦	9	36	Disraeli Gears .... *Cream*...Atco 232
⑧	11	23	Look Around .... *Sergio Mendes & Brasil '66*...A&M 4137
⑨	10	10	**Honey** .... *Andy Williams*...Columbia 9662
⑩	7	51	Are You Experienced? .... *Jimi Hendrix Experience*...Reprise 6261

Billboard — AUGUST 17, 1968 — TOP LP's

TW	LW	WK	Title	Artist...Label
1	1	6	**Wheels Of Fire**	*Cream*...Atco 700
2	3	6	Time Peace/The Rascals' Greatest Hits	*The Rascals*...Atlantic 8190
3	5	6	**Aretha Now**	*Aretha Franklin*...Atlantic 8186
4	2	23	The Graduate	*Simon & Garfunkel/Soundtrack*...Columbia 3180
5	4	15	The Beat Of The Brass	*Herb Alpert & The Tijuana Brass*...A&M 4146
6	7	37	Disraeli Gears	*Cream*...Atco 232
7	6	17	Bookends	*Simon & Garfunkel*...Columbia 9529
8	12	8	Realization	*Johnny Rivers*...Imperial 12372
9	9	11	**Honey**	*Andy Williams*...Columbia 9662
10	10	52	Are You Experienced?	*Jimi Hendrix Experience*...Reprise 6261

Billboard — AUGUST 24, 1968 — TOP LP's

TW	LW	WK	Title	Artist...Label
1	1	7	**Wheels Of Fire**	*Cream*...Atco 700
2	2	7	Time Peace/The Rascals' Greatest Hits	*The Rascals*...Atlantic 8190
3	3	7	**Aretha Now**	*Aretha Franklin*...Atlantic 8186
4	29	3	Waiting For The Sun	*The Doors*...Elektra 74024
5	5	16	The Beat Of The Brass	*Herb Alpert & The Tijuana Brass*...A&M 4146
6	6	38	Disraeli Gears	*Cream*...Atco 232
7	4	24	The Graduate	*Simon & Garfunkel/Soundtrack*...Columbia 3180
8	8	9	Realization	*Johnny Rivers*...Imperial 12372
9	7	18	Bookends	*Simon & Garfunkel*...Columbia 9529
10	28	6	Feliciano!	*Jose Feliciano*...RCA 3957

Billboard — AUGUST 31, 1968 — TOP LP's

TW	LW	WK	Title	Artist...Label
1	1	8	**Wheels Of Fire**	*Cream*...Atco 700
2	2	8	Time Peace/The Rascals' Greatest Hits	*The Rascals*...Atlantic 8190
3	4	4	Waiting For The Sun	*The Doors*...Elektra 74024
4	3	8	Aretha Now	*Aretha Franklin*...Atlantic 8186
5	8	10	**Realization**	*Johnny Rivers*...Imperial 12372
6	5	17	The Beat Of The Brass	*Herb Alpert & The Tijuana Brass*...A&M 4146
7	9	19	Bookends	*Simon & Garfunkel*...Columbia 9529
8	11	26	Steppenwolf	*Steppenwolf*...Dunhill/ABC 50029
9	10	7	Feliciano!	*Jose Feliciano*...RCA 3957
10	6	39	Disraeli Gears	*Cream*...Atco 232

Billboard — SEPTEMBER 7, 1968 — TOP LP's

TW	LW	WK	Title	Artist...Label
1	3	5	**Waiting For The Sun**	*The Doors*...Elektra 74024
2	2	9	Time Peace/The Rascals' Greatest Hits	*The Rascals*...Atlantic 8190
3	1	9	Wheels Of Fire	*Cream*...Atco 700
4	9	8	Feliciano!	*Jose Feliciano*...RCA 3957
5	5	11	**Realization**	*Johnny Rivers*...Imperial 12372
6	8	27	**Steppenwolf**	*Steppenwolf*...Dunhill/ABC 50029
7	4	9	Aretha Now	*Aretha Franklin*...Atlantic 8186
8	12	55	Are You Experienced?	*Jimi Hendrix Experience*...Reprise 6261
9	10	40	Disraeli Gears	*Cream*...Atco 232
10	7	20	Bookends	*Simon & Garfunkel*...Columbia 9529

Billboard — SEPTEMBER 14, 1968 — TOP LP's

TW	LW	WK	Title	Artist...Label
1	1	6	**Waiting For The Sun**	*The Doors*...Elektra 74024
2	2	10	Time Peace/The Rascals' Greatest Hits	*The Rascals*...Atlantic 8190
3	3	10	Wheels Of Fire	*Cream*...Atco 700
4	4	9	Feliciano!	*Jose Feliciano*...RCA 3957
5	5	12	**Realization**	*Johnny Rivers*...Imperial 12372
6	6	28	**Steppenwolf**	*Steppenwolf*...Dunhill/ABC 50029
7	9	41	Disraeli Gears	*Cream*...Atco 232
8	8	56	Are You Experienced?	*Jimi Hendrix Experience*...Reprise 6261
9	7	10	Aretha Now	*Aretha Franklin*...Atlantic 8186
10	12	27	The Graduate	*Simon & Garfunkel/Soundtrack*...Columbia 3180

Billboard — SEPTEMBER 21, 1968 — TOP LP's

TW	LW	WK	Title	Artist...Label
1	1	7	**Waiting For The Sun**	*The Doors*...Elektra 74024
2	2	11	Time Peace/The Rascals' Greatest Hits	*The Rascals*...Atlantic 8190
3	4	10	Feliciano!	*Jose Feliciano*...RCA 3957
4	3	11	Wheels Of Fire	*Cream*...Atco 700
5	5	13	**Realization**	*Johnny Rivers*...Imperial 12372
6	6	29	**Steppenwolf**	*Steppenwolf*...Dunhill/ABC 50029
7	8	57	Are You Experienced?	*Jimi Hendrix Experience*...Reprise 6261
8	10	28	The Graduate	*Simon & Garfunkel/Soundtrack*...Columbia 3180
9	7	42	Disraeli Gears	*Cream*...Atco 232
10	11	22	Bookends	*Simon & Garfunkel*...Columbia 9529

Billboard — SEPTEMBER 28, 1968 — TOP LP's

TW	LW	WK	Title	Artist...Label
1	2	12	**Time Peace/The Rascals' Greatest Hits**	*The Rascals*...Atlantic 8190
2	1	8	Waiting For The Sun	*The Doors*...Elektra 74024
3	3	11	Feliciano!	*Jose Feliciano*...RCA 3957
4	13	5	Cheap Thrills	*Big Brother & The Holding Company*...Columbia 9700
5	5	14	**Realization**	*Johnny Rivers*...Imperial 12372
6	4	12	Wheels Of Fire	*Cream*...Atco 700
7	7	58	Are You Experienced?	*Jimi Hendrix Experience*...Reprise 6261
8	15	31	Gentle On My Mind	*Glen Campbell*...Capitol 2809
9	6	30	Steppenwolf	*Steppenwolf*...Dunhill/ABC 50029
10	8	29	The Graduate	*Simon & Garfunkel/Soundtrack*...Columbia 3180

Billboard — OCTOBER 5, 1968 — TOP LP's

TW	LW	WK	Title	Artist...Label
1	2	9	**Waiting For The Sun**	*The Doors*...Elektra 74024
2	1	13	Time Peace/The Rascals' Greatest Hits	*The Rascals*...Atlantic 8190
3	3	12	Feliciano!	*Jose Feliciano*...RCA 3957
4	4	6	Cheap Thrills	*Big Brother & The Holding Company*...Columbia 9700
5	7	59	**Are You Experienced?**	*Jimi Hendrix Experience*...Reprise 6261
6	8	32	Gentle On My Mind	*Glen Campbell*...Capitol 2809
7	5	15	Realization	*Johnny Rivers*...Imperial 12372
8	6	13	Wheels Of Fire	*Cream*...Atco 700
9	9	31	Steppenwolf	*Steppenwolf*...Dunhill/ABC 50029
10	15	12	In-A-Gadda-Da-Vida	*Iron Butterfly*...Atco 250

TW	LW	WK	Billboard. OCTOBER 12, 1968 TOP LP's
1	4	7	**Cheap Thrills**......*Big Brother & The Holding Company*...Columbia 9700
2	1	10	Waiting For The Sun......*The Doors*...Elektra 74024
3	3	13	Feliciano!......*Jose Feliciano*...RCA 3957
4	2	14	Time Peace/The Rascals' Greatest Hits......*The Rascals*...Atlantic 8190
5	6	33	**Gentle On My Mind**......*Glen Campbell*...Capitol 2809
6	10	13	In-A-Gadda-Da-Vida......*Iron Butterfly*...Atco 250
7	7	16	Realization......*Johnny Rivers*...Imperial 12372
8	13	35	The Time Has Come......*The Chambers Brothers*...Columbia 9522
9	14	6	Crown Of Creation......*Jefferson Airplane*...RCA 4058
10	9	32	Steppenwolf......*Steppenwolf*...Dunhill/ABC 50029

TW	LW	WK	Billboard. OCTOBER 19, 1968 TOP LP's
1	1	8	**Cheap Thrills**......*Big Brother & The Holding Company*...Columbia 9700
2	4	15	Time Peace/The Rascals' Greatest Hits......*The Rascals*...Atlantic 8190
3	3	14	Feliciano!......*Jose Feliciano*...RCA 3957
4	2	11	Waiting For The Sun......*The Doors*...Elektra 74024
5	6	14	In-A-Gadda-Da-Vida......*Iron Butterfly*...Atco 250
6	5	34	Gentle On My Mind......*Glen Campbell*...Capitol 2809
7	9	7	Crown Of Creation......*Jefferson Airplane*...RCA 4058
8	8	36	The Time Has Come......*The Chambers Brothers*...Columbia 9522
9	12	15	Wheels Of Fire......*Cream*...Atco 700
10	18	7	The Crazy World Of Arthur Brown......*The Crazy World Of Arthur Brown*...Track 8198

TW	LW	WK	Billboard. OCTOBER 26, 1968 TOP LP's
1	1	9	**Cheap Thrills**......*Big Brother & The Holding Company*...Columbia 9700
2	2	16	Time Peace/The Rascals' Greatest Hits......*The Rascals*...Atlantic 8190
3	3	15	Feliciano!......*Jose Feliciano*...RCA 3957
4	8	37	**The Time Has Come**......*The Chambers Brothers*...Columbia 9522
5	5	15	In-A-Gadda-Da-Vida......*Iron Butterfly*...Atco 250
6	6	35	Gentle On My Mind......*Glen Campbell*...Capitol 2809
7	7	8	Crown Of Creation......*Jefferson Airplane*...RCA 4058
8	9	16	Wheels Of Fire......*Cream*...Atco 700
9	10	8	The Crazy World Of Arthur Brown......*The Crazy World Of Arthur Brown*...Track 8198
10	11	62	Are You Experienced?......*Jimi Hendrix Experience*...Reprise 6261

TW	LW	WK	Billboard. NOVEMBER 2, 1968 TOP LP's
1	1	10	**Cheap Thrills**......*Big Brother & The Holding Company*...Columbia 9700
2	3	16	**Feliciano!**......*Jose Feliciano*...RCA 3957
3	2	17	Time Peace/The Rascals' Greatest Hits......*The Rascals*...Atlantic 8190
4	4	38	**The Time Has Come**......*The Chambers Brothers*...Columbia 9522
5	5	16	In-A-Gadda-Da-Vida......*Iron Butterfly*...Atco 250
6	7	9	**Crown Of Creation**......*Jefferson Airplane*...RCA 4058
7	8	17	Wheels Of Fire......*Cream*...Atco 700
8	9	9	The Crazy World Of Arthur Brown......*The Crazy World Of Arthur Brown*...Track 8198
9	6	36	Gentle On My Mind......*Glen Campbell*...Capitol 2809
10	10	63	Are You Experienced?......*Jimi Hendrix Experience*...Reprise 6261

Billboard® NOVEMBER 9, 1968 TOP LP's

TW	LW	WK	Title	Artist	Label
①	1	11	**Cheap Thrills**	*Big Brother & The Holding Company*	Columbia 9700
❷	20	4	Electric Ladyland	*Jimi Hendrix Experience*	Reprise 6307
③	2	17	Feliciano!	*Jose Feliciano*	RCA 3957
④	3	18	Time Peace/The Rascals' Greatest Hits	*The Rascals*	Atlantic 8190
⑤	4	39	The Time Has Come	*The Chambers Brothers*	Columbia 9522
⑥	6	10	**Crown Of Creation**	*Jefferson Airplane*	RCA 4058
❼	15	6	The Second	*Steppenwolf*	Dunhill/ABC 50037
⑧	8	10	The Crazy World Of Arthur Brown	*The Crazy World Of Arthur Brown*	Track 8198
⑨	7	18	Wheels Of Fire	*Cream*	Atco 700
⑩	9	37	Gentle On My Mind	*Glen Campbell*	Capitol 2809

Billboard® NOVEMBER 16, 1968 TOP LP's

TW	LW	WK	Title	Artist	Label
①	2	5	**Electric Ladyland**	*Jimi Hendrix Experience*	Reprise 6307
②	1	12	Cheap Thrills	*Big Brother & The Holding Company*	Columbia 9700
③	4	19	Time Peace/The Rascals' Greatest Hits	*The Rascals*	Atlantic 8190
④	3	18	Feliciano!	*Jose Feliciano*	RCA 3957
⑤	7	7	The Second	*Steppenwolf*	Dunhill/ABC 50037
⑥	5	40	The Time Has Come	*The Chambers Brothers*	Columbia 9522
⑦	8	11	**The Crazy World Of Arthur Brown**	*The Crazy World Of Arthur Brown*	Track 8198
⑧	11	65	Are You Experienced?	*Jimi Hendrix Experience*	Reprise 6261
⑨	9	19	Wheels Of Fire	*Cream*	Atco 700
⑩	10	38	Gentle On My Mind	*Glen Campbell*	Capitol 2809

Billboard® NOVEMBER 23, 1968 TOP LP's

TW	LW	WK	Title	Artist	Label
①	1	6	**Electric Ladyland**	*Jimi Hendrix Experience*	Reprise 6307
②	2	13	Cheap Thrills	*Big Brother & The Holding Company*	Columbia 9700
③	4	19	Feliciano!	*Jose Feliciano*	RCA 3957
④	5	8	The Second	*Steppenwolf*	Dunhill/ABC 50037
⑤	3	20	Time Peace/The Rascals' Greatest Hits	*The Rascals*	Atlantic 8190
⑥	8	66	Are You Experienced?	*Jimi Hendrix Experience*	Reprise 6261
⑦	7	12	**The Crazy World Of Arthur Brown**	*The Crazy World Of Arthur Brown*	Track 8198
⑧	6	41	The Time Has Come	*The Chambers Brothers*	Columbia 9522
⑨	9	20	Wheels Of Fire	*Cream*	Atco 700
⑩	10	39	Gentle On My Mind	*Glen Campbell*	Capitol 2809

Billboard® NOVEMBER 30, 1968 TOP LP's

TW	LW	WK	Title	Artist	Label
①	2	14	**Cheap Thrills**	*Big Brother & The Holding Company*	Columbia 9700
②	1	7	Electric Ladyland	*Jimi Hendrix Experience*	Reprise 6307
③	3	20	Feliciano!	*Jose Feliciano*	RCA 3957
④	4	9	The Second	*Steppenwolf*	Dunhill/ABC 50037
⑤	5	21	Time Peace/The Rascals' Greatest Hits	*The Rascals*	Atlantic 8190
⑥	8	42	The Time Has Come	*The Chambers Brothers*	Columbia 9522
⑦	6	67	Are You Experienced?	*Jimi Hendrix Experience*	Reprise 6261
⑧	7	13	The Crazy World Of Arthur Brown	*The Crazy World Of Arthur Brown*	Track 8198
⑨	9	21	Wheels Of Fire	*Cream*	Atco 700
⑩	10	40	Gentle On My Mind	*Glen Campbell*	Capitol 2809

TW	LW	WK	Billboard® DECEMBER 7, 1968 TOP LP's
①	1	15	**Cheap Thrills**.................*Big Brother & The Holding Company*...Columbia 9700
②	3	21	**Feliciano!**..*Jose Feliciano*...RCA 3957
③	2	8	Electric Ladyland .... *Jimi Hendrix Experience*...Reprise 6307
④	4	10	The Second .... *Steppenwolf*...Dunhill/ABC 50037
⑤	5	22	Time Peace/The Rascals' Greatest Hits ....*The Rascals*...Atlantic 8190
⑥	9	22	Wheels Of Fire.. *Cream*...Atco 700
⑦	15	21	In-A-Gadda-Da-Vida ....*Iron Butterfly*...Atco 250
⑧	6	43	The Time Has Come...........................*The Chambers Brothers*...Columbia 9522
⑨	7	68	Are You Experienced? .... *Jimi Hendrix Experience*...Reprise 6261
⑩	10	41	Gentle On My Mind..*Glen Campbell*...Capitol 2809

TW	LW	WK	Billboard® DECEMBER 14, 1968 TOP LP's
①	1	16	**Cheap Thrills**.................*Big Brother & The Holding Company*...Columbia 9700
②	2	22	**Feliciano!**..*Jose Feliciano*...RCA 3957
③	3	9	Electric Ladyland .... *Jimi Hendrix Experience*...Reprise 6307
❹	16	5	Wichita Lineman .... *Glen Campbell*...Capitol 103
⑤	4	11	The Second .... *Steppenwolf*...Dunhill/ABC 50037
⑥	7	22	In-A-Gadda-Da-Vida ....*Iron Butterfly*...Atco 250
⑦	5	23	Time Peace/The Rascals' Greatest Hits ....*The Rascals*...Atlantic 8190
⑧	6	23	Wheels Of Fire.. *Cream*...Atco 700
⑨	10	42	Gentle On My Mind..*Glen Campbell*...Capitol 2809
⑩	8	44	The Time Has Come...........................*The Chambers Brothers*...Columbia 9522

TW	LW	WK	Billboard® DECEMBER 21, 1968 TOP LP's
❶	4	6	**Wichita Lineman** .... *Glen Campbell*...Capitol 103
❷	11	2	The Beatles [White Album] ....*The Beatles*...Apple 101
③	1	17	Cheap Thrills....................*Big Brother & The Holding Company*...Columbia 9700
④	2	23	Feliciano!..*Jose Feliciano*...RCA 3957
⑤	5	12	The Second .... *Steppenwolf*...Dunhill/ABC 50037
⑥	31	51	Wildflowers .... *Judy Collins*...Elektra 74012
⑦	3	10	Electric Ladyland .... *Jimi Hendrix Experience*...Reprise 6307
⑧	9	43	Gentle On My Mind..*Glen Campbell*...Capitol 2809
⑨	6	23	In-A-Gadda-Da-Vida ....*Iron Butterfly*...Atco 250
⑩	7	24	Time Peace/The Rascals' Greatest Hits ....*The Rascals*...Atlantic 8190

TW	LW	WK	Billboard® DECEMBER 28, 1968 TOP LP's
①	2	3	**The Beatles [White Album]**................................*The Beatles*...Apple 101
②	1	7	Wichita Lineman .... *Glen Campbell*...Capitol 103
③	3	18	Cheap Thrills....................*Big Brother & The Holding Company*...Columbia 9700
④	5	13	The Second .... *Steppenwolf*...Dunhill/ABC 50037
⑤	6	52	**Wildflowers** .... *Judy Collins*...Elektra 74012
⑥	7	11	Electric Ladyland .... *Jimi Hendrix Experience*...Reprise 6307
⑦	4	24	Feliciano!..*Jose Feliciano*...RCA 3957
⑧	9	24	In-A-Gadda-Da-Vida ....*Iron Butterfly*...Atco 250
⑨	8	44	Gentle On My Mind..*Glen Campbell*...Capitol 2809
⑩	10	25	Time Peace/The Rascals' Greatest Hits ....*The Rascals*...Atlantic 8190

Billboard — JANUARY 4, 1969 — TOP LP's

TW	LW	WK			
①	1	4	**The Beatles [White Album]**	*The Beatles*	Apple 101
②	2	8	Wichita Lineman	*Glen Campbell*	Capitol 103
③	4	14	**The Second**	*Steppenwolf*	Dunhill/ABC 50037
❹	11	5	Fool On The Hill	*Sergio Mendes & Brasil '66*	A&M 4160
❺	13	6	Diana Ross & the Supremes Join the Temptations	*Diana Ross & The Supremes & The Temptations*	Motown 679
⑥	3	19	Cheap Thrills	*Big Brother & The Holding Company*	Columbia 9700
⑦	6	12	Electric Ladyland	*Jimi Hendrix Experience*	Reprise 6307
⑧	5	53	Wildflowers	*Judy Collins*	Elektra 74012
⑨	8	25	In-A-Gadda-Da-Vida	*Iron Butterfly*	Atco 250
⑩	10	26	Time Peace/The Rascals' Greatest Hits	*The Rascals*	Atlantic 8190

Billboard — JANUARY 11, 1969 — TOP LP's

TW	LW	WK			
①	1	5	**The Beatles [White Album]**	*The Beatles*	Apple 101
❷	5	7	**Diana Ross & the Supremes Join the Temptations**	*Diana Ross & The Supremes & The Temptations*	Motown 679
③	4	6	**Fool On The Hill**	*Sergio Mendes & Brasil '66*	A&M 4160
④	2	9	Wichita Lineman	*Glen Campbell*	Capitol 103
❺	12	5	**Beggars Banquet**	*The Rolling Stones*	London 33
⑥	3	15	The Second	*Steppenwolf*	Dunhill/ABC 50037
⑦	6	20	Cheap Thrills	*Big Brother & The Holding Company*	Columbia 9700
⑧	8	54	Wildflowers	*Judy Collins*	Elektra 74012
⑨	10	27	Time Peace/The Rascals' Greatest Hits	*The Rascals*	Atlantic 8190
⑩	9	26	In-A-Gadda-Da-Vida	*Iron Butterfly*	Atco 250

Billboard — JANUARY 18, 1969 — TOP LP's

TW	LW	WK			
①	1	6	**The Beatles [White Album]**	*The Beatles*	Apple 101
❷	16	4	TCB	*Diana Ross & The Supremes with The Temptations*	Motown 682
③	2	8	Diana Ross & the Supremes Join the Temptations	*Diana Ross & The Supremes & The Temptations*	Motown 679
④	3	7	Fool On The Hill	*Sergio Mendes & Brasil '66*	A&M 4160
⑤	5	6	**Beggars Banquet**	*The Rolling Stones*	London 33
⑥	4	10	Wichita Lineman	*Glen Campbell*	Capitol 103
⑦	7	21	Cheap Thrills	*Big Brother & The Holding Company*	Columbia 9700
⑧	6	16	The Second	*Steppenwolf*	Dunhill/ABC 50037
⑨	8	55	Wildflowers	*Judy Collins*	Elektra 74012
⑩	11	14	Electric Ladyland	*Jimi Hendrix Experience*	Reprise 6307

Billboard — JANUARY 25, 1969 — TOP LP's

TW	LW	WK			
①	1	7	**The Beatles [White Album]**	*The Beatles*	Apple 101
②	2	5	TCB	*Diana Ross & The Supremes with The Temptations*	Motown 682
③	6	11	Wichita Lineman	*Glen Campbell*	Capitol 103
④	4	8	Fool On The Hill	*Sergio Mendes & Brasil '66*	A&M 4160
⑤	5	7	**Beggars Banquet**	*The Rolling Stones*	London 33
⑥	3	9	Diana Ross & the Supremes Join the Temptations	*Diana Ross & The Supremes & The Temptations*	Motown 679
⑦	12	28	In-A-Gadda-Da-Vida	*Iron Butterfly*	Atco 250
⑧	7	22	Cheap Thrills	*Big Brother & The Holding Company*	Columbia 9700
⑨	9	56	Wildflowers	*Judy Collins*	Elektra 74012
⑩	8	17	The Second	*Steppenwolf*	Dunhill/ABC 50037

Billboard — FEBRUARY 1, 1969 — TOP LP's

TW	LW	WK			
1	1	8	**The Beatles [White Album]**	*The Beatles*	Apple 101
2	2	6	TCB	*Diana Ross & The Supremes with The Temptations*	Motown 682
3	3	12	Wichita Lineman	*Glen Campbell*	Capitol 103
4	6	10	Diana Ross & the Supremes Join the Temptations	*Diana Ross & The Supremes & The Temptations*	Motown 679
5	4	9	Fool On The Hill	*Sergio Mendes & Brasil '66*	A&M 4160
6	35	6	Greatest Hits	*The Association*	Warner 1767
7	7	29	In-A-Gadda-Da-Vida	*Iron Butterfly*	Atco 250
8	10	18	The Second	*Steppenwolf*	Dunhill/ABC 50037
9	8	23	Cheap Thrills	*Big Brother & The Holding Company*	Columbia 9700
10	5	8	Beggars Banquet	*The Rolling Stones*	London 33

Billboard — FEBRUARY 8, 1969 — TOP LP's

TW	LW	WK			
1	2	7	**TCB**	*Diana Ross & The Supremes with The Temptations*	Motown 682
2	1	9	The Beatles [White Album]	*The Beatles*	Apple 101
3	3	13	Wichita Lineman	*Glen Campbell*	Capitol 103
4	6	7	**Greatest Hits**	*The Association*	Warner 1767
5	4	11	Diana Ross & the Supremes Join the Temptations	*Diana Ross & The Supremes & The Temptations*	Motown 679
6	7	30	In-A-Gadda-Da-Vida	*Iron Butterfly*	Atco 250
7	8	19	The Second	*Steppenwolf*	Dunhill/ABC 50037
8	11	8	**Elvis**	*Elvis Presley*	RCA LPM-4088
9	24	6	**Soulful Strut**	*Young-Holt Unlimited*	Brunswick 754144
10	26	2	Blood, Sweat & Tears	*Blood, Sweat & Tears*	Columbia 9720

Billboard — FEBRUARY 15, 1969 — TOP LP's

TW	LW	WK			
1	2	10	**The Beatles [White Album]**	*The Beatles*	Apple 101
2	3	14	Wichita Lineman	*Glen Campbell*	Capitol 103
3	1	8	TCB	*Diana Ross & The Supremes with The Temptations*	Motown 682
4	4	8	**Greatest Hits**	*The Association*	Warner 1767
5	5	12	Diana Ross & the Supremes Join the Temptations	*Diana Ross & The Supremes & The Temptations*	Motown 679
6	86	2	Yellow Submarine	*The Beatles/Soundtrack*	Apple 153
7	6	31	In-A-Gadda-Da-Vida	*Iron Butterfly*	Atco 250
8	8	9	**Elvis**	*Elvis Presley*	RCA LPM-4088
9	9	7	**Soulful Strut**	*Young-Holt Unlimited*	Brunswick 754144
10	10	3	Blood, Sweat & Tears	*Blood, Sweat & Tears*	Columbia 9720

Billboard — FEBRUARY 22, 1969 — TOP LP's

TW	LW	WK			
1	1	11	**The Beatles [White Album]**	*The Beatles*	Apple 101
2	2	15	Wichita Lineman	*Glen Campbell*	Capitol 103
3	6	3	Yellow Submarine	*The Beatles/Soundtrack*	Apple 153
4	3	9	TCB	*Diana Ross & The Supremes with The Temptations*	Motown 682
5	4	9	Greatest Hits	*The Association*	Warner 1767
6	10	4	Blood, Sweat & Tears	*Blood, Sweat & Tears*	Columbia 9720
7	7	32	In-A-Gadda-Da-Vida	*Iron Butterfly*	Atco 250
8	8	10	**Elvis**	*Elvis Presley*	RCA LPM-4088
9	13	4	Crimson & Clover	*Tommy James & The Shondells*	Roulette 42023
10	5	13	Diana Ross & the Supremes Join the Temptations	*Diana Ross & The Supremes & The Temptations*	Motown 679

TW	LW	WK	Billboard® MARCH 1, 1969	TOP LP's
1	1	12	**The Beatles [White Album]**	*The Beatles*...Apple 101
2	3	4	**Yellow Submarine**	*The Beatles/Soundtrack*...Apple 153
3	2	16	Wichita Lineman	*Glen Campbell*...Capitol 103
4	4	10	TCB	*Diana Ross & The Supremes with The Temptations*...Motown 682
5	5	10	Greatest Hits	*The Association*...Warner 1767
6	6	5	Blood, Sweat & Tears	*Blood, Sweat & Tears*...Columbia 9720
7	14	3	Ball	*Iron Butterfly*...Atco 280
8	9	5	**Crimson & Clover**	*Tommy James & The Shondells*...Roulette 42023
9	20	3	Goodbye	*Cream*...Atco 7001
10	7	33	In-A-Gadda-Da-Vida	*Iron Butterfly*...Atco 250

TW	LW	WK	Billboard® MARCH 8, 1969	TOP LP's
1	3	17	**Wichita Lineman**	*Glen Campbell*...Capitol 103
2	2	5	**Yellow Submarine**	*The Beatles/Soundtrack*...Apple 153
3	9	4	Goodbye	*Cream*...Atco 7001
4	1	13	The Beatles [White Album]	*The Beatles*...Apple 101
5	5	11	Greatest Hits	*The Association*...Warner 1767
6	7	4	Ball	*Iron Butterfly*...Atco 280
7	4	11	TCB	*Diana Ross & The Supremes with The Temptations*...Motown 682
8	8	6	**Crimson & Clover**	*Tommy James & The Shondells*...Roulette 42023
9	6	6	Blood, Sweat & Tears	*Blood, Sweat & Tears*...Columbia 9720
10	19	6	Help Yourself	*Tom Jones*...Parrot 71025

TW	LW	WK	Billboard® MARCH 15, 1969	TOP LP's
1	1	18	**Wichita Lineman**	*Glen Campbell*...Capitol 103
2	3	5	**Goodbye**	*Cream*...Atco 7001
3	4	14	The Beatles [White Album]	*The Beatles*...Apple 101
4	5	12	**Greatest Hits**	*The Association*...Warner 1767
5	6	5	Ball	*Iron Butterfly*...Atco 280
6	2	6	Yellow Submarine	*The Beatles/Soundtrack*...Apple 153
7	7	12	TCB	*Diana Ross & The Supremes with The Temptations*...Motown 682
8	8	7	**Crimson & Clover**	*Tommy James & The Shondells*...Roulette 42023
9	9	7	Blood, Sweat & Tears	*Blood, Sweat & Tears*...Columbia 9720
10	10	7	Help Yourself	*Tom Jones*...Parrot 71025

TW	LW	WK	Billboard® MARCH 22, 1969	TOP LP's
1	1	19	**Wichita Lineman**	*Glen Campbell*...Capitol 103
2	2	6	**Goodbye**	*Cream*...Atco 7001
3	3	15	The Beatles [White Album]	*The Beatles*...Apple 101
4	5	6	Ball	*Iron Butterfly*...Atco 280
5	9	8	Blood, Sweat & Tears	*Blood, Sweat & Tears*...Columbia 9720
6	4	13	Greatest Hits	*The Association*...Warner 1767
7	6	7	Yellow Submarine	*The Beatles/Soundtrack*...Apple 153
8	8	8	**Crimson & Clover**	*Tommy James & The Shondells*...Roulette 42023
9	10	8	Help Yourself	*Tom Jones*...Parrot 71025
10	7	13	TCB	*Diana Ross & The Supremes with The Temptations*...Motown 682

TW	LW	WK	Billboard® MARCH 29, 1969 TOP LP's	
1	5	9	**Blood, Sweat & Tears**	*Blood, Sweat & Tears*...Columbia 9720
2	1	20	Wichita Lineman	*Glen Campbell*...Capitol 103
3	2	7	Goodbye	*Cream*...Atco 7001
4	4	7	Ball	*Iron Butterfly*...Atco 280
5	3	16	The Beatles [White Album]	*The Beatles*...Apple 101
6	12	37	In-A-Gadda-Da-Vida	*Iron Butterfly*...Atco 250
7	11	6	Donovan's Greatest Hits	*Donovan*...Epic 26439
8	6	14	Greatest Hits	*The Association*...Warner 1767
9	9	9	Help Yourself	*Tom Jones*...Parrot 71025
10	10	14	TCB	*Diana Ross & The Supremes with The Temptations*...Motown 682

TW	LW	WK	Billboard® APRIL 5, 1969 TOP LP's	
1	2	21	**Wichita Lineman**	*Glen Campbell*...Capitol 103
2	1	10	Blood, Sweat & Tears	*Blood, Sweat & Tears*...Columbia 9720
3	4	8	**Ball**	*Iron Butterfly*...Atco 280
4	3	8	Goodbye	*Cream*...Atco 7001
5	6	38	In-A-Gadda-Da-Vida	*Iron Butterfly*...Atco 250
6	7	7	Donovan's Greatest Hits	*Donovan*...Epic 26439
7	8	15	Greatest Hits	*The Association*...Warner 1767
8	15	4	Cloud Nine	*The Temptations*...Gordy 939
9	9	10	Help Yourself	*Tom Jones*...Parrot 71025
10	11	9	Bayou Country	*Creedence Clearwater Revival*...Fantasy 8387

TW	LW	WK	Billboard® APRIL 12, 1969 TOP LP's	
1	2	11	**Blood, Sweat & Tears**	*Blood, Sweat & Tears*...Columbia 9720
2	1	22	Wichita Lineman	*Glen Campbell*...Capitol 103
3	11	37	Hair	*Original Cast*...RCA 1150
4	6	8	**Donovan's Greatest Hits**	*Donovan*...Epic 26439
5	9	11	**Help Yourself**	*Tom Jones*...Parrot 71025
6	5	39	In-A-Gadda-Da-Vida	*Iron Butterfly*...Atco 250
7	12	5	**At Your Birthday Party**	*Steppenwolf*...Dunhill/ABC 50053
8	8	5	Cloud Nine	*The Temptations*...Gordy 939
9	3	9	Ball	*Iron Butterfly*...Atco 280
10	4	9	Goodbye	*Cream*...Atco 7001

TW	LW	WK	Billboard® APRIL 19, 1969 TOP LP's	
1	1	12	**Blood, Sweat & Tears**	*Blood, Sweat & Tears*...Columbia 9720
2	3	38	Hair	*Original Cast*...RCA 1150
3	22	2	Galveston	*Glen Campbell*...Capitol 210
4	4	9	**Donovan's Greatest Hits**	*Donovan*...Epic 26439
5	5	12	**Help Yourself**	*Tom Jones*...Parrot 71025
6	6	40	In-A-Gadda-Da-Vida	*Iron Butterfly*...Atco 250
7	7	6	**At Your Birthday Party**	*Steppenwolf*...Dunhill/ABC 50053
8	8	6	Cloud Nine	*The Temptations*...Gordy 939
9	2	23	Wichita Lineman	*Glen Campbell*...Capitol 103
10	10	10	Goodbye	*Cream*...Atco 7001

TW	LW	WK	Billboard. APRIL 26, 1969 TOP LP's	
1	2	39	**Hair**	*Original Cast*...RCA 1150
2	1	13	Blood, Sweat & Tears	*Blood, Sweat & Tears*...Columbia 9720
3	3	3	Galveston	*Glen Campbell*...Capitol 210
4	4	10	**Donovan's Greatest Hits**	*Donovan*...Epic 26439
5	8	7	Cloud Nine	*The Temptations*...Gordy 939
6	5	13	Help Yourself	*Tom Jones*...Parrot 71025
7	9	24	Wichita Lineman	*Glen Campbell*...Capitol 103
8	6	41	In-A-Gadda-Da-Vida	*Iron Butterfly*...Atco 250
9	14	12	Bayou Country	*Creedence Clearwater Revival*...Fantasy 8387
10	12	15	**Switched-On Bach**	*Walter Carlos*...Columbia 7194

TW	LW	WK	Billboard. MAY 3, 1969 TOP LP's	
1	1	40	**Hair**	*Original Cast*...RCA 1150
2	3	4	**Galveston**	*Glen Campbell*...Capitol 210
3	2	14	Blood, Sweat & Tears	*Blood, Sweat & Tears*...Columbia 9720
4	5	8	**Cloud Nine**	*The Temptations*...Gordy 939
5	4	11	Donovan's Greatest Hits	*Donovan*...Epic 26439
6	6	14	Help Yourself	*Tom Jones*...Parrot 71025
7	8	42	In-A-Gadda-Da-Vida	*Iron Butterfly*...Atco 250
8	7	25	Wichita Lineman	*Glen Campbell*...Capitol 103
9	9	13	Bayou Country	*Creedence Clearwater Revival*...Fantasy 8387
10	15	12	Ball	*Iron Butterfly*...Atco 280

TW	LW	WK	Billboard. MAY 10, 1969 TOP LP's	
1	1	41	**Hair**	*Original Cast*...RCA 1150
2	3	15	Blood, Sweat & Tears	*Blood, Sweat & Tears*...Columbia 9720
3	2	5	Galveston	*Glen Campbell*...Capitol 210
4	5	12	**Donovan's Greatest Hits**	*Donovan*...Epic 26439
5	4	9	Cloud Nine	*The Temptations*...Gordy 939
6	22	2	Nashville Skyline	*Bob Dylan*...Columbia 9825
7	7	43	In-A-Gadda-Da-Vida	*Iron Butterfly*...Atco 250
8	6	15	Help Yourself	*Tom Jones*...Parrot 71025
9	9	14	Bayou Country	*Creedence Clearwater Revival*...Fantasy 8387
10	8	26	Wichita Lineman	*Glen Campbell*...Capitol 103

TW	LW	WK	Billboard. MAY 17, 1969 TOP LP's	
1	1	42	**Hair**	*Original Cast*...RCA 1150
2	2	16	Blood, Sweat & Tears	*Blood, Sweat & Tears*...Columbia 9720
3	3	6	Galveston	*Glen Campbell*...Capitol 210
4	6	3	Nashville Skyline	*Bob Dylan*...Columbia 9825
5	4	13	Donovan's Greatest Hits	*Donovan*...Epic 26439
6	5	10	Cloud Nine	*The Temptations*...Gordy 939
7	7	44	In-A-Gadda-Da-Vida	*Iron Butterfly*...Atco 250
8	9	15	Bayou Country	*Creedence Clearwater Revival*...Fantasy 8387
9	8	16	Help Yourself	*Tom Jones*...Parrot 71025
10	11	14	**Led Zeppelin**	*Led Zeppelin*...Atlantic 8216

TW	LW	WK	Billboard. MAY 24, 1969 TOP LP's
1	1	43	**Hair**..........*Original Cast*...RCA 1150
2	2	17	Blood, Sweat & Tears..........*Blood, Sweat & Tears*...Columbia 9720
3	4	4	**Nashville Skyline**..........*Bob Dylan*...Columbia 9825
4	3	7	Galveston..........*Glen Campbell*...Capitol 210
5	5	14	Donovan's Greatest Hits..........*Donovan*...Epic 26439
6	6	11	Cloud Nine..........*The Temptations*...Gordy 939
7	7	45	In-A-Gadda-Da-Vida..........*Iron Butterfly*...Atco 250
8	8	16	Bayou Country..........*Creedence Clearwater Revival*...Fantasy 8387
9	16	16	Romeo & Juliet..........*Soundtrack*...Capitol 2993
10	9	17	Help Yourself..........*Tom Jones*...Parrot 71025

TW	LW	WK	Billboard. MAY 31, 1969 TOP LP's
1	1	44	**Hair**..........*Original Cast*...RCA 1150
2	2	18	Blood, Sweat & Tears..........*Blood, Sweat & Tears*...Columbia 9720
3	3	5	**Nashville Skyline**..........*Bob Dylan*...Columbia 9825
4	4	8	Galveston..........*Glen Campbell*...Capitol 210
5	5	15	Donovan's Greatest Hits..........*Donovan*...Epic 26439
6	6	12	Cloud Nine..........*The Temptations*...Gordy 939
7	9	17	Romeo & Juliet..........*Soundtrack*...Capitol 2993
8	7	46	In-A-Gadda-Da-Vida..........*Iron Butterfly*...Atco 250
9	8	17	Bayou Country..........*Creedence Clearwater Revival*...Fantasy 8387
10	10	18	Help Yourself..........*Tom Jones*...Parrot 71025

TW	LW	WK	Billboard. JUNE 7, 1969 TOP LP's
1	1	45	**Hair**..........*Original Cast*...RCA 1150
2	2	19	Blood, Sweat & Tears..........*Blood, Sweat & Tears*...Columbia 9720
3	3	6	**Nashville Skyline**..........*Bob Dylan*...Columbia 9825
4	4	9	Galveston..........*Glen Campbell*...Capitol 210
5	7	18	Romeo & Juliet..........*Soundtrack*...Capitol 2993
6	8	47	In-A-Gadda-Da-Vida..........*Iron Butterfly*...Atco 250
7	9	18	**Bayou Country**..........*Creedence Clearwater Revival*...Fantasy 8387
8	32	2	The Age Of Aquarius..........*The 5th Dimension*...Soul City 92005
9	5	16	Donovan's Greatest Hits..........*Donovan*...Epic 26439
10	12	4	Happy Heart..........*Andy Williams*...Columbia 9844

TW	LW	WK	Billboard. JUNE 14, 1969 TOP LP's
1	1	46	**Hair**..........*Original Cast*...RCA 1150
2	2	20	Blood, Sweat & Tears..........*Blood, Sweat & Tears*...Columbia 9720
3	3	7	**Nashville Skyline**..........*Bob Dylan*...Columbia 9825
4	8	3	The Age Of Aquarius..........*The 5th Dimension*...Soul City 92005
5	4	10	Galveston..........*Glen Campbell*...Capitol 210
6	5	19	Romeo & Juliet..........*Soundtrack*...Capitol 2993
7	6	48	In-A-Gadda-Da-Vida..........*Iron Butterfly*...Atco 250
8	7	19	Bayou Country..........*Creedence Clearwater Revival*...Fantasy 8387
9	10	5	**Happy Heart**..........*Andy Williams*...Columbia 9844
10	9	17	Donovan's Greatest Hits..........*Donovan*...Epic 26439

Billboard — JUNE 21, 1969 — TOP LP's

TW	LW	WK	Title	Artist...Label
1	1	47	**Hair**	*Original Cast*...RCA 1150
2	2	21	Blood, Sweat & Tears	*Blood, Sweat & Tears*...Columbia 9720
3	4	4	The Age Of Aquarius	*The 5th Dimension*...Soul City 92005
4	6	20	Romeo & Juliet	*Soundtrack*...Capitol 2993
5	3	8	Nashville Skyline	*Bob Dylan*...Columbia 9825
6	7	49	In-A-Gadda-Da-Vida	*Iron Butterfly*...Atco 250
7	5	11	Galveston	*Glen Campbell*...Capitol 210
8	8	20	Bayou Country	*Creedence Clearwater Revival*...Fantasy 8387
9	9	6	**Happy Heart**	*Andy Williams*...Columbia 9844
10	10	18	Donovan's Greatest Hits	*Donovan*...Epic 26439

Billboard — JUNE 28, 1969 — TOP LP's

TW	LW	WK	Title	Artist...Label
1	1	48	**Hair**	*Original Cast*...RCA 1150
2	3	5	**The Age Of Aquarius**	*The 5th Dimension*...Soul City 92005
3	2	22	Blood, Sweat & Tears	*Blood, Sweat & Tears*...Columbia 9720
4	4	21	Romeo & Juliet	*Soundtrack*...Capitol 2993
5	6	50	In-A-Gadda-Da-Vida	*Iron Butterfly*...Atco 250
6	5	9	Nashville Skyline	*Bob Dylan*...Columbia 9825
7	10	19	Donovan's Greatest Hits	*Donovan*...Epic 26439
8	27	3	This Is Tom Jones	*Tom Jones*...Parrot 71028
9	16	4	Tommy	*The Who*...Decca 7205
10	8	21	Bayou Country	*Creedence Clearwater Revival*...Fantasy 8387

Billboard — JULY 5, 1969 — TOP LP's

TW	LW	WK	Title	Artist...Label
1	1	49	**Hair**	*Original Cast*...RCA 1150
2	2	6	**The Age Of Aquarius**	*The 5th Dimension*...Soul City 92005
3	3	23	Blood, Sweat & Tears	*Blood, Sweat & Tears*...Columbia 9720
4	4	22	Romeo & Juliet	*Soundtrack*...Capitol 2993
5	8	4	This Is Tom Jones	*Tom Jones*...Parrot 71028
6	5	51	In-A-Gadda-Da-Vida	*Iron Butterfly*...Atco 250
7	6	10	Nashville Skyline	*Bob Dylan*...Columbia 9825
8	9	5	Tommy	*The Who*...Decca 7205
9	10	22	Bayou Country	*Creedence Clearwater Revival*...Fantasy 8387
10	13	10	A Warm Shade Of Ivory	*Henry Mancini & His Orchestra*...RCA 4140

Billboard — JULY 12, 1969 — TOP LP's

TW	LW	WK	Title	Artist...Label
1	1	50	**Hair**	*Original Cast*...RCA 1150
2	4	23	**Romeo & Juliet**	*Soundtrack*...Capitol 2993
3	3	24	Blood, Sweat & Tears	*Blood, Sweat & Tears*...Columbia 9720
4	5	5	**This Is Tom Jones**	*Tom Jones*...Parrot 71028
5	2	7	The Age Of Aquarius	*The 5th Dimension*...Soul City 92005
6	10	11	A Warm Shade Of Ivory	*Henry Mancini & His Orchestra*...RCA 4140
7	7	11	Nashville Skyline	*Bob Dylan*...Columbia 9825
8	8	6	Tommy	*The Who*...Decca 7205
9	9	23	Bayou Country	*Creedence Clearwater Revival*...Fantasy 8387
10	6	52	In-A-Gadda-Da-Vida	*Iron Butterfly*...Atco 250

Billboard — JULY 19, 1969 — TOP LP's

TW	LW	WK	Title	Artist	Label
1	1	51	**Hair**	*Original Cast*	RCA 1150
2	2	24	**Romeo & Juliet**	*Soundtrack*	Capitol 2993
3	3	25	Blood, Sweat & Tears	*Blood, Sweat & Tears*	Columbia 9720
4	5	8	The Age Of Aquarius	*The 5th Dimension*	Soul City 92005
5	4	6	This Is Tom Jones	*Tom Jones*	Parrot 71028
6	6	12	A Warm Shade Of Ivory	*Henry Mancini & His Orchestra*	RCA 4140
7	8	7	Tommy	*The Who*	Decca 7205
8	7	12	Nashville Skyline	*Bob Dylan*	Columbia 9825
9	10	53	In-A-Gadda-Da-Vida	*Iron Butterfly*	Atco 250
10	17	4	Crosby, Stills & Nash	*Crosby, Stills & Nash*	Atlantic 8229

Billboard — JULY 26, 1969 — TOP LP's

TW	LW	WK	Title	Artist	Label
1	3	26	**Blood, Sweat & Tears**	*Blood, Sweat & Tears*	Columbia 9720
2	1	52	Hair	*Original Cast*	RCA 1150
3	2	25	Romeo & Juliet	*Soundtrack*	Capitol 2993
4	5	7	**This Is Tom Jones**	*Tom Jones*	Parrot 71028
5	4	9	The Age Of Aquarius	*The 5th Dimension*	Soul City 92005
6	6	13	A Warm Shade Of Ivory	*Henry Mancini & His Orchestra*	RCA 4140
7	7	8	Tommy	*The Who*	Decca 7205
8	10	5	Crosby, Stills & Nash	*Crosby, Stills & Nash*	Atlantic 8229
9	9	54	In-A-Gadda-Da-Vida	*Iron Butterfly*	Atco 250
10	8	13	Nashville Skyline	*Bob Dylan*	Columbia 9825

Billboard — AUGUST 2, 1969 — TOP LP's

TW	LW	WK	Title	Artist	Label
1	1	27	**Blood, Sweat & Tears**	*Blood, Sweat & Tears*	Columbia 9720
2	2	53	Hair	*Original Cast*	RCA 1150
3	3	26	Romeo & Juliet	*Soundtrack*	Capitol 2993
4	4	8	**This Is Tom Jones**	*Tom Jones*	Parrot 71028
5	6	14	**A Warm Shade Of Ivory**	*Henry Mancini & His Orchestra*	RCA 4140
6	9	55	In-A-Gadda-Da-Vida	*Iron Butterfly*	Atco 250
7	25	3	Best Of Cream	*Cream*	Atco 291
8	8	6	Crosby, Stills & Nash	*Crosby, Stills & Nash*	Atlantic 8229
9	14	5	Johnny Cash At San Quentin	*Johnny Cash*	Columbia 9827
10	5	10	The Age Of Aquarius	*The 5th Dimension*	Soul City 92005

Billboard — AUGUST 9, 1969 — TOP LP's

TW	LW	WK	Title	Artist	Label
1	1	28	**Blood, Sweat & Tears**	*Blood, Sweat & Tears*	Columbia 9720
2	2	54	Hair	*Original Cast*	RCA 1150
3	3	27	Romeo & Juliet	*Soundtrack*	Capitol 2993
4	6	56	**In-A-Gadda-Da-Vida**	*Iron Butterfly*	Atco 250
5	4	9	This Is Tom Jones	*Tom Jones*	Parrot 71028
6	9	6	Johnny Cash At San Quentin	*Johnny Cash*	Columbia 9827
7	7	4	Best Of Cream	*Cream*	Atco 291
8	8	7	Crosby, Stills & Nash	*Crosby, Stills & Nash*	Atlantic 8229
9	5	15	A Warm Shade Of Ivory	*Henry Mancini & His Orchestra*	RCA 4140
10	11	10	Tommy	*The Who*	Decca 7205

Billboard — AUGUST 16, 1969 — TOP LP's

TW	LW	WK	Title	Artist	Label
1	1	29	**Blood, Sweat & Tears**	*Blood, Sweat & Tears*	Columbia 9720
2	2	55	Hair	*Original Cast*	RCA 1150
3	3	28	Romeo & Juliet	*Soundtrack*	Capitol 2993
4	6	7	Johnny Cash At San Quentin	*Johnny Cash*	Columbia 9827
5	5	10	This Is Tom Jones	*Tom Jones*	Parrot 71028
6	7	5	Best Of Cream	*Cream*	Atco 291
7	8	8	Crosby, Stills & Nash	*Crosby, Stills & Nash*	Atlantic 8229
8	4	57	In-A-Gadda-Da-Vida	*Iron Butterfly*	Atco 250
9	24	2	The Soft Parade	*The Doors*	Elektra 75005
10	12	16	Nashville Skyline	*Bob Dylan*	Columbia 9825

Billboard — AUGUST 23, 1969 — TOP LP's

TW	LW	WK	Title	Artist	Label
1	4	8	**Johnny Cash At San Quentin**	*Johnny Cash*	Columbia 9827
2	1	30	Blood, Sweat & Tears	*Blood, Sweat & Tears*	Columbia 9720
3	2	56	Hair	*Original Cast*	RCA 1150
4	6	6	Best Of Cream	*Cream*	Atco 291
5	111	2	Blind Faith	*Blind Faith*	Atco 304
6	9	3	**The Soft Parade**	*The Doors*	Elektra 75005
7	3	29	Romeo & Juliet	*Soundtrack*	Capitol 2993
8	5	11	This Is Tom Jones	*Tom Jones*	Parrot 71028
9	7	9	Crosby, Stills & Nash	*Crosby, Stills & Nash*	Atlantic 8229
10	8	58	In-A-Gadda-Da-Vida	*Iron Butterfly*	Atco 250

Billboard — AUGUST 30, 1969 — TOP LP's

TW	LW	WK	Title	Artist	Label
1	1	9	**Johnny Cash At San Quentin**	*Johnny Cash*	Columbia 9827
2	2	31	Blood, Sweat & Tears	*Blood, Sweat & Tears*	Columbia 9720
3	5	3	Blind Faith	*Blind Faith*	Atco 304
4	4	7	Best Of Cream	*Cream*	Atco 291
5	3	57	Hair	*Original Cast*	RCA 1150
6	6	4	**The Soft Parade**	*The Doors*	Elektra 75005
7	7	30	Romeo & Juliet	*Soundtrack*	Capitol 2993
8	8	12	This Is Tom Jones	*Tom Jones*	Parrot 71028
9	10	59	In-A-Gadda-Da-Vida	*Iron Butterfly*	Atco 250
10	12	6	Best Of Bee Gees	*Bee Gees*	Atco 292

Billboard — SEPTEMBER 6, 1969 — TOP LP's

TW	LW	WK	Title	Artist	Label
1	1	10	**Johnny Cash At San Quentin**	*Johnny Cash*	Columbia 9827
2	3	4	Blind Faith	*Blind Faith*	Atco 304
3	2	32	Blood, Sweat & Tears	*Blood, Sweat & Tears*	Columbia 9720
4	4	8	Best Of Cream	*Cream*	Atco 291
5	5	58	Hair	*Original Cast*	RCA 1150
6	11	6	**Smash Hits**	*Jimi Hendrix Experience*	Reprise 2025
7	6	5	The Soft Parade	*The Doors*	Elektra 75005
8	9	60	In-A-Gadda-Da-Vida	*Iron Butterfly*	Atco 250
9	10	7	**Best Of Bee Gees**	*Bee Gees*	Atco 292
10	7	31	Romeo & Juliet	*Soundtrack*	Capitol 2993

TW	LW	WK	Billboard. SEPTEMBER 13, 1969	TOP LP's
1	1	11	**Johnny Cash At San Quentin**	*Johnny Cash*...Columbia 9827
2	2	5	Blind Faith	*Blind Faith*...Atco 304
3	4	9	**Best Of Cream**	*Cream*...Atco 291
4	3	33	Blood, Sweat & Tears	*Blood, Sweat & Tears*...Columbia 9720
5	10	32	Romeo & Juliet	*Soundtrack*...Capitol 2993
6	6	7	**Smash Hits**	*Jimi Hendrix Experience*...Reprise 2025
7	7	6	The Soft Parade	*The Doors*...Elektra 75005
8	5	59	Hair	*Original Cast*...RCA 1150
9	8	61	In-A-Gadda-Da-Vida	*Iron Butterfly*...Atco 250
10	9	8	Best Of Bee Gees	*Bee Gees*...Atco 292

TW	LW	WK	Billboard. SEPTEMBER 20, 1969	TOP LP's
1	2	6	**Blind Faith**	*Blind Faith*...Atco 304
2	1	12	Johnny Cash At San Quentin	*Johnny Cash*...Columbia 9827
3	4	34	Blood, Sweat & Tears	*Blood, Sweat & Tears*...Columbia 9720
4	8	60	Hair	*Original Cast*...RCA 1150
5	127	2	Green River	*Creedence Clearwater Revival*...Fantasy 8393
6	9	62	In-A-Gadda-Da-Vida	*Iron Butterfly*...Atco 250
7	3	10	Best Of Cream	*Cream*...Atco 291
8	6	8	Smash Hits	*Jimi Hendrix Experience*...Reprise 2025
9	7	7	The Soft Parade	*The Doors*...Elektra 75005
10	168	2	Through The Past, Darkly (Big Hits Vol. 2)	*The Rolling Stones*...London 3

TW	LW	WK	Billboard. SEPTEMBER 27, 1969	TOP LP's
1	1	7	**Blind Faith**	*Blind Faith*...Atco 304
2	2	13	Johnny Cash At San Quentin	*Johnny Cash*...Columbia 9827
3	5	3	Green River	*Creedence Clearwater Revival*...Fantasy 8393
4	3	35	Blood, Sweat & Tears	*Blood, Sweat & Tears*...Columbia 9720
5	10	3	Through The Past, Darkly (Big Hits Vol. 2)	*The Rolling Stones*...London 3
6	7	11	Best Of Cream	*Cream*...Atco 291
7	9	8	The Soft Parade	*The Doors*...Elektra 75005
8	8	9	Smash Hits	*Jimi Hendrix Experience*...Reprise 2025
9	4	61	Hair	*Original Cast*...RCA 1150
10	6	63	In-A-Gadda-Da-Vida	*Iron Butterfly*...Atco 250

TW	LW	WK	Billboard. OCTOBER 4, 1969	TOP LP's
1	3	4	**Green River**	*Creedence Clearwater Revival*...Fantasy 8393
2	2	14	Johnny Cash At San Quentin	*Johnny Cash*...Columbia 9827
3	1	8	Blind Faith	*Blind Faith*...Atco 304
4	5	4	Through The Past, Darkly (Big Hits Vol. 2)	*The Rolling Stones*...London 3
5	4	36	Blood, Sweat & Tears	*Blood, Sweat & Tears*...Columbia 9720
6	6	12	Best Of Cream	*Cream*...Atco 291
7	8	10	Smash Hits	*Jimi Hendrix Experience*...Reprise 2025
8	10	64	In-A-Gadda-Da-Vida	*Iron Butterfly*...Atco 250
9	7	9	The Soft Parade	*The Doors*...Elektra 75005
10	9	62	Hair	*Original Cast*...RCA 1150

Billboard — OCTOBER 11, 1969 — TOP LP's

TW	LW	WK	Title	Artist	Label
1	1	5	**Green River**	*Creedence Clearwater Revival*	Fantasy 8393
2	4	5	**Through The Past, Darkly (Big Hits Vol. 2)**	*The Rolling Stones*	London 3
3	2	15	Johnny Cash At San Quentin	*Johnny Cash*	Columbia 9827
4	3	9	Blind Faith	*Blind Faith*	Atco 304
5	5	37	Blood, Sweat & Tears	*Blood, Sweat & Tears*	Columbia 9720
6	10	63	Hair	*Original Cast*	RCA 1150
7	6	13	Best Of Cream	*Cream*	Atco 291
8	8	65	In-A-Gadda-Da-Vida	*Iron Butterfly*	Atco 250
9	9	10	The Soft Parade	*The Doors*	Elektra 75005
10	7	11	Smash Hits	*Jimi Hendrix Experience*	Reprise 2025

Billboard — OCTOBER 18, 1969 — TOP LP's

TW	LW	WK	Title	Artist	Label
1	1	6	**Green River**	*Creedence Clearwater Revival*	Fantasy 8393
2	2	6	**Through The Past, Darkly (Big Hits Vol. 2)**	*The Rolling Stones*	London 3
3	3	16	Johnny Cash At San Quentin	*Johnny Cash*	Columbia 9827
4	4	10	Blind Faith	*Blind Faith*	Atco 304
5	8	66	In-A-Gadda-Da-Vida	*Iron Butterfly*	Atco 250
6	5	38	Blood, Sweat & Tears	*Blood, Sweat & Tears*	Columbia 9720
7	6	64	Hair	*Original Cast*	RCA 1150
8	13	19	This Is Tom Jones	*Tom Jones*	Parrot 71028
9	7	14	Best Of Cream	*Cream*	Atco 291
10	11	15	Hot Buttered Soul	*Isaac Hayes*	Enterprise 1001

Billboard — OCTOBER 25, 1969 — TOP LP's

TW	LW	WK	Title	Artist	Label
1	1	7	**Green River**	*Creedence Clearwater Revival*	Fantasy 8393
2	3	17	Johnny Cash At San Quentin	*Johnny Cash*	Columbia 9827
3	2	7	Through The Past, Darkly (Big Hits Vol. 2)	*The Rolling Stones*	London 3
4	178	2	Abbey Road	*The Beatles*	Apple 383
5	4	11	Blind Faith	*Blind Faith*	Atco 304
6	5	67	In-A-Gadda-Da-Vida	*Iron Butterfly*	Atco 250
7	6	39	Blood, Sweat & Tears	*Blood, Sweat & Tears*	Columbia 9720
8	10	16	**Hot Buttered Soul**	*Isaac Hayes*	Enterprise 1001
9	9	15	Best Of Cream	*Cream*	Atco 291
10	13	7	Santana	*Santana*	Columbia 9781

Billboard — NOVEMBER 1, 1969 — TOP LP's

TW	LW	WK	Title	Artist	Label
1	4	3	**Abbey Road**	*The Beatles*	Apple 383
2	1	8	Green River	*Creedence Clearwater Revival*	Fantasy 8393
3	3	8	Through The Past, Darkly (Big Hits Vol. 2)	*The Rolling Stones*	London 3
4	5	12	Blind Faith	*Blind Faith*	Atco 304
5	2	18	Johnny Cash At San Quentin	*Johnny Cash*	Columbia 9827
6	16	4	I Got Dem Ol' Kozmic Blues Again Mama!	*Janis Joplin*	Columbia 9913
7	11	19	Crosby, Stills & Nash	*Crosby, Stills & Nash*	Atlantic 8229
8	8	17	**Hot Buttered Soul**	*Isaac Hayes*	Enterprise 1001
9	6	68	In-A-Gadda-Da-Vida	*Iron Butterfly*	Atco 250
10	10	8	Santana	*Santana*	Columbia 9781

TW	LW	WK	Billboard. NOVEMBER 8, 1969	TOP LP's
①	1	4	**Abbey Road**	*The Beatles*...Apple 383
②	2	9	Green River	*Creedence Clearwater Revival*...Fantasy 8393
③	5	19	Johnny Cash At San Quentin	*Johnny Cash*...Columbia 9827
④	4	13	Blind Faith	*Blind Faith*...Atco 304
⑤	6	5	**I Got Dem Ol' Kozmic Blues Again Mama!**	*Janis Joplin*...Columbia 9913
⑥	3	9	Through The Past, Darkly (Big Hits Vol. 2)	*The Rolling Stones*...London 3
⑦	7	20	Crosby, Stills & Nash	*Crosby, Stills & Nash*...Atlantic 8229
⑧	8	18	**Hot Buttered Soul**	*Isaac Hayes*...Enterprise 1001
⑨	10	9	Santana	*Santana*...Columbia 9781
⑩	11	41	Blood, Sweat & Tears	*Blood, Sweat & Tears*...Columbia 9720

TW	LW	WK	Billboard. NOVEMBER 15, 1969	TOP LP's
①	1	5	**Abbey Road**	*The Beatles*...Apple 383
②	2	10	Green River	*Creedence Clearwater Revival*...Fantasy 8393
③	3	20	Johnny Cash At San Quentin	*Johnny Cash*...Columbia 9827
❹	9	10	**Santana**	*Santana*...Columbia 9781
⑤	5	6	**I Got Dem Ol' Kozmic Blues Again Mama!**	*Janis Joplin*...Columbia 9913
⑥	7	21	**Crosby, Stills & Nash**	*Crosby, Stills & Nash*...Atlantic 8229
⑦	6	10	Through The Past, Darkly (Big Hits Vol. 2)	*The Rolling Stones*...London 3
❽	11	6	Puzzle People	*The Temptations*...Gordy 949
⑨	4	14	Blind Faith	*Blind Faith*...Atco 304
⑩	10	42	Blood, Sweat & Tears	*Blood, Sweat & Tears*...Columbia 9720

TW	LW	WK	Billboard. NOVEMBER 22, 1969	TOP LP's
①	1	6	**Abbey Road**	*The Beatles*...Apple 383
❷	15	3	Led Zeppelin II	*Led Zeppelin*...Atlantic 8236
③	2	11	Green River	*Creedence Clearwater Revival*...Fantasy 8393
④	4	11	**Santana**	*Santana*...Columbia 9781
⑤	5	7	**I Got Dem Ol' Kozmic Blues Again Mama!**	*Janis Joplin*...Columbia 9913
⑥	8	7	Puzzle People	*The Temptations*...Gordy 949
⑦	3	21	Johnny Cash At San Quentin	*Johnny Cash*...Columbia 9827
⑧	6	22	Crosby, Stills & Nash	*Crosby, Stills & Nash*...Atlantic 8229
❾	24	2	Tom Jones Live In Las Vegas	*Tom Jones*...Parrot 71031
⑩	9	15	Blind Faith	*Blind Faith*...Atco 304

TW	LW	WK	Billboard. NOVEMBER 29, 1969	TOP LP's
①	1	7	**Abbey Road**	*The Beatles*...Apple 383
②	2	4	Led Zeppelin II	*Led Zeppelin*...Atlantic 8236
③	3	12	Green River	*Creedence Clearwater Revival*...Fantasy 8393
❹	9	3	Tom Jones Live In Las Vegas	*Tom Jones*...Parrot 71031
⑤	6	8	**Puzzle People**	*The Temptations*...Gordy 949
⑥	8	23	**Crosby, Stills & Nash**	*Crosby, Stills & Nash*...Atlantic 8229
⑦	11	44	Blood, Sweat & Tears	*Blood, Sweat & Tears*...Columbia 9720
⑧	7	22	Johnny Cash At San Quentin	*Johnny Cash*...Columbia 9827
⑨	4	12	Santana	*Santana*...Columbia 9781
⑩	5	8	I Got Dem Ol' Kozmic Blues Again Mama!	*Janis Joplin*...Columbia 9913

TW	LW	WK	Billboard® DECEMBER 6, 1969	TOP LP's
1	1	8	**Abbey Road**	*The Beatles*...Apple 383
2	2	5	Led Zeppelin II	*Led Zeppelin*...Atlantic 8236
3	4	4	**Tom Jones Live In Las Vegas**	*Tom Jones*...Parrot 71031
4	3	13	Green River	*Creedence Clearwater Revival*...Fantasy 8393
5	5	9	**Puzzle People**	*The Temptations*...Gordy 949
6	7	45	Blood, Sweat & Tears	*Blood, Sweat & Tears*...Columbia 9720
7	6	24	Crosby, Stills & Nash	*Crosby, Stills & Nash*...Atlantic 8229
8	9	13	Santana	*Santana*...Columbia 9781
9	8	23	Johnny Cash At San Quentin	*Johnny Cash*...Columbia 9827
10	16	14	Easy Rider	*Soundtrack*...Dunhill/ABC 50063

TW	LW	WK	Billboard® DECEMBER 13, 1969	TOP LP's
1	1	9	**Abbey Road**	*The Beatles*...Apple 383
2	2	6	Led Zeppelin II	*Led Zeppelin*...Atlantic 8236
3	3	5	**Tom Jones Live In Las Vegas**	*Tom Jones*...Parrot 71031
4	4	14	Green River	*Creedence Clearwater Revival*...Fantasy 8393
5	8	14	Santana	*Santana*...Columbia 9781
6	7	25	**Crosby, Stills & Nash**	*Crosby, Stills & Nash*...Atlantic 8229
7	5	10	Puzzle People	*The Temptations*...Gordy 949
8	9	24	Johnny Cash At San Quentin	*Johnny Cash*...Columbia 9827
9	6	46	Blood, Sweat & Tears	*Blood, Sweat & Tears*...Columbia 9720
10	10	15	Easy Rider	*Soundtrack*...Dunhill/ABC 50063

TW	LW	WK	Billboard® DECEMBER 20, 1969	TOP LP's
1	1	10	**Abbey Road**	*The Beatles*...Apple 383
2	2	7	Led Zeppelin II	*Led Zeppelin*...Atlantic 8236
3	3	6	**Tom Jones Live In Las Vegas**	*Tom Jones*...Parrot 71031
4	4	15	Green River	*Creedence Clearwater Revival*...Fantasy 8393
5	29	3	Let It Bleed	*The Rolling Stones*...London 4
6	7	11	Puzzle People	*The Temptations*...Gordy 949
7	5	15	Santana	*Santana*...Columbia 9781
8	9	47	Blood, Sweat & Tears	*Blood, Sweat & Tears*...Columbia 9720
9	6	26	Crosby, Stills & Nash	*Crosby, Stills & Nash*...Atlantic 8229
10	10	16	Easy Rider	*Soundtrack*...Dunhill/ABC 50063

TW	LW	WK	Billboard® DECEMBER 27, 1969	TOP LP's
1	2	8	**Led Zeppelin II**	*Led Zeppelin*...Atlantic 8236
2	1	11	Abbey Road	*The Beatles*...Apple 383
3	5	4	**Let It Bleed**	*The Rolling Stones*...London 4
4	3	7	Tom Jones Live In Las Vegas	*Tom Jones*...Parrot 71031
5	11	3	Willy and the Poorboys	*Creedence Clearwater Revival*...Fantasy 8397
6	12	5	**Was Captured Live At The Forum**	*Three Dog Night*...Dunhill/ABC 50068
7	4	16	Green River	*Creedence Clearwater Revival*...Fantasy 8393
8	8	48	Blood, Sweat & Tears	*Blood, Sweat & Tears*...Columbia 9720
9	9	27	Crosby, Stills & Nash	*Crosby, Stills & Nash*...Atlantic 8229
10	6	12	Puzzle People	*The Temptations*...Gordy 949

Billboard — JANUARY 3, 1970 — TOP LP's

TW	LW	WK			
①	2	12	**Abbey Road**	*The Beatles*	Apple 383
②	1	9	Led Zeppelin II	*Led Zeppelin*	Atlantic 8236
③	3	5	**Let It Bleed**	*The Rolling Stones*	London 4
④	5	4	Willy and the Poorboys	*Creedence Clearwater Revival*	Fantasy 8397
⑤	4	8	Tom Jones Live In Las Vegas	*Tom Jones*	Parrot 71031
⑥	6	6	**Was Captured Live At The Forum**	*Three Dog Night*	Dunhill/ABC 50068
⑦	8	49	Blood, Sweat & Tears	*Blood, Sweat & Tears*	Columbia 9720
⑧	9	28	Crosby, Stills & Nash	*Crosby, Stills & Nash*	Atlantic 8229
⑨	10	13	Puzzle People	*The Temptations*	Gordy 949
⑩	11	17	Santana	*Santana*	Columbia 9781

Billboard — JANUARY 10, 1970 — TOP LP's

TW	LW	WK			
①	1	13	**Abbey Road**	*The Beatles*	Apple 383
②	2	10	Led Zeppelin II	*Led Zeppelin*	Atlantic 8236
③	4	5	**Willy and the Poorboys**	*Creedence Clearwater Revival*	Fantasy 8397
④	3	6	Let It Bleed	*The Rolling Stones*	London 4
⑤	5	9	Tom Jones Live In Las Vegas	*Tom Jones*	Parrot 71031
⑥	6	7	**Was Captured Live At The Forum**	*Three Dog Night*	Dunhill/ABC 50068
⑦	7	50	Blood, Sweat & Tears	*Blood, Sweat & Tears*	Columbia 9720
⑧	8	29	Crosby, Stills & Nash	*Crosby, Stills & Nash*	Atlantic 8229
⑨	10	18	Santana	*Santana*	Columbia 9781
⑩	9	14	Puzzle People	*The Temptations*	Gordy 949

Billboard — JANUARY 17, 1970 — TOP LP's

TW	LW	WK			
①	2	11	**Led Zeppelin II**	*Led Zeppelin*	Atlantic 8236
②	1	14	Abbey Road	*The Beatles*	Apple 383
③	3	6	**Willy and the Poorboys**	*Creedence Clearwater Revival*	Fantasy 8397
④	5	10	Tom Jones Live In Las Vegas	*Tom Jones*	Parrot 71031
⑤	4	7	Let It Bleed	*The Rolling Stones*	London 4
⑥	6	8	**Was Captured Live At The Forum**	*Three Dog Night*	Dunhill/ABC 50068
⑦	7	51	Blood, Sweat & Tears	*Blood, Sweat & Tears*	Columbia 9720
❽	11	3	Engelbert Humperdinck	*Engelbert Humperdinck*	Parrot 71030
⑨	9	19	Santana	*Santana*	Columbia 9781
⑩	10	15	Puzzle People	*The Temptations*	Gordy 949

Billboard — JANUARY 24, 1970 — TOP LP's

TW	LW	WK			
①	2	15	**Abbey Road**	*The Beatles*	Apple 383
②	1	12	Led Zeppelin II	*Led Zeppelin*	Atlantic 8236
③	3	7	**Willy and the Poorboys**	*Creedence Clearwater Revival*	Fantasy 8397
④	4	11	Tom Jones Live In Las Vegas	*Tom Jones*	Parrot 71031
⑤	5	8	Let It Bleed	*The Rolling Stones*	London 4
⑥	6	9	**Was Captured Live At The Forum**	*Three Dog Night*	Dunhill/ABC 50068
⑦	8	4	Engelbert Humperdinck	*Engelbert Humperdinck*	Parrot 71030
⑧	7	52	Blood, Sweat & Tears	*Blood, Sweat & Tears*	Columbia 9720
⑨	9	20	Santana	*Santana*	Columbia 9781
⑩	17	21	Easy Rider	*Soundtrack*	Dunhill/ABC 50063

Billboard — JANUARY 31, 1970 — TOP LP's

TW	LW	WK	Title	Artist...Label
1	2	13	**Led Zeppelin II**	*Led Zeppelin*...Atlantic 8236
2	1	16	Abbey Road	*The Beatles*...Apple 383
3	4	12	**Tom Jones Live In Las Vegas**	*Tom Jones*...Parrot 71031
4	5	9	Let It Bleed	*The Rolling Stones*...London 4
5	3	8	Willy and the Poorboys	*Creedence Clearwater Revival*...Fantasy 8397
6	6	10	**Was Captured Live At The Forum**	*Three Dog Night*...Dunhill/ABC 50068
7	7	5	Engelbert Humperdinck	*Engelbert Humperdinck*...Parrot 71030
8	8	53	Blood, Sweat & Tears	*Blood, Sweat & Tears*...Columbia 9720
9	9	21	Santana	*Santana*...Columbia 9781
10	14	17	Puzzle People	*The Temptations*...Gordy 949

Billboard — FEBRUARY 7, 1970 — TOP LP's

TW	LW	WK	Title	Artist...Label
1	1	14	**Led Zeppelin II**	*Led Zeppelin*...Atlantic 8236
2	2	17	Abbey Road	*The Beatles*...Apple 383
3	5	9	**Willy and the Poorboys**	*Creedence Clearwater Revival*...Fantasy 8397
4	3	13	Tom Jones Live In Las Vegas	*Tom Jones*...Parrot 71031
5	4	10	Let It Bleed	*The Rolling Stones*...London 4
6	6	11	**Was Captured Live At The Forum**	*Three Dog Night*...Dunhill/ABC 50068
7	7	6	Engelbert Humperdinck	*Engelbert Humperdinck*...Parrot 71030
8	9	22	Santana	*Santana*...Columbia 9781
9	15	17	**The Band**	*The Band*...Capitol 132
10	14	5	**The Plastic Ono Band - Live Peace In Toronto 1969**	*The Plastic Ono Band*...Apple 3362

Billboard — FEBRUARY 14, 1970 — TOP LP's

TW	LW	WK	Title	Artist...Label
1	1	15	**Led Zeppelin II**	*Led Zeppelin*...Atlantic 8236
2	2	18	Abbey Road	*The Beatles*...Apple 383
3	3	10	**Willy and the Poorboys**	*Creedence Clearwater Revival*...Fantasy 8397
4	4	14	Tom Jones Live In Las Vegas	*Tom Jones*...Parrot 71031
5	7	7	**Engelbert Humperdinck**	*Engelbert Humperdinck*...Parrot 71030
6	5	11	Let It Bleed	*The Rolling Stones*...London 4
7	6	12	Was Captured Live At The Forum	*Three Dog Night*...Dunhill/ABC 50068
8	8	23	Santana	*Santana*...Columbia 9781
9	15	5	Diana Ross Presents The Jackson 5	*The Jackson 5*...Motown 700
10	10	6	**The Plastic Ono Band - Live Peace In Toronto 1969**	*The Plastic Ono Band*...Apple 3362

Billboard — FEBRUARY 21, 1970 — TOP LP's

TW	LW	WK	Title	Artist...Label
1	1	16	**Led Zeppelin II**	*Led Zeppelin*...Atlantic 8236
2	2	19	Abbey Road	*The Beatles*...Apple 383
3	4	15	**Tom Jones Live In Las Vegas**	*Tom Jones*...Parrot 71031
4	3	11	Willy and the Poorboys	*Creedence Clearwater Revival*...Fantasy 8397
5	5	8	**Engelbert Humperdinck**	*Engelbert Humperdinck*...Parrot 71030
6	6	12	Let It Bleed	*The Rolling Stones*...London 4
7	8	24	Santana	*Santana*...Columbia 9781
8	9	6	Diana Ross Presents The Jackson 5	*The Jackson 5*...Motown 700
9	44	2	Chicago II	*Chicago*...Columbia 24
10	7	13	Was Captured Live At The Forum	*Three Dog Night*...Dunhill/ABC 50068

Billboard — FEBRUARY 28, 1970 — TOP LP's

TW	LW	WK	Title	Artist	Label
1	1	17	**Led Zeppelin II**	*Led Zeppelin*	Atlantic 8236
2	2	20	Abbey Road	*The Beatles*	Apple 383
3	4	12	**Willy and the Poorboys**	*Creedence Clearwater Revival*	Fantasy 8397
4	106	3	Bridge Over Troubled Water	*Simon & Garfunkel*	Columbia 9914
5	3	16	Tom Jones Live In Las Vegas	*Tom Jones*	Parrot 71031
6	5	9	Engelbert Humperdinck	*Engelbert Humperdinck*	Parrot 71030
7	9	3	Chicago II	*Chicago*	Columbia 24
8	8	7	Diana Ross Presents The Jackson 5	*The Jackson 5*	Motown 700
9	10	14	Was Captured Live At The Forum	*Three Dog Night*	Dunhill/ABC 50068
10	19	26	Easy Rider	*Soundtrack*	Dunhill/ABC 50063

Billboard — MARCH 7, 1970 — TOP LP's

TW	LW	WK	Title	Artist	Label
1	4	4	**Bridge Over Troubled Water**	*Simon & Garfunkel*	Columbia 9914
2	1	18	Led Zeppelin II	*Led Zeppelin*	Atlantic 8236
3	2	21	Abbey Road	*The Beatles*	Apple 383
4	3	13	Willy and the Poorboys	*Creedence Clearwater Revival*	Fantasy 8397
5	7	4	Chicago II	*Chicago*	Columbia 24
6	8	8	Diana Ross Presents The Jackson 5	*The Jackson 5*	Motown 700
7	13	4	Hello, I'm Johnny Cash	*Johnny Cash*	Columbia 9943
8	9	15	Was Captured Live At The Forum	*Three Dog Night*	Dunhill/ABC 50068
9	6	10	Engelbert Humperdinck	*Engelbert Humperdinck*	Parrot 71030
10	11	26	Santana	*Santana*	Columbia 9781

Billboard — MARCH 14, 1970 — TOP LP's

TW	LW	WK	Title	Artist	Label
1	1	5	**Bridge Over Troubled Water**	*Simon & Garfunkel*	Columbia 9914
2	2	19	Led Zeppelin II	*Led Zeppelin*	Atlantic 8236
3	3	22	Abbey Road	*The Beatles*	Apple 383
4	4	14	Willy and the Poorboys	*Creedence Clearwater Revival*	Fantasy 8397
5	5	5	Chicago II	*Chicago*	Columbia 24
6	7	5	**Hello, I'm Johnny Cash**	*Johnny Cash*	Columbia 9943
7	10	27	Santana	*Santana*	Columbia 9781
8	11	18	Tom Jones Live In Las Vegas	*Tom Jones*	Parrot 71031
9	9	11	Engelbert Humperdinck	*Engelbert Humperdinck*	Parrot 71030
10	6	9	Diana Ross Presents The Jackson 5	*The Jackson 5*	Motown 700

Billboard — MARCH 21, 1970 — TOP LP's

TW	LW	WK	Title	Artist	Label
1	1	6	**Bridge Over Troubled Water**	*Simon & Garfunkel*	Columbia 9914
2	2	20	Led Zeppelin II	*Led Zeppelin*	Atlantic 8236
3	-	1	Hey Jude	*The Beatles*	Apple 385
4	12	3	**Morrison Hotel/Hard Rock Cafe**	*The Doors*	Elektra 75007
5	4	15	Willy and the Poorboys	*Creedence Clearwater Revival*	Fantasy 8397
6	3	23	Abbey Road	*The Beatles*	Apple 383
7	7	28	Santana	*Santana*	Columbia 9781
8	5	6	Chicago II	*Chicago*	Columbia 24
9	8	19	Tom Jones Live In Las Vegas	*Tom Jones*	Parrot 71031
10	6	6	Hello, I'm Johnny Cash	*Johnny Cash*	Columbia 9943

TW	LW	WK	Billboard. MARCH 28, 1970 TOP LP's
1	1	7	**Bridge Over Troubled Water**.............. *Simon & Garfunkel*...Columbia 9914
2	3	2	**Hey Jude**.............. *The Beatles*...Apple 385
3	2	21	Led Zeppelin II.............. *Led Zeppelin*...Atlantic 8236
4	4	4	**Morrison Hotel/Hard Rock Cafe**.............. *The Doors*...Elektra 75007
5	7	29	Santana.............. *Santana*...Columbia 9781
6	8	7	Chicago II.............. *Chicago*...Columbia 24
7	6	24	Abbey Road.............. *The Beatles*...Apple 383
8	5	16	Willy and the Poorboys.............. *Creedence Clearwater Revival*...Fantasy 8397
9	9	20	Tom Jones Live In Las Vegas.............. *Tom Jones*...Parrot 71031
10	10	7	Hello, I'm Johnny Cash.............. *Johnny Cash*...Columbia 9943

TW	LW	WK	Billboard. APRIL 4, 1970 TOP LP's
1	1	8	**Bridge Over Troubled Water**.............. *Simon & Garfunkel*...Columbia 9914
2	2	3	**Hey Jude**.............. *The Beatles*...Apple 385
3	3	22	Led Zeppelin II.............. *Led Zeppelin*...Atlantic 8236
4	4	5	**Morrison Hotel/Hard Rock Cafe**.............. *The Doors*...Elektra 75007
5	5	30	Santana.............. *Santana*...Columbia 9781
6	6	8	Chicago II.............. *Chicago*...Columbia 24
7	7	25	Abbey Road.............. *The Beatles*...Apple 383
8	13	12	Diana Ross Presents The Jackson 5.............. *The Jackson 5*...Motown 700
9	-	1	Deja Vu.............. *Crosby, Stills, Nash & Young*...Atlantic 7200
10	8	17	Willy and the Poorboys.............. *Creedence Clearwater Revival*...Fantasy 8397

TW	LW	WK	Billboard. APRIL 11, 1970 TOP LP's
1	1	9	**Bridge Over Troubled Water**.............. *Simon & Garfunkel*...Columbia 9914
2	2	4	**Hey Jude**.............. *The Beatles*...Apple 385
3	9	2	Deja Vu.............. *Crosby, Stills, Nash & Young*...Atlantic 7200
4	4	6	**Morrison Hotel/Hard Rock Cafe**.............. *The Doors*...Elektra 75007
5	5	31	Santana.............. *Santana*...Columbia 9781
6	3	23	Led Zeppelin II.............. *Led Zeppelin*...Atlantic 8236
7	7	26	Abbey Road.............. *The Beatles*...Apple 383
8	8	13	Diana Ross Presents The Jackson 5.............. *The Jackson 5*...Motown 700
9	6	9	Chicago II.............. *Chicago*...Columbia 24
10	10	18	Willy and the Poorboys.............. *Creedence Clearwater Revival*...Fantasy 8397

TW	LW	WK	Billboard. APRIL 18, 1970 TOP LP's
1	1	10	**Bridge Over Troubled Water**.............. *Simon & Garfunkel*...Columbia 9914
2	2	5	**Hey Jude**.............. *The Beatles*...Apple 385
3	3	3	Deja Vu.............. *Crosby, Stills, Nash & Young*...Atlantic 7200
4	5	32	**Santana**.............. *Santana*...Columbia 9781
5	6	24	Led Zeppelin II.............. *Led Zeppelin*...Atlantic 8236
6	8	14	Diana Ross Presents The Jackson 5.............. *The Jackson 5*...Motown 700
7	4	7	Morrison Hotel/Hard Rock Cafe.............. *The Doors*...Elektra 75007
8	7	27	Abbey Road.............. *The Beatles*...Apple 383
9	9	10	Chicago II.............. *Chicago*...Columbia 24
10	16	3	Psychedelic Shack.............. *The Temptations*...Gordy 947

Billboard® — APRIL 25, 1970 — TOP LP's

TW	LW	WK	Title	Artist	Label
1	1	11	**Bridge Over Troubled Water**	*Simon & Garfunkel*	Columbia 9914
2	3	4	Deja Vu	*Crosby, Stills, Nash & Young*	Atlantic 7200
3	2	6	Hey Jude	*The Beatles*	Apple 385
4	4	33	**Santana**	*Santana*	Columbia 9781
5	6	15	**Diana Ross Presents The Jackson 5**	*The Jackson 5*	Motown 700
6	9	11	Chicago II	*Chicago*	Columbia 24
7	7	8	Morrison Hotel/Hard Rock Cafe	*The Doors*	Elektra 75007
8	5	25	Led Zeppelin II	*Led Zeppelin*	Atlantic 8236
9	8	28	Abbey Road	*The Beatles*	Apple 383
10	10	4	Psychedelic Shack	*The Temptations*	Gordy 947

Billboard® — MAY 2, 1970 — TOP LP's

TW	LW	WK	Title	Artist	Label
1	1	12	**Bridge Over Troubled Water**	*Simon & Garfunkel*	Columbia 9914
2	2	5	Deja Vu	*Crosby, Stills, Nash & Young*	Atlantic 7200
3	3	7	Hey Jude	*The Beatles*	Apple 385
4	4	34	**Santana**	*Santana*	Columbia 9781
5	6	12	Chicago II	*Chicago*	Columbia 24
6	8	26	Led Zeppelin II	*Led Zeppelin*	Atlantic 8236
7	5	16	Diana Ross Presents The Jackson 5	*The Jackson 5*	Motown 700
8	17	3	Steppenwolf 'Live'	*Steppenwolf*	Dunhill/ABC 50075
9	10	5	**Psychedelic Shack**	*The Temptations*	Gordy 947
10	15	12	American Woman	*The Guess Who*	RCA 4266

Billboard® — MAY 9, 1970 — TOP LP's

TW	LW	WK	Title	Artist	Label
1	1	13	**Bridge Over Troubled Water**	*Simon & Garfunkel*	Columbia 9914
2	2	6	Deja Vu	*Crosby, Stills, Nash & Young*	Atlantic 7200
3	3	8	Hey Jude	*The Beatles*	Apple 385
4	4	35	**Santana**	*Santana*	Columbia 9781
5	5	13	Chicago II	*Chicago*	Columbia 24
6	11	36	**Easy Rider**	*Soundtrack*	Dunhill/ABC 50063
7	7	17	Diana Ross Presents The Jackson 5	*The Jackson 5*	Motown 700
8	8	4	Steppenwolf 'Live'	*Steppenwolf*	Dunhill/ABC 50075
9	9	6	**Psychedelic Shack**	*The Temptations*	Gordy 947
10	10	13	American Woman	*The Guess Who*	RCA 4266

Billboard® — MAY 16, 1970 — TOP LP's

TW	LW	WK	Title	Artist	Label
1	2	7	**Deja Vu**	*Crosby, Stills, Nash & Young*	Atlantic 7200
2	1	14	Bridge Over Troubled Water	*Simon & Garfunkel*	Columbia 9914
3	14	2	McCartney	*Paul McCartney*	Apple 3363
4	3	9	Hey Jude	*The Beatles*	Apple 385
5	15	3	**Band Of Gypsys**	*Jimi Hendrix*	Capitol 472
6	5	14	Chicago II	*Chicago*	Columbia 24
7	8	5	**Steppenwolf 'Live'**	*Steppenwolf*	Dunhill/ABC 50075
8	18	3	**It Ain't Easy**	*Three Dog Night*	Dunhill/ABC 50078
9	10	14	**American Woman**	*The Guess Who*	RCA 4266
10	11	6	**Here Comes Bobby**	*Bobby Sherman*	Metromedia 1028

TW	LW	WK	Billboard. MAY 23, 1970	TOP LP's
①	3	3	**McCartney**	*Paul McCartney*...Apple 3363
②	2	15	Bridge Over Troubled Water	*Simon & Garfunkel*...Columbia 9914
③	1	8	Deja Vu	*Crosby, Stills, Nash & Young*...Atlantic 7200
④	6	15	**Chicago II**	*Chicago*...Columbia 24
⑤	5	4	**Band Of Gypsys**	*Jimi Hendrix*...Capitol 472
⑥	4	10	Hey Jude	*The Beatles*...Apple 385
⑦	7	6	**Steppenwolf 'Live'**	*Steppenwolf*...Dunhill/ABC 50075
⑧	8	4	**It Ain't Easy**	*Three Dog Night*...Dunhill/ABC 50078
⑨	9	15	**American Woman**	*The Guess Who*...RCA 4266
⑩	10	7	**Here Comes Bobby**	*Bobby Sherman*...Metromedia 1028

TW	LW	WK	Billboard. MAY 30, 1970	TOP LP's
①	1	4	**McCartney**	*Paul McCartney*...Apple 3363
②	3	9	Deja Vu	*Crosby, Stills, Nash & Young*...Atlantic 7200
③	2	16	Bridge Over Troubled Water	*Simon & Garfunkel*...Columbia 9914
④	4	16	**Chicago II**	*Chicago*...Columbia 24
⑤	5	5	**Band Of Gypsys**	*Jimi Hendrix*...Capitol 472
❻	11	4	**Tom**	*Tom Jones*...Parrot 71037
⑦	6	11	Hey Jude	*The Beatles*...Apple 385
⑧	12	38	Santana	*Santana*...Columbia 9781
⑨	9	16	**American Woman**	*The Guess Who*...RCA 4266
⑩	7	7	Steppenwolf 'Live'	*Steppenwolf*...Dunhill/ABC 50075

TW	LW	WK	Billboard. JUNE 6, 1970	TOP LP's
①	1	5	**McCartney**	*Paul McCartney*...Apple 3363
❷	104	2	Let It Be	*The Beatles/Soundtrack*...Apple 34001
③	2	10	Deja Vu	*Crosby, Stills, Nash & Young*...Atlantic 7200
❹	-	1	Woodstock	*Various Artists/Soundtrack*...Cotillion 500
⑤	5	6	**Band Of Gypsys**	*Jimi Hendrix*...Capitol 472
⑥	6	5	**Tom**	*Tom Jones*...Parrot 71037
⑦	3	17	Bridge Over Troubled Water	*Simon & Garfunkel*...Columbia 9914
⑧	4	17	Chicago II	*Chicago*...Columbia 24
❾	12	8	The Isaac Hayes Movement	*Isaac Hayes*...Enterprise 1010
⑩	11	6	It Ain't Easy	*Three Dog Night*...Dunhill/ABC 50078

TW	LW	WK	Billboard. JUNE 13, 1970	TOP LP's
①	2	3	**Let It Be**	*The Beatles/Soundtrack*...Apple 34001
②	1	6	McCartney	*Paul McCartney*...Apple 3363
③	4	2	Woodstock	*Various Artists/Soundtrack*...Cotillion 500
④	3	11	Deja Vu	*Crosby, Stills, Nash & Young*...Atlantic 7200
⑤	7	18	Bridge Over Troubled Water	*Simon & Garfunkel*...Columbia 9914
❻	5	7	Band Of Gypsys	*Jimi Hendrix*...Capitol 472
⑦	8	18	Chicago II	*Chicago*...Columbia 24
⑧	9	9	**The Isaac Hayes Movement**	*Isaac Hayes*...Enterprise 1010
⑨	16	18	**American Woman**	*The Guess Who*...RCA 4266
⑩	12	5	The 5th Dimension/Greatest Hits	*The 5th Dimension*...Soul City 33900

Billboard® JUNE 20, 1970 TOP LP's

TW	LW	WK	Title	Artist...Label
1	1	4	**Let It Be**	*The Beatles/Soundtrack*...Apple 34001
2	2	7	McCartney	*Paul McCartney*...Apple 3363
3	3	3	Woodstock	*Various Artists/Soundtrack*...Cotillion 500
4	4	12	Deja Vu	*Crosby, Stills, Nash & Young*...Atlantic 7200
5	10	6	**The 5th Dimension/Greatest Hits**	*The 5th Dimension*...Soul City 33900
6	14	4	Live At Leeds	*The Who*...Decca 79175
7	7	19	Chicago II	*Chicago*...Columbia 24
8	6	8	Band Of Gypsys	*Jimi Hendrix*...Capitol 472
9	5	19	Bridge Over Troubled Water	*Simon & Garfunkel*...Columbia 9914
10	9	19	American Woman	*The Guess Who*...RCA 4266

Billboard® JUNE 27, 1970 TOP LP's

TW	LW	WK	Title	Artist...Label
1	1	5	**Let It Be**	*The Beatles/Soundtrack*...Apple 34001
2	2	8	McCartney	*Paul McCartney*...Apple 3363
3	3	4	Woodstock	*Various Artists/Soundtrack*...Cotillion 500
4	4	13	Deja Vu	*Crosby, Stills, Nash & Young*...Atlantic 7200
5	5	7	**The 5th Dimension/Greatest Hits**	*The 5th Dimension*...Soul City 33900
6	6	5	Live At Leeds	*The Who*...Decca 79175
7	7	20	Chicago II	*Chicago*...Columbia 24
8	11	4	ABC	*The Jackson 5*...Motown 709
9	8	9	Band Of Gypsys	*Jimi Hendrix*...Capitol 472
10	16	11	The Isaac Hayes Movement	*Isaac Hayes*...Enterprise 1010

Billboard® JULY 4, 1970 TOP LP's

TW	LW	WK	Title	Artist...Label
1	1	6	**Let It Be**	*The Beatles/Soundtrack*...Apple 34001
2	2	9	McCartney	*Paul McCartney*...Apple 3363
3	3	5	Woodstock	*Various Artists/Soundtrack*...Cotillion 500
4	7	21	**Chicago II**	*Chicago*...Columbia 24
5	8	5	ABC	*The Jackson 5*...Motown 709
6	6	6	Live At Leeds	*The Who*...Decca 79175
7	5	8	The 5th Dimension/Greatest Hits	*The 5th Dimension*...Soul City 33900
8	4	14	Deja Vu	*Crosby, Stills, Nash & Young*...Atlantic 7200
9	10	12	The Isaac Hayes Movement	*Isaac Hayes*...Enterprise 1010
10	13	10	It Ain't Easy	*Three Dog Night*...Dunhill/ABC 50078

Billboard® JULY 11, 1970 TOP LP's

TW	LW	WK	Title	Artist...Label
1	3	6	**Woodstock**	*Various Artists/Soundtrack*...Cotillion 500
2	1	7	Let It Be	*The Beatles/Soundtrack*...Apple 34001
3	2	10	McCartney	*Paul McCartney*...Apple 3363
4	5	6	**ABC**	*The Jackson 5*...Motown 709
5	6	7	Live At Leeds	*The Who*...Decca 79175
6	8	15	Deja Vu	*Crosby, Stills, Nash & Young*...Atlantic 7200
7	200	2	Self Portrait	*Bob Dylan*...Columbia 30050
8	7	9	The 5th Dimension/Greatest Hits	*The 5th Dimension*...Soul City 33900
9	10	11	It Ain't Easy	*Three Dog Night*...Dunhill/ABC 50078
10	9	13	The Isaac Hayes Movement	*Isaac Hayes*...Enterprise 1010

TW	LW	WK	Billboard. JULY 18, 1970 TOP LP's
1	1	7	**Woodstock**.......... *Various Artists/Soundtrack*...Cotillion 500
2	2	8	Let It Be .... *The Beatles/Soundtrack*...Apple 34001
3	3	11	McCartney .... *Paul McCartney*...Apple 3363
4	4	7	**ABC**.......... *The Jackson 5*...Motown 709
5	7	3	Self Portrait.......... *Bob Dylan*...Columbia 30050
6	5	8	Live At Leeds.......... *The Who*...Decca 79175
7	13	23	Chicago II.......... *Chicago*...Columbia 24
8	11	2	Closer To Home.......... *Grand Funk Railroad*...Capitol 471
9	6	16	Deja Vu .... *Crosby, Stills, Nash & Young*...Atlantic 7200
10	10	14	The Isaac Hayes Movement .... *Isaac Hayes*...Enterprise 1010

TW	LW	WK	Billboard. JULY 25, 1970 TOP LP's
1	1	8	**Woodstock**.......... *Various Artists/Soundtrack*...Cotillion 500
2	2	9	Let It Be .... *The Beatles/Soundtrack*...Apple 34001
3	3	12	McCartney .... *Paul McCartney*...Apple 3363
4	5	4	**Self Portrait** .... *Bob Dylan*...Columbia 30050
5	18	2	Blood, Sweat & Tears 3 .... *Blood, Sweat & Tears*...Columbia 30090
6	4	8	ABC .... *The Jackson 5*...Motown 709
7	9	17	Deja Vu .... *Crosby, Stills, Nash & Young*...Atlantic 7200
8	8	3	Closer To Home.......... *Grand Funk Railroad*...Capitol 471
9	6	9	Live At Leeds.......... *The Who*...Decca 79175
10	7	24	Chicago II.......... *Chicago*...Columbia 24

TW	LW	WK	Billboard. AUGUST 1, 1970 TOP LP's
1	1	9	**Woodstock**.......... *Various Artists/Soundtrack*...Cotillion 500
2	5	3	Blood, Sweat & Tears 3 .... *Blood, Sweat & Tears*...Columbia 30090
3	14	2	Cosmo's Factory .... *Creedence Clearwater Revival*...Fantasy 8402
4	4	5	**Self Portrait** .... *Bob Dylan*...Columbia 30050
5	3	13	McCartney .... *Paul McCartney*...Apple 3363
6	2	10	Let It Be .... *The Beatles/Soundtrack*...Apple 34001
7	8	4	Closer To Home.......... *Grand Funk Railroad*...Capitol 471
8	9	10	Live At Leeds.......... *The Who*...Decca 79175
9	7	18	Deja Vu .... *Crosby, Stills, Nash & Young*...Atlantic 7200
10	6	9	ABC .... *The Jackson 5*...Motown 709

TW	LW	WK	Billboard. AUGUST 8, 1970 TOP LP's
1	2	4	**Blood, Sweat & Tears 3**.......... *Blood, Sweat & Tears*...Columbia 30090
2	3	3	Cosmo's Factory .... *Creedence Clearwater Revival*...Fantasy 8402
3	1	10	Woodstock .... *Various Artists/Soundtrack*...Cotillion 500
4	6	11	Let It Be .... *The Beatles/Soundtrack*...Apple 34001
5	5	14	McCartney .... *Paul McCartney*...Apple 3363
6	10	10	ABC .... *The Jackson 5*...Motown 709
7	9	19	Deja Vu .... *Crosby, Stills, Nash & Young*...Atlantic 7200
8	4	6	Self Portrait.......... *Bob Dylan*...Columbia 30050
9	11	26	Chicago II.......... *Chicago*...Columbia 24
10	8	11	Live At Leeds.......... *The Who*...Decca 79175

Billboard — AUGUST 15, 1970 — TOP LP's

TW	LW	WK	Title	Artist	Label
1	1	5	**Blood, Sweat & Tears 3**	*Blood, Sweat & Tears*	Columbia 30090
2	2	4	Cosmo's Factory	*Creedence Clearwater Revival*	Fantasy 8402
3	3	11	Woodstock	*Various Artists/Soundtrack*	Cotillion 500
4	10	12	**Live At Leeds**	*The Who*	Decca 79175
5	13	6	**John Barleycorn Must Die**	*Traffic*	United Artists 5504
6	6	11	ABC	*The Jackson 5*	Motown 709
7	7	20	Deja Vu	*Crosby, Stills, Nash & Young*	Atlantic 7200
8	9	27	Chicago II	*Chicago*	Columbia 24
9	8	7	Self Portrait	*Bob Dylan*	Columbia 30050
10	11	6	Closer To Home	*Grand Funk Railroad*	Capitol 471

Billboard — AUGUST 22, 1970 — TOP LP's

TW	LW	WK	Title	Artist	Label
1	2	5	**Cosmo's Factory**	*Creedence Clearwater Revival*	Fantasy 8402
2	3	12	Woodstock	*Various Artists/Soundtrack*	Cotillion 500
3	1	6	Blood, Sweat & Tears 3	*Blood, Sweat & Tears*	Columbia 30090
4	4	13	**Live At Leeds**	*The Who*	Decca 79175
5	5	7	**John Barleycorn Must Die**	*Traffic*	United Artists 5504
6	8	28	Chicago II	*Chicago*	Columbia 24
7	6	12	ABC	*The Jackson 5*	Motown 709
8	7	21	Deja Vu	*Crosby, Stills, Nash & Young*	Atlantic 7200
9	14	49	Tommy	*The Who*	Decca 7205
10	10	7	Closer To Home	*Grand Funk Railroad*	Capitol 471

Billboard — AUGUST 29, 1970 — TOP LP's

TW	LW	WK	Title	Artist	Label
1	1	6	**Cosmo's Factory**	*Creedence Clearwater Revival*	Fantasy 8402
2	2	13	Woodstock	*Various Artists/Soundtrack*	Cotillion 500
3	3	7	Blood, Sweat & Tears 3	*Blood, Sweat & Tears*	Columbia 30090
4	4	14	**Live At Leeds**	*The Who*	Decca 79175
5	6	29	Chicago II	*Chicago*	Columbia 24
6	10	8	**Closer To Home**	*Grand Funk Railroad*	Capitol 471
7	8	22	Deja Vu	*Crosby, Stills, Nash & Young*	Atlantic 7200
8	9	50	Tommy	*The Who*	Decca 7205
9	12	4	Absolutely Live	*The Doors*	Elektra 9002
10	5	8	John Barleycorn Must Die	*Traffic*	United Artists 5504

Billboard — SEPTEMBER 5, 1970 — TOP LP's

TW	LW	WK	Title	Artist	Label
1	1	7	**Cosmo's Factory**	*Creedence Clearwater Revival*	Fantasy 8402
2	2	14	Woodstock	*Various Artists/Soundtrack*	Cotillion 500
3	3	8	Blood, Sweat & Tears 3	*Blood, Sweat & Tears*	Columbia 30090
4	5	30	**Chicago II**	*Chicago*	Columbia 24
5	7	23	Deja Vu	*Crosby, Stills, Nash & Young*	Atlantic 7200
6	6	9	**Closer To Home**	*Grand Funk Railroad*	Capitol 471
7	8	51	Tommy	*The Who*	Decca 7205
8	9	5	**Absolutely Live**	*The Doors*	Elektra 9002
9	4	15	Live At Leeds	*The Who*	Decca 79175
10	10	9	John Barleycorn Must Die	*Traffic*	United Artists 5504

TW	LW	WK	Billboard. SEPTEMBER 12, 1970 TOP LP's
1	1	8	**Cosmo's Factory** ... *Creedence Clearwater Revival*...Fantasy 8402
2	2	15	Woodstock ... *Various Artists/Soundtrack*...Cotillion 500
3	3	9	Blood, Sweat & Tears 3 ... *Blood, Sweat & Tears*...Columbia 30090
4	11	2	Mad Dogs & Englishmen ... *Joe Cocker/Soundtrack*...A&M 6002
5	4	31	Chicago II ... *Chicago*...Columbia 24
6	6	10	**Closer To Home** ... *Grand Funk Railroad*...Capitol 471
7	9	16	Live At Leeds ... *The Who*...Decca 79175
8	7	52	Tommy ... *The Who*...Decca 7205
9	10	10	John Barleycorn Must Die ... *Traffic*...United Artists 5504
10	23	2	Stage Fright ... *The Band*...Capitol 425

TW	LW	WK	Billboard. SEPTEMBER 19, 1970 TOP LP's
1	1	9	**Cosmo's Factory** ... *Creedence Clearwater Revival*...Fantasy 8402
2	2	16	Woodstock ... *Various Artists/Soundtrack*...Cotillion 500
3	4	3	Mad Dogs & Englishmen ... *Joe Cocker/Soundtrack*...A&M 6002
4	8	53	**Tommy** ... *The Who*...Decca 7205
5	5	32	Chicago II ... *Chicago*...Columbia 24
6	3	10	Blood, Sweat & Tears 3 ... *Blood, Sweat & Tears*...Columbia 30090
7	10	3	Stage Fright ... *The Band*...Capitol 425
8	7	17	Live At Leeds ... *The Who*...Decca 79175
9	6	11	Closer To Home ... *Grand Funk Railroad*...Capitol 471
10	16	5	**Neil Diamond/Gold** ... *Neil Diamond*...Uni 73084

TW	LW	WK	Billboard. SEPTEMBER 26, 1970 TOP LP's
1	1	10	**Cosmo's Factory** ... *Creedence Clearwater Revival*...Fantasy 8402
2	2	17	Woodstock ... *Various Artists/Soundtrack*...Cotillion 500
3	3	4	Mad Dogs & Englishmen ... *Joe Cocker/Soundtrack*...A&M 6002
4	4	54	**Tommy** ... *The Who*...Decca 7205
5	5	33	Chicago II ... *Chicago*...Columbia 24
6	7	4	Stage Fright ... *The Band*...Capitol 425
7	9	12	Closer To Home ... *Grand Funk Railroad*...Capitol 471
8	6	11	Blood, Sweat & Tears 3 ... *Blood, Sweat & Tears*...Columbia 30090
9	12	3	A Question Of Balance ... *The Moody Blues*...Threshold 3
10	10	6	**Neil Diamond/Gold** ... *Neil Diamond*...Uni 73084

TW	LW	WK	Billboard. OCTOBER 3, 1970 TOP LP's
1	1	11	**Cosmo's Factory** ... *Creedence Clearwater Revival*...Fantasy 8402
2	2	18	Woodstock ... *Various Artists/Soundtrack*...Cotillion 500
3	3	5	Mad Dogs & Englishmen ... *Joe Cocker/Soundtrack*...A&M 6002
4	5	34	**Chicago II** ... *Chicago*...Columbia 24
5	6	5	**Stage Fright** ... *The Band*...Capitol 425
6	7	13	**Closer To Home** ... *Grand Funk Railroad*...Capitol 471
7	9	4	A Question Of Balance ... *The Moody Blues*...Threshold 3
8	4	55	Tommy ... *The Who*...Decca 7205
9	8	12	Blood, Sweat & Tears 3 ... *Blood, Sweat & Tears*...Columbia 30090
10	13	3	After The Gold Rush ... *Neil Young*...Reprise 6383

TW	LW	WK	Billboard® OCTOBER 10, 1970 TOP LP's
1	1	12	**Cosmo's Factory** ... *Creedence Clearwater Revival*...Fantasy 8402
2	3	6	**Mad Dogs & Englishmen** ... *Joe Cocker/Soundtrack*...A&M 6002
3	7	5	**A Question Of Balance** ... *The Moody Blues*...Threshold 3
4	2	19	Woodstock ... *Various Artists/Soundtrack*...Cotillion 500
5	12	3	Third Album ... *The Jackson 5*...Motown 718
6	8	56	Tommy ... *The Who*...Decca 7205
7	4	35	Chicago II ... *Chicago*...Columbia 24
8	-	1	Abraxas ... *Santana*...Columbia 30130
9	10	4	After The Gold Rush ... *Neil Young*...Reprise 6383
10	11	31	Sweet Baby James ... *James Taylor*...Warner 1843

TW	LW	WK	Billboard® OCTOBER 17, 1970 TOP LP's
1	1	13	**Cosmo's Factory** ... *Creedence Clearwater Revival*...Fantasy 8402
2	8	2	Abraxas ... *Santana*...Columbia 30130
3	2	7	Mad Dogs & Englishmen ... *Joe Cocker/Soundtrack*...A&M 6002
4	3	6	A Question Of Balance ... *The Moody Blues*...Threshold 3
5	5	4	Third Album ... *The Jackson 5*...Motown 718
6	4	20	Woodstock ... *Various Artists/Soundtrack*...Cotillion 500
7	10	32	Sweet Baby James ... *James Taylor*...Warner 1843
8	9	5	**After The Gold Rush** ... *Neil Young*...Reprise 6383
9	7	36	Chicago II ... *Chicago*...Columbia 24
10	-	1	'Get Yer Ya-Ya's Out!' ... *The Rolling Stones*...London 5

TW	LW	WK	Billboard® OCTOBER 24, 1970 TOP LP's
1	2	3	**Abraxas** ... *Santana*...Columbia 30130
2	1	14	Cosmo's Factory ... *Creedence Clearwater Revival*...Fantasy 8402
3	-	1	Led Zeppelin III ... *Led Zeppelin*...Atlantic 7201
4	5	5	**Third Album** ... *The Jackson 5*...Motown 718
5	7	33	Sweet Baby James ... *James Taylor*...Warner 1843
6	10	2	**'Get Yer Ya-Ya's Out!'** ... *The Rolling Stones*...London 5
7	6	21	Woodstock ... *Various Artists/Soundtrack*...Cotillion 500
8	8	6	**After The Gold Rush** ... *Neil Young*...Reprise 6383
9	3	8	Mad Dogs & Englishmen ... *Joe Cocker/Soundtrack*...A&M 6002
10	12	6	Close To You ... *Carpenters*...A&M 4271

TW	LW	WK	Billboard® OCTOBER 31, 1970 TOP LP's
1	3	2	**Led Zeppelin III** ... *Led Zeppelin*...Atlantic 7201
2	1	4	Abraxas ... *Santana*...Columbia 30130
3	2	15	Cosmo's Factory ... *Creedence Clearwater Revival*...Fantasy 8402
4	4	6	**Third Album** ... *The Jackson 5*...Motown 718
5	5	34	Sweet Baby James ... *James Taylor*...Warner 1843
6	6	3	**'Get Yer Ya-Ya's Out!'** ... *The Rolling Stones*...London 5
7	10	7	Close To You ... *Carpenters*...A&M 4271
8	9	9	Mad Dogs & Englishmen ... *Joe Cocker/Soundtrack*...A&M 6002
9	7	22	Woodstock ... *Various Artists/Soundtrack*...Cotillion 500
10	8	7	After The Gold Rush ... *Neil Young*...Reprise 6383

TW	LW	WK	Billboard. NOVEMBER 7, 1970 TOP LP's	
①	1	3	**Led Zeppelin III**	*Led Zeppelin*...Atlantic 7201
②	2	5	Abraxas	*Santana*...Columbia 30130
③	5	35	**Sweet Baby James**	*James Taylor*...Warner 1843
④	4	7	**Third Album**	*The Jackson 5*...Motown 718
⑤	3	16	Cosmo's Factory	*Creedence Clearwater Revival*...Fantasy 8402
⑥	7	8	Close To You	*Carpenters*...A&M 4271
⑦	6	4	'Get Yer Ya-Ya's Out!'	*The Rolling Stones*...London 5
⑧	10	8	**After The Gold Rush**	*Neil Young*...Reprise 6383
⑨	9	23	Woodstock	*Various Artists/Soundtrack*...Cotillion 500
⑩	11	9	A Question Of Balance	*The Moody Blues*...Threshold 3

TW	LW	WK	Billboard. NOVEMBER 14, 1970 TOP LP's	
①	1	4	**Led Zeppelin III**	*Led Zeppelin*...Atlantic 7201
②	2	6	Abraxas	*Santana*...Columbia 30130
③	3	36	**Sweet Baby James**	*James Taylor*...Warner 1843
④	6	9	Close To You	*Carpenters*...A&M 4271
⑤	4	8	Third Album	*The Jackson 5*...Motown 718
⑥	5	17	Cosmo's Factory	*Creedence Clearwater Revival*...Fantasy 8402
⑦	7	5	'Get Yer Ya-Ya's Out!'	*The Rolling Stones*...London 5
⑧	9	24	Woodstock	*Various Artists/Soundtrack*...Cotillion 500
⑨	8	9	After The Gold Rush	*Neil Young*...Reprise 6383
❿	48	2	Greatest Hits	*Sly & The Family Stone*...Epic 30325

TW	LW	WK	Billboard. NOVEMBER 21, 1970 TOP LP's	
①	1	5	**Led Zeppelin III**	*Led Zeppelin*...Atlantic 7201
②	2	7	Abraxas	*Santana*...Columbia 30130
③	3	37	**Sweet Baby James**	*James Taylor*...Warner 1843
④	4	10	Close To You	*Carpenters*...A&M 4271
⑤	5	9	Third Album	*The Jackson 5*...Motown 718
⑥	6	18	Cosmo's Factory	*Creedence Clearwater Revival*...Fantasy 8402
⑦	7	6	'Get Yer Ya-Ya's Out!'	*The Rolling Stones*...London 5
⑧	9	10	**After The Gold Rush**	*Neil Young*...Reprise 6383
⑨	10	3	Greatest Hits	*Sly & The Family Stone*...Epic 30325
⑩	12	20	Closer To Home	*Grand Funk Railroad*...Capitol 471

TW	LW	WK	Billboard. NOVEMBER 28, 1970 TOP LP's	
①	2	8	**Abraxas**	*Santana*...Columbia 30130
②	1	6	Led Zeppelin III	*Led Zeppelin*...Atlantic 7201
③	3	38	**Sweet Baby James**	*James Taylor*...Warner 1843
④	4	11	Close To You	*Carpenters*...A&M 4271
⑤	5	10	Third Album	*The Jackson 5*...Motown 718
❻	9	4	Greatest Hits	*Sly & The Family Stone*...Epic 30325
⑦	6	19	Cosmo's Factory	*Creedence Clearwater Revival*...Fantasy 8402
⑧	8	11	**After The Gold Rush**	*Neil Young*...Reprise 6383
❾	19	3	New Morning	*Bob Dylan*...Columbia 30290
⑩	7	7	'Get Yer Ya-Ya's Out!'	*The Rolling Stones*...London 5

Billboard — DECEMBER 5, 1970 — TOP LP's

TW	LW	WK	Title	Artist	Label
1	1	9	Abraxas	Santana	Columbia 30130
2	4	12	Close To You	Carpenters	A&M 4271
3	2	7	Led Zeppelin III	Led Zeppelin	Atlantic 7201
4	3	39	Sweet Baby James	James Taylor	Warner 1843
5	5	11	Third Album	The Jackson 5	Motown 718
6	6	5	Greatest Hits	Sly & The Family Stone	Epic 30325
7	9	4	New Morning	Bob Dylan	Columbia 30290
8	59	2	Stephen Stills	Stephen Stills	Atlantic 7202
9	7	20	Cosmo's Factory	Creedence Clearwater Revival	Fantasy 8402
10	25	3	Jesus Christ Superstar	Various Artists	Decca 7206

Billboard — DECEMBER 12, 1970 — TOP LP's

TW	LW	WK	Title	Artist	Label
1	1	10	Abraxas	Santana	Columbia 30130
2	3	8	Led Zeppelin III	Led Zeppelin	Atlantic 7201
3	2	13	Close To You	Carpenters	A&M 4271
4	4	40	Sweet Baby James	James Taylor	Warner 1843
5	6	6	Greatest Hits	Sly & The Family Stone	Epic 30325
6	5	12	Third Album	The Jackson 5	Motown 718
7	8	3	Stephen Stills	Stephen Stills	Atlantic 7202
8	11	2	Live Album	Grand Funk Railroad	Capitol 633
9	7	5	New Morning	Bob Dylan	Columbia 30290
10	10	4	Jesus Christ Superstar	Various Artists	Decca 7206

Billboard — DECEMBER 19, 1970 — TOP LP's

TW	LW	WK	Title	Artist	Label
1	1	11	Abraxas	Santana	Columbia 30130
2	5	7	Greatest Hits	Sly & The Family Stone	Epic 30325
3	2	9	Led Zeppelin III	Led Zeppelin	Atlantic 7201
4	7	4	Stephen Stills	Stephen Stills	Atlantic 7202
5	-	1	All Things Must Pass	George Harrison	Apple 639
6	3	14	Close To You	Carpenters	A&M 4271
7	8	3	Live Album	Grand Funk Railroad	Capitol 633
8	6	13	Third Album	The Jackson 5	Motown 718
9	10	5	Jesus Christ Superstar	Various Artists	Decca 7206
10	4	41	Sweet Baby James	James Taylor	Warner 1843

Billboard — DECEMBER 26, 1970 — TOP LP's

TW	LW	WK	Title	Artist	Label
1	1	12	Abraxas	Santana	Columbia 30130
2	5	2	All Things Must Pass	George Harrison	Apple 639
3	2	8	Greatest Hits	Sly & The Family Stone	Epic 30325
4	4	5	Stephen Stills	Stephen Stills	Atlantic 7202
5	7	4	Live Album	Grand Funk Railroad	Capitol 633
6	6	15	Close To You	Carpenters	A&M 4271
7	9	6	Jesus Christ Superstar	Various Artists	Decca 7206
8	3	10	Led Zeppelin III	Led Zeppelin	Atlantic 7201
9	11	9	The Partridge Family Album	The Partridge Family	Bell 6050
10	10	42	Sweet Baby James	James Taylor	Warner 1843

TW	LW	WK	Billboard. JANUARY 2, 1971 TOP LP's
1	2	3	All Things Must Pass .... *George Harrison*...Apple 639
2	1	13	Abraxas .... *Santana*...Columbia 30130
3	4	6	Stephen Stills .... *Stephen Stills*...Atlantic 7202
4	9	10	The Partridge Family Album .... *The Partridge Family*...Bell 6050
5	5	5	Live Album .... *Grand Funk Railroad*...Capitol 633
6	3	9	Greatest Hits .... *Sly & The Family Stone*...Epic 30325
7	7	7	Jesus Christ Superstar .... *Various Artists*...Decca 7206
8	6	16	Close To You .... *Carpenters*...A&M 4271
9	8	11	Led Zeppelin III .... *Led Zeppelin*...Atlantic 7201
10	15	2	Pendulum .... *Creedence Clearwater Revival*...Fantasy 8410

TW	LW	WK	Billboard. JANUARY 9, 1971 TOP LP's
1	1	4	All Things Must Pass .... *George Harrison*...Apple 639
2	2	14	Abraxas .... *Santana*...Columbia 30130
3	3	7	Stephen Stills .... *Stephen Stills*...Atlantic 7202
4	4	11	The Partridge Family Album .... *The Partridge Family*...Bell 6050
5	6	10	Greatest Hits .... *Sly & The Family Stone*...Epic 30325
6	7	8	Jesus Christ Superstar .... *Various Artists*...Decca 7206
7	10	3	Pendulum .... *Creedence Clearwater Revival*...Fantasy 8410
8	5	6	Live Album .... *Grand Funk Railroad*...Capitol 633
9	12	3	John Lennon/Plastic Ono Band ... *John Lennon/Plastic Ono Band*...Apple 3372
10	9	12	Led Zeppelin III .... *Led Zeppelin*...Atlantic 7201

TW	LW	WK	Billboard. JANUARY 16, 1971 TOP LP's
1	1	5	All Things Must Pass .... *George Harrison*...Apple 639
2	2	15	Abraxas .... *Santana*...Columbia 30130
3	3	8	Stephen Stills .... *Stephen Stills*...Atlantic 7202
4	5	11	Greatest Hits .... *Sly & The Family Stone*...Epic 30325
5	4	12	The Partridge Family Album .... *The Partridge Family*...Bell 6050
6	6	9	Jesus Christ Superstar .... *Various Artists*...Decca 7206
7	7	4	Pendulum .... *Creedence Clearwater Revival*...Fantasy 8410
8	8	7	Live Album .... *Grand Funk Railroad*...Capitol 633
9	9	4	John Lennon/Plastic Ono Band ... *John Lennon/Plastic Ono Band*...Apple 3372
10	10	13	Led Zeppelin III .... *Led Zeppelin*...Atlantic 7201

TW	LW	WK	Billboard. JANUARY 23, 1971 TOP LP's
1	1	6	All Things Must Pass .... *George Harrison*...Apple 639
2	2	16	Abraxas .... *Santana*...Columbia 30130
3	6	10	Jesus Christ Superstar .... *Various Artists*...Decca 7206
4	4	12	Greatest Hits .... *Sly & The Family Stone*...Epic 30325
5	5	13	The Partridge Family Album .... *The Partridge Family*...Bell 6050
6	7	5	Pendulum .... *Creedence Clearwater Revival*...Fantasy 8410
7	8	8	Live Album .... *Grand Funk Railroad*...Capitol 633
8	9	5	John Lennon/Plastic Ono Band ... *John Lennon/Plastic Ono Band*...Apple 3372
9	10	14	Led Zeppelin III .... *Led Zeppelin*...Atlantic 7201
10	3	9	Stephen Stills .... *Stephen Stills*...Atlantic 7202

Billboard — JANUARY 30, 1971 — TOP LP's

TW	LW	WK	Title	Artist	Label
1	1	7	**All Things Must Pass**	*George Harrison*	Apple 639
2	2	17	Abraxas	*Santana*	Columbia 30130
3	3	11	Jesus Christ Superstar	*Various Artists*	Decca 7206
4	4	13	Greatest Hits	*Sly & The Family Stone*	Epic 30325
5	6	6	**Pendulum**	*Creedence Clearwater Revival*	Fantasy 8410
6	8	6	**John Lennon/Plastic Ono Band**	*John Lennon/Plastic Ono Band*	Apple 3372
7	11	18	Elton John	*Elton John*	Uni 73090
8	10	10	Stephen Stills	*Stephen Stills*	Atlantic 7202
9	5	14	The Partridge Family Album	*The Partridge Family*	Bell 6050
10	7	9	Live Album	*Grand Funk Railroad*	Capitol 633

Billboard — FEBRUARY 6, 1971 — TOP LP's

TW	LW	WK	Title	Artist	Label
1	1	8	**All Things Must Pass**	*George Harrison*	Apple 639
2	3	12	Jesus Christ Superstar	*Various Artists*	Decca 7206
3	2	18	Abraxas	*Santana*	Columbia 30130
4	7	19	**Elton John**	*Elton John*	Uni 73090
5	4	14	Greatest Hits	*Sly & The Family Stone*	Epic 30325
6	11	3	Tumbleweed Connection	*Elton John*	Uni 73096
7	5	7	Pendulum	*Creedence Clearwater Revival*	Fantasy 8410
8	22	2	Chicago III	*Chicago*	Columbia 30110
9	9	15	The Partridge Family Album	*The Partridge Family*	Bell 6050
10	8	11	Stephen Stills	*Stephen Stills*	Atlantic 7202

Billboard — FEBRUARY 13, 1971 — TOP LP's

TW	LW	WK	Title	Artist	Label
1	1	9	**All Things Must Pass**	*George Harrison*	Apple 639
2	2	13	Jesus Christ Superstar	*Various Artists*	Decca 7206
3	8	3	Chicago III	*Chicago*	Columbia 30110
4	3	19	Abraxas	*Santana*	Columbia 30130
5	6	4	**Tumbleweed Connection**	*Elton John*	Uni 73096
6	7	8	Pendulum	*Creedence Clearwater Revival*	Fantasy 8410
7	5	15	Greatest Hits	*Sly & The Family Stone*	Epic 30325
8	13	7	Love Story	*Soundtrack*	Paramount 6002
9	14	3	Pearl	*Janis Joplin*	Columbia 30322
10	4	20	Elton John	*Elton John*	Uni 73090

Billboard — FEBRUARY 20, 1971 — TOP LP's

TW	LW	WK	Title	Artist	Label
1	2	14	**Jesus Christ Superstar**	*Various Artists*	Decca 7206
2	3	4	**Chicago III**	*Chicago*	Columbia 30110
3	1	10	All Things Must Pass	*George Harrison*	Apple 639
4	4	20	Abraxas	*Santana*	Columbia 30130
5	5	5	**Tumbleweed Connection**	*Elton John*	Uni 73096
6	8	8	Love Story	*Soundtrack*	Paramount 6002
7	9	4	Pearl	*Janis Joplin*	Columbia 30322
8	10	21	Elton John	*Elton John*	Uni 73090
9	7	16	Greatest Hits	*Sly & The Family Stone*	Epic 30325
10	6	9	Pendulum	*Creedence Clearwater Revival*	Fantasy 8410

TW	LW	WK	Billboard. FEBRUARY 27, 1971		TOP LP's
1	7	5	**Pearl**	*Janis Joplin*	Columbia 30322
2	2	5	**Chicago III**	*Chicago*	Columbia 30110
3	6	9	Love Story	*Soundtrack*	Paramount 6002
4	1	15	Jesus Christ Superstar	*Various Artists*	Decca 7206
5	4	21	Abraxas	*Santana*	Columbia 30130
6	3	11	All Things Must Pass	*George Harrison*	Apple 639
7	5	6	Tumbleweed Connection	*Elton John*	Uni 73096
8	8	22	Elton John	*Elton John*	Uni 73090
9	10	10	Pendulum	*Creedence Clearwater Revival*	Fantasy 8410
10	11	18	The Partridge Family Album	*The Partridge Family*	Bell 6050

TW	LW	WK	Billboard. MARCH 6, 1971		TOP LP's
1	1	6	**Pearl**	*Janis Joplin*	Columbia 30322
2	3	10	**Love Story**	*Soundtrack*	Paramount 6002
3	2	6	Chicago III	*Chicago*	Columbia 30110
4	4	16	Jesus Christ Superstar	*Various Artists*	Decca 7206
5	7	7	**Tumbleweed Connection**	*Elton John*	Uni 73096
6	5	22	Abraxas	*Santana*	Columbia 30130
7	6	12	All Things Must Pass	*George Harrison*	Apple 639
8	8	23	Elton John	*Elton John*	Uni 73090
9	9	11	Pendulum	*Creedence Clearwater Revival*	Fantasy 8410
10	22	3	Love Story	*Andy Williams*	Columbia 30497

TW	LW	WK	Billboard. MARCH 13, 1971		TOP LP's
1	1	7	**Pearl**	*Janis Joplin*	Columbia 30322
2	2	11	**Love Story**	*Soundtrack*	Paramount 6002
3	3	7	Chicago III	*Chicago*	Columbia 30110
4	4	17	Jesus Christ Superstar	*Various Artists*	Decca 7206
5	5	8	**Tumbleweed Connection**	*Elton John*	Uni 73096
6	6	23	Abraxas	*Santana*	Columbia 30130
7	10	4	Love Story	*Andy Williams*	Columbia 30497
8	18	2	The Cry Of Love	*Jimi Hendrix*	Reprise 2034
9	9	12	Pendulum	*Creedence Clearwater Revival*	Fantasy 8410
10	11	4	**Stoney End**	*Barbra Streisand*	Columbia 30378

TW	LW	WK	Billboard. MARCH 20, 1971		TOP LP's
1	1	8	**Pearl**	*Janis Joplin*	Columbia 30322
2	2	12	**Love Story**	*Soundtrack*	Paramount 6002
3	4	18	Jesus Christ Superstar	*Various Artists*	Decca 7206
4	3	8	Chicago III	*Chicago*	Columbia 30110
5	8	3	The Cry Of Love	*Jimi Hendrix*	Reprise 2034
6	6	24	Abraxas	*Santana*	Columbia 30130
7	7	5	Love Story	*Andy Williams*	Columbia 30497
8	5	9	Tumbleweed Connection	*Elton John*	Uni 73096
9	11	14	All Things Must Pass	*George Harrison*	Apple 639
10	10	5	**Stoney End**	*Barbra Streisand*	Columbia 30378

Billboard® — MARCH 27, 1971 — TOP LP's

TW	LW	WK	Title	Artist	Label
1	1	9	**Pearl**	*Janis Joplin*	Columbia 30322
2	2	13	**Love Story**	*Soundtrack*	Paramount 6002
3	5	4	**The Cry Of Love**	*Jimi Hendrix*	Reprise 2034
4	4	9	Chicago III	*Chicago*	Columbia 30110
5	3	19	Jesus Christ Superstar	*Various Artists*	Decca 7206
6	6	25	Abraxas	*Santana*	Columbia 30130
7	7	6	Love Story	*Andy Williams*	Columbia 30497
8	8	10	Tumbleweed Connection	*Elton John*	Uni 73096
9	9	15	All Things Must Pass	*George Harrison*	Apple 639
10	10	6	**Stoney End**	*Barbra Streisand*	Columbia 30378

Billboard® — APRIL 3, 1971 — TOP LP's

TW	LW	WK	Title	Artist	Label
1	1	10	**Pearl**	*Janis Joplin*	Columbia 30322
2	2	14	**Love Story**	*Soundtrack*	Paramount 6002
3	3	5	**The Cry Of Love**	*Jimi Hendrix*	Reprise 2034
4	5	20	Jesus Christ Superstar	*Various Artists*	Decca 7206
5	7	7	Love Story	*Andy Williams*	Columbia 30497
6	4	10	Chicago III	*Chicago*	Columbia 30110
7	11	6	Golden Bisquits	*Three Dog Night*	Dunhill/ABC 50098
8	6	26	Abraxas	*Santana*	Columbia 30130
9	8	11	Tumbleweed Connection	*Elton John*	Uni 73096
10	10	7	**Stoney End**	*Barbra Streisand*	Columbia 30378

Billboard® — APRIL 10, 1971 — TOP LP's

TW	LW	WK	Title	Artist	Label
1	1	11	**Pearl**	*Janis Joplin*	Columbia 30322
2	2	15	**Love Story**	*Soundtrack*	Paramount 6002
3	4	21	Jesus Christ Superstar	*Various Artists*	Decca 7206
4	3	6	The Cry Of Love	*Jimi Hendrix*	Reprise 2034
5	5	8	Love Story	*Andy Williams*	Columbia 30497
6	6	11	Chicago III	*Chicago*	Columbia 30110
7	7	7	Golden Bisquits	*Three Dog Night*	Dunhill/ABC 50098
8	8	27	Abraxas	*Santana*	Columbia 30130
9	11	10	Tea for the Tillerman	*Cat Stevens*	A&M 4280
10	14	30	Close To You	*Carpenters*	A&M 4271

Billboard® — APRIL 17, 1971 — TOP LP's

TW	LW	WK	Title	Artist	Label
1	1	12	**Pearl**	*Janis Joplin*	Columbia 30322
2	3	22	Jesus Christ Superstar	*Various Artists*	Decca 7206
3	5	9	**Love Story**	*Andy Williams*	Columbia 30497
4	2	16	Love Story	*Soundtrack*	Paramount 6002
5	4	7	The Cry Of Love	*Jimi Hendrix*	Reprise 2034
6	7	8	Golden Bisquits	*Three Dog Night*	Dunhill/ABC 50098
7	17	3	Up To Date	*The Partridge Family*	Bell 6059
8	9	11	**Tea for the Tillerman**	*Cat Stevens*	A&M 4280
9	8	28	Abraxas	*Santana*	Columbia 30130
10	10	31	Close To You	*Carpenters*	A&M 4271

Billboard — APRIL 24, 1971 — TOP LP's

TW	LW	WK	Title	Artist...Label
1	1	13	**Pearl**	*Janis Joplin*...Columbia 30322
2	2	23	Jesus Christ Superstar	*Various Artists*...Decca 7206
3	7	4	**Up To Date**	*The Partridge Family*...Bell 6059
4	3	10	Love Story	*Andy Williams*...Columbia 30497
5	6	9	**Golden Bisquits**	*Three Dog Night*...Dunhill/ABC 50098
6	4	17	Love Story	*Soundtrack*...Paramount 6002
7	9	29	Abraxas	*Santana*...Columbia 30130
8	5	8	The Cry Of Love	*Jimi Hendrix*...Reprise 2034
9	8	12	Tea for the Tillerman	*Cat Stevens*...A&M 4280
10	10	32	Close To You	*Carpenters*...A&M 4271

Billboard — MAY 1, 1971 — TOP LP's

TW	LW	WK	Title	Artist...Label
1	2	24	**Jesus Christ Superstar**	*Various Artists*...Decca 7206
2	1	14	Pearl	*Janis Joplin*...Columbia 30322
3	3	5	**Up To Date**	*The Partridge Family*...Bell 6059
4	14	2	4 Way Street	*Crosby, Stills, Nash & Young*...Atlantic 902
5	5	10	**Golden Bisquits**	*Three Dog Night*...Dunhill/ABC 50098
6	4	11	Love Story	*Andy Williams*...Columbia 30497
7	6	18	Love Story	*Soundtrack*...Paramount 6002
8	11	4	Woodstock Two	*Various Artists/Soundtrack*...Cotillion 400
9	9	13	Tea for the Tillerman	*Cat Stevens*...A&M 4280
10	10	33	Close To You	*Carpenters*...A&M 4271

Billboard — MAY 8, 1971 — TOP LP's

TW	LW	WK	Title	Artist...Label
1	1	25	**Jesus Christ Superstar**	*Various Artists*...Decca 7206
2	2	15	Pearl	*Janis Joplin*...Columbia 30322
3	4	3	4 Way Street	*Crosby, Stills, Nash & Young*...Atlantic 902
4	3	6	Up To Date	*The Partridge Family*...Bell 6059
5	5	11	**Golden Bisquits**	*Three Dog Night*...Dunhill/ABC 50098
6	7	19	Love Story	*Soundtrack*...Paramount 6002
7	8	5	**Woodstock Two**	*Various Artists/Soundtrack*...Cotillion 400
8	9	14	**Tea for the Tillerman**	*Cat Stevens*...A&M 4280
9	25	2	Survival	*Grand Funk Railroad*...Capitol 764
10	11	31	Abraxas	*Santana*...Columbia 30130

Billboard — MAY 15, 1971 — TOP LP's

TW	LW	WK	Title	Artist...Label
1	3	4	**4 Way Street**	*Crosby, Stills, Nash & Young*...Atlantic 902
2	1	26	Jesus Christ Superstar	*Various Artists*...Decca 7206
3	4	7	**Up To Date**	*The Partridge Family*...Bell 6059
4	2	16	Pearl	*Janis Joplin*...Columbia 30322
5	5	12	**Golden Bisquits**	*Three Dog Night*...Dunhill/ABC 50098
6	22	2	Mud Slide Slim And The Blue Horizon	*James Taylor*...Warner 2561
7	14	6	Tapestry	*Carole King*...Ode 77009
8	8	15	**Tea for the Tillerman**	*Cat Stevens*...A&M 4280
9	9	3	Survival	*Grand Funk Railroad*...Capitol 764
10	-	1	Sticky Fingers	*The Rolling Stones*...Rolling Stones 59100

Billboard — MAY 22, 1971 — TOP LP's

TW	LW	WK			
1	10	2	**Sticky Fingers**	*The Rolling Stones*	Rolling Stones 59100
2	2	27	**Jesus Christ Superstar**	*Various Artists*	Decca 7206
3	1	5	**4 Way Street**	*Crosby, Stills, Nash & Young*	Atlantic 902
4	3	8	**Up To Date**	*The Partridge Family*	Bell 6059
5	6	3	**Mud Slide Slim And The Blue Horizon**	*James Taylor*	Warner 2561
6	7	7	**Tapestry**	*Carole King*	Ode 77009
7	9	4	**Survival**	*Grand Funk Railroad*	Capitol 764
8	5	13	**Golden Bisquits**	*Three Dog Night*	Dunhill/ABC 50098
9	4	17	**Pearl**	*Janis Joplin*	Columbia 30322
10	21	3	**L.A. Woman**	*The Doors*	Elektra 75011

Billboard — MAY 29, 1971 — TOP LP's

TW	LW	WK			
1	1	3	**Sticky Fingers**	*The Rolling Stones*	Rolling Stones 59100
2	2	28	**Jesus Christ Superstar**	*Various Artists*	Decca 7206
3	3	6	**4 Way Street**	*Crosby, Stills, Nash & Young*	Atlantic 902
4	6	8	**Tapestry**	*Carole King*	Ode 77009
5	5	4	**Mud Slide Slim And The Blue Horizon**	*James Taylor*	Warner 2561
6	7	5	**Survival**	*Grand Funk Railroad*	Capitol 764
7	8	14	**Golden Bisquits**	*Three Dog Night*	Dunhill/ABC 50098
8	13	3	**Aqualung**	*Jethro Tull*	Reprise 2035
9	4	9	**Up To Date**	*The Partridge Family*	Bell 6059
10	10	4	**L.A. Woman**	*The Doors*	Elektra 75011

Billboard — JUNE 5, 1971 — TOP LP's

TW	LW	WK			
1	1	4	**Sticky Fingers**	*The Rolling Stones*	Rolling Stones 59100
2	2	29	**Jesus Christ Superstar**	*Various Artists*	Decca 7206
3	3	7	**4 Way Street**	*Crosby, Stills, Nash & Young*	Atlantic 902
4	4	9	**Tapestry**	*Carole King*	Ode 77009
5	5	5	**Mud Slide Slim And The Blue Horizon**	*James Taylor*	Warner 2561
6	-	1	**Ram**	*Paul & Linda McCartney*	Apple 3375
7	8	4	**Aqualung**	*Jethro Tull*	Reprise 2035
8	9	10	**Up To Date**	*The Partridge Family*	Bell 6059
9	10	5	**L.A. Woman**	*The Doors*	Elektra 75011
10	6	6	**Survival**	*Grand Funk Railroad*	Capitol 764

Billboard — JUNE 12, 1971 — TOP LP's

TW	LW	WK			
1	1	5	**Sticky Fingers**	*The Rolling Stones*	Rolling Stones 59100
2	4	10	**Tapestry**	*Carole King*	Ode 77009
3	2	30	**Jesus Christ Superstar**	*Various Artists*	Decca 7206
4	6	2	**Ram**	*Paul & Linda McCartney*	Apple 3375
5	5	6	**Mud Slide Slim And The Blue Horizon**	*James Taylor*	Warner 2561
6	15	2	**Carpenters**	*Carpenters*	A&M 3502
7	7	5	**Aqualung**	*Jethro Tull*	Reprise 2035
8	3	8	**4 Way Street**	*Crosby, Stills, Nash & Young*	Atlantic 902
9	8	11	**Up To Date**	*The Partridge Family*	Bell 6059
10	10	7	**Survival**	*Grand Funk Railroad*	Capitol 764

TW	LW	WK	Billboard® JUNE 19, 1971 TOP LP's
1	2	11	**Tapestry** ... *Carole King*...Ode 77009
2	1	6	Sticky Fingers ... *The Rolling Stones*...Rolling Stones 59100
3	4	3	Ram ... *Paul & Linda McCartney*...Apple 3375
4	3	31	Jesus Christ Superstar ... *Various Artists*...Decca 7206
5	6	3	Carpenters ... *Carpenters*...A&M 3502
6	5	7	Mud Slide Slim And The Blue Horizon ... *James Taylor*...Warner 2561
7	8	9	4 Way Street ... *Crosby, Stills, Nash & Young*...Atlantic 902
8	7	6	Aqualung ... *Jethro Tull*...Reprise 2035
9	14	3	Aretha Live At Fillmore West ... *Aretha Franklin*...Atlantic 7205
10	9	12	Up To Date ... *The Partridge Family*...Bell 6059

TW	LW	WK	Billboard® JUNE 26, 1971 TOP LP's
1	1	12	**Tapestry** ... *Carole King*...Ode 77009
2	2	7	Sticky Fingers ... *The Rolling Stones*...Rolling Stones 59100
3	3	4	Ram ... *Paul & Linda McCartney*...Apple 3375
4	5	4	Carpenters ... *Carpenters*...A&M 3502
5	4	32	Jesus Christ Superstar ... *Various Artists*...Decca 7206
6	6	8	Mud Slide Slim And The Blue Horizon ... *James Taylor*...Warner 2561
7	9	4	**Aretha Live At Fillmore West** ... *Aretha Franklin*...Atlantic 7205
8	8	7	Aqualung ... *Jethro Tull*...Reprise 2035
9	7	10	4 Way Street ... *Crosby, Stills, Nash & Young*...Atlantic 902
10	10	13	Up To Date ... *The Partridge Family*...Bell 6059

TW	LW	WK	Billboard® JULY 3, 1971 TOP LP's
1	1	13	**Tapestry** ... *Carole King*...Ode 77009
2	4	5	**Carpenters** ... *Carpenters*...A&M 3502
3	2	8	Sticky Fingers ... *The Rolling Stones*...Rolling Stones 59100
4	3	5	Ram ... *Paul & Linda McCartney*...Apple 3375
5	5	33	Jesus Christ Superstar ... *Various Artists*...Decca 7206
6	6	9	Mud Slide Slim And The Blue Horizon ... *James Taylor*...Warner 2561
7	7	5	**Aretha Live At Fillmore West** ... *Aretha Franklin*...Atlantic 7205
8	9	11	4 Way Street ... *Crosby, Stills, Nash & Young*...Atlantic 902
9	8	8	Aqualung ... *Jethro Tull*...Reprise 2035
10	10	14	Up To Date ... *The Partridge Family*...Bell 6059

TW	LW	WK	Billboard® JULY 10, 1971 TOP LP's
1	1	14	**Tapestry** ... *Carole King*...Ode 77009
2	2	6	**Carpenters** ... *Carpenters*...A&M 3502
3	3	9	Sticky Fingers ... *The Rolling Stones*...Rolling Stones 59100
4	4	6	Ram ... *Paul & Linda McCartney*...Apple 3375
5	5	34	Jesus Christ Superstar ... *Various Artists*...Decca 7206
6	6	10	Mud Slide Slim And The Blue Horizon ... *James Taylor*...Warner 2561
7	9	9	**Aqualung** ... *Jethro Tull*...Reprise 2035
8	7	6	Aretha Live At Fillmore West ... *Aretha Franklin*...Atlantic 7205
9	8	12	4 Way Street ... *Crosby, Stills, Nash & Young*...Atlantic 902
10	15	5	What's Going On ... *Marvin Gaye*...Tamla 310

TW	LW	WK	Billboard® JULY 17, 1971 TOP LP's
1	1	15	**Tapestry** ... *Carole King*...Ode 77009
2	3	10	Sticky Fingers ... *The Rolling Stones*...Rolling Stones 59100
3	5	35	Jesus Christ Superstar ... *Various Artists*...Decca 7206
4	2	7	Carpenters ... *Carpenters*...A&M 3502
5	4	7	Ram ... *Paul & Linda McCartney*...Apple 3375
6	6	11	Mud Slide Slim And The Blue Horizon ... *James Taylor*...Warner 2561
7	7	10	**Aqualung** ... *Jethro Tull*...Reprise 2035
8	10	6	What's Going On ... *Marvin Gaye*...Tamla 310
9	20	3	**Tarkus** ... *Emerson, Lake & Palmer*...Cotillion 9900
10	9	13	4 Way Street ... *Crosby, Stills, Nash & Young*...Atlantic 902

TW	LW	WK	Billboard® JULY 24, 1971 TOP LP's
1	1	16	**Tapestry** ... *Carole King*...Ode 77009
2	6	12	**Mud Slide Slim And The Blue Horizon** ... *James Taylor*...Warner 2561
3	2	11	Sticky Fingers ... *The Rolling Stones*...Rolling Stones 59100
4	3	36	Jesus Christ Superstar ... *Various Artists*...Decca 7206
5	5	8	Ram ... *Paul & Linda McCartney*...Apple 3375
6	4	8	Carpenters ... *Carpenters*...A&M 3502
7	8	7	What's Going On ... *Marvin Gaye*...Tamla 310
8	7	11	Aqualung ... *Jethro Tull*...Reprise 2035
9	9	4	**Tarkus** ... *Emerson, Lake & Palmer*...Cotillion 9900
10	10	14	4 Way Street ... *Crosby, Stills, Nash & Young*...Atlantic 902

TW	LW	WK	Billboard® JULY 31, 1971 TOP LP's
1	1	17	**Tapestry** ... *Carole King*...Ode 77009
2	2	13	**Mud Slide Slim And The Blue Horizon** ... *James Taylor*...Warner 2561
3	3	12	Sticky Fingers ... *The Rolling Stones*...Rolling Stones 59100
4	5	9	Ram ... *Paul & Linda McCartney*...Apple 3375
5	4	37	Jesus Christ Superstar ... *Various Artists*...Decca 7206
6	7	8	**What's Going On** ... *Marvin Gaye*...Tamla 310
7	6	9	Carpenters ... *Carpenters*...A&M 3502
8	8	12	Aqualung ... *Jethro Tull*...Reprise 2035
9	14	3	Stephen Stills 2 ... *Stephen Stills*...Atlantic 7206
10	11	7	Every Picture Tells A Story ... *Rod Stewart*...Mercury 609

TW	LW	WK	Billboard® AUGUST 7, 1971 TOP LP's
1	1	18	**Tapestry** ... *Carole King*...Ode 77009
2	2	14	**Mud Slide Slim And The Blue Horizon** ... *James Taylor*...Warner 2561
3	4	10	Ram ... *Paul & Linda McCartney*...Apple 3375
4	5	38	Jesus Christ Superstar ... *Various Artists*...Decca 7206
5	3	13	Sticky Fingers ... *The Rolling Stones*...Rolling Stones 59100
6	6	9	**What's Going On** ... *Marvin Gaye*...Tamla 310
7	7	10	Carpenters ... *Carpenters*...A&M 3502
8	9	4	**Stephen Stills 2** ... *Stephen Stills*...Atlantic 7206
9	8	13	Aqualung ... *Jethro Tull*...Reprise 2035
10	10	8	Every Picture Tells A Story ... *Rod Stewart*...Mercury 609

Billboard — AUGUST 14, 1971 — TOP LP's

TW	LW	WK	Title	Artist	Label
1	1	19	**Tapestry**	*Carole King*	Ode 77009
2	2	15	**Mud Slide Slim And The Blue Horizon**	*James Taylor*	Warner 2561
3	4	39	Jesus Christ Superstar	*Various Artists*	Decca 7206
4	3	11	Ram	*Paul & Linda McCartney*	Apple 3375
5	5	14	Sticky Fingers	*The Rolling Stones*	Rolling Stones 59100
6	7	11	Carpenters	*Carpenters*	A&M 3502
7	6	10	What's Going On	*Marvin Gaye*	Tamla 310
8	8	5	**Stephen Stills 2**	*Stephen Stills*	Atlantic 7206
9	9	14	Aqualung	*Jethro Tull*	Reprise 2035
10	10	9	Every Picture Tells A Story	*Rod Stewart*	Mercury 609

Billboard — AUGUST 21, 1971 — TOP LP's

TW	LW	WK	Title	Artist	Label
1	1	20	**Tapestry**	*Carole King*	Ode 77009
2	4	12	**Ram**	*Paul & Linda McCartney*	Apple 3375
3	2	16	Mud Slide Slim And The Blue Horizon	*James Taylor*	Warner 2561
4	3	40	Jesus Christ Superstar	*Various Artists*	Decca 7206
5	6	12	Carpenters	*Carpenters*	A&M 3502
6	7	11	**What's Going On**	*Marvin Gaye*	Tamla 310
7	9	15	**Aqualung**	*Jethro Tull*	Reprise 2035
8	5	15	Sticky Fingers	*The Rolling Stones*	Rolling Stones 59100
9	10	10	Every Picture Tells A Story	*Rod Stewart*	Mercury 609
10	11	7	**B, S & T; 4**	*Blood, Sweat & Tears*	Columbia 30590

Billboard — AUGUST 28, 1971 — TOP LP's

TW	LW	WK	Title	Artist	Label
1	1	21	**Tapestry**	*Carole King*	Ode 77009
2	2	13	**Ram**	*Paul & Linda McCartney*	Apple 3375
3	3	17	Mud Slide Slim And The Blue Horizon	*James Taylor*	Warner 2561
4	9	11	Every Picture Tells A Story	*Rod Stewart*	Mercury 609
5	5	13	Carpenters	*Carpenters*	A&M 3502
6	12	3	Who's next	*The Who*	Decca 79182
7	7	16	**Aqualung**	*Jethro Tull*	Reprise 2035
8	30	2	Every Good Boy Deserves Favour	*The Moody Blues*	Threshold 5
9	4	41	Jesus Christ Superstar	*Various Artists*	Decca 7206
10	10	8	**B, S & T; 4**	*Blood, Sweat & Tears*	Columbia 30590

Billboard — SEPTEMBER 4, 1971 — TOP LP's

TW	LW	WK	Title	Artist	Label
1	1	22	**Tapestry**	*Carole King*	Ode 77009
2	8	3	**Every Good Boy Deserves Favour**	*The Moody Blues*	Threshold 5
3	2	14	Ram	*Paul & Linda McCartney*	Apple 3375
4	4	12	Every Picture Tells A Story	*Rod Stewart*	Mercury 609
5	6	4	Who's next	*The Who*	Decca 79182
6	3	18	Mud Slide Slim And The Blue Horizon	*James Taylor*	Warner 2561
7	7	17	**Aqualung**	*Jethro Tull*	Reprise 2035
8	5	14	Carpenters	*Carpenters*	A&M 3502
9	9	42	Jesus Christ Superstar	*Various Artists*	Decca 7206
10	11	13	What's Going On	*Marvin Gaye*	Tamla 310

Billboard — SEPTEMBER 11, 1971 — TOP LP's

TW	LW	WK	Title	Artist	Label
①	1	23	**Tapestry**	Carole King	Ode 77009
②	2	4	**Every Good Boy Deserves Favour**	The Moody Blues	Threshold 5
❸	4	13	Every Picture Tells A Story	Rod Stewart	Mercury 609
❹	5	5	**Who's next**	The Who	Decca 79182
⑤	3	15	Ram	Paul & Linda McCartney	Apple 3375
⑥	6	19	Mud Slide Slim And The Blue Horizon	James Taylor	Warner 2561
⑦	8	15	Carpenters	Carpenters	A&M 3502
⑧	9	43	Jesus Christ Superstar	Various Artists	Decca 7206
⑨	7	18	Aqualung	Jethro Tull	Reprise 2035
⑩	10	14	What's Going On	Marvin Gaye	Tamla 310

Billboard — SEPTEMBER 18, 1971 — TOP LP's

TW	LW	WK	Title	Artist	Label
①	1	24	**Tapestry**	Carole King	Ode 77009
②	2	5	**Every Good Boy Deserves Favour**	The Moody Blues	Threshold 5
③	3	14	Every Picture Tells A Story	Rod Stewart	Mercury 609
④	4	6	**Who's next**	The Who	Decca 79182
⑤	5	16	Ram	Paul & Linda McCartney	Apple 3375
⑥	7	16	Carpenters	Carpenters	A&M 3502
⑦	6	20	Mud Slide Slim And The Blue Horizon	James Taylor	Warner 2561
❽	11	5	Shaft	Isaac Hayes/Soundtrack	Enterprise 5002
❾	16	3	Master Of Reality	Black Sabbath	Warner 2562
⑩	10	15	What's Going On	Marvin Gaye	Tamla 310

Billboard — SEPTEMBER 25, 1971 — TOP LP's

TW	LW	WK	Title	Artist	Label
①	1	25	**Tapestry**	Carole King	Ode 77009
②	3	15	Every Picture Tells A Story	Rod Stewart	Mercury 609
③	2	6	Every Good Boy Deserves Favour	The Moody Blues	Threshold 5
④	5	17	Ram	Paul & Linda McCartney	Apple 3375
⑤	4	7	Who's next	The Who	Decca 79182
❻	8	6	Shaft	Isaac Hayes/Soundtrack	Enterprise 5002
⑦	6	17	Carpenters	Carpenters	A&M 3502
⑧	9	4	**Master Of Reality**	Black Sabbath	Warner 2562
❾	11	5	**The Partridge Family Sound Magazine**	The Partridge Family	Bell 6064
⑩	7	21	Mud Slide Slim And The Blue Horizon	James Taylor	Warner 2561

Billboard — OCTOBER 2, 1971 — TOP LP's

TW	LW	WK	Title	Artist	Label
①	2	16	**Every Picture Tells A Story**	Rod Stewart	Mercury 609
②	1	26	Tapestry	Carole King	Ode 77009
③	3	7	Every Good Boy Deserves Favour	The Moody Blues	Threshold 5
④	6	7	Shaft	Isaac Hayes/Soundtrack	Enterprise 5002
⑤	4	18	Ram	Paul & Linda McCartney	Apple 3375
⑥	5	8	Who's next	The Who	Decca 79182
⑦	7	18	Carpenters	Carpenters	A&M 3502
⑧	8	5	**Master Of Reality**	Black Sabbath	Warner 2562
⑨	9	6	**The Partridge Family Sound Magazine**	The Partridge Family	Bell 6064
❿	134	3	Imagine	John Lennon/Plastic Ono Band	Apple 3379

Billboard — OCTOBER 9, 1971 — TOP LP's

TW	LW	WK		
1	1	17	**Every Picture Tells A Story**	*Rod Stewart*...Mercury 609
2	2	27	Tapestry	*Carole King*...Ode 77009
❸	10	4	Imagine	*John Lennon/Plastic Ono Band*...Apple 3379
4	4	8	Shaft	*Isaac Hayes/Soundtrack*...Enterprise 5002
5	3	8	Every Good Boy Deserves Favour	*The Moody Blues*...Threshold 5
6	5	19	Ram	*Paul & Linda McCartney*...Apple 3375
7	7	19	Carpenters	*Carpenters*...A&M 3502
8	6	9	Who's next	*The Who*...Decca 79182
9	8	6	Master Of Reality	*Black Sabbath*...Warner 2562
10	9	7	The Partridge Family Sound Magazine	*The Partridge Family*...Bell 6064

Billboard — OCTOBER 16, 1971 — TOP LP's

TW	LW	WK		
1	1	18	**Every Picture Tells A Story**	*Rod Stewart*...Mercury 609
2	3	5	Imagine	*John Lennon/Plastic Ono Band*...Apple 3379
3	2	28	Tapestry	*Carole King*...Ode 77009
4	4	9	Shaft	*Isaac Hayes/Soundtrack*...Enterprise 5002
5	7	20	Carpenters	*Carpenters*...A&M 3502
6	5	9	Every Good Boy Deserves Favour	*The Moody Blues*...Threshold 5
7	6	20	Ram	*Paul & Linda McCartney*...Apple 3375
8	8	10	Who's next	*The Who*...Decca 79182
9	9	7	Master Of Reality	*Black Sabbath*...Warner 2562
❿	143	2	Teaser And The Firecat	*Cat Stevens*...A&M 4313

Billboard — OCTOBER 23, 1971 — TOP LP's

TW	LW	WK		
1	1	19	**Every Picture Tells A Story**	*Rod Stewart*...Mercury 609
2	2	6	Imagine	*John Lennon/Plastic Ono Band*...Apple 3379
❸	4	10	Shaft	*Isaac Hayes/Soundtrack*...Enterprise 5002
❹	13	2	Santana III	*Santana*...Columbia 30595
5	3	29	Tapestry	*Carole King*...Ode 77009
6	6	10	Every Good Boy Deserves Favour	*The Moody Blues*...Threshold 5
7	5	21	Carpenters	*Carpenters*...A&M 3502
8	10	3	Teaser And The Firecat	*Cat Stevens*...A&M 4313
9	7	21	Ram	*Paul & Linda McCartney*...Apple 3375
10	8	11	Who's next	*The Who*...Decca 79182

Billboard — OCTOBER 30, 1971 — TOP LP's

TW	LW	WK		
1	2	7	**Imagine**	*John Lennon/Plastic Ono Band*...Apple 3379
2	1	20	Every Picture Tells A Story	*Rod Stewart*...Mercury 609
3	3	11	Shaft	*Isaac Hayes/Soundtrack*...Enterprise 5002
4	4	3	Santana III	*Santana*...Columbia 30595
5	5	30	Tapestry	*Carole King*...Ode 77009
❻	8	4	Teaser And The Firecat	*Cat Stevens*...A&M 4313
7	7	22	Carpenters	*Carpenters*...A&M 3502
8	6	11	Every Good Boy Deserves Favour	*The Moody Blues*...Threshold 5
9	9	22	Ram	*Paul & Linda McCartney*...Apple 3375
10	10	12	Who's next	*The Who*...Decca 79182

Billboard — NOVEMBER 6, 1971 — TOP LP's

TW	LW	WK	Title	Artist	Label
❶	3	12	**Shaft**	*Isaac Hayes/Soundtrack*	Enterprise 5002
❷	4	4	Santana III	*Santana*	Columbia 30595
③	2	21	Every Picture Tells A Story	*Rod Stewart*	Mercury 609
④	1	8	Imagine	*John Lennon/Plastic Ono Band*	Apple 3379
⑤	5	31	Tapestry	*Carole King*	Ode 77009
⑥	6	5	Teaser And The Firecat	*Cat Stevens*	A&M 4313
⑦	7	23	Carpenters	*Carpenters*	A&M 3502
⑧	8	12	Every Good Boy Deserves Favour	*The Moody Blues*	Threshold 5
⑨	9	23	Ram	*Paul & Linda McCartney*	Apple 3375
⑩	10	13	Who's next	*The Who*	Decca 79182

Billboard — NOVEMBER 13, 1971 — TOP LP's

TW	LW	WK	Title	Artist	Label
①	2	5	**Santana III**	*Santana*	Columbia 30595
②	1	13	Shaft	*Isaac Hayes/Soundtrack*	Enterprise 5002
③	3	22	Every Picture Tells A Story	*Rod Stewart*	Mercury 609
④	4	9	Imagine	*John Lennon/Plastic Ono Band*	Apple 3379
⑤	6	6	Teaser And The Firecat	*Cat Stevens*	A&M 4313
⑥	5	32	Tapestry	*Carole King*	Ode 77009
⑦	7	24	Carpenters	*Carpenters*	A&M 3502
⑧	8	13	Every Good Boy Deserves Favour	*The Moody Blues*	Threshold 5
⑨	9	24	Ram	*Paul & Linda McCartney*	Apple 3375
❿	16	4	Harmony	*Three Dog Night*	Dunhill/ABC 50108

Billboard — NOVEMBER 20, 1971 — TOP LP's

TW	LW	WK	Title	Artist	Label
①	1	6	**Santana III**	*Santana*	Columbia 30595
②	2	14	Shaft	*Isaac Hayes/Soundtrack*	Enterprise 5002
③	5	7	Teaser And The Firecat	*Cat Stevens*	A&M 4313
④	4	10	Imagine	*John Lennon/Plastic Ono Band*	Apple 3379
⑤	3	23	Every Picture Tells A Story	*Rod Stewart*	Mercury 609
⑥	6	33	Tapestry	*Carole King*	Ode 77009
❼	39	2	There's A Riot Goin' On	*Sly & The Family Stone*	Epic 30986
⑧	10	5	**Harmony**	*Three Dog Night*	Dunhill/ABC 50108
❾	43	2	Chicago At Carnegie Hall	*Chicago*	Columbia 30865
⑩	7	25	Carpenters	*Carpenters*	A&M 3502

Billboard — NOVEMBER 27, 1971 — TOP LP's

TW	LW	WK	Title	Artist	Label
①	1	7	**Santana III**	*Santana*	Columbia 30595
②	2	15	Shaft	*Isaac Hayes/Soundtrack*	Enterprise 5002
③	3	8	Teaser And The Firecat	*Cat Stevens*	A&M 4313
④	4	11	Imagine	*John Lennon/Plastic Ono Band*	Apple 3379
❺	7	3	There's A Riot Goin' On	*Sly & The Family Stone*	Epic 30986
⑥	6	34	Tapestry	*Carole King*	Ode 77009
❼	9	3	Chicago At Carnegie Hall	*Chicago*	Columbia 30865
⑧	8	6	**Harmony**	*Three Dog Night*	Dunhill/ABC 50108
⑨	5	24	Every Picture Tells A Story	*Rod Stewart*	Mercury 609
⑩	11	15	Every Good Boy Deserves Favour	*The Moody Blues*	Threshold 5

TW	LW	WK	Billboard. DECEMBER 4, 1971	TOP LP's
1	1	8	**Santana III**	*Santana*...Columbia 30595
2	3	9	**Teaser And The Firecat**	*Cat Stevens*...A&M 4313
3	2	16	Shaft	*Isaac Hayes/Soundtrack*...Enterprise 5002
4	5	4	There's A Riot Goin' On	*Sly & The Family Stone*...Epic 30986
5	6	35	Tapestry	*Carole King*...Ode 77009
6	4	12	Imagine	*John Lennon/Plastic Ono Band*...Apple 3379
7	7	4	Chicago At Carnegie Hall	*Chicago*...Columbia 30865
8	36	2	Led Zeppelin IV (untitled)	*Led Zeppelin*...Atlantic 7208
9	9	25	Every Picture Tells A Story	*Rod Stewart*...Mercury 609
10	8	7	Harmony	*Three Dog Night*...Dunhill/ABC 50108

TW	LW	WK	Billboard. DECEMBER 11, 1971	TOP LP's
1	1	9	**Santana III**	*Santana*...Columbia 30595
2	4	5	There's A Riot Goin' On	*Sly & The Family Stone*...Epic 30986
3	2	10	Teaser And The Firecat	*Cat Stevens*...A&M 4313
4	3	17	Shaft	*Isaac Hayes/Soundtrack*...Enterprise 5002
5	8	3	Led Zeppelin IV (untitled)	*Led Zeppelin*...Atlantic 7208
6	7	5	Chicago At Carnegie Hall	*Chicago*...Columbia 30865
7	6	13	Imagine	*John Lennon/Plastic Ono Band*...Apple 3379
8	9	26	Every Picture Tells A Story	*Rod Stewart*...Mercury 609
9	5	36	Tapestry	*Carole King*...Ode 77009
10	40	2	E Pluribus Funk	*Grand Funk Railroad*...Capitol 853

TW	LW	WK	Billboard. DECEMBER 18, 1971	TOP LP's
1	2	6	**There's A Riot Goin' On**	*Sly & The Family Stone*...Epic 30986
2	5	4	**Led Zeppelin IV (untitled)**	*Led Zeppelin*...Atlantic 7208
3	1	10	Santana III	*Santana*...Columbia 30595
4	3	11	Teaser And The Firecat	*Cat Stevens*...A&M 4313
5	6	6	Chicago At Carnegie Hall	*Chicago*...Columbia 30865
6	10	3	E Pluribus Funk	*Grand Funk Railroad*...Capitol 853
7	4	18	Shaft	*Isaac Hayes/Soundtrack*...Enterprise 5002
8	91	2	Music	*Carole King*...Ode 77013
9	7	14	Imagine	*John Lennon/Plastic Ono Band*...Apple 3379
10	9	37	Tapestry	*Carole King*...Ode 77009

TW	LW	WK	Billboard. DECEMBER 25, 1971	TOP LP's
1	1	7	**There's A Riot Goin' On**	*Sly & The Family Stone*...Epic 30986
2	2	5	**Led Zeppelin IV (untitled)**	*Led Zeppelin*...Atlantic 7208
3	8	3	Music	*Carole King*...Ode 77013
4	4	12	Teaser And The Firecat	*Cat Stevens*...A&M 4313
5	5	7	Chicago At Carnegie Hall	*Chicago*...Columbia 30865
6	6	4	E Pluribus Funk	*Grand Funk Railroad*...Capitol 853
7	3	11	Santana III	*Santana*...Columbia 30595
8	7	19	Shaft	*Isaac Hayes/Soundtrack*...Enterprise 5002
9	10	38	Tapestry	*Carole King*...Ode 77009
10	18	7	American Pie	*Don McLean*...United Artists 5535

TW	LW	WK	Billboard. JANUARY 1, 1972 TOP LP's
1	3	4	**Music** ... *Carole King*...Ode 77013
2	2	6	**Led Zeppelin IV (untitled)** ... *Led Zeppelin*...Atlantic 7208
3	4	13	Teaser And The Firecat ... *Cat Stevens*...A&M 4313
4	5	8	Chicago At Carnegie Hall ... *Chicago*...Columbia 30865
5	6	5	**E Pluribus Funk** ... *Grand Funk Railroad*...Capitol 853
6	1	8	There's A Riot Goin' On ... *Sly & The Family Stone*...Epic 30986
7	10	8	American Pie ... *Don McLean*...United Artists 5535
8	7	12	Santana III ... *Santana*...Columbia 30595
9	9	39	Tapestry ... *Carole King*...Ode 77009
10	11	7	All In The Family ... *TV Cast*...Atlantic 7210

TW	LW	WK	Billboard. JANUARY 8, 1972 TOP LP's
1	1	5	**Music** ... *Carole King*...Ode 77013
2	2	7	**Led Zeppelin IV (untitled)** ... *Led Zeppelin*...Atlantic 7208
3	7	9	American Pie ... *Don McLean*...United Artists 5535
4	4	9	Chicago At Carnegie Hall ... *Chicago*...Columbia 30865
5	5	6	**E Pluribus Funk** ... *Grand Funk Railroad*...Capitol 853
6	6	9	There's A Riot Goin' On ... *Sly & The Family Stone*...Epic 30986
7	3	14	Teaser And The Firecat ... *Cat Stevens*...A&M 4313
8	9	40	Tapestry ... *Carole King*...Ode 77009
9	10	8	All In The Family ... *TV Cast*...Atlantic 7210
10	11	5	**Black Moses** ... *Isaac Hayes*...Enterprise 5003

TW	LW	WK	Billboard. JANUARY 15, 1972 TOP LP's
1	1	6	**Music** ... *Carole King*...Ode 77013
2	3	10	American Pie ... *Don McLean*...United Artists 5535
3	4	10	**Chicago At Carnegie Hall** ... *Chicago*...Columbia 30865
4	14	2	The Concert For Bangla Desh ... *George Harrison*...Apple 3385
5	2	8	Led Zeppelin IV (untitled) ... *Led Zeppelin*...Atlantic 7208
6	7	15	Teaser And The Firecat ... *Cat Stevens*...A&M 4313
7	8	41	Tapestry ... *Carole King*...Ode 77009
8	9	9	**All In The Family** ... *TV Cast*...Atlantic 7210
9	6	10	There's A Riot Goin' On ... *Sly & The Family Stone*...Epic 30986
10	10	6	**Black Moses** ... *Isaac Hayes*...Enterprise 5003

TW	LW	WK	Billboard. JANUARY 22, 1972 TOP LP's
1	2	11	**American Pie** ... *Don McLean*...United Artists 5535
2	4	3	**The Concert For Bangla Desh** ... *George Harrison*...Apple 3385
3	1	7	Music ... *Carole King*...Ode 77013
4	3	11	Chicago At Carnegie Hall ... *Chicago*...Columbia 30865
5	5	9	Led Zeppelin IV (untitled) ... *Led Zeppelin*...Atlantic 7208
6	6	16	Teaser And The Firecat ... *Cat Stevens*...A&M 4313
7	7	42	Tapestry ... *Carole King*...Ode 77009
8	9	11	There's A Riot Goin' On ... *Sly & The Family Stone*...Epic 30986
9	13	9	Madman Across The Water ... *Elton John*...Uni 93120
10	11	5	**Wild Life** ... *Wings*...Apple 3386

TW	LW	WK	Billboard® JANUARY 29, 1972 TOP LP's
1	1	12	**American Pie**............ *Don McLean*...United Artists 5535
2	2	4	**The Concert For Bangla Desh**............ *George Harrison*...Apple 3385
3	3	8	Music............ *Carole King*...Ode 77013
4	5	10	Led Zeppelin IV (untitled)............ *Led Zeppelin*...Atlantic 7208
5	4	12	Chicago At Carnegie Hall............ *Chicago*...Columbia 30865
6	7	43	Tapestry............ *Carole King*...Ode 77009
7	12	7	A Nod Is As Good As A Wink...To A Blind Horse............ *Faces*...Warner 2574
8	18	4	Hot Rocks 1964-1971............ *The Rolling Stones*...London 606/7
9	9	10	Madman Across The Water............ *Elton John*...Uni 93120
10	10	6	**Wild Life**............ *Wings*...Apple 3386

TW	LW	WK	Billboard® FEBRUARY 5, 1972 TOP LP's
1	1	13	**American Pie**............ *Don McLean*...United Artists 5535
2	2	5	**The Concert For Bangla Desh**............ *George Harrison*...Apple 3385
3	3	9	Music............ *Carole King*...Ode 77013
4	4	11	Led Zeppelin IV (untitled)............ *Led Zeppelin*...Atlantic 7208
5	8	5	Hot Rocks 1964-1971............ *The Rolling Stones*...London 606/7
6	7	8	**A Nod Is As Good As A Wink...To A Blind Horse**............ *Faces*...Warner 2574
7	6	44	Tapestry............ *Carole King*...Ode 77009
8	9	11	**Madman Across The Water**............ *Elton John*...Uni 93120
9	5	13	Chicago At Carnegie Hall............ *Chicago*...Columbia 30865
10	11	18	Teaser And The Firecat............ *Cat Stevens*...A&M 4313

TW	LW	WK	Billboard® FEBRUARY 12, 1972 TOP LP's
1	1	14	**American Pie**............ *Don McLean*...United Artists 5535
2	2	6	**The Concert For Bangla Desh**............ *George Harrison*...Apple 3385
3	3	10	Music............ *Carole King*...Ode 77013
4	5	6	**Hot Rocks 1964-1971**............ *The Rolling Stones*...London 606/7
5	4	12	Led Zeppelin IV (untitled)............ *Led Zeppelin*...Atlantic 7208
6	6	9	**A Nod Is As Good As A Wink...To A Blind Horse**............ *Faces*...Warner 2574
7	7	45	Tapestry............ *Carole King*...Ode 77009
8	8	12	**Madman Across The Water**............ *Elton John*...Uni 93120
9	10	19	Teaser And The Firecat............ *Cat Stevens*...A&M 4313
10	9	14	Chicago At Carnegie Hall............ *Chicago*...Columbia 30865

TW	LW	WK	Billboard® FEBRUARY 19, 1972 TOP LP's
1	1	15	**American Pie**............ *Don McLean*...United Artists 5535
2	2	7	**The Concert For Bangla Desh**............ *George Harrison*...Apple 3385
3	3	11	Music............ *Carole King*...Ode 77013
4	4	7	**Hot Rocks 1964-1971**............ *The Rolling Stones*...London 606/7
5	5	13	Led Zeppelin IV (untitled)............ *Led Zeppelin*...Atlantic 7208
6	6	10	**A Nod Is As Good As A Wink...To A Blind Horse**............ *Faces*...Warner 2574
7	14	11	**The Low Spark Of High Heeled Boys**............ *Traffic*...Island 9306
8	11	5	Fragile............ *Yes*...Atlantic 7211
9	16	12	Nilsson Schmilsson............ *Nilsson*...RCA 4515
10	13	5	**Pictures At An Exhibition**............ *Emerson, Lake & Palmer*...Cotillion 66666

Billboard® — FEBRUARY 26, 1972 — TOP LP's

TW	LW	WK	Title	Artist	Label
1	1	16	**American Pie**	*Don McLean*	United Artists 5535
2	3	12	Music	*Carole King*	Ode 77013
3	2	8	The Concert For Bangla Desh	*George Harrison*	Apple 3385
4	8	6	**Fragile**	*Yes*	Atlantic 7211
5	4	8	Hot Rocks 1964-1971	*The Rolling Stones*	London 606/7
6	6	11	**A Nod Is As Good As A Wink...To A Blind Horse**	*Faces*	Warner 2574
7	7	12	**The Low Spark Of High Heeled Boys**	*Traffic*	Island 9306
8	9	13	Nilsson Schmilsson	*Nilsson*	RCA 4515
9	5	14	Led Zeppelin IV (untitled)	*Led Zeppelin*	Atlantic 7208
10	10	6	**Pictures At An Exhibition**	*Emerson, Lake & Palmer*	Cotillion 66666

Billboard® — MARCH 4, 1972 — TOP LP's

TW	LW	WK	Title	Artist	Label
1	1	17	**American Pie**	*Don McLean*	United Artists 5535
2	3	9	**The Concert For Bangla Desh**	*George Harrison*	Apple 3385
3	2	13	Music	*Carole King*	Ode 77013
4	4	7	**Fragile**	*Yes*	Atlantic 7211
5	5	9	Hot Rocks 1964-1971	*The Rolling Stones*	London 606/7
6	8	14	Nilsson Schmilsson	*Nilsson*	RCA 4515
7	6	12	A Nod Is As Good As A Wink...To A Blind Horse	*Faces*	Warner 2574
8	9	15	Led Zeppelin IV (untitled)	*Led Zeppelin*	Atlantic 7208
9	15	4	Paul Simon	*Paul Simon*	Columbia 30750
10	11	5	Baby I'm-A Want You	*Bread*	Elektra 75015

Billboard® — MARCH 11, 1972 — TOP LP's

TW	LW	WK	Title	Artist	Label
1	12	2	**Harvest**	*Neil Young*	Reprise 2032
2	1	18	American Pie	*Don McLean*	United Artists 5535
3	2	10	The Concert For Bangla Desh	*George Harrison*	Apple 3385
4	4	8	**Fragile**	*Yes*	Atlantic 7211
5	3	14	Music	*Carole King*	Ode 77013
6	6	15	Nilsson Schmilsson	*Nilsson*	RCA 4515
7	10	6	Baby I'm-A Want You	*Bread*	Elektra 75015
8	9	5	Paul Simon	*Paul Simon*	Columbia 30750
9	37	4	America	*America*	Warner 2576
10	11	7	**Phase-III**	*The Osmonds*	MGM 4796

Billboard® — MARCH 18, 1972 — TOP LP's

TW	LW	WK	Title	Artist	Label
1	1	3	**Harvest**	*Neil Young*	Reprise 2032
2	9	5	America	*America*	Warner 2576
3	2	19	American Pie	*Don McLean*	United Artists 5535
4	4	9	**Fragile**	*Yes*	Atlantic 7211
5	6	16	Nilsson Schmilsson	*Nilsson*	RCA 4515
6	8	6	Paul Simon	*Paul Simon*	Columbia 30750
7	7	7	Baby I'm-A Want You	*Bread*	Elektra 75015
8	5	15	Music	*Carole King*	Ode 77013
9	3	11	The Concert For Bangla Desh	*George Harrison*	Apple 3385
10	11	11	Hot Rocks 1964-1971	*The Rolling Stones*	London 606/7

Billboard — MARCH 25, 1972 — TOP LP's

TW	LW	WK	Title	Artist	Label
1	2	6	**America**	*America*	Warner 2576
2	1	4	Harvest	*Neil Young*	Reprise 2032
3	7	8	**Baby I'm-A Want You**	*Bread*	Elektra 75015
4	5	17	Nilsson Schmilsson	*Nilsson*	RCA 4515
5	6	7	Paul Simon	*Paul Simon*	Columbia 30750
6	4	10	Fragile	*Yes*	Atlantic 7211
7	3	20	American Pie	*Don McLean*	United Artists 5535
8	8	16	Music	*Carole King*	Ode 77013
9	10	12	Hot Rocks 1964-1971	*The Rolling Stones*	London 606/7
10	11	7	Let's Stay Together	*Al Green*	Hi 32070

Billboard — APRIL 1, 1972 — TOP LP's

TW	LW	WK	Title	Artist	Label
1	1	7	**America**	*America*	Warner 2576
2	2	5	Harvest	*Neil Young*	Reprise 2032
3	4	18	**Nilsson Schmilsson**	*Nilsson*	RCA 4515
4	5	8	**Paul Simon**	*Paul Simon*	Columbia 30750
5	3	9	Baby I'm-A Want You	*Bread*	Elektra 75015
6	6	11	Fragile	*Yes*	Atlantic 7211
7	8	17	Music	*Carole King*	Ode 77013
8	10	8	**Let's Stay Together**	*Al Green*	Hi 32070
9	13	3	Eat A Peach	*The Allman Brothers Band*	Capricorn 0102
10	7	21	American Pie	*Don McLean*	United Artists 5535

Billboard — APRIL 8, 1972 — TOP LP's

TW	LW	WK	Title	Artist	Label
1	1	8	**America**	*America*	Warner 2576
2	2	6	Harvest	*Neil Young*	Reprise 2032
3	3	19	**Nilsson Schmilsson**	*Nilsson*	RCA 4515
4	4	9	**Paul Simon**	*Paul Simon*	Columbia 30750
5	5	10	Baby I'm-A Want You	*Bread*	Elektra 75015
6	6	12	Fragile	*Yes*	Atlantic 7211
7	9	4	Eat A Peach	*The Allman Brothers Band*	Capricorn 0102
8	22	9	First Take	*Roberta Flack*	Atlantic 8230
9	10	22	American Pie	*Don McLean*	United Artists 5535
10	8	9	Let's Stay Together	*Al Green*	Hi 32070

Billboard — APRIL 15, 1972 — TOP LP's

TW	LW	WK	Title	Artist	Label
1	1	9	**America**	*America*	Warner 2576
2	2	7	Harvest	*Neil Young*	Reprise 2032
3	3	20	**Nilsson Schmilsson**	*Nilsson*	RCA 4515
4	6	13	**Fragile**	*Yes*	Atlantic 7211
5	7	5	Eat A Peach	*The Allman Brothers Band*	Capricorn 0102
6	8	10	First Take	*Roberta Flack*	Atlantic 8230
7	4	10	Paul Simon	*Paul Simon*	Columbia 30750
8	5	11	Baby I'm-A Want You	*Bread*	Elektra 75015
9	9	23	American Pie	*Don McLean*	United Artists 5535
10	10	10	Let's Stay Together	*Al Green*	Hi 32070

TW	LW	WK	Billboard. APRIL 22, 1972 TOP LP's	
1	1	10	**America**	*America*...Warner 2576
2	2	8	Harvest	*Neil Young*...Reprise 2032
3	6	11	First Take	*Roberta Flack*...Atlantic 8230
4	4	14	**Fragile**	*Yes*...Atlantic 7211
5	5	6	Eat A Peach	*The Allman Brothers Band*...Capricorn 0102
6	3	21	Nilsson Schmilsson	*Nilsson*...RCA 4515
7	7	11	Paul Simon	*Paul Simon*...Columbia 30750
8	10	11	**Let's Stay Together**	*Al Green*...Hi 32070
9	8	12	Baby I'm-A Want You	*Bread*...Elektra 75015
10	12	55	Tapestry	*Carole King*...Ode 77009

TW	LW	WK	Billboard. APRIL 29, 1972 TOP LP's	
1	3	12	**First Take**	*Roberta Flack*...Atlantic 8230
2	1	11	America	*America*...Warner 2576
3	2	9	Harvest	*Neil Young*...Reprise 2032
4	5	7	**Eat A Peach**	*The Allman Brothers Band*...Capricorn 0102
5	4	15	Fragile	*Yes*...Atlantic 7211
6	6	22	Nilsson Schmilsson	*Nilsson*...RCA 4515
7	7	12	Paul Simon	*Paul Simon*...Columbia 30750
8	9	13	Baby I'm-A Want You	*Bread*...Elektra 75015
9	12	5	Smokin'	*Humble Pie*...A&M 4342
10	10	56	Tapestry	*Carole King*...Ode 77009

TW	LW	WK	Billboard. MAY 6, 1972 TOP LP's	
1	1	13	**First Take**	*Roberta Flack*...Atlantic 8230
2	3	10	Harvest	*Neil Young*...Reprise 2032
3	2	12	America	*America*...Warner 2576
4	4	8	**Eat A Peach**	*The Allman Brothers Band*...Capricorn 0102
5	5	16	Fragile	*Yes*...Atlantic 7211
6	7	13	Paul Simon	*Paul Simon*...Columbia 30750
7	9	6	Smokin'	*Humble Pie*...A&M 4342
8	6	23	Nilsson Schmilsson	*Nilsson*...RCA 4515
9	10	57	Tapestry	*Carole King*...Ode 77009
10	16	3	Graham Nash/David Crosby	*Graham Nash/David Crosby*...Atlantic 7220

TW	LW	WK	Billboard. MAY 13, 1972 TOP LP's	
1	1	14	**First Take**	*Roberta Flack*...Atlantic 8230
2	2	11	Harvest	*Neil Young*...Reprise 2032
3	3	13	America	*America*...Warner 2576
4	5	17	**Fragile**	*Yes*...Atlantic 7211
5	10	4	Graham Nash/David Crosby	*Graham Nash/David Crosby*...Atlantic 7220
6	7	7	**Smokin'**	*Humble Pie*...A&M 4342
7	4	9	Eat A Peach	*The Allman Brothers Band*...Capricorn 0102
8	17	3	Manassas	*Stephen Stills*...Atlantic 903
9	9	58	Tapestry	*Carole King*...Ode 77009
10	6	14	Paul Simon	*Paul Simon*...Columbia 30750

TW	LW	WK	Billboard. MAY 20, 1972	TOP LP's
①	1	15	**First Take**	*Roberta Flack*...Atlantic 8230
②	2	12	Harvest	*Neil Young*...Reprise 2032
③	3	14	America	*America*...Warner 2576
❹	5	5	**Graham Nash/David Crosby**	*Graham Nash/David Crosby*...Atlantic 7220
❺	8	4	Manassas	*Stephen Stills*...Atlantic 903
⑥	7	10	Eat A Peach	*The Allman Brothers Band*...Capricorn 0102
⑦	4	18	Fragile	*Yes*...Atlantic 7211
⑧	9	59	Tapestry	*Carole King*...Ode 77009
⑨	6	8	Smokin'	*Humble Pie*...A&M 4342
⑩	12	15	Let's Stay Together	*Al Green*...Hi 32070

TW	LW	WK	Billboard. MAY 27, 1972	TOP LP's
①	1	16	**First Take**	*Roberta Flack*...Atlantic 8230
❷	13	2	Thick As A Brick	*Jethro Tull*...Reprise 2072
③	2	13	Harvest	*Neil Young*...Reprise 2032
④	4	6	**Graham Nash/David Crosby**	*Graham Nash/David Crosby*...Atlantic 7220
⑤	5	5	Manassas	*Stephen Stills*...Atlantic 903
⑥	6	11	Eat A Peach	*The Allman Brothers Band*...Capricorn 0102
⑦	7	19	Fragile	*Yes*...Atlantic 7211
⑧	3	15	America	*America*...Warner 2576
⑨	8	60	Tapestry	*Carole King*...Ode 77009
⑩	11	17	Baby I'm-A Want You	*Bread*...Elektra 75015

TW	LW	WK	Billboard. JUNE 3, 1972	TOP LP's
❶	2	3	**Thick As A Brick**	*Jethro Tull*...Reprise 2072
②	1	17	First Take	*Roberta Flack*...Atlantic 8230
③	3	14	Harvest	*Neil Young*...Reprise 2032
④	4	7	**Graham Nash/David Crosby**	*Graham Nash/David Crosby*...Atlantic 7220
⑤	5	6	Manassas	*Stephen Stills*...Atlantic 903
❻	13	4	Joplin In Concert	*Janis Joplin*...Columbia 31160
❼	11	6	A Lonely Man	*The Chi-Lites*...Brunswick 754179
⑧	6	12	Eat A Peach	*The Allman Brothers Band*...Capricorn 0102
⑨	8	16	America	*America*...Warner 2576
❿	14	8	History Of Eric Clapton	*Eric Clapton*...Atco 803

TW	LW	WK	Billboard. JUNE 10, 1972	TOP LP's
①	1	4	**Thick As A Brick**	*Jethro Tull*...Reprise 2072
②	2	18	First Take	*Roberta Flack*...Atlantic 8230
③	3	15	Harvest	*Neil Young*...Reprise 2032
④	5	7	**Manassas**	*Stephen Stills*...Atlantic 903
⑤	6	5	Joplin In Concert	*Janis Joplin*...Columbia 31160
⑥	4	8	Graham Nash/David Crosby	*Graham Nash/David Crosby*...Atlantic 7220
⑦	7	7	A Lonely Man	*The Chi-Lites*...Brunswick 754179
❽	10	9	History Of Eric Clapton	*Eric Clapton*...Atco 803
❾	11	5	Roberta Flack & Donny Hathaway	*Roberta Flack & Donny Hathaway*...Atlantic 7216
❿	-	1	Exile On Main St.	*The Rolling Stones*...Rolling Stones 2900

TW	LW	WK	Billboard® JUNE 17, 1972 TOP LP's
1	10	2	**Exile On Main St.** ... *The Rolling Stones*...Rolling Stones 2900
2	1	5	Thick As A Brick ... *Jethro Tull*...Reprise 2072
3	2	19	First Take ... *Roberta Flack*...Atlantic 8230
4	4	8	**Manassas** ... *Stephen Stills*...Atlantic 903
5	5	6	Joplin In Concert ... *Janis Joplin*...Columbia 31160
6	7	8	A Lonely Man ... *The Chi-Lites*...Brunswick 754179
7	8	10	History Of Eric Clapton ... *Eric Clapton*...Atco 803
8	9	6	Roberta Flack & Donny Hathaway ... *Roberta Flack & Donny Hathaway*...Atlantic 7216
9	3	16	Harvest ... *Neil Young*...Reprise 2032
10	6	9	Graham Nash/David Crosby ... *Graham Nash/David Crosby*...Atlantic 7220

TW	LW	WK	Billboard® JUNE 24, 1972 TOP LP's
1	1	3	**Exile On Main St.** ... *The Rolling Stones*...Rolling Stones 2900
2	2	6	Thick As A Brick ... *Jethro Tull*...Reprise 2072
3	3	20	First Take ... *Roberta Flack*...Atlantic 8230
4	5	7	**Joplin In Concert** ... *Janis Joplin*...Columbia 31160
5	6	9	**A Lonely Man** ... *The Chi-Lites*...Brunswick 754179
6	8	7	Roberta Flack & Donny Hathaway ... *Roberta Flack & Donny Hathaway*...Atlantic 7216
7	7	11	History Of Eric Clapton ... *Eric Clapton*...Atco 803
8	4	9	Manassas ... *Stephen Stills*...Atlantic 903
9	9	17	Harvest ... *Neil Young*...Reprise 2032
10	12	7	Procol Harum Live In Concert with the Edmonton Symphony Orchestra ... *Procol Harum*...A&M 4335

TW	LW	WK	Billboard® JULY 1, 1972 TOP LP's
1	1	4	**Exile On Main St.** ... *The Rolling Stones*...Rolling Stones 2900
2	2	7	Thick As A Brick ... *Jethro Tull*...Reprise 2072
3	3	21	First Take ... *Roberta Flack*...Atlantic 8230
4	4	8	**Joplin In Concert** ... *Janis Joplin*...Columbia 31160
5	6	8	Roberta Flack & Donny Hathaway ... *Roberta Flack & Donny Hathaway*...Atlantic 7216
6	7	12	**History Of Eric Clapton** ... *Eric Clapton*...Atco 803
7	37	3	Honky Chateau ... *Elton John*...Uni 93135
8	11	6	Portrait Of Donny ... *Donny Osmond*...MGM 4820
9	10	8	Procol Harum Live In Concert with the Edmonton Symphony Orchestra ... *Procol Harum*...A&M 4335
10	5	10	A Lonely Man ... *The Chi-Lites*...Brunswick 754179

Billboard — JULY 8, 1972 — TOP LP's

TW	LW	WK	Title	Artist	Label
①	1	5	**Exile On Main St.**	*The Rolling Stones*	Rolling Stones 2900
②	2	8	Thick As A Brick	*Jethro Tull*	Reprise 2072
❸	7	4	Honky Chateau	*Elton John*	Uni 93135
④	5	9	Roberta Flack & Donny Hathaway	*Roberta Flack & Donny Hathaway*	Atlantic 7216
⑤	4	9	Joplin In Concert	*Janis Joplin*	Columbia 31160
⑥	6	13	**History Of Eric Clapton**	*Eric Clapton*	Atco 803
⑦	8	7	Portrait Of Donny	*Donny Osmond*	MGM 4820
⑧	9	9	Procol Harum Live In Concert with the Edmonton Symphony Orchestra	*Procol Harum*	A&M 4335
⑨	3	22	First Take	*Roberta Flack*	Atlantic 8230
⑩	10	11	A Lonely Man	*The Chi-Lites*	Brunswick 754179

Billboard — JULY 15, 1972 — TOP LP's

TW	LW	WK	Title	Artist	Label
❶	3	5	**Honky Chateau**	*Elton John*	Uni 93135
②	1	6	Exile On Main St.	*The Rolling Stones*	Rolling Stones 2900
③	4	10	**Roberta Flack & Donny Hathaway**	*Roberta Flack & Donny Hathaway*	Atlantic 7216
④	2	9	Thick As A Brick	*Jethro Tull*	Reprise 2072
⑤	5	10	Joplin In Concert	*Janis Joplin*	Columbia 31160
⑥	8	10	Procol Harum Live In Concert with the Edmonton Symphony Orchestra	*Procol Harum*	A&M 4335
⑦	7	8	Portrait Of Donny	*Donny Osmond*	MGM 4820
❽	16	5	Amazing Grace	*Aretha Franklin*	Atlantic 906
❾	14	9	Still Bill	*Bill Withers*	Sussex 7014
⑩	11	7	Lookin' Through The Windows	*The Jackson 5*	Motown 750

Billboard — JULY 22, 1972 — TOP LP's

TW	LW	WK	Title	Artist	Label
①	1	6	**Honky Chateau**	*Elton John*	Uni 93135
②	2	7	Exile On Main St.	*The Rolling Stones*	Rolling Stones 2900
③	3	11	**Roberta Flack & Donny Hathaway**	*Roberta Flack & Donny Hathaway*	Atlantic 7216
❹	9	10	**Still Bill**	*Bill Withers*	Sussex 7014
⑤	6	11	**Procol Harum Live In Concert with the Edmonton Symphony Orchestra**	*Procol Harum*	A&M 4335
⑥	7	9	**Portrait Of Donny**	*Donny Osmond*	MGM 4820
⑦	8	6	**Amazing Grace**	*Aretha Franklin*	Atlantic 906
⑧	5	11	Joplin In Concert	*Janis Joplin*	Columbia 31160
⑨	10	8	Lookin' Through The Windows	*The Jackson 5*	Motown 750
⑩	4	10	Thick As A Brick	*Jethro Tull*	Reprise 2072

Billboard — JULY 29, 1972 — TOP LP's

TW	LW	WK	Title	Artist...Label
1	1	7	**Honky Chateau**	*Elton John*...Uni 93135
2	14	5	**School's Out**	*Alice Cooper*...Warner 2623
3	2	8	Exile On Main St.	*The Rolling Stones*...Rolling Stones 2900
4	4	11	**Still Bill**	*Bill Withers*...Sussex 7014
5	12	5	**Simon And Garfunkel's Greatest Hits**	*Simon & Garfunkel*...Columbia 31350
6	3	12	Roberta Flack & Donny Hathaway	*Roberta Flack & Donny Hathaway*...Atlantic 7216
7	11	4	A Song For You	*Carpenters*...A&M 3511
8	9	9	Lookin' Through The Windows	*The Jackson 5*...Motown 750
9	7	7	Amazing Grace	*Aretha Franklin*...Atlantic 906
10	10	11	Thick As A Brick	*Jethro Tull*...Reprise 2072

Billboard — AUGUST 5, 1972 — TOP LP's

TW	LW	WK	Title	Artist...Label
1	1	8	**Honky Chateau**	*Elton John*...Uni 93135
2	2	6	**School's Out**	*Alice Cooper*...Warner 2623
3	3	9	Exile On Main St.	*The Rolling Stones*...Rolling Stones 2900
4	4	12	**Still Bill**	*Bill Withers*...Sussex 7014
5	5	6	**Simon And Garfunkel's Greatest Hits**	*Simon & Garfunkel*...Columbia 31350
6	7	5	A Song For You	*Carpenters*...A&M 3511
7	8	10	**Lookin' Through The Windows**	*The Jackson 5*...Motown 750
8	11	6	Big Bambu	*Cheech & Chong*...Ode 77014
9	39	2	Chicago V	*Chicago*...Columbia 31102
10	14	4	Moods	*Neil Diamond*...Uni 93136

Billboard — AUGUST 12, 1972 — TOP LP's

TW	LW	WK	Title	Artist...Label
1	1	9	**Honky Chateau**	*Elton John*...Uni 93135
2	2	7	**School's Out**	*Alice Cooper*...Warner 2623
3	9	3	Chicago V	*Chicago*...Columbia 31102
4	6	6	**A Song For You**	*Carpenters*...A&M 3511
5	5	7	**Simon And Garfunkel's Greatest Hits**	*Simon & Garfunkel*...Columbia 31350
6	3	10	Exile On Main St.	*The Rolling Stones*...Rolling Stones 2900
7	8	7	Big Bambu	*Cheech & Chong*...Ode 77014
8	10	5	Moods	*Neil Diamond*...Uni 93136
9	7	11	Lookin' Through The Windows	*The Jackson 5*...Motown 750
10	14	6	Carlos Santana & Buddy Miles! Live!	*Carlos Santana & Buddy Miles*...Columbia 31308

TW	LW	WK	Billboard. AUGUST 19, 1972 TOP LP's
1	3	4	**Chicago V**......*Chicago*...Columbia 31102
2	1	10	Honky Chateau......*Elton John*...Uni 93135
3	2	8	School's Out......*Alice Cooper*...Warner 2623
4	4	7	**A Song For You**......*Carpenters*...A&M 3511
5	5	8	**Simon And Garfunkel's Greatest Hits**......*Simon & Garfunkel*...Columbia 31350
6	7	8	Big Bambu......*Cheech & Chong*...Ode 77014
7	6	11	Exile On Main St. ......*The Rolling Stones*...Rolling Stones 2900
8	8	6	Moods......*Neil Diamond*...Uni 93136
9	10	7	Carlos Santana & Buddy Miles! Live!......*Carlos Santana & Buddy Miles*...Columbia 31308
10	12	4	Trilogy......*Emerson, Lake & Palmer*...Cotillion 9903

TW	LW	WK	Billboard. AUGUST 26, 1972 TOP LP's
1	1	5	**Chicago V**......*Chicago*...Columbia 31102
2	2	11	Honky Chateau......*Elton John*...Uni 93135
3	3	9	School's Out......*Alice Cooper*...Warner 2623
4	4	8	**A Song For You**......*Carpenters*...A&M 3511
5	6	9	Big Bambu......*Cheech & Chong*...Ode 77014
6	5	9	Simon And Garfunkel's Greatest Hits ..... *Simon & Garfunkel*...Columbia 31350
7	8	7	Moods......*Neil Diamond*...Uni 93136
8	11	3	Never A Dull Moment......*Rod Stewart*...Mercury 646
9	9	8	Carlos Santana & Buddy Miles! Live!......*Carlos Santana & Buddy Miles*...Columbia 31308
10	10	5	Trilogy......*Emerson, Lake & Palmer*...Cotillion 9903

TW	LW	WK	Billboard. SEPTEMBER 2, 1972 TOP LP's
1	1	6	**Chicago V**......*Chicago*...Columbia 31102
2	2	12	Honky Chateau......*Elton John*...Uni 93135
3	5	10	Big Bambu......*Cheech & Chong*...Ode 77014
4	8	4	Never A Dull Moment......*Rod Stewart*...Mercury 646
5	3	10	School's Out......*Alice Cooper*...Warner 2623
6	7	8	Moods......*Neil Diamond*...Uni 93136
7	6	10	Simon And Garfunkel's Greatest Hits ..... *Simon & Garfunkel*...Columbia 31350
8	9	9	**Carlos Santana & Buddy Miles! Live!**......*Carlos Santana & Buddy Miles*...Columbia 31308
9	10	6	Trilogy......*Emerson, Lake & Palmer*...Cotillion 9903
10	11	8	Carney......*Leon Russell*...Shelter 8911

TW	LW	WK	Billboard® SEPTEMBER 9, 1972 TOP LP's		
1	1	7	**Chicago V**	*Chicago*	Columbia 31102
2	4	5	**Never A Dull Moment**	*Rod Stewart*	Mercury 646
3	3	11	Big Bambu	*Cheech & Chong*	Ode 77014
4	2	13	Honky Chateau	*Elton John*	Uni 93135
5	6	9	**Moods**	*Neil Diamond*	Uni 93136
6	10	9	Carney	*Leon Russell*	Shelter 8911
7	9	7	Trilogy	*Emerson, Lake & Palmer*	Cotillion 9903
8	8	10	**Carlos Santana & Buddy Miles! Live!**	*Carlos Santana & Buddy Miles*	Columbia 31308
9	11	7	Seven Separate Fools	*Three Dog Night*	Dunhill/ABC 50118
10	7	11	Simon And Garfunkel's Greatest Hits	*Simon & Garfunkel*	Columbia 31350

TW	LW	WK	Billboard® SEPTEMBER 16, 1972 TOP LP's		
1	1	8	**Chicago V**	*Chicago*	Columbia 31102
2	2	6	**Never A Dull Moment**	*Rod Stewart*	Mercury 646
3	3	12	Big Bambu	*Cheech & Chong*	Ode 77014
4	6	10	Carney	*Leon Russell*	Shelter 8911
5	5	10	**Moods**	*Neil Diamond*	Uni 93136
6	7	8	Trilogy	*Emerson, Lake & Palmer*	Cotillion 9903
7	9	8	Seven Separate Fools	*Three Dog Night*	Dunhill/ABC 50118
8	8	11	**Carlos Santana & Buddy Miles! Live!**	*Carlos Santana & Buddy Miles*	Columbia 31308
9	4	14	Honky Chateau	*Elton John*	Uni 93135
10	12	6	Gilbert O'Sullivan-Himself	*Gilbert O'Sullivan*	MAM 4

TW	LW	WK	Billboard® SEPTEMBER 23, 1972 TOP LP's		
1	1	9	**Chicago V**	*Chicago*	Columbia 31102
2	2	7	**Never A Dull Moment**	*Rod Stewart*	Mercury 646
3	3	13	Big Bambu	*Cheech & Chong*	Ode 77014
4	4	11	Carney	*Leon Russell*	Shelter 8911
5	5	11	**Moods**	*Neil Diamond*	Uni 93136
6	6	9	Trilogy	*Emerson, Lake & Palmer*	Cotillion 9903
7	7	9	Seven Separate Fools	*Three Dog Night*	Dunhill/ABC 50118
8	9	15	Honky Chateau	*Elton John*	Uni 93135
9	8	12	Carlos Santana & Buddy Miles! Live!	*Carlos Santana & Buddy Miles*	Columbia 31308
10	10	7	Gilbert O'Sullivan-Himself	*Gilbert O'Sullivan*	MAM 4

TW	LW	WK	Billboard® SEPTEMBER 30, 1972 TOP LP's		
1	1	10	**Chicago V**	*Chicago*	Columbia 31102
2	3	14	**Big Bambu**	*Cheech & Chong*	Ode 77014
3	2	8	Never A Dull Moment	*Rod Stewart*	Mercury 646
4	4	12	Carney	*Leon Russell*	Shelter 8911
5	6	10	**Trilogy**	*Emerson, Lake & Palmer*	Cotillion 9903
6	7	10	**Seven Separate Fools**	*Three Dog Night*	Dunhill/ABC 50118
7	5	12	Moods	*Neil Diamond*	Uni 93136
8	8	16	Honky Chateau	*Elton John*	Uni 93135
9	10	8	**Gilbert O'Sullivan-Himself**	*Gilbert O'Sullivan*	MAM 4
10	9	13	Carlos Santana & Buddy Miles! Live!	*Carlos Santana & Buddy Miles*	Columbia 31308

TW	LW	WK	Billboard. OCTOBER 7, 1972 TOP LP's
①	1	11	**Chicago V**..........*Chicago*...Columbia 31102
②	4	13	**Carney**..........*Leon Russell*...Shelter 8911
③	3	9	Never A Dull Moment..........*Rod Stewart*...Mercury 646
④	2	15	Big Bambu..........*Cheech & Chong*...Ode 77014
⑤	8	17	Honky Chateau..........*Elton John*...Uni 93135
⑥	6	11	**Seven Separate Fools**..........*Three Dog Night*...Dunhill/ABC 50118
⑦	7	13	Moods..........*Neil Diamond*...Uni 93136
❽	16	7	Superfly..........*Curtis Mayfield/Soundtrack*...Curtom 8014
⑨	9	9	**Gilbert O'Sullivan-Himself**..........*Gilbert O'Sullivan*...MAM 4
❿	14	18	The London Chuck Berry Sessions..........*Chuck Berry*...Chess 60020

TW	LW	WK	Billboard. OCTOBER 14, 1972 TOP LP's
①	1	12	**Chicago V**..........*Chicago*...Columbia 31102
②	2	14	**Carney**..........*Leon Russell*...Shelter 8911
③	3	10	Never A Dull Moment..........*Rod Stewart*...Mercury 646
④	5	18	Honky Chateau..........*Elton John*...Uni 93135
⑤	4	16	Big Bambu..........*Cheech & Chong*...Ode 77014
❻	8	8	Superfly..........*Curtis Mayfield/Soundtrack*...Curtom 8014
❼	14	57	Days Of Future Passed..........*The Moody Blues*...Deram 18012
⑧	6	12	Seven Separate Fools..........*Three Dog Night*...Dunhill/ABC 50118
⑨	10	19	The London Chuck Berry Sessions..........*Chuck Berry*...Chess 60020
⑩	7	14	Moods..........*Neil Diamond*...Uni 93136

TW	LW	WK	Billboard. OCTOBER 21, 1972 TOP LP's
❶	6	9	**Superfly**..........*Curtis Mayfield/Soundtrack*...Curtom 8014
②	2	15	**Carney**..........*Leon Russell*...Shelter 8911
❸	7	58	**Days Of Future Passed**..........*The Moody Blues*...Deram 18012
④	3	11	Never A Dull Moment..........*Rod Stewart*...Mercury 646
⑤	1	13	Chicago V..........*Chicago*...Columbia 31102
⑥	4	19	Honky Chateau..........*Elton John*...Uni 93135
⑦	5	17	Big Bambu..........*Cheech & Chong*...Ode 77014
❽	13	10	All Directions..........*The Temptations*...Gordy 962
⑨	9	20	The London Chuck Berry Sessions..........*Chuck Berry*...Chess 60020
❿	12	7	Rock Of Ages..........*The Band*...Capitol 11045

TW	LW	WK	Billboard. OCTOBER 28, 1972 TOP LP's
①	1	10	**Superfly**..........*Curtis Mayfield/Soundtrack*...Curtom 8014
②	2	16	**Carney**..........*Leon Russell*...Shelter 8911
③	3	59	**Days Of Future Passed**..........*The Moody Blues*...Deram 18012
④	4	12	Never A Dull Moment..........*Rod Stewart*...Mercury 646
⑤	5	14	Chicago V..........*Chicago*...Columbia 31102
❻	8	11	All Directions..........*The Temptations*...Gordy 962
❼	10	8	Rock Of Ages..........*The Band*...Capitol 11045
⑧	9	21	**The London Chuck Berry Sessions**..........*Chuck Berry*...Chess 60020
⑨	6	20	Honky Chateau..........*Elton John*...Uni 93135
❿	13	10	Ben..........*Michael Jackson*...Motown 755

Billboard — NOVEMBER 4, 1972 — TOP LP's

TW	LW	WK	Title	Artist	Label
1	1	11	**Superfly**	*Curtis Mayfield/Soundtrack*	Curtom 8014
2	21	4	Catch Bull At Four	*Cat Stevens*	A&M 4365
3	3	60	**Days Of Future Passed**	*The Moody Blues*	Deram 18012
4	4	13	Never A Dull Moment	*Rod Stewart*	Mercury 646
5	6	12	All Directions	*The Temptations*	Gordy 962
6	2	17	Carney	*Leon Russell*	Shelter 8911
7	7	9	Rock Of Ages	*The Band*	Capitol 11045
8	8	22	**The London Chuck Berry Sessions**	*Chuck Berry*	Chess 60020
9	10	11	Ben	*Michael Jackson*	Motown 755
10	11	9	**Back Stabbers**	*O'Jays*	Philadelphia I. 31712

Billboard — NOVEMBER 11, 1972 — TOP LP's

TW	LW	WK	Title	Artist	Label
1	1	12	**Superfly**	*Curtis Mayfield/Soundtrack*	Curtom 8014
2	2	5	Catch Bull At Four	*Cat Stevens*	A&M 4365
3	3	61	**Days Of Future Passed**	*The Moody Blues*	Deram 18012
4	5	13	All Directions	*The Temptations*	Gordy 962
5	9	12	**Ben**	*Michael Jackson*	Motown 755
6	7	10	**Rock Of Ages**	*The Band*	Capitol 11045
7	11	6	Close To The Edge	*Yes*	Atlantic 7244
8	8	23	**The London Chuck Berry Sessions**	*Chuck Berry*	Chess 60020
9	4	14	Never A Dull Moment	*Rod Stewart*	Mercury 646
10	10	10	**Back Stabbers**	*O'Jays*	Philadelphia I. 31712

Billboard — NOVEMBER 18, 1972 — TOP LP's

TW	LW	WK	Title	Artist	Label
1	2	6	**Catch Bull At Four**	*Cat Stevens*	A&M 4365
2	1	13	Superfly	*Curtis Mayfield/Soundtrack*	Curtom 8014
3	3	62	**Days Of Future Passed**	*The Moody Blues*	Deram 18012
4	4	14	All Directions	*The Temptations*	Gordy 962
5	5	13	**Ben**	*Michael Jackson*	Motown 755
6	6	11	**Rock Of Ages**	*The Band*	Capitol 11045
7	7	7	Close To The Edge	*Yes*	Atlantic 7244
8	20	3	Rhymes & Reasons	*Carole King*	Ode 77016
9	9	15	Never A Dull Moment	*Rod Stewart*	Mercury 646
10	8	24	The London Chuck Berry Sessions	*Chuck Berry*	Chess 60020

Billboard — NOVEMBER 25, 1972 — TOP LP's

TW	LW	WK	Title	Artist	Label
1	1	7	**Catch Bull At Four**	*Cat Stevens*	A&M 4365
2	2	14	Superfly	*Curtis Mayfield/Soundtrack*	Curtom 8014
3	4	15	All Directions	*The Temptations*	Gordy 962
4	7	8	Close To The Edge	*Yes*	Atlantic 7244
5	5	14	**Ben**	*Michael Jackson*	Motown 755
6	8	4	Rhymes & Reasons	*Carole King*	Ode 77016
7	6	12	Rock Of Ages	*The Band*	Capitol 11045
8	11	7	Phoenix	*Grand Funk Railroad*	Capitol 11099
9	19	4	Caravanserai	*Santana*	Columbia 31610
10	9	16	Never A Dull Moment	*Rod Stewart*	Mercury 646

TW	LW	WK	Billboard — DECEMBER 2, 1972 — TOP LP's
①	1	8	**Catch Bull At Four** ... *Cat Stevens*...A&M 4365
②	3	16	**All Directions** ... *The Temptations*...Gordy 962
③	4	9	**Close To The Edge** ... *Yes*...Atlantic 7244
❹	6	5	Rhymes & Reasons ... *Carole King*...Ode 77016
❺	12	3	Seventh Sojourn ... *The Moody Blues*...Threshold 7
⑥	2	15	Superfly ... *Curtis Mayfield/Soundtrack*...Curtom 8014
⑦	8	8	**Phoenix** ... *Grand Funk Railroad*...Capitol 11099
⑧	9	5	**Caravanserai** ... *Santana*...Columbia 31610
⑨	5	15	Ben ... *Michael Jackson*...Motown 755
⑩	7	13	Rock Of Ages ... *The Band*...Capitol 11045

TW	LW	WK	Billboard — DECEMBER 9, 1972 — TOP LP's
❶	5	4	**Seventh Sojourn** ... *The Moody Blues*...Threshold 7
②	2	17	**All Directions** ... *The Temptations*...Gordy 962
❸	4	6	Rhymes & Reasons ... *Carole King*...Ode 77016
④	1	9	Catch Bull At Four ... *Cat Stevens*...A&M 4365
⑤	3	10	Close To The Edge ... *Yes*...Atlantic 7244
⑥	6	16	Superfly ... *Curtis Mayfield/Soundtrack*...Curtom 8014
⑦	7	9	**Phoenix** ... *Grand Funk Railroad*...Capitol 11099
⑧	8	6	**Caravanserai** ... *Santana*...Columbia 31610
❾	12	8	I'm Still In Love With You ... *Al Green*...Hi 32074
❿	13	15	Summer Breeze ... *Seals & Crofts*...Warner 2629

TW	LW	WK	Billboard — DECEMBER 16, 1972 — TOP LP's
①	1	5	**Seventh Sojourn** ... *The Moody Blues*...Threshold 7
②	3	7	**Rhymes & Reasons** ... *Carole King*...Ode 77016
③	2	18	All Directions ... *The Temptations*...Gordy 962
④	4	10	Catch Bull At Four ... *Cat Stevens*...A&M 4365
❺	12	6	Living In The Past ... *Jethro Tull*...Chrysalis 1035
⑥	5	11	Close To The Edge ... *Yes*...Atlantic 7244
❼	9	9	I'm Still In Love With You ... *Al Green*...Hi 32074
❽	10	16	Summer Breeze ... *Seals & Crofts*...Warner 2629
⑨	6	17	Superfly ... *Curtis Mayfield/Soundtrack*...Curtom 8014
⑩	8	7	Caravanserai ... *Santana*...Columbia 31610

TW	LW	WK	Billboard — DECEMBER 23, 1972 — TOP LP's
①	1	6	**Seventh Sojourn** ... *The Moody Blues*...Threshold 7
②	2	8	**Rhymes & Reasons** ... *Carole King*...Ode 77016
❸	5	7	**Living In The Past** ... *Jethro Tull*...Chrysalis 1035
④	4	11	Catch Bull At Four ... *Cat Stevens*...A&M 4365
⑤	3	19	All Directions ... *The Temptations*...Gordy 962
❻	7	10	I'm Still In Love With You ... *Al Green*...Hi 32074
❼	8	17	**Summer Breeze** ... *Seals & Crofts*...Warner 2629
❽	16	5	One Man Dog ... *James Taylor*...Warner 2660
⑨	6	12	Close To The Edge ... *Yes*...Atlantic 7244
⑩	10	8	Caravanserai ... *Santana*...Columbia 31610

TW	LW	WK	Billboard. DECEMBER 30, 1972	TOP LP's
①	1	7	**Seventh Sojourn**	*The Moody Blues*...Threshold 7
②	2	9	**Rhymes & Reasons**	*Carole King*...Ode 77016
③	3	8	**Living In The Past**	*Jethro Tull*...Chrysalis 1035
❹	6	11	**I'm Still In Love With You**	*Al Green*...Hi 32074
❺	8	6	One Man Dog	*James Taylor*...Warner 2660
⑥	4	12	Catch Bull At Four	*Cat Stevens*...A&M 4365
⑦	7	18	**Summer Breeze**	*Seals & Crofts*...Warner 2629
⑧	5	20	All Directions	*The Temptations*...Gordy 962
⑨	10	9	Caravanserai	*Santana*...Columbia 31610
⑩	11	16	Rocky Mountain High	*John Denver*...RCA 4731

Billboard — JANUARY 6, 1973 — TOP LP's

TW	LW	WK	Title	Artist	Label
1	1	8	**Seventh Sojourn**	*The Moody Blues*	Threshold 7
2	2	10	**Rhymes & Reasons**	*Carole King*	Ode 77016
3	3	9	**Living In The Past**	*Jethro Tull*	Chrysalis 1035
4	4	12	**I'm Still In Love With You**	*Al Green*	Hi 32074
5	5	7	One Man Dog	*James Taylor*	Warner 2660
6	12	5	No Secrets	*Carly Simon*	Elektra 75049
7	7	19	**Summer Breeze**	*Seals & Crofts*	Warner 2629
8	6	13	Catch Bull At Four	*Cat Stevens*	A&M 4365
9	11	6	**Homecoming**	*America*	Warner 2655
10	10	17	Rocky Mountain High	*John Denver*	RCA 4731

Billboard — JANUARY 13, 1973 — TOP LP's

TW	LW	WK	Title	Artist	Label
1	6	6	**No Secrets**	*Carly Simon*	Elektra 75049
2	1	9	Seventh Sojourn	*The Moody Blues*	Threshold 7
3	2	11	Rhymes & Reasons	*Carole King*	Ode 77016
4	5	8	**One Man Dog**	*James Taylor*	Warner 2660
5	3	10	Living In The Past	*Jethro Tull*	Chrysalis 1035
6	11	9	The World Is A Ghetto	*War*	United Artists 5652
7	4	13	I'm Still In Love With You	*Al Green*	Hi 32074
8	8	14	Catch Bull At Four	*Cat Stevens*	A&M 4365
9	9	7	**Homecoming**	*America*	Warner 2655
10	13	6	Tommy	*London Symphony Orchestra & Chambre Choir*	Ode 99001

Billboard — JANUARY 20, 1973 — TOP LP's

TW	LW	WK	Title	Artist	Label
1	1	7	**No Secrets**	*Carly Simon*	Elektra 75049
2	3	12	**Rhymes & Reasons**	*Carole King*	Ode 77016
3	6	10	The World Is A Ghetto	*War*	United Artists 5652
4	4	9	**One Man Dog**	*James Taylor*	Warner 2660
5	5	11	Living In The Past	*Jethro Tull*	Chrysalis 1035
6	2	10	Seventh Sojourn	*The Moody Blues*	Threshold 7
7	10	7	Tommy	*London Symphony Orchestra & Chambre Choir*	Ode 99001
8	8	15	Catch Bull At Four	*Cat Stevens*	A&M 4365
9	9	8	**Homecoming**	*America*	Warner 2655
10	12	7	Hot August Night	*Neil Diamond*	MCA 8000

Billboard — JANUARY 27, 1973 — TOP LP's

TW	LW	WK	Title	Artist	Label
1	1	8	**No Secrets**	*Carly Simon*	Elektra 75049
2	3	11	The World Is A Ghetto	*War*	United Artists 5652
3	2	13	Rhymes & Reasons	*Carole King*	Ode 77016
4	11	11	Talking Book	*Stevie Wonder*	Tamla 319
5	7	8	**Tommy**	*London Symphony Orchestra & Chambre Choir*	Ode 99001
6	5	12	Living In The Past	*Jethro Tull*	Chrysalis 1035
7	4	10	One Man Dog	*James Taylor*	Warner 2660
8	10	8	Hot August Night	*Neil Diamond*	MCA 8000
9	9	9	**Homecoming**	*America*	Warner 2655
10	6	11	Seventh Sojourn	*The Moody Blues*	Threshold 7

Billboard — FEBRUARY 3, 1973 — TOP LP's

TW	LW	WK	Title	Artist...Label
1	1	9	**No Secrets**	*Carly Simon*...Elektra 75049
2	2	12	The World Is A Ghetto	*War*...United Artists 5652
3	4	12	**Talking Book**	*Stevie Wonder*...Tamla 319
4	3	14	Rhymes & Reasons	*Carole King*...Ode 77016
5	5	9	**Tommy**	*London Symphony Orchestra & Chambre Choir*...Ode 99001
6	8	9	Hot August Night	*Neil Diamond*...MCA 8000
7	6	13	Living In The Past	*Jethro Tull*...Chrysalis 1035
8	7	11	One Man Dog	*James Taylor*...Warner 2660
9	10	12	Seventh Sojourn	*The Moody Blues*...Threshold 7
10	14	11	Lady Sings The Blues	*Diana Ross/Soundtrack*...Motown 758

Billboard — FEBRUARY 10, 1973 — TOP LP's

TW	LW	WK	Title	Artist...Label
1	1	10	**No Secrets**	*Carly Simon*...Elektra 75049
2	2	13	The World Is A Ghetto	*War*...United Artists 5652
3	3	13	**Talking Book**	*Stevie Wonder*...Tamla 319
4	4	15	Rhymes & Reasons	*Carole King*...Ode 77016
5	5	10	**Tommy**	*London Symphony Orchestra & Chambre Choir*...Ode 99001
6	6	10	Hot August Night	*Neil Diamond*...MCA 8000
7	7	14	Living In The Past	*Jethro Tull*...Chrysalis 1035
8	9	13	Seventh Sojourn	*The Moody Blues*...Threshold 7
9	10	12	Lady Sings The Blues	*Diana Ross/Soundtrack*...Motown 758
10	13	7	More Hot Rocks (big hits & fazed cookies)	*The Rolling Stones*...London 626/7

Billboard — FEBRUARY 17, 1973 — TOP LP's

TW	LW	WK	Title	Artist...Label
1	2	14	**The World Is A Ghetto**	*War*...United Artists 5652
2	1	11	No Secrets	*Carly Simon*...Elektra 75049
3	3	14	**Talking Book**	*Stevie Wonder*...Tamla 319
4	4	16	Rhymes & Reasons	*Carole King*...Ode 77016
5	6	11	**Hot August Night**	*Neil Diamond*...MCA 8000
6	5	11	Tommy	*London Symphony Orchestra & Chambre Choir*...Ode 99001
7	7	15	Living In The Past	*Jethro Tull*...Chrysalis 1035
8	9	13	Lady Sings The Blues	*Diana Ross/Soundtrack*...Motown 758
9	10	8	**More Hot Rocks (big hits & fazed cookies)**	*The Rolling Stones*...London 626/7
10	8	14	Seventh Sojourn	*The Moody Blues*...Threshold 7

Billboard — FEBRUARY 24, 1973 — TOP LP's

TW	LW	WK	Title	Artist...Label
1	1	15	**The World Is A Ghetto**	*War*...United Artists 5652
2	2	12	No Secrets	*Carly Simon*...Elektra 75049
3	13	3	Don't Shoot Me I'm Only The Piano Player	*Elton John*...MCA 2100
4	3	15	Talking Book	*Stevie Wonder*...Tamla 319
5	5	12	**Hot August Night**	*Neil Diamond*...MCA 8000
6	4	17	Rhymes & Reasons	*Carole King*...Ode 77016
7	8	14	Lady Sings The Blues	*Diana Ross/Soundtrack*...Motown 758
8	11	24	Rocky Mountain High	*John Denver*...RCA 4731
9	9	9	**More Hot Rocks (big hits & fazed cookies)**	*The Rolling Stones*...London 626/7
10	23	5	Dueling Banjos	*Eric Weissberg & Steve Mandell*...Warner 2683

TW	LW	WK	Billboard. MARCH 3, 1973 TOP LP's
1	3	4	**Don't Shoot Me I'm Only The Piano Player** ...... *Elton John*...MCA 2100
2	2	13	No Secrets .... *Carly Simon*...Elektra 75049
3	1	16	The World Is A Ghetto .... *War*...United Artists 5652
4	10	6	Dueling Banjos .... *Eric Weissberg & Steve Mandell*...Warner 2683
5	5	13	**Hot August Night** .... *Neil Diamond*...MCA 8000
6	8	25	Rocky Mountain High .... *John Denver*...RCA 4731
7	7	15	Lady Sings The Blues .... *Diana Ross/Soundtrack*...Motown 758
8	4	16	Talking Book .... *Stevie Wonder*...Tamla 319
9	9	10	**More Hot Rocks (big hits & fazed cookies)** .... *The Rolling Stones*...London 626/7
10	6	18	Rhymes & Reasons .... *Carole King*...Ode 77016

TW	LW	WK	Billboard. MARCH 10, 1973 TOP LP's
1	1	5	**Don't Shoot Me I'm Only The Piano Player** ...... *Elton John*...MCA 2100
2	4	7	Dueling Banjos .... *Eric Weissberg & Steve Mandell*...Warner 2683
3	2	14	No Secrets .... *Carly Simon*...Elektra 75049
4	6	26	**Rocky Mountain High** .... *John Denver*...RCA 4731
5	7	16	Lady Sings The Blues .... *Diana Ross/Soundtrack*...Motown 758
6	3	17	The World Is A Ghetto .... *War*...United Artists 5652
7	5	14	Hot August Night .... *Neil Diamond*...MCA 8000
8	11	6	Shoot Out At The Fantasy Factory .... *Traffic*...Island 9323
9	8	17	Talking Book .... *Stevie Wonder*...Tamla 319
10	9	11	More Hot Rocks (big hits & fazed cookies)... *The Rolling Stones*...London 626/7

TW	LW	WK	Billboard. MARCH 17, 1973 TOP LP's
1	2	8	**Dueling Banjos** .... *Eric Weissberg & Steve Mandell*...Warner 2683
2	1	6	Don't Shoot Me I'm Only The Piano Player .... *Elton John*...MCA 2100
3	5	17	Lady Sings The Blues .... *Diana Ross/Soundtrack*...Motown 758
4	4	27	**Rocky Mountain High** .... *John Denver*...RCA 4731
5	3	15	No Secrets .... *Carly Simon*...Elektra 75049
6	12	9	Prelude .... *Deodato*...CTI 6021
7	8	7	Shoot Out At The Fantasy Factory .... *Traffic*...Island 9323
8	6	18	The World Is A Ghetto .... *War*...United Artists 5652
9	9	18	Talking Book .... *Stevie Wonder*...Tamla 319
10	7	15	Hot August Night .... *Neil Diamond*...MCA 8000

TW	LW	WK	Billboard. MARCH 24, 1973 TOP LP's
1	1	9	**Dueling Banjos** .... *Eric Weissberg & Steve Mandell*...Warner 2683
2	2	7	Don't Shoot Me I'm Only The Piano Player .... *Elton John*...MCA 2100
3	3	18	Lady Sings The Blues .... *Diana Ross/Soundtrack*...Motown 758
4	4	28	**Rocky Mountain High** .... *John Denver*...RCA 4731
5	6	10	Prelude .... *Deodato*...CTI 6021
6	5	16	No Secrets .... *Carly Simon*...Elektra 75049
7	7	8	Shoot Out At The Fantasy Factory .... *Traffic*...Island 9323
8	8	19	The World Is A Ghetto .... *War*...United Artists 5652
9	11	16	**The Divine Miss M** .... *Bette Midler*...Atlantic 7238
10	9	19	Talking Book .... *Stevie Wonder*...Tamla 319

Billboard — MARCH 31, 1973 — TOP LP's

TW	LW	WK			
1	1	10	**Dueling Banjos**	*Eric Weissberg & Steve Mandell*	Warner 2683
2	2	8	Don't Shoot Me I'm Only The Piano Player	*Elton John*	MCA 2100
3	3	19	Lady Sings The Blues	*Diana Ross/Soundtrack*	Motown 758
4	5	11	Prelude	*Deodato*	CTI 6021
5	4	29	Rocky Mountain High	*John Denver*	RCA 4731
6	7	9	**Shoot Out At The Fantasy Factory**	*Traffic*	Island 9323
7	8	20	The World Is A Ghetto	*War*	United Artists 5652
8	6	17	No Secrets	*Carly Simon*	Elektra 75049
9	9	17	**The Divine Miss M**	*Bette Midler*	Atlantic 7238
10	18	3	Billion Dollar Babies	*Alice Cooper*	Warner 2685

Billboard — APRIL 7, 1973 — TOP LP's

TW	LW	WK			
1	3	20	**Lady Sings The Blues**	*Diana Ross/Soundtrack*	Motown 758
2	2	9	Don't Shoot Me I'm Only The Piano Player	*Elton John*	MCA 2100
3	4	12	**Prelude**	*Deodato*	CTI 6021
4	1	11	Dueling Banjos	*Eric Weissberg & Steve Mandell*	Warner 2683
5	5	30	Rocky Mountain High	*John Denver*	RCA 4731
6	7	21	The World Is A Ghetto	*War*	United Artists 5652
7	10	4	Billion Dollar Babies	*Alice Cooper*	Warner 2685
8	6	10	Shoot Out At The Fantasy Factory	*Traffic*	Island 9323
9	27	4	The Dark Side Of The Moon	*Pink Floyd*	Harvest 11163
10	8	18	No Secrets	*Carly Simon*	Elektra 75049

Billboard — APRIL 14, 1973 — TOP LP's

TW	LW	WK			
1	1	21	**Lady Sings The Blues**	*Diana Ross/Soundtrack*	Motown 758
2	7	5	Billion Dollar Babies	*Alice Cooper*	Warner 2685
3	2	10	Don't Shoot Me I'm Only The Piano Player	*Elton John*	MCA 2100
4	3	13	Prelude	*Deodato*	CTI 6021
5	6	22	The World Is A Ghetto	*War*	United Artists 5652
6	9	5	The Dark Side Of The Moon	*Pink Floyd*	Harvest 11163
7	4	12	Dueling Banjos	*Eric Weissberg & Steve Mandell*	Warner 2683
8	8	11	Shoot Out At The Fantasy Factory	*Traffic*	Island 9323
9	12	6	Masterpiece	*The Temptations*	Gordy 965
10	11	8	Aloha from Hawaii via Satellite	*Elvis Presley*	RCA VPSX-6089

Billboard — APRIL 21, 1973 — TOP LP's

TW	LW	WK			
1	2	6	**Billion Dollar Babies**	*Alice Cooper*	Warner 2685
2	1	22	Lady Sings The Blues	*Diana Ross/Soundtrack*	Motown 758
3	6	6	The Dark Side Of The Moon	*Pink Floyd*	Harvest 11163
4	10	9	Aloha from Hawaii via Satellite	*Elvis Presley*	RCA VPSX-6089
5	5	23	The World Is A Ghetto	*War*	United Artists 5652
6	13	4	The Best Of Bread	*Bread*	Elektra 75056
7	9	7	**Masterpiece**	*The Temptations*	Gordy 965
8	3	11	Don't Shoot Me I'm Only The Piano Player	*Elton John*	MCA 2100
9	7	13	Dueling Banjos	*Eric Weissberg & Steve Mandell*	Warner 2683
10	85	2	Houses Of The Holy	*Led Zeppelin*	Atlantic 7255

TW	LW	WK	Billboard® APRIL 28, 1973 TOP LP's
1	3	7	**The Dark Side Of The Moon** ... *Pink Floyd*...Harvest 11163
2	4	10	Aloha from Hawaii via Satellite ... *Elvis Presley*...RCA VPSX-6089
3	1	7	Billion Dollar Babies ... *Alice Cooper*...Warner 2685
4	6	5	The Best Of Bread ... *Bread*...Elektra 75056
5	10	3	Houses Of The Holy ... *Led Zeppelin*...Atlantic 7255
6	5	24	The World Is A Ghetto ... *War*...United Artists 5652
7	7	8	**Masterpiece** ... *The Temptations*...Gordy 965
8	2	23	Lady Sings The Blues ... *Diana Ross/Soundtrack*...Motown 758
9	23	3	The Beatles/1962-1966 ... *The Beatles*...Apple 3403
10	24	3	The Beatles/1967-1970 ... *The Beatles*...Apple 3404

TW	LW	WK	Billboard® MAY 5, 1973 TOP LP's
1	2	11	**Aloha from Hawaii via Satellite** ... *Elvis Presley*...RCA VPSX-6089
2	5	4	Houses Of The Holy ... *Led Zeppelin*...Atlantic 7255
3	4	6	The Best Of Bread ... *Bread*...Elektra 75056
4	1	8	The Dark Side Of The Moon ... *Pink Floyd*...Harvest 11163
5	3	8	Billion Dollar Babies ... *Alice Cooper*...Warner 2685
6	9	4	The Beatles/1962-1966 ... *The Beatles*...Apple 3403
7	10	4	The Beatles/1967-1970 ... *The Beatles*...Apple 3404
8	7	9	Masterpiece ... *The Temptations*...Gordy 965
9	12	22	They Only Come Out At Night ... *The Edgar Winter Group*...Epic 31584
10	11	9	Neither One Of Us ... *Gladys Knight & The Pips*...Soul 737

TW	LW	WK	Billboard® MAY 12, 1973 TOP LP's
1	2	5	**Houses Of The Holy** ... *Led Zeppelin*...Atlantic 7255
2	3	7	**The Best Of Bread** ... *Bread*...Elektra 75056
3	1	12	Aloha from Hawaii via Satellite ... *Elvis Presley*...RCA VPSX-6089
4	6	5	The Beatles/1962-1966 ... *The Beatles*...Apple 3403
5	7	5	The Beatles/1967-1970 ... *The Beatles*...Apple 3404
6	4	9	The Dark Side Of The Moon ... *Pink Floyd*...Harvest 11163
7	9	23	They Only Come Out At Night ... *The Edgar Winter Group*...Epic 31584
8	5	9	Billion Dollar Babies ... *Alice Cooper*...Warner 2685
9	8	10	Masterpiece ... *The Temptations*...Gordy 965
10	10	10	Neither One Of Us ... *Gladys Knight & The Pips*...Soul 737

TW	LW	WK	Billboard® MAY 19, 1973 TOP LP's
1	1	6	**Houses Of The Holy** ... *Led Zeppelin*...Atlantic 7255
2	5	6	The Beatles/1967-1970 ... *The Beatles*...Apple 3404
3	4	6	**The Beatles/1962-1966** ... *The Beatles*...Apple 3403
4	2	8	The Best Of Bread ... *Bread*...Elektra 75056
5	7	24	They Only Come Out At Night ... *The Edgar Winter Group*...Epic 31584
6	6	10	The Dark Side Of The Moon ... *Pink Floyd*...Harvest 11163
7	3	13	Aloha from Hawaii via Satellite ... *Elvis Presley*...RCA VPSX-6089
8	8	10	Billion Dollar Babies ... *Alice Cooper*...Warner 2685
9	10	11	**Neither One Of Us** ... *Gladys Knight & The Pips*...Soul 737
10	12	18	Moving Waves ... *Focus*...Sire 7401

TW	LW	WK	Billboard — MAY 26, 1973 — TOP LP's
1	2	7	**The Beatles/1967-1970** .... *The Beatles*...Apple 3404
2	1	7	Houses Of The Holy .... *Led Zeppelin*...Atlantic 7255
3	3	7	**The Beatles/1962-1966** .... *The Beatles*...Apple 3403
4	5	25	They Only Come Out At Night .... *The Edgar Winter Group*...Epic 31584
5	4	9	The Best Of Bread .... *Bread*...Elektra 75056
6	6	11	The Dark Side Of The Moon .... *Pink Floyd*...Harvest 11163
7	8	11	Billion Dollar Babies .... *Alice Cooper*...Warner 2685
8	7	14	Aloha from Hawaii via Satellite .... *Elvis Presley*...RCA VPSX-6089
9	10	19	Moving Waves .... *Focus*...Sire 7401
10	9	12	Neither One Of Us .... *Gladys Knight & The Pips*...Soul 737

TW	LW	WK	Billboard — JUNE 2, 1973 — TOP LP's
1	13	4	**Red Rose Speedway** .... *Paul McCartney & Wings*...Apple 3409
2	2	8	Houses Of The Holy .... *Led Zeppelin*...Atlantic 7255
3	1	8	The Beatles/1967-1970 .... *The Beatles*...Apple 3404
4	4	26	They Only Come Out At Night .... *The Edgar Winter Group*...Epic 31584
5	3	8	The Beatles/1962-1966 .... *The Beatles*...Apple 3403
6	6	12	The Dark Side Of The Moon .... *Pink Floyd*...Harvest 11163
7	5	10	The Best Of Bread .... *Bread*...Elektra 75056
8	9	20	**Moving Waves** .... *Focus*...Sire 7401
9	11	7	Diamond Girl .... *Seals & Crofts*...Warner 2699
10	7	12	Billion Dollar Babies .... *Alice Cooper*...Warner 2685

TW	LW	WK	Billboard — JUNE 9, 1973 — TOP LP's
1	1	5	**Red Rose Speedway** .... *Paul McCartney & Wings*...Apple 3409
2	3	9	The Beatles/1967-1970 .... *The Beatles*...Apple 3404
3	4	27	**They Only Come Out At Night** .... *The Edgar Winter Group*...Epic 31584
4	2	9	Houses Of The Holy .... *Led Zeppelin*...Atlantic 7255
5	5	9	The Beatles/1962-1966 .... *The Beatles*...Apple 3403
6	7	11	The Best Of Bread .... *Bread*...Elektra 75056
7	9	8	Diamond Girl .... *Seals & Crofts*...Warner 2699
8	8	21	**Moving Waves** .... *Focus*...Sire 7401
9	6	13	The Dark Side Of The Moon .... *Pink Floyd*...Harvest 11163
10	11	8	Made In Japan .... *Deep Purple*...Warner 2701

TW	LW	WK	Billboard — JUNE 16, 1973 — TOP LP's
1	1	6	**Red Rose Speedway** .... *Paul McCartney & Wings*...Apple 3409
2	2	10	The Beatles/1967-1970 .... *The Beatles*...Apple 3404
3	4	10	Houses Of The Holy .... *Led Zeppelin*...Atlantic 7255
4	3	28	They Only Come Out At Night .... *The Edgar Winter Group*...Epic 31584
5	5	10	The Beatles/1962-1966 .... *The Beatles*...Apple 3403
6	7	9	Diamond Girl .... *Seals & Crofts*...Warner 2699
7	27	4	There Goes Rhymin' Simon .... *Paul Simon*...Columbia 32280
8	9	14	The Dark Side Of The Moon .... *Pink Floyd*...Harvest 11163
9	10	9	Made In Japan .... *Deep Purple*...Warner 2701
10	11	8	**Bloodshot** .... *The J. Geils Band*...Atlantic 7260

Billboard — JUNE 23, 1973 — TOP LP's

TW	LW	WK	Title	Artist...Label
1	11	2	**Living In The Material World**	*George Harrison*...Apple 3410
2	1	7	Red Rose Speedway	*Paul McCartney & Wings*...Apple 3409
3	3	11	Houses Of The Holy	*Led Zeppelin*...Atlantic 7255
4	7	5	There Goes Rhymin' Simon	*Paul Simon*...Columbia 32280
5	2	11	The Beatles/1967-1970	*The Beatles*...Apple 3404
6	6	10	Diamond Girl	*Seals & Crofts*...Warner 2699
7	8	15	The Dark Side Of The Moon	*Pink Floyd*...Harvest 11163
8	9	10	Made In Japan	*Deep Purple*...Warner 2701
9	4	29	They Only Come Out At Night	*The Edgar Winter Group*...Epic 31584
10	12	6	**Call Me**	*Al Green*...Hi 32077

Billboard — JUNE 30, 1973 — TOP LP's

TW	LW	WK	Title	Artist...Label
1	1	3	**Living In The Material World**	*George Harrison*...Apple 3410
2	2	8	Red Rose Speedway	*Paul McCartney & Wings*...Apple 3409
3	4	6	There Goes Rhymin' Simon	*Paul Simon*...Columbia 32280
4	3	12	Houses Of The Holy	*Led Zeppelin*...Atlantic 7255
5	7	16	The Dark Side Of The Moon	*Pink Floyd*...Harvest 11163
6	5	12	The Beatles/1967-1970	*The Beatles*...Apple 3404
7	18	5	Now & Then	*Carpenters*...A&M 3519
8	8	11	Made In Japan	*Deep Purple*...Warner 2701
9	9	30	They Only Come Out At Night	*The Edgar Winter Group*...Epic 31584
10	10	7	**Call Me**	*Al Green*...Hi 32077

Billboard — JULY 7, 1973 — TOP LP's

TW	LW	WK	Title	Artist...Label
1	1	4	**Living In The Material World**	*George Harrison*...Apple 3410
2	3	7	**There Goes Rhymin' Simon**	*Paul Simon*...Columbia 32280
3	2	9	Red Rose Speedway	*Paul McCartney & Wings*...Apple 3409
4	5	17	The Dark Side Of The Moon	*Pink Floyd*...Harvest 11163
5	7	6	Now & Then	*Carpenters*...A&M 3519
6	4	13	Houses Of The Holy	*Led Zeppelin*...Atlantic 7255
7	8	12	Made In Japan	*Deep Purple*...Warner 2701
8	6	13	The Beatles/1967-1970	*The Beatles*...Apple 3404
9	17	3	Fantasy	*Carole King*...Ode 77018
10	12	12	Diamond Girl	*Seals & Crofts*...Warner 2699

Billboard — JULY 14, 1973 — TOP LP's

TW	LW	WK	Title	Artist...Label
1	1	5	**Living In The Material World**	*George Harrison*...Apple 3410
2	2	8	**There Goes Rhymin' Simon**	*Paul Simon*...Columbia 32280
3	5	7	Now & Then	*Carpenters*...A&M 3519
4	4	18	The Dark Side Of The Moon	*Pink Floyd*...Harvest 11163
5	3	10	Red Rose Speedway	*Paul McCartney & Wings*...Apple 3409
6	6	14	Houses Of The Holy	*Led Zeppelin*...Atlantic 7255
7	9	4	Fantasy	*Carole King*...Ode 77018
8	7	13	Made In Japan	*Deep Purple*...Warner 2701
9	10	13	Diamond Girl	*Seals & Crofts*...Warner 2699
10	11	16	The Captain And Me	*The Doobie Brothers*...Warner 2694

TW	LW	WK	Billboard — JULY 21, 1973 — TOP LP's
①	1	6	**Living In The Material World** .... *George Harrison*...Apple 3410
②	3	8	**Now & Then** .... *Carpenters*...A&M 3519
③	4	19	The Dark Side Of The Moon .... *Pink Floyd*...Harvest 11163
④	2	9	There Goes Rhymin' Simon .... *Paul Simon*...Columbia 32280
⑤	5	11	Red Rose Speedway .... *Paul McCartney & Wings*...Apple 3409
⑥	7	5	**Fantasy** .... *Carole King*...Ode 77018
❼	10	17	**The Captain And Me** .... *The Doobie Brothers*...Warner 2694
⑧	6	15	Houses Of The Holy .... *Led Zeppelin*...Atlantic 7255
⑨	9	14	Diamond Girl .... *Seals & Crofts*...Warner 2699
❿	14	60	Machine Head .... *Deep Purple*...Warner 2607

TW	LW	WK	Billboard — JULY 28, 1973 — TOP LP's
❶	18	3	**Chicago VI** .... *Chicago*...Columbia 32400
②	3	20	The Dark Side Of The Moon .... *Pink Floyd*...Harvest 11163
③	1	7	Living In The Material World .... *George Harrison*...Apple 3410
④	2	9	Now & Then .... *Carpenters*...A&M 3519
⑤	4	10	There Goes Rhymin' Simon .... *Paul Simon*...Columbia 32280
⑥	6	6	**Fantasy** .... *Carole King*...Ode 77018
⑦	7	18	**The Captain And Me** .... *The Doobie Brothers*...Warner 2694
⑧	9	15	Diamond Girl .... *Seals & Crofts*...Warner 2699
⑨	10	61	Machine Head .... *Deep Purple*...Warner 2607
⑩	5	12	Red Rose Speedway .... *Paul McCartney & Wings*...Apple 3409

TW	LW	WK	Billboard — AUGUST 4, 1973 — TOP LP's
①	1	4	**Chicago VI** .... *Chicago*...Columbia 32400
②	2	21	The Dark Side Of The Moon .... *Pink Floyd*...Harvest 11163
③	4	10	Now & Then .... *Carpenters*...A&M 3519
④	3	8	Living In The Material World .... *George Harrison*...Apple 3410
❺	8	16	Diamond Girl .... *Seals & Crofts*...Warner 2699
⑥	6	7	**Fantasy** .... *Carole King*...Ode 77018
⑦	5	11	There Goes Rhymin' Simon .... *Paul Simon*...Columbia 32280
⑧	9	62	Machine Head .... *Deep Purple*...Warner 2607
❾	12	6	Fresh .... *Sly & The Family Stone*...Epic 32134
❿	14	5	Leon Live .... *Leon Russell*...Shelter 8917

TW	LW	WK	Billboard — AUGUST 11, 1973 — TOP LP's
①	1	5	**Chicago VI** .... *Chicago*...Columbia 32400
②	2	22	The Dark Side Of The Moon .... *Pink Floyd*...Harvest 11163
③	3	11	Now & Then .... *Carpenters*...A&M 3519
❹	12	4	A Passion Play .... *Jethro Tull*...Chrysalis 1040
⑤	5	17	Diamond Girl .... *Seals & Crofts*...Warner 2699
❻	11	17	**Made In Japan** .... *Deep Purple*...Warner 2701
⑦	8	63	**Machine Head** .... *Deep Purple*...Warner 2607
⑧	9	7	Fresh .... *Sly & The Family Stone*...Epic 32134
⑨	10	6	**Leon Live** .... *Leon Russell*...Shelter 8917
❿	23	3	Foreigner .... *Cat Stevens*...A&M 4391

Billboard ● AUGUST 18, 1973 ● TOP LP's

TW	LW	WK		
❶	4	5	**A Passion Play**	*Jethro Tull*...Chrysalis 1040
②	1	6	Chicago VI	*Chicago*...Columbia 32400
③	2	23	The Dark Side Of The Moon	*Pink Floyd*...Harvest 11163
④	5	18	**Diamond Girl**	*Seals & Crofts*...Warner 2699
❺	10	4	Foreigner	*Cat Stevens*...A&M 4391
⑥	6	18	**Made In Japan**	*Deep Purple*...Warner 2701
⑦	8	8	**Fresh**	*Sly & The Family Stone*...Epic 32134
❽	12	6	Touch Me In The Morning	*Diana Ross*...Motown 772
⑨	3	12	Now & Then	*Carpenters*...A&M 3519
⑩	9	7	Leon Live	*Leon Russell*...Shelter 8917

Billboard ● AUGUST 25, 1973 ● TOP LP's

TW	LW	WK		
①	2	7	**Chicago VI**	*Chicago*...Columbia 32400
②	1	6	**A Passion Play**	*Jethro Tull*...Chrysalis 1040
③	3	24	The Dark Side Of The Moon	*Pink Floyd*...Harvest 11163
④	5	5	Foreigner	*Cat Stevens*...A&M 4391
⑤	4	19	Diamond Girl	*Seals & Crofts*...Warner 2699
⑥	8	7	Touch Me In The Morning	*Diana Ross*...Motown 772
⑦	6	19	Made In Japan	*Deep Purple*...Warner 2701
⑧	7	9	Fresh	*Sly & The Family Stone*...Epic 32134
⑨	11	65	Machine Head	*Deep Purple*...Warner 2607
⑩	10	8	Leon Live	*Leon Russell*...Shelter 8917

Billboard ● SEPTEMBER 1, 1973 ● TOP LP's

TW	LW	WK		
①	1	8	**Chicago VI**	*Chicago*...Columbia 32400
②	3	25	The Dark Side Of The Moon	*Pink Floyd*...Harvest 11163
③	4	6	**Foreigner**	*Cat Stevens*...A&M 4391
❹	13	2	Brothers And Sisters	*The Allman Brothers Band*...Capricorn 0111
⑤	6	8	**Touch Me In The Morning**	*Diana Ross*...Motown 772
⑥	2	7	A Passion Play	*Jethro Tull*...Chrysalis 1040
⑦	9	66	**Machine Head**	*Deep Purple*...Warner 2607
❽	15	3	We're An American Band	*Grand Funk*...Capitol 11207
⑨	7	20	Made In Japan	*Deep Purple*...Warner 2701
⑩	8	10	Fresh	*Sly & The Family Stone*...Epic 32134

Billboard ● SEPTEMBER 8, 1973 ● TOP LP's

TW	LW	WK		
❶	4	3	**Brothers And Sisters**	*The Allman Brothers Band*...Capricorn 0111
②	1	9	Chicago VI	*Chicago*...Columbia 32400
③	2	26	The Dark Side Of The Moon	*Pink Floyd*...Harvest 11163
④	3	7	Foreigner	*Cat Stevens*...A&M 4391
❺	8	4	We're An American Band	*Grand Funk*...Capitol 11207
⑥	5	9	Touch Me In The Morning	*Diana Ross*...Motown 772
⑦	6	8	A Passion Play	*Jethro Tull*...Chrysalis 1040
❽	25	2	Killing Me Softly	*Roberta Flack*...Atlantic 7271
⑨	14	4	Innervisions	*Stevie Wonder*...Tamla 326
⑩	10	11	Fresh	*Sly & The Family Stone*...Epic 32134

TW	LW	WK	Billboard. SEPTEMBER 15, 1973	TOP LP's
①	1	4	**Brothers And Sisters**	*The Allman Brothers Band*...Capricorn 0111
②	2	10	Chicago VI	*Chicago*...Columbia 32400
③	5	5	We're An American Band	*Grand Funk*...Capitol 11207
❹	8	3	Killing Me Softly	*Roberta Flack*...Atlantic 7271
⑤	6	10	**Touch Me In The Morning**	*Diana Ross*...Motown 772
❻	9	5	Innervisions	*Stevie Wonder*...Tamla 326
⑦	3	27	The Dark Side Of The Moon	*Pink Floyd*...Harvest 11163
⑧	4	8	Foreigner	*Cat Stevens*...A&M 4391
⑨	7	9	A Passion Play	*Jethro Tull*...Chrysalis 1040
❿	22	2	Los Cochinos	*Cheech & Chong*...Ode 77019

TW	LW	WK	Billboard. SEPTEMBER 22, 1973	TOP LP's
①	1	5	**Brothers And Sisters**	*The Allman Brothers Band*...Capricorn 0111
②	3	6	**We're An American Band**	*Grand Funk*...Capitol 11207
③	4	4	**Killing Me Softly**	*Roberta Flack*...Atlantic 7271
④	6	6	**Innervisions**	*Stevie Wonder*...Tamla 326
⑤	2	11	Chicago VI	*Chicago*...Columbia 32400
❻	10	3	Los Cochinos	*Cheech & Chong*...Ode 77019
⑦	5	11	Touch Me In The Morning	*Diana Ross*...Motown 772
❽	11	7	**Long Hard Climb**	*Helen Reddy*...Capitol 11213
❾	12	4	Deliver The Word	*War*...United Artists 128
⑩	7	28	The Dark Side Of The Moon	*Pink Floyd*...Harvest 11163

TW	LW	WK	Billboard. SEPTEMBER 29, 1973	TOP LP's
①	1	6	**Brothers And Sisters**	*The Allman Brothers Band*...Capricorn 0111
②	2	7	**We're An American Band**	*Grand Funk*...Capitol 11207
③	3	5	**Killing Me Softly**	*Roberta Flack*...Atlantic 7271
❹	6	4	Los Cochinos	*Cheech & Chong*...Ode 77019
⑤	4	7	Innervisions	*Stevie Wonder*...Tamla 326
❻	11	3	Let's Get It On	*Marvin Gaye*...Tamla 329
❼	9	5	Deliver The Word	*War*...United Artists 128
⑧	8	8	**Long Hard Climb**	*Helen Reddy*...Capitol 11213
⑨	5	12	Chicago VI	*Chicago*...Columbia 32400
⑩	10	29	The Dark Side Of The Moon	*Pink Floyd*...Harvest 11163

TW	LW	WK	Billboard. OCTOBER 6, 1973	TOP LP's
①	1	7	**Brothers And Sisters**	*The Allman Brothers Band*...Capricorn 0111
②	4	5	**Los Cochinos**	*Cheech & Chong*...Ode 77019
❸	6	4	Let's Get It On	*Marvin Gaye*...Tamla 329
④	2	8	We're An American Band	*Grand Funk*...Capitol 11207
⑤	5	8	Innervisions	*Stevie Wonder*...Tamla 326
⑥	7	6	**Deliver The Word**	*War*...United Artists 128
⑦	3	6	Killing Me Softly	*Roberta Flack*...Atlantic 7271
⑧	8	9	**Long Hard Climb**	*Helen Reddy*...Capitol 11213
❾	21	2	Goats Head Soup	*The Rolling Stones*...Rolling Stones 59101
⑩	10	30	The Dark Side Of The Moon	*Pink Floyd*...Harvest 11163

TW	LW	WK	Billboard® OCTOBER 13, 1973 TOP LP's
1	9	3	**Goats Head Soup**........................ *The Rolling Stones*...Rolling Stones 59101
2	1	8	Brothers And Sisters..................... *The Allman Brothers Band*...Capricorn 0111
3	3	5	Let's Get It On .... *Marvin Gaye*...Tamla 329
4	2	6	Los Cochinos.. *Cheech & Chong*...Ode 77019
5	5	9	Innervisions .... *Stevie Wonder*...Tamla 326
6	4	9	We're An American Band.............................*Grand Funk*...Capitol 11207
7	6	7	Deliver The Word .... *War*...United Artists 128
8	7	7	Killing Me Softly .... *Roberta Flack*...Atlantic 7271
9	8	10	Long Hard Climb..*Helen Reddy*...Capitol 11213
10	11	17	The Smoker You Drink, The Player You Get..... *Joe Walsh*...Dunhill/ABC 50140

TW	LW	WK	Billboard® OCTOBER 20, 1973 TOP LP's
1	1	4	**Goats Head Soup**........................ *The Rolling Stones*...Rolling Stones 59101
2	3	6	**Let's Get It On** .... *Marvin Gaye*...Tamla 329
3	2	9	Brothers And Sisters..................... *The Allman Brothers Band*...Capricorn 0111
4	4	7	Los Cochinos.. *Cheech & Chong*...Ode 77019
5	5	10	Innervisions .... *Stevie Wonder*...Tamla 326
6	7	8	**Deliver The Word** .... *War*...United Artists 128
7	6	10	We're An American Band.............................*Grand Funk*...Capitol 11207
8	8	8	Killing Me Softly .... *Roberta Flack*...Atlantic 7271
9	11	4	Angel Clare..*Garfunkel*...Columbia 31474
10	10	18	The Smoker You Drink, The Player You Get..... *Joe Walsh*...Dunhill/ABC 50140

TW	LW	WK	Billboard® OCTOBER 27, 1973 TOP LP's
1	1	5	**Goats Head Soup**........................ *The Rolling Stones*...Rolling Stones 59101
2	3	10	Brothers And Sisters..................... *The Allman Brothers Band*...Capricorn 0111
3	4	8	Los Cochinos.. *Cheech & Chong*...Ode 77019
4	2	7	Let's Get It On .... *Marvin Gaye*...Tamla 329
5	17	2	Goodbye Yellow Brick Road..............................*Elton John*...MCA 10003
6	5	11	Innervisions .... *Stevie Wonder*...Tamla 326
7	9	5	Angel Clare..*Garfunkel*...Columbia 31474
8	6	9	Deliver The Word .... *War*...United Artists 128
9	12	8	3 + 3.. *The Isley Brothers*...T-Neck 32453
10	10	19	The Smoker You Drink, The Player You Get..... *Joe Walsh*...Dunhill/ABC 50140

TW	LW	WK	Billboard® NOVEMBER 3, 1973 TOP LP's
1	1	6	**Goats Head Soup**........................ *The Rolling Stones*...Rolling Stones 59101
2	5	3	Goodbye Yellow Brick Road..............................*Elton John*...MCA 10003
3	2	11	Brothers And Sisters..................... *The Allman Brothers Band*...Capricorn 0111
4	3	9	Los Cochinos.. *Cheech & Chong*...Ode 77019
5	4	8	Let's Get It On .... *Marvin Gaye*...Tamla 329
6	7	6	Angel Clare..*Garfunkel*...Columbia 31474
7	6	12	Innervisions .... *Stevie Wonder*...Tamla 326
8	10	20	The Smoker You Drink, The Player You Get..... *Joe Walsh*...Dunhill/ABC 50140
9	9	9	3 + 3.. *The Isley Brothers*...T-Neck 32453
10	8	10	Deliver The Word .... *War*...United Artists 128

Billboard — NOVEMBER 10, 1973 — TOP LP's

TW	LW	WK			
1	2	4	**Goodbye Yellow Brick Road**	*Elton John*	MCA 10003
2	1	7	Goats Head Soup	*The Rolling Stones*	Rolling Stones 59101
3	3	12	Brothers And Sisters	*The Allman Brothers Band*	Capricorn 0111
4	4	10	Los Cochinos	*Cheech & Chong*	Ode 77019
5	6	7	**Angel Clare**	*Garfunkel*	Columbia 31474
6	8	21	**The Smoker You Drink, The Player You Get**	*Joe Walsh*	Dunhill/ABC 50140
7	5	9	Let's Get It On	*Marvin Gaye*	Tamla 329
8	9	10	**3 + 3**	*The Isley Brothers*	T-Neck 32453
9	7	13	Innervisions	*Stevie Wonder*	Tamla 326
10	11	39	Life And Times	*Jim Croce*	ABC 769

Billboard — NOVEMBER 17, 1973 — TOP LP's

TW	LW	WK			
1	1	5	**Goodbye Yellow Brick Road**	*Elton John*	MCA 10003
2	2	8	Goats Head Soup	*The Rolling Stones*	Rolling Stones 59101
3	3	13	Brothers And Sisters	*The Allman Brothers Band*	Capricorn 0111
4	24	2	Quadrophenia	*The Who*	MCA 10004
5	4	11	Los Cochinos	*Cheech & Chong*	Ode 77019
6	6	22	**The Smoker You Drink, The Player You Get**	*Joe Walsh*	Dunhill/ABC 50140
7	5	8	Angel Clare	*Garfunkel*	Columbia 31474
8	13	39	You Don't Mess Around With Jim	*Jim Croce*	ABC 756
9	10	40	Life And Times	*Jim Croce*	ABC 769
10	7	10	Let's Get It On	*Marvin Gaye*	Tamla 329

Billboard — NOVEMBER 24, 1973 — TOP LP's

TW	LW	WK			
1	1	6	**Goodbye Yellow Brick Road**	*Elton John*	MCA 10003
2	4	3	**Quadrophenia**	*The Who*	MCA 10004
3	15	2	Ringo	*Ringo Starr*	Apple 3413
4	2	9	Goats Head Soup	*The Rolling Stones*	Rolling Stones 59101
5	8	40	You Don't Mess Around With Jim	*Jim Croce*	ABC 756
6	14	4	Jonathan Livingston Seagull	*Neil Diamond/Soundtrack*	Columbia 32550
7	3	14	Brothers And Sisters	*The Allman Brothers Band*	Capricorn 0111
8	9	41	Life And Times	*Jim Croce*	ABC 769
9	11	6	The Joker	*Steve Miller Band*	Capitol 11235
10	5	12	Los Cochinos	*Cheech & Chong*	Ode 77019

Billboard — DECEMBER 1, 1973 — TOP LP's

TW	LW	WK			
1	1	7	**Goodbye Yellow Brick Road**	*Elton John*	MCA 10003
2	3	3	**Ringo**	*Ringo Starr*	Apple 3413
3	2	4	Quadrophenia	*The Who*	MCA 10004
4	6	5	Jonathan Livingston Seagull	*Neil Diamond/Soundtrack*	Columbia 32550
5	5	41	You Don't Mess Around With Jim	*Jim Croce*	ABC 756
6	4	10	Goats Head Soup	*The Rolling Stones*	Rolling Stones 59101
7	9	7	The Joker	*Steve Miller Band*	Capitol 11235
8	7	15	Brothers And Sisters	*The Allman Brothers Band*	Capricorn 0111
9	8	42	Life And Times	*Jim Croce*	ABC 769
10	10	13	Los Cochinos	*Cheech & Chong*	Ode 77019

TW	LW	WK	Billboard® DECEMBER 8, 1973 TOP LP's
1	1	8	**Goodbye Yellow Brick Road** ... *Elton John*...MCA 10003
2	2	4	**Ringo** ... *Ringo Starr*...Apple 3413
3	4	6	Jonathan Livingston Seagull ... *Neil Diamond/Soundtrack*...Columbia 32550
4	7	8	The Joker ... *Steve Miller Band*...Capitol 11235
5	5	42	You Don't Mess Around With Jim ... *Jim Croce*...ABC 756
6	3	5	Quadrophenia ... *The Who*...MCA 10004
7	9	43	**Life And Times** ... *Jim Croce*...ABC 769
8	6	11	Goats Head Soup ... *The Rolling Stones*...Rolling Stones 59101
9	11	3	**Mind Games** ... *John Lennon*...Apple 3414
10	8	16	Brothers And Sisters ... *The Allman Brothers Band*...Capricorn 0111

TW	LW	WK	Billboard® DECEMBER 15, 1973 TOP LP's
1	1	9	**Goodbye Yellow Brick Road** ... *Elton John*...MCA 10003
2	3	7	**Jonathan Livingston Seagull** .. *Neil Diamond/Soundtrack*...Columbia 32550
3	4	9	The Joker ... *Steve Miller Band*...Capitol 11235
4	2	5	Ringo ... *Ringo Starr*...Apple 3413
5	5	43	You Don't Mess Around With Jim ... *Jim Croce*...ABC 756
6	6	6	Quadrophenia ... *The Who*...MCA 10004
7	7	44	**Life And Times** ... *Jim Croce*...ABC 769
8	30	3	The Singles 1969-1973 ... *Carpenters*...A&M 3601
9	9	4	**Mind Games** ... *John Lennon*...Apple 3414
10	8	12	Goats Head Soup ... *The Rolling Stones*...Rolling Stones 59101

TW	LW	WK	Billboard® DECEMBER 22, 1973 TOP LP's
1	1	10	**Goodbye Yellow Brick Road** ... *Elton John*...MCA 10003
2	3	10	**The Joker** ... *Steve Miller Band*...Capitol 11235
3	4	6	Ringo ... *Ringo Starr*...Apple 3413
4	2	8	Jonathan Livingston Seagull ... *Neil Diamond/Soundtrack*...Columbia 32550
5	6	7	Quadrophenia ... *The Who*...MCA 10004
6	8	4	The Singles 1969-1973 ... *Carpenters*...A&M 3601
7	5	44	You Don't Mess Around With Jim ... *Jim Croce*...ABC 756
8	7	45	Life And Times ... *Jim Croce*...ABC 769
9	9	5	**Mind Games** ... *John Lennon*...Apple 3414
10	11	9	Imagination ... *Gladys Knight & The Pips*...Buddah 5141

TW	LW	WK	Billboard® DECEMBER 29, 1973 TOP LP's
1	1	11	**Goodbye Yellow Brick Road** ... *Elton John*...MCA 10003
2	6	5	The Singles 1969-1973 ... *Carpenters*...A&M 3601
3	2	11	The Joker ... *Steve Miller Band*...Capitol 11235
4	4	9	Jonathan Livingston Seagull ... *Neil Diamond/Soundtrack*...Columbia 32550
5	7	45	You Don't Mess Around With Jim ... *Jim Croce*...ABC 756
6	3	7	Ringo ... *Ringo Starr*...Apple 3413
7	5	8	Quadrophenia ... *The Who*...MCA 10004
8	8	46	Life And Times ... *Jim Croce*...ABC 769
9	10	10	**Imagination** ... *Gladys Knight & The Pips*...Buddah 5141
10	9	6	Mind Games ... *John Lennon*...Apple 3414

TW	LW	WK	Billboard® JANUARY 5, 1974	TOP LP's
1	2	6	**The Singles 1969-1973**	*Carpenters*...A&M 3601
2	1	12	Goodbye Yellow Brick Road	*Elton John*...MCA 10003
3	5	46	You Don't Mess Around With Jim	*Jim Croce*...ABC 756
4	3	12	The Joker	*Steve Miller Band*...Capitol 11235
5	4	10	Jonathan Livingston Seagull	*Neil Diamond/Soundtrack*...Columbia 32550
6	12	4	I Got A Name	*Jim Croce*...ABC 797
7	7	9	Quadrophenia	*The Who*...MCA 10004
8	6	8	Ringo	*Ringo Starr*...Apple 3413
9	16	5	Bette Midler	*Bette Midler*...Atlantic 7270
10	11	9	**Full Sail**	*Loggins & Messina*...Columbia 32540

TW	LW	WK	Billboard® JANUARY 12, 1974	TOP LP's
1	3	47	**You Don't Mess Around With Jim**	*Jim Croce*...ABC 756
2	1	7	The Singles 1969-1973	*Carpenters*...A&M 3601
3	2	13	Goodbye Yellow Brick Road	*Elton John*...MCA 10003
4	6	5	I Got A Name	*Jim Croce*...ABC 797
5	4	13	The Joker	*Steve Miller Band*...Capitol 11235
6	5	11	Jonathan Livingston Seagull	*Neil Diamond/Soundtrack*...Columbia 32550
7	9	6	Bette Midler	*Bette Midler*...Atlantic 7270
8	7	10	Quadrophenia	*The Who*...MCA 10004
9	8	9	Ringo	*Ringo Starr*...Apple 3413
10	11	6	**Muscle Of Love**	*Alice Cooper*...Warner 2748

TW	LW	WK	Billboard® JANUARY 19, 1974	TOP LP's
1	1	48	**You Don't Mess Around With Jim**	*Jim Croce*...ABC 756
2	2	8	The Singles 1969-1973	*Carpenters*...A&M 3601
3	4	6	I Got A Name	*Jim Croce*...ABC 797
4	3	14	Goodbye Yellow Brick Road	*Elton John*...MCA 10003
5	5	14	The Joker	*Steve Miller Band*...Capitol 11235
6	7	7	**Bette Midler**	*Bette Midler*...Atlantic 7270
7	6	12	Jonathan Livingston Seagull	*Neil Diamond/Soundtrack*...Columbia 32550
8	12	7	John Denver's Greatest Hits	*John Denver*...RCA 0374
9	13	5	Band On The Run	*Paul McCartney & Wings*...Apple 3415
10	10	7	**Muscle Of Love**	*Alice Cooper*...Warner 2748

TW	LW	WK	Billboard® JANUARY 26, 1974	TOP LP's
1	1	49	**You Don't Mess Around With Jim**	*Jim Croce*...ABC 756
2	3	7	**I Got A Name**	*Jim Croce*...ABC 797
3	2	9	The Singles 1969-1973	*Carpenters*...A&M 3601
4	4	15	Goodbye Yellow Brick Road	*Elton John*...MCA 10003
5	5	15	The Joker	*Steve Miller Band*...Capitol 11235
6	8	8	John Denver's Greatest Hits	*John Denver*...RCA 0374
7	6	8	Bette Midler	*Bette Midler*...Atlantic 7270
8	9	6	Band On The Run	*Paul McCartney & Wings*...Apple 3415
9	7	13	Jonathan Livingston Seagull	*Neil Diamond/Soundtrack*...Columbia 32550
10	11	37	Behind Closed Doors	*Charlie Rich*...Epic 32247

TW	LW	WK	Billboard® FEBRUARY 2, 1974 TOP LP's	Artist	Label
1	1	50	**You Don't Mess Around With Jim**	Jim Croce	ABC 756
2	2	8	**I Got A Name**	Jim Croce	ABC 797
3	6	9	John Denver's Greatest Hits	John Denver	RCA 0374
4	4	16	Goodbye Yellow Brick Road	Elton John	MCA 10003
5	5	16	The Joker	Steve Miller Band	Capitol 11235
6	3	10	The Singles 1969-1973	Carpenters	A&M 3601
7	8	7	Band On The Run	Paul McCartney & Wings	Apple 3415
8	14	22	Under The Influence Of...	Love Unlimited	20th Century 414
9	10	38	Behind Closed Doors	Charlie Rich	Epic 32247
10	7	9	Bette Midler	Bette Midler	Atlantic 7270

TW	LW	WK	Billboard® FEBRUARY 9, 1974 TOP LP's	Artist	Label
1	1	51	**You Don't Mess Around With Jim**	Jim Croce	ABC 756
2	3	10	John Denver's Greatest Hits	John Denver	RCA 0374
3	2	9	I Got A Name	Jim Croce	ABC 797
4	8	23	Under The Influence Of...	Love Unlimited	20th Century 414
5	4	17	Goodbye Yellow Brick Road	Elton John	MCA 10003
6	5	17	The Joker	Steve Miller Band	Capitol 11235
7	6	11	The Singles 1969-1973	Carpenters	A&M 3601
8	9	39	**Behind Closed Doors**	Charlie Rich	Epic 32247
9	7	8	Band On The Run	Paul McCartney & Wings	Apple 3415
10	11	24	**American Graffiti**	Soundtrack	MCA 8001

TW	LW	WK	Billboard® FEBRUARY 16, 1974 TOP LP's	Artist	Label
1	19	2	**Planet Waves**	Bob Dylan & The Band	Asylum 1003
2	2	11	John Denver's Greatest Hits	John Denver	RCA 0374
3	4	24	**Under The Influence Of...**	Love Unlimited	20th Century 414
4	1	52	You Don't Mess Around With Jim	Jim Croce	ABC 756
5	5	18	Goodbye Yellow Brick Road	Elton John	MCA 10003
6	3	10	I Got A Name	Jim Croce	ABC 797
7	6	18	The Joker	Steve Miller Band	Capitol 11235
8	9	9	Band On The Run	Paul McCartney & Wings	Apple 3415
9	8	40	Behind Closed Doors	Charlie Rich	Epic 32247
10	13	3	Tales From Topographic Oceans	Yes	Atlantic 908

TW	LW	WK	Billboard® FEBRUARY 23, 1974 TOP LP's	Artist	Label
1	1	3	**Planet Waves**	Bob Dylan & The Band	Asylum 1003
2	2	12	John Denver's Greatest Hits	John Denver	RCA 0374
3	3	25	**Under The Influence Of...**	Love Unlimited	20th Century 414
4	14	3	Court And Spark	Joni Mitchell	Asylum 1001
5	4	53	You Don't Mess Around With Jim	Jim Croce	ABC 756
6	5	19	Goodbye Yellow Brick Road	Elton John	MCA 10003
7	16	4	Hotcakes	Carly Simon	Elektra 1002
8	10	4	Tales From Topographic Oceans	Yes	Atlantic 908
9	8	10	Band On The Run	Paul McCartney & Wings	Apple 3415
10	9	41	Behind Closed Doors	Charlie Rich	Epic 32247

Billboard — MARCH 2, 1974 — TOP LP's

TW	LW	WK	Title	Artist	Label
1	1	4	**Planet Waves**	*Bob Dylan & The Band*	Asylum 1003
2	4	4	**Court And Spark**	*Joni Mitchell*	Asylum 1001
3	2	13	John Denver's Greatest Hits	*John Denver*	RCA 0374
4	7	5	Hotcakes	*Carly Simon*	Elektra 1002
5	3	26	Under The Influence Of...	*Love Unlimited*	20th Century 414
6	5	54	You Don't Mess Around With Jim	*Jim Croce*	ABC 756
7	8	5	Tales From Topographic Oceans	*Yes*	Atlantic 908
8	6	20	Goodbye Yellow Brick Road	*Elton John*	MCA 10003
9	9	11	Band On The Run	*Paul McCartney & Wings*	Apple 3415
10	10	42	Behind Closed Doors	*Charlie Rich*	Epic 32247

Billboard — MARCH 9, 1974 — TOP LP's

TW	LW	WK	Title	Artist	Label
1	1	5	**Planet Waves**	*Bob Dylan & The Band*	Asylum 1003
2	2	5	**Court And Spark**	*Joni Mitchell*	Asylum 1001
3	4	6	**Hotcakes**	*Carly Simon*	Elektra 1002
4	3	14	John Denver's Greatest Hits	*John Denver*	RCA 0374
5	16	4	The Way We Were	*Barbra Streisand*	Columbia 32801
6	7	6	**Tales From Topographic Oceans**	*Yes*	Atlantic 908
7	6	55	You Don't Mess Around With Jim	*Jim Croce*	ABC 756
8	9	12	Band On The Run	*Paul McCartney & Wings*	Apple 3415
9	11	18	Tubular Bells	*Mike Oldfield*	Virgin 105
10	8	21	Goodbye Yellow Brick Road	*Elton John*	MCA 10003

Billboard — MARCH 16, 1974 — TOP LP's

TW	LW	WK	Title	Artist	Label
1	5	5	**The Way We Were**	*Barbra Streisand*	Columbia 32801
2	2	6	**Court And Spark**	*Joni Mitchell*	Asylum 1001
3	1	6	Planet Waves	*Bob Dylan & The Band*	Asylum 1003
4	4	15	John Denver's Greatest Hits	*John Denver*	RCA 0374
5	3	7	Hotcakes	*Carly Simon*	Elektra 1002
6	6	7	**Tales From Topographic Oceans**	*Yes*	Atlantic 908
7	9	19	Tubular Bells	*Mike Oldfield*	Virgin 105
8	8	13	Band On The Run	*Paul McCartney & Wings*	Apple 3415
9	10	22	Goodbye Yellow Brick Road	*Elton John*	MCA 10003
10	7	56	You Don't Mess Around With Jim	*Jim Croce*	ABC 756

Billboard — MARCH 23, 1974 — TOP LP's

TW	LW	WK	Title	Artist	Label
1	1	6	**The Way We Were**	*Barbra Streisand*	Columbia 32801
2	4	16	John Denver's Greatest Hits	*John Denver*	RCA 0374
3	2	7	Court And Spark	*Joni Mitchell*	Asylum 1001
4	7	20	Tubular Bells	*Mike Oldfield*	Virgin 105
5	3	7	Planet Waves	*Bob Dylan & The Band*	Asylum 1003
6	5	8	Hotcakes	*Carly Simon*	Elektra 1002
7	8	14	Band On The Run	*Paul McCartney & Wings*	Apple 3415
8	6	8	Tales From Topographic Oceans	*Yes*	Atlantic 908
9	9	23	Goodbye Yellow Brick Road	*Elton John*	MCA 10003
10	12	7	Rhapsody In White	*Love Unlimited Orchestra*	20th Century 433

Billboard — MARCH 30, 1974 — TOP LP's

TW	LW	WK	Title	Artist...Label
1	2	17	**John Denver's Greatest Hits**	*John Denver*...RCA 0374
2	3	8	**Court And Spark**	*Joni Mitchell*...Asylum 1001
3	4	21	**Tubular Bells**	*Mike Oldfield*...Virgin 105
4	1	7	The Way We Were	*Barbra Streisand*...Columbia 32801
5	7	15	Band On The Run	*Paul McCartney & Wings*...Apple 3415
6	5	8	Planet Waves	*Bob Dylan & The Band*...Asylum 1003
7	6	9	Hotcakes	*Carly Simon*...Elektra 1002
8	10	8	**Rhapsody In White**	*Love Unlimited Orchestra*...20th Century 433
9	9	24	Goodbye Yellow Brick Road	*Elton John*...MCA 10003
10	11	58	You Don't Mess Around With Jim	*Jim Croce*...ABC 756

Billboard — APRIL 6, 1974 — TOP LP's

TW	LW	WK	Title	Artist...Label
1	1	18	**John Denver's Greatest Hits**	*John Denver*...RCA 0374
2	5	16	Band On The Run	*Paul McCartney & Wings*...Apple 3415
3	2	9	Court And Spark	*Joni Mitchell*...Asylum 1001
4	3	22	Tubular Bells	*Mike Oldfield*...Virgin 105
5	4	8	The Way We Were	*Barbra Streisand*...Columbia 32801
6	13	12	Love Is The Message	*MFSB*...Philadelphia International 32707
7	9	25	Goodbye Yellow Brick Road	*Elton John*...MCA 10003
8	8	9	**Rhapsody In White**	*Love Unlimited Orchestra*...20th Century 433
9	7	10	Hotcakes	*Carly Simon*...Elektra 1002
10	14	11	The Sting	*Marvin Hamlisch/Soundtrack*...MCA 390

Billboard — APRIL 13, 1974 — TOP LP's

TW	LW	WK	Title	Artist...Label
1	2	17	**Band On The Run**	*Paul McCartney & Wings*...Apple 3415
2	1	19	John Denver's Greatest Hits	*John Denver*...RCA 0374
3	4	23	**Tubular Bells**	*Mike Oldfield*...Virgin 105
4	3	10	Court And Spark	*Joni Mitchell*...Asylum 1001
5	6	13	Love Is The Message	*MFSB*...Philadelphia International 32707
6	7	26	Goodbye Yellow Brick Road	*Elton John*...MCA 10003
7	5	9	The Way We Were	*Barbra Streisand*...Columbia 32801
8	10	12	The Sting	*Marvin Hamlisch/Soundtrack*...MCA 390
9	12	5	What Were Once Vices Are Now Habits	*The Doobie Brothers*...Warner 2750
10	11	7	Burn	*Deep Purple*...Warner 2766

Billboard — APRIL 20, 1974 — TOP LP's

TW	LW	WK	Title	Artist...Label
1	2	20	**John Denver's Greatest Hits**	*John Denver*...RCA 0374
2	1	18	Band On The Run	*Paul McCartney & Wings*...Apple 3415
3	12	4	Chicago VII	*Chicago*...Columbia 32810
4	5	14	**Love Is The Message**	*MFSB*...Philadelphia International 32707
5	8	13	The Sting	*Marvin Hamlisch/Soundtrack*...MCA 390
6	3	24	Tubular Bells	*Mike Oldfield*...Virgin 105
7	4	11	Court And Spark	*Joni Mitchell*...Asylum 1001
8	9	6	What Were Once Vices Are Now Habits	*The Doobie Brothers*...Warner 2750
9	10	8	**Burn**	*Deep Purple*...Warner 2766
10	14	4	Shinin' On	*Grand Funk*...Capitol 11278

TW	LW	WK	Billboard — APRIL 27, 1974 — TOP LP's
1	3	5	**Chicago VII** ... *Chicago*...Columbia 32810
2	1	21	John Denver's Greatest Hits ... *John Denver*...RCA 0374
3	5	14	The Sting ... *Marvin Hamlisch/Soundtrack*...MCA 390
4	2	19	Band On The Run ... *Paul McCartney & Wings*...Apple 3415
5	6	25	Tubular Bells ... *Mike Oldfield*...Virgin 105
6	4	15	Love Is The Message ... *MFSB*...Philadelphia International 32707
7	10	5	Shinin' On ... *Grand Funk*...Capitol 11278
8	8	7	What Were Once Vices Are Now Habits ... *The Doobie Brothers*...Warner 2750
9	12	32	Maria Muldaur ... *Maria Muldaur*...Reprise 2148
10	11	28	Goodbye Yellow Brick Road ... *Elton John*...MCA 10003

TW	LW	WK	Billboard — MAY 4, 1974 — TOP LP's
1	3	15	**The Sting** ... *Marvin Hamlisch/Soundtrack*...MCA 390
2	1	6	Chicago VII ... *Chicago*...Columbia 32810
3	2	22	John Denver's Greatest Hits ... *John Denver*...RCA 0374
4	11	4	Buddha And The Chocolate Box ... *Cat Stevens*...A&M 3623
5	7	6	**Shinin' On** ... *Grand Funk*...Capitol 11278
6	9	33	Maria Muldaur ... *Maria Muldaur*...Reprise 2148
7	4	20	Band On The Run ... *Paul McCartney & Wings*...Apple 3415
8	5	26	Tubular Bells ... *Mike Oldfield*...Virgin 105
9	10	29	Goodbye Yellow Brick Road ... *Elton John*...MCA 10003
10	8	8	What Were Once Vices Are Now Habits ... *The Doobie Brothers*...Warner 2750

TW	LW	WK	Billboard — MAY 11, 1974 — TOP LP's
1	1	16	**The Sting** ... *Marvin Hamlisch/Soundtrack*...MCA 390
2	4	5	**Buddha And The Chocolate Box** ... *Cat Stevens*...A&M 3623
3	3	23	John Denver's Greatest Hits ... *John Denver*...RCA 0374
4	6	34	Maria Muldaur ... *Maria Muldaur*...Reprise 2148
5	2	7	Chicago VII ... *Chicago*...Columbia 32810
6	5	7	Shinin' On ... *Grand Funk*...Capitol 11278
7	7	21	Band On The Run ... *Paul McCartney & Wings*...Apple 3415
8	9	30	Goodbye Yellow Brick Road ... *Elton John*...MCA 10003
9	8	27	Tubular Bells ... *Mike Oldfield*...Virgin 105
10	10	9	What Were Once Vices Are Now Habits ... *The Doobie Brothers*...Warner 2750

TW	LW	WK	Billboard — MAY 18, 1974 — TOP LP's
1	1	17	**The Sting** ... *Marvin Hamlisch/Soundtrack*...MCA 390
2	2	6	**Buddha And The Chocolate Box** ... *Cat Stevens*...A&M 3623
3	4	35	**Maria Muldaur** ... *Maria Muldaur*...Reprise 2148
4	3	24	John Denver's Greatest Hits ... *John Denver*...RCA 0374
5	6	8	**Shinin' On** ... *Grand Funk*...Capitol 11278
6	7	22	Band On The Run ... *Paul McCartney & Wings*...Apple 3415
7	5	8	Chicago VII ... *Chicago*...Columbia 32810
8	8	31	Goodbye Yellow Brick Road ... *Elton John*...MCA 10003
9	11	15	Court And Spark ... *Joni Mitchell*...Asylum 1001
10	9	28	Tubular Bells ... *Mike Oldfield*...Virgin 105

TW	LW	WK	Billboard — MAY 25, 1974 — TOP LP's	
①	1	18	**The Sting**	*Marvin Hamlisch/Soundtrack*...MCA 390
②	2	7	**Buddha And The Chocolate Box**	*Cat Stevens*...A&M 3623
③	3	36	**Maria Muldaur**	*Maria Muldaur*...Reprise 2148
❹	6	23	Band On The Run	*Paul McCartney & Wings*...Apple 3415
⑤	4	25	John Denver's Greatest Hits	*John Denver*...RCA 0374
⑥	5	9	Shinin' On	*Grand Funk*...Capitol 11278
⑦	7	9	Chicago VII	*Chicago*...Columbia 32810
⑧	9	16	Court And Spark	*Joni Mitchell*...Asylum 1001
⑨	8	32	Goodbye Yellow Brick Road	*Elton John*...MCA 10003
⑩	10	29	Tubular Bells	*Mike Oldfield*...Virgin 105

TW	LW	WK	Billboard — JUNE 1, 1974 — TOP LP's	
①	1	19	**The Sting**	*Marvin Hamlisch/Soundtrack*...MCA 390
❷	4	24	Band On The Run	*Paul McCartney & Wings*...Apple 3415
③	3	37	**Maria Muldaur**	*Maria Muldaur*...Reprise 2148
④	2	8	Buddha And The Chocolate Box	*Cat Stevens*...A&M 3623
⑤	5	26	John Denver's Greatest Hits	*John Denver*...RCA 0374
⑥	7	10	Chicago VII	*Chicago*...Columbia 32810
⑦	6	10	Shinin' On	*Grand Funk*...Capitol 11278
❽	13	18	Sundown	*Gordon Lightfoot*...Reprise 2177
⑨	9	33	Goodbye Yellow Brick Road	*Elton John*...MCA 10003
⑩	11	20	Bachman-Turner Overdrive II	*Bachman-Turner Overdrive*...Mercury 696

TW	LW	WK	Billboard — JUNE 8, 1974 — TOP LP's	
①	2	25	**Band On The Run**	*Paul McCartney & Wings*...Apple 3415
②	1	20	The Sting	*Marvin Hamlisch/Soundtrack*...MCA 390
③	4	9	Buddha And The Chocolate Box	*Cat Stevens*...A&M 3623
④	3	38	Maria Muldaur	*Maria Muldaur*...Reprise 2148
⑤	5	27	John Denver's Greatest Hits	*John Denver*...RCA 0374
❻	8	19	Sundown	*Gordon Lightfoot*...Reprise 2177
⑦	6	11	Chicago VII	*Chicago*...Columbia 32810
⑧	7	11	Shinin' On	*Grand Funk*...Capitol 11278
❾	11	18	Court And Spark	*Joni Mitchell*...Asylum 1001
⑩	9	34	Goodbye Yellow Brick Road	*Elton John*...MCA 10003

TW	LW	WK	Billboard — JUNE 15, 1974 — TOP LP's	
①	1	26	**Band On The Run**	*Paul McCartney & Wings*...Apple 3415
②	2	21	The Sting	*Marvin Hamlisch/Soundtrack*...MCA 390
❸	6	20	Sundown	*Gordon Lightfoot*...Reprise 2177
④	3	10	Buddha And The Chocolate Box	*Cat Stevens*...A&M 3623
⑤	4	39	Maria Muldaur	*Maria Muldaur*...Reprise 2148
⑥	5	28	John Denver's Greatest Hits	*John Denver*...RCA 0374
⑦	8	12	Shinin' On	*Grand Funk*...Capitol 11278
⑧	10	35	Goodbye Yellow Brick Road	*Elton John*...MCA 10003
⑨	9	19	Court And Spark	*Joni Mitchell*...Asylum 1001
⑩	7	12	Chicago VII	*Chicago*...Columbia 32810

Billboard — JUNE 22, 1974 — TOP LP's

TW	LW	WK	Title	Artist...Label
1	3	21	**Sundown**	*Gordon Lightfoot*...Reprise 2177
2	1	27	Band On The Run	*Paul McCartney & Wings*...Apple 3415
3	2	22	The Sting	*Marvin Hamlisch/Soundtrack*...MCA 390
4	4	11	Buddha And The Chocolate Box	*Cat Stevens*...A&M 3623
5	5	40	Maria Muldaur	*Maria Muldaur*...Reprise 2148
6	6	29	John Denver's Greatest Hits	*John Denver*...RCA 0374
7	9	20	Court And Spark	*Joni Mitchell*...Asylum 1001
8	7	13	Shinin' On	*Grand Funk*...Capitol 11278
9	8	36	Goodbye Yellow Brick Road	*Elton John*...MCA 10003
10	12	7	On Stage	*Loggins & Messina*...Columbia 32848

Billboard — JUNE 29, 1974 — TOP LP's

TW	LW	WK	Title	Artist...Label
1	1	22	**Sundown**	*Gordon Lightfoot*...Reprise 2177
2	2	28	Band On The Run	*Paul McCartney & Wings*...Apple 3415
3	3	23	The Sting	*Marvin Hamlisch/Soundtrack*...MCA 390
4	4	12	Buddha And The Chocolate Box	*Cat Stevens*...A&M 3623
5	6	30	John Denver's Greatest Hits	*John Denver*...RCA 0374
6	7	21	Court And Spark	*Joni Mitchell*...Asylum 1001
7	5	41	Maria Muldaur	*Maria Muldaur*...Reprise 2148
8	9	37	Goodbye Yellow Brick Road	*Elton John*...MCA 10003
9	10	8	On Stage	*Loggins & Messina*...Columbia 32848
10	11	11	**Apostrophe (')**	*Frank Zappa*...DiscReet 2175

Billboard — JULY 6, 1974 — TOP LP's

TW	LW	WK	Title	Artist...Label
1	2	29	**Band On The Run**	*Paul McCartney & Wings*...Apple 3415
2	1	23	Sundown	*Gordon Lightfoot*...Reprise 2177
3	3	24	The Sting	*Marvin Hamlisch/Soundtrack*...MCA 390
4	4	13	Buddha And The Chocolate Box	*Cat Stevens*...A&M 3623
5	-	1	Caribou	*Elton John*...MCA 2116
6	5	31	John Denver's Greatest Hits	*John Denver*...RCA 0374
7	7	42	Maria Muldaur	*Maria Muldaur*...Reprise 2148
8	18	4	Journey To The Centre Of The Earth	*Rick Wakeman*...A&M 3621
9	12	4	Diamond Dogs	*Bowie*...RCA 0576
10	8	38	Goodbye Yellow Brick Road	*Elton John*...MCA 10003

Billboard — JULY 13, 1974 — TOP LP's

TW	LW	WK	Title	Artist...Label
1	5	2	**Caribou**	*Elton John*...MCA 2116
2	17	3	Back Home Again	*John Denver*...RCA 0548
3	2	24	Sundown	*Gordon Lightfoot*...Reprise 2177
4	1	30	Band On The Run	*Paul McCartney & Wings*...Apple 3415
5	3	25	The Sting	*Marvin Hamlisch/Soundtrack*...MCA 390
6	6	32	John Denver's Greatest Hits	*John Denver*...RCA 0374
7	9	5	Diamond Dogs	*Bowie*...RCA 0576
8	8	5	Journey To The Centre Of The Earth	*Rick Wakeman*...A&M 3621
9	4	14	Buddha And The Chocolate Box	*Cat Stevens*...A&M 3623
10	14	10	On Stage	*Loggins & Messina*...Columbia 32848

TW	LW	WK	Billboard® JULY 20, 1974 TOP LP's
❶	1	3	**Caribou** .... *Elton John*...MCA 2116
❷	2	4	Back Home Again .... *John Denver*...RCA 0548
❸	8	6	**Journey To The Centre Of The Earth** .... *Rick Wakeman*...A&M 3621
④	4	31	Band On The Run .... *Paul McCartney & Wings*...Apple 3415
❺	7	6	**Diamond Dogs** .... *Bowie*...RCA 0576
❻	9	15	Buddha And The Chocolate Box .... *Cat Stevens*...A&M 3623
⑦	3	25	Sundown .... *Gordon Lightfoot*...Reprise 2177
❽	13	27	Bachman-Turner Overdrive II .... *Bachman-Turner Overdrive*...Mercury 696
⑨	6	33	John Denver's Greatest Hits .... *John Denver*...RCA 0374
⑩	10	11	On Stage .... *Loggins & Messina*...Columbia 32848

TW	LW	WK	Billboard® JULY 27, 1974 TOP LP's
❶	1	4	**Caribou** .... *Elton John*...MCA 2116
❷	2	5	Back Home Again .... *John Denver*...RCA 0548
③	3	7	**Journey To The Centre Of The Earth** .... *Rick Wakeman*...A&M 3621
❹	15	3	Before The Flood .... *Bob Dylan & The Band*...Asylum 201
⑤	5	7	**Diamond Dogs** .... *Bowie*...RCA 0576
⑥	6	16	Buddha And The Chocolate Box .... *Cat Stevens*...A&M 3623
⑦	4	32	Band On The Run .... *Paul McCartney & Wings*...Apple 3415
⑧	8	28	Bachman-Turner Overdrive II .... *Bachman-Turner Overdrive*...Mercury 696
⑨	10	12	On Stage .... *Loggins & Messina*...Columbia 32848
⑩	9	34	John Denver's Greatest Hits .... *John Denver*...RCA 0374

TW	LW	WK	Billboard® AUGUST 3, 1974 TOP LP's
①	1	5	**Caribou** .... *Elton John*...MCA 2116
②	2	6	Back Home Again .... *John Denver*...RCA 0548
③	4	4	**Before The Flood** .... *Bob Dylan & The Band*...Asylum 201
④	3	8	Journey To The Centre Of The Earth .... *Rick Wakeman*...A&M 3621
❺	20	3	461 Ocean Boulevard .... *Eric Clapton*...RSO 4801
❻	8	29	Bachman-Turner Overdrive II .... *Bachman-Turner Overdrive*...Mercury 696
❼	9	13	On Stage .... *Loggins & Messina*...Columbia 32848
⑧	7	33	Band On The Run .... *Paul McCartney & Wings*...Apple 3415
⑨	11	53	Tres Hombres .... *ZZ Top*...London 631
⑩	12	19	Pretzel Logic .... *Steely Dan*...ABC 808

TW	LW	WK	Billboard® AUGUST 10, 1974 TOP LP's
①	2	7	**Back Home Again** .... *John Denver*...RCA 0548
②	1	6	Caribou .... *Elton John*...MCA 2116
③	3	5	**Before The Flood** .... *Bob Dylan & The Band*...Asylum 201
❹	5	4	461 Ocean Boulevard .... *Eric Clapton*...RSO 4801
❺	7	14	**On Stage** .... *Loggins & Messina*...Columbia 32848
⑥	6	30	Bachman-Turner Overdrive II .... *Bachman-Turner Overdrive*...Mercury 696
⑦	4	9	Journey To The Centre Of The Earth .... *Rick Wakeman*...A&M 3621
⑧	9	54	**Tres Hombres** .... *ZZ Top*...London 631
⑨	10	20	Pretzel Logic .... *Steely Dan*...ABC 808
⑩	8	34	Band On The Run .... *Paul McCartney & Wings*...Apple 3415

TW	LW	WK	Billboard® AUGUST 17, 1974	TOP LP's
1	4	5	**461 Ocean Boulevard**	*Eric Clapton*...RSO 4801
2	1	8	Back Home Again	*John Denver*...RCA 0548
3	2	7	Caribou	*Elton John*...MCA 2116
4	3	6	Before The Flood	*Bob Dylan & The Band*...Asylum 201
5	5	15	**On Stage**	*Loggins & Messina*...Columbia 32848
6	79	2	Fulfillingness' First Finale	*Stevie Wonder*...Tamla 332
7	6	31	Bachman-Turner Overdrive II	*Bachman-Turner Overdrive*...Mercury 696
8	9	21	**Pretzel Logic**	*Steely Dan*...ABC 808
9	13	18	Bridge Of Sighs	*Robin Trower*...Chrysalis 1057
10	10	35	Band On The Run	*Paul McCartney & Wings*...Apple 3415

TW	LW	WK	Billboard® AUGUST 24, 1974	TOP LP's
1	1	6	**461 Ocean Boulevard**	*Eric Clapton*...RSO 4801
2	2	9	Back Home Again	*John Denver*...RCA 0548
3	3	8	Caribou	*Elton John*...MCA 2116
4	6	3	Fulfillingness' First Finale	*Stevie Wonder*...Tamla 332
5	7	32	Bachman-Turner Overdrive II	*Bachman-Turner Overdrive*...Mercury 696
6	18	5	Bad Company	*Bad Company*...Swan Song 8410
7	5	16	On Stage	*Loggins & Messina*...Columbia 32848
8	9	19	Bridge Of Sighs	*Robin Trower*...Chrysalis 1057
9	4	7	Before The Flood	*Bob Dylan & The Band*...Asylum 201
10	10	36	Band On The Run	*Paul McCartney & Wings*...Apple 3415

TW	LW	WK	Billboard® AUGUST 31, 1974	TOP LP's
1	1	7	**461 Ocean Boulevard**	*Eric Clapton*...RSO 4801
2	4	4	Fulfillingness' First Finale	*Stevie Wonder*...Tamla 332
3	2	10	Back Home Again	*John Denver*...RCA 0548
4	5	33	**Bachman-Turner Overdrive II**	*Bachman-Turner Overdrive*...Mercury 696
5	6	6	Bad Company	*Bad Company*...Swan Song 8410
6	3	9	Caribou	*Elton John*...MCA 2116
7	8	20	**Bridge Of Sighs**	*Robin Trower*...Chrysalis 1057
8	11	10	Rags To Rufus	*Rufus*...ABC 809
9	20	8	Marvin Gaye Live!	*Marvin Gaye*...Tamla 333
10	15	7	Endless Summer	*The Beach Boys*...Capitol 11307

TW	LW	WK	Billboard® SEPTEMBER 7, 1974	TOP LP's
1	1	8	**461 Ocean Boulevard**	*Eric Clapton*...RSO 4801
2	2	5	Fulfillingness' First Finale	*Stevie Wonder*...Tamla 332
3	5	7	Bad Company	*Bad Company*...Swan Song 8410
4	4	34	**Bachman-Turner Overdrive II**	*Bachman-Turner Overdrive*...Mercury 696
5	3	11	Back Home Again	*John Denver*...RCA 0548
6	6	10	Caribou	*Elton John*...MCA 2116
7	8	11	Rags To Rufus	*Rufus*...ABC 809
8	9	9	**Marvin Gaye Live!**	*Marvin Gaye*...Tamla 333
9	10	8	Endless Summer	*The Beach Boys*...Capitol 11307
10	12	24	Chicago VII	*Chicago*...Columbia 32810

Billboard — SEPTEMBER 14, 1974 — TOP LP's

TW	LW	WK	Title	Artist...Label
1	2	6	**Fulfillingness' First Finale**	*Stevie Wonder*...Tamla 332
2	3	8	Bad Company	*Bad Company*...Swan Song 8410
3	1	9	461 Ocean Boulevard	*Eric Clapton*...RSO 4801
4	9	9	Endless Summer	*The Beach Boys*...Capitol 11307
5	7	12	Rags To Rufus	*Rufus*...ABC 809
6	21	15	If You Love Me, Let Me Know	*Olivia Newton-John*...MCA 411
7	4	35	Bachman-Turner Overdrive II	*Bachman-Turner Overdrive*...Mercury 696
8	8	10	**Marvin Gaye Live!**	*Marvin Gaye*...Tamla 333
9	10	25	Chicago VII	*Chicago*...Columbia 32810
10	6	11	Caribou	*Elton John*...MCA 2116

Billboard — SEPTEMBER 21, 1974 — TOP LP's

TW	LW	WK	Title	Artist...Label
1	1	7	**Fulfillingness' First Finale**	*Stevie Wonder*...Tamla 332
2	2	9	Bad Company	*Bad Company*...Swan Song 8410
3	4	10	Endless Summer	*The Beach Boys*...Capitol 11307
4	5	13	**Rags To Rufus**	*Rufus*...ABC 809
5	6	16	If You Love Me, Let Me Know	*Olivia Newton-John*...MCA 411
6	7	36	Bachman-Turner Overdrive II	*Bachman-Turner Overdrive*...Mercury 696
7	3	10	461 Ocean Boulevard	*Eric Clapton*...RSO 4801
8	9	26	Chicago VII	*Chicago*...Columbia 32810
9	8	11	Marvin Gaye Live!	*Marvin Gaye*...Tamla 333
10	11	13	Back Home Again	*John Denver*...RCA 0548

Billboard — SEPTEMBER 28, 1974 — TOP LP's

TW	LW	WK	Title	Artist...Label
1	2	10	**Bad Company**	*Bad Company*...Swan Song 8410
2	3	11	Endless Summer	*The Beach Boys*...Capitol 11307
3	1	8	Fulfillingness' First Finale	*Stevie Wonder*...Tamla 332
4	5	17	If You Love Me, Let Me Know	*Olivia Newton-John*...MCA 411
5	12	13	Caribou	*Elton John*...MCA 2116
6	14	5	Not Fragile	*Bachman-Turner Overdrive*...Mercury 1004
7	10	14	Back Home Again	*John Denver*...RCA 0548
8	8	27	Chicago VII	*Chicago*...Columbia 32810
9	22	4	Can't Get Enough	*Barry White*...20th Century 444
10	7	11	461 Ocean Boulevard	*Eric Clapton*...RSO 4801

Billboard — OCTOBER 5, 1974 — TOP LP's

TW	LW	WK	Title	Artist...Label
1	2	12	**Endless Summer**	*The Beach Boys*...Capitol 11307
2	4	18	If You Love Me, Let Me Know	*Olivia Newton-John*...MCA 411
3	1	11	Bad Company	*Bad Company*...Swan Song 8410
4	6	6	Not Fragile	*Bachman-Turner Overdrive*...Mercury 1004
5	5	14	Caribou	*Elton John*...MCA 2116
6	9	5	Can't Get Enough	*Barry White*...20th Century 444
7	7	15	Back Home Again	*John Denver*...RCA 0548
8	8	28	Chicago VII	*Chicago*...Columbia 32810
9	14	5	Welcome back, my friends, to the show that never ends- Ladies and Gentlemen	*Emerson, Lake & Palmer*...Manticore 200
10	12	20	Body Heat	*Quincy Jones*...A&M 3617

Billboard — OCTOBER 12, 1974 — TOP LP's

TW	LW	WK	Title	Artist	Label
1	2	19	**If You Love Me, Let Me Know**	Olivia Newton-John	MCA 411
2	4	7	Not Fragile	Bachman-Turner Overdrive	Mercury 1004
3	6	6	Can't Get Enough	Barry White	20th Century 444
4	3	12	Bad Company	Bad Company	Swan Song 8410
5	5	15	Caribou	Elton John	MCA 2116
6	7	16	Back Home Again	John Denver	RCA 0548
7	12	6	So Far	Crosby, Stills, Nash & Young	Atlantic 18100
8	9	6	Welcome back, my friends, to the show that never ends- Ladies and Gentlemen	Emerson, Lake & Palmer	Manticore 200
9	10	21	Body Heat	Quincy Jones	A&M 3617
10	14	14	Holiday	America	Warner 2808

Billboard — OCTOBER 19, 1974 — TOP LP's

TW	LW	WK	Title	Artist	Label
1	2	8	**Not Fragile**	Bachman-Turner Overdrive	Mercury 1004
2	3	7	Can't Get Enough	Barry White	20th Century 444
3	6	17	Back Home Again	John Denver	RCA 0548
4	1	20	If You Love Me, Let Me Know	Olivia Newton-John	MCA 411
5	8	7	Welcome back, my friends, to the show that never ends- Ladies and Gentlemen	Emerson, Lake & Palmer	Manticore 200
6	7	7	So Far	Crosby, Stills, Nash & Young	Atlantic 18100
7	15	4	Wrap Around Joy	Carole King	Ode 77024
8	9	22	Body Heat	Quincy Jones	A&M 3617
9	10	15	Holiday	America	Warner 2808
10	14	8	Anka	Paul Anka	United Artists 314

Billboard — OCTOBER 26, 1974 — TOP LP's

TW	LW	WK	Title	Artist	Label
1	2	8	**Can't Get Enough**	Barry White	20th Century 444
2	6	8	So Far	Crosby, Stills, Nash & Young	Atlantic 18100
3	3	18	Back Home Again	John Denver	RCA 0548
4	5	8	**Welcome back, my friends, to the show that never ends- Ladies and Gentlemen**	Emerson, Lake & Palmer	Manticore 200
5	7	5	Wrap Around Joy	Carole King	Ode 77024
6	1	9	Not Fragile	Bachman-Turner Overdrive	Mercury 1004
7	8	23	Body Heat	Quincy Jones	A&M 3617
8	9	16	Holiday	America	Warner 2808
9	10	9	**Anka**	Paul Anka	United Artists 314
10	20	4	Photographs & Memories/His Greatest Hits	Jim Croce	ABC 835

Billboard — NOVEMBER 2, 1974 — TOP LP's

TW	LW	WK	Title	Artist	Label
1	2	9	**So Far**	Crosby, Stills, Nash & Young	Atlantic 18100
2	5	6	Wrap Around Joy	Carole King	Ode 77024
3	1	9	Can't Get Enough	Barry White	20th Century 444
4	12	4	Walls And Bridges	John Lennon	Apple 3416
5	6	10	Not Fragile	Bachman-Turner Overdrive	Mercury 1004
6	7	24	**Body Heat**	Quincy Jones	A&M 3617
7	8	17	Holiday	America	Warner 2808
8	10	5	Photographs & Memories/His Greatest Hits	Jim Croce	ABC 835
9	9	10	**Anka**	Paul Anka	United Artists 314
10	4	9	Welcome back, my friends, to the show that never ends- Ladies and Gentlemen	Emerson, Lake & Palmer	Manticore 200

TW	LW	WK	Billboard. NOVEMBER 9, 1974 TOP LP's
①	2	7	**Wrap Around Joy** ... *Carole King*...Ode 77024
❷	4	5	Walls And Bridges ... *John Lennon*...Apple 3416
❸	8	6	Photographs & Memories/His Greatest Hits ... *Jim Croce*...ABC 835
④	5	11	Not Fragile ... *Bachman-Turner Overdrive*...Mercury 1004
❺	7	18	Holiday ... *America*...Warner 2808
⑥	1	10	So Far ... *Crosby, Stills, Nash & Young*...Atlantic 18100
❼	18	4	Cheech & Chong's Wedding Album ... *Cheech & Chong*...Ode 77025
⑧	3	10	Can't Get Enough ... *Barry White*...20th Century 444
❾	12	11	Alice Cooper's Greatest Hits ... *Alice Cooper*...Warner 2803
❿	13	7	When The Eagle Flies ... *Traffic*...Asylum 1020

TW	LW	WK	Billboard. NOVEMBER 16, 1974 TOP LP's
①	2	6	**Walls And Bridges** ... *John Lennon*...Apple 3416
②	3	7	**Photographs & Memories/His Greatest Hits** ... *Jim Croce*...ABC 835
❸	19	3	It's Only Rock 'N Roll ... *The Rolling Stones*...Rolling Stones 79101
④	5	19	Holiday ... *America*...Warner 2808
⑤	4	12	Not Fragile ... *Bachman-Turner Overdrive*...Mercury 1004
⑥	7	5	Cheech & Chong's Wedding Album ... *Cheech & Chong*...Ode 77025
⑦	1	8	Wrap Around Joy ... *Carole King*...Ode 77024
⑧	9	12	**Alice Cooper's Greatest Hits** ... *Alice Cooper*...Warner 2803
⑨	10	8	**When The Eagle Flies** ... *Traffic*...Asylum 1020
❿	21	4	War Child ... *Jethro Tull*...Chrysalis 1067

TW	LW	WK	Billboard. NOVEMBER 23, 1974 TOP LP's
①	3	4	**It's Only Rock 'N Roll** ... *The Rolling Stones*...Rolling Stones 79101
②	2	8	**Photographs & Memories/His Greatest Hits** ... *Jim Croce*...ABC 835
③	4	20	**Holiday** ... *America*...Warner 2808
④	5	13	Not Fragile ... *Bachman-Turner Overdrive*...Mercury 1004
⑤	6	6	**Cheech & Chong's Wedding Album** ... *Cheech & Chong*...Ode 77025
⑥	1	7	Walls And Bridges ... *John Lennon*...Apple 3416
❼	10	5	War Child ... *Jethro Tull*...Chrysalis 1067
❽	15	5	Serenade ... *Neil Diamond*...Columbia 32919
❾	17	5	David Live ... *David Bowie*...RCA 0771
❿	14	8	**Sally Can't Dance** ... *Lou Reed*...RCA 0611

TW	LW	WK	Billboard. NOVEMBER 30, 1974 TOP LP's
❶	47	2	**Elton John - Greatest Hits** ... *Elton John*...MCA 2128
②	1	5	It's Only Rock 'N Roll ... *The Rolling Stones*...Rolling Stones 79101
③	4	14	Not Fragile ... *Bachman-Turner Overdrive*...Mercury 1004
❹	6	8	Walls And Bridges ... *John Lennon*...Apple 3416
⑤	2	9	Photographs & Memories/His Greatest Hits ... *Jim Croce*...ABC 835
⑥	7	6	War Child ... *Jethro Tull*...Chrysalis 1067
⑦	8	6	Serenade ... *Neil Diamond*...Columbia 32919
⑧	9	6	**David Live** ... *David Bowie*...RCA 0771
❾	11	13	Verities & Balderdash ... *Harry Chapin*...Elektra 1012
⑩	10	9	**Sally Can't Dance** ... *Lou Reed*...RCA 0611

Billboard — DECEMBER 7, 1974 — TOP LP's

TW	LW	WK	Title	Artist...Label
1	1	3	**Elton John - Greatest Hits**	*Elton John*...MCA 2128
2	2	6	It's Only Rock 'N Roll	*The Rolling Stones*...Rolling Stones 79101
3	3	15	Not Fragile	*Bachman-Turner Overdrive*...Mercury 1004
4	4	9	Walls And Bridges	*John Lennon*...Apple 3416
5	6	7	War Child	*Jethro Tull*...Chrysalis 1067
6	7	7	Serenade	*Neil Diamond*...Columbia 32919
7	5	10	Photographs & Memories/His Greatest Hits	*Jim Croce*...ABC 835
8	9	14	Verities & Balderdash	*Harry Chapin*...Elektra 1012
9	8	7	David Live	*David Bowie*...RCA 0771
10	19	5	Mother Lode	*Loggins & Messina*...Columbia 33175

Billboard — DECEMBER 14, 1974 — TOP LP's

TW	LW	WK	Title	Artist...Label
1	1	4	**Elton John - Greatest Hits**	*Elton John*...MCA 2128
2	2	7	It's Only Rock 'N Roll	*The Rolling Stones*...Rolling Stones 79101
3	3	16	Not Fragile	*Bachman-Turner Overdrive*...Mercury 1004
4	5	8	War Child	*Jethro Tull*...Chrysalis 1067
5	6	8	Serenade	*Neil Diamond*...Columbia 32919
6	11	25	Back Home Again	*John Denver*...RCA 0548
7	8	15	Verities & Balderdash	*Harry Chapin*...Elektra 1012
8	7	11	Photographs & Memories/His Greatest Hits	*Jim Croce*...ABC 835
9	10	6	Mother Lode	*Loggins & Messina*...Columbia 33175
10	12	4	Fire	*Ohio Players*...Mercury 1013

Billboard — DECEMBER 21, 1974 — TOP LP's

TW	LW	WK	Title	Artist...Label
1	1	5	**Elton John - Greatest Hits**	*Elton John*...MCA 2128
2	2	8	It's Only Rock 'N Roll	*The Rolling Stones*...Rolling Stones 79101
3	4	9	War Child	*Jethro Tull*...Chrysalis 1067
4	5	9	Serenade	*Neil Diamond*...Columbia 32919
5	7	16	Verities & Balderdash	*Harry Chapin*...Elektra 1012
6	6	26	Back Home Again	*John Denver*...RCA 0548
7	3	17	Not Fragile	*Bachman-Turner Overdrive*...Mercury 1004
8	10	5	Fire	*Ohio Players*...Mercury 1013
9	9	7	Mother Lode	*Loggins & Messina*...Columbia 33175
10	18	8	Free And Easy	*Helen Reddy*...Capitol 11348

Billboard — DECEMBER 28, 1974 — TOP LP's

TW	LW	WK	Title	Artist...Label
1	1	6	**Elton John - Greatest Hits**	*Elton John*...MCA 2128
2	3	10	**War Child**	*Jethro Tull*...Chrysalis 1067
3	4	10	**Serenade**	*Neil Diamond*...Columbia 32919
4	5	17	**Verities & Balderdash**	*Harry Chapin*...Elektra 1012
5	6	27	Back Home Again	*John Denver*...RCA 0548
6	8	6	Fire	*Ohio Players*...Mercury 1013
7	2	9	It's Only Rock 'N Roll	*The Rolling Stones*...Rolling Stones 79101
8	9	8	**Mother Lode**	*Loggins & Messina*...Columbia 33175
9	10	9	Free And Easy	*Helen Reddy*...Capitol 11348
10	13	5	Goodnight Vienna	*Ringo Starr*...Apple 3417

TW	LW	WK	Billboard® — JANUARY 4, 1975 — TOP LP's	
❶	1	7	**Elton John - Greatest Hits**	*Elton John*...MCA 2128
②	2	11	**War Child**	*Jethro Tull*...Chrysalis 1067
③	3	11	**Serenade**	*Neil Diamond*...Columbia 32919
❹	6	7	Fire	*Ohio Players*...Mercury 1013
❺	13	4	Miles Of Aisles	*Joni Mitchell*...Asylum 202
⑥	5	28	Back Home Again	*John Denver*...RCA 0548
⑦	4	18	Verities & Balderdash	*Harry Chapin*...Elektra 1012
⑧	9	10	**Free And Easy**	*Helen Reddy*...Capitol 11348
⑨	10	6	Goodnight Vienna	*Ringo Starr*...Apple 3417
⑩	11	19	Not Fragile	*Bachman-Turner Overdrive*...Mercury 1004

TW	LW	WK	Billboard® — JANUARY 11, 1975 — TOP LP's	
❶	1	8	**Elton John - Greatest Hits**	*Elton John*...MCA 2128
②	2	12	**War Child**	*Jethro Tull*...Chrysalis 1067
③	4	8	Fire	*Ohio Players*...Mercury 1013
④	5	5	Miles Of Aisles	*Joni Mitchell*...Asylum 202
⑤	6	29	Back Home Again	*John Denver*...RCA 0548
⑥	7	19	Verities & Balderdash	*Harry Chapin*...Elektra 1012
⑦	3	12	Serenade	*Neil Diamond*...Columbia 32919
⑧	9	7	**Goodnight Vienna**	*Ringo Starr*...Apple 3417
⑨	10	20	Not Fragile	*Bachman-Turner Overdrive*...Mercury 1004
❿	14	6	Heart Like A Wheel	*Linda Ronstadt*...Capitol 11358

TW	LW	WK	Billboard® — JANUARY 18, 1975 — TOP LP's	
❶	1	9	**Elton John - Greatest Hits**	*Elton John*...MCA 2128
②	3	9	Fire	*Ohio Players*...Mercury 1013
③	4	6	Miles Of Aisles	*Joni Mitchell*...Asylum 202
④	5	30	Back Home Again	*John Denver*...RCA 0548
❺	13	4	Dark Horse	*George Harrison*...Apple 3418
❻	10	7	Heart Like A Wheel	*Linda Ronstadt*...Capitol 11358
❼	11	4	Relayer	*Yes*...Atlantic 18122
⑧	8	8	**Goodnight Vienna**	*Ringo Starr*...Apple 3417
❾	14	18	AWB	*Average White Band*...Atlantic 7308
⑩	2	13	War Child	*Jethro Tull*...Chrysalis 1067

TW	LW	WK	Billboard® — JANUARY 25, 1975 — TOP LP's	
❶	1	10	**Elton John - Greatest Hits**	*Elton John*...MCA 2128
②	2	10	Fire	*Ohio Players*...Mercury 1013
③	3	7	Miles Of Aisles	*Joni Mitchell*...Asylum 202
④	5	5	**Dark Horse**	*George Harrison*...Apple 3418
⑤	6	8	Heart Like A Wheel	*Linda Ronstadt*...Capitol 11358
⑥	7	5	Relayer	*Yes*...Atlantic 18122
⑦	4	31	Back Home Again	*John Denver*...RCA 0548
⑧	9	19	AWB	*Average White Band*...Atlantic 7308
⑨	10	14	War Child	*Jethro Tull*...Chrysalis 1067
⑩	8	9	Goodnight Vienna	*Ringo Starr*...Apple 3417

Billboard — FEBRUARY 1, 1975 — TOP LP's

TW	LW	WK	Title	Artist...Label
❶	1	11	**Elton John - Greatest Hits**	*Elton John*...MCA 2128
②	2	11	Fire	*Ohio Players*...Mercury 1013
③	3	8	Miles Of Aisles	*Joni Mitchell*...Asylum 202
❹	5	9	Heart Like A Wheel	*Linda Ronstadt*...Capitol 11358
⑤	6	6	**Relayer**	*Yes*...Atlantic 18122
❻	8	20	AWB	*Average White Band*...Atlantic 7308
⑦	4	6	Dark Horse	*George Harrison*...Apple 3418
⑧	9	15	War Child	*Jethro Tull*...Chrysalis 1067
⑨	7	32	Back Home Again	*John Denver*...RCA 0548
❿	14	8	New And Improved	*Spinners*...Atlantic 18118

Billboard — FEBRUARY 8, 1975 — TOP LP's

TW	LW	WK	Title	Artist...Label
①	2	12	**Fire**	*Ohio Players*...Mercury 1013
②	3	9	**Miles Of Aisles**	*Joni Mitchell*...Asylum 202
❸	4	10	Heart Like A Wheel	*Linda Ronstadt*...Capitol 11358
❹	6	21	AWB	*Average White Band*...Atlantic 7308
⑤	1	12	Elton John - Greatest Hits	*Elton John*...MCA 2128
⑥	7	7	Dark Horse	*George Harrison*...Apple 3418
⑦	8	16	War Child	*Jethro Tull*...Chrysalis 1067
⑧	5	7	Relayer	*Yes*...Atlantic 18122
⑨	10	9	**New And Improved**	*Spinners*...Atlantic 18118
⑩	11	12	Do It ('Til You're Satisfied)	*B.T. Express*...Roadshow 5117

Billboard — FEBRUARY 15, 1975 — TOP LP's

TW	LW	WK	Title	Artist...Label
①	3	11	**Heart Like A Wheel**	*Linda Ronstadt*...Capitol 11358
❷	4	22	AWB	*Average White Band*...Atlantic 7308
③	2	10	Miles Of Aisles	*Joni Mitchell*...Asylum 202
❹	15	2	Blood On The Tracks	*Bob Dylan*...Columbia 33235
⑤	6	8	Dark Horse	*George Harrison*...Apple 3418
⑥	7	17	War Child	*Jethro Tull*...Chrysalis 1067
⑦	1	13	Fire	*Ohio Players*...Mercury 1013
❽	10	13	Do It ('Til You're Satisfied)	*B.T. Express*...Roadshow 5117
❾	14	7	Rufusized	*Rufus Featuring Chaka Khan*...ABC 837
⑩	11	13	Barry Manilow II	*Barry Manilow*...Arista 4016

Billboard — FEBRUARY 22, 1975 — TOP LP's

TW	LW	WK	Title	Artist...Label
①	2	23	**AWB**	*Average White Band*...Atlantic 7308
❷	4	3	Blood On The Tracks	*Bob Dylan*...Columbia 33235
③	1	12	Heart Like A Wheel	*Linda Ronstadt*...Capitol 11358
④	3	11	Miles Of Aisles	*Joni Mitchell*...Asylum 202
⑤	6	18	War Child	*Jethro Tull*...Chrysalis 1067
❻	8	14	Do It ('Til You're Satisfied)	*B.T. Express*...Roadshow 5117
❼	12	4	Empty Sky	*Elton John*...MCA 2130
⑧	9	8	Rufusized	*Rufus Featuring Chaka Khan*...ABC 837
⑨	10	14	**Barry Manilow II**	*Barry Manilow*...Arista 4016
⑩	11	10	**All The Girls In The World Beware!!!**	*Grand Funk*...Capitol 11356

TW	LW	WK	Billboard® MARCH 1, 1975 TOP LP's
1	2	4	**Blood On The Tracks** ... *Bob Dylan*...Columbia 33235
2	1	24	AWB ... *Average White Band*...Atlantic 7308
3	3	13	Heart Like A Wheel ... *Linda Ronstadt*...Capitol 11358
4	5	19	War Child ... *Jethro Tull*...Chrysalis 1067
5	6	15	**Do It ('Til You're Satisfied)** ... *B.T. Express*...Roadshow 5117
6	7	5	**Empty Sky** ... *Elton John*...MCA 2130
7	8	9	**Rufusized** ... *Rufus Featuring Chaka Khan*...ABC 837
8	12	26	Phoebe Snow ... *Phoebe Snow*...Shelter 2109
9	13	42	What Were Once Vices Are Now Habits ... *The Doobie Brothers*...Warner 2750
10	43	2	Have You Never Been Mellow ... *Olivia Newton-John*...MCA 2133

TW	LW	WK	Billboard® MARCH 8, 1975 TOP LP's
1	1	5	**Blood On The Tracks** ... *Bob Dylan*...Columbia 33235
2	2	25	AWB ... *Average White Band*...Atlantic 7308
3	10	3	Have You Never Been Mellow ... *Olivia Newton-John*...MCA 2133
4	3	14	Heart Like A Wheel ... *Linda Ronstadt*...Capitol 11358
5	8	27	Phoebe Snow ... *Phoebe Snow*...Shelter 2109
6	9	43	What Were Once Vices Are Now Habits ... *The Doobie Brothers*...Warner 2750
7	5	16	Do It ('Til You're Satisfied) ... *B.T. Express*...Roadshow 5117
8	7	10	Rufusized ... *Rufus Featuring Chaka Khan*...ABC 837
9	12	30	Perfect Angel ... *Minnie Riperton*...Epic 32561
10	6	6	Empty Sky ... *Elton John*...MCA 2130

TW	LW	WK	Billboard® MARCH 15, 1975 TOP LP's
1	3	4	**Have You Never Been Mellow** ... *Olivia Newton-John*...MCA 2133
2	1	6	Blood On The Tracks ... *Bob Dylan*...Columbia 33235
3	-	1	Physical Graffiti ... *Led Zeppelin*...Swan Song 200
4	5	28	**Phoebe Snow** ... *Phoebe Snow*...Shelter 2109
5	6	44	What Were Once Vices Are Now Habits ... *The Doobie Brothers*...Warner 2750
6	9	31	Perfect Angel ... *Minnie Riperton*...Epic 32561
7	4	15	Heart Like A Wheel ... *Linda Ronstadt*...Capitol 11358
8	13	13	Nightbirds ... *LaBelle*...Epic 33075
9	24	3	For Earth Below ... *Robin Trower*...Chrysalis 1073
10	2	26	AWB ... *Average White Band*...Atlantic 7308

TW	LW	WK	Billboard® MARCH 22, 1975 TOP LP's
1	3	2	**Physical Graffiti** ... *Led Zeppelin*...Swan Song 200
2	1	5	Have You Never Been Mellow ... *Olivia Newton-John*...MCA 2133
3	2	7	Blood On The Tracks ... *Bob Dylan*...Columbia 33235
4	5	45	**What Were Once Vices Are Now Habits** ... *The Doobie Brothers*...Warner 2750
5	6	32	Perfect Angel ... *Minnie Riperton*...Epic 32561
6	4	29	Phoebe Snow ... *Phoebe Snow*...Shelter 2109
7	8	14	**Nightbirds** ... *LaBelle*...Epic 33075
8	9	4	For Earth Below ... *Robin Trower*...Chrysalis 1073
9	11	3	An Evening With John Denver ... *John Denver*...RCA 0764
10	7	16	Heart Like A Wheel ... *Linda Ronstadt*...Capitol 11358

Billboard — MARCH 29, 1975 — TOP LP's

TW	LW	WK	Title	Artist...Label
①	1	3	**Physical Graffiti**	*Led Zeppelin*...Swan Song 200
②	2	6	Have You Never Been Mellow	*Olivia Newton-John*...MCA 2133
③	3	8	Blood On The Tracks	*Bob Dylan*...Columbia 33235
④	5	33	**Perfect Angel**	*Minnie Riperton*...Epic 32561
⑤	4	46	What Were Once Vices Are Now Habits	*The Doobie Brothers*...Warner 2750
❻	9	4	An Evening With John Denver	*John Denver*...RCA 0764
⑦	7	15	**Nightbirds**	*LaBelle*...Epic 33075
⑧	8	5	For Earth Below	*Robin Trower*...Chrysalis 1073
⑨	6	30	Phoebe Snow	*Phoebe Snow*...Shelter 2109
❿	12	4	Rock 'N' Roll	*John Lennon*...Apple 3419

Billboard — APRIL 5, 1975 — TOP LP's

TW	LW	WK	Title	Artist...Label
①	1	4	**Physical Graffiti**	*Led Zeppelin*...Swan Song 200
②	2	7	Have You Never Been Mellow	*Olivia Newton-John*...MCA 2133
❸	6	5	An Evening With John Denver	*John Denver*...RCA 0764
④	3	9	Blood On The Tracks	*Bob Dylan*...Columbia 33235
⑤	4	34	Perfect Angel	*Minnie Riperton*...Epic 32561
❻	8	6	For Earth Below	*Robin Trower*...Chrysalis 1073
⑦	7	16	**Nightbirds**	*LaBelle*...Epic 33075
❽	10	5	Rock 'N' Roll	*John Lennon*...Apple 3419
❾	13	9	Autobahn	*Kraftwerk*...Vertigo 2003
❿	14	3	Young Americans	*David Bowie*...RCA 0998

Billboard — APRIL 12, 1975 — TOP LP's

TW	LW	WK	Title	Artist...Label
①	1	5	**Physical Graffiti**	*Led Zeppelin*...Swan Song 200
❷	3	6	**An Evening With John Denver**	*John Denver*...RCA 0764
③	2	8	Have You Never Been Mellow	*Olivia Newton-John*...MCA 2133
④	4	10	Blood On The Tracks	*Bob Dylan*...Columbia 33235
❺	6	7	**For Earth Below**	*Robin Trower*...Chrysalis 1073
⑥	5	35	Perfect Angel	*Minnie Riperton*...Epic 32561
❼	8	6	Rock 'N' Roll	*John Lennon*...Apple 3419
❽	9	10	Autobahn	*Kraftwerk*...Vertigo 2003
❾	10	4	**Young Americans**	*David Bowie*...RCA 0998
❿	12	5	That's The Way Of The World	*Earth, Wind & Fire/Soundtrack*...Columbia 33280

Billboard — APRIL 19, 1975 — TOP LP's

TW	LW	WK	Title	Artist...Label
①	1	6	**Physical Graffiti**	*Led Zeppelin*...Swan Song 200
②	2	7	**An Evening With John Denver**	*John Denver*...RCA 0764
❸	14	2	Chicago VIII	*Chicago*...Columbia 33100
④	3	9	Have You Never Been Mellow	*Olivia Newton-John*...MCA 2133
⑤	5	8	**For Earth Below**	*Robin Trower*...Chrysalis 1073
⑥	7	7	**Rock 'N' Roll**	*John Lennon*...Apple 3419
⑦	8	11	Autobahn	*Kraftwerk*...Vertigo 2003
❽	10	6	That's The Way Of The World	*Earth, Wind & Fire/Soundtrack*...Columbia 33280
⑨	9	5	**Young Americans**	*David Bowie*...RCA 0998
❿	12	5	Crash Landing	*Jimi Hendrix*...Reprise 2204

TW	LW	WK	Billboard® — APRIL 26, 1975 — TOP LP's
①	1	7	**Physical Graffiti** ... *Led Zeppelin*...Swan Song 200
❷	3	3	Chicago VIII ... *Chicago*...Columbia 33100
③	4	10	Have You Never Been Mellow ... *Olivia Newton-John*...MCA 2133
❹	8	7	That's The Way Of The World ... *Earth, Wind & Fire/Soundtrack*...Columbia 33280
⑤	2	8	An Evening With John Denver ... *John Denver*...RCA 0764
⑥	7	12	Autobahn ... *Kraftwerk*...Vertigo 2003
❼	10	6	Crash Landing ... *Jimi Hendrix*...Reprise 2204
❽	14	5	Funny Lady ... *Barbra Streisand/Soundtrack*...Arista 9004
⑨	6	8	Rock 'N' Roll ... *John Lennon*...Apple 3419
⑩	11	9	**Cold On The Shoulder** ... *Gordon Lightfoot*...Reprise 2206

TW	LW	WK	Billboard® — MAY 3, 1975 — TOP LP's
①	2	4	**Chicago VIII** ... *Chicago*...Columbia 33100
②	1	8	Physical Graffiti ... *Led Zeppelin*...Swan Song 200
❸	4	8	That's The Way Of The World ... *Earth, Wind & Fire/Soundtrack*...Columbia 33280
④	3	11	Have You Never Been Mellow ... *Olivia Newton-John*...MCA 2133
⑤	6	13	**Autobahn** ... *Kraftwerk*...Vertigo 2003
❻	7	7	Crash Landing ... *Jimi Hendrix*...Reprise 2204
❼	8	6	Funny Lady ... *Barbra Streisand/Soundtrack*...Arista 9004
❽	14	6	Tommy ... *Soundtrack*...Polydor 9502
⑨	5	9	An Evening With John Denver ... *John Denver*...RCA 0764
❿	12	7	Welcome To My Nightmare ... *Alice Cooper*...Atlantic 18130

TW	LW	WK	Billboard® — MAY 10, 1975 — TOP LP's
①	1	5	**Chicago VIII** ... *Chicago*...Columbia 33100
❷	3	9	That's The Way Of The World ... *Earth, Wind & Fire/Soundtrack*...Columbia 33280
③	2	9	Physical Graffiti ... *Led Zeppelin*...Swan Song 200
④	4	12	Have You Never Been Mellow ... *Olivia Newton-John*...MCA 2133
⑤	6	8	**Crash Landing** ... *Jimi Hendrix*...Reprise 2204
⑥	7	7	**Funny Lady** ... *Barbra Streisand/Soundtrack*...Arista 9004
⑦	8	7	Tommy ... *Soundtrack*...Polydor 9502
❽	12	4	Straight Shooter ... *Bad Company*...Swan Song 8413
⑨	9	10	An Evening With John Denver ... *John Denver*...RCA 0764
⑩	10	8	Welcome To My Nightmare ... *Alice Cooper*...Atlantic 18130

TW	LW	WK	Billboard® — MAY 17, 1975 — TOP LP's
①	2	10	**That's The Way Of The World** ... *Earth, Wind & Fire/Soundtrack*...Columbia 33280
②	1	6	Chicago VIII ... *Chicago*...Columbia 33100
❸	7	8	Tommy ... *Soundtrack*...Polydor 9502
④	3	10	Physical Graffiti ... *Led Zeppelin*...Swan Song 200
❺	8	5	Straight Shooter ... *Bad Company*...Swan Song 8413
⑥	4	13	Have You Never Been Mellow ... *Olivia Newton-John*...MCA 2133
⑦	6	8	Funny Lady ... *Barbra Streisand/Soundtrack*...Arista 9004
⑧	9	11	An Evening With John Denver ... *John Denver*...RCA 0764
❾	10	9	Welcome To My Nightmare ... *Alice Cooper*...Atlantic 18130
❿	15	7	Hearts ... *America*...Warner 2852

TW	LW	WK	Billboard® MAY 24, 1975 TOP LP's
①	1	11	**That's The Way Of The World** .... *Earth, Wind & Fire/Soundtrack*...Columbia 33280
②	2	7	Chicago VIII .... *Chicago*...Columbia 33100
❸	3	9	Tommy .... *Soundtrack*...Polydor 9502
❹	5	6	Straight Shooter .... *Bad Company*...Swan Song 8413
⑤	4	11	Physical Graffiti .... *Led Zeppelin*...Swan Song 200
❻	14	7	Blow By Blow .... *Jeff Beck*...Epic 33409
❼	10	8	Hearts .... *America*...Warner 2852
⑧	9	10	Welcome To My Nightmare .... *Alice Cooper*...Atlantic 18130
⑨	8	12	An Evening With John Denver .... *John Denver*...RCA 0764
⑩	11	7	Nuthin' Fancy .... *Lynyrd Skynyrd*...MCA 2137

TW	LW	WK	Billboard® MAY 31, 1975 TOP LP's
①	1	12	**That's The Way Of The World** .... *Earth, Wind & Fire/Soundtrack*...Columbia 33280
②	3	10	**Tommy** .... *Soundtrack*...Polydor 9502
③	4	7	**Straight Shooter** .... *Bad Company*...Swan Song 8413
④	2	8	Chicago VIII .... *Chicago*...Columbia 33100
⑤	6	8	Blow By Blow .... *Jeff Beck*...Epic 33409
⑥	7	9	Hearts .... *America*...Warner 2852
⑦	8	11	Welcome To My Nightmare .... *Alice Cooper*...Atlantic 18130
⑧	5	12	Physical Graffiti .... *Led Zeppelin*...Swan Song 200
⑨	10	8	**Nuthin' Fancy** .... *Lynyrd Skynyrd*...MCA 2137
❿	13	5	**Playing Possum** .... *Carly Simon*...Elektra 1033

TW	LW	WK	Billboard® JUNE 7, 1975 TOP LP's
❶	-	1	**Captain Fantastic And The Brown Dirt Cowboy** .... *Elton John*...MCA 2142
②	1	13	That's The Way Of The World.... *Earth, Wind & Fire/Soundtrack*...Columbia 33280
③	2	11	Tommy .... *Soundtrack*...Polydor 9502
④	5	9	**Blow By Blow** .... *Jeff Beck*...Epic 33409
⑤	6	10	Hearts .... *America*...Warner 2852
⑥	7	12	Welcome To My Nightmare .... *Alice Cooper*...Atlantic 18130
⑦	4	9	Chicago VIII .... *Chicago*...Columbia 33100
⑧	3	8	Straight Shooter .... *Bad Company*...Swan Song 8413
⑨	9	9	**Nuthin' Fancy** .... *Lynyrd Skynyrd*...MCA 2137
⑩	10	6	**Playing Possum** .... *Carly Simon*...Elektra 1033

TW	LW	WK	Billboard® JUNE 14, 1975 TOP LP's
①	1	2	**Captain Fantastic And The Brown Dirt Cowboy** .... *Elton John*...MCA 2142
②	2	14	That's The Way Of The World.... *Earth, Wind & Fire/Soundtrack*...Columbia 33280
③	3	12	Tommy .... *Soundtrack*...Polydor 9502
④	5	11	**Hearts** .... *America*...Warner 2852
⑤	7	10	Chicago VIII .... *Chicago*...Columbia 33100
⑥	6	13	Welcome To My Nightmare .... *Alice Cooper*...Atlantic 18130
⑦	4	10	Blow By Blow .... *Jeff Beck*...Epic 33409
❽	11	5	Stampede .... *The Doobie Brothers*...Warner 2835
❾	12	3	Four Wheel Drive .... *Bachman-Turner Overdrive*...Mercury 1027
❿	13	7	Spirit Of America .... *The Beach Boys*...Capitol 11384

Billboard — JUNE 21, 1975 — TOP LP's

TW	LW	WK	Title	Artist	Label
1	1	3	**Captain Fantastic And The Brown Dirt Cowboy**	*Elton John*	MCA 2142
2	25	2	Venus And Mars	*Wings*	Capitol 11419
3	2	15	That's The Way Of The World	*Earth, Wind & Fire/Soundtrack*	Columbia 33280
4	3	13	Tommy	*Soundtrack*	Polydor 9502
5	6	14	**Welcome To My Nightmare**	*Alice Cooper*	Atlantic 18130
6	8	6	Stampede	*The Doobie Brothers*	Warner 2835
7	9	4	Four Wheel Drive	*Bachman-Turner Overdrive*	Mercury 1027
8	5	11	Chicago VIII	*Chicago*	Columbia 33100
9	10	8	Spirit Of America	*The Beach Boys*	Capitol 11384
10	4	12	Hearts	*America*	Warner 2852

Billboard — JUNE 28, 1975 — TOP LP's

TW	LW	WK	Title	Artist	Label
1	1	4	**Captain Fantastic And The Brown Dirt Cowboy**	*Elton John*	MCA 2142
2	2	3	Venus And Mars	*Wings*	Capitol 11419
3	3	16	That's The Way Of The World	*Earth, Wind & Fire/Soundtrack*	Columbia 33280
4	6	7	**Stampede**	*The Doobie Brothers*	Warner 2835
5	7	5	**Four Wheel Drive**	*Bachman-Turner Overdrive*	Mercury 1027
6	4	14	Tommy	*Soundtrack*	Polydor 9502
7	5	15	Welcome To My Nightmare	*Alice Cooper*	Atlantic 18130
8	9	9	**Spirit Of America**	*The Beach Boys*	Capitol 11384
9	8	12	Chicago VIII	*Chicago*	Columbia 33100
10	11	17	**Mister Magic**	*Grover Washington, Jr.*	Kudu 20

Billboard — JULY 5, 1975 — TOP LP's

TW	LW	WK	Title	Artist	Label
1	1	5	**Captain Fantastic And The Brown Dirt Cowboy**	*Elton John*	MCA 2142
2	2	4	Venus And Mars	*Wings*	Capitol 11419
3	3	17	That's The Way Of The World	*Earth, Wind & Fire/Soundtrack*	Columbia 33280
4	4	8	**Stampede**	*The Doobie Brothers*	Warner 2835
5	5	6	**Four Wheel Drive**	*Bachman-Turner Overdrive*	Mercury 1027
6	13	4	Love Will Keep Us Together	*The Captain & Tennille*	A&M 3405
7	6	15	Tommy	*Soundtrack*	Polydor 9502
8	8	10	**Spirit Of America**	*The Beach Boys*	Capitol 11384
9	25	2	One Of These Nights	*Eagles*	Asylum 1039
10	7	16	Welcome To My Nightmare	*Alice Cooper*	Atlantic 18130

Billboard — JULY 12, 1975 — TOP LP's

TW	LW	WK	Title	Artist	Label
1	1	6	**Captain Fantastic And The Brown Dirt Cowboy**	*Elton John*	MCA 2142
2	2	5	Venus And Mars	*Wings*	Capitol 11419
3	9	3	One Of These Nights	*Eagles*	Asylum 1039
4	6	5	Love Will Keep Us Together	*The Captain & Tennille*	A&M 3405
5	3	18	That's The Way Of The World	*Earth, Wind & Fire/Soundtrack*	Columbia 33280
6	21	3	Cut The Cake	*Average White Band*	Atlantic 18140
7	13	4	Made In The Shade	*The Rolling Stones*	Rolling Stones 79102
8	12	4	**Metamorphosis**	*The Rolling Stones*	Abkco 1
9	7	16	Tommy	*Soundtrack*	Polydor 9502
10	14	7	Gorilla	*James Taylor*	Warner 2866

Billboard — JULY 19, 1975 — TOP LP's

TW	LW	WK		
1	2	6	**Venus And Mars**	*Wings*...Capitol 11419
2	1	7	Captain Fantastic And The Brown Dirt Cowboy	*Elton John*...MCA 2142
3	3	4	One Of These Nights	*Eagles*...Asylum 1039
4	4	6	Love Will Keep Us Together	*The Captain & Tennille*...A&M 3405
5	6	4	Cut The Cake	*Average White Band*...Atlantic 18140
6	7	5	**Made In The Shade**	*The Rolling Stones*...Rolling Stones 79102
7	5	19	That's The Way Of The World	*Earth, Wind & Fire/Soundtrack*...Columbia 33280
8	8	5	**Metamorphosis**	*The Rolling Stones*...Abkco 1
9	10	8	Gorilla	*James Taylor*...Warner 2866
10	12	6	The Heat Is On	*The Isley Brothers*...T-Neck 33536

Billboard — JULY 26, 1975 — TOP LP's

TW	LW	WK		
1	3	5	**One Of These Nights**	*Eagles*...Asylum 1039
2	1	7	Venus And Mars	*Wings*...Capitol 11419
3	4	7	Love Will Keep Us Together	*The Captain & Tennille*...A&M 3405
4	2	8	Captain Fantastic And The Brown Dirt Cowboy	*Elton John*...MCA 2142
5	5	5	Cut The Cake	*Average White Band*...Atlantic 18140
6	6	6	**Made In The Shade**	*The Rolling Stones*...Rolling Stones 79102
7	10	7	The Heat Is On	*The Isley Brothers*...T-Neck 33536
8	7	20	That's The Way Of The World	*Earth, Wind & Fire/Soundtrack*...Columbia 33280
9	9	9	Gorilla	*James Taylor*...Warner 2866
10	8	6	Metamorphosis	*The Rolling Stones*...Abkco 1

Billboard — AUGUST 2, 1975 — TOP LP's

TW	LW	WK		
1	1	6	**One Of These Nights**	*Eagles*...Asylum 1039
2	3	8	**Love Will Keep Us Together**	*The Captain & Tennille*...A&M 3405
3	7	8	The Heat Is On	*The Isley Brothers*...T-Neck 33536
4	4	9	Captain Fantastic And The Brown Dirt Cowboy	*Elton John*...MCA 2142
5	2	8	Venus And Mars	*Wings*...Capitol 11419
6	5	6	Cut The Cake	*Average White Band*...Atlantic 18140
7	6	7	Made In The Shade	*The Rolling Stones*...Rolling Stones 79102
8	9	10	Gorilla	*James Taylor*...Warner 2866
9	8	21	That's The Way Of The World	*Earth, Wind & Fire/Soundtrack*...Columbia 33280
10	16	4	Greatest Hits	*Cat Stevens*...A&M 4519

Billboard — AUGUST 9, 1975 — TOP LP's

TW	LW	WK		
1	1	7	**One Of These Nights**	*Eagles*...Asylum 1039
2	3	9	The Heat Is On	*The Isley Brothers*...T-Neck 33536
3	2	9	Love Will Keep Us Together	*The Captain & Tennille*...A&M 3405
4	4	10	Captain Fantastic And The Brown Dirt Cowboy	*Elton John*...MCA 2142
5	6	7	Cut The Cake	*Average White Band*...Atlantic 18140
6	5	9	Venus And Mars	*Wings*...Capitol 11419
7	8	11	Gorilla	*James Taylor*...Warner 2866
8	10	5	Greatest Hits	*Cat Stevens*...A&M 4519
9	9	22	That's The Way Of The World	*Earth, Wind & Fire/Soundtrack*...Columbia 33280
10	11	4	Red Octopus	*Jefferson Starship*...Grunt 0999

TW	LW	WK	Billboard. AUGUST 16, 1975	TOP LP's
①	1	8	**One Of These Nights**	*Eagles*...Asylum 1039
❷	2	10	The Heat Is On	*The Isley Brothers*...T-Neck 33536
❸	10	5	Red Octopus	*Jefferson Starship*...Grunt 0999
④	5	8	**Cut The Cake**	*Average White Band*...Atlantic 18140
⑤	4	11	Captain Fantastic And The Brown Dirt Cowboy	*Elton John*...MCA 2142
⑥	7	12	**Gorilla**	*James Taylor*...Warner 2866
⑦	8	6	Greatest Hits	*Cat Stevens*...A&M 4519
❽	11	22	Between The Lines	*Janis Ian*...Columbia 33394
⑨	3	10	Love Will Keep Us Together	*The Captain & Tennille*...A&M 3405
❿	12	7	Why Can't We Be Friends?	*War*...United Artists 441

TW	LW	WK	Billboard. AUGUST 23, 1975	TOP LP's
①	1	9	**One Of These Nights**	*Eagles*...Asylum 1039
❷	2	11	The Heat Is On	*The Isley Brothers*...T-Neck 33536
❸	3	6	Red Octopus	*Jefferson Starship*...Grunt 0999
④	5	12	Captain Fantastic And The Brown Dirt Cowboy	*Elton John*...MCA 2142
⑤	4	9	Cut The Cake	*Average White Band*...Atlantic 18140
⑥	7	7	**Greatest Hits**	*Cat Stevens*...A&M 4519
⑦	8	23	Between The Lines	*Janis Ian*...Columbia 33394
⑧	9	11	Love Will Keep Us Together	*The Captain & Tennille*...A&M 3405
⑨	10	8	Why Can't We Be Friends?	*War*...United Artists 441
❿	12	5	The Basement Tapes	*Bob Dylan & The Band*...Columbia 33682

TW	LW	WK	Billboard. AUGUST 30, 1975	TOP LP's
①	4	13	**Captain Fantastic And The Brown Dirt Cowboy**	*Elton John*...MCA 2142
②	2	12	The Heat Is On	*The Isley Brothers*...T-Neck 33536
❸	3	7	Red Octopus	*Jefferson Starship*...Grunt 0999
④	1	10	One Of These Nights	*Eagles*...Asylum 1039
❺	7	24	Between The Lines	*Janis Ian*...Columbia 33394
⑥	5	10	Cut The Cake	*Average White Band*...Atlantic 18140
⑦	6	8	Greatest Hits	*Cat Stevens*...A&M 4519
⑧	9	9	**Why Can't We Be Friends?**	*War*...United Artists 441
⑨	10	6	The Basement Tapes	*Bob Dylan & The Band*...Columbia 33682
⑩	8	12	Love Will Keep Us Together	*The Captain & Tennille*...A&M 3405

TW	LW	WK	Billboard. SEPTEMBER 6, 1975	TOP LP's
①	3	8	**Red Octopus**	*Jefferson Starship*...Grunt 0999
②	1	14	Captain Fantastic And The Brown Dirt Cowboy	*Elton John*...MCA 2142
❸	5	25	Between The Lines	*Janis Ian*...Columbia 33394
④	4	11	One Of These Nights	*Eagles*...Asylum 1039
⑤	2	13	The Heat Is On	*The Isley Brothers*...T-Neck 33536
⑥	7	9	**Greatest Hits**	*Cat Stevens*...A&M 4519
❼	9	7	**The Basement Tapes**	*Bob Dylan & The Band*...Columbia 33682
⑧	6	11	Cut The Cake	*Average White Band*...Atlantic 18140
❾	11	26	That's The Way Of The World	*Earth, Wind & Fire/Soundtrack*...Columbia 33280
❿	13	3	Honey	*Ohio Players*...Mercury 1038

Billboard — SEPTEMBER 13, 1975 — TOP LP's

TW	LW	WK			
1	5	14	**The Heat Is On**	*The Isley Brothers*	T-Neck 33536
2	1	9	Red Octopus	*Jefferson Starship*	Grunt 0999
3	3	26	Between The Lines	*Janis Ian*	Columbia 33394
4	2	15	Captain Fantastic And The Brown Dirt Cowboy	*Elton John*	MCA 2142
5	4	12	One Of These Nights	*Eagles*	Asylum 1039
6	10	4	Honey	*Ohio Players*	Mercury 1038
7	7	8	**The Basement Tapes**	*Bob Dylan & The Band*	Columbia 33682
8	6	10	Greatest Hits	*Cat Stevens*	A&M 4519
9	9	27	That's The Way Of The World	*Earth, Wind & Fire/Soundtrack*	Columbia 33280
10	11	18	**Fandango!**	*ZZ Top*	London 656

Billboard — SEPTEMBER 20, 1975 — TOP LP's

TW	LW	WK			
1	3	27	**Between The Lines**	*Janis Ian*	Columbia 33394
2	1	15	The Heat Is On	*The Isley Brothers*	T-Neck 33536
3	6	5	Honey	*Ohio Players*	Mercury 1038
4	2	10	Red Octopus	*Jefferson Starship*	Grunt 0999
5	4	16	Captain Fantastic And The Brown Dirt Cowboy	*Elton John*	MCA 2142
6	5	13	One Of These Nights	*Eagles*	Asylum 1039
7	8	11	Greatest Hits	*Cat Stevens*	A&M 4519
8	84	2	Born To Run	*Bruce Springsteen*	Columbia 33795
9	9	28	That's The Way Of The World	*Earth, Wind & Fire/Soundtrack*	Columbia 33280
10	13	7	Pick Of The Litter	*Spinners*	Atlantic 18141

Billboard — SEPTEMBER 27, 1975 — TOP LP's

TW	LW	WK			
1	4	11	**Red Octopus**	*Jefferson Starship*	Grunt 0999
2	3	6	**Honey**	*Ohio Players*	Mercury 1038
3	6	14	One Of These Nights	*Eagles*	Asylum 1039
4	8	3	Born To Run	*Bruce Springsteen*	Columbia 33795
5	1	28	Between The Lines	*Janis Ian*	Columbia 33394
6	2	16	The Heat Is On	*The Isley Brothers*	T-Neck 33536
7	5	17	Captain Fantastic And The Brown Dirt Cowboy	*Elton John*	MCA 2142
8	43	3	Win, Lose Or Draw	*The Allman Brothers Band*	Capricorn 0156
9	10	8	Pick Of The Litter	*Spinners*	Atlantic 18141
10	11	9	Fleetwood Mac	*Fleetwood Mac*	Reprise 2225

Billboard — OCTOBER 4, 1975 — TOP LP's

TW	LW	WK			
1	12	2	**Wish You Were Here**	*Pink Floyd*	Columbia 33453
2	-	1	Windsong	*John Denver*	RCA 1183
3	3	15	One Of These Nights	*Eagles*	Asylum 1039
4	4	4	Born To Run	*Bruce Springsteen*	Columbia 33795
5	5	29	Between The Lines	*Janis Ian*	Columbia 33394
6	8	4	Win, Lose Or Draw	*The Allman Brothers Band*	Capricorn 0156
7	1	12	Red Octopus	*Jefferson Starship*	Grunt 0999
8	9	9	**Pick Of The Litter**	*Spinners*	Atlantic 18141
9	10	10	Fleetwood Mac	*Fleetwood Mac*	Reprise 2225
10	2	7	Honey	*Ohio Players*	Mercury 1038

TW	LW	WK	Billboard. OCTOBER 11, 1975 TOP LP's
①	1	3	**Wish You Were Here** ... *Pink Floyd*...Columbia 33453
❷	2	2	Windsong ... *John Denver*...RCA 1183
❸	4	5	**Born To Run** ... *Bruce Springsteen*...Columbia 33795
④	3	16	One Of These Nights ... *Eagles*...Asylum 1039
❺	6	5	**Win, Lose Or Draw** ... *The Allman Brothers Band*...Capricorn 0156
❻	7	13	Red Octopus ... *Jefferson Starship*...Grunt 0999
⑦	5	30	Between The Lines ... *Janis Ian*...Columbia 33394
⑧	8	10	**Pick Of The Litter** ... *Spinners*...Atlantic 18141
❾	63	2	Prisoner In Disguise ... *Linda Ronstadt*...Asylum 1045
❿	23	3	Minstrel In The Gallery ... *Jethro Tull*...Chrysalis 1082

TW	LW	WK	Billboard. OCTOBER 18, 1975 TOP LP's
①	2	3	**Windsong** ... *John Denver*...RCA 1183
②	1	4	Wish You Were Here ... *Pink Floyd*...Columbia 33453
③	3	6	**Born To Run** ... *Bruce Springsteen*...Columbia 33795
❹	6	14	Red Octopus ... *Jefferson Starship*...Grunt 0999
⑤	5	6	**Win, Lose Or Draw** ... *The Allman Brothers Band*...Capricorn 0156
⑥	4	17	One Of These Nights ... *Eagles*...Asylum 1039
❼	9	3	Prisoner In Disguise ... *Linda Ronstadt*...Asylum 1045
⑧	8	11	**Pick Of The Litter** ... *Spinners*...Atlantic 18141
❾	10	4	Minstrel In The Gallery ... *Jethro Tull*...Chrysalis 1082
❿	34	2	Extra Texture (Read All About It) ... *George Harrison*...Apple 3420

TW	LW	WK	Billboard. OCTOBER 25, 1975 TOP LP's
①	1	4	**Windsong** ... *John Denver*...RCA 1183
②	2	5	Wish You Were Here ... *Pink Floyd*...Columbia 33453
❸	4	15	Red Octopus ... *Jefferson Starship*...Grunt 0999
❹	6	18	One Of These Nights ... *Eagles*...Asylum 1039
❺	7	4	Prisoner In Disguise ... *Linda Ronstadt*...Asylum 1045
⑥	5	7	Win, Lose Or Draw ... *The Allman Brothers Band*...Capricorn 0156
❼	9	5	**Minstrel In The Gallery** ... *Jethro Tull*...Chrysalis 1082
❽	10	3	**Extra Texture (Read All About It)** ... *George Harrison*...Apple 3420
⑨	3	7	Born To Run ... *Bruce Springsteen*...Columbia 33795
❿	12	8	Atlantic Crossing ... *Rod Stewart*...Warner 2875

TW	LW	WK	Billboard. NOVEMBER 1, 1975 TOP LP's
①	3	16	**Red Octopus** ... *Jefferson Starship*...Grunt 0999
②	1	5	Windsong ... *John Denver*...RCA 1183
③	2	6	Wish You Were Here ... *Pink Floyd*...Columbia 33453
④	4	19	One Of These Nights ... *Eagles*...Asylum 1039
❺	5	5	Prisoner In Disguise ... *Linda Ronstadt*...Asylum 1045
❻	9	8	Born To Run ... *Bruce Springsteen*...Columbia 33795
⑦	7	6	**Minstrel In The Gallery** ... *Jethro Tull*...Chrysalis 1082
⑧	8	4	**Extra Texture (Read All About It)** ... *George Harrison*...Apple 3420
⑨	10	9	**Atlantic Crossing** ... *Rod Stewart*...Warner 2875
❿	14	4	Wind On The Water ... *David Crosby/Graham Nash*...ABC 902

Billboard — NOVEMBER 8, 1975 — TOP LP's

TW	LW	WK			
1	-	1	**Rock Of The Westies**	*Elton John*	MCA 2163
2	1	17	Red Octopus	*Jefferson Starship*	Grunt 0999
3	3	7	Wish You Were Here	*Pink Floyd*	Columbia 33453
4	5	6	**Prisoner In Disguise**	*Linda Ronstadt*	Asylum 1045
5	2	6	Windsong	*John Denver*	RCA 1183
6	6	9	Born To Run	*Bruce Springsteen*	Columbia 33795
7	7	7	**Minstrel In The Gallery**	*Jethro Tull*	Chrysalis 1082
8	8	5	**Extra Texture (Read All About It)**	*George Harrison*	Apple 3420
9	10	5	Wind On The Water	*David Crosby/Graham Nash*	ABC 902
10	15	3	Still Crazy After All These Years	*Paul Simon*	Columbia 33540

Billboard — NOVEMBER 15, 1975 — TOP LP's

TW	LW	WK			
1	1	2	**Rock Of The Westies**	*Elton John*	MCA 2163
2	5	7	Windsong	*John Denver*	RCA 1183
3	2	18	Red Octopus	*Jefferson Starship*	Grunt 0999
4	4	7	**Prisoner In Disguise**	*Linda Ronstadt*	Asylum 1045
5	6	10	Born To Run	*Bruce Springsteen*	Columbia 33795
6	3	8	Wish You Were Here	*Pink Floyd*	Columbia 33453
7	10	4	Still Crazy After All These Years	*Paul Simon*	Columbia 33540
8	9	6	Wind On The Water	*David Crosby/Graham Nash*	ABC 902
9	8	6	Extra Texture (Read All About It)	*George Harrison*	Apple 3420
10	11	4	The Who By Numbers	*The Who*	MCA 2161

Billboard — NOVEMBER 22, 1975 — TOP LP's

TW	LW	WK			
1	1	3	**Rock Of The Westies**	*Elton John*	MCA 2163
2	2	8	Windsong	*John Denver*	RCA 1183
3	3	19	Red Octopus	*Jefferson Starship*	Grunt 0999
4	4	8	**Prisoner In Disguise**	*Linda Ronstadt*	Asylum 1045
5	6	9	Wish You Were Here	*Pink Floyd*	Columbia 33453
6	7	5	Still Crazy After All These Years	*Paul Simon*	Columbia 33540
7	8	7	Wind On The Water	*David Crosby/Graham Nash*	ABC 902
8	5	11	Born To Run	*Bruce Springsteen*	Columbia 33795
9	10	5	The Who By Numbers	*The Who*	MCA 2161
10	13	5	Breakaway	*Art Garfunkel*	Columbia 33700

Billboard — NOVEMBER 29, 1975 — TOP LP's

TW	LW	WK			
1	3	20	**Red Octopus**	*Jefferson Starship*	Grunt 0999
2	2	9	Windsong	*John Denver*	RCA 1183
3	1	4	Rock Of The Westies	*Elton John*	MCA 2163
4	6	6	Still Crazy After All These Years	*Paul Simon*	Columbia 33540
5	5	10	Wish You Were Here	*Pink Floyd*	Columbia 33453
6	7	8	**Wind On The Water**	*David Crosby/Graham Nash*	ABC 902
7	10	6	**Breakaway**	*Art Garfunkel*	Columbia 33700
8	9	6	**The Who By Numbers**	*The Who*	MCA 2161
9	8	12	Born To Run	*Bruce Springsteen*	Columbia 33795
10	4	9	Prisoner In Disguise	*Linda Ronstadt*	Asylum 1045

Billboard — DECEMBER 6, 1975 — TOP LP's

TW	LW	WK	Title	Artist	Label
1	4	7	**Still Crazy After All These Years**	*Paul Simon*	Columbia 33540
2	1	21	Red Octopus	*Jefferson Starship*	Grunt 0999
3	2	10	Windsong	*John Denver*	RCA 1183
4	3	5	Rock Of The Westies	*Elton John*	MCA 2163
5	14	2	Chicago IX - Chicago's Greatest Hits	*Chicago*	Columbia 33900
6	6	9	**Wind On The Water**	*David Crosby/Graham Nash*	ABC 902
7	7	7	**Breakaway**	*Art Garfunkel*	Columbia 33700
8	8	7	**The Who By Numbers**	*The Who*	MCA 2161
9	24	19	KC And The Sunshine Band	*KC & The Sunshine Band*	TK 603
10	12	9	Alive!	*Kiss*	Casablanca 7020

Billboard — DECEMBER 13, 1975 — TOP LP's

TW	LW	WK	Title	Artist	Label
1	5	3	**Chicago IX - Chicago's Greatest Hits**	*Chicago*	Columbia 33900
2	2	22	Red Octopus	*Jefferson Starship*	Grunt 0999
3	4	6	Rock Of The Westies	*Elton John*	MCA 2163
4	3	11	Windsong	*John Denver*	RCA 1183
5	9	20	KC And The Sunshine Band	*KC & The Sunshine Band*	TK 603
6	1	8	Still Crazy After All These Years	*Paul Simon*	Columbia 33540
7	98	2	Gratitude	*Earth, Wind & Fire*	Columbia 33694
8	16	4	History/America's Greatest Hits	*America*	Warner 2894
9	10	10	**Alive!**	*Kiss*	Casablanca 7020
10	11	14	**Save Me**	*Silver Convention*	Midland International 1129

Billboard — DECEMBER 20, 1975 — TOP LP's

TW	LW	WK	Title	Artist	Label
1	1	4	**Chicago IX - Chicago's Greatest Hits**	*Chicago*	Columbia 33900
2	7	3	Gratitude	*Earth, Wind & Fire*	Columbia 33694
3	8	5	**History/America's Greatest Hits**	*America*	Warner 2894
4	5	21	**KC And The Sunshine Band**	*KC & The Sunshine Band*	TK 603
5	2	23	Red Octopus	*Jefferson Starship*	Grunt 0999
6	6	9	Still Crazy After All These Years	*Paul Simon*	Columbia 33540
7	3	7	Rock Of The Westies	*Elton John*	MCA 2163
8	4	12	Windsong	*John Denver*	RCA 1183
9	26	3	The Hissing Of Summer Lawns	*Joni Mitchell*	Asylum 1051
10	11	6	**Feels So Good**	*Grover Washington, Jr.*	Kudu 24

Billboard — DECEMBER 27, 1975 — TOP LP's

TW	LW	WK	Title	Artist	Label
1	1	5	**Chicago IX - Chicago's Greatest Hits**	*Chicago*	Columbia 33900
2	2	4	Gratitude	*Earth, Wind & Fire*	Columbia 33694
3	3	6	**History/America's Greatest Hits**	*America*	Warner 2894
4	4	22	**KC And The Sunshine Band**	*KC & The Sunshine Band*	TK 603
5	9	4	The Hissing Of Summer Lawns	*Joni Mitchell*	Asylum 1051
6	6	10	Still Crazy After All These Years	*Paul Simon*	Columbia 33540
7	8	13	Windsong	*John Denver*	RCA 1183
8	5	24	Red Octopus	*Jefferson Starship*	Grunt 0999
9	11	19	Honey	*Ohio Players*	Mercury 1038
10	16	4	Helen Reddy's Greatest Hits	*Helen Reddy*	Capitol 11467

TW	LW	WK	Billboard — JANUARY 3, 1976 — TOP LP's
❶	1	6	**Chicago IX - Chicago's Greatest Hits** .... *Chicago*...Columbia 33900
❷	2	5	Gratitude .... *Earth, Wind & Fire*...Columbia 33694
❸	3	7	**History/America's Greatest Hits** .... *America*...Warner 2894
❹	5	5	**The Hissing Of Summer Lawns** .... *Joni Mitchell*...Asylum 1051
⑤	6	11	Still Crazy After All These Years .... *Paul Simon*...Columbia 33540
⑥	7	14	Windsong .... *John Denver*...RCA 1183
⑦	4	23	KC And The Sunshine Band .... *KC & The Sunshine Band*...TK 603
❽	10	5	Helen Reddy's Greatest Hits .... *Helen Reddy*...Capitol 11467
⑨	9	20	Honey .... *Ohio Players*...Mercury 1038
⑩	11	6	Family Reunion .... *The O'Jays*...Philadelphia International 33807

TW	LW	WK	Billboard — JANUARY 10, 1976 — TOP LP's
❶	1	7	**Chicago IX - Chicago's Greatest Hits** .... *Chicago*...Columbia 33900
❷	2	6	Gratitude .... *Earth, Wind & Fire*...Columbia 33694
❸	3	8	**History/America's Greatest Hits** .... *America*...Warner 2894
❹	4	6	**The Hissing Of Summer Lawns** .... *Joni Mitchell*...Asylum 1051
⑤	6	15	Windsong .... *John Denver*...RCA 1183
⑥	7	24	KC And The Sunshine Band .... *KC & The Sunshine Band*...TK 603
⑦	8	6	Helen Reddy's Greatest Hits .... *Helen Reddy*...Capitol 11467
⑧	9	21	Honey .... *Ohio Players*...Mercury 1038
⑨	10	7	Family Reunion .... *The O'Jays*...Philadelphia International 33807
⑩	5	12	Still Crazy After All These Years .... *Paul Simon*...Columbia 33540

TW	LW	WK	Billboard — JANUARY 17, 1976 — TOP LP's
❶	2	7	**Gratitude** .... *Earth, Wind & Fire*...Columbia 33694
②	1	8	Chicago IX - Chicago's Greatest Hits .... *Chicago*...Columbia 33900
❸	3	9	**History/America's Greatest Hits** .... *America*...Warner 2894
④	4	7	**The Hissing Of Summer Lawns** .... *Joni Mitchell*...Asylum 1051
❺	7	7	**Helen Reddy's Greatest Hits** .... *Helen Reddy*...Capitol 11467
❻	10	13	Still Crazy After All These Years .... *Paul Simon*...Columbia 33540
⑦	5	16	Windsong .... *John Denver*...RCA 1183
⑧	9	8	Family Reunion .... *The O'Jays*...Philadelphia International 33807
⑨	6	25	KC And The Sunshine Band .... *KC & The Sunshine Band*...TK 603
❿	12	13	Breakaway .... *Art Garfunkel*...Columbia 33700

TW	LW	WK	Billboard — JANUARY 24, 1976 — TOP LP's
❶	1	8	**Gratitude** .... *Earth, Wind & Fire*...Columbia 33694
②	2	9	Chicago IX - Chicago's Greatest Hits .... *Chicago*...Columbia 33900
③	3	10	**History/America's Greatest Hits** .... *America*...Warner 2894
❹	6	14	Still Crazy After All These Years .... *Paul Simon*...Columbia 33540
❺	5	8	**Helen Reddy's Greatest Hits** .... *Helen Reddy*...Capitol 11467
❻	12	12	Tryin' To Get The Feeling .... *Barry Manilow*...Arista 4060
⑦	8	9	**Family Reunion** .... *The O'Jays*...Philadelphia International 33807
⑧	4	8	The Hissing Of Summer Lawns .... *Joni Mitchell*...Asylum 1051
❾	11	16	**Alive!** .... *Kiss*...Casablanca 7020
⑩	10	14	Breakaway .... *Art Garfunkel*...Columbia 33700

TW	LW	WK	Billboard ● JANUARY 31, 1976 ● TOP LP's
1	1	9	**Gratitude** .... *Earth, Wind & Fire*...Columbia 33694
2	23	2	Desire .... *Bob Dylan*...Columbia 33893
3	4	15	Still Crazy After All These Years .... *Paul Simon*...Columbia 33540
4	2	10	Chicago IX - Chicago's Greatest Hits .... *Chicago*...Columbia 33900
5	5	9	**Helen Reddy's Greatest Hits** .... *Helen Reddy*...Capitol 11467
6	6	13	Tryin' To Get The Feeling .... *Barry Manilow*...Arista 4060
7	3	11	History/America's Greatest Hits .... *America*...Warner 2894
8	7	10	Family Reunion .... *The O'Jays*...Philadelphia International 33807
9	9	17	**Alive!** .... *Kiss*...Casablanca 7020
10	8	9	The Hissing Of Summer Lawns .... *Joni Mitchell*...Asylum 1051

TW	LW	WK	Billboard ● FEBRUARY 7, 1976 ● TOP LP's
1	2	3	**Desire** .... *Bob Dylan*...Columbia 33893
2	3	16	Still Crazy After All These Years .... *Paul Simon*...Columbia 33540
3	1	10	Gratitude .... *Earth, Wind & Fire*...Columbia 33694
4	4	11	Chicago IX - Chicago's Greatest Hits .... *Chicago*...Columbia 33900
5	6	14	**Tryin' To Get The Feeling** .... *Barry Manilow*...Arista 4060
6	5	10	Helen Reddy's Greatest Hits .... *Helen Reddy*...Capitol 11467
7	7	12	History/America's Greatest Hits .... *America*...Warner 2894
8	8	11	Family Reunion .... *The O'Jays*...Philadelphia International 33807
9	9	18	**Alive!** .... *Kiss*...Casablanca 7020
10	11	16	Face The Music .... *Electric Light Orchestra*...United Artists 546

TW	LW	WK	Billboard ● FEBRUARY 14, 1976 ● TOP LP's
1	1	4	**Desire** .... *Bob Dylan*...Columbia 33893
2	2	17	Still Crazy After All These Years .... *Paul Simon*...Columbia 33540
3	3	11	Gratitude .... *Earth, Wind & Fire*...Columbia 33694
4	4	12	Chicago IX - Chicago's Greatest Hits .... *Chicago*...Columbia 33900
5	5	15	**Tryin' To Get The Feeling** .... *Barry Manilow*...Arista 4060
6	88	2	Station To Station .... *David Bowie*...RCA 1327
7	7	13	History/America's Greatest Hits .... *America*...Warner 2894
8	8	12	Family Reunion .... *The O'Jays*...Philadelphia International 33807
9	10	17	Face The Music .... *Electric Light Orchestra*...United Artists 546
10	11	11	Rufus featuring Chaka Khan .... *Rufus featuring Chaka Khan*...ABC 909

TW	LW	WK	Billboard ● FEBRUARY 21, 1976 ● TOP LP's
1	1	5	**Desire** .... *Bob Dylan*...Columbia 33893
2	2	18	Still Crazy After All These Years .... *Paul Simon*...Columbia 33540
3	3	12	Gratitude .... *Earth, Wind & Fire*...Columbia 33694
4	6	3	Station To Station .... *David Bowie*...RCA 1327
5	4	13	Chicago IX - Chicago's Greatest Hits .... *Chicago*...Columbia 33900
6	22	4	Frampton Comes Alive! .... *Peter Frampton*...A&M 3703
7	15	30	Fleetwood Mac .... *Fleetwood Mac*...Reprise 2225
8	9	18	**Face The Music** .... *Electric Light Orchestra*...United Artists 546
9	10	12	Rufus featuring Chaka Khan .... *Rufus featuring Chaka Khan*...ABC 909
10	13	11	Wake Up Everybody ..... *Harold Melvin & The Blue Notes*...Philadelphia Int'l. 33808

TW	LW	WK	Billboard. FEBRUARY 28, 1976	TOP LP's
1	1	6	**Desire**	*Bob Dylan*...Columbia 33893
2	2	19	Still Crazy After All These Years	*Paul Simon*...Columbia 33540
3	4	4	**Station To Station**	*David Bowie*...RCA 1327
4	6	5	Frampton Comes Alive!	*Peter Frampton*...A&M 3703
5	3	13	Gratitude	*Earth, Wind & Fire*...Columbia 33694
6	7	31	Fleetwood Mac	*Fleetwood Mac*...Reprise 2225
7	5	14	Chicago IX - Chicago's Greatest Hits	*Chicago*...Columbia 33900
8	9	13	Rufus featuring Chaka Khan	*Rufus featuring Chaka Khan*...ABC 909
9	10	12	**Wake Up Everybody**	*Harold Melvin & The Blue Notes*...Philadelphia Int'l. 33808
10	16	4	Thoroughbred	*Carole King*...Ode 77034

TW	LW	WK	Billboard. MARCH 6, 1976	TOP LP's
1	1	7	**Desire**	*Bob Dylan*...Columbia 33893
2	4	6	Frampton Comes Alive!	*Peter Frampton*...A&M 3703
3	3	5	**Station To Station**	*David Bowie*...RCA 1327
4	-	1	Eagles/Their Greatest Hits 1971-1975	*Eagles*...Asylum 1052
5	6	32	Fleetwood Mac	*Fleetwood Mac*...Reprise 2225
6	2	20	Still Crazy After All These Years	*Paul Simon*...Columbia 33540
7	8	14	**Rufus featuring Chaka Khan**	*Rufus featuring Chaka Khan*...ABC 909
8	10	5	Thoroughbred	*Carole King*...Ode 77034
9	5	14	Gratitude	*Earth, Wind & Fire*...Columbia 33694
10	11	16	History/America's Greatest Hits	*America*...Warner 2894

TW	LW	WK	Billboard. MARCH 13, 1976	TOP LP's
1	4	2	**Eagles/Their Greatest Hits 1971-1975**	*Eagles*...Asylum 1052
2	2	7	Frampton Comes Alive!	*Peter Frampton*...A&M 3703
3	1	8	Desire	*Bob Dylan*...Columbia 33893
4	5	33	Fleetwood Mac	*Fleetwood Mac*...Reprise 2225
5	3	6	Station To Station	*David Bowie*...RCA 1327
6	8	6	Thoroughbred	*Carole King*...Ode 77034
7	6	21	Still Crazy After All These Years	*Paul Simon*...Columbia 33540
8	7	15	Rufus featuring Chaka Khan	*Rufus featuring Chaka Khan*...ABC 909
9	11	5	Run With The Pack	*Bad Company*...Swan Song 8415
10	10	17	History/America's Greatest Hits	*America*...Warner 2894

TW	LW	WK	Billboard. MARCH 20, 1976	TOP LP's
1	1	3	**Eagles/Their Greatest Hits 1971-1975**	*Eagles*...Asylum 1052
2	2	8	Frampton Comes Alive!	*Peter Frampton*...A&M 3703
3	4	34	Fleetwood Mac	*Fleetwood Mac*...Reprise 2225
4	6	7	Thoroughbred	*Carole King*...Ode 77034
5	3	9	Desire	*Bob Dylan*...Columbia 33893
6	5	7	Station To Station	*David Bowie*...RCA 1327
7	7	22	Still Crazy After All These Years	*Paul Simon*...Columbia 33540
8	9	6	Run With The Pack	*Bad Company*...Swan Song 8415
9	11	13	A Night At The Opera	*Queen*...Elektra 1053
10	12	31	The Dream Weaver	*Gary Wright*...Warner 2868

Billboard — MARCH 27, 1976 — TOP LP's

TW	LW	WK			
1	1	4	**Eagles/Their Greatest Hits 1971-1975**	*Eagles*	Asylum 1052
2	2	9	Frampton Comes Alive!	*Peter Frampton*	A&M 3703
3	4	8	**Thoroughbred**	*Carole King*	Ode 77034
4	7	23	Still Crazy After All These Years	*Paul Simon*	Columbia 33540
5	5	10	Desire	*Bob Dylan*	Columbia 33893
6	6	8	Station To Station	*David Bowie*	RCA 1327
7	8	7	Run With The Pack	*Bad Company*	Swan Song 8415
8	9	14	A Night At The Opera	*Queen*	Elektra 1053
9	10	32	The Dream Weaver	*Gary Wright*	Warner 2868
10	3	35	Fleetwood Mac	*Fleetwood Mac*	Reprise 2225

Billboard — APRIL 3, 1976 — TOP LP's

TW	LW	WK			
1	1	5	**Eagles/Their Greatest Hits 1971-1975**	*Eagles*	Asylum 1052
2	2	10	Frampton Comes Alive!	*Peter Frampton*	A&M 3703
3	3	9	**Thoroughbred**	*Carole King*	Ode 77034
4	4	24	Still Crazy After All These Years	*Paul Simon*	Columbia 33540
5	5	11	Desire	*Bob Dylan*	Columbia 33893
6	7	8	Run With The Pack	*Bad Company*	Swan Song 8415
7	8	15	A Night At The Opera	*Queen*	Elektra 1053
8	9	33	The Dream Weaver	*Gary Wright*	Warner 2868
9	6	9	Station To Station	*David Bowie*	RCA 1327
10	11	9	**The Outlaws**	*Waylon Jennings/Willie Nelson/Jessi Colter/Tompall Glaser*	RCA 1321

Billboard — APRIL 10, 1976 — TOP LP's

TW	LW	WK			
1	2	11	**Frampton Comes Alive!**	*Peter Frampton*	A&M 3703
2	1	6	Eagles/Their Greatest Hits 1971-1975	*Eagles*	Asylum 1052
3	3	10	**Thoroughbred**	*Carole King*	Ode 77034
4	5	12	Desire	*Bob Dylan*	Columbia 33893
5	6	9	**Run With The Pack**	*Bad Company*	Swan Song 8415
6	7	16	A Night At The Opera	*Queen*	Elektra 1053
7	8	34	**The Dream Weaver**	*Gary Wright*	Warner 2868
8	18	5	Eargasm	*Johnnie Taylor*	Columbia 33951
9	9	10	Station To Station	*David Bowie*	RCA 1327
10	10	10	**The Outlaws**	*Waylon Jennings/Willie Nelson/Jessi Colter/Tompall Glaser*	RCA 1321

Billboard — APRIL 17, 1976 — TOP LP's

TW	LW	WK			
1	2	7	**Eagles/Their Greatest Hits 1971-1975**	*Eagles*	Asylum 1052
2	1	12	Frampton Comes Alive!	*Peter Frampton*	A&M 3703
3	32	2	Wings At The Speed Of Sound	*Wings*	Capitol 11525
4	6	17	**A Night At The Opera**	*Queen*	Elektra 1053
5	5	10	**Run With The Pack**	*Bad Company*	Swan Song 8415
6	8	6	Eargasm	*Johnnie Taylor*	Columbia 33951
7	7	35	**The Dream Weaver**	*Gary Wright*	Warner 2868
8	3	11	Thoroughbred	*Carole King*	Ode 77034
9	4	13	Desire	*Bob Dylan*	Columbia 33893
10	12	38	Fleetwood Mac	*Fleetwood Mac*	Reprise 2225

TW	LW	WK	Billboard. ● APRIL 24, 1976 ● TOP LP's		
❶	3	3	**Wings At The Speed Of Sound**................................*Wings*...Capitol 11525		
❷	-	1	Presence .... *Led Zeppelin*...Swan Song 8416		
③	1	8	Eagles/Their Greatest Hits 1971-1975 ....*Eagles*...Asylum 1052		
④	4	18	**A Night At The Opera**... *Queen*...Elektra 1053		
❺	6	7	**Eargasm**...*Johnnie Taylor*...Columbia 33951		
⑥	2	13	Frampton Comes Alive! .... *Peter Frampton*...A&M 3703		
⑦	7	36	**The Dream Weaver**.. *Gary Wright*...Warner 2868		
❽	10	39	Fleetwood Mac.. *Fleetwood Mac*...Reprise 2225		
⑨	9	14	Desire .... *Bob Dylan*...Columbia 33893		
❿	12	6	Song Of Joy .... *Captain & Tennille*...A&M 4570		

TW	LW	WK	Billboard. ● MAY 1, 1976 ● TOP LP's		
❶	2	2	**Presence**.. *Led Zeppelin*...Swan Song 8416		
②	1	4	Wings At The Speed Of Sound ....*Wings*...Capitol 11525		
③	3	9	Eagles/Their Greatest Hits 1971-1975 ....*Eagles*...Asylum 1052		
④	4	19	**A Night At The Opera**... *Queen*...Elektra 1053		
⑤	5	8	**Eargasm**...*Johnnie Taylor*...Columbia 33951		
⑥	6	14	Frampton Comes Alive! .... *Peter Frampton*...A&M 3703		
❼	12	5	I Want You..*Marvin Gaye*...Tamla 342		
⑧	8	40	Fleetwood Mac.. *Fleetwood Mac*...Reprise 2225		
⑨	10	7	**Song Of Joy**.. *Captain & Tennille*...A&M 4570		
❿	11	6	**Robin Trower Live!** .... *Robin Trower*...Chrysalis 1089		

TW	LW	WK	Billboard. ● MAY 8, 1976 ● TOP LP's		
❶	1	3	**Presence**.. *Led Zeppelin*...Swan Song 8416		
②	2	5	Wings At The Speed Of Sound ....*Wings*...Capitol 11525		
❸	6	15	Frampton Comes Alive! .... *Peter Frampton*...A&M 3703		
④	3	10	Eagles/Their Greatest Hits 1971-1975 ....*Eagles*...Asylum 1052		
❺	7	6	I Want You..*Marvin Gaye*...Tamla 342		
⑥	5	9	Eargasm...*Johnnie Taylor*...Columbia 33951		
⑦	8	41	Fleetwood Mac.. *Fleetwood Mac*...Reprise 2225		
❽	-	1	Black And Blue .... *The Rolling Stones*...Rolling Stones 79104		
⑨	9	8	**Song Of Joy**.. *Captain & Tennille*...A&M 4570		
❿	10	7	**Robin Trower Live!** .... *Robin Trower*...Chrysalis 1089		

TW	LW	WK	Billboard. ● MAY 15, 1976 ● TOP LP's		
❶	8	2	**Black And Blue**................................ *The Rolling Stones*...Rolling Stones 79104		
❷	2	6	Wings At The Speed Of Sound ....*Wings*...Capitol 11525		
❸	3	16	Frampton Comes Alive! ....*Peter Frampton*...A&M 3703		
④	1	4	Presence .... *Led Zeppelin*...Swan Song 8416		
❺	5	7	I Want You..*Marvin Gaye*...Tamla 342		
⑥	4	11	Eagles/Their Greatest Hits 1971-1975 ....*Eagles*...Asylum 1052		
⑦	7	42	Fleetwood Mac.. *Fleetwood Mac*...Reprise 2225		
⑧	6	10	Eargasm...*Johnnie Taylor*...Columbia 33951		
⑨	15	7	**Takin' It To The Streets** .... *The Doobie Brothers*...Warner 2899		
❿	11	15	**Brass Construction** ....*Brass Construction*...United Artists 545		

TW	LW	WK	Billboard — MAY 22, 1976 — TOP LP's
1	1	3	**Black And Blue** ..... *The Rolling Stones*...Rolling Stones 79104
2	2	7	Wings At The Speed Of Sound ..... *Wings*...Capitol 11525
3	3	17	Frampton Comes Alive! ..... *Peter Frampton*...A&M 3703
4	4	5	Presence ..... *Led Zeppelin*...Swan Song 8416
5	5	8	I Want You ..... *Marvin Gaye*...Tamla 342
6	6	12	Eagles/Their Greatest Hits 1971-1975 ..... *Eagles*...Asylum 1052
7	7	43	Fleetwood Mac ..... *Fleetwood Mac*...Reprise 2225
8	9	8	**Takin' It To The Streets** ..... *The Doobie Brothers*...Warner 2899
9	-	1	Here And There ..... *Elton John*...MCA 2197
10	12	12	Diana Ross ..... *Diana Ross*...Motown 861

TW	LW	WK	Billboard — MAY 29, 1976 — TOP LP's
1	2	8	**Wings At The Speed Of Sound** ..... *Wings*...Capitol 11525
2	1	4	Black And Blue ..... *The Rolling Stones*...Rolling Stones 79104
3	4	6	Presence ..... *Led Zeppelin*...Swan Song 8416
4	3	18	Frampton Comes Alive! ..... *Peter Frampton*...A&M 3703
5	5	9	I Want You ..... *Marvin Gaye*...Tamla 342
6	9	2	Here And There ..... *Elton John*...MCA 2197
7	7	44	Fleetwood Mac ..... *Fleetwood Mac*...Reprise 2225
8	10	13	Diana Ross ..... *Diana Ross*...Motown 861
9	8	9	Takin' It To The Streets ..... *The Doobie Brothers*...Warner 2899
10	11	13	Look Out For #1 ..... *The Brothers Johnson*...A&M 4567

TW	LW	WK	Billboard — JUNE 5, 1976 — TOP LP's
1	2	5	**Black And Blue** ..... *The Rolling Stones*...Rolling Stones 79104
2	1	9	Wings At The Speed Of Sound ..... *Wings*...Capitol 11525
3	3	7	Presence ..... *Led Zeppelin*...Swan Song 8416
4	5	10	**I Want You** ..... *Marvin Gaye*...Tamla 342
5	6	3	Here And There ..... *Elton John*...MCA 2197
6	7	45	Fleetwood Mac ..... *Fleetwood Mac*...Reprise 2225
7	8	14	Diana Ross ..... *Diana Ross*...Motown 861
8	4	19	Frampton Comes Alive! ..... *Peter Frampton*...A&M 3703
9	10	14	**Look Out For #1** ..... *The Brothers Johnson*...A&M 4567
10	12	9	**Amigos** ..... *Santana*...Columbia 33576

TW	LW	WK	Billboard — JUNE 12, 1976 — TOP LP's
1	1	6	**Black And Blue** ..... *The Rolling Stones*...Rolling Stones 79104
2	2	10	Wings At The Speed Of Sound ..... *Wings*...Capitol 11525
3	8	20	Frampton Comes Alive! ..... *Peter Frampton*...A&M 3703
4	5	4	**Here And There** ..... *Elton John*...MCA 2197
5	3	8	Presence ..... *Led Zeppelin*...Swan Song 8416
6	7	15	Diana Ross ..... *Diana Ross*...Motown 861
7	17	3	Rocks ..... *Aerosmith*...Columbia 34165
8	6	46	Fleetwood Mac ..... *Fleetwood Mac*...Reprise 2225
9	15	9	Breezin' ..... *George Benson*...Warner 2919
10	10	10	**Amigos** ..... *Santana*...Columbia 33576

Billboard — JUNE 19, 1976 — TOP LP's

TW	LW	WK	Title	Artist	Label
1	2	11	**Wings At The Speed Of Sound**	*Wings*	Capitol 11525
2	3	21	Frampton Comes Alive!	*Peter Frampton*	A&M 3703
3	1	7	Black And Blue	*The Rolling Stones*	Rolling Stones 79104
4	4	5	**Here And There**	*Elton John*	MCA 2197
5	7	4	Rocks	*Aerosmith*	Columbia 34165
6	6	16	Diana Ross	*Diana Ross*	Motown 861
7	8	47	Fleetwood Mac	*Fleetwood Mac*	Reprise 2225
8	9	10	Breezin'	*George Benson*	Warner 2919
9	5	9	Presence	*Led Zeppelin*	Swan Song 8416
10	12	6	Rastaman Vibration	*Bob Marley & The Wailers*	Island 9383

Billboard — JUNE 26, 1976 — TOP LP's

TW	LW	WK	Title	Artist	Label
1	1	12	**Wings At The Speed Of Sound**	*Wings*	Capitol 11525
2	2	22	Frampton Comes Alive!	*Peter Frampton*	A&M 3703
3	5	5	**Rocks**	*Aerosmith*	Columbia 34165
4	8	11	Breezin'	*George Benson*	Warner 2919
5	6	17	**Diana Ross**	*Diana Ross*	Motown 861
6	7	48	Fleetwood Mac	*Fleetwood Mac*	Reprise 2225
7	3	8	Black And Blue	*The Rolling Stones*	Rolling Stones 79104
8	-	1	Rock 'N' Roll Music	*The Beatles*	Capitol 11537
9	10	7	Rastaman Vibration	*Bob Marley & The Wailers*	Island 9383
10	12	5	Harvest For The World	*The Isley Brothers*	T-Neck 33809

Billboard — JULY 4, 1976 — TOP LP's

TW	LW	WK	Title	Artist	Label
1	1	13	**Wings At The Speed Of Sound**	*Wings*	Capitol 11525
2	2	23	Frampton Comes Alive!	*Peter Frampton*	A&M 3703
3	3	6	**Rocks**	*Aerosmith*	Columbia 34165
4	4	12	Breezin'	*George Benson*	Warner 2919
5	8	2	Rock 'N' Roll Music	*The Beatles*	Capitol 11537
6	6	49	Fleetwood Mac	*Fleetwood Mac*	Reprise 2225
7	5	18	Diana Ross	*Diana Ross*	Motown 861
8	9	8	**Rastaman Vibration**	*Bob Marley & The Wailers*	Island 9383
9	10	6	**Harvest For The World**	*The Isley Brothers*	T-Neck 33809
10	7	9	Black And Blue	*The Rolling Stones*	Rolling Stones 79104

Billboard — JULY 10, 1976 — TOP LP's

TW	LW	WK	Title	Artist	Label
1	1	14	**Wings At The Speed Of Sound**	*Wings*	Capitol 11525
2	5	3	**Rock 'N' Roll Music**	*The Beatles*	Capitol 11537
3	3	7	**Rocks**	*Aerosmith*	Columbia 34165
4	4	13	Breezin'	*George Benson*	Warner 2919
5	2	24	Frampton Comes Alive!	*Peter Frampton*	A&M 3703
6	6	50	Fleetwood Mac	*Fleetwood Mac*	Reprise 2225
7	12	2	Chicago X	*Chicago*	Columbia 34200
8	8	9	**Rastaman Vibration**	*Bob Marley & The Wailers*	Island 9383
9	9	7	**Harvest For The World**	*The Isley Brothers*	T-Neck 33809
10	11	19	Look Out For #1	*The Brothers Johnson*	A&M 4567

TW	LW	WK	Billboard. JULY 17, 1976	TOP LP's
1	1	15	**Wings At The Speed Of Sound**	*Wings*...Capitol 11525
2	2	4	**Rock 'N' Roll Music**	*The Beatles*...Capitol 11537
3	4	14	Breezin'	*George Benson*...Warner 2919
4	7	3	Chicago X	*Chicago*...Columbia 34200
5	6	51	Fleetwood Mac	*Fleetwood Mac*...Reprise 2225
6	3	8	Rocks	*Aerosmith*...Columbia 34165
7	5	25	Frampton Comes Alive!	*Peter Frampton*...A&M 3703
8	12	3	Beautiful Noise	*Neil Diamond*...Columbia 33965
9	10	20	**Look Out For #1**	*The Brothers Johnson*...A&M 4567
10	11	5	**Changesonebowie**	*David Bowie*...RCA 1732

TW	LW	WK	Billboard. JULY 24, 1976	TOP LP's
1	7	26	**Frampton Comes Alive!**	*Peter Frampton*...A&M 3703
2	1	16	Wings At The Speed Of Sound	*Wings*...Capitol 11525
3	3	15	Breezin'	*George Benson*...Warner 2919
4	4	4	Chicago X	*Chicago*...Columbia 34200
5	5	52	Fleetwood Mac	*Fleetwood Mac*...Reprise 2225
6	50	3	Spitfire	*Jefferson Starship*...Grunt 1557
7	8	4	Beautiful Noise	*Neil Diamond*...Columbia 33965
8	2	5	Rock 'N' Roll Music	*The Beatles*...Capitol 11537
9	11	9	Fly Like An Eagle	*Steve Miller Band*...Capitol 11497
10	6	9	Rocks	*Aerosmith*...Columbia 34165

TW	LW	WK	Billboard. JULY 31, 1976	TOP LP's
1	3	16	**Breezin'**	*George Benson*...Warner 2919
2	1	27	Frampton Comes Alive!	*Peter Frampton*...A&M 3703
3	2	17	Wings At The Speed Of Sound	*Wings*...Capitol 11525
4	4	5	Chicago X	*Chicago*...Columbia 34200
5	6	4	Spitfire	*Jefferson Starship*...Grunt 1557
6	7	5	Beautiful Noise	*Neil Diamond*...Columbia 33965
7	5	53	Fleetwood Mac	*Fleetwood Mac*...Reprise 2225
8	8	6	Rock 'N' Roll Music	*The Beatles*...Capitol 11537
9	9	10	Fly Like An Eagle	*Steve Miller Band*...Capitol 11497
10	16	50	The Dream Weaver	*Gary Wright*...Warner 2868

TW	LW	WK	Billboard. AUGUST 7, 1976	TOP LP's
1	1	17	**Breezin'**	*George Benson*...Warner 2919
2	2	28	Frampton Comes Alive!	*Peter Frampton*...A&M 3703
3	4	6	**Chicago X**	*Chicago*...Columbia 34200
4	5	5	Spitfire	*Jefferson Starship*...Grunt 1557
5	6	6	Beautiful Noise	*Neil Diamond*...Columbia 33965
6	3	18	Wings At The Speed Of Sound	*Wings*...Capitol 11525
7	7	54	Fleetwood Mac	*Fleetwood Mac*...Reprise 2225
8	8	7	Rock 'N' Roll Music	*The Beatles*...Capitol 11537
9	11	11	Rocks	*Aerosmith*...Columbia 34165
10	10	51	The Dream Weaver	*Gary Wright*...Warner 2868

TW	LW	WK	Billboard. AUGUST 14, 1976 TOP LP's	
1	2	29	**Frampton Comes Alive!**	*Peter Frampton*...A&M 3703
2	1	18	Breezin'	*George Benson*...Warner 2919
3	4	6	**Spitfire**	*Jefferson Starship*...Grunt 1557
4	5	7	**Beautiful Noise**	*Neil Diamond*...Columbia 33965
5	7	55	Fleetwood Mac	*Fleetwood Mac*...Reprise 2225
6	3	7	Chicago X	*Chicago*...Columbia 34200
7	8	8	Rock 'N' Roll Music	*The Beatles*...Capitol 11537
8	6	19	Wings At The Speed Of Sound	*Wings*...Capitol 11525
9	9	12	Rocks	*Aerosmith*...Columbia 34165
10	12	5	15 Big Ones	*The Beach Boys*...Brother 2251

TW	LW	WK	Billboard. AUGUST 21, 1976 TOP LP's	
1	1	30	**Frampton Comes Alive!**	*Peter Frampton*...A&M 3703
2	2	19	Breezin'	*George Benson*...Warner 2919
3	3	7	**Spitfire**	*Jefferson Starship*...Grunt 1557
4	4	8	**Beautiful Noise**	*Neil Diamond*...Columbia 33965
5	5	56	Fleetwood Mac	*Fleetwood Mac*...Reprise 2225
6	7	9	Rock 'N' Roll Music	*The Beatles*...Capitol 11537
7	8	20	Wings At The Speed Of Sound	*Wings*...Capitol 11525
8	9	13	Rocks	*Aerosmith*...Columbia 34165
9	10	6	15 Big Ones	*The Beach Boys*...Brother 2251
10	11	6	Soul Searching	*Average White Band*...Atlantic 18179

TW	LW	WK	Billboard. AUGUST 28, 1976 TOP LP's	
1	1	31	**Frampton Comes Alive!**	*Peter Frampton*...A&M 3703
2	5	57	Fleetwood Mac	*Fleetwood Mac*...Reprise 2225
3	3	8	**Spitfire**	*Jefferson Starship*...Grunt 1557
4	4	9	**Beautiful Noise**	*Neil Diamond*...Columbia 33965
5	2	20	Breezin'	*George Benson*...Warner 2919
6	7	21	Wings At The Speed Of Sound	*Wings*...Capitol 11525
7	11	24	Silk Degrees	*Boz Scaggs*...Columbia 33920
8	9	7	**15 Big Ones**	*The Beach Boys*...Brother 2251
9	10	7	**Soul Searching**	*Average White Band*...Atlantic 18179
10	13	9	Chicago X	*Chicago*...Columbia 34200

TW	LW	WK	Billboard. SEPTEMBER 4, 1976 TOP LP's	
1	2	58	**Fleetwood Mac**	*Fleetwood Mac*...Reprise 2225
2	1	32	Frampton Comes Alive!	*Peter Frampton*...A&M 3703
3	3	9	**Spitfire**	*Jefferson Starship*...Grunt 1557
4	5	21	Breezin'	*George Benson*...Warner 2919
5	7	25	Silk Degrees	*Boz Scaggs*...Columbia 33920
6	4	10	Beautiful Noise	*Neil Diamond*...Columbia 33965
7	6	22	Wings At The Speed Of Sound	*Wings*...Capitol 11525
8	12	14	All Things In Time	*Lou Rawls*...Philadelphia International 33957
9	10	10	Chicago X	*Chicago*...Columbia 34200
10	14	7	Wild Cherry	*Wild Cherry*...Sweet City 34195

TW	LW	WK	Billboard® SEPTEMBER 11, 1976	TOP LP's
1	2	33	**Frampton Comes Alive!**	*Peter Frampton*...A&M 3703
2	1	59	Fleetwood Mac	*Fleetwood Mac*...Reprise 2225
3	3	10	**Spitfire**	*Jefferson Starship*...Grunt 1557
4	4	22	Breezin'	*George Benson*...Warner 2919
5	5	26	Silk Degrees	*Boz Scaggs*...Columbia 33920
6	18	3	Hasten Down The Wind	*Linda Ronstadt*...Asylum 1072
7	8	15	**All Things In Time**	*Lou Rawls*...Philadelphia International 33957
8	10	8	Wild Cherry	*Wild Cherry*...Sweet City 34195
9	9	11	Chicago X	*Chicago*...Columbia 34200
10	14	2	Spirit	*John Denver*...RCA 1694

TW	LW	WK	Billboard® SEPTEMBER 18, 1976	TOP LP's
1	1	34	**Frampton Comes Alive!**	*Peter Frampton*...A&M 3703
2	5	27	**Silk Degrees**	*Boz Scaggs*...Columbia 33920
3	3	11	**Spitfire**	*Jefferson Starship*...Grunt 1557
4	6	4	Hasten Down The Wind	*Linda Ronstadt*...Asylum 1072
5	2	60	Fleetwood Mac	*Fleetwood Mac*...Reprise 2225
6	8	9	Wild Cherry	*Wild Cherry*...Sweet City 34195
7	7	16	**All Things In Time**	*Lou Rawls*...Philadelphia International 33957
8	10	3	Spirit	*John Denver*...RCA 1694
9	11	3	Greatest Hits	*War*...United Artists 648
10	4	23	Breezin'	*George Benson*...Warner 2919

TW	LW	WK	Billboard® SEPTEMBER 25, 1976	TOP LP's
1	1	35	**Frampton Comes Alive!**	*Peter Frampton*...A&M 3703
2	2	28	**Silk Degrees**	*Boz Scaggs*...Columbia 33920
3	4	5	**Hasten Down The Wind**	*Linda Ronstadt*...Asylum 1072
4	5	61	Fleetwood Mac	*Fleetwood Mac*...Reprise 2225
5	6	10	**Wild Cherry**	*Wild Cherry*...Sweet City 34195
6	9	4	**Greatest Hits**	*War*...United Artists 648
7	8	4	**Spirit**	*John Denver*...RCA 1694
8	3	12	Spitfire	*Jefferson Starship*...Grunt 1557
9	7	17	All Things In Time	*Lou Rawls*...Philadelphia International 33957
10	11	13	Chicago X	*Chicago*...Columbia 34200

TW	LW	WK	Billboard® OCTOBER 2, 1976	TOP LP's
1	1	36	**Frampton Comes Alive!**	*Peter Frampton*...A&M 3703
2	2	29	**Silk Degrees**	*Boz Scaggs*...Columbia 33920
3	3	6	**Hasten Down The Wind**	*Linda Ronstadt*...Asylum 1072
4	4	62	Fleetwood Mac	*Fleetwood Mac*...Reprise 2225
5	5	11	**Wild Cherry**	*Wild Cherry*...Sweet City 34195
6	6	5	**Greatest Hits**	*War*...United Artists 648
7	7	5	**Spirit**	*John Denver*...RCA 1694
8	8	13	Spitfire	*Jefferson Starship*...Grunt 1557
9	11	19	Fly Like An Eagle	*Steve Miller Band*...Capitol 11497
10	10	14	Chicago X	*Chicago*...Columbia 34200

TW	LW	WK	Billboard. OCTOBER 9, 1976 TOP LP's
1	1	37	**Frampton Comes Alive!** .... *Peter Frampton*...A&M 3703
2	2	30	**Silk Degrees** .... *Boz Scaggs*...Columbia 33920
3	3	7	**Hasten Down The Wind** .... *Linda Ronstadt*...Asylum 1072
4	4	63	Fleetwood Mac .... *Fleetwood Mac*...Reprise 2225
5	9	20	Fly Like An Eagle .... *Steve Miller Band*...Capitol 11497
6	6	6	**Greatest Hits** .... *War*...United Artists 648
7	5	12	Wild Cherry .... *Wild Cherry*...Sweet City 34195
8	8	14	Spitfire .... *Jefferson Starship*...Grunt 1557
9	7	6	Spirit .... *John Denver*...RCA 1694
10	10	15	Chicago X .... *Chicago*...Columbia 34200

TW	LW	WK	Billboard. OCTOBER 16, 1976 TOP LP's
1	-	1	**Songs In The Key Of Life** .... *Stevie Wonder*...Tamla 340
2	2	31	**Silk Degrees** .... *Boz Scaggs*...Columbia 33920
3	1	38	Frampton Comes Alive! .... *Peter Frampton*...A&M 3703
4	5	21	Fly Like An Eagle .... *Steve Miller Band*...Capitol 11497
5	3	8	Hasten Down The Wind .... *Linda Ronstadt*...Asylum 1072
6	4	64	Fleetwood Mac .... *Fleetwood Mac*...Reprise 2225
7	7	13	Wild Cherry .... *Wild Cherry*...Sweet City 34195
8	8	15	Spitfire .... *Jefferson Starship*...Grunt 1557
9	9	7	Spirit .... *John Denver*...RCA 1694
10	10	16	Chicago X .... *Chicago*...Columbia 34200

TW	LW	WK	Billboard. OCTOBER 23, 1976 TOP LP's
1	1	2	**Songs In The Key Of Life** .... *Stevie Wonder*...Tamla 340
2	3	39	Frampton Comes Alive! .... *Peter Frampton*...A&M 3703
3	4	22	**Fly Like An Eagle** .... *Steve Miller Band*...Capitol 11497
4	15	2	Spirit .... *Earth, Wind & Fire*...Columbia 34241
5	2	32	Silk Degrees .... *Boz Scaggs*...Columbia 33920
6	5	9	Hasten Down The Wind .... *Linda Ronstadt*...Asylum 1072
7	6	65	Fleetwood Mac .... *Fleetwood Mac*...Reprise 2225
8	7	14	Wild Cherry .... *Wild Cherry*...Sweet City 34195
9	10	17	Chicago X .... *Chicago*...Columbia 34200
10	11	29	Dreamboat Annie .... *Heart*...Mushroom 5005

TW	LW	WK	Billboard. OCTOBER 30, 1976 TOP LP's
1	1	3	**Songs In The Key Of Life** .... *Stevie Wonder*...Tamla 340
2	4	3	**Spirit** .... *Earth, Wind & Fire*...Columbia 34241
3	3	23	**Fly Like An Eagle** .... *Steve Miller Band*...Capitol 11497
4	2	40	Frampton Comes Alive! .... *Peter Frampton*...A&M 3703
5	6	10	Hasten Down The Wind .... *Linda Ronstadt*...Asylum 1072
6	7	66	Fleetwood Mac .... *Fleetwood Mac*...Reprise 2225
7	10	30	**Dreamboat Annie** .... *Heart*...Mushroom 5005
8	9	18	Chicago X .... *Chicago*...Columbia 34200
9	5	33	Silk Degrees .... *Boz Scaggs*...Columbia 33920
10	12	5	Children Of The World .... *Bee Gees*...RSO 3003

Billboard — NOVEMBER 6, 1976 — TOP LP's

TW	LW	WK	Title	Artist	Label
❶	1	4	Songs In The Key Of Life	Stevie Wonder	Tamla 340
②	2	4	Spirit	Earth, Wind & Fire	Columbia 34241
❸	-	1	The Soundtrack From The Film "The Song Remains The Same"	Led Zeppelin/Soundtrack	Swan Song 201
④	3	24	Fly Like An Eagle	Steve Miller Band	Capitol 11497
⑤	4	41	Frampton Comes Alive!	Peter Frampton	A&M 3703
❻	13	7	Boston	Boston	Epic 34188
⑦	7	31	Dreamboat Annie	Heart	Mushroom 5005
⑧	8	19	Chicago X	Chicago	Columbia 34200
❾	10	6	Children Of The World	Bee Gees	RSO 3003
❿	12	6	One More From The Road	Lynyrd Skynyrd	MCA 6001

Billboard — NOVEMBER 13, 1976 — TOP LP's

TW	LW	WK	Title	Artist	Label
❶	1	5	Songs In The Key Of Life	Stevie Wonder	Tamla 340
❷	3	2	The Soundtrack From The Film "The Song Remains The Same"	Led Zeppelin/Soundtrack	Swan Song 201
❸	-	1	Blue Moves	Elton John	MCA/Rocket 11004
④	5	42	Frampton Comes Alive!	Peter Frampton	A&M 3703
⑤	2	5	Spirit	Earth, Wind & Fire	Columbia 34241
❻	6	8	Boston	Boston	Epic 34188
⑦	4	25	Fly Like An Eagle	Steve Miller Band	Capitol 11497
❽	9	7	Children Of The World	Bee Gees	RSO 3003
❾	10	7	One More From The Road	Lynyrd Skynyrd	MCA 6001
❿	19	18	A Night On The Town	Rod Stewart	Warner 2938

Billboard — NOVEMBER 20, 1976 — TOP LP's

TW	LW	WK	Title	Artist	Label
❶	1	6	Songs In The Key Of Life	Stevie Wonder	Tamla 340
❷	2	3	The Soundtrack From The Film "The Song Remains The Same"	Led Zeppelin/Soundtrack	Swan Song 201
❸	3	2	Blue Moves	Elton John	MCA/Rocket 11004
❹	6	9	Boston	Boston	Epic 34188
⑤	4	43	Frampton Comes Alive!	Peter Frampton	A&M 3703
⑥	5	6	Spirit	Earth, Wind & Fire	Columbia 34241
❼	10	19	A Night On The Town	Rod Stewart	Warner 2938
⑧	8	8	Children Of The World	Bee Gees	RSO 3003
⑨	9	8	One More From The Road	Lynyrd Skynyrd	MCA 6001
⑩	7	26	Fly Like An Eagle	Steve Miller Band	Capitol 11497

Billboard — NOVEMBER 27, 1976 — TOP LP's

TW	LW	WK	Title	Artist	Label
❶	1	7	Songs In The Key Of Life	Stevie Wonder	Tamla 340
②	2	4	The Soundtrack From The Film "The Song Remains The Same"	Led Zeppelin/Soundtrack	Swan Song 201
③	3	3	Blue Moves	Elton John	MCA/Rocket 11004
④	4	10	Boston	Boston	Epic 34188
⑤	6	7	Spirit	Earth, Wind & Fire	Columbia 34241
❻	7	20	A Night On The Town	Rod Stewart	Warner 2938
⑦	5	44	Frampton Comes Alive!	Peter Frampton	A&M 3703
⑧	8	9	Children Of The World	Bee Gees	RSO 3003
⑨	9	9	One More From The Road	Lynyrd Skynyrd	MCA 6001
⑩	10	27	Fly Like An Eagle	Steve Miller Band	Capitol 11497

Billboard — DECEMBER 4, 1976 — TOP LP's

TW	LW	WK			
1	1	8	**Songs In The Key Of Life**	*Stevie Wonder*	Tamla 340
2	6	21	**A Night On The Town**	*Rod Stewart*	Warner 2938
3	4	11	**Boston**	*Boston*	Epic 34188
4	5	8	Spirit	*Earth, Wind & Fire*	Columbia 34241
5	2	5	The Soundtrack From The Film "The Song Remains The Same"	*Led Zeppelin/Soundtrack*	Swan Song 201
6	3	4	Blue Moves	*Elton John*	MCA/Rocket 11004
7	7	45	Frampton Comes Alive!	*Peter Frampton*	A&M 3703
8	10	28	Fly Like An Eagle	*Steve Miller Band*	Capitol 11497
9	39	3	The Pretender	*Jackson Browne*	Asylum 1079
10	12	6	A New World Record	*Electric Light Orchestra*	United Artists 679

Billboard — DECEMBER 11, 1976 — TOP LP's

TW	LW	WK			
1	1	9	**Songs In The Key Of Life**	*Stevie Wonder*	Tamla 340
2	2	22	**A Night On The Town**	*Rod Stewart*	Warner 2938
3	3	12	**Boston**	*Boston*	Epic 34188
4	4	9	Spirit	*Earth, Wind & Fire*	Columbia 34241
5	5	6	The Soundtrack From The Film "The Song Remains The Same"	*Led Zeppelin/Soundtrack*	Swan Song 201
6	6	5	Blue Moves	*Elton John*	MCA/Rocket 11004
7	9	4	The Pretender	*Jackson Browne*	Asylum 1079
8	8	29	Fly Like An Eagle	*Steve Miller Band*	Capitol 11497
9	10	7	A New World Record	*Electric Light Orchestra*	United Artists 679
10	7	46	Frampton Comes Alive!	*Peter Frampton*	A&M 3703

Billboard — DECEMBER 18, 1976 — TOP LP's

TW	LW	WK			
1	1	10	**Songs In The Key Of Life**	*Stevie Wonder*	Tamla 340
2	2	23	**A Night On The Town**	*Rod Stewart*	Warner 2938
3	3	13	**Boston**	*Boston*	Epic 34188
4	4	10	Spirit	*Earth, Wind & Fire*	Columbia 34241
5	7	5	**The Pretender**	*Jackson Browne*	Asylum 1079
6	5	7	The Soundtrack From The Film "The Song Remains The Same"	*Led Zeppelin/Soundtrack*	Swan Song 201
7	9	8	A New World Record	*Electric Light Orchestra*	United Artists 679
8	6	6	Blue Moves	*Elton John*	MCA/Rocket 11004
9	11	5	Best Of The Doobies	*The Doobie Brothers*	Warner 2978
10	10	47	Frampton Comes Alive!	*Peter Frampton*	A&M 3703

Billboard — DECEMBER 25, 1976 — TOP LP's

TW	LW	WK			
1	1	11	**Songs In The Key Of Life**	*Stevie Wonder*	Tamla 340
2	2	24	**A Night On The Town**	*Rod Stewart*	Warner 2938
3	3	14	**Boston**	*Boston*	Epic 34188
4	-	1	Hotel California	*Eagles*	Asylum 1084
5	5	6	**The Pretender**	*Jackson Browne*	Asylum 1079
6	7	9	A New World Record	*Electric Light Orchestra*	United Artists 679
7	-	1	Wings Over America	*Wings*	Capitol 11593
8	9	6	Best Of The Doobies	*The Doobie Brothers*	Warner 2978
9	10	48	Frampton Comes Alive!	*Peter Frampton*	A&M 3703
10	11	31	Fly Like An Eagle	*Steve Miller Band*	Capitol 11497

Billboard ● JANUARY 8, 1977 ● TOP LP's

TW	LW	WK	Title	Artist...Label
❶	1	13	**Songs In The Key Of Life**	*Stevie Wonder*...Tamla 340
❷	4	3	Hotel California	*Eagles*...Asylum 1084
③	3	16	**Boston**	*Boston*...Epic 34188
❹	7	3	Wings Over America	*Wings*...Capitol 11593
❺	6	11	**A New World Record**	*Electric Light Orchestra*...United Artists 679
⑥	2	26	A Night On The Town	*Rod Stewart*...Warner 2938
❼	8	8	Best Of The Doobies	*The Doobie Brothers*...Warner 2978
⑧	9	50	Frampton Comes Alive!	*Peter Frampton*...A&M 3703
⑨	10	33	Fly Like An Eagle	*Steve Miller Band*...Capitol 11497
⑩	13	4	Greatest Hits	*Linda Ronstadt*...Asylum 1092

Billboard ● JANUARY 15, 1977 ● TOP LP's

TW	LW	WK	Title	Artist...Label
❶	2	4	**Hotel California**	*Eagles*...Asylum 1084
②	1	14	Songs In The Key Of Life	*Stevie Wonder*...Tamla 340
❸	4	4	Wings Over America	*Wings*...Capitol 11593
④	3	17	Boston	*Boston*...Epic 34188
⑤	5	12	**A New World Record**	*Electric Light Orchestra*...United Artists 679
⑥	7	9	Best Of The Doobies	*The Doobie Brothers*...Warner 2978
⑦	8	51	Frampton Comes Alive!	*Peter Frampton*...A&M 3703
❽	10	5	Greatest Hits	*Linda Ronstadt*...Asylum 1092
⑨	9	34	Fly Like An Eagle	*Steve Miller Band*...Capitol 11497
⑩	6	27	A Night On The Town	*Rod Stewart*...Warner 2938

Billboard ● JANUARY 22, 1977 ● TOP LP's

TW	LW	WK	Title	Artist...Label
❶	3	5	**Wings Over America**	*Wings*...Capitol 11593
②	1	5	Hotel California	*Eagles*...Asylum 1084
③	2	15	Songs In The Key Of Life	*Stevie Wonder*...Tamla 340
④	4	18	Boston	*Boston*...Epic 34188
⑤	6	10	**Best Of The Doobies**	*The Doobie Brothers*...Warner 2978
❻	18	7	A Star Is Born	*Barbra Streisand/Soundtrack*...Columbia 34403
❼	8	6	Greatest Hits	*Linda Ronstadt*...Asylum 1092
⑧	7	52	Frampton Comes Alive!	*Peter Frampton*...A&M 3703
⑨	9	35	Fly Like An Eagle	*Steve Miller Band*...Capitol 11497
⑩	10	28	A Night On The Town	*Rod Stewart*...Warner 2938

Billboard ● JANUARY 29, 1977 ● TOP LP's

TW	LW	WK	Title	Artist...Label
❶	3	16	**Songs In The Key Of Life**	*Stevie Wonder*...Tamla 340
②	1	6	Wings Over America	*Wings*...Capitol 11593
③	2	6	Hotel California	*Eagles*...Asylum 1084
❹	6	8	A Star Is Born	*Barbra Streisand/Soundtrack*...Columbia 34403
⑤	4	19	Boston	*Boston*...Epic 34188
⑥	7	7	**Greatest Hits**	*Linda Ronstadt*...Asylum 1092
⑦	5	11	Best Of The Doobies	*The Doobie Brothers*...Warner 2978
❽	21	3	A Day At The Races	*Queen*...Elektra 101
⑨	8	53	Frampton Comes Alive!	*Peter Frampton*...A&M 3703
⑩	9	36	Fly Like An Eagle	*Steve Miller Band*...Capitol 11497

Billboard® — FEBRUARY 5, 1977 — TOP LP's

TW	LW	WK			
1	3	7	**Hotel California**	*Eagles*	Asylum 1084
2	4	9	A Star Is Born	*Barbra Streisand/Soundtrack*	Columbia 34403
3	1	17	Songs In The Key Of Life	*Stevie Wonder*	Tamla 340
4	2	7	Wings Over America	*Wings*	Capitol 11593
5	5	20	Boston	*Boston*	Epic 34188
6	8	4	A Day At The Races	*Queen*	Elektra 101
7	6	8	Greatest Hits	*Linda Ronstadt*	Asylum 1092
8	7	12	Best Of The Doobies	*The Doobie Brothers*	Warner 2978
9	9	54	Frampton Comes Alive!	*Peter Frampton*	A&M 3703
10	13	18	Year Of The Cat	*Al Stewart*	Janus 7022

Billboard® — FEBRUARY 12, 1977 — TOP LP's

TW	LW	WK			
1	2	10	**A Star Is Born**	*Barbra Streisand/Soundtrack*	Columbia 34403
2	1	8	Hotel California	*Eagles*	Asylum 1084
3	3	18	Songs In The Key Of Life	*Stevie Wonder*	Tamla 340
4	4	8	Wings Over America	*Wings*	Capitol 11593
5	6	5	**A Day At The Races**	*Queen*	Elektra 101
6	10	19	Year Of The Cat	*Al Stewart*	Janus 7022
7	7	9	Greatest Hits	*Linda Ronstadt*	Asylum 1092
8	5	21	Boston	*Boston*	Epic 34188
9	9	55	Frampton Comes Alive!	*Peter Frampton*	A&M 3703
10	11	38	Fly Like An Eagle	*Steve Miller Band*	Capitol 11497

Billboard® — FEBRUARY 19, 1977 — TOP LP's

TW	LW	WK			
1	1	11	**A Star Is Born**	*Barbra Streisand/Soundtrack*	Columbia 34403
2	2	9	Hotel California	*Eagles*	Asylum 1084
3	3	19	Songs In The Key Of Life	*Stevie Wonder*	Tamla 340
4	4	9	Wings Over America	*Wings*	Capitol 11593
5	6	20	**Year Of The Cat**	*Al Stewart*	Janus 7022
6	10	39	Fly Like An Eagle	*Steve Miller Band*	Capitol 11497
7	7	10	Greatest Hits	*Linda Ronstadt*	Asylum 1092
8	8	22	Boston	*Boston*	Epic 34188
9	5	6	A Day At The Races	*Queen*	Elektra 101
10	23	15	Night Moves	*Bob Seger & The Silver Bullet Band*	Capitol 11557

Billboard® — FEBRUARY 26, 1977 — TOP LP's

TW	LW	WK			
1	1	12	**A Star Is Born**	*Barbra Streisand/Soundtrack*	Columbia 34403
2	2	10	Hotel California	*Eagles*	Asylum 1084
3	3	20	Songs In The Key Of Life	*Stevie Wonder*	Tamla 340
4	4	10	Wings Over America	*Wings*	Capitol 11593
5	5	21	**Year Of The Cat**	*Al Stewart*	Janus 7022
6	6	40	Fly Like An Eagle	*Steve Miller Band*	Capitol 11497
7	8	23	Boston	*Boston*	Epic 34188
8	25	2	Animals	*Pink Floyd*	Columbia 34474
9	10	16	Night Moves	*Bob Seger & The Silver Bullet Band*	Capitol 11557
10	-	1	Rumours	*Fleetwood Mac*	Warner 3010

Billboard — MARCH 5, 1977 — TOP LP's

TW	LW	WK	Title	Artist...Label
1	1	13	**A Star Is Born**	*Barbra Streisand/Soundtrack*...Columbia 34403
2	2	11	Hotel California	*Eagles*...Asylum 1084
3	8	3	**Animals**	*Pink Floyd*...Columbia 34474
4	3	21	Songs In The Key Of Life	*Stevie Wonder*...Tamla 340
5	5	22	**Year Of The Cat**	*Al Stewart*...Janus 7022
6	6	41	Fly Like An Eagle	*Steve Miller Band*...Capitol 11497
7	7	24	Boston	*Boston*...Epic 34188
8	10	2	Rumours	*Fleetwood Mac*...Warner 3010
9	9	17	Night Moves	*Bob Seger & The Silver Bullet Band*...Capitol 11557
10	4	11	Wings Over America	*Wings*...Capitol 11593

Billboard — MARCH 12, 1977 — TOP LP's

TW	LW	WK	Title	Artist...Label
1	1	14	**A Star Is Born**	*Barbra Streisand/Soundtrack*...Columbia 34403
2	2	12	Hotel California	*Eagles*...Asylum 1084
3	3	4	**Animals**	*Pink Floyd*...Columbia 34474
4	8	3	**Rumours**	*Fleetwood Mac*...Warner 3010
5	4	22	Songs In The Key Of Life	*Stevie Wonder*...Tamla 340
6	6	42	Fly Like An Eagle	*Steve Miller Band*...Capitol 11497
7	7	25	Boston	*Boston*...Epic 34188
8	9	18	**Night Moves**	*Bob Seger & The Silver Bullet Band*...Capitol 11557
9	18	2	John Denver's Greatest Hits, Volume 2	*John Denver*...RCA 2195
10	11	25	**The Roaring Silence**	*Manfred Mann's Earth Band*...Warner 2965

Billboard — MARCH 19, 1977 — TOP LP's

TW	LW	WK	Title	Artist...Label
1	1	15	**A Star Is Born**	*Barbra Streisand/Soundtrack*...Columbia 34403
2	4	4	Rumours	*Fleetwood Mac*...Warner 3010
3	3	5	**Animals**	*Pink Floyd*...Columbia 34474
4	2	13	Hotel California	*Eagles*...Asylum 1084
5	5	23	Songs In The Key Of Life	*Stevie Wonder*...Tamla 340
6	6	43	Fly Like An Eagle	*Steve Miller Band*...Capitol 11497
7	7	26	Boston	*Boston*...Epic 34188
8	9	3	John Denver's Greatest Hits, Volume 2	*John Denver*...RCA 2195
9	11	6	**In Flight**	*George Benson*...Warner 2983
10	10	26	**The Roaring Silence**	*Manfred Mann's Earth Band*...Warner 2965

Billboard — MARCH 26, 1977 — TOP LP's

TW	LW	WK	Title	Artist...Label
1	4	14	**Hotel California**	*Eagles*...Asylum 1084
2	2	5	Rumours	*Fleetwood Mac*...Warner 3010
3	1	16	A Star Is Born	*Barbra Streisand/Soundtrack*...Columbia 34403
4	5	24	Songs In The Key Of Life	*Stevie Wonder*...Tamla 340
5	6	44	Fly Like An Eagle	*Steve Miller Band*...Capitol 11497
6	7	27	Boston	*Boston*...Epic 34188
7	8	4	John Denver's Greatest Hits, Volume 2	*John Denver*...RCA 2195
8	12	21	Leftoverture	*Kansas*...Kirshner 34224
9	9	7	**In Flight**	*George Benson*...Warner 2983
10	3	6	Animals	*Pink Floyd*...Columbia 34474

TW	LW	WK	Billboard® — APRIL 2, 1977	TOP LP's
1	2	6	**Rumours**	*Fleetwood Mac*...Warner 3010
2	1	15	Hotel California	*Eagles*...Asylum 1084
3	4	25	Songs In The Key Of Life	*Stevie Wonder*...Tamla 340
4	3	17	A Star Is Born	*Barbra Streisand/Soundtrack*...Columbia 34403
5	8	22	**Leftoverture**	*Kansas*...Kirshner 34224
6	7	5	**John Denver's Greatest Hits, Volume 2**	*John Denver*...RCA 2195
7	6	28	Boston	*Boston*...Epic 34188
8	5	45	Fly Like An Eagle	*Steve Miller Band*...Capitol 11497
9	13	6	Love At The Greek	*Neil Diamond*...Columbia 34404
10	16	33	This One's For You	*Barry Manilow*...Arista 4090

TW	LW	WK	Billboard® — APRIL 9, 1977	TOP LP's
1	1	7	**Rumours**	*Fleetwood Mac*...Warner 3010
2	2	16	Hotel California	*Eagles*...Asylum 1084
3	3	26	Songs In The Key Of Life	*Stevie Wonder*...Tamla 340
4	4	18	A Star Is Born	*Barbra Streisand/Soundtrack*...Columbia 34403
5	5	23	**Leftoverture**	*Kansas*...Kirshner 34224
6	7	29	Boston	*Boston*...Epic 34188
7	10	34	This One's For You	*Barry Manilow*...Arista 4090
8	9	7	**Love At The Greek**	*Neil Diamond*...Columbia 34404
9	8	46	Fly Like An Eagle	*Steve Miller Band*...Capitol 11497
10	12	6	Unpredictable	*Natalie Cole*...Capitol 11600

TW	LW	WK	Billboard® — APRIL 16, 1977	TOP LP's
1	2	17	**Hotel California**	*Eagles*...Asylum 1084
2	1	8	Rumours	*Fleetwood Mac*...Warner 3010
3	3	27	Songs In The Key Of Life	*Stevie Wonder*...Tamla 340
4	4	19	A Star Is Born	*Barbra Streisand/Soundtrack*...Columbia 34403
5	5	24	**Leftoverture**	*Kansas*...Kirshner 34224
6	7	35	**This One's For You**	*Barry Manilow*...Arista 4090
7	6	30	Boston	*Boston*...Epic 34188
8	8	8	**Love At The Greek**	*Neil Diamond*...Columbia 34404
9	10	7	Unpredictable	*Natalie Cole*...Capitol 11600
10	9	47	Fly Like An Eagle	*Steve Miller Band*...Capitol 11497

TW	LW	WK	Billboard® — APRIL 23, 1977	TOP LP's
1	1	18	**Hotel California**	*Eagles*...Asylum 1084
2	2	9	Rumours	*Fleetwood Mac*...Warner 3010
3	4	20	A Star Is Born	*Barbra Streisand/Soundtrack*...Columbia 34403
4	3	28	Songs In The Key Of Life	*Stevie Wonder*...Tamla 340
5	5	25	**Leftoverture**	*Kansas*...Kirshner 34224
6	6	36	**This One's For You**	*Barry Manilow*...Arista 4090
7	7	31	Boston	*Boston*...Epic 34188
8	9	8	**Unpredictable**	*Natalie Cole*...Capitol 11600
9	10	48	Fly Like An Eagle	*Steve Miller Band*...Capitol 11497
10	11	11	In Flight	*George Benson*...Warner 2983

TW	LW	WK	Billboard® — APRIL 30, 1977 — TOP LP's	Artist...Label
1	1	19	**Hotel California**	*Eagles*...Asylum 1084
2	2	10	Rumours	*Fleetwood Mac*...Warner 3010
3	3	21	A Star Is Born	*Barbra Streisand/Soundtrack*...Columbia 34403
4	4	29	Songs In The Key Of Life	*Stevie Wonder*...Tamla 340
5	12	5	Marvin Gaye Live At The London Palladium	*Marvin Gaye*...Tamla 352
6	7	32	Boston	*Boston*...Epic 34188
7	5	26	Leftoverture	*Kansas*...Kirshner 34224
8	8	9	**Unpredictable**	*Natalie Cole*...Capitol 11600
9	19	9	Rocky	*Soundtrack*...United Artists 693
10	11	9	Songs From The Wood	*Jethro Tull*...Chrysalis 1132

TW	LW	WK	Billboard® — MAY 7, 1977 — TOP LP's	Artist...Label
1	1	20	**Hotel California**	*Eagles*...Asylum 1084
2	2	11	Rumours	*Fleetwood Mac*...Warner 3010
3	3	22	A Star Is Born	*Barbra Streisand/Soundtrack*...Columbia 34403
4	5	6	Marvin Gaye Live At The London Palladium	*Marvin Gaye*...Tamla 352
5	4	30	Songs In The Key Of Life	*Stevie Wonder*...Tamla 340
6	6	33	Boston	*Boston*...Epic 34188
7	9	10	Rocky	*Soundtrack*...United Artists 693
8	11	4	Go For Your Guns	*The Isley Brothers*...T-Neck 34432
9	10	10	Songs From The Wood	*Jethro Tull*...Chrysalis 1132
10	7	27	Leftoverture	*Kansas*...Kirshner 34224

TW	LW	WK	Billboard® — MAY 14, 1977 — TOP LP's	Artist...Label
1	1	21	**Hotel California**	*Eagles*...Asylum 1084
2	2	12	Rumours	*Fleetwood Mac*...Warner 3010
3	4	7	**Marvin Gaye Live At The London Palladium**	*Marvin Gaye*...Tamla 352
4	7	11	**Rocky**	*Soundtrack*...United Artists 693
5	5	31	Songs In The Key Of Life	*Stevie Wonder*...Tamla 340
6	6	34	Boston	*Boston*...Epic 34188
7	8	5	Go For Your Guns	*The Isley Brothers*...T-Neck 34432
8	9	11	**Songs From The Wood**	*Jethro Tull*...Chrysalis 1132
9	3	23	A Star Is Born	*Barbra Streisand/Soundtrack*...Columbia 34403
10	14	7	Commodores	*Commodores*...Motown 884

TW	LW	WK	Billboard® — MAY 21, 1977 — TOP LP's	Artist...Label
1	2	13	**Rumours**	*Fleetwood Mac*...Warner 3010
2	1	22	Hotel California	*Eagles*...Asylum 1084
3	3	8	**Marvin Gaye Live At The London Palladium**	*Marvin Gaye*...Tamla 352
4	4	12	**Rocky**	*Soundtrack*...United Artists 693
5	5	32	Songs In The Key Of Life	*Stevie Wonder*...Tamla 340
6	7	6	**Go For Your Guns**	*The Isley Brothers*...T-Neck 34432
7	6	35	Boston	*Boston*...Epic 34188
8	8	12	**Songs From The Wood**	*Jethro Tull*...Chrysalis 1132
9	10	8	Commodores	*Commodores*...Motown 884
10	9	24	A Star Is Born	*Barbra Streisand/Soundtrack*...Columbia 34403

Billboard — MAY 28, 1977 — TOP LP's

TW	LW	WK	Title	Artist...Label
1	1	14	**Rumours**	*Fleetwood Mac*...Warner 3010
2	2	23	Hotel California	*Eagles*...Asylum 1084
3	3	9	**Marvin Gaye Live At The London Palladium**	*Marvin Gaye*...Tamla 352
4	4	13	**Rocky**	*Soundtrack*...United Artists 693
5	13	2	The Beatles At The Hollywood Bowl	*The Beatles*...Capitol 11638
6	6	7	**Go For Your Guns**	*The Isley Brothers*...T-Neck 34432
7	9	9	Commodores	*Commodores*...Motown 884
8	5	33	Songs In The Key Of Life	*Stevie Wonder*...Tamla 340
9	7	36	Boston	*Boston*...Epic 34188
10	-	1	Barry Manilow/Live	*Barry Manilow*...Arista 8500

Billboard — JUNE 4, 1977 — TOP LP's

TW	LW	WK	Title	Artist...Label
1	1	15	**Rumours**	*Fleetwood Mac*...Warner 3010
2	2	24	Hotel California	*Eagles*...Asylum 1084
3	5	3	The Beatles At The Hollywood Bowl	*The Beatles*...Capitol 11638
4	4	14	**Rocky**	*Soundtrack*...United Artists 693
5	3	10	Marvin Gaye Live At The London Palladium	*Marvin Gaye*...Tamla 352
6	7	10	Commodores	*Commodores*...Motown 884
7	6	8	Go For Your Guns	*The Isley Brothers*...T-Neck 34432
8	8	34	Songs In The Key Of Life	*Stevie Wonder*...Tamla 340
9	10	2	Barry Manilow/Live	*Barry Manilow*...Arista 8500
10	11	28	**Endless Flight**	*Leo Sayer*...Warner 2962

Billboard — JUNE 11, 1977 — TOP LP's

TW	LW	WK	Title	Artist...Label
1	1	16	**Rumours**	*Fleetwood Mac*...Warner 3010
2	3	4	**The Beatles At The Hollywood Bowl**	*The Beatles*...Capitol 11638
3	2	25	Hotel California	*Eagles*...Asylum 1084
4	4	15	**Rocky**	*Soundtrack*...United Artists 693
5	6	11	Commodores	*Commodores*...Motown 884
6	11	4	Book Of Dreams	*Steve Miller Band*...Capitol 11630
7	9	3	Barry Manilow/Live	*Barry Manilow*...Arista 8500
8	8	35	Songs In The Key Of Life	*Stevie Wonder*...Tamla 340
9	5	11	Marvin Gaye Live At The London Palladium	*Marvin Gaye*...Tamla 352
10	10	29	**Endless Flight**	*Leo Sayer*...Warner 2962

Billboard — JUNE 18, 1977 — TOP LP's

TW	LW	WK	Title	Artist...Label
1	1	17	**Rumours**	*Fleetwood Mac*...Warner 3010
2	2	5	**The Beatles At The Hollywood Bowl**	*The Beatles*...Capitol 11638
3	5	12	**Commodores**	*Commodores*...Motown 884
4	4	16	**Rocky**	*Soundtrack*...United Artists 693
5	3	26	Hotel California	*Eagles*...Asylum 1084
6	6	5	Book Of Dreams	*Steve Miller Band*...Capitol 11630
7	7	4	Barry Manilow/Live	*Barry Manilow*...Arista 8500
8	9	12	Marvin Gaye Live At The London Palladium	*Marvin Gaye*...Tamla 352
9	11	5	Izitso	*Cat Stevens*...A&M 4702
10	12	13	Foreigner	*Foreigner*...Atlantic 18215

TW	LW	WK	Billboard — JUNE 25, 1977 — TOP LP's	
1	1	18	**Rumours**	*Fleetwood Mac*...Warner 3010
2	6	6	**Book Of Dreams**	*Steve Miller Band*...Capitol 11630
3	3	13	**Commodores**	*Commodores*...Motown 884
4	7	5	Barry Manilow/Live	*Barry Manilow*...Arista 8500
5	-	1	I'm In You	*Peter Frampton*...A&M 4704
6	5	27	Hotel California	*Eagles*...Asylum 1084
7	8	13	Marvin Gaye Live At The London Palladium	*Marvin Gaye*...Tamla 352
8	9	6	Izitso	*Cat Stevens*...A&M 4702
9	10	14	Foreigner	*Foreigner*...Atlantic 18215
10	4	17	Rocky	*Soundtrack*...United Artists 693

TW	LW	WK	Billboard — JULY 2, 1977 — TOP LP's	
1	1	19	**Rumours**	*Fleetwood Mac*...Warner 3010
2	2	7	**Book Of Dreams**	*Steve Miller Band*...Capitol 11630
3	3	14	**Commodores**	*Commodores*...Motown 884
4	4	6	Barry Manilow/Live	*Barry Manilow*...Arista 8500
5	5	2	I'm In You	*Peter Frampton*...A&M 4704
6	7	14	Marvin Gaye Live At The London Palladium	*Marvin Gaye*...Tamla 352
7	8	7	**Izitso**	*Cat Stevens*...A&M 4702
8	9	15	Foreigner	*Foreigner*...Atlantic 18215
9	6	28	Hotel California	*Eagles*...Asylum 1084
10	12	6	Little Queen	*Heart*...Portrait 34799

TW	LW	WK	Billboard — JULY 9, 1977 — TOP LP's	
1	1	20	**Rumours**	*Fleetwood Mac*...Warner 3010
2	4	7	Barry Manilow/Live	*Barry Manilow*...Arista 8500
3	5	3	I'm In You	*Peter Frampton*...A&M 4704
4	3	15	Commodores	*Commodores*...Motown 884
5	2	8	Book Of Dreams	*Steve Miller Band*...Capitol 11630
6	6	15	Marvin Gaye Live At The London Palladium	*Marvin Gaye*...Tamla 352
7	7	8	**Izitso**	*Cat Stevens*...A&M 4702
8	8	16	Foreigner	*Foreigner*...Atlantic 18215
9	10	7	**Little Queen**	*Heart*...Portrait 34799
10	-	1	Love Gun	*Kiss*...Casablanca 7057

TW	LW	WK	Billboard — JULY 16, 1977 — TOP LP's	
1	2	8	**Barry Manilow/Live**	*Barry Manilow*...Arista 8500
2	3	4	**I'm In You**	*Peter Frampton*...A&M 4704
3	1	21	Rumours	*Fleetwood Mac*...Warner 3010
4	5	9	Book Of Dreams	*Steve Miller Band*...Capitol 11630
5	12	3	Streisand Superman	*Barbra Streisand*...Columbia 34830
6	10	2	Love Gun	*Kiss*...Casablanca 7057
7	4	16	Commodores	*Commodores*...Motown 884
8	8	17	Foreigner	*Foreigner*...Atlantic 18215
9	9	8	**Little Queen**	*Heart*...Portrait 34799
10	11	7	Here At Last...Bee Gees...Live	*Bee Gees*...RSO 3901

TW	LW	WK	Billboard — JULY 23, 1977 — TOP LP's
❶	3	22	**Rumours** .... *Fleetwood Mac*...Warner 3010
❷	2	5	**I'm In You** .... *Peter Frampton*...A&M 4704
③	1	9	Barry Manilow/Live .... *Barry Manilow*...Arista 8500
❹	5	4	Streisand Superman .... *Barbra Streisand*...Columbia 34830
❺	6	3	Love Gun .... *Kiss*...Casablanca 7057
⑥	4	10	Book Of Dreams .... *Steve Miller Band*...Capitol 11630
⑦	7	17	Commodores .... *Commodores*...Motown 884
❽	11	3	CSN .... *Crosby, Stills & Nash*...Atlantic 19104
❾	10	8	Here At Last...Bee Gees...Live .... *Bee Gees*...RSO 3901
⑩	8	18	Foreigner .... *Foreigner*...Atlantic 18215

TW	LW	WK	Billboard — JULY 30, 1977 — TOP LP's
❶	1	23	**Rumours** .... *Fleetwood Mac*...Warner 3010
❷	2	6	**I'm In You** .... *Peter Frampton*...A&M 4704
❸	4	5	**Streisand Superman** .... *Barbra Streisand*...Columbia 34830
❹	5	4	**Love Gun** .... *Kiss*...Casablanca 7057
⑤	3	10	Barry Manilow/Live .... *Barry Manilow*...Arista 8500
❻	8	4	CSN .... *Crosby, Stills & Nash*...Atlantic 19104
⑦	6	11	Book Of Dreams .... *Steve Miller Band*...Capitol 11630
⑧	9	9	**Here At Last...Bee Gees...Live** .... *Bee Gees*...RSO 3901
⑨	7	18	Commodores .... *Commodores*...Motown 884
❿	14	4	JT .... *James Taylor*...Columbia 34811

TW	LW	WK	Billboard — AUGUST 6, 1977 — TOP LP's
❶	1	24	**Rumours** .... *Fleetwood Mac*...Warner 3010
②	2	7	**I'm In You** .... *Peter Frampton*...A&M 4704
❸	3	6	**Streisand Superman** .... *Barbra Streisand*...Columbia 34830
④	4	5	**Love Gun** .... *Kiss*...Casablanca 7057
❺	6	5	CSN .... *Crosby, Stills & Nash*...Atlantic 19104
⑥	5	11	Barry Manilow/Live .... *Barry Manilow*...Arista 8500
⑦	7	12	Book Of Dreams .... *Steve Miller Band*...Capitol 11630
❽	10	5	JT .... *James Taylor*...Columbia 34811
⑨	8	10	Here At Last...Bee Gees...Live .... *Bee Gees*...RSO 3901
❿	11	7	Rejoice .... *The Emotions*...Columbia 34762

TW	LW	WK	Billboard — AUGUST 13, 1977 — TOP LP's
❶	1	25	**Rumours** .... *Fleetwood Mac*...Warner 3010
❷	5	6	**CSN** .... *Crosby, Stills & Nash*...Atlantic 19104
③	3	7	**Streisand Superman** .... *Barbra Streisand*...Columbia 34830
④	2	8	I'm In You .... *Peter Frampton*...A&M 4704
⑤	4	6	Love Gun .... *Kiss*...Casablanca 7057
⑥	7	13	Book Of Dreams .... *Steve Miller Band*...Capitol 11630
⑦	8	6	JT .... *James Taylor*...Columbia 34811
❽	12	9	Star Wars .... *Soundtrack*...20th Century 541
⑨	10	8	Rejoice .... *The Emotions*...Columbia 34762
⑩	11	20	Commodores .... *Commodores*...Motown 884

Billboard® — AUGUST 20, 1977 — TOP LP's

TW	LW	WK	Title	Artist	Label
1	1	26	Rumours	*Fleetwood Mac*	Warner 3010
2	2	7	CSN	*Crosby, Stills & Nash*	Atlantic 19104
3	3	8	Streisand Superman	*Barbra Streisand*	Columbia 34830
4	8	10	Star Wars	*Soundtrack*	20th Century 541
5	7	7	JT	*James Taylor*	Columbia 34811
6	4	9	I'm In You	*Peter Frampton*	A&M 4704
7	6	14	Book Of Dreams	*Steve Miller Band*	Capitol 11630
8	9	9	Rejoice	*The Emotions*	Columbia 34762
9	10	21	Commodores	*Commodores*	Motown 884
10	5	7	Love Gun	*Kiss*	Casablanca 7057

Billboard® — AUGUST 27, 1977 — TOP LP's

TW	LW	WK	Title	Artist	Label
1	1	27	Rumours	*Fleetwood Mac*	Warner 3010
2	2	8	CSN	*Crosby, Stills & Nash*	Atlantic 19104
3	4	11	Star Wars	*Soundtrack*	20th Century 541
4	5	8	JT	*James Taylor*	Columbia 34811
5	3	9	Streisand Superman	*Barbra Streisand*	Columbia 34830
6	9	22	Commodores	*Commodores*	Motown 884
7	8	10	Rejoice	*The Emotions*	Columbia 34762
8	6	10	I'm In You	*Peter Frampton*	A&M 4704
9	7	15	Book Of Dreams	*Steve Miller Band*	Capitol 11630
10	12	10	Shaun Cassidy	*Shaun Cassidy*	Warner/Curb 3067

Billboard® — SEPTEMBER 3, 1977 — TOP LP's

TW	LW	WK	Title	Artist	Label
1	1	28	Rumours	*Fleetwood Mac*	Warner 3010
2	2	9	CSN	*Crosby, Stills & Nash*	Atlantic 19104
3	3	12	Star Wars	*Soundtrack*	20th Century 541
4	4	9	JT	*James Taylor*	Columbia 34811
5	24	7	Moody Blue	*Elvis Presley*	RCA AFL-2428
6	6	23	Commodores	*Commodores*	Motown 884
7	7	11	Rejoice	*The Emotions*	Columbia 34762
8	8	11	I'm In You	*Peter Frampton*	A&M 4704
9	9	16	Book Of Dreams	*Steve Miller Band*	Capitol 11630
10	10	11	Shaun Cassidy	*Shaun Cassidy*	Warner/Curb 3067

Billboard® — SEPTEMBER 10, 1977 — TOP LP's

TW	LW	WK	Title	Artist	Label
1	1	29	Rumours	*Fleetwood Mac*	Warner 3010
2	3	13	Star Wars	*Soundtrack*	20th Century 541
3	2	10	CSN	*Crosby, Stills & Nash*	Atlantic 19104
4	4	10	JT	*James Taylor*	Columbia 34811
5	5	8	Moody Blue	*Elvis Presley*	RCA AFL-2428
6	6	24	Commodores	*Commodores*	Motown 884
7	7	12	Rejoice	*The Emotions*	Columbia 34762
8	10	12	Shaun Cassidy	*Shaun Cassidy*	Warner/Curb 3067
9	8	12	I'm In You	*Peter Frampton*	A&M 4704
10	11	25	Foreigner	*Foreigner*	Atlantic 18215

TW	LW	WK	Billboard® SEPTEMBER 17, 1977	TOP LP's
1	1	30	**Rumours**	*Fleetwood Mac*...Warner 3010
2	2	14	**Star Wars**	*Soundtrack*...20th Century 541
3	5	9	**Moody Blue**	*Elvis Presley*...RCA AFL-2428
4	4	11	**JT**	*James Taylor*...Columbia 34811
5	3	11	CSN	*Crosby, Stills & Nash*...Atlantic 19104
6	6	25	Commodores	*Commodores*...Motown 884
7	8	13	Shaun Cassidy	*Shaun Cassidy*...Warner/Curb 3067
8	7	13	Rejoice	*The Emotions*...Columbia 34762
9	10	26	Foreigner	*Foreigner*...Atlantic 18215
10	11	8	Going For The One	*Yes*...Atlantic 19106

TW	LW	WK	Billboard® SEPTEMBER 24, 1977	TOP LP's
1	1	31	**Rumours**	*Fleetwood Mac*...Warner 3010
2	2	15	**Star Wars**	*Soundtrack*...20th Century 541
3	3	10	**Moody Blue**	*Elvis Presley*...RCA AFL-2428
4	4	12	**JT**	*James Taylor*...Columbia 34811
5	7	14	Shaun Cassidy	*Shaun Cassidy*...Warner/Curb 3067
6	6	26	Commodores	*Commodores*...Motown 884
7	5	12	CSN	*Crosby, Stills & Nash*...Atlantic 19104
8	9	27	Foreigner	*Foreigner*...Atlantic 18215
9	10	9	Going For The One	*Yes*...Atlantic 19106
10	11	14	**Floaters**	*The Floaters*...ABC 1030

TW	LW	WK	Billboard® OCTOBER 1, 1977	TOP LP's
1	1	32	**Rumours**	*Fleetwood Mac*...Warner 3010
2	43	2	Simple Dreams	*Linda Ronstadt*...Asylum 104
3	3	11	**Moody Blue**	*Elvis Presley*...RCA AFL-2428
4	5	15	Shaun Cassidy	*Shaun Cassidy*...Warner/Curb 3067
5	2	16	Star Wars	*Soundtrack*...20th Century 541
6	4	13	JT	*James Taylor*...Columbia 34811
7	8	28	Foreigner	*Foreigner*...Atlantic 18215
8	9	10	**Going For The One**	*Yes*...Atlantic 19106
9	11	27	Anytime...Anywhere	*Rita Coolidge*...A&M 4616
10	10	15	**Floaters**	*The Floaters*...ABC 1030

TW	LW	WK	Billboard® OCTOBER 8, 1977	TOP LP's
1	1	33	**Rumours**	*Fleetwood Mac*...Warner 3010
2	2	3	Simple Dreams	*Linda Ronstadt*...Asylum 104
3	4	16	**Shaun Cassidy**	*Shaun Cassidy*...Warner/Curb 3067
4	5	17	Star Wars	*Soundtrack*...20th Century 541
5	3	12	Moody Blue	*Elvis Presley*...RCA AFL-2428
6	7	29	Foreigner	*Foreigner*...Atlantic 18215
7	9	28	Anytime...Anywhere	*Rita Coolidge*...A&M 4616
8	8	11	**Going For The One**	*Yes*...Atlantic 19106
9	6	14	JT	*James Taylor*...Columbia 34811
10	11	13	I Robot	*The Alan Parsons Project*...Arista 7002

TW	LW	WK	Billboard® OCTOBER 15, 1977 TOP LP's
1	1	34	**Rumours**........ *Fleetwood Mac*...Warner 3010
2	2	4	Simple Dreams........ *Linda Ronstadt*...Asylum 104
3	3	17	**Shaun Cassidy**........ *Shaun Cassidy*...Warner/Curb 3067
4	5	13	Moody Blue........ *Elvis Presley*...RCA AFL-2428
5	6	30	Foreigner........ *Foreigner*...Atlantic 18215
6	7	29	**Anytime...Anywhere**........ *Rita Coolidge*...A&M 4616
7	4	18	Star Wars........ *Soundtrack*...20th Century 541
8	9	15	JT........ *James Taylor*...Columbia 34811
9	10	14	**I Robot**........ *The Alan Parsons Project*...Arista 7002
10	11	6	**Livin' On The Fault Line**........ *The Doobie Brothers*...Warner 3045

TW	LW	WK	Billboard® OCTOBER 22, 1977 TOP LP's
1	1	35	**Rumours**........ *Fleetwood Mac*...Warner 3010
2	2	5	Simple Dreams........ *Linda Ronstadt*...Asylum 104
3	26	2	**Aja**........ *Steely Dan*...ABC 1006
4	5	31	**Foreigner**........ *Foreigner*...Atlantic 18215
5	3	18	Shaun Cassidy........ *Shaun Cassidy*...Warner/Curb 3067
6	6	30	**Anytime...Anywhere**........ *Rita Coolidge*...A&M 4616
7	11	3	Love You Live........ *The Rolling Stones*...Rolling Stones 9001
8	4	14	Moody Blue........ *Elvis Presley*...RCA AFL-2428
9	9	15	**I Robot**........ *The Alan Parsons Project*...Arista 7002
10	10	7	**Livin' On The Fault Line**........ *The Doobie Brothers*...Warner 3045

TW	LW	WK	Billboard® OCTOBER 29, 1977 TOP LP's
1	1	36	**Rumours**........ *Fleetwood Mac*...Warner 3010
2	2	6	Simple Dreams........ *Linda Ronstadt*...Asylum 104
3	3	3	**Aja**........ *Steely Dan*...ABC 1006
4	4	32	**Foreigner**........ *Foreigner*...Atlantic 18215
5	7	4	**Love You Live**........ *The Rolling Stones*...Rolling Stones 9001
6	6	31	**Anytime...Anywhere**........ *Rita Coolidge*...A&M 4616
7	5	19	Shaun Cassidy........ *Shaun Cassidy*...Warner/Curb 3067
8	11	5	Chicago XI........ *Chicago*...Columbia 34860
9	9	16	**I Robot**........ *The Alan Parsons Project*...Arista 7002
10	10	8	**Livin' On The Fault Line**........ *The Doobie Brothers*...Warner 3045

TW	LW	WK	Billboard® NOVEMBER 5, 1977 TOP LP's
1	1	37	**Rumours**........ *Fleetwood Mac*...Warner 3010
2	2	7	Simple Dreams........ *Linda Ronstadt*...Asylum 104
3	3	4	**Aja**........ *Steely Dan*...ABC 1006
4	4	33	**Foreigner**........ *Foreigner*...Atlantic 18215
5	5	5	**Love You Live**........ *The Rolling Stones*...Rolling Stones 9001
6	6	32	**Anytime...Anywhere**........ *Rita Coolidge*...A&M 4616
7	8	6	Chicago XI........ *Chicago*...Columbia 34860
8	7	20	Shaun Cassidy........ *Shaun Cassidy*...Warner/Curb 3067
9	18	2	Elvis In Concert........ *Elvis Presley*...RCA APL-2587
10	13	8	Barry White Sings For Someone You Love...... *Barry White*...20th Century 543

TW	LW	WK	Billboard. NOVEMBER 12, 1977	TOP LP's
1	1	38	**Rumours**	*Fleetwood Mac*...Warner 3010
2	2	8	Simple Dreams	*Linda Ronstadt*...Asylum 104
3	3	5	**Aja**	*Steely Dan*...ABC 1006
4	4	34	**Foreigner**	*Foreigner*...Atlantic 18215
5	5	6	**Love You Live**	*The Rolling Stones*...Rolling Stones 9001
6	7	7	**Chicago XI**	*Chicago*...Columbia 34860
7	9	3	Elvis In Concert	*Elvis Presley*...RCA APL-2587
8	10	9	**Barry White Sings For Someone You Love**	*Barry White*...20th Century 543
9	6	33	Anytime...Anywhere	*Rita Coolidge*...A&M 4616
10	22	5	Point Of Know Return	*Kansas*...Kirshner 34929

TW	LW	WK	Billboard. NOVEMBER 19, 1977	TOP LP's
1	1	39	**Rumours**	*Fleetwood Mac*...Warner 3010
2	2	9	Simple Dreams	*Linda Ronstadt*...Asylum 104
3	3	6	**Aja**	*Steely Dan*...ABC 1006
4	4	35	**Foreigner**	*Foreigner*...Atlantic 18215
5	7	4	**Elvis In Concert**	*Elvis Presley*...RCA APL-2587
6	6	8	**Chicago XI**	*Chicago*...Columbia 34860
7	50	3	Street Survivors	*Lynyrd Skynyrd*...MCA 3029
8	8	10	**Barry White Sings For Someone You Love**	*Barry White*...20th Century 543
9	10	6	Point Of Know Return	*Kansas*...Kirshner 34929
10	11	13	Rose Royce II/In Full Bloom	*Rose Royce*...Whitfield 3074

TW	LW	WK	Billboard. NOVEMBER 26, 1977	TOP LP's
1	1	40	**Rumours**	*Fleetwood Mac*...Warner 3010
2	2	10	Simple Dreams	*Linda Ronstadt*...Asylum 104
3	3	7	**Aja**	*Steely Dan*...ABC 1006
4	19	3	Commodores Live!	*Commodores*...Motown 894
5	5	5	**Elvis In Concert**	*Elvis Presley*...RCA APL-2587
6	7	4	Street Survivors	*Lynyrd Skynyrd*...MCA 3029
7	4	36	Foreigner	*Foreigner*...Atlantic 18215
8	9	7	Point Of Know Return	*Kansas*...Kirshner 34929
9	10	14	**Rose Royce II/In Full Bloom**	*Rose Royce*...Whitfield 3074
10	12	8	**Let's Get Small**	*Steve Martin*...Warner 3090

TW	LW	WK	Billboard. DECEMBER 3, 1977	TOP LP's
1	2	11	**Simple Dreams**	*Linda Ronstadt*...Asylum 104
2	1	41	Rumours	*Fleetwood Mac*...Warner 3010
3	3	8	**Aja**	*Steely Dan*...ABC 1006
4	4	4	Commodores Live!	*Commodores*...Motown 894
5	31	2	Foot Loose & Fancy Free	*Rod Stewart*...Warner 3092
6	6	5	Street Survivors	*Lynyrd Skynyrd*...MCA 3029
7	8	8	Point Of Know Return	*Kansas*...Kirshner 34929
8	11	6	You Light Up My Life	*Debby Boone*...Warner/Curb 3118
9	9	15	**Rose Royce II/In Full Bloom**	*Rose Royce*...Whitfield 3074
10	10	9	**Let's Get Small**	*Steve Martin*...Warner 3090

Billboard — DECEMBER 10, 1977 — TOP LP's

TW	LW	WK	Title	Artist / Label
1	1	12	**Simple Dreams**	*Linda Ronstadt*...Asylum 104
2	2	42	Rumours	*Fleetwood Mac*...Warner 3010
3	4	5	**Commodores Live!**	*Commodores*...Motown 894
4	5	3	Foot Loose & Fancy Free	*Rod Stewart*...Warner 3092
5	6	6	**Street Survivors**	*Lynyrd Skynyrd*...MCA 3029
6	76	2	All 'N All	*Earth, Wind & Fire*...Columbia 34905
7	8	7	You Light Up My Life	*Debby Boone*...Warner/Curb 3118
8	3	9	Aja	*Steely Dan*...ABC 1006
9	12	3	Out Of The Blue	*Electric Light Orchestra*...Jet 823
10	11	6	**Moonflower**	*Santana*...Columbia 34914

Billboard — DECEMBER 17, 1977 — TOP LP's

TW	LW	WK	Title	Artist / Label
1	1	13	**Simple Dreams**	*Linda Ronstadt*...Asylum 104
2	2	43	Rumours	*Fleetwood Mac*...Warner 3010
3	3	6	**Commodores Live!**	*Commodores*...Motown 894
4	4	4	Foot Loose & Fancy Free	*Rod Stewart*...Warner 3092
5	5	7	**Street Survivors**	*Lynyrd Skynyrd*...MCA 3029
6	6	3	All 'N All	*Earth, Wind & Fire*...Columbia 34905
7	7	8	You Light Up My Life	*Debby Boone*...Warner/Curb 3118
8	9	4	Out Of The Blue	*Electric Light Orchestra*...Jet 823
9	8	10	Aja	*Steely Dan*...ABC 1006
10	10	7	**Moonflower**	*Santana*...Columbia 34914

Billboard — DECEMBER 24, 1977 — TOP LP's

TW	LW	WK	Title	Artist / Label
1	1	14	**Simple Dreams**	*Linda Ronstadt*...Asylum 104
2	2	44	Rumours	*Fleetwood Mac*...Warner 3010
3	4	5	Foot Loose & Fancy Free	*Rod Stewart*...Warner 3092
4	6	4	All 'N All	*Earth, Wind & Fire*...Columbia 34905
5	8	5	Out Of The Blue	*Electric Light Orchestra*...Jet 823
6	7	9	**You Light Up My Life**	*Debby Boone*...Warner/Curb 3118
7	3	7	Commodores Live!	*Commodores*...Motown 894
8	9	11	Aja	*Steely Dan*...ABC 1006
9	11	5	Alive II	*Kiss*...Casablanca 7076
10	10	8	**Moonflower**	*Santana*...Columbia 34914

Billboard — JANUARY 7, 1978 — TOP LP's

TW	LW	WK			
1	2	46	**Rumours**	*Fleetwood Mac*	Warner 3010
2	3	7	**Foot Loose & Fancy Free**	*Rod Stewart*	Warner 3092
3	4	6	**All 'N All**	*Earth, Wind & Fire*	Columbia 34905
4	5	7	**Out Of The Blue**	*Electric Light Orchestra*	Jet 823
5	1	16	Simple Dreams	*Linda Ronstadt*	Asylum 104
6	6	11	**You Light Up My Life**	*Debby Boone*	Warner/Curb 3118
7	9	7	**Alive II**	*Kiss*	Casablanca 7076
8	18	7	Born Late	*Shaun Cassidy*	Warner/Curb 3126
9	12	7	News Of The World	*Queen*	Elektra 112
10	13	6	I'm Glad You're Here With Me Tonight	*Neil Diamond*	Columbia 34990

Billboard — JANUARY 14, 1978 — TOP LP's

TW	LW	WK			
1	1	47	**Rumours**	*Fleetwood Mac*	Warner 3010
2	2	8	**Foot Loose & Fancy Free**	*Rod Stewart*	Warner 3092
3	3	7	**All 'N All**	*Earth, Wind & Fire*	Columbia 34905
4	4	8	**Out Of The Blue**	*Electric Light Orchestra*	Jet 823
5	5	17	Simple Dreams	*Linda Ronstadt*	Asylum 104
6	8	8	**Born Late**	*Shaun Cassidy*	Warner/Curb 3126
7	7	8	**Alive II**	*Kiss*	Casablanca 7076
8	9	8	News Of The World	*Queen*	Elektra 112
9	10	7	I'm Glad You're Here With Me Tonight	*Neil Diamond*	Columbia 34990
10	22	8	Saturday Night Fever	*Bee Gees/Soundtrack*	RSO 4001

Billboard — JANUARY 21, 1978 — TOP LP's

TW	LW	WK			
1	10	9	**Saturday Night Fever**	*Bee Gees/Soundtrack*	RSO 4001
2	2	9	**Foot Loose & Fancy Free**	*Rod Stewart*	Warner 3092
3	3	8	**All 'N All**	*Earth, Wind & Fire*	Columbia 34905
4	4	9	**Out Of The Blue**	*Electric Light Orchestra*	Jet 823
5	1	48	Rumours	*Fleetwood Mac*	Warner 3010
6	6	9	**Born Late**	*Shaun Cassidy*	Warner/Curb 3126
7	8	9	News Of The World	*Queen*	Elektra 112
8	9	8	I'm Glad You're Here With Me Tonight	*Neil Diamond*	Columbia 34990
9	15	26	The Grand Illusion	*Styx*	A&M 4637
10	14	16	The Stranger	*Billy Joel*	Columbia 34987

Billboard — JANUARY 28, 1978 — TOP LP's

TW	LW	WK			
1	1	10	**Saturday Night Fever**	*Bee Gees/Soundtrack*	RSO 4001
2	2	10	**Foot Loose & Fancy Free**	*Rod Stewart*	Warner 3092
3	3	9	**All 'N All**	*Earth, Wind & Fire*	Columbia 34905
4	4	10	**Out Of The Blue**	*Electric Light Orchestra*	Jet 823
5	7	10	News Of The World	*Queen*	Elektra 112
6	6	10	**Born Late**	*Shaun Cassidy*	Warner/Curb 3126
7	5	49	Rumours	*Fleetwood Mac*	Warner 3010
8	8	9	I'm Glad You're Here With Me Tonight	*Neil Diamond*	Columbia 34990
9	9	27	The Grand Illusion	*Styx*	A&M 4637
10	10	17	The Stranger	*Billy Joel*	Columbia 34987

Billboard — FEBRUARY 4, 1978 — TOP LP's

TW	LW	WK	Title	Artist	Label
1	1	11	**Saturday Night Fever**	*Bee Gees/Soundtrack*	RSO 4001
2	2	11	**Foot Loose & Fancy Free**	*Rod Stewart*	Warner 3092
3	3	10	**All 'N All**	*Earth, Wind & Fire*	Columbia 34905
4	5	11	News Of The World	*Queen*	Elektra 112
5	4	11	Out Of The Blue	*Electric Light Orchestra*	Jet 823
6	7	50	Rumours	*Fleetwood Mac*	Warner 3010
7	8	10	I'm Glad You're Here With Me Tonight	*Neil Diamond*	Columbia 34990
8	9	28	The Grand Illusion	*Styx*	A&M 4637
9	10	18	The Stranger	*Billy Joel*	Columbia 34987
10	12	5	Running On Empty	*Jackson Browne*	Asylum 113

Billboard — FEBRUARY 11, 1978 — TOP LP's

TW	LW	WK	Title	Artist	Label
1	1	12	**Saturday Night Fever**	*Bee Gees/Soundtrack*	RSO 4001
2	2	12	**Foot Loose & Fancy Free**	*Rod Stewart*	Warner 3092
3	3	11	**All 'N All**	*Earth, Wind & Fire*	Columbia 34905
4	4	12	News Of The World	*Queen*	Elektra 112
5	9	19	The Stranger	*Billy Joel*	Columbia 34987
6	7	11	**I'm Glad You're Here With Me Tonight**	*Neil Diamond*	Columbia 34990
7	6	51	Rumours	*Fleetwood Mac*	Warner 3010
8	8	29	The Grand Illusion	*Styx*	A&M 4637
9	10	6	Running On Empty	*Jackson Browne*	Asylum 113
10	12	17	Little Criminals	*Randy Newman*	Warner 3079

Billboard — FEBRUARY 18, 1978 — TOP LP's

TW	LW	WK	Title	Artist	Label
1	1	13	**Saturday Night Fever**	*Bee Gees/Soundtrack*	RSO 4001
2	5	20	**The Stranger**	*Billy Joel*	Columbia 34987
3	4	13	**News Of The World**	*Queen*	Elektra 112
4	3	12	All 'N All	*Earth, Wind & Fire*	Columbia 34905
5	2	13	Foot Loose & Fancy Free	*Rod Stewart*	Warner 3092
6	6	12	**I'm Glad You're Here With Me Tonight**	*Neil Diamond*	Columbia 34990
7	8	30	The Grand Illusion	*Styx*	A&M 4637
8	9	7	Running On Empty	*Jackson Browne*	Asylum 113
9	10	18	**Little Criminals**	*Randy Newman*	Warner 3079
10	7	52	Rumours	*Fleetwood Mac*	Warner 3010

Billboard — FEBRUARY 25, 1978 — TOP LP's

TW	LW	WK	Title	Artist	Label
1	1	14	**Saturday Night Fever**	*Bee Gees/Soundtrack*	RSO 4001
2	2	21	**The Stranger**	*Billy Joel*	Columbia 34987
3	3	14	**News Of The World**	*Queen*	Elektra 112
4	4	13	All 'N All	*Earth, Wind & Fire*	Columbia 34905
5	5	14	Foot Loose & Fancy Free	*Rod Stewart*	Warner 3092
6	7	31	**The Grand Illusion**	*Styx*	A&M 4637
7	8	8	Running On Empty	*Jackson Browne*	Asylum 113
8	13	14	Slowhand	*Eric Clapton*	RSO 3030
9	9	19	**Little Criminals**	*Randy Newman*	Warner 3079
10	11	20	Aja	*Steely Dan*	ABC 1006

Billboard — MARCH 4, 1978 — TOP LP's

TW	LW	WK	Title	Artist	Label
1	1	15	**Saturday Night Fever**	*Bee Gees/Soundtrack*	RSO 4001
2	2	22	**The Stranger**	*Billy Joel*	Columbia 34987
3	7	9	**Running On Empty**	*Jackson Browne*	Asylum 113
4	3	15	News Of The World	*Queen*	Elektra 112
5	8	15	Slowhand	*Eric Clapton*	RSO 3030
6	6	32	**The Grand Illusion**	*Styx*	A&M 4637
7	4	14	All 'N All	*Earth, Wind & Fire*	Columbia 34905
8	10	21	Aja	*Steely Dan*	ABC 1006
9	5	15	Foot Loose & Fancy Free	*Rod Stewart*	Warner 3092
10	14	4	Weekend In L.A.	*George Benson*	Warner 3139

Billboard — MARCH 11, 1978 — TOP LP's

TW	LW	WK	Title	Artist	Label
1	1	16	**Saturday Night Fever**	*Bee Gees/Soundtrack*	RSO 4001
2	2	23	**The Stranger**	*Billy Joel*	Columbia 34987
3	3	10	**Running On Empty**	*Jackson Browne*	Asylum 113
4	5	16	Slowhand	*Eric Clapton*	RSO 3030
5	4	16	News Of The World	*Queen*	Elektra 112
6	8	22	Aja	*Steely Dan*	ABC 1006
7	7	15	All 'N All	*Earth, Wind & Fire*	Columbia 34905
8	10	5	Weekend In L.A.	*George Benson*	Warner 3139
9	9	16	Foot Loose & Fancy Free	*Rod Stewart*	Warner 3092
10	6	33	The Grand Illusion	*Styx*	A&M 4637

Billboard — MARCH 18, 1978 — TOP LP's

TW	LW	WK	Title	Artist	Label
1	1	17	**Saturday Night Fever**	*Bee Gees/Soundtrack*	RSO 4001
2	2	24	**The Stranger**	*Billy Joel*	Columbia 34987
3	4	17	Slowhand	*Eric Clapton*	RSO 3030
4	3	11	Running On Empty	*Jackson Browne*	Asylum 113
5	6	23	Aja	*Steely Dan*	ABC 1006
6	5	17	News Of The World	*Queen*	Elektra 112
7	8	6	Weekend In L.A.	*George Benson*	Warner 3139
8	11	4	Even Now	*Barry Manilow*	Arista 4164
9	10	34	The Grand Illusion	*Styx*	A&M 4637
10	7	16	All 'N All	*Earth, Wind & Fire*	Columbia 34905

Billboard — MARCH 25, 1978 — TOP LP's

TW	LW	WK	Title	Artist	Label
1	1	18	**Saturday Night Fever**	*Bee Gees/Soundtrack*	RSO 4001
2	2	25	**The Stranger**	*Billy Joel*	Columbia 34987
3	3	18	Slowhand	*Eric Clapton*	RSO 3030
4	4	12	Running On Empty	*Jackson Browne*	Asylum 113
5	5	24	Aja	*Steely Dan*	ABC 1006
6	8	5	Even Now	*Barry Manilow*	Arista 4164
7	7	7	Weekend In L.A.	*George Benson*	Warner 3139
8	6	18	News Of The World	*Queen*	Elektra 112
9	9	35	The Grand Illusion	*Styx*	A&M 4637
10	12	24	Point Of Know Return	*Kansas*	Kirshner 34929

Billboard — APRIL 1, 1978 — TOP LP's

TW	LW	WK	Title	Artist...Label
1	1	19	**Saturday Night Fever**	*Bee Gees/Soundtrack*...RSO 4001
2	3	19	**Slowhand**	*Eric Clapton*...RSO 3030
3	2	26	The Stranger	*Billy Joel*...Columbia 34987
4	6	6	Even Now	*Barry Manilow*...Arista 4164
5	5	25	Aja	*Steely Dan*...ABC 1006
6	7	8	Weekend In L.A.	*George Benson*...Warner 3139
7	4	13	Running On Empty	*Jackson Browne*...Asylum 113
8	10	25	Point Of Know Return	*Kansas*...Kirshner 34929
9	8	19	News Of The World	*Queen*...Elektra 112
10	9	36	The Grand Illusion	*Styx*...A&M 4637

Billboard — APRIL 8, 1978 — TOP LP's

TW	LW	WK	Title	Artist...Label
1	1	20	**Saturday Night Fever**	*Bee Gees/Soundtrack*...RSO 4001
2	2	20	**Slowhand**	*Eric Clapton*...RSO 3030
3	4	7	**Even Now**	*Barry Manilow*...Arista 4164
4	3	27	The Stranger	*Billy Joel*...Columbia 34987
5	5	26	Aja	*Steely Dan*...ABC 1006
6	6	9	Weekend In L.A.	*George Benson*...Warner 3139
7	8	26	Point Of Know Return	*Kansas*...Kirshner 34929
8	7	14	Running On Empty	*Jackson Browne*...Asylum 113
9	11	4	Earth	*Jefferson Starship*...Grunt 2515
10	10	37	The Grand Illusion	*Styx*...A&M 4637

Billboard — APRIL 15, 1978 — TOP LP's

TW	LW	WK	Title	Artist...Label
1	1	21	**Saturday Night Fever**	*Bee Gees/Soundtrack*...RSO 4001
2	2	21	**Slowhand**	*Eric Clapton*...RSO 3030
3	3	8	**Even Now**	*Barry Manilow*...Arista 4164
4	4	28	The Stranger	*Billy Joel*...Columbia 34987
5	6	10	**Weekend In L.A.**	*George Benson*...Warner 3139
6	7	27	Point Of Know Return	*Kansas*...Kirshner 34929
7	9	5	Earth	*Jefferson Starship*...Grunt 2515
8	5	27	Aja	*Steely Dan*...ABC 1006
9	8	15	Running On Empty	*Jackson Browne*...Asylum 113
10	11	15	Blue Lights In The Basement	*Roberta Flack*...Atlantic 19149

Billboard — APRIL 22, 1978 — TOP LP's

TW	LW	WK	Title	Artist...Label
1	1	22	**Saturday Night Fever**	*Bee Gees/Soundtrack*...RSO 4001
2	2	22	**Slowhand**	*Eric Clapton*...RSO 3030
3	3	9	**Even Now**	*Barry Manilow*...Arista 4164
4	4	29	The Stranger	*Billy Joel*...Columbia 34987
5	5	11	**Weekend In L.A.**	*George Benson*...Warner 3139
6	6	28	Point Of Know Return	*Kansas*...Kirshner 34929
7	7	6	Earth	*Jefferson Starship*...Grunt 2515
8	20	2	London Town	*Wings*...Capitol 11777
9	10	16	Blue Lights In The Basement	*Roberta Flack*...Atlantic 19149
10	8	28	Aja	*Steely Dan*...ABC 1006

TW	LW	WK	Billboard — APRIL 29, 1978 — TOP LP's	Artist	Label
1	1	23	**Saturday Night Fever**	*Bee Gees/Soundtrack*	RSO 4001
2	2	23	**Slowhand**	*Eric Clapton*	RSO 3030
3	8	3	London Town	*Wings*	Capitol 11777
4	4	30	The Stranger	*Billy Joel*	Columbia 34987
5	5	12	**Weekend In L.A.**	*George Benson*	Warner 3139
6	6	29	Point Of Know Return	*Kansas*	Kirshner 34929
7	7	7	Earth	*Jefferson Starship*	Grunt 2515
8	9	17	**Blue Lights In The Basement**	*Roberta Flack*	Atlantic 19149
9	3	10	Even Now	*Barry Manilow*	Arista 4164
10	12	17	Running On Empty	*Jackson Browne*	Asylum 113

TW	LW	WK	Billboard — MAY 6, 1978 — TOP LP's	Artist	Label
1	1	24	**Saturday Night Fever**	*Bee Gees/Soundtrack*	RSO 4001
2	3	4	**London Town**	*Wings*	Capitol 11777
3	2	24	Slowhand	*Eric Clapton*	RSO 3030
4	6	30	**Point Of Know Return**	*Kansas*	Kirshner 34929
5	7	8	**Earth**	*Jefferson Starship*	Grunt 2515
6	4	31	The Stranger	*Billy Joel*	Columbia 34987
7	5	13	Weekend In L.A.	*George Benson*	Warner 3139
8	10	18	Running On Empty	*Jackson Browne*	Asylum 113
9	13	28	Feels So Good	*Chuck Mangione*	A&M 4658
10	12	11	Excitable Boy	*Warren Zevon*	Asylum 118

TW	LW	WK	Billboard — MAY 13, 1978 — TOP LP's	Artist	Label
1	1	25	**Saturday Night Fever**	*Bee Gees/Soundtrack*	RSO 4001
2	2	5	**London Town**	*Wings*	Capitol 11777
3	3	25	Slowhand	*Eric Clapton*	RSO 3030
4	4	31	**Point Of Know Return**	*Kansas*	Kirshner 34929
5	5	9	**Earth**	*Jefferson Starship*	Grunt 2515
6	8	19	Running On Empty	*Jackson Browne*	Asylum 113
7	9	29	Feels So Good	*Chuck Mangione*	A&M 4658
8	10	12	**Excitable Boy**	*Warren Zevon*	Asylum 118
9	6	32	The Stranger	*Billy Joel*	Columbia 34987
10	12	7	Champagne Jam	*Atlanta Rhythm Section*	Polydor 6134

TW	LW	WK	Billboard — MAY 20, 1978 — TOP LP's	Artist	Label
1	1	26	**Saturday Night Fever**	*Bee Gees/Soundtrack*	RSO 4001
2	2	6	**London Town**	*Wings*	Capitol 11777
3	3	26	Slowhand	*Eric Clapton*	RSO 3030
4	7	30	Feels So Good	*Chuck Mangione*	A&M 4658
5	5	10	**Earth**	*Jefferson Starship*	Grunt 2515
6	6	20	Running On Empty	*Jackson Browne*	Asylum 113
7	4	32	Point Of Know Return	*Kansas*	Kirshner 34929
8	8	13	**Excitable Boy**	*Warren Zevon*	Asylum 118
9	10	8	Champagne Jam	*Atlanta Rhythm Section*	Polydor 6134
10	11	7	**Son Of A Son Of A Sailor**	*Jimmy Buffett*	ABC 1046

TW	LW	WK	Billboard® — MAY 27, 1978 — TOP LP's	
1	1	27	**Saturday Night Fever**	*Bee Gees/Soundtrack*...RSO 4001
2	2	7	**London Town**	*Wings*...Capitol 11777
3	4	31	Feels So Good	*Chuck Mangione*...A&M 4658
4	3	27	Slowhand	*Eric Clapton*...RSO 3030
5	5	11	**Earth**	*Jefferson Starship*...Grunt 2515
6	11	6	Showdown	*The Isley Brothers*...T-Neck 34930
7	6	21	Running On Empty	*Jackson Browne*...Asylum 113
8	9	9	Champagne Jam	*Atlanta Rhythm Section*...Polydor 6134
9	8	14	Excitable Boy	*Warren Zevon*...Asylum 118
10	10	8	**Son Of A Son Of A Sailor**	*Jimmy Buffett*...ABC 1046

TW	LW	WK	Billboard® — JUNE 3, 1978 — TOP LP's	
1	1	28	**Saturday Night Fever**	*Bee Gees/Soundtrack*...RSO 4001
2	2	8	**London Town**	*Wings*...Capitol 11777
3	3	32	Feels So Good	*Chuck Mangione*...A&M 4658
4	6	7	**Showdown**	*The Isley Brothers*...T-Neck 34930
5	5	12	**Earth**	*Jefferson Starship*...Grunt 2515
6	4	28	Slowhand	*Eric Clapton*...RSO 3030
7	8	10	**Champagne Jam**	*Atlanta Rhythm Section*...Polydor 6134
8	7	22	Running On Empty	*Jackson Browne*...Asylum 113
9	11	10	**You Light Up My Life**	*Johnny Mathis*...Columbia 35259
10	12	7	**Central Heating**	*Heatwave*...Epic 35260

TW	LW	WK	Billboard® — JUNE 10, 1978 — TOP LP's	
1	1	29	**Saturday Night Fever**	*Bee Gees/Soundtrack*...RSO 4001
2	2	9	**London Town**	*Wings*...Capitol 11777
3	3	33	Feels So Good	*Chuck Mangione*...A&M 4658
4	4	8	**Showdown**	*The Isley Brothers*...T-Neck 34930
5	5	13	**Earth**	*Jefferson Starship*...Grunt 2515
6	6	29	Slowhand	*Eric Clapton*...RSO 3030
7	7	11	**Champagne Jam**	*Atlanta Rhythm Section*...Polydor 6134
8	11	6	FM	*Soundtrack*...MCA 12000
9	9	11	**You Light Up My Life**	*Johnny Mathis*...Columbia 35259
10	10	8	**Central Heating**	*Heatwave*...Epic 35260

TW	LW	WK	Billboard® — JUNE 17, 1978 — TOP LP's	
1	1	30	**Saturday Night Fever**	*Bee Gees/Soundtrack*...RSO 4001
2	3	34	**Feels So Good**	*Chuck Mangione*...A&M 4658
3	2	10	London Town	*Wings*...Capitol 11777
4	4	9	**Showdown**	*The Isley Brothers*...T-Neck 34930
5	5	14	**Earth**	*Jefferson Starship*...Grunt 2515
6	14	7	City to City	*Gerry Rafferty*...United Artists 840
7	8	7	FM	*Soundtrack*...MCA 12000
8	11	8	So Full Of Love	*The O'Jays*...Philadelphia International 35355
9	9	12	**You Light Up My Life**	*Johnny Mathis*...Columbia 35259
10	15	4	Natural High	*Commodores*...Motown 902

Billboard® — JUNE 24, 1978 — TOP LP's

TW	LW	WK	Title	Artist	Label
1	1	31	**Saturday Night Fever**	*Bee Gees/Soundtrack*	RSO 4001
2	2	35	**Feels So Good**	*Chuck Mangione*	A&M 4658
3	6	8	City to City	*Gerry Rafferty*	United Artists 840
4	3	11	London Town	*Wings*	Capitol 11777
5	7	8	**FM**	*Soundtrack*	MCA 12000
6	8	9	**So Full Of Love**	*The O'Jays*	Philadelphia International 35355
7	10	5	Natural High	*Commodores*	Motown 902
8	12	5	Stranger in Town	*Bob Seger & The Silver Bullet Band*	Capitol 11698
9	5	15	Earth	*Jefferson Starship*	Grunt 2515
10	39	2	Darkness on the Edge of Town	*Bruce Springsteen*	Columbia 35318

Billboard® — JULY 1, 1978 — TOP LP's

TW	LW	WK	Title	Artist	Label
1	1	32	**Saturday Night Fever**	*Bee Gees/Soundtrack*	RSO 4001
2	3	9	City to City	*Gerry Rafferty*	United Artists 840
3	2	36	Feels So Good	*Chuck Mangione*	A&M 4658
4	7	6	Natural High	*Commodores*	Motown 902
5	5	9	**FM**	*Soundtrack*	MCA 12000
6	6	10	**So Full Of Love**	*The O'Jays*	Philadelphia International 35355
7	8	6	Stranger in Town	*Bob Seger & The Silver Bullet Band*	Capitol 11698
8	10	3	Darkness on the Edge of Town	*Bruce Springsteen*	Columbia 35318
9	23	3	Shadow Dancing	*Andy Gibb*	RSO 3034
10	11	11	**Boys In The Trees**	*Carly Simon*	Elektra 128

Billboard® — JULY 8, 1978 — TOP LP's

TW	LW	WK	Title	Artist	Label
1	2	10	**City to City**	*Gerry Rafferty*	United Artists 840
2	1	33	Saturday Night Fever	*Bee Gees/Soundtrack*	RSO 4001
3	4	7	**Natural High**	*Commodores*	Motown 902
4	18	3	Some Girls	*The Rolling Stones*	Rolling Stones 39108
5	7	7	Stranger in Town	*Bob Seger & The Silver Bullet Band*	Capitol 11698
6	8	4	Darkness on the Edge of Town	*Bruce Springsteen*	Columbia 35318
7	9	4	**Shadow Dancing**	*Andy Gibb*	RSO 3034
8	3	37	Feels So Good	*Chuck Mangione*	A&M 4658
9	14	8	Grease	*Soundtrack*	RSO 4002
10	10	12	**Boys In The Trees**	*Carly Simon*	Elektra 128

Billboard® — JULY 15, 1978 — TOP LP's

TW	LW	WK	Title	Artist	Label
1	4	4	**Some Girls**	*The Rolling Stones*	Rolling Stones 39108
2	1	11	City to City	*Gerry Rafferty*	United Artists 840
3	3	8	**Natural High**	*Commodores*	Motown 902
4	2	34	Saturday Night Fever	*Bee Gees/Soundtrack*	RSO 4001
5	5	8	Stranger in Town	*Bob Seger & The Silver Bullet Band*	Capitol 11698
6	6	5	Darkness on the Edge of Town	*Bruce Springsteen*	Columbia 35318
7	7	5	**Shadow Dancing**	*Andy Gibb*	RSO 3034
8	9	9	Grease	*Soundtrack*	RSO 4002
9	8	38	Feels So Good	*Chuck Mangione*	A&M 4658
10	10	13	**Boys In The Trees**	*Carly Simon*	Elektra 128

Billboard — JULY 22, 1978 — TOP LP's

TW	LW	WK	Title	Artist	Label
1	1	5	**Some Girls**	*The Rolling Stones*	Rolling Stones 39108
2	8	10	Grease	*Soundtrack*	RSO 4002
3	2	12	City to City	*Gerry Rafferty*	United Artists 840
4	5	9	**Stranger in Town**	*Bob Seger & The Silver Bullet Band*	Capitol 11698
5	3	9	Natural High	*Commodores*	Motown 902
6	6	6	Darkness on the Edge of Town	*Bruce Springsteen*	Columbia 35318
7	7	6	**Shadow Dancing**	*Andy Gibb*	RSO 3034
8	4	35	Saturday Night Fever	*Bee Gees/Soundtrack*	RSO 4001
9	13	3	Double Vision	*Foreigner*	Atlantic 19999
10	11	11	**Thank God It's Friday**	*Soundtrack*	Casablanca 7099

Billboard — JULY 29, 1978 — TOP LP's

TW	LW	WK	Title	Artist	Label
1	2	11	**Grease**	*Soundtrack*	RSO 4002
2	1	6	Some Girls	*The Rolling Stones*	Rolling Stones 39108
3	5	10	**Natural High**	*Commodores*	Motown 902
4	4	10	**Stranger in Town**	*Bob Seger & The Silver Bullet Band*	Capitol 11698
5	6	7	**Darkness on the Edge of Town**	*Bruce Springsteen*	Columbia 35318
6	3	13	City to City	*Gerry Rafferty*	United Artists 840
7	7	7	**Shadow Dancing**	*Andy Gibb*	RSO 3034
8	9	4	Double Vision	*Foreigner*	Atlantic 19999
9	8	36	Saturday Night Fever	*Bee Gees/Soundtrack*	RSO 4001
10	10	12	**Thank God It's Friday**	*Soundtrack*	Casablanca 7099

Billboard — AUGUST 5, 1978 — TOP LP's

TW	LW	WK	Title	Artist	Label
1	1	12	**Grease**	*Soundtrack*	RSO 4002
2	2	7	Some Girls	*The Rolling Stones*	Rolling Stones 39108
3	3	11	**Natural High**	*Commodores*	Motown 902
4	8	5	Double Vision	*Foreigner*	Atlantic 19999
5	5	8	**Darkness on the Edge of Town**	*Bruce Springsteen*	Columbia 35318
6	4	11	Stranger in Town	*Bob Seger & The Silver Bullet Band*	Capitol 11698
7	7	8	**Shadow Dancing**	*Andy Gibb*	RSO 3034
8	6	14	City to City	*Gerry Rafferty*	United Artists 840
9	9	37	Saturday Night Fever	*Bee Gees/Soundtrack*	RSO 4001
10	10	13	**Thank God It's Friday**	*Soundtrack*	Casablanca 7099

Billboard — AUGUST 12, 1978 — TOP LP's

TW	LW	WK	Title	Artist	Label
1	1	13	**Grease**	*Soundtrack*	RSO 4002
2	2	8	Some Girls	*The Rolling Stones*	Rolling Stones 39108
3	3	12	**Natural High**	*Commodores*	Motown 902
4	4	6	Double Vision	*Foreigner*	Atlantic 19999
5	5	9	**Darkness on the Edge of Town**	*Bruce Springsteen*	Columbia 35318
6	6	12	Stranger in Town	*Bob Seger & The Silver Bullet Band*	Capitol 11698
7	-	1	Sgt. Pepper's Lonely Hearts Club Band	*Soundtrack*	RSO 4100
8	7	9	Shadow Dancing	*Andy Gibb*	RSO 3034
9	9	38	Saturday Night Fever	*Bee Gees/Soundtrack*	RSO 4001
10	11	10	But Seriously, Folks	*Joe Walsh*	Asylum 141

TW	LW	WK	Billboard — AUGUST 19, 1978 — TOP LP's
1	1	14	**Grease** ... *Soundtrack*...RSO 4002
2	2	9	Some Girls ... *The Rolling Stones*...Rolling Stones 39108
3	3	13	**Natural High** ... *Commodores*...Motown 902
4	4	7	Double Vision ... *Foreigner*...Atlantic 19999
5	7	2	**Sgt. Pepper's Lonely Hearts Club Band** ... *Soundtrack*...RSO 4100
6	6	13	Stranger in Town ... *Bob Seger & The Silver Bullet Band*...Capitol 11698
7	13	10	Worlds Away ... *Pablo Cruise*...A&M 4697
8	8	10	Shadow Dancing ... *Andy Gibb*...RSO 3034
9	10	11	But Seriously, Folks... ... *Joe Walsh*...Asylum 141
10	9	39	Saturday Night Fever ... *Bee Gees/Soundtrack*...RSO 4001

TW	LW	WK	Billboard — AUGUST 26, 1978 — TOP LP's
1	1	15	**Grease** ... *Soundtrack*...RSO 4002
2	2	10	Some Girls ... *The Rolling Stones*...Rolling Stones 39108
3	3	14	**Natural High** ... *Commodores*...Motown 902
4	4	8	Double Vision ... *Foreigner*...Atlantic 19999
5	5	3	**Sgt. Pepper's Lonely Hearts Club Band** ... *Soundtrack*...RSO 4100
6	7	11	**Worlds Away** ... *Pablo Cruise*...A&M 4697
7	6	14	Stranger in Town ... *Bob Seger & The Silver Bullet Band*...Capitol 11698
8	9	12	**But Seriously, Folks...** ... *Joe Walsh*...Asylum 141
9	10	40	Saturday Night Fever ... *Bee Gees/Soundtrack*...RSO 4001
10	8	11	Shadow Dancing ... *Andy Gibb*...RSO 3034

TW	LW	WK	Billboard — SEPTEMBER 2, 1978 — TOP LP's
1	1	16	**Grease** ... *Soundtrack*...RSO 4002
2	2	11	Some Girls ... *The Rolling Stones*...Rolling Stones 39108
3	3	15	**Natural High** ... *Commodores*...Motown 902
4	4	9	Double Vision ... *Foreigner*...Atlantic 19999
5	5	4	**Sgt. Pepper's Lonely Hearts Club Band** ... *Soundtrack*...RSO 4100
6	6	12	**Worlds Away** ... *Pablo Cruise*...A&M 4697
7	7	15	Stranger in Town ... *Bob Seger & The Silver Bullet Band*...Capitol 11698
8	8	13	**But Seriously, Folks...** ... *Joe Walsh*...Asylum 141
9	9	41	Saturday Night Fever ... *Bee Gees/Soundtrack*...RSO 4001
10	-	1	Don't Look Back ... *Boston*...Epic 35050

TW	LW	WK	Billboard — SEPTEMBER 9, 1978 — TOP LP's
1	1	17	**Grease** ... *Soundtrack*...RSO 4002
2	2	12	Some Girls ... *The Rolling Stones*...Rolling Stones 39108
3	4	10	**Double Vision** ... *Foreigner*...Atlantic 19999
4	10	2	Don't Look Back ... *Boston*...Epic 35050
5	5	5	**Sgt. Pepper's Lonely Hearts Club Band** ... *Soundtrack*...RSO 4100
6	6	13	**Worlds Away** ... *Pablo Cruise*...A&M 4697
7	3	16	Natural High ... *Commodores*...Motown 902
8	13	5	Blam!! ... *The Brothers Johnson*...A&M 4714
9	9	42	Saturday Night Fever ... *Bee Gees/Soundtrack*...RSO 4001
10	11	49	The Stranger ... *Billy Joel*...Columbia 34987

TW	LW	WK	Billboard. SEPTEMBER 16, 1978	TOP LP's
1	4	3	**Don't Look Back**	*Boston*...Epic 35050
2	2	13	Some Girls	*The Rolling Stones*...Rolling Stones 39108
3	3	11	**Double Vision**	*Foreigner*...Atlantic 19999
4	1	18	Grease	*Soundtrack*...RSO 4002
5	5	6	**Sgt. Pepper's Lonely Hearts Club Band**	*Soundtrack*...RSO 4100
6	7	17	Natural High	*Commodores*...Motown 902
7	8	6	**Blam!!**	*The Brothers Johnson*...A&M 4714
8	20	2	Who Are You	*The Who*...MCA 3050
9	11	14	A Taste of Honey	*A Taste Of Honey*...Capitol 11754
10	10	50	The Stranger	*Billy Joel*...Columbia 34987

TW	LW	WK	Billboard. SEPTEMBER 23, 1978	TOP LP's
1	4	19	**Grease**	*Soundtrack*...RSO 4002
2	1	4	Don't Look Back	*Boston*...Epic 35050
3	3	12	**Double Vision**	*Foreigner*...Atlantic 19999
4	2	14	Some Girls	*The Rolling Stones*...Rolling Stones 39108
5	5	7	**Sgt. Pepper's Lonely Hearts Club Band**	*Soundtrack*...RSO 4100
6	8	3	Who Are You	*The Who*...MCA 3050
7	7	7	**Blam!!**	*The Brothers Johnson*...A&M 4714
8	6	18	Natural High	*Commodores*...Motown 902
9	9	15	A Taste of Honey	*A Taste Of Honey*...Capitol 11754
10	12	10	Nightwatch	*Kenny Loggins*...Columbia 35387

TW	LW	WK	Billboard. SEPTEMBER 30, 1978	TOP LP's
1	1	20	**Grease**	*Soundtrack*...RSO 4002
2	2	5	Don't Look Back	*Boston*...Epic 35050
3	3	13	**Double Vision**	*Foreigner*...Atlantic 19999
4	6	4	Who Are You	*The Who*...MCA 3050
5	4	15	Some Girls	*The Rolling Stones*...Rolling Stones 39108
6	5	8	Sgt. Pepper's Lonely Hearts Club Band	*Soundtrack*...RSO 4100
7	7	8	**Blam!!**	*The Brothers Johnson*...A&M 4714
8	9	16	A Taste of Honey	*A Taste Of Honey*...Capitol 11754
9	10	11	Nightwatch	*Kenny Loggins*...Columbia 35387
10	8	19	Natural High	*Commodores*...Motown 902

TW	LW	WK	Billboard. OCTOBER 7, 1978	TOP LP's
1	2	6	**Don't Look Back**	*Boston*...Epic 35050
2	1	21	Grease	*Soundtrack*...RSO 4002
3	3	14	**Double Vision**	*Foreigner*...Atlantic 19999
4	4	5	Who Are You	*The Who*...MCA 3050
5	5	16	Some Girls	*The Rolling Stones*...Rolling Stones 39108
6	8	17	**A Taste of Honey**	*A Taste Of Honey*...Capitol 11754
7	9	12	**Nightwatch**	*Kenny Loggins*...Columbia 35387
8	6	9	Sgt. Pepper's Lonely Hearts Club Band	*Soundtrack*...RSO 4100
9	7	9	Blam!!	*The Brothers Johnson*...A&M 4714
10	12	4	Twin Sons Of Different Mothers	*Dan Fogelberg & Tim Weisberg*...Full Moon 35339

TW	LW	WK	Billboard ® OCTOBER 14, 1978 ® TOP LP's
1	2	22	**Grease** .... *Soundtrack*...RSO 4002
2	1	7	Don't Look Back........ *Boston*...Epic 35050
3	3	15	**Double Vision**........ *Foreigner*...Atlantic 19999
4	4	6	Who Are You .... *The Who*...MCA 3050
5	5	17	Some Girls .... *The Rolling Stones*...Rolling Stones 39108
6	6	18	**A Taste of Honey** .... *A Taste Of Honey*...Capitol 11754
7	7	13	**Nightwatch**........ *Kenny Loggins*...Columbia 35387
8	10	5	**Twin Sons Of Different Mothers** .... *Dan Fogelberg & Tim Weisberg*...Full Moon 35339
9	12	5	Live And More........ *Donna Summer*...Casablanca 7119
10	30	2	Living In The USA .... *Linda Ronstadt*...Asylum 155

TW	LW	WK	Billboard ® OCTOBER 21, 1978 ® TOP LP's
1	1	23	**Grease**........ *Soundtrack*...RSO 4002
2	4	7	**Who Are You** .... *The Who*...MCA 3050
3	2	8	Don't Look Back........ *Boston*...Epic 35050
4	10	3	Living In The USA .... *Linda Ronstadt*...Asylum 155
5	3	16	Double Vision........ *Foreigner*...Atlantic 19999
6	9	6	Live And More........ *Donna Summer*...Casablanca 7119
7	7	14	**Nightwatch**........ *Kenny Loggins*...Columbia 35387
8	8	6	**Twin Sons Of Different Mothers** .... *Dan Fogelberg & Tim Weisberg*...Full Moon 35339
9	5	18	Some Girls .... *The Rolling Stones*...Rolling Stones 39108
10	15	4	Pieces of Eight........ *Styx*...A&M 4724

TW	LW	WK	Billboard ® OCTOBER 28, 1978 ® TOP LP's
1	1	24	**Grease**........ *Soundtrack*...RSO 4002
2	2	8	**Who Are You** .... *The Who*...MCA 3050
3	4	4	Living In The USA .... *Linda Ronstadt*...Asylum 155
4	3	9	Don't Look Back........ *Boston*...Epic 35050
5	6	7	Live And More........ *Donna Summer*...Casablanca 7119
6	5	17	Double Vision........ *Foreigner*...Atlantic 19999
7	7	15	**Nightwatch**........ *Kenny Loggins*...Columbia 35387
8	8	7	**Twin Sons Of Different Mothers** .... *Dan Fogelberg & Tim Weisberg*...Full Moon 35339
9	10	5	Pieces of Eight........ *Styx*...A&M 4724
10	9	19	Some Girls .... *The Rolling Stones*...Rolling Stones 39108

TW	LW	WK	Billboard ® NOVEMBER 4, 1978 ® TOP LP's
1	3	5	**Living In The USA** .... *Linda Ronstadt*...Asylum 155
2	1	25	Grease........ *Soundtrack*...RSO 4002
3	5	8	Live And More........ *Donna Summer*...Casablanca 7119
4	2	9	Who Are You........ *The Who*...MCA 3050
5	6	18	Double Vision........ *Foreigner*...Atlantic 19999
6	4	10	Don't Look Back........ *Boston*...Epic 35050
7	7	16	**Nightwatch**........ *Kenny Loggins*...Columbia 35387
8	9	6	Pieces of Eight .... *Styx*...A&M 4724
9	8	8	Twin Sons Of Different Mothers .... *Dan Fogelberg & Tim Weisberg*...Full Moon 35339
10	10	20	Some Girls .... *The Rolling Stones*...Rolling Stones 39108

TW	LW	WK	Billboard® NOVEMBER 11, 1978 TOP LP's
❶	3	9	**Live And More** ... *Donna Summer*...Casablanca 7119
②	1	6	Living In The USA ... *Linda Ronstadt*...Asylum 155
❸	2	26	Grease ... *Soundtrack*...RSO 4002
④	5	19	Double Vision ... *Foreigner*...Atlantic 19999
❺	17	3	52nd Street ... *Billy Joel*...Columbia 35609
⑥	4	10	Who Are You ... *The Who*...MCA 3050
❼	8	7	Pieces of Eight ... *Styx*...A&M 4724
⑧	6	11	Don't Look Back ... *Boston*...Epic 35050
⑨	10	21	Some Girls ... *The Rolling Stones*...Rolling Stones 39108
⑩	11	25	Stranger in Town ... *Bob Seger & The Silver Bullet Band*...Capitol 11698

TW	LW	WK	Billboard® NOVEMBER 18, 1978 TOP LP's
❶	5	4	**52nd Street** ... *Billy Joel*...Columbia 35609
②	1	10	Live And More ... *Donna Summer*...Casablanca 7119
③	4	20	**Double Vision** ... *Foreigner*...Atlantic 19999
④	2	7	Living In The USA ... *Linda Ronstadt*...Asylum 155
⑤	3	27	Grease ... *Soundtrack*...RSO 4002
❻	14	3	A Wild And Crazy Guy ... *Steve Martin*...Warner 3238
⑦	7	8	Pieces of Eight ... *Styx*...A&M 4724
⑧	6	11	Who Are You ... *The Who*...MCA 3050
⑨	9	22	Some Girls ... *The Rolling Stones*...Rolling Stones 39108
❿	11	6	**Tormato** ... *Yes*...Atlantic 19202

TW	LW	WK	Billboard® NOVEMBER 25, 1978 TOP LP's
❶	1	5	**52nd Street** ... *Billy Joel*...Columbia 35609
❷	2	11	Live And More ... *Donna Summer*...Casablanca 7119
③	3	21	**Double Vision** ... *Foreigner*...Atlantic 19999
❹	6	4	A Wild And Crazy Guy ... *Steve Martin*...Warner 3238
⑤	5	28	Grease ... *Soundtrack*...RSO 4002
⑥	4	8	Living In The USA ... *Linda Ronstadt*...Asylum 155
⑦	7	9	Pieces of Eight ... *Styx*...A&M 4724
⑧	9	23	Some Girls ... *The Rolling Stones*...Rolling Stones 39108
❾	15	6	Comes A Time ... *Neil Young*...Reprise 2266
⑩	10	7	**Tormato** ... *Yes*...Atlantic 19202

TW	LW	WK	Billboard® DECEMBER 2, 1978 TOP LP's
❶	1	6	**52nd Street** ... *Billy Joel*...Columbia 35609
②	2	12	Live And More ... *Donna Summer*...Casablanca 7119
❸	4	5	A Wild And Crazy Guy ... *Steve Martin*...Warner 3238
④	3	22	Double Vision ... *Foreigner*...Atlantic 19999
⑤	5	29	Grease ... *Soundtrack*...RSO 4002
⑥	7	10	**Pieces of Eight** ... *Styx*...A&M 4724
❼	-	1	Barbra Streisand's Greatest Hits, Volume 2 ... *Barbra Streisand*...Columbia 35679
❽	9	7	Comes A Time ... *Neil Young*...Reprise 2266
⑨	6	9	Living In The USA ... *Linda Ronstadt*...Asylum 155
⑩	8	24	Some Girls ... *The Rolling Stones*...Rolling Stones 39108

TW	LW	WK	Billboard. DECEMBER 9, 1978	TOP LP's
1	1	7	**52nd Street**	*Billy Joel*...Columbia 35609
2	3	6	**A Wild And Crazy Guy**	*Steve Martin*...Warner 3238
3	7	2	Barbra Streisand's Greatest Hits, Volume 2	*Barbra Streisand*...Columbia 35679
4	2	13	Live And More	*Donna Summer*...Casablanca 7119
5	4	23	Double Vision	*Foreigner*...Atlantic 19999
6	5	30	Grease	*Soundtrack*...RSO 4002
7	8	8	**Comes A Time**	*Neil Young*...Reprise 2266
8	6	11	Pieces of Eight	*Styx*...A&M 4724
9	9	10	Living In The USA	*Linda Ronstadt*...Asylum 155
10	10	25	Some Girls	*The Rolling Stones*...Rolling Stones 39108

TW	LW	WK	Billboard. DECEMBER 16, 1978	TOP LP's
1	1	8	**52nd Street**	*Billy Joel*...Columbia 35609
2	2	7	**A Wild And Crazy Guy**	*Steve Martin*...Warner 3238
3	3	3	Barbra Streisand's Greatest Hits, Volume 2	*Barbra Streisand*...Columbia 35679
4	4	14	Live And More	*Donna Summer*...Casablanca 7119
5	5	24	Double Vision	*Foreigner*...Atlantic 19999
6	6	31	Grease	*Soundtrack*...RSO 4002
7	7	9	**Comes A Time**	*Neil Young*...Reprise 2266
8	12	3	C'est Chic	*Chic*...Atlantic 19209
9	30	2	Jazz	*Queen*...Elektra 166
10	11	11	**Time Passages**	*Al Stewart*...Arista 4190

TW	LW	WK	Billboard. DECEMBER 23, 1978	TOP LP's
1	1	9	**52nd Street**	*Billy Joel*...Columbia 35609
2	2	8	**A Wild And Crazy Guy**	*Steve Martin*...Warner 3238
3	3	4	Barbra Streisand's Greatest Hits, Volume 2	*Barbra Streisand*...Columbia 35679
4	8	4	**C'est Chic**	*Chic*...Atlantic 19209
5	6	32	Grease	*Soundtrack*...RSO 4002
6	5	25	Double Vision	*Foreigner*...Atlantic 19999
7	9	3	Jazz	*Queen*...Elektra 166
8	4	15	Live And More	*Donna Summer*...Casablanca 7119
9	19	4	The Best Of Earth, Wind & Fire, Vol. I	*Earth, Wind & Fire*...ARC 35647
10	14	4	Backless	*Eric Clapton*...RSO 3039

Billboard — JANUARY 6, 1979 — TOP LP's

TW	LW	WK	Title	Artist	Label
1	3	6	**Barbra Streisand's Greatest Hits, Volume 2**	*Barbra Streisand*	Columbia 35679
2	2	10	**A Wild And Crazy Guy**	*Steve Martin*	Warner 3238
3	1	11	52nd Street	*Billy Joel*	Columbia 35609
4	4	6	**C'est Chic**	*Chic*	Atlantic 19209
5	5	34	Grease	*Soundtrack*	RSO 4002
6	7	5	**Jazz**	*Queen*	Elektra 166
7	70	3	Briefcase Full Of Blues	*Blues Brothers*	Atlantic 19217
8	9	6	The Best Of Earth, Wind & Fire, Vol. I	*Earth, Wind & Fire*	ARC 35647
9	10	6	Backless	*Eric Clapton*	RSO 3039
10	18	4	You Don't Bring Me Flowers	*Neil Diamond*	Columbia 35625

Billboard — JANUARY 13, 1979 — TOP LP's

TW	LW	WK	Title	Artist	Label
1	1	7	**Barbra Streisand's Greatest Hits, Volume 2**	*Barbra Streisand*	Columbia 35679
2	2	11	**A Wild And Crazy Guy**	*Steve Martin*	Warner 3238
3	3	12	52nd Street	*Billy Joel*	Columbia 35609
4	4	7	**C'est Chic**	*Chic*	Atlantic 19209
5	7	4	Briefcase Full Of Blues	*Blues Brothers*	Atlantic 19217
6	6	6	**Jazz**	*Queen*	Elektra 166
7	8	7	The Best Of Earth, Wind & Fire, Vol. I	*Earth, Wind & Fire*	ARC 35647
8	9	7	**Backless**	*Eric Clapton*	RSO 3039
9	10	5	You Don't Bring Me Flowers	*Neil Diamond*	Columbia 35625
10	5	35	Grease	*Soundtrack*	RSO 4002

Billboard — JANUARY 20, 1979 — TOP LP's

TW	LW	WK	Title	Artist	Label
1	1	8	**Barbra Streisand's Greatest Hits, Volume 2**	*Barbra Streisand*	Columbia 35679
2	3	13	52nd Street	*Billy Joel*	Columbia 35609
3	5	5	Briefcase Full Of Blues	*Blues Brothers*	Atlantic 19217
4	2	12	A Wild And Crazy Guy	*Steve Martin*	Warner 3238
5	4	8	C'est Chic	*Chic*	Atlantic 19209
6	9	6	You Don't Bring Me Flowers	*Neil Diamond*	Columbia 35625
7	7	8	The Best Of Earth, Wind & Fire, Vol. I	*Earth, Wind & Fire*	ARC 35647
8	8	8	**Backless**	*Eric Clapton*	RSO 3039
9	10	36	Grease	*Soundtrack*	RSO 4002
10	11	29	Double Vision	*Foreigner*	Atlantic 19999

Billboard — JANUARY 27, 1979 — TOP LP's

TW	LW	WK	Title	Artist	Label
1	2	14	**52nd Street**	*Billy Joel*	Columbia 35609
2	3	6	Briefcase Full Of Blues	*Blues Brothers*	Atlantic 19217
3	1	9	Barbra Streisand's Greatest Hits, Volume 2	*Barbra Streisand*	Columbia 35679
4	6	7	**You Don't Bring Me Flowers**	*Neil Diamond*	Columbia 35625
5	12	6	Blondes Have More Fun	*Rod Stewart*	Warner 3261
6	7	9	**The Best Of Earth, Wind & Fire, Vol. I**	*Earth, Wind & Fire*	ARC 35647
7	5	9	C'est Chic	*Chic*	Atlantic 19209
8	8	9	**Backless**	*Eric Clapton*	RSO 3039
9	11	9	Greatest Hits	*Barry Manilow*	Arista 8601
10	10	30	Double Vision	*Foreigner*	Atlantic 19999

Billboard FEBRUARY 3, 1979 TOP LP's

TW	LW	WK	Title	Artist...Label
1	2	7	**Briefcase Full Of Blues**	*Blues Brothers*...Atlantic 19217
2	5	7	Blondes Have More Fun	*Rod Stewart*...Warner 3261
3	1	15	52nd Street	*Billy Joel*...Columbia 35609
4	4	8	**You Don't Bring Me Flowers**	*Neil Diamond*...Columbia 35625
5	3	10	Barbra Streisand's Greatest Hits, Volume 2	*Barbra Streisand*...Columbia 35679
6	7	10	C'est Chic	*Chic*...Atlantic 19209
7	6	10	The Best Of Earth, Wind & Fire, Vol. I	*Earth, Wind & Fire*...ARC 35647
8	9	10	Greatest Hits	*Barry Manilow*...Arista 8601
9	10	31	Double Vision	*Foreigner*...Atlantic 19999
10	13	16	Cruisin'	*Village People*...Casablanca 7118

Billboard FEBRUARY 10, 1979 TOP LP's

TW	LW	WK	Title	Artist...Label
1	2	8	**Blondes Have More Fun**	*Rod Stewart*...Warner 3261
2	1	8	Briefcase Full Of Blues	*Blues Brothers*...Atlantic 19217
3	3	16	52nd Street	*Billy Joel*...Columbia 35609
4	4	9	**You Don't Bring Me Flowers**	*Neil Diamond*...Columbia 35625
5	5	11	Barbra Streisand's Greatest Hits, Volume 2	*Barbra Streisand*...Columbia 35679
6	6	11	C'est Chic	*Chic*...Atlantic 19209
7	8	11	**Greatest Hits**	*Barry Manilow*...Arista 8601
8	10	17	Cruisin'	*Village People*...Casablanca 7118
9	7	11	The Best Of Earth, Wind & Fire, Vol. I	*Earth, Wind & Fire*...ARC 35647
10	11	11	Backless	*Eric Clapton*...RSO 3039

Billboard FEBRUARY 17, 1979 TOP LP's

TW	LW	WK	Title	Artist...Label
1	1	9	**Blondes Have More Fun**	*Rod Stewart*...Warner 3261
2	2	9	Briefcase Full Of Blues	*Blues Brothers*...Atlantic 19217
3	8	18	**Cruisin'**	*Village People*...Casablanca 7118
4	-	1	Spirits Having Flown	*Bee Gees*...RSO 3041
5	3	17	52nd Street	*Billy Joel*...Columbia 35609
6	6	12	C'est Chic	*Chic*...Atlantic 19209
7	15	7	Dire Straits	*Dire Straits*...Warner 3266
8	12	11	Totally Hot	*Olivia Newton-John*...MCA 3067
9	11	18	**Toto**	*Toto*...Columbia 35317
10	10	12	Backless	*Eric Clapton*...RSO 3039

Billboard FEBRUARY 24, 1979 TOP LP's

TW	LW	WK	Title	Artist...Label
1	1	10	**Blondes Have More Fun**	*Rod Stewart*...Warner 3261
2	4	2	Spirits Having Flown	*Bee Gees*...RSO 3041
3	3	19	**Cruisin'**	*Village People*...Casablanca 7118
4	2	10	Briefcase Full Of Blues	*Blues Brothers*...Atlantic 19217
5	5	18	52nd Street	*Billy Joel*...Columbia 35609
6	7	8	Dire Straits	*Dire Straits*...Warner 3266
7	8	12	**Totally Hot**	*Olivia Newton-John*...MCA 3067
8	11	10	Minute By Minute	*The Doobie Brothers*...Warner 3193
9	9	19	**Toto**	*Toto*...Columbia 35317
10	12	8	Love Tracks	*Gloria Gaynor*...Polydor 6184

TW	LW	WK	Billboard® MARCH 3, 1979 TOP LP's	
1	2	3	**Spirits Having Flown**	*Bee Gees*...RSO 3041
2	1	11	Blondes Have More Fun	*Rod Stewart*...Warner 3261
3	3	20	**Cruisin'**	*Village People*...Casablanca 7118
4	6	9	Dire Straits	*Dire Straits*...Warner 3266
5	4	11	Briefcase Full Of Blues	*Blues Brothers*...Atlantic 19217
6	8	11	Minute By Minute	*The Doobie Brothers*...Warner 3193
7	7	13	**Totally Hot**	*Olivia Newton-John*...MCA 3067
8	10	9	Love Tracks	*Gloria Gaynor*...Polydor 6184
9	5	19	52nd Street	*Billy Joel*...Columbia 35609
10	11	14	C'est Chic	*Chic*...Atlantic 19209

TW	LW	WK	Billboard® MARCH 10, 1979 TOP LP's	
1	1	4	**Spirits Having Flown**	*Bee Gees*...RSO 3041
2	2	12	Blondes Have More Fun	*Rod Stewart*...Warner 3261
3	3	21	**Cruisin'**	*Village People*...Casablanca 7118
4	4	10	Dire Straits	*Dire Straits*...Warner 3266
5	6	12	Minute By Minute	*The Doobie Brothers*...Warner 3193
6	5	12	Briefcase Full Of Blues	*Blues Brothers*...Atlantic 19217
7	8	10	Love Tracks	*Gloria Gaynor*...Polydor 6184
8	7	14	Totally Hot	*Olivia Newton-John*...MCA 3067
9	9	20	52nd Street	*Billy Joel*...Columbia 35609
10	11	7	**Armed Forces**	*Elvis Costello*...Columbia 35709

TW	LW	WK	Billboard® MARCH 17, 1979 TOP LP's	
1	1	5	**Spirits Having Flown**	*Bee Gees*...RSO 3041
2	2	13	Blondes Have More Fun	*Rod Stewart*...Warner 3261
3	5	13	Minute By Minute	*The Doobie Brothers*...Warner 3193
4	4	11	Dire Straits	*Dire Straits*...Warner 3266
5	3	22	Cruisin'	*Village People*...Casablanca 7118
6	7	11	Love Tracks	*Gloria Gaynor*...Polydor 6184
7	6	13	Briefcase Full Of Blues	*Blues Brothers*...Atlantic 19217
8	8	15	Totally Hot	*Olivia Newton-John*...MCA 3067
9	9	21	52nd Street	*Billy Joel*...Columbia 35609
10	10	8	**Armed Forces**	*Elvis Costello*...Columbia 35709

TW	LW	WK	Billboard® MARCH 24, 1979 TOP LP's	
1	1	6	**Spirits Having Flown**	*Bee Gees*...RSO 3041
2	3	14	Minute By Minute	*The Doobie Brothers*...Warner 3193
3	4	12	Dire Straits	*Dire Straits*...Warner 3266
4	2	14	Blondes Have More Fun	*Rod Stewart*...Warner 3261
5	6	12	Love Tracks	*Gloria Gaynor*...Polydor 6184
6	5	23	Cruisin'	*Village People*...Casablanca 7118
7	7	14	Briefcase Full Of Blues	*Blues Brothers*...Atlantic 19217
8	11	18	2 Hot!	*Peaches & Herb*...Polydor 6172
9	9	22	52nd Street	*Billy Joel*...Columbia 35609
10	8	16	Totally Hot	*Olivia Newton-John*...MCA 3067

Billboard — MARCH 31, 1979 — TOP LP's

TW	LW	WK		
1	1	7	**Spirits Having Flown**	*Bee Gees*...RSO 3041
2	2	15	Minute By Minute	*The Doobie Brothers*...Warner 3193
3	3	13	Dire Straits	*Dire Straits*...Warner 3266
4	5	13	**Love Tracks**	*Gloria Gaynor*...Polydor 6184
5	4	15	Blondes Have More Fun	*Rod Stewart*...Warner 3261
6	8	19	2 Hot!	*Peaches & Herb*...Polydor 6172
7	6	24	Cruisin'	*Village People*...Casablanca 7118
8	9	23	52nd Street	*Billy Joel*...Columbia 35609
9	7	15	Briefcase Full Of Blues	*Blues Brothers*...Atlantic 19217
10	23	3	Livin' Inside Your Love	*George Benson*...Warner 3277

Billboard — APRIL 7, 1979 — TOP LP's

TW	LW	WK		
1	2	16	**Minute By Minute**	*The Doobie Brothers*...Warner 3193
2	1	8	Spirits Having Flown	*Bee Gees*...RSO 3041
3	3	14	Dire Straits	*Dire Straits*...Warner 3266
4	4	14	**Love Tracks**	*Gloria Gaynor*...Polydor 6184
5	5	16	Blondes Have More Fun	*Rod Stewart*...Warner 3261
6	6	20	2 Hot!	*Peaches & Herb*...Polydor 6172
7	8	24	52nd Street	*Billy Joel*...Columbia 35609
8	10	4	Livin' Inside Your Love	*George Benson*...Warner 3277
9	30	2	Desolation Angels	*Bad Company*...Swan Song 8506
10	13	4	Enlightened Rouges	*The Allman Brothers Band*...Capricorn 0218

Billboard — APRIL 14, 1979 — TOP LP's

TW	LW	WK		
1	1	17	**Minute By Minute**	*The Doobie Brothers*...Warner 3193
2	3	15	**Dire Straits**	*Dire Straits*...Warner 3266
3	2	9	Spirits Having Flown	*Bee Gees*...RSO 3041
4	6	21	2 Hot!	*Peaches & Herb*...Polydor 6172
5	5	17	Blondes Have More Fun	*Rod Stewart*...Warner 3261
6	4	15	Love Tracks	*Gloria Gaynor*...Polydor 6184
7	9	3	Desolation Angels	*Bad Company*...Swan Song 8506
8	8	5	Livin' Inside Your Love	*George Benson*...Warner 3277
9	10	5	**Enlightened Rouges**	*The Allman Brothers Band*...Capricorn 0218
10	11	8	Cheap Trick At Budokan	*Cheap Trick*...Epic 35795

Billboard — APRIL 21, 1979 — TOP LP's

TW	LW	WK		
1	3	10	**Spirits Having Flown**	*Bee Gees*...RSO 3041
2	1	18	Minute By Minute	*The Doobie Brothers*...Warner 3193
3	2	16	Dire Straits	*Dire Straits*...Warner 3266
4	4	22	2 Hot!	*Peaches & Herb*...Polydor 6172
5	5	18	Blondes Have More Fun	*Rod Stewart*...Warner 3261
6	7	4	Desolation Angels	*Bad Company*...Swan Song 8506
7	8	6	**Livin' Inside Your Love**	*George Benson*...Warner 3277
8	13	31	Parallel Lines	*Blondie*...Chrysalis 1192
9	9	6	**Enlightened Rouges**	*The Allman Brothers Band*...Capricorn 0218
10	6	16	Love Tracks	*Gloria Gaynor*...Polydor 6184

TW	LW	WK	Billboard® APRIL 28, 1979 TOP LP's
1	2	19	**Minute By Minute**............ *The Doobie Brothers*...Warner 3193
2	1	11	Spirits Having Flown............ *Bee Gees*...RSO 3041
3	4	23	2 Hot!............ *Peaches & Herb*...Polydor 6172
4	3	17	Dire Straits............ *Dire Straits*...Warner 3266
5	6	5	Desolation Angels............ *Bad Company*...Swan Song 8506
6	8	32	**Parallel Lines**............ *Blondie*...Chrysalis 1192
7	7	7	**Livin' Inside Your Love**............ *George Benson*...Warner 3277
8	12	5	Breakfast In America............ *Supertramp*...A&M 3708
9	9	7	**Enlightened Rouges**............ *The Allman Brothers Band*...Capricorn 0218
10	5	19	Blondes Have More Fun............ *Rod Stewart*...Warner 3261

TW	LW	WK	Billboard® MAY 5, 1979 TOP LP's
1	1	20	**Minute By Minute**............ *The Doobie Brothers*...Warner 3193
2	3	24	**2 Hot!**............ *Peaches & Herb*...Polydor 6172
3	2	12	Spirits Having Flown............ *Bee Gees*...RSO 3041
4	8	6	Breakfast In America............ *Supertramp*...A&M 3708
5	5	6	Desolation Angels............ *Bad Company*...Swan Song 8506
6	6	33	**Parallel Lines**............ *Blondie*...Chrysalis 1192
7	4	18	Dire Straits............ *Dire Straits*...Warner 3266
8	11	4	Van Halen II............ *Van Halen*...Warner 3312
9	9	8	**Enlightened Rouges**............ *The Allman Brothers Band*...Capricorn 0218
10	12	4	Go West............ *Village People*...Casablanca 7144

TW	LW	WK	Billboard® MAY 12, 1979 TOP LP's
1	1	21	**Minute By Minute**............ *The Doobie Brothers*...Warner 3193
2	2	25	**2 Hot!**............ *Peaches & Herb*...Polydor 6172
3	4	7	Breakfast In America............ *Supertramp*...A&M 3708
4	5	7	Desolation Angels............ *Bad Company*...Swan Song 8506
5	3	13	Spirits Having Flown............ *Bee Gees*...RSO 3041
6	6	34	**Parallel Lines**............ *Blondie*...Chrysalis 1192
7	8	5	Van Halen II............ *Van Halen*...Warner 3312
8	12	12	We Are Family............ *Sister Sledge*...Cotillion 5209
9	10	5	Go West............ *Village People*...Casablanca 7144
10	7	19	Dire Straits............ *Dire Straits*...Warner 3266

TW	LW	WK	Billboard® MAY 19, 1979 TOP LP's
1	3	8	**Breakfast In America**............ *Supertramp*...A&M 3708
2	2	26	**2 Hot!**............ *Peaches & Herb*...Polydor 6172
3	4	8	**Desolation Angels**............ *Bad Company*...Swan Song 8506
4	1	22	Minute By Minute............ *The Doobie Brothers*...Warner 3193
5	5	14	Spirits Having Flown............ *Bee Gees*...RSO 3041
6	7	6	**Van Halen II**............ *Van Halen*...Warner 3312
7	8	13	We Are Family............ *Sister Sledge*...Cotillion 5209
8	9	6	**Go West**............ *Village People*...Casablanca 7144
9	6	35	Parallel Lines............ *Blondie*...Chrysalis 1192
10	39	2	Bad Girls............ *Donna Summer*...Casablanca 7150

TW	LW	WK	Billboard. MAY 26, 1979	TOP LP's
1	1	9	**Breakfast In America**	*Supertramp*...A&M 3708
2	2	27	**2 Hot!**	*Peaches & Herb*...Polydor 6172
3	3	9	**Desolation Angels**	*Bad Company*...Swan Song 8506
4	4	23	Minute By Minute	*The Doobie Brothers*...Warner 3193
5	10	3	Bad Girls	*Donna Summer*...Casablanca 7150
6	6	7	**Van Halen II**	*Van Halen*...Warner 3312
7	7	14	We Are Family	*Sister Sledge*...Cotillion 5209
8	8	7	**Go West**	*Village People*...Casablanca 7144
9	5	15	Spirits Having Flown	*Bee Gees*...RSO 3041
10	11	14	Cheap Trick At Budokan	*Cheap Trick*...Epic 35795

TW	LW	WK	Billboard. JUNE 2, 1979	TOP LP's
1	1	10	**Breakfast In America**	*Supertramp*...A&M 3708
2	2	28	**2 Hot!**	*Peaches & Herb*...Polydor 6172
3	5	4	Bad Girls	*Donna Summer*...Casablanca 7150
4	4	24	Minute By Minute	*The Doobie Brothers*...Warner 3193
5	7	15	We Are Family	*Sister Sledge*...Cotillion 5209
6	6	8	**Van Halen II**	*Van Halen*...Warner 3312
7	11	9	Rickie Lee Jones	*Rickie Lee Jones*...Warner 3296
8	8	8	**Go West**	*Village People*...Casablanca 7144
9	10	15	Cheap Trick At Budokan	*Cheap Trick*...Epic 35795
10	3	10	Desolation Angels	*Bad Company*...Swan Song 8506

TW	LW	WK	Billboard. JUNE 9, 1979	TOP LP's
1	1	11	**Breakfast In America**	*Supertramp*...A&M 3708
2	2	29	**2 Hot!**	*Peaches & Herb*...Polydor 6172
3	3	5	Bad Girls	*Donna Summer*...Casablanca 7150
4	5	16	We Are Family	*Sister Sledge*...Cotillion 5209
5	7	10	Rickie Lee Jones	*Rickie Lee Jones*...Warner 3296
6	4	25	Minute By Minute	*The Doobie Brothers*...Warner 3193
7	6	9	Van Halen II	*Van Halen*...Warner 3312
8	9	16	Cheap Trick At Budokan	*Cheap Trick*...Epic 35795
9	10	11	Desolation Angels	*Bad Company*...Swan Song 8506
10	11	17	Spirits Having Flown	*Bee Gees*...RSO 3041

TW	LW	WK	Billboard. JUNE 16, 1979	TOP LP's
1	3	6	**Bad Girls**	*Donna Summer*...Casablanca 7150
2	1	12	Breakfast In America	*Supertramp*...A&M 3708
3	4	17	**We Are Family**	*Sister Sledge*...Cotillion 5209
4	5	11	Rickie Lee Jones	*Rickie Lee Jones*...Warner 3296
5	8	17	Cheap Trick At Budokan	*Cheap Trick*...Epic 35795
6	2	30	2 Hot!	*Peaches & Herb*...Polydor 6172
7	7	10	Van Halen II	*Van Halen*...Warner 3312
8	9	12	Desolation Angels	*Bad Company*...Swan Song 8506
9	10	18	Spirits Having Flown	*Bee Gees*...RSO 3041
10	11	6	**Flag**	*James Taylor*...Columbia 36058

TW	LW	WK	Billboard® JUNE 23, 1979		TOP LP's
1	2	13	**Breakfast In America**	*Supertramp*	A&M 3708
2	1	7	Bad Girls	*Donna Summer*	Casablanca 7150
3	3	18	**We Are Family**	*Sister Sledge*	Cotillion 5209
4	4	12	Rickie Lee Jones	*Rickie Lee Jones*	Warner 3296
5	5	18	Cheap Trick At Budokan	*Cheap Trick*	Epic 35795
6	8	13	Desolation Angels	*Bad Company*	Swan Song 8506
7	7	11	Van Halen II	*Van Halen*	Warner 3312
8	62	2	I Am	*Earth, Wind & Fire*	ARC 35730
9	9	19	Spirits Having Flown	*Bee Gees*	RSO 3041
10	11	5	Songs Of Love	*Anita Ward*	Juana 200,004

TW	LW	WK	Billboard® JUNE 30, 1979		TOP LP's
1	1	14	**Breakfast In America**	*Supertramp*	A&M 3708
2	2	8	Bad Girls	*Donna Summer*	Casablanca 7150
3	4	13	**Rickie Lee Jones**	*Rickie Lee Jones*	Warner 3296
4	8	3	I Am	*Earth, Wind & Fire*	ARC 35730
5	5	19	Cheap Trick At Budokan	*Cheap Trick*	Epic 35795
6	6	14	Desolation Angels	*Bad Company*	Swan Song 8506
7	3	19	We Are Family	*Sister Sledge*	Cotillion 5209
8	7	12	Van Halen II	*Van Halen*	Warner 3312
9	10	6	Songs Of Love	*Anita Ward*	Juana 200,004
10	12	4	**Monolith**	*Kansas*	Kirshner 36008

TW	LW	WK	Billboard® JULY 7, 1979		TOP LP's
1	2	9	**Bad Girls**	*Donna Summer*	Casablanca 7150
2	1	15	Breakfast In America	*Supertramp*	A&M 3708
3	3	14	**Rickie Lee Jones**	*Rickie Lee Jones*	Warner 3296
4	4	4	I Am	*Earth, Wind & Fire*	ARC 35730
5	5	20	Cheap Trick At Budokan	*Cheap Trick*	Epic 35795
6	6	15	Desolation Angels	*Bad Company*	Swan Song 8506
7	7	20	We Are Family	*Sister Sledge*	Cotillion 5209
8	9	7	**Songs Of Love**	*Anita Ward*	Juana 200,004
9	11	3	Discovery	*Electric Light Orchestra*	Jet 35769
10	10	5	**Monolith**	*Kansas*	Kirshner 36008

TW	LW	WK	Billboard® JULY 14, 1979		TOP LP's
1	1	10	**Bad Girls**	*Donna Summer*	Casablanca 7150
2	2	16	Breakfast In America	*Supertramp*	A&M 3708
3	4	5	**I Am**	*Earth, Wind & Fire*	ARC 35730
4	5	21	**Cheap Trick At Budokan**	*Cheap Trick*	Epic 35795
5	3	15	Rickie Lee Jones	*Rickie Lee Jones*	Warner 3296
6	9	4	Discovery	*Electric Light Orchestra*	Jet 35769
7	15	3	Candy-O	*The Cars*	Elektra 507
8	8	8	**Songs Of Love**	*Anita Ward*	Juana 200,004
9	17	3	Back To The Egg	*Wings*	Columbia 36057
10	11	4	Dynasty	*Kiss*	Casablanca 7152

Billboard — JULY 21, 1979 — TOP LP's

TW	LW	WK	Title	Artist	Label
1	1	11	**Bad Girls**	*Donna Summer*	Casablanca 7150
2	2	17	Breakfast In America	*Supertramp*	A&M 3708
3	3	6	**I Am**	*Earth, Wind & Fire*	ARC 35730
4	4	22	**Cheap Trick At Budokan**	*Cheap Trick*	Epic 35795
5	6	5	**Discovery**	*Electric Light Orchestra*	Jet 35769
6	7	4	Candy-O	*The Cars*	Elektra 507
7	5	16	Rickie Lee Jones	*Rickie Lee Jones*	Warner 3296
8	9	4	**Back To The Egg**	*Wings*	Columbia 36057
9	10	5	**Dynasty**	*Kiss*	Casablanca 7152
10	11	5	Teddy	*Teddy Pendergrass*	Philadelphia International 36003

Billboard — JULY 28, 1979 — TOP LP's

TW	LW	WK	Title	Artist	Label
1	1	12	**Bad Girls**	*Donna Summer*	Casablanca 7150
2	2	18	Breakfast In America	*Supertramp*	A&M 3708
3	3	7	**I Am**	*Earth, Wind & Fire*	ARC 35730
4	4	23	**Cheap Trick At Budokan**	*Cheap Trick*	Epic 35795
5	5	6	**Discovery**	*Electric Light Orchestra*	Jet 35769
6	6	5	Candy-O	*The Cars*	Elektra 507
7	10	6	Teddy	*Teddy Pendergrass*	Philadelphia International 36003
8	8	5	**Back To The Egg**	*Wings*	Columbia 36057
9	9	6	**Dynasty**	*Kiss*	Casablanca 7152
10	15	5	Get The Knack	*The Knack*	Capitol 11948

Billboard — AUGUST 4, 1979 — TOP LP's

TW	LW	WK	Title	Artist	Label
1	1	13	**Bad Girls**	*Donna Summer*	Casablanca 7150
2	2	19	Breakfast In America	*Supertramp*	A&M 3708
3	10	6	Get The Knack	*The Knack*	Capitol 11948
4	4	24	**Cheap Trick At Budokan**	*Cheap Trick*	Epic 35795
5	6	6	Candy-O	*The Cars*	Elektra 507
6	7	7	Teddy	*Teddy Pendergrass*	Philadelphia International 36003
7	3	8	I Am	*Earth, Wind & Fire*	ARC 35730
8	5	7	Discovery	*Electric Light Orchestra*	Jet 35769
9	9	7	**Dynasty**	*Kiss*	Casablanca 7152
10	8	6	Back To The Egg	*Wings*	Columbia 36057

Billboard — AUGUST 11, 1979 — TOP LP's

TW	LW	WK	Title	Artist	Label
1	3	7	**Get The Knack**	*The Knack*	Capitol 11948
2	1	14	Bad Girls	*Donna Summer*	Casablanca 7150
3	2	20	Breakfast In America	*Supertramp*	A&M 3708
4	5	7	Candy-O	*The Cars*	Elektra 507
5	6	8	**Teddy**	*Teddy Pendergrass*	Philadelphia International 36003
6	7	9	I Am	*Earth, Wind & Fire*	ARC 35730
7	8	8	Discovery	*Electric Light Orchestra*	Jet 35769
8	4	25	Cheap Trick At Budokan	*Cheap Trick*	Epic 35795
9	12	7	The Kids Are Alright	*The Who/Soundtrack*	MCA 11005
10	10	7	Back To The Egg	*Wings*	Columbia 36057

TW	LW	WK	Billboard — AUGUST 18, 1979 — TOP LP's	Artist	Label
1	1	8	**Get The Knack**	*The Knack*	Capitol 11948
2	2	15	Bad Girls	*Donna Summer*	Casablanca 7150
3	3	21	Breakfast In America	*Supertramp*	A&M 3708
4	4	8	Candy-O	*The Cars*	Elektra 507
5	5	9	**Teddy**	*Teddy Pendergrass*	Philadelphia International 36003
6	6	10	I Am	*Earth, Wind & Fire*	ARC 35730
7	7	9	Discovery	*Electric Light Orchestra*	Jet 35769
8	9	8	**The Kids Are Alright**	*The Who/Soundtrack*	MCA 11005
9	8	26	Cheap Trick At Budokan	*Cheap Trick*	Epic 35795
10	13	15	Million Mile Reflections	*Charlie Daniels Band*	Epic 35751

TW	LW	WK	Billboard — AUGUST 25, 1979 — TOP LP's	Artist	Label
1	1	9	**Get The Knack**	*The Knack*	Capitol 11948
2	3	22	Breakfast In America	*Supertramp*	A&M 3708
3	4	9	**Candy-O**	*The Cars*	Elektra 507
4	2	16	Bad Girls	*Donna Summer*	Casablanca 7150
5	6	11	I Am	*Earth, Wind & Fire*	ARC 35730
6	7	10	Discovery	*Electric Light Orchestra*	Jet 35769
7	10	16	Million Mile Reflections	*Charlie Daniels Band*	Epic 35751
8	8	9	**The Kids Are Alright**	*The Who/Soundtrack*	MCA 11005
9	12	6	Rust Never Sleeps	*Neil Young & Crazy Horse*	Reprise 2295
10	11	15	**Bombs Away Dream Babies**	*John Stewart*	RSO 3051

TW	LW	WK	Billboard — SEPTEMBER 1, 1979 — TOP LP's	Artist	Label
1	1	10	**Get The Knack**	*The Knack*	Capitol 11948
2	2	23	Breakfast In America	*Supertramp*	A&M 3708
3	3	10	**Candy-O**	*The Cars*	Elektra 507
4	5	12	I Am	*Earth, Wind & Fire*	ARC 35730
5	7	17	**Million Mile Reflections**	*Charlie Daniels Band*	Epic 35751
6	6	11	Discovery	*Electric Light Orchestra*	Jet 35769
7	32	2	Risque	*Chic*	Atlantic 16003
8	9	7	**Rust Never Sleeps**	*Neil Young & Crazy Horse*	Reprise 2295
9	4	17	Bad Girls	*Donna Summer*	Casablanca 7150
10	15	3	Midnight Magic	*Commodores*	Motown 926

TW	LW	WK	Billboard — SEPTEMBER 8, 1979 — TOP LP's	Artist	Label
1	1	11	**Get The Knack**	*The Knack*	Capitol 11948
2	2	24	Breakfast In America	*Supertramp*	A&M 3708
3	3	11	**Candy-O**	*The Cars*	Elektra 507
4	4	13	I Am	*Earth, Wind & Fire*	ARC 35730
5	5	18	**Million Mile Reflections**	*Charlie Daniels Band*	Epic 35751
6	6	12	Discovery	*Electric Light Orchestra*	Jet 35769
7	7	3	Risque	*Chic*	Atlantic 16003
8	8	8	**Rust Never Sleeps**	*Neil Young & Crazy Horse*	Reprise 2295
9	10	4	Midnight Magic	*Commodores*	Motown 926
10	-	1	In Through The Out Door	*Led Zeppelin*	Swan Song 16002

TW	LW	WK	Billboard. SEPTEMBER 15, 1979 TOP LP's
1	10	2	**In Through The Out Door**...Led Zeppelin...Swan Song 16002
2	1	12	Get The Knack...The Knack...Capitol 11948
3	3	12	**Candy-O**...The Cars...Elektra 507
4	2	25	Breakfast In America...Supertramp...A&M 3708
5	5	19	**Million Mile Reflections**...Charlie Daniels Band...Epic 35751
6	7	4	Risque...Chic...Atlantic 16003
7	4	14	I Am...Earth, Wind & Fire...ARC 35730
8	9	5	Midnight Magic...Commodores...Motown 926
9	23	3	Off The Wall...Michael Jackson...Epic 35745
10	12	9	**Reality...What A Concept**...Robin Williams...Casablanca 7162

TW	LW	WK	Billboard. SEPTEMBER 22, 1979 TOP LP's
1	1	3	**In Through The Out Door**...Led Zeppelin...Swan Song 16002
2	2	13	Get The Knack...The Knack...Capitol 11948
3	14	3	**Slow Train Coming**...Bob Dylan...Columbia 36120
4	4	26	Breakfast In America...Supertramp...A&M 3708
5	6	5	**Risque**...Chic...Atlantic 16003
6	9	4	Off The Wall...Michael Jackson...Epic 35745
7	8	6	Midnight Magic...Commodores...Motown 926
8	7	15	I Am...Earth, Wind & Fire...ARC 35730
9	3	13	Candy-O...The Cars...Elektra 507
10	10	10	**Reality...What A Concept**...Robin Williams...Casablanca 7162

TW	LW	WK	Billboard. SEPTEMBER 29, 1979 TOP LP's
1	1	4	**In Through The Out Door**...Led Zeppelin...Swan Song 16002
2	2	14	Get The Knack...The Knack...Capitol 11948
3	3	4	**Slow Train Coming**...Bob Dylan...Columbia 36120
4	4	27	Breakfast In America...Supertramp...A&M 3708
5	5	6	**Risque**...Chic...Atlantic 16003
6	6	5	Off The Wall...Michael Jackson...Epic 35745
7	7	7	Midnight Magic...Commodores...Motown 926
8	8	16	I Am...Earth, Wind & Fire...ARC 35730
9	9	14	Candy-O...The Cars...Elektra 507
10	12	9	**First Under The Wire**...Little River Band...Capitol 11954

TW	LW	WK	Billboard. OCTOBER 6, 1979 TOP LP's
1	1	5	**In Through The Out Door**...Led Zeppelin...Swan Song 16002
2	2	15	Get The Knack...The Knack...Capitol 11948
3	3	5	**Slow Train Coming**...Bob Dylan...Columbia 36120
4	7	8	Midnight Magic...Commodores...Motown 926
5	6	6	Off The Wall...Michael Jackson...Epic 35745
6	4	28	Breakfast In America...Supertramp...A&M 3708
7	5	7	Risque...Chic...Atlantic 16003
8	19	2	Head Games...Foreigner...Atlantic 29999
9	11	12	Rust Never Sleeps...Neil Young & Crazy Horse...Reprise 2295
10	10	10	**First Under The Wire**...Little River Band...Capitol 11954

TW	LW	WK	Billboard. OCTOBER 13, 1979 TOP LP's
1	1	6	**In Through The Out Door** .... *Led Zeppelin*...Swan Song 16002
2	2	16	Get The Knack........ *The Knack*...Capitol 11948
3	3	6	**Slow Train Coming** .... *Bob Dylan*...Columbia 36120
4	4	9	Midnight Magic........ *Commodores*...Motown 926
5	5	7	Off The Wall........ *Michael Jackson*...Epic 35745
6	8	3	Head Games........ *Foreigner*...Atlantic 29999
7	6	29	Breakfast In America........ *Supertramp*...A&M 3708
8	7	8	Risque .... *Chic*...Atlantic 16003
9	9	13	Rust Never Sleeps........ *Neil Young & Crazy Horse*...Reprise 2295
10	10	11	**First Under The Wire**........ *Little River Band*...Capitol 11954

TW	LW	WK	Billboard. OCTOBER 20, 1979 TOP LP's
1	1	7	**In Through The Out Door** .... *Led Zeppelin*...Swan Song 16002
2	-	1	The Long Run .... *Eagles*...Asylum 508
3	2	17	Get The Knack........ *The Knack*...Capitol 11948
4	4	10	Midnight Magic........ *Commodores*...Motown 926
5	5	8	Off The Wall........ *Michael Jackson*...Epic 35745
6	6	4	Head Games........ *Foreigner*...Atlantic 29999
7	11	3	Dream Police........ *Cheap Trick*...Epic 35773
8	3	7	Slow Train Coming........ *Bob Dylan*...Columbia 36120
9	7	30	Breakfast In America........ *Supertramp*...A&M 3708
10	21	2	Cornerstone .... *Styx*...A&M 3711

TW	LW	WK	Billboard. OCTOBER 27, 1979 TOP LP's
1	1	8	**In Through The Out Door** .... *Led Zeppelin*...Swan Song 16002
2	2	2	The Long Run .... *Eagles*...Asylum 508
3	4	11	**Midnight Magic**........ *Commodores*...Motown 926
4	10	3	Cornerstone .... *Styx*...A&M 3711
5	6	5	**Head Games** .... *Foreigner*...Atlantic 29999
6	7	4	**Dream Police** .... *Cheap Trick*...Epic 35773
7	3	18	Get The Knack........ *The Knack*...Capitol 11948
8	14	3	Rise .... *Herb Alpert*...A&M 4790
9	5	9	Off The Wall........ *Michael Jackson*...Epic 35745
10	8	8	Slow Train Coming........ *Bob Dylan*...Columbia 36120

TW	LW	WK	Billboard. NOVEMBER 3, 1979 TOP LP's
1	2	3	**The Long Run**........ *Eagles*...Asylum 508
2	1	9	In Through The Out Door .... *Led Zeppelin*...Swan Song 16002
3	3	12	**Midnight Magic**........ *Commodores*...Motown 926
4	4	4	Cornerstone .... *Styx*...A&M 3711
5	5	6	**Head Games** .... *Foreigner*...Atlantic 29999
6	6	5	**Dream Police** .... *Cheap Trick*...Epic 35773
7	-	1	Tusk .... *Fleetwood Mac*...Warner 3350
8	8	4	Rise .... *Herb Alpert*...A&M 4790
9	9	10	Off The Wall........ *Michael Jackson*...Epic 35745
10	7	19	Get The Knack........ *The Knack*...Capitol 11948

TW	LW	WK	Billboard. NOVEMBER 10, 1979 TOP LP's
1	1	4	**The Long Run** ... *Eagles*...Asylum 508
2	2	10	In Through The Out Door ... *Led Zeppelin*...Swan Song 16002
3	4	5	Cornerstone ... *Styx*...A&M 3711
4	3	13	Midnight Magic ... *Commodores*...Motown 926
5	5	7	**Head Games** ... *Foreigner*...Atlantic 29999
6	7	2	Tusk ... *Fleetwood Mac*...Warner 3350
7	8	5	Rise ... *Herb Alpert*...A&M 4790
8	53	2	On The Radio-Greatest Hits-Volumes I & II ... *Donna Summer*...Casablanca 7191
9	51	2	Wet ... *Barbra Streisand*...Columbia 36258
10	12	4	One Voice ... *Barry Manilow*...Arista 9505

TW	LW	WK	Billboard. NOVEMBER 17, 1979 TOP LP's
1	1	5	**The Long Run** ... *Eagles*...Asylum 508
2	2	11	In Through The Out Door ... *Led Zeppelin*...Swan Song 16002
3	3	6	Cornerstone ... *Styx*...A&M 3711
4	6	3	**Tusk** ... *Fleetwood Mac*...Warner 3350
5	8	3	On The Radio-Greatest Hits-Volumes I & II ... *Donna Summer*...Casablanca 7191
6	4	14	Midnight Magic ... *Commodores*...Motown 926
7	7	6	Rise ... *Herb Alpert*...A&M 4790
8	9	3	Wet ... *Barbra Streisand*...Columbia 36258
9	10	5	**One Voice** ... *Barry Manilow*...Arista 9505
10	-	1	Bee Gees Greatest ... *Bee Gees*...RSO 4200

TW	LW	WK	Billboard. NOVEMBER 24, 1979 TOP LP's
1	1	6	**The Long Run** ... *Eagles*...Asylum 508
2	3	7	**Cornerstone** ... *Styx*...A&M 3711
3	2	12	In Through The Out Door ... *Led Zeppelin*...Swan Song 16002
4	4	4	**Tusk** ... *Fleetwood Mac*...Warner 3350
5	5	4	On The Radio-Greatest Hits-Volumes I & II ... *Donna Summer*...Casablanca 7191
6	-	1	Journey Through The Secret Life of Plants ... *Stevie Wonder*...Tamla 371
7	7	7	Rise ... *Herb Alpert*...A&M 4790
8	8	4	Wet ... *Barbra Streisand*...Columbia 36258
9	9	6	**One Voice** ... *Barry Manilow*...Arista 9505
10	10	2	Bee Gees Greatest ... *Bee Gees*...RSO 4200

TW	LW	WK	Billboard. DECEMBER 1, 1979 TOP LP's
1	1	7	**The Long Run** ... *Eagles*...Asylum 508
2	5	5	On The Radio-Greatest Hits-Volumes I & II ... *Donna Summer*...Casablanca 7191
3	3	13	In Through The Out Door ... *Led Zeppelin*...Swan Song 16002
4	4	5	**Tusk** ... *Fleetwood Mac*...Warner 3350
5	6	2	Journey Through The Secret Life of Plants ... *Stevie Wonder*...Tamla 371
6	7	8	**Rise** ... *Herb Alpert*...A&M 4790
7	2	8	Cornerstone ... *Styx*...A&M 3711
8	8	5	Wet ... *Barbra Streisand*...Columbia 36258
9	9	7	**One Voice** ... *Barry Manilow*...Arista 9505
10	10	3	Bee Gees Greatest ... *Bee Gees*...RSO 4200

TW	LW	WK	Billboard. DECEMBER 8, 1979 TOP LP's
1	1	8	**The Long Run**.......... *Eagles*...Asylum 508
2	2	6	On The Radio-Greatest Hits-Volumes I & II....*Donna Summer*...Casablanca 7191
3	7	9	Cornerstone.......... *Styx*...A&M 3711
4	5	3	**Journey Through The Secret Life of Plants**.......... *Stevie Wonder*...Tamla 371
5	3	14	In Through The Out Door.......... *Led Zeppelin*...Swan Song 16002
6	10	4	Bee Gees Greatest.......... *Bee Gees*...RSO 4200
7	8	6	**Wet**.......... *Barbra Streisand*...Columbia 36258
8	4	6	Tusk.......... *Fleetwood Mac*...Warner 3350
9	6	9	Rise.......... *Herb Alpert*...A&M 4790
10	16	5	Damn The Torpedoes.......... *Tom Petty & The Heartbreakers*...Backstreet 5105

TW	LW	WK	Billboard. DECEMBER 15, 1979 TOP LP's
1	1	9	**The Long Run**.......... *Eagles*...Asylum 508
2	2	7	On The Radio-Greatest Hits-Volumes I & II....*Donna Summer*...Casablanca 7191
3	3	10	Cornerstone.......... *Styx*...A&M 3711
4	4	4	**Journey Through The Secret Life of Plants**.......... *Stevie Wonder*...Tamla 371
5	6	5	Bee Gees Greatest.......... *Bee Gees*...RSO 4200
6	5	15	In Through The Out Door.......... *Led Zeppelin*...Swan Song 16002
7	7	7	**Wet**.......... *Barbra Streisand*...Columbia 36258
8	8	7	Tusk.......... *Fleetwood Mac*...Warner 3350
9	10	6	Damn The Torpedoes.......... *Tom Petty & The Heartbreakers*...Backstreet 5105
10	12	18	Midnight Magic.......... *Commodores*...Motown 926

TW	LW	WK	Billboard. DECEMBER 22, 1979 TOP LP's
1	1	10	**The Long Run**.......... *Eagles*...Asylum 508
2	2	8	On The Radio-Greatest Hits-Volumes I & II....*Donna Summer*...Casablanca 7191
3	3	11	Cornerstone.......... *Styx*...A&M 3711
4	4	5	**Journey Through The Secret Life of Plants**.......... *Stevie Wonder*...Tamla 371
5	5	6	Bee Gees Greatest.......... *Bee Gees*...RSO 4200
6	6	16	In Through The Out Door.......... *Led Zeppelin*...Swan Song 16002
7	7	8	**Wet**.......... *Barbra Streisand*...Columbia 36258
8	8	8	Tusk.......... *Fleetwood Mac*...Warner 3350
9	9	7	Damn The Torpedoes.......... *Tom Petty & The Heartbreakers*...Backstreet 5105
10	10	19	Midnight Magic.......... *Commodores*...Motown 926

Billboard — JANUARY 5, 1980 — TOP LP's

TW	LW	WK	Title	Artist	Label
1	2	10	**On The Radio-Greatest Hits-Volumes I & II**	*Donna Summer*	Casablanca 7191
2	5	8	Bee Gees Greatest	*Bee Gees*	RSO 4200
3	3	13	Cornerstone	*Styx*	A&M 3711
4	4	7	**Journey Through The Secret Life of Plants**	*Stevie Wonder*	Tamla 371
5	1	12	The Long Run	*Eagles*	Asylum 508
6	6	18	In Through The Out Door	*Led Zeppelin*	Swan Song 16002
7	20	4	The Wall	*Pink Floyd*	Columbia 36183
8	9	9	Damn The Torpedoes	*Tom Petty & The Heartbreakers*	Backstreet 5105
9	8	10	Tusk	*Fleetwood Mac*	Warner 3350
10	11	19	Off The Wall	*Michael Jackson*	Epic 35745

Billboard — JANUARY 12, 1980 — TOP LP's

TW	LW	WK	Title	Artist	Label
1	2	9	**Bee Gees Greatest**	*Bee Gees*	RSO 4200
2	1	11	On The Radio-Greatest Hits-Volumes I & II	*Donna Summer*	Casablanca 7191
3	7	5	The Wall	*Pink Floyd*	Columbia 36183
4	5	13	The Long Run	*Eagles*	Asylum 508
5	4	8	Journey Through The Secret Life of Plants	*Stevie Wonder*	Tamla 371
6	8	10	Damn The Torpedoes	*Tom Petty & The Heartbreakers*	Backstreet 5105
7	3	14	Cornerstone	*Styx*	A&M 3711
8	15	16	Kenny	*Kenny Rogers*	United Artists 979
9	10	20	Off The Wall	*Michael Jackson*	Epic 35745
10	9	11	Tusk	*Fleetwood Mac*	Warner 3350

Billboard — JANUARY 19, 1980 — TOP LP's

TW	LW	WK	Title	Artist	Label
1	3	6	**The Wall**	*Pink Floyd*	Columbia 36183
2	2	12	On The Radio-Greatest Hits-Volumes I & II	*Donna Summer*	Casablanca 7191
3	4	14	The Long Run	*Eagles*	Asylum 508
4	1	10	Bee Gees Greatest	*Bee Gees*	RSO 4200
5	6	11	Damn The Torpedoes	*Tom Petty & The Heartbreakers*	Backstreet 5105
6	5	9	Journey Through The Secret Life of Plants	*Stevie Wonder*	Tamla 371
7	8	17	Kenny	*Kenny Rogers*	United Artists 979
8	9	21	Off The Wall	*Michael Jackson*	Epic 35745
9	7	15	Cornerstone	*Styx*	A&M 3711
10	10	12	Tusk	*Fleetwood Mac*	Warner 3350

Billboard — JANUARY 26, 1980 — TOP LP's

TW	LW	WK	Title	Artist	Label
1	1	7	**The Wall**	*Pink Floyd*	Columbia 36183
2	3	15	The Long Run	*Eagles*	Asylum 508
3	5	12	Damn The Torpedoes	*Tom Petty & The Heartbreakers*	Backstreet 5105
4	2	13	On The Radio-Greatest Hits-Volumes I & II	*Donna Summer*	Casablanca 7191
5	4	11	Bee Gees Greatest	*Bee Gees*	RSO 4200
6	7	18	Kenny	*Kenny Rogers*	United Artists 979
7	8	22	Off The Wall	*Michael Jackson*	Epic 35745
8	11	8	Phoenix	*Dan Fogelberg*	Full Moon 35634
9	9	16	Cornerstone	*Styx*	A&M 3711
10	10	13	Tusk	*Fleetwood Mac*	Warner 3350

TW	LW	WK	Billboard. FEBRUARY 2, 1980 TOP LP's
1	1	8	**The Wall** ... *Pink Floyd*...Columbia 36183
2	2	16	The Long Run ... *Eagles*...Asylum 508
3	3	13	Damn The Torpedoes ... *Tom Petty & The Heartbreakers*...Backstreet 5105
4	7	23	Off The Wall ... *Michael Jackson*...Epic 35745
5	6	19	**Kenny** ... *Kenny Rogers*...United Artists 979
6	8	9	Phoenix ... *Dan Fogelberg*...Full Moon 35634
7	4	14	On The Radio-Greatest Hits-Volumes I & II ... *Donna Summer*...Casablanca 7191
8	10	14	Tusk ... *Fleetwood Mac*...Warner 3350
9	5	12	Bee Gees Greatest ... *Bee Gees*...RSO 4200
10	11	10	**Freedom At Point Zero** ... *Jefferson Starship*...Grunt 3452

TW	LW	WK	Billboard. FEBRUARY 9, 1980 TOP LP's
1	1	9	**The Wall** ... *Pink Floyd*...Columbia 36183
2	3	14	**Damn The Torpedoes** ... *Tom Petty & The Heartbreakers*...Backstreet 5105
3	2	17	The Long Run ... *Eagles*...Asylum 508
4	4	24	Off The Wall ... *Michael Jackson*...Epic 35745
5	5	20	**Kenny** ... *Kenny Rogers*...United Artists 979
6	6	10	Phoenix ... *Dan Fogelberg*...Full Moon 35634
7	7	15	On The Radio-Greatest Hits-Volumes I & II ... *Donna Summer*...Casablanca 7191
8	8	15	Tusk ... *Fleetwood Mac*...Warner 3350
9	9	13	Bee Gees Greatest ... *Bee Gees*...RSO 4200
10	12	18	Cornerstone ... *Styx*...A&M 3711

TW	LW	WK	Billboard. FEBRUARY 16, 1980 TOP LP's
1	1	10	**The Wall** ... *Pink Floyd*...Columbia 36183
2	2	15	**Damn The Torpedoes** ... *Tom Petty & The Heartbreakers*...Backstreet 5105
3	4	25	**Off The Wall** ... *Michael Jackson*...Epic 35745
4	3	18	The Long Run ... *Eagles*...Asylum 508
5	6	11	Phoenix ... *Dan Fogelberg*...Full Moon 35634
6	5	21	Kenny ... *Kenny Rogers*...United Artists 979
7	7	16	On The Radio-Greatest Hits-Volumes I & II ... *Donna Summer*...Casablanca 7191
8	8	16	Tusk ... *Fleetwood Mac*...Warner 3350
9	10	19	Cornerstone ... *Styx*...A&M 3711
10	14	6	**September Morn** ... *Neil Diamond*...Columbia 36121

TW	LW	WK	Billboard. FEBRUARY 23, 1980 TOP LP's
1	1	11	**The Wall** ... *Pink Floyd*...Columbia 36183
2	2	16	**Damn The Torpedoes** ... *Tom Petty & The Heartbreakers*...Backstreet 5105
3	3	26	**Off The Wall** ... *Michael Jackson*...Epic 35745
4	5	12	Phoenix ... *Dan Fogelberg*...Full Moon 35634
5	4	19	The Long Run ... *Eagles*...Asylum 508
6	7	17	On The Radio-Greatest Hits-Volumes I & II ... *Donna Summer*...Casablanca 7191
7	6	22	Kenny ... *Kenny Rogers*...United Artists 979
8	15	4	Permanent Waves ... *Rush*...Mercury 4001
9	9	20	Cornerstone ... *Styx*...A&M 3711
10	10	7	**September Morn** ... *Neil Diamond*...Columbia 36121

TW	LW	WK	Billboard. MARCH 1, 1980	TOP LP's
1	1	12	The Wall	Pink Floyd...Columbia 36183
2	2	17	Damn The Torpedoes	Tom Petty & The Heartbreakers...Backstreet 5105
3	3	27	Off The Wall	Michael Jackson...Epic 35745
4	4	13	Phoenix	Dan Fogelberg...Full Moon 35634
5	8	5	Permanent Waves	Rush...Mercury 4001
6	6	18	On The Radio-Greatest Hits-Volumes I & II	Donna Summer...Casablanca 7191
7	5	20	The Long Run	Eagles...Asylum 508
8	7	23	Kenny	Kenny Rogers...United Artists 979
9	13	9	The Whispers	The Whispers...Solar 3521
10	10	8	September Morn	Neil Diamond...Columbia 36121

TW	LW	WK	Billboard. MARCH 8, 1980	TOP LP's
1	1	13	The Wall	Pink Floyd...Columbia 36183
2	2	18	Damn The Torpedoes	Tom Petty & The Heartbreakers...Backstreet 5105
3	4	14	Phoenix	Dan Fogelberg...Full Moon 35634
4	5	6	Permanent Waves	Rush...Mercury 4001
5	3	28	Off The Wall	Michael Jackson...Epic 35745
6	6	19	On The Radio-Greatest Hits-Volumes I & II	Donna Summer...Casablanca 7191
7	7	21	The Long Run	Eagles...Asylum 508
8	9	10	The Whispers	The Whispers...Solar 3521
9	8	24	Kenny	Kenny Rogers...United Artists 979
10	29	3	Fun and Games	Chuck Mangione...A&M 3715

TW	LW	WK	Billboard. MARCH 15, 1980	TOP LP's
1	1	14	The Wall	Pink Floyd...Columbia 36183
2	2	19	Damn The Torpedoes	Tom Petty & The Heartbreakers...Backstreet 5105
3	3	15	Phoenix	Dan Fogelberg...Full Moon 35634
4	4	7	Permanent Waves	Rush...Mercury 4001
5	-	1	Mad Love	Linda Ronstadt...Asylum 510
6	19	2	Bebe Le Strange	Heart...Epic 36371
7	8	11	The Whispers	The Whispers...Solar 3521
8	10	4	Fun and Games	Chuck Mangione...A&M 3715
9	9	25	Kenny	Kenny Rogers...United Artists 979
10	5	29	Off The Wall	Michael Jackson...Epic 35745

TW	LW	WK	Billboard. MARCH 22, 1980	TOP LP's
1	1	15	The Wall	Pink Floyd...Columbia 36183
2	2	20	Damn The Torpedoes	Tom Petty & The Heartbreakers...Backstreet 5105
3	5	2	Mad Love	Linda Ronstadt...Asylum 510
4	4	8	Permanent Waves	Rush...Mercury 4001
5	6	3	Bebe Le Strange	Heart...Epic 36371
6	3	16	Phoenix	Dan Fogelberg...Full Moon 35634
7	7	12	The Whispers	The Whispers...Solar 3521
8	8	5	Fun and Games	Chuck Mangione...A&M 3715
9	20	2	Against The Wind	Bob Seger & The Silver Bullet Band...Capitol 12041
10	10	30	Off The Wall	Michael Jackson...Epic 35745

TW	LW	WK	Billboard® MARCH 29, 1980		TOP LP's
❶	1	16	**The Wall**	*Pink Floyd*	Columbia 36183
❷	9	3	Against The Wind	*Bob Seger & The Silver Bullet Band*	Capitol 12041
❸	3	3	**Mad Love**	*Linda Ronstadt*	Asylum 510
④	2	21	Damn The Torpedoes	*Tom Petty & The Heartbreakers*	Backstreet 5105
⑤	5	4	**Bebe Le Strange**	*Heart*	Epic 36371
❻	11	2	Glass Houses	*Billy Joel*	Columbia 36384
⑦	7	13	The Whispers	*The Whispers*	Solar 3521
⑧	8	6	**Fun and Games**	*Chuck Mangione*	A&M 3715
⑨	6	17	Phoenix	*Dan Fogelberg*	Full Moon 35634
⑩	10	31	Off The Wall	*Michael Jackson*	Epic 35745

TW	LW	WK	Billboard® APRIL 5, 1980		TOP LP's
❶	1	17	**The Wall**	*Pink Floyd*	Columbia 36183
❷	2	4	Against The Wind	*Bob Seger & The Silver Bullet Band*	Capitol 12041
❸	3	4	**Mad Love**	*Linda Ronstadt*	Asylum 510
❹	6	3	Glass Houses	*Billy Joel*	Columbia 36384
⑤	4	22	Damn The Torpedoes	*Tom Petty & The Heartbreakers*	Backstreet 5105
⑥	5	5	Bebe Le Strange	*Heart*	Epic 36371
⑦	7	14	The Whispers	*The Whispers*	Solar 3521
⑧	8	7	**Fun and Games**	*Chuck Mangione*	A&M 3715
❾	12	5	Light Up The Night	*The Brothers Johnson*	A&M 3716
⑩	10	32	Off The Wall	*Michael Jackson*	Epic 35745

TW	LW	WK	Billboard® APRIL 12, 1980		TOP LP's
❶	1	18	**The Wall**	*Pink Floyd*	Columbia 36183
②	2	5	Against The Wind	*Bob Seger & The Silver Bullet Band*	Capitol 12041
③	3	5	**Mad Love**	*Linda Ronstadt*	Asylum 510
❹	4	4	Glass Houses	*Billy Joel*	Columbia 36384
⑤	5	23	Damn The Torpedoes	*Tom Petty & The Heartbreakers*	Backstreet 5105
⑥	7	15	**The Whispers**	*The Whispers*	Solar 3521
❼	10	33	Off The Wall	*Michael Jackson*	Epic 35745
❽	9	6	Light Up The Night	*The Brothers Johnson*	A&M 3716
❾	14	7	American Gigolo	*Soundtrack*	Polydor 6259
❿	13	4	Departure	*Journey*	Columbia 36339

TW	LW	WK	Billboard® APRIL 19, 1980		TOP LP's
①	1	19	**The Wall**	*Pink Floyd*	Columbia 36183
❷	2	6	Against The Wind	*Bob Seger & The Silver Bullet Band*	Capitol 12041
❸	4	5	Glass Houses	*Billy Joel*	Columbia 36384
④	3	6	Mad Love	*Linda Ronstadt*	Asylum 510
❺	7	34	Off The Wall	*Michael Jackson*	Epic 35745
⑥	6	16	**The Whispers**	*The Whispers*	Solar 3521
❼	8	7	Light Up The Night	*The Brothers Johnson*	A&M 3716
❽	9	8	American Gigolo	*Soundtrack*	Polydor 6259
❾	10	5	Departure	*Journey*	Columbia 36339
⑩	5	24	Damn The Torpedoes	*Tom Petty & The Heartbreakers*	Backstreet 5105

TW	LW	WK	Billboard® — APRIL 26, 1980 — TOP LP's
①	1	20	**The Wall** ... *Pink Floyd*...Columbia 36183
❷	2	7	Against The Wind... *Bob Seger & The Silver Bullet Band*...Capitol 12041
❸	3	6	Glass Houses... *Billy Joel*...Columbia 36384
④	4	7	Mad Love... *Linda Ronstadt*...Asylum 510
⑤	5	35	Off The Wall... *Michael Jackson*...Epic 35745
❻	7	8	Light Up The Night... *The Brothers Johnson*...A&M 3716
❼	8	9	**American Gigolo** ... *Soundtrack*...Polydor 6259
❽	9	6	**Departure**... *Journey*...Columbia 36339
⑨	6	17	The Whispers... *The Whispers*...Solar 3521
❿	35	2	Women and Children First... *Van Halen*...Warner 3415

TW	LW	WK	Billboard® — MAY 3, 1980 — TOP LP's
❶	2	8	**Against The Wind**... *Bob Seger & The Silver Bullet Band*...Capitol 12041
②	1	21	The Wall ... *Pink Floyd*...Columbia 36183
❸	3	7	Glass Houses... *Billy Joel*...Columbia 36384
④	4	8	Mad Love... *Linda Ronstadt*...Asylum 510
❺	6	9	**Light Up The Night** ... *The Brothers Johnson*...A&M 3716
⑥	5	36	Off The Wall... *Michael Jackson*...Epic 35745
⑦	7	10	**American Gigolo** ... *Soundtrack*...Polydor 6259
⑧	8	7	**Departure**... *Journey*...Columbia 36339
❾	10	3	Women and Children First... *Van Halen*...Warner 3415
❿	11	12	Christopher Cross... *Christopher Cross*...Warner 3383

TW	LW	WK	Billboard® — MAY 10, 1980 — TOP LP's
❶	1	9	**Against The Wind**... *Bob Seger & The Silver Bullet Band*...Capitol 12041
②	2	22	The Wall ... *Pink Floyd*...Columbia 36183
③	3	8	Glass Houses... *Billy Joel*...Columbia 36384
④	4	9	Mad Love... *Linda Ronstadt*...Asylum 510
⑤	5	10	**Light Up The Night** ... *The Brothers Johnson*...A&M 3716
⑥	6	37	Off The Wall... *Michael Jackson*...Epic 35745
⑦	7	11	**American Gigolo** ... *Soundtrack*...Polydor 6259
❽	9	4	Women and Children First... *Van Halen*...Warner 3415
❾	10	13	Christopher Cross... *Christopher Cross*...Warner 3383
⑩	8	8	Departure ... *Journey*...Columbia 36339

TW	LW	WK	Billboard® — MAY 17, 1980 — TOP LP's
❶	1	10	**Against The Wind**... *Bob Seger & The Silver Bullet Band*...Capitol 12041
②	2	23	The Wall ... *Pink Floyd*...Columbia 36183
③	3	9	Glass Houses... *Billy Joel*...Columbia 36384
④	4	10	Mad Love... *Linda Ronstadt*...Asylum 510
❺	23	3	Just One Night... *Eric Clapton*...RSO 4202
❻	8	5	**Women and Children First** ... *Van Halen*...Warner 3415
❼	9	14	Christopher Cross... *Christopher Cross*...Warner 3383
❽	11	5	**Go All The Way**... *The Isley Brothers*...T-Neck 36305
⑨	6	38	Off The Wall... *Michael Jackson*...Epic 35745
⑩	5	11	Light Up The Night... *The Brothers Johnson*...A&M 3716

TW	LW	WK	Billboard® MAY 24, 1980 TOP LP's
1	1	11	**Against The Wind** ... *Bob Seger & The Silver Bullet Band*...Capitol 12041
2	3	10	Glass Houses ... *Billy Joel*...Columbia 36384
3	2	24	The Wall ... *Pink Floyd*...Columbia 36183
4	4	11	Mad Love ... *Linda Ronstadt*...Asylum 510
5	5	4	Just One Night ... *Eric Clapton*...RSO 4202
6	6	6	**Women and Children First** ... *Van Halen*...Warner 3415
7	7	15	Christopher Cross ... *Christopher Cross*...Warner 3383
8	8	6	**Go All The Way** ... *The Isley Brothers*...T-Neck 36305
9	9	39	Off The Wall ... *Michael Jackson*...Epic 35745
10	11	18	Pretenders ... *Pretenders*...Sire 6083

TW	LW	WK	Billboard® MAY 31, 1980 TOP LP's
1	1	12	**Against The Wind** ... *Bob Seger & The Silver Bullet Band*...Capitol 12041
2	2	11	Glass Houses ... *Billy Joel*...Columbia 36384
3	3	25	The Wall ... *Pink Floyd*...Columbia 36183
4	5	5	Just One Night ... *Eric Clapton*...RSO 4202
5	11	7	**Mouth To Mouth** ... *Lipps, Inc.*...Casablanca 7197
6	6	7	**Women and Children First** ... *Van Halen*...Warner 3415
7	7	16	Christopher Cross ... *Christopher Cross*...Warner 3383
8	8	7	**Go All The Way** ... *The Isley Brothers*...T-Neck 36305
9	4	12	Mad Love ... *Linda Ronstadt*...Asylum 510
10	10	19	Pretenders ... *Pretenders*...Sire 6083

TW	LW	WK	Billboard® JUNE 7, 1980 TOP LP's
1	1	13	**Against The Wind** ... *Bob Seger & The Silver Bullet Band*...Capitol 12041
2	2	12	Glass Houses ... *Billy Joel*...Columbia 36384
3	3	26	The Wall ... *Pink Floyd*...Columbia 36183
4	4	6	Just One Night ... *Eric Clapton*...RSO 4202
5	5	8	**Mouth To Mouth** ... *Lipps, Inc.*...Casablanca 7197
6	6	8	**Women and Children First** ... *Van Halen*...Warner 3415
7	7	17	Christopher Cross ... *Christopher Cross*...Warner 3383
8	8	8	**Go All The Way** ... *The Isley Brothers*...T-Neck 36305
9	10	20	**Pretenders** ... *Pretenders*...Sire 6083
10	11	8	Middle Man ... *Boz Scaggs*...Columbia 36106

TW	LW	WK	Billboard® JUNE 14, 1980 TOP LP's
1	2	13	**Glass Houses** ... *Billy Joel*...Columbia 36384
2	1	14	Against The Wind ... *Bob Seger & The Silver Bullet Band*...Capitol 12041
3	4	7	Just One Night ... *Eric Clapton*...RSO 4202
4	3	27	The Wall ... *Pink Floyd*...Columbia 36183
5	5	9	**Mouth To Mouth** ... *Lipps, Inc.*...Casablanca 7197
6	6	9	**Women and Children First** ... *Van Halen*...Warner 3415
7	7	18	Christopher Cross ... *Christopher Cross*...Warner 3383
8	10	9	**Middle Man** ... *Boz Scaggs*...Columbia 36106
9	9	21	**Pretenders** ... *Pretenders*...Sire 6083
10	17	5	The Empire Strikes Back ... *Soundtrack*...RSO 4201

TW	LW	WK	Billboard. JUNE 21, 1980	TOP LP's
1	1	14	**Glass Houses**	*Billy Joel*...Columbia 36384
2	3	8	**Just One Night**	*Eric Clapton*...RSO 4202
3	16	2	**McCartney II**	*Paul McCartney*...Columbia 36511
4	2	15	Against The Wind	*Bob Seger & The Silver Bullet Band*...Capitol 12041
5	5	10	**Mouth To Mouth**	*Lipps, Inc.*...Casablanca 7197
6	4	28	The Wall	*Pink Floyd*...Columbia 36183
7	10	6	The Empire Strikes Back	*Soundtrack*...RSO 4201
8	8	10	**Middle Man**	*Boz Scaggs*...Columbia 36106
9	6	10	Women and Children First	*Van Halen*...Warner 3415
10	11	6	Empty Glass	*Pete Townshend*...Atco 100

TW	LW	WK	Billboard. JUNE 28, 1980	TOP LP's
1	1	15	**Glass Houses**	*Billy Joel*...Columbia 36384
2	2	9	**Just One Night**	*Eric Clapton*...RSO 4202
3	3	3	**McCartney II**	*Paul McCartney*...Columbia 36511
4	4	16	Against The Wind	*Bob Seger & The Silver Bullet Band*...Capitol 12041
5	5	11	**Mouth To Mouth**	*Lipps, Inc.*...Casablanca 7197
6	7	7	The Empire Strikes Back	*Soundtrack*...RSO 4201
7	6	29	The Wall	*Pink Floyd*...Columbia 36183
8	12	12	Let's Get Serious	*Jermaine Jackson*...Motown 928
9	10	7	Empty Glass	*Pete Townshend*...Atco 100
10	8	11	Middle Man	*Boz Scaggs*...Columbia 36106

TW	LW	WK	Billboard. JULY 5, 1980	TOP LP's
1	1	16	**Glass Houses**	*Billy Joel*...Columbia 36384
2	2	10	**Just One Night**	*Eric Clapton*...RSO 4202
3	3	4	**McCartney II**	*Paul McCartney*...Columbia 36511
4	4	17	Against The Wind	*Bob Seger & The Silver Bullet Band*...Capitol 12041
5	6	8	The Empire Strikes Back	*Soundtrack*...RSO 4201
6	9	8	Empty Glass	*Pete Townshend*...Atco 100
7	8	13	Let's Get Serious	*Jermaine Jackson*...Motown 928
8	14	2	Heroes	*Commodores*...Motown 939
9	5	12	Mouth To Mouth	*Lipps, Inc.*...Casablanca 7197
10	7	30	The Wall	*Pink Floyd*...Columbia 36183

TW	LW	WK	Billboard. JULY 12, 1980	TOP LP's
1	1	17	**Glass Houses**	*Billy Joel*...Columbia 36384
2	2	11	**Just One Night**	*Eric Clapton*...RSO 4202
3	3	5	**McCartney II**	*Paul McCartney*...Columbia 36511
4	5	9	**The Empire Strikes Back**	*Soundtrack*...RSO 4201
5	6	9	**Empty Glass**	*Pete Townshend*...Atco 100
6	7	14	**Let's Get Serious**	*Jermaine Jackson*...Motown 928
7	8	3	**Heroes**	*Commodores*...Motown 939
8	4	18	Against The Wind	*Bob Seger & The Silver Bullet Band*...Capitol 12041
9	11	9	Urban Cowboy	*Soundtrack*...Asylum 90002
10	9	13	Mouth To Mouth	*Lipps, Inc.*...Casablanca 7197

Billboard — JULY 19, 1980 — TOP LP's

TW	LW	WK		
1	1	18	**Glass Houses**	*Billy Joel*...Columbia 36384
2	2	12	**Just One Night**	*Eric Clapton*...RSO 4202
3	3	6	**McCartney II**	*Paul McCartney*...Columbia 36511
4	4	10	**The Empire Strikes Back**	*Soundtrack*...RSO 4201
5	5	10	**Empty Glass**	*Pete Townshend*...Atco 100
6	6	15	**Let's Get Serious**	*Jermaine Jackson*...Motown 928
7	7	4	**Heroes**	*Commodores*...Motown 939
8	-	1	Emotional Rescue	*The Rolling Stones*...Rolling Stones 16015
9	9	10	Urban Cowboy	*Soundtrack*...Asylum 90002
10	-	1	Hold Out	*Jackson Browne*...Asylum 511

Billboard — JULY 26, 1980 — TOP LP's

TW	LW	WK		
1	8	2	**Emotional Rescue**	*The Rolling Stones*...Rolling Stones 16015
2	2	13	**Just One Night**	*Eric Clapton*...RSO 4202
3	1	19	Glass Houses	*Billy Joel*...Columbia 36384
4	4	11	**The Empire Strikes Back**	*Soundtrack*...RSO 4201
5	5	11	**Empty Glass**	*Pete Townshend*...Atco 100
6	6	16	**Let's Get Serious**	*Jermaine Jackson*...Motown 928
7	7	5	**Heroes**	*Commodores*...Motown 939
8	9	11	Urban Cowboy	*Soundtrack*...Asylum 90002
9	10	2	Hold Out	*Jackson Browne*...Asylum 511
10	3	7	McCartney II	*Paul McCartney*...Columbia 36511

Billboard — AUGUST 2, 1980 — TOP LP's

TW	LW	WK		
1	1	3	**Emotional Rescue**	*The Rolling Stones*...Rolling Stones 16015
2	3	20	Glass Houses	*Billy Joel*...Columbia 36384
3	9	3	Hold Out	*Jackson Browne*...Asylum 511
4	4	12	**The Empire Strikes Back**	*Soundtrack*...RSO 4201
5	8	12	Urban Cowboy	*Soundtrack*...Asylum 90002
6	16	3	The Game	*Queen*...Elektra 513
7	5	12	Empty Glass	*Pete Townshend*...Atco 100
8	7	6	Heroes	*Commodores*...Motown 939
9	11	8	Diana	*Diana Ross*...Motown 936
10	10	8	McCartney II	*Paul McCartney*...Columbia 36511

Billboard — AUGUST 9, 1980 — TOP LP's

TW	LW	WK		
1	1	4	**Emotional Rescue**	*The Rolling Stones*...Rolling Stones 16015
2	3	4	Hold Out	*Jackson Browne*...Asylum 511
3	2	21	Glass Houses	*Billy Joel*...Columbia 36384
4	5	13	Urban Cowboy	*Soundtrack*...Asylum 90002
5	6	4	The Game	*Queen*...Elektra 513
6	9	9	Diana	*Diana Ross*...Motown 936
7	7	13	Empty Glass	*Pete Townshend*...Atco 100
8	4	13	The Empire Strikes Back	*Soundtrack*...RSO 4201
9	19	26	Christopher Cross	*Christopher Cross*...Warner 3383
10	11	22	Against The Wind	*Bob Seger & The Silver Bullet Band*...Capitol 12041

Billboard — AUGUST 16, 1980 — TOP LP's

TW	LW	WK		
1	1	5	**Emotional Rescue**	*The Rolling Stones*...Rolling Stones 16015
2	2	5	Hold Out	*Jackson Browne*...Asylum 511
3	3	22	Glass Houses	*Billy Joel*...Columbia 36384
4	4	14	Urban Cowboy	*Soundtrack*...Asylum 90002
5	5	5	The Game	*Queen*...Elektra 513
6	6	10	Diana	*Diana Ross*...Motown 936
7	7	14	Empty Glass	*Pete Townshend*...Atco 100
8	9	27	Christopher Cross	*Christopher Cross*...Warner 3383
9	11	11	Fame	*Soundtrack*...RSO 3080
10	10	23	Against The Wind	*Bob Seger & The Silver Bullet Band*...Capitol 12041

Billboard — AUGUST 23, 1980 — TOP LP's

TW	LW	WK		
1	1	6	**Emotional Rescue**	*The Rolling Stones*...Rolling Stones 16015
2	2	6	Hold Out	*Jackson Browne*...Asylum 511
3	3	23	Glass Houses	*Billy Joel*...Columbia 36384
4	4	15	Urban Cowboy	*Soundtrack*...Asylum 90002
5	5	6	The Game	*Queen*...Elektra 513
6	6	11	Diana	*Diana Ross*...Motown 936
7	8	28	Christopher Cross	*Christopher Cross*...Warner 3383
8	9	12	Fame	*Soundtrack*...RSO 3080
9	22	3	Give Me The Night	*George Benson*...Warner 3453
10	10	24	Against The Wind	*Bob Seger & The Silver Bullet Band*...Capitol 12041

Billboard — AUGUST 30, 1980 — TOP LP's

TW	LW	WK		
1	1	7	**Emotional Rescue**	*The Rolling Stones*...Rolling Stones 16015
2	2	7	Hold Out	*Jackson Browne*...Asylum 511
3	3	24	Glass Houses	*Billy Joel*...Columbia 36384
4	4	16	Urban Cowboy	*Soundtrack*...Asylum 90002
5	5	7	The Game	*Queen*...Elektra 513
6	6	12	Diana	*Diana Ross*...Motown 936
7	7	29	Christopher Cross	*Christopher Cross*...Warner 3383
8	8	13	Fame	*Soundtrack*...RSO 3080
9	9	4	Give Me The Night	*George Benson*...Warner 3453
10	10	25	Against The Wind	*Bob Seger & The Silver Bullet Band*...Capitol 12041

Billboard — SEPTEMBER 6, 1980 — TOP LP's

TW	LW	WK		
1	1	8	**Emotional Rescue**	*The Rolling Stones*...Rolling Stones 16015
2	2	8	Hold Out	*Jackson Browne*...Asylum 511
3	4	17	**Urban Cowboy**	*Soundtrack*...Asylum 90002
4	5	8	The Game	*Queen*...Elektra 513
5	6	13	Diana	*Diana Ross*...Motown 936
6	7	30	**Christopher Cross**	*Christopher Cross*...Warner 3383
7	8	14	**Fame**	*Soundtrack*...RSO 3080
8	9	5	Give Me The Night	*George Benson*...Warner 3453
9	3	25	Glass Houses	*Billy Joel*...Columbia 36384
10	10	26	Against The Wind	*Bob Seger & The Silver Bullet Band*...Capitol 12041

TW	LW	WK	Billboard. SEPTEMBER 13, 1980 TOP LP's
1	2	9	**Hold Out** ... *Jackson Browne*...Asylum 511
2	1	9	Emotional Rescue ... *The Rolling Stones*...Rolling Stones 16015
3	3	18	**Urban Cowboy** ... *Soundtrack*...Asylum 90002
4	4	9	The Game ... *Queen*...Elektra 513
5	5	14	Diana ... *Diana Ross*...Motown 936
6	6	31	**Christopher Cross** ... *Christopher Cross*...Warner 3383
7	7	15	**Fame** ... *Soundtrack*...RSO 3080
8	8	6	Give Me The Night ... *George Benson*...Warner 3453
9	9	26	Glass Houses ... *Billy Joel*...Columbia 36384
10	12	10	Xanadu ..... *Electric Light Orchestra Olivia Newton-John/Soundtrack*...MCA 6100

TW	LW	WK	Billboard. SEPTEMBER 20, 1980 TOP LP's
1	4	10	**The Game** ... *Queen*...Elektra 513
2	1	10	Hold Out ... *Jackson Browne*...Asylum 511
3	5	15	Diana ... *Diana Ross*...Motown 936
4	2	10	Emotional Rescue ... *The Rolling Stones*...Rolling Stones 16015
5	12	3	**Panorama** ... *The Cars*...Elektra 514
6	6	32	**Christopher Cross** ... *Christopher Cross*...Warner 3383
7	8	7	Give Me The Night ... *George Benson*...Warner 3453
8	10	11	Xanadu ..... *Electric Light Orchestra Olivia Newton-John/Soundtrack*...MCA 6100
9	3	19	Urban Cowboy ... *Soundtrack*...Asylum 90002
10	16	5	Crimes Of Passion ... *Pat Benatar*...Chrysalis 1275

TW	LW	WK	Billboard. SEPTEMBER 27, 1980 TOP LP's
1	1	11	**The Game** ... *Queen*...Elektra 513
2	2	11	Hold Out ... *Jackson Browne*...Asylum 511
3	3	16	Diana ... *Diana Ross*...Motown 936
4	4	11	Emotional Rescue ... *The Rolling Stones*...Rolling Stones 16015
5	5	4	**Panorama** ... *The Cars*...Elektra 514
6	7	8	Give Me The Night ... *George Benson*...Warner 3453
7	8	12	Xanadu ..... *Electric Light Orchestra Olivia Newton-John/Soundtrack*...MCA 6100
8	9	20	Urban Cowboy ... *Soundtrack*...Asylum 90002
9	10	6	Crimes Of Passion ... *Pat Benatar*...Chrysalis 1275
10	6	33	Christopher Cross ... *Christopher Cross*...Warner 3383

TW	LW	WK	Billboard. OCTOBER 4, 1980 TOP LP's
1	1	12	**The Game** ... *Queen*...Elektra 513
2	3	17	**Diana** ... *Diana Ross*...Motown 936
3	6	9	**Give Me The Night** ... *George Benson*...Warner 3453
4	7	13	**Xanadu** ... *Electric Light Orchestra Olivia Newton-John/Soundtrack*...MCA 6100
5	5	5	**Panorama** ... *The Cars*...Elektra 514
6	4	12	Emotional Rescue ... *The Rolling Stones*...Rolling Stones 16015
7	8	21	Urban Cowboy ... *Soundtrack*...Asylum 90002
8	9	7	Crimes Of Passion ... *Pat Benatar*...Chrysalis 1275
9	2	12	Hold Out ... *Jackson Browne*...Asylum 511
10	12	7	Back In Black ... *AC/DC*...Atlantic 16018

Billboard — OCTOBER 11, 1980 — TOP LP's

TW	LW	WK			
1	1	13	**The Game**	Queen	Elektra 513
2	2	18	**Diana**	Diana Ross	Motown 936
3	3	10	**Give Me The Night**	George Benson	Warner 3453
4	4	14	**Xanadu** ... *Electric Light Orchestra*	Olivia Newton-John/Soundtrack	MCA 6100
5	5	6	**Panorama**	The Cars	Elektra 514
6	8	8	Crimes Of Passion	Pat Benatar	Chrysalis 1275
7	7	22	Urban Cowboy	Soundtrack	Asylum 90002
8	9	13	Hold Out	Jackson Browne	Asylum 511
9	6	13	Emotional Rescue	The Rolling Stones	Rolling Stones 16015
10	10	8	Back In Black	AC/DC	Atlantic 16018

Billboard — OCTOBER 18, 1980 — TOP LP's

TW	LW	WK			
1	1	14	**The Game**	Queen	Elektra 513
2	15	2	Guilty	Barbra Streisand	Columbia 36750
3	2	19	Diana	Diana Ross	Motown 936
4	4	15	**Xanadu** ... *Electric Light Orchestra*	Olivia Newton-John/Soundtrack	MCA 6100
5	16	2	One Step Closer	The Doobie Brothers	Warner 3452
6	6	9	Crimes Of Passion	Pat Benatar	Chrysalis 1275
7	3	11	Give Me The Night	George Benson	Warner 3453
8	5	7	Panorama	The Cars	Elektra 514
9	9	14	Emotional Rescue	The Rolling Stones	Rolling Stones 16015
10	10	9	Back In Black	AC/DC	Atlantic 16018

Billboard — OCTOBER 25, 1980 — TOP LP's

TW	LW	WK			
1	2	3	**Guilty**	Barbra Streisand	Columbia 36750
2	1	15	The Game	Queen	Elektra 513
3	5	3	**One Step Closer**	The Doobie Brothers	Warner 3452
4	3	20	Diana	Diana Ross	Motown 936
5	6	10	Crimes Of Passion	Pat Benatar	Chrysalis 1275
6	4	16	Xanadu ..... *Electric Light Orchestra*	Olivia Newton-John/Soundtrack	MCA 6100
7	7	12	Give Me The Night	George Benson	Warner 3453
8	8	8	Panorama	The Cars	Elektra 514
9	10	10	Back In Black	AC/DC	Atlantic 16018
10	13	3	Paris	Supertramp	A&M 6702

Billboard — NOVEMBER 1, 1980 — TOP LP's

TW	LW	WK			
1	1	4	**Guilty**	Barbra Streisand	Columbia 36750
2	2	16	The Game	Queen	Elektra 513
3	3	4	**One Step Closer**	The Doobie Brothers	Warner 3452
4	-	1	The River	Bruce Springsteen	Columbia 36854
5	5	11	Crimes Of Passion	Pat Benatar	Chrysalis 1275
6	15	3	Kenny Rogers' Greatest Hits	Kenny Rogers	Liberty 1072
7	4	21	Diana	Diana Ross	Motown 936
8	10	4	**Paris**	Supertramp	A&M 6702
9	9	11	Back In Black	AC/DC	Atlantic 16018
10	6	17	Xanadu ..... *Electric Light Orchestra*	Olivia Newton-John/Soundtrack	MCA 6100

Billboard. NOVEMBER 8, 1980 TOP LP's

TW	LW	WK			
1	4	2	**The River**	*Bruce Springsteen*	Columbia 36854
2	1	5	Guilty	*Barbra Streisand*	Columbia 36750
3	3	5	**One Step Closer**	*The Doobie Brothers*	Warner 3452
4	2	17	The Game	*Queen*	Elektra 513
5	6	4	Kenny Rogers' Greatest Hits	*Kenny Rogers*	Liberty 1072
6	5	12	Crimes Of Passion	*Pat Benatar*	Chrysalis 1275
7	7	22	Diana	*Diana Ross*	Motown 936
8	8	5	**Paris**	*Supertramp*	A&M 6702
9	9	12	Back In Black	*AC/DC*	Atlantic 16018
10	12	4	**Triumph**	*The Jacksons*	Epic 36424

Billboard. NOVEMBER 15, 1980 TOP LP's

TW	LW	WK			
1	1	3	**The River**	*Bruce Springsteen*	Columbia 36854
2	2	6	Guilty	*Barbra Streisand*	Columbia 36750
3	5	5	Kenny Rogers' Greatest Hits	*Kenny Rogers*	Liberty 1072
4	-	1	Hotter Than July	*Stevie Wonder*	Tamla 373
5	4	18	The Game	*Queen*	Elektra 513
6	6	13	Crimes Of Passion	*Pat Benatar*	Chrysalis 1275
7	3	6	One Step Closer	*The Doobie Brothers*	Warner 3452
8	7	23	Diana	*Diana Ross*	Motown 936
9	9	13	Back In Black	*AC/DC*	Atlantic 16018
10	10	5	**Triumph**	*The Jacksons*	Epic 36424

Billboard. NOVEMBER 22, 1980 TOP LP's

TW	LW	WK			
1	1	4	**The River**	*Bruce Springsteen*	Columbia 36854
2	2	7	Guilty	*Barbra Streisand*	Columbia 36750
3	3	6	Kenny Rogers' Greatest Hits	*Kenny Rogers*	Liberty 1072
4	4	2	Hotter Than July	*Stevie Wonder*	Tamla 373
5	5	19	The Game	*Queen*	Elektra 513
6	6	14	Crimes Of Passion	*Pat Benatar*	Chrysalis 1275
7	8	24	Diana	*Diana Ross*	Motown 936
8	9	14	Back In Black	*AC/DC*	Atlantic 16018
9	7	7	One Step Closer	*The Doobie Brothers*	Warner 3452
10	10	6	**Triumph**	*The Jacksons*	Epic 36424

Billboard. NOVEMBER 29, 1980 TOP LP's

TW	LW	WK			
1	1	5	**The River**	*Bruce Springsteen*	Columbia 36854
2	2	8	Guilty	*Barbra Streisand*	Columbia 36750
3	3	7	Kenny Rogers' Greatest Hits	*Kenny Rogers*	Liberty 1072
4	4	3	Hotter Than July	*Stevie Wonder*	Tamla 373
5	5	20	The Game	*Queen*	Elektra 513
6	8	15	Back In Black	*AC/DC*	Atlantic 16018
7	6	15	Crimes Of Passion	*Pat Benatar*	Chrysalis 1275
8	7	25	Diana	*Diana Ross*	Motown 936
9	9	8	One Step Closer	*The Doobie Brothers*	Warner 3452
10	10	7	**Triumph**	*The Jacksons*	Epic 36424

TW	LW	WK	Billboard — DECEMBER 6, 1980 — TOP LP's
1	2	9	**Guilty** ... *Barbra Streisand*...Columbia 36750
2	3	8	Kenny Rogers' Greatest Hits ... *Kenny Rogers*...Liberty 1072
3	4	4	**Hotter Than July** ... *Stevie Wonder*...Tamla 373
4	1	6	The River ... *Bruce Springsteen*...Columbia 36854
5	6	16	Back In Black ... *AC/DC*...Atlantic 16018
6	5	21	The Game ... *Queen*...Elektra 513
7	7	16	Crimes Of Passion ... *Pat Benatar*...Chrysalis 1275
8	14	2	Eagles Live ... *Eagles*...Asylum 705
9	11	7	Zenyatta Mondatta ... *The Police*...A&M 4831
10	12	3	**Faces** ... *Earth, Wind & Fire*...ARC 36795

TW	LW	WK	Billboard — DECEMBER 13, 1980 — TOP LP's
1	2	9	**Kenny Rogers' Greatest Hits** ... *Kenny Rogers*...Liberty 1072
2	1	10	Guilty ... *Barbra Streisand*...Columbia 36750
3	3	5	**Hotter Than July** ... *Stevie Wonder*...Tamla 373
4	4	7	The River ... *Bruce Springsteen*...Columbia 36854
5	5	17	Back In Black ... *AC/DC*...Atlantic 16018
6	7	17	Crimes Of Passion ... *Pat Benatar*...Chrysalis 1275
7	8	3	Eagles Live ... *Eagles*...Asylum 705
8	9	8	Zenyatta Mondatta ... *The Police*...A&M 4831
9	6	22	The Game ... *Queen*...Elektra 513
10	10	4	**Faces** ... *Earth, Wind & Fire*...ARC 36795

TW	LW	WK	Billboard — DECEMBER 20, 1980 — TOP LP's
1	1	10	**Kenny Rogers' Greatest Hits** ... *Kenny Rogers*...Liberty 1072
2	2	11	Guilty ... *Barbra Streisand*...Columbia 36750
3	3	6	**Hotter Than July** ... *Stevie Wonder*...Tamla 373
4	5	18	**Back In Black** ... *AC/DC*...Atlantic 16018
5	6	18	Crimes Of Passion ... *Pat Benatar*...Chrysalis 1275
6	7	4	**Eagles Live** ... *Eagles*...Asylum 705
7	4	8	The River ... *Bruce Springsteen*...Columbia 36854
8	8	9	Zenyatta Mondatta ... *The Police*...A&M 4831
9	9	23	The Game ... *Queen*...Elektra 513
10	11	4	The Jazz Singer ... *Neil Diamond/Soundtrack*...Capitol 12120

TW	LW	WK	Billboard — DECEMBER 27, 1980 — TOP LP's
1	11	4	**Double Fantasy** ... *John Lennon/Yoko Ono*...Geffen 2001
2	2	12	Guilty ... *Barbra Streisand*...Columbia 36750
3	3	7	**Hotter Than July** ... *Stevie Wonder*...Tamla 373
4	4	19	**Back In Black** ... *AC/DC*...Atlantic 16018
5	5	19	Crimes Of Passion ... *Pat Benatar*...Chrysalis 1275
6	6	5	**Eagles Live** ... *Eagles*...Asylum 705
7	1	11	Kenny Rogers' Greatest Hits ... *Kenny Rogers*...Liberty 1072
8	8	10	Zenyatta Mondatta ... *The Police*...A&M 4831
9	10	5	The Jazz Singer ... *Neil Diamond/Soundtrack*...Capitol 12120
10	12	4	Gaucho ... *Steely Dan*...MCA 6102

TW	LW	WK	Billboard — JANUARY 10, 1981 — TOP LP's
1	1	6	**Double Fantasy** ... *John Lennon/Yoko Ono*...Geffen 2001
2	2	14	Guilty ... *Barbra Streisand*...Columbia 36750
3	3	9	**Hotter Than July** ... *Stevie Wonder*...Tamla 373
4	5	21	Crimes Of Passion ... *Pat Benatar*...Chrysalis 1275
5	4	21	Back In Black ... *AC/DC*...Atlantic 16018
6	6	7	**Eagles Live** ... *Eagles*...Asylum 705
7	7	13	Kenny Rogers' Greatest Hits ... *Kenny Rogers*...Liberty 1072
8	8	12	Zenyatta Mondatta ... *The Police*...A&M 4831
9	9	7	The Jazz Singer ... *Neil Diamond/Soundtrack*...Capitol 12120
10	10	6	Gaucho ... *Steely Dan*...MCA 6102

TW	LW	WK	Billboard — JANUARY 17, 1981 — TOP LP's
1	1	7	**Double Fantasy** ... *John Lennon/Yoko Ono*...Geffen 2001
2	4	22	**Crimes Of Passion** ... *Pat Benatar*...Chrysalis 1275
3	3	10	**Hotter Than July** ... *Stevie Wonder*...Tamla 373
4	7	14	Kenny Rogers' Greatest Hits ... *Kenny Rogers*...Liberty 1072
5	2	15	Guilty ... *Barbra Streisand*...Columbia 36750
6	5	22	Back In Black ... *AC/DC*...Atlantic 16018
7	9	8	The Jazz Singer ... *Neil Diamond/Soundtrack*...Capitol 12120
8	8	13	Zenyatta Mondatta ... *The Police*...A&M 4831
9	10	7	**Gaucho** ... *Steely Dan*...MCA 6102
10	6	8	Eagles Live ... *Eagles*...Asylum 705

TW	LW	WK	Billboard — JANUARY 24, 1981 — TOP LP's
1	1	8	**Double Fantasy** ... *John Lennon/Yoko Ono*...Geffen 2001
2	2	23	**Crimes Of Passion** ... *Pat Benatar*...Chrysalis 1275
3	4	15	Kenny Rogers' Greatest Hits ... *Kenny Rogers*...Liberty 1072
4	3	11	Hotter Than July ... *Stevie Wonder*...Tamla 373
5	7	9	The Jazz Singer ... *Neil Diamond/Soundtrack*...Capitol 12120
6	6	23	Back In Black ... *AC/DC*...Atlantic 16018
7	8	14	Zenyatta Mondatta ... *The Police*...A&M 4831
8	5	16	Guilty ... *Barbra Streisand*...Columbia 36750
9	9	8	**Gaucho** ... *Steely Dan*...MCA 6102
10	11	7	Autoamerican ... *Blondie*...Chrysalis 1290

TW	LW	WK	Billboard — JANUARY 31, 1981 — TOP LP's
1	1	9	**Double Fantasy** ... *John Lennon/Yoko Ono*...Geffen 2001
2	2	24	**Crimes Of Passion** ... *Pat Benatar*...Chrysalis 1275
3	3	16	Kenny Rogers' Greatest Hits ... *Kenny Rogers*...Liberty 1072
4	4	12	Hotter Than July ... *Stevie Wonder*...Tamla 373
5	5	10	The Jazz Singer ... *Neil Diamond/Soundtrack*...Capitol 12120
6	6	24	Back In Black ... *AC/DC*...Atlantic 16018
7	7	15	Zenyatta Mondatta ... *The Police*...A&M 4831
8	8	17	Guilty ... *Barbra Streisand*...Columbia 36750
9	9	9	**Gaucho** ... *Steely Dan*...MCA 6102
10	10	8	Autoamerican ... *Blondie*...Chrysalis 1290

TW	LW	WK	Billboard® FEBRUARY 7, 1981 TOP LP's
1	1	10	**Double Fantasy**...*John Lennon/Yoko Ono*...Geffen 2001
2	2	25	**Crimes Of Passion**...*Pat Benatar*...Chrysalis 1275
3	5	11	**The Jazz Singer**...*Neil Diamond/Soundtrack*...Capitol 12120
4	3	17	Kenny Rogers' Greatest Hits...*Kenny Rogers*...Liberty 1072
5	7	16	**Zenyatta Mondatta**...*The Police*...A&M 4831
6	6	25	Back In Black...*AC/DC*...Atlantic 16018
7	12	9	Hi Infidelity...*REO Speedwagon*...Epic 36844
8	4	13	Hotter Than July...*Stevie Wonder*...Tamla 373
9	10	9	Autoamerican...*Blondie*...Chrysalis 1290
10	18	2	Paradise Theater...*Styx*...A&M 3719

TW	LW	WK	Billboard® FEBRUARY 14, 1981 TOP LP's
1	1	11	**Double Fantasy**...*John Lennon/Yoko Ono*...Geffen 2001
2	2	26	**Crimes Of Passion**...*Pat Benatar*...Chrysalis 1275
3	3	12	**The Jazz Singer**...*Neil Diamond/Soundtrack*...Capitol 12120
4	7	10	Hi Infidelity...*REO Speedwagon*...Epic 36844
5	5	17	**Zenyatta Mondatta**...*The Police*...A&M 4831
6	10	3	Paradise Theater...*Styx*...A&M 3719
7	4	18	Kenny Rogers' Greatest Hits...*Kenny Rogers*...Liberty 1072
8	9	10	Autoamerican...*Blondie*...Chrysalis 1290
9	6	26	Back In Black...*AC/DC*...Atlantic 16018
10	8	14	Hotter Than July...*Stevie Wonder*...Tamla 373

TW	LW	WK	Billboard® FEBRUARY 21, 1981 TOP LP's
1	4	11	**Hi Infidelity**...*REO Speedwagon*...Epic 36844
2	1	12	Double Fantasy...*John Lennon/Yoko Ono*...Geffen 2001
3	3	13	**The Jazz Singer**...*Neil Diamond/Soundtrack*...Capitol 12120
4	2	27	Crimes Of Passion...*Pat Benatar*...Chrysalis 1275
5	6	4	Paradise Theater...*Styx*...A&M 3719
6	5	18	Zenyatta Mondatta...*The Police*...A&M 4831
7	8	11	**Autoamerican**...*Blondie*...Chrysalis 1290
8	7	19	Kenny Rogers' Greatest Hits...*Kenny Rogers*...Liberty 1072
9	9	27	Back In Black...*AC/DC*...Atlantic 16018
10	10	15	Hotter Than July...*Stevie Wonder*...Tamla 373

TW	LW	WK	Billboard® FEBRUARY 28, 1981 TOP LP's
1	1	12	**Hi Infidelity**...*REO Speedwagon*...Epic 36844
2	2	13	Double Fantasy...*John Lennon/Yoko Ono*...Geffen 2001
3	3	14	**The Jazz Singer**...*Neil Diamond/Soundtrack*...Capitol 12120
4	5	5	Paradise Theater...*Styx*...A&M 3719
5	6	19	**Zenyatta Mondatta**...*The Police*...A&M 4831
6	4	28	Crimes Of Passion...*Pat Benatar*...Chrysalis 1275
7	7	12	**Autoamerican**...*Blondie*...Chrysalis 1290
8	8	20	Kenny Rogers' Greatest Hits...*Kenny Rogers*...Liberty 1072
9	9	28	Back In Black...*AC/DC*...Atlantic 16018
10	10	16	Hotter Than July...*Stevie Wonder*...Tamla 373

TW	LW	WK	Billboard — MARCH 7, 1981 — TOP LP's	
1	1	13	**Hi Infidelity**	*REO Speedwagon*...Epic 36844
2	2	14	Double Fantasy	*John Lennon/Yoko Ono*...Geffen 2001
3	3	15	**The Jazz Singer**	*Neil Diamond/Soundtrack*...Capitol 12120
4	4	6	Paradise Theater	*Styx*...A&M 3719
5	5	20	**Zenyatta Mondatta**	*The Police*...A&M 4831
6	6	29	Crimes Of Passion	*Pat Benatar*...Chrysalis 1275
7	7	13	**Autoamerican**	*Blondie*...Chrysalis 1290
8	8	21	Kenny Rogers' Greatest Hits	*Kenny Rogers*...Liberty 1072
9	9	29	Back In Black	*AC/DC*...Atlantic 16018
10	11	21	**Celebrate!**	*Kool & The Gang*...De-Lite 9518

TW	LW	WK	Billboard — MARCH 14, 1981 — TOP LP's	
1	1	14	**Hi Infidelity**	*REO Speedwagon*...Epic 36844
2	4	7	Paradise Theater	*Styx*...A&M 3719
3	3	16	**The Jazz Singer**	*Neil Diamond/Soundtrack*...Capitol 12120
4	2	15	Double Fantasy	*John Lennon/Yoko Ono*...Geffen 2001
5	5	21	**Zenyatta Mondatta**	*The Police*...A&M 4831
6	6	30	Crimes Of Passion	*Pat Benatar*...Chrysalis 1275
7	7	14	**Autoamerican**	*Blondie*...Chrysalis 1290
8	8	22	Kenny Rogers' Greatest Hits	*Kenny Rogers*...Liberty 1072
9	11	4	**Captured**	*Journey*...Columbia 37016
10	10	22	**Celebrate!**	*Kool & The Gang*...De-Lite 9518

TW	LW	WK	Billboard — MARCH 21, 1981 — TOP LP's	
1	1	15	**Hi Infidelity**	*REO Speedwagon*...Epic 36844
2	2	8	Paradise Theater	*Styx*...A&M 3719
3	3	17	**The Jazz Singer**	*Neil Diamond/Soundtrack*...Capitol 12120
4	4	16	Double Fantasy	*John Lennon/Yoko Ono*...Geffen 2001
5	5	22	**Zenyatta Mondatta**	*The Police*...A&M 4831
6	6	31	Crimes Of Passion	*Pat Benatar*...Chrysalis 1275
7	7	15	**Autoamerican**	*Blondie*...Chrysalis 1290
8	15	3	Moving Pictures	*Rush*...Mercury 4013
9	9	5	**Captured**	*Journey*...Columbia 37016
10	11	24	Guilty	*Barbra Streisand*...Columbia 36750

TW	LW	WK	Billboard — MARCH 28, 1981 — TOP LP's	
1	1	16	**Hi Infidelity**	*REO Speedwagon*...Epic 36844
2	2	9	Paradise Theater	*Styx*...A&M 3719
3	8	4	**Moving Pictures**	*Rush*...Mercury 4013
4	4	17	Double Fantasy	*John Lennon/Yoko Ono*...Geffen 2001
5	3	18	The Jazz Singer	*Neil Diamond/Soundtrack*...Capitol 12120
6	12	11	Arc Of A Diver	*Steve Winwood*...Island 9576
7	5	23	Zenyatta Mondatta	*The Police*...A&M 4831
8	6	32	Crimes Of Passion	*Pat Benatar*...Chrysalis 1275
9	9	6	**Captured**	*Journey*...Columbia 37016
10	10	25	Guilty	*Barbra Streisand*...Columbia 36750

TW	LW	WK	Billboard® APRIL 4, 1981 TOP LP's
1	2	10	**Paradise Theater** .... *Styx*...A&M 3719
2	1	17	Hi Infidelity........ *REO Speedwagon*...Epic 36844
3	3	5	**Moving Pictures**........ *Rush*...Mercury 4013
4	6	12	Arc Of A Diver........ *Steve Winwood*...Island 9576
5	4	18	Double Fantasy .... *John Lennon/Yoko Ono*...Geffen 2001
6	5	19	The Jazz Singer .... *Neil Diamond/Soundtrack*...Capitol 12120
7	7	24	Zenyatta Mondatta........ *The Police*...A&M 4831
8	8	33	Crimes Of Passion .... *Pat Benatar*...Chrysalis 1275
9	9	7	**Captured** .... *Journey*...Columbia 37016
10	17	3	Another Ticket........ *Eric Clapton*...RSO 3095

TW	LW	WK	Billboard® APRIL 11, 1981 TOP LP's
1	1	11	**Paradise Theater** .... *Styx*...A&M 3719
2	2	18	Hi Infidelity........ *REO Speedwagon*...Epic 36844
3	3	6	**Moving Pictures**........ *Rush*...Mercury 4013
4	4	13	Arc Of A Diver........ *Steve Winwood*...Island 9576
5	13	22	**Winelight** .... *Grover Washington, Jr.*...Elektra 305
6	5	19	Double Fantasy .... *John Lennon/Yoko Ono*...Geffen 2001
7	7	25	Zenyatta Mondatta........ *The Police*...A&M 4831
8	28	2	Face Dances........ *The Who*...Warner 3516
9	10	4	Another Ticket........ *Eric Clapton*...RSO 3095
10	6	20	The Jazz Singer .... *Neil Diamond/Soundtrack*...Capitol 12120

TW	LW	WK	Billboard® APRIL 18, 1981 TOP LP's
1	2	19	**Hi Infidelity** .... *REO Speedwagon*...Epic 36844
2	1	12	Paradise Theater .... *Styx*...A&M 3719
3	4	14	**Arc Of A Diver** .... *Steve Winwood*...Island 9576
4	3	7	Moving Pictures .... *Rush*...Mercury 4013
5	5	23	**Winelight** .... *Grover Washington, Jr.*...Elektra 305
6	8	3	Face Dances........ *The Who*...Warner 3516
7	7	26	Zenyatta Mondatta........ *The Police*...A&M 4831
8	9	5	Another Ticket........ *Eric Clapton*...RSO 3095
9	6	20	Double Fantasy .... *John Lennon/Yoko Ono*...Geffen 2001
10	10	21	The Jazz Singer .... *Neil Diamond/Soundtrack*...Capitol 12120

TW	LW	WK	Billboard® APRIL 25, 1981 TOP LP's
1	1	20	**Hi Infidelity** .... *REO Speedwagon*...Epic 36844
2	2	13	Paradise Theater .... *Styx*...A&M 3719
3	3	15	**Arc Of A Diver** .... *Steve Winwood*...Island 9576
4	6	4	**Face Dances** .... *The Who*...Warner 3516
5	5	24	**Winelight** .... *Grover Washington, Jr.*...Elektra 305
6	4	8	Moving Pictures .... *Rush*...Mercury 4013
7	8	6	**Another Ticket**........ *Eric Clapton*...RSO 3095
8	7	27	Zenyatta Mondatta........ *The Police*...A&M 4831
9	9	21	Double Fantasy .... *John Lennon/Yoko Ono*...Geffen 2001
10	10	22	The Jazz Singer .... *Neil Diamond/Soundtrack*...Capitol 12120

TW	LW	WK	Billboard. MAY 2, 1981	TOP LP's
1	1	21	**Hi Infidelity**	*REO Speedwagon*...Epic 36844
2	2	14	Paradise Theater	*Styx*...A&M 3719
3	3	16	**Arc Of A Diver**	*Steve Winwood*...Island 9576
4	4	5	**Face Dances**	*The Who*...Warner 3516
5	5	25	**Winelight**	*Grover Washington, Jr.*...Elektra 305
6	6	9	Moving Pictures	*Rush*...Mercury 4013
7	7	7	**Another Ticket**	*Eric Clapton*...RSO 3095
8	16	3	Dirty Deeds Done Dirt Cheap	*AC/DC*...Atlantic 16033
9	9	22	Double Fantasy	*John Lennon/Yoko Ono*...Geffen 2001
10	11	7	**Dad Loves His Work**	*James Taylor*...Columbia 37009

TW	LW	WK	Billboard. MAY 9, 1981	TOP LP's
1	2	15	**Paradise Theater**	*Styx*...A&M 3719
2	1	22	Hi Infidelity	*REO Speedwagon*...Epic 36844
3	3	17	**Arc Of A Diver**	*Steve Winwood*...Island 9576
4	4	6	**Face Dances**	*The Who*...Warner 3516
5	5	26	**Winelight**	*Grover Washington, Jr.*...Elektra 305
6	8	4	Dirty Deeds Done Dirt Cheap	*AC/DC*...Atlantic 16033
7	6	10	Moving Pictures	*Rush*...Mercury 4013
8	7	8	Another Ticket	*Eric Clapton*...RSO 3095
9	9	23	Double Fantasy	*John Lennon/Yoko Ono*...Geffen 2001
10	10	8	**Dad Loves His Work**	*James Taylor*...Columbia 37009

TW	LW	WK	Billboard. MAY 16, 1981	TOP LP's
1	2	23	**Hi Infidelity**	*REO Speedwagon*...Epic 36844
2	1	16	Paradise Theater	*Styx*...A&M 3719
3	3	18	**Arc Of A Diver**	*Steve Winwood*...Island 9576
4	4	7	**Face Dances**	*The Who*...Warner 3516
5	5	27	**Winelight**	*Grover Washington, Jr.*...Elektra 305
6	6	5	Dirty Deeds Done Dirt Cheap	*AC/DC*...Atlantic 16033
7	7	11	Moving Pictures	*Rush*...Mercury 4013
8	8	9	Another Ticket	*Eric Clapton*...RSO 3095
9	9	24	Double Fantasy	*John Lennon/Yoko Ono*...Geffen 2001
10	10	9	**Dad Loves His Work**	*James Taylor*...Columbia 37009

TW	LW	WK	Billboard. MAY 23, 1981	TOP LP's
1	1	24	**Hi Infidelity**	*REO Speedwagon*...Epic 36844
2	2	17	Paradise Theater	*Styx*...A&M 3719
3	3	19	**Arc Of A Diver**	*Steve Winwood*...Island 9576
4	6	6	Dirty Deeds Done Dirt Cheap	*AC/DC*...Atlantic 16033
5	5	28	**Winelight**	*Grover Washington, Jr.*...Elektra 305
6	7	12	Moving Pictures	*Rush*...Mercury 4013
7	4	8	Face Dances	*The Who*...Warner 3516
8	8	10	Another Ticket	*Eric Clapton*...RSO 3095
9	9	25	Double Fantasy	*John Lennon/Yoko Ono*...Geffen 2001
10	11	11	Face Value	*Phil Collins*...Atlantic 16029

TW	LW	WK	Billboard — MAY 30, 1981 — TOP LP's
1	1	25	**Hi Infidelity** ... *REO Speedwagon*...Epic 36844
2	2	18	Paradise Theater ... *Styx*...A&M 3719
3	4	7	**Dirty Deeds Done Dirt Cheap** ... *AC/DC*...Atlantic 16033
4	3	20	Arc Of A Diver ... *Steve Winwood*...Island 9576
5	6	13	Moving Pictures ... *Rush*...Mercury 4013
6	5	29	Winelight ... *Grover Washington, Jr.*...Elektra 305
7	11	5	Mistaken Identity ... *Kim Carnes*...EMI America 17052
8	7	9	Face Dances ... *The Who*...Warner 3516
9	10	12	Face Value ... *Phil Collins*...Atlantic 16029
10	23	2	Hard Promises ... *Tom Petty & The Heartbreakers*...Backstreet 5160

TW	LW	WK	Billboard — JUNE 6, 1981 — TOP LP's
1	1	26	**Hi Infidelity** ... *REO Speedwagon*...Epic 36844
2	2	19	Paradise Theater ... *Styx*...A&M 3719
3	3	8	**Dirty Deeds Done Dirt Cheap** ... *AC/DC*...Atlantic 16033
4	7	6	Mistaken Identity ... *Kim Carnes*...EMI America 17052
5	4	21	Arc Of A Diver ... *Steve Winwood*...Island 9576
6	26	2	Fair Warning ... *Van Halen*...Warner 3540
7	10	3	Hard Promises ... *Tom Petty & The Heartbreakers*...Backstreet 5160
8	5	14	Moving Pictures ... *Rush*...Mercury 4013
9	9	13	Face Value ... *Phil Collins*...Atlantic 16029
10	11	13	**Being With You** ... *Smokey Robinson*...Tamla 375

TW	LW	WK	Billboard — JUNE 13, 1981 — TOP LP's
1	1	27	**Hi Infidelity** ... *REO Speedwagon*...Epic 36844
2	4	7	Mistaken Identity ... *Kim Carnes*...EMI America 17052
3	3	9	**Dirty Deeds Done Dirt Cheap** ... *AC/DC*...Atlantic 16033
4	2	20	Paradise Theater ... *Styx*...A&M 3719
5	6	3	**Fair Warning** ... *Van Halen*...Warner 3540
6	7	4	Hard Promises ... *Tom Petty & The Heartbreakers*...Backstreet 5160
7	5	22	Arc Of A Diver ... *Steve Winwood*...Island 9576
8	9	14	Face Value ... *Phil Collins*...Atlantic 16029
9	11	9	**Zebop!** ... *Santana*...Columbia 37158
10	10	14	**Being With You** ... *Smokey Robinson*...Tamla 375

TW	LW	WK	Billboard — JUNE 20, 1981 — TOP LP's
1	1	28	**Hi Infidelity** ... *REO Speedwagon*...Epic 36844
2	2	8	Mistaken Identity ... *Kim Carnes*...EMI America 17052
3	3	10	**Dirty Deeds Done Dirt Cheap** ... *AC/DC*...Atlantic 16033
4	4	21	Paradise Theater ... *Styx*...A&M 3719
5	5	4	**Fair Warning** ... *Van Halen*...Warner 3540
6	6	5	Hard Promises ... *Tom Petty & The Heartbreakers*...Backstreet 5160
7	7	23	Arc Of A Diver ... *Steve Winwood*...Island 9576
8	8	15	Face Value ... *Phil Collins*...Atlantic 16029
9	9	10	**Zebop!** ... *Santana*...Columbia 37158
10	11	16	Moving Pictures ... *Rush*...Mercury 4013

TW	LW	WK	Billboard — JUNE 27, 1981 — TOP LP's	Artist	Label
1	2	9	**Mistaken Identity**	*Kim Carnes*	EMI America 17052
2	1	29	Hi Infidelity	*REO Speedwagon*	Epic 36844
3	3	11	**Dirty Deeds Done Dirt Cheap**	*AC/DC*	Atlantic 16033
4	4	22	Paradise Theater	*Styx*	A&M 3719
5	5	5	**Fair Warning**	*Van Halen*	Warner 3540
6	6	6	Hard Promises	*Tom Petty & The Heartbreakers*	Backstreet 5160
7	16	3	Long Distance Voyager	*The Moody Blues*	Threshold 2901
8	8	16	Face Value	*Phil Collins*	Atlantic 16029
9	9	11	**Zebop!**	*Santana*	Columbia 37158
10	10	17	Moving Pictures	*Rush*	Mercury 4013

TW	LW	WK	Billboard — JULY 4, 1981 — TOP LP's	Artist	Label
1	1	10	**Mistaken Identity**	*Kim Carnes*	EMI America 17052
2	2	30	Hi Infidelity	*REO Speedwagon*	Epic 36844
3	3	12	**Dirty Deeds Done Dirt Cheap**	*AC/DC*	Atlantic 16033
4	4	23	Paradise Theater	*Styx*	A&M 3719
5	7	4	Long Distance Voyager	*The Moody Blues*	Threshold 2901
6	6	7	Hard Promises	*Tom Petty & The Heartbreakers*	Backstreet 5160
7	8	17	**Face Value**	*Phil Collins*	Atlantic 16029
8	5	6	Fair Warning	*Van Halen*	Warner 3540
9	9	12	**Zebop!**	*Santana*	Columbia 37158
10	14	9	Stars On Long Play	*Stars On*	Radio 16044

TW	LW	WK	Billboard — JULY 11, 1981 — TOP LP's	Artist	Label
1	1	11	**Mistaken Identity**	*Kim Carnes*	EMI America 17052
2	2	31	Hi Infidelity	*REO Speedwagon*	Epic 36844
3	5	5	Long Distance Voyager	*The Moody Blues*	Threshold 2901
4	4	24	Paradise Theater	*Styx*	A&M 3719
5	3	13	Dirty Deeds Done Dirt Cheap	*AC/DC*	Atlantic 16033
6	6	8	Hard Promises	*Tom Petty & The Heartbreakers*	Backstreet 5160
7	7	18	**Face Value**	*Phil Collins*	Atlantic 16029
8	11	11	Street Songs	*Rick James*	Gordy 1002
9	10	10	**Stars On Long Play**	*Stars On*	Radio 16044
10	9	13	Zebop!	*Santana*	Columbia 37158

TW	LW	WK	Billboard — JULY 18, 1981 — TOP LP's	Artist	Label
1	1	12	**Mistaken Identity**	*Kim Carnes*	EMI America 17052
2	3	6	Long Distance Voyager	*The Moody Blues*	Threshold 2901
3	2	32	Hi Infidelity	*REO Speedwagon*	Epic 36844
4	4	25	Paradise Theater	*Styx*	A&M 3719
5	8	12	Street Songs	*Rick James*	Gordy 1002
6	6	9	Hard Promises	*Tom Petty & The Heartbreakers*	Backstreet 5160
7	7	19	**Face Value**	*Phil Collins*	Atlantic 16029
8	5	14	Dirty Deeds Done Dirt Cheap	*AC/DC*	Atlantic 16033
9	9	11	**Stars On Long Play**	*Stars On*	Radio 16044
10	10	14	Zebop!	*Santana*	Columbia 37158

TW	LW	WK	Billboard® JULY 25, 1981 TOP LP's
1	2	7	**Long Distance Voyager** .... *The Moody Blues*...Threshold 2901
2	1	13	Mistaken Identity .... *Kim Carnes*...EMI America 17052
3	3	33	Hi Infidelity .... *REO Speedwagon*...Epic 36844
4	5	13	Street Songs .... *Rick James*...Gordy 1002
5	6	10	**Hard Promises** .... *Tom Petty & The Heartbreakers*...Backstreet 5160
6	4	26	Paradise Theater .... *Styx*...A&M 3719
7	7	20	**Face Value** .... *Phil Collins*...Atlantic 16029
8	14	3	Share Your Love .... *Kenny Rogers*...Liberty 1108
9	9	12	**Stars On Long Play** .... *Stars On*...Radio 16044
10	10	15	Zebop! .... *Santana*...Columbia 37158

TW	LW	WK	Billboard® AUGUST 1, 1981 TOP LP's
1	1	8	**Long Distance Voyager** .... *The Moody Blues*...Threshold 2901
2	3	34	Hi Infidelity .... *REO Speedwagon*...Epic 36844
3	4	14	**Street Songs** .... *Rick James*...Gordy 1002
4	2	14	Mistaken Identity .... *Kim Carnes*...EMI America 17052
5	5	11	**Hard Promises** .... *Tom Petty & The Heartbreakers*...Backstreet 5160
6	19	2	Precious Time .... *Pat Benatar*...Chrysalis 1346
7	8	4	Share Your Love .... *Kenny Rogers*...Liberty 1108
8	6	27	Paradise Theater .... *Styx*...A&M 3719
9	9	13	**Stars On Long Play** .... *Stars On*...Radio 16044
10	11	8	**The One That You Love** .... *Air Supply*...Arista 9551

TW	LW	WK	Billboard® AUGUST 8, 1981 TOP LP's
1	1	9	**Long Distance Voyager** .... *The Moody Blues*...Threshold 2901
2	6	3	Precious Time .... *Pat Benatar*...Chrysalis 1346
3	3	15	**Street Songs** .... *Rick James*...Gordy 1002
4	13	3	4 .... *Foreigner*...Atlantic 16999
5	4	15	Mistaken Identity .... *Kim Carnes*...EMI America 17052
6	5	12	Hard Promises .... *Tom Petty & The Heartbreakers*...Backstreet 5160
7	7	5	Share Your Love .... *Kenny Rogers*...Liberty 1108
8	2	35	Hi Infidelity .... *REO Speedwagon*...Epic 36844
9	8	28	Paradise Theater .... *Styx*...A&M 3719
10	10	9	**The One That You Love** .... *Air Supply*...Arista 9551

TW	LW	WK	Billboard® AUGUST 15, 1981 TOP LP's
1	2	4	**Precious Time** .... *Pat Benatar*...Chrysalis 1346
2	4	4	4 .... *Foreigner*...Atlantic 16999
3	1	10	Long Distance Voyager .... *The Moody Blues*...Threshold 2901
4	3	16	Street Songs .... *Rick James*...Gordy 1002
5	13	2	Escape .... *Journey*...Columbia 37408
6	7	6	**Share Your Love** .... *Kenny Rogers*...Liberty 1108
7	5	16	Mistaken Identity .... *Kim Carnes*...EMI America 17052
8	8	36	Hi Infidelity .... *REO Speedwagon*...Epic 36844
9	11	16	Don't Say No .... *Billy Squier*...Capitol 12146
10	10	10	**The One That You Love** .... *Air Supply*...Arista 9551

Billboard — AUGUST 22, 1981 — TOP LP's

TW	LW	WK	Title	Artist	Label
1	2	5	4	*Foreigner*	Atlantic 16999
2	1	5	Precious Time	*Pat Benatar*	Chrysalis 1346
3	12	2	Bella Donna	*Stevie Nicks*	Modern 139
4	5	3	Escape	*Journey*	Columbia 37408
5	3	11	Long Distance Voyager	*The Moody Blues*	Threshold 2901
6	6	7	**Share Your Love**	*Kenny Rogers*	Liberty 1108
7	9	17	Don't Say No	*Billy Squier*	Capitol 12146
8	4	17	Street Songs	*Rick James*	Gordy 1002
9	11	24	Working Class Dog	*Rick Springfield*	RCA 3697
10	10	11	**The One That You Love**	*Air Supply*	Arista 9551

Billboard — AUGUST 29, 1981 — TOP LP's

TW	LW	WK	Title	Artist	Label
1	1	6	4	*Foreigner*	Atlantic 16999
2	3	3	Bella Donna	*Stevie Nicks*	Modern 139
3	4	4	Escape	*Journey*	Columbia 37408
4	2	6	Precious Time	*Pat Benatar*	Chrysalis 1346
5	5	12	Long Distance Voyager	*The Moody Blues*	Threshold 2901
6	7	18	Don't Say No	*Billy Squier*	Capitol 12146
7	12	4	Pirates	*Rickie Lee Jones*	Warner 3432
8	9	25	Working Class Dog	*Rick Springfield*	RCA 3697
9	8	18	Street Songs	*Rick James*	Gordy 1002
10	11	38	Hi Infidelity	*REO Speedwagon*	Epic 36844

Billboard — SEPTEMBER 5, 1981 — TOP LP's

TW	LW	WK	Title	Artist	Label
1	2	4	**Bella Donna**	*Stevie Nicks*	Modern 139
2	1	7	4	*Foreigner*	Atlantic 16999
3	3	5	Escape	*Journey*	Columbia 37408
4	4	7	Precious Time	*Pat Benatar*	Chrysalis 1346
5	6	19	**Don't Say No**	*Billy Squier*	Capitol 12146
6	7	5	Pirates	*Rickie Lee Jones*	Warner 3432
7	8	26	**Working Class Dog**	*Rick Springfield*	RCA 3697
8	9	19	Street Songs	*Rick James*	Gordy 1002
9	5	13	Long Distance Voyager	*The Moody Blues*	Threshold 2901
10	10	39	Hi Infidelity	*REO Speedwagon*	Epic 36844

Billboard — SEPTEMBER 12, 1981 — TOP LP's

TW	LW	WK	Title	Artist	Label
1	3	6	**Escape**	*Journey*	Columbia 37408
2	1	5	Bella Donna	*Stevie Nicks*	Modern 139
3	2	8	4	*Foreigner*	Atlantic 16999
4	4	8	Precious Time	*Pat Benatar*	Chrysalis 1346
5	5	20	**Don't Say No**	*Billy Squier*	Capitol 12146
6	6	6	Pirates	*Rickie Lee Jones*	Warner 3432
7	7	27	**Working Class Dog**	*Rick Springfield*	RCA 3697
8	-	1	Tattoo You	*The Rolling Stones*	Rolling Stones 16052
9	8	20	Street Songs	*Rick James*	Gordy 1002
10	11	3	**Pretenders II**	*Pretenders*	Sire 3572

Billboard — SEPTEMBER 19, 1981 — TOP LP's

TW	LW	WK	Title	Artist	Label
1	8	2	**Tattoo You**	*The Rolling Stones*	Rolling Stones 16052
2	2	6	Bella Donna	*Stevie Nicks*	Modern 139
3	1	7	Escape	*Journey*	Columbia 37408
4	3	9	4	*Foreigner*	Atlantic 16999
5	5	21	**Don't Say No**	*Billy Squier*	Capitol 12146
6	6	7	Pirates	*Rickie Lee Jones*	Warner 3432
7	4	9	Precious Time	*Pat Benatar*	Chrysalis 1346
8	7	28	Working Class Dog	*Rick Springfield*	RCA 3697
9	9	21	Street Songs	*Rick James*	Gordy 1002
10	10	4	**Pretenders II**	*Pretenders*	Sire 3572

Billboard — SEPTEMBER 26, 1981 — TOP LP's

TW	LW	WK	Title	Artist	Label
1	1	3	**Tattoo You**	*The Rolling Stones*	Rolling Stones 16052
2	2	7	Bella Donna	*Stevie Nicks*	Modern 139
3	3	8	Escape	*Journey*	Columbia 37408
4	4	10	4	*Foreigner*	Atlantic 16999
5	6	8	**Pirates**	*Rickie Lee Jones*	Warner 3432
6	7	10	Precious Time	*Pat Benatar*	Chrysalis 1346
7	5	22	Don't Say No	*Billy Squier*	Capitol 12146
8	9	22	Street Songs	*Rick James*	Gordy 1002
9	11	9	**Endless Love**	*Soundtrack*	Mercury 2001
10	10	5	**Pretenders II**	*Pretenders*	Sire 3572

Billboard — OCTOBER 3, 1981 — TOP LP's

TW	LW	WK	Title	Artist	Label
1	1	4	**Tattoo You**	*The Rolling Stones*	Rolling Stones 16052
2	4	11	4	*Foreigner*	Atlantic 16999
3	3	9	Escape	*Journey*	Columbia 37408
4	2	8	Bella Donna	*Stevie Nicks*	Modern 139
5	5	9	**Pirates**	*Rickie Lee Jones*	Warner 3432
6	19	2	Nine Tonight	*Bob Seger & The Silver Bullet Band*	Capitol 12182
7	20	4	The Innocent Age	*Dan Fogelberg*	Full Moon 37393
8	6	11	Precious Time	*Pat Benatar*	Chrysalis 1346
9	9	10	**Endless Love**	*Soundtrack*	Mercury 2001
10	11	7	Breakin' Away	*Al Jarreau*	Warner 3576

Billboard — OCTOBER 10, 1981 — TOP LP's

TW	LW	WK	Title	Artist	Label
1	1	5	**Tattoo You**	*The Rolling Stones*	Rolling Stones 16052
2	2	12	4	*Foreigner*	Atlantic 16999
3	4	9	Bella Donna	*Stevie Nicks*	Modern 139
4	3	10	Escape	*Journey*	Columbia 37408
5	6	3	Nine Tonight	*Bob Seger & The Silver Bullet Band*	Capitol 12182
6	7	5	**The Innocent Age**	*Dan Fogelberg*	Full Moon 37393
7	5	10	Pirates	*Rickie Lee Jones*	Warner 3432
8	8	12	Precious Time	*Pat Benatar*	Chrysalis 1346
9	10	8	**Breakin' Away**	*Al Jarreau*	Warner 3576
10	22	2	Songs In The Attic	*Billy Joel*	Columbia 37461

Billboard® OCTOBER 17, 1981 TOP LP's

TW	LW	WK	Title	Artist / Label
1	1	6	**Tattoo You**	*The Rolling Stones*...Rolling Stones 16052
2	4	11	Escape	*Journey*...Columbia 37408
3	5	4	**Nine Tonight**	*Bob Seger & The Silver Bullet Band*...Capitol 12182
4	2	13	4	*Foreigner*...Atlantic 16999
5	3	10	Bella Donna	*Stevie Nicks*...Modern 139
6	6	6	**The Innocent Age**	*Dan Fogelberg*...Full Moon 37393
7	8	13	Precious Time	*Pat Benatar*...Chrysalis 1346
8	10	3	**Songs In The Attic**	*Billy Joel*...Columbia 37461
9	9	9	**Breakin' Away**	*Al Jarreau*...Warner 3576
10	7	11	Pirates	*Rickie Lee Jones*...Warner 3432

Billboard® OCTOBER 24, 1981 TOP LP's

TW	LW	WK	Title	Artist / Label
1	1	7	**Tattoo You**	*The Rolling Stones*...Rolling Stones 16052
2	2	12	Escape	*Journey*...Columbia 37408
3	3	5	**Nine Tonight**	*Bob Seger & The Silver Bullet Band*...Capitol 12182
4	4	14	4	*Foreigner*...Atlantic 16999
5	5	11	Bella Donna	*Stevie Nicks*...Modern 139
6	6	7	**The Innocent Age**	*Dan Fogelberg*...Full Moon 37393
7	7	14	Precious Time	*Pat Benatar*...Chrysalis 1346
8	8	4	**Songs In The Attic**	*Billy Joel*...Columbia 37461
9	9	10	**Breakin' Away**	*Al Jarreau*...Warner 3576
10	11	20	Long Distance Voyager	*The Moody Blues*...Threshold 2901

Billboard® OCTOBER 31, 1981 TOP LP's

TW	LW	WK	Title	Artist / Label
1	1	8	**Tattoo You**	*The Rolling Stones*...Rolling Stones 16052
2	2	13	Escape	*Journey*...Columbia 37408
3	3	6	**Nine Tonight**	*Bob Seger & The Silver Bullet Band*...Capitol 12182
4	4	15	4	*Foreigner*...Atlantic 16999
5	5	12	Bella Donna	*Stevie Nicks*...Modern 139
6	6	8	**The Innocent Age**	*Dan Fogelberg*...Full Moon 37393
7	16	2	Ghost In The Machine	*The Police*...A&M 3730
8	8	5	**Songs In The Attic**	*Billy Joel*...Columbia 37461
9	7	15	Precious Time	*Pat Benatar*...Chrysalis 1346
10	13	6	Private Eyes	*Daryl Hall & John Oates*...RCA 4028

Billboard® NOVEMBER 7, 1981 TOP LP's

TW	LW	WK	Title	Artist / Label
1	1	9	**Tattoo You**	*The Rolling Stones*...Rolling Stones 16052
2	2	14	Escape	*Journey*...Columbia 37408
3	3	7	**Nine Tonight**	*Bob Seger & The Silver Bullet Band*...Capitol 12182
4	4	16	4	*Foreigner*...Atlantic 16999
5	7	3	Ghost In The Machine	*The Police*...A&M 3730
6	6	9	**The Innocent Age**	*Dan Fogelberg*...Full Moon 37393
7	5	13	Bella Donna	*Stevie Nicks*...Modern 139
8	11	4	Abacab	*Genesis*...Atlantic 19313
9	10	7	Private Eyes	*Daryl Hall & John Oates*...RCA 4028
10	8	6	Songs In The Attic	*Billy Joel*...Columbia 37461

TW	LW	WK	Billboard ® NOVEMBER 14, 1981 ® TOP LP's
1	1	10	**Tattoo You**............*The Rolling Stones*...Rolling Stones 16052
2	4	17	**4**............*Foreigner*...Atlantic 16999
3	2	15	**Escape**............*Journey*...Columbia 37408
4	5	4	**Ghost In The Machine**............*The Police*...A&M 3730
5	3	8	**Nine Tonight**............*Bob Seger & The Silver Bullet Band*...Capitol 12182
6	6	10	**The Innocent Age**............*Dan Fogelberg*...Full Moon 37393
7	8	5	**Abacab**............*Genesis*...Atlantic 19313
8	9	8	**Private Eyes**............*Daryl Hall & John Oates*...RCA 4028
9	7	14	**Bella Donna**............*Stevie Nicks*...Modern 139
10	-	1	**Raise!**............*Earth, Wind & Fire*...ARC 37548

TW	LW	WK	Billboard ® NOVEMBER 21, 1981 ® TOP LP's
1	2	18	**4**............*Foreigner*...Atlantic 16999
2	1	11	**Tattoo You**............*The Rolling Stones*...Rolling Stones 16052
3	4	5	**Ghost In The Machine**............*The Police*...A&M 3730
4	3	16	**Escape**............*Journey*...Columbia 37408
5	5	9	**Nine Tonight**............*Bob Seger & The Silver Bullet Band*...Capitol 12182
6	10	2	**Raise!**............*Earth, Wind & Fire*...ARC 37548
7	9	15	**Bella Donna**............*Stevie Nicks*...Modern 139
8	8	9	**Private Eyes**............*Daryl Hall & John Oates*...RCA 4028
9	7	6	**Abacab**............*Genesis*...Atlantic 19313
10	6	11	**The Innocent Age**............*Dan Fogelberg*...Full Moon 37393

TW	LW	WK	Billboard ® NOVEMBER 28, 1981 ® TOP LP's
1	1	19	**4**............*Foreigner*...Atlantic 16999
2	2	12	**Tattoo You**............*The Rolling Stones*...Rolling Stones 16052
3	3	6	**Ghost In The Machine**............*The Police*...A&M 3730
4	4	17	**Escape**............*Journey*...Columbia 37408
5	6	3	**Raise!**............*Earth, Wind & Fire*...ARC 37548
6	5	10	**Nine Tonight**............*Bob Seger & The Silver Bullet Band*...Capitol 12182
7	7	16	**Bella Donna**............*Stevie Nicks*...Modern 139
8	8	10	**Private Eyes**............*Daryl Hall & John Oates*...RCA 4028
9	9	7	**Abacab**............*Genesis*...Atlantic 19313
10	12	5	**Physical**............*Olivia Newton-John*...MCA 5229

TW	LW	WK	Billboard ® DECEMBER 5, 1981 ® TOP LP's
1	1	20	**4**............*Foreigner*...Atlantic 16999
2	3	7	**Ghost In The Machine**............*The Police*...A&M 3730
3	2	13	**Tattoo You**............*The Rolling Stones*...Rolling Stones 16052
4	4	18	**Escape**............*Journey*...Columbia 37408
5	5	4	**Raise!**............*Earth, Wind & Fire*...ARC 37548
6	6	11	**Nine Tonight**............*Bob Seger & The Silver Bullet Band*...Capitol 12182
7	7	17	**Bella Donna**............*Stevie Nicks*...Modern 139
8	10	6	**Physical**............*Olivia Newton-John*...MCA 5229
9	9	8	**Abacab**............*Genesis*...Atlantic 19313
10	11	4	**Exit...Stage Left**............*Rush*...Mercury 7001

Billboard — DECEMBER 12, 1981 — TOP LP's

TW	LW	WK	Album	Artist...Label
1	1	21	**4**	*Foreigner*...Atlantic 16999
2	2	8	**Ghost In The Machine**	*The Police*...A&M 3730
3	3	14	Tattoo You	*The Rolling Stones*...Rolling Stones 16052
4	4	19	Escape	*Journey*...Columbia 37408
5	5	5	**Raise!**	*Earth, Wind & Fire*...ARC 37548
6	8	7	**Physical**	*Olivia Newton-John*...MCA 5229
7	7	18	Bella Donna	*Stevie Nicks*...Modern 139
8	-	1	For Those About To Rock We Salute You	*AC/DC*...Atlantic 11111
9	9	9	Abacab	*Genesis*...Atlantic 19313
10	10	5	**Exit...Stage Left**	*Rush*...Mercury 7001

Billboard — DECEMBER 19, 1981 — TOP LP's

TW	LW	WK	Album	Artist...Label
1	1	22	**4**	*Foreigner*...Atlantic 16999
2	2	9	**Ghost In The Machine**	*The Police*...A&M 3730
3	8	2	For Those About To Rock We Salute You	*AC/DC*...Atlantic 11111
4	4	20	Escape	*Journey*...Columbia 37408
5	5	6	**Raise!**	*Earth, Wind & Fire*...ARC 37548
6	6	8	**Physical**	*Olivia Newton-John*...MCA 5229
7	7	19	Bella Donna	*Stevie Nicks*...Modern 139
8	3	15	Tattoo You	*The Rolling Stones*...Rolling Stones 16052
9	11	4	**Shake It Up**	*The Cars*...Elektra 567
10	10	6	**Exit...Stage Left**	*Rush*...Mercury 7001

Billboard — DECEMBER 26, 1981 — TOP LP's

TW	LW	WK	Album	Artist...Label
1	3	3	**For Those About To Rock We Salute You**	*AC/DC*...Atlantic 11111
2	2	10	**Ghost In The Machine**	*The Police*...A&M 3730
3	1	23	**4**	*Foreigner*...Atlantic 16999
4	4	21	Escape	*Journey*...Columbia 37408
5	5	7	**Raise!**	*Earth, Wind & Fire*...ARC 37548
6	6	9	**Physical**	*Olivia Newton-John*...MCA 5229
7	7	20	Bella Donna	*Stevie Nicks*...Modern 139
8	8	16	Tattoo You	*The Rolling Stones*...Rolling Stones 16052
9	9	5	**Shake It Up**	*The Cars*...Elektra 567
10	12	3	**Memories**	*Barbra Streisand*...Columbia 37678

Billboard — JANUARY 9, 1982 — TOP LP's

TW	LW	WK	Title	Artist...Label
1	1	5	**For Those About To Rock We Salute You**	*AC/DC*...Atlantic 11111
2	2	12	**Ghost In The Machine**	*The Police*...A&M 3730
3	3	25	4	*Foreigner*...Atlantic 16999
4	4	23	Escape	*Journey*...Columbia 37408
5	5	9	**Raise!**	*Earth, Wind & Fire*...ARC 37548
6	6	11	**Physical**	*Olivia Newton-John*...MCA 5229
7	7	22	Bella Donna	*Stevie Nicks*...Modern 139
8	8	18	Tattoo You	*The Rolling Stones*...Rolling Stones 16052
9	9	7	**Shake It Up**	*The Cars*...Elektra 567
10	10	5	**Memories**	*Barbra Streisand*...Columbia 37678

Billboard — JANUARY 16, 1982 — TOP LP's

TW	LW	WK	Title	Artist...Label
1	3	26	4	*Foreigner*...Atlantic 16999
2	4	24	Escape	*Journey*...Columbia 37408
3	1	6	For Those About To Rock We Salute You	*AC/DC*...Atlantic 11111
4	13	10	**Hooked On Classics**	*The Royal Philharmonic Orchestra*...RCA 4194
5	5	10	**Raise!**	*Earth, Wind & Fire*...ARC 37548
6	8	19	Tattoo You	*The Rolling Stones*...Rolling Stones 16052
7	7	23	Bella Donna	*Stevie Nicks*...Modern 139
8	12	10	Freeze-Frame	*The J. Geils Band*...EMI America 17062
9	2	13	Ghost In The Machine	*The Police*...A&M 3730
10	10	6	**Memories**	*Barbra Streisand*...Columbia 37678

Billboard — JANUARY 23, 1982 — TOP LP's

TW	LW	WK	Title	Artist...Label
1	1	27	4	*Foreigner*...Atlantic 16999
2	2	25	Escape	*Journey*...Columbia 37408
3	3	7	For Those About To Rock We Salute You	*AC/DC*...Atlantic 11111
4	4	11	**Hooked On Classics**	*The Royal Philharmonic Orchestra*...RCA 4194
5	6	20	Tattoo You	*The Rolling Stones*...Rolling Stones 16052
6	7	24	Bella Donna	*Stevie Nicks*...Modern 139
7	8	11	Freeze-Frame	*The J. Geils Band*...EMI America 17062
8	14	18	Private Eyes	*Daryl Hall & John Oates*...RCA 4028
9	9	14	Ghost In The Machine	*The Police*...A&M 3730
10	10	7	**Memories**	*Barbra Streisand*...Columbia 37678

Billboard — JANUARY 30, 1982 — TOP LP's

TW	LW	WK	Title	Artist...Label
1	1	28	4	*Foreigner*...Atlantic 16999
2	2	26	Escape	*Journey*...Columbia 37408
3	7	12	Freeze-Frame	*The J. Geils Band*...EMI America 17062
4	4	12	**Hooked On Classics**	*The Royal Philharmonic Orchestra*...RCA 4194
5	5	21	Tattoo You	*The Rolling Stones*...Rolling Stones 16052
6	6	25	Bella Donna	*Stevie Nicks*...Modern 139
7	3	8	For Those About To Rock We Salute You	*AC/DC*...Atlantic 11111
8	8	19	Private Eyes	*Daryl Hall & John Oates*...RCA 4028
9	9	15	Ghost In The Machine	*The Police*...A&M 3730
10	10	8	**Memories**	*Barbra Streisand*...Columbia 37678

Billboard — FEBRUARY 6, 1982 — TOP LP's

TW	LW	WK	Title	Artist	Label
1	3	13	**Freeze-Frame**	*The J. Geils Band*	EMI America 17062
2	2	27	Escape	*Journey*	Columbia 37408
3	1	29	4	*Foreigner*	Atlantic 16999
4	4	13	**Hooked On Classics**	*The Royal Philharmonic Orchestra*	RCA 4194
5	5	22	Tattoo You	*The Rolling Stones*	Rolling Stones 16052
6	6	26	Bella Donna	*Stevie Nicks*	Modern 139
7	7	9	For Those About To Rock We Salute You	*AC/DC*	Atlantic 11111
8	8	20	Private Eyes	*Daryl Hall & John Oates*	RCA 4028
9	9	16	Ghost In The Machine	*The Police*	A&M 3730
10	11	11	Shake It Up	*The Cars*	Elektra 567

Billboard — FEBRUARY 13, 1982 — TOP LP's

TW	LW	WK	Title	Artist	Label
1	1	14	**Freeze-Frame**	*The J. Geils Band*	EMI America 17062
2	2	28	Escape	*Journey*	Columbia 37408
3	3	30	4	*Foreigner*	Atlantic 16999
4	4	14	**Hooked On Classics**	*The Royal Philharmonic Orchestra*	RCA 4194
5	8	21	**Private Eyes**	*Daryl Hall & John Oates*	RCA 4028
6	6	27	Bella Donna	*Stevie Nicks*	Modern 139
7	7	10	For Those About To Rock We Salute You	*AC/DC*	Atlantic 11111
8	9	17	Ghost In The Machine	*The Police*	A&M 3730
9	11	29	Beauty And The Beat	*Go-Go's*	I.R.S. 70021
10	10	12	Shake It Up	*The Cars*	Elektra 567

Billboard — FEBRUARY 20, 1982 — TOP LP's

TW	LW	WK	Title	Artist	Label
1	1	15	**Freeze-Frame**	*The J. Geils Band*	EMI America 17062
2	2	29	Escape	*Journey*	Columbia 37408
3	9	30	Beauty And The Beat	*Go-Go's*	I.R.S. 70021
4	4	15	**Hooked On Classics**	*The Royal Philharmonic Orchestra*	RCA 4194
5	5	22	**Private Eyes**	*Daryl Hall & John Oates*	RCA 4028
6	8	18	Ghost In The Machine	*The Police*	A&M 3730
7	7	11	For Those About To Rock We Salute You	*AC/DC*	Atlantic 11111
8	3	31	4	*Foreigner*	Atlantic 16999
9	11	17	Quarterflash	*Quarterflash*	Geffen 2003
10	10	13	Shake It Up	*The Cars*	Elektra 567

Billboard — FEBRUARY 27, 1982 — TOP LP's

TW	LW	WK	Title	Artist	Label
1	1	16	**Freeze-Frame**	*The J. Geils Band*	EMI America 17062
2	2	30	Escape	*Journey*	Columbia 37408
3	3	31	Beauty And The Beat	*Go-Go's*	I.R.S. 70021
4	8	32	4	*Foreigner*	Atlantic 16999
5	5	23	**Private Eyes**	*Daryl Hall & John Oates*	RCA 4028
6	6	19	Ghost In The Machine	*The Police*	A&M 3730
7	4	16	Hooked On Classics	*The Royal Philharmonic Orchestra*	RCA 4194
8	9	18	**Quarterflash**	*Quarterflash*	Geffen 2003
9	11	11	I Love Rock-n-Roll	*Joan Jett & The Blackhearts*	Boardwalk 33243
10	7	12	For Those About To Rock We Salute You	*AC/DC*	Atlantic 11111

Billboard. MARCH 6, 1982 — TOP LP's

TW	LW	WK	Title	Artist...Label
1	3	32	**Beauty And The Beat**	*Go-Go's*...I.R.S. 70021
2	2	31	Escape	*Journey*...Columbia 37408
3	1	17	Freeze-Frame	*The J. Geils Band*...EMI America 17062
4	4	33	4	*Foreigner*...Atlantic 16999
5	9	12	I Love Rock-n-Roll	*Joan Jett & The Blackhearts*...Boardwalk 33243
6	6	20	Ghost In The Machine	*The Police*...A&M 3730
7	7	17	Hooked On Classics	*The Royal Philharmonic Orchestra*...RCA 4194
8	8	19	**Quarterflash**	*Quarterflash*...Geffen 2003
9	5	24	Private Eyes	*Daryl Hall & John Oates*...RCA 4028
10	14	19	Physical	*Olivia Newton-John*...MCA 5229

Billboard. MARCH 13, 1982 — TOP LP's

TW	LW	WK	Title	Artist...Label
1	1	33	**Beauty And The Beat**	*Go-Go's*...I.R.S. 70021
2	3	18	Freeze-Frame	*The J. Geils Band*...EMI America 17062
3	5	13	I Love Rock-n-Roll	*Joan Jett & The Blackhearts*...Boardwalk 33243
4	4	34	4	*Foreigner*...Atlantic 16999
5	2	32	Escape	*Journey*...Columbia 37408
6	6	21	Ghost In The Machine	*The Police*...A&M 3730
7	7	18	Hooked On Classics	*The Royal Philharmonic Orchestra*...RCA 4194
8	8	20	**Quarterflash**	*Quarterflash*...Geffen 2003
9	9	25	Private Eyes	*Daryl Hall & John Oates*...RCA 4028
10	10	20	Physical	*Olivia Newton-John*...MCA 5229

Billboard. MARCH 20, 1982 — TOP LP's

TW	LW	WK	Title	Artist...Label
1	1	34	**Beauty And The Beat**	*Go-Go's*...I.R.S. 70021
2	2	19	Freeze-Frame	*The J. Geils Band*...EMI America 17062
3	3	14	I Love Rock-n-Roll	*Joan Jett & The Blackhearts*...Boardwalk 33243
4	4	35	4	*Foreigner*...Atlantic 16999
5	5	33	Escape	*Journey*...Columbia 37408
6	13	23	Chariots Of Fire	*Vangelis/Soundtrack*...Polydor 6335
7	6	22	Ghost In The Machine	*The Police*...A&M 3730
8	10	21	Physical	*Olivia Newton-John*...MCA 5229
9	11	11	Great White North	*Bob & Doug McKenzie*...Mercury 4034
10	12	19	Get Lucky	*Loverboy*...Columbia 37638

Billboard. MARCH 27, 1982 — TOP LP's

TW	LW	WK	Title	Artist...Label
1	1	35	**Beauty And The Beat**	*Go-Go's*...I.R.S. 70021
2	2	20	Freeze-Frame	*The J. Geils Band*...EMI America 17062
3	3	15	I Love Rock-n-Roll	*Joan Jett & The Blackhearts*...Boardwalk 33243
4	6	24	Chariots Of Fire	*Vangelis/Soundtrack*...Polydor 6335
5	5	34	Escape	*Journey*...Columbia 37408
6	7	23	Ghost In The Machine	*The Police*...A&M 3730
7	8	22	Physical	*Olivia Newton-John*...MCA 5229
8	4	36	4	*Foreigner*...Atlantic 16999
9	9	12	Great White North	*Bob & Doug McKenzie*...Mercury 4034
10	10	20	Get Lucky	*Loverboy*...Columbia 37638

TW	LW	WK	Billboard — APRIL 3, 1982 — TOP LP's		
1	1	36	**Beauty And The Beat**	*Go-Go's*	I.R.S. 70021
2	2	21	Freeze-Frame	*The J. Geils Band*	EMI America 17062
3	3	16	I Love Rock-n-Roll	*Joan Jett & The Blackhearts*	Boardwalk 33243
4	4	25	Chariots Of Fire	*Vangelis/Soundtrack*	Polydor 6335
5	5	35	Escape	*Journey*	Columbia 37408
6	7	23	**Physical**	*Olivia Newton-John*	MCA 5229
7	11	4	The Concert In Central Park	*Simon & Garfunkel*	Warner 3654
8	9	13	**Great White North**	*Bob & Doug McKenzie*	Mercury 4034
9	10	21	Get Lucky	*Loverboy*	Columbia 37638
10	6	24	Ghost In The Machine	*The Police*	A&M 3730

TW	LW	WK	Billboard — APRIL 10, 1982 — TOP LP's		
1	1	37	**Beauty And The Beat**	*Go-Go's*	I.R.S. 70021
2	3	17	**I Love Rock-n-Roll**	*Joan Jett & The Blackhearts*	Boardwalk 33243
3	4	26	Chariots Of Fire	*Vangelis/Soundtrack*	Polydor 6335
4	2	22	Freeze-Frame	*The J. Geils Band*	EMI America 17062
5	19	3	Success Hasn't Spoiled Me Yet	*Rick Springfield*	RCA 4125
6	6	24	**Physical**	*Olivia Newton-John*	MCA 5229
7	7	5	The Concert In Central Park	*Simon & Garfunkel*	Warner 3654
8	8	14	**Great White North**	*Bob & Doug McKenzie*	Mercury 4034
9	9	22	Get Lucky	*Loverboy*	Columbia 37638
10	28	2	Asia	*Asia*	Geffen 2008

TW	LW	WK	Billboard — APRIL 17, 1982 — TOP LP's		
1	3	27	**Chariots Of Fire**	*Vangelis/Soundtrack*	Polydor 6335
2	2	18	**I Love Rock-n-Roll**	*Joan Jett & The Blackhearts*	Boardwalk 33243
3	1	38	Beauty And The Beat	*Go-Go's*	I.R.S. 70021
4	5	4	Success Hasn't Spoiled Me Yet	*Rick Springfield*	RCA 4125
5	4	23	Freeze-Frame	*The J. Geils Band*	EMI America 17062
6	7	6	**The Concert In Central Park**	*Simon & Garfunkel*	Warner 3654
7	10	3	Asia	*Asia*	Geffen 2008
8	9	23	Get Lucky	*Loverboy*	Columbia 37638
9	6	25	Physical	*Olivia Newton-John*	MCA 5229
10	11	37	Escape	*Journey*	Columbia 37408

TW	LW	WK	Billboard — APRIL 24, 1982 — TOP LP's		
1	1	28	**Chariots Of Fire**	*Vangelis/Soundtrack*	Polydor 6335
2	2	19	**I Love Rock-n-Roll**	*Joan Jett & The Blackhearts*	Boardwalk 33243
3	3	39	Beauty And The Beat	*Go-Go's*	I.R.S. 70021
4	4	5	Success Hasn't Spoiled Me Yet	*Rick Springfield*	RCA 4125
5	7	4	Asia	*Asia*	Geffen 2008
6	6	7	**The Concert In Central Park**	*Simon & Garfunkel*	Warner 3654
7	5	24	Freeze-Frame	*The J. Geils Band*	EMI America 17062
8	8	24	Get Lucky	*Loverboy*	Columbia 37638
9	10	38	Escape	*Journey*	Columbia 37408
10	11	56	**The Dude**	*Quincy Jones*	A&M 3721

TW	LW	WK	Billboard. MAY 1, 1982 TOP LP's
1	1	29	**Chariots Of Fire** .... *Vangelis/Soundtrack*...Polydor 6335
2	3	40	Beauty And The Beat .... *Go-Go's*...I.R.S. 70021
3	2	20	I Love Rock-n-Roll .... *Joan Jett & The Blackhearts*...Boardwalk 33243
4	4	6	Success Hasn't Spoiled Me Yet .... *Rick Springfield*...RCA 4125
5	5	5	Asia .... *Asia*...Geffen 2008
6	7	25	Freeze-Frame .... *The J. Geils Band*...EMI America 17062
7	8	25	**Get Lucky** .... *Loverboy*...Columbia 37638
8	6	8	The Concert In Central Park .... *Simon & Garfunkel*...Warner 3654
9	9	39	Escape .... *Journey*...Columbia 37408
10	11	28	Ghost In The Machine .... *The Police*...A&M 3730

TW	LW	WK	Billboard. MAY 8, 1982 TOP LP's
1	1	30	**Chariots Of Fire** .... *Vangelis/Soundtrack*...Polydor 6335
2	5	6	Asia .... *Asia*...Geffen 2008
3	2	41	Beauty And The Beat .... *Go-Go's*...I.R.S. 70021
4	4	7	Success Hasn't Spoiled Me Yet .... *Rick Springfield*...RCA 4125
5	3	21	I Love Rock-n-Roll .... *Joan Jett & The Blackhearts*...Boardwalk 33243
6	6	26	Freeze-Frame .... *The J. Geils Band*...EMI America 17062
7	7	26	**Get Lucky** .... *Loverboy*...Columbia 37638
8	9	40	Escape .... *Journey*...Columbia 37408
9	14	8	Always On My Mind .... *Willie Nelson*...Columbia 37951
10	11	12	Aldo Nova .... *Aldo Nova*...Portrait 37498

TW	LW	WK	Billboard. MAY 15, 1982 TOP LP's
1	2	7	**Asia** .... *Asia*...Geffen 2008
2	1	31	Chariots Of Fire .... *Vangelis/Soundtrack*...Polydor 6335
3	3	42	Beauty And The Beat .... *Go-Go's*...I.R.S. 70021
4	4	8	Success Hasn't Spoiled Me Yet .... *Rick Springfield*...RCA 4125
5	5	22	I Love Rock-n-Roll .... *Joan Jett & The Blackhearts*...Boardwalk 33243
6	6	27	Freeze-Frame .... *The J. Geils Band*...EMI America 17062
7	24	2	Diver Down .... *Van Halen*...Warner 3677
8	7	27	Get Lucky .... *Loverboy*...Columbia 37638
9	9	9	Always On My Mind .... *Willie Nelson*...Columbia 37951
10	10	13	Aldo Nova .... *Aldo Nova*...Portrait 37498

TW	LW	WK	Billboard. MAY 22, 1982 TOP LP's
1	1	8	**Asia** .... *Asia*...Geffen 2008
2	4	9	**Success Hasn't Spoiled Me Yet** .... *Rick Springfield*...RCA 4125
3	15	2	Tug Of War .... *Paul McCartney*...Columbia 37462
4	2	32	Chariots Of Fire .... *Vangelis/Soundtrack*...Polydor 6335
5	7	3	Diver Down .... *Van Halen*...Warner 3677
6	3	43	Beauty And The Beat .... *Go-Go's*...I.R.S. 70021
7	6	28	Freeze-Frame .... *The J. Geils Band*...EMI America 17062
8	10	14	**Aldo Nova** .... *Aldo Nova*...Portrait 37498
9	9	10	Always On My Mind .... *Willie Nelson*...Columbia 37951
10	8	28	Get Lucky .... *Loverboy*...Columbia 37638

TW	LW	WK	Billboard® MAY 29, 1982 TOP LP's	
1	3	3	**Tug Of War**	*Paul McCartney*...Columbia 37462
2	2	10	**Success Hasn't Spoiled Me Yet**	*Rick Springfield*...RCA 4125
3	1	9	Asia	*Asia*...Geffen 2008
4	5	4	Diver Down	*Van Halen*...Warner 3677
5	-	1	Stevie Wonder's Original Musiquarium I	*Stevie Wonder*...Tamla 6002
6	4	33	Chariots Of Fire	*Vangelis/Soundtrack*...Polydor 6335
7	12	14	Dare	*The Human League*...A&M 4892
8	8	15	**Aldo Nova**	*Aldo Nova*...Portrait 37498
9	9	11	Always On My Mind	*Willie Nelson*...Columbia 37951
10	11	10	**Blackout**	*Scorpions*...Mercury 4039

TW	LW	WK	Billboard® JUNE 5, 1982 TOP LP's	
1	1	4	**Tug Of War**	*Paul McCartney*...Columbia 37462
2	2	11	**Success Hasn't Spoiled Me Yet**	*Rick Springfield*...RCA 4125
3	3	10	Asia	*Asia*...Geffen 2008
4	4	5	Diver Down	*Van Halen*...Warner 3677
5	5	2	Stevie Wonder's Original Musiquarium I	*Stevie Wonder*...Tamla 6002
6	6	34	Chariots Of Fire	*Vangelis/Soundtrack*...Polydor 6335
7	7	15	Dare	*The Human League*...A&M 4892
8	8	16	**Aldo Nova**	*Aldo Nova*...Portrait 37498
9	9	12	Always On My Mind	*Willie Nelson*...Columbia 37951
10	10	11	**Blackout**	*Scorpions*...Mercury 4039

TW	LW	WK	Billboard® JUNE 12, 1982 TOP LP's	
1	1	5	**Tug Of War**	*Paul McCartney*...Columbia 37462
2	3	11	Asia	*Asia*...Geffen 2008
3	4	6	**Diver Down**	*Van Halen*...Warner 3677
4	5	3	**Stevie Wonder's Original Musiquarium I**	*Stevie Wonder*...Tamla 6002
5	2	12	Success Hasn't Spoiled Me Yet	*Rick Springfield*...RCA 4125
6	7	16	Dare	*The Human League*...A&M 4892
7	9	13	Always On My Mind	*Willie Nelson*...Columbia 37951
8	8	17	**Aldo Nova**	*Aldo Nova*...Portrait 37498
9	11	8	Toto IV	*Toto*...Columbia 37728
10	6	35	Chariots Of Fire	*Vangelis/Soundtrack*...Polydor 6335

TW	LW	WK	Billboard® JUNE 19, 1982 TOP LP's	
1	2	12	**Asia**	*Asia*...Geffen 2008
2	1	6	Tug Of War	*Paul McCartney*...Columbia 37462
3	3	7	**Diver Down**	*Van Halen*...Warner 3677
4	4	4	**Stevie Wonder's Original Musiquarium I**	*Stevie Wonder*...Tamla 6002
5	6	17	Dare	*The Human League*...A&M 4892
6	7	14	Always On My Mind	*Willie Nelson*...Columbia 37951
7	9	9	Toto IV	*Toto*...Columbia 37728
8	8	18	**Aldo Nova**	*Aldo Nova*...Portrait 37498
9	5	13	Success Hasn't Spoiled Me Yet	*Rick Springfield*...RCA 4125
10	10	36	Chariots Of Fire	*Vangelis/Soundtrack*...Polydor 6335

Billboard — JUNE 26, 1982 — TOP LP's

TW	LW	WK	Title	Artist...Label
1	1	13	**Asia**	*Asia*...Geffen 2008
2	2	7	Tug Of War	*Paul McCartney*...Columbia 37462
3	3	8	**Diver Down**	*Van Halen*...Warner 3677
4	4	5	**Stevie Wonder's Original Musiquarium I**	*Stevie Wonder*...Tamla 6002
5	5	18	Dare	*The Human League*...A&M 4892
6	6	15	Always On My Mind	*Willie Nelson*...Columbia 37951
7	7	10	Toto IV	*Toto*...Columbia 37728
8	8	19	**Aldo Nova**	*Aldo Nova*...Portrait 37498
9	9	14	Success Hasn't Spoiled Me Yet	*Rick Springfield*...RCA 4125
10	15	8	American Fool	*John Cougar*...Riva 7501

Billboard — JULY 3, 1982 — TOP LP's

TW	LW	WK	Title	Artist...Label
1	1	14	**Asia**	*Asia*...Geffen 2008
2	2	8	Tug Of War	*Paul McCartney*...Columbia 37462
3	6	16	Always On My Mind	*Willie Nelson*...Columbia 37951
4	5	19	Dare	*The Human League*...A&M 4892
5	7	11	Toto IV	*Toto*...Columbia 37728
6	49	2	"Still Life" (American Concert 1981)	*The Rolling Stones*...*Rolling Stones 39113*
7	3	9	Diver Down	*Van Halen*...Warner 3677
8	10	9	American Fool	*John Cougar*...Riva 7501
9	4	6	Stevie Wonder's Original Musiquarium I	*Stevie Wonder*...Tamla 6002
10	12	34	Get Lucky	*Loverboy*...Columbia 37638

Billboard — JULY 10, 1982 — TOP LP's

TW	LW	WK	Title	Artist...Label
1	1	15	**Asia**	*Asia*...Geffen 2008
2	3	17	**Always On My Mind**	*Willie Nelson*...Columbia 37951
3	4	20	**Dare**	*The Human League*...A&M 4892
4	5	12	**Toto IV**	*Toto*...Columbia 37728
5	6	3	**"Still Life" (American Concert 1981)**	*The Rolling Stones*...Rolling Stones 39113
6	2	9	Tug Of War	*Paul McCartney*...Columbia 37462
7	8	10	American Fool	*John Cougar*...Riva 7501
8	7	10	Diver Down	*Van Halen*...Warner 3677
9	10	35	Get Lucky	*Loverboy*...Columbia 37638
10	37	3	Eye Of The Tiger	*Survivor*...Scotti Brothers 38062

Billboard — JULY 17, 1982 — TOP LP's

TW	LW	WK	Title	Artist...Label
1	1	16	**Asia**	*Asia*...Geffen 2008
2	2	18	**Always On My Mind**	*Willie Nelson*...Columbia 37951
3	3	21	**Dare**	*The Human League*...A&M 4892
4	4	13	**Toto IV**	*Toto*...Columbia 37728
5	5	4	**"Still Life" (American Concert 1981)**	*The Rolling Stones*...Rolling Stones 39113
6	7	11	American Fool	*John Cougar*...Riva 7501
7	10	4	Eye Of The Tiger	*Survivor*...Scotti Brothers 38062
8	9	36	Get Lucky	*Loverboy*...Columbia 37638
9	6	10	Tug Of War	*Paul McCartney*...Columbia 37462
10	11	8	**Special Forces**	*38 Special*...A&M 4888

Billboard — JULY 24, 1982 — TOP LP's

TW	LW	WK	Title	Artist	Label
1	1	17	**Asia**	*Asia*	Geffen 2008
2	2	19	**Always On My Mind**	*Willie Nelson*	Columbia 37951
3	3	22	**Dare**	*The Human League*	A&M 4892
4	4	14	**Toto IV**	*Toto*	Columbia 37728
5	5	5	**"Still Life" (American Concert 1981)**	*The Rolling Stones*	Rolling Stones 39113
6	6	12	American Fool	*John Cougar*	Riva 7501
7	7	5	Eye Of The Tiger	*Survivor*	Scotti Brothers 38062
8	8	37	Get Lucky	*Loverboy*	Columbia 37638
9	50	2	Mirage	*Fleetwood Mac*	Warner 23607
10	10	9	**Special Forces**	*38 Special*	A&M 4888

Billboard — JULY 31, 1982 — TOP LP's

TW	LW	WK	Title	Artist	Label
1	1	18	**Asia**	*Asia*	Geffen 2008
2	2	20	**Always On My Mind**	*Willie Nelson*	Columbia 37951
3	9	3	Mirage	*Fleetwood Mac*	Warner 23607
4	4	15	**Toto IV**	*Toto*	Columbia 37728
5	5	6	**"Still Life" (American Concert 1981)**	*The Rolling Stones*	Rolling Stones 39113
6	6	13	American Fool	*John Cougar*	Riva 7501
7	7	6	Eye Of The Tiger	*Survivor*	Scotti Brothers 38062
8	28	3	Pictures At Eleven	*Robert Plant*	Swan Song 8512
9	11	4	Good Trouble	*REO Speedwagon*	Epic 38100
10	10	10	**Special Forces**	*38 Special*	A&M 4888

Billboard — AUGUST 7, 1982 — TOP LP's

TW	LW	WK	Title	Artist	Label
1	3	4	**Mirage**	*Fleetwood Mac*	Warner 23607
2	1	19	Asia	*Asia*	Geffen 2008
3	7	7	Eye Of The Tiger	*Survivor*	Scotti Brothers 38062
4	6	14	American Fool	*John Cougar*	Riva 7501
5	8	4	**Pictures At Eleven**	*Robert Plant*	Swan Song 8512
6	12	7	Abracadabra	*The Steve Miller Band*	Capitol 12216
7	9	5	**Good Trouble**	*REO Speedwagon*	Epic 38100
8	4	16	Toto IV	*Toto*	Columbia 37728
9	2	21	Always On My Mind	*Willie Nelson*	Columbia 37951
10	32	4	Daylight Again	*Crosby, Stills & Nash*	Atlantic 19360

Billboard — AUGUST 14, 1982 — TOP LP's

TW	LW	WK	Title	Artist	Label
1	1	5	**Mirage**	*Fleetwood Mac*	Warner 23607
2	3	8	**Eye Of The Tiger**	*Survivor*	Scotti Brothers 38062
3	2	20	Asia	*Asia*	Geffen 2008
4	4	15	American Fool	*John Cougar*	Riva 7501
5	5	5	**Pictures At Eleven**	*Robert Plant*	Swan Song 8512
6	6	8	Abracadabra	*The Steve Miller Band*	Capitol 12216
7	7	6	**Good Trouble**	*REO Speedwagon*	Epic 38100
8	10	5	**Daylight Again**	*Crosby, Stills & Nash*	Atlantic 19360
9	8	17	Toto IV	*Toto*	Columbia 37728
10	9	22	Always On My Mind	*Willie Nelson*	Columbia 37951

TW	LW	WK	Billboard. AUGUST 21, 1982 TOP LP's
1	1	6	**Mirage** ... *Fleetwood Mac*...Warner 23607
2	2	9	**Eye Of The Tiger** ... *Survivor*...Scotti Brothers 38062
3	3	21	**Asia** ... *Asia*...Geffen 2008
4	4	16	American Fool ... *John Cougar*...Riva 7501
5	5	6	**Pictures At Eleven** ... *Robert Plant*...Swan Song 8512
6	6	9	Abracadabra ... *The Steve Miller Band*...Capitol 12216
7	7	7	**Good Trouble** ... *REO Speedwagon*...Epic 38100
8	8	6	**Daylight Again** ... *Crosby, Stills & Nash*...Atlantic 19360
9	42	2	Vacation ... *Go-Go's*...I.R.S. 70031
10	11	9	**Three Sides Live** ... *Genesis*...Atlantic 2000

TW	LW	WK	Billboard. AUGUST 28, 1982 TOP LP's
1	1	7	**Mirage** ... *Fleetwood Mac*...Warner 23607
2	2	10	**Eye Of The Tiger** ... *Survivor*...Scotti Brothers 38062
3	4	17	American Fool ... *John Cougar*...Riva 7501
4	3	22	**Asia** ... *Asia*...Geffen 2008
5	5	7	**Pictures At Eleven** ... *Robert Plant*...Swan Song 8512
6	6	10	Abracadabra ... *The Steve Miller Band*...Capitol 12216
7	7	8	**Good Trouble** ... *REO Speedwagon*...Epic 38100
8	8	7	**Daylight Again** ... *Crosby, Stills & Nash*...Atlantic 19360
9	9	3	Vacation ... *Go-Go's*...I.R.S. 70031
10	10	10	**Three Sides Live** ... *Genesis*...Atlantic 2000

TW	LW	WK	Billboard. SEPTEMBER 4, 1982 TOP LP's
1	1	8	**Mirage** ... *Fleetwood Mac*...Warner 23607
2	2	11	**Eye Of The Tiger** ... *Survivor*...Scotti Brothers 38062
3	3	18	American Fool ... *John Cougar*...Riva 7501
4	4	23	**Asia** ... *Asia*...Geffen 2008
5	5	8	**Pictures At Eleven** ... *Robert Plant*...Swan Song 8512
6	6	11	Abracadabra ... *The Steve Miller Band*...Capitol 12216
7	7	9	**Good Trouble** ... *REO Speedwagon*...Epic 38100
8	8	8	**Daylight Again** ... *Crosby, Stills & Nash*...Atlantic 19360
9	9	4	Vacation ... *Go-Go's*...I.R.S. 70031
10	10	11	**Three Sides Live** ... *Genesis*...Atlantic 2000

TW	LW	WK	Billboard. SEPTEMBER 11, 1982 TOP LP's
1	3	19	**American Fool** ... *John Cougar*...Riva 7501
2	1	9	Mirage ... *Fleetwood Mac*...Warner 23607
3	2	12	Eye Of The Tiger ... *Survivor*...Scotti Brothers 38062
4	6	12	Abracadabra ... *The Steve Miller Band*...Capitol 12216
5	5	9	**Pictures At Eleven** ... *Robert Plant*...Swan Song 8512
6	4	24	**Asia** ... *Asia*...Geffen 2008
7	7	10	**Good Trouble** ... *REO Speedwagon*...Epic 38100
8	8	9	**Daylight Again** ... *Crosby, Stills & Nash*...Atlantic 19360
9	9	5	Vacation ... *Go-Go's*...I.R.S. 70031
10	12	12	Chicago 16 ... *Chicago*...Full Moon 23689

Billboard — SEPTEMBER 18, 1982 — TOP LP's

TW	LW	WK			
1	1	20	**American Fool**	*John Cougar*	Riva 7501
2	2	10	Mirage	*Fleetwood Mac*	Warner 23607
3	4	13	**Abracadabra**	*The Steve Miller Band*	Capitol 12216
4	6	25	Asia	*Asia*	Geffen 2008
5	11	7	**Emotions in Motion**	*Billy Squier*	Capitol 12217
6	5	10	Pictures At Eleven	*Robert Plant*	Swan Song 8512
7	7	11	**Good Trouble**	*REO Speedwagon*	Epic 38100
8	9	6	**Vacation**	*Go-Go's*	I.R.S. 70031
9	10	13	**Chicago 16**	*Chicago*	Full Moon 23689
10	3	13	Eye Of The Tiger	*Survivor*	Scotti Brothers 38062

Billboard — SEPTEMBER 25, 1982 — TOP LP's

TW	LW	WK			
1	1	21	**American Fool**	*John Cougar*	Riva 7501
2	2	11	Mirage	*Fleetwood Mac*	Warner 23607
3	3	14	**Abracadabra**	*The Steve Miller Band*	Capitol 12216
4	4	26	Asia	*Asia*	Geffen 2008
5	5	8	**Emotions in Motion**	*Billy Squier*	Capitol 12217
6	6	11	Pictures At Eleven	*Robert Plant*	Swan Song 8512
7	7	12	**Good Trouble**	*REO Speedwagon*	Epic 38100
8	8	7	**Vacation**	*Go-Go's*	I.R.S. 70031
9	9	14	**Chicago 16**	*Chicago*	Full Moon 23689
10	10	14	Eye Of The Tiger	*Survivor*	Scotti Brothers 38062

Billboard — OCTOBER 2, 1982 — TOP LP's

TW	LW	WK			
1	1	22	**American Fool**	*John Cougar*	Riva 7501
2	2	12	Mirage	*Fleetwood Mac*	Warner 23607
3	3	15	**Abracadabra**	*The Steve Miller Band*	Capitol 12216
4	4	27	Asia	*Asia*	Geffen 2008
5	5	9	**Emotions in Motion**	*Billy Squier*	Capitol 12217
6	12	6	**If That's What It Takes**	*Michael McDonald*	Warner 23703
7	7	13	**Good Trouble**	*REO Speedwagon*	Epic 38100
8	8	8	**Vacation**	*Go-Go's*	I.R.S. 70031
9	9	15	**Chicago 16**	*Chicago*	Full Moon 23689
10	11	16	Eye In The Sky	*The Alan Parsons Project*	Arista 9599

Billboard — OCTOBER 9, 1982 — TOP LP's

TW	LW	WK			
1	1	23	**American Fool**	*John Cougar*	Riva 7501
2	2	13	Mirage	*Fleetwood Mac*	Warner 23607
3	3	16	**Abracadabra**	*The Steve Miller Band*	Capitol 12216
4	4	28	Asia	*Asia*	Geffen 2008
5	5	10	**Emotions in Motion**	*Billy Squier*	Capitol 12217
6	6	7	**If That's What It Takes**	*Michael McDonald*	Warner 23703
7	10	17	**Eye In The Sky**	*The Alan Parsons Project*	Arista 9599
8	8	9	**Vacation**	*Go-Go's*	I.R.S. 70031
9	9	16	**Chicago 16**	*Chicago*	Full Moon 23689
10	12	3	It's Hard	*The Who*	Warner 23731

Billboard — OCTOBER 16, 1982 — TOP LP's

TW	LW	WK			
1	1	24	**American Fool**	*John Cougar*	Riva 7501
2	2	14	Mirage	*Fleetwood Mac*	Warner 23607
3	3	17	**Abracadabra**	*The Steve Miller Band*	Capitol 12216
4	29	2	Nebraska	*Bruce Springsteen*	Columbia 38358
5	5	11	**Emotions in Motion**	*Billy Squier*	Capitol 12217
6	6	8	**If That's What It Takes**	*Michael McDonald*	Warner 23703
7	7	18	**Eye In The Sky**	*The Alan Parsons Project*	Arista 9599
8	8	10	**Vacation**	*Go-Go's*	I.R.S. 70031
9	9	17	**Chicago 16**	*Chicago*	Full Moon 23689
10	10	4	It's Hard	*The Who*	Warner 23731

Billboard — OCTOBER 23, 1982 — TOP LP's

TW	LW	WK			
1	1	25	**American Fool**	*John Cougar*	Riva 7501
2	2	15	Mirage	*Fleetwood Mac*	Warner 23607
3	3	18	**Abracadabra**	*The Steve Miller Band*	Capitol 12216
4	4	3	Nebraska	*Bruce Springsteen*	Columbia 38358
5	5	12	**Emotions in Motion**	*Billy Squier*	Capitol 12217
6	6	9	**If That's What It Takes**	*Michael McDonald*	Warner 23703
7	7	19	**Eye In The Sky**	*The Alan Parsons Project*	Arista 9599
8	10	5	**It's Hard**	*The Who*	Warner 23731
9	11	17	Business As Usual	*Men At Work*	Columbia 37978
10	12	23	**A Flock Of Seagulls**	*A Flock Of Seagulls*	Jive 66000

Billboard — OCTOBER 30, 1982 — TOP LP's

TW	LW	WK			
1	1	26	**American Fool**	*John Cougar*	Riva 7501
2	2	16	Mirage	*Fleetwood Mac*	Warner 23607
3	4	4	**Nebraska**	*Bruce Springsteen*	Columbia 38358
4	9	18	Business As Usual	*Men At Work*	Columbia 37978
5	5	13	**Emotions in Motion**	*Billy Squier*	Capitol 12217
6	6	10	**If That's What It Takes**	*Michael McDonald*	Warner 23703
7	7	20	**Eye In The Sky**	*The Alan Parsons Project*	Arista 9599
8	8	6	**It's Hard**	*The Who*	Warner 23731
9	12	3	The Nylon Curtain	*Billy Joel*	Columbia 38200
10	10	24	**A Flock Of Seagulls**	*A Flock Of Seagulls*	Jive 66000

Billboard — NOVEMBER 6, 1982 — TOP LP's

TW	LW	WK			
1	1	27	**American Fool**	*John Cougar*	Riva 7501
2	2	17	Mirage	*Fleetwood Mac*	Warner 23607
3	3	5	**Nebraska**	*Bruce Springsteen*	Columbia 38358
4	4	19	Business As Usual	*Men At Work*	Columbia 37978
5	5	14	**Emotions in Motion**	*Billy Squier*	Capitol 12217
6	6	11	**If That's What It Takes**	*Michael McDonald*	Warner 23703
7	7	21	**Eye In The Sky**	*The Alan Parsons Project*	Arista 9599
8	8	7	**It's Hard**	*The Who*	Warner 23731
9	9	4	The Nylon Curtain	*Billy Joel*	Columbia 38200
10	10	25	**A Flock Of Seagulls**	*A Flock Of Seagulls*	Jive 66000

Billboard — NOVEMBER 13, 1982 — TOP LP's

TW	LW	WK	Album	Artist	Label
1	4	20	**Business As Usual**	*Men At Work*	Columbia 37978
2	2	18	Mirage	*Fleetwood Mac*	Warner 23607
3	3	6	**Nebraska**	*Bruce Springsteen*	Columbia 38358
4	1	28	American Fool	*John Cougar*	Riva 7501
5	16	4	Lionel Richie	*Lionel Richie*	Motown 6007
6	15	20	Built For Speed	*Stray Cats*	EMI America 17070
7	7	22	**Eye In The Sky**	*The Alan Parsons Project*	Arista 9599
8	8	8	**It's Hard**	*The Who*	Warner 23731
9	9	5	The Nylon Curtain	*Billy Joel*	Columbia 38200
10	5	15	Emotions in Motion	*Billy Squier*	Capitol 12217

Billboard — NOVEMBER 20, 1982 — TOP LP's

TW	LW	WK	Album	Artist	Label
1	1	21	**Business As Usual**	*Men At Work*	Columbia 37978
2	2	19	Mirage	*Fleetwood Mac*	Warner 23607
3	3	7	**Nebraska**	*Bruce Springsteen*	Columbia 38358
4	5	5	Lionel Richie	*Lionel Richie*	Motown 6007
5	6	21	Built For Speed	*Stray Cats*	EMI America 17070
6	15	19	Night And Day	*Joe Jackson*	A&M 4906
7	9	6	**The Nylon Curtain**	*Billy Joel*	Columbia 38200
8	8	9	**It's Hard**	*The Who*	Warner 23731
9	4	29	American Fool	*John Cougar*	Riva 7501
10	12	6	Heartlight	*Neil Diamond*	Columbia 38359

Billboard — NOVEMBER 27, 1982 — TOP LP's

TW	LW	WK	Album	Artist	Label
1	1	22	**Business As Usual**	*Men At Work*	Columbia 37978
2	5	22	**Built For Speed**	*Stray Cats*	EMI America 17070
3	4	6	**Lionel Richie**	*Lionel Richie*	Motown 6007
4	6	20	**Night And Day**	*Joe Jackson*	A&M 4906
5	14	3	**...famous last words...**	*Supertramp*	A&M 3732
6	15	5	H_2O	*Daryl Hall & John Oates*	RCA 4383
7	7	7	**The Nylon Curtain**	*Billy Joel*	Columbia 38200
8	3	8	Nebraska	*Bruce Springsteen*	Columbia 38358
9	10	7	**Heartlight**	*Neil Diamond*	Columbia 38359
10	11	9	**Signals**	*Rush*	Mercury 4063

Billboard — DECEMBER 4, 1982 — TOP LP's

TW	LW	WK	Album	Artist	Label
1	1	23	**Business As Usual**	*Men At Work*	Columbia 37978
2	2	23	**Built For Speed**	*Stray Cats*	EMI America 17070
3	3	7	**Lionel Richie**	*Lionel Richie*	Motown 6007
4	4	21	**Night And Day**	*Joe Jackson*	A&M 4906
5	5	4	**...famous last words...**	*Supertramp*	A&M 3732
6	6	6	H_2O	*Daryl Hall & John Oates*	RCA 4383
7	7	8	**The Nylon Curtain**	*Billy Joel*	Columbia 38200
8	15	3	Midnight Love	*Marvin Gaye*	Columbia 38197
9	9	8	**Heartlight**	*Neil Diamond*	Columbia 38359
10	23	3	Get Nervous	*Pat Benatar*	Chrysalis 1396

TW	LW	WK	Billboard — DECEMBER 11, 1982 — TOP LP's		
1	1	24	**Business As Usual**	*Men At Work*	Columbia 37978
2	2	24	**Built For Speed**	*Stray Cats*	EMI America 17070
3	3	8	**Lionel Richie**	*Lionel Richie*	Motown 6007
4	4	22	**Night And Day**	*Joe Jackson*	A&M 4906
5	5	5	**...famous last words...**	*Supertramp*	A&M 3732
6	6	7	H_2O	*Daryl Hall & John Oates*	RCA 4383
7	7	9	**The Nylon Curtain**	*Billy Joel*	Columbia 38200
8	8	4	Midnight Love	*Marvin Gaye*	Columbia 38197
9	9	9	**Heartlight**	*Neil Diamond*	Columbia 38359
10	10	4	Get Nervous	*Pat Benatar*	Chrysalis 1396

TW	LW	WK	Billboard — DECEMBER 18, 1982 — TOP LP's		
1	1	25	**Business As Usual**	*Men At Work*	Columbia 37978
2	2	25	**Built For Speed**	*Stray Cats*	EMI America 17070
3	3	9	**Lionel Richie**	*Lionel Richie*	Motown 6007
4	4	23	**Night And Day**	*Joe Jackson*	A&M 4906
5	5	6	**...famous last words...**	*Supertramp*	A&M 3732
6	6	8	H_2O	*Daryl Hall & John Oates*	RCA 4383
7	8	5	**Midnight Love**	*Marvin Gaye*	Columbia 38197
8	10	5	Get Nervous	*Pat Benatar*	Chrysalis 1396
9	-	1	Coda	*Led Zeppelin*	Swan Song 90051
10	12	28	Combat Rock	*The Clash*	Epic 37689

TW	LW	WK	Billboard — DECEMBER 25, 1982 — TOP LP's		
1	1	26	**Business As Usual**	*Men At Work*	Columbia 37978
2	2	26	**Built For Speed**	*Stray Cats*	EMI America 17070
3	3	10	**Lionel Richie**	*Lionel Richie*	Motown 6007
4	4	24	**Night And Day**	*Joe Jackson*	A&M 4906
5	5	7	**...famous last words...**	*Supertramp*	A&M 3732
6	6	9	H_2O	*Daryl Hall & John Oates*	RCA 4383
7	7	6	**Midnight Love**	*Marvin Gaye*	Columbia 38197
8	8	6	Get Nervous	*Pat Benatar*	Chrysalis 1396
9	9	2	Coda	*Led Zeppelin*	Swan Song 90051
10	10	29	Combat Rock	*The Clash*	Epic 37689

TW	LW	WK	Billboard. JANUARY 8, 1983 TOP LP's
1	1	28	**Business As Usual**........ *Men At Work*...Columbia 37978
2	2	28	**Built For Speed**........ *Stray Cats*...EMI America 17070
3	3	12	**Lionel Richie**........ *Lionel Richie*...Motown 6007
4	6	11	H_2O........ *Daryl Hall & John Oates*...RCA 4383
5	5	9	**...famous last words...**........ *Supertramp*...A&M 3732
6	8	8	Get Nervous........ *Pat Benatar*...Chrysalis 1396
7	7	8	**Midnight Love**........ *Marvin Gaye*...Columbia 38197
8	9	4	Coda........ *Led Zeppelin*...Swan Song 90051
9	11	3	Thriller........ *Michael Jackson*...Epic 38112
10	10	31	Combat Rock........ *The Clash*...Epic 37689

TW	LW	WK	Billboard. JANUARY 15, 1983 TOP LP's
1	1	29	**Business As Usual**........ *Men At Work*...Columbia 37978
2	2	29	**Built For Speed**........ *Stray Cats*...EMI America 17070
3	4	12	**H_2O**........ *Daryl Hall & John Oates*...RCA 4383
4	6	9	**Get Nervous**........ *Pat Benatar*...Chrysalis 1396
5	3	13	Lionel Richie........ *Lionel Richie*...Motown 6007
6	8	5	**Coda**........ *Led Zeppelin*...Swan Song 90051
7	7	9	**Midnight Love**........ *Marvin Gaye*...Columbia 38197
8	9	4	Thriller........ *Michael Jackson*...Epic 38112
9	10	32	Combat Rock........ *The Clash*...Epic 37689
10	11	9	Long After Dark........ *Tom Petty & The Heartbreakers*...Backstreet 5360

TW	LW	WK	Billboard. JANUARY 22, 1983 TOP LP's
1	1	30	**Business As Usual**........ *Men At Work*...Columbia 37978
2	2	30	**Built For Speed**........ *Stray Cats*...EMI America 17070
3	3	13	**H_2O**........ *Daryl Hall & John Oates*...RCA 4383
4	4	10	**Get Nervous**........ *Pat Benatar*...Chrysalis 1396
5	8	5	Thriller........ *Michael Jackson*...Epic 38112
6	6	6	**Coda**........ *Led Zeppelin*...Swan Song 90051
7	9	33	**Combat Rock**........ *The Clash*...Epic 37689
8	16	2	The Distance........ *Bob Seger & The Silver Bullet Band*...Capitol 12254
9	10	10	**Long After Dark**........ *Tom Petty & The Heartbreakers*...Backstreet 5360
10	11	9	Hello, I Must Be Going!........ *Phil Collins*...Atlantic 80035

TW	LW	WK	Billboard. JANUARY 29, 1983 TOP LP's
1	1	31	**Business As Usual**........ *Men At Work*...Columbia 37978
2	2	31	**Built For Speed**........ *Stray Cats*...EMI America 17070
3	3	14	**H_2O**........ *Daryl Hall & John Oates*...RCA 4383
4	4	11	**Get Nervous**........ *Pat Benatar*...Chrysalis 1396
5	5	6	Thriller........ *Michael Jackson*...Epic 38112
6	6	7	**Coda**........ *Led Zeppelin*...Swan Song 90051
7	7	34	**Combat Rock**........ *The Clash*...Epic 37689
8	8	3	The Distance........ *Bob Seger & The Silver Bullet Band*...Capitol 12254
9	9	11	**Long After Dark**........ *Tom Petty & The Heartbreakers*...Backstreet 5360
10	10	10	Hello, I Must Be Going!........ *Phil Collins*...Atlantic 80035

TW	LW	WK	Billboard — FEBRUARY 5, 1983 — TOP LP's
1	1	32	**Business As Usual** ... *Men At Work*...Columbia 37978
2	2	32	**Built For Speed** ... *Stray Cats*...EMI America 17070
3	3	15	**H_2O** ... *Daryl Hall & John Oates*...RCA 4383
4	4	12	**Get Nervous** ... *Pat Benatar*...Chrysalis 1396
5	5	7	Thriller ... *Michael Jackson*...Epic 38112
6	8	4	The Distance ... *Bob Seger & The Silver Bullet Band*...Capitol 12254
7	7	35	**Combat Rock** ... *The Clash*...Epic 37689
8	10	11	**Hello, I Must Be Going!** ... *Phil Collins*...Atlantic 80035
9	9	12	**Long After Dark** ... *Tom Petty & The Heartbreakers*...Backstreet 5360
10	12	42	Toto IV ... *Toto*...Columbia 37728

TW	LW	WK	Billboard — FEBRUARY 12, 1983 — TOP LP's
1	1	33	**Business As Usual** ... *Men At Work*...Columbia 37978
2	2	33	**Built For Speed** ... *Stray Cats*...EMI America 17070
3	3	16	**H_2O** ... *Daryl Hall & John Oates*...RCA 4383
4	4	13	**Get Nervous** ... *Pat Benatar*...Chrysalis 1396
5	5	8	Thriller ... *Michael Jackson*...Epic 38112
6	6	5	The Distance ... *Bob Seger & The Silver Bullet Band*...Capitol 12254
7	7	36	**Combat Rock** ... *The Clash*...Epic 37689
8	8	12	**Hello, I Must Be Going!** ... *Phil Collins*...Atlantic 80035
9	10	43	Toto IV ... *Toto*...Columbia 37728
10	15	8	**Foreigner Records** ... *Foreigner*...Atlantic 80999

TW	LW	WK	Billboard — FEBRUARY 19, 1983 — TOP LP's
1	1	34	**Business As Usual** ... *Men At Work*...Columbia 37978
2	2	34	**Built For Speed** ... *Stray Cats*...EMI America 17070
3	3	17	**H_2O** ... *Daryl Hall & John Oates*...RCA 4383
4	5	9	Thriller ... *Michael Jackson*...Epic 38112
5	6	6	**The Distance** ... *Bob Seger & The Silver Bullet Band*...Capitol 12254
6	4	14	Get Nervous ... *Pat Benatar*...Chrysalis 1396
7	7	37	**Combat Rock** ... *The Clash*...Epic 37689
8	8	13	**Hello, I Must Be Going!** ... *Phil Collins*...Atlantic 80035
9	9	44	Toto IV ... *Toto*...Columbia 37728
10	10	9	**Foreigner Records** ... *Foreigner*...Atlantic 80999

TW	LW	WK	Billboard — FEBRUARY 26, 1983 — TOP LP's
1	4	10	**Thriller** ... *Michael Jackson*...Epic 38112
2	2	35	**Built For Speed** ... *Stray Cats*...EMI America 17070
3	3	18	**H_2O** ... *Daryl Hall & John Oates*...RCA 4383
4	1	35	Business As Usual ... *Men At Work*...Columbia 37978
5	5	7	**The Distance** ... *Bob Seger & The Silver Bullet Band*...Capitol 12254
6	23	2	Frontiers ... *Journey*...Columbia 38504
7	12	39	Rio ... *Duran Duran*...Harvest 12211
8	8	14	**Hello, I Must Be Going!** ... *Phil Collins*...Atlantic 80035
9	9	45	Toto IV ... *Toto*...Columbia 37728
10	10	10	**Foreigner Records** ... *Foreigner*...Atlantic 80999

TW	LW	WK	Billboard	MARCH 5, 1983 TOP LP's
1	1	11	**Thriller**	*Michael Jackson*...Epic 38112
2	2	36	**Built For Speed**	*Stray Cats*...EMI America 17070
3	3	19	**H_2O**	*Daryl Hall & John Oates*...RCA 4383
4	6	3	Frontiers	*Journey*...Columbia 38504
5	5	8	**The Distance**	*Bob Seger & The Silver Bullet Band*...Capitol 12254
6	4	36	Business As Usual	*Men At Work*...Columbia 37978
7	7	40	Rio	*Duran Duran*...Harvest 12211
8	8	15	**Hello, I Must Be Going!**	*Phil Collins*...Atlantic 80035
9	9	46	Toto IV	*Toto*...Columbia 37728
10	10	11	**Foreigner Records**	*Foreigner*...Atlantic 80999

TW	LW	WK	Billboard	MARCH 12, 1983 TOP LP's
1	1	12	**Thriller**	*Michael Jackson*...Epic 38112
2	4	4	**Frontiers**	*Journey*...Columbia 38504
3	3	20	**H_2O**	*Daryl Hall & John Oates*...RCA 4383
4	6	37	Business As Usual	*Men At Work*...Columbia 37978
5	5	9	**The Distance**	*Bob Seger & The Silver Bullet Band*...Capitol 12254
6	7	41	**Rio**	*Duran Duran*...Harvest 12211
7	11	21	Lionel Richie	*Lionel Richie*...Motown 6007
8	9	47	Toto IV	*Toto*...Columbia 37728
9	2	37	Built For Speed	*Stray Cats*...EMI America 17070
10	15	6	Pyromania	*Def Leppard*...Mercury 810308

TW	LW	WK	Billboard	MARCH 19, 1983 TOP LP's
1	1	13	**Thriller**	*Michael Jackson*...Epic 38112
2	2	5	**Frontiers**	*Journey*...Columbia 38504
3	3	21	**H_2O**	*Daryl Hall & John Oates*...RCA 4383
4	4	38	**Business As Usual**	*Men At Work*...Columbia 37978
5	5	10	**The Distance**	*Bob Seger & The Silver Bullet Band*...Capitol 12254
6	6	42	**Rio**	*Duran Duran*...Harvest 12211
7	7	22	Lionel Richie	*Lionel Richie*...Motown 6007
8	8	48	Toto IV	*Toto*...Columbia 37728
9	10	7	Pyromania	*Def Leppard*...Mercury 810308
10	-	1	Kilroy Was Here	*Styx*...A&M 3734

TW	LW	WK	Billboard	MARCH 26, 1983 TOP LP's
1	1	14	**Thriller**	*Michael Jackson*...Epic 38112
2	2	6	**Frontiers**	*Journey*...Columbia 38504
3	3	22	**H_2O**	*Daryl Hall & John Oates*...RCA 4383
4	4	39	**Business As Usual**	*Men At Work*...Columbia 37978
5	5	11	**The Distance**	*Bob Seger & The Silver Bullet Band*...Capitol 12254
6	6	43	**Rio**	*Duran Duran*...Harvest 12211
7	7	23	Lionel Richie	*Lionel Richie*...Motown 6007
8	8	49	Toto IV	*Toto*...Columbia 37728
9	9	8	Pyromania	*Def Leppard*...Mercury 810308
10	10	2	Kilroy Was Here	*Styx*...A&M 3734

Billboard — APRIL 2, 1983 — TOP LP's

TW	LW	WK	Title	Artist...Label
1	1	15	**Thriller**	*Michael Jackson*...Epic 38112
2	2	7	**Frontiers**	*Journey*...Columbia 38504
3	3	23	**H_2O**	*Daryl Hall & John Oates*...RCA 4383
4	4	40	Business As Usual	*Men At Work*...Columbia 37978
5	10	3	Kilroy Was Here	*Styx*...A&M 3734
6	6	44	**Rio**	*Duran Duran*...Harvest 12211
7	7	24	Lionel Richie	*Lionel Richie*...Motown 6007
8	8	50	Toto IV	*Toto*...Columbia 37728
9	9	9	Pyromania	*Def Leppard*...Mercury 810308
10	5	12	The Distance	*Bob Seger & The Silver Bullet Band*...Capitol 12254

Billboard — APRIL 9, 1983 — TOP LP's

TW	LW	WK	Title	Artist...Label
1	1	16	**Thriller**	*Michael Jackson*...Epic 38112
2	2	8	**Frontiers**	*Journey*...Columbia 38504
3	3	24	**H_2O**	*Daryl Hall & John Oates*...RCA 4383
4	4	41	Business As Usual	*Men At Work*...Columbia 37978
5	5	4	Kilroy Was Here	*Styx*...A&M 3734
6	6	45	**Rio**	*Duran Duran*...Harvest 12211
7	7	25	Lionel Richie	*Lionel Richie*...Motown 6007
8	8	51	Toto IV	*Toto*...Columbia 37728
9	9	10	Pyromania	*Def Leppard*...Mercury 810308
10	10	13	The Distance	*Bob Seger & The Silver Bullet Band*...Capitol 12254

Billboard — APRIL 16, 1983 — TOP LP's

TW	LW	WK	Title	Artist...Label
1	1	17	**Thriller**	*Michael Jackson*...Epic 38112
2	2	9	**Frontiers**	*Journey*...Columbia 38504
3	3	25	**H_2O**	*Daryl Hall & John Oates*...RCA 4383
4	4	42	Business As Usual	*Men At Work*...Columbia 37978
5	5	5	Kilroy Was Here	*Styx*...A&M 3734
6	6	46	**Rio**	*Duran Duran*...Harvest 12211
7	7	26	Lionel Richie	*Lionel Richie*...Motown 6007
8	8	52	Toto IV	*Toto*...Columbia 37728
9	9	11	Pyromania	*Def Leppard*...Mercury 810308
10	10	14	The Distance	*Bob Seger & The Silver Bullet Band*...Capitol 12254

Billboard — APRIL 23, 1983 — TOP LP's

TW	LW	WK	Title	Artist...Label
1	1	18	**Thriller**	*Michael Jackson*...Epic 38112
2	2	10	**Frontiers**	*Journey*...Columbia 38504
3	3	26	**H_2O**	*Daryl Hall & John Oates*...RCA 4383
4	4	43	Business As Usual	*Men At Work*...Columbia 37978
5	5	6	Kilroy Was Here	*Styx*...A&M 3734
6	6	47	**Rio**	*Duran Duran*...Harvest 12211
7	7	27	Lionel Richie	*Lionel Richie*...Motown 6007
8	9	12	Pyromania	*Def Leppard*...Mercury 810308
9	11	3	The Final Cut	*Pink Floyd*...Columbia 38243
10	8	53	Toto IV	*Toto*...Columbia 37728

TW	LW	WK	Billboard® APRIL 30, 1983 TOP LP's		
1	1	19	**Thriller**	*Michael Jackson*	Epic 38112
2	2	11	**Frontiers**	*Journey*	Columbia 38504
3	5	7	**Kilroy Was Here**	*Styx*	A&M 3734
4	4	44	Business As Usual	*Men At Work*	Columbia 37978
5	8	13	Pyromania	*Def Leppard*	Mercury 810308
6	3	27	H_2O	*Daryl Hall & John Oates*	RCA 4383
7	9	4	The Final Cut	*Pink Floyd*	Columbia 38243
8	7	28	Lionel Richie	*Lionel Richie*	Motown 6007
9	6	48	Rio	*Duran Duran*	Harvest 12211
10	11	6	**The Closer You Get...**	*Alabama*	RCA 4663

TW	LW	WK	Billboard® MAY 7, 1983 TOP LP's		
1	1	20	**Thriller**	*Michael Jackson*	Epic 38112
2	2	12	**Frontiers**	*Journey*	Columbia 38504
3	3	8	**Kilroy Was Here**	*Styx*	A&M 3734
4	5	14	Pyromania	*Def Leppard*	Mercury 810308
5	4	45	Business As Usual	*Men At Work*	Columbia 37978
6	7	5	**The Final Cut**	*Pink Floyd*	Columbia 38243
7	8	29	Lionel Richie	*Lionel Richie*	Motown 6007
8	6	28	H_2O	*Daryl Hall & John Oates*	RCA 4383
9	9	49	Rio	*Duran Duran*	Harvest 12211
10	12	17	The Distance	*Bob Seger & The Silver Bullet Band*	Capitol 12254

TW	LW	WK	Billboard® MAY 14, 1983 TOP LP's		
1	1	21	**Thriller**	*Michael Jackson*	Epic 38112
2	4	15	**Pyromania**	*Def Leppard*	Mercury 810308
3	2	13	Frontiers	*Journey*	Columbia 38504
4	11	2	Cargo	*Men At Work*	Columbia 38660
5	3	9	Kilroy Was Here	*Styx*	A&M 3734
6	6	6	**The Final Cut**	*Pink Floyd*	Columbia 38243
7	5	46	Business As Usual	*Men At Work*	Columbia 37978
8	8	29	H_2O	*Daryl Hall & John Oates*	RCA 4383
9	18	3	Let's Dance	*David Bowie*	EMI America 17093
10	7	30	Lionel Richie	*Lionel Richie*	Motown 6007

TW	LW	WK	Billboard® MAY 21, 1983 TOP LP's		
1	1	22	**Thriller**	*Michael Jackson*	Epic 38112
2	2	16	**Pyromania**	*Def Leppard*	Mercury 810308
3	4	3	**Cargo**	*Men At Work*	Columbia 38660
4	13	4	Flashdance	*Soundtrack*	Casablanca 811492
5	9	4	Let's Dance	*David Bowie*	EMI America 17093
6	3	14	Frontiers	*Journey*	Columbia 38504
7	5	10	Kilroy Was Here	*Styx*	A&M 3734
8	8	30	H_2O	*Daryl Hall & John Oates*	RCA 4383
9	7	47	Business As Usual	*Men At Work*	Columbia 37978
10	6	7	The Final Cut	*Pink Floyd*	Columbia 38243

TW	LW	WK	Billboard. MAY 28, 1983	TOP LP's
1	1	23	**Thriller**	*Michael Jackson*...Epic 38112
2	4	5	Flashdance	*Soundtrack*...Casablanca 811492
3	3	4	**Cargo**	*Men At Work*...Columbia 38660
4	2	17	Pyromania	*Def Leppard*...Mercury 810308
5	5	5	Let's Dance	*David Bowie*...EMI America 17093
6	6	15	Frontiers	*Journey*...Columbia 38504
7	7	11	Kilroy Was Here	*Styx*...A&M 3734
8	8	31	H_2O	*Daryl Hall & John Oates*...RCA 4383
9	13	28	**Prince **1999****	*Prince*...Warner 23720
10	11	32	Lionel Richie	*Lionel Richie*...Motown 6007

TW	LW	WK	Billboard. JUNE 4, 1983	TOP LP's
1	1	24	**Thriller**	*Michael Jackson*...Epic 38112
2	2	6	Flashdance	*Soundtrack*...Casablanca 811492
3	3	5	**Cargo**	*Men At Work*...Columbia 38660
4	4	18	Pyromania	*Def Leppard*...Mercury 810308
5	5	6	Let's Dance	*David Bowie*...EMI America 17093
6	6	16	Frontiers	*Journey*...Columbia 38504
7	7	12	Kilroy Was Here	*Styx*...A&M 3734
8	8	32	H_2O	*Daryl Hall & John Oates*...RCA 4383
9	9	29	**Prince **1999****	*Prince*...Warner 23720
10	12	16	Cuts Like A Knife	*Bryan Adams*...A&M 4919

TW	LW	WK	Billboard. JUNE 11, 1983	TOP LP's
1	1	25	**Thriller**	*Michael Jackson*...Epic 38112
2	2	7	Flashdance	*Soundtrack*...Casablanca 811492
3	3	6	**Cargo**	*Men At Work*...Columbia 38660
4	4	19	Pyromania	*Def Leppard*...Mercury 810308
5	5	7	Let's Dance	*David Bowie*...EMI America 17093
6	6	17	Frontiers	*Journey*...Columbia 38504
7	7	13	Kilroy Was Here	*Styx*...A&M 3734
8	8	33	H_2O	*Daryl Hall & John Oates*...RCA 4383
9	10	17	Cuts Like A Knife	*Bryan Adams*...A&M 4919
10	9	30	Prince **1999**	*Prince*...Warner 23720

TW	LW	WK	Billboard. JUNE 18, 1983	TOP LP's
1	1	26	**Thriller**	*Michael Jackson*...Epic 38112
2	2	8	Flashdance	*Soundtrack*...Casablanca 811492
3	3	7	**Cargo**	*Men At Work*...Columbia 38660
4	4	20	Pyromania	*Def Leppard*...Mercury 810308
5	5	8	Let's Dance	*David Bowie*...EMI America 17093
6	6	18	Frontiers	*Journey*...Columbia 38504
7	8	34	H_2O	*Daryl Hall & John Oates*...RCA 4383
8	7	14	Kilroy Was Here	*Styx*...A&M 3734
9	9	18	Cuts Like A Knife	*Bryan Adams*...A&M 4919
10	10	31	Prince **1999**	*Prince*...Warner 23720

Billboard — JUNE 25, 1983 — TOP LP's

TW	LW	WK	Title	Artist...Label
1	2	9	**Flashdance**	*Soundtrack*...Casablanca 811492
2	1	27	Thriller	*Michael Jackson*...Epic 38112
3	4	21	Pyromania	*Def Leppard*...Mercury 810308
4	5	9	**Let's Dance**	*David Bowie*...EMI America 17093
5	3	8	Cargo	*Men At Work*...Columbia 38660
6	6	19	Frontiers	*Journey*...Columbia 38504
7	7	35	H_2O	*Daryl Hall & John Oates*...RCA 4383
8	9	19	**Cuts Like A Knife**	*Bryan Adams*...A&M 4919
9	8	15	Kilroy Was Here	*Styx*...A&M 3734
10	10	32	Prince **1999**	*Prince*...Warner 23720

Billboard — JULY 2, 1983 — TOP LP's

TW	LW	WK	Title	Artist...Label
1	1	10	**Flashdance**	*Soundtrack*...Casablanca 811492
2	2	28	Thriller	*Michael Jackson*...Epic 38112
3	3	22	Pyromania	*Def Leppard*...Mercury 810308
4	5	9	Cargo	*Men At Work*...Columbia 38660
5	4	10	Let's Dance	*David Bowie*...EMI America 17093
6	6	20	Frontiers	*Journey*...Columbia 38504
7	7	36	H_2O	*Daryl Hall & John Oates*...RCA 4383
8	8	20	**Cuts Like A Knife**	*Bryan Adams*...A&M 4919
9	9	16	Kilroy Was Here	*Styx*...A&M 3734
10	10	33	Prince **1999**	*Prince*...Warner 23720

Billboard — JULY 9, 1983 — TOP LP's

TW	LW	WK	Title	Artist...Label
1	2	29	**Thriller**	*Michael Jackson*...Epic 38112
2	1	11	Flashdance	*Soundtrack*...Casablanca 811492
3	3	23	Pyromania	*Def Leppard*...Mercury 810308
4	17	2	Synchronicity	*The Police*...A&M 3735
5	5	11	Let's Dance	*David Bowie*...EMI America 17093
6	4	10	Cargo	*Men At Work*...Columbia 38660
7	6	21	Frontiers	*Journey*...Columbia 38504
8	8	21	**Cuts Like A Knife**	*Bryan Adams*...A&M 4919
9	10	34	**Prince **1999****	*Prince*...Warner 23720
10	7	37	H_2O	*Daryl Hall & John Oates*...RCA 4383

Billboard — JULY 16, 1983 — TOP LP's

TW	LW	WK	Title	Artist...Label
1	1	30	**Thriller**	*Michael Jackson*...Epic 38112
2	4	3	Synchronicity	*The Police*...A&M 3735
3	2	12	Flashdance	*Soundtrack*...Casablanca 811492
4	3	24	Pyromania	*Def Leppard*...Mercury 810308
5	5	12	Let's Dance	*David Bowie*...EMI America 17093
6	6	11	Cargo	*Men At Work*...Columbia 38660
7	12	3	The Wild Heart	*Stevie Nicks*...Modern 90084
8	18	3	Keep It Up	*Loverboy*...Columbia 38703
9	9	35	**Prince **1999****	*Prince*...Warner 23720
10	11	13	**Killer On The Rampage**	*Eddy Grant*...Portrait 38554

TW	LW	WK	Billboard. JULY 23, 1983 TOP LP's
1	2	4	**Synchronicity** ... *The Police*...A&M 3735
2	3	13	Flashdance ... *Soundtrack*...Casablanca 811492
3	1	31	Thriller ... *Michael Jackson*...Epic 38112
4	4	25	Pyromania ... *Def Leppard*...Mercury 810308
5	7	4	**The Wild Heart** ... *Stevie Nicks*...Modern 90084
6	5	13	Let's Dance ... *David Bowie*...EMI America 17093
7	8	4	**Keep It Up** ... *Loverboy*...Columbia 38703
8	6	12	Cargo ... *Men At Work*...Columbia 38660
9	9	36	**Prince **1999**** ... *Prince*...Warner 23720
10	10	14	**Killer On The Rampage** ... *Eddy Grant*...Portrait 38554

TW	LW	WK	Billboard. JULY 30, 1983 TOP LP's
1	1	5	**Synchronicity** ... *The Police*...A&M 3735
2	3	32	Thriller ... *Michael Jackson*...Epic 38112
3	2	14	Flashdance ... *Soundtrack*...Casablanca 811492
4	4	26	Pyromania ... *Def Leppard*...Mercury 810308
5	5	5	**The Wild Heart** ... *Stevie Nicks*...Modern 90084
6	6	14	Let's Dance ... *David Bowie*...EMI America 17093
7	7	5	**Keep It Up** ... *Loverboy*...Columbia 38703
8	8	13	Cargo ... *Men At Work*...Columbia 38660
9	9	37	**Prince **1999**** ... *Prince*...Warner 23720
10	10	15	**Killer On The Rampage** ... *Eddy Grant*...Portrait 38554

TW	LW	WK	Billboard. AUGUST 6, 1983 TOP LP's
1	1	6	**Synchronicity** ... *The Police*...A&M 3735
2	2	33	Thriller ... *Michael Jackson*...Epic 38112
3	3	15	Flashdance ... *Soundtrack*...Casablanca 811492
4	4	27	Pyromania ... *Def Leppard*...Mercury 810308
5	5	6	**The Wild Heart** ... *Stevie Nicks*...Modern 90084
6	6	15	Let's Dance ... *David Bowie*...EMI America 17093
7	7	6	**Keep It Up** ... *Loverboy*...Columbia 38703
8	8	14	Cargo ... *Men At Work*...Columbia 38660
9	9	38	**Prince **1999**** ... *Prince*...Warner 23720
10	11	25	Frontiers ... *Journey*...Columbia 38504

TW	LW	WK	Billboard. AUGUST 13, 1983 TOP LP's
1	1	7	**Synchronicity** ... *The Police*...A&M 3735
2	2	34	Thriller ... *Michael Jackson*...Epic 38112
3	3	16	Flashdance ... *Soundtrack*...Casablanca 811492
4	4	28	Pyromania ... *Def Leppard*...Mercury 810308
5	5	7	**The Wild Heart** ... *Stevie Nicks*...Modern 90084
6	6	16	Let's Dance ... *David Bowie*...EMI America 17093
7	7	7	**Keep It Up** ... *Loverboy*...Columbia 38703
8	8	15	Cargo ... *Men At Work*...Columbia 38660
9	10	26	Frontiers ... *Journey*...Columbia 38504
10	23	5	Staying Alive ... *Bee Gees*...RSO 813269

TW	LW	WK	Billboard® AUGUST 20, 1983	TOP LP's
❶	1	8	**Synchronicity**	*The Police*...A&M 3735
❷	2	35	Thriller	*Michael Jackson*...Epic 38112
③	3	17	Flashdance	*Soundtrack*...Casablanca 811492
④	4	29	Pyromania	*Def Leppard*...Mercury 810308
⑤	5	8	**The Wild Heart**	*Stevie Nicks*...Modern 90084
⑥	6	17	Let's Dance	*David Bowie*...EMI America 17093
❼	7	8	**Keep It Up**	*Loverboy*...Columbia 38703
❽	10	6	Staying Alive	*Bee Gees*...RSO 813269
❾	13	13	Reach The Beach	*The Fixx*...MCA 39001
❿	11	27	**Duran Duran**	*Duran Duran*...Capitol 12158

TW	LW	WK	Billboard® AUGUST 27, 1983	TOP LP's
❶	1	9	**Synchronicity**	*The Police*...A&M 3735
❷	2	36	Thriller	*Michael Jackson*...Epic 38112
③	3	18	Flashdance	*Soundtrack*...Casablanca 811492
④	4	30	Pyromania	*Def Leppard*...Mercury 810308
⑤	5	9	**The Wild Heart**	*Stevie Nicks*...Modern 90084
❻	8	7	**Staying Alive**	*Bee Gees*...RSO 813269
⑦	6	18	Let's Dance	*David Bowie*...EMI America 17093
⑧	7	9	Keep It Up	*Loverboy*...Columbia 38703
❾	11	7	**She Works Hard For The Money**	*Donna Summer*...Mercury 812265
⑩	9	14	Reach The Beach	*The Fixx*...MCA 39001

TW	LW	WK	Billboard® SEPTEMBER 3, 1983	TOP LP's
❶	1	10	**Synchronicity**	*The Police*...A&M 3735
❷	2	37	Thriller	*Michael Jackson*...Epic 38112
③	3	19	Flashdance	*Soundtrack*...Casablanca 811492
④	4	31	Pyromania	*Def Leppard*...Mercury 810308
⑤	5	10	**The Wild Heart**	*Stevie Nicks*...Modern 90084
⑥	6	8	**Staying Alive**	*Bee Gees*...RSO 813269
❼	18	3	An Innocent Man	*Billy Joel*...Columbia 38837
❽	29	2	Alpha	*Asia*...Geffen 4008
❾	13	3	Lawyers In Love	*Jackson Browne*...Asylum 60268
❿	10	15	Reach The Beach	*The Fixx*...MCA 39001

TW	LW	WK	Billboard® SEPTEMBER 10, 1983	TOP LP's
❶	2	38	**Thriller**	*Michael Jackson*...Epic 38112
②	1	11	Synchronicity	*The Police*...A&M 3735
③	3	20	Flashdance	*Soundtrack*...Casablanca 811492
④	4	32	Pyromania	*Def Leppard*...Mercury 810308
❺	7	4	An Innocent Man	*Billy Joel*...Columbia 38837
❻	8	3	**Alpha**	*Asia*...Geffen 4008
⑦	6	9	Staying Alive	*Bee Gees*...RSO 813269
❽	9	4	**Lawyers In Love**	*Jackson Browne*...Asylum 60268
⑨	5	11	The Wild Heart	*Stevie Nicks*...Modern 90084
⑩	10	16	Reach The Beach	*The Fixx*...MCA 39001

TW	LW	WK	Billboard® SEPTEMBER 17, 1983	TOP LP's
1	2	12	Synchronicity	*The Police*...A&M 3735
2	1	39	Thriller	*Michael Jackson*...Epic 38112
3	3	21	Flashdance	*Soundtrack*...Casablanca 811492
4	4	33	Pyromania	*Def Leppard*...Mercury 810308
5	5	5	An Innocent Man	*Billy Joel*...Columbia 38837
6	6	4	Alpha	*Asia*...Geffen 4008
7	7	10	Staying Alive	*Bee Gees*...RSO 813269
8	8	5	Lawyers In Love	*Jackson Browne*...Asylum 60268
9	9	12	The Wild Heart	*Stevie Nicks*...Modern 90084
10	10	17	Reach The Beach	*The Fixx*...MCA 39001

TW	LW	WK	Billboard® SEPTEMBER 24, 1983	TOP LP's
1	1	13	Synchronicity	*The Police*...A&M 3735
2	2	40	Thriller	*Michael Jackson*...Epic 38112
3	3	22	Flashdance	*Soundtrack*...Casablanca 811492
4	4	34	Pyromania	*Def Leppard*...Mercury 810308
5	5	6	An Innocent Man	*Billy Joel*...Columbia 38837
6	6	5	Alpha	*Asia*...Geffen 4008
7	9	13	The Wild Heart	*Stevie Nicks*...Modern 90084
8	8	6	Lawyers In Love	*Jackson Browne*...Asylum 60268
9	10	18	Reach The Beach	*The Fixx*...MCA 39001
10	11	9	The Principle Of Moments	*Robert Plant*...Es Paranza 90101

TW	LW	WK	Billboard® OCTOBER 1, 1983	TOP LP's
1	1	14	Synchronicity	*The Police*...A&M 3735
2	2	41	Thriller	*Michael Jackson*...Epic 38112
3	3	23	Flashdance	*Soundtrack*...Casablanca 811492
4	4	35	Pyromania	*Def Leppard*...Mercury 810308
5	5	7	An Innocent Man	*Billy Joel*...Columbia 38837
6	6	6	Alpha	*Asia*...Geffen 4008
7	12	24	Metal Health	*Quiet Riot*...Pasha 38443
8	17	9	Faster Than The Speed Of Night	*Bonnie Tyler*...Columbia 38710
9	9	19	Reach The Beach	*The Fixx*...MCA 39001
10	10	10	The Principle Of Moments	*Robert Plant*...Es Paranza 90101

TW	LW	WK	Billboard® OCTOBER 8, 1983	TOP LP's
1	1	15	Synchronicity	*The Police*...A&M 3735
2	2	42	Thriller	*Michael Jackson*...Epic 38112
3	3	24	Flashdance	*Soundtrack*...Casablanca 811492
4	5	8	An Innocent Man	*Billy Joel*...Columbia 38837
5	4	36	Pyromania	*Def Leppard*...Mercury 810308
6	7	25	Metal Health	*Quiet Riot*...Pasha 38443
7	8	10	Faster Than The Speed Of Night	*Bonnie Tyler*...Columbia 38710
8	10	11	The Principle Of Moments	*Robert Plant*...Es Paranza 90101
9	9	20	Reach The Beach	*The Fixx*...MCA 39001
10	14	8	Greatest Hits	*Air Supply*...Arista 8024

TW	LW	WK	Billboard. OCTOBER 15, 1983	TOP LP's
1	1	16	**Synchronicity**	*The Police*...A&M 3735
2	2	43	Thriller	*Michael Jackson*...Epic 38112
3	3	25	Flashdance	*Soundtrack*...Casablanca 811492
4	4	9	**An Innocent Man**	*Billy Joel*...Columbia 38837
5	5	37	Pyromania	*Def Leppard*...Mercury 810308
6	6	26	Metal Health	*Quiet Riot*...Pasha 38443
7	7	11	Faster Than The Speed Of Night	*Bonnie Tyler*...Columbia 38710
8	9	21	**Reach The Beach**	*The Fixx*...MCA 39001
9	10	9	Greatest Hits	*Air Supply*...Arista 8024
10	8	12	The Principle Of Moments	*Robert Plant*...Es Paranza 90101

TW	LW	WK	Billboard. OCTOBER 22, 1983	TOP LP's
1	1	17	**Synchronicity**	*The Police*...A&M 3735
2	2	44	Thriller	*Michael Jackson*...Epic 38112
3	6	27	Metal Health	*Quiet Riot*...Pasha 38443
4	4	10	**An Innocent Man**	*Billy Joel*...Columbia 38837
5	3	26	Flashdance	*Soundtrack*...Casablanca 811492
6	7	12	Faster Than The Speed Of Night	*Bonnie Tyler*...Columbia 38710
7	5	38	Pyromania	*Def Leppard*...Mercury 810308
8	8	22	**Reach The Beach**	*The Fixx*...MCA 39001
9	9	10	Greatest Hits	*Air Supply*...Arista 8024
10	10	13	The Principle Of Moments	*Robert Plant*...Es Paranza 90101

TW	LW	WK	Billboard. OCTOBER 29, 1983	TOP LP's
1	1	18	**Synchronicity**	*The Police*...A&M 3735
2	2	45	Thriller	*Michael Jackson*...Epic 38112
3	3	28	Metal Health	*Quiet Riot*...Pasha 38443
4	4	11	**An Innocent Man**	*Billy Joel*...Columbia 38837
5	6	13	Faster Than The Speed Of Night	*Bonnie Tyler*...Columbia 38710
6	7	39	Pyromania	*Def Leppard*...Mercury 810308
7	5	27	Flashdance	*Soundtrack*...Casablanca 811492
8	9	11	Greatest Hits	*Air Supply*...Arista 8024
9	12	6	Eyes That See In The Dark	*Kenny Rogers*...RCA 4697
10	11	5	What's New	*Linda Ronstadt*...Asylum 60260

TW	LW	WK	Billboard. NOVEMBER 5, 1983	TOP LP's
1	1	19	**Synchronicity**	*The Police*...A&M 3735
2	2	46	Thriller	*Michael Jackson*...Epic 38112
3	3	29	Metal Health	*Quiet Riot*...Pasha 38443
4	5	14	**Faster Than The Speed Of Night**	*Bonnie Tyler*...Columbia 38710
5	4	12	An Innocent Man	*Billy Joel*...Columbia 38837
6	6	40	Pyromania	*Def Leppard*...Mercury 810308
7	9	7	Eyes That See In The Dark	*Kenny Rogers*...RCA 4697
8	8	12	Greatest Hits	*Air Supply*...Arista 8024
9	7	28	Flashdance	*Soundtrack*...Casablanca 811492
10	10	6	What's New	*Linda Ronstadt*...Asylum 60260

TW	LW	WK	Billboard. NOVEMBER 12, 1983 TOP LP's
1	1	20	**Synchronicity** ... *The Police*...A&M 3735
2	3	30	Metal Health ... *Quiet Riot*...Pasha 38443
3	2	47	Thriller ... *Michael Jackson*...Epic 38112
4	5	13	**An Innocent Man** ... *Billy Joel*...Columbia 38837
5	4	15	Faster Than The Speed Of Night ... *Bonnie Tyler*...Columbia 38710
6	7	8	**Eyes That See In The Dark** ... *Kenny Rogers*...RCA 4697
7	6	41	Pyromania ... *Def Leppard*...Mercury 810308
8	8	13	Greatest Hits ... *Air Supply*...Arista 8024
9	11	30	**Eliminator** ... *ZZ Top*...Warner 23774
10	10	7	What's New ... *Linda Ronstadt*...Asylum 60260

TW	LW	WK	Billboard. NOVEMBER 19, 1983 TOP LP's
1	1	21	**Synchronicity** ... *The Police*...A&M 3735
2	2	31	Metal Health ... *Quiet Riot*...Pasha 38443
3	3	48	Thriller ... *Michael Jackson*...Epic 38112
4	15	2	Can't Slow Down ... *Lionel Richie*...Motown 6059
5	4	14	An Innocent Man ... *Billy Joel*...Columbia 38837
6	6	9	**Eyes That See In The Dark** ... *Kenny Rogers*...RCA 4697
7	8	14	**Greatest Hits** ... *Air Supply*...Arista 8024
8	7	42	Pyromania ... *Def Leppard*...Mercury 810308
9	10	8	What's New ... *Linda Ronstadt*...Asylum 60260
10	11	4	Genesis ... *Genesis*...Atlantic 80116

TW	LW	WK	Billboard. NOVEMBER 26, 1983 TOP LP's
1	2	32	**Metal Health** ... *Quiet Riot*...Pasha 38443
2	4	3	Can't Slow Down ... *Lionel Richie*...Motown 6059
3	3	49	Thriller ... *Michael Jackson*...Epic 38112
4	1	22	Synchronicity ... *The Police*...A&M 3735
5	5	15	An Innocent Man ... *Billy Joel*...Columbia 38837
6	6	10	**Eyes That See In The Dark** ... *Kenny Rogers*...RCA 4697
7	9	9	What's New ... *Linda Ronstadt*...Asylum 60260
8	7	15	Greatest Hits ... *Air Supply*...Arista 8024
9	12	4	Colour By Numbers ... *Culture Club*...Epic 39107
10	10	5	Genesis ... *Genesis*...Atlantic 80116

TW	LW	WK	Billboard. DECEMBER 3, 1983 TOP LP's
1	2	4	**Can't Slow Down** ... *Lionel Richie*...Motown 6059
2	1	33	Metal Health ... *Quiet Riot*...Pasha 38443
3	4	23	Synchronicity ... *The Police*...A&M 3735
4	3	50	Thriller ... *Michael Jackson*...Epic 38112
5	5	16	An Innocent Man ... *Billy Joel*...Columbia 38837
6	6	11	**Eyes That See In The Dark** ... *Kenny Rogers*...RCA 4697
7	7	10	What's New ... *Linda Ronstadt*...Asylum 60260
8	9	5	Colour By Numbers ... *Culture Club*...Epic 39107
9	10	6	**Genesis** ... *Genesis*...Atlantic 80116
10	11	44	Pyromania ... *Def Leppard*...Mercury 810308

TW	LW	WK	Billboard® DECEMBER 10, 1983 TOP LP's
1	1	5	**Can't Slow Down**...*Lionel Richie*...Motown 6059
2	3	24	Synchronicity...*The Police*...A&M 3735
3	4	51	Thriller...*Michael Jackson*...Epic 38112
4	13	3	**Undercover**...*The Rolling Stones*...Rolling Stones 90120
5	5	17	An Innocent Man...*Billy Joel*...Columbia 38837
6	2	34	Metal Health...*Quiet Riot*...Pasha 38443
7	7	11	What's New...*Linda Ronstadt*...Asylum 60260
8	6	12	Eyes That See In The Dark...*Kenny Rogers*...RCA 4697
9	8	6	Colour By Numbers...*Culture Club*...Epic 39107
10	14	4	Rock 'N Soul, Part 1...*Daryl Hall & John Oates*...RCA 4858

TW	LW	WK	Billboard® DECEMBER 17, 1983 TOP LP's
1	1	6	**Can't Slow Down**...*Lionel Richie*...Motown 6059
2	3	52	Thriller...*Michael Jackson*...Epic 38112
3	2	25	Synchronicity...*The Police*...A&M 3735
4	4	4	**Undercover**...*The Rolling Stones*...Rolling Stones 90120
5	7	12	What's New...*Linda Ronstadt*...Asylum 60260
6	6	35	Metal Health...*Quiet Riot*...Pasha 38443
7	8	13	Eyes That See In The Dark...*Kenny Rogers*...RCA 4697
8	9	7	Colour By Numbers...*Culture Club*...Epic 39107
9	5	18	An Innocent Man...*Billy Joel*...Columbia 38837
10	10	5	Rock 'N Soul, Part 1...*Daryl Hall & John Oates*...RCA 4858

TW	LW	WK	Billboard® DECEMBER 24, 1983 TOP LP's
1	2	53	**Thriller**...*Michael Jackson*...Epic 38112
2	1	7	Can't Slow Down...*Lionel Richie*...Motown 6059
3	5	13	**What's New**...*Linda Ronstadt*...Asylum 60260
4	3	26	Synchronicity...*The Police*...A&M 3735
5	4	5	Undercover...*The Rolling Stones*...Rolling Stones 90120
6	6	36	Metal Health...*Quiet Riot*...Pasha 38443
7	13	4	90125...*Yes*...Atco 90125
8	9	19	An Innocent Man...*Billy Joel*...Columbia 38837
9	8	8	Colour By Numbers...*Culture Club*...Epic 39107
10	10	6	Rock 'N Soul, Part 1...*Daryl Hall & John Oates*...RCA 4858

Billboard — JANUARY 7, 1984 — TOP LP's

TW	LW	WK	Title	Artist	Label
1	1	55	**Thriller**	*Michael Jackson*	Epic 38112
2	2	9	Can't Slow Down	*Lionel Richie*	Motown 6059
3	3	15	**What's New**	*Linda Ronstadt*	Asylum 60260
4	4	28	Synchronicity	*The Police*	A&M 3735
5	6	38	Metal Health	*Quiet Riot*	Pasha 38443
6	7	6	90125	*Yes*	Atco 90125
7	9	10	Colour By Numbers	*Culture Club*	Epic 39107
8	8	21	An Innocent Man	*Billy Joel*	Columbia 38837
9	14	7	**Yentl**	*Barbra Streisand/Soundtrack*	Columbia 39152
10	10	8	Rock 'N Soul, Part 1	*Daryl Hall & John Oates*	RCA 4858

Billboard — JANUARY 14, 1984 — TOP LP's

TW	LW	WK	Title	Artist	Label
1	1	56	**Thriller**	*Michael Jackson*	Epic 38112
2	2	10	Can't Slow Down	*Lionel Richie*	Motown 6059
3	3	16	**What's New**	*Linda Ronstadt*	Asylum 60260
4	4	29	Synchronicity	*The Police*	A&M 3735
5	5	39	Metal Health	*Quiet Riot*	Pasha 38443
6	6	7	90125	*Yes*	Atco 90125
7	7	11	Colour By Numbers	*Culture Club*	Epic 39107
8	8	22	An Innocent Man	*Billy Joel*	Columbia 38837
9	9	8	**Yentl**	*Barbra Streisand/Soundtrack*	Columbia 39152
10	10	9	Rock 'N Soul, Part 1	*Daryl Hall & John Oates*	RCA 4858

Billboard — JANUARY 21, 1984 — TOP LP's

TW	LW	WK	Title	Artist	Label
1	1	57	**Thriller**	*Michael Jackson*	Epic 38112
2	2	11	Can't Slow Down	*Lionel Richie*	Motown 6059
3	3	17	**What's New**	*Linda Ronstadt*	Asylum 60260
4	7	12	Colour By Numbers	*Culture Club*	Epic 39107
5	6	8	**90125**	*Yes*	Atco 90125
6	4	30	Synchronicity	*The Police*	A&M 3735
7	5	40	Metal Health	*Quiet Riot*	Pasha 38443
8	8	23	An Innocent Man	*Billy Joel*	Columbia 38837
9	10	10	Rock 'N Soul, Part 1	*Daryl Hall & John Oates*	RCA 4858
10	11	7	Seven And The Ragged Tiger	*Duran Duran*	Capitol 12310

Billboard — JANUARY 28, 1984 — TOP LP's

TW	LW	WK	Title	Artist	Label
1	1	58	**Thriller**	*Michael Jackson*	Epic 38112
2	2	12	Can't Slow Down	*Lionel Richie*	Motown 6059
3	4	13	Colour By Numbers	*Culture Club*	Epic 39107
4	3	18	What's New	*Linda Ronstadt*	Asylum 60260
5	5	9	**90125**	*Yes*	Atco 90125
6	6	31	Synchronicity	*The Police*	A&M 3735
7	9	11	**Rock 'N Soul, Part 1**	*Daryl Hall & John Oates*	RCA 4858
8	8	24	An Innocent Man	*Billy Joel*	Columbia 38837
9	12	13	**Uh-Huh**	*John Cougar Mellencamp*	Riva 7504
10	10	8	Seven And The Ragged Tiger	*Duran Duran*	Capitol 12310

Billboard — FEBRUARY 4, 1984 — TOP LP's

TW	LW	WK	Title	Artist	Label
1	1	59	**Thriller**	*Michael Jackson*	Epic 38112
2	3	14	**Colour By Numbers**	*Culture Club*	Epic 39107
3	2	13	Can't Slow Down	*Lionel Richie*	Motown 6059
4	18	2	1984 (MCMLXXXIV)	*Van Halen*	Warner 23985
5	5	10	**90125**	*Yes*	Atco 90125
6	6	32	Synchronicity	*The Police*	A&M 3735
7	7	12	**Rock 'N Soul, Part 1**	*Daryl Hall & John Oates*	RCA 4858
8	8	25	An Innocent Man	*Billy Joel*	Columbia 38837
9	4	19	What's New	*Linda Ronstadt*	Asylum 60260
10	10	9	Seven And The Ragged Tiger	*Duran Duran*	Capitol 12310

Billboard — FEBRUARY 11, 1984 — TOP LP's

TW	LW	WK	Title	Artist	Label
1	1	60	**Thriller**	*Michael Jackson*	Epic 38112
2	2	15	**Colour By Numbers**	*Culture Club*	Epic 39107
3	3	14	Can't Slow Down	*Lionel Richie*	Motown 6059
4	4	3	1984 (MCMLXXXIV)	*Van Halen*	Warner 23985
5	5	11	**90125**	*Yes*	Atco 90125
6	6	33	Synchronicity	*The Police*	A&M 3735
7	8	26	An Innocent Man	*Billy Joel*	Columbia 38837
8	10	10	**Seven And The Ragged Tiger**	*Duran Duran*	Capitol 12310
9	7	13	Rock 'N Soul, Part 1	*Daryl Hall & John Oates*	RCA 4858
10	25	2	Learning To Crawl	*The Pretenders*	Sire 23980

Billboard — FEBRUARY 18, 1984 — TOP LP's

TW	LW	WK	Title	Artist	Label
1	1	61	**Thriller**	*Michael Jackson*	Epic 38112
2	2	16	**Colour By Numbers**	*Culture Club*	Epic 39107
3	4	4	1984 (MCMLXXXIV)	*Van Halen*	Warner 23985
4	3	15	Can't Slow Down	*Lionel Richie*	Motown 6059
5	6	34	Synchronicity	*The Police*	A&M 3735
6	7	27	An Innocent Man	*Billy Joel*	Columbia 38837
7	10	3	Learning To Crawl	*The Pretenders*	Sire 23980
8	8	11	**Seven And The Ragged Tiger**	*Duran Duran*	Capitol 12310
9	5	12	90125	*Yes*	Atco 90125
10	9	14	Rock 'N Soul, Part 1	*Daryl Hall & John Oates*	RCA 4858

Billboard — FEBRUARY 25, 1984 — TOP LP's

TW	LW	WK	Title	Artist	Label
1	1	62	**Thriller**	*Michael Jackson*	Epic 38112
2	2	17	**Colour By Numbers**	*Culture Club*	Epic 39107
3	3	5	1984 (MCMLXXXIV)	*Van Halen*	Warner 23985
4	4	16	Can't Slow Down	*Lionel Richie*	Motown 6059
5	7	4	**Learning To Crawl**	*The Pretenders*	Sire 23980
6	6	28	An Innocent Man	*Billy Joel*	Columbia 38837
7	5	35	Synchronicity	*The Police*	A&M 3735
8	8	12	**Seven And The Ragged Tiger**	*Duran Duran*	Capitol 12310
9	9	13	90125	*Yes*	Atco 90125
10	11	17	Uh-Huh	*John Cougar Mellencamp*	Riva 7504

TW	LW	WK	Billboard — MARCH 3, 1984 — TOP LP's
1	1	63	**Thriller**... *Michael Jackson*...Epic 38112
2	2	18	**Colour By Numbers**... *Culture Club*...Epic 39107
3	3	6	1984 (MCMLXXXIV)... *Van Halen*...Warner 23985
4	4	17	Can't Slow Down... *Lionel Richie*...Motown 6059
5	5	5	**Learning To Crawl**... *The Pretenders*...Sire 23980
6	6	29	An Innocent Man... *Billy Joel*...Columbia 38837
7	7	36	Synchronicity... *The Police*...A&M 3735
8	8	13	**Seven And The Ragged Tiger**... *Duran Duran*...Capitol 12310
9	9	14	90125... *Yes*...Atco 90125
10	11	22	Sports... *Huey Lewis & The News*...Chrysalis 41412

TW	LW	WK	Billboard — MARCH 10, 1984 — TOP LP's
1	1	64	**Thriller**... *Michael Jackson*...Epic 38112
2	2	19	**Colour By Numbers**... *Culture Club*...Epic 39107
3	3	7	1984 (MCMLXXXIV)... *Van Halen*...Warner 23985
4	4	18	Can't Slow Down... *Lionel Richie*...Motown 6059
5	5	6	**Learning To Crawl**... *The Pretenders*...Sire 23980
6	6	30	An Innocent Man... *Billy Joel*...Columbia 38837
7	7	37	Synchronicity... *The Police*...A&M 3735
8	10	23	Sports... *Huey Lewis & The News*...Chrysalis 41412
9	9	15	90125... *Yes*...Atco 90125
10	8	14	Seven And The Ragged Tiger... *Duran Duran*...Capitol 12310

TW	LW	WK	Billboard — MARCH 17, 1984 — TOP LP's
1	1	65	**Thriller**... *Michael Jackson*...Epic 38112
2	3	8	**1984 (MCMLXXXIV)**... *Van Halen*...Warner 23985
3	2	20	Colour By Numbers... *Culture Club*...Epic 39107
4	4	19	Can't Slow Down... *Lionel Richie*...Motown 6059
5	5	7	**Learning To Crawl**... *The Pretenders*...Sire 23980
6	8	24	Sports... *Huey Lewis & The News*...Chrysalis 41412
7	7	38	Synchronicity... *The Police*...A&M 3735
8	6	31	An Innocent Man... *Billy Joel*...Columbia 38837
9	21	5	Footloose... *Soundtrack*...Columbia 39242
10	10	15	Seven And The Ragged Tiger... *Duran Duran*...Capitol 12310

TW	LW	WK	Billboard — MARCH 24, 1984 — TOP LP's
1	1	66	**Thriller**... *Michael Jackson*...Epic 38112
2	2	9	**1984 (MCMLXXXIV)**... *Van Halen*...Warner 23985
3	3	21	Colour By Numbers... *Culture Club*...Epic 39107
4	4	20	Can't Slow Down... *Lionel Richie*...Motown 6059
5	9	6	Footloose... *Soundtrack*...Columbia 39242
6	6	25	Sports... *Huey Lewis & The News*...Chrysalis 41412
7	5	8	Learning To Crawl... *The Pretenders*...Sire 23980
8	7	39	Synchronicity... *The Police*...A&M 3735
9	11	8	Touch... *Eurythmics*...RCA 4917
10	8	32	An Innocent Man... *Billy Joel*...Columbia 38837

Billboard ● MARCH 31, 1984 ● TOP LP's

TW	LW	WK	Title	Artist...Label
❶	1	67	**Thriller**	Michael Jackson...Epic 38112
❷	2	10	**1984 (MCMLXXXIV)**	Van Halen...Warner 23985
❸	5	7	**Footloose**	Soundtrack...Columbia 39242
④	3	22	**Colour By Numbers**	Culture Club...Epic 39107
⑤	4	21	**Can't Slow Down**	Lionel Richie...Motown 6059
❻	6	26	**Sports**	Huey Lewis & The News...Chrysalis 41412
⑦	7	9	**Learning To Crawl**	The Pretenders...Sire 23980
❽	9	9	**Touch**	Eurythmics...RCA 4917
⑨	8	40	**Synchronicity**	The Police...A&M 3735
⑩	12	15	**She's So Unusual**	Cyndi Lauper...Portrait 38930

Billboard ● APRIL 7, 1984 ● TOP LP's

TW	LW	WK	Title	Artist...Label
❶	1	68	**Thriller**	Michael Jackson...Epic 38112
❷	3	8	**Footloose**	Soundtrack...Columbia 39242
③	2	11	**1984 (MCMLXXXIV)**	Van Halen...Warner 23985
④	4	23	**Colour By Numbers**	Culture Club...Epic 39107
⑤	5	22	**Can't Slow Down**	Lionel Richie...Motown 6059
❻	6	27	**Sports**	Huey Lewis & The News...Chrysalis 41412
❼	8	10	**Touch**	Eurythmics...RCA 4917
⑧	7	10	**Learning To Crawl**	The Pretenders...Sire 23980
⑨	9	41	**Synchronicity**	The Police...A&M 3735
⑩	10	16	**She's So Unusual**	Cyndi Lauper...Portrait 38930

Billboard ● APRIL 14, 1984 ● TOP LP's

TW	LW	WK	Title	Artist...Label
❶	1	69	**Thriller**	Michael Jackson...Epic 38112
❷	2	9	**Footloose**	Soundtrack...Columbia 39242
❸	3	12	**1984 (MCMLXXXIV)**	Van Halen...Warner 23985
❹	5	23	**Can't Slow Down**	Lionel Richie...Motown 6059
❺	6	28	**Sports**	Huey Lewis & The News...Chrysalis 41412
⑥	4	24	**Colour By Numbers**	Culture Club...Epic 39107
⑦	7	11	**Touch**	Eurythmics...RCA 4917
❽	11	5	**Love At First Sting**	Scorpions...Mercury 814981
⑨	8	11	**Learning To Crawl**	The Pretenders...Sire 23980
⑩	10	17	**She's So Unusual**	Cyndi Lauper...Portrait 38930

Billboard ● APRIL 21, 1984 ● TOP LP's

TW	LW	WK	Title	Artist...Label
❶	2	10	**Footloose**	Soundtrack...Columbia 39242
❷	3	13	**1984 (MCMLXXXIV)**	Van Halen...Warner 23985
③	1	70	**Thriller**	Michael Jackson...Epic 38112
❹	4	24	**Can't Slow Down**	Lionel Richie...Motown 6059
❺	5	29	**Sports**	Huey Lewis & The News...Chrysalis 41412
❻	6	25	**Colour By Numbers**	Culture Club...Epic 39107
⑦	7	12	**Touch**	Eurythmics...RCA 4917
❽	8	6	**Love At First Sting**	Scorpions...Mercury 814981
⑨	13	3	**Heartbeat City**	The Cars...Elektra 60296
⑩	10	18	**She's So Unusual**	Cyndi Lauper...Portrait 38930

TW	LW	WK	Billboard®	APRIL 28, 1984	TOP LP's
1	1	11	Footloose	*Soundtrack*	Columbia 39242
2	2	14	1984 (MCMLXXXIV)	*Van Halen*	Warner 23985
3	4	25	Can't Slow Down	*Lionel Richie*	Motown 6059
4	3	71	Thriller	*Michael Jackson*	Epic 38112
5	6	26	Colour By Numbers	*Culture Club*	Epic 39107
6	5	30	Sports	*Huey Lewis & The News*	Chrysalis 41412
7	9	4	Heartbeat City	*The Cars*	Elektra 60296
8	8	7	Love At First Sting	*Scorpions*	Mercury 814981
9	7	13	Touch	*Eurythmics*	RCA 4917
10	10	19	She's So Unusual	*Cyndi Lauper*	Portrait 38930

TW	LW	WK	Billboard®	MAY 5, 1984	TOP LP's
1	1	12	Footloose	*Soundtrack*	Columbia 39242
2	3	26	Can't Slow Down	*Lionel Richie*	Motown 6059
3	2	15	1984 (MCMLXXXIV)	*Van Halen*	Warner 23985
4	4	72	Thriller	*Michael Jackson*	Epic 38112
5	5	27	Colour By Numbers	*Culture Club*	Epic 39107
6	6	31	Sports	*Huey Lewis & The News*	Chrysalis 41412
7	7	5	Heartbeat City	*The Cars*	Elektra 60296
8	8	8	Love At First Sting	*Scorpions*	Mercury 814981
9	10	20	She's So Unusual	*Cyndi Lauper*	Portrait 38930
10	11	8	Into The Gap	*Thompson Twins*	Arista 8200

TW	LW	WK	Billboard®	MAY 12, 1984	TOP LP's
1	1	13	Footloose	*Soundtrack*	Columbia 39242
2	2	27	Can't Slow Down	*Lionel Richie*	Motown 6059
3	4	73	Thriller	*Michael Jackson*	Epic 38112
4	3	16	1984 (MCMLXXXIV)	*Van Halen*	Warner 23985
5	5	28	Colour By Numbers	*Culture Club*	Epic 39107
6	7	6	Heartbeat City	*The Cars*	Elektra 60296
7	6	32	Sports	*Huey Lewis & The News*	Chrysalis 41412
8	8	9	Love At First Sting	*Scorpions*	Mercury 814981
9	9	21	She's So Unusual	*Cyndi Lauper*	Portrait 38930
10	10	9	Into The Gap	*Thompson Twins*	Arista 8200

TW	LW	WK	Billboard®	MAY 19, 1984	TOP LP's
1	1	14	Footloose	*Soundtrack*	Columbia 39242
2	2	28	Can't Slow Down	*Lionel Richie*	Motown 6059
3	3	74	Thriller	*Michael Jackson*	Epic 38112
4	4	17	1984 (MCMLXXXIV)	*Van Halen*	Warner 23985
5	7	33	Sports	*Huey Lewis & The News*	Chrysalis 41412
6	6	7	Heartbeat City	*The Cars*	Elektra 60296
7	5	29	Colour By Numbers	*Culture Club*	Epic 39107
8	8	10	Love At First Sting	*Scorpions*	Mercury 814981
9	9	22	She's So Unusual	*Cyndi Lauper*	Portrait 38930
10	13	3	Grace Under Pressure	*Rush*	Mercury 818476

TW	LW	WK	Billboard® — MAY 26, 1984 — TOP LP's	
1	1	15	**Footloose**	Soundtrack...Columbia 39242
2	2	29	Can't Slow Down	Lionel Richie...Motown 6059
3	3	75	Thriller	Michael Jackson...Epic 38112
4	5	34	Sports	Huey Lewis & The News...Chrysalis 41412
5	4	18	1984 (MCMLXXXIV)	Van Halen...Warner 23985
6	7	30	Colour By Numbers	Culture Club...Epic 39107
7	9	23	She's So Unusual	Cyndi Lauper...Portrait 38930
8	8	11	Love At First Sting	Scorpions...Mercury 814981
9	6	8	Heartbeat City	The Cars...Elektra 60296
10	10	4	**Grace Under Pressure**	Rush...Mercury 818476

TW	LW	WK	Billboard® — JUNE 2, 1984 — TOP LP's	
1	1	16	**Footloose**	Soundtrack...Columbia 39242
2	2	30	Can't Slow Down	Lionel Richie...Motown 6059
3	4	35	Sports	Huey Lewis & The News...Chrysalis 41412
4	7	24	**She's So Unusual**	Cyndi Lauper...Portrait 38930
5	9	9	Heartbeat City	The Cars...Elektra 60296
6	3	76	Thriller	Michael Jackson...Epic 38112
7	5	19	1984 (MCMLXXXIV)	Van Halen...Warner 23985
8	6	31	Colour By Numbers	Culture Club...Epic 39107
9	8	12	Love At First Sting	Scorpions...Mercury 814981
10	10	5	**Grace Under Pressure**	Rush...Mercury 818476

TW	LW	WK	Billboard® — JUNE 9, 1984 — TOP LP's	
1	1	17	**Footloose**	Soundtrack...Columbia 39242
2	2	31	Can't Slow Down	Lionel Richie...Motown 6059
3	3	36	Sports	Huey Lewis & The News...Chrysalis 41412
4	4	25	**She's So Unusual**	Cyndi Lauper...Portrait 38930
5	5	10	Heartbeat City	The Cars...Elektra 60296
6	8	32	Colour By Numbers	Culture Club...Epic 39107
7	9	13	Love At First Sting	Scorpions...Mercury 814981
8	6	77	Thriller	Michael Jackson...Epic 38112
9	7	20	1984 (MCMLXXXIV)	Van Halen...Warner 23985
10	10	6	**Grace Under Pressure**	Rush...Mercury 818476

TW	LW	WK	Billboard® — JUNE 16, 1984 — TOP LP's	
1	1	18	**Footloose**	Soundtrack...Columbia 39242
2	3	37	Sports	Huey Lewis & The News...Chrysalis 41412
3	2	32	Can't Slow Down	Lionel Richie...Motown 6059
4	4	26	**She's So Unusual**	Cyndi Lauper...Portrait 38930
5	5	11	Heartbeat City	The Cars...Elektra 60296
6	7	14	**Love At First Sting**	Scorpions...Mercury 814981
7	6	33	Colour By Numbers	Culture Club...Epic 39107
8	8	78	Thriller	Michael Jackson...Epic 38112
9	9	21	1984 (MCMLXXXIV)	Van Halen...Warner 23985
10	14	28	Seven And The Ragged Tiger	Duran Duran...Capitol 12310

TW	LW	WK	Billboard. JUNE 23, 1984 TOP LP's
1	1	19	**Footloose** ... *Soundtrack*...Columbia 39242
2	2	38	Sports ... *Huey Lewis & The News*...Chrysalis 41412
3	3	33	Can't Slow Down ... *Lionel Richie*...Motown 6059
4	4	27	**She's So Unusual** ... *Cyndi Lauper*...Portrait 38930
5	5	12	Heartbeat City ... *The Cars*...Elektra 60296
6	6	15	**Love At First Sting** ... *Scorpions*...Mercury 814981
7	9	22	1984 (MCMLXXXIV) ... *Van Halen*...Warner 23985
8	8	79	Thriller ... *Michael Jackson*...Epic 38112
9	-	1	Born In The U.S.A. ... *Bruce Springsteen*...Columbia 38653
10	10	29	Seven And The Ragged Tiger ... *Duran Duran*...Capitol 12310

TW	LW	WK	Billboard. JUNE 30, 1984 TOP LP's
1	2	39	**Sports** ... *Huey Lewis & The News*...Chrysalis 41412
2	1	20	Footloose ... *Soundtrack*...Columbia 39242
3	9	2	Born In The U.S.A. ... *Bruce Springsteen*...Columbia 38653
4	3	34	Can't Slow Down ... *Lionel Richie*...Motown 6059
5	5	13	Heartbeat City ... *The Cars*...Elektra 60296
6	4	28	She's So Unusual ... *Cyndi Lauper*...Portrait 38930
7	7	23	1984 (MCMLXXXIV) ... *Van Halen*...Warner 23985
8	8	80	Thriller ... *Michael Jackson*...Epic 38112
9	6	16	Love At First Sting ... *Scorpions*...Mercury 814981
10	10	30	Seven And The Ragged Tiger ... *Duran Duran*...Capitol 12310

TW	LW	WK	Billboard. JULY 7, 1984 TOP LP's
1	3	3	**Born In The U.S.A.** ... *Bruce Springsteen*...Columbia 38653
2	1	40	Sports ... *Huey Lewis & The News*...Chrysalis 41412
3	2	21	Footloose ... *Soundtrack*...Columbia 39242
4	5	14	Heartbeat City ... *The Cars*...Elektra 60296
5	4	35	Can't Slow Down ... *Lionel Richie*...Motown 6059
6	6	29	She's So Unusual ... *Cyndi Lauper*...Portrait 38930
7	7	24	1984 (MCMLXXXIV) ... *Van Halen*...Warner 23985
8	9	17	Love At First Sting ... *Scorpions*...Mercury 814981
9	11	32	Rebel Yell ... *Billy Idol*...Chrysalis 41450
10	10	31	Seven And The Ragged Tiger ... *Duran Duran*...Capitol 12310

TW	LW	WK	Billboard. JULY 14, 1984 TOP LP's
1	1	4	**Born In The U.S.A.** ... *Bruce Springsteen*...Columbia 38653
2	2	41	Sports ... *Huey Lewis & The News*...Chrysalis 41412
3	4	15	**Heartbeat City** ... *The Cars*...Elektra 60296
4	3	22	Footloose ... *Soundtrack*...Columbia 39242
5	5	36	Can't Slow Down ... *Lionel Richie*...Motown 6059
6	9	33	**Rebel Yell** ... *Billy Idol*...Chrysalis 41450
7	7	25	1984 (MCMLXXXIV) ... *Van Halen*...Warner 23985
8	10	32	**Seven And The Ragged Tiger** ... *Duran Duran*...Capitol 12310
9	11	7	Breakin' ... *Soundtrack*...Polydor 821919
10	13	65	Eliminator ... *ZZ Top*...Warner 23774

TW	LW	WK	Billboard	JULY 21, 1984	TOP LP's
1	1	5	**Born In The U.S.A.**	*Bruce Springsteen*	Columbia 38653
2	2	42	Sports	*Huey Lewis & The News*	Chrysalis 41412
3	11	2	Purple Rain	*Prince & The Revolution/Soundtrack*	Warner 25110
4	3	16	Heartbeat City	*The Cars*	Elektra 60296
5	5	37	Can't Slow Down	*Lionel Richie*	Motown 6059
6	6	34	**Rebel Yell**	*Billy Idol*	Chrysalis 41450
7	4	23	Footloose	*Soundtrack*	Columbia 39242
8	9	8	**Breakin'**	*Soundtrack*	Polydor 821919
9	7	26	1984 (MCMLXXXIV)	*Van Halen*	Warner 23985
10	10	66	Eliminator	*ZZ Top*	Warner 23774

TW	LW	WK	Billboard	JULY 28, 1984	TOP LP's
1	1	6	**Born In The U.S.A.**	*Bruce Springsteen*	Columbia 38653
2	3	3	Purple Rain	*Prince & The Revolution/Soundtrack*	Warner 25110
3	2	43	Sports	*Huey Lewis & The News*	Chrysalis 41412
4	4	17	Heartbeat City	*The Cars*	Elektra 60296
5	5	38	Can't Slow Down	*Lionel Richie*	Motown 6059
6	6	35	**Rebel Yell**	*Billy Idol*	Chrysalis 41450
7	17	2	Victory	*The Jacksons*	Epic 38946
8	8	9	**Breakin'**	*Soundtrack*	Polydor 821919
9	7	24	Footloose	*Soundtrack*	Columbia 39242
10	9	27	1984 (MCMLXXXIV)	*Van Halen*	Warner 23985

TW	LW	WK	Billboard	AUGUST 4, 1984	TOP LP's
1	2	4	**Purple Rain**	*Prince & The Revolution/Soundtrack*	Warner 25110
2	1	7	Born In The U.S.A.	*Bruce Springsteen*	Columbia 38653
3	3	44	Sports	*Huey Lewis & The News*	Chrysalis 41412
4	7	3	**Victory**	*The Jacksons*	Epic 38946
5	5	39	Can't Slow Down	*Lionel Richie*	Motown 6059
6	4	18	Heartbeat City	*The Cars*	Elektra 60296
7	11	20	**Out Of The Cellar**	*Ratt*	Atlantic 80143
8	19	5	Ghostbusters	*Soundtrack*	Arista 8246
9	8	10	Breakin'	*Soundtrack*	Polydor 821919
10	10	28	1984 (MCMLXXXIV)	*Van Halen*	Warner 23985

TW	LW	WK	Billboard	AUGUST 11, 1984	TOP LP's
1	1	5	**Purple Rain**	*Prince & The Revolution/Soundtrack*	Warner 25110
2	3	45	Sports	*Huey Lewis & The News*	Chrysalis 41412
3	2	8	Born In The U.S.A.	*Bruce Springsteen*	Columbia 38653
4	4	4	**Victory**	*The Jacksons*	Epic 38946
5	6	19	Heartbeat City	*The Cars*	Elektra 60296
6	5	40	Can't Slow Down	*Lionel Richie*	Motown 6059
7	7	21	**Out Of The Cellar**	*Ratt*	Atlantic 80143
8	8	6	Ghostbusters	*Soundtrack*	Arista 8246
9	13	9	Private Dancer	*Tina Turner*	Capitol 12330
10	11	37	Rebel Yell	*Billy Idol*	Chrysalis 41450

TW	LW	WK	Billboard® AUGUST 18, 1984 TOP LP's
1	1	6	**Purple Rain** ... *Prince & The Revolution/Soundtrack*...Warner 25110
2	3	9	Born In The U.S.A ... *Bruce Springsteen*...Columbia 38653
3	2	46	Sports ... *Huey Lewis & The News*...Chrysalis 41412
4	4	5	**Victory** ... *The Jacksons*...Epic 38946
5	5	20	Heartbeat City ... *The Cars*...Elektra 60296
6	8	7	**Ghostbusters** ... *Soundtrack*...Arista 8246
7	6	41	Can't Slow Down ... *Lionel Richie*...Motown 6059
8	9	10	Private Dancer ... *Tina Turner*...Capitol 12330
9	7	22	Out Of The Cellar ... *Ratt*...Atlantic 80143
10	12	70	Eliminator ... *ZZ Top*...Warner 23774

TW	LW	WK	Billboard® AUGUST 25, 1984 TOP LP's
1	1	7	**Purple Rain** ... *Prince & The Revolution/Soundtrack*...Warner 25110
2	3	47	Sports ... *Huey Lewis & The News*...Chrysalis 41412
3	2	10	Born In The U.S.A ... *Bruce Springsteen*...Columbia 38653
4	8	11	Private Dancer ... *Tina Turner*...Capitol 12330
5	5	21	Heartbeat City ... *The Cars*...Elektra 60296
6	6	8	**Ghostbusters** ... *Soundtrack*...Arista 8246
7	4	6	Victory ... *The Jacksons*...Epic 38946
8	7	42	Can't Slow Down ... *Lionel Richie*...Motown 6059
9	9	23	Out Of The Cellar ... *Ratt*...Atlantic 80143
10	14	40	Break Out ... *Pointer Sisters*...Planet 4705

TW	LW	WK	Billboard® SEPTEMBER 1, 1984 TOP LP's
1	1	8	**Purple Rain** ... *Prince & The Revolution/Soundtrack*...Warner 25110
2	3	11	Born In The U.S.A ... *Bruce Springsteen*...Columbia 38653
3	2	48	Sports ... *Huey Lewis & The News*...Chrysalis 41412
4	4	12	Private Dancer ... *Tina Turner*...Capitol 12330
5	5	22	Heartbeat City ... *The Cars*...Elektra 60296
6	6	9	**Ghostbusters** ... *Soundtrack*...Arista 8246
7	8	43	Can't Slow Down ... *Lionel Richie*...Motown 6059
8	9	24	Out Of The Cellar ... *Ratt*...Atlantic 80143
9	7	7	Victory ... *The Jacksons*...Epic 38946
10	10	41	Break Out ... *Pointer Sisters*...Planet 4705

TW	LW	WK	Billboard® SEPTEMBER 8, 1984 TOP LP's
1	1	9	**Purple Rain** ... *Prince & The Revolution/Soundtrack*...Warner 25110
2	2	12	Born In The U.S.A ... *Bruce Springsteen*...Columbia 38653
3	3	49	Sports ... *Huey Lewis & The News*...Chrysalis 41412
4	4	13	Private Dancer ... *Tina Turner*...Capitol 12330
5	5	23	Heartbeat City ... *The Cars*...Elektra 60296
6	7	44	Can't Slow Down ... *Lionel Richie*...Motown 6059
7	8	25	**Out Of The Cellar** ... *Ratt*...Atlantic 80143
8	9	8	Victory ... *The Jacksons*...Epic 38946
9	6	10	Ghostbusters ... *Soundtrack*...Arista 8246
10	41	2	1100 Bel Air Place ... *Julio Iglesias*...Columbia 39157

Billboard — SEPTEMBER 15, 1984 — TOP LP's

TW	LW	WK	Title	Artist	Label
1	1	10	**Purple Rain**	Prince & The Revolution/Soundtrack	Warner 25110
2	2	13	Born In The U.S.A.	Bruce Springsteen	Columbia 38653
3	3	50	Sports	Huey Lewis & The News	Chrysalis 41412
4	4	14	Private Dancer	Tina Turner	Capitol 12330
5	5	24	Heartbeat City	The Cars	Elektra 60296
6	6	45	Can't Slow Down	Lionel Richie	Motown 6059
7	7	26	**Out Of The Cellar**	Ratt	Atlantic 80143
8	10	3	1100 Bel Air Place	Julio Iglesias	Columbia 39157
9	9	11	Ghostbusters	Soundtrack	Arista 8246
10	8	9	Victory	The Jacksons	Epic 38946

Billboard — SEPTEMBER 22, 1984 — TOP LP's

TW	LW	WK	Title	Artist	Label
1	1	11	**Purple Rain**	Prince & The Revolution/Soundtrack	Warner 25110
2	2	14	Born In The U.S.A.	Bruce Springsteen	Columbia 38653
3	3	51	Sports	Huey Lewis & The News	Chrysalis 41412
4	4	15	Private Dancer	Tina Turner	Capitol 12330
5	5	25	Heartbeat City	The Cars	Elektra 60296
6	8	4	1100 Bel Air Place	Julio Iglesias	Columbia 39157
7	6	46	Can't Slow Down	Lionel Richie	Motown 6059
8	7	27	Out Of The Cellar	Ratt	Atlantic 80143
9	9	12	Ghostbusters	Soundtrack	Arista 8246
10	12	44	Break Out	Pointer Sisters	Planet 4705

Billboard — SEPTEMBER 29, 1984 — TOP LP's

TW	LW	WK	Title	Artist	Label
1	1	12	**Purple Rain**	Prince & The Revolution/Soundtrack	Warner 25110
2	2	15	Born In The U.S.A.	Bruce Springsteen	Columbia 38653
3	4	16	**Private Dancer**	Tina Turner	Capitol 12330
4	3	52	Sports	Huey Lewis & The News	Chrysalis 41412
5	5	26	Heartbeat City	The Cars	Elektra 60296
6	6	5	1100 Bel Air Place	Julio Iglesias	Columbia 39157
7	7	47	Can't Slow Down	Lionel Richie	Motown 6059
8	8	28	Out Of The Cellar	Ratt	Atlantic 80143
9	10	45	Break Out	Pointer Sisters	Planet 4705
10	11	12	**No Brakes**	John Waite	EMI America 17124

Billboard — OCTOBER 6, 1984 — TOP LP's

TW	LW	WK	Title	Artist	Label
1	1	13	**Purple Rain**	Prince & The Revolution/Soundtrack	Warner 25110
2	2	16	Born In The U.S.A.	Bruce Springsteen	Columbia 38653
3	4	53	Sports	Huey Lewis & The News	Chrysalis 41412
4	3	17	Private Dancer	Tina Turner	Capitol 12330
5	5	27	Heartbeat City	The Cars	Elektra 60296
6	6	6	1100 Bel Air Place	Julio Iglesias	Columbia 39157
7	7	48	Can't Slow Down	Lionel Richie	Motown 6059
8	9	46	**Break Out**	Pointer Sisters	Planet 4705
9	13	22	**Eddie And The Cruisers**	John Cafferty & The Beaver Brown Band/Soundtrack	Scotti Brothers 38929
10	12	58	Madonna	Madonna	Sire 23867

TW	LW	WK	Billboard ● OCTOBER 13, 1984 ● TOP LP's
❶	1	14	**Purple Rain**......................*Prince & The Revolution/Soundtrack*...Warner 25110
❷	2	17	Born In The U.S.A................................. *Bruce Springsteen*...Columbia 38653
❸	4	18	**Private Dancer**... *Tina Turner*...Capitol 12330
④	3	54	Sports..*Huey Lewis & The News*...Chrysalis 41412
⑤	5	28	Heartbeat City .... *The Cars*...Elektra 60296
❻	6	7	1100 Bel Air Place ....*Julio Iglesias*...Columbia 39157
⑦	7	49	Can't Slow Down...*Lionel Richie*...Motown 6059
❽	8	47	**Break Out** ....*Pointer Sisters*...Planet 4705
❾	9	23	**Eddie And The Cruisers** .... *John Cafferty & The Beaver Brown Band/Soundtrack*...Scotti Brothers 38929
⑩	10	59	Madonna ....*Madonna*...Sire 23867

TW	LW	WK	Billboard ● OCTOBER 20, 1984 ● TOP 200 ALBUMS
❶	1	15	**Purple Rain**......................*Prince & The Revolution/Soundtrack*...Warner 25110
❷	2	18	Born In The U.S.A................................. *Bruce Springsteen*...Columbia 38653
❸	3	19	**Private Dancer**... *Tina Turner*...Capitol 12330
❹	4	55	Sports...*Huey Lewis & The News*...Chrysalis 41412
❺	5	29	Heartbeat City .... *The Cars*...Elektra 60296
❻	6	8	1100 Bel Air Place ....*Julio Iglesias*...Columbia 39157
❼	12	5	The Woman in Red........................... *Stevie Wonder/Soundtrack*...Motown 6108
❽	10	60	**Madonna** ....*Madonna*...Sire 23867
⑨	7	50	Can't Slow Down...*Lionel Richie*...Motown 6059
⑩	9	24	**Eddie And The Cruisers** .... *John Cafferty & The Beaver Brown Band/Soundtrack*...Scotti Brothers 38929

TW	LW	WK	Billboard ● OCTOBER 27, 1984 ● TOP 200 ALBUMS
❶	1	16	**Purple Rain**......................*Prince & The Revolution/Soundtrack*...Warner 25110
❷	2	19	Born In The U.S.A................................. *Bruce Springsteen*...Columbia 38653
❸	3	20	**Private Dancer**... *Tina Turner*...Capitol 12330
④	4	56	Sports..*Huey Lewis & The News*...Chrysalis 41412
❺	6	9	**1100 Bel Air Place** .... *Julio Iglesias*...Columbia 39157
⑥	5	30	Heartbeat City .... *The Cars*...Elektra 60296
❼	7	6	The Woman in Red........................... *Stevie Wonder/Soundtrack*...Motown 6108
❽	8	61	**Madonna** ....*Madonna*...Sire 23867
❾	10	25	**Eddie And The Cruisers** .... *John Cafferty & The Beaver Brown Band/Soundtrack*...Scotti Brothers 38929
⑩	9	51	Can't Slow Down...*Lionel Richie*...Motown 6059

TW	LW	WK	Billboard ● NOVEMBER 3, 1984 ● TOP 200 ALBUMS
❶	1	17	**Purple Rain**......................*Prince & The Revolution/Soundtrack*...Warner 25110
❷	2	20	Born In The U.S.A................................. *Bruce Springsteen*...Columbia 38653
❸	3	21	**Private Dancer**... *Tina Turner*...Capitol 12330
❹	4	57	Sports..*Huey Lewis & The News*...Chrysalis 41412
❺	5	10	**1100 Bel Air Place** .... *Julio Iglesias*...Columbia 39157
❻	7	7	The Woman in Red........................... *Stevie Wonder/Soundtrack*...Motown 6108
⑦	6	31	Heartbeat City .... *The Cars*...Elektra 60296
❽	8	62	**Madonna** ....*Madonna*...Sire 23867
⑨	9	26	**Eddie And The Cruisers** .... *John Cafferty & The Beaver Brown Band/Soundtrack*...Scotti Brothers 38929
⑩	10	52	Can't Slow Down...*Lionel Richie*...Motown 6059

TW	LW	WK	Billboard. NOVEMBER 10, 1984 TOP 200 ALBUMS
1	1	18	**Purple Rain** ...*Prince & The Revolution/Soundtrack*...Warner 25110
2	2	21	Born In The U.S.A. ...*Bruce Springsteen*...Columbia 38653
3	3	22	**Private Dancer** ...*Tina Turner*...Capitol 12330
4	6	8	**The Woman in Red** ...*Stevie Wonder/Soundtrack*...Motown 6108
5	4	58	Sports ...*Huey Lewis & The News*...Chrysalis 41412
6	5	11	1100 Bel Air Place ...*Julio Iglesias*...Columbia 39157
7	7	32	Heartbeat City ...*The Cars*...Elektra 60296
8	10	53	Can't Slow Down ...*Lionel Richie*...Motown 6059
9	9	27	**Eddie And The Cruisers** ...*John Cafferty & The Beaver Brown Band/Soundtrack*...Scotti Brothers 38929
10	13	47	She's So Unusual ...*Cyndi Lauper*...Portrait 38930

TW	LW	WK	Billboard. NOVEMBER 17, 1984 TOP 200 ALBUMS
1	1	19	**Purple Rain** ...*Prince & The Revolution/Soundtrack*...Warner 25110
2	2	22	Born In The U.S.A. ...*Bruce Springsteen*...Columbia 38653
3	3	23	**Private Dancer** ...*Tina Turner*...Capitol 12330
4	4	9	**The Woman in Red** ...*Stevie Wonder/Soundtrack*...Motown 6108
5	5	59	Sports ...*Huey Lewis & The News*...Chrysalis 41412
6	8	54	Can't Slow Down ...*Lionel Richie*...Motown 6059
7	6	12	1100 Bel Air Place ...*Julio Iglesias*...Columbia 39157
8	18	5	Volume One ...*The Honeydrippers*...Es Paranza 90220
9	7	33	Heartbeat City ...*The Cars*...Elektra 60296
10	10	48	She's So Unusual ...*Cyndi Lauper*...Portrait 38930

TW	LW	WK	Billboard. NOVEMBER 24, 1984 TOP 200 ALBUMS
1	1	20	**Purple Rain** ...*Prince & The Revolution/Soundtrack*...Warner 25110
2	2	23	Born In The U.S.A. ...*Bruce Springsteen*...Columbia 38653
3	3	24	**Private Dancer** ...*Tina Turner*...Capitol 12330
4	4	10	**The Woman in Red** ...*Stevie Wonder/Soundtrack*...Motown 6108
5	8	6	Volume One ...*The Honeydrippers*...Es Paranza 90220
6	11	5	Big Bam Boom ...*Daryl Hall & John Oates*...RCA 5309
7	5	60	Sports ...*Huey Lewis & The News*...Chrysalis 41412
8	6	55	Can't Slow Down ...*Lionel Richie*...Motown 6059
9	14	14	**Suddenly** ...*Billy Ocean*...Jive 8213
10	10	49	She's So Unusual ...*Cyndi Lauper*...Portrait 38930

TW	LW	WK	Billboard. DECEMBER 1, 1984 TOP 200 ALBUMS
1	1	21	**Purple Rain** ...*Prince & The Revolution/Soundtrack*...Warner 25110
2	2	24	Born In The U.S.A. ...*Bruce Springsteen*...Columbia 38653
3	3	25	**Private Dancer** ...*Tina Turner*...Capitol 12330
4	5	7	**Volume One** ...*The Honeydrippers*...Es Paranza 90220
5	6	6	**Big Bam Boom** ...*Daryl Hall & John Oates*...RCA 5309
6	4	11	The Woman in Red ...*Stevie Wonder/Soundtrack*...Motown 6108
7	8	56	Can't Slow Down ...*Lionel Richie*...Motown 6059
8	7	61	Sports ...*Huey Lewis & The News*...Chrysalis 41412
9	9	15	**Suddenly** ...*Billy Ocean*...Jive 8213
10	14	27	Chicago 17 ...*Chicago*...Warner 25060

TW	LW	WK	Billboard® DECEMBER 8, 1984 TOP 200 ALBUMS
❶	1	22	**Purple Rain**...................... *Prince & The Revolution/Soundtrack*...Warner 25110
❷	2	25	Born In The U.S.A.................................... *Bruce Springsteen*...Columbia 38653
③	3	26	**Private Dancer**.. *Tina Turner*...Capitol 12330
❹	4	8	**Volume One**....................................... *The Honeydrippers*...Es Paranza 90220
❺	5	7	**Big Bam Boom**.................................... *Daryl Hall & John Oates*...RCA 5309
⑥	6	12	The Woman in Red.......................... *Stevie Wonder/Soundtrack*...Motown 6108
⑦	7	57	Can't Slow Down..*Lionel Richie*...Motown 6059
⑧	8	62	Sports... *Huey Lewis & The News*...Chrysalis 41412
❾	49	2	Arena.. *Duran Duran*...Capitol 12374
❿	70	2	Like A Virgin..*Madonna*...Sire 25157

TW	LW	WK	Billboard® DECEMBER 15, 1984 TOP 200 ALBUMS
❶	1	23	**Purple Rain**...................... *Prince & The Revolution/Soundtrack*...Warner 25110
❷	2	26	Born In The U.S.A.................................... *Bruce Springsteen*...Columbia 38653
③	3	27	**Private Dancer**.. *Tina Turner*...Capitol 12330
❹	10	3	Like A Virgin..*Madonna*...Sire 25157
⑤	4	9	Volume One .... *The Honeydrippers*...Es Paranza 90220
❻	5	8	Big Bam Boom....................................... *Daryl Hall & John Oates*...RCA 5309
❼	9	3	Arena.. *Duran Duran*...Capitol 12374
⑧	6	13	The Woman in Red.......................... *Stevie Wonder/Soundtrack*...Motown 6108
⑨	7	58	Can't Slow Down..*Lionel Richie*...Motown 6059
⑩	8	63	Sports... *Huey Lewis & The News*...Chrysalis 41412

TW	LW	WK	Billboard® DECEMBER 22, 1984 TOP 200 ALBUMS
❶	1	24	**Purple Rain**...................... *Prince & The Revolution/Soundtrack*...Warner 25110
❷	2	27	Born In The U.S.A.................................... *Bruce Springsteen*...Columbia 38653
❸	4	4	Like A Virgin..*Madonna*...Sire 25157
④	3	28	Private Dancer.. *Tina Turner*...Capitol 12330
❺	7	4	Arena.. *Duran Duran*...Capitol 12374
❻	6	9	Big Bam Boom....................................... *Daryl Hall & John Oates*...RCA 5309
⑦	5	10	Volume One .... *The Honeydrippers*...Es Paranza 90220
⑧	8	14	The Woman in Red.......................... *Stevie Wonder/Soundtrack*...Motown 6108
❾	11	30	Chicago 17 .... *Chicago*...Warner 25060
⑩	9	59	Can't Slow Down..*Lionel Richie*...Motown 6059

TW	LW	WK	Billboard® JANUARY 5, 1985 TOP POP ALBUMS
1	1	26	**Purple Rain**......*Prince & The Revolution/Soundtrack*...Warner 25110
2	3	6	Like A Virgin......*Madonna*...Sire 25157
3	2	29	Born In The U.S.A......*Bruce Springsteen*...Columbia 38653
4	5	6	**Arena**......*Duran Duran*...Capitol 12374
5	4	30	Private Dancer......*Tina Turner*...Capitol 12330
6	7	12	Volume One......*The Honeydrippers*...Es Paranza 90220
7	6	11	Big Bam Boom......*Daryl Hall & John Oates*...RCA 5309
8	9	32	Chicago 17......*Chicago*...Warner 25060
9	13	55	She's So Unusual......*Cyndi Lauper*...Portrait 38930
10	12	7	Reckless......*Bryan Adams*...A&M 5013

TW	LW	WK	Billboard® JANUARY 12, 1985 TOP POP ALBUMS
1	1	27	**Purple Rain**......*Prince & The Revolution/Soundtrack*...Warner 25110
2	3	30	Born In The U.S.A......*Bruce Springsteen*...Columbia 38653
3	2	7	Like A Virgin......*Madonna*...Sire 25157
4	4	7	**Arena**......*Duran Duran*...Capitol 12374
5	5	31	Private Dancer......*Tina Turner*...Capitol 12330
6	6	13	Volume One......*The Honeydrippers*...Es Paranza 90220
7	8	33	Chicago 17......*Chicago*...Warner 25060
8	7	12	Big Bam Boom......*Daryl Hall & John Oates*...RCA 5309
9	9	56	She's So Unusual......*Cyndi Lauper*...Portrait 38930
10	10	8	Reckless......*Bryan Adams*...A&M 5013

TW	LW	WK	Billboard® JANUARY 19, 1985 TOP POP ALBUMS
1	2	31	**Born In The U.S.A.**......*Bruce Springsteen*...Columbia 38653
2	1	28	Purple Rain......*Prince & The Revolution/Soundtrack*...Warner 25110
3	3	8	Like A Virgin......*Madonna*...Sire 25157
4	4	8	**Arena**......*Duran Duran*...Capitol 12374
5	7	34	Chicago 17......*Chicago*...Warner 25060
6	5	32	Private Dancer......*Tina Turner*...Capitol 12330
7	8	13	Big Bam Boom......*Daryl Hall & John Oates*...RCA 5309
8	10	9	Reckless......*Bryan Adams*...A&M 5013
9	6	14	Volume One......*The Honeydrippers*...Es Paranza 90220
10	9	57	She's So Unusual......*Cyndi Lauper*...Portrait 38930

TW	LW	WK	Billboard® JANUARY 26, 1985 TOP POP ALBUMS
1	1	32	**Born In The U.S.A.**......*Bruce Springsteen*...Columbia 38653
2	3	9	Like A Virgin......*Madonna*...Sire 25157
3	2	29	Purple Rain......*Prince & The Revolution/Soundtrack*...Warner 25110
4	5	35	**Chicago 17**......*Chicago*...Warner 25060
5	4	9	Arena......*Duran Duran*...Capitol 12374
6	8	10	Reckless......*Bryan Adams*...A&M 5013
7	7	14	Big Bam Boom......*Daryl Hall & John Oates*...RCA 5309
8	6	33	Private Dancer......*Tina Turner*...Capitol 12330
9	14	4	Agent Provocateur......*Foreigner*...Atlantic 81999
10	13	12	Make It Big......*Wham!*...Columbia 39595

TW	LW	WK	Billboard. FEBRUARY 2, 1985 TOP POP ALBUMS
1	1	33	**Born In The U.S.A.** ... *Bruce Springsteen*...Columbia 38653
2	2	10	Like A Virgin ... *Madonna*...Sire 25157
3	3	30	Purple Rain ... *Prince & The Revolution/Soundtrack*...Warner 25110
4	9	5	**Agent Provocateur** ... *Foreigner*...Atlantic 81999
5	4	36	Chicago 17 ... *Chicago*...Warner 25060
6	10	13	Make It Big ... *Wham!*...Columbia 39595
7	6	11	Reckless ... *Bryan Adams*...A&M 5013
8	8	34	Private Dancer ... *Tina Turner*...Capitol 12330
9	7	15	Big Bam Boom ... *Daryl Hall & John Oates*...RCA 5309
10	11	17	New Edition ... *New Edition*...MCA 5515

TW	LW	WK	Billboard. FEBRUARY 9, 1985 TOP POP ALBUMS
1	2	11	**Like A Virgin** ... *Madonna*...Sire 25157
2	1	34	Born In The U.S.A. ... *Bruce Springsteen*...Columbia 38653
3	6	14	Make It Big ... *Wham!*...Columbia 39595
4	4	6	**Agent Provocateur** ... *Foreigner*...Atlantic 81999
5	3	31	Purple Rain ... *Prince & The Revolution/Soundtrack*...Warner 25110
6	5	37	Chicago 17 ... *Chicago*...Warner 25060
7	10	18	New Edition ... *New Edition*...MCA 5515
8	7	12	Reckless ... *Bryan Adams*...A&M 5013
9	8	35	Private Dancer ... *Tina Turner*...Capitol 12330
10	21	3	Centerfield ... *John Fogerty*...Warner 25203

TW	LW	WK	Billboard. FEBRUARY 16, 1985 TOP POP ALBUMS
1	1	12	**Like A Virgin** ... *Madonna*...Sire 25157
2	2	35	Born In The U.S.A. ... *Bruce Springsteen*...Columbia 38653
3	3	15	Make It Big ... *Wham!*...Columbia 39595
4	4	7	**Agent Provocateur** ... *Foreigner*...Atlantic 81999
5	10	4	Centerfield ... *John Fogerty*...Warner 25203
6	6	38	Chicago 17 ... *Chicago*...Warner 25060
7	5	32	Purple Rain ... *Prince & The Revolution/Soundtrack*...Warner 25110
8	8	13	Reckless ... *Bryan Adams*...A&M 5013
9	7	19	New Edition ... *New Edition*...MCA 5515
10	11	17	Big Bam Boom ... *Daryl Hall & John Oates*...RCA 5309

TW	LW	WK	Billboard. FEBRUARY 23, 1985 TOP POP ALBUMS
1	1	13	**Like A Virgin** ... *Madonna*...Sire 25157
2	3	16	Make It Big ... *Wham!*...Columbia 39595
3	2	36	Born In The U.S.A. ... *Bruce Springsteen*...Columbia 38653
4	5	5	Centerfield ... *John Fogerty*...Warner 25203
5	4	8	Agent Provocateur ... *Foreigner*...Atlantic 81999
6	9	20	**New Edition** ... *New Edition*...MCA 5515
7	7	33	Purple Rain ... *Prince & The Revolution/Soundtrack*...Warner 25110
8	8	14	Reckless ... *Bryan Adams*...A&M 5013
9	6	39	Chicago 17 ... *Chicago*...Warner 25060
10	11	37	Private Dancer ... *Tina Turner*...Capitol 12330

TW	LW	WK	Billboard® — MARCH 2, 1985 — TOP POP ALBUMS	
1	2	17	**Make It Big**	*Wham!*...Columbia 39595
2	1	14	Like A Virgin	*Madonna*...Sire 25157
3	3	37	Born In The U.S.A.	*Bruce Springsteen*...Columbia 38653
4	4	6	Centerfield	*John Fogerty*...Warner 25203
5	5	9	Agent Provocateur	*Foreigner*...Atlantic 81999
6	6	21	**New Edition**	*New Edition*...MCA 5515
7	8	15	Reckless	*Bryan Adams*...A&M 5013
8	12	8	Beverly Hills Cop	*Soundtrack*...MCA 5547
9	10	38	Private Dancer	*Tina Turner*...Capitol 12330
10	9	40	Chicago 17	*Chicago*...Warner 25060

TW	LW	WK	Billboard® — MARCH 9, 1985 — TOP POP ALBUMS	
1	1	18	**Make It Big**	*Wham!*...Columbia 39595
2	4	7	Centerfield	*John Fogerty*...Warner 25203
3	2	15	Like A Virgin	*Madonna*...Sire 25157
4	3	38	Born In The U.S.A.	*Bruce Springsteen*...Columbia 38653
5	5	10	Agent Provocateur	*Foreigner*...Atlantic 81999
6	8	9	Beverly Hills Cop	*Soundtrack*...MCA 5547
7	6	22	New Edition	*New Edition*...MCA 5515
8	12	16	Wheels are turnin'	*REO Speedwagon*...Epic 39593
9	9	39	Private Dancer	*Tina Turner*...Capitol 12330
10	7	16	Reckless	*Bryan Adams*...A&M 5013

TW	LW	WK	Billboard® — MARCH 16, 1985 — TOP POP ALBUMS	
1	1	19	**Make It Big**	*Wham!*...Columbia 39595
2	2	8	Centerfield	*John Fogerty*...Warner 25203
3	4	39	Born In The U.S.A.	*Bruce Springsteen*...Columbia 38653
4	3	16	Like A Virgin	*Madonna*...Sire 25157
5	6	10	Beverly Hills Cop	*Soundtrack*...MCA 5547
6	5	11	Agent Provocateur	*Foreigner*...Atlantic 81999
7	8	17	**Wheels are turnin'**	*REO Speedwagon*...Epic 39593
8	24	2	No Jacket Required	*Phil Collins*...Atlantic 81240
9	9	40	Private Dancer	*Tina Turner*...Capitol 12330
10	10	17	Reckless	*Bryan Adams*...A&M 5013

TW	LW	WK	Billboard® — MARCH 23, 1985 — TOP POP ALBUMS	
1	2	9	**Centerfield**	*John Fogerty*...Warner 25203
2	8	3	No Jacket Required	*Phil Collins*...Atlantic 81240
3	3	40	Born In The U.S.A.	*Bruce Springsteen*...Columbia 38653
4	1	20	Make It Big	*Wham!*...Columbia 39595
5	5	11	Beverly Hills Cop	*Soundtrack*...MCA 5547
6	9	41	Private Dancer	*Tina Turner*...Capitol 12330
7	4	17	Like A Virgin	*Madonna*...Sire 25157
8	7	18	Wheels are turnin'	*REO Speedwagon*...Epic 39593
9	6	12	Agent Provocateur	*Foreigner*...Atlantic 81999
10	10	18	Reckless	*Bryan Adams*...A&M 5013

TW	LW	WK	Billboard® — MARCH 30, 1985 — TOP POP ALBUMS	
❶	2	4	**No Jacket Required**	*Phil Collins*...Atlantic 81240
②	1	10	**Centerfield**	*John Fogerty*...Warner 25203
③	3	41	**Born In The U.S.A.**	*Bruce Springsteen*...Columbia 38653
❹	5	12	**Beverly Hills Cop**	*Soundtrack*...MCA 5547
❺	6	42	**Private Dancer**	*Tina Turner*...Capitol 12330
⑥	7	18	**Like A Virgin**	*Madonna*...Sire 25157
⑦	4	21	**Make It Big**	*Wham!*...Columbia 39595
⑧	8	19	**Wheels are turnin'**	*REO Speedwagon*...Epic 39593
⑨	9	13	**Agent Provocateur**	*Foreigner*...Atlantic 81999
⑩	10	19	**Reckless**	*Bryan Adams*...A&M 5013

TW	LW	WK	Billboard® — APRIL 6, 1985 — TOP POP ALBUMS	
❶	1	5	**No Jacket Required**	*Phil Collins*...Atlantic 81240
②	2	11	**Centerfield**	*John Fogerty*...Warner 25203
③	3	42	**Born In The U.S.A.**	*Bruce Springsteen*...Columbia 38653
❹	4	13	**Beverly Hills Cop**	*Soundtrack*...MCA 5547
⑤	5	43	**Private Dancer**	*Tina Turner*...Capitol 12330
❻	6	19	**Like A Virgin**	*Madonna*...Sire 25157
⑦	7	22	**Make It Big**	*Wham!*...Columbia 39595
⑧	8	20	**Wheels are turnin'**	*REO Speedwagon*...Epic 39593
⑨	9	14	**Agent Provocateur**	*Foreigner*...Atlantic 81999
⑩	10	20	**Reckless**	*Bryan Adams*...A&M 5013

TW	LW	WK	Billboard® — APRIL 13, 1985 — TOP POP ALBUMS	
❶	1	6	**No Jacket Required**	*Phil Collins*...Atlantic 81240
②	2	12	**Centerfield**	*John Fogerty*...Warner 25203
❸	3	43	**Born In The U.S.A.**	*Bruce Springsteen*...Columbia 38653
❹	4	14	**Beverly Hills Cop**	*Soundtrack*...MCA 5547
⑤	5	44	**Private Dancer**	*Tina Turner*...Capitol 12330
⑥	6	20	**Like A Virgin**	*Madonna*...Sire 25157
⑦	7	23	**Make It Big**	*Wham!*...Columbia 39595
⑧	8	21	**Wheels are turnin'**	*REO Speedwagon*...Epic 39593
⑨	9	15	**Agent Provocateur**	*Foreigner*...Atlantic 81999
⑩	10	21	**Reckless**	*Bryan Adams*...A&M 5013

TW	LW	WK	Billboard® — APRIL 20, 1985 — TOP POP ALBUMS	
❶	1	7	**No Jacket Required**	*Phil Collins*...Atlantic 81240
❷	3	44	**Born In The U.S.A.**	*Bruce Springsteen*...Columbia 38653
❸	4	15	**Beverly Hills Cop**	*Soundtrack*...MCA 5547
④	2	13	**Centerfield**	*John Fogerty*...Warner 25203
⑤	5	45	**Private Dancer**	*Tina Turner*...Capitol 12330
⑥	6	21	**Like A Virgin**	*Madonna*...Sire 25157
⑦	7	24	**Make It Big**	*Wham!*...Columbia 39595
⑧	8	22	**Wheels are turnin'**	*REO Speedwagon*...Epic 39593
❾	-	1	**We Are The World**	*USA For Africa*...Columbia 40043
❿	12	9	**Diamond Life**	*Sade*...Portrait 39581

Billboard — APRIL 27, 1985 — TOP POP ALBUMS

TW	LW	WK		
1	9	2	**We Are The World**	*USA For Africa*...Columbia 40043
2	1	8	No Jacket Required	*Phil Collins*...Atlantic 81240
3	2	45	Born In The U.S.A.	*Bruce Springsteen*...Columbia 38653
4	3	16	Beverly Hills Cop	*Soundtrack*...MCA 5547
5	4	14	Centerfield	*John Fogerty*...Warner 25203
6	6	22	Like A Virgin	*Madonna*...Sire 25157
7	5	46	Private Dancer	*Tina Turner*...Capitol 12330
8	10	10	Diamond Life	*Sade*...Portrait 39581
9	7	25	Make It Big	*Wham!*...Columbia 39595
10	15	3	Southern Accents	*Tom Petty & The Heartbreakers*...MCA 5486

Billboard — MAY 4, 1985 — TOP POP ALBUMS

TW	LW	WK		
1	1	3	**We Are The World**	*USA For Africa*...Columbia 40043
2	2	9	No Jacket Required	*Phil Collins*...Atlantic 81240
3	3	46	Born In The U.S.A.	*Bruce Springsteen*...Columbia 38653
4	4	17	Beverly Hills Cop	*Soundtrack*...MCA 5547
5	6	23	Like A Virgin	*Madonna*...Sire 25157
6	8	11	Diamond Life	*Sade*...Portrait 39581
7	5	15	Centerfield	*John Fogerty*...Warner 25203
8	7	47	Private Dancer	*Tina Turner*...Capitol 12330
9	10	4	Southern Accents	*Tom Petty & The Heartbreakers*...MCA 5486
10	9	26	Make It Big	*Wham!*...Columbia 39595

Billboard — MAY 11, 1985 — TOP POP ALBUMS

TW	LW	WK		
1	1	4	**We Are The World**	*USA For Africa*...Columbia 40043
2	2	10	No Jacket Required	*Phil Collins*...Atlantic 81240
3	3	47	Born In The U.S.A.	*Bruce Springsteen*...Columbia 38653
4	4	18	Beverly Hills Cop	*Soundtrack*...MCA 5547
5	5	24	Like A Virgin	*Madonna*...Sire 25157
6	6	12	Diamond Life	*Sade*...Portrait 39581
7	9	5	**Southern Accents**	*Tom Petty & The Heartbreakers*...MCA 5486
8	7	16	Centerfield	*John Fogerty*...Warner 25203
9	10	27	Make It Big	*Wham!*...Columbia 39595
10	8	48	Private Dancer	*Tina Turner*...Capitol 12330

Billboard — MAY 18, 1985 — TOP POP ALBUMS

TW	LW	WK		
1	2	11	**No Jacket Required**	*Phil Collins*...Atlantic 81240
2	1	5	We Are The World	*USA For Africa*...Columbia 40043
3	4	19	Beverly Hills Cop	*Soundtrack*...MCA 5547
4	3	48	Born In The U.S.A.	*Bruce Springsteen*...Columbia 38653
5	14	2	Around the World in a Day	*Prince & The Revolution*...Paisley Park 25286
6	6	13	Diamond Life	*Sade*...Portrait 39581
7	7	6	**Southern Accents**	*Tom Petty & The Heartbreakers*...MCA 5486
8	5	25	Like A Virgin	*Madonna*...Sire 25157
9	9	28	Make It Big	*Wham!*...Columbia 39595
10	8	17	Centerfield	*John Fogerty*...Warner 25203

TW	LW	WK	Billboard® MAY 25, 1985	TOP POP ALBUMS
1	1	12	**No Jacket Required**	*Phil Collins*...Atlantic 81240
2	5	3	Around the World in a Day	*Prince & The Revolution*...Paisley Park 25286
3	3	20	Beverly Hills Cop	*Soundtrack*...MCA 5547
4	4	49	Born In The U.S.A.	*Bruce Springsteen*...Columbia 38653
5	2	6	We Are The World	*USA For Africa*...Columbia 40043
6	6	14	Diamond Life	*Sade*...Portrait 39581
7	8	26	Like A Virgin	*Madonna*...Sire 25157
8	9	29	Make It Big	*Wham!*...Columbia 39595
9	12	9	Songs From The Big Chair	*Tears For Fears*...Mercury 824300
10	7	7	Southern Accents	*Tom Petty & The Heartbreakers*...MCA 5486

TW	LW	WK	Billboard® JUNE 1, 1985	TOP POP ALBUMS
1	2	4	**Around the World in a Day**	*Prince & The Revolution*...Paisley Park 25286
2	1	13	No Jacket Required	*Phil Collins*...Atlantic 81240
3	4	50	Born In The U.S.A.	*Bruce Springsteen*...Columbia 38653
4	3	21	Beverly Hills Cop	*Soundtrack*...MCA 5547
5	6	15	**Diamond Life**	*Sade*...Portrait 39581
6	9	10	Songs From The Big Chair	*Tears For Fears*...Mercury 824300
7	7	27	Like A Virgin	*Madonna*...Sire 25157
8	8	30	Make It Big	*Wham!*...Columbia 39595
9	5	7	We Are The World	*USA For Africa*...Columbia 40043
10	11	28	Reckless	*Bryan Adams*...A&M 5013

TW	LW	WK	Billboard® JUNE 8, 1985	TOP POP ALBUMS
1	1	5	**Around the World in a Day**	*Prince & The Revolution*...Paisley Park 25286
2	2	14	No Jacket Required	*Phil Collins*...Atlantic 81240
3	4	22	Beverly Hills Cop	*Soundtrack*...MCA 5547
4	3	51	Born In The U.S.A.	*Bruce Springsteen*...Columbia 38653
5	5	16	**Diamond Life**	*Sade*...Portrait 39581
6	6	11	Songs From The Big Chair	*Tears For Fears*...Mercury 824300
7	8	31	Make It Big	*Wham!*...Columbia 39595
8	10	29	Reckless	*Bryan Adams*...A&M 5013
9	7	28	Like A Virgin	*Madonna*...Sire 25157
10	11	9	Southern Accents	*Tom Petty & The Heartbreakers*...MCA 5486

TW	LW	WK	Billboard® JUNE 15, 1985	TOP POP ALBUMS
1	1	6	**Around the World in a Day**	*Prince & The Revolution*...Paisley Park 25286
2	2	15	No Jacket Required	*Phil Collins*...Atlantic 81240
3	3	23	Beverly Hills Cop	*Soundtrack*...MCA 5547
4	6	12	Songs From The Big Chair	*Tears For Fears*...Mercury 824300
5	4	52	Born In The U.S.A.	*Bruce Springsteen*...Columbia 38653
6	7	32	Make It Big	*Wham!*...Columbia 39595
7	8	30	Reckless	*Bryan Adams*...A&M 5013
8	5	17	Diamond Life	*Sade*...Portrait 39581
9	9	29	Like A Virgin	*Madonna*...Sire 25157
10	12	10	The Power Station	*The Power Station*...Capitol 12380

Billboard — JUNE 22, 1985 — TOP POP ALBUMS

TW	LW	WK	Album	Artist	Label
1	3	24	**Beverly Hills Cop**	*Soundtrack*	MCA 5547
2	1	7	Around the World in a Day	*Prince & The Revolution*	Paisley Park 25286
3	2	16	No Jacket Required	*Phil Collins*	Atlantic 81240
4	4	13	Songs From The Big Chair	*Tears For Fears*	Mercury 824300
5	5	53	Born In The U.S.A.	*Bruce Springsteen*	Columbia 38653
6	7	31	Reckless	*Bryan Adams*	A&M 5013
7	6	33	Make It Big	*Wham!*	Columbia 39595
8	9	30	Like A Virgin	*Madonna*	Sire 25157
9	10	11	The Power Station	*The Power Station*	Capitol 12380
10	8	18	Diamond Life	*Sade*	Portrait 39581

Billboard — JUNE 29, 1985 — TOP POP ALBUMS

TW	LW	WK	Album	Artist	Label
1	1	25	**Beverly Hills Cop**	*Soundtrack*	MCA 5547
2	3	17	No Jacket Required	*Phil Collins*	Atlantic 81240
3	4	14	Songs From The Big Chair	*Tears For Fears*	Mercury 824300
4	2	8	Around the World in a Day	*Prince & The Revolution*	Paisley Park 25286
5	5	54	Born In The U.S.A.	*Bruce Springsteen*	Columbia 38653
6	6	32	Reckless	*Bryan Adams*	A&M 5013
7	7	34	Make It Big	*Wham!*	Columbia 39595
8	8	31	Like A Virgin	*Madonna*	Sire 25157
9	9	12	The Power Station	*The Power Station*	Capitol 12380
10	11	11	**Dream Into Action**	*Howard Jones*	Elektra 60390

Billboard — JULY 6, 1985 — TOP POP ALBUMS

TW	LW	WK	Album	Artist	Label
1	2	18	**No Jacket Required**	*Phil Collins*	Atlantic 81240
2	3	15	Songs From The Big Chair	*Tears For Fears*	Mercury 824300
3	1	26	Beverly Hills Cop	*Soundtrack*	MCA 5547
4	4	9	Around the World in a Day	*Prince & The Revolution*	Paisley Park 25286
5	6	33	Reckless	*Bryan Adams*	A&M 5013
6	5	55	Born In The U.S.A.	*Bruce Springsteen*	Columbia 38653
7	7	35	Make It Big	*Wham!*	Columbia 39595
8	9	13	The Power Station	*The Power Station*	Capitol 12380
9	8	32	Like A Virgin	*Madonna*	Sire 25157
10	12	7	Be Yourself Tonight	*Eurythmics*	RCA 5429

Billboard — JULY 13, 1985 — TOP POP ALBUMS

TW	LW	WK	Album	Artist	Label
1	2	16	**Songs From The Big Chair**	*Tears For Fears*	Mercury 824300
2	1	19	No Jacket Required	*Phil Collins*	Atlantic 81240
3	4	10	Around the World in a Day	*Prince & The Revolution*	Paisley Park 25286
4	5	34	Reckless	*Bryan Adams*	A&M 5013
5	3	27	Beverly Hills Cop	*Soundtrack*	MCA 5547
6	6	56	Born In The U.S.A.	*Bruce Springsteen*	Columbia 38653
7	8	14	The Power Station	*The Power Station*	Capitol 12380
8	7	36	Make It Big	*Wham!*	Columbia 39595
9	9	33	Like A Virgin	*Madonna*	Sire 25157
10	10	8	Be Yourself Tonight	*Eurythmics*	RCA 5429

TW	LW	WK	Billboard® JULY 20, 1985	TOP POP ALBUMS
1	1	17	**Songs From The Big Chair**	*Tears For Fears*...Mercury 824300
2	2	20	No Jacket Required	*Phil Collins*...Atlantic 81240
3	4	35	Reckless	*Bryan Adams*...A&M 5013
4	3	11	Around the World in a Day	*Prince & The Revolution*...Paisley Park 25286
5	6	57	Born In The U.S.A.	*Bruce Springsteen*...Columbia 38653
6	5	28	Beverly Hills Cop	*Soundtrack*...MCA 5547
7	7	15	The Power Station	*The Power Station*...Capitol 12380
8	9	34	Like A Virgin	*Madonna*...Sire 25157
9	10	9	**Be Yourself Tonight**	*Eurythmics*...RCA 5429
10	11	4	Invasion Of Your Privacy	*Ratt*...Atlantic 81257

TW	LW	WK	Billboard® JULY 27, 1985	TOP POP ALBUMS
1	1	18	**Songs From The Big Chair**	*Tears For Fears*...Mercury 824300
2	3	36	Reckless	*Bryan Adams*...A&M 5013
3	2	21	No Jacket Required	*Phil Collins*...Atlantic 81240
4	5	58	Born In The U.S.A.	*Bruce Springsteen*...Columbia 38653
5	4	12	Around the World in a Day	*Prince & The Revolution*...Paisley Park 25286
6	7	16	**The Power Station**	*The Power Station*...Capitol 12380
7	10	5	**Invasion Of Your Privacy**	*Ratt*...Atlantic 81257
8	6	29	Beverly Hills Cop	*Soundtrack*...MCA 5547
9	14	3	The Dream Of The Blue Turtles	*Sting*...A&M 3750
10	12	8	**7 Wishes**	*Night Ranger*...MCA/Camel 5593

TW	LW	WK	Billboard® AUGUST 3, 1985	TOP POP ALBUMS
1	1	19	**Songs From The Big Chair**	*Tears For Fears*...Mercury 824300
2	2	37	Reckless	*Bryan Adams*...A&M 5013
3	3	22	No Jacket Required	*Phil Collins*...Atlantic 81240
4	4	59	Born In The U.S.A.	*Bruce Springsteen*...Columbia 38653
5	5	13	Around the World in a Day	*Prince & The Revolution*...Paisley Park 25286
6	9	4	The Dream Of The Blue Turtles	*Sting*...A&M 3750
7	6	17	The Power Station	*The Power Station*...Capitol 12380
8	12	4	Theatre Of Pain	*Mötley Crüe*...Elektra 60418
9	7	6	Invasion Of Your Privacy	*Ratt*...Atlantic 81257
10	10	9	**7 Wishes**	*Night Ranger*...MCA/Camel 5593

TW	LW	WK	Billboard® AUGUST 10, 1985	TOP POP ALBUMS
1	2	38	**Reckless**	*Bryan Adams*...A&M 5013
2	1	20	Songs From The Big Chair	*Tears For Fears*...Mercury 824300
3	3	23	No Jacket Required	*Phil Collins*...Atlantic 81240
4	6	5	The Dream Of The Blue Turtles	*Sting*...A&M 3750
5	4	60	Born In The U.S.A.	*Bruce Springsteen*...Columbia 38653
6	7	18	**The Power Station**	*The Power Station*...Capitol 12380
7	8	5	Theatre Of Pain	*Mötley Crüe*...Elektra 60418
8	5	14	Around the World in a Day	*Prince & The Revolution*...Paisley Park 25286
9	9	7	Invasion Of Your Privacy	*Ratt*...Atlantic 81257
10	15	10	Brothers In Arms	*Dire Straits*...Warner 25264

TW	LW	WK	Billboard® AUGUST 17, 1985 TOP POP ALBUMS
1	1	39	**Reckless** .... *Bryan Adams*...A&M 5013
2	2	21	Songs From The Big Chair .... *Tears For Fears*...Mercury 824300
3	3	24	No Jacket Required .... *Phil Collins*...Atlantic 81240
4	4	6	The Dream Of The Blue Turtles .... *Sting*...A&M 3750
5	5	61	Born In The U.S.A. .... *Bruce Springsteen*...Columbia 38653
6	7	6	**Theatre Of Pain** .... *Mötley Crüe*...Elektra 60418
7	10	11	Brothers In Arms .... *Dire Straits*...Warner 25264
8	6	19	The Power Station .... *The Power Station*...Capitol 12380
9	8	15	Around the World in a Day .... *Prince & The Revolution*...Paisley Park 25286
10	11	11	**7 Wishes** .... *Night Ranger*...MCA/Camel 5593

TW	LW	WK	Billboard® AUGUST 24, 1985 TOP POP ALBUMS
1	2	22	**Songs From The Big Chair** .... *Tears For Fears*...Mercury 824300
2	1	40	Reckless .... *Bryan Adams*...A&M 5013
3	4	7	The Dream Of The Blue Turtles .... *Sting*...A&M 3750
4	3	25	No Jacket Required .... *Phil Collins*...Atlantic 81240
5	7	12	Brothers In Arms .... *Dire Straits*...Warner 25264
6	5	62	Born In The U.S.A. .... *Bruce Springsteen*...Columbia 38653
7	6	7	Theatre Of Pain .... *Mötley Crüe*...Elektra 60418
8	8	20	The Power Station .... *The Power Station*...Capitol 12380
9	13	6	Greatest Hits, Volume I & Volume II .... *Billy Joel*...Columbia 40121
10	11	9	Invasion Of Your Privacy .... *Ratt*...Atlantic 81257

TW	LW	WK	Billboard® AUGUST 31, 1985 TOP POP ALBUMS
1	5	13	**Brothers In Arms** .... *Dire Straits*...Warner 25264
2	1	23	Songs From The Big Chair .... *Tears For Fears*...Mercury 824300
3	3	8	The Dream Of The Blue Turtles .... *Sting*...A&M 3750
4	2	41	Reckless .... *Bryan Adams*...A&M 5013
5	6	63	Born In The U.S.A. .... *Bruce Springsteen*...Columbia 38653
6	4	26	No Jacket Required .... *Phil Collins*...Atlantic 81240
7	7	8	Theatre Of Pain .... *Mötley Crüe*...Elektra 60418
8	9	7	Greatest Hits, Volume I & Volume II .... *Billy Joel*...Columbia 40121
9	11	23	Whitney Houston .... *Whitney Houston*...Arista 8212
10	10	10	Invasion Of Your Privacy .... *Ratt*...Atlantic 81257

TW	LW	WK	Billboard® SEPTEMBER 7, 1985 TOP POP ALBUMS
1	1	14	**Brothers In Arms** .... *Dire Straits*...Warner 25264
2	3	9	**The Dream Of The Blue Turtles** .... *Sting*...A&M 3750
3	2	24	Songs From The Big Chair .... *Tears For Fears*...Mercury 824300
4	4	42	Reckless .... *Bryan Adams*...A&M 5013
5	5	64	Born In The U.S.A. .... *Bruce Springsteen*...Columbia 38653
6	6	27	No Jacket Required .... *Phil Collins*...Atlantic 81240
7	8	8	Greatest Hits, Volume I & Volume II .... *Billy Joel*...Columbia 40121
8	7	9	Theatre Of Pain .... *Mötley Crüe*...Elektra 60418
9	9	24	Whitney Houston .... *Whitney Houston*...Arista 8212
10	14	9	Heart .... *Heart*...Capitol 12410

TW	LW	WK	Billboard. ● SEPTEMBER 14, 1985 ● TOP POP ALBUMS
❶	1	15	**Brothers In Arms**...*Dire Straits*...Warner 25264
❷	2	10	**The Dream Of The Blue Turtles**....................................*Sting*...A&M 3750
③	3	25	Songs From The Big Chair.........................*Tears For Fears*...Mercury 824300
④	4	43	Reckless..*Bryan Adams*...A&M 5013
❺	5	65	Born In The U.S.A. ....*Bruce Springsteen*...Columbia 38653
⑥	6	28	No Jacket Required ....*Phil Collins*...Atlantic 81240
❼	7	9	Greatest Hits, Volume I & Volume II ....*Billy Joel*...Columbia 40121
❽	9	25	Whitney Houston.. *Whitney Houston*...Arista 8212
⑨	8	10	Theatre Of Pain...*Mötley Crüe*...Elektra 60418
⑩	10	10	Heart... *Heart*...Capitol 12410

TW	LW	WK	Billboard. ● SEPTEMBER 21, 1985 ● TOP POP ALBUMS
❶	1	16	**Brothers In Arms**...*Dire Straits*...Warner 25264
❷	2	11	**The Dream Of The Blue Turtles**....................................*Sting*...A&M 3750
③	3	26	Songs From The Big Chair.........................*Tears For Fears*...Mercury 824300
❹	5	66	Born In The U.S.A. ....*Bruce Springsteen*...Columbia 38653
⑤	4	44	Reckless..*Bryan Adams*...A&M 5013
⑥	6	29	No Jacket Required ....*Phil Collins*...Atlantic 81240
❼	7	10	Greatest Hits, Volume I & Volume II ....*Billy Joel*...Columbia 40121
❽	8	26	Whitney Houston.. *Whitney Houston*...Arista 8212
⑨	10	11	Heart... *Heart*...Capitol 12410
⑩	9	11	Theatre Of Pain...*Mötley Crüe*...Elektra 60418

TW	LW	WK	Billboard. ● SEPTEMBER 28, 1985 ● TOP POP ALBUMS
❶	1	17	**Brothers In Arms**...*Dire Straits*...Warner 25264
②	2	12	**The Dream Of The Blue Turtles**....................................*Sting*...A&M 3750
③	3	27	Songs From The Big Chair.........................*Tears For Fears*...Mercury 824300
❹	4	67	Born In The U.S.A. ....*Bruce Springsteen*...Columbia 38653
❺	8	27	Whitney Houston.. *Whitney Houston*...Arista 8212
❻	7	11	**Greatest Hits, Volume I & Volume II**............*Billy Joel*...Columbia 40121
⑦	6	30	No Jacket Required ....*Phil Collins*...Atlantic 81240
⑧	5	45	Reckless..*Bryan Adams*...A&M 5013
⑨	9	12	Heart... *Heart*...Capitol 12410
⑩	10	12	Theatre Of Pain...*Mötley Crüe*...Elektra 60418

TW	LW	WK	Billboard. ● OCTOBER 5, 1985 ● TOP POP ALBUMS
❶	1	18	**Brothers In Arms**...*Dire Straits*...Warner 25264
②	2	13	**The Dream Of The Blue Turtles**....................................*Sting*...A&M 3750
③	3	28	Songs From The Big Chair.........................*Tears For Fears*...Mercury 824300
❹	4	68	Born In The U.S.A. ....*Bruce Springsteen*...Columbia 38653
❺	5	28	Whitney Houston.. *Whitney Houston*...Arista 8212
❻	6	12	**Greatest Hits, Volume I & Volume II**............*Billy Joel*...Columbia 40121
⑦	8	46	Reckless..*Bryan Adams*...A&M 5013
⑧	7	31	No Jacket Required ....*Phil Collins*...Atlantic 81240
⑨	12	4	Scarecrow ....*John Cougar Mellencamp*...Riva 824865
⑩	9	13	Heart... *Heart*...Capitol 12410

TW	LW	WK	Billboard. OCTOBER 12, 1985 TOP POP ALBUMS
1	1	19	**Brothers In Arms** ... *Dire Straits*...Warner 25264
2	2	14	**The Dream Of The Blue Turtles** ... *Sting*...A&M 3750
3	3	29	Songs From The Big Chair ... *Tears For Fears*...Mercury 824300
4	5	29	Whitney Houston ... *Whitney Houston*...Arista 8212
5	4	69	Born In The U.S.A. ... *Bruce Springsteen*...Columbia 38653
6	9	5	Scarecrow ... *John Cougar Mellencamp*...Riva 824865
7	7	47	Reckless ... *Bryan Adams*...A&M 5013
8	10	14	Heart ... *Heart*...Capitol 12410
9	6	13	Greatest Hits, Volume I & Volume II ... *Billy Joel*...Columbia 40121
10	8	32	No Jacket Required ... *Phil Collins*...Atlantic 81240

TW	LW	WK	Billboard. OCTOBER 19, 1985 TOP POP ALBUMS
1	1	20	**Brothers In Arms** ... *Dire Straits*...Warner 25264
2	4	30	Whitney Houston ... *Whitney Houston*...Arista 8212
3	3	30	Songs From The Big Chair ... *Tears For Fears*...Mercury 824300
4	2	15	The Dream Of The Blue Turtles ... *Sting*...A&M 3750
5	5	70	Born In The U.S.A. ... *Bruce Springsteen*...Columbia 38653
6	6	6	Scarecrow ... *John Cougar Mellencamp*...Riva 824865
7	28	2	Miami Vice ... *TV Soundtrack*...MCA 6150
8	8	15	Heart ... *Heart*...Capitol 12410
9	7	48	Reckless ... *Bryan Adams*...A&M 5013
10	9	14	Greatest Hits, Volume I & Volume II ... *Billy Joel*...Columbia 40121

TW	LW	WK	Billboard. OCTOBER 26, 1985 TOP POP ALBUMS
1	1	21	**Brothers In Arms** ... *Dire Straits*...Warner 25264
2	2	31	Whitney Houston ... *Whitney Houston*...Arista 8212
3	7	3	Miami Vice ... *TV Soundtrack*...MCA 6150
4	6	7	Scarecrow ... *John Cougar Mellencamp*...Riva 824865
5	3	31	Songs From The Big Chair ... *Tears For Fears*...Mercury 824300
6	4	16	The Dream Of The Blue Turtles ... *Sting*...A&M 3750
7	5	71	Born In The U.S.A. ... *Bruce Springsteen*...Columbia 38653
8	8	16	Heart ... *Heart*...Capitol 12410
9	12	2	In Square Circle ... *Stevie Wonder*...Tamla 6134
10	9	49	Reckless ... *Bryan Adams*...A&M 5013

TW	LW	WK	Billboard. NOVEMBER 2, 1985 TOP POP ALBUMS
1	3	4	**Miami Vice** ... *TV Soundtrack*...MCA 6150
2	1	22	Brothers In Arms ... *Dire Straits*...Warner 25264
3	2	32	Whitney Houston ... *Whitney Houston*...Arista 8212
4	4	8	Scarecrow ... *John Cougar Mellencamp*...Riva 824865
5	5	32	Songs From The Big Chair ... *Tears For Fears*...Mercury 824300
6	6	17	The Dream Of The Blue Turtles ... *Sting*...A&M 3750
7	9	3	In Square Circle ... *Stevie Wonder*...Tamla 6134
8	8	17	Heart ... *Heart*...Capitol 12410
9	7	72	Born In The U.S.A. ... *Bruce Springsteen*...Columbia 38653
10	10	50	Reckless ... *Bryan Adams*...A&M 5013

TW	LW	WK	Billboard. NOVEMBER 9, 1985 TOP POP ALBUMS	
1	1	5	**Miami Vice**	*TV Soundtrack*...MCA 6150
2	2	23	**Brothers In Arms**	*Dire Straits*...Warner 25264
3	4	9	**Scarecrow**	*John Cougar Mellencamp*...Riva 824865
4	3	33	**Whitney Houston**	*Whitney Houston*...Arista 8212
5	5	33	**Songs From The Big Chair**	*Tears For Fears*...Mercury 824300
6	8	18	**Heart**	*Heart*...Capitol 12410
7	7	4	**In Square Circle**	*Stevie Wonder*...Tamla 6134
8	6	18	**The Dream Of The Blue Turtles**	*Sting*...A&M 3750
9	9	73	**Born In The U.S.A.**	*Bruce Springsteen*...Columbia 38653
10	10	51	**Reckless**	*Bryan Adams*...A&M 5013

TW	LW	WK	Billboard. NOVEMBER 16, 1985 TOP POP ALBUMS	
1	1	6	**Miami Vice**	*TV Soundtrack*...MCA 6150
2	3	10	**Scarecrow**	*John Cougar Mellencamp*...Riva 824865
3	2	24	**Brothers In Arms**	*Dire Straits*...Warner 25264
4	4	34	**Whitney Houston**	*Whitney Houston*...Arista 8212
5	6	19	**Heart**	*Heart*...Capitol 12410
6	7	5	**In Square Circle**	*Stevie Wonder*...Tamla 6134
7	5	34	**Songs From The Big Chair**	*Tears For Fears*...Mercury 824300
8	8	19	**The Dream Of The Blue Turtles**	*Sting*...A&M 3750
9	9	74	**Born In The U.S.A.**	*Bruce Springsteen*...Columbia 38653
10	10	52	**Reckless**	*Bryan Adams*...A&M 5013

TW	LW	WK	Billboard. NOVEMBER 23, 1985 TOP POP ALBUMS	
1	1	7	**Miami Vice**	*TV Soundtrack*...MCA 6150
2	2	11	**Scarecrow**	*John Cougar Mellencamp*...Riva 824865
3	3	25	**Brothers In Arms**	*Dire Straits*...Warner 25264
4	5	20	**Heart**	*Heart*...Capitol 12410
5	6	6	**In Square Circle**	*Stevie Wonder*...Tamla 6134
6	4	35	**Whitney Houston**	*Whitney Houston*...Arista 8212
7	7	35	**Songs From The Big Chair**	*Tears For Fears*...Mercury 824300
8	8	20	**The Dream Of The Blue Turtles**	*Sting*...A&M 3750
9	9	75	**Born In The U.S.A.**	*Bruce Springsteen*...Columbia 38653
10	32	2	**Afterburner**	*ZZ Top*...Warner 25342

TW	LW	WK	Billboard. NOVEMBER 30, 1985 TOP POP ALBUMS	
1	1	8	**Miami Vice**	*TV Soundtrack*...MCA 6150
2	2	12	**Scarecrow**	*John Cougar Mellencamp*...Riva 824865
3	4	21	**Heart**	*Heart*...Capitol 12410
4	3	26	**Brothers In Arms**	*Dire Straits*...Warner 25264
5	5	7	**In Square Circle**	*Stevie Wonder*...Tamla 6134
6	10	3	**Afterburner**	*ZZ Top*...Warner 25342
7	6	36	**Whitney Houston**	*Whitney Houston*...Arista 8212
8	8	21	**The Dream Of The Blue Turtles**	*Sting*...A&M 3750
9	7	36	**Songs From The Big Chair**	*Tears For Fears*...Mercury 824300
10	9	76	**Born In The U.S.A.**	*Bruce Springsteen*...Columbia 38653

TW	LW	WK	Billboard. DECEMBER 7, 1985 TOP POP ALBUMS
1	1	9	**Miami Vice**...*TV Soundtrack*...MCA 6150
2	3	22	Heart...*Heart*...Capitol 12410
3	2	13	Scarecrow...*John Cougar Mellencamp*...Riva 824865
4	6	4	**Afterburner**...*ZZ Top*...Warner 25342
5	4	27	Brothers In Arms...*Dire Straits*...Warner 25264
6	5	8	In Square Circle...*Stevie Wonder*...Tamla 6134
7	7	37	Whitney Houston...*Whitney Houston*...Arista 8212
8	9	37	Songs From The Big Chair...*Tears For Fears*...Mercury 824300
9	10	77	Born In The U.S.A...*Bruce Springsteen*...Columbia 38653
10	12	29	**Rock Me Tonight**...*Freddie Jackson*...Capitol 12404

TW	LW	WK	Billboard. DECEMBER 14, 1985 TOP POP ALBUMS
1	1	10	**Miami Vice**...*TV Soundtrack*...MCA 6150
2	2	23	Heart...*Heart*...Capitol 12410
3	3	14	Scarecrow...*John Cougar Mellencamp*...Riva 824865
4	4	5	**Afterburner**...*ZZ Top*...Warner 25342
5	5	28	Brothers In Arms...*Dire Straits*...Warner 25264
6	6	9	In Square Circle...*Stevie Wonder*...Tamla 6134
7	13	4	The Broadway Album...*Barbra Streisand*...Columbia 40092
8	9	78	Born In The U.S.A...*Bruce Springsteen*...Columbia 38653
9	7	38	Whitney Houston...*Whitney Houston*...Arista 8212
10	11	6	**Power Windows**...*Rush*...Mercury 826098

TW	LW	WK	Billboard. DECEMBER 21, 1985 TOP POP ALBUMS
1	2	24	**Heart**...*Heart*...Capitol 12410
2	1	11	Miami Vice...*TV Soundtrack*...MCA 6150
3	3	15	Scarecrow...*John Cougar Mellencamp*...Riva 824865
4	4	6	**Afterburner**...*ZZ Top*...Warner 25342
5	7	5	The Broadway Album...*Barbra Streisand*...Columbia 40092
6	5	29	Brothers In Arms...*Dire Straits*...Warner 25264
7	6	10	In Square Circle...*Stevie Wonder*...Tamla 6134
8	8	79	Born In The U.S.A...*Bruce Springsteen*...Columbia 38653
9	9	39	Whitney Houston...*Whitney Houston*...Arista 8212
10	10	7	**Power Windows**...*Rush*...Mercury 826098

TW	LW	WK	Billboard. DECEMBER 28, 1985 TOP POP ALBUMS
1	2	12	**Miami Vice**...*TV Soundtrack*...MCA 6150
2	1	25	Heart...*Heart*...Capitol 12410
3	3	16	Scarecrow...*John Cougar Mellencamp*...Riva 824865
4	5	6	The Broadway Album...*Barbra Streisand*...Columbia 40092
5	4	7	Afterburner...*ZZ Top*...Warner 25342
6	6	30	Brothers In Arms...*Dire Straits*...Warner 25264
7	7	11	In Square Circle...*Stevie Wonder*...Tamla 6134
8	8	80	Born In The U.S.A...*Bruce Springsteen*...Columbia 38653
9	15	13	Knee Deep In The Hoopla...*Starship*...Grunt 5488
10	11	40	Songs From The Big Chair...*Tears For Fears*...Mercury 824300

TW	LW	WK	Billboard. JANUARY 11, 1986 TOP POP ALBUMS
1	1	14	**Miami Vice**...*TV Soundtrack*...MCA 6150
2	4	8	The Broadway Album...*Barbra Streisand*...Columbia 40092
3	2	27	Heart...*Heart*...Capitol 12410
4	3	18	Scarecrow...*John Cougar Mellencamp*...Riva 824865
5	5	9	Afterburner...*ZZ Top*...Warner 25342
6	6	32	Brothers In Arms...*Dire Straits*...Warner 25264
7	7	13	In Square Circle...*Stevie Wonder*...Tamla 6134
8	8	82	Born In The U.S.A...*Bruce Springsteen*...Columbia 38653
9	9	15	Knee Deep In The Hoopla...*Starship*...Grunt 5488
10	10	42	Songs From The Big Chair...*Tears For Fears*...Mercury 824300

TW	LW	WK	Billboard. JANUARY 18, 1986 TOP POP ALBUMS
1	1	15	**Miami Vice**...*TV Soundtrack*...MCA 6150
2	2	9	The Broadway Album...*Barbra Streisand*...Columbia 40092
3	4	19	Scarecrow...*John Cougar Mellencamp*...Riva 824865
4	3	28	Heart...*Heart*...Capitol 12410
5	5	10	Afterburner...*ZZ Top*...Warner 25342
6	6	33	Brothers In Arms...*Dire Straits*...Warner 25264
7	11	5	Promise...*Sade*...Portrait 40263
8	8	83	Born In The U.S.A...*Bruce Springsteen*...Columbia 38653
9	9	16	Knee Deep In The Hoopla...*Starship*...Grunt 5488
10	7	14	In Square Circle...*Stevie Wonder*...Tamla 6134

TW	LW	WK	Billboard. JANUARY 25, 1986 TOP POP ALBUMS
1	2	10	**The Broadway Album**...*Barbra Streisand*...Columbia 40092
2	1	16	Miami Vice...*TV Soundtrack*...MCA 6150
3	4	29	Heart...*Heart*...Capitol 12410
4	3	20	Scarecrow...*John Cougar Mellencamp*...Riva 824865
5	7	6	Promise...*Sade*...Portrait 40263
6	6	34	Brothers In Arms...*Dire Straits*...Warner 25264
7	5	11	Afterburner...*ZZ Top*...Warner 25342
8	9	17	Knee Deep In The Hoopla...*Starship*...Grunt 5488
9	13	22	Welcome To The Real World...*Mr. Mister*...RCA 8045
10	8	84	Born In The U.S.A...*Bruce Springsteen*...Columbia 38653

TW	LW	WK	Billboard. FEBRUARY 1, 1986 TOP POP ALBUMS
1	1	11	**The Broadway Album**...*Barbra Streisand*...Columbia 40092
2	5	7	Promise...*Sade*...Portrait 40263
3	2	17	Miami Vice...*TV Soundtrack*...MCA 6150
4	3	30	Heart...*Heart*...Capitol 12410
5	4	21	Scarecrow...*John Cougar Mellencamp*...Riva 824865
6	6	35	Brothers In Arms...*Dire Straits*...Warner 25264
7	7	12	Afterburner...*ZZ Top*...Warner 25342
8	9	23	Welcome To The Real World...*Mr. Mister*...RCA 8045
9	11	45	Whitney Houston...*Whitney Houston*...Arista 8212
10	8	18	Knee Deep In The Hoopla...*Starship*...Grunt 5488

TW	LW	WK	Billboard. FEBRUARY 8, 1986 TOP POP ALBUMS
❶	1	12	**The Broadway Album**........ *Barbra Streisand*...Columbia 40092
❷	2	8	Promise........ *Sade*...Portrait 40263
③	4	31	Heart........ *Heart*...Capitol 12410
④	5	22	Scarecrow........ *John Cougar Mellencamp*...Riva 824865
⑤	3	18	Miami Vice........ *TV Soundtrack*...MCA 6150
❻	6	36	Brothers In Arms........ *Dire Straits*...Warner 25264
❼	8	24	Welcome To The Real World........ *Mr. Mister*...RCA 8045
❽	9	46	Whitney Houston........ *Whitney Houston*...Arista 8212
⑨	7	13	Afterburner........ *ZZ Top*...Warner 25342
⑩	10	19	Knee Deep In The Hoopla........ *Starship*...Grunt 5488

TW	LW	WK	Billboard. FEBRUARY 15, 1986 TOP POP ALBUMS
❶	2	9	**Promise**........ *Sade*...Portrait 40263
②	1	13	The Broadway Album........ *Barbra Streisand*...Columbia 40092
❸	7	25	Welcome To The Real World........ *Mr. Mister*...RCA 8045
④	3	32	Heart........ *Heart*...Capitol 12410
❺	8	47	Whitney Houston........ *Whitney Houston*...Arista 8212
⑥	4	23	Scarecrow........ *John Cougar Mellencamp*...Riva 824865
⑦	6	37	Brothers In Arms........ *Dire Straits*...Warner 25264
❽	10	20	Knee Deep In The Hoopla........ *Starship*...Grunt 5488
⑨	5	19	Miami Vice........ *TV Soundtrack*...MCA 6150
⑩	9	14	Afterburner........ *ZZ Top*...Warner 25342

TW	LW	WK	Billboard. FEBRUARY 22, 1986 TOP POP ALBUMS
❶	1	10	**Promise**........ *Sade*...Portrait 40263
❷	3	26	Welcome To The Real World........ *Mr. Mister*...RCA 8045
③	2	14	The Broadway Album........ *Barbra Streisand*...Columbia 40092
❹	5	48	Whitney Houston........ *Whitney Houston*...Arista 8212
⑤	4	33	Heart........ *Heart*...Capitol 12410
⑥	6	24	Scarecrow........ *John Cougar Mellencamp*...Riva 824865
⑦	7	38	Brothers In Arms........ *Dire Straits*...Warner 25264
❽	8	21	Knee Deep In The Hoopla........ *Starship*...Grunt 5488
⑨	10	15	Afterburner........ *ZZ Top*...Warner 25342
❿	11	15	**Rocky IV**........ *Soundtrack*...Scotti Brothers 40203

TW	LW	WK	Billboard. MARCH 1, 1986 TOP POP ALBUMS
❶	2	27	**Welcome To The Real World**........ *Mr. Mister*...RCA 8045
②	1	11	Promise........ *Sade*...Portrait 40263
❸	4	49	Whitney Houston........ *Whitney Houston*...Arista 8212
④	3	15	The Broadway Album........ *Barbra Streisand*...Columbia 40092
❺	6	25	Scarecrow........ *John Cougar Mellencamp*...Riva 824865
⑥	5	34	Heart........ *Heart*...Capitol 12410
❼	8	22	**Knee Deep In The Hoopla**........ *Starship*...Grunt 5488
⑧	7	39	Brothers In Arms........ *Dire Straits*...Warner 25264
⑨	9	16	Afterburner........ *ZZ Top*...Warner 25342
❿	11	17	**Once Upon A Time**........ *Simple Minds*...A&M 5092

Billboard — MARCH 8, 1986 — TOP POP ALBUMS

TW	LW	WK	Title	Artist	Label
1	3	50	**Whitney Houston**	*Whitney Houston*	Arista 8212
2	2	12	Promise	*Sade*	Portrait 40263
3	1	28	Welcome To The Real World	*Mr. Mister*	RCA 8045
4	4	16	The Broadway Album	*Barbra Streisand*	Columbia 40092
5	6	35	Heart	*Heart*	Capitol 12410
6	5	26	Scarecrow	*John Cougar Mellencamp*	Riva 824865
7	7	23	**Knee Deep In The Hoopla**	*Starship*	Grunt 5488
8	8	40	Brothers In Arms	*Dire Straits*	Warner 25264
9	13	4	The Ultimate Sin	*Ozzy Osbourne*	CBS Associated 40026
10	10	18	**Once Upon A Time**	*Simple Minds*	A&M 5092

Billboard — MARCH 15, 1986 — TOP POP ALBUMS

TW	LW	WK	Title	Artist	Label
1	1	51	**Whitney Houston**	*Whitney Houston*	Arista 8212
2	2	13	Promise	*Sade*	Portrait 40263
3	3	29	Welcome To The Real World	*Mr. Mister*	RCA 8045
4	5	36	Heart	*Heart*	Capitol 12410
5	4	17	The Broadway Album	*Barbra Streisand*	Columbia 40092
6	6	27	Scarecrow	*John Cougar Mellencamp*	Riva 824865
7	7	24	**Knee Deep In The Hoopla**	*Starship*	Grunt 5488
8	8	41	Brothers In Arms	*Dire Straits*	Warner 25264
9	9	5	The Ultimate Sin	*Ozzy Osbourne*	CBS Associated 40026
10	10	19	**Once Upon A Time**	*Simple Minds*	A&M 5092

Billboard — MARCH 22, 1986 — TOP POP ALBUMS

TW	LW	WK	Title	Artist	Label
1	1	52	**Whitney Houston**	*Whitney Houston*	Arista 8212
2	2	14	Promise	*Sade*	Portrait 40263
3	4	37	Heart	*Heart*	Capitol 12410
4	6	28	Scarecrow	*John Cougar Mellencamp*	Riva 824865
5	3	30	Welcome To The Real World	*Mr. Mister*	RCA 8045
6	5	18	The Broadway Album	*Barbra Streisand*	Columbia 40092
7	8	42	Brothers In Arms	*Dire Straits*	Warner 25264
8	9	6	The Ultimate Sin	*Ozzy Osbourne*	CBS Associated 40026
9	7	25	Knee Deep In The Hoopla	*Starship*	Grunt 5488
10	10	20	**Once Upon A Time**	*Simple Minds*	A&M 5092

Billboard — MARCH 29, 1986 — TOP POP ALBUMS

TW	LW	WK	Title	Artist	Label
1	1	53	**Whitney Houston**	*Whitney Houston*	Arista 8212
2	2	15	Promise	*Sade*	Portrait 40263
3	3	38	Heart	*Heart*	Capitol 12410
4	4	29	Scarecrow	*John Cougar Mellencamp*	Riva 824865
5	5	31	Welcome To The Real World	*Mr. Mister*	RCA 8045
6	6	19	The Broadway Album	*Barbra Streisand*	Columbia 40092
7	7	43	Brothers In Arms	*Dire Straits*	Warner 25264
8	8	7	The Ultimate Sin	*Ozzy Osbourne*	CBS Associated 40026
9	9	26	Knee Deep In The Hoopla	*Starship*	Grunt 5488
10	10	21	**Once Upon A Time**	*Simple Minds*	A&M 5092

Billboard — APRIL 5, 1986 — TOP POP ALBUMS

TW	LW	WK	Title	Artist	Label
1	1	54	**Whitney Houston**	*Whitney Houston*	Arista 8212
2	3	39	Heart	*Heart*	Capitol 12410
3	2	16	Promise	*Sade*	Portrait 40263
4	4	30	Scarecrow	*John Cougar Mellencamp*	Riva 824865
5	5	32	Welcome To The Real World	*Mr. Mister*	RCA 8045
6	8	8	**The Ultimate Sin**	*Ozzy Osbourne*	CBS Associated 40026
7	7	44	Brothers In Arms	*Dire Straits*	Warner 25264
8	11	6	Falco 3	*Falco*	A&M 5105
9	6	20	The Broadway Album	*Barbra Streisand*	Columbia 40092
10	9	27	Knee Deep In The Hoopla	*Starship*	Grunt 5488

Billboard — APRIL 12, 1986 — TOP POP ALBUMS

TW	LW	WK	Title	Artist	Label
1	1	55	**Whitney Houston**	*Whitney Houston*	Arista 8212
2	2	40	Heart	*Heart*	Capitol 12410
3	3	17	Promise	*Sade*	Portrait 40263
4	4	31	Scarecrow	*John Cougar Mellencamp*	Riva 824865
5	8	7	Falco 3	*Falco*	A&M 5105
6	6	9	**The Ultimate Sin**	*Ozzy Osbourne*	CBS Associated 40026
7	7	45	Brothers In Arms	*Dire Straits*	Warner 25264
8	11	7	Pretty In Pink	*Soundtrack*	A&M 3901
9	5	33	Welcome To The Real World	*Mr. Mister*	RCA 8045
10	9	21	The Broadway Album	*Barbra Streisand*	Columbia 40092

Billboard — APRIL 19, 1986 — TOP POP ALBUMS

TW	LW	WK	Title	Artist	Label
1	1	56	**Whitney Houston**	*Whitney Houston*	Arista 8212
2	2	41	Heart	*Heart*	Capitol 12410
3	13	2	5150	*Van Halen*	Warner 25394
4	3	18	Promise	*Sade*	Portrait 40263
5	5	8	Falco 3	*Falco*	A&M 5105
6	8	8	Pretty In Pink	*Soundtrack*	A&M 3901
7	6	10	The Ultimate Sin	*Ozzy Osbourne*	CBS Associated 40026
8	4	32	Scarecrow	*John Cougar Mellencamp*	Riva 824865
9	21	2	Dirty Work	*Rolling Stones*	Rolling Stones 40250
10	7	46	Brothers In Arms	*Dire Straits*	Warner 25264

Billboard — APRIL 26, 1986 — TOP POP ALBUMS

TW	LW	WK	Title	Artist	Label
1	3	3	**5150**	*Van Halen*	Warner 25394
2	1	57	Whitney Houston	*Whitney Houston*	Arista 8212
3	5	9	**Falco 3**	*Falco*	A&M 5105
4	2	42	Heart	*Heart*	Capitol 12410
5	9	3	Dirty Work	*Rolling Stones*	Rolling Stones 40250
6	14	2	Parade	*Prince & The Revolution/Soundtrack*	Paisley Park 25395
7	6	9	Pretty In Pink	*Soundtrack*	A&M 3901
8	4	19	Promise	*Sade*	Portrait 40263
9	47	2	Like A Rock	*Bob Seger & The Silver Bullet Band*	Capitol 12398
10	7	11	The Ultimate Sin	*Ozzy Osbourne*	CBS Associated 40026

Billboard — MAY 3, 1986 — TOP POP ALBUMS

TW	LW	WK	Title	Artist	Label
1	1	4	**5150**	*Van Halen*	Warner 25394
2	2	58	Whitney Houston	*Whitney Houston*	Arista 8212
3	6	3	**Parade**	*Prince & The Revolution/Soundtrack*	Paisley Park 25395
4	5	4	**Dirty Work**	*Rolling Stones*	Rolling Stones 40250
5	7	10	**Pretty In Pink**	*Soundtrack*	A&M 3901
6	9	3	Like A Rock	*Bob Seger & The Silver Bullet Band*	Capitol 12398
7	3	10	Falco 3	*Falco*	A&M 5105
8	4	43	Heart	*Heart*	Capitol 12410
9	13	24	Riptide	*Robert Palmer*	Island 90471
10	8	20	Promise	*Sade*	Portrait 40263

Billboard — MAY 10, 1986 — TOP POP ALBUMS

TW	LW	WK	Title	Artist	Label
1	1	5	**5150**	*Van Halen*	Warner 25394
2	2	59	Whitney Houston	*Whitney Houston*	Arista 8212
3	3	4	**Parade**	*Prince & The Revolution/Soundtrack*	Paisley Park 25395
4	4	5	**Dirty Work**	*Rolling Stones*	Rolling Stones 40250
5	5	11	**Pretty In Pink**	*Soundtrack*	A&M 3901
6	6	4	Like A Rock	*Bob Seger & The Silver Bullet Band*	Capitol 12398
7	8	44	Heart	*Heart*	Capitol 12410
8	7	11	Falco 3	*Falco*	A&M 5105
9	9	25	Riptide	*Robert Palmer*	Island 90471
10	14	23	Play Deep	*The Outfield*	Columbia 40027

Billboard — MAY 17, 1986 — TOP POP ALBUMS

TW	LW	WK	Title	Artist	Label
1	2	60	**Whitney Houston**	*Whitney Houston*	Arista 8212
2	1	6	5150	*Van Halen*	Warner 25394
3	3	5	**Parade**	*Prince & The Revolution/Soundtrack*	Paisley Park 25395
4	6	5	Like A Rock	*Bob Seger & The Silver Bullet Band*	Capitol 12398
5	5	12	**Pretty In Pink**	*Soundtrack*	A&M 3901
6	4	6	Dirty Work	*Rolling Stones*	Rolling Stones 40250
7	11	11	Control	*Janet Jackson*	A&M 5106
8	9	26	**Riptide**	*Robert Palmer*	Island 90471
9	23	2	Raised On Radio	*Journey*	Columbia 39936
10	10	24	Play Deep	*The Outfield*	Columbia 40027

Billboard — MAY 24, 1986 — TOP POP ALBUMS

TW	LW	WK	Title	Artist	Label
1	1	61	**Whitney Houston**	*Whitney Houston*	Arista 8212
2	2	7	5150	*Van Halen*	Warner 25394
3	4	6	**Like A Rock**	*Bob Seger & The Silver Bullet Band*	Capitol 12398
4	3	6	Parade	*Prince & The Revolution/Soundtrack*	Paisley Park 25395
5	5	13	**Pretty In Pink**	*Soundtrack*	A&M 3901
6	9	3	Raised On Radio	*Journey*	Columbia 39936
7	7	12	Control	*Janet Jackson*	A&M 5106
8	6	7	Dirty Work	*Rolling Stones*	Rolling Stones 40250
9	12	6	Please	*Pet Shop Boys*	EMI America 17193
10	8	27	Riptide	*Robert Palmer*	Island 90471

Billboard — MAY 31, 1986 — TOP POP ALBUMS

TW	LW	WK	Title	Artist	Label
1	1	62	**Whitney Houston**	*Whitney Houston*	Arista 8212
2	2	8	**5150**	*Van Halen*	Warner 25394
3	3	7	**Like A Rock**	*Bob Seger & The Silver Bullet Band*	Capitol 12398
4	6	4	**Raised On Radio**	*Journey*	Columbia 39936
5	4	7	Parade	*Prince & The Revolution/Soundtrack*	Paisley Park 25395
6	7	13	Control	*Janet Jackson*	A&M 5106
7	5	14	Pretty In Pink	*Soundtrack*	A&M 3901
8	14	2	Winner In You	*Patti LaBelle*	MCA 5737
9	9	7	Please	*Pet Shop Boys*	EMI America 17193
10	11	26	Play Deep	*The Outfield*	Columbia 40027

Billboard — JUNE 7, 1986 — TOP POP ALBUMS

TW	LW	WK	Title	Artist	Label
1	1	63	**Whitney Houston**	*Whitney Houston*	Arista 8212
2	2	9	**5150**	*Van Halen*	Warner 25394
3	3	8	**Like A Rock**	*Bob Seger & The Silver Bullet Band*	Capitol 12398
4	4	5	**Raised On Radio**	*Journey*	Columbia 39936
5	8	3	Winner In You	*Patti LaBelle*	MCA 5737
6	6	14	Control	*Janet Jackson*	A&M 5106
7	5	8	Parade	*Prince & The Revolution/Soundtrack*	Paisley Park 25395
8	9	8	Please	*Pet Shop Boys*	EMI America 17193
9	7	15	Pretty In Pink	*Soundtrack*	A&M 3901
10	10	27	Play Deep	*The Outfield*	Columbia 40027

Billboard — JUNE 14, 1986 — TOP POP ALBUMS

TW	LW	WK	Title	Artist	Label
1	1	64	**Whitney Houston**	*Whitney Houston*	Arista 8212
2	2	10	**5150**	*Van Halen*	Warner 25394
3	3	9	**Like A Rock**	*Bob Seger & The Silver Bullet Band*	Capitol 12398
4	5	4	Winner In You	*Patti LaBelle*	MCA 5737
5	6	15	Control	*Janet Jackson*	A&M 5106
6	4	6	Raised On Radio	*Journey*	Columbia 39936
7	7	9	Parade	*Prince & The Revolution/Soundtrack*	Paisley Park 25395
8	8	9	Please	*Pet Shop Boys*	EMI America 17193
9	10	28	**Play Deep**	*The Outfield*	Columbia 40027
10	11	49	Heart	*Heart*	Capitol 12410

Billboard — JUNE 21, 1986 — TOP POP ALBUMS

TW	LW	WK	Title	Artist	Label
1	1	65	**Whitney Houston**	*Whitney Houston*	Arista 8212
2	4	5	Winner In You	*Patti LaBelle*	MCA 5737
3	5	16	Control	*Janet Jackson*	A&M 5106
4	3	10	Like A Rock	*Bob Seger & The Silver Bullet Band*	Capitol 12398
5	2	11	5150	*Van Halen*	Warner 25394
6	6	7	Raised On Radio	*Journey*	Columbia 39936
7	8	10	**Please**	*Pet Shop Boys*	EMI America 17193
8	12	6	Love Zone	*Billy Ocean*	Jive 8409
9	7	10	Parade	*Prince & The Revolution/Soundtrack*	Paisley Park 25395
10	9	29	Play Deep	*The Outfield*	Columbia 40027

TW	LW	WK	Billboard® JUNE 28, 1986 TOP POP ALBUMS		
1	1	66	**Whitney Houston**	*Whitney Houston*	Arista 8212
2	2	6	Winner In You	*Patti LaBelle*	MCA 5737
3	3	17	Control	*Janet Jackson*	A&M 5106
4	4	11	Like A Rock	*Bob Seger & The Silver Bullet Band*	Capitol 12398
5	5	12	5150	*Van Halen*	Warner 25394
6	8	7	**Love Zone**	*Billy Ocean*	Jive 8409
7	6	8	Raised On Radio	*Journey*	Columbia 39936
8	7	11	Please	*Pet Shop Boys*	EMI America 17193
9	11	7	**The Other Side Of Life**	*The Moody Blues*	Threshold 829179
10	13	3	So	*Peter Gabriel*	Geffen 24088

TW	LW	WK	Billboard® JULY 5, 1986 TOP POP ALBUMS		
1	3	18	**Control**	*Janet Jackson*	A&M 5106
2	2	7	Winner In You	*Patti LaBelle*	MCA 5737
3	1	67	Whitney Houston	*Whitney Houston*	Arista 8212
4	4	12	Like A Rock	*Bob Seger & The Silver Bullet Band*	Capitol 12398
5	10	4	So	*Peter Gabriel*	Geffen 24088
6	6	8	**Love Zone**	*Billy Ocean*	Jive 8409
7	5	13	5150	*Van Halen*	Warner 25394
8	11	5	Top Gun	*Soundtrack*	Columbia 40323
9	9	8	**The Other Side Of Life**	*The Moody Blues*	Threshold 829179
10	23	2	Invisible Touch	*Genesis*	Atlantic 81641

TW	LW	WK	Billboard® JULY 12, 1986 TOP POP ALBUMS		
1	1	19	**Control**	*Janet Jackson*	A&M 5106
2	2	8	Winner In You	*Patti LaBelle*	MCA 5737
3	3	68	Whitney Houston	*Whitney Houston*	Arista 8212
4	5	5	So	*Peter Gabriel*	Geffen 24088
5	10	3	Invisible Touch	*Genesis*	Atlantic 81641
6	6	9	**Love Zone**	*Billy Ocean*	Jive 8409
7	4	13	Like A Rock	*Bob Seger & The Silver Bullet Band*	Capitol 12398
8	8	6	Top Gun	*Soundtrack*	Columbia 40323
9	9	9	**The Other Side Of Life**	*The Moody Blues*	Threshold 829179
10	7	14	5150	*Van Halen*	Warner 25394

TW	LW	WK	Billboard® JULY 19, 1986 TOP POP ALBUMS		
1	2	9	**Winner In You**	*Patti LaBelle*	MCA 5737
2	1	20	Control	*Janet Jackson*	A&M 5106
3	4	6	So	*Peter Gabriel*	Geffen 24088
4	8	7	Top Gun	*Soundtrack*	Columbia 40323
5	5	4	Invisible Touch	*Genesis*	Atlantic 81641
6	6	10	**Love Zone**	*Billy Ocean*	Jive 8409
7	3	69	Whitney Houston	*Whitney Houston*	Arista 8212
8	7	14	Like A Rock	*Bob Seger & The Silver Bullet Band*	Capitol 12398
9	9	10	**The Other Side Of Life**	*The Moody Blues*	Threshold 829179
10	10	15	5150	*Van Halen*	Warner 25394

TW	LW	WK	Billboard. JULY 26, 1986 TOP POP ALBUMS
1	4	8	**Top Gun**......*Soundtrack*...Columbia 40323
2	3	7	**So**......*Peter Gabriel*...Geffen 24088
3	2	21	Control......*Janet Jackson*...A&M 5106
4	5	5	Invisible Touch......*Genesis*...Atlantic 81641
5	1	10	Winner In You......*Patti LaBelle*...MCA 5737
6	6	11	**Love Zone**......*Billy Ocean*...Jive 8409
7	7	70	Whitney Houston......*Whitney Houston*...Arista 8212
8	8	15	Like A Rock......*Bob Seger & The Silver Bullet Band*...Capitol 12398
9	29	2	True Blue......*Madonna*...Sire 25442
10	9	11	The Other Side Of Life......*The Moody Blues*...Threshold 829179

TW	LW	WK	Billboard. AUGUST 2, 1986 TOP POP ALBUMS
1	1	9	**Top Gun**......*Soundtrack*...Columbia 40323
2	2	8	**So**......*Peter Gabriel*...Geffen 24088
3	4	6	**Invisible Touch**......*Genesis*...Atlantic 81641
4	3	22	Control......*Janet Jackson*...A&M 5106
5	9	3	True Blue......*Madonna*...Sire 25442
6	6	12	**Love Zone**......*Billy Ocean*...Jive 8409
7	5	11	Winner In You......*Patti LaBelle*...MCA 5737
8	7	71	Whitney Houston......*Whitney Houston*...Arista 8212
9	8	16	Like A Rock......*Bob Seger & The Silver Bullet Band*...Capitol 12398
10	10	12	The Other Side Of Life......*The Moody Blues*...Threshold 829179

TW	LW	WK	Billboard. AUGUST 9, 1986 TOP POP ALBUMS
1	1	10	**Top Gun**......*Soundtrack*...Columbia 40323
2	2	9	**So**......*Peter Gabriel*...Geffen 24088
3	5	4	True Blue......*Madonna*...Sire 25442
4	3	7	Invisible Touch......*Genesis*...Atlantic 81641
5	4	23	Control......*Janet Jackson*...A&M 5106
6	6	13	**Love Zone**......*Billy Ocean*...Jive 8409
7	7	12	Winner In You......*Patti LaBelle*...MCA 5737
8	12	3	Eat 'Em And Smile......*David Lee Roth*...Warner 25470
9	11	9	Raising Hell......*Run-D.M.C.*...Profile 1217
10	8	72	Whitney Houston......*Whitney Houston*...Arista 8212

TW	LW	WK	Billboard. AUGUST 16, 1986 TOP POP ALBUMS
1	3	5	**True Blue**......*Madonna*...Sire 25442
2	1	11	Top Gun......*Soundtrack*...Columbia 40323
3	2	10	So......*Peter Gabriel*...Geffen 24088
4	4	8	Invisible Touch......*Genesis*...Atlantic 81641
5	5	24	Control......*Janet Jackson*...A&M 5106
6	8	4	Eat 'Em And Smile......*David Lee Roth*...Warner 25470
7	6	14	Love Zone......*Billy Ocean*...Jive 8409
8	7	13	Winner In You......*Patti LaBelle*...MCA 5737
9	9	10	Raising Hell......*Run-D.M.C.*...Profile 1217
10	10	73	Whitney Houston......*Whitney Houston*...Arista 8212

Billboard — AUGUST 23, 1986 — TOP POP ALBUMS

TW	LW	WK	Title	Artist	Label
1	1	6	**True Blue**	*Madonna*	Sire 25442
2	2	12	Top Gun	*Soundtrack*	Columbia 40323
3	3	11	So	*Peter Gabriel*	Geffen 24088
4	4	9	Invisible Touch	*Genesis*	Atlantic 81641
5	6	5	Eat 'Em And Smile	*David Lee Roth*	Warner 25470
6	5	25	Control	*Janet Jackson*	A&M 5106
7	9	11	Raising Hell	*Run-D.M.C.*	Profile 1217
8	13	6	Back in the High Life	*Steve Winwood*	Island 25448
9	7	15	Love Zone	*Billy Ocean*	Jive 8409
10	12	6	**Music From The Edge Of Heaven**	*Wham!*	Columbia 40285

Billboard — AUGUST 30, 1986 — TOP POP ALBUMS

TW	LW	WK	Title	Artist	Label
1	1	7	**True Blue**	*Madonna*	Sire 25442
2	2	13	Top Gun	*Soundtrack*	Columbia 40323
3	4	10	**Invisible Touch**	*Genesis*	Atlantic 81641
4	5	6	**Eat 'Em And Smile**	*David Lee Roth*	Warner 25470
5	3	12	So	*Peter Gabriel*	Geffen 24088
6	7	12	Raising Hell	*Run-D.M.C.*	Profile 1217
7	8	7	Back in the High Life	*Steve Winwood*	Island 25448
8	6	26	Control	*Janet Jackson*	A&M 5106
9	9	16	Love Zone	*Billy Ocean*	Jive 8409
10	10	7	**Music From The Edge Of Heaven**	*Wham!*	Columbia 40285

Billboard — SEPTEMBER 6, 1986 — TOP POP ALBUMS

TW	LW	WK	Title	Artist	Label
1	1	8	**True Blue**	*Madonna*	Sire 25442
2	2	14	Top Gun	*Soundtrack*	Columbia 40323
3	7	8	**Back in the High Life**	*Steve Winwood*	Island 25448
4	4	7	**Eat 'Em And Smile**	*David Lee Roth*	Warner 25470
5	6	13	Raising Hell	*Run-D.M.C.*	Profile 1217
6	3	11	Invisible Touch	*Genesis*	Atlantic 81641
7	5	13	So	*Peter Gabriel*	Geffen 24088
8	8	27	Control	*Janet Jackson*	A&M 5106
9	11	4	The Bridge	*Billy Joel*	Columbia 40402
10	9	17	Love Zone	*Billy Ocean*	Jive 8409

Billboard — SEPTEMBER 13, 1986 — TOP POP ALBUMS

TW	LW	WK	Title	Artist	Label
1	1	9	**True Blue**	*Madonna*	Sire 25442
2	2	15	Top Gun	*Soundtrack*	Columbia 40323
3	3	9	**Back in the High Life**	*Steve Winwood*	Island 25448
4	5	14	Raising Hell	*Run-D.M.C.*	Profile 1217
5	4	8	Eat 'Em And Smile	*David Lee Roth*	Warner 25470
6	6	12	Invisible Touch	*Genesis*	Atlantic 81641
7	11	3	Dancing On The Ceiling	*Lionel Richie*	Motown 6158
8	9	5	The Bridge	*Billy Joel*	Columbia 40402
9	7	14	So	*Peter Gabriel*	Geffen 24088
10	8	28	Control	*Janet Jackson*	A&M 5106

TW	LW	WK	Billboard® SEPTEMBER 20, 1986 TOP POP ALBUMS
1	2	16	**Top Gun** .... *Soundtrack*...Columbia 40323
2	1	10	True Blue .... *Madonna*...Sire 25442
3	4	15	**Raising Hell** .... *Run-D.M.C.*...Profile 1217
4	3	10	Back in the High Life .... *Steve Winwood*...Island 25448
5	7	4	Dancing On The Ceiling .... *Lionel Richie*...Motown 6158
6	5	9	Eat 'Em And Smile .... *David Lee Roth*...Warner 25470
7	8	6	**The Bridge** .... *Billy Joel*...Columbia 40402
8	6	13	Invisible Touch .... *Genesis*...Atlantic 81641
9	10	29	Control .... *Janet Jackson*...A&M 5106
10	42	2	Fore! .... *Huey Lewis & The News*...Chrysalis 41534

TW	LW	WK	Billboard® SEPTEMBER 27, 1986 TOP POP ALBUMS
1	5	5	**Dancing On The Ceiling** .... *Lionel Richie*...Motown 6158
2	1	17	Top Gun .... *Soundtrack*...Columbia 40323
3	3	16	**Raising Hell** .... *Run-D.M.C.*...Profile 1217
4	2	11	True Blue .... *Madonna*...Sire 25442
5	4	11	Back in the High Life .... *Steve Winwood*...Island 25448
6	10	3	Fore! .... *Huey Lewis & The News*...Chrysalis 41534
7	7	7	**The Bridge** .... *Billy Joel*...Columbia 40402
8	6	10	Eat 'Em And Smile .... *David Lee Roth*...Warner 25470
9	9	30	Control .... *Janet Jackson*...A&M 5106
10	8	14	Invisible Touch .... *Genesis*...Atlantic 81641

TW	LW	WK	Billboard® OCTOBER 4, 1986 TOP POP ALBUMS
1	1	6	**Dancing On The Ceiling** .... *Lionel Richie*...Motown 6158
2	2	18	Top Gun .... *Soundtrack*...Columbia 40323
3	3	17	**Raising Hell** .... *Run-D.M.C.*...Profile 1217
4	6	4	Fore! .... *Huey Lewis & The News*...Chrysalis 41534
5	4	12	True Blue .... *Madonna*...Sire 25442
6	5	12	Back in the High Life .... *Steve Winwood*...Island 25448
7	7	8	**The Bridge** .... *Billy Joel*...Columbia 40402
8	11	4	Slippery When Wet .... *Bon Jovi*...Mercury 830264
9	10	15	Invisible Touch .... *Genesis*...Atlantic 81641
10	9	31	Control .... *Janet Jackson*...A&M 5106

TW	LW	WK	Billboard® OCTOBER 11, 1986 TOP POP ALBUMS
1	2	19	**Top Gun** .... *Soundtrack*...Columbia 40323
2	4	5	Fore! .... *Huey Lewis & The News*...Chrysalis 41534
3	1	7	Dancing On The Ceiling .... *Lionel Richie*...Motown 6158
4	8	5	Slippery When Wet .... *Bon Jovi*...Mercury 830264
5	3	18	Raising Hell .... *Run-D.M.C.*...Profile 1217
6	5	13	True Blue .... *Madonna*...Sire 25442
7	7	9	**The Bridge** .... *Billy Joel*...Columbia 40402
8	6	13	Back in the High Life .... *Steve Winwood*...Island 25448
9	9	16	Invisible Touch .... *Genesis*...Atlantic 81641
10	10	32	Control .... *Janet Jackson*...A&M 5106

TW	LW	WK	Billboard® OCTOBER 18, 1986 TOP POP ALBUMS
1	2	6	**Fore!**...*Huey Lewis & The News*...Chrysalis 41534
2	4	6	Slippery When Wet...*Bon Jovi*...Mercury 830264
3	1	20	Top Gun...*Soundtrack*...Columbia 40323
4	3	8	Dancing On The Ceiling...*Lionel Richie*...Motown 6158
5	5	19	Raising Hell...*Run-D.M.C.*...Profile 1217
6	8	14	Back in the High Life...*Steve Winwood*...Island 25448
7	6	14	True Blue...*Madonna*...Sire 25442
8	7	10	The Bridge...*Billy Joel*...Columbia 40402
9	9	17	Invisible Touch...*Genesis*...Atlantic 81641
10	10	33	Control...*Janet Jackson*...A&M 5106

TW	LW	WK	Billboard® OCTOBER 25, 1986 TOP POP ALBUMS
1	2	7	**Slippery When Wet**...*Bon Jovi*...Mercury 830264
2	1	7	Fore!...*Huey Lewis & The News*...Chrysalis 41534
3	15	2	Third Stage...*Boston*...MCA 6188
4	3	21	Top Gun...*Soundtrack*...Columbia 40323
5	4	9	Dancing On The Ceiling...*Lionel Richie*...Motown 6158
6	11	5	Break Every Rule...*Tina Turner*...Capitol 12530
7	6	15	Back in the High Life...*Steve Winwood*...Island 25448
8	5	20	Raising Hell...*Run-D.M.C.*...Profile 1217
9	7	15	True Blue...*Madonna*...Sire 25442
10	8	11	The Bridge...*Billy Joel*...Columbia 40402

TW	LW	WK	Billboard® NOVEMBER 1, 1986 TOP POP ALBUMS
1	3	3	**Third Stage**...*Boston*...MCA 6188
2	1	8	Slippery When Wet...*Bon Jovi*...Mercury 830264
3	2	8	Fore!...*Huey Lewis & The News*...Chrysalis 41534
4	4	22	Top Gun...*Soundtrack*...Columbia 40323
5	6	6	Break Every Rule...*Tina Turner*...Capitol 12530
6	7	16	Back in the High Life...*Steve Winwood*...Island 25448
7	5	10	Dancing On The Ceiling...*Lionel Richie*...Motown 6158
8	13	5	True Colors...*Cyndi Lauper*...Portrait 40313
9	8	21	Raising Hell...*Run-D.M.C.*...Profile 1217
10	9	16	True Blue...*Madonna*...Sire 25442

TW	LW	WK	Billboard® NOVEMBER 8, 1986 TOP POP ALBUMS
1	1	4	**Third Stage**...*Boston*...MCA 6188
2	2	9	Slippery When Wet...*Bon Jovi*...Mercury 830264
3	3	9	Fore!...*Huey Lewis & The News*...Chrysalis 41534
4	5	7	**Break Every Rule**...*Tina Turner*...Capitol 12530
5	8	6	True Colors...*Cyndi Lauper*...Portrait 40313
6	7	11	Dancing On The Ceiling...*Lionel Richie*...Motown 6158
7	4	23	Top Gun...*Soundtrack*...Columbia 40323
8	6	17	Back in the High Life...*Steve Winwood*...Island 25448
9	11	13	The Bridge...*Billy Joel*...Columbia 40402
10	9	22	Raising Hell...*Run-D.M.C.*...Profile 1217

Billboard — NOVEMBER 15, 1986 — TOP POP ALBUMS

TW	LW	WK	Title	Artist...Label
1	1	5	**Third Stage**	*Boston*...MCA 6188
2	2	10	Slippery When Wet	*Bon Jovi*...Mercury 830264
3	3	10	Fore!	*Huey Lewis & The News*...Chrysalis 41534
4	5	7	**True Colors**	*Cyndi Lauper*...Portrait 40313
5	4	8	Break Every Rule	*Tina Turner*...Capitol 12530
6	6	12	Dancing On The Ceiling	*Lionel Richie*...Motown 6158
7	8	18	Back in the High Life	*Steve Winwood*...Island 25448
8	7	24	Top Gun	*Soundtrack*...Columbia 40323
9	9	14	The Bridge	*Billy Joel*...Columbia 40402
10	11	18	True Blue	*Madonna*...Sire 25442

Billboard — NOVEMBER 22, 1986 — TOP POP ALBUMS

TW	LW	WK	Title	Artist...Label
1	1	6	**Third Stage**	*Boston*...MCA 6188
2	2	11	Slippery When Wet	*Bon Jovi*...Mercury 830264
3	3	11	Fore!	*Huey Lewis & The News*...Chrysalis 41534
4	4	8	**True Colors**	*Cyndi Lauper*...Portrait 40313
5	6	13	Dancing On The Ceiling	*Lionel Richie*...Motown 6158
6	5	9	Break Every Rule	*Tina Turner*...Capitol 12530
7	11	11	Graceland	*Paul Simon*...Warner 25447
8	19	3	Whiplash Smile	*Billy Idol*...Chrysalis 41514
9	9	15	The Bridge	*Billy Joel*...Columbia 40402
10	10	19	True Blue	*Madonna*...Sire 25442

Billboard — NOVEMBER 29, 1986 — TOP POP ALBUMS

TW	LW	WK	Title	Artist...Label
1	-	1	**Bruce Springsteen & The E Street Band Live/1975-85**	*Bruce Springsteen & The E Street Band*...Columbia 40558
2	1	7	Third Stage	*Boston*...MCA 6188
3	2	12	Slippery When Wet	*Bon Jovi*...Mercury 830264
4	3	12	Fore!	*Huey Lewis & The News*...Chrysalis 41534
5	5	14	Dancing On The Ceiling	*Lionel Richie*...Motown 6158
6	7	12	Graceland	*Paul Simon*...Warner 25447
7	4	9	True Colors	*Cyndi Lauper*...Portrait 40313
8	8	4	Whiplash Smile	*Billy Idol*...Chrysalis 41514
9	6	10	Break Every Rule	*Tina Turner*...Capitol 12530
10	18	24	The Way It Is	*Bruce Hornsby & The Range*...RCA 5904

Billboard — DECEMBER 6, 1986 — TOP POP ALBUMS

TW	LW	WK	Title	Artist...Label
1	1	2	**Bruce Springsteen & The E Street Band Live/1975-85**	*Bruce Springsteen & The E Street Band*...Columbia 40558
2	2	8	Third Stage	*Boston*...MCA 6188
3	3	13	Slippery When Wet	*Bon Jovi*...Mercury 830264
4	4	13	Fore!	*Huey Lewis & The News*...Chrysalis 41534
5	10	25	The Way It Is	*Bruce Hornsby & The Range*...RCA 5904
6	6	13	Graceland	*Paul Simon*...Warner 25447
7	5	15	Dancing On The Ceiling	*Lionel Richie*...Motown 6158
8	8	5	Whiplash Smile	*Billy Idol*...Chrysalis 41514
9	7	10	True Colors	*Cyndi Lauper*...Portrait 40313
10	11	11	Word Up!	*Cameo*...Atlanta Artists 830265

TW	LW	WK	Billboard. DECEMBER 13, 1986 TOP POP ALBUMS
1	1	3	**Bruce Springsteen & The E Street Band Live/1975-85** ...*Bruce Springsteen & The E Street Band*...Columbia 40558
2	3	14	Slippery When Wet...*Bon Jovi*...Mercury 830264
3	2	9	Third Stage...*Boston*...MCA 6188
4	4	14	Fore!...*Huey Lewis & The News*...Chrysalis 41534
5	5	26	The Way It Is...*Bruce Hornsby & The Range*...RCA 5904
6	8	6	**Whiplash Smile**...*Billy Idol*...Chrysalis 41514
7	7	16	Dancing On The Ceiling...*Lionel Richie*...Motown 6158
8	6	14	Graceland...*Paul Simon*...Warner 25447
9	10	12	Word Up!...*Cameo*...Atlanta Artists 830265
10	16	4	Every Breath You Take - The Singles...*The Police*...A&M 3902

TW	LW	WK	Billboard. DECEMBER 20, 1986 TOP POP ALBUMS
1	1	4	**Bruce Springsteen & The E Street Band Live/1975-85** ...*Bruce Springsteen & The E Street Band*...Columbia 40558
2	2	15	Slippery When Wet...*Bon Jovi*...Mercury 830264
3	3	10	Third Stage...*Boston*...MCA 6188
4	5	27	The Way It Is...*Bruce Hornsby & The Range*...RCA 5904
5	4	15	Fore!...*Huey Lewis & The News*...Chrysalis 41534
6	8	15	Graceland...*Paul Simon*...Warner 25447
7	10	5	**Every Breath You Take - The Singles**...*The Police*...A&M 3902
8	9	13	**Word Up!**...*Cameo*...Atlanta Artists 830265
9	6	7	Whiplash Smile...*Billy Idol*...Chrysalis 41514
10	12	23	True Blue...*Madonna*...Sire 25442

TW	LW	WK	Billboard. DECEMBER 27, 1986 TOP POP ALBUMS
1	1	5	**Bruce Springsteen & The E Street Band Live/1975-85** ...*Bruce Springsteen & The E Street Band*...Columbia 40558
2	2	16	Slippery When Wet...*Bon Jovi*...Mercury 830264
3	3	11	Third Stage...*Boston*...MCA 6188
4	4	28	The Way It Is...*Bruce Hornsby & The Range*...RCA 5904
5	5	16	Fore!...*Huey Lewis & The News*...Chrysalis 41534
6	6	16	Graceland...*Paul Simon*...Warner 25447
7	11	18	Dancing On The Ceiling...*Lionel Richie*...Motown 6158
8	10	24	True Blue...*Madonna*...Sire 25442
9	7	6	Every Breath You Take - The Singles...*The Police*...A&M 3902
10	14	24	Night Songs...*Cinderella*...Mercury 830076

TW	LW	WK	Billboard® JANUARY 10, 1987 TOP POP ALBUMS
①	1	7	**Bruce Springsteen & The E Street Band Live/1975-85** ...... *Bruce Springsteen & The E Street Band*...Columbia 40558
❷	2	18	**Slippery When Wet** ...... *Bon Jovi*...Mercury 830264
③	3	13	**Third Stage** ...... *Boston*...MCA 6188
④	4	30	**The Way It Is** ...... *Bruce Hornsby & The Range*...RCA 5904
⑤	5	18	**Fore!** ...... *Huey Lewis & The News*...Chrysalis 41534
❻	8	26	**True Blue** ...... *Madonna*...Sire 25442
❼	7	20	**Dancing On The Ceiling** ...... *Lionel Richie*...Motown 6158
❽	13	50	**Different Light** ...... *Bangles*...Columbia 40039
❾	10	26	**Night Songs** ...... *Cinderella*...Mercury 830076
⑩	6	18	**Graceland** ...... *Paul Simon*...Warner 25447

TW	LW	WK	Billboard® JANUARY 17, 1987 TOP POP ALBUMS
❶	2	19	**Slippery When Wet** ...... *Bon Jovi*...Mercury 830264
②	1	8	**Bruce Springsteen & The E Street Band Live/1975-85** ...... *Bruce Springsteen & The E Street Band*...Columbia 40558
③	3	14	**Third Stage** ...... *Boston*...MCA 6188
④	4	31	**The Way It Is** ...... *Bruce Hornsby & The Range*...RCA 5904
❺	8	51	**Different Light** ...... *Bangles*...Columbia 40039
❻	6	27	**True Blue** ...... *Madonna*...Sire 25442
⑦	5	19	**Fore!** ...... *Huey Lewis & The News*...Chrysalis 41534
❽	9	27	**Night Songs** ...... *Cinderella*...Mercury 830076
⑨	7	21	**Dancing On The Ceiling** ...... *Lionel Richie*...Motown 6158
⑩	10	19	**Graceland** ...... *Paul Simon*...Warner 25447

TW	LW	WK	Billboard® JANUARY 24, 1987 TOP POP ALBUMS
❶	1	20	**Slippery When Wet** ...... *Bon Jovi*...Mercury 830264
②	2	9	**Bruce Springsteen & The E Street Band Live/1975-85** ...... *Bruce Springsteen & The E Street Band*...Columbia 40558
③	3	15	**Third Stage** ...... *Boston*...MCA 6188
❹	5	52	**Different Light** ...... *Bangles*...Columbia 40039
⑤	4	32	**The Way It Is** ...... *Bruce Hornsby & The Range*...RCA 5904
❻	8	28	**Night Songs** ...... *Cinderella*...Mercury 830076
⑦	6	28	**True Blue** ...... *Madonna*...Sire 25442
⑧	7	20	**Fore!** ...... *Huey Lewis & The News*...Chrysalis 41534
⑨	9	22	**Dancing On The Ceiling** ...... *Lionel Richie*...Motown 6158
❿	11	47	**Control** ...... *Janet Jackson*...A&M 5106

TW	LW	WK	Billboard® JANUARY 31, 1987 TOP POP ALBUMS
①	1	21	**Slippery When Wet** ...... *Bon Jovi*...Mercury 830264
❷	4	53	**Different Light** ...... *Bangles*...Columbia 40039
③	3	16	**Third Stage** ...... *Boston*...MCA 6188
❹	6	29	**Night Songs** ...... *Cinderella*...Mercury 830076
⑤	5	33	**The Way It Is** ...... *Bruce Hornsby & The Range*...RCA 5904
⑥	2	10	**Bruce Springsteen & The E Street Band Live/1975-85** ...... *Bruce Springsteen & The E Street Band*...Columbia 40558
❼	11	10	**Licensed To Ill** ...... *Beastie Boys*...Def Jam 40238
⑧	8	21	**Fore!** ...... *Huey Lewis & The News*...Chrysalis 41534
❾	10	48	**Control** ...... *Janet Jackson*...A&M 5106
⑩	7	29	**True Blue** ...... *Madonna*...Sire 25442

Billboard® — FEBRUARY 7, 1987 — TOP POP ALBUMS

TW	LW	WK	Title	Artist...Label
1	1	22	**Slippery When Wet**	*Bon Jovi*...Mercury 830264
2	2	54	**Different Light**	*Bangles*...Columbia 40039
3	4	30	**Night Songs**	*Cinderella*...Mercury 830076
4	7	11	Licensed To Ill	*Beastie Boys*...Def Jam 40238
5	5	34	The Way It Is	*Bruce Hornsby & The Range*...RCA 5904
6	3	17	Third Stage	*Boston*...MCA 6188
7	8	22	Fore!	*Huey Lewis & The News*...Chrysalis 41534
8	6	11	Bruce Springsteen & The E Street Band Live/1975-85	*Bruce Springsteen & The E Street Band*...Columbia 40558
9	9	49	Control	*Janet Jackson*...A&M 5106
10	10	30	True Blue	*Madonna*...Sire 25442

Billboard® — FEBRUARY 14, 1987 — TOP POP ALBUMS

TW	LW	WK	Title	Artist...Label
1	1	23	**Slippery When Wet**	*Bon Jovi*...Mercury 830264
2	4	12	Licensed To Ill	*Beastie Boys*...Def Jam 40238
3	2	55	Different Light	*Bangles*...Columbia 40039
4	3	31	Night Songs	*Cinderella*...Mercury 830076
5	5	35	The Way It Is	*Bruce Hornsby & The Range*...RCA 5904
6	6	18	Third Stage	*Boston*...MCA 6188
7	9	50	Control	*Janet Jackson*...A&M 5106
8	7	23	Fore!	*Huey Lewis & The News*...Chrysalis 41534
9	12	34	Invisible Touch	*Genesis*...Atlantic 81641
10	11	25	Dancing On The Ceiling	*Lionel Richie*...Motown 6158

Billboard® — FEBRUARY 21, 1987 — TOP POP ALBUMS

TW	LW	WK	Title	Artist...Label
1	1	24	**Slippery When Wet**	*Bon Jovi*...Mercury 830264
2	2	13	Licensed To Ill	*Beastie Boys*...Def Jam 40238
3	4	32	**Night Songs**	*Cinderella*...Mercury 830076
4	5	36	The Way It Is	*Bruce Hornsby & The Range*...RCA 5904
5	3	56	Different Light	*Bangles*...Columbia 40039
6	7	51	Control	*Janet Jackson*...A&M 5106
7	9	35	Invisible Touch	*Genesis*...Atlantic 81641
8	11	17	Georgia Satellites	*Georgia Satellites*...Elektra 60496
9	6	19	Third Stage	*Boston*...MCA 6188
10	8	24	Fore!	*Huey Lewis & The News*...Chrysalis 41534

Billboard® — FEBRUARY 28, 1987 — TOP POP ALBUMS

TW	LW	WK	Title	Artist...Label
1	1	25	**Slippery When Wet**	*Bon Jovi*...Mercury 830264
2	2	14	Licensed To Ill	*Beastie Boys*...Def Jam 40238
3	3	33	**Night Songs**	*Cinderella*...Mercury 830076
4	4	37	The Way It Is	*Bruce Hornsby & The Range*...RCA 5904
5	8	18	**Georgia Satellites**	*Georgia Satellites*...Elektra 60496
6	6	52	Control	*Janet Jackson*...A&M 5106
7	7	36	Invisible Touch	*Genesis*...Atlantic 81641
8	5	57	Different Light	*Bangles*...Columbia 40039
9	9	20	Third Stage	*Boston*...MCA 6188
10	10	25	Fore!	*Huey Lewis & The News*...Chrysalis 41534

TW	LW	WK	Billboard® MARCH 7, 1987 TOP POP ALBUMS
1	2	15	**Licensed To Ill** .... *Beastie Boys*...Def Jam 40238
2	1	26	Slippery When Wet........ *Bon Jovi*...Mercury 830264
3	4	38	**The Way It Is** .... *Bruce Hornsby & The Range*...RCA 5904
4	7	37	Invisible Touch........ *Genesis*...Atlantic 81641
5	6	53	Control .... *Janet Jackson*...A&M 5106
6	5	19	Georgia Satellites........ *Georgia Satellites*...Elektra 60496
7	3	34	Night Songs .... *Cinderella*...Mercury 830076
8	9	21	Third Stage........ *Boston*...MCA 6188
9	10	26	Fore!........ *Huey Lewis & The News*...Chrysalis 41534
10	8	58	Different Light .... *Bangles*...Columbia 40039

TW	LW	WK	Billboard® MARCH 14, 1987 TOP POP ALBUMS
1	1	16	**Licensed To Ill** .... *Beastie Boys*...Def Jam 40238
2	2	27	Slippery When Wet........ *Bon Jovi*...Mercury 830264
3	3	39	**The Way It Is** .... *Bruce Hornsby & The Range*...RCA 5904
4	4	38	Invisible Touch........ *Genesis*...Atlantic 81641
5	5	54	Control .... *Janet Jackson*...A&M 5106
6	6	20	Georgia Satellites........ *Georgia Satellites*...Elektra 60496
7	11	27	Graceland........ *Paul Simon*...Warner 25447
8	7	35	Night Songs .... *Cinderella*...Mercury 830076
9	12	20	The Final Countdown........ *Europe*...Epic 40241
10	9	27	Fore!........ *Huey Lewis & The News*...Chrysalis 41534

TW	LW	WK	Billboard® MARCH 21, 1987 TOP POP ALBUMS
1	1	17	**Licensed To Ill** .... *Beastie Boys*...Def Jam 40238
2	2	28	Slippery When Wet........ *Bon Jovi*...Mercury 830264
3	3	40	**The Way It Is** .... *Bruce Hornsby & The Range*...RCA 5904
4	7	28	Graceland........ *Paul Simon*...Warner 25447
5	5	55	Control .... *Janet Jackson*...A&M 5106
6	4	39	Invisible Touch........ *Genesis*...Atlantic 81641
7	11	14	Life, Love & Pain .... *Club Nouveau*...Warner 25531
8	8	36	Night Songs .... *Cinderella*...Mercury 830076
9	9	21	The Final Countdown........ *Europe*...Epic 40241
10	6	21	Georgia Satellites........ *Georgia Satellites*...Elektra 60496

TW	LW	WK	Billboard® MARCH 28, 1987 TOP POP ALBUMS
1	1	18	**Licensed To Ill** .... *Beastie Boys*...Def Jam 40238
2	2	29	Slippery When Wet........ *Bon Jovi*...Mercury 830264
3	3	41	**The Way It Is** .... *Bruce Hornsby & The Range*...RCA 5904
4	4	29	Graceland........ *Paul Simon*...Warner 25447
5	6	40	Invisible Touch........ *Genesis*...Atlantic 81641
6	5	56	Control .... *Janet Jackson*...A&M 5106
7	7	15	Life, Love & Pain .... *Club Nouveau*...Warner 25531
8	9	22	**The Final Countdown**........ *Europe*...Epic 40241
9	8	37	Night Songs .... *Cinderella*...Mercury 830076
10	12	37	Back in the High Life .... *Steve Winwood*...Island 25448

TW	LW	WK	Billboard® APRIL 4, 1987 TOP POP ALBUMS
1	1	19	**Licensed To Ill** .... *Beastie Boys*...Def Jam 40238
2	2	30	Slippery When Wet .... *Bon Jovi*...Mercury 830264
3	4	30	**Graceland** .... *Paul Simon*...Warner 25447
4	3	42	The Way It Is .... *Bruce Hornsby & The Range*...RCA 5904
5	6	57	Control .... *Janet Jackson*...A&M 5106
6	5	41	Invisible Touch .... *Genesis*...Atlantic 81641
7	-	1	The Joshua Tree .... *U2*...Island 90581
8	7	16	Life, Love & Pain .... *Club Nouveau*...Warner 25531
9	8	23	The Final Countdown .... *Europe*...Epic 40241
10	9	38	Night Songs .... *Cinderella*...Mercury 830076

TW	LW	WK	Billboard® APRIL 11, 1987 TOP POP ALBUMS
1	1	20	**Licensed To Ill** .... *Beastie Boys*...Def Jam 40238
2	2	31	Slippery When Wet .... *Bon Jovi*...Mercury 830264
3	7	2	The Joshua Tree .... *U2*...Island 90581
4	3	31	Graceland .... *Paul Simon*...Warner 25447
5	4	43	The Way It Is .... *Bruce Hornsby & The Range*...RCA 5904
6	6	42	Invisible Touch .... *Genesis*...Atlantic 81641
7	12	37	Look What The Cat Dragged In .... *Poison*...Capitol 12523
8	5	58	Control .... *Janet Jackson*...A&M 5106
9	9	24	The Final Countdown .... *Europe*...Epic 40241
10	8	17	Life, Love & Pain .... *Club Nouveau*...Warner 25531

TW	LW	WK	Billboard® APRIL 18, 1987 TOP POP ALBUMS
1	1	21	**Licensed To Ill** .... *Beastie Boys*...Def Jam 40238
2	3	3	The Joshua Tree .... *U2*...Island 90581
3	2	32	Slippery When Wet .... *Bon Jovi*...Mercury 830264
4	4	32	Graceland .... *Paul Simon*...Warner 25447
5	5	44	The Way It Is .... *Bruce Hornsby & The Range*...RCA 5904
6	7	38	Look What The Cat Dragged In .... *Poison*...Capitol 12523
7	10	18	Life, Love & Pain .... *Club Nouveau*...Warner 25531
8	6	43	Invisible Touch .... *Genesis*...Atlantic 81641
9	8	59	Control .... *Janet Jackson*...A&M 5106
10	9	25	The Final Countdown .... *Europe*...Epic 40241

TW	LW	WK	Billboard® APRIL 25, 1987 TOP POP ALBUMS
1	2	4	**The Joshua Tree** .... *U2*...Island 90581
2	1	22	Licensed To Ill .... *Beastie Boys*...Def Jam 40238
3	3	33	Slippery When Wet .... *Bon Jovi*...Mercury 830264
4	6	39	Look What The Cat Dragged In .... *Poison*...Capitol 12523
5	4	33	Graceland .... *Paul Simon*...Warner 25447
6	7	19	**Life, Love & Pain** .... *Club Nouveau*...Warner 25531
7	5	45	The Way It Is .... *Bruce Hornsby & The Range*...RCA 5904
8	12	5	Trio .... *Dolly Parton, Linda Ronstadt, Emmylou Harris*...Warner 25491
9	10	26	The Final Countdown .... *Europe*...Epic 40241
10	9	60	Control .... *Janet Jackson*...A&M 5106

TW	LW	WK	Billboard® MAY 2, 1987 TOP POP ALBUMS
1	1	5	**The Joshua Tree** ... *U2*...Island 90581
2	2	23	Licensed To Ill ... *Beastie Boys*...Def Jam 40238
3	3	34	Slippery When Wet ... *Bon Jovi*...Mercury 830264
4	4	40	Look What The Cat Dragged In ... *Poison*...Capitol 12523
5	5	34	Graceland ... *Paul Simon*...Warner 25447
6	8	6	**Trio** ... *Dolly Parton, Linda Ronstadt, Emmylou Harris*...Warner 25491
7	6	20	Life, Love & Pain ... *Club Nouveau*...Warner 25531
8	12	3	Sign "O" The Times ... *Prince*...Paisley Park 25577
9	9	27	The Final Countdown ... *Europe*...Epic 40241
10	7	46	The Way It Is ... *Bruce Hornsby & The Range*...RCA 5904

TW	LW	WK	Billboard® MAY 9, 1987 TOP POP ALBUMS
1	1	6	**The Joshua Tree** ... *U2*...Island 90581
2	2	24	Licensed To Ill ... *Beastie Boys*...Def Jam 40238
3	3	35	Slippery When Wet ... *Bon Jovi*...Mercury 830264
4	4	41	Look What The Cat Dragged In ... *Poison*...Capitol 12523
5	5	35	Graceland ... *Paul Simon*...Warner 25447
6	8	4	**Sign "O" The Times** ... *Prince*...Paisley Park 25577
7	6	7	Trio ... *Dolly Parton, Linda Ronstadt, Emmylou Harris*...Warner 25491
8	9	28	**The Final Countdown** ... *Europe*...Epic 40241
9	12	4	Into The Fire ... *Bryan Adams*...A&M 3907
10	19	4	Whitesnake ... *Whitesnake*...Geffen 24099

TW	LW	WK	Billboard® MAY 16, 1987 TOP POP ALBUMS
1	1	7	**The Joshua Tree** ... *U2*...Island 90581
2	3	36	Slippery When Wet ... *Bon Jovi*...Mercury 830264
3	2	25	Licensed To Ill ... *Beastie Boys*...Def Jam 40238
4	4	42	Look What The Cat Dragged In ... *Poison*...Capitol 12523
5	5	36	Graceland ... *Paul Simon*...Warner 25447
6	6	5	**Sign "O" The Times** ... *Prince*...Paisley Park 25577
7	9	5	**Into The Fire** ... *Bryan Adams*...A&M 3907
8	10	5	Whitesnake ... *Whitesnake*...Geffen 24099
9	14	3	Tango In The Night ... *Fleetwood Mac*...Warner 25471
10	8	29	The Final Countdown ... *Europe*...Epic 40241

TW	LW	WK	Billboard® MAY 23, 1987 TOP POP ALBUMS
1	1	8	**The Joshua Tree** ... *U2*...Island 90581
2	2	37	Slippery When Wet ... *Bon Jovi*...Mercury 830264
3	4	43	**Look What The Cat Dragged In** ... *Poison*...Capitol 12523
4	3	26	Licensed To Ill ... *Beastie Boys*...Def Jam 40238
5	5	37	Graceland ... *Paul Simon*...Warner 25447
6	8	6	Whitesnake ... *Whitesnake*...Geffen 24099
7	9	4	**Tango In The Night** ... *Fleetwood Mac*...Warner 25471
8	7	6	Into The Fire ... *Bryan Adams*...A&M 3907
9	6	6	Sign "O" The Times ... *Prince*...Paisley Park 25577
10	13	10	**Jody Watley** ... *Jody Watley*...MCA 5898

Billboard® — MAY 30, 1987 — TOP POP ALBUMS

TW	LW	WK	Title	Artist	Label
①	1	9	**The Joshua Tree**	*U2*	Island 90581
②	2	38	Slippery When Wet	*Bon Jovi*	Mercury 830264
③	3	44	**Look What The Cat Dragged In**	*Poison*	Capitol 12523
❹	6	7	Whitesnake	*Whitesnake*	Geffen 24099
❺	5	38	Graceland	*Paul Simon*	Warner 25447
⑥	4	27	Licensed To Ill	*Beastie Boys*	Def Jam 40238
❼	7	5	**Tango In The Night**	*Fleetwood Mac*	Warner 25471
❽	14	4	Tribute	*Ozzy Osbourne/Randy Rhoads*	CBS Associated 40714
⑨	8	7	Into The Fire	*Bryan Adams*	A&M 3907
❿	17	4	One Voice	*Barbra Streisand*	Columbia 40788

Billboard® — JUNE 6, 1987 — TOP POP ALBUMS

TW	LW	WK	Title	Artist	Label
①	1	10	**The Joshua Tree**	*U2*	Island 90581
②	2	39	Slippery When Wet	*Bon Jovi*	Mercury 830264
❸	4	8	Whitesnake	*Whitesnake*	Geffen 24099
④	3	45	Look What The Cat Dragged In	*Poison*	Capitol 12523
⑤	5	39	Graceland	*Paul Simon*	Warner 25447
⑥	6	28	Licensed To Ill	*Beastie Boys*	Def Jam 40238
⑦	7	6	**Tango In The Night**	*Fleetwood Mac*	Warner 25471
❽	8	5	Tribute	*Ozzy Osbourne/Randy Rhoads*	CBS Associated 40714
❾	10	5	**One Voice**	*Barbra Streisand*	Columbia 40788
⑩	9	8	Into The Fire	*Bryan Adams*	A&M 3907

Billboard® — JUNE 13, 1987 — TOP POP ALBUMS

TW	LW	WK	Title	Artist	Label
①	1	11	**The Joshua Tree**	*U2*	Island 90581
❷	3	9	**Whitesnake**	*Whitesnake*	Geffen 24099
③	2	40	Slippery When Wet	*Bon Jovi*	Mercury 830264
④	4	46	Look What The Cat Dragged In	*Poison*	Capitol 12523
❺	-	1	Girls, Girls, Girls	*Mötley Crüe*	Elektra 60725
❻	8	6	**Tribute**	*Ozzy Osbourne/Randy Rhoads*	CBS Associated 40714
⑦	5	40	Graceland	*Paul Simon*	Warner 25447
⑧	7	7	Tango In The Night	*Fleetwood Mac*	Warner 25471
❾	9	6	**One Voice**	*Barbra Streisand*	Columbia 40788
❿	12	6	Spanish Fly	*Lisa Lisa & Cult Jam*	Columbia 40477

Billboard® — JUNE 20, 1987 — TOP POP ALBUMS

TW	LW	WK	Title	Artist	Label
①	1	12	**The Joshua Tree**	*U2*	Island 90581
❷	2	10	**Whitesnake**	*Whitesnake*	Geffen 24099
❸	5	2	Girls, Girls, Girls	*Mötley Crüe*	Elektra 60725
④	3	41	Slippery When Wet	*Bon Jovi*	Mercury 830264
⑤	4	47	Look What The Cat Dragged In	*Poison*	Capitol 12523
❻	6	7	**Tribute**	*Ozzy Osbourne/Randy Rhoads*	CBS Associated 40714
❼	10	7	**Spanish Fly**	*Lisa Lisa & Cult Jam*	Columbia 40477
❽	13	42	Duotones	*Kenny G*	Arista 8427
⑨	7	41	Graceland	*Paul Simon*	Warner 25447
⑩	8	8	Tango In The Night	*Fleetwood Mac*	Warner 25471

TW	LW	WK	Billboard. JUNE 27, 1987 TOP POP ALBUMS
1	-	1	**Whitney** ... *Whitney Houston*...Arista 8405
2	3	3	**Girls, Girls, Girls** ... *Mötley Crüe*...Elektra 60725
3	1	13	The Joshua Tree ... *U2*...Island 90581
4	2	11	Whitesnake ... *Whitesnake*...Geffen 24099
5	4	42	Slippery When Wet ... *Bon Jovi*...Mercury 830264
6	12	3	Bad Animals ... *Heart*...Capitol 12546
7	7	8	**Spanish Fly** ... *Lisa Lisa & Cult Jam*...Columbia 40477
8	6	8	Tribute ... *Ozzy Osbourne/Randy Rhoads*...CBS Associated 40714
9	5	48	Look What The Cat Dragged In ... *Poison*...Capitol 12523
10	8	43	Duotones ... *Kenny G*...Arista 8427

TW	LW	WK	Billboard. JULY 4, 1987 TOP POP ALBUMS
1	1	2	**Whitney** ... *Whitney Houston*...Arista 8405
2	3	14	The Joshua Tree ... *U2*...Island 90581
3	2	4	Girls, Girls, Girls ... *Mötley Crüe*...Elektra 60725
4	4	12	Whitesnake ... *Whitesnake*...Geffen 24099
5	6	4	Bad Animals ... *Heart*...Capitol 12546
6	5	43	Slippery When Wet ... *Bon Jovi*...Mercury 830264
7	7	9	**Spanish Fly** ... *Lisa Lisa & Cult Jam*...Columbia 40477
8	10	44	Duotones ... *Kenny G*...Arista 8427
9	8	9	Tribute ... *Ozzy Osbourne/Randy Rhoads*...CBS Associated 40714
10	9	49	Look What The Cat Dragged In ... *Poison*...Capitol 12523

TW	LW	WK	Billboard. JULY 11, 1987 TOP POP ALBUMS
1	1	3	**Whitney** ... *Whitney Houston*...Arista 8405
2	2	15	The Joshua Tree ... *U2*...Island 90581
3	3	5	Girls, Girls, Girls ... *Mötley Crüe*...Elektra 60725
4	5	5	Bad Animals ... *Heart*...Capitol 12546
5	4	13	Whitesnake ... *Whitesnake*...Geffen 24099
6	6	44	Slippery When Wet ... *Bon Jovi*...Mercury 830264
7	8	45	Duotones ... *Kenny G*...Arista 8427
8	11	4	Bigger And Deffer ... *L.L. Cool J*...Def Jam 40793
9	7	10	Spanish Fly ... *Lisa Lisa & Cult Jam*...Columbia 40477
10	10	50	Look What The Cat Dragged In ... *Poison*...Capitol 12523

TW	LW	WK	Billboard. JULY 18, 1987 TOP POP ALBUMS
1	1	4	**Whitney** ... *Whitney Houston*...Arista 8405
2	2	16	The Joshua Tree ... *U2*...Island 90581
3	5	14	Whitesnake ... *Whitesnake*...Geffen 24099
4	4	6	Bad Animals ... *Heart*...Capitol 12546
5	3	6	Girls, Girls, Girls ... *Mötley Crüe*...Elektra 60725
6	7	46	**Duotones** ... *Kenny G*...Arista 8427
7	8	5	Bigger And Deffer ... *L.L. Cool J*...Def Jam 40793
8	6	45	Slippery When Wet ... *Bon Jovi*...Mercury 830264
9	9	11	Spanish Fly ... *Lisa Lisa & Cult Jam*...Columbia 40477
10	10	51	Look What The Cat Dragged In ... *Poison*...Capitol 12523

TW	LW	WK	Billboard. JULY 25, 1987	TOP POP ALBUMS
1	1	5	**Whitney**	*Whitney Houston*...Arista 8405
2	2	17	The Joshua Tree	*U2*...Island 90581
3	5	7	Girls, Girls, Girls	*Mötley Crüe*...Elektra 60725
4	3	15	Whitesnake	*Whitesnake*...Geffen 24099
5	4	7	Bad Animals	*Heart*...Capitol 12546
6	6	47	**Duotones**	*Kenny G*...Arista 8427
7	7	6	Bigger And Deffer	*L.L. Cool J*...Def Jam 40793
8	8	46	Slippery When Wet	*Bon Jovi*...Mercury 830264
9	9	12	Spanish Fly	*Lisa Lisa & Cult Jam*...Columbia 40477
10	10	52	Look What The Cat Dragged In	*Poison*...Capitol 12523

TW	LW	WK	Billboard. AUGUST 1, 1987	TOP POP ALBUMS
1	1	6	**Whitney**	*Whitney Houston*...Arista 8405
2	5	8	**Bad Animals**	*Heart*...Capitol 12546
3	4	16	Whitesnake	*Whitesnake*...Geffen 24099
4	2	18	The Joshua Tree	*U2*...Island 90581
5	3	8	Girls, Girls, Girls	*Mötley Crüe*...Elektra 60725
6	7	7	Bigger And Deffer	*L.L. Cool J*...Def Jam 40793
7	6	48	Duotones	*Kenny G*...Arista 8427
8	8	47	Slippery When Wet	*Bon Jovi*...Mercury 830264
9	11	8	Beverly Hills Cop II	*Soundtrack*...MCA 6207
10	10	53	Look What The Cat Dragged In	*Poison*...Capitol 12523

TW	LW	WK	Billboard. AUGUST 8, 1987	TOP POP ALBUMS
1	1	7	**Whitney**	*Whitney Houston*...Arista 8405
2	2	9	**Bad Animals**	*Heart*...Capitol 12546
3	3	17	Whitesnake	*Whitesnake*...Geffen 24099
4	4	19	The Joshua Tree	*U2*...Island 90581
5	6	8	Bigger And Deffer	*L.L. Cool J*...Def Jam 40793
6	5	9	Girls, Girls, Girls	*Mötley Crüe*...Elektra 60725
7	7	49	Duotones	*Kenny G*...Arista 8427
8	9	9	**Beverly Hills Cop II**	*Soundtrack*...MCA 6207
9	12	3	In The Dark	*Grateful Dead*...Arista 8452
10	8	48	Slippery When Wet	*Bon Jovi*...Mercury 830264

TW	LW	WK	Billboard. AUGUST 15, 1987	TOP POP ALBUMS
1	1	8	**Whitney**	*Whitney Houston*...Arista 8405
2	2	10	**Bad Animals**	*Heart*...Capitol 12546
3	3	18	Whitesnake	*Whitesnake*...Geffen 24099
4	5	9	Bigger And Deffer	*L.L. Cool J*...Def Jam 40793
5	4	20	The Joshua Tree	*U2*...Island 90581
6	6	10	Girls, Girls, Girls	*Mötley Crüe*...Elektra 60725
7	9	4	In The Dark	*Grateful Dead*...Arista 8452
8	7	50	Duotones	*Kenny G*...Arista 8427
9	8	10	Beverly Hills Cop II	*Soundtrack*...MCA 6207
10	10	49	Slippery When Wet	*Bon Jovi*...Mercury 830264

Billboard — AUGUST 22, 1987 — TOP POP ALBUMS

TW	LW	WK	Title	Artist...Label
1	1	9	**Whitney**	*Whitney Houston*...Arista 8405
2	3	19	**Whitesnake**	*Whitesnake*...Geffen 24099
3	2	11	Bad Animals	*Heart*...Capitol 12546
4	4	10	Bigger And Deffer	*L.L. Cool J*...Def Jam 40793
5	5	21	The Joshua Tree	*U2*...Island 90581
6	7	5	**In The Dark**	*Grateful Dead*...Arista 8452
7	6	11	Girls, Girls, Girls	*Mötley Crüe*...Elektra 60725
8	17	5	La Bamba	*Los Lobos/Soundtrack*...Slash 25605
9	8	51	Duotones	*Kenny G*...Arista 8427
10	9	11	Beverly Hills Cop II	*Soundtrack*...MCA 6207

Billboard — AUGUST 29, 1987 — TOP POP ALBUMS

TW	LW	WK	Title	Artist...Label
1	1	10	**Whitney**	*Whitney Houston*...Arista 8405
2	2	20	**Whitesnake**	*Whitesnake*...Geffen 24099
3	4	11	**Bigger And Deffer**	*L.L. Cool J*...Def Jam 40793
4	8	6	La Bamba	*Los Lobos/Soundtrack*...Slash 25605
5	3	12	Bad Animals	*Heart*...Capitol 12546
6	6	6	**In The Dark**	*Grateful Dead*...Arista 8452
7	5	22	The Joshua Tree	*U2*...Island 90581
8	7	12	Girls, Girls, Girls	*Mötley Crüe*...Elektra 60725
9	36	2	Hysteria	*Def Leppard*...Mercury 830675
10	10	12	Beverly Hills Cop II	*Soundtrack*...MCA 6207

Billboard — SEPTEMBER 5, 1987 — TOP POP ALBUMS

TW	LW	WK	Title	Artist...Label
1	1	11	**Whitney**	*Whitney Houston*...Arista 8405
2	2	21	**Whitesnake**	*Whitesnake*...Geffen 24099
3	4	7	La Bamba	*Los Lobos/Soundtrack*...Slash 25605
4	9	3	Hysteria	*Def Leppard*...Mercury 830675
5	5	13	Bad Animals	*Heart*...Capitol 12546
6	3	12	Bigger And Deffer	*L.L. Cool J*...Def Jam 40793
7	6	7	In The Dark	*Grateful Dead*...Arista 8452
8	12	4	Who's That Girl	*Madonna/Soundtrack*...Sire 25611
9	7	23	The Joshua Tree	*U2*...Island 90581
10	10	13	Beverly Hills Cop II	*Soundtrack*...MCA 6207

Billboard — SEPTEMBER 12, 1987 — TOP POP ALBUMS

TW	LW	WK	Title	Artist...Label
1	3	8	**La Bamba**	*Los Lobos/Soundtrack*...Slash 25605
2	1	12	Whitney	*Whitney Houston*...Arista 8405
3	2	22	Whitesnake	*Whitesnake*...Geffen 24099
4	4	4	Hysteria	*Def Leppard*...Mercury 830675
5	5	14	Bad Animals	*Heart*...Capitol 12546
6	6	13	Bigger And Deffer	*L.L. Cool J*...Def Jam 40793
7	8	5	**Who's That Girl**	*Madonna/Soundtrack*...Sire 25611
8	12	14	**Crushin'**	*Fat Boys*...Tin Pan Apple 831948
9	7	8	In The Dark	*Grateful Dead*...Arista 8452
10	9	24	The Joshua Tree	*U2*...Island 90581

TW	LW	WK	Billboard. SEPTEMBER 19, 1987 TOP POP ALBUMS
1	1	9	**La Bamba** .... *Los Lobos/Soundtrack*...Slash 25605
2	2	13	Whitney .... *Whitney Houston*...Arista 8405
3	3	23	Whitesnake .... *Whitesnake*...Geffen 24099
4	4	5	Hysteria .... *Def Leppard*...Mercury 830675
5	5	15	Bad Animals .... *Heart*...Capitol 12546
6	6	14	Bigger And Deffer .... *L.L. Cool J*...Def Jam 40793
7	7	6	**Who's That Girl** .... *Madonna/Soundtrack*...Sire 25611
8	8	15	**Crushin'** .... *Fat Boys*...Tin Pan Apple 831948
9	9	9	In The Dark .... *Grateful Dead*...Arista 8452
10	10	25	The Joshua Tree .... *U2*...Island 90581

TW	LW	WK	Billboard. SEPTEMBER 26, 1987 TOP POP ALBUMS
1	-	1	**Bad** .... *Michael Jackson*...Epic 40600
2	1	10	La Bamba .... *Los Lobos/Soundtrack*...Slash 25605
3	2	14	Whitney .... *Whitney Houston*...Arista 8405
4	3	24	Whitesnake .... *Whitesnake*...Geffen 24099
5	4	6	Hysteria .... *Def Leppard*...Mercury 830675
6	5	16	Bad Animals .... *Heart*...Capitol 12546
7	6	15	Bigger And Deffer .... *L.L. Cool J*...Def Jam 40793
8	21	2	The Lonesome Jubilee .... *John Cougar Mellencamp*...Mercury 832465
9	8	16	Crushin' .... *Fat Boys*...Tin Pan Apple 831948
10	10	26	The Joshua Tree .... *U2*...Island 90581

TW	LW	WK	Billboard. OCTOBER 3, 1987 TOP POP ALBUMS
1	1	2	**Bad** .... *Michael Jackson*...Epic 40600
2	4	25	**Whitesnake** .... *Whitesnake*...Geffen 24099
3	3	15	Whitney .... *Whitney Houston*...Arista 8405
4	2	11	La Bamba .... *Los Lobos/Soundtrack*...Slash 25605
5	5	7	Hysteria .... *Def Leppard*...Mercury 830675
6	8	3	**The Lonesome Jubilee** .... *John Cougar Mellencamp*...Mercury 832465
7	6	17	Bad Animals .... *Heart*...Capitol 12546
8	9	17	**Crushin'** .... *Fat Boys*...Tin Pan Apple 831948
9	7	16	Bigger And Deffer .... *L.L. Cool J*...Def Jam 40793
10	10	27	The Joshua Tree .... *U2*...Island 90581

TW	LW	WK	Billboard. OCTOBER 10, 1987 TOP POP ALBUMS
1	1	3	**Bad** .... *Michael Jackson*...Epic 40600
2	2	26	**Whitesnake** .... *Whitesnake*...Geffen 24099
3	3	16	Whitney .... *Whitney Houston*...Arista 8405
4	4	12	La Bamba .... *Los Lobos/Soundtrack*...Slash 25605
5	5	8	Hysteria .... *Def Leppard*...Mercury 830675
6	6	4	**The Lonesome Jubilee** .... *John Cougar Mellencamp*...Mercury 832465
7	12	4	Dirty Dancing .... *Soundtrack*...RCA 6408
8	14	3	A Momentary Lapse of Reason .... *Pink Floyd*...Columbia 40599
9	10	28	The Joshua Tree .... *U2*...Island 90581
10	7	18	Bad Animals .... *Heart*...Capitol 12546

TW	LW	WK	Billboard® OCTOBER 17, 1987	TOP POP ALBUMS
❶	1	4	**Bad**	*Michael Jackson*...Epic 40600
②	2	27	**Whitesnake**	*Whitesnake*...Geffen 24099
③	3	17	**Whitney**	*Whitney Houston*...Arista 8405
❹	5	9	**Hysteria**	*Def Leppard*...Mercury 830675
❺	8	4	**A Momentary Lapse of Reason**	*Pink Floyd*...Columbia 40599
❻	7	5	**Dirty Dancing**	*Soundtrack*...RCA 6408
⑦	4	13	**La Bamba**	*Los Lobos/Soundtrack*...Slash 25605
⑧	6	5	**The Lonesome Jubilee**	*John Cougar Mellencamp*...Mercury 832465
⑨	9	29	**The Joshua Tree**	*U2*...Island 90581
⑩	10	19	**Bad Animals**	*Heart*...Capitol 12546

TW	LW	WK	Billboard® OCTOBER 24, 1987	TOP POP ALBUMS
①	1	5	**Bad**	*Michael Jackson*...Epic 40600
②	2	28	**Whitesnake**	*Whitesnake*...Geffen 24099
❸	5	5	**A Momentary Lapse of Reason**	*Pink Floyd*...Columbia 40599
❹	6	6	**Dirty Dancing**	*Soundtrack*...RCA 6408
⑤	4	10	**Hysteria**	*Def Leppard*...Mercury 830675
⑥	3	18	**Whitney**	*Whitney Houston*...Arista 8405
❼	8	6	**The Lonesome Jubilee**	*John Cougar Mellencamp*...Mercury 832465
❽	9	30	**The Joshua Tree**	*U2*...Island 90581
⑨	7	14	**La Bamba**	*Los Lobos/Soundtrack*...Slash 25605
⑩	10	20	**Bad Animals**	*Heart*...Capitol 12546

TW	LW	WK	Billboard® OCTOBER 31, 1987	TOP POP ALBUMS
❶	1	6	**Bad**	*Michael Jackson*...Epic 40600
②	2	29	**Whitesnake**	*Whitesnake*...Geffen 24099
❸	16	2	**Tunnel of Love**	*Bruce Springsteen*...Columbia 40999
❹	4	7	**Dirty Dancing**	*Soundtrack*...RCA 6408
❺	3	6	**A Momentary Lapse of Reason**	*Pink Floyd*...Columbia 40599
⑥	5	11	**Hysteria**	*Def Leppard*...Mercury 830675
⑦	6	19	**Whitney**	*Whitney Houston*...Arista 8405
⑧	7	7	**The Lonesome Jubilee**	*John Cougar Mellencamp*...Mercury 832465
⑨	8	31	**The Joshua Tree**	*U2*...Island 90581
⑩	9	15	**La Bamba**	*Los Lobos/Soundtrack*...Slash 25605

TW	LW	WK	Billboard® NOVEMBER 7, 1987	TOP POP ALBUMS
❶	3	3	**Tunnel of Love**	*Bruce Springsteen*...Columbia 40999
②	1	7	**Bad**	*Michael Jackson*...Epic 40600
❸	4	8	**Dirty Dancing**	*Soundtrack*...RCA 6408
④	2	30	**Whitesnake**	*Whitesnake*...Geffen 24099
⑤	5	7	**A Momentary Lapse of Reason**	*Pink Floyd*...Columbia 40599
⑥	6	12	**Hysteria**	*Def Leppard*...Mercury 830675
⑦	7	20	**Whitney**	*Whitney Houston*...Arista 8405
⑧	8	8	**The Lonesome Jubilee**	*John Cougar Mellencamp*...Mercury 832465
⑨	9	32	**The Joshua Tree**	*U2*...Island 90581
❿	12	7	**R.E.M. No. 5: Document**	*R.E.M.*...I.R.S. 42059

TW	LW	WK	Billboard. NOVEMBER 14, 1987 TOP POP ALBUMS
1	3	9	**Dirty Dancing** .... *Soundtrack*...RCA 6408
2	1	4	Tunnel of Love........ *Bruce Springsteen*...Columbia 40999
3	2	8	Bad .... *Michael Jackson*...Epic 40600
4	4	31	Whitesnake........ *Whitesnake*...Geffen 24099
5	5	8	A Momentary Lapse of Reason .... *Pink Floyd*...Columbia 40599
6	6	13	Hysteria .... *Def Leppard*...Mercury 830675
7	8	9	The Lonesome Jubilee .... *John Cougar Mellencamp*...Mercury 832465
8	7	21	Whitney .... *Whitney Houston*...Arista 8405
9	9	33	The Joshua Tree........ *U2*...Island 90581
10	13	6	**Vital Idol**........ *Billy Idol*...Chrysalis 41620

TW	LW	WK	Billboard. NOVEMBER 21, 1987 TOP POP ALBUMS
1	1	10	**Dirty Dancing** .... *Soundtrack*...RCA 6408
2	2	5	Tunnel of Love........ *Bruce Springsteen*...Columbia 40999
3	3	9	Bad .... *Michael Jackson*...Epic 40600
4	4	32	Whitesnake........ *Whitesnake*...Geffen 24099
5	5	9	A Momentary Lapse of Reason .... *Pink Floyd*...Columbia 40599
6	6	14	Hysteria .... *Def Leppard*...Mercury 830675
7	7	10	The Lonesome Jubilee .... *John Cougar Mellencamp*...Mercury 832465
8	8	22	Whitney .... *Whitney Houston*...Arista 8405
9	14	4	**...Nothing Like The Sun** .... *Sting*...A&M 6402
10	9	34	The Joshua Tree........ *U2*...Island 90581

TW	LW	WK	Billboard. NOVEMBER 28, 1987 TOP POP ALBUMS
1	1	11	**Dirty Dancing** .... *Soundtrack*...RCA 6408
2	3	10	Bad .... *Michael Jackson*...Epic 40600
3	2	6	Tunnel of Love........ *Bruce Springsteen*...Columbia 40999
4	4	33	Whitesnake........ *Whitesnake*...Geffen 24099
5	5	10	A Momentary Lapse of Reason .... *Pink Floyd*...Columbia 40599
6	6	15	Hysteria .... *Def Leppard*...Mercury 830675
7	7	11	The Lonesome Jubilee .... *John Cougar Mellencamp*...Mercury 832465
8	8	23	Whitney .... *Whitney Houston*...Arista 8405
9	9	5	**...Nothing Like The Sun** .... *Sting*...A&M 6402
10	10	35	The Joshua Tree........ *U2*...Island 90581

TW	LW	WK	Billboard. DECEMBER 5, 1987 TOP POP ALBUMS
1	1	12	**Dirty Dancing** .... *Soundtrack*...RCA 6408
2	2	11	Bad .... *Michael Jackson*...Epic 40600
3	4	34	Whitesnake........ *Whitesnake*...Geffen 24099
4	5	11	A Momentary Lapse of Reason .... *Pink Floyd*...Columbia 40599
5	3	7	Tunnel of Love........ *Bruce Springsteen*...Columbia 40999
6	7	12	**The Lonesome Jubilee** .... *John Cougar Mellencamp*...Mercury 832465
7	6	16	Hysteria .... *Def Leppard*...Mercury 830675
8	15	3	Faith........ *George Michael*...Columbia 40867
9	9	6	**...Nothing Like The Sun** .... *Sting*...A&M 6402
10	8	24	Whitney .... *Whitney Houston*...Arista 8405

Billboard® DECEMBER 12, 1987 TOP POP ALBUMS

TW	LW	WK	Title	Artist...Label
①	1	13	**Dirty Dancing**	*Soundtrack*...RCA 6408
②	2	12	Bad	*Michael Jackson*...Epic 40600
③	3	35	Whitesnake	*Whitesnake*...Geffen 24099
④	4	12	A Momentary Lapse of Reason	*Pink Floyd*...Columbia 40599
❺	8	4	Faith	*George Michael*...Columbia 40867
⑥	5	8	Tunnel of Love	*Bruce Springsteen*...Columbia 40999
⑦	6	13	The Lonesome Jubilee	*John Cougar Mellencamp*...Mercury 832465
⑧	7	17	Hysteria	*Def Leppard*...Mercury 830675
⑨	9	7	**...Nothing Like The Sun**	*Sting*...A&M 6402
⑩	10	25	Whitney	*Whitney Houston*...Arista 8405

Billboard® DECEMBER 19, 1987 TOP POP ALBUMS

TW	LW	WK	Title	Artist...Label
①	1	14	**Dirty Dancing**	*Soundtrack*...RCA 6408
②	2	13	Bad	*Michael Jackson*...Epic 40600
❸	5	5	Faith	*George Michael*...Columbia 40867
④	3	36	Whitesnake	*Whitesnake*...Geffen 24099
⑤	4	13	A Momentary Lapse of Reason	*Pink Floyd*...Columbia 40599
❻	13	13	Tiffany	*Tiffany*...MCA 5793
❼	7	14	The Lonesome Jubilee	*John Cougar Mellencamp*...Mercury 832465
❽	8	18	Hysteria	*Def Leppard*...Mercury 830675
⑨	6	9	Tunnel of Love	*Bruce Springsteen*...Columbia 40999
⑩	10	26	Whitney	*Whitney Houston*...Arista 8405

Billboard® DECEMBER 26, 1987 TOP POP ALBUMS

TW	LW	WK	Title	Artist...Label
①	1	15	**Dirty Dancing**	*Soundtrack*...RCA 6408
❷	2	14	Bad	*Michael Jackson*...Epic 40600
❸	3	6	Faith	*George Michael*...Columbia 40867
❹	4	37	Whitesnake	*Whitesnake*...Geffen 24099
❺	6	14	Tiffany	*Tiffany*...MCA 5793
⑥	5	14	A Momentary Lapse of Reason	*Pink Floyd*...Columbia 40599
⑦	7	15	The Lonesome Jubilee	*John Cougar Mellencamp*...Mercury 832465
⑧	9	10	Tunnel of Love	*Bruce Springsteen*...Columbia 40999
⑨	8	19	Hysteria	*Def Leppard*...Mercury 830675
⑩	10	27	Whitney	*Whitney Houston*...Arista 8405

TW	LW	WK	Billboard® JANUARY 9, 1988 TOP POP ALBUMS	
①	1	17	**Dirty Dancing**	*Soundtrack*...RCA 6408
❷	3	8	Faith	*George Michael*...Columbia 40867
③	2	16	Bad	*Michael Jackson*...Epic 40600
❹	5	16	Tiffany	*Tiffany*...MCA 5793
⑤	4	39	Whitesnake	*Whitesnake*...Geffen 24099
⑥	7	17	**The Lonesome Jubilee**	*John Cougar Mellencamp*...Mercury 832465
❼	10	29	Whitney	*Whitney Houston*...Arista 8405
⑧	6	16	A Momentary Lapse of Reason	*Pink Floyd*...Columbia 40599
❾	11	8	Cloud Nine	*George Harrison*...Dark Horse 25643
⑩	9	21	Hysteria	*Def Leppard*...Mercury 830675

TW	LW	WK	Billboard® JANUARY 16, 1988 TOP POP ALBUMS	
❶	2	9	**Faith**	*George Michael*...Columbia 40867
②	1	18	Dirty Dancing	*Soundtrack*...RCA 6408
❸	4	17	Tiffany	*Tiffany*...MCA 5793
④	3	17	Bad	*Michael Jackson*...Epic 40600
⑤	5	40	Whitesnake	*Whitesnake*...Geffen 24099
⑥	6	18	**The Lonesome Jubilee**	*John Cougar Mellencamp*...Mercury 832465
⑦	7	30	Whitney	*Whitney Houston*...Arista 8405
❽	10	22	Hysteria	*Def Leppard*...Mercury 830675
❾	12	10	Kick	*INXS*...Atlantic 81796
⑩	9	9	Cloud Nine	*George Harrison*...Dark Horse 25643

TW	LW	WK	Billboard® JANUARY 23, 1988 TOP POP ALBUMS	
❶	3	18	**Tiffany**	*Tiffany*...MCA 5793
②	1	10	Faith	*George Michael*...Columbia 40867
③	2	19	Dirty Dancing	*Soundtrack*...RCA 6408
④	4	18	Bad	*Michael Jackson*...Epic 40600
⑤	5	41	Whitesnake	*Whitesnake*...Geffen 24099
❻	9	11	Kick	*INXS*...Atlantic 81796
⑦	6	19	The Lonesome Jubilee	*John Cougar Mellencamp*...Mercury 832465
⑧	10	10	**Cloud Nine**	*George Harrison*...Dark Horse 25643
⑨	7	31	Whitney	*Whitney Houston*...Arista 8405
⑩	8	23	Hysteria	*Def Leppard*...Mercury 830675

TW	LW	WK	Billboard® JANUARY 30, 1988 TOP POP ALBUMS	
①	1	19	**Tiffany**	*Tiffany*...MCA 5793
②	2	11	Faith	*George Michael*...Columbia 40867
③	3	20	Dirty Dancing	*Soundtrack*...RCA 6408
❹	6	12	Kick	*INXS*...Atlantic 81796
⑤	4	19	Bad	*Michael Jackson*...Epic 40600
⑥	5	42	Whitesnake	*Whitesnake*...Geffen 24099
⑦	7	20	The Lonesome Jubilee	*John Cougar Mellencamp*...Mercury 832465
⑧	10	24	Hysteria	*Def Leppard*...Mercury 830675
⑨	8	11	Cloud Nine	*George Harrison*...Dark Horse 25643
⑩	11	19	A Momentary Lapse of Reason	*Pink Floyd*...Columbia 40599

Billboard — FEBRUARY 6, 1988 — TOP POP ALBUMS

TW	LW	WK	Title	Artist	Label
1	2	12	**Faith**	*George Michael*	Columbia 40867
2	1	20	Tiffany	*Tiffany*	MCA 5793
3	3	21	Dirty Dancing	*Soundtrack*	RCA 6408
4	4	13	Kick	*INXS*	Atlantic 81796
5	5	20	Bad	*Michael Jackson*	Epic 40600
6	7	21	**The Lonesome Jubilee**	*John Cougar Mellencamp*	Mercury 832465
7	6	43	Whitesnake	*Whitesnake*	Geffen 24099
8	8	25	Hysteria	*Def Leppard*	Mercury 830675
9	9	12	Cloud Nine	*George Harrison*	Dark Horse 25643
10	14	23	Out Of The Blue	*Debbie Gibson*	Atlantic 81780

Billboard — FEBRUARY 13, 1988 — TOP POP ALBUMS

TW	LW	WK	Title	Artist	Label
1	1	13	**Faith**	*George Michael*	Columbia 40867
2	2	21	Tiffany	*Tiffany*	MCA 5793
3	3	22	Dirty Dancing	*Soundtrack*	RCA 6408
4	4	14	Kick	*INXS*	Atlantic 81796
5	5	21	Bad	*Michael Jackson*	Epic 40600
6	6	22	**The Lonesome Jubilee**	*John Cougar Mellencamp*	Mercury 832465
7	8	26	Hysteria	*Def Leppard*	Mercury 830675
8	10	24	Out Of The Blue	*Debbie Gibson*	Atlantic 81780
9	7	44	Whitesnake	*Whitesnake*	Geffen 24099
10	9	13	Cloud Nine	*George Harrison*	Dark Horse 25643

Billboard — FEBRUARY 20, 1988 — TOP POP ALBUMS

TW	LW	WK	Title	Artist	Label
1	1	14	**Faith**	*George Michael*	Columbia 40867
2	3	23	Dirty Dancing	*Soundtrack*	RCA 6408
3	2	22	Tiffany	*Tiffany*	MCA 5793
4	4	15	Kick	*INXS*	Atlantic 81796
5	5	22	Bad	*Michael Jackson*	Epic 40600
6	7	27	Hysteria	*Def Leppard*	Mercury 830675
7	6	23	The Lonesome Jubilee	*John Cougar Mellencamp*	Mercury 832465
8	8	25	Out Of The Blue	*Debbie Gibson*	Atlantic 81780
9	10	14	Cloud Nine	*George Harrison*	Dark Horse 25643
10	22	2	Skyscraper	*David Lee Roth*	Warner 25671

Billboard — FEBRUARY 27, 1988 — TOP POP ALBUMS

TW	LW	WK	Title	Artist	Label
1	1	15	**Faith**	*George Michael*	Columbia 40867
2	2	24	Dirty Dancing	*Soundtrack*	RCA 6408
3	4	16	**Kick**	*INXS*	Atlantic 81796
4	3	23	Tiffany	*Tiffany*	MCA 5793
5	5	23	Bad	*Michael Jackson*	Epic 40600
6	10	3	**Skyscraper**	*David Lee Roth*	Warner 25671
7	8	26	**Out Of The Blue**	*Debbie Gibson*	Atlantic 81780
8	6	28	Hysteria	*Def Leppard*	Mercury 830675
9	7	24	The Lonesome Jubilee	*John Cougar Mellencamp*	Mercury 832465
10	9	15	Cloud Nine	*George Harrison*	Dark Horse 25643

Billboard — MARCH 5, 1988 — TOP POP ALBUMS

TW	LW	WK	Title	Artist	Label
1	1	16	**Faith**	*George Michael*	Columbia 40867
2	2	25	Dirty Dancing	*Soundtrack*	RCA 6408
3	3	17	**Kick**	*INXS*	Atlantic 81796
4	4	24	Tiffany	*Tiffany*	MCA 5793
5	5	24	Bad	*Michael Jackson*	Epic 40600
6	6	4	**Skyscraper**	*David Lee Roth*	Warner 25671
7	7	27	**Out Of The Blue**	*Debbie Gibson*	Atlantic 81780
8	8	29	Hysteria	*Def Leppard*	Mercury 830675
9	9	25	The Lonesome Jubilee	*John Cougar Mellencamp*	Mercury 832465
10	10	16	Cloud Nine	*George Harrison*	Dark Horse 25643

Billboard — MARCH 12, 1988 — TOP POP ALBUMS

TW	LW	WK	Title	Artist	Label
1	2	26	**Dirty Dancing**	*Soundtrack*	RCA 6408
2	1	17	Faith	*George Michael*	Columbia 40867
3	3	18	**Kick**	*INXS*	Atlantic 81796
4	4	25	Tiffany	*Tiffany*	MCA 5793
5	5	25	Bad	*Michael Jackson*	Epic 40600
6	6	5	**Skyscraper**	*David Lee Roth*	Warner 25671
7	8	30	Hysteria	*Def Leppard*	Mercury 830675
8	7	28	Out Of The Blue	*Debbie Gibson*	Atlantic 81780
9	9	26	The Lonesome Jubilee	*John Cougar Mellencamp*	Mercury 832465
10	17	8	**Whenever You Need Somebody**	*Rick Astley*	RCA 6822

Billboard — MARCH 19, 1988 — TOP POP ALBUMS

TW	LW	WK	Title	Artist	Label
1	1	27	**Dirty Dancing**	*Soundtrack*	RCA 6408
2	2	18	Faith	*George Michael*	Columbia 40867
3	3	19	**Kick**	*INXS*	Atlantic 81796
4	5	26	Bad	*Michael Jackson*	Epic 40600
5	4	26	Tiffany	*Tiffany*	MCA 5793
6	6	6	**Skyscraper**	*David Lee Roth*	Warner 25671
7	7	31	Hysteria	*Def Leppard*	Mercury 830675
8	8	29	Out Of The Blue	*Debbie Gibson*	Atlantic 81780
9	9	27	The Lonesome Jubilee	*John Cougar Mellencamp*	Mercury 832465
10	10	9	**Whenever You Need Somebody**	*Rick Astley*	RCA 6822

Billboard — MARCH 26, 1988 — TOP POP ALBUMS

TW	LW	WK	Title	Artist	Label
1	1	28	**Dirty Dancing**	*Soundtrack*	RCA 6408
2	2	19	Faith	*George Michael*	Columbia 40867
3	4	27	Bad	*Michael Jackson*	Epic 40600
4	3	20	Kick	*INXS*	Atlantic 81796
5	5	27	Tiffany	*Tiffany*	MCA 5793
6	6	7	**Skyscraper**	*David Lee Roth*	Warner 25671
7	7	32	Hysteria	*Def Leppard*	Mercury 830675
8	8	30	Out Of The Blue	*Debbie Gibson*	Atlantic 81780
9	9	28	The Lonesome Jubilee	*John Cougar Mellencamp*	Mercury 832465
10	11	8	**Good Morning, Vietnam**	*Soundtrack*	A&M 3913

TW	LW	WK	Billboard — APRIL 2, 1988 — TOP POP ALBUMS
①	1	29	**Dirty Dancing** ... *Soundtrack*...RCA 6408
②	2	20	Faith ... *George Michael*...Columbia 40867
❸	3	28	Bad ... *Michael Jackson*...Epic 40600
④	4	21	Kick ... *INXS*...Atlantic 81796
⑤	5	28	Tiffany ... *Tiffany*...MCA 5793
⑥	6	8	**Skyscraper** ... *David Lee Roth*...Warner 25671
⑦	7	33	Hysteria ... *Def Leppard*...Mercury 830675
⑧	8	31	Out Of The Blue ... *Debbie Gibson*...Atlantic 81780
❾	16	4	Now And Zen ... *Robert Plant*...Es Paranza 90863
❿	10	9	**Good Morning, Vietnam** ... *Soundtrack*...A&M 3913

TW	LW	WK	Billboard — APRIL 9, 1988 — TOP POP ALBUMS
①	1	30	**Dirty Dancing** ... *Soundtrack*...RCA 6408
②	2	21	Faith ... *George Michael*...Columbia 40867
③	3	29	Bad ... *Michael Jackson*...Epic 40600
④	4	22	Kick ... *INXS*...Atlantic 81796
⑤	5	29	Tiffany ... *Tiffany*...MCA 5793
❻	11	4	More Dirty Dancing ... *Soundtrack*...RCA 6965
❼	9	5	Now And Zen ... *Robert Plant*...Es Paranza 90863
⑧	6	9	Skyscraper ... *David Lee Roth*...Warner 25671
⑨	7	34	Hysteria ... *Def Leppard*...Mercury 830675
⑩	8	32	Out Of The Blue ... *Debbie Gibson*...Atlantic 81780

TW	LW	WK	Billboard — APRIL 16, 1988 — TOP POP ALBUMS
①	1	31	**Dirty Dancing** ... *Soundtrack*...RCA 6408
②	3	30	Bad ... *Michael Jackson*...Epic 40600
③	2	22	Faith ... *George Michael*...Columbia 40867
④	4	23	Kick ... *INXS*...Atlantic 81796
❺	6	5	More Dirty Dancing ... *Soundtrack*...RCA 6965
⑥	5	30	Tiffany ... *Tiffany*...MCA 5793
❼	7	6	Now And Zen ... *Robert Plant*...Es Paranza 90863
❽	13	26	Introducing The Hardline According To Terence Trent D'Arby ... *Terence Trent D'Arby*...Columbia 40964
⑨	9	35	Hysteria ... *Def Leppard*...Mercury 830675
⑩	10	33	Out Of The Blue ... *Debbie Gibson*...Atlantic 81780

TW	LW	WK	Billboard — APRIL 23, 1988 — TOP POP ALBUMS
①	1	32	**Dirty Dancing** ... *Soundtrack*...RCA 6408
②	2	31	Bad ... *Michael Jackson*...Epic 40600
❸	5	6	**More Dirty Dancing** ... *Soundtrack*...RCA 6965
④	3	23	Faith ... *George Michael*...Columbia 40867
⑤	4	24	Kick ... *INXS*...Atlantic 81796
❻	6	31	Tiffany ... *Tiffany*...MCA 5793
❼	8	27	Introducing The Hardline According To Terence Trent D'Arby ... *Terence Trent D'Arby*...Columbia 40964
❽	7	7	Now And Zen ... *Robert Plant*...Es Paranza 90863
❾	12	35	Appetite For Destruction ... *Guns N' Roses*...Geffen 24148
⑩	10	34	Out Of The Blue ... *Debbie Gibson*...Atlantic 81780

Billboard® — APRIL 30, 1988 — TOP POP ALBUMS

TW	LW	WK	Title	Artist...Label
1	1	33	**Dirty Dancing**	*Soundtrack*...RCA 6408
2	4	24	Faith	*George Michael*...Columbia 40867
3	3	7	**More Dirty Dancing**	*Soundtrack*...RCA 6965
4	2	32	Bad	*Michael Jackson*...Epic 40600
5	5	25	Kick	*INXS*...Atlantic 81796
6	7	28	Introducing The Hardline According To Terence Trent D'Arby	*Terence Trent D'Arby*...Columbia 40964
7	6	32	Tiffany	*Tiffany*...MCA 5793
8	8	8	Now And Zen	*Robert Plant*...Es Paranza 90863
9	9	36	Appetite For Destruction	*Guns N' Roses*...Geffen 24148
10	10	35	Out Of The Blue	*Debbie Gibson*...Atlantic 81780

Billboard® — MAY 7, 1988 — TOP POP ALBUMS

TW	LW	WK	Title	Artist...Label
1	1	34	**Dirty Dancing**	*Soundtrack*...RCA 6408
2	2	25	Faith	*George Michael*...Columbia 40867
3	3	8	**More Dirty Dancing**	*Soundtrack*...RCA 6965
4	6	29	**Introducing The Hardline According To Terence Trent D'Arby**	*Terence Trent D'Arby*...Columbia 40964
5	4	33	Bad	*Michael Jackson*...Epic 40600
6	5	26	Kick	*INXS*...Atlantic 81796
7	7	33	Tiffany	*Tiffany*...MCA 5793
8	8	9	Now And Zen	*Robert Plant*...Es Paranza 90863
9	9	37	Appetite For Destruction	*Guns N' Roses*...Geffen 24148
10	11	38	Hysteria	*Def Leppard*...Mercury 830675

Billboard® — MAY 14, 1988 — TOP POP ALBUMS

TW	LW	WK	Title	Artist...Label
1	2	26	**Faith**	*George Michael*...Columbia 40867
2	1	35	Dirty Dancing	*Soundtrack*...RCA 6408
3	3	9	**More Dirty Dancing**	*Soundtrack*...RCA 6965
4	4	30	**Introducing The Hardline According To Terence Trent D'Arby**	*Terence Trent D'Arby*...Columbia 40964
5	5	34	Bad	*Michael Jackson*...Epic 40600
6	6	27	Kick	*INXS*...Atlantic 81796
7	9	38	Appetite For Destruction	*Guns N' Roses*...Geffen 24148
8	8	10	Now And Zen	*Robert Plant*...Es Paranza 90863
9	7	34	Tiffany	*Tiffany*...MCA 5793
10	14	48	Let It Loose	*Gloria Estefan & Miami Sound Machine*...Epic 40769

Billboard® — MAY 21, 1988 — TOP POP ALBUMS

TW	LW	WK	Title	Artist...Label
1	1	27	**Faith**	*George Michael*...Columbia 40867
2	2	36	Dirty Dancing	*Soundtrack*...RCA 6408
3	3	10	**More Dirty Dancing**	*Soundtrack*...RCA 6965
4	5	35	Bad	*Michael Jackson*...Epic 40600
5	4	31	Introducing The Hardline According To Terence Trent D'Arby	*Terence Trent D'Arby*...Columbia 40964
6	8	11	**Now And Zen**	*Robert Plant*...Es Paranza 90863
7	6	28	Kick	*INXS*...Atlantic 81796
8	7	39	Appetite For Destruction	*Guns N' Roses*...Geffen 24148
9	10	49	Let It Loose	*Gloria Estefan & Miami Sound Machine*...Epic 40769
10	18	3	Savage Amusement	*Scorpions*...Mercury 832963

Billboard — MAY 28, 1988 — TOP POP ALBUMS

TW	LW	WK	Title	Artist	Label
1	1	28	Faith	George Michael	Columbia 40867
2	2	37	Dirty Dancing	Soundtrack	RCA 6408
3	4	36	Bad	Michael Jackson	Epic 40600
4	3	11	More Dirty Dancing	Soundtrack	RCA 6965
5	5	32	Introducing The Hardline According To Terence Trent D'Arby	Terence Trent D'Arby	Columbia 40964
6	9	50	Let It Loose	Gloria Estefan & Miami Sound Machine	Epic 40769
7	10	4	Savage Amusement	Scorpions	Mercury 832963
8	8	40	Appetite For Destruction	Guns N' Roses	Geffen 24148
9	6	12	Now And Zen	Robert Plant	Es Paranza 90863
10	11	41	Hysteria	Def Leppard	Mercury 830675

Billboard — JUNE 4, 1988 — TOP POP ALBUMS

TW	LW	WK	Title	Artist	Label
1	1	29	Faith	George Michael	Columbia 40867
2	2	38	Dirty Dancing	Soundtrack	RCA 6408
3	13	3	Open Up and Say...Ahh!	Poison	Enigma 48493
4	3	37	Bad	Michael Jackson	Epic 40600
5	7	5	Savage Amusement	Scorpions	Mercury 832963
6	6	51	Let It Loose	Gloria Estefan & Miami Sound Machine	Epic 40769
7	10	42	Hysteria	Def Leppard	Mercury 830675
8	4	12	More Dirty Dancing	Soundtrack	RCA 6965
9	5	33	Introducing The Hardline According To Terence Trent D'Arby	Terence Trent D'Arby	Columbia 40964
10	8	41	Appetite For Destruction	Guns N' Roses	Geffen 24148

Billboard — JUNE 11, 1988 — TOP POP ALBUMS

TW	LW	WK	Title	Artist	Label
1	1	30	Faith	George Michael	Columbia 40867
2	2	39	Dirty Dancing	Soundtrack	RCA 6408
3	3	4	Open Up and Say...Ahh!	Poison	Enigma 48493
4	7	43	Hysteria	Def Leppard	Mercury 830675
5	4	38	Bad	Michael Jackson	Epic 40600
6	5	6	Savage Amusement	Scorpions	Mercury 832963
7	6	52	Let It Loose	Gloria Estefan & Miami Sound Machine	Epic 40769
8	12	4	scenes from the southside	Bruce Hornsby & The Range	RCA 6686
9	11	14	Now And Zen	Robert Plant	Es Paranza 90863
10	10	42	Appetite For Destruction	Guns N' Roses	Geffen 24148

Billboard — JUNE 18, 1988 — TOP POP ALBUMS

TW	LW	WK	Title	Artist	Label
1	1	31	Faith	George Michael	Columbia 40867
2	3	5	Open Up and Say...Ahh!	Poison	Enigma 48493
3	4	44	Hysteria	Def Leppard	Mercury 830675
4	2	40	Dirty Dancing	Soundtrack	RCA 6408
5	-	1	OU812	Van Halen	Warner 25732
6	8	5	scenes from the southside	Bruce Hornsby & The Range	RCA 6686
7	6	7	Savage Amusement	Scorpions	Mercury 832963
8	7	53	Let It Loose	Gloria Estefan & Miami Sound Machine	Epic 40769
9	10	43	Appetite For Destruction	Guns N' Roses	Geffen 24148
10	5	39	Bad	Michael Jackson	Epic 40600

TW	LW	WK	Billboard® JUNE 25, 1988 TOP POP ALBUMS
1	5	2	**OU812**............ *Van Halen*...Warner 25732
2	1	32	Faith .... *George Michael*...Columbia 40867
3	3	45	Hysteria .... *Def Leppard*...Mercury 830675
4	2	6	Open Up and Say...Ahh!............ *Poison*...Enigma 48493
5	4	41	Dirty Dancing .... *Soundtrack*...RCA 6408
6	6	6	scenes from the southside .... *Bruce Hornsby & The Range*...RCA 6686
7	9	44	Appetite For Destruction............ *Guns N' Roses*...Geffen 24148
8	15	4	Stronger Than Pride............ *Sade*...Epic 44210
9	7	8	Savage Amusement............ *Scorpions*...Mercury 832963
10	13	4	Tougher Than Leather............ *Run-D.M.C.*...Profile 1265

TW	LW	WK	Billboard® JULY 2, 1988 TOP POP ALBUMS
1	1	3	**OU812**............ *Van Halen*...Warner 25732
2	2	33	Faith .... *George Michael*...Columbia 40867
3	3	46	Hysteria .... *Def Leppard*...Mercury 830675
4	5	42	Dirty Dancing .... *Soundtrack*...RCA 6408
5	4	7	Open Up and Say...Ahh!............ *Poison*...Enigma 48493
6	6	7	scenes from the southside .... *Bruce Hornsby & The Range*...RCA 6686
7	8	5	**Stronger Than Pride**............ *Sade*...Epic 44210
8	7	45	Appetite For Destruction............ *Guns N' Roses*...Geffen 24148
9	10	5	**Tougher Than Leather**............ *Run-D.M.C.*...Profile 1265
10	9	9	Savage Amusement............ *Scorpions*...Mercury 832963

TW	LW	WK	Billboard® JULY 9, 1988 TOP POP ALBUMS
1	1	4	**OU812**............ *Van Halen*...Warner 25732
2	3	47	Hysteria .... *Def Leppard*...Mercury 830675
3	2	34	Faith .... *George Michael*...Columbia 40867
4	4	43	Dirty Dancing .... *Soundtrack*...RCA 6408
5	6	8	**scenes from the southside**............ *Bruce Hornsby & The Range*...RCA 6686
6	5	8	Open Up and Say...Ahh!............ *Poison*...Enigma 48493
7	8	46	Appetite For Destruction............ *Guns N' Roses*...Geffen 24148
8	7	6	Stronger Than Pride............ *Sade*...Epic 44210
9	16	11	Tracy Chapman............ *Tracy Chapman*...Elektra 60774
10	13	17	More Dirty Dancing .... *Soundtrack*...RCA 6965

TW	LW	WK	Billboard® JULY 16, 1988 TOP POP ALBUMS
1	1	5	**OU812**............ *Van Halen*...Warner 25732
2	2	48	Hysteria .... *Def Leppard*...Mercury 830675
3	3	35	Faith .... *George Michael*...Columbia 40867
4	4	44	Dirty Dancing .... *Soundtrack*...RCA 6408
5	7	47	Appetite For Destruction............ *Guns N' Roses*...Geffen 24148
6	6	9	Open Up and Say...Ahh!............ *Poison*...Enigma 48493
7	8	7	**Stronger Than Pride**............ *Sade*...Epic 44210
8	5	9	scenes from the southside .... *Bruce Hornsby & The Range*...RCA 6686
9	9	12	Tracy Chapman............ *Tracy Chapman*...Elektra 60774
10	10	18	More Dirty Dancing .... *Soundtrack*...RCA 6965

TW	LW	WK	Billboard® JULY 23, 1988	TOP POP ALBUMS
❶	2	49	**Hysteria**	*Def Leppard*...Mercury 830675
②	1	6	**OU812**	*Van Halen*...Warner 25732
③	4	45	**Dirty Dancing**	*Soundtrack*...RCA 6408
❹	5	48	**Appetite For Destruction**	*Guns N' Roses*...Geffen 24148
⑤	3	36	**Faith**	*George Michael*...Columbia 40867
❻	15	3	**Roll With It**	*Steve Winwood*...Virgin 90946
❼	9	13	**Tracy Chapman**	*Tracy Chapman*...Elektra 60774
⑧	7	8	**Stronger Than Pride**	*Sade*...Epic 44210
⑨	6	10	**Open Up and Say...Ahh!**	*Poison*...Enigma 48493
⑩	8	10	**scenes from the southside**	*Bruce Hornsby & The Range*...RCA 6686

TW	LW	WK	Billboard® JULY 30, 1988	TOP POP ALBUMS
①	1	50	**Hysteria**	*Def Leppard*...Mercury 830675
❷	4	49	**Appetite For Destruction**	*Guns N' Roses*...Geffen 24148
③	2	7	**OU812**	*Van Halen*...Warner 25732
④	3	46	**Dirty Dancing**	*Soundtrack*...RCA 6408
❺	6	4	**Roll With It**	*Steve Winwood*...Virgin 90946
❻	7	14	**Tracy Chapman**	*Tracy Chapman*...Elektra 60774
⑦	5	37	**Faith**	*George Michael*...Columbia 40867
⑧	9	11	**Open Up and Say...Ahh!**	*Poison*...Enigma 48493
⑨	8	9	**Stronger Than Pride**	*Sade*...Epic 44210
⑩	11	20	**More Dirty Dancing**	*Soundtrack*...RCA 6965

TW	LW	WK	Billboard® AUGUST 6, 1988	TOP POP ALBUMS
❶	2	50	**Appetite For Destruction**	*Guns N' Roses*...Geffen 24148
②	1	51	**Hysteria**	*Def Leppard*...Mercury 830675
❸	5	5	**Roll With It**	*Steve Winwood*...Virgin 90946
❹	6	15	**Tracy Chapman**	*Tracy Chapman*...Elektra 60774
⑤	4	47	**Dirty Dancing**	*Soundtrack*...RCA 6408
⑥	3	8	**OU812**	*Van Halen*...Warner 25732
⑦	7	38	**Faith**	*George Michael*...Columbia 40867
❽	12	16	**He's The D.J., I'm The Rapper**	*D.J. Jazzy Jeff & The Fresh Prince*...Jive 1091
⑨	8	12	**Open Up and Say...Ahh!**	*Poison*...Enigma 48493
⑩	10	21	**More Dirty Dancing**	*Soundtrack*...RCA 6965

TW	LW	WK	Billboard® AUGUST 13, 1988	TOP POP ALBUMS
❶	2	52	**Hysteria**	*Def Leppard*...Mercury 830675
❷	3	6	**Roll With It**	*Steve Winwood*...Virgin 90946
③	1	51	**Appetite For Destruction**	*Guns N' Roses*...Geffen 24148
❹	4	16	**Tracy Chapman**	*Tracy Chapman*...Elektra 60774
⑤	5	48	**Dirty Dancing**	*Soundtrack*...RCA 6408
⑥	6	9	**OU812**	*Van Halen*...Warner 25732
⑦	7	39	**Faith**	*George Michael*...Columbia 40867
❽	8	17	**He's The D.J., I'm The Rapper**	*D.J. Jazzy Jeff & The Fresh Prince*...Jive 1091
⑨	9	13	**Open Up and Say...Ahh!**	*Poison*...Enigma 48493
⑩	11	61	**Let It Loose**	*Gloria Estefan & Miami Sound Machine*...Epic 40769

TW	LW	WK	Billboard® AUGUST 20, 1988 TOP POP ALBUMS
❶	2	7	**Roll With It**......Steve Winwood...Virgin 90946
②	1	53	Hysteria......Def Leppard...Mercury 830675
③	3	52	Appetite For Destruction......Guns N' Roses...Geffen 24148
❹	4	17	Tracy Chapman......Tracy Chapman...Elektra 60774
❺	8	18	He's The D.J., I'm The Rapper.....D.J. Jazzy Jeff & The Fresh Prince...Jive 1091
⑥	7	40	Faith......George Michael...Columbia 40867
⑦	6	10	OU812......Van Halen...Warner 25732
⑧	5	49	Dirty Dancing......Soundtrack...RCA 6408
❾	10	62	Let It Loose......Gloria Estefan & Miami Sound Machine...Epic 40769
⑩	9	14	Open Up and Say...Ahh!......Poison...Enigma 48493

TW	LW	WK	Billboard® AUGUST 27, 1988 TOP POP ALBUMS
❶	4	18	**Tracy Chapman**......Tracy Chapman...Elektra 60774
②	2	54	Hysteria......Def Leppard...Mercury 830675
③	1	8	Roll With It......Steve Winwood...Virgin 90946
④	3	53	Appetite For Destruction......Guns N' Roses...Geffen 24148
❺	5	19	He's The D.J., I'm The Rapper.....D.J. Jazzy Jeff & The Fresh Prince...Jive 1091
⑥	6	41	Faith......George Michael...Columbia 40867
⑦	7	11	OU812......Van Halen...Warner 25732
⑧	8	50	Dirty Dancing......Soundtrack...RCA 6408
⑨	11	63	Richard Marx......Richard Marx...EMI-Manhattan 53049
⑩	10	15	Open Up and Say...Ahh!......Poison...Enigma 48493

TW	LW	WK	Billboard® SEPTEMBER 3, 1988 TOP POP ALBUMS
❶	2	55	**Hysteria**......Def Leppard...Mercury 830675
②	1	19	Tracy Chapman......Tracy Chapman...Elektra 60774
③	4	54	Appetite For Destruction......Guns N' Roses...Geffen 24148
④	3	9	Roll With It......Steve Winwood...Virgin 90946
❺	5	20	He's The D.J., I'm The Rapper.....D.J. Jazzy Jeff & The Fresh Prince...Jive 1091
⑥	6	42	Faith......George Michael...Columbia 40867
❼	7	12	OU812......Van Halen...Warner 25732
⑧	9	64	**Richard Marx**......Richard Marx...EMI-Manhattan 53049
⑨	8	51	Dirty Dancing......Soundtrack...RCA 6408
⑩	12	64	Let It Loose......Gloria Estefan & Miami Sound Machine...Epic 40769

TW	LW	WK	Billboard® SEPTEMBER 10, 1988 TOP POP ALBUMS
①	1	56	**Hysteria**......Def Leppard...Mercury 830675
❷	3	55	Appetite For Destruction......Guns N' Roses...Geffen 24148
③	2	20	Tracy Chapman......Tracy Chapman...Elektra 60774
④	4	10	Roll With It......Steve Winwood...Virgin 90946
⑤	5	21	He's The D.J., I'm The Rapper.....D.J. Jazzy Jeff & The Fresh Prince...Jive 1091
⑥	6	43	Faith......George Michael...Columbia 40867
⑦	7	13	OU812......Van Halen...Warner 25732
⑧	8	65	**Richard Marx**......Richard Marx...EMI-Manhattan 53049
⑨	11	17	Open Up and Say...Ahh!......Poison...Enigma 48493
⑩	12	8	**Long Cold Winter**......Cinderella...Mercury 834612

TW	LW	WK	Billboard. SEPTEMBER 17, 1988 TOP POP ALBUMS
①	1	57	**Hysteria**......*Def Leppard*...Mercury 830675
②	2	56	**Appetite For Destruction**......*Guns N' Roses*...Geffen 24148
③	3	21	**Tracy Chapman**......*Tracy Chapman*...Elektra 60774
④	4	11	**Roll With It**......*Steve Winwood*...Virgin 90946
⑤	5	22	**He's The D.J., I'm The Rapper**.... *D.J. Jazzy Jeff & The Fresh Prince*...Jive 1091
⑥	6	44	**Faith**......*George Michael*...Columbia 40867
⑦	7	14	**OU812**......*Van Halen*...Warner 25732
⑧	9	18	**Open Up and Say...Ahh!**......*Poison*...Enigma 48493
⑨	8	66	**Richard Marx**......*Richard Marx*...EMI-Manhattan 53049
⑩	10	9	**Long Cold Winter**......*Cinderella*...Mercury 834612

TW	LW	WK	Billboard. SEPTEMBER 24, 1988 TOP POP ALBUMS
❶	2	57	**Appetite For Destruction**......*Guns N' Roses*...Geffen 24148
②	1	58	**Hysteria**......*Def Leppard*...Mercury 830675
③	3	22	**Tracy Chapman**......*Tracy Chapman*...Elektra 60774
④	5	23	**He's The D.J., I'm The Rapper**......*D.J. Jazzy Jeff & The Fresh Prince*...Jive 1091
⑤	4	12	**Roll With It**......*Steve Winwood*...Virgin 90946
⑥	6	45	**Faith**......*George Michael*...Columbia 40867
❼	12	7	**Cocktail**......*Soundtrack*...Elektra 60806
⑧	7	15	**OU812**......*Van Halen*...Warner 25732
⑨	8	19	**Open Up and Say...Ahh!**......*Poison*...Enigma 48493
⑩	10	10	**Long Cold Winter**......*Cinderella*...Mercury 834612

TW	LW	WK	Billboard. OCTOBER 1, 1988 TOP POP ALBUMS
❶	1	58	**Appetite For Destruction**......*Guns N' Roses*...Geffen 24148
②	2	59	**Hysteria**......*Def Leppard*...Mercury 830675
③	3	23	**Tracy Chapman**......*Tracy Chapman*...Elektra 60774
❹	7	8	**Cocktail**......*Soundtrack*...Elektra 60806
⑤	5	13	**Roll With It**......*Steve Winwood*...Virgin 90946
⑥	4	24	**He's The D.J., I'm The Rapper**.... *D.J. Jazzy Jeff & The Fresh Prince*...Jive 1091
⑦	6	46	**Faith**......*George Michael*...Columbia 40867
❽	12	24	**Simple Pleasures**......*Bobby McFerrin*...EMI-Manhattan 48059
❾	11	47	**Kick**......*INXS*...Atlantic 81796
⑩	8	16	**OU812**......*Van Halen*...Warner 25732

TW	LW	WK	Billboard. OCTOBER 8, 1988 TOP POP ALBUMS
①	1	59	**Appetite For Destruction**......*Guns N' Roses*...Geffen 24148
②	2	60	**Hysteria**......*Def Leppard*...Mercury 830675
③	3	24	**Tracy Chapman**......*Tracy Chapman*...Elektra 60774
❹	4	9	**Cocktail**......*Soundtrack*...Elektra 60806
❺	8	25	**Simple Pleasures**......*Bobby McFerrin*...EMI-Manhattan 48059
❻	13	3	**...And Justice For All**......*Metallica*...Elektra 60812
⑦	5	14	**Roll With It**......*Steve Winwood*...Virgin 90946
❽	-	1	**New Jersey**......*Bon Jovi*...Mercury 836345
⑨	7	47	**Faith**......*George Michael*...Columbia 40867
⑩	6	25	**He's The D.J., I'm The Rapper**.... *D.J. Jazzy Jeff & The Fresh Prince*...Jive 1091

TW	LW	WK	Billboard® OCTOBER 15, 1988 TOP POP ALBUMS	
1	8	2	**New Jersey**	*Bon Jovi*...Mercury 836345
2	1	60	Appetite For Destruction	*Guns N' Roses*...Geffen 24148
3	2	61	Hysteria	*Def Leppard*...Mercury 830675
4	4	10	Cocktail	*Soundtrack*...Elektra 60806
5	3	25	Tracy Chapman	*Tracy Chapman*...Elektra 60774
6	6	4	**...And Justice For All**	*Metallica*...Elektra 60812
7	5	26	Simple Pleasures	*Bobby McFerrin*...EMI-Manhattan 48059
8	7	15	Roll With It	*Steve Winwood*...Virgin 90946
9	11	49	Kick	*INXS*...Atlantic 81796
10	9	48	Faith	*George Michael*...Columbia 40867

TW	LW	WK	Billboard® OCTOBER 22, 1988 TOP POP ALBUMS	
1	1	3	**New Jersey**	*Bon Jovi*...Mercury 836345
2	2	61	Appetite For Destruction	*Guns N' Roses*...Geffen 24148
3	3	62	Hysteria	*Def Leppard*...Mercury 830675
4	4	11	Cocktail	*Soundtrack*...Elektra 60806
5	7	27	**Simple Pleasures**	*Bobby McFerrin*...EMI-Manhattan 48059
6	5	26	Tracy Chapman	*Tracy Chapman*...Elektra 60774
7	6	5	...And Justice For All	*Metallica*...Elektra 60812
8	12	14	Don't Be Cruel	*Bobby Brown*...MCA 42185
9	8	16	Roll With It	*Steve Winwood*...Virgin 90946
10	9	50	Kick	*INXS*...Atlantic 81796

TW	LW	WK	Billboard® OCTOBER 29, 1988 TOP POP ALBUMS	
1	1	4	**New Jersey**	*Bon Jovi*...Mercury 836345
2	2	62	Appetite For Destruction	*Guns N' Roses*...Geffen 24148
3	4	12	Cocktail	*Soundtrack*...Elektra 60806
4	3	63	Hysteria	*Def Leppard*...Mercury 830675
5	5	28	**Simple Pleasures**	*Bobby McFerrin*...EMI-Manhattan 48059
6	8	15	Don't Be Cruel	*Bobby Brown*...MCA 42185
7	6	27	Tracy Chapman	*Tracy Chapman*...Elektra 60774
8	7	6	...And Justice For All	*Metallica*...Elektra 60812
9	11	50	Faith	*George Michael*...Columbia 40867
10	13	15	**Long Cold Winter**	*Cinderella*...Mercury 834612

TW	LW	WK	Billboard® NOVEMBER 5, 1988 TOP POP ALBUMS	
1	1	5	**New Jersey**	*Bon Jovi*...Mercury 836345
2	2	63	Appetite For Destruction	*Guns N' Roses*...Geffen 24148
3	3	13	Cocktail	*Soundtrack*...Elektra 60806
4	4	64	Hysteria	*Def Leppard*...Mercury 830675
5	14	2	Rattle And Hum	*U2/Soundtrack*...Island 91003
6	6	16	Don't Be Cruel	*Bobby Brown*...MCA 42185
7	5	29	Simple Pleasures	*Bobby McFerrin*...EMI-Manhattan 48059
8	9	51	Faith	*George Michael*...Columbia 40867
9	7	28	Tracy Chapman	*Tracy Chapman*...Elektra 60774
10	8	7	...And Justice For All	*Metallica*...Elektra 60812

TW	LW	WK	Billboard. NOVEMBER 12, 1988 TOP POP ALBUMS
❶	5	3	**Rattle And Hum** ... *U2/Soundtrack*...Island 91003
②	2	64	Appetite For Destruction ... *Guns N' Roses*...Geffen 24148
③	1	6	New Jersey ... *Bon Jovi*...Mercury 836345
④	3	14	Cocktail ... *Soundtrack*...Elektra 60806
⑤	4	65	Hysteria ... *Def Leppard*...Mercury 830675
❻	6	17	Don't Be Cruel ... *Bobby Brown*...MCA 42185
❼	22	2	Giving You The Best That I Got ... *Anita Baker*...Elektra 60827
⑧	8	52	Faith ... *George Michael*...Columbia 40867
⑨	7	30	Simple Pleasures ... *Bobby McFerrin*...EMI-Manhattan 48059
⑩	11	17	**Long Cold Winter** ... *Cinderella*...Mercury 834612

TW	LW	WK	Billboard. NOVEMBER 19, 1988 TOP POP ALBUMS
❶	1	4	**Rattle And Hum** ... *U2/Soundtrack*...Island 91003
②	2	65	Appetite For Destruction ... *Guns N' Roses*...Geffen 24148
③	4	15	Cocktail ... *Soundtrack*...Elektra 60806
④	3	7	New Jersey ... *Bon Jovi*...Mercury 836345
❺	7	3	Giving You The Best That I Got ... *Anita Baker*...Elektra 60827
⑥	5	66	Hysteria ... *Def Leppard*...Mercury 830675
⑦	6	18	Don't Be Cruel ... *Bobby Brown*...MCA 42185
⑧	8	53	Faith ... *George Michael*...Columbia 40867
❾	12	5	**Any Love** ... *Luther Vandross*...Epic 44308
❿	16	5	Silhouette ... *Kenny G*...Arista 8457

TW	LW	WK	Billboard. NOVEMBER 26, 1988 TOP POP ALBUMS
①	1	5	**Rattle And Hum** ... *U2/Soundtrack*...Island 91003
❷	5	4	Giving You The Best That I Got ... *Anita Baker*...Elektra 60827
③	2	66	Appetite For Destruction ... *Guns N' Roses*...Geffen 24148
④	4	8	New Jersey ... *Bon Jovi*...Mercury 836345
⑤	3	16	Cocktail ... *Soundtrack*...Elektra 60806
⑥	6	67	Hysteria ... *Def Leppard*...Mercury 830675
⑦	7	19	Don't Be Cruel ... *Bobby Brown*...MCA 42185
⑧	8	54	Faith ... *George Michael*...Columbia 40867
❾	10	6	Silhouette ... *Kenny G*...Arista 8457
⑩	9	6	Any Love ... *Luther Vandross*...Epic 44308

TW	LW	WK	Billboard. DECEMBER 3, 1988 TOP POP ALBUMS
①	1	6	**Rattle And Hum** ... *U2/Soundtrack*...Island 91003
②	2	5	Giving You The Best That I Got ... *Anita Baker*...Elektra 60827
③	3	67	Appetite For Destruction ... *Guns N' Roses*...Geffen 24148
④	5	17	Cocktail ... *Soundtrack*...Elektra 60806
⑤	4	9	New Jersey ... *Bon Jovi*...Mercury 836345
⑥	6	68	Hysteria ... *Def Leppard*...Mercury 830675
⑦	7	20	Don't Be Cruel ... *Bobby Brown*...MCA 42185
❽	9	7	**Silhouette** ... *Kenny G*...Arista 8457
❾	12	4	Volume One ... *Traveling Wilburys*...Wilbury 25796
⑩	10	7	Any Love ... *Luther Vandross*...Epic 44308

TW	LW	WK	Billboard® DECEMBER 10, 1988	TOP POP ALBUMS
①	1	7	**Rattle And Hum**	*U2/Soundtrack*...Island 91003
②	2	6	Giving You The Best That I Got	*Anita Baker*...Elektra 60827
③	4	18	Cocktail	*Soundtrack*...Elektra 60806
④	3	68	Appetite For Destruction	*Guns N' Roses*...Geffen 24148
⑤	5	10	New Jersey	*Bon Jovi*...Mercury 836345
⑥	7	21	Don't Be Cruel	*Bobby Brown*...MCA 42185
⑦	6	69	Hysteria	*Def Leppard*...Mercury 830675
❽	9	5	Volume One	*Traveling Wilburys*...Wilbury 25796
⑨	8	8	Silhouette	*Kenny G*...Arista 8457
❿	12	5	**Till I Loved You**	*Barbra Streisand*...Columbia 40880

TW	LW	WK	Billboard® DECEMBER 17, 1988	TOP POP ALBUMS
①	1	8	**Rattle And Hum**	*U2/Soundtrack*...Island 91003
②	2	7	Giving You The Best That I Got	*Anita Baker*...Elektra 60827
③	3	19	Cocktail	*Soundtrack*...Elektra 60806
④	4	69	Appetite For Destruction	*Guns N' Roses*...Geffen 24148
⑤	5	11	New Jersey	*Bon Jovi*...Mercury 836345
❻	7	70	Hysteria	*Def Leppard*...Mercury 830675
⑦	6	22	Don't Be Cruel	*Bobby Brown*...MCA 42185
❽	8	6	Volume One	*Traveling Wilburys*...Wilbury 25796
⑨	9	9	Silhouette	*Kenny G*...Arista 8457
❿	11	31	Open Up and Say...Ahh!	*Poison*...Enigma 48493

TW	LW	WK	Billboard® DECEMBER 24, 1988	TOP POP ALBUMS
❶	2	8	**Giving You The Best That I Got**	*Anita Baker*...Elektra 60827
②	1	9	Rattle And Hum	*U2/Soundtrack*...Island 91003
③	3	20	Cocktail	*Soundtrack*...Elektra 60806
④	4	70	Appetite For Destruction	*Guns N' Roses*...Geffen 24148
⑤	5	12	New Jersey	*Bon Jovi*...Mercury 836345
❻	7	23	Don't Be Cruel	*Bobby Brown*...MCA 42185
⑦	6	71	Hysteria	*Def Leppard*...Mercury 830675
❽	8	7	Volume One	*Traveling Wilburys*...Wilbury 25796
❾	9	10	Silhouette	*Kenny G*...Arista 8457
❿	10	32	Open Up and Say...Ahh!	*Poison*...Enigma 48493

TW	LW	WK	Billboard. JANUARY 7, 1989 TOP POP ALBUMS	
1	1	10	**Giving You The Best That I Got**	*Anita Baker*...Elektra 60827
2	3	22	**Cocktail**	*Soundtrack*...Elektra 60806
3	2	11	Rattle And Hum	*U2/Soundtrack*...Island 91003
4	5	14	New Jersey	*Bon Jovi*...Mercury 836345
5	8	9	Volume One	*Traveling Wilburys*...Wilbury 25796
6	7	73	Hysteria	*Def Leppard*...Mercury 830675
7	4	72	Appetite For Destruction	*Guns N' Roses*...Geffen 24148
8	6	25	Don't Be Cruel	*Bobby Brown*...MCA 42185
9	10	34	Open Up and Say...Ahh!	*Poison*...Enigma 48493
10	9	12	Silhouette	*Kenny G*...Arista 8457

TW	LW	WK	Billboard. JANUARY 14, 1989 TOP POP ALBUMS	
1	1	11	**Giving You The Best That I Got**	*Anita Baker*...Elektra 60827
2	3	12	Rattle And Hum	*U2/Soundtrack*...Island 91003
3	2	23	Cocktail	*Soundtrack*...Elektra 60806
4	4	15	New Jersey	*Bon Jovi*...Mercury 836345
5	7	73	Appetite For Destruction	*Guns N' Roses*...Geffen 24148
6	8	26	Don't Be Cruel	*Bobby Brown*...MCA 42185
7	6	74	Hysteria	*Def Leppard*...Mercury 830675
8	5	10	Volume One	*Traveling Wilburys*...Wilbury 25796
9	9	35	Open Up and Say...Ahh!	*Poison*...Enigma 48493
10	10	13	Silhouette	*Kenny G*...Arista 8457

TW	LW	WK	Billboard. JANUARY 21, 1989 TOP POP ALBUMS	
1	6	27	**Don't Be Cruel**	*Bobby Brown*...MCA 42185
2	5	74	Appetite For Destruction	*Guns N' Roses*...Geffen 24148
3	9	36	Open Up and Say...Ahh!	*Poison*...Enigma 48493
4	4	16	New Jersey	*Bon Jovi*...Mercury 836345
5	7	75	Hysteria	*Def Leppard*...Mercury 830675
6	1	12	Giving You The Best That I Got	*Anita Baker*...Elektra 60827
7	8	11	Volume One	*Traveling Wilburys*...Wilbury 25796
8	3	24	Cocktail	*Soundtrack*...Elektra 60806
9	2	13	Rattle And Hum	*U2/Soundtrack*...Island 91003
10	12	6	G N' R Lies	*Guns N' Roses*...Geffen 24198

TW	LW	WK	Billboard. JANUARY 28, 1989 TOP POP ALBUMS	
1	1	28	**Don't Be Cruel**	*Bobby Brown*...MCA 42185
2	2	75	Appetite For Destruction	*Guns N' Roses*...Geffen 24148
3	7	12	**Volume One**	*Traveling Wilburys*...Wilbury 25796
4	5	76	Hysteria	*Def Leppard*...Mercury 830675
5	3	37	Open Up and Say...Ahh!	*Poison*...Enigma 48493
6	4	17	New Jersey	*Bon Jovi*...Mercury 836345
7	10	7	G N' R Lies	*Guns N' Roses*...Geffen 24198
8	6	13	Giving You The Best That I Got	*Anita Baker*...Elektra 60827
9	9	14	Rattle And Hum	*U2/Soundtrack*...Island 91003
10	8	25	Cocktail	*Soundtrack*...Elektra 60806

TW	LW	WK	Billboard. FEBRUARY 4, 1989 TOP POP ALBUMS
1	1	29	**Don't Be Cruel** .... *Bobby Brown*...MCA 42185
2	2	76	Appetite For Destruction .... *Guns N' Roses*...Geffen 24148
3	3	13	**Volume One** .... *Traveling Wilburys*...Wilbury 25796
4	5	38	Open Up and Say...Ahh! .... *Poison*...Enigma 48493
5	7	8	G N' R Lies .... *Guns N' Roses*...Geffen 24198
6	6	18	New Jersey .... *Bon Jovi*...Mercury 836345
7	4	77	Hysteria .... *Def Leppard*...Mercury 830675
8	8	14	Giving You The Best That I Got .... *Anita Baker*...Elektra 60827
9	11	20	Shooting Rubberbands At The Stars .... *Edie Brickell & New Bohemians*...Geffen 24192
10	9	15	Rattle And Hum .... *U2/Soundtrack*...Island 91003

TW	LW	WK	Billboard. FEBRUARY 11, 1989 TOP POP ALBUMS
1	2	77	**Appetite For Destruction** .... *Guns N' Roses*...Geffen 24148
2	1	30	Don't Be Cruel .... *Bobby Brown*...MCA 42185
3	3	14	**Volume One** .... *Traveling Wilburys*...Wilbury 25796
4	5	9	G N' R Lies .... *Guns N' Roses*...Geffen 24198
5	4	39	Open Up and Say...Ahh! .... *Poison*...Enigma 48493
6	9	21	Shooting Rubberbands At The Stars .... *Edie Brickell & New Bohemians*...Geffen 24192
7	7	78	Hysteria .... *Def Leppard*...Mercury 830675
8	6	19	New Jersey .... *Bon Jovi*...Mercury 836345
9	8	15	Giving You The Best That I Got .... *Anita Baker*...Elektra 60827
10	12	11	**Greatest Hits** .... *Journey*...Columbia 44493

TW	LW	WK	Billboard. FEBRUARY 18, 1989 TOP POP ALBUMS
1	2	31	**Don't Be Cruel** .... *Bobby Brown*...MCA 42185
2	1	78	Appetite For Destruction .... *Guns N' Roses*...Geffen 24148
3	3	15	**Volume One** .... *Traveling Wilburys*...Wilbury 25796
4	6	22	**Shooting Rubberbands At The Stars** .... *Edie Brickell & New Bohemians*...Geffen 24192
5	4	10	G N' R Lies .... *Guns N' Roses*...Geffen 24198
6	7	79	Hysteria .... *Def Leppard*...Mercury 830675
7	8	20	New Jersey .... *Bon Jovi*...Mercury 836345
8	9	16	Giving You The Best That I Got .... *Anita Baker*...Elektra 60827
9	5	40	Open Up and Say...Ahh! .... *Poison*...Enigma 48493
10	10	12	**Greatest Hits** .... *Journey*...Columbia 44493

TW	LW	WK	Billboard. FEBRUARY 25, 1989 TOP POP ALBUMS
1	1	32	**Don't Be Cruel** .... *Bobby Brown*...MCA 42185
2	2	79	Appetite For Destruction .... *Guns N' Roses*...Geffen 24148
3	3	16	**Volume One** .... *Traveling Wilburys*...Wilbury 25796
4	4	23	**Shooting Rubberbands At The Stars** .... *Edie Brickell & New Bohemians*...Geffen 24192
5	11	3	Electric Youth .... *Debbie Gibson*...Atlantic 81932
6	5	11	G N' R Lies .... *Guns N' Roses*...Geffen 24198
7	6	80	Hysteria .... *Def Leppard*...Mercury 830675
8	8	17	Giving You The Best That I Got .... *Anita Baker*...Elektra 60827
9	13	32	Forever Your Girl .... *Paula Abdul*...Virgin 90943
10	7	21	New Jersey .... *Bon Jovi*...Mercury 836345

TW	LW	WK	Billboard® MARCH 4, 1989	TOP POP ALBUMS
①	1	33	**Don't Be Cruel**	*Bobby Brown*...MCA 42185
②	2	80	Appetite For Destruction	*Guns N' Roses*...Geffen 24148
❸	5	4	Electric Youth	*Debbie Gibson*...Atlantic 81932
④	3	17	Volume One	*Traveling Wilburys*...Wilbury 25796
⑤	4	24	Shooting Rubberbands At The Stars	*Edie Brickell & New Bohemians*...Geffen 24192
⑥	6	12	G N' R Lies	*Guns N' Roses*...Geffen 24198
❼	9	33	Forever Your Girl	*Paula Abdul*...Virgin 90943
⑧	7	81	Hysteria	*Def Leppard*...Mercury 830675
⑨	8	18	Giving You The Best That I Got	*Anita Baker*...Elektra 60827
⑩	10	22	New Jersey	*Bon Jovi*...Mercury 836345

TW	LW	WK	Billboard® MARCH 11, 1989	TOP POP ALBUMS
❶	3	5	**Electric Youth**	*Debbie Gibson*...Atlantic 81932
②	1	34	Don't Be Cruel	*Bobby Brown*...MCA 42185
③	2	81	Appetite For Destruction	*Guns N' Roses*...Geffen 24148
④	4	18	Volume One	*Traveling Wilburys*...Wilbury 25796
⑤	5	25	Shooting Rubberbands At The Stars	*Edie Brickell & New Bohemians*...Geffen 24192
❻	7	34	Forever Your Girl	*Paula Abdul*...Virgin 90943
⑦	6	13	G N' R Lies	*Guns N' Roses*...Geffen 24198
❽	13	4	Mystery Girl	*Roy Orbison*...Virgin 91058
⑨	8	82	Hysteria	*Def Leppard*...Mercury 830675
⑩	9	19	Giving You The Best That I Got	*Anita Baker*...Elektra 60827

TW	LW	WK	Billboard® MARCH 18, 1989	TOP POP ALBUMS
①	1	6	**Electric Youth**	*Debbie Gibson*...Atlantic 81932
②	2	35	Don't Be Cruel	*Bobby Brown*...MCA 42185
③	3	82	Appetite For Destruction	*Guns N' Roses*...Geffen 24148
④	4	19	Volume One	*Traveling Wilburys*...Wilbury 25796
❺	6	35	Forever Your Girl	*Paula Abdul*...Virgin 90943
❻	8	5	Mystery Girl	*Roy Orbison*...Virgin 91058
⑦	5	26	Shooting Rubberbands At The Stars	*Edie Brickell & New Bohemians*...Geffen 24192
⑧	7	14	G N' R Lies	*Guns N' Roses*...Geffen 24198
❾	14	5	Loc-ed After Dark	*Tone Loc*...Delicious Vinyl 3000
⑩	9	83	Hysteria	*Def Leppard*...Mercury 830675

TW	LW	WK	Billboard® MARCH 25, 1989	TOP POP ALBUMS
①	1	7	**Electric Youth**	*Debbie Gibson*...Atlantic 81932
②	2	36	Don't Be Cruel	*Bobby Brown*...MCA 42185
③	3	83	Appetite For Destruction	*Guns N' Roses*...Geffen 24148
❹	5	36	Forever Your Girl	*Paula Abdul*...Virgin 90943
⑤	4	20	Volume One	*Traveling Wilburys*...Wilbury 25796
❻	6	6	Mystery Girl	*Roy Orbison*...Virgin 91058
❼	9	6	Loc-ed After Dark	*Tone Loc*...Delicious Vinyl 3000
⑧	7	27	Shooting Rubberbands At The Stars	*Edie Brickell & New Bohemians*...Geffen 24192
❾	12	30	Vivid	*Living Colour*...Epic 44099
❿	14	31	Hangin' Tough	*New Kids On The Block*...Columbia 40985

Billboard — APRIL 1, 1989 — TOP POP ALBUMS

TW	LW	WK	Title	Artist	Label
1	1	8	**Electric Youth**	*Debbie Gibson*	Atlantic 81932
2	2	37	Don't Be Cruel	*Bobby Brown*	MCA 42185
3	5	21	**Volume One**	*Traveling Wilburys*	Wilbury 25796
4	4	37	Forever Your Girl	*Paula Abdul*	Virgin 90943
5	3	84	Appetite For Destruction	*Guns N' Roses*	Geffen 24148
6	6	7	Mystery Girl	*Roy Orbison*	Virgin 91058
7	7	7	Loc-ed After Dark	*Tone Loc*	Delicious Vinyl 3000
8	10	32	Hangin' Tough	*New Kids On The Block*	Columbia 40985
9	9	31	Vivid	*Living Colour*	Epic 44099
10	16	4	The Raw & The Cooked	*Fine Young Cannibals*	I.R.S. 6273

Billboard — APRIL 8, 1989 — TOP POP ALBUMS

TW	LW	WK	Title	Artist	Label
1	1	9	**Electric Youth**	*Debbie Gibson*	Atlantic 81932
2	2	38	Don't Be Cruel	*Bobby Brown*	MCA 42185
3	7	8	Loc-ed After Dark	*Tone Loc*	Delicious Vinyl 3000
4	3	22	Volume One	*Traveling Wilburys*	Wilbury 25796
5	6	8	**Mystery Girl**	*Roy Orbison*	Virgin 91058
6	5	85	Appetite For Destruction	*Guns N' Roses*	Geffen 24148
7	4	38	Forever Your Girl	*Paula Abdul*	Virgin 90943
8	10	5	The Raw & The Cooked	*Fine Young Cannibals*	I.R.S. 6273
9	8	33	Hangin' Tough	*New Kids On The Block*	Columbia 40985
10	9	32	Vivid	*Living Colour*	Epic 44099

Billboard — APRIL 15, 1989 — TOP POP ALBUMS

TW	LW	WK	Title	Artist	Label
1	3	9	**Loc-ed After Dark**	*Tone Loc*	Delicious Vinyl 3000
2	1	10	Electric Youth	*Debbie Gibson*	Atlantic 81932
3	11	2	Like A Prayer	*Madonna*	Sire 25844
4	2	39	Don't Be Cruel	*Bobby Brown*	MCA 42185
5	5	9	**Mystery Girl**	*Roy Orbison*	Virgin 91058
6	8	6	The Raw & The Cooked	*Fine Young Cannibals*	I.R.S. 6273
7	4	23	Volume One	*Traveling Wilburys*	Wilbury 25796
8	6	86	Appetite For Destruction	*Guns N' Roses*	Geffen 24148
9	7	39	Forever Your Girl	*Paula Abdul*	Virgin 90943
10	9	34	Hangin' Tough	*New Kids On The Block*	Columbia 40985

Billboard — APRIL 22, 1989 — TOP POP ALBUMS

TW	LW	WK	Title	Artist	Label
1	3	3	**Like A Prayer**	*Madonna*	Sire 25844
2	1	10	Loc-ed After Dark	*Tone Loc*	Delicious Vinyl 3000
3	2	11	Electric Youth	*Debbie Gibson*	Atlantic 81932
4	4	40	Don't Be Cruel	*Bobby Brown*	MCA 42185
5	6	7	The Raw & The Cooked	*Fine Young Cannibals*	I.R.S. 6273
6	12	19	G N' R Lies	*Guns N' Roses*	Geffen 24198
7	5	10	Mystery Girl	*Roy Orbison*	Virgin 91058
8	10	35	Hangin' Tough	*New Kids On The Block*	Columbia 40985
9	9	40	Forever Your Girl	*Paula Abdul*	Virgin 90943
10	7	24	Volume One	*Traveling Wilburys*	Wilbury 25796

TW	LW	WK	Billboard® — APRIL 29, 1989 — TOP POP ALBUMS
1	1	4	**Like A Prayer** ... *Madonna*...Sire 25844
2	2	11	Loc-ed After Dark ... *Tone Loc*...Delicious Vinyl 3000
3	4	41	Don't Be Cruel ... *Bobby Brown*...MCA 42185
4	3	12	Electric Youth ... *Debbie Gibson*...Atlantic 81932
5	6	20	G N' R Lies ... *Guns N' Roses*...Geffen 24198
6	5	8	The Raw & The Cooked ... *Fine Young Cannibals*...I.R.S. 6273
7	11	35	Vivid ... *Living Colour*...Epic 44099
8	8	36	Hangin' Tough ... *New Kids On The Block*...Columbia 40985
9	7	11	Mystery Girl ... *Roy Orbison*...Virgin 91058
10	10	25	Volume One ... *Traveling Wilburys*...Wilbury 25796

TW	LW	WK	Billboard® — MAY 6, 1989 — TOP POP ALBUMS
1	1	5	**Like A Prayer** ... *Madonna*...Sire 25844
2	2	12	Loc-ed After Dark ... *Tone Loc*...Delicious Vinyl 3000
3	5	21	G N' R Lies ... *Guns N' Roses*...Geffen 24198
4	6	9	The Raw & The Cooked ... *Fine Young Cannibals*...I.R.S. 6273
5	3	42	Don't Be Cruel ... *Bobby Brown*...MCA 42185
6	7	36	**Vivid** ... *Living Colour*...Epic 44099
7	8	37	Hangin' Tough ... *New Kids On The Block*...Columbia 40985
8	4	13	Electric Youth ... *Debbie Gibson*...Atlantic 81932
9	14	16	Beaches ... *Bette Midler/Soundtrack*...Atlantic 81933
10	11	42	Forever Your Girl ... *Paula Abdul*...Virgin 90943

TW	LW	WK	Billboard® — MAY 13, 1989 — TOP POP ALBUMS
1	1	6	**Like A Prayer** ... *Madonna*...Sire 25844
2	3	22	**G N' R Lies** ... *Guns N' Roses*...Geffen 24198
3	2	13	Loc-ed After Dark ... *Tone Loc*...Delicious Vinyl 3000
4	4	10	The Raw & The Cooked ... *Fine Young Cannibals*...I.R.S. 6273
5	5	43	Don't Be Cruel ... *Bobby Brown*...MCA 42185
6	6	37	**Vivid** ... *Living Colour*...Epic 44099
7	7	38	Hangin' Tough ... *New Kids On The Block*...Columbia 40985
8	8	14	Electric Youth ... *Debbie Gibson*...Atlantic 81932
9	9	17	Beaches ... *Bette Midler/Soundtrack*...Atlantic 81933
10	10	43	Forever Your Girl ... *Paula Abdul*...Virgin 90943

TW	LW	WK	Billboard® — MAY 20, 1989 — TOP POP ALBUMS
1	1	7	**Like A Prayer** ... *Madonna*...Sire 25844
2	3	14	Loc-ed After Dark ... *Tone Loc*...Delicious Vinyl 3000
3	4	11	The Raw & The Cooked ... *Fine Young Cannibals*...I.R.S. 6273
4	2	23	G N' R Lies ... *Guns N' Roses*...Geffen 24198
5	5	44	Don't Be Cruel ... *Bobby Brown*...MCA 42185
6	9	18	Beaches ... *Bette Midler/Soundtrack*...Atlantic 81933
7	7	39	Hangin' Tough ... *New Kids On The Block*...Columbia 40985
8	6	38	Vivid ... *Living Colour*...Epic 44099
9	10	44	Forever Your Girl ... *Paula Abdul*...Virgin 90943
10	8	15	Electric Youth ... *Debbie Gibson*...Atlantic 81932

Billboard — MAY 27, 1989 — TOP POP ALBUMS

TW	LW	WK	Title	Artist	Label
①	1	8	Like A Prayer	Madonna	Sire 25844
❷	3	12	The Raw & The Cooked	Fine Young Cannibals	I.R.S. 6273
③	4	24	G N' R Lies	Guns N' Roses	Geffen 24198
❹	6	19	Beaches	Bette Midler/Soundtrack	Atlantic 81933
⑤	2	15	Loc-ed After Dark	Tone Loc	Delicious Vinyl 3000
⑥	5	45	Don't Be Cruel	Bobby Brown	MCA 42185
⑦	7	40	Hangin' Tough	New Kids On The Block	Columbia 40985
❽	9	45	Forever Your Girl	Paula Abdul	Virgin 90943
⑨	8	39	Vivid	Living Colour	Epic 44099
❿	12	5	Sonic Temple	The Cult	Sire 25871

Billboard — JUNE 3, 1989 — TOP POP ALBUMS

TW	LW	WK	Title	Artist	Label
❶	2	13	The Raw & The Cooked	Fine Young Cannibals	I.R.S. 6273
②	1	9	Like A Prayer	Madonna	Sire 25844
❸	4	20	Beaches	Bette Midler/Soundtrack	Atlantic 81933
④	3	25	G N' R Lies	Guns N' Roses	Geffen 24198
⑤	6	46	Don't Be Cruel	Bobby Brown	MCA 42185
❻	8	46	Forever Your Girl	Paula Abdul	Virgin 90943
⑦	7	41	Hangin' Tough	New Kids On The Block	Columbia 40985
⑧	5	16	Loc-ed After Dark	Tone Loc	Delicious Vinyl 3000
❾	11	4	Full Moon Fever	Tom Petty	MCA 6253
⑩	10	6	Sonic Temple	The Cult	Sire 25871

Billboard — JUNE 10, 1989 — TOP POP ALBUMS

TW	LW	WK	Title	Artist	Label
①	1	14	The Raw & The Cooked	Fine Young Cannibals	I.R.S. 6273
②	3	21	Beaches	Bette Midler/Soundtrack	Atlantic 81933
③	2	10	Like A Prayer	Madonna	Sire 25844
④	5	47	Don't Be Cruel	Bobby Brown	MCA 42185
⑤	4	26	G N' R Lies	Guns N' Roses	Geffen 24198
❻	6	47	Forever Your Girl	Paula Abdul	Virgin 90943
❼	9	5	Full Moon Fever	Tom Petty	MCA 6253
⑧	7	42	Hangin' Tough	New Kids On The Block	Columbia 40985
❾	13	3	Big Daddy	John Cougar Mellencamp	Mercury 838220
⑩	10	7	Sonic Temple	The Cult	Sire 25871

Billboard — JUNE 17, 1989 — TOP POP ALBUMS

TW	LW	WK	Title	Artist	Label
❶	1	15	The Raw & The Cooked	Fine Young Cannibals	I.R.S. 6273
❷	2	22	Beaches	Bette Midler/Soundtrack	Atlantic 81933
③	3	11	Like A Prayer	Madonna	Sire 25844
❹	4	48	Don't Be Cruel	Bobby Brown	MCA 42185
❺	6	48	Forever Your Girl	Paula Abdul	Virgin 90943
❻	7	6	Full Moon Fever	Tom Petty	MCA 6253
❼	9	4	Big Daddy	John Cougar Mellencamp	Mercury 838220
⑧	5	27	G N' R Lies	Guns N' Roses	Geffen 24198
⑨	8	43	Hangin' Tough	New Kids On The Block	Columbia 40985
⑩	10	8	Sonic Temple	The Cult	Sire 25871

TW	LW	WK	Billboard® JUNE 24, 1989 TOP POP ALBUMS		
1	1	16	**The Raw & The Cooked**	*Fine Young Cannibals*	I.R.S. 6273
2	2	23	**Beaches**	*Bette Midler/Soundtrack*	Atlantic 81933
3	4	49	Don't Be Cruel	*Bobby Brown*	MCA 42185
4	3	12	Like A Prayer	*Madonna*	Sire 25844
5	6	7	Full Moon Fever	*Tom Petty*	MCA 6253
6	5	49	Forever Your Girl	*Paula Abdul*	Virgin 90943
7	9	44	Hangin' Tough	*New Kids On The Block*	Columbia 40985
8	7	5	Big Daddy	*John Cougar Mellencamp*	Mercury 838220
9	11	14	Girl You Know It's True	*Milli Vanilli*	Arista 8592
10	10	9	**Sonic Temple**	*The Cult*	Sire 25871

TW	LW	WK	Billboard® JULY 1, 1989 TOP POP ALBUMS		
1	1	17	**The Raw & The Cooked**	*Fine Young Cannibals*	I.R.S. 6273
2	3	50	Don't Be Cruel	*Bobby Brown*	MCA 42185
3	2	24	Beaches	*Bette Midler/Soundtrack*	Atlantic 81933
4	5	8	Full Moon Fever	*Tom Petty*	MCA 6253
5	4	13	Like A Prayer	*Madonna*	Sire 25844
6	6	50	Forever Your Girl	*Paula Abdul*	Virgin 90943
7	7	45	Hangin' Tough	*New Kids On The Block*	Columbia 40985
8	9	15	Girl You Know It's True	*Milli Vanilli*	Arista 8592
9	8	6	Big Daddy	*John Cougar Mellencamp*	Mercury 838220
10	10	10	**Sonic Temple**	*The Cult*	Sire 25871

TW	LW	WK	Billboard® JULY 8, 1989 TOP POP ALBUMS		
1	1	18	**The Raw & The Cooked**	*Fine Young Cannibals*	I.R.S. 6273
2	2	51	Don't Be Cruel	*Bobby Brown*	MCA 42185
3	4	9	**Full Moon Fever**	*Tom Petty*	MCA 6253
4	5	14	Like A Prayer	*Madonna*	Sire 25844
5	3	25	Beaches	*Bette Midler/Soundtrack*	Atlantic 81933
6	7	46	Hangin' Tough	*New Kids On The Block*	Columbia 40985
7	8	16	Girl You Know It's True	*Milli Vanilli*	Arista 8592
8	6	51	Forever Your Girl	*Paula Abdul*	Virgin 90943
9	11	10	**...Twice Shy**	*Great White*	Capitol 90640
10	12	5	**The Other Side Of The Mirror**	*Stevie Nicks*	Modern 91245

TW	LW	WK	Billboard® JULY 15, 1989 TOP POP ALBUMS		
1	1	19	**The Raw & The Cooked**	*Fine Young Cannibals*	I.R.S. 6273
2	2	52	Don't Be Cruel	*Bobby Brown*	MCA 42185
3	3	10	**Full Moon Fever**	*Tom Petty*	MCA 6253
4	6	47	Hangin' Tough	*New Kids On The Block*	Columbia 40985
5	7	17	Girl You Know It's True	*Milli Vanilli*	Arista 8592
6	4	15	Like A Prayer	*Madonna*	Sire 25844
7	29	2	Batman	*Prince/Soundtrack*	Warner 25936
8	5	26	Beaches	*Bette Midler/Soundtrack*	Atlantic 81933
9	8	52	Forever Your Girl	*Paula Abdul*	Virgin 90943
10	15	3	Walking With A Panther	*L.L. Cool J.*	Def Jam 45172

Billboard — JULY 22, 1989 — TOP POP ALBUMS

TW	LW	WK	Title	Artist	Label
1	7	3	**Batman**	*Prince/Soundtrack*	Warner 25936
2	1	20	The Raw & The Cooked	*Fine Young Cannibals*	I.R.S. 6273
3	2	53	Don't Be Cruel	*Bobby Brown*	MCA 42185
4	4	48	Hangin' Tough	*New Kids On The Block*	Columbia 40985
5	3	11	Full Moon Fever	*Tom Petty*	MCA 6253
6	10	4	**Walking With A Panther**	*L.L. Cool J*	Def Jam 45172
7	5	18	Girl You Know It's True	*Milli Vanilli*	Arista 8592
8	6	16	Like A Prayer	*Madonna*	Sire 25844
9	12	10	Repeat Offender	*Richard Marx*	EMI 90380
10	9	53	Forever Your Girl	*Paula Abdul*	Virgin 90943

Billboard — JULY 29, 1989 — TOP POP ALBUMS

TW	LW	WK	Title	Artist	Label
1	1	4	**Batman**	*Prince/Soundtrack*	Warner 25936
2	2	21	The Raw & The Cooked	*Fine Young Cannibals*	I.R.S. 6273
3	4	49	Hangin' Tough	*New Kids On The Block*	Columbia 40985
4	3	54	Don't Be Cruel	*Bobby Brown*	MCA 42185
5	7	19	Girl You Know It's True	*Milli Vanilli*	Arista 8592
6	5	12	Full Moon Fever	*Tom Petty*	MCA 6253
7	6	5	Walking With A Panther	*L.L. Cool J*	Def Jam 45172
8	9	11	Repeat Offender	*Richard Marx*	EMI 90380
9	10	54	Forever Your Girl	*Paula Abdul*	Virgin 90943
10	8	17	Like A Prayer	*Madonna*	Sire 25844

Billboard — AUGUST 5, 1989 — TOP POP ALBUMS

TW	LW	WK	Title	Artist	Label
1	1	5	**Batman**	*Prince/Soundtrack*	Warner 25936
2	2	22	The Raw & The Cooked	*Fine Young Cannibals*	I.R.S. 6273
3	3	50	Hangin' Tough	*New Kids On The Block*	Columbia 40985
4	8	12	Repeat Offender	*Richard Marx*	EMI 90380
5	6	13	Full Moon Fever	*Tom Petty*	MCA 6253
6	4	55	Don't Be Cruel	*Bobby Brown*	MCA 42185
7	5	20	Girl You Know It's True	*Milli Vanilli*	Arista 8592
8	7	6	Walking With A Panther	*L.L. Cool J*	Def Jam 45172
9	9	55	Forever Your Girl	*Paula Abdul*	Virgin 90943
10	11	14	...Twice Shy	*Great White*	Capitol 90640

Billboard — AUGUST 12, 1989 — TOP POP ALBUMS

TW	LW	WK	Title	Artist	Label
1	1	6	**Batman**	*Prince/Soundtrack*	Warner 25936
2	3	51	Hangin' Tough	*New Kids On The Block*	Columbia 40985
3	4	13	Repeat Offender	*Richard Marx*	EMI 90380
4	2	23	The Raw & The Cooked	*Fine Young Cannibals*	I.R.S. 6273
5	5	14	Full Moon Fever	*Tom Petty*	MCA 6253
6	6	56	Don't Be Cruel	*Bobby Brown*	MCA 42185
7	9	56	Forever Your Girl	*Paula Abdul*	Virgin 90943
8	7	21	Girl You Know It's True	*Milli Vanilli*	Arista 8592
9	8	7	Walking With A Panther	*L.L. Cool J*	Def Jam 45172
10	10	15	...Twice Shy	*Great White*	Capitol 90640

Billboard® — AUGUST 19, 1989 — TOP POP ALBUMS

TW	LW	WK	Title	Artist	Label
1	1	7	**Batman**	*Prince/Soundtrack*	Warner 25936
2	3	14	Repeat Offender	*Richard Marx*	EMI 90380
3	2	52	Hangin' Tough	*New Kids On The Block*	Columbia 40985
4	7	57	Forever Your Girl	*Paula Abdul*	Virgin 90943
5	5	15	Full Moon Fever	*Tom Petty*	MCA 6253
6	4	24	The Raw & The Cooked	*Fine Young Cannibals*	I.R.S. 6273
7	8	22	Girl You Know It's True	*Milli Vanilli*	Arista 8592
8	6	57	Don't Be Cruel	*Bobby Brown*	MCA 42185
9	11	28	Skid Row	*Skid Row*	Atlantic 81936
10	10	16	...Twice Shy	*Great White*	Capitol 90640

Billboard® — AUGUST 26, 1989 — TOP POP ALBUMS

TW	LW	WK	Title	Artist	Label
1	1	8	**Batman**	*Prince/Soundtrack*	Warner 25936
2	2	15	Repeat Offender	*Richard Marx*	EMI 90380
3	3	53	Hangin' Tough	*New Kids On The Block*	Columbia 40985
4	4	58	Forever Your Girl	*Paula Abdul*	Virgin 90943
5	5	16	Full Moon Fever	*Tom Petty*	MCA 6253
6	7	23	Girl You Know It's True	*Milli Vanilli*	Arista 8592
7	6	25	The Raw & The Cooked	*Fine Young Cannibals*	I.R.S. 6273
8	9	29	Skid Row	*Skid Row*	Atlantic 81936
9	8	58	Don't Be Cruel	*Bobby Brown*	MCA 42185
10	12	7	The End Of The Innocence	*Don Henley*	Geffen 24217

Billboard® — SEPTEMBER 2, 1989 — TOP POP ALBUMS

TW	LW	WK	Title	Artist	Label
1	2	16	**Repeat Offender**	*Richard Marx*	EMI 90380
2	3	54	Hangin' Tough	*New Kids On The Block*	Columbia 40985
3	1	9	Batman	*Prince/Soundtrack*	Warner 25936
4	4	59	Forever Your Girl	*Paula Abdul*	Virgin 90943
5	6	24	Girl You Know It's True	*Milli Vanilli*	Arista 8592
6	5	17	Full Moon Fever	*Tom Petty*	MCA 6253
7	8	30	Skid Row	*Skid Row*	Atlantic 81936
8	7	26	The Raw & The Cooked	*Fine Young Cannibals*	I.R.S. 6273
9	11	6	Cuts Both Ways	*Gloria Estefan*	Epic 45217
10	10	8	The End Of The Innocence	*Don Henley*	Geffen 24217

Billboard® — SEPTEMBER 9, 1989 — TOP POP ALBUMS

TW	LW	WK	Title	Artist	Label
1	2	55	**Hangin' Tough**	*New Kids On The Block*	Columbia 40985
2	1	17	Repeat Offender	*Richard Marx*	EMI 90380
3	4	60	Forever Your Girl	*Paula Abdul*	Virgin 90943
4	5	25	Girl You Know It's True	*Milli Vanilli*	Arista 8592
5	3	10	Batman	*Prince/Soundtrack*	Warner 25936
6	6	18	Full Moon Fever	*Tom Petty*	MCA 6253
7	7	31	Skid Row	*Skid Row*	Atlantic 81936
8	9	7	**Cuts Both Ways**	*Gloria Estefan*	Epic 45217
9	10	9	The End Of The Innocence	*Don Henley*	Geffen 24217
10	8	27	The Raw & The Cooked	*Fine Young Cannibals*	I.R.S. 6273

Billboard — SEPTEMBER 16, 1989 — TOP POP ALBUMS

TW	LW	WK	Title	Artist...Label
1	1	56	**Hangin' Tough**	*New Kids On The Block*...Columbia 40985
2	4	26	Girl You Know It's True	*Milli Vanilli*...Arista 8592
3	2	18	Repeat Offender	*Richard Marx*...EMI 90380
4	3	61	Forever Your Girl	*Paula Abdul*...Virgin 90943
5	5	11	Batman	*Prince/Soundtrack*...Warner 25936
6	6	19	Full Moon Fever	*Tom Petty*...MCA 6253
7	7	32	Skid Row	*Skid Row*...Atlantic 81936
8	8	8	**Cuts Both Ways**	*Gloria Estefan*...Epic 45217
9	9	10	The End Of The Innocence	*Don Henley*...Geffen 24217
10	11	29	**Dirty Rotten Filthy Stinking Rich**	*Warrant*...Columbia 44383

Billboard — SEPTEMBER 23, 1989 — TOP POP ALBUMS

TW	LW	WK	Title	Artist...Label
1	2	27	**Girl You Know It's True**	*Milli Vanilli*...Arista 8592
2	1	57	Hangin' Tough	*New Kids On The Block*...Columbia 40985
3	4	62	Forever Your Girl	*Paula Abdul*...Virgin 90943
4	3	19	Repeat Offender	*Richard Marx*...EMI 90380
5	6	20	Full Moon Fever	*Tom Petty*...MCA 6253
6	7	33	**Skid Row**	*Skid Row*...Atlantic 81936
7	11	29	The Raw & The Cooked	*Fine Young Cannibals*...I.R.S. 6273
8	9	11	**The End Of The Innocence**	*Don Henley*...Geffen 24217
9	8	9	Cuts Both Ways	*Gloria Estefan*...Epic 45217
10	10	30	**Dirty Rotten Filthy Stinking Rich**	*Warrant*...Columbia 44383

Billboard — SEPTEMBER 30, 1989 — TOP POP ALBUMS

TW	LW	WK	Title	Artist...Label
1	1	28	**Girl You Know It's True**	*Milli Vanilli*...Arista 8592
2	2	58	Hangin' Tough	*New Kids On The Block*...Columbia 40985
3	3	63	Forever Your Girl	*Paula Abdul*...Virgin 90943
4	12	3	Steel Wheels	*The Rolling Stones*...Rolling Stones 45333
5	4	20	Repeat Offender	*Richard Marx*...EMI 90380
6	5	21	Full Moon Fever	*Tom Petty*...MCA 6253
7	6	34	Skid Row	*Skid Row*...Atlantic 81936
8	24	2	Dr. Feelgood	*Mötley Crüe*...Elektra 60829
9	7	30	The Raw & The Cooked	*Fine Young Cannibals*...I.R.S. 6273
10	10	31	**Dirty Rotten Filthy Stinking Rich**	*Warrant*...Columbia 44383

Billboard — OCTOBER 7, 1989 — TOP POP ALBUMS

TW	LW	WK	Title	Artist...Label
1	3	64	**Forever Your Girl**	*Paula Abdul*...Virgin 90943
2	1	29	Girl You Know It's True	*Milli Vanilli*...Arista 8592
3	4	4	**Steel Wheels**	*The Rolling Stones*...Rolling Stones 45333
4	2	59	Hangin' Tough	*New Kids On The Block*...Columbia 40985
5	8	3	Dr. Feelgood	*Mötley Crüe*...Elektra 60829
6	6	22	Full Moon Fever	*Tom Petty*...MCA 6253
7	7	35	Skid Row	*Skid Row*...Atlantic 81936
8	5	21	Repeat Offender	*Richard Marx*...EMI 90380
9	23	2	Pump	*Aerosmith*...Geffen 24254
10	9	31	The Raw & The Cooked	*Fine Young Cannibals*...I.R.S. 6273

Billboard — OCTOBER 14, 1989 — TOP POP ALBUMS

TW	LW	WK	Title	Artist...Label
1	5	4	**Dr. Feelgood**	Mötley Crüe...Elektra 60829
2	1	65	Forever Your Girl	Paula Abdul...Virgin 90943
3	3	5	**Steel Wheels**	The Rolling Stones...Rolling Stones 45333
4	2	30	Girl You Know It's True	Milli Vanilli...Arista 8592
5	4	60	Hangin' Tough	New Kids On The Block...Columbia 40985
6	9	3	Pump	Aerosmith...Geffen 24254
7	28	2	Janet Jackson's Rhythm Nation 1814	Janet Jackson...A&M 3920
8	6	23	Full Moon Fever	Tom Petty...MCA 6253
9	7	36	Skid Row	Skid Row...Atlantic 81936
10	11	13	**Heart Of Stone**	Cher...Geffen 24239

Billboard — OCTOBER 21, 1989 — TOP POP ALBUMS

TW	LW	WK	Title	Artist...Label
1	1	5	**Dr. Feelgood**	Mötley Crüe...Elektra 60829
2	7	3	Janet Jackson's Rhythm Nation 1814	Janet Jackson...A&M 3920
3	4	31	Girl You Know It's True	Milli Vanilli...Arista 8592
4	3	6	Steel Wheels	The Rolling Stones...Rolling Stones 45333
5	2	66	Forever Your Girl	Paula Abdul...Virgin 90943
6	6	4	Pump	Aerosmith...Geffen 24254
7	5	61	Hangin' Tough	New Kids On The Block...Columbia 40985
8	8	24	Full Moon Fever	Tom Petty...MCA 6253
9	9	37	Skid Row	Skid Row...Atlantic 81936
10	10	14	**Heart Of Stone**	Cher...Geffen 24239

Billboard — OCTOBER 28, 1989 — TOP POP ALBUMS

TW	LW	WK	Title	Artist...Label
1	2	4	**Janet Jackson's Rhythm Nation 1814**	Janet Jackson...A&M 3920
2	3	32	Girl You Know It's True	Milli Vanilli...Arista 8592
3	1	6	Dr. Feelgood	Mötley Crüe...Elektra 60829
4	4	7	Steel Wheels	The Rolling Stones...Rolling Stones 45333
5	5	67	Forever Your Girl	Paula Abdul...Virgin 90943
6	6	5	Pump	Aerosmith...Geffen 24254
7	7	62	Hangin' Tough	New Kids On The Block...Columbia 40985
8	11	4	**The Seeds Of Love**	Tears For Fears...Fontana 838730
9	8	25	Full Moon Fever	Tom Petty...MCA 6253
10	9	38	Skid Row	Skid Row...Atlantic 81936

Billboard — NOVEMBER 4, 1989 — TOP POP ALBUMS

TW	LW	WK	Title	Artist...Label
1	1	5	**Janet Jackson's Rhythm Nation 1814**	Janet Jackson...A&M 3920
2	2	33	Girl You Know It's True	Milli Vanilli...Arista 8592
3	3	7	Dr. Feelgood	Mötley Crüe...Elektra 60829
4	4	8	Steel Wheels	The Rolling Stones...Rolling Stones 45333
5	6	6	**Pump**	Aerosmith...Geffen 24254
6	5	68	Forever Your Girl	Paula Abdul...Virgin 90943
7	7	63	Hangin' Tough	New Kids On The Block...Columbia 40985
8	8	5	**The Seeds Of Love**	Tears For Fears...Fontana 838730
9	9	26	Full Moon Fever	Tom Petty...MCA 6253
10	15	3	Crossroads	Tracy Chapman...Elektra 60888

TW	LW	WK	Billboard. NOVEMBER 11, 1989 TOP POP ALBUMS
1	1	6	**Janet Jackson's Rhythm Nation 1814**........ *Janet Jackson*...A&M 3920
2	2	34	Girl You Know It's True .... *Milli Vanilli*...Arista 8592
3	4	9	**Steel Wheels** .... *The Rolling Stones*...Rolling Stones 45333
4	3	8	Dr. Feelgood .... *Mötley Crüe*...Elektra 60829
5	5	7	**Pump** .... *Aerosmith*...Geffen 24254
6	6	69	Forever Your Girl .... *Paula Abdul*...Virgin 90943
7	7	64	Hangin' Tough .... *New Kids On The Block*...Columbia 40985
8	8	6	**The Seeds Of Love** .... *Tears For Fears*...Fontana 838730
9	10	4	**Crossroads** .... *Tracy Chapman*...Elektra 60888
10	9	27	Full Moon Fever .... *Tom Petty*...MCA 6253

TW	LW	WK	Billboard. NOVEMBER 18, 1989 TOP POP ALBUMS
1	1	7	**Janet Jackson's Rhythm Nation 1814**........ *Janet Jackson*...A&M 3920
2	2	35	Girl You Know It's True .... *Milli Vanilli*...Arista 8592
3	3	10	**Steel Wheels** .... *The Rolling Stones*...Rolling Stones 45333
4	6	70	Forever Your Girl .... *Paula Abdul*...Virgin 90943
5	5	8	**Pump** .... *Aerosmith*...Geffen 24254
6	7	65	Hangin' Tough .... *New Kids On The Block*...Columbia 40985
7	4	9	Dr. Feelgood .... *Mötley Crüe*...Elektra 60829
8	13	3	Storm Front .... *Billy Joel*...Columbia 44366
9	9	5	**Crossroads** .... *Tracy Chapman*...Elektra 60888
10	12	18	Cosmic Thing .... *The B-52's*...Reprise 25854

TW	LW	WK	Billboard. NOVEMBER 25, 1989 TOP POP ALBUMS
1	2	36	**Girl You Know It's True** .... *Milli Vanilli*...Arista 8592
2	1	8	Janet Jackson's Rhythm Nation 1814........ *Janet Jackson*...A&M 3920
3	8	4	Storm Front .... *Billy Joel*...Columbia 44366
4	3	11	Steel Wheels .... *The Rolling Stones*...Rolling Stones 45333
5	4	71	Forever Your Girl .... *Paula Abdul*...Virgin 90943
6	5	9	Pump .... *Aerosmith*...Geffen 24254
7	6	66	Hangin' Tough .... *New Kids On The Block*...Columbia 40985
8	7	10	Dr. Feelgood .... *Mötley Crüe*...Elektra 60829
9	10	19	Cosmic Thing .... *The B-52's*...Reprise 25854
10	9	6	Crossroads .... *Tracy Chapman*...Elektra 60888

TW	LW	WK	Billboard. DECEMBER 2, 1989 TOP POP ALBUMS
1	1	37	**Girl You Know It's True** .... *Milli Vanilli*...Arista 8592
2	3	5	Storm Front .... *Billy Joel*...Columbia 44366
3	2	9	Janet Jackson's Rhythm Nation 1814........ *Janet Jackson*...A&M 3920
4	5	72	Forever Your Girl .... *Paula Abdul*...Virgin 90943
5	7	67	Hangin' Tough .... *New Kids On The Block*...Columbia 40985
6	4	12	Steel Wheels .... *The Rolling Stones*...Rolling Stones 45333
7	9	20	Cosmic Thing .... *The B-52's*...Reprise 25854
8	6	10	Pump .... *Aerosmith*...Geffen 24254
9	8	11	Dr. Feelgood .... *Mötley Crüe*...Elektra 60829
10	11	11	Stone Cold Rhymin' .... *Young M.C.*...Delicious Vinyl 91309

TW	LW	WK	Billboard® DECEMBER 9, 1989 TOP POP ALBUMS
1	1	38	**Girl You Know It's True** ... *Milli Vanilli*...Arista 8592
2	2	6	Storm Front ... *Billy Joel*...Columbia 44366
3	3	10	Janet Jackson's Rhythm Nation 1814 ... *Janet Jackson*...A&M 3920
4	4	73	Forever Your Girl ... *Paula Abdul*...Virgin 90943
5	5	68	Hangin' Tough ... *New Kids On The Block*...Columbia 40985
6	7	21	Cosmic Thing ... *The B-52's*...Reprise 25854
7	6	13	Steel Wheels ... *The Rolling Stones*...Rolling Stones 45333
8	8	11	Pump ... *Aerosmith*...Geffen 24254
9	10	12	**Stone Cold Rhymin'** ... *Young M.C.*...Delicious Vinyl 91309
10	9	12	Dr. Feelgood ... *Mötley Crüe*...Elektra 60829

TW	LW	WK	Billboard® DECEMBER 16, 1989 TOP POP ALBUMS
1	2	7	**Storm Front** ... *Billy Joel*...Columbia 44366
2	1	39	Girl You Know It's True ... *Milli Vanilli*...Arista 8592
3	3	11	Janet Jackson's Rhythm Nation 1814 ... *Janet Jackson*...A&M 3920
4	4	74	Forever Your Girl ... *Paula Abdul*...Virgin 90943
5	5	69	Hangin' Tough ... *New Kids On The Block*...Columbia 40985
6	17	3	...But Seriously ... *Phil Collins*...Atlantic 82050
7	6	22	Cosmic Thing ... *The B-52's*...Reprise 25854
8	7	14	Steel Wheels ... *The Rolling Stones*...Rolling Stones 45333
9	8	12	Pump ... *Aerosmith*...Geffen 24254
10	11	4	**Slip Of The Tongue** ... *Whitesnake*...Geffen 24249

TW	LW	WK	Billboard® DECEMBER 23, 1989 TOP POP ALBUMS
1	2	40	**Girl You Know It's True** ... *Milli Vanilli*...Arista 8592
2	1	8	Storm Front ... *Billy Joel*...Columbia 44366
3	3	12	Janet Jackson's Rhythm Nation 1814 ... *Janet Jackson*...A&M 3920
4	6	4	...But Seriously ... *Phil Collins*...Atlantic 82050
5	4	75	Forever Your Girl ... *Paula Abdul*...Virgin 90943
6	5	70	Hangin' Tough ... *New Kids On The Block*...Columbia 40985
7	9	13	Pump ... *Aerosmith*...Geffen 24254
8	7	23	Cosmic Thing ... *The B-52's*...Reprise 25854
9	14	11	**Merry, Merry Christmas** ... *New Kids On The Block*...Columbia 45280
10	15	33	Full Moon Fever ... *Tom Petty*...MCA 6253

TW	LW	WK	Billboard® JANUARY 6, 1990 TOP POP ALBUMS
1	4	6	**...But Seriously** ... *Phil Collins*...Atlantic 82050
2	1	42	Girl You Know It's True ... *Milli Vanilli*...Arista 8592
3	2	10	Storm Front ... *Billy Joel*...Columbia 44366
4	3	14	Janet Jackson's Rhythm Nation 1814 ... *Janet Jackson*...A&M 3920
5	5	77	Forever Your Girl ... *Paula Abdul*...Virgin 90943
6	6	72	Hangin' Tough ... *New Kids On The Block*...Columbia 40985
7	7	15	Pump ... *Aerosmith*...Geffen 24254
8	8	25	Cosmic Thing ... *The B-52's*...Reprise 25854
9	12	12	Cry Like A Rainstorm - Howl Like The Wind ... *Linda Ronstadt*...Elektra 60872
10	9	13	Merry, Merry Christmas ... *New Kids On The Block*...Columbia 45280

TW	LW	WK	Billboard® JANUARY 13, 1990 TOP POP ALBUMS
1	2	43	**Girl You Know It's True** ... *Milli Vanilli*...Arista 8592
2	1	7	...But Seriously ... *Phil Collins*...Atlantic 82050
3	3	11	Storm Front ... *Billy Joel*...Columbia 44366
4	4	15	Janet Jackson's Rhythm Nation 1814 ... *Janet Jackson*...A&M 3920
5	5	78	Forever Your Girl ... *Paula Abdul*...Virgin 90943
6	6	73	Hangin' Tough ... *New Kids On The Block*...Columbia 40985
7	7	16	Pump ... *Aerosmith*...Geffen 24254
8	8	26	Cosmic Thing ... *The B-52's*...Reprise 25854
9	12	36	Full Moon Fever ... *Tom Petty*...MCA 6253
10	11	18	Steel Wheels ... *The Rolling Stones*...Rolling Stones 45333

TW	LW	WK	Billboard® JANUARY 20, 1990 TOP POP ALBUMS
1	2	8	**...But Seriously** ... *Phil Collins*...Atlantic 82050
2	1	44	Girl You Know It's True ... *Milli Vanilli*...Arista 8592
3	5	79	Forever Your Girl ... *Paula Abdul*...Virgin 90943
4	3	12	Storm Front ... *Billy Joel*...Columbia 44366
5	4	16	Janet Jackson's Rhythm Nation 1814 ... *Janet Jackson*...A&M 3920
6	7	17	Pump ... *Aerosmith*...Geffen 24254
7	8	27	Cosmic Thing ... *The B-52's*...Reprise 25854
8	6	74	Hangin' Tough ... *New Kids On The Block*...Columbia 40985
9	9	37	Full Moon Fever ... *Tom Petty*...MCA 6253
10	12	18	Stone Cold Rhymin' ... *Young M.C.*...Delicious Vinyl 91309

TW	LW	WK	Billboard® JANUARY 27, 1990 TOP POP ALBUMS
1	1	9	**...But Seriously** ... *Phil Collins*...Atlantic 82050
2	3	80	Forever Your Girl ... *Paula Abdul*...Virgin 90943
3	2	45	Girl You Know It's True ... *Milli Vanilli*...Arista 8592
4	4	13	Storm Front ... *Billy Joel*...Columbia 44366
5	5	17	Janet Jackson's Rhythm Nation 1814 ... *Janet Jackson*...A&M 3920
6	6	18	Pump ... *Aerosmith*...Geffen 24254
7	7	28	Cosmic Thing ... *The B-52's*...Reprise 25854
8	9	38	Full Moon Fever ... *Tom Petty*...MCA 6253
9	8	75	Hangin' Tough ... *New Kids On The Block*...Columbia 40985
10	10	19	Stone Cold Rhymin' ... *Young M.C.*...Delicious Vinyl 91309

TW	LW	WK	Billboard® FEBRUARY 3, 1990 TOP POP ALBUMS	
❶	2	81	**Forever Your Girl**	*Paula Abdul*...Virgin 90943
②	3	46	Girl You Know It's True	*Milli Vanilli*...Arista 8592
③	1	10	...But Seriously	*Phil Collins*...Atlantic 82050
④	5	18	Janet Jackson's Rhythm Nation 1814	*Janet Jackson*...A&M 3920
⑤	4	14	Storm Front	*Billy Joel*...Columbia 44366
⑥	7	29	Cosmic Thing	*The B-52's*...Reprise 25854
⑦	6	19	Pump	*Aerosmith*...Geffen 24254
⑧	8	39	Full Moon Fever	*Tom Petty*...MCA 6253
❾	13	9	**Back On The Block**	*Quincy Jones*...Qwest 26020
⑩	12	10	Dance!...Ya Know It!	*Bobby Brown*...MCA 6342

TW	LW	WK	Billboard® FEBRUARY 10, 1990 TOP POP ALBUMS	
❶	1	82	**Forever Your Girl**	*Paula Abdul*...Virgin 90943
②	2	47	Girl You Know It's True	*Milli Vanilli*...Arista 8592
③	3	11	...But Seriously	*Phil Collins*...Atlantic 82050
❹	4	19	Janet Jackson's Rhythm Nation 1814	*Janet Jackson*...A&M 3920
⑤	6	30	Cosmic Thing	*The B-52's*...Reprise 25854
⑥	5	15	Storm Front	*Billy Joel*...Columbia 44366
⑦	7	20	Pump	*Aerosmith*...Geffen 24254
⑧	8	40	Full Moon Fever	*Tom Petty*...MCA 6253
⑨	9	10	**Back On The Block**	*Quincy Jones*...Qwest 26020
⑩	10	11	Dance!...Ya Know It!	*Bobby Brown*...MCA 6342

TW	LW	WK	Billboard® FEBRUARY 17, 1990 TOP POP ALBUMS	
❶	1	83	**Forever Your Girl**	*Paula Abdul*...Virgin 90943
❷	2	48	Girl You Know It's True	*Milli Vanilli*...Arista 8592
❸	4	20	Janet Jackson's Rhythm Nation 1814	*Janet Jackson*...A&M 3920
④	3	12	...But Seriously	*Phil Collins*...Atlantic 82050
⑤	5	31	Cosmic Thing	*The B-52's*...Reprise 25854
⑥	7	21	Pump	*Aerosmith*...Geffen 24254
⑦	6	16	Storm Front	*Billy Joel*...Columbia 44366
⑧	8	41	Full Moon Fever	*Tom Petty*...MCA 6253
❾	10	12	**Dance!...Ya Know It!**	*Bobby Brown*...MCA 6342
⑩	9	11	Back On The Block	*Quincy Jones*...Qwest 26020

TW	LW	WK	Billboard® FEBRUARY 24, 1990 TOP POP ALBUMS	
①	1	84	**Forever Your Girl**	*Paula Abdul*...Virgin 90943
❷	3	21	Janet Jackson's Rhythm Nation 1814	*Janet Jackson*...A&M 3920
③	2	49	Girl You Know It's True	*Milli Vanilli*...Arista 8592
④	4	13	...But Seriously	*Phil Collins*...Atlantic 82050
⑤	5	32	Cosmic Thing	*The B-52's*...Reprise 25854
⑥	7	17	Storm Front	*Billy Joel*...Columbia 44366
⑦	6	22	Pump	*Aerosmith*...Geffen 24254
⑧	8	42	Full Moon Fever	*Tom Petty*...MCA 6253
⑨	9	13	**Dance!...Ya Know It!**	*Bobby Brown*...MCA 6342
❿	11	32	Soul Provider	*Michael Bolton*...Columbia 45012

Billboard — MARCH 3, 1990 — TOP POP ALBUMS

TW	LW	WK	Title	Artist...Label
1	1	85	**Forever Your Girl**	*Paula Abdul*...Virgin 90943
2	2	22	Janet Jackson's Rhythm Nation 1814	*Janet Jackson*...A&M 3920
3	3	50	Girl You Know It's True	*Milli Vanilli*...Arista 8592
4	4	14	...But Seriously	*Phil Collins*...Atlantic 82050
5	5	33	Cosmic Thing	*The B-52's*...Reprise 25854
6	6	18	Storm Front	*Billy Joel*...Columbia 44366
7	7	23	Pump	*Aerosmith*...Geffen 24254
8	8	43	Full Moon Fever	*Tom Petty*...MCA 6253
9	9	14	**Dance!...Ya Know It!**	*Bobby Brown*...MCA 6342
10	10	33	Soul Provider	*Michael Bolton*...Columbia 45012

Billboard — MARCH 10, 1990 — TOP POP ALBUMS

TW	LW	WK	Title	Artist...Label
1	1	86	**Forever Your Girl**	*Paula Abdul*...Virgin 90943
2	2	23	Janet Jackson's Rhythm Nation 1814	*Janet Jackson*...A&M 3920
3	4	15	...But Seriously	*Phil Collins*...Atlantic 82050
4	5	34	**Cosmic Thing**	*The B-52's*...Reprise 25854
5	3	51	Girl You Know It's True	*Milli Vanilli*...Arista 8592
6	6	19	Storm Front	*Billy Joel*...Columbia 44366
7	8	44	Full Moon Fever	*Tom Petty*...MCA 6253
8	7	24	Pump	*Aerosmith*...Geffen 24254
9	10	34	Soul Provider	*Michael Bolton*...Columbia 45012
10	12	21	Cry Like A Rainstorm - Howl Like The Wind	*Linda Ronstadt*...Elektra 60872

Billboard — MARCH 17, 1990 — TOP POP ALBUMS

TW	LW	WK	Title	Artist...Label
1	1	87	**Forever Your Girl**	*Paula Abdul*...Virgin 90943
2	2	24	Janet Jackson's Rhythm Nation 1814	*Janet Jackson*...A&M 3920
3	3	16	...But Seriously	*Phil Collins*...Atlantic 82050
4	5	52	Girl You Know It's True	*Milli Vanilli*...Arista 8592
5	4	35	Cosmic Thing	*The B-52's*...Reprise 25854
6	9	35	Soul Provider	*Michael Bolton*...Columbia 45012
7	10	22	**Cry Like A Rainstorm - Howl Like The Wind**	*Linda Ronstadt*...Elektra 60872
8	6	20	Storm Front	*Billy Joel*...Columbia 44366
9	13	10	Alannah Myles	*Alannah Myles*...Atlantic 81956
10	8	25	Pump	*Aerosmith*...Geffen 24254

Billboard — MARCH 24, 1990 — TOP POP ALBUMS

TW	LW	WK	Title	Artist...Label
1	1	88	**Forever Your Girl**	*Paula Abdul*...Virgin 90943
2	2	25	Janet Jackson's Rhythm Nation 1814	*Janet Jackson*...A&M 3920
3	3	17	...But Seriously	*Phil Collins*...Atlantic 82050
4	6	36	Soul Provider	*Michael Bolton*...Columbia 45012
5	5	36	Cosmic Thing	*The B-52's*...Reprise 25854
6	12	50	Nick Of Time	*Bonnie Raitt*...Capitol 91268
7	4	53	Girl You Know It's True	*Milli Vanilli*...Arista 8592
8	9	11	Alannah Myles	*Alannah Myles*...Atlantic 81956
9	7	23	Cry Like A Rainstorm - Howl Like The Wind	*Linda Ronstadt*...Elektra 60872
10	8	21	Storm Front	*Billy Joel*...Columbia 44366

TW	LW	WK	Billboard® MARCH 31, 1990	TOP POP ALBUMS
1	1	89	**Forever Your Girl**	*Paula Abdul*...Virgin 90943
2	2	26	Janet Jackson's Rhythm Nation 1814	*Janet Jackson*...A&M 3920
3	6	51	Nick Of Time	*Bonnie Raitt*...Capitol 91268
4	4	37	Soul Provider	*Michael Bolton*...Columbia 45012
5	3	18	...But Seriously	*Phil Collins*...Atlantic 82050
6	8	12	Alannah Myles	*Alannah Myles*...Atlantic 81956
7	5	37	Cosmic Thing	*The B-52's*...Reprise 25854
8	9	24	Cry Like A Rainstorm - Howl Like The Wind	*Linda Ronstadt*...Elektra 60872
9	7	54	Girl You Know It's True	*Milli Vanilli*...Arista 8592
10	11	27	Pump	*Aerosmith*...Geffen 24254

TW	LW	WK	Billboard® APRIL 7, 1990	TOP POP ALBUMS
1	3	52	**Nick Of Time**	*Bonnie Raitt*...Capitol 91268
2	1	90	Forever Your Girl	*Paula Abdul*...Virgin 90943
3	2	27	Janet Jackson's Rhythm Nation 1814	*Janet Jackson*...A&M 3920
4	4	38	Soul Provider	*Michael Bolton*...Columbia 45012
5	6	13	**Alannah Myles**	*Alannah Myles*...Atlantic 81956
6	5	19	...But Seriously	*Phil Collins*...Atlantic 82050
7	7	38	Cosmic Thing	*The B-52's*...Reprise 25854
8	10	28	Pump	*Aerosmith*...Geffen 24254
9	8	25	Cry Like A Rainstorm - Howl Like The Wind	*Linda Ronstadt*...Elektra 60872
10	11	16	**Pump Up The Jam - The Album**	*Technotronic*...SBK 93422

TW	LW	WK	Billboard® APRIL 14, 1990	TOP POP ALBUMS
1	1	53	**Nick Of Time**	*Bonnie Raitt*...Capitol 91268
2	2	91	Forever Your Girl	*Paula Abdul*...Virgin 90943
3	4	39	**Soul Provider**	*Michael Bolton*...Columbia 45012
4	3	28	Janet Jackson's Rhythm Nation 1814	*Janet Jackson*...A&M 3920
5	5	14	**Alannah Myles**	*Alannah Myles*...Atlantic 81956
6	24	2	I Do Not Want What I Haven't Got	*Sinéad O'Connor*...Ensign 21759
7	6	20	...But Seriously	*Phil Collins*...Atlantic 82050
8	8	29	Pump	*Aerosmith*...Geffen 24254
9	7	39	Cosmic Thing	*The B-52's*...Reprise 25854
10	13	6	Please Hammer Don't Hurt 'Em	*M.C. Hammer*...Capitol 92857

TW	LW	WK	Billboard® APRIL 21, 1990	TOP POP ALBUMS
1	1	54	**Nick Of Time**	*Bonnie Raitt*...Capitol 91268
2	6	3	I Do Not Want What I Haven't Got	*Sinéad O'Connor*...Ensign 21759
3	4	29	Janet Jackson's Rhythm Nation 1814	*Janet Jackson*...A&M 3920
4	2	92	Forever Your Girl	*Paula Abdul*...Virgin 90943
5	3	40	Soul Provider	*Michael Bolton*...Columbia 45012
6	5	15	Alannah Myles	*Alannah Myles*...Atlantic 81956
7	10	7	Please Hammer Don't Hurt 'Em	*M.C. Hammer*...Capitol 92857
8	8	30	Pump	*Aerosmith*...Geffen 24254
9	7	21	...But Seriously	*Phil Collins*...Atlantic 82050
10	14	3	Violator	*Depeche Mode*...Sire 26081

TW	LW	WK	Billboard. APRIL 28, 1990 TOP POP ALBUMS
1	2	4	**I Do Not Want What I Haven't Got** .... *Sinéad O'Connor*...Ensign 21759
2	3	30	Janet Jackson's Rhythm Nation 1814.................. *Janet Jackson*...A&M 3920
3	5	41	**Soul Provider** .... *Michael Bolton*...Columbia 45012
4	1	55	Nick Of Time.. *Bonnie Raitt*...Capitol 91268
5	4	93	Forever Your Girl.. *Paula Abdul*...Virgin 90943
6	7	8	Please Hammer Don't Hurt 'Em .... *M.C. Hammer*...Capitol 92857
7	6	16	Alannah Myles.. *Alannah Myles*...Atlantic 81956
8	10	4	Violator.. *Depeche Mode*...Sire 26081
9	8	31	Pump.. *Aerosmith*...Geffen 24254
10	9	22	...But Seriously.. *Phil Collins*...Atlantic 82050

TW	LW	WK	Billboard. MAY 5, 1990 TOP POP ALBUMS
1	1	5	**I Do Not Want What I Haven't Got** .... *Sinéad O'Connor*...Ensign 21759
2	2	31	Janet Jackson's Rhythm Nation 1814.................. *Janet Jackson*...A&M 3920
3	3	42	**Soul Provider** .... *Michael Bolton*...Columbia 45012
4	6	9	Please Hammer Don't Hurt 'Em .... *M.C. Hammer*...Capitol 92857
5	5	94	Forever Your Girl.. *Paula Abdul*...Virgin 90943
6	4	56	Nick Of Time.. *Bonnie Raitt*...Capitol 91268
7	8	5	**Violator**.. *Depeche Mode*...Sire 26081
8	14	3	Brigade.. *Heart*...Capitol 91820
9	9	32	Pump.. *Aerosmith*...Geffen 24254
10	7	17	Alannah Myles.. *Alannah Myles*...Atlantic 81956

TW	LW	WK	Billboard. MAY 12, 1990 TOP POP ALBUMS
1	1	6	**I Do Not Want What I Haven't Got** .... *Sinéad O'Connor*...Ensign 21759
2	4	10	Please Hammer Don't Hurt 'Em .... *M.C. Hammer*...Capitol 92857
3	2	32	Janet Jackson's Rhythm Nation 1814.................. *Janet Jackson*...A&M 3920
4	8	4	Brigade.. *Heart*...Capitol 91820
5	3	43	Soul Provider .... *Michael Bolton*...Columbia 45012
6	6	57	Nick Of Time.. *Bonnie Raitt*...Capitol 91268
7	5	95	Forever Your Girl.. *Paula Abdul*...Virgin 90943
8	7	6	Violator.. *Depeche Mode*...Sire 26081
9	11	10	**Affection** .... *Lisa Stansfield*...Arista 8554
10	12	6	Poison.. *Bell Biv DeVoe*...MCA 6387

TW	LW	WK	Billboard. MAY 19, 1990 TOP POP ALBUMS
1	1	7	**I Do Not Want What I Haven't Got** .... *Sinéad O'Connor*...Ensign 21759
2	2	11	Please Hammer Don't Hurt 'Em .... *M.C. Hammer*...Capitol 92857
3	4	5	**Brigade**.. *Heart*...Capitol 91820
4	3	33	Janet Jackson's Rhythm Nation 1814.................. *Janet Jackson*...A&M 3920
5	5	44	Soul Provider .... *Michael Bolton*...Columbia 45012
6	6	58	Nick Of Time.. *Bonnie Raitt*...Capitol 91268
7	11	7	Pretty Woman .... *Soundtrack*...EMI 93492
8	7	96	Forever Your Girl.. *Paula Abdul*...Virgin 90943
9	10	7	Poison.. *Bell Biv DeVoe*...MCA 6387
10	8	7	Violator.. *Depeche Mode*...Sire 26081

TW	LW	WK	Billboard. MAY 26, 1990 TOP POP ALBUMS
①	1	8	**I Do Not Want What I Haven't Got**.........*Sinéad O'Connor*...Ensign 21759
❷	2	12	Please Hammer Don't Hurt 'Em........................ *M.C. Hammer*...Capitol 92857
③	3	6	**Brigade** .... *Heart*...Capitol 91820
④	4	34	Janet Jackson's Rhythm Nation 1814................. *Janet Jackson*...A&M 3920
⑤	5	45	Soul Provider.. *Michael Bolton*...Columbia 45012
❻	7	8	Pretty Woman.. *Soundtrack*...EMI 93492
❼	9	8	Poison .... *Bell Biv DeVoe*...MCA 6387
⑧	6	59	Nick Of Time...*Bonnie Raitt*...Capitol 91268
⑨	10	8	Violator ....*Depeche Mode*...Sire 26081
⑩	11	5	**Fear Of A Black Planet** .... *Public Enemy*...Def Jam 45413

TW	LW	WK	Billboard. JUNE 2, 1990 TOP POP ALBUMS
①	1	9	**I Do Not Want What I Haven't Got**.........*Sinéad O'Connor*...Ensign 21759
❷	2	13	Please Hammer Don't Hurt 'Em........................ *M.C. Hammer*...Capitol 92857
③	3	7	**Brigade** .... *Heart*...Capitol 91820
❹	6	9	**Pretty Woman** .... *Soundtrack*...EMI 93492
❺	7	9	**Poison**.. *Bell Biv DeVoe*...MCA 6387
⑥	5	46	Soul Provider.. *Michael Bolton*...Columbia 45012
⑦	4	35	Janet Jackson's Rhythm Nation 1814................. *Janet Jackson*...A&M 3920
⑧	9	9	Violator ....*Depeche Mode*...Sire 26081
⑨	8	60	Nick Of Time...*Bonnie Raitt*...Capitol 91268
⑩	10	6	**Fear Of A Black Planet** .... *Public Enemy*...Def Jam 45413

TW	LW	WK	Billboard. JUNE 9, 1990 TOP POP ALBUMS
❶	2	14	**Please Hammer Don't Hurt 'Em**................ *M.C. Hammer*...Capitol 92857
②	1	10	I Do Not Want What I Haven't Got ....*Sinéad O'Connor*...Ensign 21759
③	3	8	**Brigade** .... *Heart*...Capitol 91820
④	4	10	**Pretty Woman** .... *Soundtrack*...EMI 93492
⑤	5	10	**Poison**.. *Bell Biv DeVoe*...MCA 6387
⑥	6	47	Soul Provider.. *Michael Bolton*...Columbia 45012
⑦	8	10	**Violator**..*Depeche Mode*...Sire 26081
⑧	7	36	Janet Jackson's Rhythm Nation 1814................. *Janet Jackson*...A&M 3920
❾	13	3	Shut Up And Dance (The Dance Mixes) .... *Paula Abdul*...Virgin 91362
❿	12	9	Wilson Phillips.. *Wilson Phillips*...SBK 93745

TW	LW	WK	Billboard. JUNE 16, 1990 TOP POP ALBUMS
①	1	15	**Please Hammer Don't Hurt 'Em**................ *M.C. Hammer*...Capitol 92857
②	2	11	I Do Not Want What I Haven't Got ....*Sinéad O'Connor*...Ensign 21759
❸	44	2	I'm Breathless...*Madonna/Soundtrack*...Sire 26209
❹	4	11	**Pretty Woman** .... *Soundtrack*...EMI 93492
⑤	3	9	Brigade.. *Heart*...Capitol 91820
⑥	5	11	Poison .... *Bell Biv DeVoe*...MCA 6387
❼	9	4	**Shut Up And Dance (The Dance Mixes)** ...... *Paula Abdul*...Virgin 91362
⑧	7	11	Violator ....*Depeche Mode*...Sire 26081
⑨	6	48	Soul Provider.. *Michael Bolton*...Columbia 45012
❿	10	10	Wilson Phillips.. *Wilson Phillips*...SBK 93745

TW	LW	WK	Billboard® JUNE 23, 1990 TOP POP ALBUMS
1	1	16	**Please Hammer Don't Hurt 'Em**................ *M.C. Hammer*...Capitol 92857
2	3	3	**I'm Breathless** .... *Madonna/Soundtrack*...Sire 26209
3	2	12	I Do Not Want What I Haven't Got .... *Sinéad O'Connor*...Ensign 21759
4	4	12	**Pretty Woman** .... *Soundtrack*...EMI 93492
5	6	12	**Poison** .... *Bell Biv DeVoe*...MCA 6387
6	5	10	Brigade .... *Heart*...Capitol 91820
7	7	5	**Shut Up And Dance (The Dance Mixes)** .... *Paula Abdul*...Virgin 91362
8	10	11	Wilson Phillips .... *Wilson Phillips*...SBK 93745
9	8	12	Violator .... *Depeche Mode*...Sire 26081
10	9	49	Soul Provider .... *Michael Bolton*...Columbia 45012

TW	LW	WK	Billboard® JUNE 30, 1990 TOP POP ALBUMS
1	14	2	**Step By Step** .... *New Kids On The Block*...Columbia 45129
2	1	17	Please Hammer Don't Hurt 'Em .... *M.C. Hammer*...Capitol 92857
3	2	4	I'm Breathless .... *Madonna/Soundtrack*...Sire 26209
4	3	13	I Do Not Want What I Haven't Got .... *Sinéad O'Connor*...Ensign 21759
5	5	13	**Poison** .... *Bell Biv DeVoe*...MCA 6387
6	4	13	Pretty Woman .... *Soundtrack*...EMI 93492
7	8	12	Wilson Phillips .... *Wilson Phillips*...SBK 93745
8	9	13	Violator .... *Depeche Mode*...Sire 26081
9	6	11	Brigade .... *Heart*...Capitol 91820
10	7	6	Shut Up And Dance (The Dance Mixes) .... *Paula Abdul*...Virgin 91362

TW	LW	WK	Billboard® JULY 7, 1990 TOP POP ALBUMS
1	2	18	**Please Hammer Don't Hurt 'Em** .... *M.C. Hammer*...Capitol 92857
2	1	3	Step By Step .... *New Kids On The Block*...Columbia 45129
3	3	5	I'm Breathless .... *Madonna/Soundtrack*...Sire 26209
4	6	14	**Pretty Woman** .... *Soundtrack*...EMI 93492
5	4	14	I Do Not Want What I Haven't Got .... *Sinéad O'Connor*...Ensign 21759
6	5	14	Poison .... *Bell Biv DeVoe*...MCA 6387
7	7	13	Wilson Phillips .... *Wilson Phillips*...SBK 93745
8	8	14	Violator .... *Depeche Mode*...Sire 26081
9	9	12	Brigade .... *Heart*...Capitol 91820
10	11	51	Soul Provider .... *Michael Bolton*...Columbia 45012

TW	LW	WK	Billboard® JULY 14, 1990 TOP POP ALBUMS
1	1	19	**Please Hammer Don't Hurt 'Em** .... *M.C. Hammer*...Capitol 92857
2	2	4	Step By Step .... *New Kids On The Block*...Columbia 45129
3	3	6	I'm Breathless .... *Madonna/Soundtrack*...Sire 26209
4	7	14	Wilson Phillips .... *Wilson Phillips*...SBK 93745
5	6	15	**Poison** .... *Bell Biv DeVoe*...MCA 6387
6	4	15	Pretty Woman .... *Soundtrack*...EMI 93492
7	5	15	I Do Not Want What I Haven't Got .... *Sinéad O'Connor*...Ensign 21759
8	8	15	Violator .... *Depeche Mode*...Sire 26081
9	13	11	Johnny Gill .... *Johnny Gill*...Motown 6283
10	9	13	Brigade .... *Heart*...Capitol 91820

Billboard. JULY 21, 1990 — TOP POP ALBUMS

TW	LW	WK	Title	Artist...Label
1	1	20	**Please Hammer Don't Hurt 'Em**	*M.C. Hammer*...Capitol 92857
2	3	7	**I'm Breathless**	*Madonna/Soundtrack*...Sire 26209
3	2	5	Step By Step	*New Kids On The Block*...Columbia 45129
4	4	15	Wilson Phillips	*Wilson Phillips*...SBK 93745
5	6	16	Pretty Woman	*Soundtrack*...EMI 93492
6	5	16	Poison	*Bell Biv DeVoe*...MCA 6387
7	12	4	I'll Give All My Love To You	*Keith Sweat*...Vintertainment 60861
8	7	16	I Do Not Want What I Haven't Got	*Sinéad O'Connor*...Ensign 21759
9	9	12	Johnny Gill	*Johnny Gill*...Motown 6283
10	8	16	Violator	*Depeche Mode*...Sire 26081

Billboard. JULY 28, 1990 — TOP POP ALBUMS

TW	LW	WK	Title	Artist...Label
1	1	21	**Please Hammer Don't Hurt 'Em**	*M.C. Hammer*...Capitol 92857
2	2	8	**I'm Breathless**	*Madonna/Soundtrack*...Sire 26209
3	3	6	Step By Step	*New Kids On The Block*...Columbia 45129
4	4	16	Wilson Phillips	*Wilson Phillips*...SBK 93745
5	5	17	Pretty Woman	*Soundtrack*...EMI 93492
6	6	17	Poison	*Bell Biv DeVoe*...MCA 6387
7	7	5	I'll Give All My Love To You	*Keith Sweat*...Vintertainment 60861
8	9	13	**Johnny Gill**	*Johnny Gill*...Motown 6283
9	10	17	Violator	*Depeche Mode*...Sire 26081
10	8	17	I Do Not Want What I Haven't Got	*Sinéad O'Connor*...Ensign 21759

Billboard. AUGUST 4, 1990 — TOP POP ALBUMS

TW	LW	WK	Title	Artist...Label
1	1	22	**Please Hammer Don't Hurt 'Em**	*M.C. Hammer*...Capitol 92857
2	4	17	**Wilson Phillips**	*Wilson Phillips*...SBK 93745
3	3	7	Step By Step	*New Kids On The Block*...Columbia 45129
4	2	9	I'm Breathless	*Madonna/Soundtrack*...Sire 26209
5	5	18	Pretty Woman	*Soundtrack*...EMI 93492
6	7	6	**I'll Give All My Love To You**	*Keith Sweat*...Vintertainment 60861
7	6	18	Poison	*Bell Biv DeVoe*...MCA 6387
8	8	14	**Johnny Gill**	*Johnny Gill*...Motown 6283
9	12	3	Compositions	*Anita Baker*...Elektra 60922
10	13	6	Mariah Carey	*Mariah Carey*...Columbia 45202

Billboard. AUGUST 11, 1990 — TOP POP ALBUMS

TW	LW	WK	Title	Artist...Label
1	1	23	**Please Hammer Don't Hurt 'Em**	*M.C. Hammer*...Capitol 92857
2	2	18	**Wilson Phillips**	*Wilson Phillips*...SBK 93745
3	12	3	Flesh & Blood	*Poison*...Capitol 918132
4	3	8	Step By Step	*New Kids On The Block*...Columbia 45129
5	4	10	I'm Breathless	*Madonna/Soundtrack*...Sire 26209
6	10	7	Mariah Carey	*Mariah Carey*...Columbia 45202
7	6	7	I'll Give All My Love To You	*Keith Sweat*...Vintertainment 60861
8	5	19	Pretty Woman	*Soundtrack*...EMI 93492
9	9	4	Compositions	*Anita Baker*...Elektra 60922
10	7	19	Poison	*Bell Biv DeVoe*...MCA 6387

TW	LW	WK	Billboard® AUGUST 18, 1990 TOP POP ALBUMS	
1	1	24	**Please Hammer Don't Hurt 'Em**	*M.C. Hammer*...Capitol 92857
2	3	4	**Flesh & Blood**	*Poison*...Capitol 918132
3	2	19	Wilson Phillips	*Wilson Phillips*...SBK 93745
4	6	8	Mariah Carey	*Mariah Carey*...Columbia 45202
5	4	9	Step By Step	*New Kids On The Block*...Columbia 45129
6	9	5	Compositions	*Anita Baker*...Elektra 60922
7	7	8	I'll Give All My Love To You	*Keith Sweat*...Vintertainment 60861
8	5	11	I'm Breathless	*Madonna/Soundtrack*...Sire 26209
9	10	20	Poison	*Bell Biv DeVoe*...MCA 6387
10	8	20	Pretty Woman	*Soundtrack*...EMI 93492

TW	LW	WK	Billboard® AUGUST 25, 1990 TOP POP ALBUMS	
1	1	25	**Please Hammer Don't Hurt 'Em**	*M.C. Hammer*...Capitol 92857
2	3	20	**Wilson Phillips**	*Wilson Phillips*...SBK 93745
3	2	5	Flesh & Blood	*Poison*...Capitol 918132
4	4	9	Mariah Carey	*Mariah Carey*...Columbia 45202
5	6	6	**Compositions**	*Anita Baker*...Elektra 60922
6	5	10	Step By Step	*New Kids On The Block*...Columbia 45129
7	9	21	Poison	*Bell Biv DeVoe*...MCA 6387
8	7	9	I'll Give All My Love To You	*Keith Sweat*...Vintertainment 60861
9	8	12	I'm Breathless	*Madonna/Soundtrack*...Sire 26209
10	10	21	Pretty Woman	*Soundtrack*...EMI 93492

TW	LW	WK	Billboard® SEPTEMBER 1, 1990 TOP POP ALBUMS	
1	1	26	**Please Hammer Don't Hurt 'Em**	*M.C. Hammer*...Capitol 92857
2	2	21	**Wilson Phillips**	*Wilson Phillips*...SBK 93745
3	3	6	Flesh & Blood	*Poison*...Capitol 918132
4	4	10	Mariah Carey	*Mariah Carey*...Columbia 45202
5	5	7	**Compositions**	*Anita Baker*...Elektra 60922
6	7	22	Poison	*Bell Biv DeVoe*...MCA 6387
7	32	2	Blaze Of Glory/Young Guns II	*Jon Bon Jovi*...Mercury 846473
8	6	11	Step By Step	*New Kids On The Block*...Columbia 45129
9	8	10	I'll Give All My Love To You	*Keith Sweat*...Vintertainment 60861
10	10	22	Pretty Woman	*Soundtrack*...EMI 93492

TW	LW	WK	Billboard® SEPTEMBER 8, 1990 TOP POP ALBUMS	
1	1	27	**Please Hammer Don't Hurt 'Em**	*M.C. Hammer*...Capitol 92857
2	2	22	**Wilson Phillips**	*Wilson Phillips*...SBK 93745
3	7	3	**Blaze Of Glory/Young Guns II**	*Jon Bon Jovi*...Mercury 846473
4	4	11	Mariah Carey	*Mariah Carey*...Columbia 45202
5	3	7	Flesh & Blood	*Poison*...Capitol 918132
6	6	23	Poison	*Bell Biv DeVoe*...MCA 6387
7	5	8	Compositions	*Anita Baker*...Elektra 60922
8	9	11	I'll Give All My Love To You	*Keith Sweat*...Vintertainment 60861
9	8	12	Step By Step	*New Kids On The Block*...Columbia 45129
10	10	23	Pretty Woman	*Soundtrack*...EMI 93492

TW	LW	WK	Billboard. SEPTEMBER 15, 1990 TOP POP ALBUMS
①	1	28	**Please Hammer Don't Hurt 'Em** .... *M.C. Hammer*...Capitol 92857
②	2	23	**Wilson Phillips** .... *Wilson Phillips*...SBK 93745
❸	3	4	**Blaze Of Glory/Young Guns II** .... *Jon Bon Jovi*...Mercury 846473
④	4	12	Mariah Carey .... *Mariah Carey*...Columbia 45202
⑤	5	8	Flesh & Blood .... *Poison*...Capitol 918132
⑥	6	24	Poison .... *Bell Biv DeVoe*...MCA 6387
⑦	7	9	Compositions .... *Anita Baker*...Elektra 60922
⑧	8	12	I'll Give All My Love To You .... *Keith Sweat*...Vintertainment 60861
⑨	9	13	Step By Step .... *New Kids On The Block*...Columbia 45129
❿	21	2	Graffiti Bridge .... *Prince/Soundtrack*...Paisley Park 27493

TW	LW	WK	Billboard. SEPTEMBER 22, 1990 TOP POP ALBUMS
①	1	29	**Please Hammer Don't Hurt 'Em** .... *M.C. Hammer*...Capitol 92857
②	2	24	**Wilson Phillips** .... *Wilson Phillips*...SBK 93745
③	3	5	**Blaze Of Glory/Young Guns II** .... *Jon Bon Jovi*...Mercury 846473
④	4	13	Mariah Carey .... *Mariah Carey*...Columbia 45202
⑤	6	25	**Poison** .... *Bell Biv DeVoe*...MCA 6387
❻	10	3	**Graffiti Bridge** .... *Prince/Soundtrack*...Paisley Park 27493
⑦	5	9	Flesh & Blood .... *Poison*...Capitol 918132
⑧	7	10	Compositions .... *Anita Baker*...Elektra 60922
⑨	8	13	I'll Give All My Love To You .... *Keith Sweat*...Vintertainment 60861
⑩	11	62	Soul Provider .... *Michael Bolton*...Columbia 45012

TW	LW	WK	Billboard. SEPTEMBER 29, 1990 TOP POP ALBUMS
①	1	30	**Please Hammer Don't Hurt 'Em** .... *M.C. Hammer*...Capitol 92857
②	2	25	**Wilson Phillips** .... *Wilson Phillips*...SBK 93745
③	4	14	Mariah Carey .... *Mariah Carey*...Columbia 45202
④	3	6	Blaze Of Glory/Young Guns II .... *Jon Bon Jovi*...Mercury 846473
⑤	5	26	**Poison** .... *Bell Biv DeVoe*...MCA 6387
⑥	6	4	**Graffiti Bridge** .... *Prince/Soundtrack*...Paisley Park 27493
⑦	7	10	Flesh & Blood .... *Poison*...Capitol 918132
⑧	10	63	Soul Provider .... *Michael Bolton*...Columbia 45012
⑨	8	11	Compositions .... *Anita Baker*...Elektra 60922
❿	35	2	Empire .... *Queensryche*...EMI 92806

TW	LW	WK	Billboard. OCTOBER 6, 1990 TOP POP ALBUMS
①	1	31	**Please Hammer Don't Hurt 'Em** .... *M.C. Hammer*...Capitol 92857
②	2	26	**Wilson Phillips** .... *Wilson Phillips*...SBK 93745
③	3	15	Mariah Carey .... *Mariah Carey*...Columbia 45202
④	4	7	Blaze Of Glory/Young Guns II .... *Jon Bon Jovi*...Mercury 846473
❺	22	2	Listen Without Prejudice .... *George Michael*...Columbia 46898
⑥	5	27	Poison .... *Bell Biv DeVoe*...MCA 6387
❼	10	3	**Empire** .... *Queensryche*...EMI 92806
⑧	6	5	Graffiti Bridge .... *Prince/Soundtrack*...Paisley Park 27493
❾	15	6	Ghost .... *Soundtrack*...Varese Sarabande 5276
⑩	7	11	Flesh & Blood .... *Poison*...Capitol 918132

TW	LW	WK	Billboard® OCTOBER 13, 1990 TOP POP ALBUMS	
1	1	32	**Please Hammer Don't Hurt 'Em**	*M.C. Hammer*...Capitol 92857
2	2	27	**Wilson Phillips**	*Wilson Phillips*...SBK 93745
3	3	16	Mariah Carey	*Mariah Carey*...Columbia 45202
4	5	3	Listen Without Prejudice	*George Michael*...Columbia 46898
5	6	28	**Poison**	*Bell Biv DeVoe*...MCA 6387
6	4	8	Blaze Of Glory/Young Guns II	*Jon Bon Jovi*...Mercury 846473
7	14	3	**Cherry Pie**	*Warrant*...Columbia 45487
8	9	7	**Ghost**	*Soundtrack*...Varese Sarabande 5276
9	7	4	Empire	*Queensryche*...EMI 92806
10	10	12	Flesh & Blood	*Poison*...Capitol 918132

TW	LW	WK	Billboard® OCTOBER 20, 1990 TOP POP ALBUMS	
1	1	33	**Please Hammer Don't Hurt 'Em**	*M.C. Hammer*...Capitol 92857
2	4	4	**Listen Without Prejudice**	*George Michael*...Columbia 46898
3	3	17	Mariah Carey	*Mariah Carey*...Columbia 45202
4	2	28	Wilson Phillips	*Wilson Phillips*...SBK 93745
5	13	3	X	*INXS*...Atlantic 82140
6	19	3	The Razors Edge	*AC/DC*...Atco 91413
7	23	5	To The Extreme	*Vanilla Ice*...SBK 95325
8	5	29	Poison	*Bell Biv DeVoe*...MCA 6387
9	7	4	Cherry Pie	*Warrant*...Columbia 45487
10	9	5	Empire	*Queensryche*...EMI 92806

TW	LW	WK	Billboard® OCTOBER 27, 1990 TOP POP ALBUMS	
1	1	34	**Please Hammer Don't Hurt 'Em**	*M.C. Hammer*...Capitol 92857
2	6	4	**The Razors Edge**	*AC/DC*...Atco 91413
3	2	5	Listen Without Prejudice	*George Michael*...Columbia 46898
4	3	18	Mariah Carey	*Mariah Carey*...Columbia 45202
5	7	6	To The Extreme	*Vanilla Ice*...SBK 95325
6	5	4	X	*INXS*...Atlantic 82140
7	4	29	Wilson Phillips	*Wilson Phillips*...SBK 93745
8	14	3	Family Style	*The Vaughan Brothers*...Epic/Associated 46225
9	8	30	Poison	*Bell Biv DeVoe*...MCA 6387
10	9	5	Cherry Pie	*Warrant*...Columbia 45487

TW	LW	WK	Billboard® NOVEMBER 3, 1990 TOP POP ALBUMS	
1	1	35	**Please Hammer Don't Hurt 'Em**	*M.C. Hammer*...Capitol 92857
2	5	7	To The Extreme	*Vanilla Ice*...SBK 95325
3	2	5	The Razors Edge	*AC/DC*...Atco 91413
4	4	19	Mariah Carey	*Mariah Carey*...Columbia 45202
5	3	6	Listen Without Prejudice	*George Michael*...Columbia 46898
6	6	5	X	*INXS*...Atlantic 82140
7	7	30	Wilson Phillips	*Wilson Phillips*...SBK 93745
8	8	4	Family Style	*The Vaughan Brothers*...Epic/Associated 46225
9	10	6	Cherry Pie	*Warrant*...Columbia 45487
10	9	31	Poison	*Bell Biv DeVoe*...MCA 6387

TW	LW	WK	Billboard. NOVEMBER 10, 1990 TOP POP ALBUMS
1	2	8	**To The Extreme**........ *Vanilla Ice*...SBK 95325
2	1	36	Please Hammer Don't Hurt 'Em........ *M.C. Hammer*...Capitol 92857
3	3	6	The Razors Edge........ *AC/DC*...Atco 91413
4	4	20	Mariah Carey........ *Mariah Carey*...Columbia 45202
5	7	31	Wilson Phillips........ *Wilson Phillips*...SBK 93745
6	6	6	X........ *INXS*...Atlantic 82140
7	8	5	**Family Style**........ *The Vaughan Brothers*...Epic/Associated 46225
8	5	7	Listen Without Prejudice........ *George Michael*...Columbia 46898
9	33	2	Recycler........ *ZZ Top*...Warner 26265
10	10	32	Poison........ *Bell Biv DeVoe*...MCA 6387

TW	LW	WK	Billboard. NOVEMBER 17, 1990 TOP POP ALBUMS
1	1	9	**To The Extreme**........ *Vanilla Ice*...SBK 95325
2	2	37	Please Hammer Don't Hurt 'Em........ *M.C. Hammer*...Capitol 92857
3	4	21	Mariah Carey........ *Mariah Carey*...Columbia 45202
4	3	7	The Razors Edge........ *AC/DC*...Atco 91413
5	11	3	The Rhythm Of The Saints........ *Paul Simon*...Warner 26098
6	9	3	**Recycler**........ *ZZ Top*...Warner 26265
7	5	32	Wilson Phillips........ *Wilson Phillips*...SBK 93745
8	6	7	X........ *INXS*...Atlantic 82140
9	7	6	Family Style........ *The Vaughan Brothers*...Epic/Associated 46225
10	8	8	Listen Without Prejudice........ *George Michael*...Columbia 46898

TW	LW	WK	Billboard. NOVEMBER 24, 1990 TOP POP ALBUMS
1	1	10	**To The Extreme**........ *Vanilla Ice*...SBK 95325
2	2	38	Please Hammer Don't Hurt 'Em........ *M.C. Hammer*...Capitol 92857
3	3	22	Mariah Carey........ *Mariah Carey*...Columbia 45202
4	5	4	**The Rhythm Of The Saints**........ *Paul Simon*...Warner 26098
5	4	8	The Razors Edge........ *AC/DC*...Atco 91413
6	6	4	**Recycler**........ *ZZ Top*...Warner 26265
7	7	33	Wilson Phillips........ *Wilson Phillips*...SBK 93745
8	12	7	Some People's Lives........ *Bette Midler*...Atlantic 82129
9	10	9	Listen Without Prejudice........ *George Michael*...Columbia 46898
10	8	8	X........ *INXS*...Atlantic 82140

TW	LW	WK	Billboard. DECEMBER 1, 1990 TOP POP ALBUMS
1	1	11	**To The Extreme**........ *Vanilla Ice*...SBK 95325
2	2	39	Please Hammer Don't Hurt 'Em........ *M.C. Hammer*...Capitol 92857
3	3	23	Mariah Carey........ *Mariah Carey*...Columbia 45202
4	4	5	**The Rhythm Of The Saints**........ *Paul Simon*...Warner 26098
5	22	2	I'm Your Baby Tonight........ *Whitney Houston*...Arista 8616
6	6	5	**Recycler**........ *ZZ Top*...Warner 26265
7	5	9	The Razors Edge........ *AC/DC*...Atco 91413
8	7	34	Wilson Phillips........ *Wilson Phillips*...SBK 93745
9	8	8	Some People's Lives........ *Bette Midler*...Atlantic 82129
10	9	10	Listen Without Prejudice........ *George Michael*...Columbia 46898

Billboard® DECEMBER 8, 1990 TOP POP ALBUMS

TW	LW	WK	Title	Artist	Label
1	1	12	**To The Extreme**	*Vanilla Ice*	SBK 95325
2	2	40	Please Hammer Don't Hurt 'Em	*M.C. Hammer*	Capitol 92857
3	5	3	**I'm Your Baby Tonight**	*Whitney Houston*	Arista 8616
4	3	24	Mariah Carey	*Mariah Carey*	Columbia 45202
5	4	6	The Rhythm Of The Saints	*Paul Simon*	Warner 26098
6	6	6	**Recycler**	*ZZ Top*	Warner 26265
7	7	10	The Razors Edge	*AC/DC*	Atco 91413
8	8	35	Wilson Phillips	*Wilson Phillips*	SBK 93745
9	9	9	Some People's Lives	*Bette Midler*	Atlantic 82129
10	10	11	Listen Without Prejudice	*George Michael*	Columbia 46898

Billboard® DECEMBER 15, 1990 TOP POP ALBUMS

TW	LW	WK	Title	Artist	Label
1	1	13	**To The Extreme**	*Vanilla Ice*	SBK 95325
2	2	41	Please Hammer Don't Hurt 'Em	*M.C. Hammer*	Capitol 92857
3	4	25	Mariah Carey	*Mariah Carey*	Columbia 45202
4	3	4	I'm Your Baby Tonight	*Whitney Houston*	Arista 8616
5	12	3	The Immaculate Collection	*Madonna*	Sire 26440
6	5	7	The Rhythm Of The Saints	*Paul Simon*	Warner 26098
7	9	10	Some People's Lives	*Bette Midler*	Atlantic 82129
8	8	36	Wilson Phillips	*Wilson Phillips*	SBK 93745
9	7	11	The Razors Edge	*AC/DC*	Atco 91413
10	10	12	Listen Without Prejudice	*George Michael*	Columbia 46898

Billboard® DECEMBER 22, 1990 TOP POP ALBUMS

TW	LW	WK	Title	Artist	Label
1	1	14	**To The Extreme**	*Vanilla Ice*	SBK 95325
2	2	42	Please Hammer Don't Hurt 'Em	*M.C. Hammer*	Capitol 92857
3	5	4	The Immaculate Collection	*Madonna*	Sire 26440
4	4	5	I'm Your Baby Tonight	*Whitney Houston*	Arista 8616
5	3	26	Mariah Carey	*Mariah Carey*	Columbia 45202
6	6	8	The Rhythm Of The Saints	*Paul Simon*	Warner 26098
7	7	11	Some People's Lives	*Bette Midler*	Atlantic 82129
8	8	37	Wilson Phillips	*Wilson Phillips*	SBK 93745
9	9	12	The Razors Edge	*AC/DC*	Atco 91413
10	10	13	Listen Without Prejudice	*George Michael*	Columbia 46898

Billboard — JANUARY 5, 1991 — TOP POP ALBUMS

TW	LW	WK	Title	Artist	Label
1	1	16	**To The Extreme**	*Vanilla Ice*	SBK 95325
2	2	44	Please Hammer Don't Hurt 'Em	*M.C. Hammer*	Capitol 92857
3	3	6	The Immaculate Collection	*Madonna*	Sire 26440
4	4	7	I'm Your Baby Tonight	*Whitney Houston*	Arista 8616
5	5	28	Mariah Carey	*Mariah Carey*	Columbia 45202
6	7	13	**Some People's Lives**	*Bette Midler*	Atlantic 82129
7	6	10	The Rhythm Of The Saints	*Paul Simon*	Warner 26098
8	8	39	Wilson Phillips	*Wilson Phillips*	SBK 93745
9	9	14	The Razors Edge	*AC/DC*	Atco 91413
10	42	3	The Simpsons Sing The Blues	*The Simpsons*	Geffen 24308

Billboard — JANUARY 12, 1991 — TOP POP ALBUMS

TW	LW	WK	Title	Artist	Label
1	1	17	**To The Extreme**	*Vanilla Ice*	SBK 95325
2	2	45	Please Hammer Don't Hurt 'Em	*M.C. Hammer*	Capitol 92857
3	3	7	The Immaculate Collection	*Madonna*	Sire 26440
4	5	29	Mariah Carey	*Mariah Carey*	Columbia 45202
5	4	8	I'm Your Baby Tonight	*Whitney Houston*	Arista 8616
6	6	14	**Some People's Lives**	*Bette Midler*	Atlantic 82129
7	10	4	The Simpsons Sing The Blues	*The Simpsons*	Geffen 24308
8	8	40	Wilson Phillips	*Wilson Phillips*	SBK 93745
9	7	11	The Rhythm Of The Saints	*Paul Simon*	Warner 26098
10	9	15	The Razors Edge	*AC/DC*	Atco 91413

Billboard — JANUARY 19, 1991 — TOP POP ALBUMS

TW	LW	WK	Title	Artist	Label
1	1	18	**To The Extreme**	*Vanilla Ice*	SBK 95325
2	2	46	Please Hammer Don't Hurt 'Em	*M.C. Hammer*	Capitol 92857
3	3	8	The Immaculate Collection	*Madonna*	Sire 26440
4	7	5	The Simpsons Sing The Blues	*The Simpsons*	Geffen 24308
5	4	30	Mariah Carey	*Mariah Carey*	Columbia 45202
6	5	9	I'm Your Baby Tonight	*Whitney Houston*	Arista 8616
7	8	41	Wilson Phillips	*Wilson Phillips*	SBK 93745
8	6	15	Some People's Lives	*Bette Midler*	Atlantic 82129
9	10	16	The Razors Edge	*AC/DC*	Atco 91413
10	9	12	The Rhythm Of The Saints	*Paul Simon*	Warner 26098

Billboard — JANUARY 26, 1991 — TOP POP ALBUMS

TW	LW	WK	Title	Artist	Label
1	1	19	**To The Extreme**	*Vanilla Ice*	SBK 95325
2	3	9	**The Immaculate Collection**	*Madonna*	Sire 26440
3	4	6	**The Simpsons Sing The Blues**	*The Simpsons*	Geffen 24308
4	2	47	Please Hammer Don't Hurt 'Em	*M.C. Hammer*	Capitol 92857
5	5	31	Mariah Carey	*Mariah Carey*	Columbia 45202
6	6	10	I'm Your Baby Tonight	*Whitney Houston*	Arista 8616
7	7	42	Wilson Phillips	*Wilson Phillips*	SBK 93745
8	9	17	The Razors Edge	*AC/DC*	Atco 91413
9	8	16	Some People's Lives	*Bette Midler*	Atlantic 82129
10	10	13	The Rhythm Of The Saints	*Paul Simon*	Warner 26098

TW	LW	WK	Billboard® FEBRUARY 2, 1991	TOP POP ALBUMS
①	1	20	**To The Extreme**	*Vanilla Ice*...SBK 95325
②	2	10	**The Immaculate Collection**	*Madonna*...Sire 26440
❸	5	32	Mariah Carey	*Mariah Carey*...Columbia 45202
④	3	7	The Simpsons Sing The Blues	*The Simpsons*...Geffen 24308
⑤	4	48	Please Hammer Don't Hurt 'Em	*M.C. Hammer*...Capitol 92857
⑥	6	11	I'm Your Baby Tonight	*Whitney Houston*...Arista 8616
⑦	8	18	The Razors Edge	*AC/DC*...Atco 91413
⑧	7	43	Wilson Phillips	*Wilson Phillips*...SBK 93745
⑨	9	17	Some People's Lives	*Bette Midler*...Atlantic 82129
⑩	10	14	The Rhythm Of The Saints	*Paul Simon*...Warner 26098

TW	LW	WK	Billboard® FEBRUARY 9, 1991	TOP POP ALBUMS
①	1	21	**To The Extreme**	*Vanilla Ice*...SBK 95325
❷	3	33	Mariah Carey	*Mariah Carey*...Columbia 45202
③	2	11	The Immaculate Collection	*Madonna*...Sire 26440
④	4	8	The Simpsons Sing The Blues	*The Simpsons*...Geffen 24308
⑤	5	49	Please Hammer Don't Hurt 'Em	*M.C. Hammer*...Capitol 92857
⑥	6	12	I'm Your Baby Tonight	*Whitney Houston*...Arista 8616
⑦	9	18	Some People's Lives	*Bette Midler*...Atlantic 82129
⑧	7	19	The Razors Edge	*AC/DC*...Atco 91413
⑨	8	44	Wilson Phillips	*Wilson Phillips*...SBK 93745
⑩	10	15	The Rhythm Of The Saints	*Paul Simon*...Warner 26098

TW	LW	WK	Billboard® FEBRUARY 16, 1991	TOP POP ALBUMS
❶	1	22	**To The Extreme**	*Vanilla Ice*...SBK 95325
❷	2	34	Mariah Carey	*Mariah Carey*...Columbia 45202
③	3	12	The Immaculate Collection	*Madonna*...Sire 26440
④	4	9	The Simpsons Sing The Blues	*The Simpsons*...Geffen 24308
❺	5	50	Please Hammer Don't Hurt 'Em	*M.C. Hammer*...Capitol 92857
⑥	6	13	I'm Your Baby Tonight	*Whitney Houston*...Arista 8616
❼	9	45	Wilson Phillips	*Wilson Phillips*...SBK 93745
⑧	7	19	Some People's Lives	*Bette Midler*...Atlantic 82129
⑨	8	20	The Razors Edge	*AC/DC*...Atco 91413
❿	30	2	The Soul Cages	*Sting*...A&M 6405

TW	LW	WK	Billboard® FEBRUARY 23, 1991	TOP POP ALBUMS
❶	1	23	**To The Extreme**	*Vanilla Ice*...SBK 95325
❷	2	35	Mariah Carey	*Mariah Carey*...Columbia 45202
❸	10	3	The Soul Cages	*Sting*...A&M 6405
④	5	51	Please Hammer Don't Hurt 'Em	*M.C. Hammer*...Capitol 92857
⑤	6	14	I'm Your Baby Tonight	*Whitney Houston*...Arista 8616
⑥	4	10	The Simpsons Sing The Blues	*The Simpsons*...Geffen 24308
⑦	3	13	The Immaculate Collection	*Madonna*...Sire 26440
⑧	7	46	Wilson Phillips	*Wilson Phillips*...SBK 93745
⑨	9	21	The Razors Edge	*AC/DC*...Atco 91413
⑩	8	20	Some People's Lives	*Bette Midler*...Atlantic 82129

Billboard® MARCH 2, 1991 — TOP POP ALBUMS

TW	LW	WK	Album	Artist...Label
1	2	36	**Mariah Carey**	*Mariah Carey*...Columbia 45202
2	1	24	To The Extreme	*Vanilla Ice*...SBK 95325
3	3	4	The Soul Cages	*Sting*...A&M 6405
4	4	52	Please Hammer Don't Hurt 'Em	*M.C. Hammer*...Capitol 92857
5	5	15	I'm Your Baby Tonight	*Whitney Houston*...Arista 8616
6	8	47	Wilson Phillips	*Wilson Phillips*...SBK 93745
7	12	3	Into The Light	*Gloria Estefan*...Epic 46988
8	6	11	The Simpsons Sing The Blues	*The Simpsons*...Geffen 24308
9	7	14	The Immaculate Collection	*Madonna*...Sire 26440
10	10	21	Some People's Lives	*Bette Midler*...Atlantic 82129

Billboard® MARCH 9, 1991 — TOP POP ALBUMS

TW	LW	WK	Album	Artist...Label
1	1	37	**Mariah Carey**	*Mariah Carey*...Columbia 45202
2	2	25	To The Extreme	*Vanilla Ice*...SBK 95325
3	3	5	The Soul Cages	*Sting*...A&M 6405
4	5	16	I'm Your Baby Tonight	*Whitney Houston*...Arista 8616
5	7	4	**Into The Light**	*Gloria Estefan*...Epic 46988
6	6	48	Wilson Phillips	*Wilson Phillips*...SBK 93745
7	4	53	Please Hammer Don't Hurt 'Em	*M.C. Hammer*...Capitol 92857
8	12	51	Shake Your Money Maker	*The Black Crowes*...Def American 24278
9	10	22	Some People's Lives	*Bette Midler*...Atlantic 82129
10	9	15	The Immaculate Collection	*Madonna*...Sire 26440

Billboard® MARCH 16, 1991 — TOP POP ALBUMS

TW	LW	WK	Album	Artist...Label
1	1	38	**Mariah Carey**	*Mariah Carey*...Columbia 45202
2	2	26	To The Extreme	*Vanilla Ice*...SBK 95325
3	3	6	The Soul Cages	*Sting*...A&M 6405
4	6	49	Wilson Phillips	*Wilson Phillips*...SBK 93745
5	4	17	I'm Your Baby Tonight	*Whitney Houston*...Arista 8616
6	7	54	Please Hammer Don't Hurt 'Em	*M.C. Hammer*...Capitol 92857
7	9	23	Some People's Lives	*Bette Midler*...Atlantic 82129
8	5	5	Into The Light	*Gloria Estefan*...Epic 46988
9	8	52	Shake Your Money Maker	*The Black Crowes*...Def American 24278
10	11	10	Gonna Make You Sweat	*C & C Music Factory*...Columbia 47093

Billboard® MARCH 23, 1991 — TOP POP ALBUMS

TW	LW	WK	Album	Artist...Label
1	1	39	**Mariah Carey**	*Mariah Carey*...Columbia 45202
2	3	7	**The Soul Cages**	*Sting*...A&M 6405
3	4	50	Wilson Phillips	*Wilson Phillips*...SBK 93745
4	2	27	To The Extreme	*Vanilla Ice*...SBK 95325
5	10	11	Gonna Make You Sweat	*C & C Music Factory*...Columbia 47093
6	9	53	Shake Your Money Maker	*The Black Crowes*...Def American 24278
7	5	18	I'm Your Baby Tonight	*Whitney Houston*...Arista 8616
8	8	6	Into The Light	*Gloria Estefan*...Epic 46988
9	6	55	Please Hammer Don't Hurt 'Em	*M.C. Hammer*...Capitol 92857
10	7	24	Some People's Lives	*Bette Midler*...Atlantic 82129

Billboard® — MARCH 30, 1991 — TOP POP ALBUMS

TW	LW	WK	Title	Artist...Label
①	1	40	**Mariah Carey**	*Mariah Carey*...Columbia 45202
❷	5	12	**Gonna Make You Sweat**	*C & C Music Factory*...Columbia 47093
③	2	8	The Soul Cages	*Sting*...A&M 6405
④	3	51	Wilson Phillips	*Wilson Phillips*...SBK 93745
⑤	6	54	Shake Your Money Maker	*The Black Crowes*...Def American 24278
⑥	4	28	To The Extreme	*Vanilla Ice*...SBK 95325
⑦	8	7	Into The Light	*Gloria Estefan*...Epic 46988
⑧	11	23	Heart Shaped World	*Chris Isaak*...Reprise 25837
⑨	7	19	I'm Your Baby Tonight	*Whitney Houston*...Arista 8616
⑩	9	56	Please Hammer Don't Hurt 'Em	*M.C. Hammer*...Capitol 92857

Billboard® — APRIL 6, 1991 — TOP POP ALBUMS

TW	LW	WK	Title	Artist...Label
①	1	41	**Mariah Carey**	*Mariah Carey*...Columbia 45202
❷	2	13	**Gonna Make You Sweat**	*C & C Music Factory*...Columbia 47093
❸	4	52	Wilson Phillips	*Wilson Phillips*...SBK 93745
④	5	55	**Shake Your Money Maker**	*The Black Crowes*...Def American 24278
⑤	3	9	The Soul Cages	*Sting*...A&M 6405
⑥	6	29	To The Extreme	*Vanilla Ice*...SBK 95325
⑦	8	24	**Heart Shaped World**	*Chris Isaak*...Reprise 25837
⑧	7	8	Into The Light	*Gloria Estefan*...Epic 46988
⑨	9	20	I'm Your Baby Tonight	*Whitney Houston*...Arista 8616
⑩	10	57	Please Hammer Don't Hurt 'Em	*M.C. Hammer*...Capitol 92857

Billboard® — APRIL 13, 1991 — TOP POP ALBUMS

TW	LW	WK	Title	Artist...Label
①	1	42	**Mariah Carey**	*Mariah Carey*...Columbia 45202
②	2	14	**Gonna Make You Sweat**	*C & C Music Factory*...Columbia 47093
❸	3	53	Wilson Phillips	*Wilson Phillips*...SBK 93745
❹	4	56	**Shake Your Money Maker**	*The Black Crowes*...Def American 24278
❺	16	3	Out Of Time	*R.E.M.*...Warner 26496
⑥	5	10	The Soul Cages	*Sting*...A&M 6405
⑦	7	25	**Heart Shaped World**	*Chris Isaak*...Reprise 25837
❽	11	4	**The Doors**	*The Doors/Soundtrack*...Elektra 61047
⑨	6	30	To The Extreme	*Vanilla Ice*...SBK 95325
⑩	8	9	Into The Light	*Gloria Estefan*...Epic 46988

Billboard® — APRIL 20, 1991 — TOP POP ALBUMS

TW	LW	WK	Title	Artist...Label
①	1	43	**Mariah Carey**	*Mariah Carey*...Columbia 45202
②	2	15	**Gonna Make You Sweat**	*C & C Music Factory*...Columbia 47093
③	3	54	Wilson Phillips	*Wilson Phillips*...SBK 93745
❹	5	4	Out Of Time	*R.E.M.*...Warner 26496
⑤	4	57	Shake Your Money Maker	*The Black Crowes*...Def American 24278
❻	11	22	I'm Your Baby Tonight	*Whitney Houston*...Arista 8616
⑦	7	26	**Heart Shaped World**	*Chris Isaak*...Reprise 25837
⑧	8	5	**The Doors**	*The Doors/Soundtrack*...Elektra 61047
❾	12	8	MCMXC a.D.	*Enigma*...Charisma 91642
⑩	6	11	The Soul Cages	*Sting*...A&M 6405

Billboard — APRIL 27, 1991 — TOP POP ALBUMS

TW	LW	WK	Title	Artist	Label
1	1	44	**Mariah Carey**	*Mariah Carey*	Columbia 45202
2	2	16	**Gonna Make You Sweat**	*C & C Music Factory*	Columbia 47093
3	3	55	Wilson Phillips	*Wilson Phillips*	SBK 93745
4	4	5	Out Of Time	*R.E.M.*	Warner 26496
5	5	58	Shake Your Money Maker	*The Black Crowes*	Def American 24278
6	6	23	I'm Your Baby Tonight	*Whitney Houston*	Arista 8616
7	9	9	MCMXC a.D.	*Enigma*	Charisma 91642
8	7	27	Heart Shaped World	*Chris Isaak*	Reprise 25837
9	13	32	Empire	*Queensryche*	EMI 92806
10	8	6	The Doors	*The Doors/Soundtrack*	Elektra 61047

Billboard — MAY 4, 1991 — TOP POP ALBUMS

TW	LW	WK	Title	Artist	Label
1	1	45	**Mariah Carey**	*Mariah Carey*	Columbia 45202
2	2	17	**Gonna Make You Sweat**	*C & C Music Factory*	Columbia 47093
3	4	6	Out Of Time	*R.E.M.*	Warner 26496
4	3	56	Wilson Phillips	*Wilson Phillips*	SBK 93745
5	5	59	Shake Your Money Maker	*The Black Crowes*	Def American 24278
6	7	10	**MCMXC a.D.**	*Enigma*	Charisma 91642
7	8	28	**Heart Shaped World**	*Chris Isaak*	Reprise 25837
8	6	24	I'm Your Baby Tonight	*Whitney Houston*	Arista 8616
9	12	7	New Jack City	*Soundtrack*	Giant 24409
10	9	33	Empire	*Queensryche*	EMI 92806

Billboard — MAY 11, 1991 — TOP POP ALBUMS

TW	LW	WK	Title	Artist	Label
1	1	46	**Mariah Carey**	*Mariah Carey*	Columbia 45202
2	2	18	**Gonna Make You Sweat**	*C & C Music Factory*	Columbia 47093
3	3	7	Out Of Time	*R.E.M.*	Warner 26496
4	4	57	Wilson Phillips	*Wilson Phillips*	SBK 93745
5	5	60	Shake Your Money Maker	*The Black Crowes*	Def American 24278
6	6	11	**MCMXC a.D.**	*Enigma*	Charisma 91642
7	9	8	New Jack City	*Soundtrack*	Giant 24409
8	7	29	Heart Shaped World	*Chris Isaak*	Reprise 25837
9	10	34	Empire	*Queensryche*	EMI 92806
10	11	5	**Vagabond Heart**	*Rod Stewart*	Warner 26300

Billboard — MAY 18, 1991 — TOP POP ALBUMS

TW	LW	WK	Title	Artist	Label
1	3	8	**Out Of Time**	*R.E.M.*	Warner 26496
2	1	47	Mariah Carey	*Mariah Carey*	Columbia 45202
3	2	19	Gonna Make You Sweat	*C & C Music Factory*	Columbia 47093
4	4	58	Wilson Phillips	*Wilson Phillips*	SBK 93745
5	5	61	Shake Your Money Maker	*The Black Crowes*	Def American 24278
6	7	9	New Jack City	*Soundtrack*	Giant 24409
7	6	12	MCMXC a.D.	*Enigma*	Charisma 91642
8	38	2	Time, Love & Tenderness	*Michael Bolton*	Columbia 46771
9	11	11	Coolin' At The Playground Ya' Know!	*Another Bad Creation*	Motown 6318
10	10	6	**Vagabond Heart**	*Rod Stewart*	Warner 26300

TW	LW	WK	Billboard® MAY 25, 1991 TOP POP ALBUMS
1	8	3	**Time, Love & Tenderness** ...... *Michael Bolton*...Columbia 46771
2	6	10	**New Jack City** ...... *Soundtrack*...Giant 24409
3	2	48	Mariah Carey ...... *Mariah Carey*...Columbia 45202
4	16	36	No Fences ...... *Garth Brooks*...Capitol 93866
5	1	9	Out Of Time ...... *R.E.M.*...Warner 26496
6	3	20	Gonna Make You Sweat ...... *C & C Music Factory*...Columbia 47093
7	41	2	**Power Of Love** ...... *Luther Vandross*...Epic 46789
8	9	12	Coolin' At The Playground Ya' Know! ...... *Another Bad Creation*...Motown 6318
9	4	59	Wilson Phillips ...... *Wilson Phillips*...SBK 93745
10	10	7	**Vagabond Heart** ...... *Rod Stewart*...Warner 26300

TW	LW	WK	Billboard® JUNE 1, 1991 TOP POP ALBUMS
1	5	10	**Out Of Time** ...... *R.E.M.*...Warner 26496
2	1	4	Time, Love & Tenderness ...... *Michael Bolton*...Columbia 46771
3	3	49	Mariah Carey ...... *Mariah Carey*...Columbia 45202
4	2	11	New Jack City ...... *Soundtrack*...Giant 24409
5	-	1	Spellbound ...... *Paula Abdul*...Captive/Virgin 91611
6	4	37	No Fences ...... *Garth Brooks*...Capitol 93866
7	6	21	Gonna Make You Sweat ...... *C & C Music Factory*...Columbia 47093
8	8	13	Coolin' At The Playground Ya' Know! ...... *Another Bad Creation*...Motown 6318
9	11	63	Shake Your Money Maker ...... *The Black Crowes*...Def American 24278
10	9	60	Wilson Phillips ...... *Wilson Phillips*...SBK 93745

TW	LW	WK	Billboard® JUNE 8, 1991 TOP POP ALBUMS
1	5	2	**Spellbound** ...... *Paula Abdul*...Captive/Virgin 91611
2	2	5	Time, Love & Tenderness ...... *Michael Bolton*...Columbia 46771
3	1	11	Out Of Time ...... *R.E.M.*...Warner 26496
4	3	50	Mariah Carey ...... *Mariah Carey*...Columbia 45202
5	7	22	Gonna Make You Sweat ...... *C & C Music Factory*...Columbia 47093
6	4	12	New Jack City ...... *Soundtrack*...Giant 24409
7	6	38	No Fences ...... *Garth Brooks*...Capitol 93866
8	9	64	Shake Your Money Maker ...... *The Black Crowes*...Def American 24278
9	8	14	Coolin' At The Playground Ya' Know! ...... *Another Bad Creation*...Motown 6318
10	11	26	**Pornograffitti** ...... *Extreme*...A&M 5313

TW	LW	WK	Billboard® JUNE 15, 1991 TOP POP ALBUMS
1	1	3	**Spellbound** ...... *Paula Abdul*...Captive/Virgin 91611
2	-	1	EFIL4ZAGGIN ...... *N.W.A.*...Ruthless 57126
3	3	12	Out Of Time ...... *R.E.M.*...Warner 26496
4	2	6	Time, Love & Tenderness ...... *Michael Bolton*...Columbia 46771
5	5	23	Gonna Make You Sweat ...... *C & C Music Factory*...Columbia 47093
6	4	51	Mariah Carey ...... *Mariah Carey*...Columbia 45202
7	6	13	New Jack City ...... *Soundtrack*...Giant 24409
8	7	39	No Fences ...... *Garth Brooks*...Capitol 93866
9	9	15	Coolin' At The Playground Ya' Know! ...... *Another Bad Creation*...Motown 6318
10	10	27	**Pornograffitti** ...... *Extreme*...A&M 5313

TW	LW	WK	Billboard. JUNE 22, 1991 TOP POP ALBUMS
1	2	2	**EFIL4ZAGGIN** .... *N.W.A.*...Ruthless 57126
2	1	4	Spellbound........ *Paula Abdul*...Captive/Virgin 91611
3	3	13	Out Of Time........ *R.E.M.*...Warner 26496
4	5	24	Gonna Make You Sweat........ *C & C Music Factory*...Columbia 47093
5	4	7	Time, Love & Tenderness ....*Michael Bolton*...Columbia 46771
6	6	52	Mariah Carey .... *Mariah Carey*...Columbia 45202
7	9	16	**Coolin' At The Playground Ya' Know!** ....*Another Bad Creation*...Motown 6318
8	8	40	No Fences ....*Garth Brooks*...Capitol 93866
9	7	14	New Jack City........ *Soundtrack*...Giant 24409
10	11	66	Shake Your Money Maker .... *The Black Crowes*...Def American 24278

TW	LW	WK	Billboard. JUNE 29, 1991 TOP POP ALBUMS
1	-	1	**Slave To The Grind**........*Skid Row*...Atlantic 82278
2	2	5	Spellbound........ *Paula Abdul*...Captive/Virgin 91611
3	1	3	EFIL4ZAGGIN........ *N.W.A.*...Ruthless 57126
4	8	41	No Fences ....*Garth Brooks*...Capitol 93866
5	4	25	Gonna Make You Sweat........ *C & C Music Factory*...Columbia 47093
6	3	14	Out Of Time........ *R.E.M.*...Warner 26496
7	5	8	Time, Love & Tenderness ....*Michael Bolton*...Columbia 46771
8	6	53	Mariah Carey .... *Mariah Carey*...Columbia 45202
9	10	67	Shake Your Money Maker .... *The Black Crowes*...Def American 24278
10	7	17	Coolin' At The Playground Ya' Know!..... *Another Bad Creation*...Motown 6318

TW	LW	WK	Billboard. JULY 6, 1991 TOP POP ALBUMS
1	-	1	**For Unlawful Carnal Knowledge**........ *Van Halen*...Warner 26594
2	1	2	Slave To The Grind ....*Skid Row*...Atlantic 82278
3	2	6	Spellbound........ *Paula Abdul*...Captive/Virgin 91611
4	4	42	No Fences ....*Garth Brooks*...Capitol 93866
5	5	26	Gonna Make You Sweat........ *C & C Music Factory*...Columbia 47093
6	3	4	EFIL4ZAGGIN........ *N.W.A.*...Ruthless 57126
7	6	15	Out Of Time........ *R.E.M.*...Warner 26496
8	8	54	Mariah Carey .... *Mariah Carey*...Columbia 45202
9	9	68	Shake Your Money Maker .... *The Black Crowes*...Def American 24278
10	7	9	Time, Love & Tenderness ....*Michael Bolton*...Columbia 46771

TW	LW	WK	Billboard. JULY 13, 1991 TOP POP ALBUMS
1	1	2	**For Unlawful Carnal Knowledge**........ *Van Halen*...Warner 26594
2	2	3	Slave To The Grind ....*Skid Row*...Atlantic 82278
3	3	7	Spellbound........ *Paula Abdul*...Captive/Virgin 91611
4	11	3	Unforgettable With Love .... *Natalie Cole*...Elektra 61049
5	5	27	Gonna Make You Sweat........ *C & C Music Factory*...Columbia 47093
6	7	16	Out Of Time........ *R.E.M.*...Warner 26496
7	6	5	EFIL4ZAGGIN........ *N.W.A.*...Ruthless 57126
8	4	43	No Fences ....*Garth Brooks*...Capitol 93866
9	-	1	Luck Of The Draw .... *Bonnie Raitt*...Capitol 96111
10	9	69	Shake Your Money Maker .... *The Black Crowes*...Def American 24278

TW	LW	WK	Billboard. JULY 20, 1991 TOP POP ALBUMS
1	1	3	**For Unlawful Carnal Knowledge** .... *Van Halen*...Warner 26594
2	4	4	Unforgettable With Love.......................................*Natalie Cole*...Elektra 61049
3	2	4	Slave To The Grind.. *Skid Row*...Atlantic 82278
4	3	8	Spellbound .... *Paula Abdul*...Captive/Virgin 91611
5	5	28	Gonna Make You Sweat .... *C & C Music Factory*...Columbia 47093
6	9	2	Luck Of The Draw...*Bonnie Raitt*...Capitol 96111
7	-	1	Robin Hood: Prince Of Thieves..................... *Soundtrack*...Morgan Creek 20004
8	6	17	Out Of Time .... *R.E.M.*...Warner 26496
9	7	6	EFIL4ZAGGIN .... *N.W.A.*...Ruthless 57126
10	8	44	No Fences .... *Garth Brooks*...Capitol 93866

TW	LW	WK	Billboard. JULY 27, 1991 TOP POP ALBUMS
1	2	5	**Unforgettable With Love** ....*Natalie Cole*...Elektra 61049
2	1	4	For Unlawful Carnal Knowledge............................ *Van Halen*...Warner 26594
3	4	9	Spellbound .... *Paula Abdul*...Captive/Virgin 91611
4	5	29	Gonna Make You Sweat .... *C & C Music Factory*...Columbia 47093
5	3	5	Slave To The Grind.. *Skid Row*...Atlantic 82278
6	7	2	Robin Hood: Prince Of Thieves..................... *Soundtrack*...Morgan Creek 20004
7	8	18	Out Of Time .... *R.E.M.*...Warner 26496
8	10	45	No Fences .... *Garth Brooks*...Capitol 93866
9	6	3	Luck Of The Draw...*Bonnie Raitt*...Capitol 96111
10	9	7	EFIL4ZAGGIN .... *N.W.A.*...Ruthless 57126

TW	LW	WK	Billboard. AUGUST 3, 1991 TOP POP ALBUMS
1	1	6	**Unforgettable With Love** ....*Natalie Cole*...Elektra 61049
2	2	5	For Unlawful Carnal Knowledge............................ *Van Halen*...Warner 26594
3	3	10	Spellbound .... *Paula Abdul*...Captive/Virgin 91611
4	4	30	Gonna Make You Sweat .... *C & C Music Factory*...Columbia 47093
5	6	3	**Robin Hood: Prince Of Thieves**............. *Soundtrack*...Morgan Creek 20004
6	9	4	Luck Of The Draw...*Bonnie Raitt*...Capitol 96111
7	5	6	Slave To The Grind.. *Skid Row*...Atlantic 82278
8	7	19	Out Of Time .... *R.E.M.*...Warner 26496
9	11	13	Time, Love & Tenderness............................ *Michael Bolton*...Columbia 46771
10	16	10	Cooleyhighharmony...*Boyz II Men*...Motown 6320

TW	LW	WK	Billboard. AUGUST 10, 1991 TOP POP ALBUMS
1	1	7	**Unforgettable With Love** ....*Natalie Cole*...Elektra 61049
2	2	6	For Unlawful Carnal Knowledge............................ *Van Halen*...Warner 26594
3	3	11	Spellbound .... *Paula Abdul*...Captive/Virgin 91611
4	4	31	Gonna Make You Sweat .... *C & C Music Factory*...Columbia 47093
5	6	5	Luck Of The Draw...*Bonnie Raitt*...Capitol 96111
6	8	20	Out Of Time .... *R.E.M.*...Warner 26496
7	5	4	Robin Hood: Prince Of Thieves..................... *Soundtrack*...Morgan Creek 20004
8	10	11	Cooleyhighharmony...*Boyz II Men*...Motown 6320
9	9	14	Time, Love & Tenderness............................ *Michael Bolton*...Columbia 46771
10	11	47	No Fences .... *Garth Brooks*...Capitol 93866

Billboard — AUGUST 17, 1991 — TOP POP ALBUMS

TW	LW	WK	Title	Artist / Label
1	1	8	**Unforgettable With Love**	*Natalie Cole*...Elektra 61049
2	5	6	**Luck Of The Draw**	*Bonnie Raitt*...Capitol 96111
3	2	7	For Unlawful Carnal Knowledge	*Van Halen*...Warner 26594
4	4	32	Gonna Make You Sweat	*C & C Music Factory*...Columbia 47093
5	8	12	Cooleyhighharmony	*Boyz II Men*...Motown 6320
6	6	21	Out Of Time	*R.E.M.*...Warner 26496
7	3	12	Spellbound	*Paula Abdul*...Captive/Virgin 91611
8	7	5	Robin Hood: Prince Of Thieves	*Soundtrack*...Morgan Creek 20004
9	10	48	No Fences	*Garth Brooks*...Capitol 93866
10	9	15	Time, Love & Tenderness	*Michael Bolton*...Columbia 46771

Billboard — AUGUST 24, 1991 — TOP POP ALBUMS

TW	LW	WK	Title	Artist / Label
1	1	9	**Unforgettable With Love**	*Natalie Cole*...Elektra 61049
2	2	7	**Luck Of The Draw**	*Bonnie Raitt*...Capitol 96111
3	5	13	**Cooleyhighharmony**	*Boyz II Men*...Motown 6320
4	4	33	Gonna Make You Sweat	*C & C Music Factory*...Columbia 47093
5	11	3	C.M.B.	*Color Me Badd*...Giant 24429
6	3	8	For Unlawful Carnal Knowledge	*Van Halen*...Warner 26594
7	10	16	Time, Love & Tenderness	*Michael Bolton*...Columbia 46771
8	7	13	Spellbound	*Paula Abdul*...Captive/Virgin 91611
9	8	6	Robin Hood: Prince Of Thieves	*Soundtrack*...Morgan Creek 20004
10	6	22	Out Of Time	*R.E.M.*...Warner 26496

Billboard — AUGUST 31, 1991 — TOP POP ALBUMS

TW	LW	WK	Title	Artist / Label
1	-	1	**Metallica**	*Metallica*...Elektra 61113
2	1	10	Unforgettable With Love	*Natalie Cole*...Elektra 61049
3	5	4	**C.M.B.**	*Color Me Badd*...Giant 24429
4	2	8	Luck Of The Draw	*Bonnie Raitt*...Capitol 96111
5	3	14	Cooleyhighharmony	*Boyz II Men*...Motown 6320
6	4	34	Gonna Make You Sweat	*C & C Music Factory*...Columbia 47093
7	6	9	For Unlawful Carnal Knowledge	*Van Halen*...Warner 26594
8	7	17	Time, Love & Tenderness	*Michael Bolton*...Columbia 46771
9	8	14	Spellbound	*Paula Abdul*...Captive/Virgin 91611
10	11	24	**Heart In Motion**	*Amy Grant*...A&M 5321

Billboard — SEPTEMBER 7, 1991 — THE BILLBOARD 200

TW	LW	WK	Title	Artist / Label
1	1	2	**Metallica**	*Metallica*...Elektra 61113
2	2	11	Unforgettable With Love	*Natalie Cole*...Elektra 61049
3	3	5	**C.M.B.**	*Color Me Badd*...Giant 24429
4	7	10	For Unlawful Carnal Knowledge	*Van Halen*...Warner 26594
5	4	9	Luck Of The Draw	*Bonnie Raitt*...Capitol 96111
6	5	15	Cooleyhighharmony	*Boyz II Men*...Motown 6320
7	6	35	Gonna Make You Sweat	*C & C Music Factory*...Columbia 47093
8	8	18	Time, Love & Tenderness	*Michael Bolton*...Columbia 46771
9	9	15	Spellbound	*Paula Abdul*...Captive/Virgin 91611
10	13	24	Out Of Time	*R.E.M.*...Warner 26496

Billboard® — SEPTEMBER 14, 1991 — THE BILLBOARD 200®

TW	LW	WK	Title	Artist...Label
1	1	3	**Metallica**	*Metallica*...Elektra 61113
2	2	12	Unforgettable With Love	*Natalie Cole*...Elektra 61049
3	5	10	Luck Of The Draw	*Bonnie Raitt*...Capitol 96111
4	3	6	C.M.B.	*Color Me Badd*...Giant 24429
5	6	16	Cooleyhighharmony	*Boyz II Men*...Motown 6320
6	4	11	For Unlawful Carnal Knowledge	*Van Halen*...Warner 26594
7	-	1	**The Fire Inside**	*Bob Seger & The Silver Bullet Band*...Capitol 91134
8	8	19	Time, Love & Tenderness	*Michael Bolton*...Columbia 46771
9	7	36	Gonna Make You Sweat	*C & C Music Factory*...Columbia 47093
10	9	16	Spellbound	*Paula Abdul*...Captive/Virgin 91611

Billboard® — SEPTEMBER 21, 1991 — THE BILLBOARD 200®

TW	LW	WK	Title	Artist...Label
1	1	4	**Metallica**	*Metallica*...Elektra 61113
2	2	13	Unforgettable With Love	*Natalie Cole*...Elektra 61049
3	-	1	**Roll The Bones**	*Rush*...Atlantic 82293
4	3	11	Luck Of The Draw	*Bonnie Raitt*...Capitol 96111
5	4	7	C.M.B.	*Color Me Badd*...Giant 24429
6	5	17	Cooleyhighharmony	*Boyz II Men*...Motown 6320
7	7	2	**The Fire Inside**	*Bob Seger & The Silver Bullet Band*...Capitol 91134
8	6	12	For Unlawful Carnal Knowledge	*Van Halen*...Warner 26594
9	8	20	Time, Love & Tenderness	*Michael Bolton*...Columbia 46771
10	9	37	Gonna Make You Sweat	*C & C Music Factory*...Columbia 47093

Billboard® — SEPTEMBER 28, 1991 — THE BILLBOARD 200®

TW	LW	WK	Title	Artist...Label
1	-	1	**Ropin' The Wind**	*Garth Brooks*...Capitol 96330
2	1	5	Metallica	*Metallica*...Elektra 61113
3	2	14	Unforgettable With Love	*Natalie Cole*...Elektra 61049
4	5	8	C.M.B.	*Color Me Badd*...Giant 24429
5	4	12	Luck Of The Draw	*Bonnie Raitt*...Capitol 96111
6	6	18	Cooleyhighharmony	*Boyz II Men*...Motown 6320
7	10	38	Gonna Make You Sweat	*C & C Music Factory*...Columbia 47093
8	9	21	Time, Love & Tenderness	*Michael Bolton*...Columbia 46771
9	11	27	Out Of Time	*R.E.M.*...Warner 26496
10	3	2	Roll The Bones	*Rush*...Atlantic 82293

Billboard® — OCTOBER 5, 1991 — THE BILLBOARD 200®

TW	LW	WK	Title	Artist...Label
1	-	1	**Use Your Illusion II**	*Guns N' Roses*...Geffen 24420
2	-	1	**Use Your Illusion I**	*Guns N' Roses*...Geffen 24415
3	1	2	Ropin' The Wind	*Garth Brooks*...Capitol 96330
4	-	1	**Emotions**	*Mariah Carey*...Columbia 47980
5	2	6	Metallica	*Metallica*...Elektra 61113
6	3	15	Unforgettable With Love	*Natalie Cole*...Elektra 61049
7	-	1	**No More Tears**	*Ozzy Osbourne*...Epic/Associated 46795
8	21	4	**The Commitments**	*Soundtrack*...MCA 10286
9	5	13	Luck Of The Draw	*Bonnie Raitt*...Capitol 96111
10	4	9	C.M.B.	*Color Me Badd*...Giant 24429

Billboard — OCTOBER 12, 1991 — THE BILLBOARD 200

TW	LW	WK	Title	Artist...Label
1	1	2	**Use Your Illusion II**	*Guns N' Roses*...Geffen 24420
2	2	2	**Use Your Illusion I**	*Guns N' Roses*...Geffen 24415
3	3	3	Ropin' The Wind	*Garth Brooks*...Capitol 96330
4	4	2	**Emotions**	*Mariah Carey*...Columbia 47980
5	5	7	Metallica	*Metallica*...Elektra 61113
6	-	1	**Waking Up The Neighbours**	*Bryan Adams*...A&M 5367
7	6	16	Unforgettable With Love	*Natalie Cole*...Elektra 61049
8	8	5	**The Commitments**	*Soundtrack*...MCA 10286
9	9	14	Luck Of The Draw	*Bonnie Raitt*...Capitol 96111
10	11	20	Cooleyhighharmony	*Boyz II Men*...Motown 6320

Billboard — OCTOBER 19, 1991 — THE BILLBOARD 200

TW	LW	WK	Title	Artist...Label
1	3	4	**Ropin' The Wind**	*Garth Brooks*...Capitol 96330
2	-	1	**Decade Of Decadence - '81-'91**	*Mötley Crüe*...Elektra 61204
3	1	3	Use Your Illusion II	*Guns N' Roses*...Geffen 24420
4	-	1	**Apocalypse 91...The Enemy Strikes Black**	*Public Enemy*...Def Jam 47374
5	-	1	Diamonds And Pearls	*Prince & The New Power Generation*...Paisley Park 25379
6	2	3	Use Your Illusion I	*Guns N' Roses*...Geffen 24415
7	4	3	Emotions	*Mariah Carey*...Columbia 47980
8	5	8	Metallica	*Metallica*...Elektra 61113
9	6	2	Waking Up The Neighbours	*Bryan Adams*...A&M 5367
10	15	57	No Fences	*Garth Brooks*...Capitol 93866

Billboard — OCTOBER 26, 1991 — THE BILLBOARD 200

TW	LW	WK	Title	Artist...Label
1	1	5	**Ropin' The Wind**	*Garth Brooks*...Capitol 96330
2	3	4	Use Your Illusion II	*Guns N' Roses*...Geffen 24420
3	2	2	Decade Of Decadence - '81-'91	*Mötley Crüe*...Elektra 61204
4	4	2	**Apocalypse 91...The Enemy Strikes Black**	*Public Enemy*...Def Jam 47374
5	5	2	Diamonds And Pearls	*Prince & The New Power Generation*...Paisley Park 25379
6	7	4	Emotions	*Mariah Carey*...Columbia 47980
7	6	4	Use Your Illusion I	*Guns N' Roses*...Geffen 24415
8	8	9	Metallica	*Metallica*...Elektra 61113
9	9	3	Waking Up The Neighbours	*Bryan Adams*...A&M 5367
10	10	58	No Fences	*Garth Brooks*...Capitol 93866

Billboard — NOVEMBER 2, 1991 — THE BILLBOARD 200

TW	LW	WK	Title	Artist...Label
1	1	6	**Ropin' The Wind**	*Garth Brooks*...Capitol 96330
2	2	5	Use Your Illusion II	*Guns N' Roses*...Geffen 24420
3	3	3	Decade Of Decadence - '81-'91	*Mötley Crüe*...Elektra 61204
4	5	3	Diamonds And Pearls	*Prince & The New Power Generation*...Paisley Park 25379
5	8	10	Metallica	*Metallica*...Elektra 61113
6	4	3	Apocalypse 91...The Enemy Strikes Black	*Public Enemy*...Def Jam 47374
7	6	5	Emotions	*Mariah Carey*...Columbia 47980
8	7	5	Use Your Illusion I	*Guns N' Roses*...Geffen 24415
9	9	4	Waking Up The Neighbours	*Bryan Adams*...A&M 5367
10	10	59	No Fences	*Garth Brooks*...Capitol 93866

TW	LW	WK	Billboard® NOVEMBER 9, 1991 THE BILLBOARD 200®
①	1	7	**Ropin' The Wind** ... *Garth Brooks*...Capitol 96330
②	2	6	Use Your Illusion II ... *Guns N' Roses*...Geffen 24420
③	4	4	**Diamonds And Pearls** ... *Prince & The New Power Generation*...Paisley Park 25379
④	5	11	Metallica ... *Metallica*...Elektra 61113
❺	8	6	Use Your Illusion I ... *Guns N' Roses*...Geffen 24415
⑥	3	4	Decade Of Decadence - '81-'91 ... *Mötley Crüe*...Elektra 61204
⑦	7	6	Emotions ... *Mariah Carey*...Columbia 47980
⑧	6	4	Apocalypse 91...The Enemy Strikes Black ... *Public Enemy*...Def Jam 47374
❾	11	27	Time, Love & Tenderness ... *Michael Bolton*...Columbia 46771
⑩	10	60	No Fences ... *Garth Brooks*...Capitol 93866

TW	LW	WK	Billboard® NOVEMBER 16, 1991 THE BILLBOARD 200®
①	1	8	**Ropin' The Wind** ... *Garth Brooks*...Capitol 96330
❷	-	1	**Death Certificate** ... *Ice Cube*...Priority 57155
❸	-	1	Too Legit To Quit ... *Hammer*...Capitol 98151
④	2	7	Use Your Illusion II ... *Guns N' Roses*...Geffen 24420
⑤	4	12	Metallica ... *Metallica*...Elektra 61113
⑥	3	5	Diamonds And Pearls ... *Prince & The New Power Generation*...Paisley Park 25379
⑦	5	7	Use Your Illusion I ... *Guns N' Roses*...Geffen 24415
⑧	7	7	Emotions ... *Mariah Carey*...Columbia 47980
❾	17	6	Nevermind ... *Nirvana*...DGC 24425
⑩	12	25	Cooleyhighharmony ... *Boyz II Men*...Motown 6320

TW	LW	WK	Billboard® NOVEMBER 23, 1991 THE BILLBOARD 200®
❶	1	9	**Ropin' The Wind** ... *Garth Brooks*...Capitol 96330
❷	3	2	**Too Legit To Quit** ... *Hammer*...Capitol 98151
❸	2	2	Death Certificate ... *Ice Cube*...Priority 57155
❹	9	7	Nevermind ... *Nirvana*...DGC 24425
⑤	4	8	Use Your Illusion II ... *Guns N' Roses*...Geffen 24420
❻	5	13	Metallica ... *Metallica*...Elektra 61113
⑦	6	6	Diamonds And Pearls .. *Prince & The New Power Generation*...Paisley Park 25379
❽	10	26	Cooleyhighharmony ... *Boyz II Men*...Motown 6320
⑨	7	8	Use Your Illusion I ... *Guns N' Roses*...Geffen 24415
❿	-	1	**The Sky Is Crying** ... *Stevie Ray Vaughan & Double Trouble*...Epic 47390

TW	LW	WK	Billboard® NOVEMBER 30, 1991 THE BILLBOARD 200®
①	1	10	**Ropin' The Wind** ... *Garth Brooks*...Capitol 96330
❷	2	3	**Too Legit To Quit** ... *Hammer*...Capitol 98151
③	3	3	Death Certificate ... *Ice Cube*...Priority 57155
❹	-	1	**We Can't Dance** ... *Genesis*...Atlantic 82344
❺	4	8	Nevermind ... *Nirvana*...DGC 24425
⑥	5	9	Use Your Illusion II ... *Guns N' Roses*...Geffen 24420
⑦	6	14	Metallica ... *Metallica*...Elektra 61113
❽	13	30	Time, Love & Tenderness ... *Michael Bolton*...Columbia 46771
❾	12	63	No Fences ... *Garth Brooks*...Capitol 93866
⑩	8	27	Cooleyhighharmony ... *Boyz II Men*...Motown 6320

Billboard® — DECEMBER 7, 1991 — THE BILLBOARD 200®

TW	LW	WK	Title	Artist	Label
❶	-	1	**Achtung Baby**	*U2*	Island 10347
②	1	11	Ropin' The Wind	*Garth Brooks*	Capitol 96330
③	2	4	Too Legit To Quit	*Hammer*	Capitol 98151
❹	5	9	Nevermind	*Nirvana*	DGC 24425
❺	8	31	Time, Love & Tenderness	*Michael Bolton*	Columbia 46771
⑥	6	10	Use Your Illusion II	*Guns N' Roses*	Geffen 24420
❼	7	15	Metallica	*Metallica*	Elektra 61113
⑧	4	2	We Can't Dance	*Genesis*	Atlantic 82344
⑨	3	4	Death Certificate	*Ice Cube*	Priority 57155
❿	11	10	Emotions	*Mariah Carey*	Columbia 47980

Billboard® — DECEMBER 14, 1991 — THE BILLBOARD 200®

TW	LW	WK	Title	Artist	Label
❶	-	1	**Dangerous**	*Michael Jackson*	Epic 45400
②	2	12	Ropin' The Wind	*Garth Brooks*	Capitol 96330
③	1	2	Achtung Baby	*U2*	Island 10347
④	3	5	Too Legit To Quit	*Hammer*	Capitol 98151
⑤	5	32	Time, Love & Tenderness	*Michael Bolton*	Columbia 46771
⑥	4	10	Nevermind	*Nirvana*	DGC 24425
❼	6	11	Use Your Illusion II	*Guns N' Roses*	Geffen 24420
❽	7	16	Metallica	*Metallica*	Elektra 61113
❾	13	29	Cooleyhighharmony	*Boyz II Men*	Motown 6320
❿	10	11	Emotions	*Mariah Carey*	Columbia 47980

Billboard® — DECEMBER 21, 1991 — THE BILLBOARD 200®

TW	LW	WK	Title	Artist	Label
❶	1	2	**Dangerous**	*Michael Jackson*	Epic 45400
❷	2	13	Ropin' The Wind	*Garth Brooks*	Capitol 96330
❸	4	6	Too Legit To Quit	*Hammer*	Capitol 98151
④	3	3	Achtung Baby	*U2*	Island 10347
❺	5	33	Time, Love & Tenderness	*Michael Bolton*	Columbia 46771
⑥	6	11	Nevermind	*Nirvana*	DGC 24425
❼	13	26	Unforgettable With Love	*Natalie Cole*	Elektra 61049
❽	9	30	Cooleyhighharmony	*Boyz II Men*	Motown 6320
⑨	8	17	Metallica	*Metallica*	Elektra 61113
⑩	7	12	Use Your Illusion II	*Guns N' Roses*	Geffen 24420

Billboard® — JANUARY 4, 1992 — THE BILLBOARD 200®

TW	LW	WK	Title	Artist	Label
①	1	4	**Dangerous**	*Michael Jackson*	Epic 45400
②	2	15	Ropin' The Wind	*Garth Brooks*	Capitol 96330
❸	3	8	Too Legit To Quit	*Hammer*	Capitol 98151
❹	5	35	Time, Love & Tenderness	*Michael Bolton*	Columbia 46771
❺	8	32	Cooleyhighharmony	*Boyz II Men*	Motown 6320
❻	6	13	Nevermind	*Nirvana*	DGC 24425
⑦	4	5	Achtung Baby	*U2*	Island 10347
⑧	7	28	Unforgettable With Love	*Natalie Cole*	Elektra 61049
⑨	9	19	Metallica	*Metallica*	Elektra 61113
❿	10	14	Use Your Illusion II	*Guns N' Roses*	Geffen 24420

Billboard® — JANUARY 11, 1992 — THE BILLBOARD 200®

TW	LW	WK	Title	Artist	Label
❶	6	14	**Nevermind**	*Nirvana*	DGC 24425
②	2	16	Ropin' The Wind	*Garth Brooks*	Capitol 96330
③	3	9	Too Legit To Quit	*Hammer*	Capitol 98151
❹	7	6	Achtung Baby	*U2*	Island 10347
⑤	1	5	Dangerous	*Michael Jackson*	Epic 45400
❻	5	33	Cooleyhighharmony	*Boyz II Men*	Motown 6320
❼	10	15	Use Your Illusion II	*Guns N' Roses*	Geffen 24420
❽	12	15	Use Your Illusion I	*Guns N' Roses*	Geffen 24415
❾	9	20	Metallica	*Metallica*	Elektra 61113
⑩	4	36	Time, Love & Tenderness	*Michael Bolton*	Columbia 46771

Billboard® — JANUARY 18, 1992 — THE BILLBOARD 200®

TW	LW	WK	Title	Artist	Label
❶	2	17	**Ropin' The Wind**	*Garth Brooks*	Capitol 96330
②	5	6	Dangerous	*Michael Jackson*	Epic 45400
③	3	10	Too Legit To Quit	*Hammer*	Capitol 98151
④	1	15	Nevermind	*Nirvana*	DGC 24425
❺	9	21	Metallica	*Metallica*	Elektra 61113
⑥	10	37	Time, Love & Tenderness	*Michael Bolton*	Columbia 46771
⑦	4	7	Achtung Baby	*U2*	Island 10347
⑧	6	34	Cooleyhighharmony	*Boyz II Men*	Motown 6320
⑨	11	16	Emotions	*Mariah Carey*	Columbia 47980
⑩	7	16	Use Your Illusion II	*Guns N' Roses*	Geffen 24420

Billboard® — JANUARY 25, 1992 — THE BILLBOARD 200®

TW	LW	WK	Title	Artist	Label
①	1	18	**Ropin' The Wind**	*Garth Brooks*	Capitol 96330
②	2	7	Dangerous	*Michael Jackson*	Epic 45400
③	3	11	Too Legit To Quit	*Hammer*	Capitol 98151
❹	4	16	Nevermind	*Nirvana*	DGC 24425
⑤	6	38	Time, Love & Tenderness	*Michael Bolton*	Columbia 46771
⑥	7	8	Achtung Baby	*U2*	Island 10347
⑦	5	22	Metallica	*Metallica*	Elektra 61113
⑧	8	35	Cooleyhighharmony	*Boyz II Men*	Motown 6320
⑨	9	17	Emotions	*Mariah Carey*	Columbia 47980
⑩	12	71	No Fences	*Garth Brooks*	Capitol 93866

TW	LW	WK	Billboard®	FEBRUARY 1, 1992 — THE BILLBOARD 200®
1	4	17	**Nevermind**	*Nirvana*...DGC 24425
2	1	19	**Ropin' The Wind**	*Garth Brooks*...Capitol 96330
3	2	8	**Dangerous**	*Michael Jackson*...Epic 45400
4	3	12	**Too Legit To Quit**	*Hammer*...Capitol 98151
5	10	72	**No Fences**	*Garth Brooks*...Capitol 93866
6	6	9	**Achtung Baby**	*U2*...Island 10347
7	8	36	**Cooleyhighharmony**	*Boyz II Men*...Motown 6320
8	7	23	**Metallica**	*Metallica*...Elektra 61113
9	5	39	**Time, Love & Tenderness**	*Michael Bolton*...Columbia 46771
10	9	18	**Emotions**	*Mariah Carey*...Columbia 47980

TW	LW	WK	Billboard®	FEBRUARY 8, 1992 — THE BILLBOARD 200®
1	2	20	**Ropin' The Wind**	*Garth Brooks*...Capitol 96330
2	1	18	**Nevermind**	*Nirvana*...DGC 24425
3	5	73	**No Fences**	*Garth Brooks*...Capitol 93866
4	3	9	**Dangerous**	*Michael Jackson*...Epic 45400
5	4	13	**Too Legit To Quit**	*Hammer*...Capitol 98151
6	6	10	**Achtung Baby**	*U2*...Island 10347
7	7	37	**Cooleyhighharmony**	*Boyz II Men*...Motown 6320
8	9	40	**Time, Love & Tenderness**	*Michael Bolton*...Columbia 46771
9	8	24	**Metallica**	*Metallica*...Elektra 61113
10	11	17	**Diamonds And Pearls**	*Prince & The New Power Generation*...Paisley Park 25379

TW	LW	WK	Billboard®	FEBRUARY 15, 1992 — THE BILLBOARD 200®
1	1	21	**Ropin' The Wind**	*Garth Brooks*...Capitol 96330
2	2	19	**Nevermind**	*Nirvana*...DGC 24425
3	3	74	**No Fences**	*Garth Brooks*...Capitol 93866
4	4	10	**Dangerous**	*Michael Jackson*...Epic 45400
5	7	38	**Cooleyhighharmony**	*Boyz II Men*...Motown 6320
6	11	28	**C.M.B.**	*Color Me Badd*...Giant 24429
7	5	14	**Too Legit To Quit**	*Hammer*...Capitol 98151
8	8	41	**Time, Love & Tenderness**	*Michael Bolton*...Columbia 46771
9	6	11	**Achtung Baby**	*U2*...Island 10347
10	9	25	**Metallica**	*Metallica*...Elektra 61113

TW	LW	WK	Billboard®	FEBRUARY 22, 1992 — THE BILLBOARD 200®
1	1	22	**Ropin' The Wind**	*Garth Brooks*...Capitol 96330
2	4	11	**Dangerous**	*Michael Jackson*...Epic 45400
3	2	20	**Nevermind**	*Nirvana*...DGC 24425
4	3	75	**No Fences**	*Garth Brooks*...Capitol 93866
5	6	29	**C.M.B.**	*Color Me Badd*...Giant 24429
6	5	39	**Cooleyhighharmony**	*Boyz II Men*...Motown 6320
7	8	42	**Time, Love & Tenderness**	*Michael Bolton*...Columbia 46771
8	7	15	**Too Legit To Quit**	*Hammer*...Capitol 98151
9	9	12	**Achtung Baby**	*U2*...Island 10347
10	14	13	**We Can't Dance**	*Genesis*...Atlantic 82344

TW	LW	WK	Billboard ● FEBRUARY 29, 1992 ● THE BILLBOARD 200®
①	1	23	**Ropin' The Wind** ....*Garth Brooks*...Capitol 96330
②	2	12	**Dangerous**...*Michael Jackson*...Epic 45400
③	3	21	**Nevermind**...*Nirvana*...DGC 24425
④	4	76	**No Fences** ....*Garth Brooks*...Capitol 93866
❺	7	43	**Time, Love & Tenderness** ....*Michael Bolton*...Columbia 46771
⑥	5	30	**C.M.B.**..*Color Me Badd*...Giant 24429
❼	10	14	**We Can't Dance**... *Genesis*...Atlantic 82344
❽	9	13	**Achtung Baby** ....*U2*...Island 10347
⑨	6	40	**Cooleyhighharmony** ....*Boyz II Men*...Motown 6320
⑩	8	16	**Too Legit To Quit** ....*Hammer*...Capitol 98151

TW	LW	WK	Billboard ● MARCH 7, 1992 ● THE BILLBOARD 200®
①	1	24	**Ropin' The Wind** ....*Garth Brooks*...Capitol 96330
②	2	13	**Dangerous**...*Michael Jackson*...Epic 45400
③	3	22	**Nevermind**...*Nirvana*...DGC 24425
④	4	77	**No Fences** ....*Garth Brooks*...Capitol 93866
⑤	5	44	**Time, Love & Tenderness** ....*Michael Bolton*...Columbia 46771
❻	9	41	**Cooleyhighharmony** ....*Boyz II Men*...Motown 6320
⑦	6	31	**C.M.B.**..*Color Me Badd*...Giant 24429
⑧	10	17	**Too Legit To Quit** ....*Hammer*...Capitol 98151
⑨	8	14	**Achtung Baby** ....*U2*...Island 10347
⑩	7	15	**We Can't Dance**... *Genesis*...Atlantic 82344

TW	LW	WK	Billboard ● MARCH 14, 1992 ● THE BILLBOARD 200®
①	1	25	**Ropin' The Wind** ....*Garth Brooks*...Capitol 96330
❷	16	38	**Unforgettable With Love** .... *Natalie Cole*...Elektra 61049
③	3	23	**Nevermind**...*Nirvana*...DGC 24425
❹	12	36	**Luck Of The Draw** .... *Bonnie Raitt*...Capitol 96111
⑤	4	78	**No Fences** ....*Garth Brooks*...Capitol 93866
⑥	2	14	**Dangerous**...*Michael Jackson*...Epic 45400
❼	5	45	**Time, Love & Tenderness** ....*Michael Bolton*...Columbia 46771
⑧	6	42	**Cooleyhighharmony** ....*Boyz II Men*...Motown 6320
⑨	7	32	**C.M.B.**..*Color Me Badd*...Giant 24429
⑩	11	29	**Metallica** ....*Metallica*...Elektra 61113

TW	LW	WK	Billboard ● MARCH 21, 1992 ● THE BILLBOARD 200®
①	1	26	**Ropin' The Wind** ....*Garth Brooks*...Capitol 96330
②	3	24	**Nevermind**...*Nirvana*...DGC 24425
③	2	39	**Unforgettable With Love** .... *Natalie Cole*...Elektra 61049
④	4	37	**Luck Of The Draw** .... *Bonnie Raitt*...Capitol 96111
⑤	7	46	**Time, Love & Tenderness** ....*Michael Bolton*...Columbia 46771
⑥	6	15	**Dangerous**...*Michael Jackson*...Epic 45400
⑦	5	79	**No Fences** ....*Garth Brooks*...Capitol 93866
❽	11	3	**Wayne's World**.. *Soundtrack*...Reprise 26805
⑨	8	43	**Cooleyhighharmony** ....*Boyz II Men*...Motown 6320
⑩	10	30	**Metallica** ....*Metallica*...Elektra 61113

Billboard — MARCH 28, 1992 — THE BILLBOARD 200

TW	LW	WK	Title	Artist / Label
1	1	27	**Ropin' The Wind**	*Garth Brooks*...Capitol 96330
2	2	25	Nevermind	*Nirvana*...DGC 24425
3	8	4	Wayne's World	*Soundtrack*...Reprise 26805
4	3	40	Unforgettable With Love	*Natalie Cole*...Elektra 61049
5	7	80	No Fences	*Garth Brooks*...Capitol 93866
6	6	16	Dangerous	*Michael Jackson*...Epic 45400
7	4	38	Luck Of The Draw	*Bonnie Raitt*...Capitol 96111
8	5	47	Time, Love & Tenderness	*Michael Bolton*...Columbia 46771
9	10	31	Metallica	*Metallica*...Elektra 61113
10	12	17	Achtung Baby	*U2*...Island 10347

Billboard — APRIL 4, 1992 — THE BILLBOARD 200

TW	LW	WK	Title	Artist / Label
1	3	5	**Wayne's World**	*Soundtrack*...Reprise 26805
2	1	28	Ropin' The Wind	*Garth Brooks*...Capitol 96330
3	2	26	Nevermind	*Nirvana*...DGC 24425
4	5	81	No Fences	*Garth Brooks*...Capitol 93866
5	9	32	Metallica	*Metallica*...Elektra 61113
6	13	9	As Ugly As They Want To Be	*Ugly Kid Joe*...Stardog 868823
7	10	18	Achtung Baby	*U2*...Island 10347
8	4	41	Unforgettable With Love	*Natalie Cole*...Elektra 61049
9	6	17	Dangerous	*Michael Jackson*...Epic 45400
10	8	48	Time, Love & Tenderness	*Michael Bolton*...Columbia 46771

Billboard — APRIL 11, 1992 — THE BILLBOARD 200

TW	LW	WK	Title	Artist / Label
1	1	6	**Wayne's World**	*Soundtrack*...Reprise 26805
2	2	29	Ropin' The Wind	*Garth Brooks*...Capitol 96330
3	3	27	Nevermind	*Nirvana*...DGC 24425
4	6	10	**As Ugly As They Want To Be**	*Ugly Kid Joe*...Stardog 868823
5	4	82	No Fences	*Garth Brooks*...Capitol 93866
6	5	33	Metallica	*Metallica*...Elektra 61113
7	7	19	Achtung Baby	*U2*...Island 10347
8	-	1	**Funky Divas**	*En Vogue*...EastWest 92121
9	12	3	Classic Queen	*Queen*...Hollywood 61311
10	10	49	Time, Love & Tenderness	*Michael Bolton*...Columbia 46771

Billboard — APRIL 18, 1992 — THE BILLBOARD 200

TW	LW	WK	Title	Artist / Label
1	-	1	**Adrenalize**	*Def Leppard*...Mercury 512185
2	-	1	**Human Touch**	*Bruce Springsteen*...Columbia 53000
3	-	1	**Lucky Town**	*Bruce Springsteen*...Columbia 53001
4	-	1	**Wynonna**	*Wynonna*..Curb/MCA 10529
5	1	7	Wayne's World	*Soundtrack*...Reprise 26805
6	2	30	Ropin' The Wind	*Garth Brooks*...Capitol 96330
7	3	28	Nevermind	*Nirvana*...DGC 24425
8	4	11	As Ugly As They Want To Be	*Ugly Kid Joe*...Stardog 868823
9	-	1	Totally Krossed Out	*Kris Kross*...Ruffhouse 48710
10	8	2	Funky Divas	*En Vogue*...EastWest 92121

TW	LW	WK	Billboard® APRIL 25, 1992	THE BILLBOARD 200®
①	1	2	**Adrenalize**	*Def Leppard*...Mercury 512185
②	2	2	**Human Touch**	*Bruce Springsteen*...Columbia 53000
❸	9	2	Totally Krossed Out	*Kris Kross*...Ruffhouse 48710
④	3	2	Lucky Town	*Bruce Springsteen*...Columbia 53001
⑤	4	2	Wynonna	*Wynonna*...Curb/MCA 10529
⑥	5	8	Wayne's World	*Soundtrack*...Reprise 26805
⑦	6	31	Ropin' The Wind	*Garth Brooks*...Capitol 96330
⑧	7	29	Nevermind	*Nirvana*...DGC 24425
⑨	10	3	Funky Divas	*En Vogue*...EastWest 92121
⑩	8	12	As Ugly As They Want To Be	*Ugly Kid Joe*...Stardog 868823

TW	LW	WK	Billboard® MAY 2, 1992	THE BILLBOARD 200®
①	1	3	**Adrenalize**	*Def Leppard*...Mercury 512185
❷	3	3	Totally Krossed Out	*Kris Kross*...Ruffhouse 48710
③	2	3	Human Touch	*Bruce Springsteen*...Columbia 53000
❹	6	9	Wayne's World	*Soundtrack*...Reprise 26805
❺	11	30	Blood Sugar Sex Magik	*Red Hot Chili Peppers*...Warner 26681
⑥	5	3	Wynonna	*Wynonna*...Curb/MCA 10529
⑦	8	30	Nevermind	*Nirvana*...DGC 24425
⑧	7	32	Ropin' The Wind	*Garth Brooks*...Capitol 96330
⑨	10	13	As Ugly As They Want To Be	*Ugly Kid Joe*...Stardog 868823
❿	13	22	Achtung Baby	*U2*...Island 10347

TW	LW	WK	Billboard® MAY 9, 1992	THE BILLBOARD 200®
①	1	4	**Adrenalize**	*Def Leppard*...Mercury 512185
❷	-	1	**Wish**	*The Cure*...Fiction 61309
③	2	4	Totally Krossed Out	*Kris Kross*...Ruffhouse 48710
❹	13	7	**Classic Queen**	*Queen*...Hollywood 61311
⑤	5	31	Blood Sugar Sex Magik	*Red Hot Chili Peppers*...Warner 26681
⑥	4	10	Wayne's World	*Soundtrack*...Reprise 26805
⑦	8	33	Ropin' The Wind	*Garth Brooks*...Capitol 96330
❽	-	1	**The Wild Life**	*Slaughter*...Chrysalis 21911
⑨	7	31	Nevermind	*Nirvana*...DGC 24425
❿	-	1	**Check Your Head**	*Beastie Boys*...Capitol 98938

TW	LW	WK	Billboard® MAY 16, 1992	THE BILLBOARD 200®
①	1	5	**Adrenalize**	*Def Leppard*...Mercury 512185
②	3	5	Totally Krossed Out	*Kris Kross*...Ruffhouse 48710
③	5	32	**Blood Sugar Sex Magik**	*Red Hot Chili Peppers*...Warner 26681
④	4	8	**Classic Queen**	*Queen*...Hollywood 61311
❺	7	34	Ropin' The Wind	*Garth Brooks*...Capitol 96330
⑥	2	2	Wish	*The Cure*...Fiction 61309
❼	15	87	No Fences	*Garth Brooks*...Capitol 93866
⑧	9	32	Nevermind	*Nirvana*...DGC 24425
⑨	11	5	Wynonna	*Wynonna*...Curb/MCA 10529
⑩	6	11	Wayne's World	*Soundtrack*...Reprise 26805

TW	LW	WK	Billboard. MAY 23, 1992 — THE BILLBOARD 200.
1	2	6	**Totally Krossed Out** .... *Kris Kross*...Ruffhouse 48710
2	1	6	Adrenalize........ *Def Leppard*...Mercury 512185
3	3	33	**Blood Sugar Sex Magik** .... *Red Hot Chili Peppers*...Warner 26681
4	5	35	Ropin' The Wind........ *Garth Brooks*...Capitol 96330
5	4	9	Classic Queen .... *Queen*...Hollywood 61311
6	7	88	No Fences .... *Garth Brooks*...Capitol 93866
7	6	3	Wish .... *The Cure*...Fiction 61309
8	8	33	Nevermind........ *Nirvana*...DGC 24425
9	9	6	Wynonna .... *Wynonna*...Curb/MCA 10529
10	12	4	Greatest Hits........ *ZZ Top*...Warner 26846

TW	LW	WK	Billboard. MAY 30, 1992 — THE BILLBOARD 200.
1	-	1	**The Southern Harmony and Musical Companion** .... *The Black Crowes*...Def American 26916
2	1	7	Totally Krossed Out........ *Kris Kross*...Ruffhouse 48710
3	2	7	Adrenalize........ *Def Leppard*...Mercury 512185
4	3	34	Blood Sugar Sex Magik........ *Red Hot Chili Peppers*...Warner 26681
5	4	36	Ropin' The Wind........ *Garth Brooks*...Capitol 96330
6	6	89	No Fences .... *Garth Brooks*...Capitol 93866
7	5	10	Classic Queen .... *Queen*...Hollywood 61311
8	16	22	Ten........ *Pearl Jam*...Epic/Associated 47857
9	10	5	**Greatest Hits**........ *ZZ Top*...Warner 26846
10	7	4	Wish .... *The Cure*...Fiction 61309

TW	LW	WK	Billboard. JUNE 6, 1992 — THE BILLBOARD 200.
1	2	8	**Totally Krossed Out** .... *Kris Kross*...Ruffhouse 48710
2	1	2	The Southern Harmony and Musical Companion .... *The Black Crowes*...Def American 26916
3	4	35	**Blood Sugar Sex Magik** .... *Red Hot Chili Peppers*...Warner 26681
4	-	1	Some Gave All........ *Billy Ray Cyrus*...Mercury 510635
5	3	8	Adrenalize........ *Def Leppard*...Mercury 512185
6	-	1	**Revenge** .... *Kiss*...Mercury 848037
7	5	37	Ropin' The Wind........ *Garth Brooks*...Capitol 96330
8	8	23	Ten........ *Pearl Jam*...Epic/Associated 47857
9	7	11	Classic Queen .... *Queen*...Hollywood 61311
10	6	90	No Fences .... *Garth Brooks*...Capitol 93866

TW	LW	WK	Billboard. JUNE 13, 1992 — THE BILLBOARD 200.
1	4	2	**Some Gave All** .... *Billy Ray Cyrus*...Mercury 510635
2	1	9	Totally Krossed Out........ *Kris Kross*...Ruffhouse 48710
3	3	36	**Blood Sugar Sex Magik** .... *Red Hot Chili Peppers*...Warner 26681
4	2	3	The Southern Harmony and Musical Companion .... *The Black Crowes*...Def American 26916
5	5	9	Adrenalize........ *Def Leppard*...Mercury 512185
6	8	24	Ten........ *Pearl Jam*...Epic/Associated 47857
7	7	38	Ropin' The Wind........ *Garth Brooks*...Capitol 96330
8	9	12	Classic Queen .... *Queen*...Hollywood 61311
9	16	17	**Mack Daddy**........ *Sir Mix-A-Lot*...Def American 26765
10	11	7	Greatest Hits........ *ZZ Top*...Warner 26846

TW	LW	WK	Billboard. JUNE 20, 1992 THE BILLBOARD 200.
1	1	3	**Some Gave All** ... *Billy Ray Cyrus*...Mercury 510635
2	2	10	Totally Krossed Out ... *Kris Kross*...Ruffhouse 48710
3	3	37	**Blood Sugar Sex Magik** ... *Red Hot Chili Peppers*...Warner 26681
4	-	1	**Shadows And Light** ... *Wilson Phillips*...SBK 98924
5	4	4	The Southern Harmony and Musical Companion ... *The Black Crowes*...Def American 26916
6	5	10	Adrenalize ... *Def Leppard*...Mercury 512185
7	6	25	Ten ... *Pearl Jam*...Epic/Associated 47857
8	-	1	MTV Unplugged EP ... *Mariah Carey*...Columbia 52758
9	7	39	Ropin' The Wind ... *Garth Brooks*...Capitol 96330
10	9	18	Mack Daddy ... *Sir Mix-A-Lot*...Def American 26765

TW	LW	WK	Billboard. JUNE 27, 1992 THE BILLBOARD 200.
1	1	4	**Some Gave All** ... *Billy Ray Cyrus*...Mercury 510635
2	2	11	Totally Krossed Out ... *Kris Kross*...Ruffhouse 48710
3	3	38	**Blood Sugar Sex Magik** ... *Red Hot Chili Peppers*...Warner 26681
4	4	2	**Shadows And Light** ... *Wilson Phillips*...SBK 98924
5	8	2	MTV Unplugged EP ... *Mariah Carey*...Columbia 52758
6	7	26	Ten ... *Pearl Jam*...Epic/Associated 47857
7	5	5	The Southern Harmony and Musical Companion ... *The Black Crowes*...Def American 26916
8	6	11	Adrenalize ... *Def Leppard*...Mercury 512185
9	9	40	Ropin' The Wind ... *Garth Brooks*...Capitol 96330
10	10	19	Mack Daddy ... *Sir Mix-A-Lot*...Def American 26765

TW	LW	WK	Billboard. JULY 4, 1992 THE BILLBOARD 200.
1	1	5	**Some Gave All** ... *Billy Ray Cyrus*...Mercury 510635
2	2	12	Totally Krossed Out ... *Kris Kross*...Ruffhouse 48710
3	5	3	**MTV Unplugged EP** ... *Mariah Carey*...Columbia 52758
4	3	39	Blood Sugar Sex Magik ... *Red Hot Chili Peppers*...Warner 26681
5	6	27	Ten ... *Pearl Jam*...Epic/Associated 47857
6	4	3	Shadows And Light ... *Wilson Phillips*...SBK 98924
7	9	41	Ropin' The Wind ... *Garth Brooks*...Capitol 96330
8	7	6	The Southern Harmony and Musical Companion ... *The Black Crowes*...Def American 26916
9	8	12	Adrenalize ... *Def Leppard*...Mercury 512185
10	-	1	**Angel Dust** ... *Faith No More*...Slash 26785

TW	LW	WK	Billboard. JULY 11, 1992 THE BILLBOARD 200.
1	1	6	**Some Gave All** ... *Billy Ray Cyrus*...Mercury 510635
2	2	13	Totally Krossed Out ... *Kris Kross*...Ruffhouse 48710
3	3	4	**MTV Unplugged EP** ... *Mariah Carey*...Columbia 52758
4	4	40	Blood Sugar Sex Magik ... *Red Hot Chili Peppers*...Warner 26681
5	5	28	Ten ... *Pearl Jam*...Epic/Associated 47857
6	7	42	Ropin' The Wind ... *Garth Brooks*...Capitol 96330
7	9	13	Adrenalize ... *Def Leppard*...Mercury 512185
8	6	4	Shadows And Light ... *Wilson Phillips*...SBK 98924
9	13	95	No Fences ... *Garth Brooks*...Capitol 93866
10	8	7	The Southern Harmony and Musical Companion ... *The Black Crowes*...Def American 26916

Billboard® — JULY 18, 1992 — THE BILLBOARD 200®

TW	LW	WK	Title	Artist	Label
1	1	7	**Some Gave All**	*Billy Ray Cyrus*	Mercury 510635
2	2	14	Totally Krossed Out	*Kris Kross*	Ruffhouse 48710
3	3	5	**MTV Unplugged EP**	*Mariah Carey*	Columbia 52758
4	5	29	Ten	*Pearl Jam*	Epic/Associated 47857
5	4	41	Blood Sugar Sex Magik	*Red Hot Chili Peppers*	Warner 26681
6	6	43	Ropin' The Wind	*Garth Brooks*	Capitol 96330
7	9	96	No Fences	*Garth Brooks*	Capitol 93866
8	-	1	Boomerang	*Soundtrack*	LaFace 26006
9	11	22	**Mack Daddy**	*Sir Mix-A-Lot*	Def American 26765
10	7	14	Adrenalize	*Def Leppard*	Mercury 512185

Billboard® — JULY 25, 1992 — THE BILLBOARD 200®

TW	LW	WK	Title	Artist	Label
1	1	8	**Some Gave All**	*Billy Ray Cyrus*	Mercury 510635
2	2	15	Totally Krossed Out	*Kris Kross*	Ruffhouse 48710
3	3	6	**MTV Unplugged EP**	*Mariah Carey*	Columbia 52758
4	8	2	**Boomerang**	*Soundtrack*	LaFace 26006
5	4	30	Ten	*Pearl Jam*	Epic/Associated 47857
6	5	42	Blood Sugar Sex Magik	*Red Hot Chili Peppers*	Warner 26681
7	6	44	Ropin' The Wind	*Garth Brooks*	Capitol 96330
8	7	97	No Fences	*Garth Brooks*	Capitol 93866
9	10	15	Adrenalize	*Def Leppard*	Mercury 512185
10	9	23	Mack Daddy	*Sir Mix-A-Lot*	Def American 26765

Billboard® — AUGUST 1, 1992 — THE BILLBOARD 200®

TW	LW	WK	Title	Artist	Label
1	1	9	**Some Gave All**	*Billy Ray Cyrus*	Mercury 510635
2	-	1	**Countdown To Extinction**	*Megadeth*	Capitol 98531
3	2	16	Totally Krossed Out	*Kris Kross*	Ruffhouse 48710
4	3	7	MTV Unplugged EP	*Mariah Carey*	Columbia 52758
5	4	3	Boomerang	*Soundtrack*	LaFace 26006
6	-	1	**Shorty The Pimp**	*Too $hort*	Jive 41467
7	5	31	Ten	*Pearl Jam*	Epic/Associated 47857
8	7	45	Ropin' The Wind	*Garth Brooks*	Capitol 96330
9	6	43	Blood Sugar Sex Magik	*Red Hot Chili Peppers*	Warner 26681
10	-	1	The Hard Way	*Clint Black*	RCA 66003

Billboard® — AUGUST 8, 1992 — THE BILLBOARD 200®

TW	LW	WK	Title	Artist	Label
1	1	10	**Some Gave All**	*Billy Ray Cyrus*	Mercury 510635
2	3	17	Totally Krossed Out	*Kris Kross*	Ruffhouse 48710
3	4	8	**MTV Unplugged EP**	*Mariah Carey*	Columbia 52758
4	5	4	**Boomerang**	*Soundtrack*	LaFace 26006
5	7	32	Ten	*Pearl Jam*	Epic/Associated 47857
6	2	2	Countdown To Extinction	*Megadeth*	Capitol 98531
7	6	2	Shorty The Pimp	*Too $hort*	Jive 41467
8	10	2	**The Hard Way**	*Clint Black*	RCA 66003
9	8	46	Ropin' The Wind	*Garth Brooks*	Capitol 96330
10	-	1	**Way 2 Fonky**	*DJ Quik*	Profile 1430

TW	LW	WK	Billboard® AUGUST 15, 1992 THE BILLBOARD 200®	
1	1	11	**Some Gave All**	*Billy Ray Cyrus*...Mercury 510635
2	2	18	Totally Krossed Out	*Kris Kross*...Ruffhouse 48710
3	5	33	Ten	*Pearl Jam*...Epic/Associated 47857
4	3	9	MTV Unplugged EP	*Mariah Carey*...Columbia 52758
5	4	5	Boomerang	*Soundtrack*...LaFace 26006
6	12	6	**Mo' Money**	*Soundtrack*...Perspective 1004
7	6	3	Countdown To Extinction	*Megadeth*...Capitol 98531
8	9	47	Ropin' The Wind	*Garth Brooks*...Capitol 96330
9	11	45	Blood Sugar Sex Magik	*Red Hot Chili Peppers*...Warner 26681
10	8	3	The Hard Way	*Clint Black*...RCA 66003

TW	LW	WK	Billboard® AUGUST 22, 1992 THE BILLBOARD 200®	
1	1	12	**Some Gave All**	*Billy Ray Cyrus*...Mercury 510635
2	3	34	**Ten**	*Pearl Jam*...Epic/Associated 47857
3	2	19	Totally Krossed Out	*Kris Kross*...Ruffhouse 48710
4	5	6	**Boomerang**	*Soundtrack*...LaFace 26006
5	4	10	MTV Unplugged EP	*Mariah Carey*...Columbia 52758
6	7	4	Countdown To Extinction	*Megadeth*...Capitol 98531
7	6	7	Mo' Money	*Soundtrack*...Perspective 1004
8	8	48	Ropin' The Wind	*Garth Brooks*...Capitol 96330
9	9	46	Blood Sugar Sex Magik	*Red Hot Chili Peppers*...Warner 26681
10	12	52	Metallica	*Metallica*...Elektra 61113

TW	LW	WK	Billboard® AUGUST 29, 1992 THE BILLBOARD 200®	
1	1	13	**Some Gave All**	*Billy Ray Cyrus*...Mercury 510635
2	2	35	**Ten**	*Pearl Jam*...Epic/Associated 47857
3	3	20	Totally Krossed Out	*Kris Kross*...Ruffhouse 48710
4	4	7	**Boomerang**	*Soundtrack*...LaFace 26006
5	6	5	Countdown To Extinction	*Megadeth*...Capitol 98531
6	5	11	MTV Unplugged EP	*Mariah Carey*...Columbia 52758
7	11	10	Temple Of The Dog	*Temple Of The Dog*...A&M 5350
8	9	47	Blood Sugar Sex Magik	*Red Hot Chili Peppers*...Warner 26681
9	7	8	Mo' Money	*Soundtrack*...Perspective 1004
10	8	49	Ropin' The Wind	*Garth Brooks*...Capitol 96330

TW	LW	WK	Billboard® SEPTEMBER 5, 1992 THE BILLBOARD 200®	
1	1	14	**Some Gave All**	*Billy Ray Cyrus*...Mercury 510635
2	2	36	**Ten**	*Pearl Jam*...Epic/Associated 47857
3	3	21	Totally Krossed Out	*Kris Kross*...Ruffhouse 48710
4	4	8	**Boomerang**	*Soundtrack*...LaFace 26006
5	7	11	**Temple Of The Dog**	*Temple Of The Dog*...A&M 5350
6	5	6	Countdown To Extinction	*Megadeth*...Capitol 98531
7	6	12	MTV Unplugged EP	*Mariah Carey*...Columbia 52758
8	11	9	**The One**	*Elton John*...MCA 10614
9	8	48	Blood Sugar Sex Magik	*Red Hot Chili Peppers*...Warner 26681
10	10	50	Ropin' The Wind	*Garth Brooks*...Capitol 96330

TW	LW	WK	Billboard. SEPTEMBER 12, 1992 THE BILLBOARD 200.
①	1	15	**Some Gave All** .... *Billy Ray Cyrus*...Mercury 510635
❷	-	1	**Bobby** .... *Bobby Brown*...MCA 10417
③	2	37	Ten .... *Pearl Jam*...Epic/Associated 47857
❹	-	1	Unplugged .... *Eric Clapton*...Duck 45024
❺	-	1	Beyond The Season .... *Garth Brooks*...Liberty 98742
⑥	3	22	Totally Krossed Out .... *Kris Kross*...Ruffhouse 48710
⑦	4	9	Boomerang .... *Soundtrack*...LaFace 26006
⑧	5	12	Temple Of The Dog .... *Temple Of The Dog*...A&M 5350
⑨	8	10	The One .... *Elton John*...MCA 10614
⑩	6	7	Countdown To Extinction .... *Megadeth*...Capitol 98531

TW	LW	WK	Billboard. SEPTEMBER 19, 1992 THE BILLBOARD 200.
①	1	16	**Some Gave All** .... *Billy Ray Cyrus*...Mercury 510635
❷	5	2	**Beyond The Season** .... *Garth Brooks*...Liberty 98742
❸	4	2	Unplugged .... *Eric Clapton*...Duck 45024
④	3	38	Ten .... *Pearl Jam*...Epic/Associated 47857
⑤	2	2	Bobby .... *Bobby Brown*...MCA 10417
⑥	7	10	Boomerang .... *Soundtrack*...LaFace 26006
⑦	6	23	Totally Krossed Out .... *Kris Kross*...Ruffhouse 48710
⑧	8	13	Temple Of The Dog .... *Temple Of The Dog*...A&M 5350
❾	20	6	What's The 411? .... *Mary J. Blige*...Uptown/MCA 10681
❿	11	24	Funky Divas .... *En Vogue*...EastWest 92121

TW	LW	WK	Billboard. SEPTEMBER 26, 1992 THE BILLBOARD 200.
①	1	17	**Some Gave All** .... *Billy Ray Cyrus*...Mercury 510635
②	3	3	Unplugged .... *Eric Clapton*...Duck 45024
③	4	39	Ten .... *Pearl Jam*...Epic/Associated 47857
④	2	3	Beyond The Season .... *Garth Brooks*...Liberty 98742
⑤	5	3	Bobby .... *Bobby Brown*...MCA 10417
⑥	9	7	**What's The 411?** .... *Mary J. Blige*...Uptown/MCA 10681
⑦	6	11	Boomerang .... *Soundtrack*...LaFace 26006
⑧	7	24	Totally Krossed Out .... *Kris Kross*...Ruffhouse 48710
⑨	10	25	Funky Divas .... *En Vogue*...EastWest 92121
❿	23	2	**I Still Believe In You** .... *Vince Gill*...MCA 10630

TW	LW	WK	Billboard. OCTOBER 3, 1992 THE BILLBOARD 200.
❶	1	18	**Some Gave All** .... *Billy Ray Cyrus*...Mercury 510635
❷	3	40	**Ten** .... *Pearl Jam*...Epic/Associated 47857
③	2	4	Unplugged .... *Eric Clapton*...Duck 45024
④	4	4	Beyond The Season .... *Garth Brooks*...Liberty 98742
⑤	5	4	Bobby .... *Bobby Brown*...MCA 10417
❻	6	8	**What's The 411?** .... *Mary J. Blige*...Uptown/MCA 10681
❼	16	12	Singles .... *Soundtrack*...Epic 52476
❽	8	25	Totally Krossed Out .... *Kris Kross*...Ruffhouse 48710
❾	9	26	Funky Divas .... *En Vogue*...EastWest 92121
⑩	7	12	Boomerang .... *Soundtrack*...LaFace 26006

TW	LW	WK	Billboard. OCTOBER 10, 1992 THE BILLBOARD 200.
❶	-	1	**The Chase** .... *Garth Brooks*...Liberty 98743
❷	3	5	Unplugged........ *Eric Clapton*...Duck 45024
③	1	19	Some Gave All .... *Billy Ray Cyrus*...Mercury 510635
④	2	41	Ten .... *Pearl Jam*...Epic/Associated 47857
⑤	4	5	Beyond The Season........ *Garth Brooks*...Liberty 98742
❻	7	13	**Singles**........ *Soundtrack*...Epic 52476
❼	-	1	**Broken**........ *Nine Inch Nails*...Nothing/TVT 92213
⑧	5	5	Bobby........ *Bobby Brown*...MCA 10417
⑨	6	9	What's The 411?........ *Mary J. Blige*...Uptown/MCA 10681
❿	-	1	**III Sides To Every Story**........ *Extreme*...A&M 40006

TW	LW	WK	Billboard. OCTOBER 17, 1992 THE BILLBOARD 200.
❶	1	2	**The Chase** .... *Garth Brooks*...Liberty 98743
❷	-	1	**Us** .... *Peter Gabriel*...Geffen 24473
❸	3	20	Some Gave All .... *Billy Ray Cyrus*...Mercury 510635
④	2	6	Unplugged........ *Eric Clapton*...Duck 45024
❺	-	1	Timeless (The Classics)........ *Michael Bolton*...Columbia 52783
❻	-	1	**Dirt**........ *Alice In Chains*...Columbia 52475
⑦	4	42	Ten .... *Pearl Jam*...Epic/Associated 47857
⑧	5	6	Beyond The Season........ *Garth Brooks*...Liberty 98742
⑨	9	10	What's The 411?........ *Mary J. Blige*...Uptown/MCA 10681
⑩	6	14	Singles .... *Soundtrack*...Epic 52476

TW	LW	WK	Billboard. OCTOBER 24, 1992 THE BILLBOARD 200.
①	1	3	**The Chase** .... *Garth Brooks*...Liberty 98743
❷	-	1	**Automatic For The People**........ *R.E.M.*...Warner 45138
❸	3	21	Some Gave All .... *Billy Ray Cyrus*...Mercury 510635
❹	4	7	Unplugged........ *Eric Clapton*...Duck 45024
❺	5	2	Timeless (The Classics)........ *Michael Bolton*...Columbia 52783
⑥	2	2	Us........ *Peter Gabriel*...Geffen 24473
⑦	7	43	Ten .... *Pearl Jam*...Epic/Associated 47857
⑧	6	2	Dirt........ *Alice In Chains*...Columbia 52475
⑨	8	7	Beyond The Season........ *Garth Brooks*...Liberty 98742
⑩	9	11	What's The 411?........ *Mary J. Blige*...Uptown/MCA 10681

TW	LW	WK	Billboard. OCTOBER 31, 1992 THE BILLBOARD 200.
①	1	4	**The Chase** .... *Garth Brooks*...Liberty 98743
②	2	2	**Automatic For The People**........ *R.E.M.*...Warner 45138
❸	4	8	Unplugged........ *Eric Clapton*...Duck 45024
④	3	22	Some Gave All .... *Billy Ray Cyrus*...Mercury 510635
❺	-	1	**(untitled)**........ *Prince & The New Power Generation*...Paisley Park 45037
⑥	5	3	Timeless (The Classics)........ *Michael Bolton*...Columbia 52783
⑦	7	44	Ten .... *Pearl Jam*...Epic/Associated 47857
⑧	6	3	Us........ *Peter Gabriel*...Geffen 24473
⑨	10	12	What's The 411?........ *Mary J. Blige*...Uptown/MCA 10681
⑩	8	3	Dirt........ *Alice In Chains*...Columbia 52475

Billboard — NOVEMBER 7, 1992 — THE BILLBOARD 200

TW	LW	WK	Title	Artist	Label
1	1	5	**The Chase**	Garth Brooks	Liberty 98743
2	-	1	**Erotica**	Madonna	Maverick/Sire 45154
3	3	9	Unplugged	Eric Clapton	Duck 45024
4	4	23	Some Gave All	Billy Ray Cyrus	Mercury 510635
5	2	3	Automatic For The People	R.E.M.	Warner 45138
6	6	4	Timeless (The Classics)	Michael Bolton	Columbia 52783
7	7	45	Ten	Pearl Jam	Epic/Associated 47857
8	5	2	(untitled)	Prince & The New Power Generation	Paisley Park 45037
9	22	6	Pure Country	George Strait/Soundtrack	MCA 10651
10	9	13	What's The 411?	Mary J. Blige	Uptown/MCA 10681

Billboard — NOVEMBER 14, 1992 — THE BILLBOARD 200

TW	LW	WK	Title	Artist	Label
1	1	6	**The Chase**	Garth Brooks	Liberty 98743
2	6	5	Timeless (The Classics)	Michael Bolton	Columbia 52783
3	3	10	Unplugged	Eric Clapton	Duck 45024
4	2	2	Erotica	Madonna	Maverick/Sire 45154
5	4	24	Some Gave All	Billy Ray Cyrus	Mercury 510635
6	5	4	Automatic For The People	R.E.M.	Warner 45138
7	9	7	Pure Country	George Strait/Soundtrack	MCA 10651
8	7	46	Ten	Pearl Jam	Epic/Associated 47857
9	10	14	What's The 411?	Mary J. Blige	Uptown/MCA 10681
10	8	3	(untitled)	Prince & The New Power Generation	Paisley Park 45037

Billboard — NOVEMBER 21, 1992 — THE BILLBOARD 200

TW	LW	WK	Title	Artist	Label
1	2	6	**Timeless (The Classics)**	Michael Bolton	Columbia 52783
2	1	7	The Chase	Garth Brooks	Liberty 98743
3	-	1	**Love Deluxe**	Sade	Epic 53178
4	3	11	Unplugged	Eric Clapton	Duck 45024
5	-	1	**Keep The Faith**	Bon Jovi	Jambco 514045
6	5	25	Some Gave All	Billy Ray Cyrus	Mercury 510635
7	7	8	Pure Country	George Strait/Soundtrack	MCA 10651
8	6	5	Automatic For The People	R.E.M.	Warner 45138
9	4	3	Erotica	Madonna	Maverick/Sire 45154
10	8	47	Ten	Pearl Jam	Epic/Associated 47857

Billboard — NOVEMBER 28, 1992 — THE BILLBOARD 200

TW	LW	WK	Title	Artist	Label
1	2	8	**The Chase**	Garth Brooks	Liberty 98743
2	1	7	Timeless (The Classics)	Michael Bolton	Columbia 52783
3	4	12	Unplugged	Eric Clapton	Duck 45024
4	6	26	Some Gave All	Billy Ray Cyrus	Mercury 510635
5	3	2	Love Deluxe	Sade	Epic 53178
6	7	9	**Pure Country**	George Strait/Soundtrack	MCA 10651
7	5	2	Keep The Faith	Bon Jovi	Jambco 514045
8	8	6	Automatic For The People	R.E.M.	Warner 45138
9	10	48	Ten	Pearl Jam	Epic/Associated 47857
10	9	4	Erotica	Madonna	Maverick/Sire 45154

TW	LW	WK	Billboard. ● DECEMBER 5, 1992 ● THE BILLBOARD 200.
❶	-	1	**The Predator** ....*Ice Cube*...Priority 57185
❷	-	1	The Bodyguard .... *Whitney Houston/Soundtrack*...Arista 18699
③	1	9	The Chase ....*Garth Brooks*...Liberty 98743
④	2	8	Timeless (The Classics) ....*Michael Bolton*...Columbia 52783
❺	3	13	Unplugged...*Eric Clapton*...Duck 45024
❻	4	27	Some Gave All ....*Billy Ray Cyrus*...Mercury 510635
❼	6	10	Pure Country......................................*George Strait/Soundtrack*...MCA 10651
⑧	5	3	Love Deluxe ....*Sade*...Epic 53178
❾	-	1	Breathless ....*Kenny G*...Arista 18646
⑩	8	7	Automatic For The People .... *R.E.M*....Warner 45138

TW	LW	WK	Billboard. ● DECEMBER 12, 1992 ● THE BILLBOARD 200.
❶	2	2	**The Bodyguard** .... *Whitney Houston/Soundtrack*...Arista 18699
❷	5	14	Unplugged...*Eric Clapton*...Duck 45024
③	1	2	The Predator ....*Ice Cube*...Priority 57185
④	4	9	Timeless (The Classics) ....*Michael Bolton*...Columbia 52783
⑤	3	10	The Chase ....*Garth Brooks*...Liberty 98743
❻	14	8	Home For Christmas...*Amy Grant*...A&M 31454
⑦	6	28	Some Gave All ....*Billy Ray Cyrus*...Mercury 510635
❽	9	2	Breathless ....*Kenny G*...Arista 18646
❾	18	5	A Very Special Christmas 2................................*Various Artists*...A&M 31454
⑩	11	14	Beyond The Season... *Garth Brooks*...Liberty 98742

TW	LW	WK	Billboard. ● DECEMBER 19, 1992 ● THE BILLBOARD 200.
❶	1	3	**The Bodyguard** .... *Whitney Houston/Soundtrack*...Arista 18699
❷	4	10	Timeless (The Classics) ....*Michael Bolton*...Columbia 52783
❸	5	11	The Chase ....*Garth Brooks*...Liberty 98743
❹	7	29	Some Gave All ....*Billy Ray Cyrus*...Mercury 510635
❺	6	9	Home For Christmas...*Amy Grant*...A&M 31454
⑥	2	15	Unplugged...*Eric Clapton*...Duck 45024
❼	9	6	**A Very Special Christmas 2** ....*Various Artists*...A&M 31454
❽	14	9	**The Christmas Album** .... *Neil Diamond*...Columbia 52914
⑨	8	3	Breathless ....*Kenny G*...Arista 18646
⑩	10	15	Beyond The Season..*Garth Brooks*...Liberty 98742

TW	LW	WK	Billboard. ● DECEMBER 26, 1992 ● THE BILLBOARD 200.
❶	1	4	**The Bodyguard** .... *Whitney Houston/Soundtrack*...Arista 18699
❷	5	10	**Home For Christmas** ....*Amy Grant*...A&M 31454
③	2	11	Timeless (The Classics) ....*Michael Bolton*...Columbia 52783
❹	3	12	The Chase ....*Garth Brooks*...Liberty 98743
⑤	4	30	Some Gave All ....*Billy Ray Cyrus*...Mercury 510635
❻	6	16	Unplugged...*Eric Clapton*...Duck 45024
❼	7	7	**A Very Special Christmas 2** ....*Various Artists*...A&M 31454
❽	8	10	**The Christmas Album** .... *Neil Diamond*...Columbia 52914
❾	9	4	Breathless ....*Kenny G*...Arista 18646
⑩	10	16	Beyond The Season..*Garth Brooks*...Liberty 98742

Billboard® JANUARY 2, 1993 — THE BILLBOARD 200®

TW	LW	WK	Title	Artist...Label
1	1	5	The Bodyguard	*Whitney Houston/Soundtrack*...Arista 18699
2	6	17	Unplugged	*Eric Clapton*...Duck 45024
3	3	12	Timeless (The Classics)	*Michael Bolton*...Columbia 52783
4	4	13	The Chase	*Garth Brooks*...Liberty 98743
5	9	5	Breathless	*Kenny G*...Arista 18646
6	5	31	Some Gave All	*Billy Ray Cyrus*...Mercury 510635
7	2	11	Home For Christmas	*Amy Grant*...A&M 31454
8	7	8	A Very Special Christmas 2	*Various Artists*...A&M 31454
9	8	11	The Christmas Album	*Neil Diamond*...Columbia 52914
10	10	17	Beyond The Season	*Garth Brooks*...Liberty 98742

Billboard® JANUARY 9, 1993 — THE BILLBOARD 200®

TW	LW	WK	Title	Artist...Label
1	1	6	The Bodyguard	*Whitney Houston/Soundtrack*...Arista 18699
2	2	18	Unplugged	*Eric Clapton*...Duck 45024
3	5	6	Breathless	*Kenny G*...Arista 18646
4	3	13	Timeless (The Classics)	*Michael Bolton*...Columbia 52783
5	4	14	The Chase	*Garth Brooks*...Liberty 98743
6	11	54	Ten	*Pearl Jam*...Epic/Associated 47857
7	6	32	Some Gave All	*Billy Ray Cyrus*...Mercury 510635
8	12	12	Automatic For The People	*R.E.M.*...Warner 45138
9	7	12	Home For Christmas	*Amy Grant*...A&M 31454
10	18	5	Hard Or Smooth	*Wreckx-N-Effect*...MCA 10566

Billboard® JANUARY 16, 1993 — THE BILLBOARD 200®

TW	LW	WK	Title	Artist...Label
1	1	7	The Bodyguard	*Whitney Houston/Soundtrack*...Arista 18699
2	5	15	The Chase	*Garth Brooks*...Liberty 98743
3	4	14	Timeless (The Classics)	*Michael Bolton*...Columbia 52783
4	2	19	Unplugged	*Eric Clapton*...Duck 45024
5	7	33	Some Gave All	*Billy Ray Cyrus*...Mercury 510635
6	3	7	Breathless	*Kenny G*...Arista 18646
7	6	55	Ten	*Pearl Jam*...Epic/Associated 47857
8	17	2	...If I Ever Fall In Love	*Shai*...Gasoline Alley 10762
9	12	3	It's Your Call	*Reba McEntire*...MCA 10673
10	10	6	Hard Or Smooth	*Wreckx-N-Effect*...MCA 10566

Billboard® JANUARY 23, 1993 — THE BILLBOARD 200®

TW	LW	WK	Title	Artist...Label
1	1	8	The Bodyguard	*Whitney Houston/Soundtrack*...Arista 18699
2	2	16	The Chase	*Garth Brooks*...Liberty 98743
3	5	34	Some Gave All	*Billy Ray Cyrus*...Mercury 510635
4	4	20	Unplugged	*Eric Clapton*...Duck 45024
5	3	15	Timeless (The Classics)	*Michael Bolton*...Columbia 52783
6	6	8	Breathless	*Kenny G*...Arista 18646
7	7	56	Ten	*Pearl Jam*...Epic/Associated 47857
8	9	4	It's Your Call	*Reba McEntire*...MCA 10673
9	12	17	Pure Country	*George Strait/Soundtrack*...MCA 10651
10	20	59	Brand New Man	*Brooks & Dunn*...Arista 18658

Billboard. JANUARY 30, 1993 — THE BILLBOARD 200.

TW	LW	WK	Title	Artist...Label
1	1	9	**The Bodyguard**	*Whitney Houston/Soundtrack*...Arista 18699
2	6	9	**Breathless**	*Kenny G*...Arista 18646
3	4	21	Unplugged	*Eric Clapton*...Duck 45024
4	3	35	Some Gave All	*Billy Ray Cyrus*...Mercury 510635
5	2	17	The Chase	*Garth Brooks*...Liberty 98743
6	5	16	Timeless (The Classics)	*Michael Bolton*...Columbia 52783
7	12	5	The Chronic	*Dr. Dre*...Death Row 57128
8	11	4	...If I Ever Fall In Love	*Shai*...Gasoline Alley 10762
9	7	57	Ten	*Pearl Jam*...Epic/Associated 47857
10	14	8	Hard Or Smooth	*Wreckx-N-Effect*...MCA 10566

Billboard. FEBRUARY 6, 1993 — THE BILLBOARD 200.

TW	LW	WK	Title	Artist...Label
1	1	10	**The Bodyguard**	*Whitney Houston/Soundtrack*...Arista 18699
2	2	10	**Breathless**	*Kenny G*...Arista 18646
3	3	22	Unplugged	*Eric Clapton*...Duck 45024
4	7	6	The Chronic	*Dr. Dre*...Death Row 57128
5	4	36	Some Gave All	*Billy Ray Cyrus*...Mercury 510635
6	8	5	**...If I Ever Fall In Love**	*Shai*...Gasoline Alley 10762
7	6	17	Timeless (The Classics)	*Michael Bolton*...Columbia 52783
8	11	11	Aladdin	*Soundtrack*...Disney 60846
9	10	9	**Hard Or Smooth**	*Wreckx-N-Effect*...MCA 10566
10	9	58	Ten	*Pearl Jam*...Epic/Associated 47857

Billboard. FEBRUARY 13, 1993 — THE BILLBOARD 200.

TW	LW	WK	Title	Artist...Label
1	1	11	**The Bodyguard**	*Whitney Houston/Soundtrack*...Arista 18699
2	2	11	**Breathless**	*Kenny G*...Arista 18646
3	4	7	**The Chronic**	*Dr. Dre*...Death Row 57128
4	3	23	Unplugged	*Eric Clapton*...Duck 45024
5	5	37	Some Gave All	*Billy Ray Cyrus*...Mercury 510635
6	7	18	Timeless (The Classics)	*Michael Bolton*...Columbia 52783
7	10	59	Ten	*Pearl Jam*...Epic/Associated 47857
8	6	6	...If I Ever Fall In Love	*Shai*...Gasoline Alley 10762
9	8	12	Aladdin	*Soundtrack*...Disney 60846
10	13	33	Pocket Full Of Kryptonite	*Spin Doctors*...Epic/Associated 47461

Billboard. FEBRUARY 20, 1993 — THE BILLBOARD 200.

TW	LW	WK	Title	Artist...Label
1	1	12	**The Bodyguard**	*Whitney Houston/Soundtrack*...Arista 18699
2	2	12	**Breathless**	*Kenny G*...Arista 18646
3	3	8	**The Chronic**	*Dr. Dre*...Death Row 57128
4	5	38	Some Gave All	*Billy Ray Cyrus*...Mercury 510635
5	4	24	Unplugged	*Eric Clapton*...Duck 45024
6	8	7	**...If I Ever Fall In Love**	*Shai*...Gasoline Alley 10762
7	10	34	Pocket Full Of Kryptonite	*Spin Doctors*...Epic/Associated 47461
8	7	60	Ten	*Pearl Jam*...Epic/Associated 47857
9	9	13	Aladdin	*Soundtrack*...Disney 60846
10	6	19	Timeless (The Classics)	*Michael Bolton*...Columbia 52783

Billboard — FEBRUARY 27, 1993 — THE BILLBOARD 200

TW	LW	WK	Title	Artist...Label
1	1	13	**The Bodyguard**	*Whitney Houston/Soundtrack*...Arista 18699
2	2	13	**Breathless**	*Kenny G*...Arista 18646
3	3	9	**The Chronic**	*Dr. Dre*...Death Row 57128
4	5	25	Unplugged	*Eric Clapton*...Duck 45024
5	4	39	Some Gave All	*Billy Ray Cyrus*...Mercury 510635
6	9	14	**Aladdin**	*Soundtrack*...Disney 60846
7	7	35	Pocket Full Of Kryptonite	*Spin Doctors*...Epic/Associated 47461
8	10	20	Timeless (The Classics)	*Michael Bolton*...Columbia 52783
9	6	8	...If I Ever Fall In Love	*Shai*...Gasoline Alley 10762
10	15	9	It's Your Call	*Reba McEntire*...MCA 10673

Billboard — MARCH 6, 1993 — THE BILLBOARD 200

TW	LW	WK	Title	Artist...Label
1	1	14	**The Bodyguard**	*Whitney Houston/Soundtrack*...Arista 18699
2	2	14	**Breathless**	*Kenny G*...Arista 18646
3	3	10	**The Chronic**	*Dr. Dre*...Death Row 57128
4	5	40	Some Gave All	*Billy Ray Cyrus*...Mercury 510635
5	4	26	Unplugged	*Eric Clapton*...Duck 45024
6	7	36	Pocket Full Of Kryptonite	*Spin Doctors*...Epic/Associated 47461
7	6	15	Aladdin	*Soundtrack*...Disney 60846
8	10	10	**It's Your Call**	*Reba McEntire*...MCA 10673
9	13	62	Ten	*Pearl Jam*...Epic/Associated 47857
10	12	65	Dangerous	*Michael Jackson*...Epic 45400

Billboard — MARCH 13, 1993 — THE BILLBOARD 200

TW	LW	WK	Title	Artist...Label
1	5	27	**Unplugged**	*Eric Clapton*...Duck 45024
2	1	15	The Bodyguard	*Whitney Houston/Soundtrack*...Arista 18699
3	-	1	**19 Naughty III**	*Naughty By Nature*...Tommy Boy 1069
4	2	15	Breathless	*Kenny G*...Arista 18646
5	-	1	**LIVE: Right here, right now.**	*Van Halen*...Warner 45198
6	4	41	Some Gave All	*Billy Ray Cyrus*...Mercury 510635
7	-	1	**Duran Duran**	*Duran Duran*...Capitol 98876
8	3	11	The Chronic	*Dr. Dre*...Death Row 57128
9	11	48	3 Years, 5 Months & 2 Days In The Life Of	*Arrested Development*...Chrysalis 21929
10	6	37	Pocket Full Of Kryptonite	*Spin Doctors*...Epic/Associated 47461

Billboard — MARCH 20, 1993 — THE BILLBOARD 200

TW	LW	WK	Title	Artist...Label
1	1	28	**Unplugged**	*Eric Clapton*...Duck 45024
2	2	16	The Bodyguard	*Whitney Houston/Soundtrack*...Arista 18699
3	4	16	Breathless	*Kenny G*...Arista 18646
4	3	2	19 Naughty III	*Naughty By Nature*...Tommy Boy 1069
5	8	12	The Chronic	*Dr. Dre*...Death Row 57128
6	6	42	Some Gave All	*Billy Ray Cyrus*...Mercury 510635
7	9	49	**3 Years, 5 Months & 2 Days In The Life Of**	*Arrested Development*...Chrysalis 21929
8	10	38	Pocket Full Of Kryptonite	*Spin Doctors*...Epic/Associated 47461
9	19	2	**Hard Workin' Man**	*Brooks & Dunn*...Arista 18716
10	13	11	Lose Control	*Silk*...Elektra 61394

TW	LW	WK	Billboard® MARCH 27, 1993 THE BILLBOARD 200®
①	1	29	**Unplugged**......Eric Clapton...Duck 45024
❷	-	1	**Ten Summoner's Tales**......Sting...A&M 0070
③	2	17	The Bodyguard......Whitney Houston/Soundtrack...Arista 18699
④	3	17	Breathless......Kenny G...Arista 18646
⑤	8	39	Pocket Full Of Kryptonite......Spin Doctors...Epic/Associated 47461
⑥	5	13	The Chronic......Dr. Dre...Death Row 57128
⑦	4	3	19 Naughty III......Naughty By Nature...Tommy Boy 1069
⑧	6	43	Some Gave All......Billy Ray Cyrus...Mercury 510635
⑨	7	50	3 Years, 5 Months & 2 Days In The Life Of ......Arrested Development...Chrysalis 21929
⑩	10	12	Lose Control......Silk...Elektra 61394

TW	LW	WK	Billboard® APRIL 3, 1993 THE BILLBOARD 200®
❶	3	18	**The Bodyguard**......Whitney Houston/Soundtrack...Arista 18699
②	4	18	**Breathless**......Kenny G...Arista 18646
③	1	30	Unplugged......Eric Clapton...Duck 45024
④	2	2	Ten Summoner's Tales......Sting...A&M 0070
❺	-	1	**Coverdale•Page**......Coverdale • Page...Geffen 24487
❻	5	40	Pocket Full Of Kryptonite......Spin Doctors...Epic/Associated 47461
⑦	6	14	The Chronic......Dr. Dre...Death Row 57128
❽	10	13	Lose Control......Silk...Elektra 61394
⑨	7	4	19 Naughty III......Naughty By Nature...Tommy Boy 1069
❿	14	9	12 Inches Of Snow......Snow...EastWest 92207

TW	LW	WK	Billboard® APRIL 10, 1993 THE BILLBOARD 200®
❶	-	1	**Songs Of Faith And Devotion**......Depeche Mode...Sire 45243
②	1	19	The Bodyguard......Whitney Houston/Soundtrack...Arista 18699
③	2	19	Breathless......Kenny G...Arista 18646
④	3	31	Unplugged......Eric Clapton...Duck 45024
⑤	4	3	Ten Summoner's Tales......Sting...A&M 0070
⑥	6	41	Pocket Full Of Kryptonite......Spin Doctors...Epic/Associated 47461
❼	10	10	12 Inches Of Snow......Snow...EastWest 92207
⑧	7	15	The Chronic......Dr. Dre...Death Row 57128
⑨	8	14	Lose Control......Silk...Elektra 61394
⑩	5	2	Coverdale•Page......Coverdale • Page...Geffen 24487

TW	LW	WK	Billboard® APRIL 17, 1993 THE BILLBOARD 200®
❶	2	20	**The Bodyguard**......Whitney Houston/Soundtrack...Arista 18699
②	3	20	**Breathless**......Kenny G...Arista 18646
③	4	32	Unplugged......Eric Clapton...Duck 45024
④	6	42	Pocket Full Of Kryptonite......Spin Doctors...Epic/Associated 47461
❺	-	1	**14 Shots To The Dome**......L.L. Cool J...Def Jam 53325
⑥	1	2	Songs Of Faith And Devotion......Depeche Mode...Sire 45243
⑦	5	4	Ten Summoner's Tales......Sting...A&M 0070
⑧	7	11	12 Inches Of Snow......Snow...EastWest 92207
❾	8	16	The Chronic......Dr. Dre...Death Row 57128
❿	9	15	Lose Control......Silk...Elektra 61394

Billboard — APRIL 24, 1993 — THE BILLBOARD 200

TW	LW	WK	Title	Artist...Label
1	1	21	**The Bodyguard**	*Whitney Houston/Soundtrack*...Arista 18699
2	2	21	**Breathless**	*Kenny G*...Arista 18646
3	4	43	**Pocket Full Of Kryptonite**	*Spin Doctors*...Epic/Associated 47461
4	3	33	Unplugged	*Eric Clapton*...Duck 45024
5	8	12	**12 Inches Of Snow**	*Snow*...EastWest 92207
6	7	5	Ten Summoner's Tales	*Sting*...A&M 0070
7	9	17	The Chronic	*Dr. Dre*...Death Row 57128
8	10	16	Lose Control	*Silk*...Elektra 61394
9	6	3	Songs Of Faith And Devotion	*Depeche Mode*...Sire 45243
10	12	22	Aladdin	*Soundtrack*...Disney 60846

Billboard — MAY 1, 1993 — THE BILLBOARD 200

TW	LW	WK	Title	Artist...Label
1	1	22	**The Bodyguard**	*Whitney Houston/Soundtrack*...Arista 18699
2	2	22	**Breathless**	*Kenny G*...Arista 18646
3	3	44	**Pocket Full Of Kryptonite**	*Spin Doctors*...Epic/Associated 47461
4	4	34	Unplugged	*Eric Clapton*...Duck 45024
5	5	13	**12 Inches Of Snow**	*Snow*...EastWest 92207
6	7	18	The Chronic	*Dr. Dre*...Death Row 57128
7	8	17	**Lose Control**	*Silk*...Elektra 61394
8	6	6	Ten Summoner's Tales	*Sting*...A&M 0070
9	12	24	Love Deluxe	*Sade*...Epic 53178
10	9	4	Songs Of Faith And Devotion	*Depeche Mode*...Sire 45243

Billboard — MAY 8, 1993 — THE BILLBOARD 200

TW	LW	WK	Title	Artist...Label
1	-	1	**Get A Grip**	*Aerosmith*...Geffen 24455
2	1	23	The Bodyguard	*Whitney Houston/Soundtrack*...Arista 18699
3	2	23	Breathless	*Kenny G*...Arista 18646
4	3	45	Pocket Full Of Kryptonite	*Spin Doctors*...Epic/Associated 47461
5	4	35	Unplugged	*Eric Clapton*...Duck 45024
6	6	19	The Chronic	*Dr. Dre*...Death Row 57128
7	-	1	**Pork Soda**	*Primus*...Interscope 92257
8	5	14	12 Inches Of Snow	*Snow*...EastWest 92207
9	7	18	Lose Control	*Silk*...Elektra 61394
10	9	25	Love Deluxe	*Sade*...Epic 53178

Billboard — MAY 15, 1993 — THE BILLBOARD 200

TW	LW	WK	Title	Artist...Label
1	2	24	**The Bodyguard**	*Whitney Houston/Soundtrack*...Arista 18699
2	1	2	Get A Grip	*Aerosmith*...Geffen 24455
3	-	1	**Porno For Pyros**	*Porno For Pyros*...Warner 45228
4	3	24	Breathless	*Kenny G*...Arista 18646
5	4	46	Pocket Full Of Kryptonite	*Spin Doctors*...Epic/Associated 47461
6	5	36	Unplugged	*Eric Clapton*...Duck 45024
7	6	20	The Chronic	*Dr. Dre*...Death Row 57128
8	8	15	12 Inches Of Snow	*Snow*...EastWest 92207
9	13	17	It's About Time	*SWV*...RCA 66074
10	9	19	Lose Control	*Silk*...Elektra 61394

TW	LW	WK	Billboard. MAY 22, 1993 THE BILLBOARD 200.
1	1	25	**The Bodyguard** ... *Whitney Houston/Soundtrack*...Arista 18699
2	4	25	**Breathless** ... *Kenny G*...Arista 18646
3	2	3	Get A Grip ... *Aerosmith*...Geffen 24455
4	5	47	Pocket Full Of Kryptonite ... *Spin Doctors*...Epic/Associated 47461
5	7	21	The Chronic ... *Dr. Dre*...Death Row 57128
6	6	37	Unplugged ... *Eric Clapton*...Duck 45024
7	-	1	**Down With The King** ... *Run-D.M.C.*...Profile 1440
8	9	18	**It's About Time** ... *SWV*...RCA 66074
9	11	27	Love Deluxe ... *Sade*...Epic 53178
10	8	16	12 Inches Of Snow ... *Snow*...EastWest 92207

TW	LW	WK	Billboard. MAY 29, 1993 THE BILLBOARD 200.
1	1	26	**The Bodyguard** ... *Whitney Houston/Soundtrack*...Arista 18699
2	3	4	Get A Grip ... *Aerosmith*...Geffen 24455
3	2	26	Breathless ... *Kenny G*...Arista 18646
4	4	48	Pocket Full Of Kryptonite ... *Spin Doctors*...Epic/Associated 47461
5	-	1	**Tell Me Why** ... *Wynonna*...Curb/MCA 10822
6	5	22	The Chronic ... *Dr. Dre*...Death Row 57128
7	6	38	Unplugged ... *Eric Clapton*...Duck 45024
8	8	19	**It's About Time** ... *SWV*...RCA 66074
9	9	28	Love Deluxe ... *Sade*...Epic 53178
10	11	10	Ten Summoner's Tales ... *Sting*...A&M 0070

TW	LW	WK	Billboard. JUNE 5, 1993 THE BILLBOARD 200.
1	-	1	**janet.** ... *Janet Jackson*...Virgin 87825
2	1	27	The Bodyguard ... *Whitney Houston/Soundtrack*...Arista 18699
3	2	5	Get A Grip ... *Aerosmith*...Geffen 24455
4	4	49	Pocket Full Of Kryptonite ... *Spin Doctors*...Epic/Associated 47461
5	3	27	Breathless ... *Kenny G*...Arista 18646
6	5	2	Tell Me Why ... *Wynonna*...Curb/MCA 10822
7	6	23	The Chronic ... *Dr. Dre*...Death Row 57128
8	8	20	**It's About Time** ... *SWV*...RCA 66074
9	-	1	**Alive III** ... *Kiss*...Mercury 514777
10	10	11	Ten Summoner's Tales ... *Sting*...A&M 0070

TW	LW	WK	Billboard. JUNE 12, 1993 THE BILLBOARD 200.
1	1	2	**janet.** ... *Janet Jackson*...Virgin 87825
2	-	1	**Unplugged...And Seated** ... *Rod Stewart*...Warner 45289
3	2	28	The Bodyguard ... *Whitney Houston/Soundtrack*...Arista 18699
4	5	28	Breathless ... *Kenny G*...Arista 18646
5	4	50	Pocket Full Of Kryptonite ... *Spin Doctors*...Epic/Associated 47461
6	3	6	Get A Grip ... *Aerosmith*...Geffen 24455
7	-	1	**Sound Of White Noise** ... *Anthrax*...Elektra 61430
8	7	24	The Chronic ... *Dr. Dre*...Death Row 57128
9	8	21	It's About Time ... *SWV*...RCA 66074
10	-	1	**Kamakiriad** ... *Donald Fagen*...Reprise 45230

Billboard — JUNE 19, 1993 — THE BILLBOARD 200

TW	LW	WK	Title	Artist...Label
1	1	3	**janet.**	*Janet Jackson*...Virgin 87825
2	2	2	**Unplugged...And Seated**	*Rod Stewart*...Warner 45289
3	8	25	**The Chronic**	*Dr. Dre*...Death Row 57128
4	3	29	The Bodyguard	*Whitney Houston/Soundtrack*...Arista 18699
5	4	29	Breathless	*Kenny G*...Arista 18646
6	6	7	Get A Grip	*Aerosmith*...Geffen 24455
7	5	51	Pocket Full Of Kryptonite	*Spin Doctors*...Epic/Associated 47461
8	-	1	Never Let Me Go	*Luther Vandross*...Epic/LV 53231
9	9	22	It's About Time	*SWV*...RCA 66074
10	12	24	Core	*Stone Temple Pilots*...Atlantic 82418

Billboard — JUNE 26, 1993 — THE BILLBOARD 200

TW	LW	WK	Title	Artist...Label
1	1	4	**janet.**	*Janet Jackson*...Virgin 87825
2	2	3	**Unplugged...And Seated**	*Rod Stewart*...Warner 45289
3	3	26	**The Chronic**	*Dr. Dre*...Death Row 57128
4	4	30	The Bodyguard	*Whitney Houston/Soundtrack*...Arista 18699
5	10	25	Core	*Stone Temple Pilots*...Atlantic 82418
6	5	30	Breathless	*Kenny G*...Arista 18646
7	7	52	Pocket Full Of Kryptonite	*Spin Doctors*...Epic/Associated 47461
8	6	8	Get A Grip	*Aerosmith*...Geffen 24455
9	8	2	Never Let Me Go	*Luther Vandross*...Epic/LV 53231
10	9	23	It's About Time	*SWV*...RCA 66074

Billboard — JULY 3, 1993 — THE BILLBOARD 200

TW	LW	WK	Title	Artist...Label
1	1	5	**janet.**	*Janet Jackson*...Virgin 87825
2	2	4	**Unplugged...And Seated**	*Rod Stewart*...Warner 45289
3	5	26	**Core**	*Stone Temple Pilots*...Atlantic 82418
4	3	27	The Chronic	*Dr. Dre*...Death Row 57128
5	6	31	Breathless	*Kenny G*...Arista 18646
6	9	3	**Never Let Me Go**	*Luther Vandross*...Epic/LV 53231
7	4	31	The Bodyguard	*Whitney Houston/Soundtrack*...Arista 18699
8	7	53	Pocket Full Of Kryptonite	*Spin Doctors*...Epic/Associated 47461
9	12	2	Last Action Hero	*Soundtrack*...Columbia 57127
10	10	24	It's About Time	*SWV*...RCA 66074

Billboard — JULY 10, 1993 — THE BILLBOARD 200

TW	LW	WK	Title	Artist...Label
1	1	6	**janet.**	*Janet Jackson*...Virgin 87825
2	2	5	**Unplugged...And Seated**	*Rod Stewart*...Warner 45289
3	3	27	**Core**	*Stone Temple Pilots*...Atlantic 82418
4	5	32	Breathless	*Kenny G*...Arista 18646
5	4	28	The Chronic	*Dr. Dre*...Death Row 57128
6	-	1	It Won't Be The Last	*Billy Ray Cyrus*...Mercury 514758
7	9	3	**Last Action Hero**	*Soundtrack*...Columbia 57127
8	7	32	The Bodyguard	*Whitney Houston/Soundtrack*...Arista 18699
9	8	54	Pocket Full Of Kryptonite	*Spin Doctors*...Epic/Associated 47461
10	10	25	It's About Time	*SWV*...RCA 66074

Billboard — JULY 17, 1993 — THE BILLBOARD 200

TW	LW	WK	Title	Artist...Label
1	-	1	**Back To Broadway**	*Barbra Streisand*...Columbia 44189
2	1	7	janet.	*Janet Jackson*...Virgin 87825
3	6	2	**It Won't Be The Last**	*Billy Ray Cyrus*...Mercury 514758
4	3	28	Core	*Stone Temple Pilots*...Atlantic 82418
5	2	6	Unplugged...And Seated	*Rod Stewart*...Warner 45289
6	5	29	The Chronic	*Dr. Dre*...Death Row 57128
7	4	33	Breathless	*Kenny G*...Arista 18646
8	7	4	Last Action Hero	*Soundtrack*...Columbia 57127
9	54	2	Sleepless In Seattle	*Soundtrack*...Epic Soundtrax 53764
10	10	26	It's About Time	*SWV*...RCA 66074

Billboard — JULY 24, 1993 — THE BILLBOARD 200

TW	LW	WK	Title	Artist...Label
1	-	1	**Zooropa**	*U2*...Island 518047
2	1	2	Back To Broadway	*Barbra Streisand*...Columbia 44189
3	2	8	janet.	*Janet Jackson*...Virgin 87825
4	9	3	Sleepless In Seattle	*Soundtrack*...Epic Soundtrax 53764
5	3	3	It Won't Be The Last	*Billy Ray Cyrus*...Mercury 514758
6	4	29	Core	*Stone Temple Pilots*...Atlantic 82418
7	5	7	Unplugged...And Seated	*Rod Stewart*...Warner 45289
8	6	30	The Chronic	*Dr. Dre*...Death Row 57128
9	8	5	Last Action Hero	*Soundtrack*...Columbia 57127
10	7	34	Breathless	*Kenny G*...Arista 18646

Billboard — JULY 31, 1993 — THE BILLBOARD 200

TW	LW	WK	Title	Artist...Label
1	1	2	**Zooropa**	*U2*...Island 518047
2	4	4	Sleepless In Seattle	*Soundtrack*...Epic Soundtrax 53764
3	2	3	Back To Broadway	*Barbra Streisand*...Columbia 44189
4	3	9	janet.	*Janet Jackson*...Virgin 87825
5	6	30	Core	*Stone Temple Pilots*...Atlantic 82418
6	7	8	Unplugged...And Seated	*Rod Stewart*...Warner 45289
7	5	4	It Won't Be The Last	*Billy Ray Cyrus*...Mercury 514758
8	8	31	The Chronic	*Dr. Dre*...Death Row 57128
9	11	28	It's About Time	*SWV*...RCA 66074
10	10	35	Breathless	*Kenny G*...Arista 18646

Billboard — AUGUST 7, 1993 — THE BILLBOARD 200

TW	LW	WK	Title	Artist...Label
1	-	1	**Black Sunday**	*Cypress Hill*...Ruffhouse 53931
2	1	3	Zooropa	*U2*...Island 518047
3	2	5	Sleepless In Seattle	*Soundtrack*...Epic Soundtrax 53764
4	4	10	janet.	*Janet Jackson*...Virgin 87825
5	3	4	Back To Broadway	*Barbra Streisand*...Columbia 44189
6	5	31	Core	*Stone Temple Pilots*...Atlantic 82418
7	6	9	Unplugged...And Seated	*Rod Stewart*...Warner 45289
8	11	36	The Bodyguard	*Whitney Houston/Soundtrack*...Arista 18699
9	8	32	The Chronic	*Dr. Dre*...Death Row 57128
10	7	5	It Won't Be The Last	*Billy Ray Cyrus*...Mercury 514758

TW	LW	WK	Billboard. AUGUST 14, 1993 THE BILLBOARD 200.
①	1	2	**Black Sunday**......*Cypress Hill*...Ruffhouse 53931
❷	3	6	Sleepless In Seattle......*Soundtrack*...Epic Soundtrax 53764
③	2	4	Zooropa......*U2*...Island 518047
④	4	11	janet......*Janet Jackson*...Virgin 87825
❺	6	32	Core......*Stone Temple Pilots*...Atlantic 82418
⑥	5	5	Back To Broadway......*Barbra Streisand*...Columbia 44189
❼	-	1	Promises and Lies......*UB40*...Virgin 88229
❽	8	37	The Bodyguard......*Whitney Houston/Soundtrack*...Arista 18699
⑨	7	10	Unplugged...And Seated......*Rod Stewart*...Warner 45289
❿	-	1	**Siamese Dream**......*The Smashing Pumpkins*...Virgin 88267

TW	LW	WK	Billboard. AUGUST 21, 1993 THE BILLBOARD 200.
❶	2	7	**Sleepless In Seattle**......*Soundtrack*...Epic Soundtrax 53764
②	1	3	Black Sunday......*Cypress Hill*...Ruffhouse 53931
③	4	12	janet......*Janet Jackson*...Virgin 87825
④	3	5	Zooropa......*U2*...Island 518047
⑤	5	33	Core......*Stone Temple Pilots*...Atlantic 82418
❻	7	2	**Promises and Lies**......*UB40*...Virgin 88229
⑦	8	38	The Bodyguard......*Whitney Houston/Soundtrack*...Arista 18699
⑧	9	11	Unplugged...And Seated......*Rod Stewart*...Warner 45289
❾	13	16	Get A Grip......*Aerosmith*...Geffen 24455
❿	28	5	Blind Melon......*Blind Melon*...Capitol 96585

TW	LW	WK	Billboard. AUGUST 28, 1993 THE BILLBOARD 200.
❶	-	1	**River Of Dreams**......*Billy Joel*...Columbia 53003
②	1	8	Sleepless In Seattle......*Soundtrack*...Epic Soundtrax 53764
③	2	4	Black Sunday......*Cypress Hill*...Ruffhouse 53931
④	3	13	janet......*Janet Jackson*...Virgin 87825
⑤	5	34	Core......*Stone Temple Pilots*...Atlantic 82418
⑥	4	6	Zooropa......*U2*...Island 518047
❼	10	6	Blind Melon......*Blind Melon*...Capitol 96585
⑧	6	3	Promises and Lies......*UB40*...Virgin 88229
❾	9	17	Get A Grip......*Aerosmith*...Geffen 24455
⑩	7	39	The Bodyguard......*Whitney Houston/Soundtrack*...Arista 18699

TW	LW	WK	Billboard. SEPTEMBER 4, 1993 THE BILLBOARD 200.
①	1	2	**River Of Dreams**......*Billy Joel*...Columbia 53003
②	2	9	Sleepless In Seattle......*Soundtrack*...Epic Soundtrax 53764
③	3	5	Black Sunday......*Cypress Hill*...Ruffhouse 53931
④	4	14	janet......*Janet Jackson*...Virgin 87825
❺	7	7	Blind Melon......*Blind Melon*...Capitol 96585
⑥	5	35	Core......*Stone Temple Pilots*...Atlantic 82418
❼	-	1	**The World Is Yours**......*Scarface*...Rap-A-Lot 53861
❽	8	4	Promises and Lies......*UB40*...Virgin 88229
❾	10	40	The Bodyguard......*Whitney Houston/Soundtrack*...Arista 18699
⑩	6	7	Zooropa......*U2*...Island 518047

Billboard — SEPTEMBER 11, 1993 — THE BILLBOARD 200

TW	LW	WK	Title	Artist	Label
1	1	3	**River Of Dreams**	*Billy Joel*	Columbia 53003
2	2	10	Sleepless In Seattle	*Soundtrack*	Epic Soundtrax 53764
3	5	8	**Blind Melon**	*Blind Melon*	Capitol 96585
4	4	15	janet.	*Janet Jackson*	Virgin 87825
5	3	6	Black Sunday	*Cypress Hill*	Ruffhouse 53931
6	6	36	Core	*Stone Temple Pilots*	Atlantic 82418
7	9	41	The Bodyguard	*Whitney Houston/Soundtrack*	Arista 18699
8	8	5	Promises and Lies	*UB40*	Virgin 88229
9	11	19	Get A Grip	*Aerosmith*	Geffen 24455
10	12	14	Unplugged...And Seated	*Rod Stewart*	Warner 45289

Billboard — SEPTEMBER 18, 1993 — THE BILLBOARD 200

TW	LW	WK	Title	Artist	Label
1	-	1	**In Pieces**	*Garth Brooks*	Liberty 80857
2	-	1	Music Box	*Mariah Carey*	Columbia 53205
3	1	4	River Of Dreams	*Billy Joel*	Columbia 53003
4	3	9	Blind Melon	*Blind Melon*	Capitol 96585
5	2	11	Sleepless In Seattle	*Soundtrack*	Epic Soundtrax 53764
6	4	16	janet.	*Janet Jackson*	Virgin 87825
7	6	37	Core	*Stone Temple Pilots*	Atlantic 82418
8	5	7	Black Sunday	*Cypress Hill*	Ruffhouse 53931
9	8	6	Promises and Lies	*UB40*	Virgin 88229
10	7	42	The Bodyguard	*Whitney Houston/Soundtrack*	Arista 18699

Billboard — SEPTEMBER 25, 1993 — THE BILLBOARD 200

TW	LW	WK	Title	Artist	Label
1	1	2	**In Pieces**	*Garth Brooks*	Liberty 80857
2	2	2	Music Box	*Mariah Carey*	Columbia 53205
3	3	5	River Of Dreams	*Billy Joel*	Columbia 53003
4	4	10	Blind Melon	*Blind Melon*	Capitol 96585
5	5	12	Sleepless In Seattle	*Soundtrack*	Epic Soundtrax 53764
6	6	17	janet.	*Janet Jackson*	Virgin 87825
7	-	1	**Human Wheels**	*John Mellencamp*	Mercury 518088
8	7	38	Core	*Stone Temple Pilots*	Atlantic 82418
9	31	2	**Barney's Favorites - Volume 1**	*Barney*	SBK 27114
10	8	8	Black Sunday	*Cypress Hill*	Ruffhouse 53931

Billboard — OCTOBER 2, 1993 — THE BILLBOARD 200

TW	LW	WK	Title	Artist	Label
1	1	3	**In Pieces**	*Garth Brooks*	Liberty 80857
2	2	3	Music Box	*Mariah Carey*	Columbia 53205
3	-	1	Bat Out Of Hell II: Back Into Hell	*Meat Loaf*	MCA 10699
4	3	6	River Of Dreams	*Billy Joel*	Columbia 53003
5	4	11	Blind Melon	*Blind Melon*	Capitol 96585
6	5	13	Sleepless In Seattle	*Soundtrack*	Epic Soundtrax 53764
7	6	18	janet.	*Janet Jackson*	Virgin 87825
8	8	39	Core	*Stone Temple Pilots*	Atlantic 82418
9	7	2	Human Wheels	*John Mellencamp*	Mercury 518088
10	10	9	Black Sunday	*Cypress Hill*	Ruffhouse 53931

TW	LW	WK	Billboard. OCTOBER 9, 1993 THE BILLBOARD 200.
1	-	1	**In Utero** ... *Nirvana*...DGC 24607
2	1	4	In Pieces ... *Garth Brooks*...Liberty 80857
3	2	4	Music Box ... *Mariah Carey*...Columbia 53205
4	3	2	Bat Out Of Hell II: Back Into Hell ... *Meat Loaf*...MCA 10699
5	4	7	River Of Dreams ... *Billy Joel*...Columbia 53003
6	5	12	Blind Melon ... *Blind Melon*...Capitol 96585
7	7	19	janet. ... *Janet Jackson*...Virgin 87825
8	6	14	Sleepless In Seattle ... *Soundtrack*...Epic Soundtrax 53764
9	8	40	Core ... *Stone Temple Pilots*...Atlantic 82418
10	10	10	Black Sunday ... *Cypress Hill*...Ruffhouse 53931

TW	LW	WK	Billboard. OCTOBER 16, 1993 THE BILLBOARD 200.
1	2	5	**In Pieces** ... *Garth Brooks*...Liberty 80857
2	1	2	In Utero ... *Nirvana*...DGC 24607
3	4	3	Bat Out Of Hell II: Back Into Hell ... *Meat Loaf*...MCA 10699
4	3	5	Music Box ... *Mariah Carey*...Columbia 53205
5	-	1	**Easy Come, Easy Go** ... *George Strait*...MCA 10907
6	5	8	River Of Dreams ... *Billy Joel*...Columbia 53003
7	7	20	janet. ... *Janet Jackson*...Virgin 87825
8	-	1	Greatest Hits Volume Two ... *Reba McEntire*...MCA 10906
9	6	13	Blind Melon ... *Blind Melon*...Capitol 96585
10	-	1	**187 He Wrote** ... *Spice 1*...Jive 41513

TW	LW	WK	Billboard. OCTOBER 23, 1993 THE BILLBOARD 200.
1	1	6	**In Pieces** ... *Garth Brooks*...Liberty 80857
2	3	4	Bat Out Of Hell II: Back Into Hell ... *Meat Loaf*...MCA 10699
3	2	3	In Utero ... *Nirvana*...DGC 24607
4	4	6	Music Box ... *Mariah Carey*...Columbia 53205
5	8	2	**Greatest Hits Volume Two** ... *Reba McEntire*...MCA 10906
6	7	21	janet. ... *Janet Jackson*...Virgin 87825
7	6	9	River Of Dreams ... *Billy Joel*...Columbia 53003
8	5	2	Easy Come, Easy Go ... *George Strait*...MCA 10907
9	-	1	**Retro Active** ... *Def Leppard*...Mercury 518305
10	9	14	Blind Melon ... *Blind Melon*...Capitol 96585

TW	LW	WK	Billboard. OCTOBER 30, 1993 THE BILLBOARD 200.
1	2	5	**Bat Out Of Hell II: Back Into Hell** ... *Meat Loaf*...MCA 10699
2	1	7	In Pieces ... *Garth Brooks*...Liberty 80857
3	3	4	In Utero ... *Nirvana*...DGC 24607
4	7	10	River Of Dreams ... *Billy Joel*...Columbia 53003
5	4	7	Music Box ... *Mariah Carey*...Columbia 53205
6	6	22	janet. ... *Janet Jackson*...Virgin 87825
7	5	3	Greatest Hits Volume Two ... *Reba McEntire*...MCA 10906
8	8	3	Easy Come, Easy Go ... *George Strait*...MCA 10907
9	10	15	Blind Melon ... *Blind Melon*...Capitol 96585
10	-	1	Common Thread: The Songs Of The Eagles ... *Various Artists*...Giant 24531

NOVEMBER 6, 1993 — THE BILLBOARD 200

TW	LW	WK	Title	Artist	Label
1	-	1	**Vs.**	*Pearl Jam*	Epic/Associated 53136
2	-	1	**Counterparts**	*Rush*	Atlantic 82528
3	1	6	Bat Out Of Hell II: Back Into Hell	*Meat Loaf*	MCA 10699
4	3	5	In Utero	*Nirvana*	DGC 24607
5	-	1	**It's On (Dr. Dre) 187um Killa**	*Eazy-E*	Ruthless 5503
6	10	2	Common Thread: The Songs Of The Eagles	*Various Artists*	Giant 24531
7	5	8	Music Box	*Mariah Carey*	Columbia 53205
8	4	11	River Of Dreams	*Billy Joel*	Columbia 53003
9	2	8	In Pieces	*Garth Brooks*	Liberty 80857
10	6	23	janet.	*Janet Jackson*	Virgin 87825

NOVEMBER 13, 1993 — THE BILLBOARD 200

TW	LW	WK	Title	Artist	Label
1	1	2	**Vs.**	*Pearl Jam*	Epic/Associated 53136
2	3	7	Bat Out Of Hell II: Back Into Hell	*Meat Loaf*	MCA 10699
3	6	3	**Common Thread: The Songs Of The Eagles**	*Various Artists*	Giant 24531
4	-	1	**Get In Where You Fit In**	*Too $hort*	Jive 41526
5	7	9	Music Box	*Mariah Carey*	Columbia 53205
6	8	12	River Of Dreams	*Billy Joel*	Columbia 53003
7	5	2	It's On (Dr. Dre) 187um Killa	*Eazy-E*	Ruthless 5503
8	10	24	janet.	*Janet Jackson*	Virgin 87825
9	11	5	Greatest Hits Volume Two	*Reba McEntire*	MCA 10906
10	4	6	In Utero	*Nirvana*	DGC 24607

NOVEMBER 20, 1993 — THE BILLBOARD 200

TW	LW	WK	Title	Artist	Label
1	1	3	**Vs.**	*Pearl Jam*	Epic/Associated 53136
2	-	1	**Duets**	*Frank Sinatra*	Capitol 89611
3	2	8	Bat Out Of Hell II: Back Into Hell	*Meat Loaf*	MCA 10699
4	3	4	Common Thread: The Songs Of The Eagles	*Various Artists*	Giant 24531
5	5	10	Music Box	*Mariah Carey*	Columbia 53205
6	8	25	janet.	*Janet Jackson*	Virgin 87825
7	6	13	River Of Dreams	*Billy Joel*	Columbia 53003
8	7	3	It's On (Dr. Dre) 187um Killa	*Eazy-E*	Ruthless 5503
9	4	2	Get In Where You Fit In	*Too $hort*	Jive 41526
10	12	17	Toni Braxton	*Toni Braxton*	LaFace 26007

NOVEMBER 27, 1993 — THE BILLBOARD 200

TW	LW	WK	Title	Artist	Label
1	1	4	**Vs.**	*Pearl Jam*	Epic/Associated 53136
2	2	2	**Duets**	*Frank Sinatra*	Capitol 89611
3	3	9	Bat Out Of Hell II: Back Into Hell	*Meat Loaf*	MCA 10699
4	4	5	Common Thread: The Songs Of The Eagles	*Various Artists*	Giant 24531
5	5	11	Music Box	*Mariah Carey*	Columbia 53205
6	6	26	janet.	*Janet Jackson*	Virgin 87825
7	7	14	River Of Dreams	*Billy Joel*	Columbia 53003
8	-	1	**Midnight Marauders**	*A Tribe Called Quest*	Jive 41490
9	-	1	So Far So Good	*Bryan Adams*	A&M 0157
10	12	7	Greatest Hits Volume Two	*Reba McEntire*	MCA 10906

TW	LW	WK	Billboard® DECEMBER 4, 1993 THE BILLBOARD 200®
1	1	5	**Vs.** ... *Pearl Jam*...Epic/Associated 53136
2	2	3	**Duets** ... *Frank Sinatra*...Capitol 89611
3	-	1	**The One Thing** ... *Michael Bolton*...Columbia 53567
4	3	10	Bat Out Of Hell II: Back Into Hell ... *Meat Loaf*...MCA 10699
5	4	6	Common Thread: The Songs Of The Eagles ... *Various Artists*...Giant 24531
6	5	12	Music Box ... *Mariah Carey*...Columbia 53205
7	9	2	So Far So Good ... *Bryan Adams*...A&M 0157
8	-	1	Greatest Hits ... *Tom Petty & The Heartbreakers*...MCA 10813
9	6	27	janet. ... *Janet Jackson*...Virgin 87825
10	7	15	River Of Dreams ... *Billy Joel*...Columbia 53003

TW	LW	WK	Billboard® DECEMBER 11, 1993 THE BILLBOARD 200®
1	-	1	**Doggy Style** ... *Snoop Doggy Dogg*...Death Row 92279
2	1	6	Vs. ... *Pearl Jam*...Epic/Associated 53136
3	6	13	Music Box ... *Mariah Carey*...Columbia 53205
4	-	1	**The Spaghetti Incident?** ... *Guns N' Roses*...Geffen 24617
5	-	1	**The Beavis & Butt-head Experience** ... *Beavis & Butt-head*...Geffen 24613
6	2	4	Duets ... *Frank Sinatra*...Capitol 89611
7	4	11	Bat Out Of Hell II: Back Into Hell ... *Meat Loaf*...MCA 10699
8	3	2	The One Thing ... *Michael Bolton*...Columbia 53567
9	5	7	Common Thread: The Songs Of The Eagles ... *Various Artists*...Giant 24531
10	9	28	janet. ... *Janet Jackson*...Virgin 87825

TW	LW	WK	Billboard® DECEMBER 18, 1993 THE BILLBOARD 200®
1	1	2	**Doggy Style** ... *Snoop Doggy Dogg*...Death Row 92279
2	3	14	Music Box ... *Mariah Carey*...Columbia 53205
3	2	7	Vs. ... *Pearl Jam*...Epic/Associated 53136
4	8	3	The One Thing ... *Michael Bolton*...Columbia 53567
5	7	12	Bat Out Of Hell II: Back Into Hell ... *Meat Loaf*...MCA 10699
6	6	5	Duets ... *Frank Sinatra*...Capitol 89611
7	5	2	The Beavis & Butt-head Experience ... *Beavis & Butt-head*...Geffen 24613
8	10	29	janet. ... *Janet Jackson*...Virgin 87825
9	9	8	Common Thread: The Songs Of The Eagles ... *Various Artists*...Giant 24531
10	4	2	The Spaghetti Incident? ... *Guns N' Roses*...Geffen 24617

TW	LW	WK	Billboard® DECEMBER 25, 1993 THE BILLBOARD 200®
1	2	15	**Music Box** ... *Mariah Carey*...Columbia 53205
2	1	3	Doggy Style ... *Snoop Doggy Dogg*...Death Row 92279
3	3	8	Vs. ... *Pearl Jam*...Epic/Associated 53136
4	5	13	Bat Out Of Hell II: Back Into Hell ... *Meat Loaf*...MCA 10699
5	-	1	**Lethal Injection** ... *Ice Cube*...Priority 53876
6	4	4	The One Thing ... *Michael Bolton*...Columbia 53567
7	6	6	Duets ... *Frank Sinatra*...Capitol 89611
8	8	30	janet. ... *Janet Jackson*...Virgin 87825
9	9	9	Common Thread: The Songs Of The Eagles ... *Various Artists*...Giant 24531
10	12	18	River Of Dreams ... *Billy Joel*...Columbia 53003

TW	LW	WK	Billboard® JANUARY 1, 1994 THE BILLBOARD 200®
1	1	16	**Music Box** .... *Mariah Carey*...Columbia 53205
2	3	9	Vs. .... *Pearl Jam*...Epic/Associated 53136
3	2	4	Doggy Style .... *Snoop Doggy Dogg*...Death Row 92279
4	7	7	Duets .... *Frank Sinatra*...Capitol 89611
5	4	14	Bat Out Of Hell II: Back Into Hell .... *Meat Loaf*...MCA 10699
6	6	5	The One Thing .... *Michael Bolton*...Columbia 53567
7	8	31	janet. .... *Janet Jackson*...Virgin 87825
8	9	10	Common Thread: The Songs Of The Eagles .... *Various Artists*...Giant 24531
9	10	19	River Of Dreams .... *Billy Joel*...Columbia 53003
10	12	4	The Beavis & Butt-head Experience .... *Beavis & Butt-head*...Geffen 24613

TW	LW	WK	Billboard® JANUARY 8, 1994 THE BILLBOARD 200®
1	1	17	**Music Box** .... *Mariah Carey*...Columbia 53205
2	2	10	Vs. .... *Pearl Jam*...Epic/Associated 53136
3	3	5	Doggy Style .... *Snoop Doggy Dogg*...Death Row 92279
4	6	6	The One Thing .... *Michael Bolton*...Columbia 53567
5	4	8	Duets .... *Frank Sinatra*...Capitol 89611
6	5	15	Bat Out Of Hell II: Back Into Hell .... *Meat Loaf*...MCA 10699
7	7	32	janet. .... *Janet Jackson*...Virgin 87825
8	10	5	The Beavis & Butt-head Experience .... *Beavis & Butt-head*...Geffen 24613
9	8	11	Common Thread: The Songs Of The Eagles .... *Various Artists*...Giant 24531
10	9	20	River Of Dreams .... *Billy Joel*...Columbia 53003

TW	LW	WK	Billboard® JANUARY 15, 1994 THE BILLBOARD 200®
1	3	6	**Doggy Style** .... *Snoop Doggy Dogg*...Death Row 92279
2	1	18	Music Box .... *Mariah Carey*...Columbia 53205
3	2	11	Vs. .... *Pearl Jam*...Epic/Associated 53136
4	7	33	janet. .... *Janet Jackson*...Virgin 87825
5	4	7	The One Thing .... *Michael Bolton*...Columbia 53567
6	6	16	Bat Out Of Hell II: Back Into Hell .... *Meat Loaf*...MCA 10699
7	11	8	So Far So Good .... *Bryan Adams*...A&M 0157
8	27	2	Diary Of A Mad Band .... *Jodeci*...Uptown/MCA 10915
9	13	7	Greatest Hits .... *Tom Petty & The Heartbreakers*...MCA 10813
10	17	37	Get A Grip .... *Aerosmith*...Geffen 24455

TW	LW	WK	Billboard® JANUARY 22, 1994 THE BILLBOARD 200®
1	2	19	**Music Box** .... *Mariah Carey*...Columbia 53205
2	3	12	Vs. .... *Pearl Jam*...Epic/Associated 53136
3	5	8	**The One Thing** .... *Michael Bolton*...Columbia 53567
4	1	7	Doggy Style .... *Snoop Doggy Dogg*...Death Row 92279
5	6	17	Bat Out Of Hell II: Back Into Hell .... *Meat Loaf*...MCA 10699
6	4	34	janet. .... *Janet Jackson*...Virgin 87825
7	7	9	So Far So Good .... *Bryan Adams*...A&M 0157
8	8	3	Diary Of A Mad Band .... *Jodeci*...Uptown/MCA 10915
9	15	15	Greatest Hits Volume Two .... *Reba McEntire*...MCA 10906
10	9	8	Greatest Hits .... *Tom Petty & The Heartbreakers*...MCA 10813

TW	LW	WK	Billboard. JANUARY 29, 1994 THE BILLBOARD 200.
1	1	20	**Music Box** ..... *Mariah Carey*...Columbia 53205
2	4	8	Doggy Style ..... *Snoop Doggy Dogg*...Death Row 92279
3	2	13	Vs. ..... *Pearl Jam*...Epic/Associated 53136
4	3	9	The One Thing ..... *Michael Bolton*...Columbia 53567
5	8	4	Diary Of A Mad Band ..... *Jodeci*...Uptown/MCA 10915
6	7	10	**So Far So Good** ..... *Bryan Adams*...A&M 0157
7	6	35	janet. ..... *Janet Jackson*...Virgin 87825
8	5	18	Bat Out Of Hell II: Back Into Hell ..... *Meat Loaf*...MCA 10699
9	10	9	Greatest Hits ..... *Tom Petty & The Heartbreakers*...MCA 10813
10	12	27	Toni Braxton ..... *Toni Braxton*...LaFace 26007

TW	LW	WK	Billboard. FEBRUARY 5, 1994 THE BILLBOARD 200.
1	1	21	**Music Box** ..... *Mariah Carey*...Columbia 53205
2	2	9	Doggy Style ..... *Snoop Doggy Dogg*...Death Row 92279
3	5	5	**Diary Of A Mad Band** ..... *Jodeci*...Uptown/MCA 10915
4	7	36	janet. ..... *Janet Jackson*...Virgin 87825
5	9	10	**Greatest Hits** ..... *Tom Petty & The Heartbreakers*...MCA 10813
6	6	11	**So Far So Good** ..... *Bryan Adams*...A&M 0157
7	3	14	Vs. ..... *Pearl Jam*...Epic/Associated 53136
8	4	10	The One Thing ..... *Michael Bolton*...Columbia 53567
9	8	19	Bat Out Of Hell II: Back Into Hell ..... *Meat Loaf*...MCA 10699
10	12	15	Very Necessary ..... *Salt-N-Pepa*...Next Plateau 828392

TW	LW	WK	Billboard. FEBRUARY 12, 1994 THE BILLBOARD 200.
1	-	1	**Jar Of Flies** ..... *Alice In Chains*...Columbia 57628
2	1	22	Music Box ..... *Mariah Carey*...Columbia 53205
3	-	1	Kickin' It Up ..... *John Michael Montgomery*...Atlantic 82559
4	2	10	Doggy Style ..... *Snoop Doggy Dogg*...Death Row 92279
5	5	11	**Greatest Hits** ..... *Tom Petty & The Heartbreakers*...MCA 10813
6	3	6	Diary Of A Mad Band ..... *Jodeci*...Uptown/MCA 10915
7	10	16	Very Necessary ..... *Salt-N-Pepa*...Next Plateau 828392
8	6	12	So Far So Good ..... *Bryan Adams*...A&M 0157
9	12	12	12 Play ..... *R. Kelly*...Jive 41527
10	11	29	Toni Braxton ..... *Toni Braxton*...LaFace 26007

TW	LW	WK	Billboard. FEBRUARY 19, 1994 THE BILLBOARD 200.
1	3	2	**Kickin' It Up** ..... *John Michael Montgomery*...Atlantic 82559
2	2	23	Music Box ..... *Mariah Carey*...Columbia 53205
3	4	11	Doggy Style ..... *Snoop Doggy Dogg*...Death Row 92279
4	1	2	Jar Of Flies ..... *Alice In Chains*...Columbia 57628
5	9	13	12 Play ..... *R. Kelly*...Jive 41527
6	7	17	Very Necessary ..... *Salt-N-Pepa*...Next Plateau 828392
7	10	30	Toni Braxton ..... *Toni Braxton*...LaFace 26007
8	6	7	Diary Of A Mad Band ..... *Jodeci*...Uptown/MCA 10915
9	5	12	Greatest Hits ..... *Tom Petty & The Heartbreakers*...MCA 10813
10	15	8	August and Everything After ..... *Counting Crows*...DGC 24528

TW	LW	WK	Billboard. FEBRUARY 26, 1994 THE BILLBOARD 200.
1	7	31	**Toni Braxton** ... *Toni Braxton*...LaFace 26007
2	2	24	Music Box ... *Mariah Carey*...Columbia 53205
3	3	12	Doggy Style ... *Snoop Doggy Dogg*...Death Row 92279
4	1	3	Kickin' It Up ... *John Michael Montgomery*...Atlantic 82559
5	5	14	12 Play ... *R. Kelly*...Jive 41527
6	6	18	Very Necessary ... *Salt-N-Pepa*...Next Plateau 828392
7	10	9	August and Everything After ... *Counting Crows*...DGC 24528
8	9	13	Greatest Hits ... *Tom Petty & The Heartbreakers*...MCA 10813
9	4	3	Jar Of Flies ... *Alice In Chains*...Columbia 57628
10	14	14	The Colour Of My Love ... *Celine Dion*...550 Music/Epic 57555

TW	LW	WK	Billboard. MARCH 5, 1994 THE BILLBOARD 200.
1	2	25	**Music Box** ... *Mariah Carey*...Columbia 53205
2	1	32	Toni Braxton ... *Toni Braxton*...LaFace 26007
3	5	15	12 Play ... *R. Kelly*...Jive 41527
4	6	19	**Very Necessary** ... *Salt-N-Pepa*...Next Plateau 828392
5	3	13	Doggy Style ... *Snoop Doggy Dogg*...Death Row 92279
6	4	4	Kickin' It Up ... *John Michael Montgomery*...Atlantic 82559
7	7	10	August and Everything After ... *Counting Crows*...DGC 24528
8	10	15	The Colour Of My Love ... *Celine Dion*...550 Music/Epic 57555
9	13	13	The Sign ... *Ace Of Base*...Arista 18740
10	8	14	Greatest Hits ... *Tom Petty & The Heartbreakers*...MCA 10813

TW	LW	WK	Billboard. MARCH 12, 1994 THE BILLBOARD 200.
1	1	26	**Music Box** ... *Mariah Carey*...Columbia 53205
2	3	16	**12 Play** ... *R. Kelly*...Jive 41527
3	9	14	The Sign ... *Ace Of Base*...Arista 18740
4	5	14	Doggy Style ... *Snoop Doggy Dogg*...Death Row 92279
5	4	20	Very Necessary ... *Salt-N-Pepa*...Next Plateau 828392
6	8	16	The Colour Of My Love ... *Celine Dion*...550 Music/Epic 57555
7	7	11	August and Everything After ... *Counting Crows*...DGC 24528
8	2	33	Toni Braxton ... *Toni Braxton*...LaFace 26007
9	10	15	Greatest Hits ... *Tom Petty & The Heartbreakers*...MCA 10813
10	16	3	ENIGMA 2 the CROSS of changes ... *Enigma*...Charisma 39236

TW	LW	WK	Billboard. MARCH 19, 1994 THE BILLBOARD 200.
1	8	34	**Toni Braxton** ... *Toni Braxton*...LaFace 26007
2	3	15	The Sign ... *Ace Of Base*...Arista 18740
3	2	17	12 Play ... *R. Kelly*...Jive 41527
4	6	17	**The Colour Of My Love** ... *Celine Dion*...550 Music/Epic 57555
5	1	27	Music Box ... *Mariah Carey*...Columbia 53205
6	16	68	The Bodyguard ... *Whitney Houston/Soundtrack*...Arista 18699
7	7	12	August and Everything After ... *Counting Crows*...DGC 24528
8	4	15	Doggy Style ... *Snoop Doggy Dogg*...Death Row 92279
9	5	21	Very Necessary ... *Salt-N-Pepa*...Next Plateau 828392
10	10	4	ENIGMA 2 the CROSS of changes ... *Enigma*...Charisma 39236

TW	LW	WK	Billboard. MARCH 26, 1994 THE BILLBOARD 200.
1	-	1	**Superunknown**......Soundgarden...A&M 0198
2	-	1	**The Downward Spiral**......Nine Inch Nails...Nothing/TVT 92346
3	2	16	The Sign......Ace Of Base...Arista 18740
4	3	18	12 Play......R. Kelly...Jive 41527
5	1	35	Toni Braxton......Toni Braxton...LaFace 26007
6	5	28	Music Box......Mariah Carey...Columbia 53205
7	7	13	August and Everything After......Counting Crows...DGC 24528
8	4	18	The Colour Of My Love......Celine Dion...550 Music/Epic 57555
9	8	16	Doggy Style......Snoop Doggy Dogg...Death Row 92279
10	10	5	ENIGMA 2 the CROSS of changes......Enigma...Charisma 39236

TW	LW	WK	Billboard. APRIL 2, 1994 THE BILLBOARD 200.
1	3	17	**The Sign**......Ace Of Base...Arista 18740
2	1	2	Superunknown......Soundgarden...A&M 0198
3	4	19	12 Play......R. Kelly...Jive 41527
4	7	14	**August and Everything After**......Counting Crows...DGC 24528
5	6	29	Music Box......Mariah Carey...Columbia 53205
6	5	36	Toni Braxton......Toni Braxton...LaFace 26007
7	-	1	**Motley Crue**......Motley Crue...Elektra 61534
8	8	19	The Colour Of My Love......Celine Dion...550 Music/Epic 57555
9	9	17	Doggy Style......Snoop Doggy Dogg...Death Row 92279
10	12	23	Very Necessary......Salt-N-Pepa...Next Plateau 828392

TW	LW	WK	Billboard. APRIL 9, 1994 THE BILLBOARD 200.
1	-	1	**Far Beyond Driven**......Pantera...EastWest 92302
2	-	1	Longing In Their Hearts......Bonnie Raitt...Capitol 81427
3	1	18	The Sign......Ace Of Base...Arista 18740
4	-	1	Above The Rim......Soundtrack...Death Row 92359
5	11	4	**Live At The Acropolis**......Yanni...Private Music 82116
6	3	20	12 Play......R. Kelly...Jive 41527
7	4	15	August and Everything After......Counting Crows...DGC 24528
8	2	3	Superunknown......Soundgarden...A&M 0198
9	5	30	Music Box......Mariah Carey...Columbia 53205
10	8	20	The Colour Of My Love......Celine Dion...550 Music/Epic 57555

TW	LW	WK	Billboard. APRIL 16, 1994 THE BILLBOARD 200.
1	2	2	**Longing In Their Hearts**......Bonnie Raitt...Capitol 81427
2	3	19	The Sign......Ace Of Base...Arista 18740
3	4	2	Above The Rim......Soundtrack...Death Row 92359
4	7	16	**August and Everything After**......Counting Crows...DGC 24528
5	6	21	12 Play......R. Kelly...Jive 41527
6	9	31	Music Box......Mariah Carey...Columbia 53205
7	10	21	The Colour Of My Love......Celine Dion...550 Music/Epic 57555
8	19	2	Not A Moment Too Soon......Tim McGraw...Curb 77659
9	1	2	Far Beyond Driven......Pantera...EastWest 92302
10	5	5	Live At The Acropolis......Yanni...Private Music 82116

Billboard — APRIL 23, 1994 — THE BILLBOARD 200

TW	LW	WK	Title	Artist	Label
1	-	1	**The Division Bell**	*Pink Floyd*	Columbia 64200
2	3	3	**Above The Rim**	*Soundtrack*	Death Row 92359
3	2	20	The Sign	*Ace Of Base*	Arista 18740
4	1	3	Longing In Their Hearts	*Bonnie Raitt*	Capitol 81427
5	4	17	August and Everything After	*Counting Crows*	DGC 24528
6	5	22	12 Play	*R. Kelly*	Jive 41527
7	8	3	Not A Moment Too Soon	*Tim McGraw*	Curb 77659
8	10	6	Live At The Acropolis	*Yanni*	Private Music 82116
9	6	32	Music Box	*Mariah Carey*	Columbia 53205
10	7	22	The Colour Of My Love	*Celine Dion*	550 Music/Epic 57555

Billboard — APRIL 30, 1994 — THE BILLBOARD 200

TW	LW	WK	Title	Artist	Label
1	1	2	**The Division Bell**	*Pink Floyd*	Columbia 64200
2	3	21	The Sign	*Ace Of Base*	Arista 18740
3	2	4	Above The Rim	*Soundtrack*	Death Row 92359
4	7	4	Not A Moment Too Soon	*Tim McGraw*	Curb 77659
5	5	18	August and Everything After	*Counting Crows*	DGC 24528
6	12	5	Chant	*The Benedictine Monks Of Santo Domingo de Silos*	Angel 55138
7	4	4	Longing In Their Hearts	*Bonnie Raitt*	Capitol 81427
8	6	23	12 Play	*R. Kelly*	Jive 41527
9	9	33	Music Box	*Mariah Carey*	Columbia 53205
10	10	23	The Colour Of My Love	*Celine Dion*	550 Music/Epic 57555

Billboard — MAY 7, 1994 — THE BILLBOARD 200

TW	LW	WK	Title	Artist	Label
1	1	3	**The Division Bell**	*Pink Floyd*	Columbia 64200
2	2	22	The Sign	*Ace Of Base*	Arista 18740
3	4	5	Not A Moment Too Soon	*Tim McGraw*	Curb 77659
4	3	5	Above The Rim	*Soundtrack*	Death Row 92359
5	6	6	Chant	*The Benedictine Monks Of Santo Domingo de Silos*	Angel 55138
6	5	19	August and Everything After	*Counting Crows*	DGC 24528
7	8	24	12 Play	*R. Kelly*	Jive 41527
8	7	5	Longing In Their Hearts	*Bonnie Raitt*	Capitol 81427
9	12	15	**God Shuffled His Feet**	*Crash Test Dummies*	Arista 16531
10	10	24	The Colour Of My Love	*Celine Dion*	550 Music/Epic 57555

Billboard — MAY 14, 1994 — THE BILLBOARD 200

TW	LW	WK	Title	Artist	Label
1	1	4	**The Division Bell**	*Pink Floyd*	Columbia 64200
2	3	6	Not A Moment Too Soon	*Tim McGraw*	Curb 77659
3	2	23	The Sign	*Ace Of Base*	Arista 18740
4	5	7	Chant	*The Benedictine Monks Of Santo Domingo de Silos*	Angel 55138
5	-	1	Read My Mind	*Reba McEntire*	MCA 10994
6	6	20	August and Everything After	*Counting Crows*	DGC 24528
7	4	6	Above The Rim	*Soundtrack*	Death Row 92359
8	7	25	12 Play	*R. Kelly*	Jive 41527
9	14	12	**ENIGMA 2 the CROSS of changes**	*Enigma*	Charisma 39236
10	8	6	Longing In Their Hearts	*Bonnie Raitt*	Capitol 81427

TW	LW	WK	Billboard. MAY 21, 1994 THE BILLBOARD 200.
1	2	7	**Not A Moment Too Soon** ... *Tim McGraw*...Curb 77659
2	5	2	**Read My Mind** ... *Reba McEntire*...MCA 10994
3	3	24	The Sign ... *Ace Of Base*...Arista 18740
4	1	5	The Division Bell ... *Pink Floyd*...Columbia 64200
5	4	8	Chant... *The Benedictine Monks Of Santo Domingo de Silos*...Angel 55138
6	6	21	August and Everything After... *Counting Crows*...DGC 24528
7	7	7	Above The Rim... *Soundtrack*...Death Row 92359
8	8	26	12 Play... *R. Kelly*...Jive 41527
9	10	7	Longing In Their Hearts... *Bonnie Raitt*...Capitol 81427
10	11	43	Toni Braxton... *Toni Braxton*...LaFace 26007

TW	LW	WK	Billboard. MAY 28, 1994 THE BILLBOARD 200.
1	1	8	**Not A Moment Too Soon** ... *Tim McGraw*...Curb 77659
2	3	25	The Sign ... *Ace Of Base*...Arista 18740
3	5	9	**Chant**... *The Benedictine Monks Of Santo Domingo de Silos*...Angel 55138
4	4	6	The Division Bell ... *Pink Floyd*...Columbia 64200
5	2	3	Read My Mind... *Reba McEntire*...MCA 10994
6	15	7	The Crow ... *Soundtrack*...Atlantic 82519
7	6	22	August and Everything After... *Counting Crows*...DGC 24528
8	7	8	Above The Rim... *Soundtrack*...Death Row 92359
9	-	1	**Swamp Ophelia** ... *Indigo Girls*...Epic 57621
10	8	27	12 Play... *R. Kelly*...Jive 41527

TW	LW	WK	Billboard. JUNE 4, 1994 THE BILLBOARD 200.
1	6	8	**The Crow**... *Soundtrack*...Atlantic 82519
2	1	9	Not A Moment Too Soon... *Tim McGraw*...Curb 77659
3	2	26	The Sign ... *Ace Of Base*...Arista 18740
4	3	10	Chant... *The Benedictine Monks Of Santo Domingo de Silos*...Angel 55138
5	8	9	Above The Rim... *Soundtrack*...Death Row 92359
6	7	23	August and Everything After... *Counting Crows*...DGC 24528
7	4	7	The Division Bell ... *Pink Floyd*...Columbia 64200
8	10	28	12 Play... *R. Kelly*...Jive 41527
9	5	4	Read My Mind... *Reba McEntire*...MCA 10994
10	14	6	All-4-One... *All-4-One*...Blitzz/Atlantic 82588

TW	LW	WK	Billboard. JUNE 11, 1994 THE BILLBOARD 200.
1	3	27	**The Sign** ... *Ace Of Base*...Arista 18740
2	1	9	The Crow ... *Soundtrack*...Atlantic 82519
3	2	10	Not A Moment Too Soon... *Tim McGraw*...Curb 77659
4	4	11	Chant... *The Benedictine Monks Of Santo Domingo de Silos*...Angel 55138
5	-	1	**Fruitcakes**... *Jimmy Buffett*...Margaritaville 11043
6	6	24	August and Everything After... *Counting Crows*...DGC 24528
7	5	10	Above The Rim... *Soundtrack*...Death Row 92359
8	7	8	The Division Bell ... *Pink Floyd*...Columbia 64200
9	8	29	12 Play... *R. Kelly*...Jive 41527
10	10	7	All-4-One... *All-4-One*...Blitzz/Atlantic 82588

TW	LW	WK	Billboard. JUNE 18, 1994	THE BILLBOARD 200.
1	-	1	**Ill Communication**	*Beastie Boys*...Grand Royal 28599
2	1	28	The Sign	*Ace Of Base*...Arista 18740
3	2	10	The Crow	*Soundtrack*...Atlantic 82519
4	3	11	Not A Moment Too Soon	*Tim McGraw*...Curb 77659
5	7	11	Above The Rim	*Soundtrack*...Death Row 92359
6	6	25	August and Everything After	*Counting Crows*...DGC 24528
7	4	12	Chant	*The Benedictine Monks Of Santo Domingo de Silos*...Angel 55138
8	8	9	The Division Bell	*Pink Floyd*...Columbia 64200
9	5	2	Fruitcakes	*Jimmy Buffett*...Margaritaville 11043
10	10	8	All-4-One	*All-4-One*...Blitzz/Atlantic 82588

TW	LW	WK	Billboard. JUNE 25, 1994	THE BILLBOARD 200.
1	-	1	**Purple**	*Stone Temple Pilots*...Atlantic 82607
2	-	1	**Regulate...G Funk Era**	*Warren G*...Violator/RAL 523364
3	2	29	The Sign	*Ace Of Base*...Arista 18740
4	1	2	Ill Communication	*Beastie Boys*...Grand Royal 28599
5	4	12	Not A Moment Too Soon	*Tim McGraw*...Curb 77659
6	3	11	The Crow	*Soundtrack*...Atlantic 82519
7	-	1	**Walk On**	*Boston*...MCA 10973
8	5	12	Above The Rim	*Soundtrack*...Death Row 92359
9	6	26	August and Everything After	*Counting Crows*...DGC 24528
10	-	1	When Love Finds You	*Vince Gill*...MCA 11047

TW	LW	WK	Billboard. JULY 2, 1994	THE BILLBOARD 200.
1	1	2	**Purple**	*Stone Temple Pilots*...Atlantic 82607
2	3	30	The Sign	*Ace Of Base*...Arista 18740
3	2	2	Regulate...G Funk Era	*Warren G*...Violator/RAL 523364
4	5	13	Not A Moment Too Soon	*Tim McGraw*...Curb 77659
5	14	3	The Lion King	*Soundtrack*...Walt Disney 60858
6	10	2	**When Love Finds You**	*Vince Gill*...MCA 11047
7	9	27	August and Everything After	*Counting Crows*...DGC 24528
8	6	12	The Crow	*Soundtrack*...Atlantic 82519
9	8	13	Above The Rim	*Soundtrack*...Death Row 92359
10	4	3	Ill Communication	*Beastie Boys*...Grand Royal 28599

TW	LW	WK	Billboard. JULY 9, 1994	THE BILLBOARD 200.
1	1	3	**Purple**	*Stone Temple Pilots*...Atlantic 82607
2	5	4	The Lion King	*Soundtrack*...Walt Disney 60858
3	2	31	The Sign	*Ace Of Base*...Arista 18740
4	3	3	Regulate...G Funk Era	*Warren G*...Violator/RAL 523364
5	4	14	Not A Moment Too Soon	*Tim McGraw*...Curb 77659
6	7	28	August and Everything After	*Counting Crows*...DGC 24528
7	11	11	**All-4-One**	*All-4-One*...Blitzz/Atlantic 82588
8	8	13	The Crow	*Soundtrack*...Atlantic 82519
9	6	3	When Love Finds You	*Vince Gill*...MCA 11047
10	9	14	Above The Rim	*Soundtrack*...Death Row 92359

TW	LW	WK	Billboard — JULY 16, 1994 — THE BILLBOARD 200	
1	2	5	**The Lion King**	*Soundtrack*...Walt Disney 60858
2	1	4	Purple	*Stone Temple Pilots*...Atlantic 82607
3	3	32	The Sign	*Ace Of Base*...Arista 18740
4	4	4	Regulate...G Funk Era	*Warren G*...Violator/RAL 523364
5	5	15	Not A Moment Too Soon	*Tim McGraw*...Curb 77659
6	6	29	August and Everything After	*Counting Crows*...DGC 24528
7	-	1	Who I Am	*Alan Jackson*...Arista 18759
8	-	1	**Get Up On It**	*Keith Sweat*...Elektra 61550
9	7	12	All-4-One	*All-4-One*...Blitzz/Atlantic 82588
10	11	17	Superunknown	*Soundgarden*...A&M 0198

TW	LW	WK	Billboard — JULY 23, 1994 — THE BILLBOARD 200	
1	1	6	**The Lion King**	*Soundtrack*...Walt Disney 60858
2	2	5	Purple	*Stone Temple Pilots*...Atlantic 82607
3	3	33	The Sign	*Ace Of Base*...Arista 18740
4	4	5	Regulate...G Funk Era	*Warren G*...Violator/RAL 523364
5	7	2	**Who I Am**	*Alan Jackson*...Arista 18759
6	6	30	August and Everything After	*Counting Crows*...DGC 24528
7	5	16	Not A Moment Too Soon	*Tim McGraw*...Curb 77659
8	9	13	All-4-One	*All-4-One*...Blitzz/Atlantic 82588
9	10	18	Superunknown	*Soundgarden*...A&M 0198
10	8	2	Get Up On It	*Keith Sweat*...Elektra 61550

TW	LW	WK	Billboard — JULY 30, 1994 — THE BILLBOARD 200	
1	1	7	**The Lion King**	*Soundtrack*...Walt Disney 60858
2	-	1	**Voodoo Lounge**	*The Rolling Stones*...Virgin 39782
3	3	34	The Sign	*Ace Of Base*...Arista 18740
4	2	6	Purple	*Stone Temple Pilots*...Atlantic 82607
5	6	31	August and Everything After	*Counting Crows*...DGC 24528
6	4	6	Regulate...G Funk Era	*Warren G*...Violator/RAL 523364
7	34	2	Forrest Gump	*Soundtrack*...Epic Soundtrax 66329
8	9	19	Superunknown	*Soundgarden*...A&M 0198
9	7	17	Not A Moment Too Soon	*Tim McGraw*...Curb 77659
10	5	3	Who I Am	*Alan Jackson*...Arista 18759

TW	LW	WK	Billboard — AUGUST 6, 1994 — THE BILLBOARD 200	
1	1	8	**The Lion King**	*Soundtrack*...Walt Disney 60858
2	3	35	The Sign	*Ace Of Base*...Arista 18740
3	7	3	Forrest Gump	*Soundtrack*...Epic Soundtrax 66329
4	4	7	Purple	*Stone Temple Pilots*...Atlantic 82607
5	-	1	**We Come Strapped**	*MC Eiht Featuring CMW*...Epic Street 57696
6	2	2	Voodoo Lounge	*The Rolling Stones*...Virgin 39782
7	5	32	August and Everything After	*Counting Crows*...DGC 24528
8	-	1	**It Takes A Thief**	*Coolio*...Tommy Boy 1083
9	6	7	Regulate...G Funk Era	*Warren G*...Violator/RAL 523364
10	8	20	Superunknown	*Soundgarden*...A&M 0198

Billboard® — AUGUST 13, 1994 — THE BILLBOARD 200®

TW	LW	WK	Title	Artist	Label
①	1	9	**The Lion King**	*Soundtrack*	Walt Disney 60858
❷	3	4	**Forrest Gump**	*Soundtrack*	Epic Soundtrax 66329
③	2	36	The Sign	*Ace Of Base*	Arista 18740
④	4	8	Purple	*Stone Temple Pilots*	Atlantic 82607
❺	7	33	August and Everything After	*Counting Crows*	DGC 24528
❻	9	8	Regulate...G Funk Era	*Warren G.*	Violator/RAL 523364
⑦	10	21	Superunknown	*Soundgarden*	A&M 0198
⑧	6	3	Voodoo Lounge	*The Rolling Stones*	Virgin 39782
⑨	12	16	All-4-One	*All-4-One*	Blitzz/Atlantic 82588
❿	13	38	Candlebox	*Candlebox*	Maverick/Sire 45313

Billboard® — AUGUST 20, 1994 — THE BILLBOARD 200®

TW	LW	WK	Title	Artist	Label
①	1	10	**The Lion King**	*Soundtrack*	Walt Disney 60858
②	2	5	**Forrest Gump**	*Soundtrack*	Epic Soundtrax 66329
③	3	37	The Sign	*Ace Of Base*	Arista 18740
❹	6	9	Regulate...G Funk Era	*Warren G.*	Violator/RAL 523364
⑤	4	9	Purple	*Stone Temple Pilots*	Atlantic 82607
⑥	5	34	August and Everything After	*Counting Crows*	DGC 24528
❼	8	4	Voodoo Lounge	*The Rolling Stones*	Virgin 39782
⑧	7	22	Superunknown	*Soundgarden*	A&M 0198
⑨	10	39	Candlebox	*Candlebox*	Maverick/Sire 45313
❿	13	20	Not A Moment Too Soon	*Tim McGraw*	Curb 77659

Billboard® — AUGUST 27, 1994 — THE BILLBOARD 200®

TW	LW	WK	Title	Artist	Label
①	1	11	**The Lion King**	*Soundtrack*	Walt Disney 60858
②	2	6	**Forrest Gump**	*Soundtrack*	Epic Soundtrax 66329
③	3	38	The Sign	*Ace Of Base*	Arista 18740
④	5	10	Purple	*Stone Temple Pilots*	Atlantic 82607
⑤	4	10	Regulate...G Funk Era	*Warren G.*	Violator/RAL 523364
⑥	6	35	August and Everything After	*Counting Crows*	DGC 24528
❼	9	40	**Candlebox**	*Candlebox*	Maverick/Sire 45313
❽	13	27	Dookie	*Green Day*	Reprise 45529
⑨	7	5	Voodoo Lounge	*The Rolling Stones*	Virgin 39782
⑩	8	23	Superunknown	*Soundgarden*	A&M 0198

Billboard® — SEPTEMBER 3, 1994 — THE BILLBOARD 200®

TW	LW	WK	Title	Artist	Label
①	1	12	**The Lion King**	*Soundtrack*	Walt Disney 60858
②	2	7	**Forrest Gump**	*Soundtrack*	Epic Soundtrax 66329
③	3	39	The Sign	*Ace Of Base*	Arista 18740
❹	4	11	Purple	*Stone Temple Pilots*	Atlantic 82607
❺	8	28	Dookie	*Green Day*	Reprise 45529
⑥	6	36	August and Everything After	*Counting Crows*	DGC 24528
⑦	5	11	Regulate...G Funk Era	*Warren G.*	Violator/RAL 523364
❽	7	41	Candlebox	*Candlebox*	Maverick/Sire 45313
❾	-	1	**Sleeps With Angels**	*Neil Young & Crazy Horse*	Reprise 45749
❿	11	14	Smash	*Offspring*	Epitaph 86432

Billboard® — SEPTEMBER 10, 1994 — THE BILLBOARD 200®

TW	LW	WK	Title	Artist...Label
1	1	13	**The Lion King**	*Soundtrack*...Walt Disney 60858
2	2	8	**Forrest Gump**	*Soundtrack*...Epic Soundtrax 66329
3	4	12	Purple	*Stone Temple Pilots*...Atlantic 82607
4	5	29	Dookie	*Green Day*...Reprise 45529
5	3	40	The Sign	*Ace Of Base*...Arista 18740
6	6	37	August and Everything After	*Counting Crows*...DGC 24528
7	7	12	Regulate...G Funk Era	*Warren G*...Violator/RAL 523364
8	8	42	Candlebox	*Candlebox*...Maverick/Sire 45313
9	10	15	Smash	*Offspring*...Epitaph 86432
10	11	25	Superunknown	*Soundgarden*...A&M 0198

Billboard® — SEPTEMBER 17, 1994 — THE BILLBOARD 200®

TW	LW	WK	Title	Artist...Label
1	-	1	II	*Boyz II Men*...Motown 0323
2	1	14	The Lion King	*Soundtrack*...Walt Disney 60858
3	2	9	Forrest Gump	*Soundtrack*...Epic Soundtrax 66329
4	-	1	**The 3 Tenors In Concert 1994**	*Carreras Domingo Pavarotti*...Atlantic 82614
5	4	30	Dookie	*Green Day*...Reprise 45529
6	3	13	Purple	*Stone Temple Pilots*...Atlantic 82607
7	5	41	The Sign	*Ace Of Base*...Arista 18740
8	8	43	Candlebox	*Candlebox*...Maverick/Sire 45313
9	6	38	August and Everything After	*Counting Crows*...DGC 24528
10	7	13	Regulate...G Funk Era	*Warren G*...Violator/RAL 523364

Billboard® — SEPTEMBER 24, 1994 — THE BILLBOARD 200®

TW	LW	WK	Title	Artist...Label
1	1	2	II	*Boyz II Men*...Motown 0323
2	2	15	The Lion King	*Soundtrack*...Walt Disney 60858
3	3	10	Forrest Gump	*Soundtrack*...Epic Soundtrax 66329
4	5	31	Dookie	*Green Day*...Reprise 45529
5	6	14	Purple	*Stone Temple Pilots*...Atlantic 82607
6	11	17	Smash	*Offspring*...Epitaph 86432
7	4	2	The 3 Tenors In Concert 1994	*Carreras Domingo Pavarotti*...Atlantic 82614
8	8	44	Candlebox	*Candlebox*...Maverick/Sire 45313
9	9	39	August and Everything After	*Counting Crows*...DGC 24528
10	7	42	The Sign	*Ace Of Base*...Arista 18740

Billboard® — OCTOBER 1, 1994 — THE BILLBOARD 200®

TW	LW	WK	Title	Artist...Label
1	-	1	**From The Cradle**	*Eric Clapton*...Duck 45735
2	1	3	II	*Boyz II Men*...Motown 0323
3	-	1	**Rhythm Of Love**	*Anita Baker*...Elektra 61555
4	2	16	The Lion King	*Soundtrack*...Walt Disney 60858
5	4	32	Dookie	*Green Day*...Reprise 45529
6	3	11	Forrest Gump	*Soundtrack*...Epic Soundtrax 66329
7	6	18	Smash	*Offspring*...Epitaph 86432
8	11	29	Tuesday Night Music Club	*Sheryl Crow*...A&M 0126
9	5	15	Purple	*Stone Temple Pilots*...Atlantic 82607
10	8	45	Candlebox	*Candlebox*...Maverick/Sire 45313

TW	LW	WK	Billboard® — OCTOBER 8, 1994 — THE BILLBOARD 200®
1	2	4	**II** ... *Boyz II Men*...Motown 0323
2	1	2	From The Cradle ... *Eric Clapton*...Duck 45735
3	3	2	**Rhythm Of Love** ... *Anita Baker*...Elektra 61555
4	4	17	The Lion King ... *Soundtrack*...Walt Disney 60858
5	-	1	**Songs** ... *Luther Vandross*...Epic/LV 57775
6	5	33	Dookie ... *Green Day*...Reprise 45529
7	7	19	Smash ... *Offspring*...Epitaph 86432
8	8	30	Tuesday Night Music Club ... *Sheryl Crow*...A&M 0126
9	6	12	Forrest Gump ... *Soundtrack*...Epic Soundtrax 66329
10	9	16	Purple ... *Stone Temple Pilots*...Atlantic 82607

TW	LW	WK	Billboard® — OCTOBER 15, 1994 — THE BILLBOARD 200®
1	-	1	**Monster** ... *R.E.M.*...Warner 45740
2	1	5	II ... *Boyz II Men*...Motown 0323
3	2	3	From The Cradle ... *Eric Clapton*...Duck 45735
4	3	3	Rhythm Of Love ... *Anita Baker*...Elektra 61555
5	5	2	**Songs** ... *Luther Vandross*...Epic/LV 57775
6	4	18	The Lion King ... *Soundtrack*...Walt Disney 60858
7	7	20	Smash ... *Offspring*...Epitaph 86432
8	-	1	**Divine Intervention** ... *Slayer*...American 45522
9	6	34	Dookie ... *Green Day*...Reprise 45529
10	-	1	**The Concert** ... *Barbra Streisand*...Columbia 66109

TW	LW	WK	Billboard® — OCTOBER 22, 1994 — THE BILLBOARD 200®
1	1	2	**Monster** ... *R.E.M.*...Warner 45740
2	2	6	II ... *Boyz II Men*...Motown 0323
3	3	4	From The Cradle ... *Eric Clapton*...Duck 45735
4	-	1	**Pisces Iscariot** ... *The Smashing Pumpkins*...Virgin 39834
5	7	21	Smash ... *Offspring*...Epitaph 86432
6	4	4	Rhythm Of Love ... *Anita Baker*...Elektra 61555
7	6	19	The Lion King ... *Soundtrack*...Walt Disney 60858
8	9	35	Dookie ... *Green Day*...Reprise 45529
9	5	3	Songs ... *Luther Vandross*...Epic/LV 57775
10	-	1	**Stones In The Road** ... *Mary Chapin Carpenter*...Columbia 64327

TW	LW	WK	Billboard® — OCTOBER 29, 1994 — THE BILLBOARD 200®
1	2	7	**II** ... *Boyz II Men*...Motown 0323
2	1	3	Monster ... *R.E.M.*...Warner 45740
3	3	5	From The Cradle ... *Eric Clapton*...Duck 45735
4	5	22	**Smash** ... *Offspring*...Epitaph 86432
5	8	36	Dookie ... *Green Day*...Reprise 45529
6	7	20	The Lion King ... *Soundtrack*...Walt Disney 60858
7	6	5	Rhythm Of Love ... *Anita Baker*...Elektra 61555
8	11	33	Tuesday Night Music Club ... *Sheryl Crow*...A&M 0126
9	12	2	No Need To Argue ... *The Cranberries*...Island 524050
10	4	2	Pisces Iscariot ... *The Smashing Pumpkins*...Virgin 39834

TW	LW	WK	Billboard® NOVEMBER 5, 1994 THE BILLBOARD 200®	
1	-	1	**Murder Was The Case**	*Soundtrack*...Death Row 92484
2	-	1	**The Diary**	*Scarface*...Rap-A-Lot 39946
3	-	1	**Promised Land**	*Queensryche*...EMI 30711
4	1	8	II	*Boyz II Men*...Motown 0323
5	4	23	Smash	*Offspring*...Epitaph 86432
6	2	4	Monster	*R.E.M.*...Warner 45740
7	3	6	From The Cradle	*Eric Clapton*...Duck 45735
8	-	1	**Cross Road**	*Bon Jovi*...Mercury 526013
9	5	37	Dookie	*Green Day*...Reprise 45529
10	8	34	Tuesday Night Music Club	*Sheryl Crow*...A&M 0126

TW	LW	WK	Billboard® NOVEMBER 12, 1994 THE BILLBOARD 200®	
1	1	2	**Murder Was The Case**	*Soundtrack*...Death Row 92484
2	4	9	II	*Boyz II Men*...Motown 0323
3	-	1	**Bedtime Stories**	*Madonna*...Maverick/Sire 45767
4	5	24	**Smash**	*Offspring*...Epitaph 86432
5	6	5	Monster	*R.E.M.*...Warner 45740
6	7	7	From The Cradle	*Eric Clapton*...Duck 45735
7	2	2	The Diary	*Scarface*...Rap-A-Lot 39946
8	-	1	**Greatest Hits**	*Bob Seger & The Silver Bullet Band*...Capitol 30334
9	11	2	**Hold Me, Thrill Me, Kiss Me**	*Gloria Estefan*...Epic 66205
10	9	38	Dookie	*Green Day*...Reprise 45529

TW	LW	WK	Billboard® NOVEMBER 19, 1994 THE BILLBOARD 200®	
1	-	1	**MTV Unplugged In New York**	*Nirvana*...DGC 24727
2	2	10	II	*Boyz II Men*...Motown 0323
3	1	3	Murder Was The Case	*Soundtrack*...Death Row 92484
4	-	1	**Youthanasia**	*Megadeth*...Capitol 29004
5	4	25	Smash	*Offspring*...Epitaph 86432
6	-	1	**Big Ones**	*Aerosmith*...Geffen 24716
7	3	2	Bedtime Stories	*Madonna*...Maverick/Sire 45767
8	-	1	**Wildflowers**	*Tom Petty*...Warner 45759
9	5	6	Monster	*R.E.M.*...Warner 45740
10	6	8	From The Cradle	*Eric Clapton*...Duck 45735

TW	LW	WK	Billboard® NOVEMBER 26, 1994 THE BILLBOARD 200®	
1	-	1	**Hell Freezes Over**	*Eagles*...Geffen 24725
2	1	2	MTV Unplugged In New York	*Nirvana*...DGC 24727
3	2	11	II	*Boyz II Men*...Motown 0323
4	-	1	**No Quarter**	*Jimmy Page & Robert Plant*...Atlantic 82706
5	3	4	Murder Was The Case	*Soundtrack*...Death Row 92484
6	5	26	Smash	*Offspring*...Epitaph 86432
7	-	1	**Fields Of Gold - The Best Of Sting 1984-1994**	*Sting*...A&M 0269
8	6	2	Big Ones	*Aerosmith*...Geffen 24716
9	-	1	**Best Of Sade**	*Sade*...Epic 66686
10	8	2	Wildflowers	*Tom Petty*...Warner 45759

Billboard — DECEMBER 3, 1994 — THE BILLBOARD 200

TW	LW	WK	Title	Artist / Label
1	1	2	**Hell Freezes Over**	*Eagles*...Geffen 24725
2	3	12	II	*Boyz II Men*...Motown 0323
3	2	3	MTV Unplugged In New York	*Nirvana*...DGC 24727
4	-	1	**Tical**	*Method Man*...Def Jam 523839
5	6	27	Smash	*Offspring*...Epitaph 86432
6	18	3	Miracles - The Holiday Album	*Kenny G*...Arista 18767
7	13	3	Merry Christmas	*Mariah Carey*...Columbia 64222
8	8	3	Big Ones	*Aerosmith*...Geffen 24716
9	11	25	The Lion King	*Soundtrack*...Walt Disney 60858
10	10	3	Wildflowers	*Tom Petty*...Warner 45759

Billboard — DECEMBER 10, 1994 — THE BILLBOARD 200

TW	LW	WK	Title	Artist / Label
1	6	4	**Miracles - The Holiday Album**	*Kenny G*...Arista 18767
2	2	13	II	*Boyz II Men*...Motown 0323
3	1	3	Hell Freezes Over	*Eagles*...Geffen 24725
4	7	4	Merry Christmas	*Mariah Carey*...Columbia 64222
5	3	4	MTV Unplugged In New York	*Nirvana*...DGC 24727
6	5	28	Smash	*Offspring*...Epitaph 86432
7	9	26	The Lion King	*Soundtrack*...Walt Disney 60858
8	10	4	**Wildflowers**	*Tom Petty*...Warner 45759
9	16	2	**Duets II**	*Frank Sinatra*...Capitol 28103
10	20	42	Dookie	*Green Day*...Reprise 45529

Billboard — DECEMBER 17, 1994 — THE BILLBOARD 200

TW	LW	WK	Title	Artist / Label
1	1	5	**Miracles - The Holiday Album**	*Kenny G*...Arista 18767
2	2	14	II	*Boyz II Men*...Motown 0323
3	4	5	**Merry Christmas**	*Mariah Carey*...Columbia 64222
4	3	4	Hell Freezes Over	*Eagles*...Geffen 24725
5	5	5	MTV Unplugged In New York	*Nirvana*...DGC 24727
6	7	27	The Lion King	*Soundtrack*...Walt Disney 60858
7	6	29	Smash	*Offspring*...Epitaph 86432
8	10	43	Dookie	*Green Day*...Reprise 45529
9	-	1	My Life	*Mary J. Blige*...Uptown/MCA 11156
10	9	3	Duets II	*Frank Sinatra*...Capitol 28103

Billboard — DECEMBER 24, 1994 — THE BILLBOARD 200

TW	LW	WK	Title	Artist / Label
1	173	3	**Vitalogy**	*Pearl Jam*...Epic 66900
2	1	6	Miracles - The Holiday Album	*Kenny G*...Arista 18767
3	-	1	**Live At The BBC**	*The Beatles*...Apple 31796
4	3	6	Merry Christmas	*Mariah Carey*...Columbia 64222
5	2	15	II	*Boyz II Men*...Motown 0323
6	4	5	Hell Freezes Over	*Eagles*...Geffen 24725
7	8	44	Dookie	*Green Day*...Reprise 45529
8	5	6	MTV Unplugged In New York	*Nirvana*...DGC 24727
9	6	28	The Lion King	*Soundtrack*...Walt Disney 60858
10	7	30	Smash	*Offspring*...Epitaph 86432

TW	LW	WK	Billboard. DECEMBER 31, 1994 THE BILLBOARD 200.
❶	2	7	**Miracles - The Holiday Album** .... *Kenny G*...Arista 18767
②	1	4	**Vitalogy** .... *Pearl Jam*...Epic 66900
❸	-	1	**The Hits** .... *Garth Brooks*...Liberty 29689
❹	6	6	**Hell Freezes Over** .... *Eagles*...Geffen 24725
⑤	4	7	**Merry Christmas** .... *Mariah Carey*...Columbia 64222
⑥	5	16	**II** .... *Boyz II Men*...Motown 0323
⑦	3	2	**Live At The BBC** .... *The Beatles*...Apple 31796
❽	7	45	**Dookie** .... *Green Day*...Reprise 45529
⑨	10	31	**Smash** .... *Offspring*...Epitaph 86432
⑩	8	7	**MTV Unplugged In New York** .... *Nirvana*...DGC 24727

TW	LW	WK	Billboard® — JANUARY 7, 1995 — THE BILLBOARD 200®		
1	3	2	**The Hits**	*Garth Brooks*	Liberty 29689
2	1	8	Miracles - The Holiday Album	*Kenny G*	Arista 18767
3	2	5	Vitalogy	*Pearl Jam*	Epic 66900
4	6	17	II	*Boyz II Men*	Motown 0323
5	4	7	Hell Freezes Over	*Eagles*	Geffen 24725
6	5	8	Merry Christmas	*Mariah Carey*	Columbia 64222
7	8	46	Dookie	*Green Day*	Reprise 45529
8	10	8	MTV Unplugged In New York	*Nirvana*	DGC 24727
9	9	32	Smash	*Offspring*	Epitaph 86432
10	7	3	Live At The BBC	*The Beatles*	Apple 31796

TW	LW	WK	Billboard® — JANUARY 14, 1995 — THE BILLBOARD 200®		
1	1	3	**The Hits**	*Garth Brooks*	Liberty 29689
2	3	6	Vitalogy	*Pearl Jam*	Epic 66900
3	4	18	II	*Boyz II Men*	Motown 0323
4	7	47	Dookie	*Green Day*	Reprise 45529
5	5	8	Hell Freezes Over	*Eagles*	Geffen 24725
6	9	33	Smash	*Offspring*	Epitaph 86432
7	8	9	MTV Unplugged In New York	*Nirvana*	DGC 24727
8	15	9	Big Ones	*Aerosmith*	Geffen 24716
9	11	9	Wildflowers	*Tom Petty*	Warner 45759
10	12	13	No Need To Argue	*The Cranberries*	Island 524050

TW	LW	WK	Billboard® — JANUARY 21, 1995 — THE BILLBOARD 200®		
1	1	4	**The Hits**	*Garth Brooks*	Liberty 29689
2	3	19	II	*Boyz II Men*	Motown 0323
3	2	7	Vitalogy	*Pearl Jam*	Epic 66900
4	5	9	Hell Freezes Over	*Eagles*	Geffen 24725
5	4	48	Dookie	*Green Day*	Reprise 45529
6	6	34	Smash	*Offspring*	Epitaph 86432
7	7	10	MTV Unplugged In New York	*Nirvana*	DGC 24727
8	8	10	Big Ones	*Aerosmith*	Geffen 24716
9	12	8	CrazySexyCool	*TLC*	LaFace 26009
10	9	10	Wildflowers	*Tom Petty*	Warner 45759

TW	LW	WK	Billboard® — JANUARY 28, 1995 — THE BILLBOARD 200®		
1	1	5	**The Hits**	*Garth Brooks*	Liberty 29689
2	5	49	**Dookie**	*Green Day*	Reprise 45529
3	2	20	II	*Boyz II Men*	Motown 0323
4	4	10	Hell Freezes Over	*Eagles*	Geffen 24725
5	3	8	Vitalogy	*Pearl Jam*	Epic 66900
6	6	35	Smash	*Offspring*	Epitaph 86432
7	15	7	**My Life**	*Mary J. Blige*	Uptown/MCA 11156
8	9	9	CrazySexyCool	*TLC*	LaFace 26009
9	7	11	MTV Unplugged In New York	*Nirvana*	DGC 24727
10	12	15	No Need To Argue	*The Cranberries*	Island 524050

TW	LW	WK	Billboard. FEBRUARY 4, 1995 THE BILLBOARD 200.
1	1	6	**The Hits** ... *Garth Brooks*...Liberty 29689
2	2	50	**Dookie** ... *Green Day*...Reprise 45529
3	4	11	Hell Freezes Over ... *Eagles*...Geffen 24725
4	3	21	II ... *Boyz II Men*...Motown 0323
5	5	9	Vitalogy ... *Pearl Jam*...Epic 66900
6	10	16	**No Need To Argue** ... *The Cranberries*...Island 524050
7	8	10	CrazySexyCool ... *TLC*...LaFace 26009
8	7	8	My Life ... *Mary J. Blige*...Uptown/MCA 11156
9	6	36	Smash ... *Offspring*...Epitaph 86432
10	9	12	MTV Unplugged In New York ... *Nirvana*...DGC 24727

TW	LW	WK	Billboard. FEBRUARY 11, 1995 THE BILLBOARD 200.
1	-	1	**Balance** ... *Van Halen*...Warner 45760
2	1	7	The Hits ... *Garth Brooks*...Liberty 29689
3	2	51	Dookie ... *Green Day*...Reprise 45529
4	3	12	Hell Freezes Over ... *Eagles*...Geffen 24725
5	4	22	II ... *Boyz II Men*...Motown 0323
6	-	1	**Cocktails** ... *Too $hort*...Jive 41553
7	5	10	Vitalogy ... *Pearl Jam*...Epic 66900
8	7	11	CrazySexyCool ... *TLC*...LaFace 26009
9	6	17	No Need To Argue ... *The Cranberries*...Island 524050
10	8	9	My Life ... *Mary J. Blige*...Uptown/MCA 11156

TW	LW	WK	Billboard. FEBRUARY 18, 1995 THE BILLBOARD 200.
1	2	8	**The Hits** ... *Garth Brooks*...Liberty 29689
2	1	2	Balance ... *Van Halen*...Warner 45760
3	5	23	II ... *Boyz II Men*...Motown 0323
4	3	52	Dookie ... *Green Day*...Reprise 45529
5	4	13	Hell Freezes Over ... *Eagles*...Geffen 24725
6	8	12	CrazySexyCool ... *TLC*...LaFace 26009
7	6	2	Cocktails ... *Too $hort*...Jive 41553
8	7	11	Vitalogy ... *Pearl Jam*...Epic 66900
9	10	10	My Life ... *Mary J. Blige*...Uptown/MCA 11156
10	9	18	No Need To Argue ... *The Cranberries*...Island 524050

TW	LW	WK	Billboard. FEBRUARY 25, 1995 THE BILLBOARD 200.
1	1	9	**The Hits** ... *Garth Brooks*...Liberty 29689
2	3	24	II ... *Boyz II Men*...Motown 0323
3	2	3	Balance ... *Van Halen*...Warner 45760
4	4	53	Dookie ... *Green Day*...Reprise 45529
5	5	14	Hell Freezes Over ... *Eagles*...Geffen 24725
6	6	13	CrazySexyCool ... *TLC*...LaFace 26009
7	11	31	Cracked Rear View ... *Hootie & The Blowfish*...Atlantic 82613
8	8	12	Vitalogy ... *Pearl Jam*...Epic 66900
9	10	19	No Need To Argue ... *The Cranberries*...Island 524050
10	12	39	Smash ... *Offspring*...Epitaph 86432

Billboard. MARCH 4, 1995 — THE BILLBOARD 200.

TW	LW	WK	Title	Artist	Label
1	1	10	**The Hits**	*Garth Brooks*	Liberty 29689
2	2	25	II	*Boyz II Men*	Motown 0323
3	4	54	Dookie	*Green Day*	Reprise 45529
4	3	4	Balance	*Van Halen*	Warner 45760
5	5	15	Hell Freezes Over	*Eagles*	Geffen 24725
6	7	32	Cracked Rear View	*Hootie & The Blowfish*	Atlantic 82613
7	6	14	CrazySexyCool	*TLC*	LaFace 26009
8	12	43	Throwing Copper	*Live*	Radioactive 10997
9	9	20	No Need To Argue	*The Cranberries*	Island 524050
10	8	13	Vitalogy	*Pearl Jam*	Epic 66900

Billboard. MARCH 11, 1995 — THE BILLBOARD 200.

TW	LW	WK	Title	Artist	Label
1	2	26	**II**	*Boyz II Men*	Motown 0323
2	1	11	The Hits	*Garth Brooks*	Liberty 29689
3	3	55	Dookie	*Green Day*	Reprise 45529
4	5	16	Hell Freezes Over	*Eagles*	Geffen 24725
5	7	15	CrazySexyCool	*TLC*	LaFace 26009
6	6	33	Cracked Rear View	*Hootie & The Blowfish*	Atlantic 82613
7	4	5	Balance	*Van Halen*	Warner 45760
8	8	44	Throwing Copper	*Live*	Radioactive 10997
9	12	52	Tuesday Night Music Club	*Sheryl Crow*	A&M 0126
10	9	21	No Need To Argue	*The Cranberries*	Island 524050

Billboard. MARCH 18, 1995 — THE BILLBOARD 200.

TW	LW	WK	Title	Artist	Label
1	-	1	**Greatest Hits**	*Bruce Springsteen*	Columbia 67060
2	1	27	II	*Boyz II Men*	Motown 0323
3	2	12	The Hits	*Garth Brooks*	Liberty 29689
4	9	53	Tuesday Night Music Club	*Sheryl Crow*	A&M 0126
5	3	56	Dookie	*Green Day*	Reprise 45529
6	6	34	Cracked Rear View	*Hootie & The Blowfish*	Atlantic 82613
7	5	16	CrazySexyCool	*TLC*	LaFace 26009
8	4	17	Hell Freezes Over	*Eagles*	Geffen 24725
9	8	45	Throwing Copper	*Live*	Radioactive 10997
10	7	6	Balance	*Van Halen*	Warner 45760

Billboard. MARCH 25, 1995 — THE BILLBOARD 200.

TW	LW	WK	Title	Artist	Label
1	1	2	**Greatest Hits**	*Bruce Springsteen*	Columbia 67060
2	14	41	The Lion King	*Soundtrack*	Walt Disney 60858
3	4	54	**Tuesday Night Music Club**	*Sheryl Crow*	A&M 0126
4	8	18	Hell Freezes Over	*Eagles*	Geffen 24725
5	2	28	II	*Boyz II Men*	Motown 0323
6	6	35	Cracked Rear View	*Hootie & The Blowfish*	Atlantic 82613
7	3	13	The Hits	*Garth Brooks*	Liberty 29689
8	5	57	Dookie	*Green Day*	Reprise 45529
9	9	46	Throwing Copper	*Live*	Radioactive 10997
10	7	17	CrazySexyCool	*TLC*	LaFace 26009

Billboard — APRIL 1, 1995 — THE BILLBOARD 200

TW	LW	WK	Title	Artist	Label
1	-	1	**Me Against The World**	*2 Pac*	Interscope 92399
2	1	3	Greatest Hits	*Bruce Springsteen*	Columbia 67060
3	4	19	Hell Freezes Over	*Eagles*	Geffen 24725
4	6	36	Cracked Rear View	*Hootie & The Blowfish*	Atlantic 82613
5	2	42	The Lion King	*Soundtrack*	Walt Disney 60858
6	5	29	II	*Boyz II Men*	Motown 0323
7	3	55	Tuesday Night Music Club	*Sheryl Crow*	A&M 0126
8	7	14	The Hits	*Garth Brooks*	Liberty 29689
9	9	47	Throwing Copper	*Live*	Radioactive 10997
10	8	58	Dookie	*Green Day*	Reprise 45529

Billboard — APRIL 8, 1995 — THE BILLBOARD 200

TW	LW	WK	Title	Artist	Label
1	1	2	**Me Against The World**	*2 Pac*	Interscope 92399
2	2	4	Greatest Hits	*Bruce Springsteen*	Columbia 67060
3	4	37	Cracked Rear View	*Hootie & The Blowfish*	Atlantic 82613
4	3	20	Hell Freezes Over	*Eagles*	Geffen 24725
5	5	43	The Lion King	*Soundtrack*	Walt Disney 60858
6	9	48	Throwing Copper	*Live*	Radioactive 10997
7	7	56	Tuesday Night Music Club	*Sheryl Crow*	A&M 0126
8	6	30	II	*Boyz II Men*	Motown 0323
9	10	59	Dookie	*Green Day*	Reprise 45529
10	8	15	The Hits	*Garth Brooks*	Liberty 29689

Billboard — APRIL 15, 1995 — THE BILLBOARD 200

TW	LW	WK	Title	Artist	Label
1	1	3	**Me Against The World**	*2 Pac*	Interscope 92399
2	5	44	The Lion King	*Soundtrack*	Walt Disney 60858
3	3	38	Cracked Rear View	*Hootie & The Blowfish*	Atlantic 82613
4	2	5	Greatest Hits	*Bruce Springsteen*	Columbia 67060
5	6	49	Throwing Copper	*Live*	Radioactive 10997
6	4	21	Hell Freezes Over	*Eagles*	Geffen 24725
7	-	1	**Return To The 36 Chambers: The Dirty Version**	*Ol' Dirty Bastard*	Elektra 61659
8	7	57	Tuesday Night Music Club	*Sheryl Crow*	A&M 0126
9	8	31	II	*Boyz II Men*	Motown 0323
10	-	1	John Michael Montgomery	*John Michael Montgomery*	Atlantic 82728

Billboard — APRIL 22, 1995 — THE BILLBOARD 200

TW	LW	WK	Title	Artist	Label
1	1	4	**Me Against The World**	*2 Pac*	Interscope 92399
2	2	45	The Lion King	*Soundtrack*	Walt Disney 60858
3	3	39	Cracked Rear View	*Hootie & The Blowfish*	Atlantic 82613
4	5	50	Throwing Copper	*Live*	Radioactive 10997
5	4	6	Greatest Hits	*Bruce Springsteen*	Columbia 67060
6	10	2	John Michael Montgomery	*John Michael Montgomery*	Atlantic 82728
7	6	22	Hell Freezes Over	*Eagles*	Geffen 24725
8	8	58	Tuesday Night Music Club	*Sheryl Crow*	A&M 0126
9	9	32	II	*Boyz II Men*	Motown 0323
10	13	21	CrazySexyCool	*TLC*	LaFace 26009

TW	LW	WK	Billboard® APRIL 29, 1995 THE BILLBOARD 200®
1	2	46	**The Lion King** .... *Soundtrack*...Walt Disney 60858
2	-	1	Friday .... *Soundtrack*...Priority 53959
3	3	40	Cracked Rear View .... *Hootie & The Blowfish*...Atlantic 82613
4	4	51	Throwing Copper .... *Live*...Radioactive 10997
5	1	5	Me Against The World .... *2 Pac*...Interscope 92399
6	-	1	**Astro-Creep: 2000-Songs Of Love, Destruction And Other Synthetic Delusions Of The Electric Head** .... *White Zombie*...Geffen 24806
7	9	33	II .... *Boyz II Men*...Motown 0323
8	7	23	Hell Freezes Over .... *Eagles*...Geffen 24725
9	8	59	Tuesday Night Music Club .... *Sheryl Crow*...A&M 0126
10	5	7	Greatest Hits .... *Bruce Springsteen*...Columbia 67060

TW	LW	WK	Billboard® MAY 6, 1995 THE BILLBOARD 200®
1	4	52	**Throwing Copper** .... *Live*...Radioactive 10997
2	2	2	Friday .... *Soundtrack*...Priority 53959
3	3	41	Cracked Rear View .... *Hootie & The Blowfish*...Atlantic 82613
4	1	47	The Lion King .... *Soundtrack*...Walt Disney 60858
5	5	6	Me Against The World .... *2 Pac*...Interscope 92399
6	7	34	II .... *Boyz II Men*...Motown 0323
7	13	4	John Michael Montgomery .... *John Michael Montgomery*...Atlantic 82728
8	8	24	Hell Freezes Over .... *Eagles*...Geffen 24725
9	6	2	Astro-Creep: 2000-Songs Of Love, Destruction And Other Synthetic Delusions Of The Electric Head .... *White Zombie*...Geffen 24806
10	12	23	CrazySexyCool .... *TLC*...LaFace 26009

TW	LW	WK	Billboard® MAY 13, 1995 THE BILLBOARD 200®
1	2	3	**Friday** .... *Soundtrack*...Priority 53959
2	1	53	Throwing Copper .... *Live*...Radioactive 10997
3	3	42	Cracked Rear View .... *Hootie & The Blowfish*...Atlantic 82613
4	5	7	Me Against The World .... *2 Pac*...Interscope 92399
5	4	48	The Lion King .... *Soundtrack*...Walt Disney 60858
6	6	35	II .... *Boyz II Men*...Motown 0323
7	8	25	Hell Freezes Over .... *Eagles*...Geffen 24725
8	7	5	John Michael Montgomery .... *John Michael Montgomery*...Atlantic 82728
9	9	3	Astro-Creep: 2000-Songs Of Love, Destruction And Other Synthetic Delusions Of The Electric Head .... *White Zombie*...Geffen 24806
10	10	24	CrazySexyCool .... *TLC*...LaFace 26009

Billboard® — MAY 20, 1995 — THE BILLBOARD 200®

TW	LW	WK	Title	Artist	Label
1	1	4	**Friday**	*Soundtrack*	Priority 53959
2	3	43	Cracked Rear View	*Hootie & The Blowfish*	Atlantic 82613
3	2	54	Throwing Copper	*Live*	Radioactive 10997
4	22	44	Forrest Gump	*Soundtrack*	Epic Soundtrax 66329
5	4	8	Me Against The World	*2 Pac*	Interscope 92399
6	6	36	II	*Boyz II Men*	Motown 0323
7	7	26	Hell Freezes Over	*Eagles*	Geffen 24725
8	9	4	Astro-Creep: 2000-Songs Of Love, Destruction And Other Synthetic Delusions Of The Electric Head	*White Zombie*	Geffen 24806
9	8	6	John Michael Montgomery	*John Michael Montgomery*	Atlantic 82728
10	5	49	The Lion King	*Soundtrack*	Walt Disney 60858

Billboard® — MAY 27, 1995 — THE BILLBOARD 200®

TW	LW	WK	Title	Artist	Label
1	2	44	**Cracked Rear View**	*Hootie & The Blowfish*	Atlantic 82613
2	3	55	Throwing Copper	*Live*	Radioactive 10997
3	1	5	Friday	*Soundtrack*	Priority 53959
4	4	45	Forrest Gump	*Soundtrack*	Epic Soundtrax 66329
5	7	27	Hell Freezes Over	*Eagles*	Geffen 24725
6	5	9	Me Against The World	*2 Pac*	Interscope 92399
7	6	37	II	*Boyz II Men*	Motown 0323
8	9	7	John Michael Montgomery	*John Michael Montgomery*	Atlantic 82728
9	8	5	Astro-Creep: 2000-Songs Of Love, Destruction And Other Synthetic Delusions Of The Electric Head	*White Zombie*	Geffen 24806
10	15	22	The Hits	*Garth Brooks*	Liberty 29689

Billboard® — JUNE 3, 1995 — THE BILLBOARD 200®

TW	LW	WK	Title	Artist	Label
1	1	45	**Cracked Rear View**	*Hootie & The Blowfish*	Atlantic 82613
2	2	56	Throwing Copper	*Live*	Radioactive 10997
3	3	6	Friday	*Soundtrack*	Priority 53959
4	4	46	Forrest Gump	*Soundtrack*	Epic Soundtrax 66329
5	8	8	**John Michael Montgomery**	*John Michael Montgomery*	Atlantic 82728
6	7	38	II	*Boyz II Men*	Motown 0323
7	6	10	Me Against The World	*2 Pac*	Interscope 92399
8	5	28	Hell Freezes Over	*Eagles*	Geffen 24725
9	9	6	Astro-Creep: 2000-Songs Of Love, Destruction And Other Synthetic Delusions Of The Electric Head	*White Zombie*	Geffen 24806
10	10	23	The Hits	*Garth Brooks*	Liberty 29689

Billboard® — JUNE 10, 1995 — THE BILLBOARD 200®

TW	LW	WK	Title	Artist	Label
1	1	46	**Cracked Rear View**	*Hootie & The Blowfish*	Atlantic 82613
2	2	57	Throwing Copper	*Live*	Radioactive 10997
3	3	7	Friday	*Soundtrack*	Priority 53959
4	6	39	II	*Boyz II Men*	Motown 0323
5	5	9	**John Michael Montgomery**	*John Michael Montgomery*	Atlantic 82728
6	4	47	Forrest Gump	*Soundtrack*	Epic Soundtrax 66329
7	9	7	Astro-Creep: 2000-Songs Of Love, Destruction And Other Synthetic Delusions Of The Electric Head	*White Zombie*	Geffen 24806
8	7	11	Me Against The World	*2 Pac*	Interscope 92399
9	8	29	Hell Freezes Over	*Eagles*	Geffen 24725
10	11	28	CrazySexyCool	*TLC*	LaFace 26009

Billboard — JUNE 17, 1995 — THE BILLBOARD 200

TW	LW	WK	Title	Artist	Label
1	1	47	**Cracked Rear View**	*Hootie & The Blowfish*	Atlantic 82613
2	2	58	Throwing Copper	*Live*	Radioactive 10997
3	-	1	**Poverty's Paradise**	*Naughty By Nature*	Tommy Boy 1111
4	-	1	Pocahontas	*Soundtrack*	Walt Disney 60874
5	3	8	Friday	*Soundtrack*	Priority 53959
6	4	40	II	*Boyz II Men*	Motown 0323
7	10	29	CrazySexyCool	*TLC*	LaFace 26009
8	5	10	John Michael Montgomery	*John Michael Montgomery*	Atlantic 82728
9	7	8	Astro-Creep: 2000-Songs Of Love, Destruction And Other Synthetic Delusions Of The Electric Head	*White Zombie*	Geffen 24806
10	8	12	Me Against The World	*2 Pac*	Interscope 92399

Billboard — JUNE 24, 1995 — THE BILLBOARD 200

TW	LW	WK	Title	Artist	Label
1	-	1	**Pulse**	*Pink Floyd*	Columbia 67065
2	1	48	Cracked Rear View	*Hootie & The Blowfish*	Atlantic 82613
3	4	2	Pocahontas	*Soundtrack*	Walt Disney 60874
4	2	59	Throwing Copper	*Live*	Radioactive 10997
5	7	30	CrazySexyCool	*TLC*	LaFace 26009
6	-	1	**Let Your Dim Light Shine**	*Soul Asylum*	Columbia 57616
7	8	11	John Michael Montgomery	*John Michael Montgomery*	Atlantic 82728
8	-	1	**Tales From The Punchbowl**	*Primus*	Interscope 92553
9	6	41	II	*Boyz II Men*	Motown 0323
10	5	9	Friday	*Soundtrack*	Priority 53959

Billboard — JULY 1, 1995 — THE BILLBOARD 200

TW	LW	WK	Title	Artist	Label
1	2	49	**Cracked Rear View**	*Hootie & The Blowfish*	Atlantic 82613
2	3	3	Pocahontas	*Soundtrack*	Walt Disney 60874
3	1	2	Pulse	*Pink Floyd*	Columbia 67065
4	5	31	CrazySexyCool	*TLC*	LaFace 26009
5	4	60	Throwing Copper	*Live*	Radioactive 10997
6	15	2	Batman Forever	*Soundtrack*	Atlantic 82759
7	7	12	John Michael Montgomery	*John Michael Montgomery*	Atlantic 82728
8	6	2	Let Your Dim Light Shine	*Soul Asylum*	Columbia 57616
9	9	42	II	*Boyz II Men*	Motown 0323
10	14	29	four	*Blues Traveler*	A&M 0265

Billboard — JULY 8, 1995 — THE BILLBOARD 200

TW	LW	WK	Title	Artist	Label
1	-	1	**HIStory: Past, Present And Future - Book I**	*Michael Jackson*	Epic 59000
2	2	4	Pocahontas	*Soundtrack*	Walt Disney 60874
3	1	50	Cracked Rear View	*Hootie & The Blowfish*	Atlantic 82613
4	4	32	CrazySexyCool	*TLC*	LaFace 26009
5	6	3	**Batman Forever**	*Soundtrack*	Atlantic 82759
6	5	61	Throwing Copper	*Live*	Radioactive 10997
7	3	3	Pulse	*Pink Floyd*	Columbia 67065
8	7	13	John Michael Montgomery	*John Michael Montgomery*	Atlantic 82728
9	9	43	II	*Boyz II Men*	Motown 0323
10	11	17	The Woman In Me	*Shania Twain*	Mercury 522886

TW	LW	WK	Billboard. JULY 15, 1995 THE BILLBOARD 200.
①	1	2	**HIStory: Past, Present And Future - Book I** ... *Michael Jackson*...Epic 59000
❷	2	5	Pocahontas ... *Soundtrack*...Walt Disney 60874
③	3	51	Cracked Rear View ... *Hootie & The Blowfish*...Atlantic 82613
④	4	33	CrazySexyCool ... *TLC*...LaFace 26009
❺	-	1	**Mirror Ball** ... *Neil Young*...Reprise 45934
⑥	5	4	Batman Forever ... *Soundtrack*...Atlantic 82759
⑦	6	62	Throwing Copper ... *Live*...Radioactive 10997
❽	20	29	The Hits ... *Garth Brooks*...Liberty 29689
❾	-	1	**These Days** ... *Bon Jovi*...Mercury 528181
⑩	8	14	John Michael Montgomery ... *John Michael Montgomery*...Atlantic 82728

TW	LW	WK	Billboard. JULY 22, 1995 THE BILLBOARD 200.
❶	2	6	**Pocahontas** ... *Soundtrack*...Walt Disney 60874
②	1	3	HIStory: Past, Present And Future - Book I ... *Michael Jackson*...Epic 59000
③	3	52	Cracked Rear View ... *Hootie & The Blowfish*...Atlantic 82613
❹	4	34	CrazySexyCool ... *TLC*...LaFace 26009
⑤	6	5	**Batman Forever** ... *Soundtrack*...Atlantic 82759
⑥	7	63	Throwing Copper ... *Live*...Radioactive 10997
❼	11	19	The Woman In Me ... *Shania Twain*...Mercury 522886
⑧	8	30	The Hits ... *Garth Brooks*...Liberty 29689
⑨	12	32	four ... *Blues Traveler*...A&M 0265
⑩	10	15	John Michael Montgomery ... *John Michael Montgomery*...Atlantic 82728

TW	LW	WK	Billboard. JULY 29, 1995 THE BILLBOARD 200.
❶	3	53	**Cracked Rear View** ... *Hootie & The Blowfish*...Atlantic 82613
②	1	7	Pocahontas ... *Soundtrack*...Walt Disney 60874
③	4	35	**CrazySexyCool** ... *TLC*...LaFace 26009
④	2	4	HIStory: Past, Present And Future - Book I ... *Michael Jackson*...Epic 59000
⑤	5	6	**Batman Forever** ... *Soundtrack*...Atlantic 82759
❻	7	20	The Woman In Me ... *Shania Twain*...Mercury 522886
⑦	6	64	Throwing Copper ... *Live*...Radioactive 10997
❽	10	16	John Michael Montgomery ... *John Michael Montgomery*...Atlantic 82728
❾	9	33	four ... *Blues Traveler*...A&M 0265
⑩	8	31	The Hits ... *Garth Brooks*...Liberty 29689

TW	LW	WK	Billboard. AUGUST 5, 1995 THE BILLBOARD 200.
❶	-	1	**Dreaming Of You** ... *Selena*...EMI Latin 34123
❷	-	1	**The Show - The After-Party - The Hotel** ... *Jodeci*...Uptown/MCA 11258
❸	1	54	Cracked Rear View ... *Hootie & The Blowfish*...Atlantic 82613
❹	3	36	CrazySexyCool ... *TLC*...LaFace 26009
⑤	2	8	Pocahontas ... *Soundtrack*...Walt Disney 60874
❻	6	21	The Woman In Me ... *Shania Twain*...Mercury 522886
⑦	5	7	Batman Forever ... *Soundtrack*...Atlantic 82759
⑧	4	5	HIStory: Past, Present And Future - Book I ... *Michael Jackson*...Epic 59000
⑨	7	65	Throwing Copper ... *Live*...Radioactive 10997
❿	14	6	Jagged Little Pill ... *Alanis Morissette*...Maverick 45901

Billboard — AUGUST 12, 1995 — THE BILLBOARD 200

TW	LW	WK	Title	Artist...Label
1	-	1	**E. 1999 Eternal**	*Bone Thugs-N-Harmony*...Ruthless 5539
2	3	55	Cracked Rear View	*Hootie & The Blowfish*...Atlantic 82613
3	1	2	Dreaming Of You	*Selena*...EMI Latin 34123
4	4	37	CrazySexyCool	*TLC*...LaFace 26009
5	2	2	The Show - The After-Party - The Hotel	*Jodeci*...Uptown/MCA 11258
6	5	9	Pocahontas	*Soundtrack*...Walt Disney 60874
7	10	7	Jagged Little Pill	*Alanis Morissette*...Maverick 45901
8	6	22	The Woman In Me	*Shania Twain*...Mercury 522886
9	14	2	Games Rednecks Play	*Jeff Foxworthy*...Warner 45856
10	7	8	Batman Forever	*Soundtrack*...Atlantic 82759

Billboard — AUGUST 19, 1995 — THE BILLBOARD 200

TW	LW	WK	Title	Artist...Label
1	1	2	**E. 1999 Eternal**	*Bone Thugs-N-Harmony*...Ruthless 5539
2	2	56	Cracked Rear View	*Hootie & The Blowfish*...Atlantic 82613
3	3	3	Dreaming Of You	*Selena*...EMI Latin 34123
4	-	1	**Only Built 4 Cuban Linx...**	*Raekwon*...Loud/RCA 66663
5	4	38	CrazySexyCool	*TLC*...LaFace 26009
6	-	1	**Barometer Soup**	*Jimmy Buffett*...Margaritaville 11247
7	7	8	Jagged Little Pill	*Alanis Morissette*...Maverick 45901
8	5	3	The Show - The After-Party - The Hotel	*Jodeci*...Uptown/MCA 11258
9	8	23	The Woman In Me	*Shania Twain*...Mercury 522886
10	6	10	Pocahontas	*Soundtrack*...Walt Disney 60874

Billboard — AUGUST 26, 1995 — THE BILLBOARD 200

TW	LW	WK	Title	Artist...Label
1	2	57	**Cracked Rear View**	*Hootie & The Blowfish*...Atlantic 82613
2	1	3	E. 1999 Eternal	*Bone Thugs-N-Harmony*...Ruthless 5539
3	7	9	Jagged Little Pill	*Alanis Morissette*...Maverick 45901
4	22	3	Dangerous Minds	*Soundtrack*...MCA 11228
5	5	39	CrazySexyCool	*TLC*...LaFace 26009
6	3	4	Dreaming Of You	*Selena*...EMI Latin 34123
7	9	24	The Woman In Me	*Shania Twain*...Mercury 522886
8	8	4	The Show - The After-Party - The Hotel	*Jodeci*...Uptown/MCA 11258
9	11	68	Throwing Copper	*Live*...Radioactive 10997
10	4	2	Only Built 4 Cuban Linx	*Raekwon*...Loud/RCA 66663

Billboard — SEPTEMBER 2, 1995 — THE BILLBOARD 200

TW	LW	WK	Title	Artist...Label
1	4	4	**Dangerous Minds**	*Soundtrack*...MCA 11228
2	1	58	Cracked Rear View	*Hootie & The Blowfish*...Atlantic 82613
3	3	10	Jagged Little Pill	*Alanis Morissette*...Maverick 45901
4	-	1	**The Show**	*Soundtrack*...Def Jam 529021
5	2	4	E. 1999 Eternal	*Bone Thugs-N-Harmony*...Ruthless 5539
6	5	40	CrazySexyCool	*TLC*...LaFace 26009
7	7	25	The Woman In Me	*Shania Twain*...Mercury 522886
8	6	5	Dreaming Of You	*Selena*...EMI Latin 34123
9	14	5	Games Rednecks Play	*Jeff Foxworthy*...Warner 45856
10	15	38	four	*Blues Traveler*...A&M 0265

Billboard — SEPTEMBER 9, 1995 — THE BILLBOARD 200

TW	LW	WK	Title	Artist	Label
1	1	5	**Dangerous Minds**	*Soundtrack*	MCA 11228
2	2	59	Cracked Rear View	*Hootie & The Blowfish*	Atlantic 82613
3	3	11	Jagged Little Pill	*Alanis Morissette*	Maverick 45901
4	4	2	**The Show**	*Soundtrack*	Def Jam 529021
5	5	5	E. 1999 Eternal	*Bone Thugs-N-Harmony*	Ruthless 5539
6	6	41	CrazySexyCool	*TLC*	LaFace 26009
7	7	26	The Woman In Me	*Shania Twain*	Mercury 522886
8	10	39	**four**	*Blues Traveler*	A&M 0265
9	8	6	Dreaming Of You	*Selena*	EMI Latin 34123
10	9	6	Games Rednecks Play	*Jeff Foxworthy*	Warner 45856

Billboard — SEPTEMBER 16, 1995 — THE BILLBOARD 200

TW	LW	WK	Title	Artist	Label
1	1	6	**Dangerous Minds**	*Soundtrack*	MCA 11228
2	2	60	Cracked Rear View	*Hootie & The Blowfish*	Atlantic 82613
3	3	12	Jagged Little Pill	*Alanis Morissette*	Maverick 45901
4	4	3	**The Show**	*Soundtrack*	Def Jam 529021
5	5	6	E. 1999 Eternal	*Bone Thugs-N-Harmony*	Ruthless 5539
6	6	42	CrazySexyCool	*TLC*	LaFace 26009
7	7	27	The Woman In Me	*Shania Twain*	Mercury 522886
8	-	1	**Conspiracy**	*Junior M.A.F.I.A.*	Undeas/Big Beat 92614
9	10	7	Games Rednecks Play	*Jeff Foxworthy*	Warner 45856
10	8	40	four	*Blues Traveler*	A&M 0265

Billboard — SEPTEMBER 23, 1995 — THE BILLBOARD 200

TW	LW	WK	Title	Artist	Label
1	1	7	**Dangerous Minds**	*Soundtrack*	MCA 11228
2	2	61	Cracked Rear View	*Hootie & The Blowfish*	Atlantic 82613
3	3	13	Jagged Little Pill	*Alanis Morissette*	Maverick 45901
4	6	43	CrazySexyCool	*TLC*	LaFace 26009
5	5	7	E. 1999 Eternal	*Bone Thugs-N-Harmony*	Ruthless 5539
6	4	4	The Show	*Soundtrack*	Def Jam 529021
7	7	28	The Woman In Me	*Shania Twain*	Mercury 522886
8	9	8	**Games Rednecks Play**	*Jeff Foxworthy*	Warner 45856
9	12	11	**Frogstomp**	*Silverchair*	Epic 67247
10	15	3	**Mortal Kombat**	*Soundtrack*	TVT 6110

Billboard — SEPTEMBER 30, 1995 — THE BILLBOARD 200

TW	LW	WK	Title	Artist	Label
1	2	62	**Cracked Rear View**	*Hootie & The Blowfish*	Atlantic 82613
2	1	8	Dangerous Minds	*Soundtrack*	MCA 11228
3	3	14	Jagged Little Pill	*Alanis Morissette*	Maverick 45901
4	-	1	**One Hot Minute**	*Red Hot Chili Peppers*	Warner 45733
5	4	44	CrazySexyCool	*TLC*	LaFace 26009
6	5	8	E. 1999 Eternal	*Bone Thugs-N-Harmony*	Ruthless 5539
7	7	29	The Woman In Me	*Shania Twain*	Mercury 522886
8	6	5	The Show	*Soundtrack*	Def Jam 529021
9	9	12	**Frogstomp**	*Silverchair*	Epic 67247
10	-	1	**Circus**	*Lenny Kravitz*	Virgin 40696

TW	LW	WK	Billboard® OCTOBER 7, 1995	THE BILLBOARD 200®	
1	3	15	**Jagged Little Pill**	*Alanis Morissette*	Maverick 45901
2	2	9	Dangerous Minds	*Soundtrack*	MCA 11228
3	1	63	Cracked Rear View	*Hootie & The Blowfish*	Atlantic 82613
4	-	1	**All I Want**	*Tim McGraw*	Curb 77800
5	-	1	**Greatest Hits 1985-1995**	*Michael Bolton*	Columbia 67300
6	4	2	One Hot Minute	*Red Hot Chili Peppers*	Warner 45733
7	5	45	CrazySexyCool	*TLC*	LaFace 26009
8	6	9	E. 1999 Eternal	*Bone Thugs-N-Harmony*	Ruthless 5539
9	9	13	**Frogstomp**	*Silverchair*	Epic 67247
10	7	30	The Woman In Me	*Shania Twain*	Mercury 522886

TW	LW	WK	Billboard® OCTOBER 14, 1995	THE BILLBOARD 200®	
1	1	16	**Jagged Little Pill**	*Alanis Morissette*	Maverick 45901
2	2	10	Dangerous Minds	*Soundtrack*	MCA 11228
3	3	64	Cracked Rear View	*Hootie & The Blowfish*	Atlantic 82613
4	-	1	**Ballbreaker**	*AC/DC*	EastWest 61780
5	4	2	All I Want	*Tim McGraw*	Curb 77800
6	-	1	**The Gold Experience**		Warner 45999
7	5	2	Greatest Hits 1985-1995	*Michael Bolton*	Columbia 67300
8	7	46	CrazySexyCool	*TLC*	LaFace 26009
9	8	10	E. 1999 Eternal	*Bone Thugs-N-Harmony*	Ruthless 5539
10	6	3	One Hot Minute	*Red Hot Chili Peppers*	Warner 45733

TW	LW	WK	Billboard® OCTOBER 21, 1995	THE BILLBOARD 200®	
1	-	1	**Daydream**	*Mariah Carey*	Columbia 66700
2	1	17	Jagged Little Pill	*Alanis Morissette*	Maverick 45901
3	2	11	Dangerous Minds	*Soundtrack*	MCA 11228
4	3	65	Cracked Rear View	*Hootie & The Blowfish*	Atlantic 82613
5	-	1	**Starting Over**	*Reba McEntire*	MCA 11264
6	5	3	All I Want	*Tim McGraw*	Curb 77800
7	7	3	Greatest Hits 1985-1995	*Michael Bolton*	Columbia 67300
8	8	47	CrazySexyCool	*TLC*	LaFace 26009
9	4	2	Ballbreaker	*AC/DC*	EastWest 61780
10	11	32	The Woman In Me	*Shania Twain*	Mercury 522886

TW	LW	WK	Billboard® OCTOBER 28, 1995	THE BILLBOARD 200®	
1	1	2	**Daydream**	*Mariah Carey*	Columbia 66700
2	-	1	**Insomniac**	*Green Day*	Reprise 46046
3	2	18	Jagged Little Pill	*Alanis Morissette*	Maverick 45901
4	-	1	Design Of A Decade 1986/1996	*Janet Jackson*	A&M 0399
5	3	12	Dangerous Minds	*Soundtrack*	MCA 11228
6	4	66	Cracked Rear View	*Hootie & The Blowfish*	Atlantic 82613
7	5	2	Starting Over	*Reba McEntire*	MCA 11264
8	6	4	All I Want	*Tim McGraw*	Curb 77800
9	10	33	The Woman In Me	*Shania Twain*	Mercury 522886
10	8	48	CrazySexyCool	*TLC*	LaFace 26009

TW	LW	WK	Billboard® NOVEMBER 4, 1995	THE BILLBOARD 200®	
①	1	3	**Daydream**	*Mariah Carey*	Columbia 66700
②	3	19	Jagged Little Pill	*Alanis Morissette*	Maverick 45901
③	4	2	**Design Of A Decade 1986/1996**	*Janet Jackson*	A&M 0399
④	6	67	Cracked Rear View	*Hootie & The Blowfish*	Atlantic 82613
⑤	5	13	Dangerous Minds	*Soundtrack*	MCA 11228
⑥	2	2	Insomniac	*Green Day*	Reprise 46046
❼	11	5	Greatest Hits 1985-1995	*Michael Bolton*	Columbia 67300
⑧	10	49	CrazySexyCool	*TLC*	LaFace 26009
⑨	8	5	All I Want	*Tim McGraw*	Curb 77800
⑩	9	34	The Woman In Me	*Shania Twain*	Mercury 522886

TW	LW	WK	Billboard® NOVEMBER 11, 1995	THE BILLBOARD 200®	
❶	-	1	**Mellon Collie And The Infinite Sadness**	*The Smashing Pumpkins*	Virgin 40861
②	1	4	Daydream	*Mariah Carey*	Columbia 66700
③	2	20	Jagged Little Pill	*Alanis Morissette*	Maverick 45901
❹	-	1	**Ozzmosis**	*Ozzy Osbourne*	Epic 67091
❺	-	1	**The Greatest Hits Collection**	*Alan Jackson*	Arista 18801
⑥	4	68	Cracked Rear View	*Hootie & The Blowfish*	Atlantic 82613
❼	7	6	Greatest Hits 1985-1995	*Michael Bolton*	Columbia 67300
⑧	5	14	Dangerous Minds	*Soundtrack*	MCA 11228
⑨	3	3	Design Of A Decade 1986/1996	*Janet Jackson*	A&M 0399
⑩	6	3	Insomniac	*Green Day*	Reprise 46046

TW	LW	WK	Billboard® NOVEMBER 18, 1995	THE BILLBOARD 200®	
❶	-	1	**Dogg Food**	*Tha Dogg Pound*	Death Row 50546
❷	2	5	Daydream	*Mariah Carey*	Columbia 66700
❸	-	1	**Cypress Hill III (Temples Of Boom)**	*Cypress Hill*	Ruffhouse 66991
④	3	21	Jagged Little Pill	*Alanis Morissette*	Maverick 45901
⑤	1	2	Mellon Collie And The Infinite Sadness	*The Smashing Pumpkins*	Virgin 40861
❻	5	2	The Greatest Hits Collection	*Alan Jackson*	Arista 18801
⑦	6	69	Cracked Rear View	*Hootie & The Blowfish*	Atlantic 82613
❽	-	1	**On Top Of The World**	*Eightball & MJG*	Suave House 1521
⑨	8	15	Dangerous Minds	*Soundtrack*	MCA 11228
⑩	9	4	Design Of A Decade 1986/1996	*Janet Jackson*	A&M 0399

TW	LW	WK	Billboard® NOVEMBER 25, 1995	THE BILLBOARD 200®	
❶	-	1	**Alice In Chains**	*Alice In Chains*	Columbia 67248
❷	2	6	Daydream	*Mariah Carey*	Columbia 66700
❸	4	22	Jagged Little Pill	*Alanis Morissette*	Maverick 45901
④	1	2	Dogg Food	*Tha Dogg Pound*	Death Row 50546
⑤	5	3	Mellon Collie And The Infinite Sadness	*The Smashing Pumpkins*	Virgin 40861
❻	-	1	**Something To Remember**	*Madonna*	Maverick/Sire 46100
⑦	6	3	The Greatest Hits Collection	*Alan Jackson*	Arista 18801
❽	7	70	Cracked Rear View	*Hootie & The Blowfish*	Atlantic 82613
❾	-	1	**Liquid Swords**	*Genius/GZA*	Geffen 24813
⑩	3	2	Cypress Hill III (Temples Of Boom)	*Cypress Hill*	Ruffhouse 66991

Billboard® DECEMBER 2, 1995 THE BILLBOARD 200®

TW	LW	WK	Title	Artist	Label
1	-	1	**R. Kelly**	*R. Kelly*	Jive 41579
2	2	7	Daydream	*Mariah Carey*	Columbia 66700
3	-	1	Waiting To Exhale	*Soundtrack*	Arista 18796
4	3	23	Jagged Little Pill	*Alanis Morissette*	Maverick 45901
5	7	4	**The Greatest Hits Collection**	*Alan Jackson*	Arista 18801
6	-	1	**Your Little Secret**	*Melissa Etheridge*	Island 524154
7	5	4	Mellon Collie And The Infinite Sadness	*The Smashing Pumpkins*	Virgin 40861
8	8	71	Cracked Rear View	*Hootie & The Blowfish*	Atlantic 82613
9	-	1	**Stripped**	*The Rolling Stones*	Virgin 41040
10	15	10	Christmas In The Aire	*Mannheim Steamroller*	American Grammaphone 1995

Billboard® DECEMBER 9, 1995 THE BILLBOARD 200®

TW	LW	WK	Title	Artist	Label
1	-	1	**Anthology 1**	*The Beatles*	Apple 34445
2	-	1	**Fresh Horses**	*Garth Brooks*	Capitol 32080
3	2	8	Daydream	*Mariah Carey*	Columbia 66700
4	10	11	Christmas In The Aire	*Mannheim Steamroller*	American Grammaphone 1995
5	3	2	Waiting To Exhale	*Soundtrack*	Arista 18796
6	4	24	Jagged Little Pill	*Alanis Morissette*	Maverick 45901
7	1	2	R. Kelly	*R. Kelly*	Jive 41579
8	8	72	Cracked Rear View	*Hootie & The Blowfish*	Atlantic 82613
9	7	5	Mellon Collie And The Infinite Sadness	*The Smashing Pumpkins*	Virgin 40861
10	5	5	The Greatest Hits Collection	*Alan Jackson*	Arista 18801

Billboard® DECEMBER 16, 1995 THE BILLBOARD 200®

TW	LW	WK	Title	Artist	Label
1	1	2	**Anthology 1**	*The Beatles*	Apple 34445
2	2	2	**Fresh Horses**	*Garth Brooks*	Capitol 32080
3	3	9	Daydream	*Mariah Carey*	Columbia 66700
4	4	12	Christmas In The Aire	*Mannheim Steamroller*	American Grammaphone 1995
5	5	3	Waiting To Exhale	*Soundtrack*	Arista 18796
6	6	25	Jagged Little Pill	*Alanis Morissette*	Maverick 45901
7	8	73	Cracked Rear View	*Hootie & The Blowfish*	Atlantic 82613
8	7	3	R. Kelly	*R. Kelly*	Jive 41579
9	10	6	The Greatest Hits Collection	*Alan Jackson*	Arista 18801
10	9	6	Mellon Collie And The Infinite Sadness	*The Smashing Pumpkins*	Virgin 40861

Billboard® DECEMBER 23, 1995 THE BILLBOARD 200®

TW	LW	WK	Title	Artist	Label
1	1	3	**Anthology 1**	*The Beatles*	Apple 34445
2	3	10	Daydream	*Mariah Carey*	Columbia 66700
3	2	3	Fresh Horses	*Garth Brooks*	Capitol 32080
4	4	13	Christmas In The Aire	*Mannheim Steamroller*	American Grammaphone 1995
5	5	4	Waiting To Exhale	*Soundtrack*	Arista 18796
6	6	26	Jagged Little Pill	*Alanis Morissette*	Maverick 45901
7	7	74	Cracked Rear View	*Hootie & The Blowfish*	Atlantic 82613
8	9	7	The Greatest Hits Collection	*Alan Jackson*	Arista 18801
9	10	7	Mellon Collie And The Infinite Sadness	*The Smashing Pumpkins*	Virgin 40861
10	12	56	CrazySexyCool	*TLC*	LaFace 26009

TW	LW	WK	Billboard. DECEMBER 30, 1995 THE BILLBOARD 200.
❶	2	11	**Daydream**........ *Mariah Carey*...Columbia 66700
②	1	4	Anthology 1 .... *The Beatles*...Apple 34445
③	4	14	**Christmas In The Aire**.... *Mannheim Steamroller*...American Grammphone 1995
❹	5	5	Waiting To Exhale .... *Soundtrack*...Arista 18796
⑤	3	4	Fresh Horses........ *Garth Brooks*...Capitol 32080
❻	7	75	Cracked Rear View........ *Hootie & The Blowfish*...Atlantic 82613
⑦	6	27	Jagged Little Pill........ *Alanis Morissette*...Maverick 45901
⑧	8	8	The Greatest Hits Collection .... *Alan Jackson*...Arista 18801
⑨	9	8	Mellon Collie And The Infinite Sadness .... *The Smashing Pumpkins*...Virgin 40861
⑩	10	57	CrazySexyCool........ *TLC*...LaFace 26009

Billboard® — JANUARY 6, 1996 — THE BILLBOARD 200®

TW	LW	WK	Title	Artist	Label
1	1	12	**Daydream**	*Mariah Carey*	Columbia 66700
2	4	6	Waiting To Exhale	*Soundtrack*	Arista 18796
3	2	5	Anthology 1	*The Beatles*	Apple 34445
4	5	5	Fresh Horses	*Garth Brooks*	Capitol 32080
5	6	76	Cracked Rear View	*Hootie & The Blowfish*	Atlantic 82613
6	7	28	Jagged Little Pill	*Alanis Morissette*	Maverick 45901
7	3	15	Christmas In The Aire	*Mannheim Steamroller*	American Grammaphone 1995
8	9	9	Mellon Collie And The Infinite Sadness	*The Smashing Pumpkins*	Virgin 40861
9	8	9	The Greatest Hits Collection	*Alan Jackson*	Arista 18801
10	10	58	CrazySexyCool	*TLC*	LaFace 26009

Billboard® — JANUARY 13, 1996 — THE BILLBOARD 200®

TW	LW	WK	Title	Artist	Label
1	1	13	**Daydream**	*Mariah Carey*	Columbia 66700
2	2	7	Waiting To Exhale	*Soundtrack*	Arista 18796
3	6	29	Jagged Little Pill	*Alanis Morissette*	Maverick 45901
4	4	6	Fresh Horses	*Garth Brooks*	Capitol 32080
5	5	77	Cracked Rear View	*Hootie & The Blowfish*	Atlantic 82613
6	9	10	The Greatest Hits Collection	*Alan Jackson*	Arista 18801
7	8	10	Mellon Collie And The Infinite Sadness	*The Smashing Pumpkins*	Virgin 40861
8	10	59	CrazySexyCool	*TLC*	LaFace 26009
9	3	6	Anthology 1	*The Beatles*	Apple 34445
10	11	51	Sixteen Stone	*Bush*	Trauma 92531

Billboard® — JANUARY 20, 1996 — THE BILLBOARD 200®

TW	LW	WK	Title	Artist	Label
1	2	8	**Waiting To Exhale**	*Soundtrack*	Arista 18796
2	1	14	Daydream	*Mariah Carey*	Columbia 66700
3	3	30	Jagged Little Pill	*Alanis Morissette*	Maverick 45901
4	5	78	Cracked Rear View	*Hootie & The Blowfish*	Atlantic 82613
5	4	7	Fresh Horses	*Garth Brooks*	Capitol 32080
6	6	11	The Greatest Hits Collection	*Alan Jackson*	Arista 18801
7	12	45	The Woman In Me	*Shania Twain*	Mercury 522886
8	8	60	CrazySexyCool	*TLC*	LaFace 26009
9	7	11	Mellon Collie And The Infinite Sadness	*The Smashing Pumpkins*	Virgin 40861
10	10	52	Sixteen Stone	*Bush*	Trauma 92531

Billboard® — JANUARY 27, 1996 — THE BILLBOARD 200®

TW	LW	WK	Title	Artist	Label
1	1	9	**Waiting To Exhale**	*Soundtrack*	Arista 18796
2	2	15	Daydream	*Mariah Carey*	Columbia 66700
3	3	31	Jagged Little Pill	*Alanis Morissette*	Maverick 45901
4	4	79	Cracked Rear View	*Hootie & The Blowfish*	Atlantic 82613
5	10	53	Sixteen Stone	*Bush*	Trauma 92531
6	7	46	The Woman In Me	*Shania Twain*	Mercury 522886
7	6	12	The Greatest Hits Collection	*Alan Jackson*	Arista 18801
8	9	12	Mellon Collie And The Infinite Sadness	*The Smashing Pumpkins*	Virgin 40861
9	18	15	(What's The Story) Morning Glory?	*Oasis*	Epic 67351
10	12	9	R. Kelly	*R. Kelly*	Jive 41579

Billboard — FEBRUARY 3, 1996 — THE BILLBOARD 200

TW	LW	WK	Title	Artist	Label
1	1	10	**Waiting To Exhale**	*Soundtrack*	Arista 18796
2	2	16	Daydream	*Mariah Carey*	Columbia 66700
3	3	32	Jagged Little Pill	*Alanis Morissette*	Maverick 45901
4	5	54	**Sixteen Stone**	*Bush*	Trauma 92531
5	9	16	(What's The Story) Morning Glory?	*Oasis*	Epic 67351
6	4	80	Cracked Rear View	*Hootie & The Blowfish*	Atlantic 82613
7	6	47	The Woman In Me	*Shania Twain*	Mercury 522886
8	8	13	Mellon Collie And The Infinite Sadness	*The Smashing Pumpkins*	Virgin 40861
9	7	13	The Greatest Hits Collection	*Alan Jackson*	Arista 18801
10	10	10	R. Kelly	*R. Kelly*	Jive 41579

Billboard — FEBRUARY 10, 1996 — THE BILLBOARD 200

TW	LW	WK	Title	Artist	Label
1	1	11	**Waiting To Exhale**	*Soundtrack*	Arista 18796
2	-	1	**Boys For Pele**	*Tori Amos*	Atlantic 82862
3	3	33	Jagged Little Pill	*Alanis Morissette*	Maverick 45901
4	2	17	Daydream	*Mariah Carey*	Columbia 66700
5	5	17	(What's The Story) Morning Glory?	*Oasis*	Epic 67351
6	4	55	Sixteen Stone	*Bush*	Trauma 92531
7	7	48	The Woman In Me	*Shania Twain*	Mercury 522886
8	6	81	Cracked Rear View	*Hootie & The Blowfish*	Atlantic 82613
9	11	8	**The Memory Of Trees**	*Enya*	Reprise 46106
10	8	14	Mellon Collie And The Infinite Sadness	*The Smashing Pumpkins*	Virgin 40861

Billboard — FEBRUARY 17, 1996 — THE BILLBOARD 200

TW	LW	WK	Title	Artist	Label
1	1	12	**Waiting To Exhale**	*Soundtrack*	Arista 18796
2	3	34	Jagged Little Pill	*Alanis Morissette*	Maverick 45901
3	-	1	**Str8 Off Tha Streetz Of Muthaphukkin Compton**	*Eazy-E*	Ruthless 5504
4	4	18	Daydream	*Mariah Carey*	Columbia 66700
5	5	18	(What's The Story) Morning Glory?	*Oasis*	Epic 67351
6	7	49	The Woman In Me	*Shania Twain*	Mercury 522886
7	6	56	Sixteen Stone	*Bush*	Trauma 92531
8	8	82	Cracked Rear View	*Hootie & The Blowfish*	Atlantic 82613
9	2	2	Boys For Pele	*Tori Amos*	Atlantic 82862
10	9	9	The Memory Of Trees	*Enya*	Reprise 46106

Billboard — FEBRUARY 24, 1996 — THE BILLBOARD 200

TW	LW	WK	Title	Artist	Label
1	2	35	**Jagged Little Pill**	*Alanis Morissette*	Maverick 45901
2	1	13	Waiting To Exhale	*Soundtrack*	Arista 18796
3	4	19	Daydream	*Mariah Carey*	Columbia 66700
4	5	19	**(What's The Story) Morning Glory?**	*Oasis*	Epic 67351
5	6	50	**The Woman In Me**	*Shania Twain*	Mercury 522886
6	7	57	Sixteen Stone	*Bush*	Trauma 92531
7	8	83	Cracked Rear View	*Hootie & The Blowfish*	Atlantic 82613
8	3	2	Str8 Off Tha Streetz Of Muthaphukkin Compton	*Eazy-E*	Ruthless 5504
9	10	10	**The Memory Of Trees**	*Enya*	Reprise 46106
10	12	26	The Presidents Of The United States Of America	*The Presidents of The United States of America*	Columbia 67291

Billboard® — MARCH 2, 1996 — THE BILLBOARD 200®

TW	LW	WK	Title	Artist...Label
1	-	1	**All Eyez On Me**	*2Pac*...Death Row 524204
2	1	36	Jagged Little Pill	*Alanis Morissette*...Maverick 45901
3	2	14	Waiting To Exhale	*Soundtrack*...Arista 18796
4	3	20	Daydream	*Mariah Carey*...Columbia 66700
5	4	20	(What's The Story) Morning Glory?	*Oasis*...Epic 67351
6	5	51	The Woman In Me	*Shania Twain*...Mercury 522886
7	7	84	Cracked Rear View	*Hootie & The Blowfish*...Atlantic 82613
8	6	58	Sixteen Stone	*Bush*...Trauma 92531
9	-	1	**Revelations**	*Wynonna*...Curb/MCA 11090
10	-	1	**Congratulations I'm Sorry**	*Gin Blossoms*...A&M 0469

Billboard® — MARCH 9, 1996 — THE BILLBOARD 200®

TW	LW	WK	Title	Artist...Label
1	1	2	**All Eyez On Me**	*2Pac*...Death Row 524204
2	2	37	Jagged Little Pill	*Alanis Morissette*...Maverick 45901
3	3	15	Waiting To Exhale	*Soundtrack*...Arista 18796
4	4	21	Daydream	*Mariah Carey*...Columbia 66700
5	5	21	(What's The Story) Morning Glory?	*Oasis*...Epic 67351
6	11	28	**The Presidents Of The United States Of America**	*The Presidents of The United States of America*...Columbia 67291
7	12	2	The Score	*Fugees (Refugee Camp)*...Ruffhouse 67147
8	6	52	The Woman In Me	*Shania Twain*...Mercury 522886
9	8	59	Sixteen Stone	*Bush*...Trauma 92531
10	9	2	Revelations	*Wynonna*...Curb/MCA 11090

Billboard® — MARCH 16, 1996 — THE BILLBOARD 200®

TW	LW	WK	Title	Artist...Label
1	2	38	**Jagged Little Pill**	*Alanis Morissette*...Maverick 45901
2	1	3	All Eyez On Me	*2Pac*...Death Row 524204
3	7	3	The Score	*Fugees (Refugee Camp)*...Ruffhouse 67147
4	3	16	Waiting To Exhale	*Soundtrack*...Arista 18796
5	4	22	Daydream	*Mariah Carey*...Columbia 66700
6	8	53	The Woman In Me	*Shania Twain*...Mercury 522886
7	6	29	The Presidents Of The United States Of America	*The Presidents of The United States of America*...Columbia 67291
8	5	22	(What's The Story) Morning Glory?	*Oasis*...Epic 67351
9	13	28	**Relish**	*Joan Osborne*...Blue Gorilla 526699
10	11	86	Cracked Rear View	*Hootie & The Blowfish*...Atlantic 82613

Billboard® — MARCH 23, 1996 — THE BILLBOARD 200®

TW	LW	WK	Title	Artist...Label
1	1	39	**Jagged Little Pill**	*Alanis Morissette*...Maverick 45901
2	2	4	All Eyez On Me	*2Pac*...Death Row 524204
3	3	4	The Score	*Fugees (Refugee Camp)*...Ruffhouse 67147
4	5	23	Daydream	*Mariah Carey*...Columbia 66700
5	4	17	Waiting To Exhale	*Soundtrack*...Arista 18796
6	6	54	The Woman In Me	*Shania Twain*...Mercury 522886
7	7	30	The Presidents Of The United States Of America	*The Presidents of The United States of America*...Columbia 67291
8	8	23	(What's The Story) Morning Glory?	*Oasis*...Epic 67351
9	12	18	**Gangsta's Paradise**	*Coolio*...Tommy Boy 1141
10	9	29	Relish	*Joan Osborne*...Blue Gorilla 526699

Billboard® — MARCH 30, 1996 — THE BILLBOARD 200®

TW	LW	WK	Title	Artist	Label
1	1	40	**Jagged Little Pill**	*Alanis Morissette*	Maverick 45901
2	-	1	Falling Into You	*Celine Dion*	550 Music 67541
3	3	5	The Score	*Fugees (Refugee Camp)*	Ruffhouse 67147
4	2	5	All Eyez On Me	*2Pac*	Death Row 524204
5	-	1	**Mercury Falling**	*Sting*	A&M 0483
6	4	24	Daydream	*Mariah Carey*	Columbia 66700
7	5	18	Waiting To Exhale	*Soundtrack*	Arista 18796
8	6	55	The Woman In Me	*Shania Twain*	Mercury 522886
9	8	24	(What's The Story) Morning Glory?	*Oasis*	Epic 67351
10	7	31	The Presidents Of The United States Of America	*The Presidents of The United States of America*	Columbia 67291

Billboard® — APRIL 6, 1996 — THE BILLBOARD 200®

TW	LW	WK	Title	Artist	Label
1	-	1	**Anthology 2**	*The Beatles*	Apple 34448
2	1	41	Jagged Little Pill	*Alanis Morissette*	Maverick 45901
3	2	2	Falling Into You	*Celine Dion*	550 Music 67541
4	3	6	The Score	*Fugees (Refugee Camp)*	Ruffhouse 67147
5	4	6	All Eyez On Me	*2Pac*	Death Row 524204
6	6	25	Daydream	*Mariah Carey*	Columbia 66700
7	7	19	Waiting To Exhale	*Soundtrack*	Arista 18796
8	9	25	(What's The Story) Morning Glory?	*Oasis*	Epic 67351
9	5	2	Mercury Falling	*Sting*	A&M 0483
10	8	56	The Woman In Me	*Shania Twain*	Mercury 522886

Billboard® — APRIL 13, 1996 — THE BILLBOARD 200®

TW	LW	WK	Title	Artist	Label
1	2	42	**Jagged Little Pill**	*Alanis Morissette*	Maverick 45901
2	1	2	Anthology 2	*The Beatles*	Apple 34448
3	3	3	Falling Into You	*Celine Dion*	550 Music 67541
4	-	1	**Tiny Music...Songs From The Vatican Gift Shop**	*Stone Temple Pilots*	Atlantic 82871
5	4	7	The Score	*Fugees (Refugee Camp)*	Ruffhouse 67147
6	-	1	**The Coming**	*Busta Rhymes*	Elektra 61742
7	6	26	Daydream	*Mariah Carey*	Columbia 66700
8	5	7	All Eyez On Me	*2Pac*	Death Row 524204
9	8	26	(What's The Story) Morning Glory?	*Oasis*	Epic 67351
10	7	20	Waiting To Exhale	*Soundtrack*	Arista 18796

Billboard® — APRIL 20, 1996 — THE BILLBOARD 200®

TW	LW	WK	Title	Artist	Label
1	1	43	**Jagged Little Pill**	*Alanis Morissette*	Maverick 45901
2	3	4	Falling Into You	*Celine Dion*	550 Music 67541
3	5	8	The Score	*Fugees (Refugee Camp)*	Ruffhouse 67147
4	2	3	Anthology 2	*The Beatles*	Apple 34448
5	4	2	Tiny Music...Songs From The Vatican Gift Shop	*Stone Temple Pilots*	Atlantic 82871
6	-	1	**The Resurrection**	*The Geto Boys*	Rap-A-Lot 41555
7	7	27	Daydream	*Mariah Carey*	Columbia 66700
8	9	27	(What's The Story) Morning Glory?	*Oasis*	Epic 67351
9	8	8	All Eyez On Me	*2Pac*	Death Row 524204
10	10	21	Waiting To Exhale	*Soundtrack*	Arista 18796

TW	LW	WK	Billboard®	APRIL 27, 1996	THE BILLBOARD 200®
1	1	44	**Jagged Little Pill**	*Alanis Morissette*	Maverick 45901
2	3	9	The Score	*Fugees (Refugee Camp)*	Ruffhouse 67147
3	2	5	Falling Into You	*Celine Dion*	550 Music 67541
4	5	3	**Tiny Music...Songs From The Vatican Gift Shop**	*Stone Temple Pilots*	Atlantic 82871
5	7	28	Daydream	*Mariah Carey*	Columbia 66700
6	8	28	(What's The Story) Morning Glory?	*Oasis*	Epic 67351
7	12	66	Sixteen Stone	*Bush*	Trauma 92531
8	4	4	Anthology 2	*The Beatles*	Apple 34448
9	6	2	The Resurrection	*The Geto Boys*	Rap-A-Lot 41555
10	14	23	Gangsta's Paradise	*Coolio*	Tommy Boy 1141

TW	LW	WK	Billboard®	MAY 4, 1996	THE BILLBOARD 200®
1	-	1	**Evil Empire**	*Rage Against The Machine*	Epic 57523
2	1	45	Jagged Little Pill	*Alanis Morissette*	Maverick 45901
3	2	10	The Score	*Fugees (Refugee Camp)*	Ruffhouse 67147
4	3	6	Falling Into You	*Celine Dion*	550 Music 67541
5	-	1	**Borderline**	*Brooks & Dunn*	Arista 18810
6	4	4	Tiny Music...Songs From The Vatican Gift Shop	*Stone Temple Pilots*	Atlantic 82871
7	7	67	Sixteen Stone	*Bush*	Trauma 92531
8	5	29	Daydream	*Mariah Carey*	Columbia 66700
9	6	29	(What's The Story) Morning Glory?	*Oasis*	Epic 67351
10	18	23	New Beginning	*Tracy Chapman*	Elektra 61850

TW	LW	WK	Billboard®	MAY 11, 1996	THE BILLBOARD 200®
1	-	1	**Fairweather Johnson**	*Hootie & The Blowfish*	Atlantic 82886
2	3	11	The Score	*Fugees (Refugee Camp)*	Ruffhouse 67147
3	2	46	Jagged Little Pill	*Alanis Morissette*	Maverick 45901
4	-	1	**Sunset Park**	*Soundtrack*	Flavor Unit 61904
5	4	7	Falling Into You	*Celine Dion*	550 Music 67541
6	1	2	Evil Empire	*Rage Against The Machine*	Epic 57523
7	-	1	**Blue Clear Sky**	*George Strait*	MCA 11428
8	5	2	Borderline	*Brooks & Dunn*	Arista 18810
9	-	1	**New Beginning**	*SWV*	RCA 66487
10	7	68	Sixteen Stone	*Bush*	Trauma 92531

TW	LW	WK	Billboard®	MAY 18, 1996	THE BILLBOARD 200®
1	1	2	**Fairweather Johnson**	*Hootie & The Blowfish*	Atlantic 82886
2	-	1	**Crash**	*Dave Matthews Band*	RCA 66904
3	2	12	The Score	*Fugees (Refugee Camp)*	Ruffhouse 67147
4	-	1	**To The Faithful Departed**	*The Cranberries*	Island 524234
5	3	47	Jagged Little Pill	*Alanis Morissette*	Maverick 45901
6	5	8	Falling Into You	*Celine Dion*	550 Music 67541
7	4	2	Sunset Park	*Soundtrack*	Flavor Unit 61904
8	8	3	Borderline	*Brooks & Dunn*	Arista 18810
9	6	3	Evil Empire	*Rage Against The Machine*	Epic 57523
10	7	2	Blue Clear Sky	*George Strait*	MCA 11428

Billboard — MAY 25, 1996 — THE BILLBOARD 200

TW	LW	WK			
1	3	13	**The Score**	*Fugees (Refugee Camp)*	Ruffhouse 67147
2	1	3	Fairweather Johnson	*Hootie & The Blowfish*	Atlantic 82886
3	5	48	Jagged Little Pill	*Alanis Morissette*	Maverick 45901
4	-	1	**The Great Southern Trendkill**	*Pantera*	EastWest 61908
5	6	9	Falling Into You	*Celine Dion*	550 Music 67541
6	2	2	Crash	*Dave Matthews Band*	RCA 66904
7	4	2	To The Faithful Departed	*The Cranberries*	Island 524234
8	11	26	New Beginning	*Tracy Chapman*	Elektra 61850
9	8	4	Borderline	*Brooks & Dunn*	Arista 18810
10	9	4	Evil Empire	*Rage Against The Machine*	Epic 57523

Billboard — JUNE 1, 1996 — THE BILLBOARD 200

TW	LW	WK			
1	1	14	**The Score**	*Fugees (Refugee Camp)*	Ruffhouse 67147
2	3	49	Jagged Little Pill	*Alanis Morissette*	Maverick 45901
3	5	10	Falling Into You	*Celine Dion*	550 Music 67541
4	2	4	Fairweather Johnson	*Hootie & The Blowfish*	Atlantic 82886
5	6	3	Crash	*Dave Matthews Band*	RCA 66904
6	-	1	**Older**	*George Michael*	DreamWorks 50000
7	8	27	New Beginning	*Tracy Chapman*	Elektra 61850
8	7	3	To The Faithful Departed	*The Cranberries*	Island 524234
9	9	5	Borderline	*Brooks & Dunn*	Arista 18810
10	10	5	Evil Empire	*Rage Against The Machine*	Epic 57523

Billboard — JUNE 8, 1996 — THE BILLBOARD 200

TW	LW	WK			
1	1	15	**The Score**	*Fugees (Refugee Camp)*	Ruffhouse 67147
2	-	1	**Down On The Upside**	*Soundgarden*	A&M 0526
3	-	1	**Gettin' It (Album Number Ten)**	*Too $hort*	Jive 41584
4	2	50	Jagged Little Pill	*Alanis Morissette*	Maverick 45901
5	3	11	Falling Into You	*Celine Dion*	550 Music 67541
6	7	28	New Beginning	*Tracy Chapman*	Elektra 61850
7	4	5	Fairweather Johnson	*Hootie & The Blowfish*	Atlantic 82886
8	5	4	Crash	*Dave Matthews Band*	RCA 66904
9	6	2	Older	*George Michael*	DreamWorks 50000
10	8	4	To The Faithful Departed	*The Cranberries*	Island 524234

Billboard — JUNE 15, 1996 — THE BILLBOARD 200

TW	LW	WK			
1	1	16	**The Score**	*Fugees (Refugee Camp)*	Ruffhouse 67147
2	4	51	Jagged Little Pill	*Alanis Morissette*	Maverick 45901
3	5	12	Falling Into You	*Celine Dion*	550 Music 67541
4	6	29	**New Beginning**	*Tracy Chapman*	Elektra 61850
5	2	2	Down On The Upside	*Soundgarden*	A&M 0526
6	3	2	Gettin' It (Album Number Ten)	*Too $hort*	Jive 41584
7	8	5	Crash	*Dave Matthews Band*	RCA 66904
8	7	6	Fairweather Johnson	*Hootie & The Blowfish*	Atlantic 82886
9	15	45	E. 1999 Eternal	*Bone Thugs-N-Harmony*	Ruthless 5539
10	10	5	To The Faithful Departed	*The Cranberries*	Island 524234

TW	LW	WK	Billboard. JUNE 22, 1996 THE BILLBOARD 200.
1	-	1	**Load** .... *Metallica*...Elektra 61923
2	1	17	The Score .... *Fugees (Refugee Camp)*...Ruffhouse 67147
3	2	52	Jagged Little Pill .... *Alanis Morissette*...Maverick 45901
4	-	1	**Banana Wind** .... *Jimmy Buffett*...Margaritaville 11451
5	3	13	Falling Into You .... *Celine Dion*...550 Music 67541
6	-	1	**Legal Drug Money** .... *Lost Boyz*...Universal 53010
7	4	30	New Beginning .... *Tracy Chapman*...Elektra 61850
8	5	3	Down On The Upside .... *Soundgarden*...A&M 0526
9	6	3	Gettin' It (Album Number Ten) .... *Too $hort*...Jive 41584
10	8	7	Fairweather Johnson .... *Hootie & The Blowfish*...Atlantic 82886

TW	LW	WK	Billboard. JUNE 29, 1996 THE BILLBOARD 200.
1	1	2	Load .... *Metallica*...Elektra 61923
2	2	18	The Score .... *Fugees (Refugee Camp)*...Ruffhouse 67147
3	3	53	Jagged Little Pill .... *Alanis Morissette*...Maverick 45901
4	5	14	Falling Into You .... *Celine Dion*...550 Music 67541
5	7	31	New Beginning .... *Tracy Chapman*...Elektra 61850
6	4	2	Banana Wind .... *Jimmy Buffett*...Margaritaville 11451
7	13	47	E. 1999 Eternal .... *Bone Thugs-N-Harmony*...Ruthless 5539
8	10	8	Fairweather Johnson .... *Hootie & The Blowfish*...Atlantic 82886
9	12	7	Crash .... *Dave Matthews Band*...RCA 66904
10	9	4	Gettin' It (Album Number Ten) .... *Too $hort*...Jive 41584

TW	LW	WK	Billboard. JULY 6, 1996 THE BILLBOARD 200.
1	1	3	Load .... *Metallica*...Elektra 61923
2	-	1	**Secrets** .... *Toni Braxton*...LaFace 26020
3	2	19	The Score .... *Fugees (Refugee Camp)*...Ruffhouse 67147
4	3	54	Jagged Little Pill .... *Alanis Morissette*...Maverick 45901
5	4	15	Falling Into You .... *Celine Dion*...550 Music 67541
6	5	32	New Beginning .... *Tracy Chapman*...Elektra 61850
7	7	48	E. 1999 Eternal .... *Bone Thugs-N-Harmony*...Ruthless 5539
8	11	3	**The Nutty Professor** .... *Soundtrack*...Def Jam 531911
9	8	9	Fairweather Johnson .... *Hootie & The Blowfish*...Atlantic 82886
10	9	8	Crash .... *Dave Matthews Band*...RCA 66904

TW	LW	WK	Billboard. JULY 13, 1996 THE BILLBOARD 200.
1	1	4	Load .... *Metallica*...Elektra 61923
2	4	55	Jagged Little Pill .... *Alanis Morissette*...Maverick 45901
3	3	20	The Score .... *Fugees (Refugee Camp)*...Ruffhouse 67147
4	2	2	Secrets .... *Toni Braxton*...LaFace 26020
5	-	1	**Keith Sweat** .... *Keith Sweat*...Elektra 61707
6	6	33	New Beginning .... *Tracy Chapman*...Elektra 61850
7	7	49	E. 1999 Eternal .... *Bone Thugs-N-Harmony*...Ruthless 5539
8	5	16	Falling Into You .... *Celine Dion*...550 Music 67541
9	8	4	The Nutty Professor .... *Soundtrack*...Def Jam 531911
10	11	26	Tragic Kingdom .... *No Doubt*...Trauma 92580

TW	LW	WK	Billboard. JULY 20, 1996 THE BILLBOARD 200.
1	-	1	**It Was Written** ... *Nas*...Columbia 67015
2	1	5	**Load** ... *Metallica*...Elektra 61923
3	2	56	**Jagged Little Pill** ... *Alanis Morissette*...Maverick 45901
4	3	21	**The Score** ... *Fugees (Refugee Camp)*...Ruffhouse 67147
5	4	3	**Secrets** ... *Toni Braxton*...LaFace 26020
6	7	50	**E. 1999 Eternal** ... *Bone Thugs-N-Harmony*...Ruthless 5539
7	6	34	**New Beginning** ... *Tracy Chapman*...Elektra 61850
8	5	2	**Keith Sweat** ... *Keith Sweat*...Elektra 61707
9	8	17	**Falling Into You** ... *Celine Dion*...550 Music 67541
10	9	5	**The Nutty Professor** ... *Soundtrack*...Def Jam 531911

TW	LW	WK	Billboard. JULY 27, 1996 THE BILLBOARD 200.
1	1	2	**It Was Written** ... *Nas*...Columbia 67015
2	3	57	**Jagged Little Pill** ... *Alanis Morissette*...Maverick 45901
3	2	6	**Load** ... *Metallica*...Elektra 61923
4	-	1	**Blue** ... *LeAnn Rimes*...MCG/Curb 77821
5	4	22	**The Score** ... *Fugees (Refugee Camp)*...Ruffhouse 67147
6	5	4	**Secrets** ... *Toni Braxton*...LaFace 26020
7	6	51	**E. 1999 Eternal** ... *Bone Thugs-N-Harmony*...Ruthless 5539
8	9	18	**Falling Into You** ... *Celine Dion*...550 Music 67541
9	7	35	**New Beginning** ... *Tracy Chapman*...Elektra 61850
10	8	3	**Keith Sweat** ... *Keith Sweat*...Elektra 61707

TW	LW	WK	Billboard. AUGUST 3, 1996 THE BILLBOARD 200.
1	1	3	**It Was Written** ... *Nas*...Columbia 67015
2	2	58	**Jagged Little Pill** ... *Alanis Morissette*...Maverick 45901
3	4	2	**Blue** ... *LeAnn Rimes*...MCG/Curb 77821
4	3	7	**Load** ... *Metallica*...Elektra 61923
5	7	52	**E. 1999 Eternal** ... *Bone Thugs-N-Harmony*...Ruthless 5539
6	6	5	**Secrets** ... *Toni Braxton*...LaFace 26020
7	5	23	**The Score** ... *Fugees (Refugee Camp)*...Ruffhouse 67147
8	8	19	**Falling Into You** ... *Celine Dion*...550 Music 67541
9	9	36	**New Beginning** ... *Tracy Chapman*...Elektra 61850
10	11	29	**Tragic Kingdom** ... *No Doubt*...Trauma 92580

TW	LW	WK	Billboard. AUGUST 10, 1996 THE BILLBOARD 200.
1	1	4	**It Was Written** ... *Nas*...Columbia 67015
2	2	59	**Jagged Little Pill** ... *Alanis Morissette*...Maverick 45901
3	3	3	**Blue** ... *LeAnn Rimes*...MCG/Curb 77821
4	4	8	**Load** ... *Metallica*...Elektra 61923
5	5	53	**E. 1999 Eternal** ... *Bone Thugs-N-Harmony*...Ruthless 5539
6	8	20	**Falling Into You** ... *Celine Dion*...550 Music 67541
7	7	24	**The Score** ... *Fugees (Refugee Camp)*...Ruffhouse 67147
8	6	6	**Secrets** ... *Toni Braxton*...LaFace 26020
9	9	37	**New Beginning** ... *Tracy Chapman*...Elektra 61850
10	10	30	**Tragic Kingdom** ... *No Doubt*...Trauma 92580

Billboard — AUGUST 17, 1996 — THE BILLBOARD 200

TW	LW	WK	Title	Artist	Label
1	-	1	**Beats, Rhymes And Life**	*A Tribe Called Quest*	Jive 41587
2	2	60	Jagged Little Pill	*Alanis Morissette*	Maverick 45901
3	-	1	**MTV Unplugged**	*Alice In Chains*	Columbia 67703
4	1	5	It Was Written	*Nas*	Columbia 67015
5	6	21	Falling Into You	*Celine Dion*	550 Music 67541
6	5	54	E. 1999 Eternal	*Bone Thugs-N-Harmony*	Ruthless 5539
7	8	7	Secrets	*Toni Braxton*	LaFace 26020
8	4	9	Load	*Metallica*	Elektra 61923
9	10	31	Tragic Kingdom	*No Doubt*	Trauma 92580
10	3	4	Blue	*LeAnn Rimes*	MCG/Curb 77821

Billboard — AUGUST 24, 1996 — THE BILLBOARD 200

TW	LW	WK	Title	Artist	Label
1	2	61	**Jagged Little Pill**	*Alanis Morissette*	Maverick 45901
2	4	6	It Was Written	*Nas*	Columbia 67015
3	5	22	Falling Into You	*Celine Dion*	550 Music 67541
4	9	32	Tragic Kingdom	*No Doubt*	Trauma 92580
5	7	8	Secrets	*Toni Braxton*	LaFace 26020
6	3	2	MTV Unplugged	*Alice In Chains*	Columbia 67703
7	1	2	Beats, Rhymes And Life	*A Tribe Called Quest*	Jive 41587
8	6	55	E. 1999 Eternal	*Bone Thugs-N-Harmony*	Ruthless 5539
9	11	26	The Score	*Fugees (Refugee Camp)*	Ruffhouse 67147
10	8	10	Load	*Metallica*	Elektra 61923

Billboard — AUGUST 31, 1996 — THE BILLBOARD 200

TW	LW	WK	Title	Artist	Label
1	1	62	**Jagged Little Pill**	*Alanis Morissette*	Maverick 45901
2	3	23	Falling Into You	*Celine Dion*	550 Music 67541
3	2	7	It Was Written	*Nas*	Columbia 67015
4	11	6	Blue	*LeAnn Rimes*	MCG/Curb 77821
5	4	33	Tragic Kingdom	*No Doubt*	Trauma 92580
6	9	27	The Score	*Fugees (Refugee Camp)*	Ruffhouse 67147
7	5	9	Secrets	*Toni Braxton*	LaFace 26020
8	12	3	**The Crow - City Of Angels**	*Soundtrack*	Miramax/Hollywood 62047
9	10	11	Load	*Metallica*	Elektra 61923
10	8	56	E. 1999 Eternal	*Bone Thugs-N-Harmony*	Ruthless 5539

Billboard — SEPTEMBER 7, 1996 — THE BILLBOARD 200

TW	LW	WK	Title	Artist	Label
1	1	63	**Jagged Little Pill**	*Alanis Morissette*	Maverick 45901
2	2	24	Falling Into You	*Celine Dion*	550 Music 67541
3	3	8	It Was Written	*Nas*	Columbia 67015
4	5	34	Tragic Kingdom	*No Doubt*	Trauma 92580
5	4	7	Blue	*LeAnn Rimes*	MCG/Curb 77821
6	6	28	The Score	*Fugees (Refugee Camp)*	Ruffhouse 67147
7	7	10	Secrets	*Toni Braxton*	LaFace 26020
8	8	4	**The Crow - City Of Angels**	*Soundtrack*	Miramax/Hollywood 62047
9	13	9	Keith Sweat	*Keith Sweat*	Elektra 61707
10	9	12	Load	*Metallica*	Elektra 61923

Billboard — SEPTEMBER 14, 1996 — THE BILLBOARD 200

TW	LW	WK	Title	Artist	Label
1	-	1	**No Code**	*Pearl Jam*	Epic 67500
2	-	1	**ATLiens**	*OutKast*	LaFace 26029
3	2	25	Falling Into You	*Celine Dion*	550 Music 67541
4	1	64	Jagged Little Pill	*Alanis Morissette*	Maverick 45901
5	4	35	Tragic Kingdom	*No Doubt*	Trauma 92580
6	3	9	It Was Written	*Nas*	Columbia 67015
7	5	8	Blue	*LeAnn Rimes*	MCG/Curb 77821
8	7	11	Secrets	*Toni Braxton*	LaFace 26020
9	8	5	The Crow - City Of Angels	*Soundtrack*	Miramax/Hollywood 62047
10	9	10	Keith Sweat	*Keith Sweat*	Elektra 61707

Billboard — SEPTEMBER 21, 1996 — THE BILLBOARD 200

TW	LW	WK	Title	Artist	Label
1	1	2	No Code	*Pearl Jam*	Epic 67500
2	3	26	Falling Into You	*Celine Dion*	550 Music 67541
3	2	2	ATLiens	*OutKast*	LaFace 26029
4	4	65	Jagged Little Pill	*Alanis Morissette*	Maverick 45901
5	7	9	Blue	*LeAnn Rimes*	MCG/Curb 77821
6	5	36	Tragic Kingdom	*No Doubt*	Trauma 92580
7	10	11	Keith Sweat	*Keith Sweat*	Elektra 61707
8	12	59	E. 1999 Eternal	*Bone Thugs-N-Harmony*	Ruthless 5539
9	6	10	It Was Written	*Nas*	Columbia 67015
10	8	12	Secrets	*Toni Braxton*	LaFace 26020

Billboard — SEPTEMBER 28, 1996 — THE BILLBOARD 200

TW	LW	WK	Title	Artist	Label
1	-	1	**Home Again**	*New Edition*	MCA 11480
2	-	1	**New Adventures In Hi-Fi**	*R.E.M.*	Warner 46320
3	-	1	**Another Level**	*Blackstreet*	Interscope 90071
4	2	27	Falling Into You	*Celine Dion*	550 Music 67541
5	-	1	**Test For Echo**	*Rush*	Atlantic 82925
6	4	66	Jagged Little Pill	*Alanis Morissette*	Maverick 45901
7	1	3	No Code	*Pearl Jam*	Epic 67500
8	3	3	ATLiens	*OutKast*	LaFace 26029
9	-	1	**Mr. Happy Go Lucky**	*John Mellencamp*	Mercury 532896
10	6	37	Tragic Kingdom	*No Doubt*	Trauma 92580

Billboard — OCTOBER 5, 1996 — THE BILLBOARD 200

TW	LW	WK	Title	Artist	Label
1	4	28	**Falling Into You**	*Celine Dion*	550 Music 67541
2	1	2	Home Again	*New Edition*	MCA 11480
3	2	2	New Adventures In Hi-Fi	*R.E.M.*	Warner 46320
4	6	67	Jagged Little Pill	*Alanis Morissette*	Maverick 45901
5	3	2	Another Level	*Blackstreet*	Interscope 90071
6	18	32	All Eyez On Me	*2Pac*	Death Row 524204
7	7	4	No Code	*Pearl Jam*	Epic 67500
8	11	13	Keith Sweat	*Keith Sweat*	Elektra 61707
9	8	4	ATLiens	*OutKast*	LaFace 26029
10	15	5	**ESPN Presents Jock Jams Volume 2**	*Various Artists*	Tommy Boy 1163

Billboard® — OCTOBER 12, 1996 — THE BILLBOARD 200®

TW	LW	WK	Title	Artist...Label
1	1	29	**Falling Into You**	*Celine Dion*...550 Music 67541
2	2	3	Home Again	*New Edition*...MCA 11480
3	4	68	Jagged Little Pill	*Alanis Morissette*...Maverick 45901
4	-	1	**Set It Off**	*Soundtrack*...EastWest 61951
5	5	3	Another Level	*Blackstreet*...Interscope 90071
6	-	1	**Sheryl Crow**	*Sheryl Crow*...A&M 0587
7	3	3	New Adventures In Hi-Fi	*R.E.M.*...Warner 46320
8	8	14	Keith Sweat	*Keith Sweat*...Elektra 61707
9	6	33	All Eyez On Me	*2Pac*...Death Row 524204
10	7	5	No Code	*Pearl Jam*...Epic 67500

Billboard® — OCTOBER 19, 1996 — THE BILLBOARD 200®

TW	LW	WK	Title	Artist...Label
1	-	1	**From The Muddy Banks Of The Wishkah**	*Nirvana*...DGC 25105
2	-	1	**Ænima**	*Tool*...Zoo 31087
3	1	30	Falling Into You	*Celine Dion*...550 Music 67541
4	-	1	The Moment	*Kenny G*...Arista 18935
5	11	13	Blue	*LeAnn Rimes*...MCG/Curb 77821
6	2	4	Home Again	*New Edition*...MCA 11480
7	4	2	Set It Off	*Soundtrack*...EastWest 61951
8	3	69	Jagged Little Pill	*Alanis Morissette*...Maverick 45901
9	-	1	**Your Secret Love**	*Luther Vandross*...Epic/LV 67553
10	5	4	Another Level	*Blackstreet*...Interscope 90071

Billboard® — OCTOBER 26, 1996 — THE BILLBOARD 200®

TW	LW	WK	Title	Artist...Label
1	3	31	**Falling Into You**	*Celine Dion*...550 Music 67541
2	4	2	**The Moment**	*Kenny G*...Arista 18935
3	-	1	**Antichrist Superstar**	*Marilyn Manson*...Nothing 90086
4	1	2	From The Muddy Banks Of The Wishkah	*Nirvana*...DGC 25105
5	5	14	Blue	*LeAnn Rimes*...MCG/Curb 77821
6	8	70	Jagged Little Pill	*Alanis Morissette*...Maverick 45901
7	16	41	Tragic Kingdom	*No Doubt*...Trauma 92580
8	6	5	Home Again	*New Edition*...MCA 11480
9	11	16	Keith Sweat	*Keith Sweat*...Elektra 61707
10	7	3	Set It Off	*Soundtrack*...EastWest 61951

Billboard® — NOVEMBER 2, 1996 — THE BILLBOARD 200®

TW	LW	WK	Title	Artist...Label
1	-	1	**Recovering The Satellites**	*Counting Crows*...DGC 24975
2	1	32	Falling Into You	*Celine Dion*...550 Music 67541
3	-	1	**Life Is Peachy**	*Korn*...Immortal 67554
4	2	3	The Moment	*Kenny G*...Arista 18935
5	6	71	Jagged Little Pill	*Alanis Morissette*...Maverick 45901
6	7	42	Tragic Kingdom	*No Doubt*...Trauma 92580
7	-	1	**Billy Breathes**	*Phish*...Elektra 61971
8	5	15	Blue	*LeAnn Rimes*...MCG/Curb 77821
9	9	17	Keith Sweat	*Keith Sweat*...Elektra 61707
10	4	3	From The Muddy Banks Of The Wishkah	*Nirvana*...DGC 25105

Billboard — NOVEMBER 9, 1996 — THE BILLBOARD 200

TW	LW	WK			
1	-	1	**Best Of Volume 1**	*Van Halen*	Warner 46332
2	-	1	**Bow Down**	*Westside Connection*	Priority 50583
3	-	1	**Trial By Fire**	*Journey*	Columbia 67514
4	2	33	Falling Into You	*Celine Dion*	550 Music 67541
5	1	2	Recovering The Satellites	*Counting Crows*	DGC 24975
6	4	4	The Moment	*Kenny G*	Arista 18935
7	6	43	Tragic Kingdom	*No Doubt*	Trauma 92580
8	5	72	Jagged Little Pill	*Alanis Morissette*	Maverick 45901
9	12	19	Secrets	*Toni Braxton*	LaFace 26020
10	9	18	Keith Sweat	*Keith Sweat*	Elektra 61707

Billboard — NOVEMBER 16, 1996 — THE BILLBOARD 200

TW	LW	WK			
1	-	1	**Anthology 3**	*The Beatles*	Apple 46332
2	-	1	**Ironman**	*Ghostface Killah*	Razor Sharp 67729
3	1	2	Best Of Volume 1	*Van Halen*	Warner 46332
4	-	1	**Tha Hall Of Game**	*E40*	Jive 41591
5	4	34	Falling Into You	*Celine Dion*	550 Music 67541
6	-	1	**The Day**	*Babyface*	Epic 67293
7	7	44	Tragic Kingdom	*No Doubt*	Trauma 92580
8	6	5	The Moment	*Kenny G*	Arista 18935
9	2	2	Bow Down	*Westside Connection*	Priority 50583
10	3	2	Trial By Fire	*Journey*	Columbia 67514

Billboard — NOVEMBER 23, 1996 — THE BILLBOARD 200

TW	LW	WK			
1	-	1	**The Don Killuminati - The 7 Day Theory**	*Makaveli*	Death Row 90039
2	-	1	**Family Scriptures**	*Mo Thugs Family*	Mo Thugs 1561
3	5	35	Falling Into You	*Celine Dion*	550 Music 67541
4	7	45	Tragic Kingdom	*No Doubt*	Trauma 92580
5	1	2	Anthology 3	*The Beatles*	Apple 46332
6	3	3	Best Of Volume 1	*Van Halen*	Warner 46332
7	8	6	The Moment	*Kenny G*	Arista 18935
8	16	7	Set It Off	*Soundtrack*	EastWest 61951
9	6	2	The Day	*Babyface*	Epic 67293
10	2	2	Ironman	*Ghostface Killah*	Razor Sharp 67729

Billboard — NOVEMBER 30, 1996 — THE BILLBOARD 200

TW	LW	WK			
1	-	1	**Tha Doggfather**	*Snoop Doggy Dogg*	Death Row 90038
2	1	2	The Don Killuminati - The 7 Day Theory	*Makaveli*	Death Row 90039
3	4	46	Tragic Kingdom	*No Doubt*	Trauma 92580
4	3	36	Falling Into You	*Celine Dion*	550 Music 67541
5	2	2	Family Scriptures	*Mo Thugs Family*	Mo Thugs 1561
6	-	1	Evita	*Soundtrack*	Warner 46346
7	7	7	The Moment	*Kenny G*	Arista 18935
8	8	8	Set It Off	*Soundtrack*	EastWest 61951
9	11	22	Secrets	*Toni Braxton*	LaFace 26020
10	6	4	Best Of Volume 1	*Van Halen*	Warner 46332

TW	LW	WK	Billboard® DECEMBER 7, 1996 THE BILLBOARD 200®	
1	-	1	**Razorblade Suitcase**	*Bush*...Trauma 90091
2	1	2	Tha Doggfather	*Snoop Doggy Dogg*...Death Row 90038
3	3	47	Tragic Kingdom	*No Doubt*...Trauma 92580
4	2	3	The Don Killuminati - The 7 Day Theory	*Makaveli*...Death Row 90039
5	4	37	Falling Into You	*Celine Dion*...550 Music 67541
6	-	1	**Hell On Earth**	*Mobb Deep*...Loud/RCA 66992
7	-	1	**Ill Na Na**	*Foxy Brown*...Violator 533684
8	13	2	Space Jam	*Soundtrack*...Warner Sunset 82961
9	7	8	The Moment	*Kenny G*...Arista 18935
10	9	23	Secrets	*Toni Braxton*...LaFace 26020

TW	LW	WK	Billboard® DECEMBER 14, 1996 THE BILLBOARD 200®	
1	1	2	**Razorblade Suitcase**	*Bush*...Trauma 90091
2	3	48	Tragic Kingdom	*No Doubt*...Trauma 92580
3	5	38	Falling Into You	*Celine Dion*...550 Music 67541
4	2	3	Tha Doggfather	*Snoop Doggy Dogg*...Death Row 90038
5	8	3	Space Jam	*Soundtrack*...Warner Sunset 82961
6	-	1	**Dr. Dre Presents...The Aftermath**	*Various Artists*...Aftermath 90044
7	4	4	The Don Killuminati - The 7 Day Theory	*Makaveli*...Death Row 90039
8	12	5	Romeo & Juliet	*Soundtrack*...Capitol 37715
9	9	9	The Moment	*Kenny G*...Arista 18935
10	10	24	Secrets	*Toni Braxton*...LaFace 26020

TW	LW	WK	Billboard® DECEMBER 21, 1996 THE BILLBOARD 200®	
1	2	49	**Tragic Kingdom**	*No Doubt*...Trauma 92580
2	3	39	Falling Into You	*Celine Dion*...550 Music 67541
3	1	3	Razorblade Suitcase	*Bush*...Trauma 90091
4	12	2	The Preacher's Wife	*Whitney Houston/Soundtrack*...Arista 18951
5	5	4	Space Jam	*Soundtrack*...Warner Sunset 82961
6	9	10	The Moment	*Kenny G*...Arista 18935
7	8	6	Romeo & Juliet	*Soundtrack*...Capitol 37715
8	14	22	Blue	*LeAnn Rimes*...MCG/Curb 77821
9	10	25	Secrets	*Toni Braxton*...LaFace 26020
10	11	78	Jagged Little Pill	*Alanis Morissette*...Maverick 45901

TW	LW	WK	Billboard® DECEMBER 28, 1996 THE BILLBOARD 200®	
1	1	50	**Tragic Kingdom**	*No Doubt*...Trauma 92580
2	2	40	Falling Into You	*Celine Dion*...550 Music 67541
3	4	3	**The Preacher's Wife**	*Whitney Houston/Soundtrack*...Arista 18951
4	3	4	Razorblade Suitcase	*Bush*...Trauma 90091
5	5	5	Space Jam	*Soundtrack*...Warner Sunset 82961
6	7	7	Romeo & Juliet	*Soundtrack*...Capitol 37715
7	8	23	Blue	*LeAnn Rimes*...MCG/Curb 77821
8	9	26	Secrets	*Toni Braxton*...LaFace 26020
9	6	11	The Moment	*Kenny G*...Arista 18935
10	10	79	Jagged Little Pill	*Alanis Morissette*...Maverick 45901

Billboard® JANUARY 4, 1997 — THE BILLBOARD 200®

TW	LW	WK	Title	Artist...Label
1	1	51	**Tragic Kingdom**	*No Doubt*...Trauma 92580
2	2	41	Falling Into You	*Celine Dion*...550 Music 67541
3	3	4	**The Preacher's Wife**	*Whitney Houston/Soundtrack*...Arista 18951
4	4	5	Razorblade Suitcase	*Bush*...Trauma 90091
5	6	8	Romeo & Juliet	*Soundtrack*...Capitol 37715
6	8	27	Secrets	*Toni Braxton*...LaFace 26020
7	5	6	Space Jam	*Soundtrack*...Warner Sunset 82961
8	7	24	Blue	*LeAnn Rimes*...MCG/Curb 77821
9	9	12	The Moment	*Kenny G*...Arista 18935
10	15	6	Evita	*Soundtrack*...Warner 46346

Billboard® JANUARY 11, 1997 — THE BILLBOARD 200®

TW	LW	WK	Title	Artist...Label
1	1	52	**Tragic Kingdom**	*No Doubt*...Trauma 92580
2	2	42	Falling Into You	*Celine Dion*...550 Music 67541
3	4	6	Razorblade Suitcase	*Bush*...Trauma 90091
4	5	9	Romeo & Juliet	*Soundtrack*...Capitol 37715
5	3	5	The Preacher's Wife	*Whitney Houston/Soundtrack*...Arista 18951
6	7	7	Space Jam	*Soundtrack*...Warner Sunset 82961
7	6	28	Secrets	*Toni Braxton*...LaFace 26020
8	8	25	Blue	*LeAnn Rimes*...MCG/Curb 77821
9	11	81	Jagged Little Pill	*Alanis Morissette*...Maverick 45901
10	9	13	The Moment	*Kenny G*...Arista 18935

Billboard® JANUARY 18, 1997 — THE BILLBOARD 200®

TW	LW	WK	Title	Artist...Label
1	1	53	**Tragic Kingdom**	*No Doubt*...Trauma 92580
2	4	10	**Romeo & Juliet**	*Soundtrack*...Capitol 37715
3	2	43	Falling Into You	*Celine Dion*...550 Music 67541
4	5	6	The Preacher's Wife	*Whitney Houston/Soundtrack*...Arista 18951
5	6	8	Space Jam	*Soundtrack*...Warner Sunset 82961
6	3	7	Razorblade Suitcase	*Bush*...Trauma 90091
7	7	29	Secrets	*Toni Braxton*...LaFace 26020
8	8	26	Blue	*LeAnn Rimes*...MCG/Curb 77821
9	9	82	Jagged Little Pill	*Alanis Morissette*...Maverick 45901
10	12	17	**Did I Shave My Legs For This?**	*Deana Carter*...Capitol 37514

Billboard® JANUARY 25, 1997 — THE BILLBOARD 200®

TW	LW	WK	Title	Artist...Label
1	1	54	**Tragic Kingdom**	*No Doubt*...Trauma 92580
2	2	11	**Romeo & Juliet**	*Soundtrack*...Capitol 37715
3	3	44	Falling Into You	*Celine Dion*...550 Music 67541
4	8	27	Blue	*LeAnn Rimes*...MCG/Curb 77821
5	7	30	Secrets	*Toni Braxton*...LaFace 26020
6	4	7	The Preacher's Wife	*Whitney Houston/Soundtrack*...Arista 18951
7	12	9	Evita	*Soundtrack*...Warner 46346
8	5	9	Space Jam	*Soundtrack*...Warner Sunset 82961
9	6	8	Razorblade Suitcase	*Bush*...Trauma 90091
10	9	83	Jagged Little Pill	*Alanis Morissette*...Maverick 45901

Billboard — FEBRUARY 1, 1997 — THE BILLBOARD 200

TW	LW	WK	Title	Artist / Label
1	1	55	**Tragic Kingdom**	*No Doubt*...Trauma 92580
2	7	10	**Evita**	*Soundtrack*...Warner 46346
3	2	12	Romeo & Juliet	*Soundtrack*...Capitol 37715
4	3	45	Falling Into You	*Celine Dion*...550 Music 67541
5	8	10	Space Jam	*Soundtrack*...Warner Sunset 82961
6	5	31	Secrets	*Toni Braxton*...LaFace 26020
7	6	8	The Preacher's Wife	*Whitney Houston/Soundtrack*...Arista 18951
8	4	28	Blue	*LeAnn Rimes*...MCG/Curb 77821
9	11	11	The Don Killuminati - The 7 Day Theory	*Makaveli*...Death Row 90039
10	9	9	Razorblade Suitcase	*Bush*...Trauma 90091

Billboard — FEBRUARY 8, 1997 — THE BILLBOARD 200

TW	LW	WK	Title	Artist / Label
1	1	56	**Tragic Kingdom**	*No Doubt*...Trauma 92580
2	2	11	**Evita**	*Soundtrack*...Warner 46346
3	3	13	Romeo & Juliet	*Soundtrack*...Capitol 37715
4	4	46	Falling Into You	*Celine Dion*...550 Music 67541
5	5	11	Space Jam	*Soundtrack*...Warner Sunset 82961
6	6	32	Secrets	*Toni Braxton*...LaFace 26020
7	8	29	Blue	*LeAnn Rimes*...MCG/Curb 77821
8	7	9	The Preacher's Wife	*Whitney Houston/Soundtrack*...Arista 18951
9	9	12	The Don Killuminati - The 7 Day Theory	*Makaveli*...Death Row 90039
10	10	10	Razorblade Suitcase	*Bush*...Trauma 90091

Billboard — FEBRUARY 15, 1997 — THE BILLBOARD 200

TW	LW	WK	Title	Artist / Label
1	-	1	**Gridlock'd**	*Soundtrack*...Death Row 90114
2	1	57	Tragic Kingdom	*No Doubt*...Trauma 92580
3	2	12	Evita	*Soundtrack*...Warner 46346
4	4	47	Falling Into You	*Celine Dion*...550 Music 67541
5	6	33	Secrets	*Toni Braxton*...LaFace 26020
6	7	30	Blue	*LeAnn Rimes*...MCG/Curb 77821
7	3	14	Romeo & Juliet	*Soundtrack*...Capitol 37715
8	-	1	**West Coast Bad Boyz II**	*Various Artists*...No Limit 50658
9	5	12	Space Jam	*Soundtrack*...Warner Sunset 82961
10	12	51	Pieces Of You	*Jewel*...Atlantic 82700

Billboard — FEBRUARY 22, 1997 — THE BILLBOARD 200

TW	LW	WK	Title	Artist / Label
1	2	58	**Tragic Kingdom**	*No Doubt*...Trauma 92580
2	1	2	Gridlock'd	*Soundtrack*...Death Row 90114
3	5	34	Secrets	*Toni Braxton*...LaFace 26020
4	3	13	Evita	*Soundtrack*...Warner 46346
5	4	48	Falling Into You	*Celine Dion*...550 Music 67541
6	-	1	Spice	*Spice Girls*...Virgin 42174
7	10	52	Pieces Of You	*Jewel*...Atlantic 82700
8	6	31	Blue	*LeAnn Rimes*...MCG/Curb 77821
9	-	1	**Ixnay On The Hombre**	*The Offspring*...Columbia 67810
10	7	15	Romeo & Juliet	*Soundtrack*...Capitol 37715

Billboard. MARCH 1, 1997 — THE BILLBOARD 200.

TW	LW	WK	Title	Artist...Label
1	-	1	**Unchained Melody/The Early Years**	*LeAnn Rimes*...Curb 77856
2	-	1	**Baduizm**	*Erykah Badu*...Kedar/Universal 53027
3	1	59	Tragic Kingdom	*No Doubt*...Trauma 92580
4	7	53	**Pieces Of You**	*Jewel*...Atlantic 82700
5	3	35	Secrets	*Toni Braxton*...LaFace 26020
6	6	2	Spice	*Spice Girls*...Virgin 42174
7	5	49	Falling Into You	*Celine Dion*...550 Music 67541
8	4	14	Evita	*Soundtrack*...Warner 46346
9	10	16	Romeo & Juliet	*Soundtrack*...Capitol 37715
10	8	32	Blue	*LeAnn Rimes*...MCG/Curb 77821

Billboard. MARCH 8, 1997 — THE BILLBOARD 200.

TW	LW	WK	Title	Artist...Label
1	-	1	**Secret Samadhi**	*Live*...Radioactive 11590
2	1	2	Unchained Melody/The Early Years	*LeAnn Rimes*...Curb 77856
3	2	2	Baduizm	*Erykah Badu*...Kedar/Universal 53027
4	3	60	Tragic Kingdom	*No Doubt*...Trauma 92580
5	6	3	Spice	*Spice Girls*...Virgin 42174
6	4	54	Pieces Of You	*Jewel*...Atlantic 82700
7	-	1	**Lost Highway**	*Soundtrack*...Nothing 90090
8	-	1	**Tru 2 Da Game**	*Tru*...No Limit 50660
9	5	36	Secrets	*Toni Braxton*...LaFace 26020
10	7	50	Falling Into You	*Celine Dion*...550 Music 67541

Billboard. MARCH 15, 1997 — THE BILLBOARD 200.

TW	LW	WK	Title	Artist...Label
1	-	1	**Private Parts**	*Soundtrack*...Warner 46477
2	1	2	Secret Samadhi	*Live*...Radioactive 11590
3	2	3	Unchained Melody/The Early Years	*LeAnn Rimes*...Curb 77856
4	10	51	Falling Into You	*Celine Dion*...550 Music 67541
5	4	61	Tragic Kingdom	*No Doubt*...Trauma 92580
6	6	55	Pieces Of You	*Jewel*...Atlantic 82700
7	5	4	Spice	*Spice Girls*...Virgin 42174
8	3	3	Baduizm	*Erykah Badu*...Kedar/Universal 53027
9	16	34	Blue	*LeAnn Rimes*...MCG/Curb 77821
10	11	35	Bringing Down The Horse	*The Wallflowers*...Interscope 90055

Billboard. MARCH 22, 1997 — THE BILLBOARD 200.

TW	LW	WK	Title	Artist...Label
1	-	1	**Pop**	*U2*...Island 524334
2	3	4	Unchained Melody/The Early Years	*LeAnn Rimes*...Curb 77856
3	4	52	Falling Into You	*Celine Dion*...550 Music 67541
4	6	56	**Pieces Of You**	*Jewel*...Atlantic 82700
5	5	62	Tragic Kingdom	*No Doubt*...Trauma 92580
6	7	5	Spice	*Spice Girls*...Virgin 42174
7	2	3	Secret Samadhi	*Live*...Radioactive 11590
8	10	36	Bringing Down The Horse	*The Wallflowers*...Interscope 90055
9	8	4	Baduizm	*Erykah Badu*...Kedar/Universal 53027
10	9	35	Blue	*LeAnn Rimes*...MCG/Curb 77821

TW	LW	WK	Billboard® MARCH 29, 1997	THE BILLBOARD 200®
1	-	1	**The Untouchable**	*Scarface*...Rap-A-Lot 42799
2	1	2	Pop	*U2*...Island 524334
3	2	5	Unchained Melody/The Early Years	*LeAnn Rimes*...Curb 77856
4	6	6	Spice	*Spice Girls*...Virgin 42174
5	4	57	Pieces Of You	*Jewel*...Atlantic 82700
6	14	18	Space Jam	*Soundtrack*...Warner Sunset 82961
7	3	53	Falling Into You	*Celine Dion*...550 Music 67541
8	8	37	Bringing Down The Horse	*The Wallflowers*...Interscope 90055
9	5	63	Tragic Kingdom	*No Doubt*...Trauma 92580
10	9	5	Baduizm	*Erykah Badu*...Kedar/Universal 53027

TW	LW	WK	Billboard® APRIL 5, 1997	THE BILLBOARD 200®
1	-	1	**Nine Lives**	*Aerosmith*...Columbia 67547
2	6	19	**Space Jam**	*Soundtrack*...Warner Sunset 82961
3	1	2	The Untouchable	*Scarface*...Rap-A-Lot 42799
4	3	6	Unchained Melody/The Early Years	*LeAnn Rimes*...Curb 77856
5	4	7	Spice	*Spice Girls*...Virgin 42174
6	7	54	Falling Into You	*Celine Dion*...550 Music 67541
7	5	58	Pieces Of You	*Jewel*...Atlantic 82700
8	2	3	Pop	*U2*...Island 524334
9	8	38	Bringing Down The Horse	*The Wallflowers*...Interscope 90055
10	9	64	Tragic Kingdom	*No Doubt*...Trauma 92580

TW	LW	WK	Billboard® APRIL 12, 1997	THE BILLBOARD 200®
1	176	2	**Life After Death**	*The Notorious B.I.G.*...Bad Boy 73011
2	6	55	Falling Into You	*Celine Dion*...550 Music 67541
3	5	8	Spice	*Spice Girls*...Virgin 42174
4	2	20	Space Jam	*Soundtrack*...Warner Sunset 82961
5	1	2	Nine Lives	*Aerosmith*...Columbia 67547
6	7	59	Pieces Of You	*Jewel*...Atlantic 82700
7	12	3	**Selena**	*Selena/Soundtrack*...EMI Latin 55535
8	9	39	Bringing Down The Horse	*The Wallflowers*...Interscope 90055
9	4	7	Unchained Melody/The Early Years	*LeAnn Rimes*...Curb 77856
10	10	65	Tragic Kingdom	*No Doubt*...Trauma 92580

TW	LW	WK	Billboard® APRIL 19, 1997	THE BILLBOARD 200®
1	1	3	**Life After Death**	*The Notorious B.I.G.*...Bad Boy 73011
2	3	9	Spice	*Spice Girls*...Virgin 42174
3	4	21	Space Jam	*Soundtrack*...Warner Sunset 82961
4	2	56	Falling Into You	*Celine Dion*...550 Music 67541
5	8	40	Bringing Down The Horse	*The Wallflowers*...Interscope 90055
6	6	60	Pieces Of You	*Jewel*...Atlantic 82700
7	7	4	**Selena**	*Selena/Soundtrack*...EMI Latin 55535
8	5	3	Nine Lives	*Aerosmith*...Columbia 67547
9	9	8	Unchained Melody/The Early Years	*LeAnn Rimes*...Curb 77856
10	10	66	Tragic Kingdom	*No Doubt*...Trauma 92580

Billboard — APRIL 26, 1997 — THE BILLBOARD 200

TW	LW	WK			
1	1	4	**Life After Death**	*The Notorious B.I.G.*	Bad Boy 73011
2	2	10	Spice	*Spice Girls*	Virgin 42174
3	3	22	Space Jam	*Soundtrack*	Warner Sunset 82961
4	4	57	Falling Into You	*Celine Dion*	550 Music 67541
5	5	41	Bringing Down The Horse	*The Wallflowers*	Interscope 90055
6	6	61	Pieces Of You	*Jewel*	Atlantic 82700
7	7	5	**Selena**	*Selena/Soundtrack*	EMI Latin 55535
8	12	9	Baduizm	*Erykah Badu*	Kedar/Universal 53027
9	9	9	Unchained Melody/The Early Years	*LeAnn Rimes*	Curb 77856
10	11	31	Another Level	*Blackstreet*	Interscope 90071

Billboard — MAY 3, 1997 — THE BILLBOARD 200

TW	LW	WK			
1	1	5	**Life After Death**	*The Notorious B.I.G.*	Bad Boy 73011
2	2	11	Spice	*Spice Girls*	Virgin 42174
3	3	23	Space Jam	*Soundtrack*	Warner Sunset 82961
4	5	42	**Bringing Down The Horse**	*The Wallflowers*	Interscope 90055
5	-	1	**Ultra**	*Depeche Mode*	Mute 46522
6	4	58	Falling Into You	*Celine Dion*	550 Music 67541
7	6	62	Pieces Of You	*Jewel*	Atlantic 82700
8	8	10	Baduizm	*Erykah Badu*	Kedar/Universal 53027
9	10	32	Another Level	*Blackstreet*	Interscope 90071
10	7	6	Selena	*Selena/Soundtrack*	EMI Latin 55535

Billboard — MAY 10, 1997 — THE BILLBOARD 200

TW	LW	WK			
1	-	1	**Share My World**	*Mary J. Blige*	MCA 11606
2	-	1	Carrying Your Love With Me	*George Strait*	MCA 11584
3	2	12	Spice	*Spice Girls*	Virgin 42174
4	1	6	Life After Death	*The Notorious B.I.G.*	Bad Boy 73011
5	3	24	Space Jam	*Soundtrack*	Warner Sunset 82961
6	4	43	Bringing Down The Horse	*The Wallflowers*	Interscope 90055
7	7	63	Pieces Of You	*Jewel*	Atlantic 82700
8	6	59	Falling Into You	*Celine Dion*	550 Music 67541
9	-	1	**Waterbed Hev**	*Heavy D*	Uptown 53033
10	8	11	Baduizm	*Erykah Badu*	Kedar/Universal 53027

Billboard — MAY 17, 1997 — THE BILLBOARD 200

TW	LW	WK			
1	2	2	**Carrying Your Love With Me**	*George Strait*	MCA 11584
2	1	2	Share My World	*Mary J. Blige*	MCA 11606
3	3	13	Spice	*Spice Girls*	Virgin 42174
4	4	7	Life After Death	*The Notorious B.I.G.*	Bad Boy 73011
5	5	25	Space Jam	*Soundtrack*	Warner Sunset 82961
6	6	44	Bringing Down The Horse	*The Wallflowers*	Interscope 90055
7	-	1	**Shaming Of The Sun**	*Indigo Girls*	Epic 67891
8	7	64	Pieces Of You	*Jewel*	Atlantic 82700
9	11	43	Blue	*LeAnn Rimes*	MCG/Curb 77821
10	10	12	Baduizm	*Erykah Badu*	Kedar/Universal 53027

TW	LW	WK	Billboard. MAY 24, 1997 THE BILLBOARD 200.
1	3	14	**Spice** ... *Spice Girls*...Virgin 42174
2	1	3	Carrying Your Love With Me ... *George Strait*...MCA 11584
3	2	3	Share My World ... *Mary J. Blige*...MCA 11606
4	4	8	Life After Death ... *The Notorious B.I.G.*...Bad Boy 73011
5	5	26	Space Jam ... *Soundtrack*...Warner Sunset 82961
6	11	61	Falling Into You ... *Celine Dion*...550 Music 67541
7	6	45	Bringing Down The Horse ... *The Wallflowers*...Interscope 90055
8	8	65	Pieces Of You ... *Jewel*...Atlantic 82700
9	-	1	Middle Of Nowhere ... *Hanson*...Mercury 534615
10	10	13	Baduizm ... *Erykah Badu*...Kedar/Universal 53027

TW	LW	WK	Billboard. MAY 31, 1997 THE BILLBOARD 200.
1	1	15	**Spice** ... *Spice Girls*...Virgin 42174
2	95	4	Butterfly Kisses (Shades Of Grace) ... *Bob Carlisle*...Diadem/Jive 41613
3	4	9	Life After Death ... *The Notorious B.I.G.*...Bad Boy 73011
4	3	4	Share My World ... *Mary J. Blige*...MCA 11606
5	2	4	Carrying Your Love With Me ... *George Strait*...MCA 11584
6	9	2	Middle Of Nowhere ... *Hanson*...Mercury 534615
7	5	27	Space Jam ... *Soundtrack*...Warner Sunset 82961
8	8	66	Pieces Of You ... *Jewel*...Atlantic 82700
9	7	46	Bringing Down The Horse ... *The Wallflowers*...Interscope 90055
10	10	14	Baduizm ... *Erykah Badu*...Kedar/Universal 53027

TW	LW	WK	Billboard. JUNE 7, 1997 THE BILLBOARD 200.
1	1	16	**Spice** ... *Spice Girls*...Virgin 42174
2	2	5	Butterfly Kisses (Shades Of Grace) ... *Bob Carlisle*...Diadem/Jive 41613
3	-	1	**I Got Next** ... *KRS-One*...Jive 41601
4	-	1	**I'm Bout It** ... *Soundtrack*...No Limit 50643
5	3	10	Life After Death ... *The Notorious B.I.G.*...Bad Boy 73011
6	6	3	Middle Of Nowhere ... *Hanson*...Mercury 534615
7	5	5	Carrying Your Love With Me ... *George Strait*...MCA 11584
8	4	5	Share My World ... *Mary J. Blige*...MCA 11606
9	-	1	**Hourglass** ... *James Taylor*...Columbia 67912
10	-	1	**The Colour And The Shape** ... *Foo Fighters*...Roswell/Capitol 55832

TW	LW	WK	Billboard. JUNE 14, 1997 THE BILLBOARD 200.
1	1	17	**Spice** ... *Spice Girls*...Virgin 42174
2	-	1	**Flaming Pie** ... *Paul McCartney*...Capitol 56500
3	-	1	**God's Property** ... *God's Property*...B-Rite 90093
4	6	4	Middle Of Nowhere ... *Hanson*...Mercury 534615
5	2	6	Butterfly Kisses (Shades Of Grace) ... *Bob Carlisle*...Diadem/Jive 41613
6	5	11	Life After Death ... *The Notorious B.I.G.*...Bad Boy 73011
7	8	6	Share My World ... *Mary J. Blige*...MCA 11606
8	7	6	Carrying Your Love With Me ... *George Strait*...MCA 11584
9	11	48	Bringing Down The Horse ... *The Wallflowers*...Interscope 90055
10	12	29	Space Jam ... *Soundtrack*...Warner Sunset 82961

TW	LW	WK	Billboard® JUNE 21, 1997	THE BILLBOARD 200®
1	-	1	**Wu-Tang Forever**	*Wu-Tang Clan*...Loud/RCA 66905
2	-	1	**Everywhere**	*Tim McGraw*...Curb 77886
3	1	18	Spice	*Spice Girls*...Virgin 42174
4	5	7	Butterfly Kisses (Shades Of Grace)	*Bob Carlisle*...Diadem/Jive 41613
5	4	5	Middle Of Nowhere	*Hanson*...Mercury 534615
6	3	2	God's Property	*God's Property*...B-Rite 90093
7	6	12	Life After Death	*The Notorious B.I.G.*...Bad Boy 73011
8	2	2	Flaming Pie	*Paul McCartney*...Capitol 56500
9	9	49	Bringing Down The Horse	*The Wallflowers*...Interscope 90055
10	8	7	Carrying Your Love With Me	*George Strait*...MCA 11584

TW	LW	WK	Billboard® JUNE 28, 1997	THE BILLBOARD 200®
1	4	8	**Butterfly Kisses (Shades Of Grace)**	*Bob Carlisle*...Diadem/Jive 41613
2	1	2	Wu-Tang Forever	*Wu-Tang Clan*...Loud/RCA 66905
3	2	2	Everywhere	*Tim McGraw*...Curb 77886
4	3	19	Spice	*Spice Girls*...Virgin 42174
5	5	6	Middle Of Nowhere	*Hanson*...Mercury 534615
6	6	3	God's Property	*God's Property*...B-Rite 90093
7	9	50	Bringing Down The Horse	*The Wallflowers*...Interscope 90055
8	10	8	Carrying Your Love With Me	*George Strait*...MCA 11584
9	-	1	Batman & Robin	*Soundtrack*...Warner Sunset 46620
10	14	66	Falling Into You	*Celine Dion*...550 Music 67541

TW	LW	WK	Billboard® JULY 5, 1997	THE BILLBOARD 200®
1	1	9	**Butterfly Kisses (Shades Of Grace)**	*Bob Carlisle*...Diadem/Jive 41613
2	4	20	Spice	*Spice Girls*...Virgin 42174
3	3	3	Everywhere	*Tim McGraw*...Curb 77886
4	2	3	Wu-Tang Forever	*Wu-Tang Clan*...Loud/RCA 66905
5	5	7	Middle Of Nowhere	*Hanson*...Mercury 534615
6	9	2	Batman & Robin	*Soundtrack*...Warner Sunset 46620
7	6	4	God's Property	*God's Property*...B-Rite 90093
8	-	1	**EV3**	*En Vogue*...EastWest 62057
9	-	1	**Love, Peace And Nappiness**	*Lost Boyz*...Universal 53080
10	-	1	**Cryptic Writings**	*Megadeth*...Capitol 38262

TW	LW	WK	Billboard® JULY 12, 1997	THE BILLBOARD 200®
1	2	21	**Spice**	*Spice Girls*...Virgin 42174
2	5	8	**Middle Of Nowhere**	*Hanson*...Mercury 534615
3	3	4	Everywhere	*Tim McGraw*...Curb 77886
4	-	1	**Generation Swine**	*Mötley Crüe*...Elektra 61901
5	6	3	**Batman & Robin**	*Soundtrack*...Warner Sunset 46620
6	1	10	Butterfly Kisses (Shades Of Grace)	*Bob Carlisle*...Diadem/Jive 41613
7	7	5	God's Property	*God's Property*...B-Rite 90093
8	4	4	Wu-Tang Forever	*Wu-Tang Clan*...Loud/RCA 66905
9	11	52	Bringing Down The Horse	*The Wallflowers*...Interscope 90055
10	13	72	Pieces Of You	*Jewel*...Atlantic 82700

TW	LW	WK	Billboard® JULY 19, 1997	THE BILLBOARD 200®
❶	-	1	**The Fat Of The Land**	*Prodigy*...Maverick 46606
❷	-	1	Men In Black - The Album	*Soundtrack*...Columbia 68169
❸	1	22	Spice	*Spice Girls*...Virgin 42174
④	2	9	Middle Of Nowhere	*Hanson*...Mercury 534615
❺	3	5	Everywhere	*Tim McGraw*...Curb 77886
❻	7	6	God's Property	*God's Property*...B-Rite 90093
⑦	6	11	Butterfly Kisses (Shades Of Grace)	*Bob Carlisle*...Diadem/Jive 41613
❽	9	53	Bringing Down The Horse	*The Wallflowers*...Interscope 90055
⑨	5	4	Batman & Robin	*Soundtrack*...Warner Sunset 46620
❿	13	11	Carrying Your Love With Me	*George Strait*...MCA 11584

TW	LW	WK	Billboard® JULY 26, 1997	THE BILLBOARD 200®
❶	2	2	**Men In Black - The Album**	*Soundtrack*...Columbia 68169
②	3	23	Spice	*Spice Girls*...Virgin 42174
③	1	2	The Fat Of The Land	*Prodigy*...Maverick 46606
④	4	10	Middle Of Nowhere	*Hanson*...Mercury 534615
⑤	6	7	God's Property	*God's Property*...B-Rite 90093
⑥	8	54	Bringing Down The Horse	*The Wallflowers*...Interscope 90055
⑦	5	6	Everywhere	*Tim McGraw*...Curb 77886
⑧	7	12	Butterfly Kisses (Shades Of Grace)	*Bob Carlisle*...Diadem/Jive 41613
⑨	13	74	Pieces Of You	*Jewel*...Atlantic 82700
❿	16	11	**Pure Moods**	*Various Artists*...Virgin 42186

TW	LW	WK	Billboard® AUGUST 2, 1997	THE BILLBOARD 200®
①	1	3	**Men In Black - The Album**	*Soundtrack*...Columbia 68169
❷	-	1	**Surfacing**	*Sarah McLachlan*...Arista 18970
❸	-	1	**Supa Dupa Fly**	*Missy "Misdemeanor" Elliott*...EastWest 62062
④	2	24	Spice	*Spice Girls*...Virgin 42174
⑤	3	3	The Fat Of The Land	*Prodigy*...Maverick 46606
❻	4	11	Middle Of Nowhere	*Hanson*...Mercury 534615
⑦	5	8	God's Property	*God's Property*...B-Rite 90093
⑧	7	7	Everywhere	*Tim McGraw*...Curb 77886
⑨	6	55	Bringing Down The Horse	*The Wallflowers*...Interscope 90055
❿	9	75	Pieces Of You	*Jewel*...Atlantic 82700

TW	LW	WK	Billboard® AUGUST 9, 1997	THE BILLBOARD 200®
❶	-	1	**No Way Out**	*Puff Daddy & The Family*...Bad Boy 73012
②	1	4	Men In Black - The Album	*Soundtrack*...Columbia 68169
❸	4	25	Spice	*Spice Girls*...Virgin 42174
❹	6	12	Middle Of Nowhere	*Hanson*...Mercury 534615
⑤	2	2	Surfacing	*Sarah McLachlan*...Arista 18970
⑥	5	4	The Fat Of The Land	*Prodigy*...Maverick 46606
⑦	3	2	Supa Dupa Fly	*Missy "Misdemeanor" Elliott*...EastWest 62062
❽	10	76	Pieces Of You	*Jewel*...Atlantic 82700
❾	11	21	Yourself Or Someone Like You	*Matchbox 20*...Lava/Atlantic 92721
⑩	7	9	God's Property	*God's Property*...B-Rite 90093

TW	LW	WK	Billboard® AUGUST 16, 1997 THE BILLBOARD 200®
1	-	1	**The Art Of War** .... *Bone Thugs-N-Harmony*...Ruthless 6340
2	1	2	No Way Out .... *Puff Daddy & The Family*...Bad Boy 73012
3	2	5	Men In Black - The Album .... *Soundtrack*...Columbia 68169
4	3	26	Spice .... *Spice Girls*...Virgin 42174
5	4	13	Middle Of Nowhere .... *Hanson*...Mercury 534615
6	5	3	Surfacing .... *Sarah McLachlan*...Arista 18970
7	-	1	**Spawn - The Album** .... *Soundtrack*...Immortal/Epic 68494
8	6	5	The Fat Of The Land .... *Prodigy*...Maverick 46606
9	9	22	Yourself Or Someone Like You .... *Matchbox 20*...Lava/Atlantic 92721
10	8	77	Pieces Of You .... *Jewel*...Atlantic 82700

TW	LW	WK	Billboard® AUGUST 23, 1997 THE BILLBOARD 200®
1	2	3	**No Way Out** .... *Puff Daddy & The Family*...Bad Boy 73012
2	1	2	The Art Of War .... *Bone Thugs-N-Harmony*...Ruthless 6340
3	3	6	Men In Black - The Album .... *Soundtrack*...Columbia 68169
4	-	1	**Transistor** .... *311*...Capricorn 536181
5	4	27	Spice .... *Spice Girls*...Virgin 42174
6	5	14	Middle Of Nowhere .... *Hanson*...Mercury 534615
7	-	1	**Def Jam's How To Be A Player** .... *Soundtrack*...Def Jam 537973
8	6	4	Surfacing .... *Sarah McLachlan*...Arista 18970
9	9	23	Yourself Or Someone Like You .... *Matchbox 20*...Lava/Atlantic 92721
10	8	6	The Fat Of The Land .... *Prodigy*...Maverick 46606

TW	LW	WK	Billboard® AUGUST 30, 1997 THE BILLBOARD 200®
1	1	4	**No Way Out** .... *Puff Daddy & The Family*...Bad Boy 73012
2	3	7	Men In Black - The Album .... *Soundtrack*...Columbia 68169
3	2	3	The Art Of War .... *Bone Thugs-N-Harmony*...Ruthless 6340
4	5	28	Spice .... *Spice Girls*...Virgin 42174
5	6	15	Middle Of Nowhere .... *Hanson*...Mercury 534615
6	9	24	Yourself Or Someone Like You .... *Matchbox 20*...Lava/Atlantic 92721
7	11	79	Pieces Of You .... *Jewel*...Atlantic 82700
8	8	5	Surfacing .... *Sarah McLachlan*...Arista 18970
9	7	2	Def Jam's How To Be A Player .... *Soundtrack*...Def Jam 537973
10	10	7	The Fat Of The Land .... *Prodigy*...Maverick 46606

TW	LW	WK	Billboard® SEPTEMBER 6, 1997 THE BILLBOARD 200®
1	-	1	**The Dance** .... *Fleetwood Mac*...Reprise 46702
2	1	5	No Way Out .... *Puff Daddy & The Family*...Bad Boy 73012
3	4	29	Spice .... *Spice Girls*...Virgin 42174
4	2	8	Men In Black - The Album .... *Soundtrack*...Columbia 68169
5	6	25	**Yourself Or Someone Like You** .... *Matchbox 20*...Lava/Atlantic 92721
6	5	16	Middle Of Nowhere .... *Hanson*...Mercury 534615
7	3	4	The Art Of War .... *Bone Thugs-N-Harmony*...Ruthless 6340
8	7	80	Pieces Of You .... *Jewel*...Atlantic 82700
9	-	1	**Greatest Hits Volume III** .... *Billy Joel*...Columbia 67347
10	8	6	Surfacing .... *Sarah McLachlan*...Arista 18970

TW	LW	WK	Billboard. ● SEPTEMBER 13, 1997 ● THE BILLBOARD 200.
①	2	6	**No Way Out**.............................*Puff Daddy & The Family*...Bad Boy 73012
❷	-	1	**Be Here Now** .... *Oasis*...Epic 68530
③	1	2	The Dance ....*Fleetwood Mac*...Reprise 46702
❹	-	1	**Songbook - A Collection Of Hits** .... *Trisha Yearwood*...MCA 70011
⑤	3	30	Spice.. *Spice Girls*...Virgin 42174
⑥	4	9	Men In Black - The Album .... *Soundtrack*...Columbia 68169
⑦	5	26	Yourself Or Someone Like You...................... *Matchbox 20*...Lava/Atlantic 92721
⑧	8	81	Pieces Of You..*Jewel*...Atlantic 82700
⑨	6	17	Middle Of Nowhere...*Hanson*...Mercury 534615
⑩	7	5	The Art Of War...............................*Bone Thugs-N-Harmony*...Ruthless 6340

TW	LW	WK	Billboard. ● SEPTEMBER 20, 1997 ● THE BILLBOARD 200.
❶	137	2	**Ghetto D** .... *Master P*...No Limit 50659
②	1	7	No Way Out ....*Puff Daddy & The Family*...Bad Boy 73012
③	3	3	The Dance ....*Fleetwood Mac*...Reprise 46702
④	4	2	**Songbook - A Collection Of Hits** .... *Trisha Yearwood*...MCA 70011
❺	8	82	Pieces Of You..*Jewel*...Atlantic 82700
⑥	5	31	Spice.. *Spice Girls*...Virgin 42174
⑦	7	27	Yourself Or Someone Like You..................... *Matchbox 20*...Lava/Atlantic 92721
⑧	6	10	Men In Black - The Album .... *Soundtrack*...Columbia 68169
⑨	2	2	Be Here Now... *Oasis*...Epic 68530
❿	12	10	The Fat Of The Land .... *Prodigy*...Maverick 46606

TW	LW	WK	Billboard. ● SEPTEMBER 27, 1997 ● THE BILLBOARD 200.
❶	-	1	**You Light Up My Life - Inspirational Songs**...*LeAnn Rimes*...Curb 77885
②	1	3	Ghetto D .... *Master P*...No Limit 50659
③	2	8	No Way Out ....*Puff Daddy & The Family*...Bad Boy 73012
④	3	4	The Dance ....*Fleetwood Mac*...Reprise 46702
❺	5	83	Pieces Of You..*Jewel*...Atlantic 82700
⑥	4	3	Songbook - A Collection Of Hits .... *Trisha Yearwood*...MCA 70011
⑦	6	32	Spice.. *Spice Girls*...Virgin 42174
❽	-	1	**Behind The Eyes** ....*Amy Grant*...A&M 0760
⑨	7	28	Yourself Or Someone Like You................... *Matchbox 20*...Lava/Atlantic 92721
⑩	10	11	The Fat Of The Land .... *Prodigy*...Maverick 46606

TW	LW	WK	Billboard. ● OCTOBER 4, 1997 ● THE BILLBOARD 200.
❶	-	1	**Butterfly** .... *Mariah Carey*...Columbia 67835
❷	1	2	You Light Up My Life - Inspirational Songs......... *LeAnn Rimes*...Curb 77885
❸	-	1	**When Disaster Strikes...** .... *Busta Rhymes*...Elektra 62064
④	2	4	Ghetto D .... *Master P*...No Limit 50659
⑤	3	9	No Way Out ....*Puff Daddy & The Family*...Bad Boy 73012
⑥	4	5	The Dance ....*Fleetwood Mac*...Reprise 46702
❼	-	1	The Greatest Hits Collection .... *Brooks & Dunn*...Arista 18852
❽	-	1	**Much Afraid** .... *Jars Of Clay*...Essential 41612
⑨	5	84	Pieces Of You..*Jewel*...Atlantic 82700
⑩	6	4	Songbook - A Collection Of Hits .... *Trisha Yearwood*...MCA 70011

Billboard. OCTOBER 11, 1997 — THE BILLBOARD 200.

TW	LW	WK	Title	Artist...Label
1	-	1	**Evolution**	*Boyz II Men*...Motown 0819
2	2	3	You Light Up My Life - Inspirational Songs	*LeAnn Rimes*...Curb 77885
3	1	2	Butterfly	*Mariah Carey*...Columbia 67835
4	7	2	**The Greatest Hits Collection**	*Brooks & Dunn*...Arista 18852
5	4	5	Ghetto D	*Master P*...No Limit 50659
6	6	6	The Dance	*Fleetwood Mac*...Reprise 46702
7	3	2	When Disaster Strikes...	*Busta Rhymes*...Elektra 62064
8	5	10	No Way Out	*Puff Daddy & The Family*...Bad Boy 73012
9	-	1	**The Big Picture**	*Elton John*...Rocket 536266
10	11	3	Aquarium	*Aqua*...MCA 11705

Billboard. OCTOBER 18, 1997 — THE BILLBOARD 200.

TW	LW	WK	Title	Artist...Label
1	2	4	**You Light Up My Life - Inspirational Songs**	*LeAnn Rimes*...Curb 77885
2	1	2	Evolution	*Boyz II Men*...Motown 0819
3	-	1	**Bridges To Babylon**	*The Rolling Stones*...Virgin 44712
4	11	3	**Soul Food**	*Soundtrack*...LaFace 26041
5	3	3	Butterfly	*Mariah Carey*...Columbia 67835
6	5	6	Ghetto D	*Master P*...No Limit 50659
7	10	4	**Aquarium**	*Aqua*...MCA 11705
8	6	7	The Dance	*Fleetwood Mac*...Reprise 46702
9	12	6	Songbook - A Collection Of Hits	*Trisha Yearwood*...MCA 70011
10	-	1	**Time Out Of Mind**	*Bob Dylan*...Columbia 68556

Billboard. OCTOBER 25, 1997 — THE BILLBOARD 200.

TW	LW	WK	Title	Artist...Label
1	-	1	**The Velvet Rope**	*Janet*...Virgin 44762
2	-	1	**Gang Related**	*Soundtrack*...Death Row 53509
3	1	5	You Light Up My Life - Inspirational Songs	*LeAnn Rimes*...Curb 77885
4	2	3	Evolution	*Boyz II Men*...Motown 0819
5	4	4	Soul Food	*Soundtrack*...LaFace 26041
6	5	4	Butterfly	*Mariah Carey*...Columbia 67835
7	8	8	The Dance	*Fleetwood Mac*...Reprise 46702
8	7	5	Aquarium	*Aqua*...MCA 11705
9	6	7	Ghetto D	*Master P*...No Limit 50659
10	9	7	Songbook - A Collection Of Hits	*Trisha Yearwood*...MCA 70011

Billboard. NOVEMBER 1, 1997 — THE BILLBOARD 200.

TW	LW	WK	Title	Artist...Label
1	3	6	**You Light Up My Life - Inspirational Songs**	*LeAnn Rimes*...Curb 77885
2	1	2	The Velvet Rope	*Janet*...Virgin 44762
3	2	2	Gang Related	*Soundtrack*...Death Row 53509
4	7	9	The Dance	*Fleetwood Mac*...Reprise 46702
5	5	5	Soul Food	*Soundtrack*...LaFace 26041
6	6	5	Butterfly	*Mariah Carey*...Columbia 67835
7	-	1	**Phenomenon**	*L.L. Cool J*...Def Jam 539186
8	4	4	Evolution	*Boyz II Men*...Motown 0819
9	8	6	Aquarium	*Aqua*...MCA 11705
10	-	1	**Nimrod**	*Green Day*...Reprise 46794

TW	LW	WK	Billboard. NOVEMBER 8, 1997 — THE BILLBOARD 200.
❶	-	1	**The Firm - The Album**... *The Firm*...Aftermath 90136
②	1	7	You Light Up My Life - Inspirational Songs... *LeAnn Rimes*...Curb 77885
③	4	10	The Dance... *Fleetwood Mac*...Reprise 46702
④	6	6	Butterfly... *Mariah Carey*...Columbia 67835
⑤	2	3	The Velvet Rope... *Janet*...Virgin 44762
⑥	5	6	Soul Food... *Soundtrack*...LaFace 26041
⑦	8	5	Evolution... *Boyz II Men*...Motown 0819
⑧	9	7	Aquarium... *Aqua*...MCA 11705
⑨	11	9	Ghetto D... *Master P*...No Limit 50659
⑩	13	89	Pieces Of You... *Jewel*...Atlantic 82700

TW	LW	WK	Billboard. NOVEMBER 15, 1997 — THE BILLBOARD 200.
❶	-	1	**Harlem World**... *Mase*...Bad Boy 73017
②	2	8	You Light Up My Life - Inspirational Songs... *LeAnn Rimes*...Curb 77885
❸	-	1	**Live At Red Rocks 8.15.95**... *Dave Matthews Band*...Bama Rags 67587
④	4	7	Butterfly... *Mariah Carey*...Columbia 67835
⑤	1	2	The Firm - The Album... *The Firm*...Aftermath 90136
⑥	3	11	The Dance... *Fleetwood Mac*...Reprise 46702
⑦	8	8	**Aquarium**... *Aqua*...MCA 11705
❽	15	6	Tubthumper... *Chumbawamba*...Republic 53099
⑨	6	7	Soul Food... *Soundtrack*...LaFace 26041
⑩	7	6	Evolution... *Boyz II Men*...Motown 0819

TW	LW	WK	Billboard. NOVEMBER 22, 1997 — THE BILLBOARD 200.
①	1	2	**Harlem World**... *Mase*...Bad Boy 73017
❷	-	1	**Come On Over**... *Shania Twain*...Mercury 536003
❸	-	1	**In My Lifetime, Vol. 1**... *Jay-Z*...Roc-A-Fella 536392
❹	-	1	**The 18th Letter**... *Rakim*...Universal 53113
❺	2	9	You Light Up My Life - Inspirational Songs... *LeAnn Rimes*...Curb 77885
❻	8	7	Tubthumper... *Chumbawamba*...Republic 53099
⑦	4	8	Butterfly... *Mariah Carey*...Columbia 67835
❽	-	1	Spiceworld... *Spice Girls/Soundtrack*...Virgin 45111
⑨	6	12	The Dance... *Fleetwood Mac*...Reprise 46702
⑩	7	9	Aquarium... *Aqua*...MCA 11705

TW	LW	WK	Billboard. NOVEMBER 29, 1997 — THE BILLBOARD 200.
❶	-	1	**Higher Ground**... *Barbra Streisand*...Columbia 66181
②	2	2	**Come On Over**... *Shania Twain*...Mercury 536003
❸	-	1	**Unpredictable**... *Mystikal*...No Limit 41620
❹	-	1	**Levert - Sweat - Gill**... *LSG*...EastWest 62125
⑤	1	3	Harlem World... *Mase*...Bad Boy 73017
⑥	5	10	You Light Up My Life - Inspirational Songs... *LeAnn Rimes*...Curb 77885
❼	6	8	Tubthumper... *Chumbawamba*...Republic 53099
❽	8	2	Spiceworld... *Spice Girls/Soundtrack*...Virgin 45111
❾	7	9	Butterfly... *Mariah Carey*...Columbia 67835
❿	11	37	Yourself Or Someone Like You... *Matchbox 20*...Lava/Atlantic 92721

TW	LW	WK	Billboard® DECEMBER 6, 1997 THE BILLBOARD 200®
❶	-	1	**Reload** ... *Metallica*...Elektra 62126
❷	-	1	Let's Talk About Love ... *Celine Dion*...550 Music 68861
❸	1	2	Higher Ground ... *Barbra Streisand*...Columbia 66181
❹	-	1	**Live** ... *Erykah Badu*...Kedar/Universal 53109
⑤	2	3	Come On Over ... *Shania Twain*...Mercury 536003
❻	6	11	You Light Up My Life - Inspirational Songs ... *LeAnn Rimes*...Curb 77885
❼	-	1	**Snowed In** ... *Hanson*...Mercury 536717
❽	7	9	Tubthumper ... *Chumbawamba*...Republic 53099
⑨	5	4	Harlem World ... *Mase*...Bad Boy 73017
⑩	4	2	Levert - Sweat - Gill ... *LSG*...EastWest 62125

TW	LW	WK	Billboard® DECEMBER 13, 1997 THE BILLBOARD 200®
❶	-	1	**Sevens** ... *Garth Brooks*...Capitol 56599
❷	-	1	**R U Still Down? [Remember Me]** ... *2 Pac*...Amaru 41628
③	2	2	Let's Talk About Love ... *Celine Dion*...550 Music 68861
④	3	3	Higher Ground ... *Barbra Streisand*...Columbia 66181
⑤	1	2	Reload ... *Metallica*...Elektra 62126
❻	6	12	You Light Up My Life - Inspirational Songs ... *LeAnn Rimes*...Curb 77885
⑦	5	4	Come On Over ... *Shania Twain*...Mercury 536003
❽	8	10	Tubthumper ... *Chumbawamba*...Republic 53099
❾	11	4	Spiceworld ... *Spice Girls/Soundtrack*...Virgin 45111
⑩	7	2	Snowed In ... *Hanson*...Mercury 536717

TW	LW	WK	Billboard® DECEMBER 20, 1997 THE BILLBOARD 200®
①	1	2	**Sevens** ... *Garth Brooks*...Capitol 56599
②	3	3	Let's Talk About Love ... *Celine Dion*...550 Music 68861
③	4	4	Higher Ground ... *Barbra Streisand*...Columbia 66181
❹	6	13	You Light Up My Life - Inspirational Songs ... *LeAnn Rimes*...Curb 77885
⑤	2	2	R U Still Down? [Remember Me] ... *2 Pac*...Amaru 41628
❻	9	5	Spiceworld ... *Spice Girls/Soundtrack*...Virgin 45111
❼	8	11	Tubthumper ... *Chumbawamba*...Republic 53099
⑧	5	3	Reload ... *Metallica*...Elektra 62126
⑨	7	5	Come On Over ... *Shania Twain*...Mercury 536003
❿	14	31	Middle Of Nowhere ... *Hanson*...Mercury 534615

TW	LW	WK	Billboard® DECEMBER 27, 1997 THE BILLBOARD 200®
①	1	3	**Sevens** ... *Garth Brooks*...Capitol 56599
❷	2	4	Let's Talk About Love ... *Celine Dion*...550 Music 68861
❸	3	5	Higher Ground ... *Barbra Streisand*...Columbia 66181
❹	4	14	You Light Up My Life - Inspirational Songs ... *LeAnn Rimes*...Curb 77885
❺	7	12	Tubthumper ... *Chumbawamba*...Republic 53099
❻	6	6	Spiceworld ... *Spice Girls/Soundtrack*...Virgin 45111
❼	9	6	Come On Over ... *Shania Twain*...Mercury 536003
⑧	8	4	Reload ... *Metallica*...Elektra 62126
❾	10	32	Middle Of Nowhere ... *Hanson*...Mercury 534615
⑩	11	13	Butterfly ... *Mariah Carey*...Columbia 67835

Billboard® — JANUARY 3, 1998 — THE BILLBOARD 200®

TW	LW	WK	Title	Artist	Label
1	1	4	**Sevens**	*Garth Brooks*	Capitol 56599
2	2	5	Let's Talk About Love	*Celine Dion*	550 Music 68861
3	3	6	Higher Ground	*Barbra Streisand*	Columbia 66181
4	4	15	You Light Up My Life - Inspirational Songs	*LeAnn Rimes*	Curb 77885
5	5	13	Tubthumper	*Chumbawamba*	Republic 53099
6	7	7	Come On Over	*Shania Twain*	Mercury 536003
7	6	7	Spiceworld	*Spice Girls/Soundtrack*	Virgin 45111
8	9	33	Middle Of Nowhere	*Hanson*	Mercury 534615
9	8	5	Reload	*Metallica*	Elektra 62126
10	10	14	Butterfly	*Mariah Carey*	Columbia 67835

Billboard® — JANUARY 10, 1998 — THE BILLBOARD 200®

TW	LW	WK	Title	Artist	Label
1	1	5	**Sevens**	*Garth Brooks*	Capitol 56599
2	2	6	Let's Talk About Love	*Celine Dion*	550 Music 68861
3	3	7	Higher Ground	*Barbra Streisand*	Columbia 66181
4	4	16	You Light Up My Life - Inspirational Songs	*LeAnn Rimes*	Curb 77885
5	5	14	Tubthumper	*Chumbawamba*	Republic 53099
6	6	8	Come On Over	*Shania Twain*	Mercury 536003
7	9	6	Reload	*Metallica*	Elektra 62126
8	10	15	Butterfly	*Mariah Carey*	Columbia 67835
9	7	8	Spiceworld	*Spice Girls/Soundtrack*	Virgin 45111
10	16	9	Harlem World	*Mase*	Bad Boy 73017

Billboard® — JANUARY 17, 1998 — THE BILLBOARD 200®

TW	LW	WK	Title	Artist	Label
1	2	7	**Let's Talk About Love**	*Celine Dion*	550 Music 68861
2	1	6	Sevens	*Garth Brooks*	Capitol 56599
3	5	15	**Tubthumper**	*Chumbawamba*	Republic 53099
4	10	10	Harlem World	*Mase*	Bad Boy 73017
5	4	17	You Light Up My Life - Inspirational Songs	*LeAnn Rimes*	Curb 77885
6	6	9	Come On Over	*Shania Twain*	Mercury 536003
7	11	44	Yourself Or Someone Like You	*Matchbox 20*	Lava/Atlantic 92721
8	13	24	No Way Out	*Puff Daddy & The Family*	Bad Boy 73012
9	12	21	Backstreet Boys	*Backstreet Boys*	Jive 41589
10	15	17	Aquarium	*Aqua*	MCA 11705

Billboard® — JANUARY 24, 1998 — THE BILLBOARD 200®

TW	LW	WK	Title	Artist	Label
1	11	5	**Titanic**	*Soundtrack*	Sony Classical 63213
2	1	8	Let's Talk About Love	*Celine Dion*	550 Music 68861
3	3	16	**Tubthumper**	*Chumbawamba*	Republic 53099
4	12	17	**My Way**	*Usher*	LaFace 26043
5	2	7	Sevens	*Garth Brooks*	Capitol 56599
6	4	11	Harlem World	*Mase*	Bad Boy 73017
7	9	22	Backstreet Boys	*Backstreet Boys*	Jive 41589
8	7	45	Yourself Or Someone Like You	*Matchbox 20*	Lava/Atlantic 92721
9	5	18	You Light Up My Life - Inspirational Songs	*LeAnn Rimes*	Curb 77885
10	8	25	No Way Out	*Puff Daddy & The Family*	Bad Boy 73012

Billboard — JANUARY 31, 1998 — THE BILLBOARD 200

TW	LW	WK	Title	Artist...Label
1	1	6	**Titanic**	*Soundtrack*...Sony Classical 63213
2	2	9	Let's Talk About Love	*Celine Dion*...550 Music 68861
3	-	1	**Money, Power & Respect**	*The Lox*...Bad Boy 73015
4	7	23	**Backstreet Boys**	*Backstreet Boys*...Jive 41589
5	4	18	My Way	*Usher*...LaFace 26043
6	13	11	Spiceworld	*Spice Girls/Soundtrack*...Virgin 45111
7	3	17	Tubthumper	*Chumbawamba*...Republic 53099
8	8	46	Yourself Or Someone Like You	*Matchbox 20*...Lava/Atlantic 92721
9	5	8	Sevens	*Garth Brooks*...Capitol 56599
10	9	19	You Light Up My Life - Inspirational Songs	*LeAnn Rimes*...Curb 77885

Billboard — FEBRUARY 7, 1998 — THE BILLBOARD 200

TW	LW	WK	Title	Artist...Label
1	1	7	**Titanic**	*Soundtrack*...Sony Classical 63213
2	2	10	Let's Talk About Love	*Celine Dion*...550 Music 68861
3	6	12	**Spiceworld**	*Spice Girls/Soundtrack*...Virgin 45111
4	5	19	**My Way**	*Usher*...LaFace 26043
5	4	24	Backstreet Boys	*Backstreet Boys*...Jive 41589
6	8	47	Yourself Or Someone Like You	*Matchbox 20*...Lava/Atlantic 92721
7	7	18	Tubthumper	*Chumbawamba*...Republic 53099
8	18	41	Savage Garden	*Savage Garden*...Columbia 67954
9	17	19	Soul Food	*Soundtrack*...LaFace 26041
10	-	1	**All I Have In This World, Are...My Balls And My Word**	*Young Bleed*...No Limit 50738

Billboard — FEBRUARY 14, 1998 — THE BILLBOARD 200

TW	LW	WK	Title	Artist...Label
1	1	8	**Titanic**	*Soundtrack*...Sony Classical 63213
2	2	11	Let's Talk About Love	*Celine Dion*...550 Music 68861
3	3	13	**Spiceworld**	*Spice Girls/Soundtrack*...Virgin 45111
4	4	20	**My Way**	*Usher*...LaFace 26043
5	6	48	**Yourself Or Someone Like You**	*Matchbox 20*...Lava/Atlantic 92721
6	5	25	Backstreet Boys	*Backstreet Boys*...Jive 41589
7	8	42	Savage Garden	*Savage Garden*...Columbia 67954
8	7	19	Tubthumper	*Chumbawamba*...Republic 53099
9	15	14	Harlem World	*Mase*...Bad Boy 73017
10	11	52	Spice	*Spice Girls*...Virgin 42174

Billboard — FEBRUARY 21, 1998 — THE BILLBOARD 200

TW	LW	WK	Title	Artist...Label
1	1	9	**Titanic**	*Soundtrack*...Sony Classical 63213
2	-	1	**Yield**	*Pearl Jam*...Epic 68164
3	2	12	Let's Talk About Love	*Celine Dion*...550 Music 68861
4	3	14	Spiceworld	*Spice Girls/Soundtrack*...Virgin 45111
5	4	21	My Way	*Usher*...LaFace 26043
6	5	49	Yourself Or Someone Like You	*Matchbox 20*...Lava/Atlantic 92721
7	6	26	Backstreet Boys	*Backstreet Boys*...Jive 41589
8	7	43	Savage Garden	*Savage Garden*...Columbia 67954
9	9	15	Harlem World	*Mase*...Bad Boy 73017
10	14	11	Big Willie Style	*Will Smith*...Columbia 68683

TW	LW	WK	Billboard® FEBRUARY 28, 1998 THE BILLBOARD 200®
1	1	10	**Titanic** .... *Soundtrack*...Sony Classical 63213
2	3	13	Let's Talk About Love .... *Celine Dion*...550 Music 68861
3	2	2	Yield .... *Pearl Jam*...Epic 68164
4	24	12	Sevens .... *Garth Brooks*...Capitol 56599
5	4	15	Spiceworld .... *Spice Girls/Soundtrack*...Virgin 45111
6	8	44	Savage Garden........ *Savage Garden*...Columbia 67954
7	5	22	My Way........ *Usher*...LaFace 26043
8	7	27	Backstreet Boys........ *Backstreet Boys*...Jive 41589
9	6	50	Yourself Or Someone Like You........ *Matchbox 20*...Lava/Atlantic 92721
10	16	35	Love Always........ *K-Ci & JoJo*...MCA 11613

TW	LW	WK	Billboard® MARCH 7, 1998 THE BILLBOARD 200®
1	1	11	**Titanic** .... *Soundtrack*...Sony Classical 63213
2	2	14	Let's Talk About Love .... *Celine Dion*...550 Music 68861
3	-	1	**Charge It 2 Da Game**........ *Silkk The Shocker*...No Limit 50716
4	6	45	Savage Garden........ *Savage Garden*...Columbia 67954
5	3	3	Yield .... *Pearl Jam*...Epic 68164
6	8	28	Backstreet Boys........ *Backstreet Boys*...Jive 41589
7	7	23	My Way........ *Usher*...LaFace 26043
8	5	16	Spiceworld .... *Spice Girls/Soundtrack*...Virgin 45111
9	26	3	The Wedding Singer .... *Soundtrack*...Maverick 46840
10	9	51	Yourself Or Someone Like You........ *Matchbox 20*...Lava/Atlantic 92721

TW	LW	WK	Billboard® MARCH 14, 1998 THE BILLBOARD 200®
1	1	12	**Titanic** .... *Soundtrack*...Sony Classical 63213
2	2	15	Let's Talk About Love .... *Celine Dion*...550 Music 68861
3	3	2	**Charge It 2 Da Game**........ *Silkk The Shocker*...No Limit 50716
4	4	46	Savage Garden........ *Savage Garden*...Columbia 67954
5	9	4	**The Wedding Singer** .... *Soundtrack*...Maverick 46840
6	6	29	Backstreet Boys........ *Backstreet Boys*...Jive 41589
7	7	24	My Way........ *Usher*...LaFace 26043
8	11	37	Love Always........ *K-Ci & JoJo*...MCA 11613
9	10	52	Yourself Or Someone Like You........ *Matchbox 20*...Lava/Atlantic 92721
10	5	4	Yield .... *Pearl Jam*...Epic 68164

TW	LW	WK	Billboard® MARCH 21, 1998 THE BILLBOARD 200®
1	1	13	**Titanic** .... *Soundtrack*...Sony Classical 63213
2	-	1	**Ray Of Light** .... *Madonna*...Maverick 46847
3	2	16	Let's Talk About Love .... *Celine Dion*...550 Music 68861
4	-	1	**My Homies**........ *Scarface*...Rap-A-Lot 45471
5	4	47	Savage Garden........ *Savage Garden*...Columbia 67954
6	3	3	Charge It 2 Da Game .... *Silkk The Shocker*...No Limit 50716
7	8	38	Love Always........ *K-Ci & JoJo*...MCA 11613
8	6	30	Backstreet Boys........ *Backstreet Boys*...Jive 41589
9	5	5	The Wedding Singer .... *Soundtrack*...Maverick 46840
10	7	25	My Way........ *Usher*...LaFace 26043

TW	LW	WK	Billboard. MARCH 28, 1998 THE BILLBOARD 200.	
1	1	14	**Titanic**	*Soundtrack*...Sony Classical 63213
2	2	2	**Ray Of Light**	*Madonna*...Maverick 46847
3	3	17	Let's Talk About Love	*Celine Dion*...550 Music 68861
4	-	1	**Pilgrim**	*Eric Clapton*...Duck 46577
5	5	48	Savage Garden	*Savage Garden*...Columbia 67954
6	7	39	**Love Always**	*K-Ci & JoJo*...MCA 11613
7	9	6	The Wedding Singer	*Soundtrack*...Maverick 46840
8	8	31	Backstreet Boys	*Backstreet Boys*...Jive 41589
9	4	2	My Homies	*Scarface*...Rap-A-Lot 45471
10	-	1	**Left Of The Middle**	*Natalie Imbruglia*...RCA 67634

TW	LW	WK	Billboard. APRIL 4, 1998 THE BILLBOARD 200.	
1	1	15	**Titanic**	*Soundtrack*...Sony Classical 63213
2	3	18	Let's Talk About Love	*Celine Dion*...550 Music 68861
3	-	1	**Life Or Death**	*C-Murder*...No Limit 50723
4	-	1	**Van Halen 3**	*Van Halen*...Warner 46662
5	2	3	Ray Of Light	*Madonna*...Maverick 46847
6	5	49	Savage Garden	*Savage Garden*...Columbia 67954
7	4	2	Pilgrim	*Eric Clapton*...Duck 46577
8	8	32	Backstreet Boys	*Backstreet Boys*...Jive 41589
9	6	40	Love Always	*K-Ci & JoJo*...MCA 11613
10	-	1	**The Players Club**	*Soundtrack*...A&M 540886

TW	LW	WK	Billboard. APRIL 11, 1998 THE BILLBOARD 200.	
1	1	16	**Titanic**	*Soundtrack*...Sony Classical 63213
2	2	19	Let's Talk About Love	*Celine Dion*...550 Music 68861
3	-	1	**The Pillage**	*Cappadonna*...Razor Sharp 67947
4	5	4	Ray Of Light	*Madonna*...Maverick 46847
5	6	50	Savage Garden	*Savage Garden*...Columbia 67954
6	8	33	Backstreet Boys	*Backstreet Boys*...Jive 41589
7	3	2	Life Or Death	*C-Murder*...No Limit 50723
8	7	3	Pilgrim	*Eric Clapton*...Duck 46577
9	9	41	Love Always	*K-Ci & JoJo*...MCA 11613
10	12	28	My Way	*Usher*...LaFace 26043

TW	LW	WK	Billboard. APRIL 18, 1998 THE BILLBOARD 200.	
1	1	17	**Titanic**	*Soundtrack*...Sony Classical 63213
2	2	20	Let's Talk About Love	*Celine Dion*...550 Music 68861
3	5	51	**Savage Garden**	*Savage Garden*...Columbia 67954
4	4	5	Ray Of Light	*Madonna*...Maverick 46847
5	6	34	Backstreet Boys	*Backstreet Boys*...Jive 41589
6	-	1	**Moment Of Truth**	*Gang Starr*...Noo Trybe 45585
7	8	4	Pilgrim	*Eric Clapton*...Duck 46577
8	-	1	**Retaliation, Revenge And Get Back**	*Daz Dillinger*...Death Row 53524
9	9	42	Love Always	*K-Ci & JoJo*...MCA 11613
10	7	3	Life Or Death	*C-Murder*...No Limit 50723

Billboard — APRIL 25, 1998 — THE BILLBOARD 200®

TW	LW	WK	Title	Artist...Label
1	1	18	**Titanic**	*Soundtrack*...Sony Classical 63213
2	2	21	Let's Talk About Love	*Celine Dion*...550 Music 68861
3	-	1	**I Got The Hook-Up!**	*Soundtrack*...No Limit 50745
4	5	35	**Backstreet Boys**	*Backstreet Boys*...Jive 41589
5	3	52	Savage Garden	*Savage Garden*...Columbia 67954
6	-	1	**Still Standing**	*Goodie Mob*...LaFace 26047
7	23	2	City Of Angels	*Soundtrack*...Warner Sunset 46867
8	9	43	Love Always	*K-Ci & JoJo*...MCA 11613
9	4	6	Ray Of Light	*Madonna*...Maverick 46847
10	11	5	**Left Of The Middle**	*Natalie Imbruglia*...RCA 67634

Billboard — MAY 2, 1998 — THE BILLBOARD 200®

TW	LW	WK	Title	Artist...Label
1	1	19	**Titanic**	*Soundtrack*...Sony Classical 63213
2	2	22	Let's Talk About Love	*Celine Dion*...550 Music 68861
3	7	3	City Of Angels	*Soundtrack*...Warner Sunset 46867
4	5	53	Savage Garden	*Savage Garden*...Columbia 67954
5	4	36	Backstreet Boys	*Backstreet Boys*...Jive 41589
6	3	2	I Got The Hook-Up!	*Soundtrack*...No Limit 50745
7	8	44	Love Always	*K-Ci & JoJo*...MCA 11613
8	9	7	Ray Of Light	*Madonna*...Maverick 46847
9	17	24	Come On Over	*Shania Twain*...Mercury 536003
10	10	6	**Left Of The Middle**	*Natalie Imbruglia*...RCA 67634

Billboard — MAY 9, 1998 — THE BILLBOARD 200®

TW	LW	WK	Title	Artist...Label
1	1	20	**Titanic**	*Soundtrack*...Sony Classical 63213
2	-	1	**One Step At A Time**	*George Strait*...MCA 70020
3	3	4	City Of Angels	*Soundtrack*...Warner Sunset 46867
4	2	23	Let's Talk About Love	*Celine Dion*...550 Music 68861
5	4	54	Savage Garden	*Savage Garden*...Columbia 67954
6	5	37	Backstreet Boys	*Backstreet Boys*...Jive 41589
7	-	1	**Faith**	*Faith Hill*...Warner 46790
8	-	1	**Walking Into Clarksdale**	*Jimmy Page & Robert Plant*...Atlantic 83092
9	7	45	Love Always	*K-Ci & JoJo*...MCA 11613
10	9	25	Come On Over	*Shania Twain*...Mercury 536003

Billboard — MAY 16, 1998 — THE BILLBOARD 200®

TW	LW	WK	Title	Artist...Label
1	-	1	**Before These Crowded Streets**	*Dave Matthews Band*...RCA 67660
2	3	5	City Of Angels	*Soundtrack*...Warner Sunset 46867
3	1	21	Titanic	*Soundtrack*...Sony Classical 63213
4	2	2	One Step At A Time	*George Strait*...MCA 70020
5	-	1	**Capital Punishment**	*Big Punisher*...Loud 67512
6	4	24	Let's Talk About Love	*Celine Dion*...550 Music 68861
7	6	38	Backstreet Boys	*Backstreet Boys*...Jive 41589
8	5	55	Savage Garden	*Savage Garden*...Columbia 67954
9	7	2	Faith	*Faith Hill*...Warner 46790
10	10	26	Come On Over	*Shania Twain*...Mercury 536003

TW	LW	WK	Billboard. MAY 23, 1998	THE BILLBOARD 200.
1	-	1	**The Limited Series**	*Garth Brooks*...Capitol 94572
2	1	2	Before These Crowded Streets	*Dave Matthews Band*...RCA 67660
3	2	6	City Of Angels	*Soundtrack*...Warner Sunset 46867
4	-	1	Sittin' On Top Of The World	*LeAnn Rimes*...Curb 77901
5	-	1	**From The Choirgirl Hotel**	*Tori Amos*...Atlantic 83095
6	3	22	Titanic	*Soundtrack*...Sony Classical 63213
7	-	1	**Songs From Ally McBeal**	*Vonda Shepard*...550 Music 69365
8	-	1	**There's One In Every Family**	*Fiend*...No Limit 50715
9	6	25	Let's Talk About Love	*Celine Dion*...550 Music 68861
10	7	39	Backstreet Boys	*Backstreet Boys*...Jive 41589

TW	LW	WK	Billboard. MAY 30, 1998	THE BILLBOARD 200.
1	1	2	**The Limited Series**	*Garth Brooks*...Capitol 94572
2	3	7	City Of Angels	*Soundtrack*...Warner Sunset 46867
3	4	2	**Sittin' On Top Of The World**	*LeAnn Rimes*...Curb 77901
4	2	3	Before These Crowded Streets	*Dave Matthews Band*...RCA 67660
5	6	23	Titanic	*Soundtrack*...Sony Classical 63213
6	-	1	**3 Car Garage: The Indie Recordings '95-'96**	*Hanson*...Mercury 558399
7	7	2	**Songs From Ally McBeal**	*Vonda Shepard*...550 Music 69365
8	10	40	Backstreet Boys	*Backstreet Boys*...Jive 41589
9	13	4	One Step At A Time	*George Strait*...MCA 70020
10	9	26	Let's Talk About Love	*Celine Dion*...550 Music 68861

TW	LW	WK	Billboard. JUNE 6, 1998	THE BILLBOARD 200.
1	-	1	**It's Dark And Hell Is Hot**	*DMX*...Def Jam 558227
2	2	8	City Of Angels	*Soundtrack*...Warner Sunset 46867
3	-	1	**Sparkle**	*Sparkle*...Rock Land 90149
4	-	1	Godzilla	*Soundtrack*...Epic 69338
5	-	1	**Lost**	*Eightball*...Suave 53127
6	1	3	The Limited Series	*Garth Brooks*...Capitol 94572
7	4	4	Before These Crowded Streets	*Dave Matthews Band*...RCA 67660
8	-	1	**Ophelia**	*Natalie Merchant*...Elektra 62196
9	7	3	Songs From Ally McBeal	*Vonda Shepard*...550 Music 69365
10	3	3	Sittin' On Top Of The World	*LeAnn Rimes*...Curb 77901

TW	LW	WK	Billboard. JUNE 13, 1998	THE BILLBOARD 200.
1	2	9	**City Of Angels**	*Soundtrack*...Warner Sunset 46867
2	4	2	**Godzilla**	*Soundtrack*...Epic 69338
3	1	2	It's Dark And Hell Is Hot	*DMX*...Def Jam 558227
4	6	4	The Limited Series	*Garth Brooks*...Capitol 94572
5	11	42	Backstreet Boys	*Backstreet Boys*...Jive 41589
6	7	5	Before These Crowded Streets	*Dave Matthews Band*...RCA 67660
7	3	2	Sparkle	*Sparkle*...Rock Land 90149
8	9	4	Songs From Ally McBeal	*Vonda Shepard*...550 Music 69365
9	14	30	Come On Over	*Shania Twain*...Mercury 536003
10	12	25	Titanic	*Soundtrack*...Sony Classical 63213

TW	LW	WK	Billboard® JUNE 20, 1998 THE BILLBOARD 200®	
1	112	2	**MP Da Last Don**	*Master P*...No Limit 53538
2	-	1	**Adore**	*The Smashing Pumpkins*...Virgin 45879
3	1	10	City Of Angels	*Soundtrack*...Warner Sunset 46867
4	2	3	Godzilla	*Soundtrack*...Epic 69338
5	14	3	Hope Floats	*Soundtrack*...Capitol 93402
6	3	3	It's Dark And Hell Is Hot	*DMX*...Def Jam 558227
7	5	43	Backstreet Boys	*Backstreet Boys*...Jive 41589
8	-	1	**If You See Him**	*Reba McEntire*...MCA 70019
9	4	5	The Limited Series	*Garth Brooks*...Capitol 94572
10	-	1	**Shut 'Em Down**	*Onyx*...Def Jam 536988

TW	LW	WK	Billboard® JUNE 27, 1998 THE BILLBOARD 200®	
1	1	3	**MP Da Last Don**	*Master P*...No Limit 53538
2	3	11	City Of Angels	*Soundtrack*...Warner Sunset 46867
3	-	1	Never S-a-y Never	*Brandy*...Atlantic 83039
4	4	4	Godzilla	*Soundtrack*...Epic 69338
5	5	4	Hope Floats	*Soundtrack*...Capitol 93402
6	9	6	The Limited Series	*Garth Brooks*...Capitol 94572
7	7	44	Backstreet Boys	*Backstreet Boys*...Jive 41589
8	2	2	Adore	*The Smashing Pumpkins*...Virgin 45879
9	13	32	Come On Over	*Shania Twain*...Mercury 536003
10	6	4	It's Dark And Hell Is Hot	*DMX*...Def Jam 558227

TW	LW	WK	Billboard® JULY 4, 1998 THE BILLBOARD 200®	
1	2	12	**City Of Angels**	*Soundtrack*...Warner Sunset 46867
2	3	2	**Never S-a-y Never**	*Brandy*...Atlantic 83039
3	1	4	MP Da Last Don	*Master P*...No Limit 53538
4	5	5	**Hope Floats**	*Soundtrack*...Capitol 93402
5	4	5	Godzilla	*Soundtrack*...Epic 69338
6	6	7	The Limited Series	*Garth Brooks*...Capitol 94572
7	7	45	Backstreet Boys	*Backstreet Boys*...Jive 41589
8	9	33	Come On Over	*Shania Twain*...Mercury 536003
9	12	30	Big Willie Style	*Will Smith*...Columbia 68683
10	8	3	Adore	*The Smashing Pumpkins*...Virgin 45879

TW	LW	WK	Billboard® JULY 11, 1998 THE BILLBOARD 200®	
1	1	13	**City Of Angels**	*Soundtrack*...Warner Sunset 46867
2	3	5	MP Da Last Don	*Master P*...No Limit 53538
3	2	3	Never S-a-y Never	*Brandy*...Atlantic 83039
4	-	1	Armageddon	*Soundtrack*...Columbia 69440
5	4	6	Hope Floats	*Soundtrack*...Capitol 93402
6	5	6	Godzilla	*Soundtrack*...Epic 69338
7	7	46	Backstreet Boys	*Backstreet Boys*...Jive 41589
8	9	31	**Big Willie Style**	*Will Smith*...Columbia 68683
9	8	34	Come On Over	*Shania Twain*...Mercury 536003
10	12	10	**Bulworth**	*Soundtrack*...Interscope 90160

TW	LW	WK	Billboard — JULY 18, 1998 — THE BILLBOARD 200	
1	4	2	**Armageddon**	*Soundtrack*...Columbia 69440
2	-	1	**El Niño**	*Def Squad*...Def Jam 558343
3	-	1	**Embrya**	*Maxwell*...Columbia 68968
4	1	14	City Of Angels	*Soundtrack*...Warner Sunset 46867
5	3	4	Never S-a-y Never	*Brandy*...Atlantic 83039
6	5	7	Hope Floats	*Soundtrack*...Capitol 93402
7	2	6	MP Da Last Don	*Master P*...No Limit 53538
8	8	32	**Big Willie Style**	*Will Smith*...Columbia 68683
9	7	47	Backstreet Boys	*Backstreet Boys*...Jive 41589
10	18	3	Dr. Dolittle	*Soundtrack*...Blackground 83113

TW	LW	WK	Billboard — JULY 25, 1998 — THE BILLBOARD 200	
1	1	3	**Armageddon**	*Soundtrack*...Columbia 69440
2	4	15	City Of Angels	*Soundtrack*...Warner Sunset 46867
3	-	1	**Stunt**	*Barenaked Ladies*...Reprise 46963
4	5	5	Never S-a-y Never	*Brandy*...Atlantic 83039
5	-	1	**Am I My Brothers Keeper**	*Kane & Abel*...No Limit 50720
6	6	8	Hope Floats	*Soundtrack*...Capitol 93402
7	7	7	MP Da Last Don	*Master P*...No Limit 53538
8	8	33	**Big Willie Style**	*Will Smith*...Columbia 68683
9	3	2	Embrya	*Maxwell*...Columbia 68968
10	10	4	Dr. Dolittle	*Soundtrack*...Blackground 83113

TW	LW	WK	Billboard — AUGUST 1, 1998 — THE BILLBOARD 200	
1	-	1	**Hello Nasty**	*Beastie Boys*...Grand Royal 37716
2	1	4	Armageddon	*Soundtrack*...Columbia 69440
3	136	2	**N.O.R.E.**	*Noreaga*...Penalty 3077
4	2	16	City Of Angels	*Soundtrack*...Warner Sunset 46867
5	4	6	Never S-a-y Never	*Brandy*...Atlantic 83039
6	3	2	Stunt	*Barenaked Ladies*...Reprise 46963
7	10	5	Dr. Dolittle	*Soundtrack*...Blackground 83113
8	-	1	**The Boy Is Mine**	*Monica*...Arista 19011
9	11	49	Backstreet Boys	*Backstreet Boys*...Jive 41589
10	8	34	Big Willie Style	*Will Smith*...Columbia 68683

TW	LW	WK	Billboard — AUGUST 8, 1998 — THE BILLBOARD 200	
1	1	2	**Hello Nasty**	*Beastie Boys*...Grand Royal 37716
2	2	5	Armageddon	*Soundtrack*...Columbia 69440
3	-	1	**Jermaine Dupri Presents Life In 1472 - The Original Soundtrack**	*Jermaine Dupri*...So So Def 69087
4	-	1	**The Swarm**	*Wu-Tang Killa Bees*...Wu-Tang 50013
5	4	17	City Of Angels	*Soundtrack*...Warner Sunset 46867
6	-	1	**Confessions Of Fire**	*Cam'ron*...Untertainment 68976
7	7	6	Dr. Dolittle	*Soundtrack*...Blackground 83113
8	5	7	Never S-a-y Never	*Brandy*...Atlantic 83039
9	9	50	Backstreet Boys	*Backstreet Boys*...Jive 41589
10	6	3	Stunt	*Barenaked Ladies*...Reprise 46963

Billboard — AUGUST 15, 1998 — THE BILLBOARD 200

TW	LW	WK			
1	1	3	**Hello Nasty**	*Beastie Boys*	Grand Royal 37716
2	2	6	Armageddon	*Soundtrack*	Columbia 69440
3	5	18	City Of Angels	*Soundtrack*	Warner Sunset 46867
4	3	2	Jermaine Dupri Presents Life In 1472 - The Original Soundtrack	*Jermaine Dupri*	So So Def 69087
5	7	7	Dr. Dolittle	*Soundtrack*	Blackground 83113
6	10	4	Stunt	*Barenaked Ladies*	Reprise 46963
7	8	8	Never S-a-y Never	*Brandy*	Atlantic 83039
8	9	51	Backstreet Boys	*Backstreet Boys*	Jive 41589
9	12	19	'N Sync	*'N Sync*	RCA 67613
10	13	36	Big Willie Style	*Will Smith*	Columbia 68683

Billboard — AUGUST 22, 1998 — THE BILLBOARD 200

TW	LW	WK			
1	-	1	**Da Game Is To Be Sold, Not To Be Told**	*Snoop Dogg*	No Limit 50000
2	2	7	Armageddon	*Soundtrack*	Columbia 69440
3	1	4	Hello Nasty	*Beastie Boys*	Grand Royal 37716
4	5	8	**Dr. Dolittle**	*Soundtrack*	Blackground 83113
5	6	5	Stunt	*Barenaked Ladies*	Reprise 46963
6	3	19	City Of Angels	*Soundtrack*	Warner Sunset 46867
7	8	52	Backstreet Boys	*Backstreet Boys*	Jive 41589
8	4	3	Jermaine Dupri Presents Life In 1472 - The Original Soundtrack	*Jermaine Dupri*	So So Def 69087
9	9	20	'N Sync	*'N Sync*	RCA 67613
10	7	9	Never S-a-y Never	*Brandy*	Atlantic 83039

Billboard — AUGUST 29, 1998 — THE BILLBOARD 200

TW	LW	WK			
1	1	2	**Da Game Is To Be Sold, Not To Be Told**	*Snoop Dogg*	No Limit 50000
2	2	8	Armageddon	*Soundtrack*	Columbia 69440
3	3	5	Hello Nasty	*Beastie Boys*	Grand Royal 37716
4	-	1	**Funkmaster Flex: The Mix Tape Volume III**	*Various Artists*	Loud 67647
5	5	6	Stunt	*Barenaked Ladies*	Reprise 46963
6	9	21	'N Sync	*'N Sync*	RCA 67613
7	4	9	Dr. Dolittle	*Soundtrack*	Blackground 83113
8	6	20	City Of Angels	*Soundtrack*	Warner Sunset 46867
9	7	53	Backstreet Boys	*Backstreet Boys*	Jive 41589
10	-	1	How Stella Got Her Groove Back	*Soundtrack*	Flyte Tyme 11806

Billboard — SEPTEMBER 5, 1998 — THE BILLBOARD 200

TW	LW	WK			
1	-	1	**Follow The Leader**	*Korn*	Immortal 69001
2	3	6	Hello Nasty	*Beastie Boys*	Grand Royal 37716
3	1	3	Da Game Is To Be Sold, Not To Be Told	*Snoop Dogg*	No Limit 50000
4	2	9	Armageddon	*Soundtrack*	Columbia 69440
5	6	22	'N Sync	*'N Sync*	RCA 67613
6	5	7	Stunt	*Barenaked Ladies*	Reprise 46963
7	7	10	Dr. Dolittle	*Soundtrack*	Blackground 83113
8	10	2	**How Stella Got Her Groove Back**	*Soundtrack*	Flyte Tyme 11806
9	9	54	Backstreet Boys	*Backstreet Boys*	Jive 41589
10	8	21	City Of Angels	*Soundtrack*	Warner Sunset 46867

Billboard® SEPTEMBER 12, 1998 — THE BILLBOARD 200®

TW	LW	WK			
1	-	1	**The Miseducation Of Lauryn Hill**	*Lauryn Hill*	Ruffhouse 69035
2	2	7	Hello Nasty	*Beastie Boys*	Grand Royal 37716
3	4	10	Armageddon	*Soundtrack*	Columbia 69440
4	6	8	Stunt	*Barenaked Ladies*	Reprise 46963
5	-	1	**Hellbilly Deluxe**	*Rob Zombie*	Geffen 25212
6	5	23	'N Sync	*'N Sync*	RCA 67613
7	-	1	Back To Titanic	*Soundtrack*	Sony Classical 60691
8	3	4	Da Game Is To Be Sold, Not To Be Told	*Snoop Dogg*	No Limit 50000
9	1	2	Follow The Leader	*Korn*	Immortal 69001
10	7	11	Dr. Dolittle	*Soundtrack*	Blackground 83113

Billboard® SEPTEMBER 19, 1998 — THE BILLBOARD 200®

TW	LW	WK			
1	1	2	**The Miseducation Of Lauryn Hill**	*Lauryn Hill*	Ruffhouse 69035
2	7	2	**Back To Titanic**	*Soundtrack*	Sony Classical 60691
3	6	24	'N Sync	*'N Sync*	RCA 67613
4	-	1	**High Mileage**	*Alan Jackson*	Arista 18864
5	2	8	Hello Nasty	*Beastie Boys*	Grand Royal 37716
6	4	9	Stunt	*Barenaked Ladies*	Reprise 46963
7	-	1	**Don Cartagena**	*Fat Joe*	Mystic 92805
8	3	11	Armageddon	*Soundtrack*	Columbia 69440
9	11	56	Backstreet Boys	*Backstreet Boys*	Jive 41589
10	8	5	Da Game Is To Be Sold, Not To Be Told	*Snoop Dogg*	No Limit 50000

Billboard® SEPTEMBER 26, 1998 — THE BILLBOARD 200®

TW	LW	WK			
1	1	3	**The Miseducation Of Lauryn Hill**	*Lauryn Hill*	Ruffhouse 69035
2	-	1	**Can-I-Bus**	*Canibus*	Universal 53136
3	3	25	'N Sync	*'N Sync*	RCA 67613
4	5	9	Hello Nasty	*Beastie Boys*	Grand Royal 37716
5	2	3	Back To Titanic	*Soundtrack*	Sony Classical 60691
6	6	10	Stunt	*Barenaked Ladies*	Reprise 46963
7	8	12	Armageddon	*Soundtrack*	Columbia 69440
8	9	57	Backstreet Boys	*Backstreet Boys*	Jive 41589
9	-	1	**Celebrity Skin**	*Hole*	DGC 25164
10	4	2	High Mileage	*Alan Jackson*	Arista 18864

Billboard® OCTOBER 3, 1998 — THE BILLBOARD 200®

TW	LW	WK			
1	-	1	**Mechanical Animals**	*Marilyn Manson*	Nothing 90273
2	1	4	The Miseducation Of Lauryn Hill	*Lauryn Hill*	Ruffhouse 69035
3	4	10	Hello Nasty	*Beastie Boys*	Grand Royal 37716
4	-	1	**Musical Chairs**	*Hootie & The Blowfish*	Atlantic 83136
5	3	26	'N Sync	*'N Sync*	RCA 67613
6	6	11	Stunt	*Barenaked Ladies*	Reprise 46963
7	-	1	Rush Hour	*Soundtrack*	Def Jam 558663
8	8	58	Backstreet Boys	*Backstreet Boys*	Jive 41589
9	11	13	**The Dirty Boogie**	*The Brian Setzer Orchestra*	Interscope 90183
10	9	2	Celebrity Skin	*Hole*	DGC 25164

Billboard® OCTOBER 10, 1998 — THE BILLBOARD 200®

TW	LW	WK	Title	Artist...Label
1	2	5	**The Miseducation Of Lauryn Hill**	*Lauryn Hill*...Ruffhouse 69035
2	5	27	**'N Sync**	*'N Sync*...RCA 67613
3	-	1	**Psycho-Circus**	*Kiss*...Mercury 558992
4	-	1	**Supernatural**	*DC Talk*...ForeFront 46525
5	1	2	Mechanical Animals	*Marilyn Manson*...Nothing 90273
6	-	1	**Still In The Game**	*Keith Sweat*...Elektra 62262
7	3	11	Hello Nasty	*Beastie Boys*...Grand Royal 37716
8	7	2	Rush Hour	*Soundtrack*...Def Jam 558663
9	6	12	Stunt	*Barenaked Ladies*...Reprise 46963
10	12	47	Come On Over	*Shania Twain*...Mercury 536003

Billboard® OCTOBER 17, 1998 — THE BILLBOARD 200®

TW	LW	WK	Title	Artist...Label
1	-	1	**Vol. 2...Hard Knock Life**	*Jay-Z*...Roc-A-Fella 558902
2	-	1	**Aquemini**	*OutKast*...LaFace 26053
3	-	1	**The Love Movement**	*A Tribe Called Quest*...Jive 41638
4	1	6	The Miseducation Of Lauryn Hill	*Lauryn Hill*...Ruffhouse 69035
5	-	1	**The Globe Sessions**	*Sheryl Crow*...A&M 540959
6	2	28	'N Sync	*'N Sync*...RCA 67613
7	-	1	**The Nu Nation Project**	*Kirk Franklin*...GospoCentric 90178
8	10	48	Come On Over	*Shania Twain*...Mercury 536003
9	-	1	**Mean Green - Major Players Compilation**	*Various Artists*...No Limit 53505
10	9	13	Stunt	*Barenaked Ladies*...Reprise 46963

Billboard® OCTOBER 24, 1998 — THE BILLBOARD 200®

TW	LW	WK	Title	Artist...Label
1	1	2	**Vol. 2...Hard Knock Life**	*Jay-Z*...Roc-A-Fella 558902
2	4	7	The Miseducation Of Lauryn Hill	*Lauryn Hill*...Ruffhouse 69035
3	-	1	**Heaven'z Movie**	*Bizzy Bone*...Mo Thugs 1670
4	6	29	'N Sync	*'N Sync*...RCA 67613
5	2	2	Aquemini	*OutKast*...LaFace 26053
6	5	2	The Globe Sessions	*Sheryl Crow*...A&M 540959
7	8	49	Come On Over	*Shania Twain*...Mercury 536003
8	-	1	**Kuruption!**	*Kurupt*...A&M 540963
9	7	2	The Nu Nation Project	*Kirk Franklin*...GospoCentric 90178
10	10	14	Stunt	*Barenaked Ladies*...Reprise 46963

Billboard® OCTOBER 31, 1998 — THE BILLBOARD 200®

TW	LW	WK	Title	Artist...Label
1	1	3	**Vol. 2...Hard Knock Life**	*Jay-Z*...Roc-A-Fella 558902
2	2	8	The Miseducation Of Lauryn Hill	*Lauryn Hill*...Ruffhouse 69035
3	7	50	Come On Over	*Shania Twain*...Mercury 536003
4	4	30	'N Sync	*'N Sync*...RCA 67613
5	5	3	Aquemini	*OutKast*...LaFace 26053
6	6	3	The Globe Sessions	*Sheryl Crow*...A&M 540959
7	10	15	Stunt	*Barenaked Ladies*...Reprise 46963
8	14	5	Rush Hour	*Soundtrack*...Def Jam 558663
9	13	62	Backstreet Boys	*Backstreet Boys*...Jive 41589
10	17	38	Wide Open Spaces	*Dixie Chicks*...Monument 68195

TW	LW	WK	Billboard. NOVEMBER 7, 1998 THE BILLBOARD 200.
❶	1	4	**Vol. 2...Hard Knock Life** .... *Jay-Z*...Roc-A-Fella 558902
②	2	9	The Miseducation Of Lauryn Hill .... *Lauryn Hill*...Ruffhouse 69035
③	3	51	Come On Over .... *Shania Twain*...Mercury 536003
④	4	31	'N Sync .... *'N Sync*...RCA 67613
❺	8	6	**Rush Hour** .... *Soundtrack*...Def Jam 558663
⑥	5	4	Aquemini .... *OutKast*...LaFace 26053
⑦	7	16	Stunt .... *Barenaked Ladies*...Reprise 46963
⑧	6	4	The Globe Sessions .... *Sheryl Crow*...A&M 540959
⑨	9	63	Backstreet Boys .... *Backstreet Boys*...Jive 41589
⑩	10	39	Wide Open Spaces .... *Dixie Chicks*...Monument 68195

TW	LW	WK	Billboard. NOVEMBER 14, 1998 THE BILLBOARD 200.
①	1	5	**Vol. 2...Hard Knock Life** .... *Jay-Z*...Roc-A-Fella 558902
❷	-	1	**Enter The Dru** .... *Dru Hill*...Island 524542
❸	-	1	**Up** .... *R.E.M.*...Warner 47112
④	2	10	The Miseducation Of Lauryn Hill .... *Lauryn Hill*...Ruffhouse 69035
⑤	3	52	Come On Over .... *Shania Twain*...Mercury 536003
❻	-	1	**Keep The Faith** .... *Faith Evans*...Bad Boy 73016
⑦	4	32	'N Sync .... *'N Sync*...RCA 67613
❽	-	1	**The Story Of The Ghost** .... *Phish*...Elektra 62297
⑨	5	7	Rush Hour .... *Soundtrack*...Def Jam 558663
❿	9	64	Backstreet Boys .... *Backstreet Boys*...Jive 41589

TW	LW	WK	Billboard. NOVEMBER 21, 1998 THE BILLBOARD 200.
❶	-	1	**Supposed Former Infatuation Junkie** .... *Alanis Morissette*...Maverick 47094
❷	-	1	**The Best Of 1980-1990/The B-Sides** .... *U2*...Island 524612
③	1	6	Vol. 2...Hard Knock Life .... *Jay-Z*...Roc-A-Fella 558902
❹	-	1	These Are Special Times .... *Celine Dion*...550 Music 69523
❺	-	1	**Belly** .... *Soundtrack*...Def Jam 558925
❻	7	33	'N Sync .... *'N Sync*...RCA 67613
❼	-	1	**Mama Drama** .... *Mia X*...No Limit 53502
⑧	2	2	Enter The Dru .... *Dru Hill*...Island 524542
❾	5	53	Come On Over .... *Shania Twain*...Mercury 536003
⑩	4	11	The Miseducation Of Lauryn Hill .... *Lauryn Hill*...Ruffhouse 69035

TW	LW	WK	Billboard. NOVEMBER 28, 1998 THE BILLBOARD 200.
①	1	2	**Supposed Former Infatuation Junkie** .... *Alanis Morissette*...Maverick 47094
❷	-	1	**R.** .... *R. Kelly*...Jive 41625
❸	4	2	These Are Special Times .... *Celine Dion*...550 Music 69523
④	3	7	Vol. 2...Hard Knock Life .... *Jay-Z*...Roc-A-Fella 558902
⑤	2	2	The Best Of 1980-1990/The B-Sides .... *U2*...Island 524612
❻	6	34	'N Sync .... *'N Sync*...RCA 67613
❼	-	1	**Home For Christmas** .... *'N sync*...RCA 67726
❽	9	54	Come On Over .... *Shania Twain*...Mercury 536003
⑨	8	3	Enter The Dru .... *Dru Hill*...Island 524542
❿	11	66	Backstreet Boys .... *Backstreet Boys*...Jive 41589

Billboard · DECEMBER 5, 1998 · THE BILLBOARD 200

TW	LW	WK	Title	Artist	Label
1	-	1	**Double Live**	*Garth Brooks*	Capitol 97424
2	-	1	**Tical 2000: Judgement Day**	*Method Man*	Def Jam 558920
3	-	1	**Spirit**	*Jewel*	Atlantic 82950
4	-	1	#1's	*Mariah Carey*	Columbia 69670
5	3	3	These Are Special Times	*Celine Dion*	550 Music 69523
6	-	1	Americana	*The Offspring*	Columbia 69661
7	-	1	**War & Peace Vol. I (The War Disc)**	*Ice Cube*	Priority 50700
8	1	3	Supposed Former Infatuation Junkie	*Alanis Morissette*	Maverick 47094
9	6	35	'N Sync	*'N Sync*	RCA 67613
10	4	8	Vol. 2...Hard Knock Life	*Jay-Z*	Roc-A-Fella 558902

Billboard · DECEMBER 12, 1998 · THE BILLBOARD 200

TW	LW	WK	Title	Artist	Label
1	1	2	**Double Live**	*Garth Brooks*	Capitol 97424
2	-	1	**Garage Inc.**	*Metallica*	Elektra 62299
3	5	4	These Are Special Times	*Celine Dion*	550 Music 69523
4	3	2	Spirit	*Jewel*	Atlantic 82950
5	-	1	Greatest Hits	*2Pac*	Amaru 90301
6	9	36	'N Sync	*'N Sync*	RCA 67613
7	4	2	#1's	*Mariah Carey*	Columbia 69670
8	10	9	Vol. 2...Hard Knock Life	*Jay-Z*	Roc-A-Fella 558902
9	15	68	Backstreet Boys	*Backstreet Boys*	Jive 41589
10	12	3	Home For Christmas	*'N sync*	RCA 67726

Billboard · DECEMBER 19, 1998 · THE BILLBOARD 200

TW	LW	WK	Title	Artist	Label
1	1	3	**Double Live**	*Garth Brooks*	Capitol 97424
2	3	5	**These Are Special Times**	*Celine Dion*	550 Music 69523
3	6	37	'N Sync	*'N Sync*	RCA 67613
4	4	3	Spirit	*Jewel*	Atlantic 82950
5	2	2	Garage Inc.	*Metallica*	Elektra 62299
6	5	2	Greatest Hits	*2Pac*	Amaru 90301
7	7	3	#1's	*Mariah Carey*	Columbia 69670
8	9	69	Backstreet Boys	*Backstreet Boys*	Jive 41589
9	10	4	Home For Christmas	*'N sync*	RCA 67726
10	14	57	Come On Over	*Shania Twain*	Mercury 536003

Billboard · DECEMBER 26, 1998 · THE BILLBOARD 200

TW	LW	WK	Title	Artist	Label
1	1	4	**Double Live**	*Garth Brooks*	Capitol 97424
2	2	6	**These Are Special Times**	*Celine Dion*	550 Music 69523
3	3	38	'N Sync	*'N Sync*	RCA 67613
4	4	4	Spirit	*Jewel*	Atlantic 82950
5	8	70	Backstreet Boys	*Backstreet Boys*	Jive 41589
6	7	4	#1's	*Mariah Carey*	Columbia 69670
7	9	5	**Home For Christmas**	*'N sync*	RCA 67726
8	10	58	Come On Over	*Shania Twain*	Mercury 536003
9	11	4	Americana	*The Offspring*	Columbia 69661
10	5	3	Garage Inc.	*Metallica*	Elektra 62299

THE ARTISTS

This section lists alphabetically, by artist, all Top 10 albums listed in the chart section of this book. The peak date and peak positiion are shown to the left of each album title. A superior number is shown to the right of all #1 and #2 albums which indicates the total weeks the album held that position.

Significant artist name variations (duo recordings, etc.) are shown in bold capital letters below the album title.

◆ All albums listed on the first Top 10 chart of 1963 (August 17, 1963) are included in this section. Some of these albums peaked on the earlier monaural and stereo charts (see page 8 for an explanation). A small bold diamond is shown after the date (ex.: 8/17/63◆) of these albums. The date shown is the first date the album appeared in the Top 10 in this book.

• All albums listed on the last Top 10 chart of 1998 (December 26, 1998) are included in this section. Some of these albums peaked in 1999. A small bold bullet is shown after the date (ex.: 12/5/98•) of these albums. The date shown is the first date the album appeared in the Top 10 in this book.

A

ABDUL, Paula
10/7/89 1^{10} Forever Your Girl
6/16/90 7 Shut Up And Dance
6/8/91 1^{2} Spellbound

AC/DC
12/20/80 4 Back In Black
5/30/81 3 Dirty Deeds Done Dirt Cheap
12/26/81 1^{3} For Those About To Rock We Salute You
10/27/90 2^{1} The Razors Edge
10/14/95 4 Ballbreaker

ACE OF BASE
4/2/94 1^{2} The Sign

ADAMS, Bryan
6/25/83 8 Cuts Like A Knife
8/10/85 1^{2} Reckless
5/16/87 7 Into The Fire
10/12/91 6 Waking Up The Neighbours
1/29/94 6 So Far So Good

AEROSMITH
6/26/76 3 Rocks
11/4/89 5 Pump
5/8/93 1^{1} Get A Grip
11/19/94 6 Big Ones
4/5/97 1^{1} Nine Lives

AIR SUPPLY
8/1/81 10 The One That You Love
11/19/83 7 Greatest Hits

ALABAMA
4/30/83 10 The Closer You Get...

ALICE IN CHAINS
10/17/92 6 Dirt
2/12/94 1^{1} Jar Of Flies
11/25/95 1^{1} Alice In Chains
8/17/96 3 MTV Unplugged

ALL-4-ONE
7/9/94 7 All-4-One

ALLMAN BROTHERS BAND, The
4/29/72 4 Eat A Peach
9/8/73 1^{5} Brothers And Sisters
10/11/75 5 Win, Lose Or Draw
4/14/79 9 Enlightened Rouges

ALPERT, Herb, & The Tijuana Brass
11/27/65 1^{8} Whipped Cream & Other Delights
3/5/66 1^{6} Going Places
3/26/66 10 The Lonely Bull
4/16/66 6 South Of The Border
5/28/66 1^{9} What Now My Love
12/31/66 2^{6} S.R.O.
6/17/67 1^{1} Sounds Like
2/10/68 4 Herb Alpert's Ninth
7/27/68 1^{2} The Beat Of The Brass
12/1/79 6 Rise

AMERICA
3/25/72 1^{5} America
1/6/73 9 Homecoming
11/23/74 3 Holiday
6/14/75 4 Hearts
12/20/75 3 History/America's Greatest Hits

AMES, Ed
4/22/67 4 My Cup Runneth Over

AMOS, Tori
2/10/96 2^{1} Boys For Pele
5/23/98 5 From The Choirgirl Hotel

ANIMALS, The
10/31/64 7 The Animals
3/26/66 6 The Best Of The Animals

ANKA, Paul
10/26/74 9 Anka

ANOTHER BAD CREATION
6/22/91 7 Coolin' At The Playground Ya' Know!

ANTHRAX
6/12/93 7 Sound Of White Noise

AQUA
10/18/97 7 Aquarium

ARMSTRONG, Louis
6/13/64 1^{6} Hello, Dolly!

ARNOLD, Eddy
1/8/66 7 My World

ARRESTED DEVELOPMENT
3/20/93 7 3 Years, 5 Months & 2 Days In The Life Of ...

ASIA
5/15/82 1^{9} Asia
9/10/83 6 Alpha

ASSOCIATION, The
11/12/66 5 And Then...Along Comes The Association
9/2/67 8 Insight Out
2/8/69 4 Greatest Hits

ASTLEY, Rick
3/12/88 10 Whenever You Need Somebody

ATLANTA RHYTHM SECTION
6/3/78 7 Champagne Jam

AVERAGE WHITE BAND
2/22/75 1^{1} AWB
8/16/75 4 Cut The Cake
8/28/76 9 Soul Searching

B

BABYFACE
11/16/96 6 The Day

BACHMAN-TURNER OVERDRIVE
8/31/74 4 Bachman-Turner Overdrive II
10/19/74 1^{1} Not Fragile
6/28/75 5 Four Wheel Drive

BACKSTREET BOYS
1/31/98 4 Backstreet Boys

BAD COMPANY
9/28/74 1^{1} Bad Company
5/31/75 3 Straight Shooter
4/10/76 5 Run With The Pack
5/19/79 3 Desolation Angels

BADU, Erykah
3/1/97 2^{1} Baduizm
12/6/97 4 Live

BAEZ, Joan
12/21/63◆ 10 Joan Baez In Concert
1/18/64 7 Joan Baez In Concert, Part 2
12/11/65 10 Farewell, Angelina

BAKER, Anita
12/24/88 1^{4} Giving You The Best That I Got
8/25/90 5 Compositions
10/1/94 3 Rhythm Of Love

BAND, The
2/7/70 9 The Band
10/3/70 5 Stage Fright
11/11/72 6 Rock Of Ages
2/16/74 1^{4} Planet Waves
8/3/74 3 Before The Flood
9/6/75 7 The Basement Tapes
BOB DYLAN & THE BAND (above 3)

BANGLES
1/31/87 2^{2} Different Light

BARENAKED LADIES
7/25/98 3 Stunt

BEACH BOYS, The
11/23/63 7 Surfer Girl
2/8/64 4 Little Deuce Coupe
8/22/64 4 All Summer Long
12/5/64 1^{4} Beach Boys Concert
5/1/65 4 The Beach Boys Today!
9/4/65 2^{1} Summer Days (And Summer Nights!!)
1/1/66 6 Beach Boys' Party!
7/2/66 10 Pet Sounds
9/24/66 8 Best Of The Beach Boys
10/5/74 1^{1} Endless Summer
6/28/75 8 Spirit Of America
8/28/76 8 15 Big Ones

BEASTIE BOYS
3/7/87 1^{7} Licensed To Ill
5/9/92 10 Check Your Head
6/18/94 1^{1} Ill Communication
8/1/98 1^{3} Hello Nasty

BEATLES, The
2/15/64 1^{11} Meet The Beatles!
2/29/64 2^{9} Introducing...The Beatles
5/2/64 1^{5} The Beatles' Second Album
7/25/64 1^{14} A Hard Day's Night
8/22/64 2^{9} Something New
1/2/65 7 The Beatles' Story
1/9/65 1^{9} Beatles '65

BEATLES, The — Cont'd

7/10/65 1^{6} Beatles VI
9/11/65 1^{9} Help!
1/8/66 1^{6} Rubber Soul
7/30/66 1^{5} "Yesterday"...And Today
9/10/66 1^{6} Revolver
7/1/67 1^{15} Sgt. Pepper's Lonely Hearts Club Band
1/6/68 1^{8} Magical Mystery Tour
12/28/68 1^{9} The Beatles [White Album]
3/1/69 2^{2} Yellow Submarine
11/1/69 1^{11} Abbey Road
3/28/70 2^{4} Hey Jude
6/13/70 1^{4} Let It Be
5/19/73 3 The Beatles/ 1962-1966
5/26/73 1^{1} The Beatles/ 1967-1970
7/10/76 2^{2} Rock 'N' Roll Music
6/11/77 2^{2} The Beatles At The Hollywood Bowl
12/24/94 3 Live At The BBC
12/9/95 1^{3} Anthology 1
4/6/96 1^{1} Anthology 2
11/16/96 1^{1} Anthology 3

BECK, Jeff

6/7/75 4 Blow By Blow

BEE GEES

12/2/67 7 Bee Gees' 1st
9/6/69 9 Best Of Bee Gees
11/13/76 8 Children Of The World
7/30/77 8 Here At Last...Bee Gees...Live
1/21/78 1^{24} Saturday Night Fever
3/3/79 1^{6} Spirits Having Flown
1/12/80 1^{1} Bee Gees Greatest
8/27/83 6 Staying Alive

BELL BIV DeVOE

6/2/90 5 Poison

BENATAR, Pat

1/17/81 2^{5} Crimes Of Passion
8/15/81 1^{1} Precious Time
1/15/83 4 Get Nervous

BENEDICTINE MONKS OF SANTO DOMINGO DE SILOS, The

5/28/94 3 Chant

BENSON, George

7/31/76 1^{2} Breezin'
3/19/77 9 In Flight
4/15/78 5 Weekend In L.A.
4/21/79 7 Livin' Inside Your Love
10/4/80 3 Give Me The Night

BERRY, Chuck

10/28/72 8 The London Chuck Berry Sessions

B-52's, The

3/10/90 4 Cosmic Thing

BIG BROTHER & THE HOLDING COMPANY

10/12/68 1^{8} Cheap Thrills

BIG PUNISHER

5/16/98 5 Capital Punishment

BIZZY BONE

10/24/98 3 Heaven'z Movie

BLACK, Clint

8/8/92 8 The Hard Way

BLACK CROWES, The

4/6/91 4 Shake Your Money Maker
5/30/92 1^{1} The Southern Harmony and Musical Companion

BLACK SABBATH

9/25/71 8 Master Of Reality

BLACKSTREET

9/28/96 3 Another Level

BLIGE, Mary J.

9/26/92 6 What's The 411?
1/28/95 7 My Life
5/10/97 1^{1} Share My World

BLIND FAITH

9/20/69 1^{2} Blind Faith

BLIND MELON

9/11/93 3 Blind Melon

BLONDIE

4/28/79 6 Parallel Lines
2/21/81 7 Autoamerican

BLOOD, SWEAT & TEARS

3/29/69 1^{7} Blood, Sweat & Tears
8/8/70 1^{2} Blood, Sweat & Tears 3
8/21/71 10 B, S & T; 4

BLUES BROTHERS

2/3/79 1^{1} Briefcase Full Of Blues

BLUES TRAVELER

9/9/95 8 four

BOLTON, Michael

4/14/90 3 Soul Provider
5/25/91 1^{1} Time, Love & Tenderness
11/21/92 1^{1} Timeless (The Classics)
12/4/93 3 The One Thing
10/7/95 5 Greatest Hits 1985-1995

BONE THUGS-N-HARMONY

8/12/95 1^{2} E. 1999 Eternal
8/16/97 1^{1} The Art Of War

BON JOVI

10/25/86 1^{8} Slippery When Wet
10/15/88 1^{4} New Jersey
9/8/90 3 Blaze Of Glory/Young Guns II
11/21/92 5 Keep The Faith
11/5/94 8 Cross Road
7/15/95 9 These Days

BOONE, Debby

12/24/77 6 You Light Up My Life

BOSTON

12/4/76 3 Boston
9/16/78 1^{2} Don't Look Back
11/1/86 1^{4} Third Stage
6/25/94 7 Walk On

BOWIE, David

7/20/74 5 Diamond Dogs
11/30/74 8 David Live
4/12/75 9 Young Americans
2/28/76 3 Station To Station
7/17/76 10 Changesonebowie
6/25/83 4 Let's Dance

BOYZ II MEN

8/24/91 3 Cooleyhighharmony
9/17/94 1^{5} II
10/11/97 1^{1} Evolution

BRANDY

7/4/98 2^{1} Never S-a-y Never

BRASS CONSTRUCTION

5/15/76 10 Brass Construction

BRAXTON, Toni

2/26/94 1^{2} Toni Braxton
7/6/96 2^{1} Secrets

BREAD

3/25/72 3 Baby I'm-A Want You
5/12/73 2^{1} The Best Of Bread

BRICKELL, Edie, & New Bohemians

2/18/89 4 Shooting Rubberbands At The Stars

BROOKS, Garth

9/28/91 1^{18} Ropin' The Wind
2/8/92 3 No Fences
9/19/92 2^{1} Beyond The Season
10/10/92 1^{7} The Chase
9/18/93 1^{5} In Pieces
1/7/95 1^{8} The Hits
12/9/95 2^{2} Fresh Horses
12/13/97 1^{5} Sevens
5/23/98 1^{2} The Limited Series
12/5/98 1^{5} Double Live

BROOKS & DUNN

1/23/93 10 Brand New Man
3/20/93 9 Hard Workin' Man
5/4/96 5 Borderline
10/11/97 4 The Greatest Hits Collection

BROTHERS JOHNSON, The

6/5/76 9 Look Out For #1
9/16/78 7 Blam!!
5/3/80 5 Light Up The Night

BROWN, Arthur, The Crazy World Of

11/16/68 7 The Crazy World Of Arthur Brown

BROWN, Bobby

1/21/89 1^{6} Don't Be Cruel
2/17/90 9 Dance!...Ya Know It!
9/12/92 2^{1} Bobby

BROWN, Foxy

12/7/96 7 Ill Na Na

BROWN, James

8/17/63◆ 2^{2} Live At The Apollo
4/18/64 10 Pure Dynamite! Live At The Royal

BROWNE, Jackson
12/18/76 **5** The Pretender
3/4/78 **3** Running On Empty
9/13/80 **1^{1}** Hold Out
9/10/83 **8** Lawyers In Love

B.T. EXPRESS
3/1/75 **5** Do It ('Til You're Satisfied)

BUFFETT, Jimmy
5/20/78 **10** Son Of A Son Of A Sailor
6/11/94 **5** Fruitcakes
8/19/95 **6** Barometer Soup
6/22/96 **4** Banana Wind

BUSH
2/3/96 **4** Sixteen Stone
12/7/96 **1^{2}** Razorblade Suitcase

BUSTA RHYMES
4/13/96 **6** The Coming
10/4/97 **3** When Disaster Strikes...

BYRDS, The
8/7/65 **6** Mr. Tambourine Man
10/14/67 **6** The Byrds' Greatest Hits

C

CAFFERTY, John, & The Beaver Brown Band
10/6/84 **9** Eddie And The Cruisers

CAMEO
12/20/86 **8** Word Up!

CAMPBELL, Glen
10/12/68 **5** Gentle On My Mind
12/21/68 **1^{5}** Wichita Lineman
5/3/69 **2^{1}** Galveston

CAM'RON
8/8/98 **6** Confessions Of Fire

C & C MUSIC FACTORY
3/30/91 **2^{7}** Gonna Make You Sweat

CANDLEBOX
8/27/94 **7** Candlebox

CANIBUS
9/26/98 **2^{1}** Can-I-Bus

CAPPADONNA
4/11/98 **3** The Pillage

CAPTAIN & TENNILLE
8/2/75 **2^{1}** Love Will Keep Us Together
5/1/76 **9** Song Of Joy

CAREY, Mariah
3/2/91 **1^{11}** Mariah Carey
10/5/91 **4** Emotions
7/4/92 **3** MTV Unplugged EP
12/25/93 **1^{8}** Music Box
12/17/94 **3** Merry Christmas
10/21/95 **1^{6}** Daydream
10/4/97 **1^{1}** Butterfly
12/5/98 **4** #1's

CARLISLE, Bob
6/28/97 **1^{2}** Butterfly Kisses (Shades Of Grace)

CARLOS, Walter
4/26/69 **10** Switched-On Bach

CARNES, Kim
6/27/81 **1^{4}** Mistaken Identity

CARPENTER, Mary Chapin
10/22/94 **10** Stones In The Road

CARPENTERS
12/5/70 **2^{1}** Close To You
7/3/71 **2^{2}** Carpenters
8/12/72 **4** A Song For You
7/21/73 **2^{1}** Now & Then
1/5/74 **1^{1}** The Singles 1969-1973

CARRERAS, DOMINGO, PAVAROTTI
9/17/94 **4** The 3 Tenors In Concert 1994

CARS, The
8/25/79 **3** Candy-O
9/20/80 **5** Panorama
12/19/81 **9** Shake It Up
7/14/84 **3** Heartbeat City

CARTER, Deana
1/18/97 **10** Did I Shave My Legs For This?

CASH, Johnny
8/23/69 **1^{4}** Johnny Cash At San Quentin
3/14/70 **6** Hello, I'm Johnny Cash

CASSIDY, Shaun
10/8/77 **3** Shaun Cassidy
1/14/78 **6** Born Late

CHAMBERS BROTHERS, The
10/26/68 **4** The Time Has Come

CHAPIN, Harry
12/28/74 **4** Verities & Balderdash

CHAPMAN, Tracy
8/27/88 **1^{1}** Tracy Chapman
11/11/89 **9** Crossroads
6/15/96 **4** New Beginning

CHARLES, Ray
10/12/63 **2^{2}** Ingredients In A Recipe For Soul
4/18/64 **9** Sweet & Sour Tears

CHEAP TRICK
7/14/79 **4** Cheap Trick At Budokan
10/27/79 **6** Dream Police

CHEECH & CHONG
9/30/72 **2^{1}** Big Bambu
10/6/73 **2^{1}** Los Cochinos
11/23/74 **5** Cheech & Chong's Wedding Album

CHER
10/14/89 **10** Heart Of Stone

CHIC
12/23/78 **4** C'est Chic
9/22/79 **5** Risque

CHICAGO
5/23/70 **4** Chicago II
2/20/71 **2^{2}** Chicago III
1/15/72 **3** Chicago At Carnegie Hall
8/19/72 **1^{9}** Chicago V
7/28/73 **1^{5}** Chicago VI
4/27/74 **1^{1}** Chicago VII
5/3/75 **1^{2}** Chicago VIII
12/13/75 **1^{5}** Chicago IX - Chicago's Greatest Hits
8/7/76 **3** Chicago X
11/12/77 **6** Chicago XI
9/18/82 **9** Chicago 16
1/26/85 **4** Chicago 17

CHI-LITES, The
6/24/72 **5** A Lonely Man

CHUMBAWAMBA
1/17/98 **3** Tubthumper

CINDERELLA
2/7/87 **3** Night Songs
9/10/88 **10** Long Cold Winter

CLAPTON, Eric
7/1/72 **6** History Of Eric Clapton
8/17/74 **1^{4}** 461 Ocean Boulevard
4/1/78 **2^{5}** Slowhand
1/13/79 **8** Backless
6/21/80 **2^{6}** Just One Night
4/25/81 **7** Another Ticket
3/13/93 **1^{3}** Unplugged
10/1/94 **1^{1}** From The Cradle
3/28/98 **4** Pilgrim

CLARK, Dave, Five
5/23/64 **3** Glad All Over
7/18/64 **5** The Dave Clark Five Return!
2/27/65 **6** Coast To Coast
4/30/66 **9** The Dave Clark Five's Greatest Hits

CLASH, The
1/22/83 **7** Combat Rock

CLUB NOUVEAU
4/25/87 **6** Life, Love & Pain

CMW — see MC EIHT

C-MURDER
4/4/98 **3** Life Or Death

COCKER, Joe
10/10/70 **2^{1}** Mad Dogs & Englishmen

COLE, Natalie
4/23/77 **8** Unpredictable
7/27/91 **1^{5}** Unforgettable With Love

COLE, Nat "King"
3/27/65 **4** L-O-V-E
4/24/65◆ **3** Ramblin' Rose

COLLINS, Judy
12/28/68 **5** Wildflowers

COLLINS, Phil
7/4/81 **7** Face Value
2/5/83 **8** Hello, I Must Be Going!
3/30/85 **1^{7}** No Jacket Required
1/6/90 **1^{3}** ...But Seriously

COLOR ME BADD
8/31/91 **3** C.M.B.

COLTER, Jessi — see JENNINGS, Waylon

COMMODORES
6/18/77 **3** Commodores
12/10/77 **3** Commodores Live!
7/8/78 **3** Natural High
10/27/79 **3** Midnight Magic
7/12/80 **7** Heroes

CONNIFF, Ray
9/24/66 **3** Somewhere My Love

COOLIDGE, Rita
10/15/77 **6** Anytime...Anywhere

COOLIO
8/6/94 **8** It Takes A Thief
3/23/96 **9** Gangsta's Paradise

COOPER, Alice
7/29/72 **2^{3}** School's Out
4/21/73 **1^{1}** Billion Dollar Babies
1/12/74 **10** Muscle Of Love
11/16/74 **8** Alice Cooper's Greatest Hits
6/21/75 **5** Welcome To My Nightmare

COSBY, Bill
7/30/66 **7** Wonderfulness
6/17/67 **2^{1}** Revenge
5/4/68 **7** To Russell, My Brother, Whom I Slept With

COSTELLO, Elvis
3/10/79 **10** Armed Forces

COUNTING CROWS
4/2/94 **4** August And Everything After
11/2/96 **1^{1}** Recovering The Satellites

COVERDALE•PAGE
4/3/93 **5** Coverdale•Page

CRANBERRIES, The
2/4/95 **6** No Need To Argue
5/18/96 **4** To The Faithful Departed

CRASH TEST DUMMIES
5/7/94 **9** God Shuffled His Feet

CREAM
6/29/68 **4** Disraeli Gears
8/10/68 **1^{4}** Wheels Of Fire
3/15/69 **2^{2}** Goodbye
9/13/69 **3** Best Of Cream

CREEDENCE CLEARWATER REVIVAL
6/7/69 **7** Bayou Country
10/4/69 **1^{4}** Green River
1/10/70 **3** Willy and the Poorboys
8/22/70 **1^{9}** Cosmo's Factory
1/30/71 **5** Pendulum

CROCE, Jim
12/8/73 **7** Life And Times
1/12/74 **1^{5}** You Don't Mess Around With Jim
1/26/74 **2^{2}** I Got A Name
11/16/74 **2^{2}** Photographs & Memories/His Greatest Hits

CROSBY, David — see NASH, Graham

CROSBY, STILLS & NASH
11/15/69 **6** Crosby, Stills & Nash
5/16/70 **1^{1}** Deja Vu
5/15/71 **1^{1}** 4 Way Street
11/2/74 **1^{1}** So Far
CROSBY, STILLS, NASH & YOUNG (above 3)
8/13/77 **2^{4}** CSN
8/14/82 **8** Daylight Again

CROSS, Christopher
9/6/80 **6** Christopher Cross

CROW, Sheryl
3/25/95 **3** Tuesday Night Music Club
10/12/96 **6** Sheryl Crow
10/17/98 **5** The Globe Sessions

CULT, The
5/27/89 **10** Sonic Temple

CULTURE CLUB
2/4/84 **2^{6}** Colour By Numbers

CURE, The
5/9/92 **2^{1}** Wish

CYPRESS HILL
8/7/93 **1^{2}** Black Sunday
11/18/95 **3** Cypress Hill III (Temples Of Boom)

CYRUS, Billy Ray
6/13/92 **1^{17}** Some Gave All
7/17/93 **3** It Won't Be The Last

D

DANIELS, Charlie, Band
9/1/79 **5** Million Mile Reflections

D'ARBY, Terence Trent
5/7/88 **4** Introducing The Hardline According To Terence Trent D'Arby

DC TALK
10/10/98 **4** Supernatural

DEEP PURPLE
8/11/73 **6** Made In Japan
8/11/73 **7** Machine Head
4/20/74 **9** Burn

DEF LEPPARD
5/14/83 **2^{2}** Pyromania
7/23/88 **1^{6}** Hysteria
4/18/92 **1^{5}** Adrenalize
10/23/93 **9** Retro Active

DEF SQUAD
7/18/98 **2^{1}** El Niño

DENVER, John
3/10/73 **4** Rocky Mountain High
3/30/74 **1^{3}** John Denver's Greatest Hits
8/10/74 **1^{1}** Back Home Again
4/12/75 **2^{2}** An Evening With John Denver
10/18/75 **1^{2}** Windsong
9/25/76 **7** Spirit
4/2/77 **6** John Denver's Greatest Hits, Volume 2

DEODATO
4/7/73 **3** Prelude

DEPECHE MODE
5/5/90 **7** Violator
4/10/93 **1^{1}** Songs Of Faith And Devotion
5/3/97 **5** Ultra

DIAMOND, Neil
9/19/70 **10** Neil Diamond/Gold
9/9/72 **5** Moods
2/17/73 **5** Hot August Night
12/15/73 **2^{1}** Jonathan Livingston Seagull
12/28/74 **3** Serenade
8/14/76 **4** Beautiful Noise
4/9/77 **8** Love At The Greek
2/11/78 **6** I'm Glad You're Here With Me Tonight
1/27/79 **4** You Don't Bring Me Flowers
2/16/80 **10** September Morn
2/7/81 **3** The Jazz Singer
11/27/82 **9** Heartlight
12/19/92 **8** The Christmas Album

DILLINGER, Daz
4/18/98 **8** Retaliation, Revenge And Get Back

DION, Celine
3/19/94 **4** The Colour Of My Love
10/5/96 **1^{3}** Falling Into You
1/17/98 **1^{1}** Let's Talk About Love
12/19/98 **2^{2}** These Are Special Times

DIRE STRAITS
4/14/79 **2^{1}** Dire Straits
8/31/85 **1^{9}** Brothers In Arms

DIXIE CHICKS
10/31/98● **4** Wide Open Spaces

D.J. JAZZY JEFF & THE FRESH PRINCE
9/24/88 **4** He's The D.J., I'm The Rapper

DJ QUIK
8/8/92 **10** Way 2 Fonky

DMX
6/6/98 **1^{1}** It's Dark And Hell Is Hot

DR. DRE
2/13/93 **3** The Chronic

DOGG POUND, Tha
11/18/95 **1^{1}** Dogg Food

DOMINGO, Plácido — see CARRERAS

DONOVAN
4/12/69 **4** Donovan's Greatest Hits

DOOBIE BROTHERS, The
7/21/73 **7** The Captain And Me
3/22/75 **4** What Were Once Vices Are Now Habits
6/28/75 **4** Stampede
5/22/76 **8** Takin' It To The Streets
1/22/77 **5** Best Of The Doobies
10/15/77 **10** Livin' On The Fault Line
4/7/79 **1^{5}** Minute By Minute
10/25/80 **3** One Step Closer

DOORS, The
9/16/67 **2^{2}** The Doors
11/18/67 **3** Strange Days
9/7/68 **1^{4}** Waiting For The Sun
8/23/69 **6** The Soft Parade
3/21/70 **4** Morrison Hotel/Hard Rock Cafe
9/5/70 **8** Absolutely Live
6/5/71 **9** L.A. Woman
4/13/91 **8** The Doors

DRU HILL
11/14/98 **2^{1}** Enter The Dru

DUPRI, Jermaine
8/8/98 **3** Jermaine Dupri Presents Life In 1472 - The Original Soundtrack

DURAN DURAN
3/12/83 **6** Rio
8/20/83 **10** Duran Duran
2/11/84 **8** Seven And The Ragged Tiger
1/5/85 **4** Arena
3/13/93 **7** Duran Duran

DYLAN, Bob
10/9/65 **6** Bringing It All Back Home
11/6/65 **3** Highway 61 Revisited
10/1/66 **9** Blonde On Blonde
6/17/67 **10** Bob Dylan's Greatest Hits
2/17/68 **2^{4}** John Wesley Harding
5/24/69 **3** Nashville Skyline
7/25/70 **4** Self Portrait
12/5/70 **7** New Morning
2/16/74 **1^{4}** Planet Waves
8/3/74 **3** Before The Flood
BOB DYLAN & THE BAND (above 2)
3/1/75 **1^{2}** Blood On The Tracks
9/6/75 **7** The Basement Tapes
BOB DYLAN & THE BAND
2/7/76 **1^{5}** Desire
9/22/79 **3** Slow Train Coming
10/18/97 **10** Time Out Of Mind

E

EAGLES
7/26/75 **1^{5}** One Of These Nights
3/13/76 **1^{5}** Eagles/Their Greatest Hits 1971-1975
1/15/77 **1^{8}** Hotel California
11/3/79 **1^{9}** The Long Run
12/20/80 **6** Eagles Live
11/26/94 **1^{2}** Hell Freezes Over

EARTH, WIND & FIRE
5/17/75 **1^{3}** That's The Way Of The World
1/17/76 **1^{3}** Gratitude
10/30/76 **2^{2}** Spirit
1/7/78 **3** All 'N All
1/27/79 **6** The Best Of Earth, Wind & Fire, Vol. I
7/14/79 **3** I Am
12/6/80 **10** Faces
11/28/81 **5** Raise!

EAZY-E
11/6/93 **5** It's On (Dr. Dre) 187um Killa
2/17/96 **3** Str8 Off Tha Streetz Of Muthaphukkin Compton

E-40
11/16/96 **4** Tha Hall Of Game

EIGHTBALL & MJG
11/18/95 **8** On Top Of The World
6/6/98 **5** Lost
EIGHTBALL

ELECTRIC LIGHT ORCHESTRA
2/21/76 **8** Face The Music
1/8/77 **5** A New World Record
1/7/78 **4** Out Of The Blue
7/21/79 **5** Discovery
10/4/80 **4** Xanadu
ELECTRIC LIGHT ORCHESTRA OLIVIA NEWTON-JOHN

ELLIOTT, Missy Misdemeanor
8/2/97 **3** Supa Dupa Fly

EMERSON, LAKE & PALMER
7/17/71 **9** Tarkus
2/19/72 **10** Pictures At An Exhibition
9/30/72 **5** Trilogy
10/26/74 **4** Welcome back, my friends, to the show that never ends- Ladies and Gentlemen

EMOTIONS, The
8/27/77 **7** Rejoice

ENIGMA
5/4/91 **6** MCMXC a.D.
5/14/94 **9** ENIGMA 2 the CROSS of changes

EN VOGUE
4/11/92 **8** Funky Divas
7/5/97 **8** EV3

ENYA
2/10/96 **9** The Memory Of Trees

ESTEFAN, Gloria
5/28/88 **6** Let It Loose
GLORIA ESTEFAN & MIAMI SOUND MACHINE
9/9/89 **8** Cuts Both Ways
3/9/91 **5** Into The Light
11/12/94 **9** Hold Me, Thrill Me, Kiss Me

ETHERIDGE, Melissa
12/2/95 **6** Your Little Secret

EUROPE
3/28/87 **8** The Final Countdown

EURYTHMICS
4/7/84 **7** Touch
7/20/85 **9** Be Yourself Tonight

EVANS, Faith
11/14/98 **6** Keep The Faith

EXTREME
6/8/91 **10** Pornograffitti
10/10/92 **10** III Sides To Every Story

F

FACES
2/5/72 **6** A Nod Is As Good As A Wink...To A Blind Horse

FAGEN, Donald
6/12/93 **10** Kamakiriad

FAITH NO MORE
7/4/92 **10** Angel Dust

FALCO
4/26/86 **3** Falco 3

FAT BOYS
9/12/87 **8** Crushin'

FAT JOE
9/19/98 **7** Don Cartagena

FELICIANO, Jose
11/2/68 **2^{3}** Feliciano!

FIEND
5/23/98 **8** There's One In Every Family

5TH DIMENSION, The
8/12/67 **8** Up, Up And Away
6/28/69 **2^{2}** The Age Of Aquarius
6/20/70 **5** The 5th Dimension/ Greatest Hits

FINE YOUNG CANNIBALS
6/3/89 **1^{7}** The Raw & The Cooked

FIRM, The
11/8/97 **1^{1}** The Firm - The Album

FIXX, The
10/15/83 **8** Reach The Beach

FLACK, Roberta
4/29/72 **1^{5}** First Take
7/15/72 **3** Roberta Flack & Donny Hathaway
9/22/73 **3** Killing Me Softly
4/29/78 **8** Blue Lights In The Basement

FLEETWOOD MAC
9/4/76 **1^{1}** Fleetwood Mac
4/2/77 **1^{31}** Rumours
11/17/79 **4** Tusk
8/7/82 **1^{5}** Mirage
5/23/87 **7** Tango In The Night
9/6/97 **1^{1}** The Dance

FLOATERS, The
9/24/77 **10** Floaters

FLOCK OF SEAGULLS, A
10/23/82 **10** A Flock Of Seagulls

FOCUS
6/2/73 **8** Moving Waves

FOGELBERG, Dan
10/14/78 **8** Twin Sons Of Different Mothers
DAN FOGELBERG & TIM WEISBERG
3/8/80 **3** Phoenix
10/10/81 **6** The Innocent Age

FOGERTY, John
3/23/85 **1^{1}** Centerfield

FOO FIGHTERS
6/7/97 **10** The Colour And The Shape

FOREIGNER
10/22/77 **4** Foreigner
9/9/78 **3** Double Vision
10/27/79 **5** Head Games
8/22/81 **1^{10}** 4
2/12/83 **10** Foreigner Records
2/2/85 **4** Agent Provocateur

4 SEASONS, The
4/18/64 **6** Dawn (Go Away) and 11 other great songs
9/19/64 **7** Rag Doll
2/19/66 **10** The 4 Seasons' Gold Vault of Hits

FOUR TOPS
11/25/67 **4** The Four Tops Greatest Hits

FOXWORTHY, Jeff
9/23/95 **8** Games Rednecks Play

FRAMPTON, Peter
4/10/76 **1^{10}** Frampton Comes Alive!
7/16/77 **2^{4}** I'm In You

FRANKLIN, Aretha
5/27/67 **2^{3}** I Never Loved A Man The Way I Love You
10/7/67 **5** Aretha Arrives
3/16/68 **2^{2}** Aretha: Lady Soul
8/17/68 **3** Aretha Now
6/26/71 **7** Aretha Live At Fillmore West
7/22/72 **7** Amazing Grace

FRANKLIN, Kirk
10/17/98 **7** The Nu Nation Project

FUGEES
5/25/96 **1^{4}** The Score

G

GABRIEL, Peter
7/26/86 **2^{3}** So
10/17/92 **2^{1}** Us

GANG STARR
4/18/98 **6** Moment Of Truth

GARFUNKEL, Art
11/10/73 **5** Angel Clare
11/29/75 **7** Breakaway

GAYE, Marvin
7/31/71 **6** What's Going On
10/20/73 **2^{1}** Let's Get It On
9/7/74 **8** Marvin Gaye Live!
6/5/76 **4** I Want You
5/14/77 **3** Marvin Gaye Live At The London Palladium
12/18/82 **7** Midnight Love

GAYNOR, Gloria
3/31/79 **4** Love Tracks

GEILS, J., Band
6/16/73 **10** Bloodshot
2/6/82 **1^{4}** Freeze-Frame

GENESIS
11/14/81 **7** Abacab
8/21/82 **10** Three Sides Live
12/3/83 **9** Genesis
8/2/86 **3** Invisible Touch
11/30/91 **4** We Can't Dance

GENIUS/GZA
11/25/95 **9** Liquid Swords

GENTRY, Bobbie
10/14/67 **1^{2}** Ode To Billie Joe

GEORGIA SATELLITES
2/28/87 **5** Georgia Satellites

GETO BOYS, The
4/20/96 **6** The Resurrection

GETZ, Stan/Joao Gilberto
8/8/64 **2^{2}** Getz/Gilberto

GHOSTFACE KILLAH
11/16/96 **2^{1}** Ironman

GIBB, Andy
7/8/78 **7** Shadow Dancing

GIBSON, Debbie
2/27/88 **7** Out Of The Blue
3/11/89 **1^{5}** Electric Youth

GILL, Johnny
7/28/90 **8** Johnny Gill

GILL, Vince
9/26/92 **10** I Still Believe In You
7/2/94 **6** When Love Finds You

GIN BLOSSOMS
3/2/96 **10** Congratulations I'm Sorry

GLASER, Tompall — see JENNINGS, Waylon

GOD'S PROPERTY
6/14/97 **3** God's Property

GO-GO'S
3/6/82 **1^{6}** Beauty And The Beat
9/18/82 **8** Vacation

GOLDSBORO, Bobby
6/15/68 **5** Honey

GOODIE MOB
4/25/98 **6** Still Standing

GOULET, Robert
2/27/65 **5** My Love Forgive Me

GRAND FUNK RAILROAD
8/29/70 **6** Closer To Home
12/26/70 **5** Live Album
5/29/71 **6** Survival
1/1/72 **5** E Pluribus Funk
12/2/72 **7** Phoenix
9/22/73 **2^{2}** We're An American Band
5/4/74 **5** Shinin' On
2/22/75 **10** All The Girls In The World Beware!!!

GRANT, Amy
8/31/91 **10** Heart In Motion
12/26/92 **2^{1}** Home For Christmas
9/27/97 **8** Behind The Eyes

GRANT, Eddy
7/16/83 **10** Killer On The Rampage

GRATEFUL DEAD
8/22/87 **6** In The Dark

GREAT WHITE
7/8/89 **9** ...Twice Shy

GREEN, Al
4/1/72 **8** Let's Stay Together
12/30/72 **4** I'm Still In Love With You
6/23/73 **10** Call Me

GREEN DAY
1/28/95 **2^{2}** Dookie
10/28/95 **2^{1}** Insomniac
11/1/97 **10** Nimrod

GUESS WHO, The
5/16/70 **9** American Woman

GUNS N' ROSES
8/6/88 **1^{5}** Appetite For Destruction
5/13/89 **2^{1}** G N' R Lies
10/5/91 **1^{2}** Use Your Illusion II
10/5/91 **2^{2}** Use Your Illusion I
12/11/93 **4** The Spaghetti Incident?

H

HALL, Daryl, & John Oates
2/13/82 **5** Private Eyes
1/15/83 **3** H_2O
1/28/84 **7** Rock 'N Soul, Part 1
12/1/84 **5** Big Bam Boom

HAMLISCH, Marvin
5/4/74 **1^{5}** The Sting

HAMMER — see M.C.

HANSON
7/12/97 **2^{1}** Middle Of Nowhere
12/6/97 **7** Snowed In
5/30/98 **6** 3 Car Garage: The Indie Recordings '95-'96

HARRIS, Emmylou — see PARTON, Dolly

HARRIS, Richard
7/13/68 **4** A Tramp Shining

HARRISON, George
1/2/71 **1^{7}** All Things Must Pass
1/22/72 **2^{6}** The Concert For Bangla Desh
6/23/73 **1^{5}** Living In The Material World
1/25/75 **4** Dark Horse
10/25/75 **8** Extra Texture (Read All About It)
1/23/88 **8** Cloud Nine

HATHAWAY, Donny — see FLACK, Roberta

HAYES, Isaac
10/25/69 **8** Hot Buttered Soul
6/13/70 **8** The Isaac Hayes Movement
11/6/71 **1^{1}** Shaft
1/8/72 **10** Black Moses

HEART
10/30/76 **7** Dreamboat Annie
7/9/77 **9** Little Queen
3/22/80 **5** Bebe Le Strange
12/21/85 **1^{1}** Heart
8/1/87 **2^{3}** Bad Animals
5/19/90 **3** Brigade

HEATWAVE
6/3/78 **10** Central Heating

HEAVY D
5/10/97 **9** Waterbed Hev

HENDRIX, Jimi
3/9/68 **3** Axis: Bold As Love
10/5/68 **5** Are You Experienced?
11/16/68 **1^{2}** Electric Ladyland
9/6/69 **6** Smash Hits
5/16/70 **5** Band Of Gypsys
3/27/71 **3** The Cry Of Love
5/10/75 **5** Crash Landing

HENLEY, Don
9/23/89 **8** The End Of The Innocence

HERMAN'S HERMITS
4/24/65 **2^{4}** Introducing Herman's Hermits
7/10/65 **2^{6}** Herman's Hermits On Tour
12/25/65 **5** The Best Of Herman's Hermits

HILL, Faith
5/9/98 **7** Faith

HILL, Lauryn
9/12/98 **1^{4}** The Miseducation Of Lauryn Hill

HIRT, Al
3/7/64 **3** Honey In The Horn
6/27/64 **6** Cotton Candy
11/21/64 **9** Sugar Lips

HOLE
9/26/98 **9** Celebrity Skin

HONEYDRIPPERS, The
12/1/84 **4** Volume One

HOOTIE & THE BLOWFISH
5/27/95 **1^{8}** Cracked Rear View
5/11/96 **1^{2}** Fairweather Johnson
10/3/98 **4** Musical Chairs

HORNSBY, Bruce, & The Range
3/7/87 **3** The Way It Is
7/9/88 **5** scenes from the southside

HOUSTON, Whitney
3/8/86 **1^{14}** Whitney Houston
6/27/87 **1^{11}** Whitney
12/8/90 **3** I'm Your Baby Tonight
12/12/92 **1^{20}** The Bodyguard
12/28/96 **3** The Preacher's Wife

HUMAN LEAGUE, The
7/10/82 **3** Dare

HUMBLE PIE
5/13/72 **6** Smokin'

HUMPERDINCK, Engelbert
9/9/67 **7** Release Me
2/3/68 **10** The Last Waltz
2/14/70 **5** Engelbert Humperdinck

I

IAN, Janis
9/20/75 **1^{1}** Between The Lines

ICE CUBE
11/16/91 **2^{1}** Death Certificate
12/5/92 **1^{1}** The Predator
12/25/93 **5** Lethal Injection
12/5/98 **7** War & Peace Vol. I (The War Disc)

IDOL, Billy
7/14/84 **6** Rebel Yell
12/13/86 **6** Whiplash Smile
11/14/87 **10** Vital Idol

IGLESIAS, Julio
10/27/84 **5** 1100 Bel Air Place

IMBRUGLIA, Natalie
3/28/98 **10** Left Of The Middle

IMPRESSIONS, The
10/10/64 **8** Keep On Pushing

INDIGO GIRLS
5/28/94 **9** Swamp Ophelia
5/17/97 **7** Shaming Of The Sun

INXS
2/27/88 **3** Kick
10/20/90 **5** X

IRON BUTTERFLY
4/5/69 **3** Ball
8/9/69 **4** In-A-Gadda-Da-Vida

ISAAK, Chris
4/6/91 **7** Heart Shaped World

ISLEY BROTHERS, The
11/10/73 **8** 3 + 3
9/13/75 **1^{1}** The Heat Is On
7/4/76 **9** Harvest For The World
5/21/77 **6** Go For Your Guns
6/3/78 **4** Showdown
5/17/80 **8** Go All The Way

J

JACKSON, Alan
7/23/94 **5** Who I Am
11/11/95 **5** The Greatest Hits Collection
9/19/98 **4** High Mileage

JACKSON, Freddie
12/7/85 **10** Rock Me Tonight

JACKSON, Janet
7/5/86 **1^{2}** Control
10/28/89 **1^{4}** Janet Jackson's Rhythm Nation 1814
6/5/93 **1^{6}** janet.
11/4/95 **3** Design Of A Decade 1986/1996
10/25/97 **1^{1}** The Velvet Rope

JACKSON, Jermaine
7/12/80 **6** Let's Get Serious

JACKSON, Joe
11/27/82 **4** Night And Day

JACKSON, Michael
11/11/72 **5** Ben
2/16/80 **3** Off The Wall
2/26/83 **1^{37}** Thriller
9/26/87 **1^{6}** Bad
12/14/91 **1^{4}** Dangerous
7/8/95 **1^{2}** HIStory: Past, Present And Future - Book I

JACKSON 5/JACKSONS
THE JACKSON 5:
4/25/70 **5** Diana Ross Presents The Jackson 5
7/11/70 **4** ABC
10/24/70 **4** Third Album
8/5/72 **7** Lookin' Through The Windows

THE JACKSONS:
11/8/80 **10** Triumph
8/4/84 **4** Victory

JAMES, Rick
8/1/81 **3** Street Songs

JAMES, Tommy, & The Shondells
3/1/69 **8** Crimson & Clover

JARREAU, Al
10/10/81 **9** Breakin' Away

JARS OF CLAY
10/4/97 **8** Much Afraid

JAY-Z
11/22/97 **3** In My Lifetime, Vol. 1
10/17/98 **1^{5}** Vol. 2...Hard Knock Life

JEFFERSON AIRPLANE/ STARSHIP
JEFFERSON AIRPLANE:
8/5/67 **3** Surrealistic Pillow
11/2/68 **6** Crown Of Creation
JEFFERSON STARSHIP:
9/6/75 **1^{4}** Red Octopus
8/14/76 **3** Spitfire
5/6/78 **5** Earth
2/2/80 **10** Freedom At Point Zero
STARSHIP:
3/1/86 **7** Knee Deep In The Hoopla

JENNINGS, Waylon/ Willie Nelson/ Jessi Colter/ Tompall Glaser
4/3/76 **10** The Outlaws

JETHRO TULL
6/5/71 **7** Aqualung
6/3/72 **1^{2}** Thick As A Brick
12/23/72 **3** Living In The Past
8/18/73 **1^{1}** A Passion Play
12/28/74 **2^{3}** War Child
10/25/75 **7** Minstrel In The Gallery
5/14/77 **8** Songs From The Wood

JETT, Joan, & The Blackhearts
4/10/82 **2^{3}** I Love Rock-n-Roll

JEWEL
3/1/97 **4** Pieces Of You
12/5/98 **3** Spirit

JODECI
2/5/94 **3** Diary Of A Mad Band
8/5/95 **2^{1}** The Show - The After-Party - The Hotel

JOEL, Billy
2/18/78 **2^{6}** The Stranger
11/18/78 **1^{8}** 52nd Street
6/14/80 **1^{6}** Glass Houses
10/17/81 **8** Songs In The Attic
11/20/82 **7** The Nylon Curtain
10/8/83 **4** An Innocent Man
9/28/85 **6** Greatest Hits, Volume I & Volume II
9/20/86 **7** The Bridge
12/16/89 **1^{1}** Storm Front
8/28/93 **1^{3}** River Of Dreams
9/6/97 **9** Greatest Hits Volume III

JOHN, Elton
2/6/71 **4** Elton John
2/13/71 **5** Tumbleweed Connection
2/5/72 **8** Madman Across The Water
7/15/72 **1^{5}** Honky Chateau
3/3/73 **1^{2}** Don't Shoot Me I'm Only The Piano Player
11/10/73 **1^{8}** Goodbye Yellow Brick Road
7/13/74 **1^{4}** Caribou
11/30/74 **1^{10}** Elton John - Greatest Hits
3/1/75 **6** Empty Sky
6/7/75 **1^{7}** Captain Fantastic And The Brown Dirt Cowboy
11/8/75 **1^{3}** Rock Of The Westies
6/12/76 **4** Here And There
11/13/76 **3** Blue Moves
9/5/92 **8** The One
10/11/97 **9** The Big Picture

JONES, Howard
6/29/85 **10** Dream Into Action

JONES, Jack
10/29/66 **9** The Impossible Dream

JONES, Quincy
11/2/74 **6** Body Heat
4/24/82 **10** The Dude
2/3/90 **9** Back On The Block

JONES, Rickie Lee
6/30/79 **3** Rickie Lee Jones
9/26/81 **5** Pirates

JONES, Tom
4/12/69 **5** Help Yourself
7/12/69 **4** This Is Tom Jones
12/6/69 **3** Tom Jones Live In Las Vegas
5/30/70 **6** Tom

JOPLIN, Janis
11/8/69 **5** I Got Dem Ol' Kozmic Blues Again Mama!
2/27/71 **1^{9}** Pearl
6/24/72 **4** Joplin In Concert

JOURNEY
4/26/80 **8** Departure
3/14/81 **9** Captured
9/12/81 **1^{1}** Escape
3/12/83 **2^{9}** Frontiers
5/31/86 **4** Raised On Radio
2/11/89 **10** Greatest Hits
11/9/96 **3** Trial By Fire

JUNIOR M.A.F.I.A.
9/16/95 **8** Conspiracy

K

KAEMPFERT, Bert
4/17/65 **5** Blue Midnight

KANE & ABEL
7/25/98 **5** Am I My Brothers Keeper

KANSAS
4/2/77 **5** Leftoverture
5/6/78 **4** Point Of Know Return
6/30/79 **10** Monolith

KC & The SUNSHINE BAND
12/20/75 **4** KC And The Sunshine Band

K-CI & JOJO
3/28/98 **6** Love Always

KELLY, R.
3/12/94 **2^{1}** 12 Play
12/2/95 **1^{1}** R. Kelly
11/28/98 **2^{1}** R.

KENNEDY, John Fitzgerald
2/1/64 **8** The Presidential Years 1960-1963
2/8/64 **5** That Was The Week That Was

KENNY G
7/25/87 **6** Duotones
12/3/88 **8** Silhouette
1/30/93 **2^{11}** Breathless
12/10/94 **1^{3}** Miracles - The Holiday Album
10/26/96 **2^{1}** The Moment

KING, Carole
6/19/71 **1^{15}** Tapestry
1/1/72 **1^{3}** Music
12/16/72 **2^{5}** Rhymes & Reasons
7/21/73 **6** Fantasy
11/9/74 **1^{1}** Wrap Around Joy
3/27/76 **3** Thoroughbred

KINGSTON TRIO, The
9/21/63 **7** Sunny Side!

KINKS, The
11/19/66 **9** The Kinks Greatest Hits!

KISS
12/13/75 **9** Alive!
7/30/77 **4** Love Gun
1/7/78 **7** Alive II
7/21/79 **9** Dynasty
6/6/92 **6** Revenge
6/5/93 **9** Alive III
10/10/98 **3** Psycho-Circus

KNACK, The
8/11/79 **1^{5}** Get The Knack

KNIGHT, Gladys, & The Pips
5/19/73 **9** Neither One Of Us
12/29/73 **9** Imagination

KOOL & THE GANG
3/7/81 **10** Celebrate!

KORN
11/2/96 **3** Life Is Peachy
9/5/98 **1^{1}** Follow The Leader

KRAFTWERK
5/3/75 **5** Autobahn

KRAVITZ, Lenny
9/30/95 **10** Circus

KRIS KROSS
5/23/92 **1^{2}** Totally Krossed Out

KRS-ONE
6/7/97 **3** I Got Next

KURUPT
10/24/98 **8** Kuruption!

L

LaBELLE, Patti
3/22/75 **7** Nightbirds
LaBELLE
7/19/86 **1^{1}** Winner In You

LAUPER, Cyndi
6/2/84 **4** She's So Unusual
11/15/86 **4** True Colors

LED ZEPPELIN
5/17/69 **10** Led Zeppelin
12/27/69 **1^{7}** Led Zeppelin II
10/31/70 **1^{4}** Led Zeppelin III
12/18/71 **2^{4}** Led Zeppelin IV (untitled)
5/12/73 **1^{2}** Houses Of The Holy
3/22/75 **1^{6}** Physical Graffiti
5/1/76 **1^{2}** Presence
11/13/76 **2^{3}** The Soundtrack From The Film "The Song Remains The Same"
9/15/79 **1^{7}** In Through The Out Door
1/15/83 **6** Coda

LENNON, John
2/7/70 **10** The Plastic Ono Band - Live Peace In Toronto 1969
1/30/71 **6** John Lennon/Plastic Ono Band
10/30/71 **1^{1}** Imagine
12/8/73 **9** Mind Games
11/16/74 **1^{1}** Walls And Bridges
4/19/75 **6** Rock 'N' Roll
12/27/80 **1^{8}** Double Fantasy

LETTERMEN, The
3/9/68 **10** The Lettermen!!!...and "Live!"

LEWIS, Gary, & The Playboys
12/31/66 **10** Golden Greats

LEWIS, Huey, & the News
6/30/84 **1^{1}** Sports
10/18/86 **1^{1}** Fore!

LEWIS, Ramsey, Trio
11/6/65 **2^{1}** The In Crowd

LIGHTFOOT, Gordon
6/22/74 **1^{2}** Sundown
4/26/75 **10** Cold On The Shoulder

LIPPS, INC.
5/31/80 **5** Mouth To Mouth

LISA LISA & CULT JAM
6/20/87 **7** Spanish Fly

LITTLE RIVER BAND
9/29/79 **10** First Under The Wire

LIVE
5/6/95 **1^{1}** Throwing Copper
3/8/97 **1^{1}** Secret Samadhi

LIVING COLOUR
5/6/89 **6** Vivid

LL COOL J
8/29/87 **3** Bigger And Deffer
7/22/89 **6** Walking With A Panther
4/17/93 **5** 14 Shots To The Dome
11/1/97 **7** Phenomenon

LOGGINS, Kenny
10/7/78 **7** Nightwatch

LOGGINS & MESSINA
1/5/74 **10** Full Sail
8/10/74 **5** On Stage
12/28/74 **8** Mother Lode

LOPEZ, Trini
8/24/63 **2^{6}** Trini Lopez At PJ'S

LOS INDIOS TABAJARAS
1/4/64 **7** Maria Elena

LOS LOBOS
9/12/87 **1^{2}** La Bamba

LOST BOYZ
6/22/96 **6** Legal Drug Money
7/5/97 **9** Love, Peace And Nappiness

LOVERBOY
5/1/82 **7** Get Lucky
7/23/83 **7** Keep It Up

LOVE UNLIMITED
2/16/74 **3** Under The Influence Of...

LOVE UNLIMITED ORCHESTRA
3/30/74 **8** Rhapsody In White

LOVIN' SPOONFUL, The
6/11/66 **10** Daydream
5/6/67 **3** The Best Of The Lovin' Spoonful

LOX, The
1/31/98 **3** Money, Power & Respect

LSG
11/29/97 **4** Levert - Sweat - Gill

LYNYRD SKYNYRD
5/31/75 **9** Nuthin' Fancy
11/13/76 **9** One More From The Road
12/10/77 **5** Street Survivors

M

MADONNA
10/20/84 **8** Madonna
2/9/85 **1^{3}** Like A Virgin
8/16/86 **1^{5}** True Blue
9/12/87 **7** Who's That Girl
4/22/89 **1^{6}** Like A Prayer
6/23/90 **2^{3}** I'm Breathless
1/26/91 **2^{2}** The Immaculate Collection
11/7/92 **2^{1}** Erotica
11/12/94 **3** Bedtime Stories
11/25/95 **6** Something To Remember
3/21/98 **2^{2}** Ray Of Light

MAMAS & THE PAPAS, The
5/21/66 **1^{1}** If You Can Believe Your Eyes And Ears
10/22/66 **4** The Mamas & The Papas
4/8/67 **2^{7}** The Mamas & The Papas Deliver
12/9/67 **5** Farewell To The First Golden Era

MANCINI, Henry
2/22/64 **6** Charade
8/15/64 **8** The Pink Panther
8/2/69 **5** A Warm Shade Of Ivory

MANDELL, Steve — see WEISSBERG, Eric

MANFRED MANN'S EARTH BAND
3/12/77 **10** The Roaring Silence

MANGIONE, Chuck
6/17/78 **2^{2}** Feels So Good
3/15/80 **8** Fun and Games

MANILOW, Barry
2/22/75 **9** Barry Manilow II
2/7/76 **5** Tryin' To Get The Feeling
4/16/77 **6** This One's For You
7/16/77 **1^{1}** Barry Manilow/Live
4/8/78 **3** Even Now
2/10/79 **7** Greatest Hits
11/17/79 **9** One Voice

MANNHEIM STEAMROLLER
12/30/95 **3** Christmas In The Aire

MARILYN MANSON
10/26/96 **3** Antichrist Superstar
10/3/98 **1^{1}** Mechanical Animals

MARLEY, Bob, & The Wailers
7/4/76 **8** Rastaman Vibration

MARTIN, Dean
10/31/64 **2^{4}** Everybody Loves Somebody
12/19/64 **9** The Door Is Still Open To My Heart

MARTIN, Steve
11/26/77 **10** Let's Get Small
12/9/78 **2^{6}** A Wild And Crazy Guy

MARTINO, Al
11/30/63 **9** Painted, Tainted Rose
4/16/66 **8** Spanish Eyes

MARX, Richard
9/3/88 **8** Richard Marx
9/2/89 **1^1** Repeat Offender

MASE
11/15/97 **1^2** Harlem World

MASTER P
9/20/97 **1^1** Ghetto D
6/20/98 **1^2** MP Da Last Don

MATCHBOX 20
9/6/97 **5** Yourself Or Someone Like You

MATHIS, Johnny
6/25/66 **9** The Shadow Of Your Smile
6/3/78 **9** You Light Up My Life

MATTHEWS, Dave, Band
5/18/96 **2^1** Crash
11/15/97 **3** Live At Red Rocks 8.15.95
5/16/98 **1^1** Before These Crowded Streets

MAURIAT, Paul
3/2/68 **1^5** Blooming Hits

MAXWELL
7/18/98 **3** Embrya

MAYFIELD, Curtis
10/21/72 **1^4** Superfly

MC EIHT Featuring CMW
8/6/94 **5** We Come Strapped

M.C. HAMMER
6/9/90 **1^{21}** Please Hammer Don't Hurt 'Em
11/23/91 **2^2** Too Legit To Quit
HAMMER

McCARTNEY, Paul/ Wings
5/23/70 **1^3** McCartney
8/21/71 **2^2** Ram
1/22/72 **10** Wild Life
6/2/73 **1^3** Red Rose Speedway
4/13/74 **1^4** Band On The Run
7/19/75 **1^1** Venus And Mars
4/24/76 **1^7** Wings At The Speed Of Sound
1/22/77 **1^1** Wings Over America
5/6/78 **2^6** London Town
7/21/79 **8** Back To The Egg
6/21/80 **3** McCartney II
5/29/82 **1^3** Tug Of War
6/14/97 **2^1** Flaming Pie

McDONALD, Michael
10/2/82 **6** If That's What It Takes

McENTIRE, Reba
1/23/93 **8** It's Your Call
10/23/93 **5** Greatest Hits Volume Two
5/21/94 **2^1** Read My Mind
10/21/95 **5** Starting Over
6/20/98 **8** If You See Him

McFERRIN, Bobby
10/8/88 **5** Simple Pleasures

McGRAW, Tim
5/21/94 **1^2** Not A Moment Too Soon
10/7/95 **4** All I Want
6/21/97 **2^1** Everywhere

McKENZIE, Bob & Doug
4/3/82 **8** Great White North

McLACHLAN, Sarah
8/2/97 **2^1** Surfacing

McLEAN, Don
1/22/72 **1^7** American Pie

MEAT LOAF
10/30/93 **1^1** Bat Out Of Hell II: Back Into Hell

MEGADETH
8/1/92 **2^1** Countdown To Extinction
11/19/94 **4** Youthanasia
7/5/97 **10** Cryptic Writings

MELLENCAMP, John Cougar
9/11/82 **1^9** American Fool
1/28/84 **9** Uh-Huh
11/16/85 **2^3** Scarecrow
10/3/87 **6** The Lonesome Jubilee
6/17/89 **7** Big Daddy
9/25/93 **7** Human Wheels
9/28/96 **9** Mr. Happy Go Lucky

MELVIN, Harold, & The Blue Notes
2/28/76 **9** Wake Up Everybody

MEN AT WORK
11/13/82 **1^{15}** Business As Usual
5/21/83 **3** Cargo

MENDES, Sergio, & Brasil '66
12/10/66 **7** Sergio Mendes & Brasil '66
7/13/68 **5** Look Around
1/11/69 **3** Fool On The Hill

MERCHANT, Natalie
6/6/98 **8** Ophelia

METALLICA
10/8/88 **6** ...And Justice For All
8/31/91 **1^4** Metallica
6/22/96 **1^4** Load
12/6/97 **1^1** Reload
12/12/98 **2^1** Garage Inc.

METHOD MAN
12/3/94 **4** Tical
12/5/98 **2^1** Tical 2000: Judgement Day

MFSB
4/20/74 **4** Love Is The Message

MIAMI SOUND MACHINE — see ESTEFAN, Gloria

MIA X
11/21/98 **7** Mama Drama

MICHAEL, George/ Wham!
WHAM!:
3/2/85 **1^3** Make It Big
8/23/86 **10** Music From The Edge Of Heaven
GEORGE MICHAEL:
1/16/88 **1^{12}** Faith
10/20/90 **2^1** Listen Without Prejudice
6/1/96 **6** Older

MIDLER, Bette
3/24/73 **9** The Divine Miss M
1/19/74 **6** Bette Midler
6/10/89 **2^3** Beaches
1/5/91 **6** Some People's Lives

MILES, Buddy — see SANTANA, Carlos

MILLER, Roger
4/17/65 **4** The Return Of Roger Miller
2/26/66 **6** Golden Hits

MILLER, Steve, Band
12/22/73 **2^1** The Joker
10/23/76 **3** Fly Like An Eagle
6/25/77 **2^2** Book Of Dreams
9/18/82 **3** Abracadabra

MILLI VANILLI
9/23/89 **1^8** Girl You Know It's True

MIRACLES, The
2/26/66 **8** Going To A Go-Go
3/23/68 **7** Greatest Hits, Vol. 2

MR. MISTER
3/1/86 **1^1** Welcome To The Real World

MITCHELL, Joni
3/2/74 **2^4** Court And Spark
2/8/75 **2^1** Miles Of Aisles
1/3/76 **4** The Hissing Of Summer Lawns

MOBB DEEP
12/7/96 **6** Hell On Earth

MONICA
8/1/98 **8** The Boy Is Mine

MONKEES, The
11/12/66 **1^{13}** The Monkees
2/11/67 **1^{18}** More Of The Monkees
6/24/67 **1^1** Headquarters
12/2/67 **1^5** Pisces, Aquarius, Capricorn & Jones Ltd.
5/18/68 **3** The Birds, The Bees & The Monkees

MONTENEGRO, Hugo
6/29/68 **9** Music From "A Fistful Of Dollars" & "For A Few Dollars More" & "The Good, The Bad And The Ugly"

MONTGOMERY, John Michael
2/19/94 **1^1** Kickin' It Up
6/3/95 **5** John Michael Montgomery

MOODY BLUES, The
10/10/70 **3** A Question Of Balance
9/4/71 **2^{3}** Every Good Boy Deserves Favour
10/21/72 **3** Days Of Future Passed
12/9/72 **1^{5}** Seventh Sojourn
7/25/81 **1^{3}** Long Distance Voyager
6/28/86 **9** The Other Side Of Life

MORISSETTE, Alanis
10/7/95 **1^{12}** Jagged Little Pill
11/21/98 **1^{2}** Supposed Former Infatuation Junkie

MO THUGS FAMILY
11/23/96 **2^{1}** Family Scriptures

MÖTLEY CRÜE
8/17/85 **6** Theatre Of Pain
6/27/87 **2^{1}** Girls, Girls, Girls
10/14/89 **1^{2}** Dr. Feelgood
10/19/91 **2^{1}** Decade Of Decadence - '81-'91
4/2/94 **7** Motley Crue
7/12/97 **4** Generation Swine

MULDAUR, Maria
5/18/74 **3** Maria Muldaur

MYLES, Alannah
4/7/90 **5** Alannah Myles

MYSTIKAL
11/29/97 **3** Unpredictable

N

NAS
7/20/96 **1^{4}** It Was Written

NASH, Graham/David Crosby
5/20/72 **4** Graham Nash/David Crosby
11/29/75 **6** Wind On The Water

NAUGHTY BY NATURE
3/13/93 **3** 19 Naughty III
6/17/95 **3** Poverty's Paradise

NELSON, Willie
4/3/76 **10** The Outlaws
WAYLON JENNINGS/ WILLIE NELSON/ JESSI COLTER/ TOMPALL GLASER
7/10/82 **2^{4}** Always On My Mind

NEW CHRISTY MINSTRELS, The
6/6/64 **9** Today

NEW EDITION
2/23/85 **6** New Edition
9/28/96 **1^{1}** Home Again

NEW KIDS ON THE BLOCK
9/9/89 **1^{2}** Hangin' Tough
12/23/89 **9** Merry, Merry Christmas
6/30/90 **1^{1}** Step By Step

NEWMAN, Randy
2/18/78 **9** Little Criminals

NEWTON-JOHN, Olivia
10/12/74 **1^{1}** If You Love Me, Let Me Know
3/15/75 **1^{1}** Have You Never Been Mellow
2/24/79 **7** Totally Hot
10/4/80 **4** Xanadu
ELECTRIC LIGHT ORCHESTRA OLIVIA NEWTON-JOHN
12/12/81 **6** Physical

NEW VAUDEVILLE BAND, The
1/21/67 **5** Winchester Cathedral

NICKS, Stevie
9/5/81 **1^{1}** Bella Donna
7/23/83 **5** The Wild Heart
7/8/89 **10** The Other Side Of The Mirror

NIGHT RANGER
7/27/85 **10** 7 Wishes

NILSSON
4/1/72 **3** Nilsson Schmilsson

NINE INCH NAILS
10/10/92 **7** Broken
3/26/94 **2^{1}** The Downward Spiral

NIRVANA
1/11/92 **1^{2}** Nevermind
10/9/93 **1^{1}** In Utero
11/19/94 **1^{1}** MTV Unplugged In New York
10/19/96 **1^{1}** From The Muddy Banks Of The Wishkah

NO DOUBT
12/21/96 **1^{9}** Tragic Kingdom

NOREAGA
8/1/98 **3** N.O.R.E.

NOTORIOUS B.I.G., The
4/12/97 **1^{4}** Life After Death

NOVA, Aldo
5/22/82 **8** Aldo Nova

'N SYNC
10/10/98 **2^{3}** 'N Sync
11/28/98 **7** Home For Christmas

N.W.A.
6/22/91 **1^{1}** EFIL4ZAGGIN

O

OASIS
2/24/96 **4** (What's The Story) Morning Glory?
9/13/97 **2^{1}** Be Here Now

OCEAN, Billy
11/24/84 **9** Suddenly
6/28/86 **6** Love Zone

O'CONNOR, Sinéad
4/28/90 **1^{6}** I Do Not Want What I Haven't Got

OFFSPRING, The
10/29/94 **4** Smash
2/22/97 **9** Ixnay On The Hombre
12/5/98● **2^{2}** Americana

OHIO PLAYERS
2/8/75 **1^{1}** Fire
9/27/75 **2^{1}** Honey

O'JAYS, The
11/4/72 **10** Back Stabbers
1/24/76 **7** Family Reunion
6/24/78 **6** So Full Of Love

OLDFIELD, Mike
3/30/74 **3** Tubular Bells

OL DIRTY BASTARD
4/15/95 **7** Return To The 36 Chambers: The Dirty Version

ONYX
6/20/98 **10** Shut 'Em Down

ORBISON, Roy
4/8/89 **5** Mystery Girl

OSBORNE, Joan
3/16/96 **9** Relish

OSBOURNE, Ozzy
4/5/86 **6** The Ultimate Sin
6/13/87 **6** Tribute
OZZY OSBOURNE/ RANDY RHOADS
10/5/91 **7** No More Tears
11/11/95 **4** Ozzmosis

OSMOND, Donny
7/22/72 **6** Portrait Of Donny

OSMONDS, The
3/11/72 **10** Phase-III

O'SULLIVAN, Gilbert
9/30/72 **9** Gilbert O'Sullivan-Himself

OUTFIELD, The
6/14/86 **9** Play Deep

OUTKAST
9/14/96 **2^{1}** ATLiens
10/17/98 **2^{1}** Aquemini

P

PABLO CRUISE
8/26/78 **6** Worlds Away

PAGE, Jimmy, & Robert Plant
11/26/94 **4** No Quarter
5/9/98 **8** Walking Into Clarksdale

PALMER, Robert
5/17/86 **8** Riptide

PANTERA
4/9/94 **1^{1}** Far Beyond Driven
5/25/96 **4** The Great Southern Trendkill

PARSONS, Alan, Project

10/15/77 9 I Robot
10/9/82 7 Eye In The Sky

PARTON, Dolly/ Linda Ronstadt/ Emmylou Harris

5/2/87 6 Trio

PARTRIDGE FAMILY, The

1/2/71 4 The Partridge Family Album
4/24/71 3 Up To Date
9/25/71 9 The Partridge Family Sound Magazine

PAVAROTTI, Luciano — see CARRERAS

PEACHES & HERB

5/5/79 2^{6} 2 Hot!

PEARL JAM

8/22/92 2^{4} Ten
11/6/93 1^{5} Vs.
12/24/94 1^{1} Vitalogy
9/14/96 1^{2} No Code
2/21/98 2^{1} Yield

PENDERGRASS, Teddy

8/11/79 5 Teddy

PETER, PAUL & MARY

8/17/63◆ 1^{7} Peter, Paul and Mary
8/17/63◆ 2^{8} (Moving)
11/2/63 1^{5} In The Wind
9/26/64 4 Peter, Paul and Mary In Concert
5/22/65 8 A Song Will Rise

PET SHOP BOYS

6/21/86 7 Please

PETTY, Tom, &The Heartbreakers

2/9/80 2^{7} Damn The Torpedoes
7/25/81 5 Hard Promises
1/22/83 9 Long After Dark
5/11/85 7 Southern Accents
7/8/89 3 Full Moon Fever
2/5/94 5 Greatest Hits
11/19/94 8 Wildflowers

PHISH

11/2/96 7 Billy Breathes
11/14/98 8 The Story Of The Ghost

PINK FLOYD

4/28/73 1^{1} The Dark Side Of The Moon
10/4/75 1^{2} Wish You Were Here
3/5/77 3 Animals
1/19/80 1^{15} The Wall
5/7/83 6 The Final Cut
10/24/87 3 A Momentary Lapse of Reason
4/23/94 1^{4} The Division Bell
6/24/95 1^{1} Pulse

PLANT, Robert

8/7/82 5 Pictures At Eleven
10/8/83 8 The Principle Of Moments
5/21/88 6 Now And Zen

POINTER SISTERS

10/6/84 8 Break Out

POISON

5/23/87 3 Look What The Cat Dragged In
6/18/88 2^{1} Open Up and Say...Ahh!
8/18/90 2^{1} Flesh & Blood

POLICE, The

2/7/81 5 Zenyatta Mondatta
12/5/81 2^{6} Ghost In The Machine
7/23/83 1^{17} Synchronicity
12/20/86 7 Every Breath You Take - The Singles

PORNO FOR PYROS

5/15/93 3 Porno For Pyros

POWER STATION, The

7/27/85 6 The Power Station

PRESIDENTS OF THE UNITED STATES OF AMERICA, The

3/9/96 6 The Presidents Of The United States Of America

PRESLEY, Elvis

11/16/63 3 Elvis' Golden Records, Volume 3
1/18/64 3 Fun in Acapulco
5/2/64 6 Kissin' Cousins
1/2/65 1^{1} Roustabout
6/12/65 8 Girl Happy
10/23/65 10 Elvis For Everyone!
1/1/66 8 Harum Scarum
2/8/69 8 Elvis
5/5/73 1^{1} Aloha from Hawaii via Satellite
9/17/77 3 Moody Blue
11/19/77 5 Elvis In Concert

PRETENDERS

6/7/80 9 Pretenders
9/12/81 10 Pretenders II
2/25/84 5 Learning To Crawl

PRIMUS

5/8/93 7 Pork Soda
6/24/95 8 Tales From The Punchbowl

PRINCE

5/28/83 9 Prince **1999**
8/4/84 1^{24} Purple Rain
6/1/85 1^{3} Around the World in a Day
5/3/86 3 Parade
5/9/87 6 Sign "O" The Times
7/22/89 1^{6} Batman
9/22/90 6 Graffiti Bridge
11/9/91 3 Diamonds And Pearls
10/31/92 5 (untitled)
10/14/95 6 The Gold Experience

PROCOL HARUM

7/22/72 5 Procol Harum Live In Concert with the Edmonton Symphony Orchestra

PRODIGY

7/19/97 1^{1} The Fat Of The Land

PUBLIC ENEMY

5/26/90 10 Fear Of A Black Planet
10/19/91 4 Apocalypse 91...The Enemy Strikes Black

PUFF DADDY & THE FAMILY

8/9/97 1^{4} No Way Out

Q

QUARTERFLASH

2/27/82 8 Quarterflash

QUEEN

4/17/76 4 A Night At The Opera
2/12/77 5 A Day At The Races
2/18/78 3 News Of The World
1/6/79 6 Jazz
9/20/80 1^{5} The Game
5/9/92 4 Classic Queen

QUEENSRYCHE

10/6/90 7 Empire
11/5/94 3 Promised Land

QUIET RIOT

11/26/83 1^{1} Metal Health

R

RAEKWON

8/19/95 4 Only Built 4 Cuban Linx...

RAFFERTY, Gerry

7/8/78 1^{1} City to City

RAGE AGAINST THE MACHINE

5/4/96 1^{1} Evil Empire

RAITT, Bonnie

4/7/90 1^{3} Nick Of Time
8/17/91 2^{2} Luck Of The Draw
4/16/94 1^{1} Longing In Their Hearts

RAKIM

11/22/97 4 The 18th Letter

RASCALS, The

9/23/67 5 Groovin'
3/30/68 9 Once Upon A Dream
9/28/68 1^{1} Time Peace/The Rascals' Greatest Hits

RATT

8/4/84 7 Out Of The Cellar
7/27/85 7 Invasion Of Your Privacy

RAWLS, Lou

7/23/66 4 Lou Rawls Live!
11/12/66 7 Lou Rawls Soulin'
9/11/76 7 All Things In Time

REDDING, Otis

3/16/68 9 History Of Otis Redding
4/13/68 4 The Dock Of The Bay

REDDY, Helen

9/22/73	**8**	Long Hard Climb
1/4/75	**8**	Free And Easy
1/17/76	**5**	Helen Reddy's Greatest Hits

RED HOT CHILI PEPPERS

5/16/92	**3**	Blood Sugar Sex Magik
9/30/95	**4**	One Hot Minute

REED, Lou

11/23/74	**10**	Sally Can't Dance

REEVES, Jim

11/14/64	**9**	The Best Of Jim Reeves

R.E.M.

11/7/87	**10**	R.E.M. No. 5: Document
5/18/91	1^{2}	Out Of Time
10/24/92	2^{2}	Automatic For The People
10/15/94	1^{2}	Monster
9/28/96	2^{1}	New Adventures In Hi-Fi
11/14/98	**3**	Up

REO SPEEDWAGON

2/21/81	1^{15}	Hi Infidelity
8/7/82	**7**	Good Trouble
3/16/85	**7**	Wheels are turnin'

REVERE, Paul, & The Raiders

4/2/66	**5**	Just Like Us!
8/6/66	**9**	Midnight Ride
2/11/67	**9**	The Spirit Of '67
6/10/67	**9**	Greatest Hits

RICH, Charlie

2/9/74	**8**	Behind Closed Doors

RICHIE, Lionel

11/27/82	**3**	Lionel Richie
12/3/83	1^{3}	Can't Slow Down
9/27/86	1^{2}	Dancing On The Ceiling

RIGHTEOUS BROTHERS, The

2/27/65	**4**	You've Lost That Lovin' Feelin'
8/14/65	**9**	Just Once In My Life...
5/21/66	**7**	Soul & Inspiration

RIMES, LeAnn

8/3/96	**3**	Blue
3/1/97	1^{1}	Unchained Melody/ The Early Years
9/27/97	1^{3}	You Light Up My Life - Inspirational Songs
5/30/98	**3**	Sittin' On Top Of The World

RIPERTON, Minnie

3/29/75	**4**	Perfect Angel

RIVERS, Johnny

8/31/68	**5**	Realization

ROBINSON, Smokey

6/6/81	**10**	Being With You

ROGERS, Kenny

2/2/80	**5**	Kenny
12/13/80	1^{2}	Kenny Rogers' Greatest Hits
8/15/81	**6**	Share Your Love
11/12/83	**6**	Eyes That See In The Dark

ROLLING STONES, The

12/12/64	**3**	12 x 5
4/24/65	**5**	The Rolling Stones, Now!
8/21/65	1^{3}	Out Of Our Heads
1/8/66	**4**	December's Children (and everybody's)
5/14/66	**3**	Big Hits (High Tide And Green Grass)
8/13/66	2^{2}	Aftermath
1/21/67	**6**	got Live if you want it!
3/11/67	2^{4}	Between The Buttons
8/12/67	**3**	Flowers
1/6/68	2^{6}	Their Satanic Majesties Request
1/11/69	**5**	Beggars Banquet
10/11/69	2^{2}	Through The Past, Darkly (Big Hits Vol. 2)
12/27/69	**3**	Let It Bleed
10/24/70	**6**	'Get Yer Ya-Ya's Out!'
5/22/71	1^{4}	Sticky Fingers
2/12/72	**4**	Hot Rocks 1964-1971
6/17/72	1^{4}	Exile On Main St.
2/17/73	**9**	More Hot Rocks (big hits & fazed cookies)
10/13/73	1^{4}	Goats Head Soup
11/23/74	1^{1}	It's Only Rock 'N Roll
7/12/75	**8**	Metamorphosis
7/19/75	**6**	Made In The Shade
5/15/76	1^{4}	Black And Blue
10/29/77	**5**	Love You Live
7/15/78	1^{2}	Some Girls
7/26/80	1^{7}	Emotional Rescue
9/19/81	1^{9}	Tattoo You
7/10/82	**5**	"Still Life" (American Concert 1981)
12/10/83	**4**	Undercover
5/3/86	**4**	Dirty Work
10/7/89	**3**	Steel Wheels
7/30/94	2^{1}	Voodoo Lounge
12/2/95	**9**	Stripped
10/18/97	**3**	Bridges To Babylon

RONSTADT, Linda

2/15/75	1^{1}	Heart Like A Wheel
11/8/75	**4**	Prisoner In Disguise
9/25/76	**3**	Hasten Down The Wind
1/29/77	**6**	Greatest Hits
12/3/77	1^{5}	Simple Dreams
11/4/78	1^{1}	Living In The USA
3/22/80	**3**	Mad Love
12/24/83	**3**	What's New
5/2/87	**6**	Trio **DOLLY PARTON/ LINDA RONSTADT/ EMMYLOU HARRIS**
3/17/90	**7**	Cry Like A Rainstorm - Howl Like The Wind

ROSE ROYCE

11/26/77	**9**	Rose Royce II/In Full Bloom

ROSS, Diana

4/7/73	1^{2}	Lady Sings The Blues
9/1/73	**5**	Touch Me In The Morning
6/26/76	**5**	Diana Ross
10/4/80	2^{2}	Diana

ROTH, David Lee

8/30/86	**4**	Eat 'Em And Smile
2/27/88	**6**	Skyscraper

ROYAL PHILHARMONIC ORCHESTRA

1/16/82	**4**	Hooked On Classics

RUFUS Featuring Chaka Khan

9/21/74	**4**	Rags To Rufus
3/1/75	**7**	Rufusized
3/6/76	**7**	Rufus featuring Chaka Khan

RUN-D.M.C.

9/20/86	**3**	Raising Hell
7/2/88	**9**	Tougher Than Leather
5/22/93	**7**	Down With The King

RUSH

3/8/80	**4**	Permanent Waves
3/28/81	**3**	Moving Pictures
12/5/81	**10**	Exit...Stage Left
11/27/82	**10**	Signals
5/19/84	**10**	Grace Under Pressure
12/14/85	**10**	Power Windows
9/21/91	**3**	Roll The Bones
11/6/93	2^{1}	Counterparts
9/28/96	**5**	Test For Echo

RUSSELL, Leon

10/7/72	2^{4}	Carney
8/11/73	**9**	Leon Live

S

SADE

6/1/85	**5**	Diamond Life
2/15/86	1^{2}	Promise
7/2/88	**7**	Stronger Than Pride
11/21/92	**3**	Love Deluxe
11/26/94	**9**	Best Of Sade

SADLER, SSgt Barry

3/12/66	1^{5}	Ballads of the Green Berets

SALT-N-PEPA

3/5/94	**4**	Very Necessary

SANTANA

11/15/69	**4**	Santana
10/24/70	1^{6}	Abraxas
11/13/71	1^{5}	Santana III
12/2/72	**8**	Caravanserai
6/5/76	**10**	Amigos
12/10/77	**10**	Moonflower
6/13/81	**9**	Zebop!

SANTANA, Carlos, & Buddy Miles

9/2/72	**8**	Carlos Santana & Buddy Miles! Live!

SAVAGE GARDEN

4/18/98	**3**	Savage Garden

SAYER, Leo
6/4/77 **10** Endless Flight

SCAGGS, Boz
9/18/76 **2^{5}** Silk Degrees
6/14/80 **8** Middle Man

SCARFACE
9/4/93 **7** The World Is Yours
11/5/94 **2^{1}** The Diary
3/29/97 **1^{1}** The Untouchable
3/21/98 **4** My Homies

SCORPIONS
5/29/82 **10** Blackout
6/16/84 **6** Love At First Sting
6/4/88 **5** Savage Amusement

SEALS & CROFTS
12/23/72 **7** Summer Breeze
8/18/73 **4** Diamond Girl

SEEKERS, The
4/8/67 **10** Georgy Girl

SEGER, Bob, & The Silver Bullet Band
3/12/77 **8** Night Moves
7/22/78 **4** Stranger in Town
5/3/80 **1^{6}** Against The Wind
10/17/81 **3** Nine Tonight
2/19/83 **5** The Distance
5/24/86 **3** Like A Rock
9/14/91 **7** The Fire Inside
11/12/94 **8** Greatest Hits

SELENA
8/5/95 **1^{1}** Dreaming Of You
4/12/97 **7** Selena

SETZER, Brian, Orchestra
10/3/98 **9** The Dirty Boogie

SHAI
2/6/93 **6** ...If I Ever Fall In Love

SHEPARD, Vonda
5/23/98 **7** Songs From Ally McBeal

SHERMAN, Allan
8/31/63 **1^{8}** My Son, The Nut

SHERMAN, Bobby
5/16/70 **10** Here Comes Bobby

SILK
5/1/93 **7** Lose Control

SILKK THE SHOCKER
3/7/98 **3** Charge It 2 Da Game

SILVERCHAIR
9/23/95 **9** Frogstomp

SILVER CONVENTION
12/13/75 **10** Save Me

SIMON, Carly
1/13/73 **1^{5}** No Secrets
3/9/74 **3** Hotcakes
5/31/75 **10** Playing Possum
7/1/78 **10** Boys In The Trees

SIMON, Paul
4/1/72 **4** Paul Simon
7/7/73 **2^{2}** There Goes Rhymin' Simon
12/6/75 **1^{1}** Still Crazy After All These Years
4/4/87 **3** Graceland
11/24/90 **4** The Rhythm Of The Saints

SIMON & GARFUNKEL
12/24/66 **4** Parsley, Sage, Rosemary and Thyme
4/6/68 **1^{9}** The Graduate
5/25/68 **1^{7}** Bookends
3/7/70 **1^{10}** Bridge Over Troubled Water
7/29/72 **5** Simon And Garfunkel's Greatest Hits
4/17/82 **6** The Concert In Central Park

SIMPLE MINDS
3/1/86 **10** Once Upon A Time

SIMPSONS, The
1/26/91 **3** The Simpsons Sing The Blues

SINATRA, Frank
11/30/63 **8** Sinatra's Sinatra
5/9/64 **10** Days Of Wine And Roses, Moon River, and other academy award winners
9/11/65 **9** Sinatra '65
2/19/66 **9** A Man And His Music
2/26/66 **5** September Of My Years
7/23/66 **1^{1}** Strangers In The Night
10/15/66 **9** Sinatra At The Sands
2/25/67 **6** That's Life
11/20/93 **2^{3}** Duets
12/10/94 **9** Duets II

SINATRA, Nancy
4/9/66 **5** Boots

SINGING NUN, The
12/7/63 **1^{10}** The Singing Nun

SIR MIX-A-LOT
6/13/92 **9** Mack Daddy

SISTER SLEDGE
6/16/79 **3** We Are Family

SKID ROW
9/23/89 **6** Skid Row
6/29/91 **1^{1}** Slave To The Grind

SLAUGHTER
5/9/92 **8** The Wild Life

SLAYER
10/15/94 **8** Divine Intervention

SLY & THE FAMILY STONE
12/19/70 **2^{1}** Greatest Hits
12/18/71 **1^{2}** There's A Riot Goin' On
8/18/73 **7** Fresh

SMASHING PUMPKINS, The
8/14/93 **10** Siamese Dream
10/22/94 **4** Pisces Iscariot
11/11/95 **1^{1}** Mellon Collie And The Infinite Sadness
6/20/98 **2^{1}** Adore

SMITH, Will
7/11/98 **8** Big Willie Style

SNOOP DOGGY DOGG
12/11/93 **1^{3}** Doggy Style
11/30/96 **1^{1}** Tha Doggfather
8/22/98 **1^{2}** Da Game Is To Be Sold, Not To Be Told

SNOW
4/24/93 **5** 12 Inches Of Snow

SNOW, Phoebe
3/15/75 **4** Phoebe Snow

SONNY & CHÉR
9/11/65 **2^{8}** Look At Us

SOUL ASYLUM
6/24/95 **6** Let Your Dim Light Shine

SOUNDGARDEN
3/26/94 **1^{1}** Superunknown
6/8/96 **2^{1}** Down On The Upside

SPARKLE
6/6/98 **3** Sparkle

SPICE GIRLS
5/24/97 **1^{5}** Spice
2/7/98 **3** Spiceworld

SPICE 1
10/16/93 **10** 187 He Wrote

SPIN DOCTORS
4/24/93 **3** Pocket Full Of Kryptonite

SPINNERS
2/8/75 **9** New And Improved
10/4/75 **8** Pick Of The Litter

SPRINGFIELD, Rick
9/5/81 **7** Working Class Dog
5/22/82 **2^{3}** Success Hasn't Spoiled Me Yet

SPRINGSTEEN, Bruce
10/11/75 **3** Born To Run
7/29/78 **5** Darkness on the Edge of Town
11/8/80 **1^{4}** The River
10/30/82 **3** Nebraska
7/7/84 **1^{7}** Born In The U.S.A.
11/29/86 **1^{7}** Bruce Springsteen & The E Street Band Live/1975-85
11/7/87 **1^{1}** Tunnel of Love
4/18/92 **2^{2}** Human Touch
4/18/92 **3** Lucky Town
3/18/95 **1^{2}** Greatest Hits

SQUIER, Billy
9/5/81 **5** Don't Say No
9/18/82 **5** Emotions in Motion

STANSFIELD, Lisa
5/12/90 **9** Affection

STARR, Ringo
12/1/73 **2^{2}** Ringo
1/11/75 **8** Goodnight Vienna

STARS ON
7/11/81 **9** Stars On Long Play

STEELY DAN

8/17/74	8	Pretzel Logic
10/22/77	3	Aja
1/17/81	9	Gaucho

STEPPENWOLF

9/7/68	6	Steppenwolf
1/4/69	3	The Second
4/12/69	7	At Your Birthday Party
5/16/70	7	Steppenwolf 'Live'

STEVENS, Cat

4/17/71	8	Tea for the Tillerman
12/4/71	2^{1}	Teaser And The Firecat
11/18/72	1^{3}	Catch Bull At Four
9/1/73	3	Foreigner
5/11/74	2^{3}	Buddha And The Chocolate Box
8/23/75	6	Greatest Hits
7/2/77	7	Izitso

STEWART, Al

2/19/77	5	Year Of The Cat
12/16/78	10	Time Passages

STEWART, John

8/25/79	10	Bombs Away Dream Babies

STEWART, Rod

10/2/71	1^{4}	Every Picture Tells A Story
9/9/72	2^{3}	Never A Dull Moment
11/1/75	9	Atlantic Crossing
12/4/76	2^{5}	A Night On The Town
1/7/78	2^{6}	Foot Loose & Fancy Free
2/10/79	1^{3}	Blondes Have More Fun
5/11/91	10	Vagabond Heart
6/12/93	2^{5}	Unplugged...And Seated

STILLS, Stephen

1/2/71	3	Stephen Stills
8/7/71	8	Stephen Stills 2
6/10/72	4	Manassas

STING

9/7/85	2^{6}	The Dream Of The Blue Turtles
11/21/87	9	...Nothing Like The Sun
3/23/91	2^{1}	The Soul Cages
3/27/93	2^{1}	Ten Summoner's Tales
11/26/94	7	Fields Of Gold - The Best Of Sting 1984-1994
3/30/96	5	Mercury Falling

STONE TEMPLE PILOTS

7/3/93	3	Core
6/25/94	1^{3}	Purple
4/13/96	4	Tiny Music...Songs From The Vatican Gift Shop

STRAIT, George

11/28/92	6	Pure Country
10/16/93	5	Easy Come, Easy Go
5/11/96	7	Blue Clear Sky
5/17/97	1^{1}	Carrying Your Love With Me
5/9/98	2^{1}	One Step At A Time

STRAY CATS

11/27/82	2^{15}	Built For Speed

STREISAND, Barbra

11/9/63◆	8	The Barbra Streisand Album
11/9/63	2^{3}	The Second Barbra Streisand Album
3/21/64	5	The Third Album
6/6/64	2^{3}	Funny Girl
10/31/64	1^{5}	People
6/19/65	2^{3}	My Name Is Barbra
11/27/65	2^{3}	My Name Is Barbra, Two...
4/30/66	3	Color Me Barbra
1/7/67	5	Je m'appelle Barbra
3/13/71	10	Stoney End
3/16/74	1^{2}	The Way We Were
5/10/75	6	Funny Lady
2/12/77	1^{6}	A Star Is Born
7/30/77	3	Streisand Superman
1/6/79	1^{3}	Barbra Streisand's Greatest Hits, Volume 2
12/8/79	7	Wet
10/25/80	1^{3}	Guilty
12/26/81	10	Memories
1/7/84	9	Yentl
1/25/86	1^{3}	The Broadway Album
6/6/87	9	One Voice
12/10/88	10	Till I Loved You
7/17/93	1^{1}	Back To Broadway
10/15/94	10	The Concert
11/29/97	1^{1}	Higher Ground

STYX

2/25/78	6	The Grand Illusion
12/2/78	6	Pieces of Eight
11/24/79	2^{1}	Cornerstone
4/4/81	1^{3}	Paradise Theater
4/30/83	3	Kilroy Was Here

SUMMER, Donna

11/11/78	1^{1}	Live And More
6/16/79	1^{6}	Bad Girls
1/5/80	1^{1}	On The Radio-Greatest Hits-Volumes I & II
8/27/83	9	She Works Hard For The Money

SUPERTRAMP

5/19/79	1^{6}	Breakfast In America
11/1/80	8	Paris
11/27/82	5	...famous last words...

SUPREMES, The

1/16/65	2^{4}	Where Did Our Love Go
10/16/65	6	More Hits By The Supremes
4/30/66	8	I Hear A Symphony
10/22/66	1^{2}	The Supremes A' Go-Go
3/18/67	6	The Supremes sing Holland-Dozier-Holland
10/28/67	1^{5}	Diana Ross and the Supremes Greatest Hits
1/11/69	2^{1}	Diana Ross & the Supremes Join the Temptations
2/8/69	1^{1}	TCB

DIANA ROSS & THE SUPREMES with THE TEMPTATIONS
(above 2)

SURVIVOR

8/14/82	2^{4}	Eye Of The Tiger

SWEAT, Keith

8/4/90	6	I'll Give All My Love To You
7/16/94	8	Get Up On It
7/13/96	5	Keith Sweat
10/10/98	6	Still In The Game

SWV

5/22/93	8	It's About Time
5/11/96	9	New Beginning

T

TASTE OF HONEY, A

10/7/78	6	A Taste of Honey

TAYLOR, James

11/7/70	3	Sweet Baby James
7/24/71	2^{4}	Mud Slide Slim And The Blue Horizon
1/13/73	4	One Man Dog
8/16/75	6	Gorilla
8/27/77	4	JT
6/16/79	10	Flag
5/2/81	10	Dad Loves His Work
6/7/97	9	Hourglass

TAYLOR, Johnnie

4/24/76	5	Eargasm

TEARS FOR FEARS

7/13/85	1^{5}	Songs From The Big Chair
10/28/89	8	The Seeds Of Love

TECHNOTRONIC

4/7/90	10	Pump Up The Jam - The Album

TEMPLE OF THE DOG

9/5/92	5	Temple Of The Dog

TEMPTATIONS, The

2/11/67	5	The Temptations Greatest Hits
5/20/67	10	Temptations Live!
9/30/67	7	With A Lot O' Soul
1/11/69	2^{1}	Diana Ross & the Supremes Join the Temptations
2/8/69	1^{1}	TCB

DIANA ROSS & THE SUPREMES with THE TEMPTATIONS
(above 2)

5/3/69	4	Cloud Nine
11/29/69	5	Puzzle People
5/2/70	9	Psychedelic Shack
12/2/72	2^{2}	All Directions
4/21/73	7	Masterpiece

38 SPECIAL

7/17/82	10	Special Forces

THOMPSON TWINS
- 5/5/84 **10** Into The Gap

THREE DOG NIGHT
- 12/27/69 **6** Was Captured Live At The Forum
- 5/16/70 **8** It Ain't Easy
- 4/24/71 **5** Golden Bisquits
- 11/20/71 **8** Harmony
- 9/30/72 **6** Seven Separate Fools

311
- 8/23/97 **4** Transistor

TIFFANY
- 1/23/88 **1^{2}** Tiffany

TINY TIM
- 7/13/68 **7** God Bless Tiny Tim

TLC
- 7/29/95 **3** CrazySexyCool

TONE LOC
- 4/15/89 **1^{1}** Loc-ed After Dark

TOOL
- 10/19/96 **2^{1}** Ænima

TOO $HORT
- 8/1/92 **6** Shorty The Pimp
- 11/13/93 **4** Get In Where You Fit In
- 2/11/95 **6** Cocktails
- 6/8/96 **3** Gettin' It (Album Number Ten)

TOTO
- 2/17/79 **9** Toto
- 7/10/82 **4** Toto IV

TOWNSHEND, Pete
- 7/12/80 **5** Empty Glass

TRAFFIC
- 8/15/70 **5** John Barleycorn Must Die
- 2/19/72 **7** The Low Spark Of High Heeled Boys
- 3/31/73 **6** Shoot Out At The Fantasy Factory
- 11/16/74 **9** When The Eagle Flies

TRAVELING WILBURYS
- 1/28/89 **3** Volume One

TRIBE CALLED QUEST, A
- 11/27/93 **8** Midnight Marauders
- 8/17/96 **1^{1}** Beats, Rhymes And Life
- 10/17/98 **3** The Love Movement

TROWER, Robin
- 8/31/74 **7** Bridge Of Sighs
- 4/12/75 **5** For Earth Below
- 5/1/76 **10** Robin Trower Live!

TRU
- 3/8/97 **8** Tru 2 Da Game

TURNER, Tina
- 9/29/84 **3** Private Dancer
- 11/8/86 **4** Break Every Rule

TURTLES, The
- 2/3/68 **7** The Turtles! Golden Hits

TWAIN, Shania
- 2/24/96 **5** The Woman In Me
- 11/22/97 **2^{2}** Come On Over

2 PAC
- 4/1/95 **1^{4}** Me Against The World
- 3/2/96 **1^{2}** All Eyez On Me
- 11/23/96 **1^{1}** The Don Killuminati - The 7 Day Theory **MAKAVELI**
- 12/13/97 **2^{1}** R U Still Down? [Remember Me]
- 12/12/98● **3** Greatest Hits

TYLER, Bonnie
- 11/5/83 **4** Faster Than The Speed Of Night

U

UB40
- 8/21/93 **6** Promises and Lies

UGLY KID JOE
- 4/11/92 **4** As Ugly As They Want To Be

USA FOR AFRICA
- 4/27/85 **1^{3}** We Are The World

USHER
- 1/24/98 **4** My Way

U2
- 4/25/87 **1^{9}** The Joshua Tree
- 11/12/88 **1^{6}** Rattle And Hum
- 12/7/91 **1^{1}** Achtung Baby
- 7/24/93 **1^{2}** Zooropa
- 3/22/97 **1^{1}** Pop
- 11/21/98 **2^{1}** The Best Of 1980-1990/The B-Sides

V

VANDROSS, Luther
- 11/19/88 **9** Any Love
- 5/25/91 **7** Power Of Love
- 7/3/93 **6** Never Let Me Go
- 10/8/94 **5** Songs
- 10/19/96 **9** Your Secret Love

VANGELIS
- 4/17/82 **1^{4}** Chariots Of Fire

VAN HALEN
- 5/19/79 **6** Van Halen II
- 5/17/80 **6** Women and Children First
- 6/13/81 **5** Fair Warning
- 6/12/82 **3** Diver Down
- 3/17/84 **2^{5}** 1984 (MCMLXXXIV)
- 4/26/86 **1^{3}** 5150
- 6/25/88 **1^{4}** OU812
- 7/6/91 **1^{3}** For Unlawful Carnal Knowledge
- 3/13/93 **5** LIVE: Right here, right now.
- 2/11/95 **1^{1}** Balance
- 11/9/96 **1^{1}** Best Of Volume 1
- 4/4/98 **4** Van Halen 3

VANILLA FUDGE
- 11/18/67 **6** Vanilla Fudge

VANILLA ICE
- 11/10/90 **1^{16}** To The Extreme

VAUGHAN, Stevie Ray, & Double Trouble
- 11/23/91 **10** The Sky Is Crying

VAUGHAN BROTHERS, The
- 11/10/90 **7** Family Style

VILLAGE PEOPLE
- 2/17/79 **3** Cruisin'
- 5/19/79 **8** Go West

VILLAGE STOMPERS, The
- 12/28/63 **5** Washington Square

VINTON, Bobby
- 10/26/63 **10** Blue Velvet
- 3/28/64 **8** There! I've Said It Again

W

WAITE, John
- 9/29/84 **10** No Brakes

WAKEMAN, Rick
- 7/20/74 **3** Journey To The Centre Of The Earth

WALLFLOWERS, The
- 5/3/97 **4** Bringing Down The Horse

WALSH, Joe
- 11/10/73 **6** The Smoker You Drink, The Player You Get
- 8/26/78 **8** But Seriously, Folks...

WAR
- 2/17/73 **1^{2}** The World Is A Ghetto
- 10/6/73 **6** Deliver The Word
- 8/30/75 **8** Why Can't We Be Friends?
- 9/25/76 **6** Greatest Hits

WARD, Anita
- 7/7/79 **8** Songs Of Love

WARRANT
- 9/16/89 **10** Dirty Rotten Filthy Stinking Rich
- 10/13/90 **7** Cherry Pie

WARREN G
- 6/25/94 **2^{1}** Regulate...G Funk Era

WARWICK, Dionne
- 12/23/67 **10** Dionne Warwick's Golden Hits, Part One
- 4/13/68 **6** Valley of the Dolls

WASHINGTON, Grover Jr.
- 6/28/75 **10** Mister Magic
- 12/20/75 **10** Feels So Good
- 4/11/81 **5** Winelight

WATLEY, Jody
- 5/30/87 **10** Jody Watley

WEISBERG, Tim — see FOGELBERG, Dan

WEISSBERG, Eric, & Steve Mandell

3/17/73 1^{3} Dueling Banjos

WESTSIDE CONNECTION

11/9/96 2^{1} Bow Down

WHISPERS, The

4/12/80 **6** The Whispers

WHITE, Barry

10/26/74 1^{1} Can't Get Enough
11/12/77 **8** Barry White Sings For Someone You Love

WHITESNAKE

6/13/87 2^{10} Whitesnake
12/16/89 **10** Slip Of The Tongue

WHITE ZOMBIE

4/29/95 **6** Astro-Creep: 2000-Songs Of Love, Destruction And Other Synthetic Delusions Of The Electric Head

WHO, The

8/15/70 **4** Live At Leeds
9/19/70 **4** Tommy
9/11/71 **4** Who's next
11/24/73 2^{1} Quadrophenia
11/29/75 **8** The Who By Numbers
10/21/78 2^{2} Who Are You
8/18/79 **8** The Kids Are Alright
4/25/81 **4** Face Dances
10/23/82 **8** It's Hard

WILD CHERRY

9/25/76 **5** Wild Cherry

WILLIAMS, Andy

8/17/63◆ 1^{16} Days of Wine and Roses
2/29/64 **9** The Wonderful World Of Andy Williams
6/6/64 **5** The Academy Award Winning "Call Me Irresponsible"
12/12/64 **5** The Great Songs From "My Fair Lady" and other Broadway hits
5/29/65 **4** Dear Heart
6/25/66 **6** The Shadow of Your Smile
6/17/67 **5** Born Free
1/20/68 **8** Love, Andy
8/10/68 **9** Honey
6/14/69 **9** Happy Heart
4/17/71 **3** Love Story

WILLIAMS, Robin

9/15/79 **10** Reality...What A Concept

WILLIAMS, Roger

1/14/67 **7** Born Free

WILSON, Nancy

3/14/64 **4** Yesterday's Love Songs/Today's Blues
6/27/64 **10** Today, Tomorrow, Forever
11/14/64 **4** How Glad I Am
6/26/65 **7** Today-My Way

WILSON PHILLIPS

8/4/90 2^{10} Wilson Phillips
6/20/92 **4** Shadows And Light

WINTER, Edgar, Group

6/9/73 **3** They Only Come Out At Night

WINWOOD, Steve

4/18/81 **3** Arc Of A Diver
9/6/86 **3** Back in the High Life
8/20/88 1^{1} Roll With It

WITHERS, Bill

7/22/72 **4** Still Bill

WONDER, Stevie

8/24/63 1^{1} Little Stevie Wonder/ The 12 Year Old Genius
2/3/73 **3** Talking Book
9/22/73 **4** Innervisions
9/14/74 1^{2} Fulfillingness' First Finale
10/16/76 1^{14} Songs In The Key Of Life
12/8/79 **4** Journey Through The Secret Life of Plants
12/6/80 **3** Hotter Than July
6/12/82 **4** Stevie Wonder's Original Musiquarium I
11/10/84 **4** The Woman in Red
11/23/85 **5** In Square Circle

WRECKX-N-EFFECT

2/6/93 **9** Hard Or Smooth

WRIGHT, Gary

4/10/76 **7** The Dream Weaver

WU-TANG CLAN

6/21/97 1^{1} Wu-Tang Forever

WU-TANG KILLA BEES

8/8/98 **4** The Swarm

WYNONNA

4/18/92 **4** Wynonna
5/29/93 **5** Tell Me Why
3/2/96 **9** Revelations

Y

YANNI

4/9/94 **5** Live At The Acropolis

YEARWOOD, Trisha

9/13/97 **4** Songbook - A Collection Of Hits

YES

2/26/72 **4** Fragile
10/21/72 **3** Close To The Edge
3/9/74 **6** Tales From Topographic Oceans
2/1/75 **5** Relayer
10/1/77 **8** Going For The One
11/18/78 **10** Tormato
1/21/84 **5** 90125

YOUNG, Neil

10/17/70 **8** After The Gold Rush
3/11/72 1^{2} Harvest
12/9/78 **7** Comes A Time
9/1/79 **8** Rust Never Sleeps
9/3/94 **9** Sleeps With Angels
7/15/95 **5** Mirror Ball

YOUNG BLEED

2/7/98 **10** All I Have In This World, Are...My Balls And My Word

YOUNG-HOLT UNLIMITED

2/8/69 **9** Soulful Strut

YOUNG M.C.

12/9/89 **9** Stone Cold Rhymin'

Z

ZAPPA, Frank

6/29/74 **10** Apostrophe (')

ZEVON, Warren

5/13/78 **8** Excitable Boy

ZOMBIE, Rob

9/12/98 **5** Hellbilly Deluxe

ZZ TOP

8/10/74 **8** Tres Hombres
9/13/75 **10** Fandango!
11/12/83 **9** Eliminator
12/7/85 **4** Afterburner
11/17/90 **6** Recycler
5/30/92 **9** Greatest Hits

SOUNDTRACKS

4/23/94 2^{1} Above The Rim
2/27/93 **6** Aladdin
4/26/80 **7** American Gigolo
2/9/74 **10** American Graffiti
7/18/98 1^{2} Armageddon
9/19/98 2^{1} Back To Titanic
7/12/97 **5** Batman & Robin
7/8/95 **5** Batman Forever
11/21/98 **5** Belly
6/22/85 1^{2} Beverly Hills Cop
8/8/87 **8** Beverly Hills Cop II
7/25/92 **4** Boomerang
7/21/84 **8** Breakin'
7/11/98 **10** Bulworth
10/5/63 2^{2} Bye Bye Birdie
6/13/98 1^{3} City Of Angels
8/17/63◆ 2^{3} Cleopatra
1/7/89 2^{1} Cocktail
10/5/91 **8** Commitments, The
6/4/94 1^{1} Crow, The
8/31/96 **8** Crow - City Of Angels, The
9/2/95 1^{4} Dangerous Minds
8/23/97 **7** Def Jam's How To Be A Player
11/14/87 1^{18} Dirty Dancing
4/23/88 **3** Dirty Dancing, More
8/22/98 **4** Dr. Dolittle
11/5/66 1^{1} Doctor Zhivago
5/9/70 **6** Easy Rider
7/12/80 **4** Empire Strikes Back, The

SOUNDTRACKS — Cont'd

9/26/81	9	Endless Love
2/1/97	2^{2}	Evita
9/6/80	7	Fame
6/25/83	1^{2}	Flashdance
6/24/78	5	FM
4/21/84	1^{10}	Footloose
8/13/94	2^{5}	Forrest Gump
5/13/95	1^{2}	Friday
10/25/97	2^{1}	Gang Related
10/13/90	8	Ghost
8/18/84	6	Ghostbusters
6/13/98	2^{1}	Godzilla
3/20/65	1^{3}	Goldfinger
3/26/88	10	Good Morning, Vietnam
5/11/68	4	Good, The Bad And The Ugly, The
7/29/78	1^{12}	Grease
2/15/97	1^{1}	Gridlock'd
7/4/98	4	Hope Floats
9/5/98	8	How Stella Got Her Groove Back
4/25/98	3	I Got The Hook-Up!
6/7/97	4	I'm Bout It
7/10/93	7	Last Action Hero
9/7/63◆	2^{2}	Lawrence Of Arabia
7/16/94	1^{10}	Lion King, The
3/8/97	7	Lost Highway
3/6/71	2^{6}	Love Story
5/6/67	10	Man And A Woman, A
3/13/65	1^{14}	Mary Poppins
7/26/97	1^{2}	Men In Black - The Album
8/15/92	6	Mo' Money
9/23/95	10	Mortal Kombat
11/5/94	1^{2}	Murder Was The Case
2/6/65	4	My Fair Lady
5/25/91	2^{1}	New Jack City
7/6/96	8	Nutty Professor, The
4/4/98	10	Players Club, The
7/22/95	1^{1}	Pocahontas
5/3/86	5	Pretty In Pink
6/2/90	4	Pretty Woman
3/15/97	1^{1}	Private Parts
8/3/91	5	Robin Hood: Prince Of Thieves
5/14/77	4	Rocky
2/22/86	10	Rocky IV
7/12/69	2^{2}	Romeo & Juliet
1/18/97	2^{2}	Romeo & Juliet
11/7/98	5	Rush Hour
10/12/96	4	Set It Off
8/19/78	5	Sgt. Pepper's Lonely Hearts Club Band
9/2/95	4	Show, The
10/10/92	6	Singles
8/21/93	1^{1}	Sleepless In Seattle
10/18/97	4	Soul Food
11/13/65	1^{2}	Sound Of Music, The
4/5/97	2^{1}	Space Jam
8/16/97	7	Spawn - The Album
9/10/77	2^{3}	Star Wars
5/11/96	4	Sunset Park
7/22/78	10	Thank God It's Friday
3/5/66	10	Thunderball
1/24/98	1^{16}	Titanic
5/31/75	2^{1}	Tommy
7/26/86	1^{5}	Top Gun
9/6/80	3	Urban Cowboy
1/20/96	1^{5}	Waiting To Exhale
4/4/92	1^{2}	Wayne's World
3/14/98	5	Wedding Singer, The
5/5/62	1^{54}	West Side Story

ORIGINAL CASTS

1/30/65	7	Fiddler On The Roof
4/26/69	1^{13}	Hair
6/6/64	1^{1}	Hello, Dolly!

VARIOUS ARTISTS

1/15/72	8	All In The Family
9/25/93	9	Barney's Favorites - Volume 1
12/11/93	5	Beavis & Butt-head Experience, The
11/13/93	3	Common Thread: The Songs Of The Eagles
12/14/96	6	Dr. Dre Presents ...The Aftermath
10/5/96	10	ESPN Presents Jock Jams Volume 2
8/29/98	4	Funkmaster Flex: The Mix Tape Volume III
2/20/71	1^{3}	Jesus Christ Superstar
10/17/98	9	Mean Green - Major Players Compilation
11/2/85	1^{11}	Miami Vice
1/23/99	10	Now
7/26/97	10	Pure Moods
8/24/63	7	Shut Down
1/27/73	5	Tommy
12/19/92	7	Very Special Christmas 2, A
12/18/65	3	Welcome to the LBJ Ranch!
2/15/97	8	West Coast Bad Boyz II
7/11/70	1^{4}	Woodstock
5/8/71	7	Woodstock Two
11/27/65	9	You Don't Have To Be Jewish

NOTABLE #1s

SLOWEST MOVERS TO #1

Weeks*	Title	Artist	Debut Date	Peak Date
118	First Take	*Roberta Flack*	1/31/70	4/29/72
	(fell off chart on 6/13/70 and re-entered on 3/18/72 after a 91-week absence)			
81	You Don't Mess Around With Jim	*Jim Croce*	7/1/72	1/12/74
	(fell off chart on 2/3/73 and re-entered on 10/6/73 after a 34-week absence)			
64	Forever Your Girl	*Paula Abdul*	7/23/88	10/7/89
58	Fleetwood Mac	*Fleetwood Mac*	8/2/75	9/4/76
55	Hangin' Tough	*New Kids On The Block*	8/27/88	9/9/89
52	Throwing Copper	*Live*	5/14/94	5/6/95
52	Nick Of Time	*Bonnie Raitt*	4/15/89	4/7/90
50	Appetite For Destruction	*Guns N' Roses*	8/29/87	8/6/88
50	Whitney Houston	*Whitney Houston*	3/30/85	3/8/86
49	Hysteria	*Def Leppard*	8/22/87	7/23/88
49	Tragic Kingdom	*No Doubt*	1/20/96	12/21/96
45	Cracked Rear View	*Hootie & The Blowfish*	7/23/94	5/27/95

BIGGEST JUMPS TO #1

Position From - To	Title	Artist	Date First Hit #1
176 - 1	Life After Death	*The Notorious B.I.G.*	4/12/97
173 - 1	Vitalogy	*Pearl Jam*	12/24/94
137 - 1	Ghetto D	*Master P*	9/20/97
122 - 1	More Of The Monkees	*The Monkees*	2/11/67
112 - 1	MP Da Last Don	*Master P*	6/20/98
98 - 1	Beatles '65	*The Beatles*	1/9/65
61 - 1	Help!	*The Beatles/Soundtrack*	9/11/65
60 - 1	Rubber Soul	*The Beatles*	1/8/66
53 - 1	Ballads of the Green Berets	*SSgt Barry Sadler*	3/12/66
48 - 1	Beatles VI	*The Beatles*	7/10/65
47 - 1	Elton John – Greatest Hits	*Elton John*	11/30/74
45 - 1	Revolver	*The Beatles*	9/10/66

BIGGEST FALLS FROM #1

Position From - To	Title	Artist	Date Last Hit #1
1 - 13	Endless Summer	*The Beach Boys*	10/5/74
1 - 12	Alice In Chains	*Alice In Chains*	11/25/95
1 - 11	Private Parts	*Soundtrack*	3/15/97
1 - 9	Far Beyond Driven	*Pantera*	4/9/94
1 - 9	Follow The Leader	*Korn*	9/5/98
1 - 8	Supposed Former Infatuation Junkie	*Alanis Morissette*	11/28/98
1 - 7	Wrap Around Joy	*Carole King*	11/9/74
1 - 7	Fire	*Ohio Players*	2/8/75
1 - 7	Kenny Rogers' Greatest Hits	*Kenny Rogers*	12/20/80
1 - 7	R. Kelly	*R. Kelly*	12/2/95
1 - 7	No Code	*Pearl Jam*	9/21/96
1 - 7	Beats, Rhymes And Life	*A Tribe Called Quest*	8/17/96

TOP 50 ALBUMS

With The:

MOST WEEKS AT #1

PK YR	WKS CH	WKS T40	WKS T10	WKS @ #1	RANK	TITLE	ARTIST
83	122	91	78	37	1.	**Thriller**	*Michael Jackson*
77	134	60	52	31	2.	**Rumours**	*Fleetwood Mac*
78	120	54	35	24	3.	**Saturday Night Fever**	*Bee Gees/Soundtrack*
84	72	42	32	24	4.	**Purple Rain**	*Prince & The Revolution/Soundtrack*
90	108	70	52	21	5.	**Please Hammer Don't Hurt 'Em**	*M.C. Hammer*
92	141	76	40	20	6.	**The Bodyguard**	*Whitney Houston/Soundtrack*
91	132	70	50	18	7.	**Ropin' The Wind**	*Garth Brooks*
87	96	68	48	18	8.	**Dirty Dancing**	*Soundtrack*
67	70	45	25	18	9.	**More Of The Monkees**	*The Monkees*
92	97	59	43	17	10.	**Some Gave All**	*Billy Ray Cyrus*
83	75	50	40	17	11.	**Synchronicity**	*The Police*
90	67	39	26	16	12.	**To The Extreme**	*Vanilla Ice*
98	66 +	33	20	16	13.	**Titanic**	*Soundtrack*
71	302	68	46	15	14.	**Tapestry**	*Carole King*
67	175	63	33	15	15.	**Sgt. Pepper's Lonely Hearts Club Band**	*The Beatles*
82	90	48	31	15	16.	**Business As Usual**	*Men At Work*
81	101	50	30	15	17.	**Hi Infidelity**	*REO Speedwagon*
80	123	35	27	15	18.	**The Wall**	*Pink Floyd*
65	114	78	48	14	19.	**Mary Poppins**	*Soundtrack*
86	162	78	46	14	20.	**Whitney Houston**	*Whitney Houston*
76	80	44	35	14	21.	**Songs In The Key Of Life**	*Stevie Wonder*
64	51	40	28	14	22.	**A Hard Day's Night**	*The Beatles/Soundtrack*
66	78	49	32	13	23.	**The Monkees**	*The Monkees*
69	151	59	28	13	24.	**Hair**	*Original Cast*
95	113	89	72	12	25.	**Jagged Little Pill**	*Alanis Morissette*
88	87	69	51	12	26.	**Faith**	*George Michael*
78	77	39	29	12	27.	**Grease**	*Soundtrack*
91	113	66	49	11	28.	**Mariah Carey**	*Mariah Carey*
87	85	51	31	11	29.	**Whitney**	*Whitney Houston*
69	129	32	27	11	30.	**Abbey Road**	*The Beatles*
64	71	27	21	11	31.	**Meet The Beatles!**	*The Beatles*
85	34	22	18	11	32.	**Miami Vice**	*TV Soundtrack*
89	175	78	64	10	33.	**Forever Your Girl**	*Paula Abdul*
76	97	55	52	10	34.	**Frampton Comes Alive!**	*Peter Frampton*
81	81	52	34	10	35.	**4**	*Foreigner*
94	88	56	31	10	36.	**The Lion King**	*Soundtrack*
84	61	27	20	10	37.	**Footloose**	*Soundtrack*
63	39	22	18	10	38.	**The Singing Nun**	*The Singing Nun*
70	85	24	17	10	39.	**Bridge Over Troubled Water**	*Simon & Garfunkel*
74	104	20	11	10	40.	**Elton John – Greatest Hits**	*Elton John*
85	97	55	37	9	41.	**Brothers In Arms**	*Dire Straits*
96	90	70	36	9	42.	**Tragic Kingdom**	*No Doubt*
87	103	58	35	9	43.	**The Joshua Tree**	*U2*
66	129	59	32	9	44.	**What Now My Love**	*Herb Alpert & The Tijuana Brass*
82	64	35	27	9	45.	**Asia**	*Asia*
68	69	47	26	9	46.	**The Graduate**	*Simon & Garfunkel/Soundtrack*
82	106	40	22	9	47.	**American Fool**	*John Cougar*
81	58	30	22	9	48.	**Tattoo You**	*The Rolling Stones*
79	57	36	21	9	49.	**The Long Run**	*Eagles*
70	69	26	19	9	50.	**Cosmo's Factory**	*Creedence Clearwater Revival*

PK YR: Peak Year   WKS CH: Weeks Charted   T40 WKS: Top 40 Weeks   T10 WKS: Top 10 Weeks   WKS @ #1: Weeks At #1

+ still charted as of the 3/27/99 cut-off date

TOP 50 ALBUMS

With The:

MOST WEEKS IN THE TOP 10

PK YR	T40 WKS	PK WKS	PK POS	T10 WKS	RANK	TITLE	ARTIST
65	161	2	1	109	1.	**The Sound Of Music**	*Soundtrack*
84	96	7	1	84	2.	**Born In The U.S.A.**	*Bruce Springsteen*
83	91	37	1	78	3.	**Thriller**	*Michael Jackson*
88	96	6	1	78	4.	**Hysteria**	*Def Leppard*
95	89	12	1	72	5.	**Jagged Little Pill**	*Alanis Morissette*
66	115	1	1	71	6.	**Doctor Zhivago**	*Soundtrack*
89	78	10	1	64	7.	**Forever Your Girl**	*Paula Abdul*
65	141	8	1	61	8.	**Whipped Cream & Other Delights**	*Herb Alpert*
96	73	3	1	61	9.	**Falling Into You**	*Celine Dion*
83	78	3	1	59	10.	**Can't Slow Down**	*Lionel Richie*
95	73	8	1	55	11.	**Cracked Rear View**	*Hootie & The Blowfish*
77	60	31	1	52	12.	**Rumours**	*Fleetwood Mac*
90	70	21	1	52	13.	**Please Hammer Don't Hurt 'Em**	*M.C. Hammer*
76	55	10	1	52	14.	**Frampton Comes Alive!**	*Peter Frampton*
88	78	5	1	52	15.	**Appetite For Destruction**	*Guns N' Roses*
90	69	10	2	52	16.	**Wilson Phillips**	*Wilson Phillips*
88	69	12	1	51	17.	**Faith**	*George Michael*
91	70	18	1	50	18.	**Ropin' The Wind**	*Garth Brooks*
69	66	7	1	50	19.	**Blood, Sweat & Tears**	*Blood, Sweat & Tears*
91	66	11	1	49	20.	**Mariah Carey**	*Mariah Carey*
69	87	1	4	49	21.	**In-A-Gadda-Da-Vida**	*Iron Butterfly*
87	68	18	1	48	22.	**Dirty Dancing**	*Soundtrack*
65	78	14	1	48	23.	**Mary Poppins**	*Soundtrack*
66	107	6	1	48	24.	**Going Places**	*Herb Alpert*
71	68	15	1	46	25.	**Tapestry**	*Carole King*
86	78	14	1	46	26.	**Whitney Houston**	*Whitney Houston*
86	60	8	1	46	27.	**Slippery When Wet**	*Bon Jovi*
89	69	6	1	45	28.	**Don't Be Cruel**	*Bobby Brown*
89	71	2	1	45	29.	**Hangin' Tough**	*New Kids On The Block*
98	80+	2	4	45	30.	**Backstreet Boys**	*Backstreet Boys*
92	59	17	1	43	31.	**Some Gave All**	*Billy Ray Cyrus*
94	56	5	1	43	32.	**II**	*Boyz II Men*
84	71	1	1	42	33.	**Sports**	*Huey Lewis & The News*
89	61	8	1	41	34.	**Girl You Know It's True**	*Milli Vanilli*
71	65	3	1	41	35.	**Jesus Christ Superstar**	*Various Artists*
87	54	10	2	41	36.	**Whitesnake**	*Whitesnake*
92	76	20	1	40	37.	**The Bodyguard**	*Whitney Houston/Soundtrack*
83	50	17	1	40	38.	**Synchronicity**	*The Police*
85	66	2	1	40	39.	**Reckless**	*Bryan Adams*
95	75	1	3	40	40.	**CrazySexyCool**	*TLC*
87	54	6	1	39	41.	**Bad**	*Michael Jackson*
84	71	11	3	39	42.	**Private Dancer**	*Tina Turner*
93	52	3	1	38	43.	**Unplugged**	*Eric Clapton*
91	77	1	1	38	44.	**Time, Love & Tenderness**	*Michael Bolton*
81	58	1	1	38	45.	**Escape**	*Journey*
83	58	2	2	38	46.	**Pyromania**	*Def Leppard*
85	55	9	1	37	47.	**Brothers In Arms**	*Dire Straits*
86	77	2	1	37	48.	**Control**	*Janet Jackson*
76	68	1	1	37	49.	**Fleetwood Mac**	*Fleetwood Mac*
85	58	1	1	37	50.	**Heart**	*Heart*

PK YR: Peak Year T40 WKS: Top 40 Weeks PK WKS: Peak Weeks PK POS: Peak Position T10 WKS: Top 10 Weeks

+ still in the Top 40 as of the 3/27/99 cut-off date

TOP ALBUM ARTISTS
With The:
MOST #1 ALBUMS

The Beatles	18
The Rolling Stones	9
Barbra Streisand	8
Garth Brooks	7
Elton John	7
Paul McCartney	7
Led Zeppelin	6
Herb Alpert	5
Chicago	5
Eagles	5
Pink Floyd	5
Bruce Springsteen	5
U2	5
Van Halen	5
Mariah Carey	4
Fleetwood Mac	4
Janet Jackson	4
Michael Jackson	4
Billy Joel	4
The Monkees	4
Nirvana	4
Beastie Boys	3
Bee Gees	3
Eric Clapton	3
Crosby, Stills & Nash	3
John Denver	3
Bob Dylan	3
Whitney Houston	3
Carole King	3
John Lennon	3
Madonna	3
Metallica	3
Pearl Jam	3
Prince	3
Linda Ronstadt	3
Simon & Garfunkel	3
Snoop Doggy Dogg	3
Donna Summer	3
The Supremes	3
2 Pac	3
Stevie Wonder	3

MOST TOP 10 ALBUMS

The Rolling Stones	34
The Beatles	27
Barbra Streisand	24
Bob Dylan	15
Elton John	15
Neil Diamond	13
Paul McCartney	13
The Beach Boys	12
Chicago	12
Van Halen	12
Billy Joel	11
Madonna	11
Elvis Presley	11
Andy Williams	11
Herb Alpert	10
Garth Brooks	10
Led Zeppelin	10
Prince	10
Linda Ronstadt	10
Frank Sinatra	10
Bruce Springsteen	10
The Temptations	10
Stevie Wonder	10
Eric Clapton	9
Rush	9
The Who	9
Bee Gees	8
Mariah Carey	8
The Doobie Brothers	8
The Doors	8
Earth, Wind & Fire	8
Grand Funk Railroad	8
Pink Floyd	8
Bob Seger	8
Rod Stewart	8
The Supremes	8
James Taylor	8
John Denver	7
Jimi Hendrix	7
Jefferson Airplane/Starship	7
Jethro Tull	7
Journey	7
Kiss	7
John Lennon	7
Barry Manilow	7
John Cougar Mellencamp	7
Tom Petty	7
Santana	7
Cat Stevens	7
Yes	7

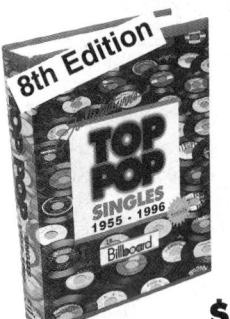

POP HITS 1940-1954

A Treasure Trove For Fans Of One Of The Richest Eras In American Popular Music. From Big Band Swing To The Stirrings Of Rock & Roll, **Pop Hits 1940-1954** Is An Artist-By-Artist Listing & A Year-By-Year Ranking Of The Over 3,500 Records That Appeared On Billboard's Pop Singles Charts ("Best Sellers in Stores," "Most Played by Disk Jockeys" And "Most Played in Juke Boxes") From 1940 Through 1954.

$44.95 #PH4054H Hardcover

2 BOOKS IN 1!

ARRANGED BY ARTIST...

SHOWS EACH RECORD'S:

• **Peak chart position** on Billboard's multiple weekly Pop singles charts • **Chart debut date** • **Total weeks charted** • **Original label/record number** • **Complete record price guide** • Record number prefixes for both 45 rpm & 78 rpm versions • Total weeks at #1 or #2 • And more

Plus: • Detailed Artist Biographies • Expansive Title Trivia Notes

RANKED BY YEAR...

BY PEAK CHART POSITION, WITH EACH RECORD'S:

• **Peak chart position** • **Total peak weeks** • **Peak chart date** • **Final ranking for the year** • Original label/record number • Total weeks in the Top 5, in the Top 10 and on the charts • Week-by-week chart positions on all three Pop charts for each #1 record's entire chart life • And more

Plus:

- Yearly Time Capsules of news, sports and entertainment
- Yearly Top Artists Rankings & Photos
- Yearly Top New Artists Debuts
- Alphabetical Song Title List
- And Other Special Artist & Record Achievement Sections

Size: 7" x 9". 416 pages.

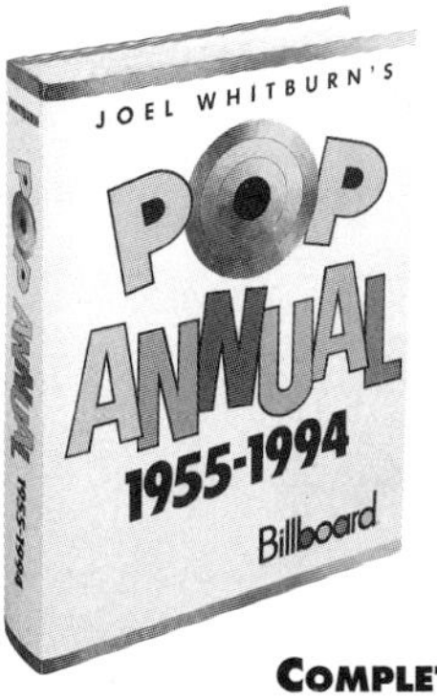

POP ANNUAL 1955-1994

Planning A Class Reunion Or A Movie Soundtrack, Then You Need This **Year-By-Year Ranking** According To Highest Chart Position Reached, Of The 20,520 Singles That Peaked On Billboard's Pop Singles Charts ("Hot 100," "Best Sellers in Stores," "Most Played by Jockeys," "Most Played in Juke Boxes" And "Top 100") From January, 1955 Through December, 1994.

$69.95 #PSA501H Hardcover

$59.95 #PSA501S Softcover

40 Complete Yearly Rankings!

COMPLETE CHART DATA SHOWS EACH SINGLE'S:

• **Peak chart position** • **Total weeks at peak position** • **Date peaked** • **Yearly rank** • **Total weeks in Top 10 and Top 40** • Total weeks charted • Peak positions on Billboard's multiple weekly '55-'58 Pop singles charts

Plus:

• Original label and number • Playing time • RIAA platinum/gold certifications • **Complete record price guide** • **Complete picture sleeve & cassette picture box guide** • And more

Also Features:

- Week-by-week chart positions for every #1 through #5 hit's entire chart life
- Songwriter(s) of every Top 5 hit
- Yearly "Tag-Along" Sections list B-side chart hits
- Yearly Time Capsules of news, sports and entertainment
- Yearly Top 20 Artists Rankings
- Yearly Top Artist Debuts
- Top 500 Artists Ranking
- Complete research of Billboard's Christmas Singles Charts
- List of Academy and Grammy Award-winning Songs and Records
- Complete Alphabetical Song Title List
- And Other Special Artist, Songwriter & Record Achievement Sections

Size: 7" x 9". 880 pages.

TOP COUNTRY SINGLES 1944 - 1997

An Artist-By-Artist Listing Of More Than 2,100 Artists And 16,693 Songs That Appeared On Billboard's "Country" Singles Charts From January, 1944 Through December, 1997.

$64.95
#TCS401H
Hardcover

COMPLETE CHART DATA SHOWS EACH TITLE'S:

• **Peak chart position** • **Chart debut date** • **Total weeks charted** • Total weeks at #1 or #2 • Original label and record number • Peak Pop chart position (for crossover hits) • Peak positions on Billboard's multiple weekly '48-'58 "Country" charts

Plus: • The B-sides of all charted singles • RIAA platinum/gold certifications • Complete record price guide • Every Top 200 artist's picture is shown next to their name • Every Top 400 artist's all-time ranking is shown next to their name • Comprehensive, fact-packed biographies • Interesting title trivia notes • And more

Special Sections: • Complete Alphabetical Song Title List • Top Artist & Record Achievements • Year-By-Year Listing Of All #1 Records

Size: 7" x 9". 624 pages.

COUNTRY ANNUAL 1944 - 1997

A Country First - A Year-by-Year Ranking Of The 16,054 Songs That Peaked On Billboard's "Top Country Singles" Charts From January 8, 1944 through December 27, 1997 — All Arranged In Numerical Order According To The Highest Chart Position Each Reached.

$64.95
#CA101H
Hardcover

COMPLETE CHART DATA SHOWS EACH SINGLE'S:

• **Peak chart position** • **Total weeks at the peak position** • **Date Peaked** • **Yearly Rank** • **Original label and record/cassette/CD single number** • Total weeks in the Top 10, Top 40 and on the charts • Week-by-week chart positions for every Top 5 hit • Peak position reached on Billboard's "Hot 100" • Every Top 5 hit's songwriter(s) • RIAA Gold or Platinum certification • Complete Record Price Guide lists each single's current dealer price

Plus: • Yearly Top Artist Rankings • Yearly Top Artist Debuts • "Tag-Along" Sections list B-sides that were also chart hits • Year-By-Year Listing Of All #1 Records • Top 400 Artists Ranking • Song Title Section alphabetically lists all titles with peak position, peak year and artist's name • Other Record Achievements

Size: 7" x 9". 704 pages.

TOP COUNTRY ALBUMS 1964 - 1997

A Music Industry First And A Record Research Exclusive, **Top Country Albums 1964-1997** Is An Artist-By-Artist Listing Of Every Album To Appear On Billboard's "Top Country Albums" Chart From Its First Appearance In 1964 Through September, 1997.

$49.95
#TCA101H
Hardcover

COMPREHENSIVE DATA ON EVERY CHARTED COUNTRY ALBUM:

• **Peak chart position** • **Chart debut date** • **Total weeks charted** • **Original label and number** • **Total weeks at #1 or #2** • Peak position on Billboard's Pop albums charts • Comprehensive artist biographies • Title notes indicate duet partners, guest artists, special recording sites and much more • RIAA platinum/gold certifications • Current prices for all near-mint-condition albums and CDs

Top 10 Albums Track Lists show individual tracks from each Top 10 Album below the album title and each "Country Singles"-charted track from album is shown in bold type along with its peak position.

Complete A-Z Track Section lists every track from every Top 10 album alphabetically with an indication of the album on which each track is found and the year the album charted.

PLUS: • Top 50 Artists Pictures • Ranking of Top 200 Artists and Top 100 Albums • Top Artist & bum Achievements • Chronological Listing of All #1 Albums

Size: 7" x 9". 304 pages.

TOP R&B SINGLES 1942-1995

From Doo-Woppers To Hip-Hoppers, The Complete Chart History Of Rhythm & Blues Is Chronicled In This Artist-By-Artist Listing Of The Over 16,500 Records That Appeared On Billboard's R&B Singles Charts From 1942 through 1995.

$64.95
#RBS301H
Hardcover

COMPLETE CHART DATA SHOWS EACH SINGLE'S:

• **Peak chart position** • **Chart debut date** • **Total weeks charted** • Original label and record number • Total weeks at #1 or #2 • Peak Pop chart position (for crossover hits)

Plus: • Complete record price guide • RIAA platinum/gold certifications • Updated artist biographies and expanded title notes • Complete Alphabetical Song Title List • Year-By-Year Listing Of All #1 Records • Artists & Singles Record Holders • And more

Size: 7" x 9". 704 pages.

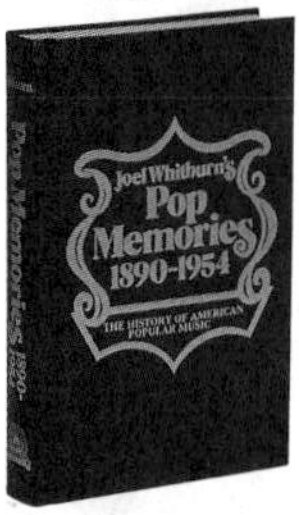

POP MEMORIES 1890-1954

The Beginning Of The Record Industry To The Dawn Of The Rock Era Is Chronicled In This Artist-By-Artist Listing Of The Over 12,000 Records That Appeared On America's Popular Music Charts, Surveys & Record Listings From 1890 Through 1954.

$59.95
#MEM101H
Hardcover

COMPLETE DATA SHOWS EACH RECORD'S:

• **Peak chart position** • **Chart debut date** • **Total weeks charted** • **Original label and record number** • Total weeks at #1 or #2 • And more

Plus: In-Depth Artist Biographies • Title Trivia Notes • Complete A-Z Song Title List • Top 100 Artists • Top 100 Hits • Top Artist & Record Achievements • Academy Award Winners • Billboard Disc Jockey Poll & College Survey Results • Year-By-Year Listing Of All #1 Records

Size: 6" x 9". 660 pages.

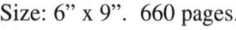

HOT 100/POP CHART BOOKS

4 Volumes:

Pop Charts 1955-1959 - Hardcover/#PSCH50H - **$59.95**
Hot 100 Charts 1960-1969 - Hardcover/#PSCH60H - **$79.95**
Hot 100 Charts 1970-1979 - Hardcover/#PSCH70H - **$79.95**
Hot 100 Charts 1980-1989 - Hardcover/#PSCH80H - **$79.95**

If You Love The Charts, Here They Are! Complete Collections Of Picture-Perfect Reproductions Of Actual, Mint-Condition Billboard Pop Singles Charts, Each Shown In Its Entirety, In Black And White, At About 70% Of Original Size. **Complete Alphabetical Title Section** (all books) lists all charted titles with artist name and chart debut date.

Size: 9" x 12". Various page lengths.

BILLBOARD® TOP 10 CHARTS 1958-1997

2,027 Weeks Of The Hottest Of The "Hot 100" Is Detailed In This Week-By-Week Listing Of The Top 10 From Every Billboard "Hot 100" Chart From Its Debut On August 4, 1958 Through 1997.

$39.95
#TEN301H
Hardcover

ARRANGED IN THE ORIGINAL "HOT 100" CHART FORMAT & PACKED WITH PERTINENT DATA ON EACH TOP 10 RECORD

Includes: • **This week and last week chart positions** • **Total number of weeks on the "Hot 100"** as of chart date • Original label/record number • **Records at their peak Top 10 positions** are shown in boldface type • **Billboard's original chart bullets** denote the week's hottest movers • **The "Highest Debut"** highlights record debuting at the highest "Hot 100" position each week • **The "Biggest Mover"** highlights record advancing the most "Hot 100" positions each week • Several special sections of significant chart achievements.

Size: 6" x 9". 780 pages.

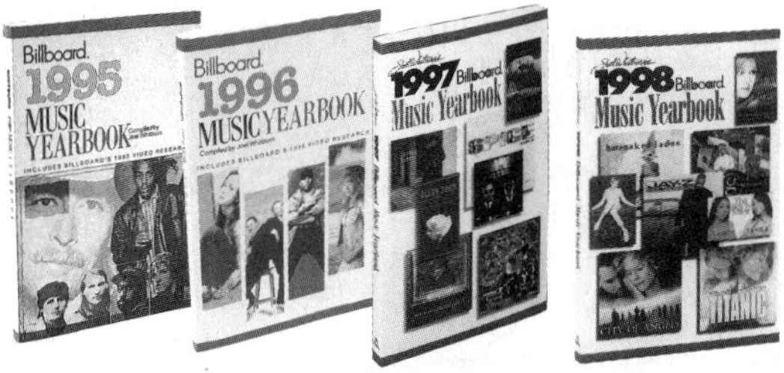

Billboard®
1998 MUSIC YEARBOOK
1997 MUSIC YEARBOOK
1996 MUSIC YEARBOOK
1995 MUSIC YEARBOOK

Get The Full Story On *Everything* That Hit Billboard's Charts During The Year.

Each Book Contains Ten Complete Sections, Arranged By Artist Within Each Chart Category, Listing The Over 2,500 Titles That Debuted During The Year On Billboard's Major Singles & Albums Charts: "Hot 100," Country Singles, R&B Singles, Adult Contemporary Singles, Mainstream Rock Tracks, Modern Rock Tracks, Bubbling Under The Hot 100 Singles, "The Billboard 200" (Pop Albums), Country Albums And R&B Albums.

1998 Music Yearbook: 272 pages. #YB1998 Softcover
1997 Music Yearbook: 256 pages. #YB1997 Softcover
1996 Music Yearbook: 264 pages. #YB1996 Softcover
1995 Music Yearbook: 256 pages. #YB1995 Softcover

Size: 6" x 9" (all yearbooks)

$34.95 each

1990 through 1994 Music Yearbooks are also available at $29.95 each.

TOP ADULT CONTEMPORARY 1961-1993

Neil Diamond To Celine Dion...Mantovani To Mariah Carey...**Top Adult Contemporary 1961-1993** Is An Artist-By-Artist Listing Of The 7,226 Records That Appeared On Billboard's Easy Listening And Top Adult Contemporary Singles Charts From July, 1961 Through July, 1993.
Size: 7" x 9". 368 pages.

$39.95
#ACN201H
Hardcover

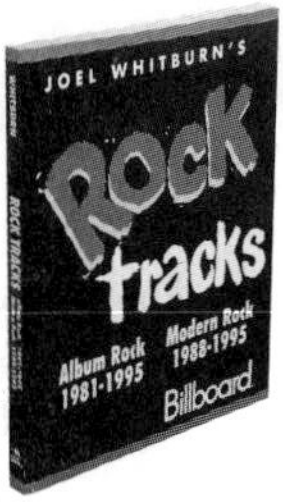

ROCK TRACKS — Album Rock 1981-1995 / Modern Rock 1988-1995

The Stadium-Packing Rock Legends Appear With The Underground College Bands In These Two Separate Artist-By-Artist Listings Of The 3,749 Titles & 926 Artists That Appeared On Billboard's Album (Mainstream) Rock Tracks Charts And The 1,282 Titles & 544 Artists That Appeared On Billboard's Modern Rock Tracks Charts Through August 1985.
Size: 7" x 9". 288 pages.

$34.95
#ROK101S
Softcover

1998 Edition

BUBBLING UNDER SINGLES AND ALBUMS

All Bubbling Under The Hot 100 (1959-1997) and Bubbling Under The Top Pop Albums (1970-1985) chart hits that did not proceed to the Hot 100 or Top Pop Albums charts, respectively, are covered in full and organized artist by artist. Also features a photo section of all 131 EPs that hit Billboard's Best Selling Pop EP's chart (1957-1960). Size: 7" x 9". 416 pages.

$49.95
#BUB301S
Softcover

TOP 1000 x 5 1996 Edition

Five separate rankings of the All-Time #1-#1,000 hits that appeared on each of Billboard's "Hot 100," Early Pop, Adult Contemporary, R&B and Country singles charts — plus two bonus rankings of the All-Time Top 200 Hits from each of Billboard's "Modern Rock Tracks" and "Album (Mainstream) Rock Tracks" charts.
Size: 7" x 9". 288 pages.

$29.95
#TXF201S
Softcover

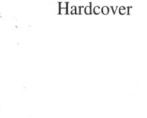